From left to right:

Joanne R. Moss, M.A. (Cantab), LL.M. (Lond), F.C.I. Arb.; **Catherine L. Taskis**, B.C.L., M.A. (Oxon); **James Muir Watt**, O.B.E., M.A. (Oxon).

Property and Conveyancing Library

AGRICULTURAL HOLDINGS

AUSTRALIA
LBC Information Services
Sydney

CANADA
Carswell
Toronto

NEW ZEALAND
Brooker's
Auckland

SINGAPORE AND MALAYSIA
Thomson Information (S.E. Asia)
Singapore

PROPERTY AND CONVEYANCING LIBRARY

MUIR WATT AND MOSS
AGRICULTURAL HOLDINGS

FOURTEENTH EDITION

by

Editor
JAMES MUIR WATT, O.B.E., M.A. (Oxon)
Hon. Assoc. R.I.C.S.
F.A.A.V.
of the Inner Temple, Barrister

Editor
JOANNE R. MOSS, M.A. (Cantab), LL.M. (Lond), F.C.I.Arb.
of the Inner Temple, Barrister

Assistant Editor
CATHERINE L. TASKIS, B.C.L., M.A. (Oxon)
of the Inner Temple, Barrister

LONDON
SWEET & MAXWELL
1998

First edition	(1912)	by T.C. Jackson
Second edition	(1914)	"
Third edition	(1917)	"
Fourth edition	(1920)	"
Fifth edition	(1921)	by W. Hanbury Aggs
Sixth edition	(1924)	"
Seventh edition	(1928)	"
Eighth edition	(1934)	"
Ninth edition	(1939)	"
Tenth edition	(1949)	"
Eleventh edition	(1959)	by J. Muir Watt
Twelfth edition	(1967)	"
Thirteenth edition	(1987)	"
Fourteenth edition	(1998)	by J. Muir Watt, J.R. Moss

Published in 1998 by
Sweet & Maxwell Ltd of
100 Avenue Road, Swiss Cottage, London NW3 3PF
(http://www.smlawpub.co.uk)
Computerset by Tradespools Ltd, Frome, Somerset
Printed and bound in Great Britain by
MPG Books Ltd, Bodmin, Cornwall.

No natural forests were destroyed to make this product;
only farmed timber was used and replanted.

A C.I.P. Catalogue record for this book is available from the British Library

ISBN 0421 444 908

All rights reserved. U.K. statutory material in this publication is
acknowledged as Crown Copyright.

No part of this publication may be reproduced or transmitted in any form or by any means, or stored in any retrieval system of any nature without prior written permission, except for permitted fair dealing under the Copyright, Designs and Patents Act 1988, or in accordance with the terms of a licence issued by the Copyright Licensing Agency in respect of photocopying and/or reprographic reproduction. Precedent material in this publication may be used as a guide for the drafting of legal documents specifically for particular clients, though no liability is accepted in relation to their use. Application for permission for other use of copyright material including permission to reproduce extracts in other published works shall be made to the publishers. Full acknowledgement of author, publisher and source must be given.

©Sweet & Maxwell 1998

FOREWORD

by James Muir Watt

Before anything else it is essential for me to make absolutely clear that the credit for the authorship of this new reconstructed edition belongs entirely to Joanne Moss and her able assistant, Catherine Taskis. Although I have brazenly used the excuse of extreme old age to avoid my fair share of the hard work on the reconstructed book which my colleagues have carried out, I have read carefully through enough of the text to appreciate fully the merits of the excellent work which they have done.

PREFACE

In this edition we have endeavoured to state the law as at April 2 1998. The current work is a restructured and updated version of the previous Edition: all comment on the statutes is now to be found in the main text. In this we have shamelessly copied the clear format of Gill's *Law of Agricultural Holdings in Scotland* (2nd edition, W. Green, Edinburgh). To compensate for any unfamiliarities with definitions (which previously were cross-linked in by the separate statutory gloss) there is now in Chapter 8 a single complete alphabetical list of definitions used in the Agricultural Holdings Act 1986. We have tried to devise a paragraph layout which enables the key statutes to be worked through in sequence, and to assist with the complex requirements of procedures relating to notices to quit there is now a collection of procedural tables in Part VI identifying not only the relevant steps with time limits and forms but also the consequences where those steps are not taken. The Precedents Division has been overhauled and new forms provided for the Agricultural Tenancies Act 1995. We have tried to focus on areas and issues of anxious practitioner concern such as changes in the construction of notices to quit (Chapter 12), succession (Chapter 14) and milk quotas (Chapters 18 and 19). Our treatment of the 1995 Act is necessarily to some extent speculative in the absence of reported litigation. We have taken a policy decision to avoid reference to unreported material as far as is possible. Our aim is to provide a tool for practitioners and we have expanded the use of footnotes to allow more detailed reasons to be given without cluttering the main text. Finally, although we had not originally intended to reproduce it in full, the Arbitration Act 1996 is such a model of clarity and is so fundamental to the disputes resolutions procedures under the 1995 Agricultural Tenancies Act that we decided the reader would find it indispensable; it is now to be found in full in Part VII.

Special thanks are due to those who have been kind enough to read and comment on Chapters of the text in draft—in relation to Chapter 18, milk quotas, Mr David Carter FRICS, FAAV, of P.D. Carter & Co., Nailsworth, Gloucestershire and Mr Graham Holmes, FRICS, FAAV, of Berry Bros & Holmes, Shrewsbury, Shropshire; in relation to Chapter 14, succession, and Chapters 3 and 5, dealing with farm business tenancies, Mrs Angela Sydenham of Birketts, Solicitors, of Ipswich. These are sophisticated and trenchant readers and we are grateful for that. But if there are mistakes Joanne Moss claims them as hers.

The editorial and production team at Sweet & Maxwell have been truly patient, helpful and hardworking. Their many tasks include the preparation of indexes. We also take the opportunity to thank Margaret Mitchell and Carolyn Wren who have endlessly typed and corrected the text: without them there would be no new edition at all. Joanne Moss wishes to thank Dr Jeremy Horder of Worcester College, Oxford for his cheerful help with baby Alice whilst the text was completed.

Lastly, we have enjoyed the project as we hope is obvious from the portrait which appears by courtesy of Robert Stewart, photographers, of Ayr, Scotland.

James Muir Watt	Ayr, Scotland
Joanne R. Moss	Falcon Chambers, London
Catherine Taskis	Falcon Chambers, London

CONTENTS

	Page
Foreword	v
Preface	vii
Table of Cases	xi
Table of Statutes	xliii
Table of Statutory Instruments	lxxiii
Table of Rules of the Supreme Court	lxxxi
Table of EEC Regulations	lxxxi

PART I: COMMENTARY

Introduction: an overview   3

Section 1: Tenancies Governed by the Agricultural Tenancies Act 1995

Chapter 1:	Creation and meaning of farm business tenancy	9
Chapter 2:	Rent review	39
Chapter 3:	Removal of fixtures and buildings	67
Chapter 4:	Termination of tenancy by notice	77
Chapter 5:	Compensation on termination of farm business tenancy	85
Chapter 6:	Dispute resolution	109
Chapter 7:	Miscellaneous	141

Section 2: Tenancies Governed by the Agricultural Holdings Act 1986

Chapter 8:	General principles and definitions	149
Chapter 9:	Statutory control over interests granted	169
Chapter 10:	Provisions affecting tenancy during its continuance	191
Chapter 11:	Rent review	239
Chapter 12:	Termination of tenancy by notice to quit	269
Chapter 13:	Compensation and custom	353
Chapter 14:	Succession on death or retirement	421
Chapter 15:	Sub-tenancies, market gardens smallholdings	491
Chapter 16:	Dispute resolution	509
Chapter 17:	Miscellaneous	575

Section 3: Milk Quotas and the Agriculture Act 1986

Chapter 18:	Milk quotas generally	593
Chapter 19:	The Agriculture Act 1986	625

PART II: STATUTES 647

PART III: STATUTORY INSTRUMENTS 833

PART IV: EUROPEAN UNION MATERIALS 965

PART V: FORMS 993

PART VI: PROCEDURAL TABLES 1123

PART VII: THE ARBITRATION ACT 1996 1153

TABLE OF DERIVATIONS 1219

TABLE OF DESTINATIONS 1233

INDEX 1243

TABLE OF CASES

Absolem v. Knight (1742) Bull. N.P. 181 .... 10.70
Ackland v. Lutley (1839) 9 A. & E. 879; 1 Per. & Dav. 636; 8 L.J.Q.B. 164; 112 E.R. 1446 ... 12.14
Adam v. Smyth 1948 S.C. 445 .... 13.119
Addin v. Secretary of State for the Environment [1997] 1 E.G.L.R. 99; [1997] 14 E.G. 132, Ch.
    D 2.10.2
Addington v. Sims [1952] E.G.D. 1; (1952) 159 E.G. 663 .... 12.39
Addis v. Burrows [1948] 1 K.B. 444; [1948] 4 L.J.R. 1033; 64 T.L.R. 169; 92 S.J. 124; [1948] 1
    All E.R. 177 .... 12.26
Adsetts v. Heath (1951) 95 S.J. 620 .... 8.13
Agip (Africa) Ltd. v. Jackson [1991] Ch. 547; [1991] 3 W.L.R. 116; (1992) 4 All E.R. 451;
    (1991) 135 S.J. 117; *The Times*, January 9, 1991; *Financial Times*, January 18, 1991, CA;
    affirming [1990] Ch. 265; [1989] 3 W.L.R. 1367; [1992] 4 All E.R. 385; (1990) 134 S.J.
    198; [1989] L.S. Gaz. January 17, 34 .... 12.47
Albyn Properties Ltd. v. Knox 1977 S.L.T. 41 .... 16.56
Aldin v. Latimer Clark, Muirhead & Co. [1894] 2 Ch. 437 .... 1.44
Allen and Matthews' Arbitration, *Re* [1971] 2 C.B. 518; [1971] 2 W.L.R. 1249; [1971] 2 All
    E.R. 1259; 22 P. & C.R. 576; *sub nom.* Allen v. Mathews, 115 S.J. 304 .... 16.68
Al Saloom v. James (Shirley) Travel Services (1981) 125 S.J. 397; (1981) 42 P. & C.R. 181,
    CA; *affirming* (1980) 255 E.G. 541 .... 2.10.1
Amalgamated Estates Limited v. Joystretch Manufacturing Limited [1980] 257 E.G. 489, CA ...5.21,
    12.81.1, 13.11.9, 19.19
Amalgamated Investment and Property Co. Ltd. v. Texas Commerce International Bank Ltd
    [1982] Q.B. 84; [1981] 3 W.L.R. 565; (1981) 125 S.J. 623; [1981] 3 All E.R. 577; [1981]
    Com. L.R. 236, CA; *affirming* [1981] 2 W.L.R. 554; (1980) 125 S.J. 133; [1981] 1 All E.R.
    923; [1981] Com. L.R. 37 .... 12.32, 12.76.1
Aman v. Southern Railway Company [1926] 1 K.B. 59 .... 12.55
Amego Litho Ltd v. Scanway Ltd [1994] 1 E.G.L.R. 15, [1994] 02 E.G. 110 .... 11.33
Amherst v. Walker (James) Goldsmith and Silversmith [1983] Ch. 305; [1983] 3 W.L.R. 334;
    (1983) 127 S.J. 391; [1983] 2 All E.R. 1067; (1984) 47 P. & C.R. 85; (1982) 267 E.G. 163,
    CA 2.10.1
Andrea v. British Italian Trading Co. *See* Giacomo Costa Fu Andrea v. British Italian Trading
    Co.
Anisminic Ltd. v. Foreign Compensation Commission [1969] 2 A.C. 147; [1969] 2 W.L.R. 163;
    (1968) 113 S.J. 55; [1969] 1 All E.R. 208, H.L.; *reversing* [1968] 2 Q.B. 862; [1967] 3
    W.L.R. 382; 111 S.J. 374; [1967] 3 All E.R. 986, CA 12.41, 16.68
Anstruther-Gough-Calthorpe v. McOscar [1924] 1 K.B. 716; 130 L.T. 691; *sub nom.* Calthorpe
    v. McOscar, 93 L.J.K.B. 273; 40 T.L.R. 223; 68 S.J. 367 .... 10.28
Anthony v. Brecon Markets Company [1867] L.R. 2 Ex. 167 .... 1.44
Arden and Rutter, *Re* [1923] 2 K.B. 865; 130 L.T.S. 1; *sub nom.* Arden v. Rutter, 92 L.J.K.B.
    894 .... 8.22, 13.83, 13.122, 16.15
Arenson v. Arenson. *See* Arenson v. Casson Beckman Rutley & Co.
—— v. Casson Beckman Rutley & Co. [1977] A.C. 405; [1975] 3 W.L.R. 815; 119 S.J. 810;
    [1975] 3 All E.R. 901; [1976] 1 Lloyd's Rep. 179, H.L.; *reversing sub nom.* Arenson v.
    Arenson [1973] Ch. 346; [1973] 2 W.L.R. 553; 117 S.J. 247; [1973] 2 All E.R. 235; *sub
    nom.* Arenson v. Arenson and Casson Beckman, Rutley & Co. [1973] 2 Lloyd's Rep. 104,
    CA 6.83
Arlesford Trading Co. Ltd. v. Servansingh [1971] 1 W.L.R. 1080; 115 S.J. 507; [1971] 3 All
    E.R. 113; 22 P. & C.R. 848, CA 13.97
Armitage v. Nurse [1997] 2 All E.R. 705; *The Times*, March 31, 1997, CA 12.47
A/S Tankexpress v. Compagnie Financiére Belge de Pétroles SA [1949] A.C. 76; [1949] L.J.R.
    170; 93 S.J. 26; [1948] 2 All E.R. 939; 82 Ll.L. Rep. 43, HL; *affirming* (1947) 80 Ll.L. Rep.
    365, CA 12.55, 12.56
Ashbridge Investments Ltd v. Minister of Housing and Local Government [1965] 1 W.L.R.
    1320; 129 J.P. 580; 109 S.J. 595; [1965] 3 All E.R. 371; 63 L.G.R. 400, CA.; *reversing*
    (1965) 109 S.J. 474 .... 12.41, 16.61
Ashdale Land and Property Co. Ltd v. Manners [1992] 2 E.G.L.R. 5; [1992] 34 E.G. 76 .... 9.15
Ashworth Frazer Ltd v. Gloucester City Council [1997] 1 E.G.L.R. 104; [1997] E.G.C.S. 7,
    CA 2.7

TABLE OF CASES

Aspinall, *Re*, Aspinall v. Aspinall [1961] Ch. 526; [1961] 3 W.L.R. 235; 105 S.J. 529; [1961] 2 All E.R. 751 .... 10.69
Atkins v. Temple (1625) 1 Rep. Ch. 13; Toth. 143; 21 E.R. 493 .... 10.55
Atkyns v. Baldwyn (1816) 1 Stark. 209 .... 16.38
Att.-Gen. v. Davison (1825) McCl. & Y. 160; 148 E.R. 366 .... 16.37
Att.-Gen. (Duchy of Lancaster) v. Simcock [1966] Ch. 1; [1965] 2 W.L.R. 1126; [1965] 2 All E.R. 32 .... 12.45, 12.56, 12.61.9
Avon County Council v. Clothier (1977) 75 L.G.R. 344; (1977) 242 E.G. CA 8.17, 9.10

Bache v. Billingham [1894] 1 Q.B. 107; 63 L.J.M.C. 1; 69 L.T. 648; 58 J.P. 181; 9 R. 79; 42 W.R. 217 .... 16.34
Bahamas International Trust Co. Ltd. v. Threadgold [1974] 1 W.L.R. 1514; 118 S.J. 832; [1974] 3 All E.R. 881; HL.; *affirming for different reasons* [1974] 3 All E.R. 428, CA 8.17, 9.4, 9.5
Bailey v. Purser. *See* Purser v. Bailey.
—— v. Sitwell [1986] 2 E.G.L.R. 7; (1986) 279 E.G. 1092 .... 14.37, 14.39, 14.45, 14.47
Bairstow Eves (Securities) v. Ripley (1992) 65 P. & C.R. 220; [1992] 32 E.G. 52; [1992] N.P.C. 78; [1992] E.G.C.S. 83, CA 10.37
Baker v. Merckel, Anson (Third Party) [1960] 1 Q.B. 657; [1960] 2 W.L.R. 492; 104 S.J. 231; [1960] 1 All E.R. 668; [104 S.J. 264; 24 Conv. 250], CA; *affirming* (1958) 173 E.G. 133; [103 S.J. 345]; [1959] C.L.Y. 1847 .... 1.13, 14.8
Balls Brothers Ltd v. Sinclair [1931] 2 Ch. 325 .... 5.4, 11.21
Barbour v. M'Douall 1914 S.C. 844 .... 10.76, 13.27, 13.29
Barclays Bank Plc v. Prudential Assurance Co. Ltd [1998] 10 E.G. 159, Ch. D. 15.16
Barff v. Probyn (1895) 64 L.J.Q.B. 557; 73 L.T. 118; 11 T.L.R. 467 .... 15.24
Barns Graham v. Lamont 1971 S.C. 170; 1971 S.L.T. 341 .... 13.20
Barrett v. Morgan [1997] 1 E.G.L.R. 1; [1997] 12 E.G. 155, Ch. D. 15.17
Barrow v. Ashburnham (Lord) (1835) 4 L.J.K.B. 146 .... 10.74
Barrow Green Estate Co. v. Walker (Exors. of decd.) [1954] 1 W.L.R. 231; 98 S.J. 78; [1954] 1 All E.R. 204; 52 L.G.R. 130 .... 10.10, 13.81
Bass Holdings Ltd v. Morton Music Ltd (1988) Ch. 493; [1987] 3 W.L.R. 543; (1987) 131 S.J. 473; [1987] 2 All E.R. 1001; (1987) 54 P. & C.R. 135; [1987] 1 E.G.L.R. 214; (1987) 84 L.S. Gaz. 1414, CA; *reversing* [1987] 2 W.L.R. 397; (1987) 131 S.J. 224; [1987] 1 All E.R. 389; (1987) 53 P. & C.R. 155; (1986) 280 E.G. 1435; [1986] 2 E.G.L.R. 50; (1987) 84 L.S. Gaz. 742 .... 9.22, 10.37, 12.76.1
Bathavon R.D.C. v. Carlile [1958] 1 Q.B. 461; [1958] 2 W.L.R. 545; 122 J.P. 240; 102 S.J. 230; [1958] 1 All E.R. 801; 56 L.G.R. 139 .... 12.14
Batt v. London City and Westcliff Properties Ltd [1967] 111 S.J. 684; [1967] R.V.R. 412; 203 E.G. 337, DC 11.14
Bebington's Tenancy, *Re*, Bebington v. Wildman [1921] 1 Ch. 559; 90 L.J. Ch. 269; 124 L.T. 661; 37 T.L.R. 409; 65 S.J. 343 .... 12.17, 14.82
Becker, Shillan & Co and Barry Bros., *Re* [1921] 1 K.B. 391; 90 L.J.K.B. 316; 124 L.T. 604 .. 16.66, 16.72
Beckett v. South Devon Homes (Teignmouth) Ltd; Weston v. South Devon Homes (Teignmouth) (1971) 220 E.G. 33 .... 16.34
Bedding v. McCarthy [1995] 27 H.L.R. 103; [1994] 41 E.G. 151, CA 9.29
Bedfordshire County Council v. Clarke (1974) 230 E.G. 1587 .... 9.6, 9.29
Beer v. Davies [1958] 2 Q.B. 187; [1958] 2 W.L.R. 920; 122 J.P. 344; 102 S.J. 383; [1958] 2 All E.R. 255; 56 L.G.R. 261; 42 Cr. App. R. 198 .... 17.20
Beevers v. Mason (1978) 37 P. & C.R. 452; (1978) 122 S.J. 610; (1978) 248 E.G. 781, CA ... 12.56
Behren v. Bremer (1854) 3 C.L.R. 40 .... 16.49
Bell v. Franks (Alfred) & Bartlett Co. [1980] 1 W.L.R. 340; (1979) 123 S.J. 804; [1980] 1 All E.R. 356; (1979) 39 P. & C.R. 591; (1979) 253 E.G. 903, CA 8.20
Bell v. McCubbin [1990] 1 Q.B. 976; [1989] 3 W.L.R. 1306; [1990] 1 All E.R. 54; (1989) 133 S.J. 1514; [1989] 40 E.G. 100; (1990) 59 P. & C.R. 352, CA 12.50
Belmont Farm Ltd. v. Minister of Housing and Local Government (1962) 106 S.J. 469; (1962) 13 P. & C.R. 417; 60 L.G.R. 319; [1963] J.P.L. 256 .... 8.18
Belmont Finance Corp. v. Williams Furniture [1979] Ch. 250; [1978] 3 W.L.R. 712; (1977) 122 S.J. 743; [1979] 1 All E.R. 118, CA 12.47
Belsfield Court Construction Co. Ltd v. Pywell [1970] 2 Q.B. 47; [1969] 3 W.L.R. 1051; 113 S.J. 940; [1970] 1 All E.R. 453 .... 16.68
Belvedere Motors Ltd v. King [1981] 260 E.G. 813 .... 6.84

TABLE OF CASES

Bendall v. McWhirter [1952] 2 Q.B. 466; [1952] 1 T.L.R. 1332; 96 S.J. 344; [1952] 1 All E.R. 1307 .... 15.13
Bennett v. Stone [1902] 1 Ch. 226; 71 L.J.Ch. 60; 85 L.T. 753; 46 S.J. 151; 50 W.R. 118 .... 13.51, 13.113, 17.6
Bennion and National Provincial Bank's Arbitration, Re (1965) 115 L.J. 302 .... 16.30
Bernays v. Prosser [1963] 2 Q.B. 592; [1963] 2 W.L.R. 1255; 107 S.J. 271; [1963] 2 All E.R. 321 .... 9.2, 9.3, 9.8, 9.9
Bevan v. Chambers [1896] 12 T.L.R. 417 .... 8.22
Bew, Re, ex p. Bull (1887) 18 Q.B.D. 642; 56 L.J.Q.B. 270; 56 L.T. 571; 51 J.P. 710; 4 Morr. 94; 35 W.R. 455 .... 10.69
Bickerdike v. Lucy [1920] 1 K.B. 707; 89 L.J.K.B. 558; 84 J.P. 61; 18 L.G.R. 207 .... 15.20, 15.27
Billson v. Residential Apartments Ltd [1992] 1 A.C. 494; [1992] 2 W.L.R. 15; [1992] 1 All E.R. 141; (1991) 63 P. & C.R. 122; (1991) 24 H.L.R. 218; [1992] 1 E.G.L.R. 43; [1992] 01 E.G. 91; (1992) 136 S.J.L.B. 10; [1992] N.P.C. 133; [1992] N.P.C. 133; [1992] *Gazette*, January 22, 31; *The Times*, December 13, 1991; *The Independent*, January 8, 1992, HL; *reversing* [1991] 3 W.L.R. 264; [1991] 3 All E.R. 265; (1991) 62 P. & C.R. 505; [1991] 1 E.G.L.R. 70; [1991] 18 E.G. 169 and [1991] 19 E.G. 122; [1991] E.G.C.S. 17; *The Times*, February 26, 1991, CA; *affirming* (1990) 60 P. & C.R. 392 ....12.76.2
Birch v. Stephenson (1811) 3 Taunt. 469; 128 E.R. 186 .... 10.55
Birkbeck v. Paget (1862) 31 Beav. 403; 54 E.R. 1194 .... 10.74
Birmingham Dudley & District Banking Co. v. Ross [1887] 38 Ch. D. 295, CA 1.44
Birtley & District Co-operative Society Ltd v. Windy Nook and District Industrial Co-operative Society [1959] 1 W.L.R. 142; 103 S.J. 112; [1959] 1 All E.R. 43 .... 16.66
Black v. Clay [1894] A.C. 368 .... 8.22
Blackmore v. Butler [1954] 2 Q.B. 171; [1954] 3 W.L.R. 62; 98 S.J. 405; [1954] 2 All E.R. 403; 52 L.G.R. 345 .... 8.14, 8.16, 8.18
Blanchard v. Sun Fire Office (1890) 6 T.L.R. 365 .... 16.35
Blewett v. Blewett [1936] 2 All E.R. 188, CA 17.23
Bliss v. Collins (1822) 5 B. & Ald. 876; 1 Dow. & Ry.K.B. 291; 106 E.R. 1411 .... 12.32
Blizzard v. Kennett ref. S.E. 87/1960 .... 12.39
Blundell v. Obsdale Ltd [1958] E.G.D. 144 .... 10.12
Bolesworth Estate Co. Ltd. v. Cook (1966) 116 New L.J. 1318; (1966) 116 L.J. 739n., Cty. Ct. . 11.29, 11.44
Bolnore Properties Ltd v. Cobb (1996) 29 H.L.R. 202; [1996] E.G.C.S. 42; [1996] N.P.C. 37, CA 1.20
Bolton's (House Furnishers) v. Oppenheim [1959] 1 W.L.R. 913; 103 S.J. 634; [1959] 3 All E.R. 90, CA; *affirming* [1959] 1 W.L.R. 685; [1959] 2 All E.R. 473; *sub nom.* Brixton Road, No. 395, Re Brixton Bolton's (House Furnishers) v. Oppenheim, 103 S.J. 52 ...... 12.60
Bonnett and Fowler, Re [1913] 2 K.B. 537; 82 L.J.K.B. 713; 108 L.T. 497; 77 J.P. 281 .... 16.65
Boston's Will Trusts, Re Inglis v. Boston [1956] Ch. 395; [1956] 2 W.L.R. 700; 100 S.J. 209; [1956] 1 All E.R. 593 .... 17.15
Boswell v. Crucible Steel Co. of America [1925] 1 K.B. 119 .... 10.12, 10.31
Bourgoin SA v. Ministry of Agriculture Fisheries and Food [1986] Q.B. 716; [1985] 3 W.L.R. 1027; [1985] 3 All E.R. 585; [1986] 1 C.M.L.R. 267; (1985) 82 L.S. Gaz. 3534, CA; *reversing in part* [1985] 1 C.M.L.R. 528, DC 6.22
Bowers v. Nixon (1848) 12 Q.B. 558; 18 L.J.Q.B. 35; 13 Jur. 334; 116 E.R. 978 .... 10.59
Boyce v. Rendells [1983] E.G.D. 26; (1983) 268 E.G. 268, CA 9.9, 9.10, 9.15
Boyd v. Wilton [1957] 2 Q.B. 277; [1957] 2 W.L.R. 636; 101 S.J. 301; [1957] 2 All E.R. 102 13.87
Bracegirdle v. Oxley, Bracegirdle v. Cobley [1947] 1 K.B. 349; [1947] L.J.R. 815; 176 L.T. 187; 63 T.L.R. 98; 111 J.P. 131; 91 S.J. 27; [1947] 1 All E.R. 126 .... 16.61
Bracey v. Read [1963] Ch. 88; [1962] 3 W.L.R. 1194; 106 S.J. 878; [1962] 3 All E.R. 472 .... 8.18
Bradburn v. Foley (1878) 3 C.P.D. 129; 47 L.J.Q.B. 331; 38 L.T. 421; 42 J.P. 344; 26 W.R. 423 . 10.59, 13.48, 13.71, 13.108, 13.113
Bradshaw v. Bird [1920] 3 K.B. 144; 90 L.J.K.B. 221; 123 L.T. 703 .... 13.13
—— v. Pawley [1980] 1 W.L.R. 10; [1979] 3 All E.R. 273; (1979) 40 P. & C.R. 496; (1979) 253 E.G. 693 .... 1.21, 1.43, 9.21
Breadalbane (Marquess) v. Stewart [1904] A.C. 217 .... 13.113
Brett v. Brett Essex Golf Club, The (1986) 52 P. & C.R. 330; [1986] 1 E.G.L.R. 154; (1986) 278 E.G. 1476, CA; reversing (1984) 49 P. & C.R. 315; (1985) 273 E.G. 507; (1985) 82 L.S. Gaz. 518 .... 2.19
Brew Bros. Ltd. v. Snax (Ross) Ltd. [1970] 1 Q.B. 612; [1969] 3 W.L.R. 657; 113 S.J. 795;

TABLE OF CASES

[1970] 1 All E.R. 587; 20 P. & C.R. 829; CA; *affirming* (1968) 19 P. & C.R. 702; 207 E.G. 341 .... 10.28
Brien and Brien, *Re* [1910] 2 Ir.R. 84 .... 16.34
Brimnes, The; Tenax Steamship Co. v. Brimnes, The (Owners) [1975] Q.B. 929; [1974] 3 W.L.R. 613; 118 S.J. 808; *sub nom.* Brimnes, The; Tenax Steamship Co. v. Owners of the Motor Vessel Brimnes [1974] 3 All E.R. 88; *sub nom.* Tenax Steamship Co. v. Brimnes, The (Owners); Brimnes, The [1974] 2 Lloyd's Rep. 241, CA; *affirming sub nom.* Tenax Steamship Co. v. Reinante Transoceanica Navegacion SA; Brimnes, The [1973] 1 W.L.R. 386; 117 S.J. 244; *sub nom.* Tenax Steamship Co. v. Brimnes, The (Owners) [1972] 2 Lloyd's Rep. 465; [1973] 1 All E.R. 769 .... 12.56
British Anzani (Felixstowe) Limited v. International Marine Management (U.K.) Ltd [1980] Q.B. 637; [1979] 3 W.L.R. 451; (1978) 123 S.J. 64; [1979] 2 All E.R. 1063; (1978) 39 P. & C.R. 189; (1978) 250 E.G. 1183 .... 12.58
British Launderers Research Association v. Hendon Borough Rating Authority [1949] 1 K.B. 462; [1949] L.J.R. 416; 65 T.L.R. 103; 93 S.J. 58; *sub nom.* British Launderers' Research Association v. Central Middlesex Assessment Committee and Hendon Rating Authority, 113 J.P. 72; [1949] 1 All E.R. 21 .... 16.61
British Petroleum Pension Trust Ltd. v. Behrendt (1986) 52 P. & C.R. 117; (1985) 18 H.L.R. 42; (1985) 276 E.G. 199, CA 12.61.12
British Shipbuilders v. VSEL Consortium Plc *The Times*, February 14, 1996, Ch.D. 6.87
Brodie v. Ker, McCallum v. McNair 1952 S.C. 216 .... 16.15
Brooker Settled Estates Ltd. v. Ayers (1987) 19 H.L.R. 246; (1987) 282 E.G. 325, CA 9.4
Brooks v. Brown, 50 Conv. (N.S.) 320 .... 14.62
Brougham and Vaux's (Lord) Settled Estates, *Re* [1954] Ch. 24; [1953] 3 W.L.R. 465; 97 S.J. 540; [1953] 2 All E.R. 655 .... 17.15
Brown v. Leicester Corp. [1892] 57 J.P. 70 .... 3.11
Brown v. Trumper (1858) 26 Beav. 11; 53 E.R. 800 .... 10.28
—— v. Wilson (1949) 208 L.T. 144; (1949) 93 S.J. 640; (1950) 156 E.G. 45 .... 12.76.2, 15.14
BSC Pension Fund Trustees Limited v. Downing [1990] 1 E.G.L.R. 10, [1990] 19 E.G. 87 ...... 5.21, 12.32, 12.81.1
B.T.E. Limited v. Merseyside and Cheshire Rent Assessment Committee and Jones (1991) 24 H.L.R. 514; [1992] 1 E.G.L.R. 116; [1992] 16 E.G. 111 .... 11.18
Buchanan v. Taylor 1916 S.C. 129; S.L.R. 86; 2 S.L.T. 455 .... 11.21, 13.68, 16.32
Buckinghamshire County Council v. Gordon [1986] 2 E.G.L.R. 8; (1986) 279 E.G. 853, Cty.Ct. 11.1
Budd-Scott v. Daniell [1902] 2 K.B. 351 .... 1.44
Budge v. Hicks [1951] 2 K.B. 335; 95 S.J. 501; [1951] 2 All E.R. 245; *sub nom.* Hicks v. Budge [1951] 2 T.L.R. 349 .... 12.61.10, 12.76, 12.83
Bulk Oil (Zug) A.G. v. Sun International and Sun Oil Trading Co. [1984] 1 W.L.R. 147; [1984] 1 All E.R. 386; [1983] 2 Lloyd's Rep. 587; (1984) 81 L.S. Gaz. 36, CA; *affirming* (1983) 127 S.J. 857; [1983] 1 Lloyd's Rep. 655; [1983] Com. L.R. 68 .... 6.78
Bungalows (Maidenhead) v. Mason [1954] 1 W.L.R. 769; 98 S.J. 334; [1954] 1 All E.R. 1002; [98 S.J. 347; 104 L.J. 423; 18 Conv. 323], CA 9.12
Burden v. Hannaford [1956] 1 Q.B. 142; [1955] 3 W.L.R. 606; 99 S.J. 780; [1955] 3 All E.R. 401 .... 10.9, 10.10, 10.25, 10.27, 13.81, 13.91
Burgess v. Purchase & Sons (Farms) Ltd [1983] Ch. 216; [1983] 2 W.L.R. 361; [1983] 2 All E.R. 4 .... 6.86
Burgoyne v. Ainsworth (1885) 79 L.T.J. 377 .... 12.22
Burton v. Timmis (1986) 281 E.G. 795 .... 16.68
Butterfield v. Burniston (1961) 180 E.G. 597 .... 9.9

Cadogan v. McCarthy & Stone (Developments) Ltd [1996] E.G.C.S. 94; [1996] N.P.C. 77; *The Independent*, June 17, 1996 (C.S.), CA 12.50
Calcott v. J.S. Bloor (Measham) Ltd (1998) E.G.C.S. 25; *The Times*, March 5, 1998, CA 9.4
Caldecott v. Smythies (1837) 7 C. & P. 808 .... 13.41, 13.51, 13.108
Calderbank v. Calderbank [1976] Fam. 93; [1975] 3 W.L.R. 586; 119 S.J. 490; [1975] 3 All E.R. 333; (1975) 5 Fam. Law. 190, CA 16.41
Caledonian Ry. v. Turcan [1898] A.C. 256; 67 L.J.P.C. 69 .... 16.58
Calthorpe v. McOscar. *See* Anstruther-Gough-Calthorpe v. McOscar.
Cameron v. Nicol 1930 S.C. 1 .... 13.116
Campbell v. Edwards [1976] 1 W.L.R. 403; (1975) 119 S.J. 845; [1976] 1 All E.R. 785; [1976] 1 Lloyd's Rep. 522, CA 6.83, 6.86

TABLE OF CASES

Canas Property Co. Ltd. v. K.L. Television Services Ltd. [1970] 2 C.B. 433; [1970] 2 W.L.R.
  1133; 114 S.J. 337; [1970] 2 All E.R. 795; 21 P. & C.R. 601, CA 13.90
Cardshops Ltd v. Davies [1971] 1 W.L.R. 591; 115 S.J. 265; [1971] 2 All E.R. 721; 22 P. & C.R.
  499, CA 11.8
Carnarvon v. Villebois [1844] 13 M. & W. 313 .... 1.13
Carnegie v. Davidson 1966 S.L.T. (Land Ct.) 3 .... 12.41
Carradine Properties Ltd. v. Aslam [1976] 1 W.L.R. 442; (1975) 120 S.J. 166; [1976] 1 All E.R.
  573; (1975) 32 P. & C.R. 12 .... 12.29
Carson v. Cornwall County Council [1993] 1 E.G.L.R. 21; [1993] 03 E.G. 119 ... 18.11, 18.23, 19.17
Cary v. Cary (1862) 10 W.R. 669 .... 13.51, 13.113
"Catalina" v. "Norma" (1938) 61 Ll.L.R. 360; 82 S.J. 698 .... 16.66
Cathcart v. Chalmers [1911] A.C. 246; 80 L.J.P.C. 143; 104 L.T. 355 .... 13.2, 13.120
Cattan (L.E.) Ltd. v. Michaelides (A.) & Co. [1958] 1 W.L.R. 717; 102 S.J. 470; [1958] 2 All
  E.R. 125; [1958] 1 Lloyd's Rep. 479 .... 16.68
Cave v. Page [1923] W.N. 178; (1923) 67 S.J. 659 .... 13.22
Cawley v. Pratt [1988] 2 E.G.L.R. 6; [1988] 33 E.G. 54, CA 12.46, 12.50
Central Estates Ltd v. Secretary of State for the Environment [1997] 1 E.G.L.R. 239, CA 2.10.1
Ceylon (Government of) v. Chandris [1963] 2 Q.B. 327; [1963] 2 W.L.R. 1097; 107 S.J. 316;
  [1963] 2 All E.R. 1; [1963] 1 Lloyd's Rep. 214 .... 16.66
Chalmers Property Investment Co. Ltd v. MacColl 1951 S.C. 24; 1951 S.L.T. 50 .... 16.22
Chaloner v. Bower (1983) 269 E.G. 725, CA 9.8, 9.9, 9.15
Champsey Bhara & Co. v. Jivraj Balloo Spinning and Weaving Co. Ltd [1923] A.C. 480; 92
  L.J.P.C. 163; 129 L.T. 166; 39 T.L.R. 253 .... 16.68
Channon v. Patch (1826) 5 B. & C. 897 .... 10.31
Chapman v. Smith [1907] 2 Ch. 97; 76 L.J.Ch. 394; 96 L.T. 662; 51 S.J. 428 .... 10.59
Chatwood Safe and Engineering Co. Ltd v. Frank [1952] C.P.L. 532 .... 11.37
Cheshire County Council v. Hopley (1923) 130 L.T. 123; 21 L.G.R. 524 .... 13.48, 13.71
Cheshire County Council v. Woodward [1962] 2 Q.B. 126; [1962] 2 W.L.R. 636; 126 J.P. 186;
  106 S.J. 222; [1962] 1 All E.R. 517; 13 P. & C.R. 157; 60 L.G.R. 180; [1962] R.V.R. 148;
  [112 L.J. 484; 126 J.P.J. 251; 26 Conv. 480; [1962] R.V.R. 727], DC 3.11
Cheshire v. Elwes and the Colesbourne Estate Co. (1979) *Hamilton* No. 76, p. 97 .... 14.84
Chester v. Buckingham Travel [1981] 1 W.L.R. 96; (1980) 125 S.J. 99; [1981] 1 All E.R. 386;
  (1981) 42 P. & C.R. 221 .... 1.45
Chetwynd (Viscountess) v. Edwards (1967) 204 E.G. 822 .... 12.39
Chicago, Burlington and Quincy Railway Co. v. Babcock 204 U.S. 585 (1907) 16.44
Childers (J.W.) Trustees v. Anker. *See* Trustees of J.W. Childers Will Trust v. Anker
Chilton v. Saga Holidays plc [1986] 1 All E.R. 841, CA 16.47
Christison's Trustees v. Callender Brodie (1906) 8 F. 928 .... 16.23
Church Commissioners for England v. Ibrahim [1997] 1 E.G.L.R. 13; [1997] 03 E.G. 136, CA   6.30
Church Commissioners for England v. Mathews (1979) 251 E.G. 1074 .... 16.27, 16.28
CIL Securities Ltd v. Briant Champion Long [1993] 2 E.G.L.R. 164; [1993] 42 E.G. 281; [1993]
  E.G.C.S. 22 .... 6.84
Clarke v. Grant [1950] 1 K.B. 104; [1949] L.J.R. 1450; 65 T.L.R. 241; 93 S.J. 249; [1949] 1 All
  E.R. 768; [93 S.J. 284; 13 Conv. 314] 1.43
Clarke v. Hall [1961] 2 Q.B. 331; [1961] 2 W.L.R. 836; 105 S.J. 366; [1961] 2 All E.R. 365 ..   9.25,
                                                                                              12.80
Clarke-Jervoise v. Scutt [1920] 1 Ch. 382; 89 L.J. Ch. 218; 122 L.T. 581 .... 10.55
Clays Lane Housing Co-operative v. Patrick (1984) 49 P. & C.R. 72; (1984) 17 H.L.R. 188 ...   3.9
Clegg v. Fraser (1982) 264 E.G. 144 .... 12.41, 12.74
Coates v. Diment [1951] 1 All E.R. 890 .... 12.7, 13.2, 13.5
Codd v. Brown (1867) 15 L.T. 536 .... 13.48, 13.113
Cohen v. Hale [1878] 3 Q.B.D. 371 .... 12.56
Colchester Borough Council v. Smith [1992] Ch. 421; [1992] 2 W.L.R. 728; [1992] 2 All E.R.
  561, CA; *affirming* [1991] Ch. 448; [1991] 2 W.L.R. 540; [1991] 2 All E.R. 29; (1990) 62
  P. & C.R. 242 .... 9.4
Coldman v. Hill [1919] 1 K.B. 443; 88 L.J.K.B. 491; 120 L.J. 412; 35 T.L.R. 146; 63 S.J. 166   10.71
Collett v. Deeley (1950) 100 L.J. 108 .... 16.30
Collier v. Hicks (1831) 2 B. & A. 663; 9 L.J.O.S.M.C. 138; 109 E.R. 1290 .... 16.36
—— v. Hollinshead (1984) 272 E.G. 941 .... 9.3, 9.4, 9.15
Collins v. Claughton [1959] 1 W.L.R. 145; 103 S.J. 111; [1959] 1 All E.R. 95; [103 S.J. 104; 23
  Conv. 144], CA 9.12
Collins v. Flynn [1963] 2 All E.R. 1068 .... 10.28

—— v. Spurway (1967) 204 E.G. 801 .... 12.41
Collyer-Bristow & Co., *Re* [1901] 2 K.B. 839 .... 16.49
Combey v. Gumbrill [1990] 2 E.G.L.R. 7 .... 12.29
Computer Machinery Co. Ltd v. Drescher [1983] 1 W.L.R. 1379; (1983) 127 S.J. 823; [1983] 3 All E.R. 153 .... 16.42
Congreve v. I.R.C. [1948] W.N. 197; [1948] L.J.R. 1229; 92 S.J. 407; [1948] 1 All E.R. 948; 41 R. & I.T. 319; 30 T.C. 163; [48 Tax. 47; 64 L.Q.R. 459; 13 Conv. 153], HL; *affirming* [1947] 1 All E.R. 168; [10 M.L.R. 429; 11 Conv. 301], CA; *reversing* [1946] 2 All E.R. 170; [11 Conv. 71] 3.12
Constable & Cranswick, *Re* (1899) 80 L.T. 164; 43 S.J. 208 .... 13.107
Control Securities plc v. Spencer [1989] 1 E.G.L.R. 136; [1989] 07 E.G. 82 ..... 16.46
Cooke v. Talbot (1977) 243 E.G. 831 .... 12.39, 12.41, 12.51
Cooke-Bourne (E.D. & A.D.) (Farms) Ltd v. Mellows [1983] Q.B. 104; [1982] 3 W.L.R. 783; (1982) 126 S.J. 481; [1982] 2 All E.R. 208; (1983) 45P. & C.R. 264; (1982) 262 E.G. 229, CA 13.119, 16.27, 16.28
Coombes, *Re* (1850) 4 Ex. 839 .... 16.26
Cooper v. Scott-Farnell [1969] 1 W.L.R. 120; (1968) 112 S.J. 945; [1969] 1 All E.R. 1781, CA   17.20
Co-operative Insurance Society Ltd v. Argyll Stores (Holdings) Ltd [1997] 2 W.L.R. 893; [1997] 3 All E.R. 297, HL 1.19, 10.33, 18.24
Cope v. Sharpe (No. 2) [1912] 1 K.B. 496; 81 L.J.K.B. 346; 106 L.T. 57; 28 T.L.R. 157; 56 S.J. 187 .... 10.74
Copeland v. McQuaker 1973 S.L.T. 186 .... 12.48, 13.20
Cork v. Cork (1997) 16 E.G. 130, Ch. D. 12.32
Cormack v. McIldowie's Executors 1972 S.L.T. (Notes) 40 .... 16.32
Cornwall Coast Country Club v. Cardgrange (1987) 282 E.G. 1664; [1987] 1 E.G.L.R. 146 ... 2.23
Corporation of the City of Victoria v. Bishop of Vancouver Island [1921] 2 A.C. 384 .... 3.11
Cory Brothers & Co. Ltd v. Owners of the Turkish Steamship "Mecca" [1897], A.C. 286 ..... 12.56
Costagliogla v. Bunting [1958] 1 W.L.R. 580; 102 S.J. 364; [1958] 1 All E.R. 846; 56 L.G.R. 292 .... 12.79
Coutts v. Barclay-Harvey 1956 S.L.T. (Sh.Ct.) 54; 72 Sh.Ct.Rep. 105 .... 13.122
Cowan v. Wrayford [1953] 1 W.L.R. 1340; 97 S.J. 780; [1953] 2 All E.R. 1138; 51 L.G.R. 659 . 12.28, 12.48, 12.61.8
Cox v. Hurst (1976) 239 E.G. 123 .... 9.3, 9.11
Cox v. Husk [1976] 2 E.G.L.R. 1 .... 9.15
Crabb v. Arun District Council [1976] Ch. 179; [1975] 3 W.L.R. 847; 119 S.J. 711; [1975] 3 All E.R. 865; (1975) 32 P. & C.R. 70, CA 1.19
Crate v. Miller [1947] K.B. 946; [1947] L.J.R. 1341; 177 L.T. 29; 63 T.L.R. 389; 91 S.J. 396; [1947] 2 All E.R. 45 .... 12.14
Crawford v. McKinlay 1954 S.L.C.R. 39 .... 12.29, 12.39
Creear v. Fearon [1994] 2 E.G.L.R. 12; [1994] 46 E.G. 202; [1994] E.G.C.S. 114, CA ... 19.15, 19.17
Cresswell (Valuation Officer) v. British Oxygen Co. Ltd [1980] 1 W.L.R. 1556; (1980) 124 S.J. 497; [1980] 3 All E.R. 443; [1981] J.P.L. 355; (1980) 255 E.G. 1101, CA; *reversing* (LVC/923/1976) [1980] J.P.L. 187; (1979) 250 E.G. 1195 .... 8.18
Cristina v. Seear [1985] 2 E.G.L.R. 128; (1985) 275 E.G. 898, CA 5.4, 19.9.1
Croft v. Brocklesby (1972) 224 E.G. 1405 .... 16.66
Crown Estates Commissioners v. Allingham (1973) 226 E.G. 2153 .... 12.45, 12.55
Cuff v. Stone (J. & F.) Property Co. [1979] A.C. 87; (1973) 38 P. & C.R. 288; [1978] 3 W.L.R. 256 (W.); [1978] 2 All E.R. 833 .... 2.16
Cunliffe v. Goodwan [1950] 2 K.B. 237; 66 T.L.R. (Pt. 2) 109; 94 S.J. 179; [1950] 1 All E.R. 720 .... 13.94
Curtis v. Wheeler [1830] Moo & M. 493 .... 15.2
Cutting v. Derby (1776) 2 W.Bl. 1075; 96 E.R. 633 .... 10.69
Cutts v. Head [1984] Ch. 290; [1984] 2 W.L.R. 349; [1984] 1 All E.R. 597; (1984) 128 S.J. 117, CA 16.41

DAF Motoring Centre (Gosport) v. Hatfield & Wheeler (1982) 2 E.G.L.R. 59; (1982) 263 E.G. 976, CA 12.50
Dagg v. Lovett (1980) 256 E.G. 491, CA; *reversing* (1980) 254 E.G. 993; *restoring* (1979) *Hamilton* No. 72, p. 88 (1979) 251 E.G. 75 .... 14.70, 14.74
Daintry, *Re ex p.* Holt [1893] 2 Q.B. 116; 62 L.J.Q.B. 511; 10 Morr. 158; 69 L.T. 257; 9 T.L.R. 452; 37 S.J. 480; 41 W.R. 590; 5 R.414 .... 16.41
Dalby v. Hirst (1819) 1 Brod. & Bing. 224; 3 Moo.P.C. 536; 129 E.R. 708 .... 13.108

TABLE OF CASES

Dale v. Hatfield Chase Corporation [1922] 2 K.B. 282; 92 L.J.K.B. 237; 128 L.T. 194; 87 J.P. 11; 20 L.G.R. 765 .... 10.76, 13.12, 13.29, 13.51, 13.113, 16.61
Dallhold Estates (U.K.) Pty (In Administration) v. Lindsey Trading Properties Inc. (1995) 70 P. & C.R. 332; [1993] E.G.C.S. 195; [1994] 17 E.G. 148; [1993] E.G.C.S. 195; [1993] N.P.C. 158; *The Times*, December 15, 1993, CA; *reversing* [1992] 1 E.G.L.R. 88; [1992] 23 E.G. 112; [1992] E.G.C.S. 29; [1992] N.P.C. 36 .... 7.16, 12.23, 12.54, 12.55
Dalton v. Pickard (1911), reported in note at [1926] 2 K.B. 545n.; 95 L.J.K.B. 1052n.; 136 L.T. 21n. 13.113
Darby v. Williams (1974) 232 E.G. 579, CA 8.14, 8.16
Darlington Borough Council v. Waring & Gillow (Holdings) plc [1988] 2 E.G.L.R. 159 ...... 6.86
Dashwood v. Magniac [1891] 3 Ch. 306; 60 L.J.Ch. 210; 64 L.T. 99; 7 T.L.R. 189 .... 13.108
Datnow v. Jones [1985] 2 E.GL.R. 1; (1985) 275 E.G. 145, CA 7.10, 12.5, 17.19
Davies, *ex p*. [1953] 1 W.L.R. 722 .... 12.35
—— v. Ecroyd (H. & R.) Ltd [1996] 30 E.G. 97; [1996] E.G.C.S. 77; [1996] 2 E.G.L.R. 5; [1996] N.P.C. 67, Ch. D. 18.28, 18.29
—— v. Price [1958] 1 W.L.R. 434; 102 S.J. 290; [1958] 1 All E.R. 671 .... 12.35, 16.7, 16.8
Davis v. Connop (1814) 1 Price 53; 145 E.R. 1328 .... 13.113
—— v. Witney U.D.C. (1899) 15 T.L.R. 275; 63 J.P. 279 .... 16.74
Dean v. Prince [1954] Ch. 409; [1954] 2 W.L.R. 538; 98 S.J. 215; [1954] 1 All E.R. 749; 47 R. & I.T. 494; [9 Sec. Jo. 382; 18 Conv. 206], CA; *reversing* [1953] Ch. 590; [1953] 3 W.L.R. 271; 97 S.J. 490; [1953] 2 All E.R. 636; [Sec. Jo., July, 1953, p. 62; Accty., Sept., 1953, p. 286; 103 L.J. 615; 17 Conv. 320] [1953] C.L.Y. 525 .... 6.87
Deen v. Andrews [1986] 1 E.G.L.R. 262; (1986) 52 P. & C.R. 17 .... 3.11
Deith v. Brown [1956] J.P.L. 736 .... 8.19
De La Warr's (Earl) Cooden Beach Settled Estate, *Re* [1913] 1 Ch. 142; 82 L.J. Ch. 174; 107 L.T. 671 .... 17.11
Dennis v. McDonald [1982] Fam. 63; [1982] 2 W.L.R. 275; (1982) 126 S.J. 16; [1982] 1 All E.R. 590; (1982) 12 Fam. Law 84, CA; *affirming* [1981] 1 W.L.R. 810; (1981) 125 S.J. 308; [1981] 2 All E.R. 632 .... 14.62
Dennis & Robinson Ltd. v. Kiossos Establishment (1987) 282 E.G. 857, CA 11.6
Derby (Earl) and Fergusson's Contract, *Re* [1912] 1 Ch. 479; 81 L.J. Ch. 567; 105 L.T. 943 ... 13.51, 13.61, 13.113
Derry v. Peak (1889) 14 App. Cas. 337 .... 12.47
DHN Food Distributors v. Tower Hamlets London Borough Council; Bronze Investments v. Same; DHN Food Transport v. Same [1976] 1 W.L.R. 852; 120 S.J. 215; [1976] J.P.L. 363; 74 L.G.R. 506; *sub nom.* DHN Food Distributors v. London Borough of Tower Hamlets [1976] 3 All E.R. 462; *sub nom.* DHN Food Distributors (in Liquidation) v. Tower Hamlets London Borough Council; Bronze Investments (in Liquidation) v. Same; DHN Food Transport (in Liquidation) v. Same (1976) 32 P. & C.R. 240, CA; *reversing sub nom.* D.H.N. Food Distributors, Bronze Investments and D.H.N. Food Transport v. London Borough of Tower Hamlets (Ref. Nos. 36, 37 and 38/1974) (1975) 30 P. & C.R. 251, Lands Tribunal 19.91
Dibble v. Bowater (1853) 2 E. & B. 564; 1 C.L.R. 877; 22 L.J.Q.B. 396; 17 J.P. 792; 17 Jur. 1054; 1 W.R. 435; 118 E.R. 879; *sub nom.* Biddle v. Bowater 21 L.T. (o.s.) 165 .... 10.69
Dibble (H.E.) v. Moore, West, Third Party [1970] 2 Q.B. 181; [1969] 3 W.L.R. 748; 20 P. & C.R. 898; *sub nom.* Dibble (H.E.) v. Moore, 113 S.J. 853; [34 Conv. 50; 86 L.Q.R. 19]; *sub nom.* Dibble (H.E.) (Trading as Mill Lane Nurseries) v. Moore (West, Third Party) [1969] 3 All E.R. 465, CA 3.11
Dickinson v. Boucher (1983) 269 E.G. 1159, CA 12.53, 12.54
Disraili Agreement, *Re*, Cleasby v. Park Estates (Hughenden) Ltd. [1939] Ch. 382; 108 L.J. Ch. 100; 160 L.T. 156; 55 T.L.R. 204; 82 S.J. 1031; [1938] 4 All E.R. 658 ... 12.7, 12.22, 13.2, 13.5, 16.15
Divall v. Harrison [1992] 2 E.G.L.R. 64; [1992] 38 E.G. 147; [1992] N.P.C. 25; [1991] 14 E.G. 108, CA 12.29
Dobson v. Groves, R. v. Dobson (1844) 6 C.B. 637; 14 L.J.Q.B. 17; 1 New Pract. Cas. 101; 4 L.T. (o.s.) 155; 9 Jur. 86; 115 E.R. 239 .... 16.49
Dodds v. Walker [1981] 1 W.L.R. 1027; (1981) 125 S.J. 463; [1981] 2 All E.R. 609; (1981) 42 P. & C.R. 131, HL; *affirming* [1980] 1 W.L.R. 1061; (1980) 124 S.J. 575; [1980] 2 All E.R. 507; (1980) 40 P. & C.R. 487; (1980) 255 E.G. 53, CA 10.37, 12.32, 13.28, 14.24, 14.109
Dodson Bull Carpet Co. Ltd v. City of London Corporation [1975] 1 W.L.R. 781; (1974) 119 S.J. 320; [1975] 2 All E.R. 497; (1974) 29 P. & C.R. 311 .... 12.20
Doe *d*. Aslin v. Summersett (1830) 1 B. & A.D. 135; 109 E.R. 738 .... 12.24

xvii

TABLE OF CASES

—— *d.* Bradford v. Watkins (1806) 7 East 551; 3 Smith K.B. 255; 102 E.R. 1232 .... 12.54
—— *d.* Cheny v. Batten (1775) 1 Cowp. 423 .... 12.16
—— *d.* Dagget v. Snowdon (1779) 2 Wm. Bl. 1224; 96 E.R. 720 .... 13.108
—— *d.* Heapy v. Howard (1809) 11 East 498; 103 E.R. 1096 .... 12.15
—— *d.* Macartney v. Crick (1805) 5 Esp. 196 .... 12.54
—— *d.* Rodd v. Archer (1811) 14 East 244; 104 E.R. 595 .... 12.17
—— *d.* Spicer v. Lea [1809] 11 East 312 .... 12.29
—— *d.* Winnall v. Broad (1841) 2 Man. & G. 523; Drinkwater 113; 2 Scott N.R. 685; 10 L.J.C.P. 80; 133 E.R. 855 .... 10.59
Donaldson's Hospital Trustees v. Esslemont 1926 S.L.T. 526 .... 13.116
Dow Agrochemicals v. E.A. Lane (North Lynn) Ltd [1965] E.G.D. 295; (1965) 192 E.G. 737; 115 L.J. 76 .... 8.18, 12.7, 12.50
Dowse v. Coxe (1825) 3 Bing. 20; 10 Moore C.P. 272; 3 L.J. (o.s.) C.P. 127; 130 E.R. 420 ... 16.52
Dreyfus (Louis) & Co. v. Arunachala Ayya (1931) L.R. 58 ind. App. 381, P.C. 16.49, 16.56
Drury v. Molins (1801) 6 Ves. 328; 31 E.R. 1076 .... 10.55
Duke of Westminster v. Guild [1985] Q.B. 688; [1984] 3 W.L.R. 630; (1984) 128 S.J. 581; [1984] 3 All E.R. 144; (1984) 48 P. & C.R. 42; (1983) 267 E.G. 763, CA 1.44
Dundee Corporation v. Guthrie 1969 S.L.T. 93 .... 11.3.7, 16.24
Dunn v. Fidoe [1950] W.N. 419; 66 T.L.R. (Pt. 2) 611; 94 S.J. 579; [1950] 2 All E.R. 685 . 8.16, 8.19
Dunstan v. Benney [1938] K.B. 1; 107 L.J.K.B. 311; 158 L.T. 34; 54 T.L.R. 167; 81 S.J. 1039; [1937] 4 All E.R. 510 .... 13.27

Eagle Star Insurance Co. v. Yuval Insurance Co. [1978] 1 Lloyd's Rep. 357 .... 6.23
Earl of Plymouth v. Glamorgan County Council (1974) 232 E.G. 1235, CC 8.13
East Coast Amusement Co. Ltd v. British Transport Board [1965] A.C. 58; [1963] 2 W.L.R. 1426; *sub nom.* "Wonderland", Cleethorpes, *Re'* East Coast Amusement Co. Ltd v. British Railways Board, 107 S.J. 455; [1963] 2 All E.R. 775, HL; *affirming* [1962] Ch. 696; [1962] 2 W.L.R. 776; 106 S.J. 175; [1962] 2 All E.R. 92, CA; *affirming* [1962] 2 W.L.R. 165; 106 S.J. 15; [1962] 1 All E.R. 68 .... 11.21
Eastern Counties Ry. and Eastern Union Ry., *Re* (1863) 3 De G.J. & S. 610; 2 New Rep. 538; 46 E.R. 773 .... 16.66
Eastham v. Tyler (1847) 2 Saund. & C. 136; 9 L.T (o.s.) 250 .... 16.35
Eaton v. Swetenham [1912] E.G.D. 98 .... 13.6
Ecclesiastical Commissioners for England v. National Provincial Bank Ltd. [1935] 1 K.B. 566; 104 L.J.K.B. 352; 153 L.T. 23; 51 T.L.R. 377; 79 S.J. 305 .... 13.116
Edell v. Dulieu [1924] A.C. 38; 93 L.J.K.B. 286; 130 L.T. 390; 40 T.L.R. 84; 68 S.J. 183; HL; *affirming* [1923] 2 K.B. 247 .... 9.21, 12.5, 13.12
Edinburgh Corporation v. Gray 1948 S.C. 538 .... 13.119
Edinburgh Magistrates v. Lowine (1903) 5 F. 711; 40 Sc.L.R. 741 .... 16.35
Edwards v. Bairstow [1956] A.C. 14; [1955] 3 W.L.R. 410; 99 S.J. 558; [1955] 3 All E.R. 48; [1955] T.R. 209; 48 R. & I.T. 534; 36 T.C. 207; 34 A.T.C. 198; HL; *reversing* [1954] T.R. 155; 47 R. & I.T. 340; 33 A.T.C. 131; T.C. Leaflet No. 1692, CA; *restoring* [1954] T.R. 65; 4 R. & I.T.177; 33 A.T.C. 58; T.C. Leaflet No. 1680 .... 16.61
Edwin Jones v. Thyssen (Great Britain) Limited [1991] 57 B.L.R. 116, CA 6.17
Egerton v. Rutter [1951] 1 K.B. 472; [1951] 1 T.L.R. 58 .... 7.13, 12.81.2, 17.4, 17.23
Eldon (Lord) v. Hedley Bros. [1935] 2 K.B. 1; 104 L.J.K.B. 334; 152 L.T. 507; 51 T.L.R. 313; 79 S.J. 270 .... 10.60, 10.67
Electricity Supply Nominees Ltd v. London Clubs Ltd [1988] 2 E.G.L.R. 152; [1988] 34 E.G. 71 .... 11.7
Elite Investments Ltd v. Bainbridge Silencers Ltd [1986] 2 E.G.L.R. 43; (1986) 280 E.G. 1001 10.28
Elitestone Ltd v. Morris [1997] 1 W.L.R. 687; [1997] 27 E.G. 116, HL 2.12, 3.10, 19.15
Ellerby v. March [1954] 2 Q.B. 357; [1954] 3 W.L.R. 53; 118 J.P. 382; 98 S.J. 404; [1954] 2 All E.R. 375; 47 R. & I.T. 335; 52 L.G.R. 397; CA; *affirming* [1953] C.P.L. 674; 46 R. & I.T. 718; 162 E.G. 424 .... 11.33
Ellis v. Lewin (1963) 107 S.J. 851; [1963] E.G.D. 434; (1963) 188 E.G. 493 .... 16.48, 16.66
Ellison v. Bray (1864) 9 L.T. 730 .... 16.49
Elmcroft Developments Ltd. v. Tankersley-Sawyer (1984) 15 H.L.R. 63; (1984) 270 E.G. 140, CA 10.28
Elsden v. Pick [1980] 1 W.L.R. 898; (1980) 124 S.J. 312; [1980] 3 All E.R. 235; (1980) 40 P. & C.R. 550; (1980) 254 E.G. 503, CA 4.14, 11.44, 12.4, 12.60, 13.17
Elwes v. Maw (1802) 3 East 38; 102 E.R. 510 .... 10.34
Enfield London Borough Council v. Pott [1990] 2 E.G.L.R. 7 .... 11.9, 11.15

TABLE OF CASES

England v. Shearburn (1884) 52 L.T. 22; 49 J.P. 86 .... 13.113
Enoch and Zaretsky, Bock & Co., *Re* [1910] 1 K.B. 327; 79 L.J.K.B. 363; 101 L.T. 801   16.37, 16.39, 16.66
Epps v. Ledger (1972) 225 E.G. 1373 .... 9.4, 10.3
Epsom and Ewell Borough Council v. Bell (C.) (Tadworth) Ltd [1983] 1 W.L.R. 379; (1983) 127 S.J. 121; [1983] 2 All E.R. 59; (1983) 46 P. & C.R. 143; (1983) 81 L.G.R. 613; (1983) 266 E.G. 808 .... 9.6, 9.12, 9.29
Erich Schroeder, The [1974] 1 Lloyd's Rep. 192 .... 16.66
Errington v. Errington and Woods [1952] 1 K.B. 290; [1952] 1 T.L.R. 231; 96 S.J. 119; [1952] 1 All E.R. 149; [214 L.T. 35; 96 S.J. 67; 97 S.J. 220, 255, 273, 364; 102 L.J. 355; 15 M.L.R. 236; 16 M.L.R. 1, 215; 68 L.Q.R. 337; 69 L.Q.R. 466; 16 Conv. 54, 71; 19 Sol. 75], CA   9.4
Erskine v. Adeane, Bennett's Claim (1873) 8 Ch. App. 756; 42 L.J. Ch. 835; 29 L.T. 234; 38 J.P. 20; 21 W.R. 802 .... 10.74
Esselte A.B. v. Pearl Assurance plc (1997) 1 E.G.L.R. 73 .... 4.5
Estates Projects Ltd v. Greenwich London Borough (1979) 251 E.G. 851 .... 11.21, 19.6
European Central Railway, *Re* [1876] 4 Ch. D. 33 .... 12.55
Evans v. Jones [1955] 2 Q.B. 58; [1955] 2 W.L.R. 936; 99 S.J. 305; [1955] 2 All E.R. 118; 53 L.G.R. 377 .... 10.10, 10.83, 13.81, 13.85, 13.92, 13.99
—— v. Lloyd [1912] E.G.D. 392 .... 13.27
—— v. Rees (1839) 10 A. & E. 151; 2 Per. & Dav. 626; 113 E.R. 58 .... 16.58
—— v. Roberts (1826) 5 B. & C. 829 .... 10.78
—— v. Roper [1960] 1 W.L.R. 814; 124 J.P. 371; 104 S.J. 604; [1960] 2 All E.R. 507 .. 12.33, 12.36, 12.41, 16.11
—— v. Tompkins [1993] 2 E.G.L.R. 6; [1993] 33 E.G. 86; [1993] E.G.C.S. 18, CA 9.4, 9.15
Evans (F.R.) (Leeds) Ltd v. English Electric Co. Ltd (1977) 36 P. & C.R. 185; (1977) 245 E.G. 657 .... 2.16, 11.6, 16.21, 16.32
Evans and Glamorgan County Council, *Re* (1912) 76 J.P. 468; 56 S.J. 668; 10 L.G.R. 805 .... 13.27
Everglade Maritime Inc. v. Schiffahrts-gesellschaft Detlef von Appen GmbH; Maria, The [1993] Q.B. 780; [1993] 3 W.L.R. 176; [1993] 3 All E.R. 748; [1993] 2 Lloyd's Rep. 168, CA; *affirming* [1993] 1 W.L.R. 33; [1992] 3 All E.R. 851; [1992] 2 Lloyd's Rep. 167 .... 16.72
Evers' Trust, *Re*, Papps v. Evers [1980] 1 W.L.R. 1327; (1980) 124 S.J. 562; [1980] 3 All E.R. 399; (1980) 10 Fam. Law 245, CA 14.62
E.W.P. Ltd v. Moore [1992] Q.B. 460; [1992] 2 W.L.R. 184; [1992] 1 All E.R. 880; (1991) 135 S.J. 135; [1992] I.C.R. 109; [1992] 2 E.G.L.R. 4; [1991] 45 E.G. 180; [1991] E.G.C.S. 90; [1991] N.P.C. 101; *The Times*, September 10, 1991, CA 9.20, 14.12
Expert Clothing Service & Sales v. Hillgate House [1986] Ch. 340; [1985] 3 W.L.R. 359; (1985) 129 S.J. 484; [1985] 2 All E.R. 998; (1985) 50 P. & C.R. 317; (1985) 275 E.G. 1011, 1129, CA 2.24, 12.61.12, 12.76.1

Fahy's Will Trusts, *Re* [1962] 1 W.L.R. 17; 106 S.J. 15; [1962] 1 All E.R. 73 .... 16.72
Fairclough Building Ltd v. Vale of Belvoir Superstore Ltd [1990] 56 B.L.R. 74; 28 Con. L.R. 1   16.47
Fairmount Investments Ltd. v. Secretary of State for the Environment [1976] 1 W.L.R. 1255; (1976) 120 S.J. 801; [1976] 2 All E.R. 865, HL; *affirming* (1975) 119 S.J. 866; [1976] J.P.L. 161, CA; *reversing* [1975] J.P.L. 285 .... 16.48
Fairweather v. St. Marylebone Property Company Ltd [1963] A.C. 510; [1962] 2 W.L.R. 1020; 106 S.J. 368; [1962] 2 All E.R. 288; [233 L.T. 298; 78 L.Q.R. 541; 106 S.J. 639; 26 Conv. 316; 112 L.J. 470, 563; 97 I.L.T.R. 1], HL; *affirming sub nom.* St. Marylebone Property Co v. Fairweather [1962] 1 Q.B. 498; [1961] 3 W.L.R. 1083; 105 S.J. 947; [1961] 3 All E.R. 560; [78 L.Q.R. 33; 25 M.L.R. 249; 26 Conv. 81]; [1961] C.L.Y. 4967, CA 15.15
Falconar v. South Shields Corporation (1895) 11 T.L.R. 223 .... 10.13
Fallon v. Calvert [1960] 2 Q.B. 201; [1960] 2 W.L.R. 346; 104 S.J. 106; [1960] 1 All E.R. 281   16.39
Family Management v. Gray (1979) 253 E.G. 369, CA 13.94
Farimani v. Gates (1984) 128 S.J. 615; (1984) 271 E.G. 887, CA 12.61.16
Farrer v. Nelson (1885) 15 Q.B.D. 258; 54 L.J.Q.B. 385; 52 L.T. 766; 1 T.L.R. 483; 49 J.P. 725; 33 W.R. 80 .... 10.74, 10.75, 10.77
Farrow v. Orttewell [1933] Ch. 480; 102 L.J. Ch. 133; 149 L.T. 101; 49 T.L.R. 251 ..... 13.12, 13.22, 13.116, 16.15
Faulks v. Faulks [1992] 1 E.G.L.R. 9; [1992] 15 E.G. 82 .... 18.28
Faure Fairclough Ltd v. Premier Oil and Cake Mills Ltd (1967) 112 S.J. 86; [1968] 1 Lloyd's Rep. 237; 118 New L.J. 325 .... 16.66
Faviell v. Gaskoin (1852) 7 Exch. 273; 21 L.J. Ex. 85; 18 L.T. (o.s.) 226; 15 J.P. 360; 155 E.R. 949 .... 13.51, 13.113

TABLE OF CASES

Fawcett (Thomas) & Sons Ltd v. Thompson [1954] E.G.D. 5 .... 9.7, 12.61.16
Fawke v. Viscount Chelsea [1980] Q.B. 441; [1979] 3 W.L.R. 508; (1979) 123 S.J. 387; [1979]
    3 All E.R. 568; (1979) 38 P. & C.R. 504; (1979) 250 E.G. 855, CA 2.24
Featherstone v. Staples [1986] 1 W.L.R. 861; (1986) 130 S.J. 482; [1986] 2 All E.R. 461; (1986)
    52 P. & C.R. 287; [1986] 1 E.G.L.R. 6; (1986) 278 E.G. 867, CA, *affirming* (1985) 129 S.J.
    66; (1984) 49 P. & C.R. 273; (1984) 273 E.G. 193 .... 12.32, 12.76, 13.36, 14.8
Fenceline Ltd v. Simms (W.J.) Sons & Cooke Ltd (1972) 224 E.G. 1041 .... 16.72
Fenner v. Blake [1900] 1 Q.B. 426 .... 1.13
Fermier v. Maund (1638) 1 Rep. Ch. 116; 21 E.R. 524 .... 10.55
Field v. Barkworth (1985) 129 S.J. 891; [1986] 1 All E.R. 362; (1985) 51 P. & C.R. 182; [1986]
    1 E.G.L.R. 46; (1985) 277 E.G. 189 .... 12.76.1
Finbow v. Air Ministry [1963] 1 W.L.R. 697; 107 S.J. 535; [1963] 2 All E.R. 647 .... 9.4, 9.6
Findlay v. Munro 1917 S.C. 419; 54 Sc.L.R. 316; 15 L.T. 203 .... 11.21, 13.68
Fisher v. Wellfair (P.G.) Ltd, Fox v. Wellfair (P.G.) Ltd (1981) 125 S.J. 413; [1981] 2 Lloyd's
    Rep. 514; [1981] Com. L.R. 140; [1982] 19 Build. L.R. 52; (1981) 263 E.G. 589, 657, CA;
    (1979) 124 S.J. 15 .... 11.33, 12.61.12, 16.34, 16.44, 16.47, 16.66, 16.67
Fleming v. Snook (1842) 5 Beav. 250; 49 E.R. 574 .... 10.59, 12.5
Fletcher v. Robertson 1919 56 S.L.R. 305; 1919 1 S.L.T. 260 .... 11.33
Flexman v. Corbett [1930] 1 Ch. 672 .... 1.45
Flight v. Bentley (1835) 7 Sim. 149; 4 L.J. Ch. 262; 58 E.R. 793 .... 13.97
Flint v. Fox (1956) 106 L.J. 828 .... 12.56
Forbes-Sempill's Trustees v. Brown 1954 S.L.C.R. 36 .... 12.61.14
Forsyth-Grant v. Salmon 1961 S.L.T. 262 .... 16.64
Forte & Co. v. General Accident Life Assurance (1987) 54 P. & C.R. 9; [1986] 2 E.G.L.R. 115;
    (1986) 279 E.G. 1227 .... 2.16, 2.19, 3.5
Foster v. Great Western Railway (1882) 8 Q.B.D. 515; 51 L.J.Q.B. 233; 46 L.T. 74; 30 W.R.
    398; 4 Ry. & Can. Tr. Cas. 58 .... 16.72
Fox v. Wellfair (P.G.) Ltd. *See* Fisher v. Wellfair (P.G.) Ltd; Fox v. Wellfair (P.G.) Ltd
Fox and Widley v. Guram [1998] 03 E.G. 142, Q.B.D. 6.9, 6.12
Francovich v. Haly (C-6/90) [1991] E.C.R.I. - 5357; [1993] 2 C.M.L.R. 66 .... 12.56
Frankland v. Capstick [1959] 1 W.L.R. 205; 227 L.T. 64; [1959] 1 All E.R. 209 .... 12.29
Freeman v. Evans [1922] 1 Ch. 36; 91 L.J. Ch. 195; 125 L.T. 722 .... 12.16
French v. Elliott [1960] 1 W.L.R. 40; 104 S.J. 52; [1959] 3 All E.R. 866 .... 12.28, 12.57, 12.61.8,
    12.61.11, 16.21
Friends Provident Life Office v. British Railways Board [1996] 1 All E.R. 336; [1995] 2
    E.G.L.R. 55; [1995] 48 E.G. 106; [1995] N.P.C. 143; *The Times*, July 31, 1995; *The
    Independent*, September 14, 1995, CA 1.13
Fuller v. Judy Properties (1991) 64 P. & C.R. 176; [1992] 1 E.G.L.R. 75; [1992] 14 E.G. 106;
    [1991] N.P.C. 142; *The Times*, December 30, 1991, CA; *reversing* [1991] 2 E.G.L.R. 41;
    [1991] 31 E.G. 63 .... 10.7

Gairneybridge Farm Ltd and King 1974 S.L.T. (Land Ct.) 8 .... 9.9
Gale v. Bates (1864) 3 H. & C. 84; 4 New Rep. 66; 33 L.J. Ex. 235; 10 L.T. 304; 10 Jur.
    (N.S.) 734; 12 W.R. 715; 159 E.R. 457 .... 10.59, 10.60
Galloway v. Keyworth (1854) 15 C.B. 228; 23 L.J.C.P. 218; 2 C.L.R. 860; 139 E.R. 408 ...... 16.49
Galloway (Earl) v. McClelland 1915 S.C. 1062; 52 Sc.L.R. 822; 2 S.L.T. 128 .... 11.21, 13.68, 13.69
Gardner v. Beck [1947] E.G.D. 169; (1947) 150 E.G. 458 .... 13.46, 13.61
Garton v. Hunter [1969] 2 Q.B. 37; [1968] 2 W.L.R. 86; 133 J.P. 162; (1968) S.J. 924; [1969] 1
    All E.R. 451; 67 L.G.R. 229; 15 R.R.C. 145; CA; *reversing* 13 R.R.C. 375; [1968] J.P.L.
    97; 204 E.G. 1285; [1967] R.A. 448 .... 16.66
Gartside v. Gartside (1796) 3 Anst. 735; 145 E.R. 1023 .... 16.66
Gas Light & Coke Co. v. Holloway (1885) 52 L.T. 434; 49 J.P. 344 .... 13.116, 16.15
Gatliffe v. Dunn (1738) Barnes 55; 94 E.R. 804 .... 16.56
Germax Securities Ltd v. Spiegal (1978) 123 S.J. 164; (1978) 37 P. & C.R. 204; (1978) 250 E.G.
    449, CA 12.29
Giacomo Costa Fu Andrea v. British Italian Trading Co. [1963] 1 Q.B. 201; [1962] 3 W.L.R.
    512; 106 S.J. 219; [1962] 2 All E.R. 53; *sub nom.* Andrea v. British Italian Trading Co.
    [1962] 1 Lloyd's Rep. 151, CA; *affirming* [1961] 2 Lloyd's Rep. 392 .... 16.49, 16.68
Gisbourne v. Burton [1989] Q.B. 390; (1989) 57 P. & C.R. 192, CA 15.18
Givaudan & Co. Ltd v. Minister of Housing and Local Government [1967] 1 W.L.R. 250; 131
    J.P. 79; 110 S.J. 371; [1966] 3 All E.R. 696; 18 P. & C.R. 88; 64 L.G.R. 352; 198 E.G. 585 . 16.56,
    16.68

TABLE OF CASES

Gladstone v. Bower [1960] 2 Q.B. 384; [1960] 3 W.L.R. 575; 104 S.J. 763 [1960] 3 All E.R. 353; 58 L.G.R. 313, CA; *affirming* [1960] 1 Q.B. 170; [1959] 3 W.L.R. 815; 103 S.J. 835; [1959] 3 All E.R. 475; 58 L.G.R. 75 ... 8.5, 9.1–9.3, 9.20, 9.21, 12.5, 13.17, 14.12, 14.62, 18.21, 19.3, 19.17
Gladwin v. Chilcote (1841) 9 Dowl. 550; Woll. 189; 5 J.P. 531; 5 Jur. 749 .... 16.34
Glasgow Heritable Trust Ltd 1977 S.L.T. 44 .... 16.56
Glass v. Inland Revenue 1915 S.C. 449 .... 11.6
Glendyne (Lord) v. Rapley [1978] 1 W.L.R. 601; (1978) 122 S.J. 247; [1978] 2 All E.R. 110; (1978) 246 E.G. 573, CA 1.20, 8.18
Godbold v. Martin (the Newsagents) [1983] 2 E.G.L.R. 128; (1983) 268 E.G. 1202 .... 2.19, 3.5
Godfrey v. Waite [1951] E.G.D. 9; (1951) 157 E.G. 582 .... 8.14, 8.20
Gold v. Jacques Amand Ltd [1992] 2 E.G.L.R. 1; (1991) 63 P. & C.R. 1; [1992] 27 E.G. 140 . 9.4
Goldsack v. Shore [1950] 1 K.B. 708; 66 T.L.R. (Pt. 1) 636; 94 S.J. 192; [1950] 1 All E.R. 276 ...8.17, 9.4, 9.5, 9.9, 9.16, 13.116, 16.15
Goldsworthy v. Brickell [1987] Ch. 378; [1987] 2 W.L.R. 133; (1987) 131 S.J. 102; [1987] 1 All E.R. 853; (1987) 84 L.S. Gaz. 654, CA 12.42
Gordon v. Selico Co. [1986] 1 E.G.L.R. 71; (1986) 18 H.L.R. 219; (1986) 278 E.G. 53, CA; *affirming* (1985) 129 S.J. 347; [1985] 2 E.G.L.R. 79; (1984) 275 E.G. 841; (1985) 82 L.S. Gaz. 2087 .... 1.44
Gough v. Gough [1891] 2 Q.B. 665; 60 L.J.Q.B. 726; 65 L.T. 110; 7 T.L.R. 608; 39 W.R. 593   17.6
—— v. Howard (1801) Peake Add Cas. 197 .... 10.59
Gould v. Staffordshire Potteries Waterworks Co. (1850) 5 Ex. 214; 1 L.M. & P. 264; 6 Ry. & Can. Cas. 568; 19 L.J. Ex. 281; 15 L.T. (o.s.) 117; 14 Jur. 528; 155 E.R. 92 .... 16.52
Government of Ceylon v. Chandris. *See* Ceylon (Government of) v. Chandris
Governors of Peabody Donation Fund v. Parkinson (Sir Lindsay) & Co. *See* Peabody Donation Fund v. Sir Lindsay Parkinson
Graham v. Lamont 1971 S.C. 170; 1970 S.L.T. 10 .... 12.39, 12.48
Grant, *ex p. See* R. v. Agricultural Land Tribunal (Eastern Province), *ex p.* Grant.
Graves v. Weld (1833) 3 B. & Ad. 105 .... 10.78
Gray v. Ashburton (Lord) [1917] A.C. 26; 86 L.J.K.B. 224; 115 L.T. 729; 81 J.P. 17; 61 S.J. 129 .... 16.72
Grayless v. Watkinson [1990] 1 E.G.L.R. 6; [1990] 21 E.G. 163, CA 10.18
GREA Real Property Investments Ltd v. Williams (1979) 250 E.G. 651 .... 11.21, 19.6
Great Western Railway Co. v. Smith. *See* Smith v. Great Western Railway Co.
Greaves v. Mitchell (1971) 222 E.G. 1395 .... 12.35, 12.36
Greenshields v. Roger 1922 S.C. (H.L.) 140 .... 13.48, 13.116
Greenwich London Borough Council v. McGrady (1983) 46 P. & C.R. 223; (1983) 81 L.G.R. 288; (1982) 267 E.G. 515, CA 12.54
Gregson and Armstrong, *Re* (1894) 70 L.T. 106; 38 S.J. 237; 10 R. 408 .... 16.34
Grewar v. Moncur's Curator Bonis 1916 S.C. 764; 2 S.L.T. 20 .... 15.20
Grieve & Sons v. Barr 1954 S.C. 414 .... 10.3
Griffiths v. Morris [1895] 1 Q.B. 866; 64 L.J.Q.B. 386; 15 R. 301; 43 W.R. 652 .... 16.72
—— v. Tombs (1833) 7 C. & P. 810 .... 13.108
Grounds v. Att.-Gen. of the Duchy of Lancaster [1989] 1 E.G.L.R. 6 [1989] 21 E.G. 73, CA . 19.14.1, 19.4.3
Grundy v. Hewson [1933] 1 K.B. 787; 102 L.J.K.B. 398; 149 L.T. 212; 49 T.L.R. 346; 77 S.J. 216 .... 17.2, 17.4
Gulliver v. Catt [1952] 2 Q.B. 308; [1952] 1 T.L.R. 956; 96 S.J. 245; [1952] 1 All E.R. 929; 50 L.G.R. 342; CA; *affirming* [1952] 1 T.L.R. 6; [1952] 1 All E.R. 97 .... 13.22, 13.83
Gunter (V.O.) v. New Town Oyster Fishery Co. Ltd (LVC/300–301/1976) (1977) 244 E.G. 140 .... 8.18
—— v.—— (No. 2) (1979) 124 S.J. 81; [1982] 1 H.L.R. 30; (1979) 253 E.G. 907 .... 16.56
—— v.—— (No. 3) (1981) 258 E.G. 1083 .... 16.56
Guthe v. Broatch 1956 S.C. 132; 1956 S.L.T. 170 .... 11.28
Gwillim v. Stone (1807), (1811) 3 Taunt. 433 .... 1.44

Hadley (Felix) & Co. v. Hadley [1898] 2 Ch. 680 .... 12.56
Hagee (London) v. Erikson (A.B.) and Larson [1976] Q.B. 209; [1975] 3 W.L.R. 272; 119 S.J. 354; [1975] 3 All E.R. 234; 29 P. & C.R. 512, CA 1.16
Haigh, *Re* Haigh v. Haigh (1861) 3 De G.F. & J. 157; 31 L.J. Ch. 420; 5 L.T. 507; 8 Jur (N.S.) 983; 45 E.R. 838 .... 16.36, 16.66
Haines v. Welch & Marriott (1868) L.R. 4 C.P. 91; 38 L.J.C.P. 118; 19 L.T. 422; 17 W.R. 163   10.78

TABLE OF CASES

Halfdan Greig & Co. A/S v. Sterling Coal & Navigation Corporation [1973] Q.B. 843; [1973] 2 W.L.R. 904; 117 S.J. 415; [1973] 2 All E.R. 1073; [1973] 1 Lloyd's Rep. 296, CA; *reversing* [1973] 2 W.L.R. 237; (1972) 117 S.J. 122; [1973] 1 All E.R. 545 .... 16.62
Halki Shipping Corp. v. Sopex Oils Ltd [1998] 2 All E.R. 23; *The Times*, January 19, 1998, CA 10.24
Halliday v. Fergusson (Wm.) & Sons 1961 S.C. 24; 1961 S.L.T. 176 ....12.61.14
—— v. Semple (1959) 110 L.J. 352; 75 Sh.Ct.Rep. 188; 1960 S.L.T. (Sh.Ct.) 11 .... 16.51, 16.66
Hallinan (Lady) v. Jones (1984) 272 E.G. 1081 .... 13.37, 13.100, 13.119, 17.18, 17.20
Hambros Bank Executor and Trustee Co. Ltd v. Superdrug Stores Ltd (1985) 274 E.G. 590 ... 11.21
Hamilton v. Peeke [1926] E.G.D. 175; (1926) L.J.C.C.R. 54 .... 16.55, 16.66
Hammersmith and Fulham London Borough Council v. Monk; Barnet London Borough Council v. Smith [1992] 1 A.C. 478; [1990] 3 W.L.R. 1144; [1992] 1 All E.R.I.; (1992) 136 S.J.L.B. 10; 90 L.G.R. 38; (1992) 24 H.L.R. 207; (1991) 63 P. & C.R. 373; [1992] 1 F.L.R. 465; [1992] 1 E.G.L.R. 65; [1992] 09 E.G. 135; [1992] Fam. Law 292; [1991] E.G.C.S. 130; (1991) 141 N.L.J. 1697; (1992) 156 L.G. Rev. 481; [1992] *Gazette*, 22 January, 32 [1991] N.P.C. 132; *The Times*, December 6, 1991; *The Independent*, December 10, 1991, HL; *affirming* (1990) 61 P. & C.R. 414; 89 L.G.R. 357; [1991] 1 E.G.L.R. 263; (1990) 23 H.L.R. 114; *The Times*, November 5, 1990, CA 4.6, 4.19, 12.24, 12.32
Hammon v. Fairbrother [1956] 1 W.L.R. 490; 100 S.J. 322; [1956] 2 All E.R. 108; 54 L.G.R. 271 .... 12.28
Hammond, *Re, ex p.* Hammond (1844) De G. 93; 14 L.J.Q.By. 14; 4 L.T. (o.s.) 215; 9 Jur. 358 15.20
—— v. Allen [1994] 1 All E.R. 307; (1992) 65 P. & C.R. 18; [1993] 08 E.G. 122; *The Times*, July 21, 1992 ....10.21, 10.24
Hampshire v. Wickens [1877] 7 Ch. D. 55 .... 1.45
Hanak v. Green [1958] 2 Q.B. 9; [1958] 2 W.L.R. 755; 102 S.J. 329; [1958] 2 All E.R. 141; [108 L.J. 500], CA 12.58
Hankey v. Clavering [1942] 2 K.B. 326 ....12.29, 12.30
Hanmer v. King (1887) 51 J.P. 804; 57 L.T. 367; 3 T.L.R. 526 .... 10.72
Hannaford v. Smallacombe [1994] 1 E.G.L.R. 9; (1995) 69 P. & C.R. 339; [1994] 15 E.G. 155; [1993] E.G.C.S. 204; [1993] N.P.C. 168; *The Times*, December 30, 1993, CA 12.56, 12.57, 12.61.9, 16.22
Harding v. Marshall (1983) 267 E.G. 161, CA 12.45, 12.53
Hare, *Re* (1839) 6 Bing. N.C. 158; 8 Dowl. 71; 8 Scott, 367; 133 E.R. 62 .... 16.49
Harley v. Moss [1962] E.G.D. 403; (1962) 181 E.G. 707 .... 12.28
Harmer v. Jumbil (Nigeria) Tin Areas [1921] 1 Ch. 200 .... 1.44
Harmsworth Pension Funds Trustees Ltd v. Charringtons Industrial Holdings Ltd [1985] 49 P. & C.R. 297; [1985] 1 E.G.L.R. 97; (1985) 274 E.G. 588 .... 2.24
Harper v. Taylor (1950) 100 L.J. 108; Cty. Ct. 12.81.2
Harries v. Barclays Bank [1997] 2 E.G.L.R. 14, CA 18.1, 18.16, 18.19, 18.21, 18.22, 18.31
Harris v. Black (1983) 46 P. & C.R. 366, CA 12.33
Harrison v. Ridgeway (1925) 133 L.T. 238; 23 L.G.R. 434 .... 13.116
Harrison-Broadley v. Smith [1964] 1 W.L.R. 456; 108 S.J. 136; [1964] 1 All E.R. 867, CA; *reversing* [1963] 1 W.L.R. 1262; 107 S.J. 618; [1963] 3 All E.R. 586 .... 9.4, 9.5, 9.17
Harrowby v. Snelson [1951] W.N. 11; 95 S.J. 108; [1951] 1 All E.R. 140 ....12.81.2, 17.23
Harte v. Frampton [1948] 1 K.B. 73; [1948] L.J.R. 1125; 63 T.L.R. 554; 91 S.J. 625; [1947] 2 All E.R. 604 .... 12.39
Harvey v. Shelton (1844) 7 Beav. 455; 13 L.J. Ch. 466; 3 L.T. (o.s.) 279; 49 R. 1141 .... 16.34
Harvey and Mann's Arbitration, *Re* (1920) 89 L.J.K.B. 687; 123 L.T. 242 .... 10.37, 13.27
Hasell v. McAulay, 116 J.P. 606; [1952] 2 All E.R. 825; 51 L.G.R. 96 .... 8.14, 14.42
Hassall v. Cholmondeley (1935) 79 S.J. 522; [1935] E.G.D. 82 .... 16.66
Hastie and Jenkerson v. McMahon [1990] 1 W.L.R. 1575; [1991] 1 All E.R. 255; (1990) 134 S.J. 725; [1990] R.V.R. 172, CA 17.22
Hayter v. Nelson Home Insurance [1990] 2 Lloyd's Rep. 265; 23 Con. L.R. 88; *The Times*, March 29, 1990 .... 10.24
Heap v. Wilkes, *The Times*, October 29, 1910 .... 10.64
Heaven and Kesterton Ltd v. Sven Widaeus A/B [1958] 1 W.L.R. 248; 102 S.J. 161; [1958] 1 All E.R. 420; [1958] 1 Lloyd's Rep. 101 .... 16.66, 16.67, 16.69, 16.72
Hegarty v. Winters (1953) 162 E.G. 89 .... 16.48
Hemns v. Wheeler [1948] 2 K.B. 61; [1948] L.J.R. 1024; 64 T.L.R. 236; 92 S.J. 194 .... 16.61
Hendry v. Walker 1927 S.L.T. 333 .... 13.22
Henn and Darby v. D.P.P. [1980] 2 W.L.R. 597; (1980) 124 S.J. 290; (1980) 71 Cr. App. R. 44; *sub nom.* R. v. Henn; R. v. Darby [1980] 2 All E.R. 166; *sub nom.* D.P.P. v. Henn and Darby [1980] 2 C.M.L.R. 229, HL; *affirming sub nom.* R. v. Henn; R. v. Darby [1978] 1

TABLE OF CASES

W.L.R. 1031; (1978) 122 S.J. 555; [1978] 3 All E.R. 1190; (1978) 69 Cr. App. R. 137; [1979] Crim. L.R. 113; [1978] 2 C.M.L.R. 688, CA; *affirming sub nom.* R. v. Darby, Henn and Thornton [1977] Crim. L.R. 743, Ipswich Crown Ct. 18.7
Hereford and Worcester County Council v. Newman [1975] 1 W.L.R. 901; 119 S.J. 354; [1975] 2 All E.R. 673; 73 L.G.R. 461; 30 P. & C.R. 381, CA; *affirming in part* [1974] 1 W.L.R. 938; 118 S.J. 330; [1974] 2 All E.R. 867; 72 L.G.R. 616 .... 12.60
Hewetson and Pennington-Ramsden's Arbitration, *Re* (1966) 116 New L.J. 1613, Cty.Ct. 13.119
Heyes (J.) v. (Earl of) Derby (1984) 2 E.G.L.R. 87; (1984) 272 E.G. 939, CA 6.87
Hickmott v. Dorset County Council (1977) 35 P. & C.R. 195; [1977] J.P.L. 715; 243 E.G. 671, CA 16.48
Hicks v. Richardson (1797) 1 Bos. & P. 93; 126 E.R. 796 .... 16.53
Hickson & Welch Ltd v. Cann (Note) (1977) 40 P. & C.R. 218, CA. 1.17, 8.15
Hill v. Barclay [1810] 16 Ves. Jun. 402; (1811) 18 Ves. 56 .... 10.33
Hill v. Booth [1930] 1 K.B. 381 .... 2.2
Hill Samuel Life Assurance v. Preston Borough Council [1990] 2 E.G.L.R. 127; [1990] 36 E.G. 111 .... 2.16
Hilton v. Green (1862) 2 F. & F. 821 .... 10.74
Historic House Hotels v. Cadogan Estates [1995] 11 E.G. 140; [1994] E.G.C.S. 142; [1994] N.P.C. 119, CA; *affirming* [1993] 2 E.G.L.R. 151; [1993] 30 E.G. 94; [1993] N.P.C. 28 .... 2.19, 3.5
Holdcroft v. Staffordshire County Council [1994] 2 E.G.L.R. 1 ..... 18.11, 18.14, 18.16, 18.18, 18.21
Holder v. Holder [1968] Ch. 353; [1968] 2 W.L.R. 237; (1967) 112 S.J. 17; [1968] 1 All E.R. 665, CA; *reversing in part* [1966] 3 W.L.R. 229; 110 S.J. 569; [1966] 2 All E.R. 116 .. 9.4, 9.17
Holding and Management v. Property Holding and Investment Trust [1989] 1 W.L.R. 1313; [1990] 1 E.G.L.R. 65; [1990] 1 All E.R. 938; (1990) 134 S.J. 262; (1989) 21 H.L.R. 596; [1990] 05 E.G. 75; [1989] L.S. Gaz. November 29, 38, CA 10.28
Holding v. Pigott (1831) 7 Bing. 465; 5 Moo. & P. 427; 9 L.J. (o.s.) C.P. 125; 131 E.R. 180 .. 13.113
Holiday Fellowship v. Hereford [1959] 1 W.L.R. 211; 103 S.J. 156; [1959] 1 All E.R. 433; [103 S.J. 231; 109 L.J. 196; 75 L.Q.R. 153; 23 Conv. 144], CA 10.12
Hollings v. Swindell [1950] E.G.D. 11; (1950) 155 E.G. 269 .... 10.6
Hollington Brothers v. Rhodes [1951] W.N. 437, [1951] 2 T.L.R. 691; [1951] 2 All E.R. 578n.; [18 Sol. 243; 212 L.T. 264; 95 S.J. 606, 722; 15 Conv. 355] 1.43
Holme v. Brunskill [1878] 3 Q.B.D. 495 .... 1.13
Hood Barrs v. Howard (1967) 201 E.G. 768; 13 R.R.C. 164, CA; *affirming* LVC/354/1965 [1966] R.V.R. 224; 12 R.R.C. 118; [1966] R.A. 212; 116 New L.J. 1118 .... 15.20
Hooper, *Re* (1867) L.R. 2 Q.B. 367; 8 B. & S. 100; 36 L.J.Q.B. 97; 15 W.R. 443 . 16.22, 16.35, 16.66
Horn v. Sunderland Corporation [1941] 2 K.B. 26; 110 L.J.K.B. 353; 165 L.T. 298; 105 J.P. 223; 57 T.L.R. 404; 85 S.J. 212 [1941] 1 All E.R. 480; 39 L.G.R. 367 .... 11.6
Horrell v. St. John of Bletso (Lord) [1928] 2 K.B. 616; *sub nom.* Horrell v. Bletso, 97 L.J.K.B. 653; 139 L.T. 400 .... 17.4
Horton v. Kurzke [1971] 1 W.L.R. 769; (1970) 115 S.J. 287; [1971] 2 All E.R. 577; 22 P. & C.R. 661 .... 16.32
Hosier v. Goodall [1962] 2 Q.B. 401; [1962] 2 W.L.R. 157; 126 J.P. 52; 105 S.J. 1085; [1962] 1 All E.R. 30; 60 L.G.R. 500 .... 17.18
Hotchkin v. Leggott (1966) 197 E.G. 669 .... 13.99
Houison-Craufurd's Trustees v. Davies 1951 S.C. 1 .... 16.15
Howell's Application, *Re* [1972] Ch. 509; [1972] 2 W.L.R. 1346; 116 S.J. 446; [1972] 3 All E.R. 662; (1971) 23 P. & C.R. 266 .... 13.24
Howkins v. Jardine [1951] 1 K.B. 614; [1951] 1 T.L.R. 135; 95 S.J. 75; [1951] 1 All E.R. 320 ...8.16, 8.17–8.19
Howson v. Buxton (1928) 97 L.J.K.B. 749; 139 L.T. 504 .... 13.28, 13.36, 19.9.1
Hudson (A.) Pty Ltd v. Legal & General Life of Australia Ltd [1986] 2 E.G.L.R. 130; (1986) 280 E.G. 1434, PC 6.86
Hughes v. Homewood [1963] E.G.D. 670; (1963) 188 E.G. 875 .... 16.56, 16.68
—— Taylor [1950] E.G.D. 13; (1950)156 E.G. 141 .... 12.61.8
Hull and Meux (Lady), *Re* [1905] 1 K.B. 588; 74 L.J.K.B. 252; 92 L.T. 74; 21 T.L.R. 220; 49 S.J. 222; 53 W.R. 389 .... 10.4, 10.59
Hulme v. Brigham [1943] 1 K.B. 152 .... 3.10

Imperial Metal Industries (Kynoch) Ltd v. AUEW [1979] I.C.R. 23; [1979] 1 All E.R. 847; [1978] I.R.L.R. 407; CA 16.70
Inchiquin (Lord) v. Lyons (1887) 20 L.R.Ir. 474 .... 12.16

TABLE OF CASES

Inglewood Investment Co. Ltd v. Forestry Commission [1988] 1 W.L.R. 1278; (1988) 132 S.J. 1670; [1988] E.G.C.S. 137, CA; *affirming* [1988] 1 W.L.R. 959; (1988) 132 S.J. 933; [1988] 1 All E.R. 783 .... 10.75
Inglis v. Moir's Tutors (1871) 10M. (Ct. of Sess.) 204 .... 10.77
Inland Revenue Commissioners v. Clay [1914] 3 K.B. 466 .... 2.16
I.R.C. v. Luke. See Luke v. I.R.C.
Iredell v. Brocklehurst [1950] E.G.D. 15; (1950) 155 E.G. 268 .... 8.20
Irvine v. Elnon (1806) 8 East. 54; 103 E.R. 264 .... 16.58
Italica Holdings S.A. v. Bayadea [1985] 1 E.G.L.R. 70; (1985) 273 E.G. 888 .... 17.19
Itex Shipping Pte Ltd v. China Ocean Shipping Co. (The "Jing Hong Hai") [1989] 2 Lloyd's Rep. 522 .... 16.22

Jackson v. Hall; Williamson v. Thompson [1980] A.C. 854; [1980] 2 W.L.R. 118; (1979) 124 S.J. 62; [1980] 1 All E.R. 177; (1979) 39 P. & C.R. 436; (1979) 253 E.G. 145, HL; *reversing* Jackson v. Hall [1979] 2 W.L.R. 505; (1978) 123 S.J. 64; [1979] 1 All E.R. 449; (1978) 30 P. & C.R. 293, CA *and affirming* Williamson v. Thompson (1979) 251 E.G. 955 .... 14.8, 14.24, 14.53
Jacobs v. Chaudhuri [1968] 2 Q.B. 470 [1968] 2 W.L.R. 1098; (1968) 112 S.J. 135; [1968] 2 All E.R. 124; 19 P. & C.R. 286, CA 13.36
Jager v. Tolme & Runge & London Produce Clearing House [1916] 1 K.B. 939; 85 L.J.K.B. 1116; 114 L.T. 647; 32 T.L.R. 291 .... 16.56
James v. Lock (1977) 246 E.G. 395, CA 9.4, 9.15, 9.16
Jaquin v. Holland [1960] 1 W.L.R. 258; 104 S.J. 248; [1960] 1 All E.R. 402 .... 10.28
Javad v. Aqil [1991] 1 W.L.R. 1007; [1991] 1 All E.R. 243; [1990] 41 E.G. 61; (1991) 61 P. & C.R. 164; (1990) 140 N.L.J. 1232, CA 1.43
Jeffryes v. Evans (1865) 19 C.B. (N.S.) 246; 34 L.J.C.P. 261; 13 L.T. 72; 11 Jur. (N.S.) 584; 13 W.R. 864; 144 E.R. 781 .... 10.75
Jelley v. Buckman [1974] Q.B. 488; [1973] 3 W.L.R. 585; [1973] 3 All E.R. 853; 26 P. & C.R. 215; *sub nom.* Jelly v. Buckman, 117 S.J. 728, CA 11.31, 12.20
Jeune v. Queens Cross Properties [1974] Ch. 97; [1973] 3 W.L.R. 378; 117 S.J. 680; [1973] 3 All E.R. 97; 26 P. & C.R. 98; [118 S.J. 212] 10.33
Joel's Lease, *Re*, Berwick v. Baird 2 Ch. 359; 99 L.J.Ch. 529; 143 L.T. 765; 46 T.L.R. 424 ... 8.18
John v. George and Walton (1996) 71 P. & C.R. 375; [1996] 1 E.G.L.R. 7; [1996] 8 E.G. 140; [1995] N.P.C. 147, CA; *reversing* [1995] 22 E.G. 146; [1995] 1 E.G.L.R. 9, Ch. D . 1.19, 12.20, 12.50
Johnson v. Latham (1850) 19 L.J.Q.B. 329; 1 L.M. & P. 348; 15 L.T. (o.s.) 211 .... 16.56
—— v. Moreton [1980] A.C. 37; [1978] 3 W.L.R. 538; (1978) 122 S.J. 697; [1978] 3 All E.R. 37; (1978) 37 P. & C.R. 243; (1978) 247 E.G. 895; HL; *affirming* (1977) 35 P. & C.R. 378; 241 E.G. 759, CA 9.19, 9.24, 10.39, 10.53, 11.44, 12.3, 12.4, 12.32, 12.76, 13.46, 13.68, 13.82
Johnston & Sons v. Holland [1988] 1 E.G.L.R. 264, CA 1.44
Johnston v. Malcolm 1923 S.L.T. (Sh. Ct.) 81 .... 13.22
Jolly v. Brown. *See* Fox v. Jolly.
Jones v. Burgoyne [1963] E.G.D. 435; (1963) 188 E.G. 497 .... 12.39, 12.41
Jones v. Challenger [1961] 1 Q.B. 176; [1960] 2 W.L.R. 695; 104 S.J. 328; [1960] 1 All E.R. 785; [23 M.L.R. 703; 24 Conv. 240; 27 Sol. 321; [1960] C.L.J. 167], CA 14.62
—— v. Davies [1979] J.P.L. 317; (1977) 244 E.G. 897 .... 8.18
—— v. Evans [1923] 1 K.B. 12; 92 L.J.K.B. 35; 128 L.T. 228 .... 13.119
—— v. Gates [1954] 1 W.L.R. 222; 98 S.J. 61; [1954] 1 All E.R. 158; 52 L.G.R. 5 ...... 12.50, 12.83
—— v. Herxheimer [1950] 2 K.B. 106; 66 T.L.R. (Pt. 1) 403; 94 S.J. 97; [1950] 1 All E.R. 323 13.93
—— v. Lewis (1973) 117 S.J. 373; (1973) 25 P. & C.R. 375, CA 12.53, 12.54, 17.23
—— v. Owen [1997] 32 E.G. 85, Ch. D. 9.30
—— v. Pembrokeshire County Council [1967] 1 Q.B. 181; [1966] 2 W.L.R. 938; 110 S.J. 172; [1966] 1 All E.R. 1027; 64 L.G.R. 179 .... 16.23, 16.32, 16.68, 17.4
—— v. Sherwood Computer Services plc [1992] 1 W.L.R. 277; [1992] 2 All E.R. 170; *The Times*, December 14, 1989, CA 6.86
—— v. West Midlands Agricultural Land Tribunal (1962) 184 E.G. 78 .... 12.42
Jones and Carter, *Re* [1922] 2 Ch. 599; 91 L.J. Ch. 824; 127 L.T. 622; 38 T.L.R. 779; 66 S.J. 611 .... 16.32, 16.68, 17.4
Joyner v. Weeks [1891] 2 Q.B. 31; 60 L.J.Q.B. 510; 65 L.T. 16; 7 T.L.R. 509; 55 J.P. 725; 39 W.R. 583 .... 13.93
J.T. Sydenham & Co. Ltd v. Enichem Elastomers Ltd [1989] 1 E.G.L.R. 257 .... 6.87

TABLE OF CASES

Kammins Ballrooms Co. Ltd v. Zenith Investments (Torquay) Ltd [1971] A.C. 850; [1970] 3 W.L.R. 287; 114 S.J. 590; [1970] 2 All E.R. 871; 22 P. & C.R. 74, HL; *affirming* [1970] 1 Q.B. 673; [1969] 3 W.L.R. 799; 113 S.J. 640; [1969] 3 All E.R. 1268; 20 P. & C.R. 1087, CA 13.121, 14.24, 14.32
Katholische Kirchengemeinde St. Martinus Elten v. Landwirtschaftskammer Rheinland (C–463/93) January 23, 1997 .... 18.11, 18.14
Kaye v. Sutherland (1887) 20 Q.B.D. 147 .... 13.113
Keen v. Holland [1984] 1 W.L.R. 251; (1983) 127 S.J. 764; [1984] 1 All E.R. 75; (1984) 47 P. & C.R. 639; (1983) 269 E.G. 1043, CA 1.21, 1.43, 2.11, 4.16, 9.3, 9.17, 9.19, 9.21
—— v. Priest (1859) 4 H. & N. 236; 28 L.J. Ex. 157; 32 L.T. (o.s.) 319; 23 J.P. 216; 7 W.R. 376; 157 E.R. 829 .... 10.71
Kellett v. Alexander, Kellett v. Cady (1980) 257 E.G. 494; *sub nom.* Kellett v. Steel's Estate (1979) *Hamilton* No. 97, p. 140 .... 14.24, 14.25, 14.29
—— v. Steel's Estate. *See* Kellett v. Alexander.
Kempe v. Dillon-Trenchard (1951) 101 L.J. 417 .... 8.20
Kendall v. Hamilton (1879) 4 App. Cas. 504 .... 12.55
Kenny v. Preen [1963] 1 Q.B. 499; [1962] 3 W.L.R. 1233; 106 S.J. 854; [1962] 3 All E.R. 814; [79 L.Q.R. 21; 27 Conv. 75; 97 I.L.T. 113; 3 Osgoode Hall L.J. 132], CA 1.44
Kent v. Conniff [1953] 1 Q.B. 361; [1953] 2 W.L.R. 41; 97 S.J. 46; [1953] 1 All E.R. 155; 51 L.G.R. 77 .... 10.32, 10.64, 13.2, 13.83, 13.88, 13.90, 13.93, 13.116, 16.15
Kestell v. Langmaid [1950] 1 K.B. 233; 65 T.L.R. 699; 93 S.J. 726; [1949] 2 All E.R. 749 .... 12.4, 13.22
Keswick v. Wright 1924 S.C. 766 .... 13.27
King v. Earl Cadogan [1915] 3 K.B. 485 .... 2.2
King v. McKenna (Thomas) [1991] 2 Q.B. 480; [1991] 2 W.L.R. 1234; [1991] 1 All E.R. 653; 54 B.L.R. 48, *The Times*, January 30, 1991, CA 16.67
King v. Turner [1954] E.G.D. 7 .... 9.4, 13.27
——, decd. *Re*, Robinson v. Gray [1963] Ch. 459; [1963] 2 W.L.R. 629; 107 S.J. 134; [1963] 1 All E.R. 781; [1963] R.V.R. 245, CA; *reversing* [1962] 1 W.L.R. 632; 106 S.J. 509; [1962] 2 All E.R. 66; [1962] R.V.R. 621 .... 13.97
Kingswood Estate Co. Ltd v. Anderson [1963] 2 Q.B. 169; [1962] 3 W.L.R. 1102; 106 S.J. 651; [1962] 3 All E.R. 593, CA 12.9
Kinson Brothers v. Swinnerton (1961) 179 E.G. 691 .... 12.39
Kirby v. Robinson [1965] E.G.D. 236; (1965) 195 E.G. 363 .... 11.35, 16.32

K/S Norjarl A/S v. Hyundai Heavy Industries Co. [1992] Q.B. 863; [1991] 3 W.L.R. 1025; [1991] 3 All E.R. 211; [1991] 1 Lloyd's Rep. 524; [1991] E.G.C.S. 20; (1991) 141 N.L.J. 343; *The Independent*, February 22, 1991; *The Times*, March 12, 1991; *Financial Times*, March 5, 1991, CA; *affirming* [1991] 1 Lloyd's Rep. 260; *The Times*, November 8, 1990 . 16.26, 16.66
Kursell v. Timber Operators and Contractors Ltd [1923] 2 K.B. 202; 92 L.J.K.B. 607; 129 L.T. 21; 39 T.L.R. 419; 87 J.P. 79; 67 S.J. 557; 28 Conv. Cas. 376 .... 16.38

Ladds Radio and Television Service Ltd v. Docker (1973) 226 E.G. 1565 ...... 12.45, 12.61.15, 12.66
Ladyman v. Wirral Estates Limited [1968] 2 All E.R. 197; 19 P. & C.R. 781; [32 Conv. 297] . 12.14
Lambert v. F.W. Woolworth and Co. [1938] 1 Ch. 883; [1938] 2 All E.R. 664, CA 5.4, 11.21
Lampard v. Barker (1984) 272 E.G. 783, CA 9.3, 9.4, 9.9, 9.15
Lancaster and Macnamara, *Re* [1918] 2 K.B. 472; 87 L.J.K.B. 1250; 119 L.T. 440; 62 S.J. 681   13.44
Land v. Sykes [1992] 1 E.G.L.R. 1; [1992] 03 E.G. 115; [1991] E.G.C.S. 98, CA; *affirming* [1992] 1 E.G.L.R. 18; [1991] 16 E.G. 125 .... 12.16, 12.20, 12.29, 12.30
Land Securities v. Westminster City Council [1993] 1 W.L.R. 286; [1993] 4 All E.R. 124; (1992) 65 P. & C.R. 387; [1992] 44 E.G. 153; [1992] N.P.C. 125 .... 11.10
Land Settlement Association Ltd v. Carr [1944] K.B. 657; 114 L.J.K.B. 33; 171 L.T. 121; 60 T.L.R. 488; [1944] 2 All E.R. 126 .... 9.2, 9.3
Langham House Developments Ltd v. Brompton Securities Ltd [1980] 2 E.G.L.R. 117; (1980) 256 E.G. 719 .... 6.83
Latham v. Atwood (1638) Cro. Car. 515 .... 10.78
Laura Investments Co. v. Havering London Borough Council (No. 2) [1993] 1 E.G.L.R. 124; [1993] 08 E.G. 120; [1992] N.P.C. 117 .... 2.16
Law v. National Greyhound Racing Club Ltd [1983] 1 W.L.R. 1302; (1983) 127 S.J. 619; [1983] 3 All E.R. 300, CA 16.70
Law Land Co. Ltd. v. Consumers' Association Ltd (1980) 225 E.G. 617, CA 11.6

TABLE OF CASES

Lazarus Estates Limited v. Beasley [1956] 1 Q.B. 702; [1956] 2 W.L.R. 502; 100 S.J. 131; [1956] 1 All E.R. 341; [100 S.J. 240; 72 L.Q.R. 171; 20 Conv. 168; [1956] C.L.J. 143], CA; *reversing* [1955] J.P.L. 880; 105 L.J. 476; [1955] C.L.Y. 2362 .... 12.42
Learmonth Property Investment Co. Ltd v. Amos Hinton & Sons plc [1985] 1 E.G.L.R. 13; (1984) 274 E.G. 725 .... 16.56
Leavey (J.) and Co. v. Hirst (George H.) & Co. [1944] K.B. 24, CA 16.27
Leek & Moorlands Building Society v. Clark [1952] 2 Q.B. 788; [1952] 2 T.L.R. 401; 96 S.J. 561; [1952] 2 All E.R. 492 .... 4.12, 12.24
Lees v. Tatchell [1990] 1 E.G.L.R. 10; [1990] 23 E.G. 62; (1990) 60 P. & C.R. 228, CA . 5.21, 12.32, 12.81.1
Leeson v. Leeson [1936] 2 K.B. 156 .... 12.56
Legal and General Assurance (Pension Management) v. Cheshire County Council (1984) 269 E.G. 40, CA; *affirming* (1983) 46 P. & C.R. 160; (1983) 265 E.G. 781 .... 2.10.1
Legh v. Hewitt (1803) 4 East 154; 102 E.R. 789 .... 13.108
—— v. Lillie (1860) 6 H. & N. 165; 30 L.J. Ex. 25; 25 J.P. 118; 9 W.R. 55; 158 E.R. 69 ...... 10.59
Lendon v. Keen [1916] 1 K.B. 994; 85 L.J.K.B. 1237; 114 L.T. 847; 60 S.J. 619 .... 16.66, 16.74
Leschallas v. Woolf [1908] 1 Ch. 641; 77 L.J. Ch. 345; 98 L.T. 558 .... 10.35
Lester v. Ridd [1990] 2 Q.B. 430; [1989] 3 W.L.R. 173; (1989) 133 S.J. 849; [1989] 1 All E.R. 1111; (1989) 21 H.L.R. 248; [1989] 22 E.G. 101; (1989) 56 P. & C.R. 210, CA 8.14, 8.17, 12.20
Leveson v. Parfums Marcel Rochas [1966] 200 E.G. 407 .... 1.43
Lewis v. Haverfordwest R.D.C. [1953] 1 W.L.R. 1486; 97 S.J. 877; [1953] 2 All E.R. 1599; 52 L.G.R. 44 .... 16.66, 16.72
—— v. Moss (1962) 181 E.G. 685 .... 12.35, 12.36
Lewis (Jenkin R.) & Son v. Kerman [1971] Ch. 477; [1970] 3 W.L.R. 673; 114 S.J. 769; [1970] 3 All E.R. 414; 21 P. & C.R. 941, CA; *reversing* [1970] 2 W.L.R. 378; 114 S.J. 88; [1970] 1 All E.R. 833; 21 P. & C.R. 210 .... 1.13, 11.32, 11.34, 12.81.3, 14.8
Lilley and Skinner Ltd v. Crump [1929] 73 S.J. 366 .... 5.4, 11.21
Lister v. Forth Dry Dock and Engineering Co. [1990] 1 A.C. 546; [1989] 2 W.L.R. 634; [1989] 1 C.R. 341; (1989) 133 S.J. 455; [1989] 1 All E.R. 1134; [1989] I.R.L.R. 161; (1989) 139 N.L.J. 400; [1989] 2 C.M.L.R. 194; [1989] L.S. Gaz. June 14, 18, HL 18.7
Lister v. Lane & Nesham [1893] 2 Q.B. 212; 62 L.J.Q.B. 583; 69 L.J. 176; 9 T.L.R. 503; 57 J.P. 725; 37 S.J. 558; 41 W.R. 626; 4 R. 474, CA 10.28
Littlewood v. Rolfe [1980] 2 All E.R. 51; (1980) 258 E.G. 168; (1982) 43 P. & C.R. 262 14.70, 14.71
Liverpool City Council v. Irwin (1977) A.C. 239; (1976) 238 E.G. 879; (1984) 13 H.L.R. 38, HL 1.44
Lloyd v. Sadler [1978] Q.B. 774; [1978] 2 W.L.R. 721; (1978) 122 S.J. 111; [1978] 2 All E.R. 529; (1978) 35 P. & C.R. 78; (1978) 245 E.G. 479, CA 13.36
Lloyds Bank Ltd v. Jones [1955] 2 Q.B. 298; [1955] 3 W.L.R. 5; 99 S.J. 398; 53 L.G.R. 433; *sub nom.* Lower Onibury Farm, *Re*, Onibury, Shropshire, Lloyds Bank v. Jones [1955] 2 All E.R. 409 .... 12.61.16, 12.75, 16.63, 16.68
London and County Ltd v. Sportsman (W.) Ltd [1971] Ch. 764; [1970] 3 W.L.R. 418; 114 S.J. 666; [1970] 2 All E.R. 600; 21 P. & C.R. 788, CA; *reversing* [1969] 1 W.L.R. 1215; 113 S.J. 383; [1969] 3 All E.R. 621; 20 P. & C.R. 613 .... 13.97
London and Leeds Estates Ltd v. Paribus Ltd (No. 2) [1995] 1 E.G.L.R. 102; [1995] 02 E.G. 134, Q.B.D. 16.39
London and Manchester Assurance Co. v. Dunn and Co. (G.A.) [1983] 1 E.G.L.R. 111; (1983) 265 E.G. 39, 131, CA; *affirming* (1982) 262 E.G. 143 .... 2.10.1
London and Yorkshire Bank v. Belton (1885) 15 Q.B.D. 457; 54 L.J.Q.B. 568; 50 J.P. 86; 34 W.R. 31 .... 10.71
London Export Corporation Ltd v. Jubilee Coffee Roasting Co. Ltd [1958] 1 W.L.R. 661; 102 S.J. 452; [1958] 2 All E.R. 411; [1958] 1 Lloyd's Rep. 367, CA; *affirming* [1958] 1 W.L.R. 271; 102 S.J. 178; [1958] 1 All E.R. 494; [1958] 1 Lloyd's Rep. 197 .... 16.44
London Hilton Jewellers v. Hilton International Hotels (1990) 1 E.G.L.R. 112; [1990] 20 E.G. 69, CA 12.50
London Supplementary Benefits Appeal Tribunal, *ex p.* Bullen (1976) 120 S.J. 437 .... 16.35
Long (Nevill) & Co. (Boards) Ltd v. Firmenich & Co. (1984) 47 P. & C.R. 59; (1983) 268 E.G. 572, CA; *affirming* (1981) 44 P. & C.R. 12; (1981) 261 E.G. 461 .... 12.20
Look v. Davies [1952] E.G.D. 17; (1952) 160 E.G. 147, Cty.Ct. 8.13
Lord v. Lord (1857) 5 E. & B. 404; 26 L.J.Q.B. 34; 1 Jur. (N.S.) 893; 3 W.R. 553; 119 E.R. 531 16.22
Lory v. Brent London Borough Council [1971] 1 W.L.R. 823; 115 S.J. 245; 22 P. & C.R. 393; 69 L.G.R. 317; *sub nom.* Lory v. London Borough of Brent [1971] 1 All E.R. 1042 ... 9.10, 9.16

TABLE OF CASES

Lowe v. Dorling [1905] 2 K.B. 501; 74 L.J.K.B. 794; 93 L.T. 398; 54 W.R. 28; *sub nom.* Lucy v.
  Dorling, 21 T.L.R. 616; 49 S.J. 582 .... 10.72
Lowenthal v. Vanhoute [1947] K.B. 342; [1947] L.J.R. 421; 177 L.T. 180; 63 T.L.R. 54; [1947]
  1 All E.R. 116 .... 12.16, 12.28
Lower Street Properties Ltd (formerly Mirod Estates) v. Jones (1996) 28 H.L.R. 877; [1996] 48
  E.G. 154; [1996] E.G.C.S. 37; [1996] 2 E.G.L.R. 67; [1996] N.P.C. 29, CA March 6, 1995;
  Assistant Recorder Phillips; CC (Worthing) (Ex rel. Mark James, Barrister) 2.13
Lower v. Sorrell [1963] 1 Q.B. 959; [1963] 2 W.L.R. 1; [1962] 3 All E.R. 1074 .... 9.2, 12.5, 12.16
Lower Onibury Farm, *Re. See* Lloyds Bank Ltd v. Jones.
Lowther v. Clifford [1927] 1 K.B. 130; 95 L.J.K.B. 576; 135 L.T. 200; 42 T.L.R. 432; 90 J.P.
  113; 70 S.J. 544; 24 L.G.R. 231 .... 15.20, 16.15
Luke v. I.R.C. [1963] A.C. 557; [1963] 2 W.L.R. 559; 107 S.J. 174; [1963] 1 All E.R. 655;
  [1963] T.R. 21; 42 A.T.C. 21; *sub nom.* I.R.C. v. Luke 40 T.C. 630; 1963 S.C. (H.L.) 65;
  1963 S.L.T. 129, HL; *reversing sub nom.* I.R.C. v. Luke [1962] T.R. 153; 41 A.T.C. 152;
  1962 S.C. 218; 1962 S.L.T. 253 .... 11.15
Lurcott v. Wakeley & Wheeler [1911] 1 K.B. 905; 80 L.J.K.B. 713; 104 L.T. 290; 55 S.J. 290   10.28
Luton v. Tinsey (1978) 249 E.G. 239, CA 9.7, 9.9, 9.11, 9.15
Luttenberger v. North Thoresby Farms Limited [1993] 1 E.G.L.R. 3; [1993] 17 E.G. 102 .... 12.30,
  12.48, 12.56, 12.61.9
Lyttleton Times Company v. Warners [1907] A.C. 476 .... 1.44

MacArthur v. Campbell (1833) 5 B. & Ad. 518; 2 Nev. & M.K.B. 444; 4 L.J.K.B. 25; 110 E.R.
  882 .... 16.53
McCallum v. Arthur 1955 S.C. 188 .... 16.2
McClinton v. McFall (1974) 232 E.G. 707, CA 8.18, 9.10
McGill v. Bury Management Ltd (1986) S.L. Ct., Strath, R.N. 293 .... 19.4
McGreal v. Wake (1984) 128 S.J. 116; (1984) 13 H.L.R. 107; (1984) 269 E.G. 1254, CA 10.86
Macgregor v. Board of Agriculture for Scotland 1925 S.C. 613 .... 13.27
Mackenzie v. Laird 1959 S.C. 266; 1959 S.L.T. 268 .... 9.9
—— v. Macgillivray 1921 S.C. 722; 58 Sc.L.R. 488 .... 11.21, 13.68
McKenzie v. McKenzie [1971] P. 33; [1970] 3 W.L.R. 472; 114 S.J. 667; [1970] 3 All E.R.
  1034, CA 16.36
McLaren v. Turnbull 1942 S.C. 179 .... 13.27, 13.119
Maclean v. Chalmers Property Investment Co. Ltd. 1951 S.L.T. (Sh.Ct.) 71 .... 16.38
McMorran v. Marrison (A.E.) (Contractors) Ltd. [1944] 2 All E.R. 448 .... 12.7
Macnab v. Anderson (A. & J.) 1955 S.C. 38 .... 12.57
Macnab of Macnab v. Anderson 1957 S.C. 213; 1958 S.L.T. 8 .... 12.53, 12.61.3, 12.61.10,
  12.76
M'Quater v. Fergusson 1911 S.C. 640; 48 Sc.L.R. 560; 1 S.L.T. 295 .... 11.21, 13.45, 13.68, 16.73
Macon (Michel) v. Préfet de l'Aisne (C–152/95) E.C.J., October 9, 1997 .... 18.11
Magdalen College, Oxford v. Heritage [1974] 1 W.L.R. 441; 118 S.J. 243; [1974] 1 All E.R.
  1065; 27 P. & C.R. 169 (1974) 230 E.G. 219, CA; *affirming* [1973] 1 W.L.R. 1225; 117 S.J.
  747; [1973] 3 All E.R. 891; 26 P. & C.R. 226 .... 12.45–12.47, 12.53–12.55, 12.61.15, 16.15
Maier v. Freistaat Bayern (–236/90) [1992] E.C.R.I–4483 .... 18.11
Malloch v. Aberdeen Corporation [1971] 1 W.L.R. 1578; 115 S.J. 756; [1971] 2 All E.R. 1278;
  1971 S.C. 85, HL 16.34
Malmesbury Ry. v. Budd (1876) 2 Ch. D. 113; 45 L.J. Ch. 271 .... 16.35
Mancetter Developments v. Garmanson and Givertz [1986] Q.B. 1212; [1986] W.L.R. 871;
  (1986) 130 S.J. 129; [1986] 1 All E.R. 449; [1986] 1 E.G.L.R. 240; (1985) 83 L.S. Gaz.
  612, CA 1.44
Manchester Bonded Warehouse v. Carr (1880) 5 C.P.D. 507 .... 10.31
Manchester's (Duke of) Settlement, *Re* [1910] 1 Ch. 106; 79 L.J. Ch. 48; 101 L.T. 892; 26
  T.L.R. 5; 53 S.J. 868 .... 17.14
Manfield & Sons v. Botchin [1970] 2 Q.B. 612; [1970] 3 W.L.R. 120; 114 S.J. 338; [1970] 3 All
  E.R. 143; 21 P. & C.R. 587; [34 Conv. 360] 1.16
Mann v. Gardner (1990) 61 P. & C.R. 1; [1991] 1 E.G.L.R. 9; [1991] 11 E.G. 107; *The Times*,
  June 22, 1990, CA 8.18, 11.30, 19.4.3
Mannai Investment Co. Limited v. Eagle Star Life Assurance Co. Ltd [1997] 3 All E.R. 352,
  [1997] 2 W.L.R. 945, HL 12.24, 12.29, 12.32, 12.54
Manorlike Ltd v. Le Vitas Travel Agency & Consultancy Services Ltd [1986] 1 All E.R. 573;
  (1986) 278 E.G. 412, CA 13.28
Mansel v. Norton (1883) 22 Ch.D. 769; 52 L.J.Ch. 357; 48 L.T. 654; 31 W.R. 325 ...... 13.51, 13.113

TABLE OF CASES

Mansfield v. Robinson [1928] 2 K.B. 353; 97 L.J.K.B. 466; 139 L.T. 349; 44 T.L.R. 518; 92 J.P. 126 .... 16.72
Martin v. Boulanger (1883) 8 App. Cas. 296; 52 L.J.P.C. 31; 49 L.T. 62 .... 16.58
—— v. Coggan (1824) 1 Hog. 120 .... 10.55
Martin-Smith v. Smale [1954] 1 W.L.R. 247; 98 S.J. 92; [1954] 1 All E.R. 237; 52 L.G.R. 136   12.42
Mason v. Clarke [1955] A.C. 778; [1955] 2 W.L.R. 853; 99 S.J. 274; [1955] 1 All E.R. 914 .... 10.74, 10.77
—— v. Skilling [1974] 1 W.L.R. 1437; (1973) 118 S.J. 810; [1974] 3 All E.R. 977; (1973) 29 P. & C.R. 88; *sub nom.* Skilling v. Acari's Exrx, 1974, S.L.T. 46, HL 11.14
Masters v. Green (1888) 20 Q.B.D. 807; 59 L.T. 476; 52 J.P. 597; 36 W.R. 591 ....9.7, 10.71
Masters and Duveen, *Re* [1923] 2 K.B. 729; 68 S.J. 11 ....13.2, 15.27
Maunder, *Re* (1883) 49 L.T. 535 .... 16.35
Maunsell v. Olins [1974] 3 W.L.R. 835; 118 S.J. 882; [1975] 1 All E.R. 16; (1974) 30 P. & C.R. 1, HL; *affirming* [1974] 1 W.L.R. 830; 118 S.J. 278; [1974] 2 All E.R. 250; 27 P. & C.R. 460, CA 12.23
Maxwell-Lefroy v. Bracey (1956) 100 S.J. 201; [1956] E.G.D. 305 .... 16.68
Mears v. Callender [1901] 2 Ch. 388; 70 L.J.Ch. 621; 84 L.T. 618; 17 T.L.R. 518; 65 J.P. 615; 49 W.R. 584 .... 10.34, 10.39, 13.46, 13.61, 13.68, 15.28
Mecca Leisure v. Renown Investments (Holdings) [1985] 49 P. & C.R. 12; (1984) 271 E.G. 989, CA 2.10.1, 2.10.2
Mediterranean and Eastern Export Co. Ltd v. Fortress Fabrics (Manchester) Ltd [1948] W.N. 244; [1948] L.J.R. 1536; 64 T.L.R. 337; 92 S.J. 362; [1948] 2 All E.R. 186; 81 Ll.L.Rep. 401 .... 16.44
Meggeson v. Groves [1917] 1 Ch. 158; 86 L.J.Ch. 145; 115 L.T. 683; 61 S.J. 115 .... 10.59, 10.60
Mellor v. Watkins (1874) L.R. 9 Q.B. 400; 23 W.R. 55 .... 15.14
Melluish (Inspector of Taxes) v. B.M.I. (No. 3) Ltd; Melluish (Inspector of Taxes) v. B.M.I. (No. 6) Ltd; Melluish (Inspector of Taxes) v. B.M.I. (No. 9) Ltd; Melluish (Inspector of Taxes) v. Barclays Mercantile Business Finance Ltd; Melluish (Inspector of Taxes) v. Fitzroy Finance Ltd [1996] 1 A.C. 454; [1995] 3 W.L.R. 630; [1995] 4 All E.R. 453; [1995] S.T.C. 964; 68 T.C.I.; (1995) 139 S.J.L.B. 220; (1995) 92(40) L.S.G. 22; [1995] E.G.C.S. 150; *The Times*, October 16, 1995; *The Independent*, November 6, 1995 (C.S.), HL; *affirming in part* [1995] Ch. 90; [1994] 3 W.L.R. 1032; [1994] S.T.C. 802; [1994] S.T.I. 1921; (1994) 138 S.J.L.B. 200; (1994) 91(38) L.S.G. 46; [1994] E.G.C.S. 147; *The Times*, August 17, 1994; *The Independent*, September 5, 1994 (C.S.), CA; *reversing* [1994] 2 W.L.R. 795; [1994] S.T.C. 315; [1994] S.T.I. 128; (1995) 69 P. & C.R. 517; [1994] E.G.C.S. 16; (1994) 91(9) L.S.G. 41; (1994) 138 S.J.L.B. 40; *The Times*, February 15, 1994; *The Independent*, March 28, 1994 (C.S.), Ch. D. 3.9
Melton Medes v. Securities & Investments Board [1995] Ch. 137; [1995] 2 W.L.R. 247; [1995] 3 All E.R. 880; *The Times*, July 27, 1994; *The Independent*, August 8, 1994 (C.S.), Ch. D.   6.22
Mercantile and General Reinsurance Co. Ltd v. Groves [1974] Q.B. 43; [1973] 3 W.L.R. 248; 117 S.J. 566; [1973] 3 All E.R. 330; 26 P. & C.R. 71; [1973] J.P.L. 427, CA 12.60
Mercury Communications v. Director General of Telecommunications [1996] 1 W.L.R. 48; [1996] 1 All E.R. 575; [1996] Masons C.L.R. 2; *The Times*, February 10, 1995; *The Independent*, February 16, 1995, HL; *reversing* [1995] Masons C.L.R. 2; (1994) 138 S.J.L.B. 183; (1994) 91(36) L.S.G. 36; *The Times*, June 29, 1995, PC 6.86, 6.87
Merstham Manor Ltd v. Maiklem [1967] Journal of the Chartered Land Agents' Society, 362   12.36
Metcalf v. Ives (1737) 1 Atk. 63 .... 16.66
Methodist Secondary Schools Trust Deed Trustees v. O'Leary (1992) 66 P. & C.R. 364; (1993) 25 H.L.R. 364; [1993] 16 E.G. 119; [1992] E.G.C.S. 144; [1992] N.P.C. 149, CA 1.19
Metropolitan Properties Ltd v. Wooldridge (1968) 112 S.J. 862; 20 P. & C.R. 64; [1968] R.V.R. 734; 208 E.G. 733 .... 11.25
Metropolitan Properties Co. (F.G.C.) Ltd v. Lannon [1969] 1 Q.B. 577; [1968] 3 W.L.R. 694; 112 S.J. 585; [1968] 3 All E.R. 304; 19 P. & C.R. 858; [1968] R.V.R. 490, CA; *reversing in part* [1968] 1 W.L.R. 815; [1968] 1 All E.R. 354; [1968] R.V.R. 236 .... 11.33, 16.23, 16.35, 16.66
Metropolitan Property Holdings Ltd v. Finegold [1975] 1 W.L.R. 349; (1974) 119 S.J. 151; [1975] 1 All E.R. 389; (1974) 29 P. & C.R. 161 .... 11.13
—— v. Laufer (1974) 29 P. & C.R. 172 .... 16.44
Meux v. Cobley [1892] 2 Ch. 253; 61 L.J. Ch. 449; 66 L.T. 86; 8 T.L.R. 173 .... 15.27
Midgley v. Stott (1977) 244 E.G. 883, CA 9.4, 9.15, 9.16
Midland Railway Co.'s Agreement, *Re*, Charles Clay & Sons Ltd v. British Railways Board [1971] Ch. 725; [1971] 2 W.L.R. 625; 115 S.J. 126; 22 P. & C.R. 360; *sub nom.* Clay

TABLE OF CASES

(Charles) & Sons v. British Railways Board [1971] 1 All E.R. 1007, CA; *affirming* [1970] 1 Ch. 568; [1970] 2 W.L.R. 1328; 114 S.J. 473; 21 P. & C.R. 521; *sub nom.* Clay (Charles) & Sons v. British Railways Board [1970] 2 All E.R. 463 .... 12.5
Miles v. Clarke [1953] 1 W.L.R. 537; 97 S.J. 209; [1953] 1 All E.R. 779 .... 18.28
—— v. Furber (1873) L.R. 8 Q.B. 77; 42 L.J.Q.B. 41; 27 L.T. 756; 37 J.P. 516; 21 W.R. 262 10.71
Miller v. Emcer Products [1956] Ch. 304; [1956] 2 W.L.R. 267; 100 S.J. 74; [1956] 1 All E.R. 237; [72 L.Q.R. 172; 20 Conv. 161, 170; 221 L.T. 81; 100 S.J. 1223; 223 Sol. 119], CA . 1.44
Miller v. Lakefield Estates Limited [1989] 1 E.G.L.R.; [1989] 19 E.G. 67, CA 1.44
Million Pigs Ltd v. Parry (No. 2) (1983) 46 P. & C.R. 333; (1983) 268 E.G. 809 .... 11.1
Mills v. Edwards [1971] 1 Q.B. 379; [1971] 2 W.L.R. 418; (1970) 114 S.J. 973; [1971] 1 All E.R. 922; 22 P. & C.R. 171, CA 12.28, 13.48, 13.30
—— v. Rose (1923) 68 S.J. 420 .... 13.22
Milverton Group v. Warner World (1995) 2 E.G.L.R. 28; (1994) P. & C.R. D9; [1995] 32 E.G. 70; [1994] N.P.C. 64; [1994] E.G.C.S. 88, *The Independent*, May 30, 1994 (C.S.), CA ... 12.56
Minister of Agriculture and Fisheries v. Dean [1924] 1 K.B. 851; 93 L.J.K.B. 374; 130 L.T. 709; 40 T.L.R. 285; 68 S.J. 401 .... 13.27
Minister of Agriculture, Fisheries and Food v. Appleton [1970] 1 Q.B. 221; [1969] 3 W.L.R. 755; 113 S.J. 738; [1969] 3 All E.R. 105; 7 K.I.R. 232 .... 8.18
—— v. Jenkins [1963] 2 Q.B. 317; [1963] 2 W.L.R. 906; 107 S.J. 234; [1963] 2 All E.R. 147 12.50
Mint v. Good [1951] 1 K.B. 517; 94 S.J. 822; [1950] 2 All E.R. 1159; 49 L.G.R. 495; *reversing* 155 E.G. 409 .... 10.86
Mitchell-Gill v. Buchan 1921 S.C. 390 .... 16.62, 16.66
Mitton v. Farrow (1980) 255 E.G. 449, CA 1.43, 9.4
Moir v. Williams [1892] 1 Q.B. 264 .... 3.11
Molton Builders v. City of Westminster London Borough Council (1975) 119 S.J. 627; 30 P. & C.R. 182, CA; *affirming* [1974] J.P.L. 600 .... 1.44
Monk v. Noyes (1824) 1 C. & P. 265 .... 10.12
Monson v. Bound [1954] 1 W.L.R. 1321; 98 S.J. 751; [1954] 3 All E.R. 228; 52 L.G.R. 511 .. 8.19
Montgomery Jones & Co. and Liebenthal, *Re* (1898) 78 L.T. 406, CA 16.61
Moody v. Godstone Rural District Council [1966] 1 W.L.R. 1085; 130 J.P. 332; 110 S.J. 687; [1966] 2 All E.R. 696 .... 17.20
Moore v. Lambeth County Court Registrar [1969] 1 W.L.R. 141; [1969] 1 All E.R. 782, CA . 16.36
—— v. Plymouth (Lord) (1819) 3 B. & Ald. 66; *affirming* (1817) 7 Taunt. 614; 1 Moore C.P. 346; 129 E.R. 245 .... 10.74
Moore, Stephens and Co. v. Local Authorities' Mutual Investment Trust [1992] 1 E.G.L.R. 33; [1992] 04 E.G. 135 .... 16.47
Moore and Hulm's Contract, *Re* [1912] 2 Ch. 105; 81 L.J.Ch. 503; 106 L.T. 330; 56 S.J. 89 .. 15.5
Moran v. Lloyd's [1983] Q.B. 542; [1983] 2 W.L.R. 672; [1983] 2 All E.R. 200; [1983] 1 Lloyd's Rep. 472; [1983] Com.L.R. 132, CA; *affirming* [1983] 1 Lloyd's Rep. 51; [1982] Com.L.R. 258 .... 16.66
Mordue v. Palmer (1870) L.R. 6 Ch. 22; 40 L.J. Ch. 8; 23 L.T. 752; 35 J.P. 196; 19 W.R. 86 ... 16.58, 16.61
Morecambe and Heysham Corporation v. Robinson [1961] 1 W.L.R. 373; 125 J.P. 259; 105 S.J. 152; [1961] 1 All E.R. 721; 59 L.G.R. 160; [1961] R.V.R. 137; 8 R.R.C. 33, CA; *affirming* (1959) 52 R. & I.T. 577; 5 R.R.C. 164; 174 E.G. 203 .... 11.33
Morgan v. William Harrison [1907] 2 Ch. 137 .... 1.16
Morley v. Carter [1898] 1 Q.B. 8 .... 8.22
Morris v. Morris (1825) 1 Hog. 238 .... 10.55
—— v. Muirhead 1969 S.L.T. 70 .... 12.60
—— v. Redland Bricks Limited. *See* Redland Bricks Limited v. Morris
Morris Marks v. British Waterways Board [1963] 1 W.L.R. 1008 .... 2.11, 11.38
Morrison v. Chadwick [1849] 7 C.B. 266 .... 1.13
Morse and Dixon, *Re* (1917) 87 L.J.K.B. 1; 117 L.T. 590 .... 13.46, 13.61, 15.27
Morton's (Earl) Trustees v. Macdougall 1944 S.C. 410 .... 10.76
Moseley v. Simpson (1873) L.R. 16 Eq. 226; 42 L.J.Ch. 739; 28 L.T. 727; 37 J.P. 789; 21 W.R. 694 .... 16.35, 16.66
Moss v. National Coal Board (1982) 264 E.G. 52 .... 14.29, 16.7
Mount Charlotte Investments plc v. Prudential Assurance Co. (1995) 1 E.G.L.R. 15; [1995] 10 E.G. 129; [1994] N.P.C. 110, Ch. D. 16.46
Mountford v. Hodkinson [1956] 1 W.L.R. 422; 100 S.J. 301; [1956] 2 All E.R. 17 .... 12.32
Mountview Court Properties Ltd v. Devlin (1970) 114 S.J. 474; (1970) 21 P. & C.R. 689; [1971] J.P.L. 113 .... 16.68

TABLE OF CASES

Mulder (J.) v. Minister van Landbouw en Visserij (120/86) [1988] E.C.R. 2321; [1989] 2 C.M.L.R. 1 .... 18.8, 18.10, 18.11, 18.15
Myron, The [1970] 1 Q.B. 527; [1969] 3 W.L.R. 292; 113 S.J. 404; [1969] 2 All E.R. 1263; [1969] 1 Lloyd's Rep. 411 .... 16.34, 16.66

National Coal Board v. Naylor [1972] 1 W.L.R. 908; (1971) 116 S.J. 507; [1972] 1 All E.R. 1153; (1971) 23 P. & C.R. 129; 71 L.G.R. 403 *sub nom.* Naylor v. National Coal Board (1972) 221 E.G. 1285 .... 12.36, 12.42
National Labour Relations Board v. Seven-Up Bottling Co. of Miami Inc. 344 U.S. 343 (1953) 16.44
National Trust for Places of Historic Interest or Natural Beauty v. Knipe [1997] 40 E.G. 151; *The Times*, June 21, 1997, CA 4.18, 12.23
Naylor v. National Coal Board. *See* National Coal Board v. Naylor.
New Zealand Government Property Corporation v. H.M. & S. Ltd. [1982] Q.B. 1145; [1982] 2 W.L.R. 837; [1982] 1 All E.R. 624; (1982) 44 P. & C.R. 329; (1982) 263 E.G. 765, CA; *affirming* [1981] 1 W.L.R. 870; (1980) 125 S.J. 343; [1981] 1 All E.R. 759; (1981) 42 P. & C.R. 50; (1980) 257 E.G. 606 .... 2.18, 2.23, 5.6, 10.34, 10.35
Newborough (Lord) v. Jones [1975] Ch. 90; [1974] 3 W.L.R. 52; 118 S.J. 479; [1974] 3 All E.R. 17; 28 P. & C.R. 215, CA 7.10, 13.119, 17.19
Newman v. Keedwell (1977) 35 P. & C.R. 393; (1977) 244 E.G. 469 .... 13.36
Nickels v. Hancock (1855) 7 De G.M. & G. 300; 3 Eq. Rep. 689; 1 Jur. (N.S.) 1149; 44 E.R. 117 .... 16.56
99 Bishopsgate Ltd. v. Prudential Assurance Co. Ltd [1985] 1 E.G.L.R. 72 (1985) 273 E.G. 984, CA; *affirming* (1984) 270 E.G. 950 .... 11.15
Nikko Hotels (U.K.) Limited v. MEPC Plc [1991] 2 E.G.L.R. 103; [1991] 28 E.G. 86 .... 6.86
Nocton v. Lord Ashburton [1914] A.C. 932, HL 12.47
Nokes v. Doncaster Amalgamated Collieries Ltd [1940] A.C. 1014; 109 L.J.K.B. 865; 163 L.T. 343; 56 T.L.R. 988; 85 S.J. 45; [1940] 3 All E.R. 549, HL 11.15
North Eastern Co-operative Society Ltd v. Newcastle upon Tyne City Council (1987) 282 E.G. 1409 .... 6.83
Northern Electric plc v. Addison [1997] 39 E.G. 175, CA 2.16
Northern Press and Engineering Co. v. Shepherd [1908] 52 S.J. 715 .... 3.10
Northumberland (Duke of), *Re* Halifax v. Northumberland [1951] Ch. 202; 66 T.L.R. (Pt. 2) 1045; 94 S.J. 805; [1950] 2 All E.R. 1181 .... 17.10, 17.15
Northumberland and Durham Property Trust v. London Rent Assessment Committee [1997] 1 E.G.L.R. 236 .... 11.14, 11.18
Norwich Union Life Insurance Society v. P. & O. Property Holdings. *See* P. & O. Property Holdings v. Norwich Union Life Insurance Society
Norwich Union Life Insurance Society v. Trustee Savings Banks Central Board [1986] 1 E.G.L.R. 136; (1985) 278 E.G. 162 .... 2.16
Nozari-Zadeh v. Pearl Assurance plc [1987] 2 E.G.L.R. 91; (1987) 283 E.G. 457, CA 5.4

Oades v. Spafford [1948] 2 K.B. 74; [1948] L.J.R. 1201; 64 T.L.R. 253; 92 S.J. 180; [1948] 1 All E.R. 607 .... 13.113
Oakstead Garages Ltd v. Leach Pension Scheme (Trustees) Ltd (1996) 1 E.G.L.R. 26; [1996] 24 E.G. 147, Ch. D 16.46
Ocean Accident and Guarantee Corp. v. Next Plc; Commercial Union Assurance Co. Plc v. Next Plc [1996] 33 E.G. 91; [1996] 2 E.G.L.R. 84; [1995] N.P.C. 185; [1995] E.G.C.S. 187; *The Times*, December 5, 1995, Ch. D. 2.23
O'Connor and Brewin's Arbitration, *Re* [1933] 1 K.B. 20; 101 L.J.K.B. 706; *sub nom. Re* Agricultural Holdings Act 1923, O'Connor v. Brewin, 147 L.T. 386; 76 S.J. 511 . 13.27, 13.119, 16.28
O'Connor and Whitlaw's Arbitration, *Re* (1919) 88 L.J.K.B. 1242 .... 16.66
Official Solicitor v. Thomas [1986] 2 E.G.L.R. 1; (1986) 279 E.G. 407 .... 12.54–12.56
Old Grovebury Manor Farm Ltd v. Seymour (W.) Plant Sales and Hire Ltd (No. 2) [1979] 1 W.L.R. 1397; (1979) 123 S.J. 719; [1979] 3 All E.R. 504; (1979) 39 P. & C.R. 99; (1979) 252 E.G. 1103, CA; *affirming* (1979) 38 P. & C.R. 374 .... 10.7, 12.61.16, 12.77
O'May v. City of London Real Property Co. Ltd [1983] 2 A.C. 726; [1982] 2 W.L.R. 407; [1982] 1 All E.R. 660; (1982) 43 P. & C.R. 351; (1982) 261 E.G. 1185, HL; *affirming* [1981] Ch. 216; [1980] 3 W.L.R. 881; (1980) 124 S.J. 847; [1980] 3 All E.R. 466; (1980) 40 P. & C.R. 310; (1980) 255 E.G. 151, CA; *reversing* (1978) 249 E.G. 1065 .... 11.8
O'Reilly v. Mackman; Millbanks v. Secretary of State for the Home Department [1983] 2 A.C. 237; [1982] 3 W.L.R. 1096; (1982) 126 S.J. 820; [1982] 3 All E.R. 1124, HL; *affirming*

[1982] 3 W.L.R. 604; (1982) 126 S.J. 578; [1982] 3 All E.R. 680, CA; *reversing* (1982) 126 S.J. 312 .... 16.70
Oscroft v. Benabo [1967] 1 W.L.R. 1087; 111 S.J. 520; [1967] 2 All E.R. 548; [31 Conv. 372], CA 2.16
Ostreicher v. Secretary of State for the Environment [1978] 1 W.L.R. 810; (1978) 122 S.J. 194; [1978] 3 All E.R. 82; (1978) 76 L.G.R. 445; (1978) 37 P. & C.R. 9; [1978] J.P.L. 539, CA; *affirming* (1977) 121 S.J. 618; [1978] 1 All E.R. 591; (1977) 34 P. & C.R. 86; (1977) 76 L.G.R. 94; [1977] J.P.L. 716 .... 16.35
Oswald v.Grey (Earl) (1855) 24 L.J.Q.B. 69 .... 16.34
Owen v. Nicholl [1948] W.N. 138; 12 S.J. 244; [1948] 1 All E.R. 707 .... 16.44
Oxley v. James (1844) 13 M. & W. 209 .... 15.2

P. & O. Property Holdings v. Norwich Union Life Insurance Society; *sub nom.* Norwich Union Life Insurance Society v. P. & O. Property Holdings (1994) 68 P. & C.R. 261, HL; *affirming* [1993] 13 E.G. 108; [1993] E.G.C.S. 69; [1993] N.P.C. 1, CA 6.87
Paczy v. Haendler & Natermann GmbH [1981] F.S.R. 250; [1981] 1 Lloyd's Rep. 302; [1981] Com. L.R. 12, CA; *reversing* [1980] F.S.R. 526; [1979] F.S.R. 420 .... 6.17
Padbury v. York (1990) 2 E.G.L.R. 3; [1990] 41 E.G. 65 .... 9.4, 9.19
Paddock Investments Ltd v. Lory (1975) 236 E.G. 803, CA .. 12.7, 12.18, 12.19, 12.37, 12.50, 12.83, 13.116, 16.15
Pahl v. Trevor [1992] 1 E.G.L.R. 22; [1992] 25 E.G. 130; [1991] E.G.C.S. 131, CA . 1.21, 1.43, 4.16, 9.21, 9.30
Palmer & Co. and Hosken & Co., *Re* [1898] 1 Q.B. 131; 67 L.J.Q.B. 1; 77 L.T. 350; 14 T.L.R. 28; 42 S.J. 32; 46 W.R. 49 .... 16.61, 16.62, 16.66
Pannell v. City of London Brewery Co. [1900] 1 Ch. 496; 69 L.J.Ch. 244; 82 L.T. 53; 16 T.L.R. 152; 48 W.R. 264; 44 S.J. 195 .... 12.61.12
Panther Shop Investments v. Keith Pople (1987) 282 E.G. 594; [1987] 1 E.G.L.R. 131 .... 2.19
Parrish v. Kinsey (1983) 268 E.G. 1113, CA 12.45, 12.53
Parry v. Million Pigs Ltd (1980) 260 E.G. 281 .. 1.46, 3.14, 9.21, 10.4, 12.7, 12.22, 13.2, 13.5, 13.90, 16.15
Paul v. Caldwell (1960) 110 L.J. 704; (1960) 176 E.G. 743 .... 12.20
Paul, *Re, ex p.* Portarlington (Earl) [1889] 24 Q.B.D. 247 .... 8.22
Paultons Square Properties Ltd v. London County Council (1965) 63 L.G.R. 158 .... 16.68
Pawsey v. Armstrong (1881) 18 Ch. D. 698 .... 18.28
Pazgate Ltd v. McGrath (1984) 17 H.L.R. 127; (1984) 272 E.G. 1069, CA 10.7
Peabody Donation Fund Governors v. Parkinson (Sir Lindsay) & Co. [1985] A.C. 210; [1984] 3 W.L.R. 953; (1984) 128 S.J. 753; [1984] 3 All E.R. 529; [1985] 83 L.G.R. 1; (1984) 28 Build. L.R. 1; [1984] C.I.L.L. 128; (1984) 81 L.S. Gaz. 3179, HL; *affirming* [1983] 3 W.L.R. 754; (1983) 127 S.J. 749; [1983] 3 All E.R. 417; (1984) 47 P. & C.R. 402; [1984] 82 L.G.R. 138; (1984) 25 Build. L.R. 108, CA [(1984–85) 1 Const. L.J. 175] 10.7, 12.61.16, 12.77
Pearl Assurance v. Shaw [1985] 1 E.G.L.R. 92; (1984) 274 E.G. 490 .... 2.16
Pearsons and l'Anson [1899] 2 Q.B. 618; 68 L.J.Q.B. 878; 81 L.T. 289; 15 T.L.R. 452; 63 J.P. 677; 48 W.R. 154 .... 13.61, 15.27
Pedler v. Hardy (1902) 18 T.L.R. 591 .... 16.58
Pelly's Will Trusts, *Re*, Ransome v. Pelly [1957] Ch. 1 [1956] 3 W.L.R. 26; 100 S.J. 379; [1956] T.R. 139; 35 A.T.C. 98; *sub nom. Re* Pelly, Ransome v. Pelly [1956] 2 All E.R. 326; 49 R. & I.T. 452 .... 17.15
Pembery v. Landin [1940] 2 All E.R. 434, CA 10.28
Pennell v. Payne [1995] Q.B. 192; [1995] 2 W.L.R. 261; [1995] 2 All E.R. 592; [1995] 06 E.G. 152; [1994] E.G.C.S. 196; (1995) 139 S.J.L.B. 17; [1994] N.P.C. 151; *The Times,* December 13, 1994; *The Independent,* January 23, 1995, CA 12.76.2, 12.77, 15.14
Pennington-Ramsden v. McWilliam [1982] C.L.Y. 218 .... 16.24
Penton v. Robart (1801) 2 East 88; 102 E.R. 302 .... 10.34
Pepys v. London Transport Executive [1975] 1 W.L.R. 234; (1974) 118 S.J. 882; [1975] 1 All E.R. 748; (1974) 29 P. & C.R. 248, CA 16.66
Perkins (H.G.) Ltd v. Brent-Shaw [1973] 1 W.L.R. 975; 117 S.J. 527; *sub nom.* Perkins (H.G.) Ltd v. Best-Shaw [1973] 2 All E.R. 924 .... 16.72
Perry v. Stopher [1959] 1 W.L.R. 415; 103 S.J. 311; [1959] 1 All E.R. 713 .... 16.56
Persey v. Bazley (1983) 127 S.J. 579; (1984) 47 P. & C.R. 37; (1983) 267 E.G. 519, CA 12.20
Petch v. Tutin (1846) 15 M. & W. 110; 15 L.J. Ex. 280; 153 E.R. 782 .... 13.51, 13.113
Petrie v. Daniel (1804) 1 Smith K.B. 199 .... 13.48, 13.113

TABLE OF CASES

Phillips v. Smith (1845) 14 M. & W. 589 .... 10.31
Phipps v. Ingram (1835) 3 Dowl. 669 .... 16.66
Phipps (P.) and Son (Northampton and Towcester Breweries) Ltd v. Rogers [1925] 1 K.B. 14   12.26
Pickard v. Bishop (1975) 119 S.J. 407; (1975) 31 P. & C.R. 108; 235 E.G. 133, CA 12.30, 12.53,
12.55, 12.58
Pike v. Eyre [1829] 9 B. & C. 909 .... 15.2
Piper v. Harvey [1958] 1 Q.B. 439; [1958] 2 W.L.R. 408; 102 S.J. 174; [1958] 1 All E.R. 454   12.39
Plews and Middleton, Re (1845); 6 Q.B. 845; 1 New Pract. Cas. 158; 14 L.J.Q.B. 139; 4 L.T.
(o.s.) 155; 9 Jur. 160; 115 E.R. 319 .... 16.66
Plumb Brothers v. Dolmac (Agriculture) Ltd (1984) 271 E.G. 373, CA 11.10, 11.37
Plymouth (Earl of) v. Glamorgan County Council (1974) 232 E.G. 1235 .... 16.28
Plymouth Corporation v. Harvey [1971] 1 W.L.R. 549; (1970) 115 S.J. 13; [1971] 1 All E.R.
623; 22 P. & C.R. 475; 69 L.G.R. 310 .... 13.90
Pochin v. Smith (1887) 52 J.P. 4; 3 T.L.R. 647 .... 10.74
Ponsford v. H.M.S. Aerosols [1979] A.C. 63; [1978] 3 W.L.R. 241; (1978) 122 S.J. 487; [1978]
2 All E.R. 837; (1978) 38 P. & C.R. 270; (1978) 247 E.G. 1171, HL; *affirming* [1977] 1
W.L.R. 1029; (1977) 121 S.J. 240; [1977] 3 All E.R. 651; (1977) 33 P. & C.R. 465; (1977)
243 E.G. 742, CA 2.16, 2.24
Ponsford v. Swaine (1861) J. & H. 433; 4 L.T. 15; 70 E.R. 816 .... 16.26
Pontsarn Investments Ltd v. Kansallis-Osake-Pankki [1992] 1 E.G.L.R. 148; [1992] 22 E.G.
103; [1992] N.P.C. 56; [1992] Gazette, 22 July, 33 .... 6.86
Poole v. Warren (1838) 8 A. & E. 582; 3 Nev. & P.K.B. 693; 1 Will. Woll. & H. 518; 3 Jur. 23;
112 E.R. 959 .... 12.14
Port Arthur Shipbuilding Co. Ltd v. Arthurs [1969] S.C.R. 85 .... 16.70
Port Sudan Cotton Co. Ltd v. Govindaswamy Chettiar & Sons [1977] 2 Lloyd's Rep. 5, CA;
reversing [1977] 1 Lloyd's Rep. 166 .... 16.66
Postel Properties Ltd and Daichi Line (London) Ltd v. Greenwell [1992] 65 P. & C.R. 239 and
244; [1992] 47 E.G. 106; [1992] E.G.C.S. 105; [1992] N.P.C. 97 .... 6.87
Post Office v. Aquarius Properties Ltd [1987] 1 All E.R. 1055; (1987) 54 P. & C.R. 61; (1987)
281 E.G. 798; [1987] 1 E.G.L.R. 40; (1987) 84 L.S. Gaz. 820, CA; [1985] 2 E.G.L.R. 105;
(1985) 276 E.G. 923 .... 10.28
Powell v. Stevens (1951) 101 L.J. 109, Cty.Ct. 9.16, 10.28
Poyser and Mills' Arbitration, Re [1964] 2 Q.B. 467; [1963] 2 W.L.R. 1309; [1963] 1 All E.R.
612; *sub nom.* Poyser v. Mills, 107 S.J. 115 .... 12.33, 16.56, 16.68, 17.20
Pratt v. Keith (1864) 3 New Rep. 406; 33 L.J.Ch. 528; 10 L.T. 15; 10 Jur. (N.S.) 305; 12 W.R.
394 .... 10.70
Premier Dairies Ltd v. Garlick [1920] 2 Ch. 17; 89 L.J.Ch. 332; 123 L.T. 44; 64 S.J. 375 ...... 10.39
Prenn v. Simmonds [1971] 1 W.L.R. 1381; 115 S.J. 654; [1971] 3 All E.R. 237, HL 12.29
President of India v. Jadranska Slobodna Plovidba (1922) 2 Ll. Rep. 274 .... 16.72
Preston v. Norfolk County Council [1947] K.B. 775; [1947] L.J.R. 1301; 177 L.T. 390; 63
T.L.R. 441; [1947] 2 All E.R. 124 .... 13.22
Price v. Evans (1872) 29 L.T. 835 .... 12.17
―― v. Popkin (1839) 10 A. & E. 139; 2 Per. & Dav. 304; 8 L.J.Q.B. 198; 3 Jur. 433; 113 E.R.
53 .... 16.66
―― v. Romilly [1960] 1 W.L.R. 1360; 104 S.J. 1060; [1960] 3 All E.R. 429 .. 12.56, 12.57, 12.61.2,
12.61.4, 12.61.9, 16.56, 16.68
―― v. West London Investment Building Society [1964] 1 W.L.R. 616; 108 S.J. 276; [1964] 2
All E.R. 318 .... 17.19
―― v. Williams (1967) 201 E.G. 863 .... 16.68
Proudfoot v. Hart (1890) 25 Q.B.D. 42 .... 10.12, 10.28, 10.83, 13.92, 16.49
Prudential Assurance Co. v. Grand Metropolitan Estates [1993] 2 E.G.L.R. 153; 32 E.G. 74 ..   2.23
Prudential Assurance Co. Limited v. Mount Eden Land Limited [1977] 1 E.G.L.R. 37, CA ..5.9, 5.10
Public Trustee v. Randag [1966] Ch. 649; [1965] 3 W.L.R. 1156; 109 S.J. 935; [1965] 3 All E.R.
88 .... 16.52, 16.53, 16.56, 16.61
Pugh v. Arton [1869] L.R. 8 Eq. 626 .... 1.46
Puncknowle Farms Ltd v. Kane [1985] 3 All E.R. 790; [1986] 1 C.M.L.R. 27; [1985] 2 E.G.L.R.
8; (1985) 275 E.G. 1283 .... 18.18
Purkiss' Application, Re [1962] 1 W.L.R. 902; 106 S.J. 308; [1962] 2 All E.R. 690; 13 P. & C.R.
277; 60 L.G.R. 349; [1962] R.V.R. 455, CA; *affirming* 178 E.G. 761; 111 L.J. 408 .... 16.32
Purser v. Bailey [1967] 2 Q.B. 500; [1967] 2 W.L.R. 1500; 111 S.J. 353; *sub nom.* Bailey v.
Purser [1967] 2 All E.R. 189, CA; *affirming* [1967] 1 Q.B. 526; [1967] 2 W.L.R. 146; 110
S.J. 909; *sub nom.* Bailey v. Purser [1967] 1 All E.R. 188 .... 12.36, 12.39, 16.4

xxxii

—— v. Worthing Local Board (1887) 18 Q.B.D. 818; 56 L.J.M.C. 78; 3 T.L.R. 636; 51 J.P. 596; 35 W.R. 682 .... 15.20

R. v. Agricultural Land Tribunal for the Eastern Area, *ex p.* Moses; Moses v. Hurst (1983) 269 E.G. 168 .... 16.7
—— v. Agricultural Land Tribunal for the Eastern Province, *ex p.* Grant [1956] 1 W.L.R. 1240; 100 S.J. 650; [1956] 3 All E.R. 321; 54 L.G.R. 567 .... 12.33, 12.35, 12.36, 16.7
—— v. Agricultural Land Tribunal for the South Eastern Area, *ex p.* Boucher [1952] C.P.L. 188; [1952] E.G.D. 20; (1952) 159 E.G. 191 .... 12.42, 16.7
—— v.——, *ex p.* Bracey [1960] 1 W.L.R. 911; 104 S.J. 643; [1960] 2 All E.R. 518 .... 12.39, 16.7, 16.70
—— v.——, *ex p.* Hooker [1952] 1 K.B. 1; [1951] 2 T.L.R. 824; [1951] 2 All E.R. 801 ...... 16.7
—— v.——, *ex p.* Palmer [154] J.P.L. 181 .... 16.7
—— v.——, *ex p.* Parslow (1979) 251 E.G. 667 .... 12.39, 16.7
—— v. Agricultural Land Tribunal Wales and Monmouth area, *ex p.* Davies [1953] 1 W.L.R. 722; 97 S.J. 335; [1953] 1 All E.R. 1182; 51 L.G.R. 368 .... 12.33, 12.36, 16.7
—— v. Agricultural Land Tribunal for Wales, *ex. p.* Hughes (1980) 255 E.G. 703 .... 14.60
—— v. Birkenhead J.J., *ex p.* Fisher (Practice Note) [1962] 1 W.L.R. 1410; 127 J.P. 15; 106 S.J. 856; [1962] 3 All E.R. 837 .... 16.34
—— v. Chester City Council, *ex p.* Quietlynn; R. v. Havant Borough Council, *ex p.* Quietlynn; R. v. Preston Borough Council, *ex p.* Quietlynn; R. v. Swansea City Council, *ex p.* Quietlynn; R. v. Trafford Borough Council, *ex p.* Quietlynn; R. v. Watford Borough Council, *ex p.* Quietlynn (1985) 83 L.G.R. 308, CA; *affirming The Times*, October 19, 1983 .... 13.37
—— v. County of London Quarter Sessions Appeals Committee, *ex p.* Rossi [1956] 1 Q.B. 682; [1956] 2 W.L.R. 800; 120 J.P. 239; 100 S.J. 225; [1956] 1 All E.R. 670, CA 17.20
—— v. Cripps, *ex p.* Muldoon [1984] Q.B. 686; [1984] 3 W.L.R. 53; (1984) 128 S.J. 431; [1984] 2 All E.R. 705; (1984) 82 L.G.R. 439, CA; *affirming* [1984] Q.B. 68; [1983] 3 W.L.R. 465; (1983) 127 S.J. 427; [1983] 3 All E.R. 72; (1983) 133 New L.J. 848 .... 16.58
—— v. Dairy Produce Quota Tribunal for England and Wales, *ex p.* Hall & Sons (Dairy Farmers) Ltd (174/88) [1990] E.C.R.I–2237 .... 18.6
—— v. Fulham, Hammersmith & Kensington Rent Tribunal, *ex p.* Zerek [1951] 2 K.B. 1; [1951] 1 T.L.R. 423; 115 J.P. 132; 95 S.J. 237; [1951] 1 All E.R. 482; 49 L.G.R. 275 .... 16.32
—— v. Gravesend J.J., *ex p.* Sheldon [1968] 1 W.L.R. 1699; 132 J.P. 553; 112 S.J. 838; [1968] 3 All E.R. 466n.; [1968] Crim. L.R. 506 .... 16.34
—— v. Henn; R. v. Darby. *See* Henn and Darby v. D.P.P.
—— v. Kensington and Chelsea Rent Tribunal, *ex p.* MacFarlane [1974] 1 W.L.R. 1486; 118 S.J. 700 [1974] 3 All E.R. 390; 29 P. & C.R. 13 .... 16.58
—— v. Kingston-upon-Hull Rent Tribunal, *ex p.* Black [1949] W.N. 51; (1949) 65 T.L.R. 209; 113 J.P. 123; 93 S.J. 199; [1949] 1 All E.R. 260; 47 L.G.R. 262 .... 16.34
—— v. Liverpool Justices, *ex p.* Roberts [1960] 1 W.L.R. 585; 124 J.P. 336; 104 S.J. 450; [1960] 2 All E.R. 384n. 16.23
—— v. L.C.C. [1894] 1 Q.B. 453; 63 L.J.Q.B. 301; 70 L.T. 148; 10 T.L.R. 189; 58 J.P. 380; 9 R. 148; 42 W.R. 225 .... 16.23
—— v. Ministry of Agriculture, Fisheries & Food, *ex p.* Bostock (C–2/92) [1994] E.C.R.I.–955; [1994] 3 C.M.L.R. 547 .... 18.11, 19.1, 19.7, 19.17
—— v. Ministry of Agriculture, Fisheries and Food, *ex p.* Cox (1994) 6 Admin. L.R. 421; [1993] 1 E.G.L.R. 17; [1993] 22 E.G. 111; [1993] E.G.C.S. 27; *The Times*, February 16, 1993, Q.B.D. 18.21
—— v. Nat Bell Liquors Ltd [1922] 2 A.C. 128; 91 L.J.P.C. 146; 127 L.T. 437; 38 T.L.R. 541; 27 Cox C.C. 253 .... 16.7, 16.68
—— v. National Joint Council for the Craft of Dental Technicians (Disputes Committee) *ex p.* Neate [1953] 1 Q.B. 704; [1953] 2 W.L.R. 342; 97 S.J. 116; [1953] 1 All E.R. 327 .... 16.70
—— v. Northumberland Compensation Appeal Tribunal, *ex p.* Shaw [1952] 1 K.B. 338; [1952] 1 T.L.R. 161; 116 J.P. 54; 96 S.J. 29; [1952] 1 All E.R. 122; 2 P. & C.R. 361; 50 L.G.R. 193 .... 16.7
—— v. Paddington and St. Marylebone Rent Tribunal, *ex p.* Bell, London and Provincial Properties Ltd [1949] 1 K.B. 666; 65 T.L.R. 200; 113 J.P. 209; 93 S.J. 219 [1949] 1 All E.R. 720; 47 L.G.R. 306 .... 16.48
—— v. Powell, *ex p.* Camden [1925] 1 K.B. 641; 94 L.J.K.B. 433; 132 L.T. 766; 41 T.L.R. 277; 89 J.P. 64; 23 L.G.R. 391 .... 13.116, 16.15, 16.23, 16.70
—— v. Preston Borough Council, *ex p.* Quietlynn Ltd *The Times*, March 22, 1984, CA 13.37

xxxiii

TABLE OF CASES

—— v. Preston Borough Council and others, *ex p.* Quietlynn. *See* R. v. Chester City Council, *ex p.* Quietlynn
—— v. Pugh (Judge), *ex p.* Graham [1951] 2 K.B. 623; [1951] 2 T.L.R. 253; 115 J.P. 425; 95 S.J. 431; [1951] 2 All E.R. 307; 49 L.G.R. 659 .... 16.32
—— v. Rent Assessment Committee for London, *ex p.* Ellis-Rees (1982) 262 E.G. 1298 16.35, 16.66
—— v. Secretary of State for the Environment, *ex p.* Greater London Council, *The Times*, December 30, 1985 .... 16.70
—— v. Secretary of State for the Home Department, *ex p.* Brind [1991] 1 A.C. 696; [1991] 2 W.L.R. 588; [1991] 1 All E.R. 720; (1991) 135 S.J. 250; (1991) 141 N.L.J. 199; (1991) 3 Admin. L.R. 486, *The Times*, February 8, 1991; *The Independent*, February 8, 1991; *The Guardian*, February 8, 1991, HL; *affirming* [1990] 2 W.L.R. 787; [1990] 1 All E.R. 469; [1990] C.O.D. 190; (1989) 139 N.L.J. 1751, CA; *affirming* (1989) 2 Admin. L.R. 169; [1990] C.O.D. 49, *The Times*, May 30, 1989, DC 18.6
—— v. Smith (Joan) [1968] 1 W.L.R. 636; (1968) 132 J.P. 312; [1968] 2 All E.R. 115; 52 Cr. App. R. 224; *sub nom.* R. v. Smith, 112 S.J. 231, CA 16.36
—— v. South Devon Ry. (1850) 15 Q.B. 1043; 20 L.J.Q.B. 145; 16 L.T. (o.s.) 149; 15 Jur. 464; 117 E.R. 754 .... 16.26
—— v. Sussex Justices, *ex p.* McCarthy [1924] 1 K.B. 256; 93 L.J.K.B. 129; 88 J.P. 3; 68 S.J. 253; 22 L.G.R. 46 .... 16.23
—— v. Thames Magistrates, *ex p.* Polemis [1974] 1 W.L.R. 1371; 118 S.J. 734; [1974] 2 All E.R. 1219; [1974] 2 Lloyd's Rep. 16 .... 16.35
Racecourse Betting Control Board v. Secretary of State for Air [1944] Ch. 114; 113 L.J.Ch. 129; 170 L.T. 29; 60 T.L.R. 147; 88 S.J. 58; [1944] 1 All E.R. 60 .... 16.68
Radio Publicity v. Cie Luxembourgeoise [1936] 2 All E.R. 721 .... 6.17
Railtrack Plc v. Gojra [1998] 08 E.G. 158, CA 7.14, 17.24
Raine (James) (Senior), (Trustees of) v. Raine (1985) 275 E.G. 374 .... 14.70, 14.71
Ramsay v. McLaren 1936 S.L.T. 35 .... 16.23
Ravenseft Properties Ltd v. Davstone (Holdings) Ltd [1980] 1 Q.B. 12; [1979] 2 W.L.R. 898; (1978) 123 S.J. 320; [1979] 1 All E.R. 929; (1978) 37 P. & C.R. 502; (1978) 249 E.G. 51 .... 10.28
Reardon Smith Line Ltd v. Hansen-Tangen. *See* Reardon Smith Line Ltd v. Yngrar Hansen-Tangen
—— v. Yngrar Hansen-Tangen; Yngrar Hansen-Tangen v. Sanko Steamship Co. [1976] 1 W.L.R. 989; 120 S.J. 719; *sub nom.* Reardon Smith Line v. Hansen-Tangen; Hansen-Tangen v. Sanko Steamship Co. [1976] 3 All E.R. 570, HL; *affirming sub nom.*Reardon Smith Line v. Yngrar Hansen-Tangen Sanko Steamship Co. (third party), 120 S.J. 329; *sub nom.* Reardon Smith Line v. Yngrar Hansen-Tangen and Sanko Steamship Co.; Diana Prosperity, The [1976] 2 Lloyd's Rep. 60, CA 12.29
Redland Bricks v. Morris [1970] A.C. 652; [1969] 2 W.L.R. 1437; 113 S.J. 405; [1969] 2 All E.R. 576, HL; *reversing sub nom.* Morris v. Redland Bricks [1967] 1 W.L.R. 967; 111 S.J. 373; [1967] 3 All E.R. 1, CA 10.33
Reeve v. Atterby [1978] C.L.Y. 73 .... 8.18
Regional Properties v. City of London Real Property; Sedgwick Forbes Bland Payne Group v. Regional Properties (1980) E.G. 64 .... 10.33
Regis Property Co. Ltd v. Dudley [1959] A.C. 370; [1958] 3 W.L.R. 647; 102 S.J. 844; [1958] 3 All E.R. 491 .... 10.31
Regor Estates v. Wright [1951] 1 K.B. 689; [1951] 1 T.L.R. 242; 115 J.P. 61; 95 S.J. 106; [1951] 1 All E.R. 219; 49 L.G.R. 241; [15 Conv. 126], CA 2.2
Reid v. Dawson [1955] 1 Q.B. 214; [1954] 3 W.L.R. 810; 98 S.J. 818; [1954] 3 All E.R. 498; 53 L.G.R. 24 .... 9.3, 9.9, 9.11
Rena K, The [1979] Q.B. 377; [1978] 3 W.L.R. 431; [1979] 1 All E.R. 397; (1978) 122 S.J. 315; [1978] 1 Lloyd's Rep. 545 .... 6.17
Richards v. Allinson (1978) 249 E.G. 59 .... 9.7, 11.3.4, 16.27
—— v. Davies [1921] 1 Ch. 90; 89 L.J.Ch. 601; 124 L.T. 238; 65 S.J. 44 .... 10.71, 13.107
Richards (C.) and Son v. Karenita [1972] 221 E.G. 25 .... 2.10.1
—— v. Pryse [1927] 2 K.B. 76; 96 L.J.K.B. 743; 137 L.T. 170 .... 13.12
Richardson v. Worsley (1850) 5 Ex. 613; 19 L.J. Ex. 317; 15 L.T. (o.s.) 282; 155 E.R. 268 .... 16.72
Rickett v. Green [1910] 1 K.B. 253; 79 L.J.K.B. 193; 102 L.T. 16 .... 13.97
Right *d.* Fisher v. Cuthell (1804) 5 East 491; 2 Smith K.B. 83; 102 E.R. 1158 .... 12.17
Riley (E.J.) Investments v. Eurostile Holdings [1985] 1 W.L.R. 1139; (1985) 129 S.J. 523; [1985] 3 All E.R. 181; (1985) 51 P. & C.R. 36; [1985] 2 E.G.L.R. 124; (1985) 135 New L.J. 887, CA 13.28
Ritz Hotel (London) Ltd v. Ritz Casino Ltd [1989] 2 E.G.L.R. 135; [1989] 46 E.G. 95 .... 2.16

TABLE OF CASES

Roberts v. Barker (1833) 1 C. & M. 808; 3 Tyr. 945; 2 L.J. Ex. 268; 149 E.R. 625 .... 13.107
—— v. Church Commissioners for England [1972] 1 Q.B. 278; [1971] 3 W.L.R. 566; 115 S.J. 792; [1971] 3 All E.R. 703, CA 1.43, 9.3, 9.21
—— v. Magor [1953] E.G.D. 18; (1953) 103 L.J. 703, Cty.Ct. 10.37
Robertson's Trustees v. Cunningham 1951 S.L.T. 89, Sh.Ct. 16.27
Robertson-Ackerman v. George (1953) 103 L.J. 496 .... 10.10, 10.12
Robinson v. Moody [1994] 2 E.G.L.R. 16; [1994] 37 E.G. 154; [1994] N.P.C. 10; *The Times*, February 23, 1994, CA 16.22
Romer & Haslam, *Re* [1893] 2 Q.B. 286 .... 12.56
Roper v. Prudential Assurance Co. Limited (1992) 1 E.G.L.R. 5; [1992] 09 E.G. 141; [1991] N.P.C. 78 .... 10.10, 10.19
Rosen & Co. v. Dowley and Selby [1943] 2 All E.R. 172 .... 16.72
Ross v. Boards (1838) 8 A. & E. 290; 3 Nev. & P.K.B. 382; 1 Will.Woll. & H. 376; 7 L.J.Q.B. 209; 2 Jur. 567; 112 E.R. 847 .... 16.56
Ross v. Watson 1943 S.C. 406 .... 10.76
Ross-Clunis v. Papadopoullos [1958] 1 W.L.R. 546; 122 J.P. 362; 102 S.J. 362; [1958] 2 All E.R. 23 .... 12.34
Rotheray (E.) & Sons v. Carlo Bedarida & Co. [1961] 1 Lloyd's Rep. 220 .... 16.33
Rous v. Mitchell; *sub nom.* Earl of Stradbroke v. Mitchell [1991] 1 W.L.R. 469; [1991] 1 All E.R. 676; (1990) 61 P. & C.R. 314; [1991] 1 E.G.L.R. 1; [1991] 03 E.G. 128; (1990) 140 N.L.J. 1386, CA; *affirming* [1989] 50 E.G. 45 .... 12.47
Royal Bank of Scotland v. Jennings [1997] 1 E.G.L.R. 101; [1996] E.G.C.S. 168, CA 2.10.2
Royal Brunei Airlines Sdn Bhd v. Tan (Philip Kok Ming) [1995] 2 A.C. 378; [1995] 3 W.L.R. 64; [1995] 3 All E.R. 97; [1995] B.C.C. 899; (1995) 145 N.L.J. Rep. 888; [1995] 139 S.J.L.B. 146; [1995] 92(27) L.S. Gaz. 33; *The Times*, May 29, 1995; *The Independent*, June 22, 1995, PC 12.47
Royal Trust International Ltd v. Nordbanken [1993] 1 E.G.L.R. 169E 6.87
Rugby Joint Water Board v. Foottit. *See* Rugby Joint Water Board v. Fox; Rugby Joint Water Board v. Foottit.
—— v. Shaw Fox; Rugby Joint Water Board v. Foottit [1973] A.C. 202; [1972] 2 W.L.R. 757; 116 S.J. 240; [1972] 1 All E.R. 1057; 71 L.G.R. 339; 24 P. & C.R. 256; [1972] R.V.R. 112, 135, HL; *reversing in part* [1971] 2 Q.B. 14; [1971] 2 W.L.R. 154; 114 S.J. 911; [1971] 1 All E.R. 373; 22 P. & C.R. 275, CA 12.7, 12.50
Rush v. Lucas [1910] 1 Ch. 437; 79 L.J.Ch. 172; 101 L.T. 851; 54 S.J. 200 .... 10.55
Russell v. Booker (1982) 263 E.G. 513, CA 8.15
Rutherford v. Maurer [1962] 1 Q.B. 16; [1961] 3 W.L.R. 5; 105 S.J. 404; [1961] 2 All E.R. 755 ...8.18, 9.2, 9.8, 9.10

Safeway Food Stores Ltd v. Banderway Ltd [1983] 2 E.G.L.R. 116; (1983) 267 E.G. 850 ..... 6.87
Salisbury v. Gilmore [1942] 2 K.B. 38; 111 L.J.K.B. 593; 166 L.T. 329; [1942] 1 All E.R. 457 13.94
Sampson and Horsfall, *Re* (1921) 10 L.J.C.C.R. 90 .... 13.27
Samuel v. Cooper (1835) 2 A. & E. 752; 1 Har. & W. 86; 4 Nev. & M.K.B. 520; 111 E.R. 290 16.66
Samuel v. Salmon and Gluckstein [1946] Ch. 8 .... 2.2
Sanctuary Housing Association v. Baker [1998] 09 E.G. 150, CA 12.42, 12.61.16, 12.77
Saner v. Bilton (1878) 7 Ch. D. 815; 47 L.J.Ch. 267; 38 L.T. 281; 26 W.R. 394 .... 10.31, 10.86
Saul v. Norfolk County Council [1984] Q.B. 559; [1984] 3 W.L.R. 84; (1984) 128 S.J. 433; [1984] 2 All E.R. 489; (1984) 82 L.G.R. 601; (1985) 49 P. & C.R. 1, CA 12.49, 14.22, 15.39
Saunders Dec'd. Trustees v. Ralph. *See* Trustees of Saunders v. Ralph
Saunders-Jacobs v. Yates [1933] 2 K.B. 240; 102 L.J.K.B. 417; 149 L.T. 209, CA; *affirming* [1933] 1 K.B. 392 .... 15.27
Savile Settled Estates, *Re* [1931] 2 Ch. 210 .... 1.13, 14.8
Savva v. Hussein [1997] 73 P. & C.R. 150 ....12.76.1
Sawyer and Withall, *Re* [1919] 2 Ch. 333; 88 L.J.Ch. 474; 122 L.T. 158; 35 T.L.R. 611; 63 S.J. 662 .... 10.78
Sayers v. Collyer [1884] 28 Ch. D. 103 .... 1.19
Scala House and District Property Co. Ltd v. Forbes [1974] Q.B. 575; [1973] 3 W.L.R. 14; 117 S.J. 467; [1973] 3 All E.R. 308; 26 P. & C.R. 164, CA 12.61.16, 12.76.1
Scene Estate Ltd v. Amos [1957] 2 Q.B. 205; [1957] 2 W.L.R. 1017; 101 S.J. 445; [1957] 2 All E.R. 325; 56 L.G.R. 14 .... 9.8, 9.9, 9.11, 9.15, 9.16
Schnabel v. Allard [1967] 1 Q.B. 627; [1966] 3 W.L.R. 1295; 110 S.J. 831; [1966] 3 All E.R. 816, CA 12.14
Schofield v. Allen (1904) 48 S.J. 176; 116 L.T. 239 .... 16.66

TABLE OF CASES

—— v. Hincks (1888) 58 L.J.Q.B. 147; 60 L.T. 573; 5 T.L.R. 101; 37 W.R. 157 .... 13.116, 16.15
Sclater v. Horton [1954] 2 Q.B. 1; [1954] 2 W.L.R. 566; 98 S.J. 213; [1954] 1 All E.R. 712; 52 L.G.R. 217 .... 11.3, 11.3.3, 11.3.4
—— v. Scott [1921] p. 107; 90 L.J.P. 171; 124 L.T. 619; 37 T.L.R. 158, CA 16.56
Scottish and Newcastle Breweries plc v. Sir Richard Sutton's Settled Estates [1985] 2 E.G.L.R. 130; (1985) 276 E.G. 77 .... 2.16, 2.20, 2.23
Scrimgeour v. Waller (1980) 257 E.G. 61, CA 9.12
Seccombe v. Babb (1840) 6 M. & W. 129; 8 Dowl. 167; 9 L.J.Ex. 65; 4 J. 90; 151 E.R. 351 ... 16.72
Secretary of State for the Environment v. Reed International plc [1994] 1 E.G.L.R. 22; [1994] 06 E.G. 137 .... 16.44
Secretary of State for Social Services v. Beavington (1981) 262 E.G. 551 .... 9.4, 9.6
Secretary of State for Wales v. Pugh (1970) 120 L.J. 357, Cty.Ct. 8.18, 12.18, 12.50
Segama N.V. v. Penny le Roy Ltd (1983) 269 E.G. 322 .... 2.16
Seligman v. Docker [1949] Ch. 53; [1949] L.J.R. 188; 92 S.J. 647; [1948] 2 All E.R. 887 ..... 10.74
Sellar v. Highland Ry. 1919 56 S.L.R. 216 (H.L.); S.C.(H.L.)19 .... 16.35
—— v. Reid [1965] E.G.D. 4; (1965) 193 E.G. 19 .... 11.34
Sharpe v. Bickerdyke (1815) 3 Dowl H.L. 102; 3 E.R. 1003 .... 16.66
Sharpley v. Manby [1942] 1 K.B. 217; 111 L.J.K.B. 82; 166 L.T. 44; 58 T.L.R. 91; *sub nom.* Re Sharpley & Manby's Arbitration [1942] 1 All E.R. 66 .... 12.55
Sheerness Steel Co. plc v. Medway Ports Authority [1992] 1 E.G.L.R. 133; [1992] 12 E.G. 138; [1991] E.G.C.S. 121, CA 2.24
The Sheffield and South Yorkshire Permanent Benefit Building Society v. Harrison [1884] 15 Q.B.D. 358, CA 3.10
Shepherd v. Lomas [1963] 1 W.L.R. 962; 107 S.J. 435; [1963] 2 All E.R. 902 .... 12.61.4, 12.61.6, 12.61.13
Shepton Mallet Transport Co. Ltd. v. Clarke [1953] C.P. L. 343; (1953) 161 E.G. 518 .... 12.61.17
Sherwood (Baron) v. Moody [1952] 1 T.L.R. 450; 96 S.J. 105; [1952] 1 All E.R. 389; 50 L.G.R. 180; *sub nom.* Sheerwood v. Moody [1952] W.N. 95 ....12.76.2, 13.33, 15.13
Shield Properties & Investments Ltd v. Anglo-Overseas Transport Co. Ltd. [1985] 1 E.G.L.R. 7; (1984) 273 E.G. 69; (1984) 134 New L.J. 705 .... 16.41
Short v. Greeves [1988] 1 E.G.L.R. 1; [1988] 08 E.G. 109, CA 8.15, 8.16, 8.19
Short Bros. (Plant) Ltd v. Edwards (1978) 249 E.G. 539, CA 9.8, 9.12, 9.15
Sidebothom v. Holland [1895] 1 Q.B. 378; 64 L.J.Q.B. 200; 72 L.T. 62; 11 T.L.R. 154; 39 S.J. 165; 14 R. 135; 43 W.R. 228 .... 12.14, 12.29
Silvester v. Ostrowska [1959] 1 W.L.R. 1060; 103 S.J. 940; [1959] 3 All E.R. 642 ....12.61.12
Simmons v. Norton (1831) 7 Bing. 640; 5 Moo. & P. 645; 9 L.J. (o.s.) C.P. 185; 131 E.R. 247   10.55
Simpson v. Batey [1924] 2 K.B. 666; 93 L.J.K.B. 919; 131 L.T. 724; 68 S.J. 754 ....13.116, 16.15
—— v. Henderson 1944 S.C. 365 .... 13.119
Skelton (William) & Son Ltd v. Harrison & Pinder Ltd [1975] Q.B. 361; [1975] 2 W.L.R. 238; (1974) 119 S.J. 98; [1975] 1 All E.R. 182; (1974) 29 P. & C.R. 113 .... 12.20
Slade v. Manton's Executors (Lord) (1923) 12 L.J.C.C.R. 83, Cty.Ct. 16.62
Sloan Stanley Estate Trustees v. Barribal [1994] 2 E.G.L.R. 8 .... 12.58
Smeaton Hanscomb & Co. Ltd v. Setty (Sassoon I.), Son & Co. (No. 2) [1953] 1 W.L.R. 1481; 97 S.J. 876; [1953] 2 All E.R. 1588; [1953] 2 Lloyd's Rep. 580 .... 16.66, 16.72
Smith v. Callander [1901] A.C. 297; 70 L.J.P.C. 53; 84 L.T. 801 .... 15.28
—— v. Great Western Railway Co. (1877) 3 App. Cas. 165, HL; *affirming sub nom.* Great Western Railway Co. v. Smith (1876) 2 Ch. D. 235; 45 L.J.Ch. 235; 34 L.T. 267; 40 J.P. 469; 24 W.R. 443, CA 3.9
—— v. Gronow [1891] 2 Q.B. 394 .... 12.78
—— v. Harwich [1857] 2 C.B. (N.S.) 651 .... 1.44
—— v. Hughes (1871) L.R. 6 Q.B. 597; 40 L.J.Q.B. 221; 25 L.T. 329; 19 W.R. 1059 ....9.8, 9.15
—— v. Morgan [1971] 1 W.L.R. 803; 115 S.J. 288; [1971] 2 All E.R. 1500; 22 P. & C.R. 618; [68 L.S. Gaz. 484] 1.44
—— v. Richmond [1899] A.C. 448; 68 L.J.Q.B. 898; 81 L.T. 269; 15 T.L.R. 523; 63 J.P. 804; 48 W.R. 115; 4 T.C. 131 .... 15.20
Snell v. Snell [1964] E.G.D. 294; (1964) 191 E.G. 361 .... 9.4
Snook v. London and West Riding Investments [1967] 2 Q.B. 786; [1967] 2 W.L.R. 1020; 111 S.J. 71; [1967] 1 All E.R. 518; [30 M.L.R. 697], CA 9.15
Sociedad Iberica de Molturacion SA v. Nidera Handelscompagnie BV [1990] 2 Lloyd's Rep. 240 .... 16.47

TABLE OF CASES

Société Franco-Tunisienne d'Armement Tunis v. Government of Ceylon (The "Massalia") [1959] 1 W.L.R. 787; 103 S.J. 675; [1959] 3 All E.R. 25; [1959] 2 Lloyd's Rep. 1, CA; *reversing* [1959] 1 Lloyd's Rep. 244 .... 11.33, 16.35, 16.66
Soho Square Syndicate Ltd v. Pollard (E.) & Co. Ltd [1940] Ch. 638; 109 L.J.Ch. 266; 162 L.T. 372; 56 T.L.R. 764; [1940] 2 All E.R. 601 .... 10.53
Somerset County Council v. Pearse [1977] C.L.Y. 53 .... 9.12
South Sea Co. v. Bumstead (1734) 2 Eq. Cas. Ab. 80; 22 E.R. 70 .... 16.66
South Shropshire District Council v. Amos [1986] 1 W.L.R. 1271; (1986) 130 S.J. 803; [1987] 1 All E.R. 340; [1986] 2 E.G.L.R. 194; (1986) 280 E.G. 635; (1986) 26 R.V.R. 235; (1986) 136 New L.J. 800 .... 16.41
South West Water Authority v. Palmer (1983) 268 E.G. 357, 443, CA; (1982) 263 E.G. 438 ...... 9.9, 9.11, 9.15
Southern Livestock Producers Ltd, *Re* [1964] 1 W.L.R. 24; 108 S.J. 15; [1963] 3 All E.R. 801   10.71
Sparkes v. Smart [1990] 2 E.G.L.R. 245, CA 15.17
Spath Holme Limited v. Greater Manchester and Lancashire Rent Assessment Committee [1995] 2 E.G.L.R. 80; [1995] 49 E.G. 128; [1995] N.P.C. 138; *The Times*, August 9, 1995; *The Independent*, August 28, 1995 (C.S.), CA; *reversing* (1995) 27 H.L.R. 243; *The Times*, July 13, 1994, Q.B.D. 11.14, 11.18
Spiller and Baker Ltd and Leetham & Sons Arbitration, *Re* [1897] 1 Q.B. 312; 66 L.J.Q.B. 326; 76 L.T. 35; 13 T.L.R. 152; 41 S.J. 208; 45 W.R. 241 .... 16.62
Spreckley v. Leicestershire County Council [1934] 1 K.B. 366; 103 L.J.K.B. 200; 150 L.T. 9 .. 13.27, 13.119, 16.28
Spyer v. Phillipson [1931] 2 Ch. 183; 100 L.J. Ch. 245; 144 L.T. 626; 74 S,J. 787, CA 10.31
Stafford v. Gardner (1872) L.R. 7 C.P. 242; 25 L.T. 876; 36 J.P. 566; 20 W.R. 299 ..... 13.48, 13.113
Staines Warehousing Co. Ltd v. Montagu Executor & Trustee Co. Ltd (1985) 51 P. & C.R. 211; [1986] 1 E.G.L.R. 101; (1985) 277 E.G. 305 .... 16.23
Stent v. Monmouth District Council (1987) 19 H.L.R. 269; (1987) 54 P. & C.R. 193; (1987) 282 E.G. 705; [1987] 1 E.G.L.R. 59, CA 10.28
Stephens v. Balls (1957) 107 L.J. 764; [1957] E.G.D. 237, Cty.Ct. 10.78
Sterling Land Office Developments v. Lloyds Bank plc [1984] 2 E.G.L.R. 135; (1984) 271 E.G. 894 .... 2.16
Stevenage Development Corporation v. Ivory (1960), unreported 12.40
Stevens v. Feoffes of the Poor Lands in the Parish of Downham [1926] W.N. 168 .... 16.62, 16.63
—— v. Gourley [1859] 7 C.B.(N.S.) 99 .... 3.11
—— v. Sedgeman [1951] 2 K.B. 434; [1951] 2 T.L.R. 16; 95 S.J. 367; [1951] 2 All E.R. 33; 49 L.G.R. 524 .... 8.13, 8.18, 12.38
Stewart v. Brims 1969 S.L.T. 2 .... 16.30
Steyning and Littlehampton Building Society v. Wilson [1951] Ch. 1018; [1951] 2 T.L.R. 424; 95 S.J. 514; [1951] 2 All E.R. 452 .... 8.17, 8.19, 9.17, 12.5
Stiles v. Farrow (1977) 241 E.G. 623 .... 12.20
Stocker v. Planet Building Society (1879) 27 W.R. 877 .... 10.86
Stone v. Whitcombe (1980) 40 P. & C.R. 296; (1980) 257 E.G. 929 .... 9.8, 9.9, 9.15
Stoneman v. Brown [1973] 1 W.L.R. 459; 117 S.J. 109; [1973] 2 All E.R. 225; 25 P. & C.R. 297, CA 12.57, 12.61.9
Stotesbury v. Turner [1943] K.B. 370; 112 L.J.K.B. 365; 168 L.T. 355 .... 16.41
Strachan v. Hunter 1916 S.C. 901 .... 16.72
Stradbroke v. Mitchell [1991] 1 E.G.L.R. 1 .... 12.47
Stradbrooke (Lord) v. Mulcahy (1852) 2 Ir. C.L.R. 406 .... 10.78
Strang v. Stuart [1887] 14 R. 637 .... 8.22
Stranks v. St. John (1867) L.R. 2 C.P. 376 .... 1.44
Strathclyde Regional Council v. Arnell 1987 S.L.C.R. 44 .... 11.25
Streat v. Cottey [1947] E.G.D. 136; [1947] L.J.N.C.C.R. 156 .... 8.22, 13.22
Street v. Mountford [1985] A.C. 809; [1985] 2 W.L.R. 877; (1985) 129 S.J. 348; [1985] 2 All E.R. 289; (1985) 50 P. & C.R. 258; (1985) 274 E.G. 821; (1985) 17 H.L.R. 402; (1985) 135 New L.J. 460, HL; *reversing* (1984) 128 S.J. 483; (1984) 49 P. & C.R. 324; (1984) 16 H.L.R. 27; (1984) 271 E.G. 1153, CA 9.3, 9.4, 18.21
Strickland v. Maxwell (1834) 2 Cr. & M. 539; 4 Tyr. 346; 3 L.J.Ex. 161; 149 E.R. 875 .... 13.113
Sucksmith v. Wilson (1866) 4 F. & F. 1083 .... 13.113
Sudbrook Trading Estate v. Eggleton [1983] 1 A.C. 444; [1982] 3 W.L.R. 315; (1982) 126 S.J. 512; [1982] 3 All E.R. 1; (1982) 44 P. & C.R. 153; (1982) 79 L.S. Gaz. 1175; [1983] 1 E.G.L.R. 47; (1983) 265 E.G. 215, HL; *reversing* [1981] 3 W.L.R. 361; (1981) 125 S.J. 513; [1981] 3 All E.R. 105; (1981) 260 E.G. 1033, CA 2.9

TABLE OF CASES

Suggett v. Shaw 1987 S.L.T. (Land Ct.) 5; (1985) Sutherland R.N. 392 .... 16.27
Sumnall v. Stott (1984) 49 P. & C.R. 367; (1984) 271 E.G. 628, CA 12.61.5, 12.75, 12.76.1
Sun Alliance Insurance Ltd v. I.R.C. [1972] Ch. 133; [1971] 2 W.L.R. 432; (1970) 115 S.J. 32;
    [1971] 1 All E.R. 135; [1970] T.R. 411 .... 16.43
Sunderland v. Newton (1830) 3 Sim. 450 .... 3.6
Sunderland Steamship P. and I. Association v. Gatoil International; Lorenzo Halcoussi, The
    [1988] 1 Lloyd's Rep. 180 .... 16.39
Sutcliffe v. Thackrah [1974] A.C. 727; [1974] 2 W.L.R. 295; 118 S.J. 148; [1974] 1 All E.R.
    859; [1974] 1 Lloyd's Rep. 318; HL; *reversing* [1973] 1 W.L.R. 888; 117 S.J. 509; [1973]
    2 All E.R. 1047; [1973] 2 Lloyd's Rep. 115, CA 6.83, 6.84
Sutherland v. Hannevig [1921] 1 K.B. 336; 90 L.J.K.B. 225; 37 T.L.R. 102 .... 16.58
Sutherland Settlement Trusts, *Re* [1953] Ch. 792 [1953] 2 W.L.R. 1163; 97 S.J. 387; [1953] 2
    All E.R. 27 .... 17.15
Swansea Corporation v. Thomas (1882) 10 Q.B.D.48; 52 L.J.Q.B. 340; 47 L.T. 657; 47 J.P.
    135; 31 W.R. 506 .... 12.22
Sweeny v. Sweeny (1876) I.R. 10 C.L. 375 ....12.81.2
Swinburne v. Andrews [1923] 2 K.B. 483; 92 L.J.K.B. 889; 129 L.T. 650; 39 T.L.R. 545; 67 S.J.
    726 .... 8.22, 13.122
Sykes v. Land (1984) 271 E.G. 1264, CA 12.32
—— v. Secretary of State for the Environment; South Oxfordshire District Council v. Secretary
    of State for the Environment [1981] 1 W.L.R. 1092; (1980) 125 S.J. 444; [1981] 2 All E.R.
    954; (1981) 42 P. & C.R. 19; (1981) 257 E.G. 821; [1981] J.P.L. 285 .... 8.18, 8.19, 9.10

Tabernacle Permanent Building Society v. Knight [1892] A.C. 298; 62 L.J.Q.B. 50; 67 L.T.
    483; 8 T.L.R. 616; 56 J.P. 709; 36 S.J. 538; 41 W.R. 207 .... 16.61
Take Harvest v. Lin [1993] A.C. 552; [1993] 2 W.L.R. 785; [1993] 2 All E.R. 459; (1993) 67 P.
    & C.R. 150; (1993) 137 S.J.L.B. 92; [1993] N.P.C. 43; (1993) 143 N.L.J. 617, PC 1.13
Tankexpress v. Compagnie Financière Belge des Pétroles S/A *See* Tankexpress v. Compagnie
    Financière Belge de Pétroles S.A.
Tassell v. Hallen [1892] 1 Q.B. 321; 61 L.J.Q.B. 159; 66 L.T. 196; 8 T.L.R. 210; 56 J.P. 520; 36
    S.J. 202; 40 W.R. 221 .... 13.113
Tayleur v. Wildin (1868) L.R. 3 Exch. 303; 37 L.J.Ex. 173; 18 L.T. 655; 32 J.P. 630; 16 W.R.
    1018 .... 12.16
Taylor v. Steel-Maitland 1913 S.C. 562; 50 Sc.L.R. 395; 1 S.L.T. 224 .... 15.28
Techno Ltd v. Allied Dunbar Assurance plc [1993] 1 E.G.L.R. 29; [1993] 22 E.G. 109; [1993]
    E.G.C.S. 47; [1993] N.P.C. 42 .... 16.45
Tersons Ltd v. Stevenage Development Corporation [1965] 1 Q.B. 37; [1964] 2 W.L.R. 225;
    107 S.J. 852; [1963] 3 All E.R. 863; [1963] 2 Lloyd's Rep. 333; [1963] R.A. 393 .. 16.61, 16.64,
    16.69
Tew v. Harris (1847) 11 Q.B. 7; 17 L.J.Q.B. 1; 10 L.T. (o.s.) 87; 11 Jur. 947; 116 E.R. 376 ... 16.22
Thomas v. Countryside Council for Wales [1994] 4 All E.R. 853; [1994] 1 E.G.L.R. 17; [1994]
    04 E.G. 138; [1994] R.V.R. 66; [1993] E.G.C.S. 145; [1993] N.P.C. 119; *The Times*,
    August 24, 1993; *The Independent*, September 29, 1993 .... 16.56
Thomas v. National Farmers Union Mutual Insurance Society Ltd [1961] 1 W.L.R. 386; 105
    S.J. 233; [1961] 1 All E.R. 363; [1960] 2 Lloyd's Rep. 444 .... 13.22
—— v. Official Solicitor (1982) 265 E.G. 601, CA 16.33, 16.66
Thompson v. McCullogh [1947] K.B. 447; 176 L.T. 493; 63 T.L.R. 95; 91 S.J. 147; [1947] 1 All
    E.R. 265 .... 12.16
Thomson v. Anderson (1870) L.R. 9 Eq. 523; 39 L.J.Ch. 468; 22 L.T. 570; 34 J.P. 500; 18 W.R.
    445 .... 11.33
—— v. Galloway (Earl) 1919 S.C. 611; 56 Sc.L.R. 521 .... 10.75, 10.77
Thorlby v. Olivant [1960] E.G.D. 257 .... 12.81.2, 17.23
Threlfall v. Fanshawe (1851) 19 L.J.Q.B. 334; 1 L.M. & P. 340; 15 L.T. (o.s.) 210 .... 16.49
Tidswell, *Re* (1863) 33 Beav. 213; 3 New Pre. 281; 10 Jur. (N.S.) 143; 55 E.R. 349 .... 16.56
Tillam v. Copp (1847) 5 C.B. 211; 136 E.R. 857 .... 16.39
Tilling v. Whiteman [1980] A.C. 1; [1979] 2 W.L.R. 401; (1979) 123 S.J. 202; [1979] 1 All E.R.
    737; (1979) 38 P. & C.R. 341; (1979) 250 E.G. 51; [1979] J.P.L. 834; HL; *reversing*
    [1978] 3 W.L.R. 137; (1978) 37 P. & C.R. 427; (1978) 246 E.G. 1107, CA 13.36
Tombs v. Turvey (1923) 93 L.J.K.B. 785; 131 L.T. 330; 68 S.J. 385 .... 13.12
Tomlin v. Standard Telephones and Cables [1969] 1 W.L.R. 1378; 113 S.J. 641; [1969] 3 All
    E.R. 201; [1969] 1 Lloyd's Rep. 309, CA 16.41
Tomlinson v. Plymouth Argyle Football Co. Limited. *See* Tomlinson v. Plymouth Corporation

TABLE OF CASES

Tomlinson v. Plymouth Corporation and Plymouth Argyle Football Co. and Plymouth City Council (1960) 53 R. & I.T. 297; 175 E.G 1023; 6 R.R.C. 173, CA; *reversing* LVC/1134/1957 [1959] J.P.L. 62; 51 R. & I.T. 815; 4 R.R.C. 272; 172 E.G. 761; [1958] C.L.Y. 2831, Lands Tribunal 2.16
Top Shop Estates Ltd v. Danino (C.) [1985] 1 E.G.L.R. 9; (1984) 273 E.G. 197 .. 11.33, 16.34, 16.44, 16.48, 16.66
Tottenham Hotspur Football & Athletic Co. Ltd v. Princegrove Publishers Ltd [1974] 1 W.L.R. 113; (1973) 118 S.J. 35; [1974] 1 All E.R. 17; (1973) 27 P. & C.R. 101 .... 9.31
Town and City Properties (Development) Ltd v. Wiltshier Southern Ltd and Gilbert Powell [1988] 44 B.L.R. 109 .... 16.47
Tracomin S.A. v. Gibbs Nathaniel (Canada) Ltd [1985] 1 Lloyd's Rep. 586 .... 16.35, 16.66
Tradax Export S.A. v. Volkswagenwerk A.G. [1970] 1 Q.B. 537; [1970] 2 W.L.R. 339; 113 S.J. 978; [1970] 1 All E.R. 420; [1970] 1 Lloyd's Rep. 62, CA; *affirming* [1969] 2 Q.B. 599; [1969] 2 W.L.R. 498; [1969] 2 All E.R. 144 .... 16.22
Trane (U.K.) Ltd v. Provident Mutual Life Assurance Association [1995] 1 E.G.L.R. 33; [1995] 03 E.G. 122; [1994] E.G.C.S. 121, Ch. D. 10.37
Trinity College, Cambridge v. Caines (1983) 272 E.G. 1287 .... 5.4, 14.38, 14.41, 14.42, 14.47, 14.61
Troop v. Gibson [1986] 1 E.G.L.R. 1; (1985) 277 E.G. 1134 .... 1.19, 12.61.16, 12.76.1
Trustees of Smith's (Henry) Charity v. A.W.A.D.A. Trading and Promotion Services (1984) 128 S.J. 130; (1984) 47 P. & C.R. 607; (1984) 269 E.G. 729; (1984) 81 L.S. Gaz. 118, CA; *reversing* (1983) 46 P. & C.R. 74 ....2.10.1, 2.10.2
Trustees of J.W. Childers Will Trust v. Anker (1996) 71 P. & C.R. D5; [1996] 1 E.G.L.R. 1; [1996] 01 E.G. 102; [1995] N.P.C. 113; [1995] E.G.C.S. 116, CA ... 2.23, 5.4, 11.7, 11.8, 11.15, 11.17, 11.27, 14.8
Trustees of Saunders v. Ralph (1983) 66 P. & C.R. 335; [1993] 28 E.G. 129; [1993] N.P.C. 46; [1993] E.G.C.S. 44 .... 1.13, 14.17, 14.99
Tucker v. Linger (1883) 8 App. Cas. 508, HL; *affirming* (1882) 21 Ch.D. 18; 51 L.J.Ch. 713; 46 L.T. 894; 30 W.R. 578 .... 10.59, 13.108
Tummon v. Barclay's Bank Trust Co. Ltd (1979) 39 P. & C.R. 300; (1979) 250 E.G. 980 ...... 11.21, 11.28
Tunbridge Wells Local Board v. Ackroyd (1880) 5 Ex.D. 199; 49 L.J.Q.B. 403; 42 L.T. 640; 44 J.P. 504; 28 W.R. 450 .... 16.58
Turnbull v. Millar 1942 S.C. 521 .... 13.46, 13.68
Turner v. Stevenage Borough Council [1995] N.P.C. 186; [1995] W.L.R., CA, E.G.C.S. 181; *The Times*, December 7, 1995, Ch. D. 16.26, 16.66
Turner (East Asia) Pte v. Builders Federal (Hong Kong) Ltd [1988] 42 B.L.R. 122 (High Court of the Republic of Singapore) 16.47
Turton v. Turnbull [1934] 2 K.B. 197; 103 L.J.K.B. 598; 151 L.T. 265; 78 S.J. 367 ...... 12.48, 13.20
Tustian v. Johnstone (Note) [1993] 3 All E.R. 534; [1993] 47 E.G. 139, CA; *reversing* [1993] 2 All E.R. 673; [1992] N.P.C. 80 .... 10.11, 10.24
Tyson v. Smith (1838) 9 A. & E. 406; 3 J.P. 65; 112 E.R. 1265 .... 13.108

Underwood and the Bedford and Cambridge Ry., *Re* (1861) 11 C.B. (N.S.) 442; 31 L.J.C.P. 10; 5 L.T. 581; 10 W.R. 106; 142 E.R. 868 .... 16.49, 16.56
Unit Four Cinemas v. Tosara Investment Ltd [1993] 2 E.G.L.R. 11; [1993] 44 E.G. 121 .... 16.44
United Bank of Kuwait v. Sohib [1996] 3 W.L.R. 372; [1996] 3 All E.R. 215; (1996) 73 P. & C.R. 177; [1996] 2 F.L.R. 666; [1996] E.G.C.S. 19; [1996] N.P.C. 12; *The Times*, February 13, 1996, CA; *affirming* [1995] 2 W.L.R. 94; [1995] 2 All E.R. 973; [1996] 1 F.L.R. 379; [1996] Fam. Law 87; *The Times*, July 7, 1994, Ch. D. 1.45
United Co-operative Ltd v. Sun Alliance & London Assurance Co. Ltd [1987] 1 E.G.L.R. 126; (1986) 282 E.G. 91 .... 16.23
United Scientific Holdings v. Burnley Borough Council; Cheapside Land Development Co. v. Messels Service Co. [1978] A.C. 904; [1977] 2 W.L.R. 806; (1977) 121 S.J. 223; (1977) 33 P. & C.R. 220; (1977) 75 L.G.R. 407; (1977) 243 E.G. 43, HL; *reversing sub nom.* United Scientific Holdings v. Burnley Corp. (1976) 238 E.G. 487, CA 2.10.1, 2.13
Universal Cargo Carriers Corporation v. Citati (No. 2) [1958] 2 Q.B. 254; [1958] 3 W.L.R. 109; 102 S.J. 509; [1958] 2 All E.R. 563 .... 16.65
University College Oxford v. Durdy [1982] Ch. 413; [1982] 3 W.L.R. 94; [1982] 1 All E.R. 1108; (1982) 43 P. & C.R. 399; (1981) 262 E.G. 338, CA 6.82, 11.3, 11.33, 11.34, 16.22, 16.23, 16.25
University of Reading v. Johnson-Houghton [1985] 2 E.G.L.R. 113; (1985) 276 E.G. 1353 ... 8.18

TABLE OF CASES

Urban Small Space Ltd v. Burford Investment Co. Ltd [1990] 2 E.G.L.R. 120; [1990] 28 E.G. 116 .... 2.25
Urwick v. Taylor [1969] E.G.D. 1106 .... 12.55

Van Grutten v. Trevenen [1902] 2 K.B. 82; 71 L.J.K.B. 544; 87 L.T. 344; 18 T.L.R. 575; 46 S.J. 482; 50 W.R. 516 .... 17.20
Verrall v. Farnes [1966] 1 W.L.R. 1254; 110 S.J. 406; [1966] 2 All E.R. 808 .... 8.16, 9.4, 9.5
Von Deetzen v. Hauptzollamt Oldenburg (–44/89) [1991] E.C.R.I.–5119; [1994] 2 C.M.L.R. 487 .... 18.16
Vyrichera Narayani Gajapatiraju v. Revenue Divisional Officer, Vizagapatam [1939] A.C. 302; 108 L.J.P.C. 51; 55 T.L.R. 563; 83 S.J. 336; [1939] 2 All E.R. 317 .... 11.6

Wachauf v. Bundesamt fuer Ernaehrung und Forstwirtschaft (5/88) [1989] E.C.R. 2609; [1991] 1 C.M.L.R. 328 .... 18.11, 18.16, 19.17
Waddell v. Howat 1925 S.C. 484 .... 13.12
Wadsley, Re, Bettinson's Representative v. Trustee (1925) 94 L.J.Ch. 215; [1925] B. & C.R. 76 .... 13.113
Walford, Baker & Co. v. Macfie & Sons (1915) 84 L.J.K.B. 2221; 113 L.T. 180 .... 16.66
Walker v. Crocker [1992] 1 E.G.L.R. 29; [1992] 23 E.G. 123 .... 19.19
Walker v. Titterton, December 23, 1993, unreported, Case No. 9304964 .... 18.25
Walker v. Wilsher (1889) 23 Q.B.D. 335; 58 L.J.Q.B. 501; 5 T.L.R. 649; 54 J.P. 213; 37 W.R. 723 .... 16.41
Wallace v. C. Brian Barratt & Son Ltd [1997] 31 E.G. 97; [1997] E.G.C.S. 40, CA 5.4
Waller v. Legh [1955] E.G.D. 6; (1955) 166 E.G. 201 ....12.61.3
Wallingford Estates Ltd v. Tench [1951] E.G.D. 22, Cty.Ct. 11.3.1
Wallis, Re, ex p. Sully 14 Q.B.D. 950; 33 W.R. 733 .... 15.20
Wallshire Ltd v. Aarons [1989] 260 E.G. 81 .... 6.84
Walsh v. Lonsdale (1882) 21 Ch.D. 9; 52 L.J.Ch. 2; 46 L.T. 858; 31 W.R. 109, CA 9.31
Walters v. Roberts (1980) 41 P. & C.R. 210; (1980) 258 E.G. 965 .... 9.5, 9.17
Ward v. Scott [1950] W.N. 76; 66 T.L.R. (Pt. 1) 340; 94 S.J. 97 .... 12.32
—— v. Space Design Ltd (1969) 213 E.G. 893 .... 16.15
Ware v. Davies [1931] 101 L.J.K.B. 1 .... 8.22
Warren v. Keen [1954] 1 Q.B. 15; [1953] 3 W.L.R. 702; 97 S.J. 742; [1953] 2 All E.R. 1118 .... 10.9, 10.31
Wates v. Rowland [1952] 2 Q.B. 12; [1952] 1 T.L.R. 488; [1952] 1 All E.R. 470; CA 10.28
Wattters v. Hunter 1927 S.C. 310 .... 15.20
Watts v. Yeend [1987] 1 W.L.R. 323; [1987] 1 All E.R. 744; (1986) 281 E.G. 912 ..... 9.9, 9.15, 9.16
Webb v. Bevis [1940] 1 All E.R. 247, CA 10.34
—— v. Plummer (1819) 2 B. & Ald. 746; 106 E.R. 537 .... 13.107
Webb v. Russell [1789] 3 T.R. 393 .... 15.15
Wedd v. Porter [1916] 2 K.B. 91; 85 L.J.K.B. 1298; 115 L.T. 243 .... 1.44, 10.9
Welby v. Casswell [1995] 2 E.G.L.R. 1; [1995] 42 E.G. 134; (1995) 92(17) L.S. Gaz. 48; (1995) 139 S.J.L.B. 118; [1995] E.G.C.S. 50; [1995] N.P.C. 53; *The Times*, April 18, 1995; *The Independent*, April 14, 1995, CA; *reversing* [1994] 35 E.G. 126; [1994] E.G.C.S. 43; [1994] N.P.C. 42; *The Independent*, March 28, 1994 (C.S.); *The Times*, April 1, 1994, Q.B.D. 14.38, 14.39
Wellington (Duke)'s Parliamentary Estates, Re, King v. Wellesley [1972] Ch. 374, [1971] 3 W.L.R. 184; 115 S.J. 549; [1971] 2 All E.R. 1140; 22 P. & C.R. 867 .... 17.11, 17.12, 17.15
Wenlock v. River Dee Co. (1883) 53 L.J.Q.B. 208; 49 L.T. 617; 32 W.R. 220 .... 16.34
West Country Cleaners (Falmouth) Ltd v. Saly [1966] 1 W.L.R. 1485; 110 S.J. 634; [1966] 3 All E.R. 210; 119 E.G. 563 .... 10.37
West Ham Central Charity Board v. East London Waterworks Co. [1900] 1 Ch. 624; 10.31, 18.27
Western Heritable Investment Co. Ltd v. Husband [1983] 2 A.C. 849; [1983] 3 W.L.R. 429; (1983) 127 S.J. 551; [1983] 3 All E.R. 65; (1983) 268 E.G. 266; (1983) 133 New L.J. 847, HL 11.14, 11.15
West Middlesex Golf Club v. Ealing London Borough Council (1994) 68 P. & C.R. 461; [1993] E.G.C.S. 136; [1993] N.P.C. 109, Ch. D 10.37
Wheeler v. Mercer [1957] A.C. 416; [1956] 3 W.L.R. 841; 100 S.J. 836; [1956] 3 All E.R. 631; [21 Conv. 78], HL; *reversing* [1956] 1 Q.B. 274; [1955] 3 W.L.R. 714; 99 S.J. 794; [1955] 3 All E.R. 455; [99 S.J. 754; 100 S.J. 66, 923; 105 L.J. 803; [1956] C.L.J. 30; 20 Conv. 73]; [1955] C.L.Y. 1519, CA 1.16
Westlake v. Page [1926] 1 K.B. 298; 95 L.J.K.B. 456; 134 L.T. 612 .... 12.4, 13.22

TABLE OF CASES

Weston v. Devonshire (Duke) (1923) 12 L.J.C.C.R. 74 .... 13.6
Westwood v. Barnett 1925 S.C. 624 .... 16.24
Wetherall v. Smith [1980] 1 W.L.R. 1290; (1980) 124 S.J. 543; [1980] 2 All E.R. 530; (1980) 40
 P. & C.R. 205; (1980) 256 E.G. 163, CA. 8.15
Whatley v. Morland (1834) 2 Dowl. 249; 2 Cr. & M. 347; 4 Tyr. 255; 3 L.J.Ex. 58 .... 16.35, 16.66
Whelton Sinclair v. Hyland [1992] 2 E.G.L.R. 158; 41 E.G. 112, CA 12.14
Whittaker v. Barker (1832) 1 Cr. & M. 113; 3 Tyr. 135; 149 E.R. 336 .... 13.113
Wickington v. Bonney (1982) 47 P. & C.R. 655; (1983) 266 E.G. 434 .... 12.33
Whitsbury Farm and Stud Ltd v. Hemens (Valuation Officer) [1988] 1 E.G.L.R. 159, HL 8.18
Wickington v. Bonney (1984) 47 P. & C.R. 655; (1983) 266 E.G. 434 .... 12.36, 12.39
Wigglesworth v. Dallison (1779) 1 Dougl. 201; 99 E.R. 132 .... 13.41, 13.107, 13.108
Wilbraham v. Colclough [1952] 1 All E.R. 979 .... 12.81.2, 17.23
Wilkins v. Wood (1848) 17 L.J.K.B. 319; 11 L.T. (o.s.) 291; 12 Jur. 583 .... 13.107
—— v. Lewis [1915] 3 K.B. 493; 85 L.J.K.B. 40; 113 L.T. 1161; 32 T.L.R. 42 .... 13.92, 13.108
Williams v. Minister of Agriculture, *The Times*, October 17, 1986; (1985) 275 E.G. 1082n. HL;
 reversing The Times, July 11, 1985 .... 10.65, 15.38
—— v. Wallis & Cox [1914] 2 K.B. 478; 83 L.J.K.B. 1296; 110 L.T. 999; 78 J.P. 337; 58 S.J.
 536; 12 L.G.R. 726 .... 16.37, 16.42, 16.66
Williamson v. Thompson. *See* Jackson v. Hall; Williamson v. Thompson.
Willson v. Davenport (1833) 5 C. & P. 531 .... 10.70
—— v. Love [1896] 1 Q.B. 626; 65 L.J.Q.B. 474; 74 L.T. 580; 44 W.R. 450 .... 10.59
Wilmot v. Rose (1854) 3 E. & B. 563; 23 L.J.Q.B. 281; 23 L.T. (o.s.) 76; 18 J.P. 600; 18 Jur.
 518; 2 C.L.R. 677; 2 W.R. 378; 118 E.R. 1253 .... 10.60
Wilson v. Earl Spencer's Settlement Trustees [1985] 1 E.G.L.R. 3; (1984) 274 E.G. 1254 ...... 14.43,
 14.46, 14.47, 14.70, 16.11
—— *Re, ex p.* Hastings (1893) 62 L.J.Q.B. 628; 10 Morr. 219; 5 R. 455 .... 13.113
Wilts County Council v. Habershon [1952] E.G.D. 23; (1952) 159 E.G. 157 .... 12.57
Wolfe v. Hogan [1949] 2 K.B. 194; [1949] 1 All E.R. 570; [93 S.J. 233; 13 Conv. 307], CA .. 1.19
Wolverhampton Corp. v. Emmon [1901] 1 K.B. 514 .... 10.33
Wombwell U.D.C. v. Burke [1966] 2 Q.B. 149; [1966] 2 W.L.R. 669; 130 J.P. 282; 110 S.J.
 311; [1966] 1 All E.R. 911; 64 L.G.R. 151 .... 8.13
Womersley v. Dally (1857) 26 L.J.Ex. 219 .... 10.59, 13.51, 13.108, 13.113
Wood v. Durose [1958] E.G.D. 344; (1958) 172 E.G. 295 .... 16.66
—— v. East Sussex County Council [1954–55] A.L.R. 159 .... 12.37
—— v. Leake (1806) 12 Ves 412; 33 E.R. 156 .... 16.34
Woodward v. Dudley (Earl of) [1954] Ch. 283; [1954] 1 W.L.R. 476; 98 S.J. 162; [1954] 1 All
 E.R. 559; 52 L.G.R. 269 .... 12.17, 12.81.3
Woolfson v. Strathclyde Regional Council (1978) 38 P. & C.R. 521; [1979] J.P.L. 169; (1978)
 248 E.G. 777; 1978 S.L.T. 159, HL 12.14
Wrightson v. Bywater (1838) 3 M. & W. 199; 6 Dowl. 359; 1 Horn. & H. 50; 7 L.J.Ex. 83; 150
 E.R. 1114 .... 9.4
Wykes v. Davis [1975] Q.B. 843; [1975] 2 W.L.R. 131; (1974) 119 S.J. 84; [1975] 1 All E.R.
 399; (1974) 30 P. & C.R. 338; (1974) 233 E.G. 265, CA. 12.60, 12.61.4, 12.61.7, 12.61.12,
 12.67
Wynn, *Re* [1955] 1 W.L.R. 940; 99 S.J. 542; [1955] 2 All E.R. 865 .... 17.14, 17.15

Yellowly v. Gower (1855) 11 Ex. 274; 24 L.J.Ex. 289; 156 E.R. 833 .... 10.31
Young v. Dalgety plc [1987] 1 E.G.L.R. 116; (1986) 281 E.G. 42; (1986) 130 S.J. 985; [1987] 1
 E.G.L.R. 116; (1987) 84 L.S. Gaz. 189, CA 2.23, 10.34
—— v. Hopkins (1968) 12.5

Zermalt Holdings S.A. v. Nu-Life Upholstery Repairs Ltd [1985] 2 E.G.L.R. 14; (1985) 275
 E.G. 1134 .... 16.44, 16.66
Zubaida v. Hargreaves [1995] 1 E.G.L.R. 127; [1995] 09 E.G. 320, CA; *affirming* [1993] 43
 E.G. 111, Q.B.D. 6.84

TABLE OF STATUTES

[Reference in **bold** type denote where the text of the statute is printed.]

1816 Sale of Farming Stock Act (56 Geo. 3, c. 50)
    s. 11 .... 10.67
1817 Duchy of Lancaster Act (57 Geo. 3, c. 97)–
    s. 25 .... A.8, A.9, A.10
1831 Game Act (1 & 2 Will. 4, c. 22) .. 10.74
1838 Judgments Act (1 & 2 Vict., c. 110)
    s. 17 .... A.9
1845 Real Property Act (7 and 8 Vict. c. 27)
    s. 9 .... 15.15
1851 Landlord and Tenant Act (14 & 15 Vict. c. 25)
    s. 1 .... 10.78
1863 Duchy of Cornwall Management Act (26 & 27 Vict. c. 49)–
    s. 8 .... A.8, A.9, A.10
1870 Apportionment Act (33 & 34 Vict. c. 35) 10.78
1875 Agricultural Holdings (England) Act (38 & 39 Vict. c. 92) 10.36
    s. 52 .... 12.18
1880 Ground Game Act (43 & 44 Vict. c. 47) 10.74
1882 Married Women's Property Act (45 and 46 Vict. c. 75)
    s. 17 .... 14.62
1883 Agricultural Holdings (England) Act (46 & 47 Vict. c. 61) 10.36, 10.68, 12.1, 13.41, 13.116, 15.23
    s. 34 .... 10.39, 17.20
    s. 44 .... 10.69
1889 Interpretation Act (52 & 53 Vict. c. 63)– 17.20, A.12, A.13, A.14, A.15, A.16, A.17
1891 Stamp Act (54 & 55 Vict. C.39)–
    s. 14 .... **16.43**
    (1) (4) 16.43
    Sched. 1 .... 16.43
1894 Arbitration (Scotland) Act (57 & 58 Vict., c. 13) A.28
    Merchant Shipping Act (57 & 58 Vict., c. 60)
    s. 496(5) **A.174**
1895 Market Gardeners Compensation Act (58 & 59 Vict. c. 27) 15.27, 15.28

1896 Stannaries Court (Abolition) Act (59 & 60 Vict., c. 45)
    s. 4(1) A.174
1900 Agricultural Holdings Act (63 & 64 Vict. c. 50) ... 10.36, 13.2, 15.23
    s. 4 .... 10.36, 15.23
    s. 6 .... 10.87
    s. 13 .... 15.23
1906 Ground Game (Amendment) Act (6 Edw. 7, c. 21) 10.74
    Agricultural Holdings Act (6 Edw. 7, c. 56) 13.11, 13.90
    s. 3 .... 13.90
    s. 4 .... 13.11
1908 Agricultural Holdings Act (8 Edw. 7, c. 28) .. 13.27, 13.41, 13.45, 13.90, A.9
    s. 11 .... 13.11
1908 Agricultural Holdings (Scotland) Act (c.) 13.116
    s. 11 (1) 13.116
    s. 21 .... 10.39
    Sched. 1, Pt. III A.9
    Sched. 2 .... A.9
    Small Holdings and Allotments Act (8 Edw. 7, c. 36)
    s. 47 .... 1.26, A.9, A.10
    (1) A.9
    (3) A.9
    s. 58 .... A.9
    Sched. 1, Pt. II, para. 3 .... A.9
    Law of Distress Amendment Act (8 Edw. 7, c. 53)–
    s. 4 (1) 1.27, A.9, A.10
1911 Small Landholders (Scotland) Act (1 & 2 Geo. 5, c. 49)
    ss. 2, 32 .... A.28
1914 Bankruptcy Act (4 & 5 Geo. 5, c. 59)–
    s. 35 (1)
1917 Chequers Estate Act (7 & 8 Geo. 5, c. 55)–
    Sched A.9
1919 Land Settlement (Facilities) Act (9 & 10 Geo. 5, c. 59)–
    ss. 2 (3), 11 (4) A.9
    Agricultural Land Sales (Restriction of Notices to Quit) Act (9 & 10 Geo. 5, c. 63) 12.91

TABLE OF STATUTES

Year	Statute	
1920	Agricultural Act (10 & 11 Geo. 5, c. 76)	9.22, 12.5, 13.45, 13.75
	s. 13	9.22
	s. 14	10.78
	s. 15 (3)	15.31
	s. 16	13.75
	s. 17	13.6
	s. 18 (1)	13.119
	s. 20	13.44
1921	Railways Act (11 & 12 Geo. 5, c. 55)	A.9
1922	Allotments Act (12 & 13 Geo. 5, c. 51)	8.13, A.9, A.10
	s. 3(5)	A.9
	(7)	1.28, A.10
	s. 6 (1)	1.28, A.10
	s. 11(2)	A.9
	s. 22 (1)	8.13, 12.38
	(3)	A.174
1923	Agricultural Holdings Act (13 & 14 Geo. 5, c. 9)	8.22, 9.2, 10.55, 10.87, 13.2, 13.27, 13.41, 13.42, 13.43, 13.44, 13.116, 13.119, A.9
	s. 3	A.9
	s. 23	A.9
	s. 25(2) (b)	A.9
1923	Agricultural Holdings (Scotland) Act.13 and 14 Geo. 6 c. 11	13.27, 13.119
	s. 3	13.46
	s. 9	13.75
	s. 12	13.11
	s. 16 (1)	13.116
	(2)	13.119
	s. 18	13.6
	s. 23	13.79
	s. 25	12.5
	s. 27	12.18
	(2)	13.5
	s. 28	10.86
	s. 29	10.87
	s. 30	10.59
	s. 33	13.44
	s. 57 (1)	13.44, 15.20
	Sched. 1	13.42, 13.46, A.9
	Pts. I, II	13.49, A.9
1925	Settled Land Act (15 & 16 Geo. 5, c. 18)	7.3, 10.78, 17.10, 17.14, A.9
	s. 71	A.10
	s. 73	17.12, A.10
	(1)	A.9
	(ii)	17.12, 17.13, 17.14
	(iv)	17.10, 17.11, 17.15
	Sched. 3, Pt. I	17.10, 17.15, A.9
	Law of Property Act (15 & 16 Geo. 5, c. 20)	12.20, 12.24, 12.25, 17.8, 17.10, 18.16, A.2, A.9
	s. 13	18.31
	s. 13A	**18.31**
	s. 13B	18.31
	s. 28 (1)	17.10
	s. 30	14.64
1925	Law of Property Act—*cont.*	
	s. 34, 36	14.65
	s. 52 (1)	1.24
	s. 62	1.44, 3.11
	s. 99	7.2, 18.31, 18.32, A.9, A.10
	s. 99 (13)	18.31, A.9, A.10
	(19)	18.31
	s. 139	15.15
	s. 140	4.9, 5.24, 11.31, 12.17, 12.20, 12.21, 13.5, 13.16, 13.98, 19.20, **A.2**, A.8, A.9, A.10
	(1)	12.20
	(2)	4.9, 4.15, 12.20, 12.21, A.10
	s. 141	13.97
	s. 146	1.29, 1.46, 3.9, 3.14, 12.61.12, 12.76.1, 12.76.2, 13.90, 17.23
	(4)	15.16
	(9) (10)	12.78
	(9) (*a*), (*b*)	1.46
	s. 147	1.46
	s. 149	
	(6)	1.43, 4.10, 8.17, 9.22, 10.78, 12.5, 12.9, A.9, A.10, A.35, A.136
	Land Registration Act (15 & 16 Geo. 5, c. 21)	1.24
	Allotments Act (15 & 16 Geo. 5, c. 61)	8.13
	Administration of Estates Act (15 & 16 Geo. 5, c. 23)–	
	s. 9	7.13
	Universities and College Estates Act (15 & 16 Geo. 5, c. 24)	7.3, 17.8, 17.10, A.9, A.10
	s. 26	A.10
	(1)	17.10, A.9
	(5)	17.10, A.9
1926	Law of Property (Amendment) Act (16 & 17 Geo. 5, c. 11)–	
	s. 2	12.20
1927	Landlord and Tenant Act (17 & 18 Geo. 5, c. 36)–	17.11, A.9, A.10
	Pt. I	1.29
	s. 13	17.11
	s. 17	1.29
	(1)	A.9, A.10
	s. 18	1.29, 2.2, 13.93, 13.94
	(1)	10.87, 13.94
	s. 19	1.29, 2.2, 5.2, 5.9
	(1) (4)	1.29
	(3)	2.2, 5.2
	(4)	A.9, A.10
	s. 20	12.22
	s. 23 (2)	7.14
1928	Agricultural Credits Act (18 & 19 Geo. 5, c. 43)	3.9, 18.31, A.9, A.10
	s. 5 (7)	1.30, 13.113, 18.16, A.9, A.10
1930	Road Traffic Act (20 and 21 Geo. 5, c. 43)	
	s. 21 (2)	17.20

TABLE OF STATUTES

1930	Administration of Justice (appeals) Act (24 & 25 Geo. 5, c. 40) 16.63		1947	Agriculture Act—*cont.*
1936	Tithe Act (26 Geo. 5 & 1 Edw. 8, c. 43)			Sched. 1, para. 16 (1) 16.2
	s. 39(1) A.174			Sched. 2, paras. 1, 3 .... A.9
1937	Arbitration (Northern Ireland) Act (1 & 2 Geo. 6, c. 8) A.174			Sched. 7, para. 6 .... 12.18
1938	Leasehold property (Repairs) Act (1 & 2 Geo. 5, c. 34) 1.31, 1.46, 10.29, 13.101, A.9, A.10			para. 7 .... 10.87
				Sched. 9 .... 16.2, A.5
				para. 13 .... 16.2, **A.5**
				paras. 14, 15 .... 16.2, **A.5**
	s. 7 .... 10.29			para. 16 .... 16.2, **A.5**
	(1) A.9, A.10			(1) (*a*) A.12, A.18
1944	Education Act (7 & 8 Geo. 6, c. 31) A.174			(2) (3) 16.2
				para. 16A 16.2, **A.5**, A.12, A.18
1946	Statutory Instruments Act (9 & 10 Geo. 6, c. 36)			para. 17 .... 16.2, **A.5**
				para. 18 .... 16.2, **A.5**
	s. 5 .... A.174			paras. 19, 20 .... 16.2, **A.5**
1946	Hill Farming Act (9 & 10 Geo. 6, c. 73)			paras. 21–23 .... **A.5**
				para. 24 .... 16.13, **A.5**
	s. 1 .... 13.73, A.9			Transport Act (10 & 11 Geo. 6, c. 49)–
	s. 9 .... A.9			Pt. II A.9
	s. 21 .... A.18		1948	Agricultural Holdings Act (11 & 12 Geo. 6, c. 63) 1.45, 8.2, 8.5, 10.3, 10.76, 10.87, 11.1, 12.1, 12.51, 13.2, 13.5, 13.22, 13.27, 13.41, 13.42, 13.50, 13.55, 13.83, 13.102, 13.116, 15.20, 16.19, A.9, A.12, A.13, A.14, A.15, A.18, A.24, A.97
1947	Agriculture Act (10 & 11 Geo. 6, c. 48) 8.18, 10.52, 10.87, 12.1, 12.82, 13.27, 13.51, 13.54, 13.69, 13.82, 13.91, 13.110,13.111, 14.42, 15.20, 15.22, 16.4, 16.12, 18.31, A.3, A.3, A.4, A.9, A.10			
	s. 10 . 8.23, 10.21, 10.25, 10.52, 12.36, **A.3**, A.9			s. 1 .... 8.16
				(1) A.175, A.176
	(3) 13.81, 13.85, 13.91			(1A) (1B) A.175, A.176
	s. 11 . 8.23, 10.25, 10.52, 12.35, 13.82, 18.27, **A.3**, A.9			(2) A.9, A.175
				s. 2 ....8.5, 9.2, 9.7, 9.29, 13.116
	(2) 13.82			(1) A.9, A.83, A.90, A.175, A.176
	(3) 13.81, 13.85, 13.91			
	s. 21			2 (3) (*a*) 8.5
	(2) (*b*) A.18			s. 3 ....A.83, A.90
	s. 25 (2) 13.67			(1) (2) A.175, A.176
	s. 27 ....13.107, 13.110			s. 3A 14.11
	s. 34 (2) 13.110			(1)–(4) A.175, A.176
	s. 43 .... 10.86			s. 3B A.83, A.90, A.175, A.176
	s. 73 .... 16.2, **A.4**, A.12, A.19			s. 5 .... A.13
	(1) 16.2, A.19			(1) (2) A.15, A.175, A.176
	(3) . 14.109, 16.4, A.6, A.9, A.17, A.20			(3) A.175, A.176
				(4) (6) A.175, A.176
	(*a*) A.9			s. 6 .... A.13
	(4) 16.4, A.17, A.20			(1) A.14
	(5) 16.2			(2) A.14
	s. 74 .... **A.4**			s. 7 (1) (2) A.13, A.175, A.176
	s. 75 .... 16.2			(3) (5) A.175, A.176
	s. 86 .... A.17			(4) A.15, A.175, A.176
	s. 95 .... 13.69			s. 8 ..2.16, 11.1, 11.3, 11.6, 11.7, 11.8, 11.21, 11.28, A.9
	s. 108 (3) A.20			
	s. 109 ....8.23, 14.42, **A.4**			(1)–(13) A.175, A.176
	(1) 8.18, 9.18, A.9			(1) 11.3.1
	(2) 9.18, 12.18, **14.42**			(2) (*b*) 11.28
	(3) 8.13, 10.25, 14.42			(13) 11.3.3
	(5) **14.42**			s. 8A 11.3, 11.28
	Pt. III A.9			(1)–(5) A.175, A.176
	Pt. V A.9			(4) 11.21
				s. 9 .... A.9
				(1) (2) (4) A.175, A.176

xlv

1948	Agricultural Holdings Act—*cont.*	1948	Agricultural Holdings Act—*cont.*
	s. 10 .... 10.55		ss. 52, 53 .... A.175, A.176
	(1) (2) (*a*) (*b*) A.175, A.176		s. 54 .... A.9
	s. 11 (1)–(5) A.175, A.176		s. 55 .... A.9
	s. 12 (1) (2) A.175, A.176		(1) (2) A.175, A.176
	s. 13 .... 10.34, 10.39, A.9		s. 56 .... 13.75, 13.79, A.9
	(1)–(4) A.175, A.176		(1)–(4) A.175, A.176
	(2) (*b*) A.9		s. 57 .... 13.99, 13.102, A.9
	(4A) (4B) A.175, A.176		(1) (3) 13.93, A.175, A.176
	s. 14 .... 10.75, A.9		(2) (4) A.175, A.176
	(1) 10.75, A.175, A.176		s. 58 .... 13.99, 13.102, A.9,
	(*a*) (2) (3) A.175, A.176		A.175, A.176
	s. 15 .... 10.87, A.175, A.176		s. 59 .... A.175, A.176
	s. 16 .... 10.79, A.9		s. 60 .... 13.5
	(1) (3) A.175, A.176		(1)–(3) A.175, A.176
	(2) A.9, A.175, A.176		s. 61 .... 13.6, A.175, A.176
	s. 17 .... A.9		s. 63 (1) (2) A.175, A.176
	s. 18 .... A.175, A.176		s. 64 .... 13.107, 13.110, A.175,
	s. 19 (1)–(4) A.175, A.176		A.176
	s. 20 (1) (2) A.175, A.176		s. 65 (1) (2) A.175, A.176
	s. 21 (1)–(4) A.175, A.176		s. 66 .... 13.9, 17.7
	s. 22 .... A.175, A.176		s. 67 .... A.9
	s. 23 .... 12.4		(1) (*b*) A.9, A.175, A.176
	s. 24 .... A.9		(2) (3) A.175, A.176
	(1) 12.86, 13.30, A.12		s. 68 .... A.18, A.109, A.110
	(2) 12.86		(1)–(6) A.175, A.176
	(*g*) 9.25, 12.80, A.16		(1) A.9
	s. 25 (1) 12.41		s. 69 .... A.175, A.176
	(*e*) 12.40		s. 70 .... 13.119, 13.121
	s. 30 (2) A.13		(1)–(5) A.175, A.176
	(*a*) A.13		(3) 16.67, A.9
	s. 31 .... 12.7		ss. 71–73 .... A.175, A.176
	s. 32 .... 12.20		s. 74 .... 17.7, A.9
	(*b*) 13.5		s. 77 .... A.9
	s. 34 .... 13.11, A.9		(1)–(6) A.175, A.176
	(1) A.175, A.176		s. 78 .... A.9
	(1) (*b*) 12.20, A.175, A.176		(1) A.175, A.176
	(2) (*a*)–(*d*) A.175, A.176		s. 79 .... 13.67, A.175, A.176
	(2A) A.175, A.176		s. 80 .... 17.9, A.175, A.176
	(3) 13.33, A.175, A.176		s. 81 (1) (2) A.175, A.176
	(4) 13.35, A.175, A.176		s. 82 .... 17.12
	ss. 35, 36 (1) (2) A.175, A.176		(1) (2) A.175, A.176
	s. 37 .... 13.45, A.175, A.176		s. 87 .... A.14, A.175, A.176
	ss. 38–45 .... A.175, A.176		ss. 83, 86, 89 .... A.175, A.176
	s. 39 (1) (2) A.175, A.176		(1) (2) A.9
	s. 43 (1) (3) A.175, A.176		s. 92 .... 17.22, 17.23
	s. 44 .... A.9		(1)–(5) A.175, A.176
	s. 45 .... A.9		(3) 17.23
	s. 46 (1) (2) A.175, A.176		s. 93 .... 17.7
	s. 47 (1) A.9		s. 94 (1) A.13, A.175, A.176
	(*a*) (*b*) A.175, A.176		(1)–(5) A.175, A.176
	(*c*) 13.55, A.175, A.176		s. 96 (2) A.175, A.176
	(2) A.175, A.176		s. 100 .... A.13
	s. 48 .... 13.45, A.175, A.176		s. 101 .... A.175, A.176
	s. 49 (1) (2) A.175, A.176		Sched. 1
	s. 50 .... A.100, A.101		paras. 1–10 .... A.175, A.176
	(1)–(4) A.175, A.176		Sched. 2 .... 13.49
	(1) A.18		paras. 1, 2, 4–11, 13–17 ..... A.175,
	(3) A.17, A.18		A.176
	(4) (*b*) A.18, A.103		Pts. I–III 13.46
	s. 51 (1) A.175, A.176		Sched. 3 ...... 13.50, 13.58, 17.15, A.9
	(2) (3) A.175, A.176		paras. 1–25 .... A.175, A.176

Year	Statute	Reference
1948	Agricultural Holdings Act—*cont.*	
	Sched. 4	13.58, 13.112, A.9
	paras. 1–12	A.175, A.176
	Pt. I	13.50
	Pt. II	13.112
	Sched. 5	A.9
	paras. 1–5	A.175, A.176
	Sched. 6	16.19
	paras. 1–28	A.175, A.176
	paras. 15, 27	A.9
	Sched. 7, para. 2	18.31, A.175, A.176
	para. 4	A.175, A.176
	Sched. 8	
	paras. 98–100	A.2
1949	Agriculture (Miscellaneous Provisions) Act (12, 13 & 14 Geo. 6, c. 37)–	
	s. 10 (1) (2)	A.175, A.176
	Commonwealth Telegraphs Act (12, 13 & 14 Geo. 6, c. 39)	
	s. 8 (2)	A.174
	Lands Tribunal Act (12, 13 & 14 Geo. 6, c. 42)	
	s. 3	A.174
	Wireless Telegraphy Act (12, 13 & 14 Geo. 6, c. 54)	A.174
	Sched. 2, para. 3 (1)	A.174
	Finance Act (12, 13 & 14 Geo. 6., c. 47)	16.59
	Consolidation of Enactments (Procedure) Act (12, 13 and 14 Geo. 6, c. 33)	8.2
	Agricultural Holdings (Scotland) Act (12, 13 & 14 Geo. 6, c. 75)	16.15
	s. 2 (1)	A.9
	ss. 7, 8	A.9
	s. 14 (2) (3)	A.9
	s. 18	A.9
	ss. 25, 26	A.9
	s. 44	11.21
	s. 45	A.9
	s. 46	A.9
	s. 54	A.9
	s. 55 (1) (2)	A.9
	s. 56	A.9
	s. 65 (1) (*b*)	A.9
	s. 68 (3)	A.9
	s. 75	A.9
	Sched. 1, Pts I, II	A.9
	Patents Act (12, 13 & 14 Geo. 6, c. 87)	
	s. 67	A.174
	National Health Service (Amendment) Act (12, 13 & 14 Geo. 6, c. 93)	
	s. 7 (8)	A.174
	National Parks and Access to the Countryside Act (12, 13 & 14 Geo. 6, c. 97)	
	s. 18 (4)	A.174
1950	Arbitration Act (14 Geo. 6, c. 27)	6.1, 16.14, 16.20, 16.61, 16.65, 16.66, 16.72, A.112
	s. 36 (1)	A.174
	s. 42 (3)	A.174
	s. 44 (3)	A.175, A.176
	Pt. II	A.174
	Allotments Act (14 Geo. 6, c. 31)	8.13
1951	Leasehold Property (Temporary Provisions) Act (14 & 15 Geo. 6, c. 38)	
	Mineral Workings Act (14 & 15 Geo. 6, c. 60)–	
	s. 20	10.66
	(5)	A.18
	Reserve and Auxiliary Forces (Protection of Civil Interests) Act (14 & 15 Geo. 6, c. 65)	1.2, A.9, A.10, A.12
	s. 21 (1)	A.12
	(5)	A.12
	s. 27 (1)	1.32, A.9, A.10
	(5) (5A) (6)	A.10
	s. 64 (1)	12.92, A.9
	Sched. 1	12.92, A.9
1954	Interpretation Act (Northern Ireland) (2 & 3 Eliz. 2, c. 33)	
	s. 1 (*f*)	A.174
	s. 41 (6)	A.174
	s. 46 (2)	A.174
	Agriculture (Miscellaneous Provisions) Act (2 & 3 Eliz. 2, c. 39)	16.12
	s. 4	16.2
	s. 5	16.2, 16.12, 16.13, **A.6**, A.18
	(1)	16.12
	(2)	16.13
	(3) (4)	16.13
	s. 6	12.33, 14.78, 14.122, 16.7, 16.8, **A.6**, A.18, A.123, A.124
	(1)	16.8
	(2)	16.9, 6.10
	(4)	16.13, A.4, A.17
	(5)	16.11, A.18
	(6)	6.11, A.4, A.17
	Sched. 1	16.2
	Landlord and Tenant Act (2 & 3 Eliz. 2, c. 56)	1.5, 1.33, 1.45, 2.3, 2.11, 2.16, 3.10, 4.1, 4.5, 4.17, 5.4, 8.20, 9.18, 9.20, 10.29, 11.38, 12.50, 13.28, 19.9.1, A.9, A.10
	s. 23 (1)	1.5, 8.18, 15.2
	(4)	1.19, 8.20
	s. 30 (1) (*f*)	12.50
	s. 34	11.24
	(1)	11.8
	s. 38	2.3, 9.31
	s. 43	9.18, 9.20
	(1) (*a*)	8.5, 9.18, A.9, A.10
	(*aa*)	1.5, A.10

xlvii

TABLE OF STATUTES

1954	Landlord and Tenant Act—*cont.*
	s. 51 .... 10.29
	(1) (*c*) 10.29, A.10
	s. 69 (1) A.9, A.10
	Pt. II 8.5, 9.18, 9.20, 12.20
1956	Agriculture (Safety, Health and Welfare Provisions) Act (4 & 5 Eliz. 2, c. 49) A.9
	s. 3 .... 11.41
1956	Crown Estate Act (4 & 5 Eliz. 2, c. 73)
	s. 95 .... A.175, A.176
1957	House of Commons Disqualification Act (5 & 6 Eliz. 2, c. 20)
	Sched. 4, Pt I A.5
1958	Agricultural Marketing Act (6 & 7 Eliz. 2, c. 47)
	s. 12 (1) A.174
	s. 47 (2) A.27
	s. 53 (8) A.174
	Opencast Coal Act (6 & 7 Eliz. 2, c. 69) ...1.34, 8.3, 8.6, 10.41, 11.36, 13.102, A.9, A.10
	s. 14 .... 11.36, 11.40, A.9, A.10
	(1) (*b*) A.10
	(2) 8.6, A.9, A.10
	(3) 12.51, 13.82, A.9
	(4) 12.40, A.9
	(5) A.9
	(6) A.9
	(7) 11.44, A.9
	(8) A.9
	(9) A.9
	s. 14A A.10
	s. 14B **A.10**
	s. 24 .... 13.102, A.9, A.10
	(1)–(10) A.9
	s. 25 .... **13.102**, A.9, A.10
	s. 25A **A.10**
	s. 26 ....A.9, A.10
	(3), (5), (6) A.9
	s. 27 .... A.9
	(1)–(3) A.9
	(1) 10.41
	s. 28 ....A.9, A.10
	(1)–(6) A.10
	(3)–(6) A.9
	(4) 10.41
	s. 51 (1) A.9, A.10
	Sched. 6 .... A.9
	para. 20 (*a*) A.9
	para. 24, 25 .... A.9
	para. 31 .... A.9
	paras. 20–25
	Sched. 7
	paras. 1 (2), 2, 3, 4, 5, 6 (2), 25 .... A.9
	para. 1A, 2A, 3A, 4A, 7A ... **A.10**
	para. 4 .... 11.36, A.9

1958	Agriculture Act (6 & 7 Eliz. 2, c. 71) 8.2, 8.5, 11.1, 16.2, A.100, A.103, A.109
	s. 2 .... 11.7
	s. 4 .... 10.46, A.9
	(1)–(8) A.175, A.176
	(1) A.18, A.49
	(4) A.18
	(6) (*b*) 13.72
	s. 8 .... 8.5, 9.18, 16.2, 16.12, A.12
	(1) A.17
	s. 9 (1) A.9, A.175, A.176
	s. 10 .... 16.2
	Sched. 1 .... A.12
	para. 3 .... 16.2, 16.4, A.17, A.20
	(*a*) (*e*) 16.2, A.4
	para. 4 .... 16.2
	para. 5 .... 16.2
	(1) A.5
	(2) 16.2, A.5
	(3) A.5
	para. 6 .... 10.55, A.9, A.175, A.176
	paras. 7, 14–18, 20 ..... A.9, A.175, A.176
	para. 15 .... A.17
	para. 21 .. 16.75, A.9, A.175, A.176
	(1)
	para. 26 .... 16.12, A.6
	para. 27 .... A.17
	para. 29 .... 8.5, 9.18
	Sched. 2, Pt. I 16.2, A.5, A.6
	Sched. 4, paras, 5, 9, 11 .... A.9
1959	Chevening Estate Act (7 & 8 Eliz. 2, c. 49)– A.9
	Sched. A.9
1960	Horticulture Act (8 & 9 Eliz. 2, c. 22)– A.9
1961	Carriage by Air Act (9 & 10 Eliz. 2, c. 27)
	s. 5 (3) A.174
	s. 11 (*c*) A.174
	Factories Act (9 & 10 Eliz. 2, c. 34)
	s. 171 .... A.174
	Crown Estate Act (9 & 10 Eliz. 2, c. 55)
	s. 95 .... A.175, A.176
	Clergy Pensions Measure (1961) No. 3
	s. 38 (4) A.174
	Housing Act (9 & 10 Eliz. 2, c. 65)–
	s. 32 .... 8.11, 10.30
	s. 33 .... 10.30
1962	Town and Country Planning Act (10 and 11 Eliz. 2, c. 38)
	s. 45 .... 17.20
	s. 214 .... 17.20
	Transport Act (10 & 11 Eliz. 2, c. 65)–
	s. 31 .... A.9
	s. 74 (6) (*f*) A.174

TABLE OF STATUTES

1962 Transport Act—*cont.*
    Sched. 11, para. 7 .... A.174
1963 Agriculture (Miscellaneous Provisions) Act (c. 11)– A.9, A.10
    s. 19 .... A.14
        (1) (3) A.14
    s. 20 (*b*) A.9, A.175, A.176
    s. 22 .... 1.41, A.10
        (1) (*a*), (*b*) (c) A.9, A.10
    Sched., Pt 1 .... A.5
    Corn Rents Act (c. 14)
        s. 1 (5) A.174
1964 Plant Varieties and Seeds Act (c. 14)
    s. 10 (4) (6) A.174
    s. 39 (3) (*b*) (i) A.174
    Lands Tribunal and Compensation Act (Northern Ireland) (c. 29)
        s. 9 (3) A.174
    Harbours Act (c. 40)
        ss. 14 and 16 .... 12.50, A.9, A.68
    Universities and College Estates Act (c. 51) 17.10
        s. 2 .... A.9
        Sched. 1 .... 17.10, A.9
        Sched. 3, Pt. I A.9, A.175, A.176
1965 Industrial and Provident Societies Act (c. 12)
    s. 60 (8) (9) A.174
    New Towns Act (Northern Ireland) (c. 13)
        s. 27 (2) A.174
    Carriage of Goods by Road Act (c. 37)
        s. 7 (2) (*b*) A.174
    Factories Act (Northern Ireland) (c. 20 (N.I.))
        s. 171 .... A.174
    Compulsory Purchase Act (c. 56)–
        s. 7
1966 Commonwealth Secretariat Act (c. 10)
    s. 1 (3) A.174
    Arbitration (International Investment Disputes) (c. 41)
        s. 3 .... A.174
1967 Poultry Improvement Act (Northern Ireland) (c. 12 (N.I.))
    Sched. para. 10 (4) A.174
    Agriculture Act (c. 22)–
        s. 26 (1) 8.23, 12.82, A.9
        ss. 27 (5B) (*a*), 28 (1) (*a*) A.9
        s. 29 .... 12.82, A.9
            (3) (*a*) A.9
            (4) 12.82
        s. 40 (2) (*a*) 14.60
        s. 48 .... A.9
            (2) (*a*) A.9
            (4) A.9
        s. 109

1967 Agriculture Act—*cont.*
    Sched. 3, para. 7 (4) A.9
    Leasehold Reform, Act (c. 88) .1.35, 8.7, 12.20, A.10
    s. 1 (3) (*b*) 8.7, A.10
        (3) 1.35, A.10
    Pt. I 8.7
1968 Agriculture (Miscellaneous Provisions) Act (c. 34) 8.2, 12.48, A.9, A.10
    s. 9 .... 13.11, 13.30, 17.9, A.9
        (1) A.175, A.176
        (1A) A.175, A.176
        (2) A.9, A.175, A.176
    s. 10 .... 17.9, A.9
        (1) (*b*)–(*e*) A.175, A.176
        (2)–(5) (8) A.175, A.176
    s. 11 .... 17.9
    s. 12 .... 1.41, 17.9, A.9, A.10
        (1) A.9, A.10
        (1A) **A.10**
    s. 13 .... 17.9
    s. 13 .... 17.9
    s. 14 .... 17.9
    s. 15 .... 17.9
        (1) (2) A.9
        (2) (4) (5) A.175, A.176
    s. 17 .... A.9
        (1) (3) A.9
        (1) (2) A.175, A.176
    s. 42 (2) A.9
    Sched. 3 .... A.9
        paras. 2, 3 .... A.9
    Transport Act (c. 73)
        s. 7 .... A.9
1969 Industrial and Provident Societies Act (Northern Ireland) (c. 24 (N.I.))
    s. 69 (7) (8) A.174
    Transport (London) Act (c. 35)–
        s. 16 .... A.9
    Law of Property Act (c.59)–
        s. 1 .... 11.21
1970 Administration of Justice Act (c. 31)
    s. 4, Sched. 3 .... A.174
    Agriculture Act (c. 40) 14.22, 15.36
    s. 38 .... 15.37
    s. 45 .... 15.39
    s. 64 (2) 12.18
    s. 68
        Pt. III 12.18, 12.49, 14.22, A.9
    Sched. 4 .....12.18, A.9, A.175, A.176
1971 Courts Act (c. 23)–s. 56 (2)
    Sched. 9 .... A.9
    Pt. I A.9, A.175, A.176
    Tribunals and Inquiries Act (c. 62) 12.33, 16.2, 16.6, 16.56, A.9
    s. 10 ....A.17, A.20, A.22, A.24
    s. 12 . 12.33, 16.6, 16.49, 16.55, 16.56, 16.68, A.122

il

TABLE OF STATUTES

1971	Tribunals and Inquiries Act— cont.	
	s. 12—cont.	
	(2)	16.56
	Sched. 1, Pt. I, para. 1	
	(a)	12.33, 16.2
	(b)	16.71
	Town and Country Planning Act (c. 78)–	A.9
	s.27 (7)	A.9
1972	Civil Evidence Act (c. 30)	
	Land Charges Act (c. 61)	17.7, A.9
	Sched. 2	
	para. 1	17.7
	(g)	A.9
	(h)	A.9
	para. 3	A.9
	Agriculture (Miscellaneous Provisions) Act (c. 62)–	
	s. 15	16.56, A.9
	(1)	16.68, A.175, A.176
	(2)	A.14, A.175, A.176
	Sched. 6	A.5
	European Communities Act (c. 68)	10.44
	s. 2 (2)	18.5, A.27
	s. 6 (1)	A.27
1973	Land Compensation Act (c. 26)–	
	s. 34 (3) (c)	A.9, A.10
	s. 48	1.41, 12.7, A.10
	(1) (1A)	A.10
	(2) (3) (6)	A.9
	ss. 56, 59, 87 (1)	A.9
	Fair Trading Act (c. 41)	
	s. 33 (2) (d)	A.174
1974	Consumer Credit Act (c. 39)	
	s. 146 (2) (4)	A.174
	Housing Act (c. 44)–	11.41
	s. 98	
	(3)	13.58
	Pt. VIII	11.41, A.9
	Friendly Societies Act (c. 46)	
	s. 78 (1)	A.174
	s. 83 (3)	A.174
	Solicitors Act (c. 47)	6.59
	s. 19	6.59
	s. 20	6.59
	s. 22	1.24, A.10
	(2)	1.24, A.10
	(3)	1.24
	(3A)	1.24, A.10
	s. 73	A.174
	s. 87 (1)	A.174
	Industry Act (c. 68)	
	Sched. 3	A.174
1975	Arbitration Act (c. 3)	16.20, A.174
	Children Act (c. 72)–	
	Sched. 3, para. 3 (5)	14.34
	Petroleum and Submarine Pipe-Lines Act (c. 74)	
	Sched. 2, Pt II	A.174

1976	Agriculture (Miscellaneous Provisions) Act (c. 55) ...	12.72, 12.80, 14.1, 14.52, 14.82, 14.100, A.16, A.20
	s. 12	12.72
	(4)	12.74
	s. 16	12.80, A.16
	s. 17	10.4, A.9, A.16, A.175, A.176
	ss. 18–23	A.20
	s. 18	A.9, A.16
	(1)–(8)	A.175, A.176
	(1)	A.16, A.20
	(b)	
	(1A)	**A.16**
	(2)	A.20, A.83, A.175
	(2) (c)	14.60, 14.62
	(4)	
	(f)	12.49, 14.22
	(7)	A.20
	s. 19	A.9, A.16, A.175, A.176
	s. 19A	**A.16**
	s. 20	A.8, A.9, A.16, A.20, A.83
	(1)–(15)	A.175, A.176
	(1)	A.83, A.85
	(3)	A.20
	(5)	A.16, A.20
	(6)	A.16, A.20
	(7)	A.20, A.84
	(9)	A.16, A.20
	(9A)	A.20
	(10)	A.20
	(14)	A.4
	s. 21 ...	A.9, A.16, A.20, A.175, A.176
	(2)	A.83
	s. 22	A.9, A.16, A.20
	(1)	A.85
	(2)	A.18, A.85
	(6)	A.20
	s. 23	14.84, A.9, A.16, A.83
	(1)–(9)	A,175, A.176
	(1)	A.16
	(1A)	14.84
	(2)	A.16, A.20
	(2A)	A.16, A.20
	(3)	A.16
	(6)	A.8, A.9
	(8)	A.16
	(9)	A.16
	s. 24	A.9, A.16
	(1)–(9)	A.175, A.176
	s. 25 (5) (a)	A.16
	s. 27 (5)	A.9
	Pt. II	8.2, 17.9, A.9, A.16, A.17, A.18, A.20, A.83, A.85, A.87
	Sched. 3	A.9
	Sched. 3A	A.9
	paras. 1–7	A.175, A.176
	para. 2 (1) (a)–(f)	A.83, A.90
	paras. 4 (2), 6 (2)	A.83, A.90

1

TABLE OF STATUTES

1976 Land Drainage Act (c. 70)
    s. 40 .... A.18
    s. 41 .... A.18
    s. 42 (1) (2) A.5
    s. 72 (5) (*d*) **12.58**
    Rent (Agriculture) Act (c. 80) ... 8.2, 8.4,
        8.8, A.10
    s. 9 .... 1.41, A.10
        (3) (4) A.10
    Sched. 2 .... 1.41, A.10
    Sched. 2. para. 2 .... 8.8, A.10
1977 Aircraft and Shipbuilding Industries Act (c. 3)
    Sched. 7 .... A.174
    Agricultural Holdings (Notices to Quit) Act (c. 12) . 8.2, 12.37, 12.44,
        A.9, A.18
    s. 1 (1)–(7) A.175, A.176
    s. 2
        (1) 12.86, A.18, A.78, A.175, A.176
        (2) ... 12.80, 12.86, A.175, A.176
        (3) 12.49, 12.82, A.9, A.18, A.78, A.85, A.175, A.176
        (4) A.18, A.63
        (4)–(6) A.175, A.176
    s. 3 .... A.175, A.176
        (3) A.18, A.78, A.85
        (*c*) .... 12.
        (*e*) A.9
        (4) A.80
        (5) A.18, A.80
    s. 4 (1)–(5) A.175, A.176
        (2) (3) A.18, A.78
        (4) 12.74
    s. 5 (1) (2) A.175, A.176
    s. 6 .... A.18
        (1)–(4) A.175, A.176
    s. 7 .... 12.91, A.9
    s. 8 (1) (2) A.175, A.176
        (2) (*a*) (*b*) 12.37
    s. 9 .... 12.20, A.9, A.175, A.176
    s. 10 (1) (1A) (2) A.175, A.176
    s. 11 .... A.78
        (1)–(10) A.175, A.176
    s. 12 (1) (1A), (2) (*a*) A.175, A.176
    Sched. 1, para. 1 (6) 16.19, A.9
        para. 3 (3) A.9, A.175, A.176
        para. 5 .... A.175, A.176
        para. 7 (2)–(5) A.175, A.176
    Sched. 1A, paras. 1–6 ... A.175, A.176
    Patents Act (c. 37)
    s. 52 (4) A.174
    s. 130 (8) A.174
    Administration of Justice Act (c. 38)
    s. 17 (2) A.174
    Rent Act (c. 42) 4.5, 8.9, 8.15, 11.15, 11.18, 12.39, A.9, A.10
    s. 6 .... 8.8, 8.9
    s. 10 ...1.36, 8.8, 8.9, 12.93, A.9, A.10
    s. 26 ....8.8, 8.9

1977 Rent Act—*cont.*
    s. 70 (1) 11.14
    s. (2) 11.13, 11.14, 11.16
    (3)
    s. 98 .... 12.39
    s. 137 .... A.10
        (3) (4) (*c*) A.9, A.10
    Pt. VII A.9
    Sched. 15 .... 12.39
        Pt. III, para. 1 .... 12.39, 14.112
        Sched. 15, Pt. IV 12.49
    Protection from Eviction Act (c. 43)– 4.18, 12.23, A.10
    s. 5 ....4.18, 12.23
    s. 8 (1) 1.41, A.10
        (*d*) A.9, A.10
        (*g*) A.10
1978 Judicature (Northern Ireland) Act (c. 23)
    s. 35 (2) A.174
    s. 55 (2) A.174
    Sched. 5 .... A.174
    Interpretation Act (c. 30)– A.174
    s. 7 .... 17.20, A.8, A.9
    s. 16 .... A.9
    s. 17 .... A.9
    s. 25 (2) A.175, A.176
    s. 78 (3) A.175, A.176
1979 Arbitration Act (c. 42) 16.14, 16.20, 16.61, A.112, A.174
    s. 1 ....6.78, 16.53
1980 Limitation Act (c. 58)– A.174
    s. 19 .... 10.69
    s. 34 .... A.174
1981 Animal Health Act (c. 22) A.27
    s. 17 .... A.27
    s. 32 (1) (*b*) A.27
    Supreme Court Act (c. 54)–
    s. 18 (1) A.174
    s. 31 .... 16.7
    s. 68 (1) (*a*) A.174
    s. 148 .... A.174
    s. 151 .... A.174
    Wildlife and Countryside Act (c. 69)–
    Sched. 1–7 .... 10.75
    Transport Act (c. 56)
    s. 5 .... A.175, A.176
1982 Civil Jurisdiction and Judgments Act (c. 27)
    s. 25 (3) (*c*), (5) A.174
    s. 26 .... A.174
    Merchant Shipping (Liner Conferences) Act (c. 37)
    s. 7 (5) A.174
    Duchy of Cornwall Management Act (c. 47) A.9, A.10
    Administration of Justice Act (c. 53)
    s. 15 (6) A.174
    Sched. 1, Pt IV A.174

TABLE OF STATUTES

1983	Mental Health Act (c. 20)
	s. 78 .... A.174
1984	Merchant Shipping Act (c. 5)
	s. 4 (8) A.174
	Telecommunications Act (c. 12)
	Sched. 2, para. 13 (8) A.174
	Foreign Limitation Periods Act (c. 16) A.174
	Registered Homes Act (c. 23)
	s. 43 .... A.174
	County Courts Act (c. 28)–
	s. 55 .... A.9, A.28
	s. 64 .... A.174
	s. 77 .... 10.72, 16.63
	Sched. 2, para. 70 .... A.174
	London Regional Transport Act (c. 32) A.9
	ss. 4, 5 .... A.9
	Sched. 6, para. 13 .... A.9, A.175, A.176
	Cycle Tracks Act (c. 38)– A.9
	s. 3 (2) A.9
	Agricultural Holdings Act (c. 41) 8.2, 8.20, 10.34, 10.79, 11.1, 11.3, 11.3.3, 11.6, 11.7, 11.28, 12.37, 12.49, 12.80, 12.81, 12.91, 13.5, 13.6, 13.9, 13.35, 13.41, 13.45, 13.58, 13.66, 13.98, 13.121, 14.52, 14.84, 16.14, 16.19, 16.66, 16.67, 17.7, A.9, A.20
	s. 1 ... 11.3.3, 11.6, 11.7, 11.21, 11.28, A.175, A.176
	s. 2 .... 14.1
	(1) 14.7, A.175, A.176
	(2) (3) A.175, A.176
	s. 3 .... 14.52, A.20
	(1) 14.84, A.175, A.176
	(2)(b) A.175, A.176
	(3) A.175, A.176
	(4) A.175, A.176
	s. 4 .... 14.52
	s. 5 ....12.10, A.175, A.176
	s. 6 .... 12.44
	(3) ... 10.37, 12.51, A.175, A.176
	(4)–(9) A.175, A.176
	(5) 12.80, 12.81
	(6) 12.49
	s. 7 ....12.74, A.175, A.176
	s. 8 .... 16.22
	(1)–(5) A.175, A.176
	s. 9 (2) (3) A.175, A.176
	s. 10 (1) 10.34, 16.14
	(2) 12.91, 13.9
	s. 11
	(2) 14.11, A.175, A.176
	(6)
	s. 91 .... 10.81
	Sched. 1 .... 14.52, A.20
	para. 1 (a) A.175, A.176
	paras. 2–8 ....A.175, A.176
	para. 2 (6) 12.49, 14.22 (7)

1984	Agricultural Holdings Act—cont.
	Sched. 2 ..... 14.52, 14.100, 17.9, A.9, A.17, A.20, A.92
	para. 1 .... A.20
	(1)–(7) A.175, A.176
	(1) (2) A.20
	(4) (b) A.90
	para. 2 .... A.20
	(1) (a)–(g) A.175, A.176
	(2) (4)–(6) A.175, A.176
	(3) A.20
	para. 3 .... A.20
	(1)–(4) A.175, A.176
	para. 4 ....A.9, A.20, A.175, A.176
	para. 5 .... A.20
	(1)–(10) A.175, A.176
	(1) A.20, A.90
	(3) (a) (b) A.20
	(5) A.8
	(6) A.20
	para. 6 .... A.20
	(1)–(7) A.175, A.176
	(7) A.20
	Sched. 3, para. 1 (3) A.175, A.176
	paras. 7 (1)–(3), 8, 9 ....A.175, A.176
	para. 10 (1) (a) (b), (2) A.175, A.176
	Sched. 3, para. 2 .... 9.25
	(1) (a) (b) A.175, A.176
	(2) 14.11, A.175, A.176
	para. 4 .... A.175, A.176
	para. 5 (2) (b) (c) A.175, A.176
	(3) A.175, A.176
	para. 6 .... 10.34
	(2) (3) A.175, A.176
	para. 7 .... 10.75
	(2) (3) A.175, A.176
	para. 8 .... 10.79, 10.81
	(a) (b) A.175, A.176
	para. 9
	(2) 13.33, A.175, A.176
	(3) 13.35
	(a) (b) (c) A.175, A.176
	para. 10 .... 13.42, 13.45, A.175, A.176
	para. 11 .... 13.69, A.175, A.176
	para. 12 .... A.175, A.176
	para. 13 .... 13.81, 13, 87, 13.93
	(a) (b) A.175, A.176
	para. 14 .... 13.5, 13.16, 13.98
	(a) (b) A.175, A.176
	para. 15 ....13.6, A.175, A.176
	para. 16 .... A.175, A.176
	para. 17 (a) (b) A.175, A.176
	para. 18 .... 13.121
	para. 18 (a) (b) A.175, A.176
	para. 19 .... 16.14, 16.19, A.9
	(2) (3) A.175, A.176
	para. 21 .... A.175, A.176
	para. 23 .... A.175, A.176

TABLE OF STATUTES

1984 Agricultural Holdings Act—*cont.*
    Sched. 3, para. 2—*cont.*
      para. 25 .... 13.50, 13.58
        (1) (*b*)–(*d*) A.175, A.176
        (2) (*b*) A.175, A.176
      para. 26 .... A.175, A.176
      para. 27 .... 13.46
        (*b*) A.175, A.176
      para. 28 .... 16.14
        (2)–(10) A.175, A.176
        (2) 16.24
        (3) 11.3.7
        (4) 16.25
        (7) 16.56, 16.57
        (9) 16.58, 16.66, 16.67
        (10) 11.34
      para. 29 .... A.9
      para. 30, 31 .... A.175, A.176
      para. 32 (*a*) (*b*) A.175, A.176
      paras. 33–39 ....A.175, A.176
      para. 39 .... 12.18
      para. 40 (*a*) (*b*) (*c*) A.175, A.176
      paras. 41–43 ....A.175, A.176
    Sched. 4 .... 12.91, 13.9
    Sched. 5, para. 14 .... A.9
      para. 2 (2) (*a*) (*b*) A.175, A.176
      para. 4 (*d*) A.175, A.176
      paras. 5, 7, 8, 10, 14 .. A.175, A.176

1985 Mineral Workings Act (c. 12)
    ss. 1, 4, 10 .... 10.66
    Sched. 2 .... 10.66
  Food and Environment Protection
    Act (c. 48)
    s. 1 .... A.27
  Administration of Justice Act (c. 61)
    s. 58 .... A.174
  Insolvency Act (c. 65)– A.9
    s. 80 .... 10.69
    s. 180
      Pt. III A.9
    Sched. 8, paras. 9, 30 .... A.9, A.175, A.176
    Sched. 9, para. 11 ....A.175, A.176
  Housing Act (c. 68) 1.37, 8.10, 13.64, A.9, A.10
    s. 8 .... 1.37
    s. 14 (3) 8.11
    s. 47 (3) A.174
    s. 112 .... 8.10
    s. 231 .... 13.64, A.9
      (2) 13.58
    Pts. IV, V 8.10
    Pt. VII 11.41, A.9
    Pt. X A.9
    Sched. 1, para. 8 .... 8.10, A.9, A.10
    Sched. 18, para. 6 (2) A.174
  Landlord and Tenant Act (c. 70)– ...8.11, 10.30, A.10, A.174
    s. 11–16 .... 10.30
    s. 11 .... 1.38, 8.11, 13.101
    ss. 12, 13 .... 13.101

1985 Landlord and Tenant Act—*cont.*
    s. 14 .... 13.101
      (3) 1.38, 10.30, A.9, A.10
    ss. 15, 16 .... 13.101
  Housing (Consequential Provisions) Act (c. 71)– 11.41
    s. 3 .... 11.41
    Sched. 1 .... 11.41
    Sched. 2, para. 34 .... A.9, A.175, A.176

1986 Agricultural Holdings Act (c. 5) 1.1, 1.3, 1.6, 1.7, 1.8, 1.9, 1.10, 1.11, 1.12, 1.13, 1.14, 1.24, 1.28, 1.29, 1.30, 1.31, 1.35, 1.36, 1.37, 1.38, 1.40, 1.45, 1.46, 2.4, 2.7, 3.1, 4.7, 4.14, 4.16, 4.18, 5.2, 5.7, 6.3, 6.82, 7.1, 7.3, 7.10, 8.1, 8.2, 8.3, 8.5, 8.8, 8.9, 8.12, 8.13, 8.15, 8.16, 8.18, 8.19, 8.20, 8.21, 8.23, 9.17, 9.18, 9.19, 9.20, 9.22, 10.1, 10.3, 10.15, 10.16, 10.17, 10.18, 10.20, 10.24, 10.30, 10.36, 10.37, 10.44, 10.49, 10.52, 10.58, 10.72, 10.75, 10.77, 10.82, 10.87, 11.1, 11.7, 11.10, 11.14, 11.15, 11.18, 12.1, 12.2, 12.3, 12.8, 12.20, 12.22, 12.44, 12.63, 12.92, 13.2, 13.5, 13.6, 13.11, 13.16, 13.17, 13.41, 13.46, 13.54, 13.56, 13.68, 13.71, 13.72, 13.82, 13.83, 13.91, 13.98, 13.102, 13.103, 13.106, 13.115, 13.116, 13.119, 13.128, 14.5, 14.12, 14.86, 14.91, 14.95, 14.97, 15.1, 15.2, 15.3, 15.10, 15.15, 15.18, 15.19, 15.20, 15.32, 15.33, 15.36, 15.39, 16.1, 16.4, 16.14, 16.15, 16.17, 16.18, 16.35, 16.55, 16.66, 16.70, 17.3, 17.4, 17.5, 17.7, 17.9, 17.10, 17.17, 17.18, 17.19, 17.20, 17.23, 17.25, 18.14, 18.21, 18.24, 18.31, 19.2, 19.10, 19.18, 19.24, A.7, **A.9**, A.10, A.22, A.23, A.24, A.35, A.42, A.44, A.51, A.52, A.59, A.60, A.61, A.66, A.68, A.69, A.70, A.71, A.74, A.76, A.77, A.93, A.97, A.111, A.112, A.113, A.114, A.120, A.121, A.122, A.170, A.171
    Pt. II 4.1, A.9
    Pt. IV 1.11, A.10, A.89, A.93
    s. 1 .... 8.16, 8.18, 8.25, A.113, A.114, A.175, A.176
      (1) . 8.4, **8.16**, 9.17, 10.78, 15.20, A.175, A.176
      (2) . 1.20, 8.16, 8.19, 8.23, A.175, A.176
      (3) 8.20, A.175, A.176
      (4) 8.16, 8.23, 15.20, A.175, A.176
      (5) . 8.16, 8.23, 9.3, A.175, A.176
    s. 2 .. 1.71, 4.1, 4.7, 8.1, 8.5, 8.8, 8.16, 8.17, 9.1, 9.2, 9.3, 9.4, 9.6, 9.7, 9.13, 9.14, 9.15, 9.16, 9.18, 9.20,

1986 Agricultural Holdings Act—*cont.*
s. 2—*cont.*
9.21, 9.33, 10.24, 12.2, 15.17, A.8,
A.10, A.35, A.175, A.176
(1) .. 9.2, 9.4, 9.5, 9.6, 9.17, 9.18,
14.62, A.35
(2) 9.2, 9.3, 9.4, 9.8
(*a*) 9.2, 9.3, 9.9
(*b*) 9.4
(3) 9.2, 9.16, 9.20, 14.62
(*a*) 8.19, 9.3, 9.7, 9.8, 9.9,
9.10, 9.11
(*b*) 9.13, 14.62
(4) 9.16, 13.116, A.114
s. 3 ... 8.23, 9.1, 9.15, 9.21, 9.22, 9.23,
9.24, 9.25, 9.27, 9.28, 9.29, 9.30,
9.31, 9.32, 12.5, 12.9, 13.12, 19.3,
A.8, A.35, A.65
(1) 9.22, 9.26, A.65, A.175,
A.176
(2) 9.22, 13.11, 13.17, A.175,
A.176
(3) 9.22, A.175, A.176
(4) 8.23, 9.22, 9.25, A.175,
A.176
s. 4 .... 8.18, 8.21, 8.23, 9.1, 9.15,
9.22, 9.25, 9.26, 9.27, 13.13,
14.11
(1) A.175, A.176
(*a*) 1.17, 9.25
(*b*) 9.25
(*c*) 9.25, 9.26
(2) 9.27, A.175, A.176
(*a*), (*b*) 9.26
(3) 9.25, 9.28, 13.13, 13.17,
A.175, A.176
(4) 8.23, 9.25, A.175, A.176
s. 5 ..... 8.17, 9.1, 9.6, 9.15, 9.22, 9.24,
9.28, 9.30, 9.31, 9.32, 9.33, 19.3,
A.8
(1) 9.24, 9.28, 9.32, A.175,
A.176
(2) 9.28, 9.29, 9.32, A.175,
A.176
(*a*)–(*c*) 9.29
(3) 9.28, 9.31, 9.32, A.175,
A.176
ss. 6–24 .... 10.1
s. 6 .. 1.16, 8.21, 9.16, 10.1, 10.2, 10.3,
10.4, 10.5, 10.6, 10.7, 10.27,
12.25, 12.77, 13.86, A.35, A.39,
A.43, A.114
(1) .. 13.116, A.35, A.175, A.176
(2) A.175, A.176
(*b*) 10.5
(*c*) 10.5
(3) 10.4, 10.6, 11.30, A.175,
A.176
(4) 10.6, 10.26, 16.59, A.175,
A.176
(5) 10.4, 10.7, A.175, A.176
(6) 10.7, A.175, A.176

1986 Agricultural Holdings Act—*cont.*
s. 7 .. 1.16, 1.38, 8.21, 10.1, 10.3, 10.4,
10.8, 10.9, 10.27, 10.37, 10.86,
13.85, 13.86, A.43, A.114
(1) 8.23, 10.9, A.114, A.175
(2) 10.9, A.175, A.176
(3) 10.9, 13.85, A.175, A.176
s. 8 ..... 10.1, 10.8, 10.9, 10.26, 10.27,
11.34, 12.61.17, 13.86, A.35,
A.40, A.41, A.43
(1) .. 10.25, A.114, A.175, A.176
(2) ... 10.25, 11.29, 13.116, A.40,
A.41, A.114, A.175
(3) 10.25, A.175, A.176
(4) ... 10.25, 11.30, A.175, A.176
(5) 10.26, A.175, A.176
(6) ... 10.26, 11.29, A.175, A.176
s. 9 ..... 10.1, 10.8, 10.27, 13.87, A.43
(1) .. 10.27, 13.86, A.114, A.175,
A.176
(2) 8.23, 10.27, 13.86, A.175
(3) . 10.27, 13.116, A.114, A.175,
A.176
(4) 10.27, A.175, A.176
s. 10 .... 3.1, 3.4, 10.1, 10.8, 10.34,
10.35, 10.36, 10.37, 10.38, 10.39,
10.40, 10.41, 10.43, 10.79, 15.23,
A.57, A.114, A.118
(1) .. 10.35, A.170, A.175, A.176
(*a*) (*b*) 10.35
(2) 12.44, A.175, A.176
(*a*) (*b*) 10.36
(*c*) 10.36, 15.23
(*d*) 10.36, 15.23
(3) A.35, A.45, A.175, A.176
(*a*) 10.37
(*b*) 10.37, A.170
(4) 10.37, 10.38, A.35, A.46,
A.170, A.175, A.176
(5) 10.37, A.175, A.176
(6) . 10.37, 13.113, A.175, A.176
(7) ... 10.35, 10.40, A.175, A.176
(8) 10.35, A.175, A.176
s. 11 .. 10.1, 10.8, 10.19, 10.44, 10.45,
10.46, 10.47, 10.48, 10.49,
10.50, 10.51, 10.52, 10.53,
10.54, 11.41, 13.71, 16.9, 16.10,
A.35, A.47, A.48, A.49, A.50
(1) 10.46, 10.48, 10.52, 13.82,
A.175, A.176
(2) 10.46, A.175, A.176
(3) 10.52, A.47, A.175, A.176
(*a*) (*b*) 10.46
(4) 10.47, A.175, A.176
(5) 10.49, A.175, A.176
(6) ... 10.44, 10.49, 11.41, A.175,
A.176
(7) 10.48, A.175, A.176
(8) 8.23, 10.49, 11.41, 13.72,
A.175, A.176
s. 12 ..2.13, 2.15, 2.16, 2.25, 8.1, 10.1,
10.6, 10.26, 10.30, 11.1, 11.2,

1986 Agricultural Holdings Act—*cont.*
    s. 12—*cont.*
        11.4, 11.7, 11.10, 11.20, 11.29,
        11.31, 11.37, 11.40, 11.43, 11.44,
        12.61.17, 13.30, 13.55, 14.90,
        15.39, 16.22, 16.23, 19.2, 19.6,
        19.15, A.8, A.35, A.51, A.113,
        A.117, A.122, A.170
      (1) .. 11.1, 11.3.1, 13.116, A.171,
        A.175, A.176
      (2) 2.15, 11.1, 11.3.2, 11.3.6,
        11.7, 11.30, 16.24, A.171,
        A.175, A.176
      (3) 2.14, 11.2, 11.3.3, 16.23,
        A.171, A.175, A.176
      (4) 8.23, 11.1, 11.3.1, 16.23,
        A.175, A.176
      (5) A.175, A.176
    s. 13 .... 10.50, 11.40, 11.41, 11.44,
        13.62, A.10, A.35, A.52, A.114
      (1) ... 11.30, 11.40, 11.42, A.175,
        A.176
      (2) 11.40, A.175, A.176
       (*b*) 10.50, 10.51
       (*c*) 13.62
      (3) ... 11.42, 11.43, 11.44, A.175,
        A.176
      (4) 11.43, A.175, A.176
       (*a*) 10.50
      (5) ... 10.50, 11.41, A.175, A.176
      (6) 11.41, A.175, A.176
      (7) . 11.40, 13.116, A.175, A.176
      (8) A.175, A.176
    s. 14 . 10.1, 10.55, 10.56, 10.57, 10.59,
        13.3, A.35, A.53, A.114
      (1) 10.55, A.175, A.176
      (2) . 10.55, 10.57, 13.116, A.175,
        A.176
      (3) 10.57, A.175, A.176
      (4) 10.57, 13.3, 13.69, A.175,
        A.176
      (5) ... 10.57, 12.40, A.175, A.176
    s. 15 .. 8.23, 10.1, 10.59, 10.60, 10.61,
        10.62, 10.63, 10.64, 10.66,
        13.90, 15.37, 19.6, A.35, A.54,
        A.114
      (1) 9.24, 10.59, 10.60, 10.61,
        10.63, 10.64, 10.65, 10.66,
        10.67, 15.37, 15.38, 19,
        A.175, A.176
       (*b*) 10.59
      (2) ... 10.60, 13.79, A.175, A.176
      (3) ... 10.60, 10.61, 10.62, A.175,
        A.176
      (4) ... 10.59, 10.63, 13.74, A.175,
        A.176
      (5) 10.59, 10.63, 10.64, 13.90,
        A.114, A.175, A.176
       (*a*) 10.32
       (*b*) 10.64, 13.90
      (6) . 10.63, 10.64, 13.112, A.114,
        A.175, A.176

1986 Agricultural Holdings Act—*cont.*
    s. 15—*cont.*
      (7) 8.23, 10.55, 10.59, A.175,
        A.176
    s. 16 . 10.1, 10.62, 10.68, 10.69, 10.73,
        A.175, A.176
      (1) 10.69
      (2) 10.69
    s. 17 10.1, 10.68, 10.70, 10.73, A.175,
        A.176
    s. 18 .... 1.27, 1.29, 10.1, 10.68, 10.71,
        10.73
      (1) A.175, A.176
       (*a*) (*b*) 10.71
      (2) 10.71, A.175, A.176
      (3) 10.71, A.175, A.176
      (4) 10.71, A.175, A.176
      (5) 8.23, 10.71, A.175, A.176
    s. 19 .... 10.1, 10.68, 10.72, 10.73
      (1) (2) 10.72, A.175, A.176
      (3) 8.23, 10.72, A.175, A.176
    s. 20 . 10.1, 10.70, 10.74, 10.75, 10.76,
        10.77, A.55, A.56, A.114
      (1) 10.75, A.55, A.56, A.175,
        A.176
      (2) 8.23, A.175, A.176
       (*a*) 10.76, A.35, A.55
       (*b*) 10.76
       (*c*) A.35, A.56
      (3) A.175, A.176
       (*a*) 10.76
       (*b*) 8.23, 10.76
      (4) . 10.77, 13.116, A.175, A.176
      (5) . 10.75, 10.77, 13.116, A.175,
        A.176
    s. 21 .... 10.1, 10.78
      (1) 10.78, A.175, A.176
      (2) 10.78, A.175, A.176
       (*b*) 14.70
      (3) 10.78, A.175, A.176
    s. 22 .. 8.23, 10.1, 10.43, 10.79, 10.80,
        10.81, 10.82, 10.83, 10.84,
        10.85, 13.77, 13.99, 13.103,
        16.42, A.35, A.57, A.114
      (1) A.175, A.176
       (*a*) (*b*) 10.79
      (2) 8.23, 10.80, 10.82, A.25,
        A.175, A.176
      (3) 10.43, A.175, A.176
      (4) 10.80, A.25, A.175, A.176
      (5) A.175, A.176
    s. 23 .... 10.86, A.175, A.176
    s. 24 10.1, 10.87, 13.95, A.175, A.176
      (2) (*b*) 12.40
    s. 25 .. 9.21, 10.60, 12.5, 12.17, 12.25,
        15.7, A.160
      (1) ... 9.24, 12.5, 12.6, 12.7, 12.8,
        12.9, 12.10, 12.11, 12.12,
        12.29, 12.51, 12.71, A.175,
        A.176
      (2) 10.60, 12.6, 16.5
       (*a*) 12.5, 12.6, 12.78

TABLE OF STATUTES

1986 Agricultural Holdings Act—*cont.*
s. 25—*cont.*
(2)—*cont.*
(b) 12.5, 12.7, 12.19, A.35,
A.73
(c) 12.5, 12.8, 12.17, 15.7
(d) 12.5, 12.9
(3) 12.10, A.175, A.176
(4) 12.5, 12.11, 12.51, A.175,
A.176
(5) ... 12.10, 12.11, 12.51, A.175,
A.176
s. 26 . 12.2, 12.17, 12.25, 12.41, 13.54,
14.19, 15.8
(1) . 9.21, 10.78, 12.2, 12.3, 12.5,
12.28, 12.32, 12.33, 12.48,
12.49, 12.51, 12.61.19,
12.81.5, 12.82, 12.86,
12.89.5, 12.90, 12.94.1,
12.94.5, 13.39, 14.19, 15.6,
15.8, 15.10, 15.12, 15.13,
16.5, A.22, A.27, A.35, A.70,
A.74, A.78, A.114, A.175,
A.176
(b) 12.32, 13.20, A.160
(2) 8.23, 10.32, 12.25, 12.27,
12.32, 12.86, 15.10, A.22,
A.70, A.71, A.175, A.176
(3) A.175
s. 27 . 10.32, 12.2, 12.17, 12.33, 12.34,
12.41, 13.54, 14.83, 14.112,
14.120, 16.12, A.166
(1) 12.33, 12.34, A.175,
A.176
(2) 12.33, 12.34, 12.41, 12.74,
14.2, A.175, A.176
(3) 12.2, 12.34, 12.39, 12.74,
12.94.2, A.175, A.176
(a) 12.33, **12.35**, 12.41,
12.94.1, 13.20, 13.82
(b) 12.33, **12.36**, 12.41,
12.94.1, 13.20, 13.21,
13.82
(c) 12.33, 12.37, 12.94.1,
13.20, 15.39
(d) 12.33, 12.37, **12.38**,
12.94.1, 13.20
(e) . 12.33, 12.36, **12.39**, 12.41,
12.42, 12.50.3, 12.94.1,
13.20
(f) 12.33, **12.40**, 12.94.1,
13.21, 13.39
(4) (5) 12.42, A.35, A.80,
A.175, A.176
(6) 14.83, A.175, A.176
(7) 12.42, 16.12, A.175,
A.176
(9) 12.42, A.175, A.176
s. 28 .... 8.23, 12.17, 12.32, 12.33,
12.71, 12.72, 12.73, 12.74
(b) 12.73, 12.90
(1) A.175, A.176

1986 Agricultural Holdings Act—*cont.*
s. 28—*cont.*
(2) 12.72, 12.73, 12.74, 12.90,
A.22, A.35, A.74, A.78,
A.175, A.176
(3) 12.73, 12.90, A.35, A.175,
A.176
(4) ... 12.73, 12.90, 13.116, A.35,
A.164, A.175, A.176
(b) 12.32, 12.73
(5) ... 12.41, 12.74, 12.90, A.175,
A.176
(6) 8.23, 12.60, 12.63, 12.72,
A.175, A.176
s. 29 .... 12.62, 13.116, 15.6, A.23,
A.175, A.176
s. 30 .... A.175, A.176
s. 31 .. 12.2, 12.7, 12.17, 12.18, 12.21,
13.5, 13.15, 19.20, A.8, A.35,
A.72
(1) 11.30, 12.18, 13.5,
13.16, A.175, A.176
(2) ... 12.19, 13.16, A.175, A.176
(a) (b) 12.37
(d) 15.39
s. 32 .... 12.2, 12.18, 12.19, 12.20,
12.21, 13.5, 13.14, 13.15, 13.16,
13.17, 13.32, 15.8, A.22, A.35,
A.75, A.94, A.114, A.175,
A.176
(1)(b) 13.5
(2) 12.21, 13.116
(b) 12.21
s. 33 .... 11.30, 12.22, A.114
(1) 12.22, A.175, A.176
(2) 12.22, A.175, A.176
(3) 12.22, A.175, A.176
s. 34 .... 8.21, 12.80, 14.10, 14.13
(1) 14.10, A.175, A.176
(a) 14.1, 14.3
(b) 14.1, 14.3, 14.4, 14.16,
14.17, 14.80, 14.102
(i) 14.4
(ii) 14.4, 14.11, 14.80
(iii) 14.4, 14.7, 14.11,
14.16
(iv) 1.13, 14.4, 14.8,
14.10, 14.11
(2) 8.23, 14.9, 14.10, A.175,
A.176
s. 35
(1) 12.81.3, A.175, A.176
(b) 14.33, 14.34
(2) 1.14, 8.23, 14.16, 14.17,
14.34, 14.97, A.10, A.175,
A.176
(3) 12.81.3
ss. 36–48 .... A.166, A.167
s. 36 .... 12.80, 14.71, 14.117
(1) 14.34, A.175, A.176
(2) A.175, A.176
(a) 14.9, 14.11

TABLE OF STATUTES

1986 Agricultural Holdings Act—*cont.*
   s. 36—*cont.*
     (2)—*cont.*
      (*b*) 14.9, 14.12
     (3) 8.23, 14.34, A.26, A.29,
                   A.30, A.175, A.176
      (*a*) . 12.82, 14.33, 14.36, 14.39,
                 14.41, 14.42, 14.70
      (*b*) 14.33, 14.52, 14.119
     (4) 14.44, A.175, A.176
     (5) A.175, A.176
   s. 37 .... 12.80, 14.13, 14.17, 14.71,
              14.99, 14.105, 14.117
     (1) 14.17, 14.97, A.10, A.175,
                           A.176
      (*a*) 1.11, 14.9, 14.14, 14.15,
                 14.80, 14.97, A.10
      (*b*) 1.11, 14.9, 14.16, 14.80,
                 14.97, A.8, A.10
     (2) 1.11, 14.9, 14.17, 14.84,
           14.100, 14.117, A.8, A.175,
                           A.176
     (3) A.175, A.176
     (4) 14.14, 14.15, 14.16, 14.17,
                      A.175, A.176
      (*a*) (*b*) 14.14, 14.15, 14.17
     (5) A.175, A.176
     (6) 14.9, 14.17, 14.18, A.175,
                         A.176
     (7) 14.17, A.175, A.176
      (*a*) 14.17
     (8) 14.14, 14.15, 14.16, 14.17,
                      A.175, A.176
     (9) 8.23, 14.13, A.175, A.176
   s. 38 .... 12.80, 14.71, 14.105, 14.108,
              14.117, A.168, A.176
     (1) 14.9, 14.19, A.175, A.176
     (2) 14.20, A.175, A.176
     (3) ... 14.9, 14.21, 14.105, A.175,
                         A.176
     (4) 12.49, 14.9, 14.22, 15.39,
                    A.175, A.176
     (5) 14.9, 14.23, A.175, A.176
   ss. 39–46 .... A.166, A.167
   s. 39 .... 1.9, 1.10, 12.79, 14.5, 14.6,
              14.14, 14.15, 14.17, 14.24,
              14.30, 14.69, 14.70, 14.71,
              14.72, 14.82, 14.83, 14.94,
            14.97, 14.117, 19.19, A.8, A.10,
                          A.114
     (1) .. 14.24, A.166, A.167, A.175,
                           A.176
     (2) ... 14.24, 14.52, 14.53, A.175,
                           A.176
      (*b*) 14.72
     (3) ... 14.71, 14.75, A.175, A.176
     (4) ... 14.75, 14.76, A.175, A.176
     (5) .. 14.72, 14.75, A.166, A.167,
                    A.175, A.176
     (6) ... 14.72, 14.75, A.175, A.176
     (7) 12.81, 14.27, 14.72, 14.78,
           A.166, A.167, A.175, A.176

1986 Agricultural Holdings Act—*cont.*
   s. 39—*cont.*
     (8) 14.72, A.166, A.175,
                         A.176
      (*a*) 14.74
     (9) 14.80, A.175, A.176
     (10) 14.94, A.175, A.176
   s. 40 .... 14.76, 14.117
     (1) 8.23, A.175, A.176
      (*a*) (*b*) 14.76
     (2) (3) 14.76, A.175, A.176
     (4) 14.24, A.175, A.176
     (5) .. 12.79, 14.77, A.166, A.167,
                    A.175, A.176
   s. 41 .... 12.79, 14.28, 14.30, 14.31,
           14.70, 14.110, 14.111, 14.117,
              14.120, A.175, A.176
     (1) 14.30, 14.32
      (*a*) (*b*) 14.70
     (2) ... 14.30, 14.32, A.166, A.167
     (3) 14.71
      (*b*) 14.71
     (4) 14.71
     (5) 14.71
     (6) 14.70
   s. 42 ..... 14.77, 14.117, A.175, A.176
     (1) 14.77
     (2) 14.77
     (3) 14.77
   s. 43 . 12.81, 13.5, 13.16, 14.82, 14.84,
          14.87, 14.117, A.175, A.176
     (1)(*a*) A.166
      (*a*) (*b*) (i) (ii) 14.82
     (2) 13.5, 14.82, 19.20, A.8
   s. 44 .... 12.81, 14.82, 14.83, 14.94,
           14.112, 14.117, 19.20
     (1) 14.83, A.175, A.176
     (2) . 14.83, 14.112, A.175, A.176
     (3)–(5) 14.83, A.175, A.176
     (4) A.166, A.167
     (6) .. 14.78, 14.83, A.166, A.175,
                         A.176
     (7) .. 14.83, A.166, A.175, A.176
   s. 45 .. 14.84, 14.94, 14.115, 14.117
     (1) ... 14.84, 14.85, A.175, A.176
     (2)–(4) 14.84, 14.115, 15.5,
                    A.175, A.176
     (5) . 14.80, 14.92, 14.115, A.175,
                         A.176
     (6) 1.10, 14.6, 14.15, 14.85,
            14.86, 14.95, 14.96, 14.97,
            A.8, A.10, A.166, A.167,
                    A.175, A.176
     (7) . 14.85, 14.93, 14.115, A.175,
                         A.176
     (8) 14.84, 14.115, A.175,
                         A.176
   s. 46 .... 8.23, 14.80, 14.84, 14.91,
              14.115, 14.117, 19.19, A.8
     (1) .. 14.78, 14.84, A.169, A.175,
                         A.176
      (*a*) (*b*) A.166, A.167

lvii

TABLE OF STATUTES

1986 Agricultural Holdings Act—*cont.*
   s. 46—*cont.*
     (1)—*cont.*
     (2) ... 14.78, 14.84, 14.87, A.114, A.166, A.167, A.169, A.175, A.176
     (3) 14.94, A.175, A.176
     (6) 14.15, 14.80
   s. 47 .... 14.85, 14.117
     (1) . 14.85, 14.91, 14.116, A.175, A.176
     (2) 14.85, A.175, A.176
     (3) . 14.85, 14.93, 14.116, A.175, A.176
   s. 48 ...... 13.116, 14.80, 14.84, 14.85, 14.86, 14.90, 14.94, 14.96, 14.116, 14.117
     (1) 14.86, A.175, A.176
     (2) 8.23, 14.84, 14.87, A.93, A.169, A.175, A.176
     (3) ..14.88, A.114, A.169, A.175, A.176
     (4) 8.23, 14.88, A.114, A.175, A.176
     (5) .. 14.89, 14.91, A.169, A.175, A.176
       (*a*) 14.96
       (*b*) 14.96, 17.4
     (6) ... 14.89, 14.91, A.175, A.176
     (7) ... 14.89, 14.91, A.175, A.176
     (8) 14.89, A.175, A.176
       (*a*) 14.96
       (*b*) 14.96, A.93
     (9) ... 8.23, 14.90, 14.116, A.175, A.176
     (10) . 14.90, A.169, A.175, A.176
     (11) (12) 14.91, A.175, A.176
   s. 49 ....14.1, 14.100, 14.122, A.35
     (1) 14.103, 14.105, 14.115, A.89, A.175, A.176
       (*a*) 14.1, 14.102
       (*b*) 14.104, A.114
     (2) 8.23, A.175, A.176
     (3) .. 8.23, 14.13, 14.103, 14.105, 14.113, A.175, A.176
     (6) A.168
   s. 50 .... 14.1, 14.100, 14.122
     (2) 8.23, 14.103, A.26, A.29, A.30
     (4) 14.110
   s. 51 .... 14.1, 14.100, 14.108, 14.122, A.168
     (1) 14.105, 14.108, A.175, A.176
     (2) 14.105, 14.108, 14.113, 14.114, A.175, A.176
     (3) . 14.103, 14.105, A.89, A.175, A.176
       (*a*) 13.82, 14.105, 14.106
     (4) 14.105, A.175, A.176
     (5) 14.105, A.175, A.176
     (6) . 8.23, 14.105, 14.109, A.175, A.176

1986 Agricultural Holdings Act—*cont.*
   s. 52 .... 14.1, 14.100, 14.108, 14.122, A.168
     (1) 14.105, A.175, A.176
       (*a*) (*b*) 14.107
     (2) 14.105, 14.107, A.175, A.176
     (3) 14.107, A.175, A.176
     (4) 14.107, 14.109, A.175, A.176
     (5) 14.105, A.175, A.176
   s. 53 .... 1.9, 14.1, 14.5, 14.97, 14.100, 14.105, 14.108, 14.109, 14.113, 14.122, A.8, A.10
     (1) . 14.109, A.168, A.175, A.176
     (2) .. 8.23, 14.109, A.168, A.175, A.176
     (3) 14.109, A.175, A.176
     (4) 14.109, A.175, A.176
     (5) 14.103, 14.110, A.175, A.176
     (6) 14.103, 14.109, 14.110, A.175, A.176
     (7) 14.18, 14.103, 14.112, A.114, A.168, A.175, A.176
     (8) . 14.112, A.168, A.175, A.176
     (9) . 14.114, A.168, A.175, A.176
     (10) 14.105, 14.113, A.175, A.176
     (11) 14.109, A.175, A.176
   s. 54 ..... 14.1, 14.100, 14.108, 14.122
     (1) A.175, A.176
     (2) ... 8.23, 14.108, A.175, A.176
     (3) A.175, A.176
   s. 55 ..... 14.1, 14.100, 14.115, 14.122
     (1) A.168, A.175, A.176
     (2)–(4) 14.115, 15.5, A.175, A.176
     (5) 14.115, A.175, A.176
     (6) 14.115, 14.116, A.175, A.176
     (7) 14.115, A.175, A.176
     (8) .8.23, 14.115, 14.117, 14.118, A.114, A.168, A.175, A.176
       (*a*) 14.115, 14.118, 14.122
       (*b*) 14.115, 14.118
   s. 56 .... 14.1, 14.100, 14.122
     (1) . 14.116, A.114, A.175, A.176
     (2) 14.116, A.175, A.176
     (3) . 13.116, 14.116, 17.4, A.114, A.169, A.175, A.176
     (4) .. 8.23, 14.116, A.169, A.175, A.176
   s. 57 .... 14.1, 14.100, 14.117, 14.122, A.175, A.176
     (1) 14.117
     (2) 14.117
     (3) 14.117
     (4) 14.106, 14.117
   s. 58 .... 14.1, 14.100, 14.119, 14.122, A.175, A.176
   s. 59 .... 14.1, 14.119, A.175, A.176
   s. 60 . 9.21, 12.40, 13.12, 13.13, 13.17, 13.22, 13.26, 13.31, 13.33, 17.9, A.114
       (*a*) 13.11

TABLE OF STATUTES

1986 Agricultural Holdings Act—*cont.*
    s. 60—*cont.*
        (*b*) 13.15
        (1) A.175, A.176
        (2) 8.23, 12.19, 12.20, 13.11,
            13.23, 13.30, 13.38, 17.4,
            A.175, A.176
        (*b*) 13.5
        (3) 8.23, 13.11, 13.23, A.175,
            A.176
        (*a*) .13.23, 13.24, 13.36, 13.38,
            A.111, A.114, A.118,
            A.170
        (*b*) .. 12.7, 13.16, 13.23, 13.25,
            13.36, 13.37, 13.38, A.35,
            A.111
        (4) 8.23, 12.28, 13.11, 13.30,
            13.36, 13.38, A.111, A.118,
            A.175, A.176
        (5) 8.23, 13.26, 13.29, 13.38,
            A.175, A.176
        (6) 13.23, 13.25, 13.28, 13.29,
            A.175, A.176
        (*a*) 12.3, 12.7, 12.19, 13.2,
            13.5, 13.28, 13.36, 13.37,
            13.38, 13.90, 13.100,
            13.117, A.170
        (*b*) 13.28, 13.29
        (7) ... 13.25, 13.31, A.175, A.176
    s. 61 .... 13.26, 17.9
        (1) 12.19, 12.50, 12.51, 12.61.19,
            12.78, 12.81.5, 13.18, A.175,
            A.176
        (2) 12.19, 12.49, 12.82, 13.19,
            A.175, A.176
        (3) 12.25, 12.28, 12.48, 13.20,
            13.40, A.35, A.67, A.70,
            A.175, A.176
        (*a*) 13.20, 13.40
        (*b*) 13.20, A.94
        (4) ... 12.28, 13.21, 13.40, A.175,
            A.176
        (5) ... 13.21, 13.40, A.175, A.176
        (6) 8.23, A.175, A.176
    s. 62 .. 12.7, 13.16, 13.32, 13.33, 17.4,
        17.9
        (1)–(3) 13.32, A.175, A.176
    s. 63 .... 17.9
        (1) 13.33, 15.3, A.175, A.176
        (2) 13.33, 15.3, A.175, A.176
        (3) 12.20, 12.21, 13.15, 13.34,
            13.35, A.175, A.176
        (*a*) (*b*) 13.34
        (4) 8.23, 12.20, 13.15, 13.34,
            13.35, A.175, A.176
    s. 64 .... 10.51, A.111, A.118
        (1) 8.23, 13.2, 13.42, 13.50,
            13.52, A.97, A.175, A.176
        (2) 8.23, 13.42, 13.50, 13.78,
            15.34, A.175, A.176
        (3) ... 13.42, 13.50, A.175, A.176
        (4) A.175, A.176

1986 Agricultural Holdings Act—*cont.*
    s. 65 .... A.111, A.170
        (1) 13.51, 13.52, 13.54, A.95,
            A.96, A.118, A.175, A.176
        (2) 13.69, A.175, A.176
        (*b*) 13.82
        (3) 13.52, A.175, A.176
    s. 66 .... 13.64
        (1) 13.61, 13.66, 13.68, 13.76,
            13.99, 13.123, A.175, A.176
        (2) ... 13.67, 13.68, 13.76, A.175,
            A.176
        (3) A.175, A.176
        (4) 13.3, 13.51, 13.52, 13.68,
            A.175, A.176
        (5) 10.51, 13.69, A.175,
            A.176
    s. 67 ....10.36, 10.51, 13.72, A.35,
        A.98, A.99, A.100, A.102,
        A.109
        (1) 13.61, A.175, A.176
        (2) ... 13.3, 13.68, 13.123, A.175,
            A.176
        (3) ... 13.62, A.35, A.101, A.175,
            A.176
        (4) ... 13.62, A.35, A.102, A.103,
            A.104, A.175, A.176
        (5) 8.23, 10.46, 11.41, 13.62,
            16.4, 17.5, A.35, A.102,
            A.175, A.176
        (6) ... 13.2, 13.62, 13.122, A.175,
            A.176
        (7) 8.23, 13.62, A.175, A.176
    s. 68(1) ... 13.63, A.35, A.105, A.175,
        A.176
        (2) 13.65, 13.72, A.175,
            A.176
        (*a*) 10.51, 13.72
        (*b*) 10.51, 13.72
        (3) (4) 13.73, A.175, A.176
        (5) A.175, A.176
    s. 69 .... 8.22
        (1) . 13.70, 13.75, 13.104, A.175,
            A.176
        (2) 13.71, 15.25, A.35, A.97,
            A.175, A.176
        (*a*) A.97
        (3) 13.71, A.175, A.176
    s. 70 ....10.83, 11.22, 12.3, 13.75,
        13.77, 13.78, 13.79, A.106
        (1) ... 13.75, 13.76, 13.99, A.170,
            A.175, A.176
        (2) ... 13.77, 13.93, A.175, A.176
        (*a*) 12.3, 12.7, 12.19, 13.2,
            13.5, 13.37, 13.77, 13.90,
            13.100, 13.117, A.170
        (*b*) 10.83, 13.77
        (3) ... 13.77, 13.93, A.175, A.176
        (4) 12.3, 13.78, A.175, A.176
        (5) 13.78, A.175, A.176
    s. 71 .... 10.87, 13.80, 13.81. 13.99,
        13.102, 13.103, 18.27

TABLE OF STATUTES

1986 Agricultural Holdings Act—*cont.*
s. 71—*cont.*
(1) 10.32, 13.81, 13.82, 13.83,
13.85, 13.86, 13.87, 13.89,
13.91, 13.93, 13.94, 13.97,
13.99, A.107, A.111, A.175,
A.176
(2) A.175, A.176
(3) 10.32, 13.3, 13.83, 13.84,
13.85, 13.86, 13.87, 13.88,
13.89, 13.91, 13.93, 13.94,
13.97, 13.99, A.111, A.175,
A.176
(4) ... 13.83, 13.87, A.175, A.176
(*a*) 13.86
(*b*) 13.87
(5) ... 13.81, 13.87, 13.94, A.175,
A.176
s. 72 .... 10.32, 13.80, 13.81, 13.99,
13.100, 13.102, 13.103, 18.27,
A.35, A.107, A.111, A.175,
A.176
(1) 13.82, 13.99, A.170
(2) (3) 13.99
(4) 13.100, 13.117, A.170
s. 73 ..... 13.80, 13.104, A.175, A.176
s. 74 ..... 5.24, 8.22, 8.23, 12.22, 13.5,
13.30
(1) 13.16, A.175, A.176
(2) A.175, A.176
(*a*) (*b*) 13.5, 13.16
(3) 12.20, 13.5, 13.6, 13.16,
13.98, A.175, A.176
(4) 8.22, 8.23, 13.5, 13.16,
A.175, A.176
s. 75 ..5.25, 13.6, 13.98, 16.76, A.175,
A.176
(1) (2) 13.6, 16.76
s. 76 .... 8.23, 13.74
(1) ... 13.69, 13.74, A.175, A.176
(*a*) 10.58, 13.3
(*b*) 10.58
(2) 8.23, 10.58, 13.74, A.175,
A.176
(3) 13.74, A.175, A.176
s. 77 . 10.39, 13.4, 13.8, 13.10, 13.107,
13.109, 13.110, 13.111, 13.112,
13.116, A.175, A.176
(1) 13.54
s. 78 . 10.75, 12.19, 13.2, 13.48, 13.68,
13.120, 13.123
(1) 9.24, 10.58, 12.7, 13.2, 13.30,
13.77, 13.83, 13.89, 13.90,
19.8, A.175, A.176
(2) 10.58, 13.3, A.175, A.176
(3) 13.4, 13.51, 13.68, A.175,
A.176
s. 79 .... 15.19, 15.29, 15.35, A.35,
A.108, A.175, A.176
(1) 15.20, 15.27
(2) 15.22, 15.34, A.108
(3) 10.42, A.108

1986 Agricultural Holdings Act—*cont.*
s. 79—*cont.*
(3) (*a*) 15.23
(*b*) 15.23
(4) 15.24, A.108
(5) 15.25, A.108
s. 80 .... 15.19, 15.30, 15.35, A.35,
A.108, A.109
(1) 15.29, A.175, A.176
(2) 1.12, 15.29, 15.31, A.17.5,
A.176
(3) (4) .. 1.12, 8.23, 15.30, 15.31,
15.32, 15.33, 15.35, A.10,
A.175, A.176
(5) 1.12, 8.23, 15.30, 15.31,
15.33, 15.35, A.10, A.175,
A.176
(6) 15.30, A.175, A.176
(7) 15.30, A.175, A.176
(8) 15.33, A.175, A.176
(9) 8.23, A.175, A.176
s. 81 .... 15.19, A.175, A.176
(1) 13.3, 15.35
(2) 8.23, 15.30, 15.35
s. 82 ....10.65, 15.38
(1) ... 10.64, 10.65, 15.37, A.175,
A.176
(2) 10.65, A.175, A.176
(3) ... 10.65, 15.38, A.175, A.176
(*a*) (*b*) 15.38
s. 83 .... 3.14, 13.117, 13.120, 13.122,
19.19, A.114
(1) .. 13.83, 13.88, 13.89, 13.115,
13.116, 13.117, 13.120,
A.175, A.176
(2) 5.21, 13.28, 13.36, 13.37,
13.38, 13.77, 13.100, 13.117,
13.119, 13.122, 16.28, A.35,
A.111, A.118, A.170, A.175,
A.176
(3) **13.119**, A.175, A.176
(4) . 13.120, A.170, A.175, A.176
(5) 13.121, 13.122, A.170,
A.175, A.176
(6) . 8.22, 13.121, 13.122, A.175,
A.176
s. 84 ..... 5.15, 8.23, 9.16, 14.86, 16.1,
16.14, 16.17, 16.19, 16.30,
19.19, A.8
(1) A.174, A.175, A.176
(2) 16.19, A.25, A.175, A.176
(3) (4) 16.19, A.175, A.176
(*c*) A.24
(5) 8.23, 16.19, A.175, A.176
s. 85 17.1, 17.4, 17.6, 17.7, 19.23, A.8
(1) 12.70, 16.60, 17.1, 17.2, 17.4,
A.22, A.175, A.176
(2) . 17.1, 17.3, 17.4, 17.7, A.175,
A.176
(3) 17.1, 17.2, 17.4, A.175,
A.176
(*a*) (*b*) 17.4

TABLE OF STATUTES

1986 Agricultural Holdings Act—cont.
  s. 86 ...... 17.1, 17.5, 17.6, 17.7, 17.12
    (1) 17.1, 17.4, 17.6, 17.7,
      17.13, 19.23, A.8, A.175,
      A.176
    (a) 17.1, 17.5, 17.6, 17.12
    (b) 17.1, 17.5
    (2) 17.1, 17.5, 17.6, A.175,
      A.176
    (3) 17.1, 17.5, 17.6, 17.12, 19.23,
      A.8, A.175, A.176
    (4) . 17.1, 17.5, 17.12, 19.23, A.8,
      A.175, A.176
  s. 87 .... 17.1, A.175, A.176
    (1) 17.1, 17.7
    (2) 17.1, 17.7
    (3) 17.1, 17.7
    (4) 17.1, 17.7
    (5) 17.1, 17.7
    (6) 17.1, 17.4, 17.7
    (8) 17.1, 17.7
  s. 88 ... 7.4, 10.54, 17.9, 19.23, A.175,
    A.176
  s. 89 .... 7.5, 17.1, 17.8, 17.10
    (1) 17.1, 17.10, 17.14, A.175,
      A.176
    (2) 17.1, 17.10, A.175, A.176
  s. 90 ..... 7.6, 17.1, 17.8, 17.16, A.175,
    A.176
  s. 91 .... A.175, A.176
  s. 92 .... 13.67, A.175, A.176
  s. 93 . 12.25, 12.29, 17.1, 17.17, 17.20,
    17.22, 19.22
    (1) 7.10, 17.18, 17.19, 17.20,
      17.22, A.175, A.176
    (2) 17.18, A.175, A.176
    (3) 7.13, 12.25, 12.29, 17.18,
      17.20, 17.23, A.175, A.176
    (4) ... 17.19, 17.20, A.175, A.176
    (5) 12.25, 17.20, 17.24, A.35,
      A.58, A.175, A.176
    (a) 8.23
  s. 94(1) (3) 16.23, A.175, A.176
    (2) (4) A.175, A.176
  s. 95 .... 8.23, 17.25, A.7
    (1) 17.25
    (3) 17.25
    (7) 8.23
  s. 96(1) ... 1.17, 1.20, 5.21, 8.16, 8.17,
    8.18, 8.20, 8.22, 8.23, 9.28,
    10.8, 10.9, 10.36, 10.80,
    11.21, 12.18, 12.82, 13.12,
    13.44, 13.69, 14.10, 14.42,
    15.3, 19.3, A.25, A.26,
    A.29, A.31, A.68, A.175,
    A.176
    (2) 8.23, 12.78, 15.31, A.175,
      A.176
    (3) 8.23, 10.25, 10.52, 10.86,
      12.35, 12.36, 12.51, 12.76,
      13.69, 13.81, 13.82, 13.85,
      13.91, A.175, A.176

1986 Agricultural Holdings Act—cont.
  s. 96—cont.
    (4) 8.18, 8.23, A.175, A.176
    (5) 8.18, 8.23, A.175, A.176
    (6) ... 8.23, 13.106, 16.38, A.175,
      A.176
  s. 97 ...... 10.39, 13.10, 13.51, 13.116,
    16.15, A.175, A.176
  s. 98 .... 8.21, A.175, A.176
  s. 99 .... A.4, A.175, A.176
  s. 100 .... A.4, A.175, A.176
  s. 101 .... A.175, A.176
  s. 102 .... A.175, A.176
  s. 109 (5) 14.61
  Pt. IV . 8.1, 12.49, 14.2, 14.3, 14.74,
    14.97, 15.5, 17.9, 19.10
  Pt. V 11.40, 12.81, 13.1, 14.119
  Pt. VI 11.40
  Sched. 1 .... 5.7, 9.16, 10.3, 10.4, 10.5,
    10.7, A.10, A.35, A.39
    para. 1 .... 10.4, 11.7, A.175, A.176
    para. 2 ... 10.4, 14.98, A.175, A.176
    para. 3 .... 10.4, A.175, A.176
    para. 4 .... 10.4, A.175, A.176
    para. 5 .... 10.4, A.175, A.176
    para. 6 ... 10.4, 13.82, A.175, A.176
    para. 7 .... 10.4, A.175, A.176
    para. 9 ...... 1.29, 10.4, 10.7, A.175,
      A.176
  Sched. 2 .... 11.1, 11.3.1, 11.4, 11.7,
    11.21, 14.90, 15.33, 15.39,
    19.4
    para. 1 .... 11.11
    (1) ... 11.4, 11.5, 11.6, 11.7, 11.8,
      11.9, 11.10, 14.90,
      19.4, A.175, A.176
    (2) . 11.4, 11.5, 11.7, 11.9, 11.11,
      14.90, 19.4, 19.6, A.175,
      A.176
    (a) 8.23
    (b) 8.23
    (3) 2.25, 11.10, 11.11, 11.18,
      14.90, A.175, A.176
    (a) 11.7, 11.13, 11.15
    (b) 11.16, 11.17
    (c) 11.19
    para. 2 .... 8.23, 11.20, A.7
    (1) 11.17, 19.10, A.8, A.175,
      A.176
    (a) 2.19, 2.23, 11.21
    (b) 11.23
    (2) A.175, A.176
    (a) 8.23
    (b) 8.23, 11.21
    (c) 8.23, 11.23
    (3) 11.21, A.7, A.175, A.176
    (a) 8.23
    (b) 8.23
    (4) 11.22, A.175, A.176
    para. 3 .... 11.20, A.175, A.176
    (a) 11.17, 11.24
    (b) 11.25

lxi

TABLE OF STATUTES

1986 Agricultural Holdings Act—*cont.*
Sched. 2—*cont.*
para. 4
(1) A.171, A.175, A.176
   (*a*) 11.29
   (*b*) 11.29, 11.30
(2) 11.29, 11.30, A.175, A.176
   (*a*) 10.6, 10.26
   (*b*) 11.40
para. 5 .... 11.31
(1) 8.23, A.175, A.176
   (*a*) 8.23
(2) 11.31, A.175, A.176
   (*b*) 8.23
para. 6 . 11.29, 11.32, A.175, A.176
para. 8 .... 8.23
Sched. 3 ... 12.25, 12.27, 12.28, 12.32,
12.44, 12.47, 12.48, 12.80,
12.82, 13.54, 14.20, 14.21,
15.39, A.22, A.27, A.68,
A.70, A.71, A.74, A.161,
A.164
Pt. I 12.49, 12.50, 12.52, 12.76,
12.78, 12.80, 12.82, 13.82,
A.22, A.165
Case A ... 12.2, 12.44, 12.46, 12.49,
12.76, 12.79, 12.81.4,
12.83, 13.19, 14.100, A.35,
A.68, A.71, A.114, A.175,
A.176
Case B 8.2, 12.2, 12.19, 12.40,
12.44, 12.46, 12.50,
12.50.1, 12.50.2, 12.50.3,
12.50.4, 12.76, 12.81.4,
12.83, 12.94.1, 12.94.2,
12.94.4, 13.21, 13.39,
14.21, 14.107, A.22, A.35,
A.68, A.71, A.72, A.73,
A.78, A.114, A.175, A.176
Case C ... 10.32, 12.2, 12.44, 12.50,
12.51, 12.76, 12.94.1,
12.94.2, 13.18, 13.82,
14.20, 14.107, A.22, A.35,
A.68, A.71, A.162, A.175,
A.176
Case D ... 10.32, 12.2, 12.27, 12.29,
12.44, 12.46, 12.50, 12.51,
12.52, 12.53, 12.56, 12.58,
12.59, 12.60, 12.61.2,
12.61.9, 12.61.10, 12.61.12,
12.61.13, 12.61.14,
12.61.18, 12.61.19, 12.73,
12.75, 12.76, 12.76.1,
12.81.4, 12.83, 12.89.5,
12.89.6, 12.94.1, 12.94.2,
12.94.4, 13.18, 13.82,
14.21, 14.107, 17.23, 18.27,
A.22, A.23, A.35, A.59,
A.60, A.61, A.68, A.71,
A.78, A.114, A.175, A.176
para. (*b*) 12.60, 12.72

1986 Agricultural Holdings Act—*cont.*
Sched. 3—*cont.*
Case E 12.2, 12.3, 12.27, 12.44,
12.46, 12.50, 12.51,
12.61.10, 12.76, 12.76.1,
12.76.2, 12.77, 12.81.1,
12.81.4, 12.83, 12.94.1,
12.94.2, 12.94.4, 13.18,
13.82, 14.21, 15.39,
18.27, A.22, A.35, A.68,
A.71, A.78, A.114, A.175,
A.176
Case F ... 12.2, 12.50, 12.76, 12.78,
12.94.1, 12.94.2, 13.18,
14.20, 14.107, A.22, A.68,
A.175, A.176
Case G 1.29, 8.23, 12.2, 12.25,
12.39, 12.44, 12.46, 12.50,
12.76, 12.77, 12.80, 12.81,
12.81.1, 12.81.2, 12.81.3,
12.81.4, 12.81.5, 12.94.1,
12.94.2, 13.5, 13.16, 13.18,
14.2, 14.10, 14.82, 14.83,
14.84, 14.87, 19.19, A.22,
A.68, A.69, A.175, A.176
Case H ... 12.2, 12.44, 12.76, 12.82,
13.19, A.68, A.175, A.176
para. (*b*) 12.82
Pt. II, para. 1 .. 12.49, A.175, A.176
para. 2 .... 12.49, A.175, A.176
para. 3 .... 12.49, A.175, A.176
para. 4 .... 12.49, A.175, A.176
para. 5 .... 12.49, A.175, A.176
para. 6 .... 12.49, A.175, A.176
para. 7 .... 10.76, 12.49, A.175, A.176
(1) 8.23
(2) 8.23
para. 8 ... 8.23, 12.50, A.175, A.176
(2) 8.23
para. 8A (2) 12.50
para. 9 .... 12.11, 12.51, A.35, A.68
(1) ... 12.51, 13.82, A.175, A.176
   (*d*) 13.82
(2) 11.32, 12.51, 12.61.18, A.175, A.176
para. 10 .... 12.52, A.164
(1) A.175, A.176
   (*a*) . 12.53, A.23, A.163, A.165
   (*b*) (*c*) 12.60
   (*d*) 12.51, 12.61.18
(2) 12.60, A.23, A.175, A.176
para. 11 .... 12.76
(1) 12.76, A.175, A.176
(2) ... 12.51, 12.76, 13.82, A.175, A.176
para. 12 ...... 12.81.1, 12.79, 14.10, A.175, A.176
   (*a*) 8.23, 12.79, 12.80
   (*b*) . 8.23, 12.79, 12.80, A.166, A.167
para. 12 (3) 12.81.1

1986 Agricultural Holdings Act—*cont.*
  Sched. 4 .. 12.44, 13.116, 15.6, A.175,
      A.176
    paras. 1–4 .... A.22
    para. 5 .... 12.43, A.22
    para. 6 .... A.22
    paras. 8–13 .... 12.62, A.22
  Sched. 5 .... 12.2, 12.92, 12.93, A.175,
      A.176
    para. 1 ... 8.23, 12.92, 12.93, A.175,
      A.176
    para. 2 .... 12.93, A.175, A.176
    para. 2 (1) (*a*) (*b*) 12.93
         (2) (*a*) (*b*) 12.93
    para. 3 .... A.175, A.176
      (1) 12.94
      (2) 12.94
    para. 4 .... 12.94.3, A.175, A.176
    para. 5 .... A.22, A.175, A.176
    para. 6 .... 12.32, A.175, A.176
  Sched. 6 .... 1.29, 8.23, 14.2, 14.52,
      14.59, 14.61, 14.103, 14.110,
      A.10
    Pt. I A.175, A.176
    para. 1 ... 8.23, 14.62, A.175, A.176
      (1) 14.119
      (2) 8.23, 14.63
    para. 2 . 14.45, 14.70, A.175, A.176
    para. 3 ..... 8.23, 14.54, A.26, A.29,
      A.30, A.175, A.176
      (1) 14.57, A.26, A.29, A.30
      (2) 14.54, 14.56
    para. 4 ... 8.23, 14.54, 14.56, 14.60,
      A.26, A.29, A.30, A.175,
      A.176
      (1) (*b*) and (*c*) 8.23
    para. 5 .... 14.54
      (1) (2) A.175, A.176
      (3) 14.60, A.175, A.176
        (*a*) 14.58
        (*b*) 14.60
      (4) 14.60, A.175, A.176
      (5) 14.60, A.175, A.176
    para. 6 .. 14.59, 14.61, 14.62, 14.65,
      A.10, A.175, A.176
      (1) 14.63, 14.64
      (1) (*a*)–(*f*) 14.62, 14.64
        (*d*) (*dd*) A.10
      (2) 14.63
      (3) 14.62
    para. 7 .. 14.59, 14.61, 14.62, 14.65,
      14.68, 14.69, A.175, A.176
      (1) 14.65
      (2) 14.65, 14.67
      (3) 14.65, 14.67, 14.68
        (*a*) 14.67
    para. 8 .... 14.59, 14.62, 14.69
      (1) (2) 14.69, A.175, A.176
    para. 9 . 14.59, 14.62, 14.65, A.175,
      A.176
      (2) 14.61
    para. 10. 14.59, 14.62, A.175, A.176

1986 Agricultural Holdings Act—*cont.*
  Sched. 6—*cont.*
    para. 10—*cont.*
      (1) 14.68
      (2) 14.64, 14.68
      (3) 8.23, 14.64
    Pt. II 14.110, A.175, A.176
  Sched. 7 .... 5.13, 10.51, 13.42, 13.45,
      13.50, 13.57, 13.66, 13.68,
      13.69, 13.72, 13.78, 13.112,
      13.123, 17.10, 17.13, 17.14,
      17.15, A.98
    paras. 1–8 .... A.175, A.176
    para. 9 .... 13.64, A.175, A.176
    paras. 10–28 .... A.175, A.176
    para. 12 .... A.111, A.118
    para. 23 .... A.111
    para. 26 .... 17.15
    Pt. I 5.13, 13.4, 13.50, 13.58, 13.59,
      13.61, 13.78, A.175, A.176
    Pt. II 5.13, 13.56, 13.58, 13.59,
      13.61, 13.62, A.100, A.101
  Sched. 8 ...... 5.13, 5.14, 10.55, 13.54,
      13.57, 13.76, 13.112
    Pt. I 5.13, 13.2, 13.42, 13.50, 13.57,
      13.66, 13.67, 13.68, 13.69,
      13.78, 13.112, 15.22, 15.34,
      17.13, A.175, A.176
    paras. 1–11 .... A.175, A.176
    para. 1 .... A.35, A.105, A.118
    paras. 5, 6 .... 13.112, A.111
    Pt. II 5.14, 13.3, 13.4, 13.42, 13.50,
      13.51, 13.52, 13.67, 13.68,
      13.71, 13.78, 13.112, 17.13,
      A.35, A.96
    para. 7 .... 5.13, 13.112, A.95, A.96,
      A.111, A.118
    para. 8 .... 5.13, 13.112, A.95, A.96,
      A.111
    para. 9 ... 5.13, 10.55, 13.56, 13.71,
      13.112, A.95, A.96, A.118
    para. 10 .... 13.54, 13.55, 13.112,
      15.22, A.95, A.96, A.111
      (2) 8.23
    para. 11 .5.13, 13.54, 13.112, A.111
      (3) 8.23
  Sched. 9 .... 13.46, 13.48
    Pt. I 13.42
    para. 1 (2) 8.23, 13.44, A.175,
      A.176
    para. 1 (1) (3) . 13.44, A.175, A.176
      (4) 13.44, A.175, A.176
      (5) 13.44, A.175, A.176
    para. 2
      (1) 13.45, A.175, A.176
      (2) 13.45, A.175, A.176
    para. 3 (1) 13.46, 13.61, A.175,
      A.176
      (2) 13.46
    para. 4 (1)–(3) 13.46, A.175, A.176
    para. 5 .... 8.22
    para. 5 (1) 13.47, A.175, A.176

1986 Agricultural Holdings Act—*cont.*	1986 Agricultural Holdings Act—*cont.*
Sched. 9—*cont.*	Sched. 11—*cont.*
(2) 13.48, A.175, A.176	para. 18 .. 16.55, 16.77, 17.2, 19.19, A.8, A.170
Pt. II 13.42, 13.46, 13.49, 15.22	para. 19 . 16.19, 16.38, 16.56, 16.58
paras. 1–16 .... A.175, A.176	para. 20 ....12.69, 16.58
Sched. 10 .. 15.28, 15.29, 15.34, 17.12	para. 21 .... 12.69, 16.19, 16.58
paras. 1–5 ....A.175, A.176	para. 22 ....16.19, 16.57
para. 1 .... 15.24	para. 23 .... 12.69, 16.72, 16.73
para. 5 .... 15.22	para. 24 .... 16.72
Sched. 11 ...9.16, 10.84, 12.69, 13.38, 14.86, 16.1, 16.14, 16.17, 16.19, 16.20, 16.22, 16.23, 16.53, 16.75, 17.25, 18.17, 19.19, A.28	para. 25 .... 16.72
	para. 26 ...... 12.50.4, 16.19, 16.23, 16.32, 16.61
	para. 27 ....16.32, 16.66
para. 1 .. 12.85, 12.87, 16.19, 16.22, A.22, A.59, A.60, A.61, A.175, A.176	(1) A.175, A.176
	(2) ... 16.56, 16.66, 16.67, A.175, A.176
(1) 8.23, 16.21, A.25, A.170, A.175, A.176	para. 28 .... 16.66
	(1) ... 16.58, 16.67, 16.68, A.175, A.176
(2) 11.3.8, 16.23, A.25, A.28, A.175, A.176	(2) ... 16.58, 16.67, A.175, A.176
(3) . 11.3.5, 11.3.8, 16.23, A.171, A.175, A.176	(3) (4) 16.67, A.175, A.176
	para. 29 ....16.19, 16.26
(4) 16.23, A.175, A.176	para. 30 ....11.3.8, 16.23, 16.26, 16.75
(5) 10.84, 16.23, A.29, A.175, A.176	para. 31 .... 6.82, 11.3.4, 16.23
paras. 2–32 .... A.175, A.176	para. 32 ....16.19, 16.23
para. 2 ... 16.19, 16.24, A.35, A.115	Sched. 12 .... 8.21
para. 3 .... 16.19, 16.24	paras. 1–10 .... A.175, A.176
para. 4 ... 16.19, 16.25, A.35, A.116	para. 1 .... 9.14, 9.22
para. 5 .... 16.19, 16.22, 16.25	para. 2 ....9.23, 13.41
para. 6 .... 16.19, 16.26	para. 3 .... 10.35, 10.36, 13.41, 15.23
(*a*) 16.26	para. 4 .... 12.5, 12.12, 13.41
(*b*) 16.26	(3) 8.23
para. 7 .. 16.23, 16.27, A.35, A.113, A.114, A.117, A.118, A.161, A.163, A.164, A.165, A.169, A.171	(5) 8.23
	para. 5 .... 13.41, 13.69
	para. 6 ... 13.41, 13.52, 13.78, A.35, A.95, A.170
(*a*) 16.27	(1) 13.54
(*b*) 16.27, 16.30	(2) 13.54, A.35, A.96
para. 8 .... 16.38, A.35, A.120	para. 7 13.41, 13.52, 13.78, 13.112, A.35, A.95, A.170
para. 9 .... 16.38, 16.39	
para. 10 .... 16.39	(1) (2) 13.55
para. 11 .... 16.19	(3) 13.55
(1) (3) (4) 16.39, A.175, A.176	para. 8 .. 13.41, 13.52, 13.54, 13.78, 13.112, A.35, A.95, A.170
para. 12 .... 8.23, 16.19, 16.39	(2) 8.23
(1)–(4) A.175, A.176	(*a*) 13.78
(1) 8.23	(*c*) 13.4
para. 13 ....16.19, 16.39	para. 9 .... 13.4, 13.41, 13.52, A.35, A.95, A.170
para. 14 .... 16.23	
(1) 12.50.4, 16.51, 16.66, A.161, A.163, A.164, A.165, A.169, A.170, A.171, A.175, A.176	(*a*) 13.78
	para. 10
	(1) 15.27
	(2) 15.28
(2) . 12.50.4, 16.19, 16.51, 16.66, A.161, A.163, A.164, A.165, A.169, A.170, A.171, A.175, A.176	(3) (4) 15.28
	Sched. 13
	paras. 1–16 .... A.175, A.176
para. 15 ....16.52, 16.58	para. 1(1) .. 14.5, 14.6, 14.14, 14.15
para. 16 .... 16.66	(2) 14.7
para. 17 ....16.19, 16.55	para. 15 .... A.24

TABLE OF STATUTES

1986 Agricultural Holdings Act—*cont.*
   Sched. 14
      para. 11 ....17.10, 17.13
      para. 12 ... 7.2, 18.31, A.175, A.176
      para. 13 .... 17.10
      para. 17 .... 10.29
      para. 18 .... 16.4
      para. 21 .... 8.5, 9.19
      para. 27 .... 13.102
      para. 29 .... 10.41
      para. 44 .... A.175
      para. 49 .... 16.71
      para. 53 (4) A.175, A.176
      para. 64 .... 10.30
   Sched. 17, para. 51 .... 17.7
      Pt. II ... 13.55, 13.56, 13.58, 13.112
   Insolvency Act (c. 45)
      s. 349 .... A.174
      s. 349A A.174
      Sched. 14 .... A.174
   Agriculture Act (c. 49) 5, 5.3, 8.2, 11.26,
      13.1, 13.31, 14.98, 15.3, 16.18, 18.1,
      18.23, 18.24, 18.27, 18.29, 18.30,
      19.1, 19.2, 19.3, 19.6, 19.6.1, 19.18,
      A.7, A.111, A.112, A.114, A.115,
      A.118
      s. 13 19.1, 19.7, 19.8, 19.17, **A.7**, A.9,
      A.111, A.118
      s. 15 ..... 11.20, 19.1, 19.3, 19.4, 19.5,
      19.6, 19.8, **A.7**
      (1) 11.26, 19.6, 19.6.1, 19.6.2
         (*b*) 19.9.4
      (2) (*a*)–(*c*) 19.6.1
      (3) 19.3
      (4) A.9
   Sched. 1 ..... 14.98, 19.3, 19.6.1, 19.7,
      19.9.1, 19.21, **A.8**, A.21,
      A.111, A.114, A.118
      para. 1 .... 19.9, 19.10, 19.18
      (1) 19.9.1, 19.12, 19.14
         (*a*) 19.9.3, 19.9.4
      (2) 11.26, 19.6, 19.9.2, 19.9.4
      (3) 19.9.5
      para. 2 .... 19.6.1, 19.9.4, 19.10
      (2)
         (*a*) 19.10
         (*b*) (i) (ii) 19.10
         (3) 19.10
      para. 3 .... 19.6.1, 19.9.4, 19.11
         (*a*) 19.11
         (*b*) (i) (ii) 19.11
      para. 4 ... 15.3, 19.6.1, 19.9.4, 19.12
         (*a*) 19.12
         (*b*) (i) (ii) 19.12
         (*c*) 19.12
      para. 5 ....19.13.1
      (1)–(3) 19.13, 19.13.1
      para. 6 .... 19.14, A.21
      (1) 19.14, 19.14.3
         (*a*) 19.14, 19.14.1, 19.14.3
         (*b*) 19.14, 19.14.2, 19.14.3,
         A.21

1986 Agriculture Act—*cont.*
   Sched. 1—*cont.*
      (2) 19.14, 19.14.3,
      A.21
      (3) (4) 19.14.4
      (5) (*a*) (*b*) 19.14.1
      para. 7 .... 19.15
      (1)(*b*) 19.14.1
      (2) 19.15
      (3) (4) 19.15
      para. 8 .... 19.14.4, 19.15, 19.16
         (*a*) (*b*) 19.16
      para. 9 .... 19.17
   Building Societies Act (c. 53)
      Sched. 14, Pt II A.174
      para. 10 .... 19.18, A.114, A.170
      para. 11 ...... 13.119, 19.19, A.111,
      A.114, A.118
      (1) 14.98, 16.18, A.170
      (2)–(5) 19.19, A.9, A.170
      (6)–(7) 19.18, 19.19
      paras. 12, 15, 17 .... 19.23
      para. 13 .... 19.20
      (1) (2) 19.21
      para. 14 .... 19.21
      para. 16 .... 19.22
      (5) 19.22
      para. 18 .... 19.3
      (1) 19.9.1, 19.14.2
   Sched. 6
      para. 1 ....19.14.3
      para. 8 ....19.14.1
   Financial Services Act (c. 60)
      s. 187 .... 6.23
   Housing and Planning Act (c. 63–
      s. 39 (3) (4) A.9
      Sched. 8, para. 5 ....11.40, 11.45,
      12.40, 12.51,
      A.9
      Sched. 12, Pt II A.9
1987 Coal Industry Act (c. 3)
      s. 1 (2) 11.36
      Sched. 1, para. 7 (*c*) 11.36
   Landlord and Tenant Act (c. 31)
      .... 7.16
      s. 47 .... 7.8, 7.16, 17.17, A.35, A.138,
      A.139
      s. 48 ....7.8, 7.16, 12.54, 12.55, 17.17,
      A.35, A.138, A.139
      (1) 12.55
      (2) 12.55
1988 Multilateral Investment Guarantee Agency Act (c. 8)
      s. 6, 8 (3) A.174
   Consumer Arbitration Agreements Act (c. 21) A.174
   Landlord and Tenant Act (c. 26) 1.29,
      1.39
      s. 1 (5) 2.7
      s. 4 .... 1.29
   Education Reform Act (c. 40)
      s. 231 (7) A.9

TABLE OF STATUTES

1988 Education Reform Act—*cont.*
 s. 235 (6) A.9
 s. 237 .... A.9
 Sched. 12, para. 96 .... A.9
 Copyright, Designs and Patents Act (c. 48)
 s.150 (2) A.174
 Housing Act (c. 50) 1.37, 8.4, 8.12
  Pt. I A.9
  s. 34 .... 1.20
  s. 101 .... A.9
  s. 140 .... A.9
  Sched. 1 .... 1.37. A10
   para. 6 .... 8.12
   para. 7 .... 8.12, **A.10**
  Sched. 17, para. 69 (1) (2) A.9
 Local Government and Housing Act (c. 42)
  s. 165 (2) 11.41
  s. 194 (4) 11.41
  Sched. 12, Pt II 11.41
1989 Water Act (c. 15)
  s. 58 (7) A.9
  s. 101 (1) A.9
  s. 141 (6) A.9
  s. 160 (1) (2) (4) A.9
  s. 189 (4)–(10) A.9
  s. 190 .... A.9
  s. 193 (1) A.9
  Sched. 25, para. 75 (*a*), (*b*) A.9
  Sched. 26, para. 3 (1) (2) A.9
   para. 17 .... A.9
   para. 40 (4) A.9
   para. 57 (6) A.9
   para. 58 .... A.9
 Fair Employment (Northern Ireland) Act (c. 32)
  s.5 (7) A.174
1990 Town and Country Planning Act (c. 8) 12.50, A.9, A.10
  Pt III A.9
  s. 59 .... 12.50
  s. 65 .... 1.41, A.10
   (2) (8) A.10
  s. 336 (1) 12.50, A.9, A.10
 Planning (Consequential provisions) Act (c. 11)
  s. 4, Sched. 2, para. 72 .... A.9
 Agricultural Holdings (Amendment) Act (c. 15) 8.2, 12.50
 Courts and Legal Services Act (c. 41)
  s. 71 (2) A.5
  ss. 99, 101–103 .... A.174
  Sched. 10, para. 6 (1) A.5
  ss. 1 (1) (2), 2 .... A.9
1991 Coal Mining Subsidence Act (c. 45) .A.10
  s. 21 .... 1.41, A.10
   (3) (*a*), (*aa*) A.10
  s. 53 (2) A.9
  Sched. 3 .... 1.41, A.10
   para. 1 (2) (*b*), (*bb*) A.10

1991 Coal Mining Subsidence Act—*cont.*
  Sched. 8 .... A.9
 Agricultural Holdings (Scotland) Act (c. 55)
  s. 1 .... A.28
  s. 88 .... A.9
  Sched. 13 Pt. II A.9
 Water Resources Act (c. 57)
  ss. 94, 95 .... A.9
 Water Consolidation (Consequential Provisions) Act (c. 60)
  s. 2, Sched. 1, para. 43 .... A.9
1992 Social Security Administration Act (c. 5)
  s. 59 .... A.174
 Social Security Administration (Northern Ireland) Act (c. 8)
  s. 57 .... A.174
 Friendly Societies Act (c. 40)
  Sched. 16, para. 31 .... A.174
 Trade Union and Labour Relations (Consolidation) Act (c. 52)
  s. 212 (5) A.174
  s. 263 (6) A.174
 Tribunals and Inquiries Act (c. 53)
  s. 18 (1) (2) A.9
  Sched. 1, para. 1 (*b*) A.9
  Sched. 3, para. 18 .... A.9
  Sched. 4 .... A.9
1993 Judicial Pensions and Retirement Act (c. 8)
  s. 26 .... A.5, A.9
   (4)–(6) A.5, A.9
  Sched. 6, para. 45 .... A.9
 Education Act (c. 35) A.174
 Crofters (Scotland) Act (c. 44)
  s. 3 .... A.28
 Statute Law (Repeals Act) (c. 50)
  Sched. 1, Pt II A.9
1994 Coal Industry Act (c. 21)
  s. 52 .... 11.36
   (1) 11.36
   (3) 11.36
  s. 67 .... A.9
  Sched. 8 .... 11.36
   Pt I, para. 5 .... 11.36
  Sched. 9, para. 35 .... A.9
  Sched. 11, Pt. II A.9
 Criminal Justice and Public Order Act (c. 33)
  s. 44 .... A.9
  Sched. 4, para. 63 .... A.9
1995 Agricultural Tenancies Act (c. 8) 1.1, 1.2, 1.3, 1.5, 1.6, 1.7, 1.24, 1.42, 2.3, 3.1, 4.1, 4.2, 4.3, 4.4, 4.11, 5.2, 5.3, 5.7, 5.13, 5.15, 5.20, 6.1, 6.3, 6.10, 6.11, 6.12, 6.14, 6.16, 6.38, 6.39, 6.40, 6.41, 6.42, 6.44, 6.45, 6.46, 6.49, 6.50, 6.52, 6.53, 6.56, 6.57, 6.58, 6.60, 6.63, 6.64, 6.65, 6.66, 6.68,

TABLE OF STATUTES

1995 Agricultural Tenancies Act—
cont.
6.70, 6.71, 6.72, 6.74, 6.75, 6.76,
6.77, 6.78, 6.79, 6.81, 6.82,
6.83, 7.1, 7.3, 7.8, 7.9, 7.10,
7.11, 7.12, 7.13, 7.14, 7.15,
7.16, 11.10, 11.18, 11.21,
11.24, 11.25, 13.70, 14.97,
14.121, 16.37, 18.32, 19.24,
A.9, **A.10**, A.35, A.125,
A.137
Pt I 1.22
Pt II 1.45, 2.1, 2.3, 2.5, 2.6, 2.7, 2.9,
2.10
Pt III ... 1.22, 1.47, 2.17, 2.18, 2.21,
3.2, 5.1, 5.2, 5.3, 5.4, 5.6, 5.7,
5.8, 5.10, 5.11, 5.25, 6.1, 6.3,
6.10, 6.14, 6.49, 6.65, 6.67
Pt IV 6.1, 6.11
s. 1
(1) 1.15
(2) 1.5, 1.17
(3) **1.20**, 1.22
(4) **1.21**, 1.23, A.35, A.125
(5) 1.20
(6) 1.20
(7) 1.18, 8.20
(8) 1.19, A.126
s. 2 .... 1.15
(1)
(a) 1.4, 1.6
(b) 1.6, 1.7
s. 3 .... 1.20
(1)
(a) 1.20
(c) 1.20
(2) 1.20
(3) 1.20
s. 4 ....1.4, 1.5, 1.7, 14.97, 18.31
(1) 14.97
(a) 1.6, 1.8, 14.97
(b) 1.9, 1.11, 14.97
(c) 1.10, 1.11, 14.97
(d) 1.11, 14.97
(e) 1.12, 14.97
(f) 1.13
(2) 1.11, 14.97
(3) 1.14
(a) 1.14
(b) 1.14
s. 5 ....3.9, 4.1, 4.4, 4.5, 4.6, 4.7,
4.13, 4.14, 4.16, 4.17, 4.20, A.35,
A.127
(1) 4.5, 4.7, 4.14
(2) 4.5
(3) 4.5
(4) 4.7
s. 6 .....4.1, 4.4, 4.13, 4.14, 4.15, 4.17,
4.19, 4.20, A.35, A.132, A.133,
A.134, A.135
(1) 4.7, 4.13, 4.14, 4.15
(2) 4.6, 4.14

1995 Agricultural Tenancies Act—
cont.
s. 7 . 4.1, 4.4, 4.8, 4.9, 4.12, 4.14, 4.16,
4.17, 4.20, A.35, A.128, A.129,
A.130, A.131
(1) 4.7, 4.8, 4.9, 4.10
(2) 4.9
(3) 4.10, A.35, A.136
s. 8 3.1, 3.2, 3.3, 3.4, 3.5, 3.6, 3.7, 3.8,
3.9, 3.10, 3.11, 3.12, 3.13, 3.14,
5.4, 5.6, 5.7, 5.16, 10.36
(1) 3.1, 3.9, 3.1
(a) 3.10
(b) 3.11
(2) 3.1
(a) 3.2, 3.5, 3.6
(c) 3.7
(d) 3.1, 3.2, 3.6, 3.8, 5.6
(3) 3.1, 3.13
(4) 3.1, 3.13
(5) 3.1, 3.5, 3.11, 3.12, 5.4
(6) 3.1, 3.2, 3.4, 3.5
(7) 3.1, 3.2
s. 9 .... 2.1, 2.3, 2.6, 2.8, 2.11, 2.12
(a) 2.2, 2.5, 2.6, 2.8
(b) 2.8
(i) 2.2, 2.6, 2.8
(ii) 2.6, 2.7, 2.8, 2.15
ss. 10–14 .... 6.14
s. 10 .....2.1, 2.3, 2.9, 2.10, 2.11, 2.12,
2.14, 6.3, 6.10, 6.14, 16.37,
A.35, A.140, A.141
(1) 2.10.2, 2.11, 2.12, 2.13
(2) 2.13
(a) 2.13
(3) 2.10, 2.10.2, 2.13
(4) . 2.1, 2.9, **2.10**, 2.10.1, 2.10.2,
2.13, 2.16
(5) 2.1, **2.10**, 2.10.1, 2.10.2, 2.13,
2.16
(6) 2.5, 2.9, 2.10, 2.11, 2.13, 2.16
(a) 2.10, 2.13
(b) 2.9, 2.13
s. 11 ....2.1, 2.13, 16.37
s. 12 ....2.1, 2.11, 2.14, 6.82, 19.24
(a) 2.11, 2.14
(b) . 2.1, 2.10.2, 2.11, 2.12, 6.1
s. 13 .... 2.1, 2.11, 2.12, 2.15, 2.16,
19.24
(1) 2.13, 2.15, 2.16, 6.49
(2) 2.3, 2.15, **2.16**
(a) 2.19, 19.24
(b) 2.20, 2.21, 2.22, 19.24
(c) 2.21, 2.22, 19.24
(4) 2.15
(a) 2.16, 2.17, 2.18, 2.23
(b) 2.24
(5) 2.15, 2.17
s. 15 ...... 2.17, 3.10, 5.1, 5.4, 5.6, 5.9,
5.10, 5.14, 5.24, 19.24
(a) ... 2.17, 3.10, A.149, A.151
(b) 2.17, 3.10, 5.4, 5.7

lxvii

TABLE OF STATUTES

1995 Agricultural Tenancies Act—
cont.
s. 16 ...... 1.30, 3.7, 5.1, 5.7, 5.21, 7.5,
7.15, A.152, A.153
   (1) 3.7
   (2) 3.7
     (a) 5.7
     (b) 5.4, 5.7
   (3) 5.7, 19.24
   (5) 16.37
s. 17–19 .... 5.1, 5.8
s. 17 .. 3.8, 5.1, 5.2, 5.6, 5.8, 5.9, 5.10,
5.11, A.35, A.142, A.144, A.147,
A.148, A.149, A.150
   (1) 5.10, 5.11, A.145, A.146
   (2) 5.10
   (3) 5.10, 5.16
   (4) 5.10, 5.11
   (5) 5.4, 5.10
s. 18 ...... 1.22, 2.17, 5.1, 5.2, 5.8, 5.9,
5.10, 5.17, A.35, A.143, A.149,
A.150, A.151, A.152
   (1) 5.9
     (a) 5.9
     (b) 5.9
       (i) 5.9
       (ii) 5.9
     (c) 5.8
   (2) 5.9
   (3) 5.9, 5.10
s. 19 . 3.8, 5.1, 5.2, 5.4, 5.8, 5.10, 5.11,
5.12, 5.15, 6.3, 6.10, 6.14, 6.38,
6.49, 6.66, 6.67, A.35, A.145,
A.146, A.147
s. 19 (1) 5.11, 5.13, 5.15, 6.1
     (a) 5.11
     (b) 5.11
     (c) 5.9, 5.10, 5.11
   (2) 5.2, 5.3, 5.11, 5.12, 5.13
   (3) 5.11
     (a) 5.11
     (b) 5.11
   (4) 5.15, 5.22
   (5) 5.2, 5.10, 5.13, 5.16
   (6) 5.12, 5.16, 6.38
   (7) 5.2, 5.10, 5.16
   (8) 5.16
   (9) 5.12
     (a) 5.12
     (b) 5.12
     (c) 5.12
   (10) 2.17, 2.18, 5.2, 5.6, 5.10,
5.12, 5.13, 5.22
s. 20 .... 5.1, 5.18, 5.25, 6.3
   (1) 5.18
   (2) 5.18, 5.19, 5.24
   (3) 5.3, 5.18
   (4) 5.18
   (5) 5.18
s. 21 .... 5.1, 5.17, 5.18, 5.25
   (1) 5.17
   (2) 5.17

1995 Agricultural Tenancies Act—
cont.
s. 21—cont.
   (3) 5.3, 5.17, 5.18, 5.19, 5.24
s. 22 5.1, 5.20, 5.21, 5.22, A.35, A.152
   (1) 5.20
   (2) 3.9, 5.7, 5.21, 5.22
   (3) 5.22
   (3) (a) 3.7
   (4) 5.22, 5.23
   (5) 5.7, 5.21, 5.22
s. 23 .. 2.21, 3.7, 3.9, 5.1, 5.3, 5.4, 5.23
   (1) 5.23, 13.70
   (2) 5.23, A.35, A.153
   (3) 5.23
s. 24 .... 5.1, 5.3, 5.24, 5.25
   (1) 5.24
     (a) 5.24
     (b) 5.24
   (2) 5.24
   (3) 5.24
   (5) 5.24
s. 25 .... 5.1, 5.3, 5.25
   (1) 5.25
s. 26 .... 5.1, 5.2, 6.72
   (1) 2.21, 5.2, 5.10
   (2) 5.2, 5.4, 5.5
s. 28 . 4.20, 5.20, 6.1, 6.2, 6.3, 6.5, 6.7,
6.10, 6.11, 6.12, 6.14, 6.41, 6.61,
6.63, 6.65, 6.66
   (1) 6.2
   (2) 6.2, 6.5, 6.7, 6.10, A.35,
A.158
   (3) 6.2, 6.10
   (4) 6.1, 6.12, A.174
   (5) 6.1, 6.12
     (a) 2.11, 6.1
     (b) 6.1
     (c) 5.20, 6.1
s. 29 .. 2.11, 6.1, 6.2, 6.3, 6.4, 6.5, 6.6,
6.7, 6.9, 6.10, 6.11, 6.13, 6.14,
6.16, 6.38, 6.83, A.156
   (1) 6.5, A.155, A.157
     (a) 6.5, A.154
       (i) 6.5
       (ii) 6.5
     (b) 6.5
       (i) 6.5
       (ii) 6.5
   (2) 2.11, 6.6
s. 30 ...... 5.15, 5.20, 6.1, 6.2, 6.3, 6.4,
6.10, 6.11, 6.14, 6.35, 6.37,
6.38, 6.43, 6.44, 6.45, 6.47, 6.51,
6.52
   (1) 6.2, 6.3
   (2) 2.14, 5.22, 6.3
   (3) 2.14, 6.3, 6.51
   (4) 6.51
   (5) 6.51
s. 31 .... 7.2, 18.31
   (4) A.9
ss. 32–34 .... 7.3

1995	Agricultural Tenancies Act—*cont.*		1995	Agricultural Tenancies Act—*cont.*	
	s. 32	7.4		Sched.—*cont.*	
	s. 33	7.3, 7.5		para. 28	1.36
	s. 34	7.6		para. 29	1.41
	s. 35	1.24, 7.7		para. 30	1.37
	s. 36	6.37, 6.79, 6.80, 7.8		para. 31	1.38
	(1)	7.8		para. 32	A.9
	(2)	7.12		para. 34	1.37
	(*a*)	7.9		para. 35	1.41
	(*b*)	7.10		para. 36	1.41
	(*c*)	7.11, 7.12		para. 37	1.41
	(3)	7.11, 17.22		Landlord and Tenant (Covenants) Act (c. 30)	1.44
	(4)	7.12		s. 1	1.40
	(5)	7.13		(3)	1.40
	(*a*)	7.13		ss. 3–16	1.40
	(*b*)	7.13		ss. 17–20, 21	1.40
	(6)	7.10		s. 29	1.40
	(7)	7.14, 17.16, 17.24, A.35, A.138		s. 31	1.40
				Merchant Shipping Act (c.21)	
	(*a*)	7.14		s. 96 (10)	A.174
	(*b*)	7.14		s. 264 (9)	A.174
	s. 37	1.42, 7.15		Sched. 6, Pt. 11, para. 7	A.174
	(2)	7.15	1995	Civil Evidence Act (c. 38)	2.25, 11.10, 16.20
	(3)	7.15			
	(5)	7.15		Private International Law (Miscellaneous Provisions) Act (c.42)	
	(6)	7.15			
	s. 38	3.9, 3.10, 6.11		s. 3	A.174
	(1)	1.16, 1.17, 1.20, 1.22, 2.3, 2.13, 2.16, 2.17, 3.9, 3.10, 3.11, 5.2, 5.4, 5.21, 6.32, 6.50		s. 4	A.9
			1996	Industrial Tribunals Act (c.17)	
				s. 6 (2)	A.174
	(2)	1.17		Arbitration Act (c. 23)	1.48, 2.11, 2.14, 2.25, 5.15, 5.20, 6.1, 6.4, 6.7, 6.8, 6.9, 6.10, 6.11, 6.12, 6.14, 6.15, 6.16, 6.17, 6.38, 6.65, 6.71, 6.81, 6.82, 16.1, 16.4, 16.16, 16.17, 16.18, 16.19, 16.20, 16.35, 16.53, 18.17, A.28, A.173, **A.174**
	(3)	1.6, 1.8, 4.16			
	(4)	1.6, 1.8, 1.17, 1.21, 2.9, 2.13, 4.16			
	(5)	3.9, 4.5, 5.7			
	s. 40	A.9			
	s. 41 (2)	1.4, 1.8, 18.32			
	(3)	1.2			
				Pt. I	6.10, 6.13, 6.15, 6.73, 6.81, A.9, A.29
	(4)	1.2			
	s. 82 (1)	6.18		Pt. II	6.13, 6.29
	s. 93 (3)	7.13		Pt. IV	A.29
	Sched.	1.2, 1.41		Pt VII	6.9, 6.40
	para. 1	1.26		ss. 1–84	6.10, 6.12, 6.14
	para. 2	1.27		s. 1	6.12
	para. 3	1.28		(*c*)	**6.12**
	para. 4	1.28		s. 2	6.10
	para. 5	1.29		s. 4	6.9, 6.39
	para. 6	1.29		(1)	6.9
	para. 7	1.30		(2)	6.9
	para. 8	1.31		s. 5	6.15, 6.40, 6.82, A.29
	para. 9	1.2, 1.32		(1)	A.29
	para. 10	1.33		s. 6	6.15, 6.41, A.29
	paras. 13–20	1.34		s. 7	6.41
	para. 21	1.41		s. 8	6.11, 6.14
	para. 22	1.35		s. 9–11	6.17
	para. 23	1.41		s. 9	6.1, 6.9, 6.12
	para. 24	1.41		ss. (1)–(4)	6.12
	para. 25	1.41		(3)	6.17, 6.37
	para. 26	1.41		(5)	6.11, 6.14, 6.17
	para. 27	1.36			

TABLE OF STATUTES

1996 Arbitration Act—*cont.*
- s. 10 .... 6.9, 6.11
  - (2) 6.11, 6.14
- s. 11 .... 6.9
- s. 12 .... 6.9, 6.11, 6.14, 6.44
  - (*a*) 6.48
- s. 13 .... 6.9, 6.18
  - (2) 6.53
- s. 14 .... 6.42
- s. 15 .... 6.43
- s. 16 .... 6.44, 6.46, 6.51
  - (3) 6.44
- s. 17 .... 6.45
  - (1) 6.45
- s. 18 .... 6.44, 6.46
  - (2) 6.37
- s. 19 .... 6.40, 6.44, 6.46, 6.52
  - (4) 6.44
  - (9) 6.44
- ss. 20–22 .... 6.47
- s. 21 (5) 6.37
- s. 22 (2) 6.53
  - (4) 6.44
- s. 23 .... 6.48
- s. 24 .... 6.9, 6.19, 6.25
  - (2) 6.19, 6.37
- s. 25 .... 6.49
  - (1) 6.49
  - (3) 6.49
- s. 26 (1) 6.9, 6.20
  - (2) 6.50
- s. 27 .... 6.51
- s. 28 .... 6.9, 6.21, 6.40, 6.52, 6.88
  - (2) 6.21
  - (3) 6.44
- s. 29 .... 6.9, 6.22, 6.83, 6.88
- s. 30 .... 6.19
  - (1) 6.11, 6.23, 6.34, 6.38
    - (*a*) 6.23
  - (3) 6.20, 6.49
- s. 31 .... 6.9, 6.23, 6.34
  - (2) 6.23
- s. 32 .... 6.9, 6.24
  - (3) 6.37
- s. 33 .... 6.9, 6.19, 6.25, 6.53
- s. 34 .... 6.9, 6.25, 6.53
  - (1) 6.53
  - (2) 6.53
    - (*b*) 6.53
    - (*d*) 6.53
    - (*e*) 6.53
    - (*f*) 2.25
    - (*g*) 6.53
- s. 35 .... 6.9, 6.11, 6.38, 6.54
- s. 36 .... 6.9, 6.55, 17.17
- s. 37 (1) 6.56, 6.62
  - (*b*) 6.56
  - (2) 6.9, 6.26, 6.56
- s. 38 .... 6.57
- s. 39 .... 6.58
- s. 40 .... 6.9, 6.27, 6.53

1996 Arbitration Act—*cont.*
- s. 41 .... 6.27, 6.59
  - (1) 6.59
- s. 42 .... 6.27, 6.60
  - (3) 6.37
- s. 43 .... 6.9, 6.28
- s. 44 .... 6.61
  - (4) 6.37
  - (5) 6.37
  - (6) 6.61
- s. 45 .... 6.62
  - (2) 6.62
    - (*b*) 6.62
  - (3) 6.37
- s. 46 .... 6.11, 6.25, 6.38, 6.63
  - (1) (*b*) 6.8, 6.25, 6.38, 6.63
- s. 47 .... 6.58, 6.64
- s. 48 .... 6.38, 6.65
  - (2) 6.38
  - (3) 6.38
  - (4) 6.38
  - (5) 6.38
- s. 49 .... 6.66
- s. 50 .... 6.67
  - (2) 6.37
- s. 51 .... 6.68
- s. 52 .... 6.69
  - (5) 6.69
- s. 53 .... 6.70
- s. 54 .... 6.70
- s. 55 .... 6.70
- s. 56 .... 6.9, 6.29, 16.26
  - (4) 6.29, 6.37
- s. 57 .... 6.71
- s. 58 .... 6.72
  - (1) 6.72
- ss. 59–65 .... 6.26
- s. 59 .... 6.73
- s. 60 .... 6.9, 6.30
- s. 61 .... 6.74
- s. 62 .... 6.74
- s. 63 .... 6.73, 6.75
  - (5) 6.75
- s. 64 .... 6.21, 6.76
- s. 65 .... 6.77
- s. 66 .... 6.9, 6.31, 6.38
- s. 67 .... 6.9, 6.23, 6.32
- s. 68 .... 6.9, 6.32
- s. 69 .... 6.78
  - (2) 6.37
  - (4) 6.37
- s. 70 .... 6.9, 6.32, 6.78
  - (2) 6.37
  - (3) 6.32, 6.37
- s. 71 .... 6.9, 6.32
  - (4) 6.11, 6.14, 6.32
- s. 72 .... 6.9, 6.33
- s. 73 .... 6.9, 6.23, 6.33
- s. 74 .... 6.9, 6.35
- s. 75 .... 6.9, 6.36
- s. 76 .... 6.79, 6.80

1996	Arbitration Act—*cont.*	
	s. 77	6.80
	(3)	6.37
	ss. 78–84	6.81
	s. 80	6.21, 6.29
	(1)	6.28, 6.29
	(2)	6.55
	ss. 85–87	6.8, 6.13
	ss. 85–88	6.13, 6.14
	s. 85	6.10
	(2)	6.13
	s. 86 (2)	6.13
	(4)	6.13
	(6)	6.13
	s. 87	6.13
	s. 91	6.8
	ss. 94–98	6.10
	s. 94	
	(1)	6.10
	(2) (*a*)	6.10, 6.38
	(*b*)	6.10
	(3)	6.10
	s. 95 (1)	6.10, 6.13
	(2)	6.10, 6.69
	ss. 96–98	6.11
	s. 96	6.11, 6.14, 6.23, 6.38, 6.52
	(4)	6.63
1996	Arbitration Act—*cont.*	
	s. 97	6.11, 6.17, 6.32
	s. 97—*cont.*	
	(*b*)	6.44
	(*c*)	6.12
	s. 98	6.8, 6.12
	s. 105	6.8, 6.18, 6.21, 6.23, 6.29, 6.36
	s. 107	6.8
	(1)	6.8, A.9
	(2)	6.8, A.10
	ss. 108–110	6.8
	s. 109	6.8
	Sched. 1	1.48, 6.9, 6.14
	Sched. 3, para. 45	A.9
	Sched. 4	A.10
1996	Trust of Land and Appointment of Trustees Act (c. 47)	7.3, 17.8, 17.15
	s. 6 (1)	7.3, 17.8
	s. 12	9.13, **14.62**, 14.65
	s. 13	14.62
	s. 25 (2)	A.9, A.10
	Sched. 2	14.65
	Sched. 4	A.9, A.10
	Housing Act (c.52)	
	s. 227	A.10
	Sched. 19, Pt. IX	A.10

TABLE OF STATUTORY INSTRUMENTS

[References in **bold** type denote where the text of the Instrument is printed]

1948 Agriculture (Maintenance, Repair and Insurance of Fixed Equipment) Regulations (S.I. 1948 No. 184) 10.9, 13.81, A.14
Agriculture (Miscellaneous Time-Limits) Regulations (S.I. 1948 No. 188) A.13
Agriculture (Control of Notices to Quit) Regulations (S.I. 1948 No. 190)
reg. 4 .... 12.83
Agricultural Holdings (England and Wales) Rules (S.I.1948 No. 1943) A.24

1951 Reserve and Auxiliary Forces (Protection of Civil Interests) (Agricultural Tenants' Representation) Regulations (S.I. 1951 No. 1787) A.12
Agricultural Holdings Act (Variation of Fourth Schedule) Order (S.I. 1951 No. 2168) 13.55, 13.112, A.9, A.175, A.176

1954 (Procedure of Agricultural Land Tribunals) Order (S.I. 1954 No. 1138) A.17

1955 Transfer of Functions (Ministry of Food) Order (S.I. 1955 No. 554)
art. 3 .... A.6, A.175, A.176

1959 Agricultural Land Tribunals and Notices to Quit Order (S.I. 1959 No. 81) A.17
art. 7 .... 12.86

1959 Reserve and Auxiliary Forces (Agricultural Tenants) Regulations (S.I. 1959 No. 84) 12.32, 12.94.5, A.9, A.11, **A.12**
Agriculture (Miscellaneous Time-Limits) Regulations (S.I. 1959 No. 171) 10.27, A.11, **A.13**
reg. 2
(2) (3) A.114
Agricultural Land Tribunals (Amendment) Order (S.I. 1959 No. 359) A.17

1961 Agricultural Land Tribunals (Amendment) Order (S.I. 1961 No. 1755) A.17

1964 Agricultural (Notices to Remedy and Notices to Quit) Order (S.I. 1964 No. 706)
art. 7 .... 12.86
art. 10 .... 12.28, 12.86

1970 Secretary of State for the Environment Order (S.I. 1970 No. 1681) 12.22

1971 Northern Pennines Rural Development Board (Dissolution) Order (S.I. 1971 No. 224) 12.82
The Minister for the Civil Service Order (S.I. 1971 No. 2099)
arts 2, 3, 6 (5) A.5

1972 Agriculture (Notices to Quit) (Miscellaneous Provisions) Order (S.I. 1972 No. 1207)–
art. 5 (2) 12.86
The European Communities (Designation) Order 1972 (S.I. 1972 No. 1811) A.28
Health and Personal Social Services (Northern Ireland) Order 1265
art. 105 (6) A.174

1973 Agriculture (Maintenance, Repair and Insurance of Fixed Equipment) Regulations (S.I. 1973 No. 1473) 8.11, 10.3, 10.4, 10.9, 10.11, 10.12, 10.13, 10.14, 10.17, 10.18, 10.19, 10.23, 10.24, 10.25, 10.44, 10.47, 10.86, 12.65, 13.81, 13.85, 13.91, A.9, A.11, **A.14**, A.15, A.35, A.40, A.41, A.42, A.44, A.114
Sched., para. 1 .... 10.12
(1) 10.12
(2) 10.12, 10.13
(3) 10.12, 10.19
para. 2 .... 10.12
para. 3 .... 10.12, 10.14
para. 4 .... 10.12
(2) 10.15, 10.32, 10.86, 12.61.14, A.114

lxxiii

1973	Agriculture (Maintenance, Repair and Insurance of Fixed Equipment) Regulations—*cont.*		1976	Smallholdings (Selection of Tenants) (Amendment) Regulations (S.I. 1976 No. 2001) 14.22
	Sched.—*cont.*			Agricultural Land Tribunals (Succession to Agricultural Tenancies) Order (S.I. 1976 No. 2183) A.17, A.18, A.20
	para. 4—*cont.*			
	(3)			
	(*a*) 10.15, A.114			
	(*c*) 10.15			
	para. 5 .... 10.12, 10.13, 10.15			Sched., r. 1 (2) A.18
	(1) 10.12, 10.13, 10.19			r. 10 .... **A.18**
	(2), (3), (4) 10.13			rr. 13, 14 (2), 19 .... **A.18**
	para. 6 .... 10.12, 10.13, 10.15			Appendix A.18
	(2) 10.19			Form 2 .... A.18
	para. 7 ... 10.12, 10.13, 10.14, 10.15			Solicitors (Northern Ireland) Order (S.I. 1976 No. 582)
	para. 8 .... 10.12, 10.13, 10.15			
	paras. 9, 10 .... 10.12, 10.13			art. 3 (2) A.174
	para. 11 .... 10.12, 10.14			art. 71H A.74
	(3) 10.14		1977	Agriculture (Miscellaneous Provisions) Act 1976 (Application of Provisions) Regulations (S.I. 1977 No. 1215) 14.84, 14.93, A.9, A.11, A.16
	para. 12 .... 10.18, 10.21, 10.24, 10.44			
	(1) 10.16, A.114			
	(2) 10.17, A.114			
	(3) 10.18			
	(*a*) A.114			Health and Safety at Work (Northern Ireland) Order (N.I. 9)
	(5) (*a*) 10.16, 10.17, 10.18			
				Sched. 4 .... A.174
	(*b*) 10.16, 10.18		1978	Agricultural Holdings (Arbitration on Notices) Order (S.I. 1978 No. 257) A.18, A.22
	(*c*) 10.16, 10.17			
	(*d*) 10.18			
	para. 13 .... 10.20, A.114			Agricultural Land Tribunals (Rules) Order (S.I. 1978 No. 259) 13.62, 14.78, 14.109, 15.6, 16.4, 16.5, A.11, **A.17**. A.20
	(1) 10.20			
	(2) 10.20			
	(*a*) (i) **10.20**			
	(ii) **10.20**			
	(*b*) **10.20**			Sched. 1 .... **A.18**
	para. 14 (1), (2) 10.20, 10.22, 10.23			r. 1
				(2) 16.2
	para. 15 .... 10.11, 10.18, 10.24, A.114			r. 2 .... 12.33, 16.4
				(2) 16.4, A.160, A.164
	para. 16			
	Pt. I 10.24			(3) 16.4
	Pt. II 10.12, 10.24			r. 3 .... 12.33, 16.4, A.160
	Pt. III			
	Agriculture (Time-Limit) Regulations (S.I. 1973 No. 1482) .. A.11, **A.15**			r. 4 .... 16.4, A.162
				r. 5 .... 16.4
				r. 6 .... 10.45, 16.4
1973	Drainage (Northern Ireland) Order (N.I. 1)			r. 7 .... 13.62, 16.4, A.9
				(2) 16.4, A.102
	art. 15 (4) A.174			(3) 13.62
	art. 40 (4) A.174			r. 8 .... 16.4
	Sched. 7, para. 9 (2) A.174			r. 9 .... 16.4
1974	Agricultural Land Tribunals (Areas) Order (S.I. 1974 No. 66) A.19			r. 10 .... 16.4
				r. 11 .... 16.4
				r. 12 .... 10.51, 16.4
	Agricultural Land Tribunals (Amendment) Order (S.I. 1974 No. 67) A.17			r. 13 .... 15.6
				r. 15 .... A.162
				(1) A.160, A.164
1975	(S.I. 1975 No. 447) 10.76			(2) 14.78, 16.4, A.160, A.164
1976	Agricultural Land Tribunals (Areas) (Amendment) Order (S.I. 1976 No. 208) A.19			
				r. 16 .... 14.78, 14.109
				(5) 14.78, 14.109

TABLE OF STATUTORY INSTRUMENTS

1978 Agricultural Land Tribunals (Rules) Order—*cont.*
 r. 18 .... 14.78, 14.109, 16.4
  (2) 14.78, 14.109
 r. 19 .... 14.48, 14.78, 14.122
 r. 20 .... 14.48, 14.78, 14.122, 16.4
 r. 23
  (2) 14.78, 14.122
  (4) 14.78, 14.122
 r. 24 .... 14.78, 14.122, 16.4
 r. 25 .... 14.78, 14.79, 14.122, 16.4
 r. 26
  (2) (3) 14.78, 14.79, 14.122
 r. 27 .... 14.78, 14.122, 16.4
 r. 28 .... 14.78, 14.122, 16.37
  (1) 14.79
  (2) (*b*) 14.79
  (3) 14.79, 16.4
 r. 29 .... 14.78, 14.79, 14.122
  (2) 14.60, 16.4
  (3) 14.79, 16.4
  (4) 16.4
 r. 30 .... 14.78, 14.79, 14.122, 16.4
 r. 31 .... 14.78, 14.122, 16.4, 16.6
  (1) 12.33
 r. 33 .... 14.78, 14.122
  (1) 16.9
  (2) 14.122
 r. 34 .... 14.78, 14.122, A.6
 r. 35 .... 14.78, 14.122
  (1) 16.4
 r. 36 ......14.78, 14.122, A.166, A.167
 r. 37 . 14.25, 14.29, 14.122, 16.4, 16.7, A.160, A.162, A.164, A.166, A.167, A.168
 r. 38 .... 12.33, 12.51, 14.25, 14.29, 14.78, 14.122, 16.4, A.166, A.167
 Appendix
  Form 1 .... 16.4
  Form 1R 14.72
  Form 3 .... 12.51
  form 3R 12.51
  Form R 16.4
  Form 8 .... 15.29
  Form 8R 15.29
Transfer of Functions (Wales) (No. 1) Order (S.I. 1978 No. 272)
 art. 2 (1) A.175, A.176
Agricultural Holdings (England and Wales) (Amendment) Rules (S.I. 1978 No. 444) ... A.24
The Agriculture Act 1947 (Amendment) Regulations (S.I. 1978 No. 446)
 reg. 2 (1) A.4
Agricultural Holdings Act 1948 (Amendment) Regulations (S.I. 1978 No. 447) A.9, A.175, A.176
 reg. 2 (2) A.175, A.176

1978 Agricultural Holdings Act 1948 (Variation of Fourth Schedule) Order (S.I. 1978 No. 742) 13.56, 13.58, 13.112, A.9, A.175, A.176
 art. 4 .... 13.56
 Sched. para. 1, 2 .... A.175, A.176
 para. 5, 6 .... A.175, A.176
Agriculture (Calculation of Value for Compensation) Regulations (S.I. 1978 No. 809) ... 13.56, 13.67, A.9
 reg. 4
  (2) 10.4
 Sched., Pt. II
  para. 11 .... 13.55
  para. 12 .... 13.56
1979 Statutory Rules (Northern Ireland) Order 1573 .... A.174
1980 Agriculture (Calculation of Value for Compensation) (Amendment) Regulations (S.I. 1980 No. 751) 13.56, 13.67
 reg. 3 (2) (*a*) 13.55
Country Courts (Northern Ireland) Order (N.I. 3)
 art. 30, 31 (3) A.174
 art. 61 .... A.174
 art. 61A **A.174**
1981 Agriculture (Calculation of Value for Compensation) (Amendment) Regulations (S.I. 1981 No. 822) 13.67
Diseases of Animals (Northern Ireland) Order (S.I. 1981 No. 1115) A.27
 art. 12 (1) A.27
County Court Rules (S.I. 1981 No. 1687)– 14.122, 16.4, 16.61
 Ord. 3, r. 4 .... 16.61
 Ord. 20,
  r. 11 .... 16.4
  r. 12 .... 16.4
  rr. 00 .... 14.28
 Ord. 25,
  r. 12 .... 16.13, 16.26, 16.60
  Ord. 38, r. 1 .... 16.73
  r. 22 .... 16.13, 16.26
 Ord. 44
  r. 1 .... 16.61
  r. 2 .... 16.61
  (5) 16.64, 16.65
  r. 3 .... 16.53, 16.66
1982 Agricultural Land Tribunals (Areas) Order (S.I. 1982 No. 97) 16.2, 16.3, A.11, **A.19**

lxxv

1982	Agricultural Marketing (Northern Ireland) Order (S.I. 1981 No. 1080)
	art. 14 .... A.174
	art. 29 .... A.27
1983	Agriculture (Calculation of Value for Compensation) (Amendment) Regulations (S.I. 1983 No. 1475) 13.67
	reg. 3 .... 13.56
	(2) 13.55
	(d) 13.56
1984	Dairy Produce Quotas Regulations (S.I. 1984 No. 1047) . 14.98, 18.5, 19.9.3, A.27
	Agricultural Holdings (Arbitration on Notices) (Variation) Order (S.I. 1984 No. 1300) A.22
	Agricultural Land Tribunals (Succession to Agricultural Tenancies) Order (S.I. 1984 No. 1301) 14.29, 14.30, 14.75, 14.77, 14.78, 14.122, 16.4, A.9, A.11, A.17, **A.20**, A.83, A.91
	Sched., Pt. I, r. 1
	(3) 14.25
	(b) 14.30, 14.78
	r. 3 .... 14.29, 14.78, A.167
	(1) 14.25, 14.83
	(2) 14.30, A.166, A.167
	r. 4 .... 14.78
	(1) 14.83, A.166
	(3) 14.83, A.166
	(4) 14.83
	(5) 14.78
	r. 5 .... 14.25, 14.78, A.166, A.167
	(2) A.83
	r. 6 .... 14.27, 14.78, A.166, A.167
	r. 7 .... 14.78, 14.83, A.166
	r. 8 .... 14.78
	r. 10 .... 14.78
	r. 11 .... 14.78
	(1) A.83, A.84, A.86, A.87
	r. 13 .... 14.75
	(1) A.166
	(2) (3) A.166
	r. 14 .... 14.78
	r. 15 .... 14.28, 14.78, 14.83
	(1) 14.78, A.166, A.167
	(2) (3) 14.78
	r. 16 .... 14.75
	r. 17 .... 14.75
	(1) (3) (4) (5) 14.75
	r. 18 .... 14.29, 14.75
	r. 20 .... 14.78
	(2) 14.78
	r. 21 .... 14.78, 14.83
	(1) (2) 14.78, A.166, A.167
	Agricultural Land Tribunals (Succession to Agricultural Tenancies) Order—*cont.*
	Sched.—*cont.*
	r. 21—*cont.*
	Pt. III 14.122, 16.4
	r. 23
	(1) 14.109
	(2) 14.109
	r. 24 .... 14.109, A.9, A.168
	r. 25 .... 14.109, A.168
	r. 27 .... 14.109
	r. 28 .... 14.109, A.90
	r. 29 .... 14.122
	r. 30 .... 14.48, 14.122
	r. 31 .... 14.109, A.168
	r. 32
	(1) 14.110
	(2) 14.110
	r. 33 .... 14.60, A.168
	r. 34 .... 14.122, A.168
	Appendix
	Form 1 .... 14.25, 14.30, 14.83, A.166, A.167
	Form 1R 14.27, A.166, A.167
	Form 2 .... 14.78, 14.82, A.166
	Form 2R 14.78, 14.83, A.166
	Form 3 .... 14.25, A.166, A.167
	Form 4 .... 14.78
	Form 5R 14.109, A.168
	Form 6 .... 14.109, A.168
	Agricultural Holdings (Forms of Notice to Pay Rent or to Remedy) Regulations (S.I. 1984 No. 1308) A.23, A.114
	The Dairy Produce Quotas (Amendment) Regulations (S.I. 1984 No. 1538) A.27
	Agricultural Holdings Act 1984 (Commencement) Order (S.I. 1984 No. 1644) 16.22
	The Dairy Produce Quotas (Amendment) (No. 2) regulations (S.I. 1984 No. 1787) A.27
1985	Dairy Produce Quotas Regulations (S.I. 1985 No. 509) 18.5, A.27
	Agricultural Holdings (England and Wales) (Rules (Variation) Order (S.I. 1985 No. 1829) A.9, A.24
	Agricultural Holdings Act 1948 (Variation of Fourth Schedule) Order (S.I. 1985 No. 1947) 13.56, 13.58, 13.112, A.9
	art. 3 (2) (3) A.175, A.176
	art. 4 (2) (a) (b) 13.56
	Agricultural Holdings (Fee) Regulations (S.I. 1985 No. 1967) 16.23, A.9, A.25

TABLE OF STATUTORY INSTRUMENTS

1985 Credit Unions (Northern Ireland) Order (N.I. 12)
    art. 72 (7) (8) A.174
1986 Dairy Produce Quotas Regulations (S.I. 1986 No. 470) 18.5, 19.3, 19.6, A.8, A.27
    Milk Quota (Calculation of Standard Quota) Order (S.I. 1986 No. 1530) 19.14.2, 19.14.3, A.8, A.11, **A.21**
    Milk (Community Outgoers Scheme) (England and Wales) Regulations (S.I. 1986 No. 1611) A.9
    reg. 16 (3) (4) A.9
1987 Agricultural Holdings (Arbitration on Notices) Order (S.I. 1987 No. 710) ... 12.43, 12.47, 13.116, 15.6, 15.8, 16.21, 16.23, A.9 **A.22**, A,60, A.61, A.114
    Pt. II 12.60, A.35
    art. 2 .... 12.87
        (1) 12.69, 12.86
    art. 3 ...... 12.62, 12.68, 16.21, A.114, A.164
        (1) 12.63, 12.64, 12.65, A.60
            (*a*) 12.65
            (*b*) 12.60
        (2) (3) 12.63
    art. 4 ...... 12.62, 12.68, 16.21, A.114, A.164
        (1) 12.60, 12.63, 12.65
        (2) 12.60, 12.63, 12.64, A.60
            (*a*) A.60
        (3) 12.64, 12.67
    art. 5 .... 12.62, A.164
    art. 6 .... 12.62, 12.67, 12.89
        (1) 12.68, A.164
        (2) 12.68, 12.69, A.60, A.164
    art. 7 .... 12.62, 16.58, A.60, A.164
        (1) 12.69, 12.71
        (2) (3) 12.69
        (4) 12.5, 12.13, 12.69, A.164
    art. 8 .... 12.62, 12.66, 12.70, A.60
    art. 9 .... 12.29, 12.45, 12.47, 12.49, 12.50, 12.53, 12.61.15, 12.62, 12.64, 12.67, 12.76, 12.83, 12.84, 12.85, 12.86, 12.89, 12.94.4, 16.21, 16.23, A.59, A.60, A.61, A.71, A.114, A.161, A.163, A.164
    art. 10 ...... 12.53, 12.85, 12.87, A.59, A.60, A.61, A.161, A.163, A.164, A.165
    art. 11 ... 12.28, 12.32, 12.86, 12.89.5, 12.94.4, A.9
    art. 12 ..... 12.28, 12.87, 12.88, A.161, A.163, A.164, A.165
        (1) (2) A.81
    art. 13 .... 12.33, 12.43, 12.88, 16.5, A.160, A.161, A.163, A.164, A.165

1987 Agricultural Holdings (Arbitration on Notices) Order—*cont.*
    art. 13—*cont.*
        (1) 12.88
        (2) 12.88
    art. 14 .... 12.71, 12.89, A.164, A.165
    art. 15 . 12.71, 12.89.1, 12.89.7, 16.58, A.164, A.165
        (1) (2) 12.71
        (3) 12.71
        (4) 12.5, 12.13, 12.71, 12.89.7
        (5) (6) 12.71, 12.90
    art. 16 12.21, 15.6, **15.8**, 15.12, 15.13, A.9
    art. 17 .... 12.92, A.9
        (2) 12.94.4
        (3)–(4) 12.94.4
        (4) A.9
    Agricultural Holdings (Forms of Notice to Pay Rent or to Remedy) Regulations (S.I. 1987 No. 711) . 11.44, 12.53, 12.60, A.9, A.11, **A.23**
    reg. 2
        (2) 12.60
    reg. 3 .... A.163
    reg. 4 .... A.164, A.165
    reg. 5
    Sched.
        Form 2 .... 12.66
        Form 3 .... A.164, A.165
    Mental Health (Northern Ireland) Order (N.I. 4)
    art. 83 .... A.174
1988 Agriculture (Maintenance, Repair and Insurance of Fixed Equipment) (Amendment) Regulations (S.I. 1988 No.. 281) ... 10.9, A.9, A.14
    Agriculture (Time Limits) Regulations (S.I. 1988 No. 282) 10.9, A.9
    Dairy Produce Quotas Regulations (S.I. 1988 No. 534) 18.5
1989 Dairy Produce Quotas Regulations (S.I. 1989 No. 380) 18.5
    Dairy Produce Quotas (Amendment) Regulations (S.I. 1990 No. 132) 18.15
    Limitation (Northern Ireland) Order (S.I. 1989 No. 1339) . A.174
    art. 2 (2) A.174
    Sched. 3, para. 1 .... A.174
    Local Government and Housing Act 1989 (Commencement No. 5 and Transitional Provisions) Order 1990 (S.I. 1990 No. 431)

TABLE OF STATUTORY INSTRUMENTS

1989 Dairy Produce Quotas Regulations—*cont.*
    Sched. 1
        para. 12 .... 11.41
    Insolvency (Northern Ireland) Order
        art. 320 .... A.174
        art. 320A **A.174**

1990 Agricultural Holdings (Form of Award in Arbitration Proceedings) Order
    (S.I. 1990 No. 1472) 13.124, 16.53, A.9, A.11, **A.24**

1991 Food Safety (Northern Ireland) Order (S.I. 1991 No. 762)
        arts. 8 (8), 11 (10) A.174
    Dairy Produce Quotas Regulations
        (S.I. 1991 No. 2232) 18.5

1992 Milk Quota (Calculation of Standard Quota) (Amendment) Order
    (S.I. 1992 No. 1225) 19.14.2, 19.14.3, A.8
        art. 2 (2) (3) A.21
    Industrial Relations (Northern Ireland) Order (N.I. 5)
        art. 84 (9) A.174
        art. 92 (5) A.174
    Registered Homes (Northern Ireland) Order (N.I. 20)
        art. 33 (3) A.174

1993 Hill Livestock (Compensatory Allowances) Regulations (S.I. 1992 No. 269) A.21, **A.26**
    Dairy Produce Quotas Regulations
    (S.I. 1993 No. 923)
        reg. 14 .... 18.5
        reg. 32 .... 18.5
    Agricultural Holdings (Units of Production) Order
        (S.I. 1993 No. 2037) 14.56
    Roads (Northern Ireland) Order
        art. 131 .... A.174
        Sched. 4 .... A.174

1994 Dairy Produce Quotas Regulations
    (S.I. 1994 No. 672) A.27
        reg. 6 .... A.27
        reg. 13 .... 18.5
    Dairy Produce Quotas (Amendments) Regulations A.27
    Dairy Produce Quotas (Amendments) (No.2) Regulations .. A.27
    Unfair Terms in Consumer Contracts Regulations (S.I. 1994 No. 3159) A.174
    Foreign Limitation Periods (Northern Ireland) Order A.174

1995 Dairy Produce Quotas (Amendment) Regulations (S.I. 1995 No. 254) A.27
    Agricultural Holdings (Units of Production) Order (S.I. 1995 No. 2125) A.26
    Landlord and Tenant (Covenants) Act 1995 (Commencement) Order
        (S.I. 1995 No. 2963) 1.40

1996 Agricultural Holdings (Fee) Regulations
    (S.I. 1996 No. 337) . 6.3, 10.80, 16.23, **A.25**
    Hill Livestock (Compensatory Allowances) Regulations (S.I. 1996 No. 1500) A.26
    Agriculture Holdings (Units of Production) Order (S.I. 1996 No. 2163) A.9, A.10, A.29
    Dairy Produce Quotas (Amendment) Regulations (S.I. 1996 No. 2657) A.26
    Trusts of Land and Appointment of Trustees Act 1996 (Commencement) Order
        (S.I. 1996 No. 2974) 7.3, 17.8
    Civil Evidence Act 1995 (Commencement No. 1) Order
        (S.I. 1996 No. 3217) 16.37
    Arbitration Act (Commencement No. 1) Order
        (S.I. 1996 No. 3146) 6.8
        Sched. 2 .... 6.8
        Sched. 3
            para. 36 .... 6.8
        Sched. 4 .... 6.8

1997 Dairy Produce Quotas Regulations
    (S.I. 1997 No. 733) 5.4, 5.7, 16.1, 16.18, 18.5, 18.10, 18.12, 18.13, 18.16, 18.17, 18.19, 18.20, 19.3, A.10, **A.27**, A.28
        reg. 1 .... 18.15
        reg. 2 .... 18.5, 18.16
        (1) 18.11, 18.13, 18.14, 18.16, 18.18, 18.19, 18.20, 19.3, **A.28**
        reg. 3 .... 18.10
        reg. 4 .... 18.10
        reg. 5 .... 18.10
        reg. 7 ...... 18.10, 18.17, 18.21, 18.23, 18.26
        (1) (*a*) A.28
        (2) 18.18
        (5) 18.21
        reg. 8 .... 18.10, 18.17, A.28, A.172
        (*a*) (*b*) 18.18
        reg. 9 .... 18.10, A.28

TABLE OF STATUTORY INSTRUMENTS

1997 Dairy Produce Quotas Regulations—*cont.*	
reg. 9—*cont.*	
(1)	18.17
(*b*)	18.17
reg. 10	18.10, 18.17, 18.18, A.28
reg. 11	18.10, 18.20
(1)	18.20
(2)	18.20
(*a*)	18.20
(*c*)	18.20
(*d*)	18.20
(3)	18.20
(7)	18.20
(8)	18.20
(9)	18.20
reg. 12	18.10
reg. 13	18.10, 18.12, 18.16, 18.19
(3)	18.19
(4)	18.19
(5)	18.19
reg. 14	18.19
(2) (*b*) (i), (ii)	A.28
(7)	A.28
reg. 16	A.28
16 (3) (*b*), (4)	A.28
(5)	A.28
reg. 25	18.19
reg. 26	18.19
reg. 24	18.19
(*b*)	18.19
regs. 20–30	18.10
reg. 30 (4) (5)	A.28
reg. 31	18.10, A.28
reg. 31 (1) (*a*), (*b*), (*c*)	A.28
reg. 32	18.10, 18.12, 18.16, 18.19, 18.26, A.28
(5)	18.17, 18.18, A.28
(*b*) (ii)	18.17, A.28
(*b*) (iii)	18.17
reg. 33	18.15
reg. 34	**A.28**
Sched. 1–6	**A.28**
Sched. 2	16.1, 16.18, 18.10, 18.17, 18.18, 18.21, 18.26, **A.28**

1997 Dairy Produce Quotas Regulations—*cont.*	
Sched. 2—*cont.*	
para. 1	
(1)	18.17, A.172
(2)	18.17, A.172
(3)	18.17, A.172
(4)	A.172
(5)	A.172
para. 2	18.17
(1) (*b*)	A.172
(2)	A.172
para. 3	
(1)	18.18
(3)	18.5, 18.18
para. 4	18.17
para. 5	18.17
para. 6	18.17
para. 9	18.17
para. 10	18.17
para. 11	18.17
para. 12	18.17
para. 13	18.17
(1)	18.17
(2)	18.17
para. 14	18.17, A.172
paras. 15–21	18.17
para. 22	18.17
(1)	18.17, A.172
(2)	18.17, A.172
(3)	18.17, A.172
(4)	18.17, A.172
paras. 23–35	18.17
Sched. 4	A.28
para. 5 (3)	18.5
(S.I. 1997 No. 1093)	
reg. 2 (2) (3)	A.27
Agricultural Holdings (Units of Production) Order (S.I. 1997 No. 1962)	A.10, **A.29**, A.30
1998 The Hill Livestock (Compensatory Allowances) (Amendment) Regulations (S.I. 1998 No. 206)	A.30
Agricultural Holdings (Units of Production) Order (S.I. 1998 No. 2025)	**A.30**

TABLE OF RULES OF THE SUPREME COURT

Rules of the Supreme Court . 6.59, 17.20	(4) 16.9
Ord. 3 .... 13.28	r. 11 .... 16.8
Ord. 11 .... 13.113	Ord. 57
Ord. 14 ....6.87, 10.24	r. 2 .... 16.9
Ord. 20, r. 5 .... 16.27	(2) 16.9
Ord. 20, r. 11 .... 16.58	Ord. 59, r. 19 .... 16.63
Ord. 38, r. 20 .... 16.37	Ord. 65 .... 7.9, 17.17, 17.18, 17.22
Ord. 53 .... 16.7	Ord. 73 .... 6.16, 6.17, 6.19, 6.24, 6.27
Ord. 56	Ord. 73 ... 6.29, 6.32, 6.37, 6.60, 6.61,
r. 8 .... 16.10	6.62, 6.67, 6.78, 6.80
r. 9 .... 16.10	Pt I 6.37
(3) 16.9	Ord. 94, r. 7 .... 16.10
r. 10 .... 16.10	(2) 10.45
Ord. 56, r. 10 (3) 16.8	(3) 10.45

TABLE OF EEC REGULATIONS

Reg. 804/68, O.J. 1968, L148/	Reg. 2776/88
13 .... 18.2, A.28	art. 3 (3) (4) (5) A.33
art. 5c 18.2, A.29, A.32, A.33	Reg. 764/89, O.J. 1989, L 84/2 . 18.15,
Reg. 805/68, O.J/S.E. 1968,	A.28
p.187 ....A.26, A.29, A.30	Reg. 3013/89, O.J. 1989,
art. 4b A.26, A.29, A.30	L289/1 .... A.26, A.29, A.30
art. 4d A.26, A.30	art. 5 .... A.26, A.29, A.30
art. 4h A.26, A.29, A.30	Reg. 4045/89 .... A.33
Reg. 729/70	Reg. 1639/91, O.J. 1991, L150/35 A.28
art. 3 .... A.32	Reg. 1765/92, O.J. 1992, L181/
Reg. 1079/77, O.J. 1977,	12 .... A.26, A.29, A.30
L131/6 .... 18.2	art. 2 .... A.26, A.29, A.30
Reg. 856/84, O.J. 1984, L10/	(5) A.26, A.29
10 .... 18.2, A.32	(6) A.30
art. 1 (1) 18.2	art. 7 (4) A.26, A.29, A.30
Reg. 857/84, O.J. 1984, L090/	Reg. 2066/92 .... A.26
13 .... 18.2, A.32, A.33	Reg. 2074/92 .... A.32
art. 1 (1) 18.2	Reg. 3813/92
art. 3 (*a*) (i) 18.15, A.32	art. 1 .... A.33
art. 7 .... 18.18, 19.7, 19.17	Reg. 3950/92, O.J. 1992,
art. 12 .... 19.3	L405/1 .... 18.4, 18.9, 18.10, 18.11,
Reg. 1371/84, O.J. 1984, L132/	18.18, 18.24, A.27, A.28,
11 .... 18.4	**A.32**, A.33
Reg. 590/85, O.J. 1985, L 68/1 18.18	art. 1 .... 18.9, A.27, A.28, A.33
Reg. 1546/88, O.J. 1988, L	art. 2 .... 18.9, A.27
139/12 .... A.33	(1)–(4) A.27, A.33
art. 7.2 .... 18.18	(2) A.33

lxxxi

art. 3	A.33	Reg. 1756/93 O.J. 1993, L161/48	A.28
(2)	A.27	Reg. 2055/93, O.J. 1993	
art. 4 (2) (3)	18.15, A.27, A.33	art. 1 (1)	18.15, A.27, A.28
art. 5	18.9, 18.11, A.27, A.33	Reg. 2187/93 O.J. 1993, L196/6	A.28
art. 6	18.9, 18.11, 18.12, 18.19, 18.20, A.27, A.33	Reg. 2562/93 O.J. 1993, L253	A.28
(2)	A.33	Reg. 2648/93 O.J. 1993, L243	A.28
art. 7	18.9, 18.16, 18.18, A.33	Reg. 647/94	A.32
7.1 (*a*) (*b*)	18.9	Reg. 647/94, O.J. 1994, L 80/16	18.4
7.2	18.9, 19.7	Reg. 1883/94, O.J. 1994, L 197/25	18.4, A.32
art. 7	18.9, 18.18	Reg. 630/95, O.J. 1995, L 66/11	18.4, A.32
(1)	18.18, A.27	Reg. 1265/95	A.26
art. 8	18.9, 18.20, A.27, A.33	Reg. 1552/95, O.J. 1995, L 148/43	18.4, A.32
art. 9 (*a*) (*b*)	18.9	Reg. 82/96	A.33
(*c*)	18.11, A.27	Reg. 204/96	A.32
(*d*)	**18.14**, A.27	Reg. 614/96	A.32
(*e*)	18.13, A.27	Reg. 635/96, O.J. 1996, L 90/17	18.4, A.32
(*g*)	A.27	Reg. 894/96	A.26
(*h*)	A.27	Reg. 1109/96, O.J. 1996, L 148/13	18.4, A.27, A.32
art. 11	A.33	Reg. 1357/96	A.26
Reg. 536/93, O.J. 1993, L 57/12	18.4, 18.9, A.27, A.28, **A.33**	Reg. 1552/96	A.32
art. 2	A.27	Reg. 1589/96	A.29
(1) (*e*)	A.27	Reg. 2186/96, O.J. 1996, L 292/6	18.4
(2)	A.27, A.28	Reg. 2222/96	A.29
art. 3	A.27	194NN01/05/B1	A.32
(2)	A.27		
art. 4 (2)	A.27		
art. 7.1 (*a*)	**18.13**, A.27		
(*b*)	A.27		
Reg. 748/93	A.32		
Reg. 1560/93, O.J. 1993, L 154/30	18.4, 18.11, 18.14, A.32		

EEC Directives

75/268/EEC	A.32
art. 3 (3)	A.33
92/102/EEC	
art. 4 (1)	A.33

PART 1

COMMENTARY

Introduction: An Overview

Two separate codes

There are now two completely separate codes dealing with agricultural tenancies namely the Agricultural Holdings Act 1986 and the Agricultural Tenancies Act 1995. Tenancies governed by the 1986 Act are "agricultural holdings" and tenancies governed by the 1995 Act are "farm business tenancies". The 1995 Act marked a dramatic break with the increasingly protectionist policies formulated from the late nineteenth century onwards. The 1986 Act is a consolidation and much light is thrown on its meaning by cases decided under earlier legislation: the 1995 Act is an entirely new departure and is motivated by a return to the open market and commercial bargaining. It represents very considerable deregulation except in essential areas.

Which code applies

This is relatively straightforwardly ascertained by reference to the beginning of the relevant tenancy. In very broad terms tenancies beginning on or after September 1, 1995 are under the new legislation with a few exceptions including for statutory succession tenancies where rights exist under Part IV of the 1986 Act.[1] 1986 Act tenancies continue unaffected and it is likely that for many years there will be a need to understand two distinct and parallel codes. For this reason each code has been dealt with by a separate section in this book.

Treatment of the 1995 Act

It is in the nature of a deregulatory Act that it is likely to be shorter than a statute imposing detailed control over contracting parties. The 1995 Act, although short, is treated first in this work since it is, increasingly, likely to be the more important of the two codes. Each of the main areas where the 1995 Act imposes requirements or restrictions is separately treated:

Chapter 1: Creation and meaning of farm business tenancy.
Chapter 2: Rent review.
Chapter 3: Removal of fixtures and buildings.
Chapter 4: Termination of tenancy by notice.
Chapter 5: Compensation on termination of farm business tenancy.
Chapter 6: Dispute resolution.

Where the statute prescribes no special regime, the general law will apply and practitioners in this area will increasingly have to familiarise themselves with the large general works dealing with landlord and tenant law.[2] A decision has been taken not to attempt to reproduce the general law in a specialist work of this kind but to refer readers on to other works where full treatment is given to matters of general interest. Conversely, and this is particularly evident in Chapter 1, a decision has been made to pinpoint those statutes which operate on tenancies

---

[1] The detail is dealt with in Chapter 1.
[2] e.g. Woodfall, *Landlord and Tenant*, Volume 1; Hill and Redman's *Law of Landlord and Tenant*, Division A.

generally so as to identify the treatment of farm business tenancies. This sort of material is usually scattered throughout the general works and it is convenient to a practitioner to find it collected in one place. There is necessarily a speculative element in the treatment of rent review in Chapter 2 since there is at this stage no litigation to assist on issues of interpretation. The rent review provisions are not as straightforward as at first they may appear. Because the statute makes special provision in relation to termination of the tenancy by notice, this is treated separately in Chapter 4. However this does not mean that other methods of termination of the tenancy cannot be used: rather it is the case that termination by surrender or forfeiture, etc., now falls to be dealt with as part of the general law, there being no special feature of treatment in relation to farm business tenancies. Dispute resolution in relation to the 1995 Act is likely in practice to involve consideration of the workings of and case law under the new Arbitration Act 1996. This statute, the application of which to 1986 Act tenancies is negligible, is itself a complete and upgraded arbitration code which is the subject of specialist works. For that reason this book does not give the 1996 Arbitration Act detailed coverage, although some broad outline is provided and the text of the Act is set out in Part VII. In one sense the "balance" of treatment of the 1995 Act is experimental: it may be that in subsequent editions of this work, in response to readers' opinions, some subjects will be expanded and others cut back.

4 Treatment of the 1986 Act

The 13th edition of this work was, of course, exclusively concerned with the 1986 Agricultural Holdings Act which received very detailed coverage. The decision to restructure the old edition and incorporate statutory comment into discussion in the Chapters is part of a more general policy to make the subject matter more accessible to readers. Increasingly as time goes by there will be a generation of practitioners who will normally be operating in relation to the grant of 1995 Act tenancies and who will depend on textbooks to a significant extent for their ability to deal with 1986 Act tenancies. To that end the number of small Chapters has been cut down and there are now three very lengthy Chapters at the heart of the work. They are Chapters 12 (termination of tenancy by notice to quit), 13 (compensation and custom) and 14 (succession on death or retirement). Chapter 12 is now supplemented by a number of Procedural Tables which hopefully will allow practitioners to move more confidently between the statute, the various statutory instruments and an assortment of forms, some prescribed and others simply following the wording of a section in the statute. This Chapter is also materially affected by a volume of new case law. Chapter 13 incorporates no less than six Chapters from the previous edition and, owing to the antiquity of some of the case law, a decision has been taken to give the reader a little more detail in the footnotes as to what is contained in cases which may be useful but obscurely reported. Chapter 14 covers very difficult material and has been designed to guide the practitioner through the entire process of preparing assessing and presenting a succession claim. Such claims, though they nearly always settle, have to be approached with a keen eye for what documents may be relevant and what arguments may be available on the facts of any individual case. The arbitration code contained within Schedule 11 of the 1986 Act remains untouched by the

Arbitration Act 1996 and accordingly more detailed treatment of Schedule 11 is considered justified.

Milk quotas 5

Milk quotas are creatures of Community law and impact upon dairy farms whether they are held in freehold or on a tenanted basis. The general rules which establish the conditions for transfer of milk quotas are extremely important for all types of dairy land and in the overwhelming majority of cases the movement of the quota is determined by underlying land transactions. For this reason there is a separate section in the book (Chapter 18) which covers the overall position in relation to milk quotas. Additionally there are special provisions in the Agriculture Act 1986 which affect rent reviews under the Agricultural Holdings Act 1986 and, in certain circumstances, provide that compensation should be payable to an outgoing tenant. Both the Community Regulations and the corresponding domestic Regulations have been the subject of frequent change and there is increasingly a body of case law which is sometimes directly and often indirectly relevant to issues arising in relation to the treatment of milk quota in the United Kingdom. It has been decided to deal with milk quota in some detail and to do so from a practitioner perspective rather than a wholly academic one. Practitioners deal with milk quotas on an almost daily basis but it is alarming how often lawyers will simply leave legal aspects to be dealt with by surveyors, often the explanation being that the relevant legal materials are too difficult to obtain or are not properly understood. We hope that Section 3 goes some way to clarifying the issues and identifying the materials.

How to use the book 6

The contents page and the Index in combination should direct attention to the relevant treatment in each Chapter. We have not primarily designed the book for people who are able to go straight to the statutory section as this pre-supposes a level of knowledge which many readers may not have. The statutes and statutory instruments stand free of commentary in Parts II and III. Readers consulting Section 3 in relation to milk quotas will find in Part IV the European Union Materials relevant to that subject. Part V contains all the forms required for taking steps under the Agricultural Holdings Act 1986 and certain suggested precedents in relation to the Agricultural Tenancies Act 1995; there is no commentary provided with the forms. Deadlines can be ascertained, hopefully, from the discussion in the relevant Chapter and/or the relevant Procedural Table. These Tables are especially designed for following through the complex sequence of, in particular, the notice to quit procedures in Chapter 12 and they are mentioned at the beginning of each relevant Chapter as a reminder. The Agricultural Holdings Act 1986 should be read using the definitions (alphabetically listed and cross-referred to sections) in Chapter 8. The authors are, themselves, surprised at how many of these definitions there are.

SECTION ONE

TENANCIES GOVERNED BY THE AGRICULTURAL TENANCIES ACT 1995

Chapter I

CREATION AND MEANING OF FARM BUSINESS TENANCY

1.1   General

1.4   Importance of commencement date of tenancy

1.5   Relationship to Landlord and Tenant Act 1954

1.6   Exclusions from the 1995 Act

1.15 Definition of farm business tenancy

1.17 The business conditions

1.20 The agriculture condition

1.21 The notice conditions

1.22 Diversification

1.23 Failure to serve notices

1.24 Preparation of documents by valuers and surveyors

1.25 Content of farm business tenancy

1.26 Relationship to other statutes

1.42 Application to Crown land

1.43 Length of term

1.44 Implied covenants

1.45 The usual covenants

1.46 Relative freedom of contract

1.47 Supplementary compensation and arbitration provisions

Farm business tenancies: general background   1.1

The Agricultural Holdings Act 1986, with its detailed regulation over almost every aspect of activity, established almost insurmountable barriers to a landlord gaining possession by means of serving a notice to quit.[1] Even where the tenant died or wished to retire members of his close family were entitled, subject to compliance with various statutory tests, to demand a grant to themselves of a further protected tenancy.[2] Such demand would be satisfied on two occasions, thereby extending the application of the restrictive 1986 Act code to, effectively, a further two generations beyond the current tenant. Perhaps not surprisingly landlords became increasingly reluctant to let land, a state of affairs not generally thought to be in the

---

[1] See generally Chapter 12 below.
[2] See generally Chapter 14 below.

public interest. In consequence the orthodoxies of almost 50 years were overturned by the passage of the Agricultural Tenancies Act 1995 which gave statutory sanction to the principle that landlords should indeed be entitled to vacant possession, subject only to the very minimum of control and, further, should in large measure be entitled to bargain on the open market with tenants as to the terms of the tenancy. This breathtaking reversal of previous policy, achieved with apparent consensus throughout the industry and virtually no opposition in principle in Parliament, no doubt recognises the fact that the modern farmer, in the decades of protection by the old legislation, has evolved into a profit-motivated businessman with access, when necessary, to sophisticated and detailed technical, valuation, veterinerary and legal advice.[3] The 1995 Act establishes basic rules as to the duration of a notice to quit,[4] but otherwise provides no barriers to the landlord obtaining possession. There are special statutory provisions as to rent review[5] but which also recognise a scope for the parties to make their own agreement. Finally there are simple rules relating to the removal of fixtures and buildings[6] and fairly elaborate provisions for compensation on termination of farm business tenancies.[7] This latter is doubtless motivated by the expectation that tenants who successfully conclude a farm business tenancy will wish to invest and ought to some extent to be protected in that investment. The statute also makes a somewhat complex provision for dispute resolution[8] and deals with a number of miscellaneous matters.[9] References to section numbers, without a further specific reference to a statute, in Chapters 1–7 inclusive of this work are references to the Agricultural Tenancies Act 1995 since those chapters are predominantly concerned with that statute.[10]

1.2 Territorial extent of the Agricultural Tenancies Act 1995

Essentially the Agricultural Tenancies Act 1995 is one which extends to England and Wales only.[11] This general provision is qualified only in two specific respects:

---

[3] The Central Association of Agricultural Valuers' Annual Tenanted Farms Survey 1997 (published February 1998) suggests that the policy of liberalisation is reinvigorating the tenanted sector. The survey concludes (i) there is a net inflow of land into the tenanted sector (ii) almost one in four farm business tenancies were on land not previously let (iii) 85% of the old full tenancies that ended were relet as farm business tenancies (iv) over 95% of units previously let on short term lettings had been let on farm business tenancies (v) the average length for all farm business tenancies is almost four years (vi) sales to sitting tenants are the major reason for land leaving the let sector. [Copies from CAAV Secretary: telephone 01594 832979.]
[4] See generally Chapter 4 below.
[5] See generally Chapter 2 below.
[6] See generally Chapter 3 below.
[7] See generally Chapter 5 below.
[8] See generally Chapter 6 below.
[9] See generally Chapter 7.
[10] Conversely references in Chapters 8–17 of this work to section numbers without any further reference to a statute are references to the Agricultural Holdings Act 1986, since those chapters deal predominantly with that statute.
[11] s. 41(3).

(i) where the 1995 Act by the Schedule amends a statute which already extends to Scotland or Northern Ireland, the amendment will also apply in those territories;

(ii) paragraph 9 of the Schedule (which amends the Reserve and Auxillary Forces (Protection of Civil Interests) Act 1951 does not extend to Northern Ireland.[12]

No qualification as to size of farm business tenancy 1.3

Like the Agricultural Holdings Act 1986, the 1995 statute does not require a tenancy to comprise a minimum amount of land before protection is available or the relevant statute should apply.

Importance of commencement date of tenancy 1.4

A tenancy beginning before the September 1, 1995 cannot be a farm business tenancy[13] because the statute is not retrospective.[14] The reader is referred elsewhere[15] for a more detailed consideration as to when a particular tenancy may begin: identification of that date is crucial since tenancies granted before it, if they are protected by an agricultural code, can only fall within the 1986 Act. As to tenancies beginning on or after September 1, 1995, these will fall[16] to be considered under the 1995 Act, the only exceptions being those referred to in section 4.[17]

Relationship between the Agricultural Tenancies Act 1995 and the Landlord and Tenant Act 1954 1.5

Both the 1995 Act and the 1954 Act deal with premises occupied by a tenant for the purpose of a business.[18] However the 1954 Act will not apply if the tenancy is a farm business tenancy.[19] In the case of a tenancy granted on or after September 1, 1995 but falling neither within section 4 of the 1995 Act[20] nor within the 1995 Act, there is the possibility that it may be protected by the 1954 Act.[21]

Exclusions from the scope of the Agricultural Tenancies Act 1995: tenancy beginning before September 1, 1995: section 2(1)((a) 1.6

A tenancy beginning before September 1, 1995 cannot be a farm business tenancy.[22] By section 38(4) it is provided that for the purposes of the Act a tenancy begins on the day on which, under the terms of the tenancy, the tenant is entitled to

---

[12] See, for both qualifications, s. 41(4).
[13] See s. 2(1)(a) and para. 1.6 below.
[14] The Act was passed on May 9, 1995 and by s. 41(2) came into force on September 1, 1995.
[15] para. 1.6 below.
[16] Subject to compliance with the various tests in the 1995 Act.
[17] See generally paras 1.7–1.14 below.
[18] Compare s. 23(1) of the 1954 Act and s. 1(2) of the 1995 Act.
[19] s. 43(1)(aa) of the 1954 Act.
[20] See paras 1.7–1.14 below.
[21] The reader is referred to standard works covering that statute in particular *Woodfall, Landlord and Tenant*, Vol. II, and Hill and Redman's *Law of Landlord and Tenant*, Vol. I. Both works are looseleaf.
[22] s. 2(1)(a).

possession under that tenancy and references to the beginning of the tenancy are references to that day. For tenancies created prior to September 1, 1995 there are, therefore, three possible situations:

(i) Where the contract is entered into before September 1, 1995 and it stipulates possession as being available before September 1, 1995. This tenancy is protected by the Agricultural Holdings Act 1986.

(ii) Where the contract is entered into before September 1, 1995 but possession is not available until on or after September 1, 1995. This tenancy is covered by the Agricultural Tenancies Act 1995.[23]

(iii) Where the contract is entered into before the September 1, 1995 but stipulates for possession to be available to the tenant only on or after the September 1, 1995 but in circumstances where the tenancy is granted by a written contract indicating (in whatever terms) that the Agricultural Holdings Act 1986 is to apply to the tenancy.[24] This tenancy is protected by the 1986 Act.

For the purposes of the 1995 Act a tenancy is regarded as granted at the point "when the contract was entered into".[25] It is submitted that this means that an agreement to grant a tenancy is for these purposes the grant of the tenancy and the tenancy is regarded as beginning only when the tenant is entitled to possession. It is accordingly further submitted that in section 38(4) the reference to rights of possession under the terms of the tenancy means under the terms of any relevant contract to grant that tenancy, having regard to the contents of section 38(3). These somewhat cumbersome and detailed provisions were necessary in order to deal clearly with the transitional situation in 1995 since September is in many parts of the country the traditional time of year for new tenancies to be granted. The 1995 Act is, accordingly, not retrospective and agreements already protected by, for example, the Agricultural Holdings Act 1986, are not affected at all. Similarly any tenancy beginning before the September 1, 1995 which happens not to be protected by the 1986 Act[26] is also unaffected by the 1995 Act.

1.7 Exclusions from the scope of the Agricultural Tenancies Act 1995: tenancies beginning on or after September 1, 1995 protected by the Agricultural Holdings Act 1986 by virtue of section 4 of the 1995 Act

Where a tenancy is granted beginning on or after September 1, 1995, it may only fall within the Agricultural Holdings Act 1986 if it does so under the scope of section 4 of the 1995 Act.[27] Such a tenancy is governed by the 1986 Act and cannot be a farm business tenancy.[28] This exclusion relates to a tenancy of an agricultural holding, an expression defined and discussed in the context of the 1986 Act in this

---

[23] s. 38(4).
[24] *i.e.* falling within ss. 2(1)(b) and 4(1)(a) of the 1995 Act.
[25] s. 38(3).
[26] For example because it was granted pursuant to a Ministerial consent.
[27] See paras 1.8–1.13 below.
[28] s. 2(1)(b) of the 1995 Act.

EXCLUSIONS FROM THE SCOPE OF THE AGRICULTURAL TENANCIES ACT 1995

work.[29] There is a general disapplication of the 1986 Act in relation to all tenancies beginning on or after the September 1, 1995[30] except those falling within section 4 of the 1995 Act.

1986 Act applicable to written tenancy beginning on or after September 1, 1995 where parties prior to that date agree the 1986 Act shall apply: section 4(1)(a)   1.8

A tenancy beginning on or after the September 1, 1995 will be governed by the Agricultural Holdings Act 1986 where the tenancy is of an agricultural holding[31] granted by a written contract of tenancy entered into[32] before September 1, 1995 and indicating (in whatever terms) that the 1986 Act is to apply in relation to the tenancy.[33] It follows that where the contract of tenancy is not written but is oral the 1995 Act will apply even though documentation may demonstrate that the parties intended the 1986 Act to apply. It is submitted that, probably, this particular provision is limited in its scope as it appears likely only to cover transitional arrangements granted between May 9, 1995, when the 1995 Act was passed, and September 1, 1995 when it came into force.[34] Prior to the passage of the 1995 Act it is unlikely in the extreme that any tenancy agreement would specifically opt for protection by the 1986 Act since that statute applied to all tenancies of agricultural holdings unless special steps had been taken to avoid the Act.

1986 Act applicable to tenancies beginning on or after September 1, 1995 being obtained by virtue of an Agricultural Land Tribunal succession direction: section 4(1)(b)   1.9

Where a tenancy begins on or after September 1, 1995[35] the Agricultural Holdings Act 1986 will apply to it if it is obtained by virtue of a direction of an Agricultural Land Tribunal under section 39 (succession on death of the previous tenant) or 53 (retirement of the previous tenant) of the 1986 Act.[36] The effect of this exemption is to ensure that succession tenancies, where the original tenant was protected by the 1986 Act, continue to be protected by that Act. Effectively accrued rights under the succession provisions of the 1986 Act are therefore untouched by the 1995 legislation.

1986 Act applicable to agreed succession tenancies beginning on or after September 1, 1995 which are granted following a direction in the Applicant's favour: section 4(1)(c)   1.10

The Agricultural Holdings Act 1986 will apply to any tenancy beginning[37] on or after September 1, 1995 where that tenancy is granted following a direction under

---

[29] See paras 8.16–8.20 below.
[30] Including any agreement to which s. 2 of the 1986 Act would otherwise apply beginning on or after that date.
[31] See paras 8.16–8.20 below.
[32] See s. 38(3) and (4) and para. 1.6 above.
[33] s. 4(1)(a).
[34] s. 41(2).
[35] See para. 1.6 above.
[36] See generally Chapter 14 below.
[37] See para. 1.6 above.

section 39 of the 1986 Act[38] in circumstances falling within section 45(6)[39] of that Act.[40] In short this covers the case of a successful application following the death of the original tenant being one where the landlord then acts to grant the tenancy prior to any vesting by virtue of that direction. This provision assimilates voluntary grants made in the shadow of a direction to tenancies arising through the machinery of a succession direction.[41]

1.11 1986 Act applicable to tenancies beginning on or after September 1, 1995 granted on an agreed succession by written agreement opting for the 1986 Act: section 4(1)(d)

The Agricultural Holdings Act 1986 applies to any tenancy beginning[42] on or after September 1, 1995 which is granted on an agreed succession by a written contract of tenancy indicating (in whatever terms) that Part IV of the 1986 Act is to apply to the tenancy.[43] The new tenancy is granted on an agreed succession only where section 4(2) so provides.[44] Essentially there is only an agreed succession if (a) the previous tenancy was one which carried succession rights under Part IV of the 1986 Act and (b) the grant of the present tenancy would fall within section 37(1)(a) or (b) of the 1986 Act even though section 4(1)(b) and (c) of the 1995 Act does not apply.[45] For the avoidance of doubt it should be pointed out that a succession occasion falling within section 37(2) is deemed by that section to fall within section 37(1)(a).

1.12 1986 Act applicable to tenancies beginning on or after September 1, 1995 where the tenant comes in by virtue of the "Evesham custom": section 4(1)(e)

The Agricultural Holdings Act 1986 applies to any tenancy beginning on or after September 1, 1995 where that tenancy is created by the acceptance of a tenant in accordance with the provisions as to compensation known as the "Evesham custom" set out in section 80(3)-(5) of the 1986 Act[46] on the terms and conditions of the previous tenancy. The "Evesham custom" relates to compensation for investment in market gardens. If a market garden tenancy ends either by reason of a tenant's notice to quit or by reason of the tenant's insolvency, the tenant is not entitled to compensation for improvements specified by a Tribunal direction under section 80(2) unless the conditions in section 80(4) are satisfied.[47] The exemption in the 1995 Act enables a market garden tenant protected by the 1986 Act to secure

---

[38] Succession on death: see Chapter 14 below.
[39] See para. 14.6 below.
[40] s. 4(1)(c).
[41] See previous paragraph.
[42] See para. 1.6 above.
[43] s. 4(1)(d).
[44] Readers are referred to the full, somewhat convoluted, terms of s. 4(2) printed in Part II.
[45] For commentary on s. 37(1)(a) and (b) see paras 14.13–14.16 below. Particular care should be taken to check the status of any grant to joint tenants since the status of a joint tenancy will depend on the date of grant.
[46] See generally paras 15.31–15.35 below.
[47] See generally para. 15.32 below.

a successor under that Act thereby enabling himself to be paid out for improvements.

1986 Act applicable to tenancies beginning on or after September 1, 1995 by virtue of surrender and regrant in favour of a tenant already protected by the 1986 Act: section 4(1)(f) 1.13

The Agricultural Holdings Act 1986 applies in relation to any tenancy beginning[48] on or after September 1, 1995 where that tenancy:

> "is granted to a person who, immediately before the grant of the tenancy, was the tenant of the holding, or of any agricultural holding which comprises the whole or a substantial part of the land comprised in the holding, under a tenancy in relation to which the 1986 Act applied ('the previous tenancy') and is so granted merely because a purported variation of the previous tenancy (not being an agreement expressed to take effect as a new tenancy between the parties) has effect as an implied surrender followed by the grant of the tenancy."

This sub-paragraph is designed to allow, in certain circumstances, the doctrine of surrender and regrant to take effect without impugning the protected status of a tenancy under the Agricultural Holdings Act 1986. The circumstances in which section 4(1)(f) applies are extremely limited and narrower than, for example, in other areas of the law where surrender and regrant has been singled out for special treatment.[49] This sub-section appears applicable only to circumstances where, in effect, an "accidental" surrender took place. It covers only a situation where a tenant protected by the 1986 Act enters into what appears to be a variation of the terms of his existing tenancy but which, as a matter of law, takes effect as an implied surrender followed by the grant of a new tenancy. Specifically excluded from the contents of this paragraph is any agreement which is "expressed to take effect as a new tenancy between the parties": where the parties deliberately express themselves as creating a new tenancy the sub-paragraph is not applicable. What appears to be protected here is the expectation of the original tenant as to maintenance of his fully protected status in circumstances where, having regard to any expression of agreement, it would not be clear to him that a new tenancy would be granted.[50] It follows that where an express deed of surrender is used and a new tenancy, a farm business tenancy on the face of it, is created then the arrangement will indeed give rise to a farm business tenancy and the old Agricultural Holdings Act tenancy will come to an end. There appears nothing inconsistent with statutory policy in allowing this to occur, given the wording of section 4(1)(f). In these circumstances the erstwhile 1986 Act tenancy will be formally terminated with

---

[48] See para. 1.6 above.

[49] *e.g.* in s. 34(1)(b)(iv) of the Agricultural Holdings Act 1986: see discussion at para. 14.8 below.

[50] For purposes of capital taxation landlords have attempted to trigger the terms of s. 4(1)(f) intending not to disturb the protected status of an existing tenant. Probably such a window of opportunity does exist but clearly there is considerable scope for the documentation to take an incorrect form. Well advised tenants should probably regard these schemes with very great caution.

every opportunity for the tenant to make his usual end of tenancy claims. Clearly this type of procedure could only take effect where the tenant actually agreed to it under a code whereby he enjoys a very high degree of protection from unilateral termination by the landlord. An implied surrender may perhaps occur where there is a variation of the tenancy terms but this must be rare.[51] The addition of land to the tenancy will normally automatically result in the surrender of the old tenancy and the grant of a new one by operation of law.[52] A situation often encountered is the informal amalgamation of the rent of two separate holdings: does this involve a surrender and regrant? In lengthy discussion on this topic the Court of Appeal concluded that surrender and regrant was not necessarily the result, that is to say, two separate holdings might technically survive as such despite the amalgamation of the rent.[53] This resolution allows each tenancy, despite the rent amalgamation to be treated separately for all purposes including, for instance, succession and ascertainment of commencement dates. It is as yet unknown whether this paragraph requires inclusion or exclusion of the situation where the original tenant was comprised of two persons and only one of them is involved in the new grant.[54] If it is desired definitely to exclude application of this section in such circumstances the obvious remedy is to execute an express surrender and deliberately grant a new tenancy. If the converse is intended then it may be appropriate to vary the tenancy terms so as to fall within the sub-paragraph but subsequently allow the joint tenant to assign to one of the two tenants.

---

[51] See *Jenkin R. Lewis & Son Ltd v. Kerman* [1971] Ch. 477.

[52] See *Baker v. Merckel* (1960) 1 Q.B. 657; *Re Savile Settled Estates* (1931) 2 Ch. 210.

[53] *Childers v. Anker* [1996] 1 E.G.L.R. 1. As can be seen from the discussion in that case determination of the issue as to whether a tenancy variation is so fundamental that a new tenancy must come into existence is extremely difficult: it appears that the intention of the parties is an important ingredient (*Take Harvest Ltd v. Liu* [1993] A.C. 552, [1993] 2 All E.R. 459) but even so dramatic a step as adding a new tenant will not necessarily effect a surrender of the original tenancy (*Saunders' Trustees v. Ralph* [1993] 28 E.G. 127). However there is considerable authority that a surrender by operation of law will take place despite the intention of the parties: for a full discussion of this topic with many illustrations from the old cases see *Woodfall Landlord and Tenant*, Vol. I, Chapter 17, Section 3(C). In *Friends Provident v. British Railways Board* [1996] 1 All E.R. 336 there was no surrender despite a variation of the rent and significant changes as to the covenants relating to alterations. A change in the term date of the tenancy is likely to effect a surrender (*Fenner v. Blake* [1900] 1 Q.B. 426). Surrendering part of the land within the tenancy does not effect a surrender of the retained part nor does any new tenancy come into existence (*Holme v. Brunskill* [1878] 3 Q.B.D. 495; *Carnarvon v. Villebois* [1844] 13 M.&W. 313; *Morrison v. Chadwick* [1849] 7 CB 266).

[54] It is suggested on balance that the new tenant, in order to be included within this paragraph, must have been the only previous tenant. In the sub-paragraph the words "the tenant" appear to contrast with "a person". Furthermore the selection of one out of more than one original tenants seems to go much further than "a purported variation of the previous tenancy".

Definitions in section 4(3) 1.14
"Agricultural holding"[55] and "contract of tenancy"[56] bear the same meaning as in the Agricultural Holdings Act 1986.[57] "Close relative"[58] and "related holding"[59] have the same meaning as in section 35(2) of the 1986 Act.[60]

"Farm business tenancy" 1.15
A tenancy is a "farm business tenancy" where, provided it does not fall within the exceptions in section 2,[61] that tenancy either:

(i) satisfies "the business conditions"[62] and "the agriculture condition"[63]; or

(ii) satisfies the business conditions and "the notice conditions".[64]

This general definition is established by section 1(1) in an alternative form. Thus if the notice conditions are not satisfied parties may seek to rely on proving the agriculture condition in order to bring the tenancy within this section. In contrast with much housing legislation, the absence of appropriate notices is not fatal.

Meaning of tenancy 1.16
"Tenancy" is defined[65] to mean any tenancy other than a tenancy at will,[66] and includes a sub-tenancy and an agreement for a tenancy or sub-tenancy". This wide definition embraces all tenancies, whether or not created by writing or by deed. There is additionally provided, for particular purposes, a separate definition of "fixed term tenancy".[67] Although "the notice conditions" are one way of satisfying the essential ingredients of a farm business tenancy,[68] it is neither essential to serve those notices nor to create the tenancy by written document.[69] There is no provision for a minimum length of term.

---

[55] See paras 8.16–8.20 below.
[56] See para. 8.17 below.
[57] s. 4(3)(a).
[58] See paras 14.34–14.35 below. "'Close relative' of a deceased tenant means—(a) the wife or husband or the deceased; (b) a brother or sister of the deceased; (c) a child of the deceased; (d) any person (not within (b) or (c) above) who, in the case of any marriage to which the deceased was at any time a party, was treated by the deceased as a child of the family in relation to that marriage."
[59] "Related holding" means, in relation to the holding, any agricultural holding comprising the whole or a substantial part of the land comprised in the holding.
[60] s. 4(3)(b).
[61] See paras 1.6–1.14 above.
[62] See paras 1.17–1.19 below.
[63] See para. 1.20 below.
[64] See para. 1.21 below.
[65] s. 38(1).
[66] As to tenancies at will, this term covers those which arise as a matter of legal construction (see ***Wheeler v. Mercer*** [1957] A.C. 416) and those expressly so created (see ***Hagee (London) v. AB Erikson & Larson*** [1975] 29 P.&C.R. 512; ***Manfield & Sons v. Botchin*** [1970] 2 QB 612; ***Morgan v. William Harrison*** [1907] 2 Ch. 137).
[67] s. 38(1): "any tenancy other than a periodic tenancy".
[68] See para. 1.21 below.
[69] The 1995 Act is liberal in this respect, as is the 1986 Act. However there is this contrast

1.17 The business conditions

These are established in a cumulative form.[70] They are:

(a) That all or part of the land comprised in the tenancy is farmed for the purposes of a trade or business, and

(b) that, since the beginning of the tenancy, all or part of the land so comprised has been so farmed.

The first condition requires the situation to be examined as at the present time.[71] Farming is defined by section 38(2).[72] "Agriculture" is defined by section 38(1) in terms which mirror those applicable to the Agricultural Holdings Act 1986.[73] The section excludes purely recreational use of land.[74] The phrase "trade or business" again reflects established language familiar from the Agricultural Holdings Act 1986.[75]

In relation to the second condition, a retrospective test is applied as to the continuity of use. It is necessary to establish that at least some part of the land within the tenancy has always been used for the purposes of a trade or business. The "beginning of the tenancy" means the time from which the tenant is entitled to possession.[76]

1.18 Rebuttable presumption as to use

Where there is litigation as to whether or not a tenancy was a farm business tenancy at any time, there is a rebuttable presumption, if it can be proved that all or part of the land was at any time farmed for the purposes of a trade or business, that such land has been so farmed since the beginning of the tenancy.[77] This is an extremely important presumption since although the first business condition is directed to the present time, the second requires continuity of use to be established over what may one day prove to be many years. Quite how generously this presumption is to be construed remains open to question. It appears, since the presumption relates to a question as to whether a tenancy "was" a farm business tenancy, that it is available only in aid of the second business condition. If it can be demonstrated that at some point in the past there was business use it does not follow from that that business use to the present time is presumed. It appears that the presumption only extends backwards in time not forwards (*i.e.* if, for example, business use at the middle point in the tenancy can be demonstrated it would be presumed to have been there

---

namely that the 1986 Act allows the statute to provide very significant supplementation to what the parties have agreed (*e.g.* ss. 6 and 7 of the 1986 Act). By contrast the 1995 Act provides minimal supplementation to the contract and provides no machinery whereby the tenancy terms can be reduced to writing.

[70] s. 1(2).
[71] "Is" farmed.
[72] References in this Act to the farming of land include references to the carrying on in relation to land of any agricultural activity.
[73] s. 96(1): see commentary at para. 8.18 below.
[74] Compare *Hickson & Welch Ltd v. Cann* (1977) 40 P.&C.R. 218.
[75] s. 1(4)(a): see commentary at para. 8.18 below.
[76] s. 38(4).
[77] s. 1(7).

since the beginning of the tenancy but is not presumed to have extended forwards to the present time). It is submitted that, in the usual way, it is for the person seeking to displace the presumption to demonstrate that, on a balance of probabilities, it has been displaced.

Use of land in breach of the terms of the tenancy 1.19

In determining whether at any time the tenancy satisfies the business or agriculture conditions use of the land in breach of the terms of the tenancy, commercial activities carried on in breach of those terms, and any cessation of such activities in breach of those terms must be disregarded.[78] It is only where the landlord or his predecessor in title has consented to the breach or where the landlord has acquiesced in it that regard will be had to such unlawful activities or use. This provision bears comparison with analogous provisions in the Landlord and Tenant Act 1954.[79] In summary it is only lawful use of the tenanted land which will be regarded and where a tenant who is obliged to conduct a business fails to do so, such failure has no effect on the classification of the tenancy. A distinction is drawn between consenting to a breach and acquiescing in it. In neither case is there any requirement as to such consent or acquiescence being demonstrated by writing. Consent clearly involves communication of assent to the tenant intending or apparently intending that the use should be regarded as legitimate. Acquiescence is limited to acquiescence by the present landlord[80] and connotes long-term knowledge of and lack of action over the particular breach. In practice, the distinction between these two categories in some cases is likely to be blurred and although there is no mention of it in the section it is difficult to imagine that the tenant would not be able to rely on an estoppel as establishing a form of consent.[81] Although there are as yet no cases on "acquiescence" in the context of the 1995 Act it is submitted that the term in principle requires the landlord to know the facts which are said to establish the breach.[82] Section 1(8) is particularly useful given that the Courts have now set their face against enforcement of covenants to carry on a business.[83]

The agriculture condition: section 1(3) 1.20

"The agriculture condition is that, having regard to—

    (a) the terms of the tenancy,

    (b) the use of the land comprised in the tenancy,

---

[78] s. 1(8).
[79] s. 23(4) of the 1954 Act.
[80] By necessary contrast with consent.
[81] See *Troop v. Gibson* [1986] 1 E.G.L.R. 1 (estoppel by convention) and, more generally, *Crabb v. Arun District Council* [1976] Ch. 179. More recently, *John v. George* [1996] 1 E.G.L.R. 7, though dealing with estoppel by convention, usefully reviews the authorities.
[82] See *Methodist Secondary Schools Trust Deed Trustees v. O'Leary* [1992] 66 P.&C.R. 364 and see as to the doctrine of acquiescence in equity *Sayers v. Collyer* [1884] 28 Ch.D. 103, *Wolfe v. Hogan* [1949] 2 K.B. 194.
[83] See *Co-op Insurance Society Ltd v. Argyll Stores (Holdings) Ltd* [1997] 3 All E.R. 297.

(c) the nature of any commercial activities carried on on that land, and

(d) any other relevant circumstances,

the character of the tenancy is primarily or wholly agricultural."

The agriculture condition is one which must be satisfied, where it is relied on, as at the time of reliance. The condition is phrased using the present tense although a consideration of the historic situation is not precluded, since regard may be had to "any other relevant circumstances". Attention is specifically directed to the tenancy terms, the use of the land and the nature of any commercial activities as well as the general situation. It is an exercise similar in broad terms to that required for the purposes of section 1(2) of the Agricultural Holdings Act 1986,[84] but is directed to a different objective.[85] The 1995 Act contrasts strongly in its objective namely to establish whether or not "the character of the tenancy is primarily or wholly agricultural". It is submitted that the character of the tenancy may be substantially affected by non-agricultural use whilst still remaining primarily agricultural in character.[86] It is submitted that the 1995 Act clearly intends to allow uses within its scope which are diversified away from agriculture.[87] The "character" of the tenancy may be primarily agricultural despite substantial commercial activity: such a situation can occur quite easily.[88] There is no definition of "character" and it is submitted that this is a matter for general assessment by the Court. "Agricultural" is to be construed in accordance with the definition of agriculture.[89] It is submitted that a number of commonly encountered countryside activities are not agricultural, although some may be so ancillary to or consistent with agricultural use that their impact on the character of the tenancy is not very great where there is other agricultural use.[90] It is essential that the written notices to be served by the landlord and the tenant should be separate from any instrument which creates the tenancy.[91]

There is a deemed compliance with the notice conditions where section 3

---

[84] See para. 8.19 below.

[85] The 1986 Act requires consideration as to whether "the whole of the land comprised in the contract, subject to such exceptions only as do not substantially affect the character of the tenancy, is let for use as agricultural land".

[86] There appears to be a subtle change of emphasis and it is submitted that the section should not be construed as though it read "wholly or primarily agricultural".

[87] See generally para. 1.22 below.

[88] For example working farms where substantial income is derived from visits by members of the public to see animals or walk along nature trails. It is also evident where seasonal bed and breakfast provides a large contribution to income from a smallholding, the "character" of which is primarily agricultural but the economics of which may be seriously dependent on the commercial cash flow.

[89] s. 38(1). This definition is co-terminous with that provided by section 96(1) of the 1986 Act (see commentary at para. 8.18 below). "Livestock", an incorporated definition for these purposes, is also identical in s. 38(1) of the 1995 Act and s. 96(1) of the 1986 Act. Accordingly the treatment of horses under both statutes is the same: see para. 8.18 below.

[90] Compare **Normanton v. Giles** [1980] 1 W.L.R. 28 and **Glendyne v. Rapley** [1978] 1 W.L.R. 601 (keeping fish or birds for sport).

[91] s. 1(6).

THE AGRICULTURE CONDITION: SECTION 1(3)

applies. Essentially this section operates in circumstances where[92] a fixed term farm business tenancy is replaced by another fixed term farm business tenancy, the termination date of which is earlier than under the original agreement, alternatively where[93] the area within the tenancies remains significantly the same and the character of each holding is unchanged. In either case the terms of the new tenancy must be substantially the same as under the old.[94] Where the notice conditions are satisfied in relation to the first tenancy, the benefit of this is deemed to accrue to the second tenancy.[95]

The notice conditions: section 1(4)   1.21

"The notice conditions are-

    (a)   that, on or before the relevant day,[96] the landlord and the tenant each gave the other a written notice—

---

[92] s. 3(3).
[93] s. 3(2).
[94] s. 3(1)(c)
[95] There appears to be some disagreement in the literature as to whether or not it is necessary to serve further notices in circumstances where there is a series of farm business tenancies. Scammell & Densham's *Law of Agricultural Holdings*, (8th ed.), page 923, apparently considers that s. 3 extends beyond the application of the doctrine of surrender and re-grant: "Whilst s. 3 is headed 'Compliance with notice conditions in cases of surrender and re-grant' it is clearly wide enough (through the s. 3(2) condition) to cover some situations where a fixed-term tenancy comes to an end and a new tenancy is granted to the same tenant of the same holding on essentially the same terms". In contrast Sydenham & Mainwaring, *Farm Business Tenancies*, page 127 states: "A series of fixed term tenancies which expire by effluxion of time would need new notices." As to the position quoted in Scamell & Densham, it is submitted that this wrongly concludes that s. 3 is available beyond the scope of surrender and re-grant. It is respectfully suggested that their view fails to accord sufficient importance to the words in s. 3(1)(a) "a tenancy ... is granted to a person who, immediately before the grant, was the tenant under a farm business tenancy". These words restrict the operation of s. 3, as the notes to the section indicate, to the circumstance that the previous tenancy had not been determined at the point when the new arrangement came into effect: see ***Bolnore Properties Ltd v. Cobb*** (1996) 29 H.L.R. 202 where, on materially identical wording contained within section 34 of the Housing Act 1988, it was held that the Housing Act did not stipulate the minimum period which must elapse before it can be said that the grantee of the new tenancy was not a statutory or protected tenant "immediately before" the grant (Millett L.J. at 212). It was integral to the reasoning in that case that the appellant was unable to demonstrate that he had a continuing protected or statutory status prior to the new tenancy coming into force. The issue for the purposes of s. 3 of the 1995 Act is not whether the arrangement in question has expired but whether in fact it has been brought to an end. If it has, these authors agree with Sydenham & Mainwaring that new notices are required. But it must be remembered that fixed term tenancies of more than two years must be brought to an end by notice and without such notice of termination the tenant continues to enjoy an interest which would trigger the provisions of s. 3.
[96] s. 1(5) defines this to mean whichever is the earlier of (a) the day on which the parties enter into any instrument creating the tenancy, other than an agreement to enter into a tenancy on a future date, or (b) the beginning of the tenancy. The latter is defined by s. 38(4) to mean the day on which under the terms of the tenancy the tenant is entitled to possession. In short, therefore, the relevant day means the earliest point at which the tenant is entitled to possession. It should be noted that the tenancy does not begin until it has been created:

(i) identifying (by name or otherwise) the land to be comprised in the tenancy or proposed tenancy, and

(ii) containing a statement to the effect that the person giving the notice intends that the tenancy or proposed tenancy is to be, and remain, a farm business tenancy, and

(b) that, at the beginning of the tenancy, having regard to the terms of the tenancy and any other relevant circumstances, the character of the tenancy was primarily or wholly agricultural.[97]"

The first notice condition requires the landlord and the tenant each to give the other a written notice. There is no prescribed form for either notice.[98] The relevant notices may be given before the tenancy is created or on the same day and these notices must be given whether the tenancy agreement is to be in writing or not. It should be noted that each person, in his own notice, gives a statement as to his own intention, not the intention of the other party.

The second of the notice conditions requires that, at the beginning of the tenancy,[99] it should be the case that the character of the tenancy was primarily or wholly agricultural.[1]

1.22 Diversification

The 1995 Act does not define diversification nor refer to it. Diversification is the process by which, increasingly in recent years, agricultural activities have been supplemented by compatible non-agricultural use of farms. Examples of this are many.[2] The need to supplement farm income from non-traditional farming activities may be particularly acute as the efficiency of traditional farm businesses requires expansion of individual farms and as the towns increasingly encroach on the countryside. It is submitted that the terms of the 1995 Act are designed to allow significant elements of diversification which do affect the character of the tenancy whilst permitting the character of that tenancy to be regarded as still primarily agricultural.[3] This concern of the statute is evident in relation to compensation on

---

the obviousness of this statement belies the complexity of the case law regarding backdated agreements. It is submitted that it is the real situation which is the subject of assessment as to whether the tenancy has begun (compare **Keen v. Holland** [1984] 1 W.L.R. 251) and not backdated provisions (see **Bradshaw v. Pawley** [1980] 1 W.L.R. 10 and other cases explained in **Pahl v. Trevor** [1992] 1 E.G.L.R. 22).

[97] s. 1(4).
[98] For a suggested form see Part V Form 101 below.
[99] As to the beginning of the tenancy see the notes at para. 1.6 above. Part V Form 102 contains a form of recital for use in the tenancy agreement.
[1] See above comments as to the agriculture condition para. 1.20.
[2] Nature trails, paint-ball 'war games', bed and breakfast, breeding novelty animals such as shire horses, even office use in converted buildings, storage of non-agricultural equipment, food processing and packing where the raw materials and products are imported, farm shops (*i.e.* retail activities using imported food), arguably "pick your own" enterprises, selling postcards, craft shops, potteries, farm implement museums, caravans, allowing fairs, shows or racing events, filming, etc.
[3] See comments in relation to s. 1(3), "the agriculture condition" para. 1.20 above.

termination of a farm business tenancy,[4] with provisions dealing with the benefit of planning permission. This may be particularly important where the tenant has spotted a business opportunity which the landlord may subsequently exploit himself. The business conditions[5] require that a farm business tenancy always demonstrates some agricultural use. It is then necessary to satisfy either the agriculture condition, which requires a current demonstration of primarily agricultural character in the tenancy; or satisfaction of the notice conditions[6] which relates to the original primarily agricultural character of the tenancy and the intention of the parties at the outset. It may well be that, in the second case (*i.e.* reliance on the notice conditions) the primacy of the agricultural use will have been displaced by the dates at which the investigation takes place. It is not as such a condition of qualification as a farm business tenancy that as at the present time it must always be shown that the character of the tenancy is primarily agricultural: if this were the case it may be thought that there would be little point in establishing a different test by way of contrast in terms of the agriculture condition and the notice conditions. In this sense, therefore, the statute allows it would seem an opportunity for very substantial diversification to take place even displacing the original agricultural character of the farm business tenancy. Finally, it is submitted that there is clearly no severance as to different uses of the tenanted land and this is demonstrable in relation to the ascertainment of rent in relation to "the holding".[7] In this there is a clear parallel with the approach of the 1986 Act.[8]

Failure to serve notices 1.23

For completeness it is pointed out that there is no penalty for failure to serve the appropriate notices required for satisfaction of the notice conditions in section 1(4). A farm business tenancy may be such where there is reliance in the alternative on satisfaction of the agriculture condition.[9]

Preparation of documents etc. by valuers and surveyors 1.24

Section 35 of the 1995 Act amends section 22 of the Solicitors Act 1974 which prohibits unqualified persons from preparing certain legal instruments. The instruments in question include transfers or charges for the purposes of the Land Registration Act 1925, applications under that Act at the registry and any other instrument relating to real or personal estate and any legal proceedings. The only exception is where the person creating the instrument proves that he acted otherwise than for or in expectation of any fee gain or reward.[10] Persons exempt from the general prohibition are set out in section 22(2) of the 1974 Act which has now been expanded to authorise "any accredited person"[11] to draw or prepare any instrument:

---

[4] See Part III of the Act and in particular s. 18.
[5] See paras. 1.17–1.19 above.
[6] See para. 1.21 above.
[7] An expression which is not used in Part I of the 1995 Act but which is defined by s. 38(1) to mean "the aggregate of the land comprised in the tenancy".
[8] See para. 8.16 below.
[9] See para. 1.20 above.
[10] The section in fact creates a criminal offence where its terms are transgressed.
[11] Now defined by s. 22(3A) as amended by s. 35 of the 1995 Act to mean any Associate or

(i) which creates, or which he believes on reasonable grounds will create, a farm business tenancy (within the meaning of the Agricultural Tenancies Act 1995), or

(ii) which relates to an existing tenancy which is, or which he believes on reasonable grounds to be, such a tenancy.

Valuers and surveyors should consider carefully the terms of the amended section 22. It was probably passed because, in the context of the Agricultural Holdings Act 1986, it was common for valuers and surveyors to act for clients in preparing and drawing up annual tenancy agreements.[12] Therefore under the Agricultural Holdings Act 1986 it was always and remains an offence for a valuer or surveyor to draw a lease for more than three years which must be executed by deed.[13] When the 1995 Act was passed it was perceived to be desirable to continue to allow valuers and surveyors to draw yearly agreements and in addition to extend the power of preparation and drafting to leases which are or which the valuer or surveyor reasonably believes will be farm business tenancies. In relation to farm business tenancies the valuer or surveyor is entitled not only to facilitate creation of the arrangement but in addition to prepare any variation of an existing farm business tenancy (or a tenancy which on reasonable grounds he believes to be such a tenancy). This is an important change which authorises, for example, the preparation of deeds of variation to cover desired changes to alterations or user covenants.

1.25 Content of the farm business tenancy agreement

Subject to the matters expressly required by the 1995 Act, the general law applies. This work is not the place for a general treatise and there are many good and detailed books on this subject.[14] Nor does this work provide drafting precedents for the creation of a farm business tenancy. Once again, there are many available precedents easily available which provide a convenient starting point for discussion between the intending landlord and tenant.[15] Henceforth case law

---

Fellow of the Incorporated Society of Valuers and Auctioneers or of the Royal Institution of Chartered Surveyors (RICS) or any Full Member of the Central Association of Agricultural Valuers.

[12] The definition of "instrument" in s. 22(3) of the 1974 Act is such as to exclude agreements not intended to be executed as a deed, other than those expressly included elsewhere in the section (which did not include reference to yearly tenancies).

[13] s. 52(1) of the Law of Property Act 1925.

[14] The most comprehensive is probably *Woodfall, Law of Landlord and Tenant* Vol. 1 and, though seriously out of date, the lucidity of Megarry and Wade, *The Law of Real Property*, (5th Ed.) is unrivalled.

[15] For commentary on and provision of suitable precedents for business leases see *Lewison Drafting Business Leases* (5th ed.), F.T. Law and Tax. Kim Lewison Q.C. is the general editor of *Woodfall* Volume 1 and the smaller book benefits from this wider connection. In addition, various professional bodies provide specialist agricultural precedents such as the Royal Institution of Chartered Surveyors and the Central Association of Agricultural Valuers. The National Farmers' Union and the Country Landowners' Association also have specimen clauses. A good general text with discussion as to the effect of particular forms is Ross, *Drafting and Negotiating Commercial Leases*, (4th ed., Butterworths, 1994).

arising in relation to farm business tenancies will, apart from where it concerns specific parts of the 1995 Act, once more enhance our understanding of the general law. There are a number of points where the 1995 Act establishes the relationship between farm business tenancies and other statutory codes or provisions. The most important of these are highlighted below.

Farm business tenancies and the Small Holdings and Allotments Act 1908 1.26
Farm business tenants are excluded from the compensation rights provided for by section 47 of the Small Holdings and Allotments Act 1908.[16]

Law of Distress Amendment Act 1908 1.27
Farm business tenancies are not the subject of any special exclusion. The amendment provided by the Schedule, paragraph 2, of the 1995 Act operates to confine an exemption within section 4(1) of the 1908 Act in favour of agisted livestock within the meaning of section 18 of the Agricultural Holdings Act 1986 on land comprised within a tenancy governed by the 1986 Act. In other words, the exception has not been extended to assimilate agisted livestock on holdings governed by the 1986 and 1995 Acts.

The Allotments Act 1922 1.28
Farm business tenancies are expressly excluded from the definition of allotment.[17] They are further expressly excluded from the compensation provisions contained in section 6(1) of the 1922 Act.[18] As to the inter-relationship of allotments and smallholdings with the Agricultural Holdings Act 1986, attention is drawn to chapter 15 below.

The Landlord and Tenant Act 1927 1.29
The Landlord and Tenant Act 1927 Part I contains important access to compensation for improvements for business tenants. By section 17 of the 1927 Act[19] agricultural holdings within the Agricultural Holdings Act 1986 and farm business tenancies are both treated in the same way and are both excluded from access to the compensation rights within Part I. This exclusion is, of course, because each of the agricultural codes has its own mandatory compensation scheme.[20] Section 18 of the 1927 Act[21] applies to tenancies protected by the

---

[16] See the Schedule to the 1995 Act, para. 1.
[17] Amendment by the Schedule, para. 3 to the 1995 Act to s. 3(7) of the 1922 Act.
[18] para. 4 of the 1995 Act.
[19] As amended by the Schedule, para. 5 to the 1995 Act.
[20] See in relation to the 1995 Act, Chapter 5, and in relation to the 1986 Act, Chapter 13.
[21] s.18 (1) Damages for a breach of a covenant or agreement to keep or put premises in repair during the currency of a lease, or to leave or put premises in repair at the termination of a lease, whether such covenant or agreement is expressed or implied, and whether general or specific, shall in no case exceed the amount (if any) by which the value of the reversion (whether immediate or not) in the premises is diminished owing to the breach of such covenant or agreement as aforesaid, and in particular no damage shall be recovered for a breach of any such covenant or agreement to leave or put premises in repair at the termination of a lease, if it is shown that the premises, in whatever state of repair they might be, would at or shortly after the termination of the tenancy have been or be pulled down, or such structural alterations made therein as would render valueless the repairs

Agricultural Holdings Act 1986 and also to farm business tenancies. Probably the importance to 1986 Act tenancies is relatively small because of the large variety of express statutory enforcement procedures relative to the doing of works and failure to repair.[22] It may be that section 18 will prove more important to farm business tenancies and attention is drawn to the body of learning under this section.[23] Section 19 of the 1927 Act deals with a variety of covenants deemed to be included in leases. Section 19(1), in the case of a covenant prohibiting assignment, etc. without licence or consent, deems the covenant to be subject to the qualification that such licence or consent is not to be unreasonably withheld; section 19(2), in the case of a covenant against the making of improvements without licence or consent, deems that covenant to be subject to a proviso that such licence or consent is not to be unreasonably withheld; section 19(3), in a case where a lease contains a covenant against alterations in the user of the demised premises without licence or consent, deems (where the alteration does not involve any structural alteration) the covenant to be subject to a proviso that no fine or sum of money in the nature of a fine (including by way of increase of the rent) is to be payable for such licence or consent. There is a saving for the landlord requiring payment of a reasonable sum for diminution of the value of the premises belonging to him and legal, etc., expenses. By section 19(4)[24] the terms of section 19 do not apply either to holdings protected by the Agricultural Holdings Act 1986 or to farm business tenancies. For reasons connected with the desire to retain the opportunity to serve a notice on the

---

covered by the covenant or agreement.

(2) A right of re-entry or forfeiture for a breach of any such covenant or agreement as aforesaid shall not be enforceable, by action or otherwise, unless the lessor proves that the fact that such a notice as is required by section 146 of the Law of Property Act, 1925, has been served on the lessee was known either –

(a) to the lessee; or

(b) to an under-lessee holding under an under-lease which reserved a nominal reversion only to the lessee; or

(c) to the person who last paid the rent due under the lease either on his own behalf or as agent for the lessee or under-lessee,

and that a time reasonably sufficient to enable the repairs to be executed had elapsed since the time when the fact of the service of the notice came to the knowledge of any such person.

Where a notice has been sent by registered post addressed to a person at his last known place of abode in the United Kingdom, then, for the purposes of this subsection, that person shall be deemed, unless the contrary is proved, to have had knowledge of the fact that the notice had been served as from the time at which the letter would have been delivered in the ordinary course of post.

This subsection shall be construed as one with section 146 of the Law of Property Act, 1925.

(3) This section applies whether the lease was created before or after the commencement of the Act.

[22] See for example procedures under Case D discussed in Chapter 12 below.
[23] See further *Woodfall, Landlord and Tenant* Vol. 1, para. 13.082.
[24] As amended by the Schedule, para. 6 of the 1995 Act.

tenant's death[25] qualified covenants on assignment of holdings protected by the 1986 Act are extremely rare. If they are found in the form which requires landlord's consent to an assignment or underletting[26] the landlord may, if he wishes, unreasonably or for no reason, withhold his consent. The position in regard to farm business tenancies is likely to be more complex. It is, of course, the case that the landlord may have an absolute bar on assignment.[27] If in a farm business tenancy there is a covenant not to assign, etc. without the landlord's consent, there is no statutory implication that this consent will not unreasonably be withheld. However, if, as a matter of contract,[28] there is an express provision that the tenant shall not assign without the landlord's consent, such consent not to be unreasonably withheld, then there will arise an obligation on the landlord's part to comply with the Landlord and Tenant Act 1988. In the case of a breach of duty by the landlord he will be liable for damages under section 4 of the 1988 Act. As to the making of improvements, in the case of a farm business tenancy the reader is referred to Chapter 5 below.[29]

The Agricultural Credits Act 1928 1.30

This statute authorises farmers, in favour of certain lending bodies, to create floating charges over farming stock and statutory compensation/tenant right. Section 5(7) authorised such a charge over a tenant's right to compensation under the Agricultural Holdings Act 1986, and this is now extended to the compensation available to a farm business tenant under section 16 of the 1995 Act.[30]

The Leasehold Property (Repairs) Act 1938 1.31

The 1938 Act applies, in the case of certain leases with at least three years or more of the term unexpired, to require a landlord forfeiting for breach of a repairing covenant to include prescribed information and also requires that landlord to secure the leave of the Court for enforcement of the forfeiture. The 1938 Act does not apply to leases within the Agricultural Holdings Act 1986; nor does it apply to farm business tenancies.[31] The removal of this particular hurdle to landlords does not, of course, guarantee possession when forfeiture proceedings are taken in view of the courts' general jurisdiction to grant relief from forfeiture.

The Reserve and Auxiliary Forces Protection of Civil Interests Act 1951 1.32

Section 27(1) has been amended to assimilate the position of a farm business tenancy to that of an agricultural holding protected by the Agricultural Holdings Act 1986.[32]

---

[25] An incontestable Case G notice to quit, as to which Chapter 12 below.
[26] For example because they have been inserted under arbitration in accordance with Sched. 6 to the 1986 Act in the terms of Sched. 1, para. 9 of that Act.
[27] But of course this will be likely to depress the rent.
[28] And it is increasingly likely that commercially tenants will negotiate this.
[29] Compensation on termination.
[30] Schedule, para. 7 of the 1995 Act.
[31] Schedule, para. 8 of the 1995 Act.
[32] Schedule, para. 9 of the 1995 Act. As to the 1986 Act see further para. 12.92 below.

CREATION AND MEANING OF FARM BUSINESS TENANCY

1.33 The Landlord and Tenant Act 1954
Amendments to the Landlord and Tenant Act 1954 are contained within the Schedule paragraph 10 of the 1995 Act. The general relationship between farm business tenancies and business tenancies protected by the 1954 Act has been discussed already.[33]

1.34 The Opencast Coal Act 1958
Extensive amendments to the Opencast Coal Act 1958 are contained within the Schedule at paragraphs 13–20 of the 1995 Act.

1.35 Leasehold Reform Act 1967
Neither an agricultural holding protected by the Agricultural Holdings Act 1986 nor a farm business tenancy is capable of enfranchisement.[34]

1.36 The Rent Act 1977
Section 10 of the Rent Act 1977[35] excludes the protection of the Rent Act for both farm business tenancies and tenancies protected by the Agricultural Holdings Act 1986 where the dwelling-house is occupied by the person responsible for the control of the farming of the holding (whether as tenant or as servant or agent of the tenant). The position of tenancies under the 1986 Act and 1995 Acts is generally for the purposes of the 1977 Act assimilated.[36]

1.37 The Housing Acts 1985 and 1988
A farm business tenancy and a tenancy protected by the Agricultural Holdings Act 1986 are precluded from being a secure tenancy.[37] Tenancies within the 1986 Act or the 1995 Act are incapable of being assured tenancies under the Housing Act 1988.[38]

1.38 Exclusion of repairing obligations contained in section 11 of the Landlord and Tenant Act 1985
The repairing obligations implied by statute in the terms of section 11 of the Landlord and Tenant Act 1985 do not apply to tenancies protected by the Agricultural Holdings Act 1986 or to farm business tenancies.[39] This is an important exclusion and it is perhaps surprising that farm business tenancies have been assimilated to agricultural holdings protected by the 1986 Act in view of the terms incorporated by section 7[40] of the 1986 Act. That section has no equivalent in relation to farm business tenancies.

---

[33] See para. 1.5 above.
[34] s. 1(3) of the Leasehold Reform Act 1967 as amended by the Schedule, para. 22 of the 1995 Act.
[35] As amended by the Schedule, para. 27 of the 1995 Act.
[36] See the Schedule, paras 27–28 of the 1995 Act.
[37] s. 8 of the Housing Act 1985 as amended by the Schedule, para. 30 of the 1995 Act.
[38] See Sched. 1 to the 1988 Act as amended by the Schedule at para. 34 of the 1995 Act.
[39] See amendments to s. 14(3) of the 1985 Act by the Schedule, para. 31 of the 1995 Act.
[40] See generally paras 10.8–10.29 below.

Landlord and Tenant Act 1988 1.39
The terms of this statute operate where a covenant as to assigning underletting etc. is qualified as being subject to landlord's consent such consent not to be unreasonably withheld. Although such a covenant is not implied by statute in the case of a farm business tenancy,[41] contractual inclusion of a covenant in those terms will bring into play the 1988 statute.[42]

Landlord and Tenant (Covenants) Act 1995 1.40
This statute deals with the transmission and enforcement of covenants in particular following assignment. Sections 3–16 and 21 apply[43] only to what are described as "new" tenancies.[44] All farm business tenancies entered into on or after January 1, 1996 will be regarded as "new" tenancies. Sections 17–20 of the Landlord and Tenant (Covenants) Act 1995 (restrictions on the liability of former tenants/guarantors and rights to overriding leases) apply to both new and other tenancies. There are no special exemptions for the Agricultural Holdings Act 1986 or for farm business tenancies. The rights and liabilities created by this statute are the subject of considerable specialist learning.[45]

Other statutes 1.41
The Schedule to the 1995 Act also makes amendments to the following:

(i) section 22 of the Agriculture (Miscellaneous Provisions) Act 1963 (allowances to persons displaced from agricultural land)[46]

(ii) section 12 of the Agriculture (Miscellaneous Provisions) Act 1968 (additional payments in consequence of compulsory acquisition, etc., of agricultural holdings)[47]

(iii) section 48 of the Land Compensation Act 1973 (compensation in respect of agricultural holdings)[48]

(iv) section 9 and Schedule 2 of the Rent (Agriculture) Act 1976[49]

(v) section 8(1) of the Protection from Eviction Act 1977[50]

---

[41] See para. 1.29 above.
[42] Printed in full in *Woodfall, Landlord and Tenant*, Vol. 1, Appendices.
[43] s. 1 of the Landlord and Tenant (Covenants) Act 1995.
[44] By s. 1(3) tenancies granted on or after the date on which that Act comes into force otherwise than in pursuance of an agreement entered into before that date or an order of court made before that date. Readers are referred to the full terms of s. 1(3). The Act binds the Crown (s. 29) and the entire Act came into force on January 1, 1996 (s. 31 of that Act brought into force by the Landlord and Tenant (Covenants) Act 1995 (Commencement) Order 1995/2963).
[45] See Fancourt, *Enforceability of Landlord and Tenant Covenants*, (1st ed., Sweet & Maxwell, 1997).
[46] Schedule, para. 21 of the 1995 Act.
[47] Schedule, para. 23 of the 1995 Act.
[48] Schedule, para. 24 of the 1995 Act.
[49] Schedule, paras 25 and 26 of the 1995 Act.
[50] Schedule, para. 29 of the 1995 Act.

(vi) section 65 of the Town and Country Planning Act 1990[51]

(vii) section 21 and Schedule 3 of the Coal Mining Subsidence Act 1991.[52]

1.42 Application to Crown land
The Agricultural Tenancies Act 1995 applies to all Crown land in the same way as it would to any other land.[53] For these purposes this includes land forming part of the Crown Estate, land held by government departments and land within the Duchies of Lancaster and Cornwall. Section 37 contains as necessary certain compensation and management provisions.

1.43 Length of term
There is no statutory minimum for a farm business tenancy. Parties are free to choose either a periodic form or a fixed term form for their tenancy. However there is no relaxation of the usual formalities associated with the creation of leases by deed, the only relaxation provided for by the 1995 Act being the ability of valuers and surveyors to create a farm business tenancy.[54] Note should be taken of the fact that the creation of a term of years determinable with the tenant's life operates in law as the grant of a fixed term of 90 years determinable after the original tenant's death or marriage.[55] The choice as to what length of term to make is essentially a commercial matter for the proposed landlord and tenant to fix, each bearing in mind their own commercial objectives. Because there is effectively now no long term security of tenure for periodic interests, it is really only with the grant of substantial fixed terms that any complex drafting is likely to be required. The inadvertent creation of a periodic tenancy arising by entry by the negotiating tenant coupled with payment of money is a distinct possibility. Although historically the assessment of such a situation has always been the same, namely a matter of legal inference arising from the facts and the actual or presumed intention of the parties, there is some indication that the willingness of the Courts to infer a periodic tenancy is diminishing.[56] The essential question as to what may be inferred as the intention of the parties[57] is one which can only be resolved as a matter of contemporaneous evidence. The best advice must be not to allow any negotiating would-be tenant into possession and certainly not to accept money from such a person if no risk of rights being created is to be run. It is, regrettably, notorious that negotiations never proceed as quickly as parties might wish but the farming season requires attention in any case. Consequently farming arrangements are more prone than other types of arrangement to informal entry and uncertainty in the interim

---

[51] Schedule, para. 35 of the 1995 Act.
[52] Schedule, paras 36 and 37 of the 1995 Act.
[53] s. 37.
[54] See para. 1.24.
[55] See s. 149(6) of the Law of Property Act 1925.
[56] Contrast **Hollington Brothers v. Rhodes** [1951] W.N. 437, [1951] 2 T.L.R. 691 and **Leveson v. Parfum Marcel Rochas** [1966] 200 E.G. 407 where negotiations for the grant of fixed terms were never concluded but in the interim occupation was taken and annual rent paid, as a result of which annual periodic tenancies were inferred. See however now **Javad v. Aqil** [1991] 1 All E.R. 243 and in particular Nicholls L.J. at 248.
[57] The classic question being as posed in **Clarke v. Grant** [1950] 1 K.B. 104.

pending negotiations as to what if any interest might be inferred. In circumstances where it cannot be avoided that occupation will be taken it is extremely important that contemporaneous documentation of some sort is entered into which will establish what the parties intended at the time. This is particularly the case where money is to change hands. Practitioners will also be familiar with the phenomenon whereby consideration may be given by an occupier in a non-monetary form, for example the doing of reclamation or other physical works.[58]

If it is contemplated that the occupier will do something on the land which may be construed as consideration, although this also forms part of the occupier's business activities, this is something which again ought to be documented prior to entry being permitted.[59] Terms of two years or less expire without the need for service of any notice and accordingly a short term is a suitable vehicle for, for example, a grazing arrangement.[60] For long term leases it is anticipated that considerable care will be given to the drafting of the essential terms such as user, assignment and the making of alterations. Care should be taken to ensure that no confusion is caused by "backdating" the term.[61]

Implied covenants 1.44

It is likely that the need to imply covenants will arise only in relation to periodic agreements and fixed terms orally created. It is to be hoped that all written leases nowadays would displace the need to rely on the so-called "usual" covenants.[62] In this context it should be noted that the terms which will be implied in relation to a yearly tenancy may be very different from those which will be implied in relation to a fixed term lease. Furthermore, implied covenants will not be inferred if the subject matter is already the subject of an express covenant.[63] Courts are reluctant to imply covenants at all or to import an obligation which did not arise by necessary implication from the parties' own chosen language.[64] Statute will occasionally intervene to impose obligations on parties, although such intervention is very limited in relation to farm business tenancies.[65] A tenancy or lease will always

---

[58] *Mitton v. Farrow* [1980] 255 E.G. 449.

[59] There is a compounding danger here that the occupier may at some point assert a proprietary estoppel. Such an estoppel may or may not take the form of asserting a claim to a fixed term tenancy, the terms of which should be settled by the court.

[60] In such a case the only added complexity is whether or not it is intended that the short lease will carry milk quota consequences: see Chapter 18 below.

[61] The actual term will run from the date the tenancy is entered into, assuming that the tenant has possession: *Keen v. Holland* [1984] 1 W.L.R. 251. Other obligations may be referable to the expressed commencement date for the internal convenience of the lease and the parties' mutual obligations: see *Roberts v. Church Commissioners for England* [1972] 1 Q.B. 278; *Bradshaw v. Pawley* [1980] 1 W.L.R. 10; *Pahl v. Trevor* [1992] 1 E.G.L.R. 22. As to the beginning of a farm business tenancy, see para. 1.6 above.

[62] See the next paragraph.

[63] *e.g.* the implied covenant for quiet enjoyment is displaced by an express covenant in relation to that subject matter: *Miller v. Emcer Products* [1956] Ch. 304.

[64] See Lewison, *The Interpretation of Contracts*. This reluctance is of some antiquity: *Smith v. Harwich* [1857] 2 C.B. (N.S.) 651. The reluctance is all the greater where the parties already have a detailed contract dealing with other matters: *Duke of Westminster v. Guild* [1985] Q.B. 688 and *Gordon v. Selico* [1986] 1 E.G.L.R. 71.

[65] See paras 1.27–1.41 above.

imply a covenant for quiet enjoyment arising from the relationship of landlord or tenant.[66] The implied covenant protects the tenant against lawful entry, but not against unlawful entry for which his remedy lies in tort.[67] The content of the implied covenant is as to part a covenant as to the landlord's title and as to part a covenant for the quiet enjoyment of the demised premises. Purporting to let property at a time when the landlord does not have possession will breach the first part of the implied covenant. It includes an implied covenant that the landlord has the power to grant the lease in question[68] but does not go so far as to require the landlord to prove his title by delivery of documents.[69] Whereas the implied covenant for quiet enjoyment offers the tenant a remedy if the landlord purports to authorise others to interfere with the tenant's possession, the law will also imply into all tenancy agreements an additional covenant by the landlord not to derogate from his grant. This is a covenant which protects the tenant where the landlord acts so as to frustrate the purpose for which the land was let.[70] The covenant protects not only the use of property but the enjoyment of easements which were granted to the tenant either expressly or by virtue of section 62 of the Law of Property Act 1925.[71] The principle would, for example, stop the landlord from authorising others to act in such a way as to frustrate the purpose of the letting.[72] It has been used to establish a valid complaint that a landlord erected buildings in such a way as to prevent the ingress of air into the tenant's drying sheds.[73] Finally, there is an implied covenant by the tenant not to derogate from the reservations of the landlord.[74] The principal obligations imposed by implication are those contained in the Landlord and Tenant (Covenants) Act 1995.[75] All other covenants, if implied, will only be implied where necessary to give business efficacy to what has been expressly agreed.[76]

---

[66] ***Budd-Scott v. Daniell*** [1902] 2 K.B. 351, ***Kenny v. Preen*** [1963] 1 Q.B. 499. This covenant applies even to oral tenancies and is unaffected by the form of letting.
[67] See the ancient cases cited in *Woodfall, Landlord and Tenant*, Vol. I, para. 11.267 and following.
[68] ***Stranks v. St. John*** [1867] L.R. 376, ***Anthony v. Brecon Market Company*** [1867] L.R. 2 Ex. 167.
[69] Such an extension is not necessary and confers no extra protection on the tenant. The cause usually cited in support of this obvious proposition is ***Gwillim v. Stone*** [1811] 3 Taunt 433 but it appears to represent trite law.
[70] See ***Molton Builders v. City of Westminster*** [1975] 30 P.&C.R. 182; ***Johnston & Sons v. Holland*** [1988] 1 E.G.L.R. 264. Older cases are good illustrations of the principle: ***Birmingham Dudley & District Banking Co. v. Ross*** [1887] 38 Ch.D. 295, ***Lyttleton Times Company v. Warners*** [1907] A.C. 476 and ***Harmer v. Jumbil (Nigeria) Tin Areas*** [1921] 1 Ch. 200.
[71] See ***Johnson & Sons v. Holland*** (above) and other cases cited in *Woodfall, Landlord and Tenant*, Vol. I, para. 11.083 *et. seq.*
[72] ***Harmer v. Jumbil*** (above).
[73] ***Aldin v. Latimer Clark*** [1894] 2 Ch. 437.
[74] This would include rights of access and shooting. For an instance of this see ***Johnson v. Holland*** (above).
[75] See *Fancourt, Enforceability of Landlord and Tenant Covenants*, (1st ed., Sweet & Maxwell, 1997).
[76] This is a narrow formulation although how narrow may well vary over a period of time: see ***Liverpool City Council v. Irwin*** [1977] A.C. 239. The current trend appears towards the narrow direction: see ***Miller v. Lakefield Estates Limited*** [1989] 1 E.G.L.R., CA refusing, in an option, to imply the words "such price to be a reasonable price" or "such

Certain terms which have been alleged on an implied basis have been held, as a matter of law, to be repugnant to the nature of a yearly tenancy. These mainly relate to what terms are regarded as suitable for an implied yearly tenancy.[77] An agricultural tenant is subject to an implied obligation to use the land in a husband-like manner according to the custom of the country and to preserve buildings wind and watertight.[78] Finally the tenant is bound not to commit waste and, where the tenancy provides nothing express, the obligation arises in the form of a tort committed by the tenant, actionable by the landlord under the law of tort, not contract.[79]

The usual covenants 1.45

The "usual covenants" are of very limited interest and should not be confused with implied covenants generally. The "usual" covenants are those which will be implied into a contract where the parties themselves agree that a lease should be granted on the usual covenants and, in the alternative, where it has been decided by the Court that there is an agreement for a lease but the terms themselves have not been further identified. The latter must be rare indeed and it is suspected that the former is also relatively rare. For that reason it is not proposed to pursue the detail of such covenants.[80] The purpose of the "usual covenants" is really to save an identifiable agreement from being void for uncertainty. The content of the usual covenants is a question of fact, according to the better view.[81] What is included under the heading of a "usual" covenant is, rather straightforwardly, whatever happens to be usual in that particular type of lease and perhaps in the location in question: there is clearly a contrast with the strict and limited basis on which terms will be implied into contracts on the basis discussed in the preceding paragraph. A

---

price to be the market price" after "at a price to be agreed" (in itself a formulation incapable of enforcement), casting doubt on *Smith v. Morgan* [1971] 1 W.L.R. 803, Brightman J.

[77] Classically restrictions on termination by the landlord being restrictions as to the exercise of his right to serve notice to quit or break clauses operable dependant on public events. There is a considerable body of law, although one probably very infrequently consulted, on this: see *Woodfall, Landlord and Tenant*, Vol. I, paras 6.046–6.047.

[78] *Wedd v. Porters* [1916] 2 K.B. 91. These authors agree with the comment in *Farm Business Tenancies* by Sydenham & Mainwaring (Jordans, 1995), p. 39 that this is "not a very onerous requirement and somewhat vague". As a matter of fact, we might go further and suggest that in many instances it would be extremely difficult to imply content into such an obligation if one looked to an established custom of the country. Not only has custom almost disappeared in the traditional sense during the long period of protection by the agricultural holdings legislation but in addition to that farming practice has lost, in a significant way, any homogeneity. Routine features of farm budgeting such as planning land to go into set aside or entering into special management covenants for environmental reasons are impossible or at least extremely difficult to reconcile with any earlier notion of husband-like cultivation. Even the obligation to keep buildings wind and watertight may be subject to attack where the buildings are redundant (compare the 1973 Regulations governing agricultural holdings under the 1986 Act: para. 10.20 below).

[79] See *Mancetter Developments v. Garmanson* [1986] 1 All E.R. 449 and further para. 10.31 below.

[80] Such detail is available in *Woodfall, Landlord and Tenant*, Vol. I, para. 4.029 *et seq.*

[81] See *Woodfall, op. cit.*, para. 4.030 and in particular n. 47.

very few covenants appear to be universally regarded as "usual", for example the covenant to pay rent[82] and the covenant by the tenant to pay taxes excluding only those which are usually payable by the landlord.[83] It is assumed that covenants implied by law will normally be regarded as "usual" covenants. Beyond this it is submitted that the content of "usual" covenants must be proved and such content may vary considerably according to what is normal at any particular time.[84] Although a covenant to repair is regarded as "usual", such covenants nowadays take many forms and the content of such a covenant will be the subject of evidence. Covenants against making alterations or stopping up windows have also been regarded, in particular circumstances, as "usual",[85] although it is questionable whether either would necessarily be applicable to a farm. Restrictions on use and on assignment or underletting appear particularly difficult to assert in this context. Even a proviso for re-entry will take its colour from normal practice. Although historically limited to re-entry for non-payment of rent, re-entry for breach of other covenants is probably now usual.[86] A proviso for re-entry on the tenant's insolvency is more contentious.[87] Lastly, and perhaps more daringly, it is suggested that the inclusion of a rent review clause is likely nowadays to be a "usual" provision for a fixed term lease of any significant length.[88]

---

[82] *Hampshire v. Wickens* [1877] 7 Ch.D. 55.

[83] *Hampshire v. Wickens* (above).

[84] For example the contrast in even so basic a matter as a covenant against nuisance which in the 1930s was not regarded as usual (*Flexman v. Corbett* [1930] 1 Ch. 672) but was so regarded by 1971 (*Chester v. Buckingham Travel* [1981] 1 W.L.R. 96), a contrast pointed out in *Woodfall* at paragraph 4.038.

[85] *Chester v. Buckingham Travel* (above).

[86] *Chester v. Buckingham Travel* (above).

[87] Although refused in a number of cases including in a 19th century lease of farm land and despite the opinion of the learned editor of *Woodfall*, Vol. I, para. 4.043, it may be possible in connection with a farm business tenancy to establish, where a non-farming enterprise is intended, that similar businesses would normally contain provisions for re-entry on the insolvency of the tenant and perhaps some comfort can be drawn from the ability of the landlord under the Agricultural Holdings Act 1986 to serve an incontestable notice to quit on the tenant's insolvency. Although the latter does not directly impact on what parties may choose to do, it indirectly establishes the opportunity of a landlord to retake possession in such a way as to show what Parliament regarded as his essential interests: it is submitted that the statutory framework, in substance much stronger than, although consistent with, commercial conveyancing, should not be ignored when considering what the reasonable expectation would be as to a "usual" covenant. The likely problem in implementing this concept as regards farm business tenancies is simply the novelty of the statute and accordingly it is submitted that the search for relevant materials may legitimately at any rate for the time being be widened.

[88] The overwhelming commercial application of this type of provision is everywhere visible— in normal commercial conveyancing relating to businesses, embedded in the Landlord and Tenant Act 1954 and the practice of the Court in granting renewals; in the mandatory provisions of the Agricultural Holdings Acts 1948–1986; in the terms of Part II of the Agricultural Tenancies Act 1995. The grant of a lease on "arm's length commercial terms" (perhaps the modern language for "the usual covenants") includes a rent review clause, but not an upwards only one: *United Bank of Kuwait v. Sahib* [1996] 3 W.L.R. 372. It is therefore suggested that, in the context of a farm business tenancy "the usual covenants" would authorise the inclusion of a rent review provision, in all probability following the statutory form.

Relative freedom of contract 1.46

Since the scope for use of the "usual covenants" is so very limited and since the content of implied obligations is likely to be restricted, the application of the 1995 Act allows very considerable scope for the parties to contract as they wish. Subject to limited statutory intervention from other codes[89] parties may make such provision as they choose. If they make no provision, it is at their own risk. Specifically it is worthwhile noting the following areas where contractual agreement is essential:

  (i)   break clauses;

  (ii) repairs;

  (iii) assignment, etc.;

  (iv) user;

  (v)   forfeiture.

With the single exception of break clauses (regulated as to length of termination notice) and subject to extremely limited interference from other statutory codes, all of the above matters are entirely such as the parties may choose to agree. A break clause of the correct length[90] can be operable, if the parties choose, on any ground desired.[91] There is almost infinite variety as to the way in which parties may choose to draft and share or dispose of repairing responsibilities and no doubt they would do so bearing in mind the likely impact on any rent review. There is nothing comparable to the 1973 Regulations[92] in relation to tenancies protected by the Agricultural Holdings Act 1986 and although it is possible as a matter of contract to import the substantive content of covenants, it is suggested that great care be given in the drafting of any "importation", in particular taking care that matters such as obsolete buildings are dealt with by writing in, where necessary, valid arbitration clauses. Without express contractual provision there is no restriction on the tenant's ability to assign or sub-let and/or franchise out parts of the property. There is limited statutory interference, depending on the contractual terms chosen to express a qualified covenant[93] but the matter is generally one for contract. The lawful use of land is also as the parties wish and there is a large body of case law as to how particular variants of covenant should be construed or applied, particularly

---

[89] See paras 1.27–1.41 above.
[90] See para. 4.8 below.
[91] Although it is usual that such a ground would be a purpose rather than simply breach by the tenant of all or any of the tenancy clauses. The latter would probably amount, as a matter of drafting, to a forfeiture clause which would then only be exercisable on service of a notice under s. 146 of the Law of Property Act 1925.
[92] See paras 10.8–10.25 below.
[93] See para. 1.29 above.

where reasonableness is relevant.[94] Forfeiture clauses must be agreed and are not implied. There are a few special provisions in section 146 of the Law of Property Act 1925 relating to agricultural leases.[95] Section 147 of the same statute may restrict the landlord where he intends to forfeit for internal decorative disrepair to a house or other building, but in general terms the restrictions experienced by business tenants in the operation of section 146 are not applicable.[96] It is not considered necessary that a proviso for re-entry should be exercisable only on service of prior warning because there is no requirement in the 1995 Act for the tenant to serve notice in advance of termination of the tenancy in order to claim his compensation[97]: such drafting was necessary under the Agricultural Holdings Act 1986.[98]

1.47 Supplementary compensation provisions

Part III of the Act contains a mandatory code governing compensation to the tenant for specified types of improvement.[99] However the terms of Part III leave entirely unregulated a considerable range of matters which may be relevant, depending on the type of farming and the tenancy clauses. Thus when drafting a farm business tenancy it will be prudent to enquire of the tenant what type of enterprises will be carried out on the holding and in particular what types of investment he intends to make. Certain types of investment, previously regulated by the compensation provisions of the Agricultural Holding Acts 1986 are no longer included within Part III. Furthermore, if sub-letting or assignment is a possibility it will be necessary by contract to make provision for compensation in that event. In Chapter 5 there is a list of suggested matters to be considered in respect of which the tenant may find it desirable to insert contractual compensation provisions in the absence of any in the statute.[1]

---

[94] See *Woodfall, Landlord and Tenant* Vol. I, paras 11.113–11.177.
[95] By s. 146(9)(a) and (b) the section is not applicable to exercise of a right of re-entry on bankruptcy of the tenant where contained in a lease of agricultural or pastoral land or in a lease of mines or minerals.
[96] See the disapplication of the Leasehold Property (Repairs) Act 1938 and para. 1.31 above.
[97] These authors agree with the view expressed in Sydenham & Mainwaring, *Farm Business Tenancies*, (above) p. 44 that the tenant's right to remove fixtures under the 1995 Act corresponds, in terms of the timing of the exercise of any right, to that available at common law (*i.e.* fixtures must be removed on or prior to termination of the tenancy: **Pugh v. Arton** [1869] L.R. 8 Eq.626) and despite this the general law does not impose on forfeiture clauses the need for prior service of notice. Therefore it is considered that the tenant's statutory rights to take fixtures does not affect the drafting of a proper re-entry clause. A similar view is expressed, though perhaps less confidently, in Scammell & Densham, *Law of Agricultural Holdings* (8th ed.), p. 982.
[98] See the problem illustrated by **Parry v. Million Pigs Limited** [1980] 260 E.G. 281 discussed at para. 13.2 below.
[99] See generally Chapter 5 below.
[1] See para. 5.3 below.

Tailoring a dispute resolution provision 1.48

Where the 1995 Act allows or requires the parties to have an arbitration under the Arbitration Act 1996[2] some thought should be given as to how these particular parties wish the arbitration to be run. There are many matters which the 1996 Act deals with on a fallback footing: it is perhaps appropriate to remind draftsman of arbitration provisions to consider taking advantage of their contractual freedom.[3]

---

[2] See generally Chapter 16 below.
[3] See for the limited compulsory element under the 1996 Act the list in Sched. 1, printed in Part VII of this work.

CHAPTER 2

RENT REVIEW

2.1 Rent review: general

2.5 Exemptions from statutory rent review

2.9 Initial rent

2.10 Enforceable contractual timetable for statutory rent review

2.11 Scope for contractual rent review

2.12 Implementing a statutory rent review: procedures

2.15 Basis of valuation under section 13

2.25 Evidence in relation to rent reviews

Rent review: general 2.1

Rent review under a farm business tenancy is dealt with in the terms of Part II of the Agricultural Tenancies Act 1995. The scheme contained within that Part is a curious compromise between on the one hand imposing a mandatory statutory rent review scheme and, on the other, allowing the parties a measure of freedom in which to contract. Critics may disagree as to whether or not the balance is struck correctly but the overall effect is to direct attention more to the statutory scheme than away from it. Apart from the specific exemptions or disapplications provided for by statute[1] Part II and the rent review provided by it will apply "notwithstanding any agreement to the contrary".[2] The machinery of review is triggered by the service of a "statutory review notice"[3] which, failing appointment of an expert, will give rise to an arbitration[4] based on the statutory criteria.[5] Special provisions to ascertain the review date apply where there is a new tenancy of a severed part of the reversion.[6] The timing of a statutory rent review is something the parties may decide for themselves[7] but where a statutory review applies, it applies in its totality subject to one exception only. That exception is where the parties, after a statutory rent review has been triggered, then agree the appointment of an expert to

---

[1] See paras 2.5–2.11 below.
[2] s. 9.
[3] s. 10 and see para. 2.13 below.
[4] See s. 12 and para. 2.14 below.
[5] s. 13 and paras 2.15–2.24 below.
[6] s. 11 and see para. 2.13 below.
[7] s. 10(4) and (5) and see para. 2.13 below.

determine what the rent shall be on a basis which the parties have also agreed.[8] Perhaps because of the way in which the statute itself is drafted, farm business tenancy rent review provisions of the type familiar in commercial lettings generally (*i.e.* involving a formula with assessment requiring skill) appear so far to be relatively uncommon. The statute effectively buries the possibility of a "normal" commercial rent review clause by denying its availability until after a statutory review notice has been given and referring only obliquely to it by the words "on a basis agreed by the parties" in section 12(b).

2.2 Fine or premium

There is nothing in relation to farm business tenancies which prohibits the taking of a capital sum by way of fine or premium. Such payments may be made for the granting of the lease[9] whether or not the payment is staged over a period of time in instalments.[10] Sometimes the fine or premium will have been calculated as it was on the basis that the rent was below market rent[11]: perhaps this possibility is linked to the exemption from statutory rent review for leases which stipulate there is to be no rent review[12] or provide in advance the amount of any change to the rent.[13] However practitioners will be aware that labelling does not establish the character of a payment[14] and for that reason care must be taken to ensure that there is no risk of mislabelling or confusion as between staged premium payments and the reservation of true rent. It is also worth noting at this point that only some (not all) of the limited provisions prohibiting the taking of a fine or premium in the context of a normal commercial tenancy apply to farm business tenancies. Only section 18 of the Landlord and Tenant Act 1927 applies to a farm business tenancy and section 19 does not.[15] Specifically section 19(3) does not apply so as to prevent the taking of a premium where the landlord agrees to a change in the user of the property in circumstances where there is a prohibition as to changing the user without his licence or consent.[16]

2.3 Different rents for different parts of the holding

It is of the essence of many farm business tenancies that, whilst agricultural activities may be important, diversification is contemplated and realised.[17] One result of this is that parties may at the outset intend not only that different activities should be permitted on the holding but may even go so far as to identify the location of such activities. The statutory rent review may pose a threat to many leases drafted on the footing that some enterprises will be subject to one type of rent review whereas others may be subject to a different type of rent review or even

---

[8] See s. 12(b) and para. 2.11 below.
[9] See *Hill v. Booth* [1930] 1 K.B. 381.
[10] *Regor Estates v. Wright* [1951] 1 K.B. 689.
[11] *King v. Earl Cadogan* [1915] 3 K.B. 485.
[12] s. 9(a).
[13] s. 9(b)(i).
[14] *Samuel v. Salmon and Gluckstein* [1946] Ch. 8.
[15] See para. 1.29 above.
[16] See also the provisions as to compensation on termination in regard to contemplated changes of use.
[17] See para. 1.29 above.

to no rent review. This is a problem simply not contemplated by Part II of the 1995 Act. Section 9 refers to "the rent"; section 10 refers to "rent to be payable in respect of the holding". The wording of section 10 and in particular the definition of "holding"[18] suggest that a statutory rent review must be in respect of the entire holding, including non-agricultural elements.[19] There is a distinction, although established only by ancient and not ideally reported cases, between a rent reserved as an entire sum but assuming a demise of several different parcels or activities in the same lease on the one hand and, on the other hand, a reservation of rent which is several and severally apportioned to areas demised.[20] This raises the possibility that, for example where section 9 exempts "rent" stated to be reviewed on a particular footing[21] that footing may withstand or be incorporated into any general review of other parts of the demise under the statutory provisions.[22] Whilst this possibility survives, it cannot be said with any real confidence that differently reserved rents within the same overall lease will be treated according to the lease when the statutory review is available. Where parties in fact wish to deal with different enterprises or areas by using completely different rent formulae then it is suggested that the prudent course is to separate the areas for each activity, examine each separately so as to decide which statutory code may be applicable and, if it is desired that a straightforward commercial activity should not be protected by the Landlord and Tenant Act 1954, to seek an order of the Court under section 38 of that Act exempting a lease from that code. Other parts of the property might then fall under the Agricultural Tenancies Act 1995 but would be let separately.[23]

Notice to quit or break clause following rent review 2.4

Nothing in the statute prevents a landlord or a tenant from terminating a lease in circumstances where that party has the contractual opportunity to do so. In

---

[18] "'Holding', in relation to a farm business tenancy, means the aggregate of the land comprised in the tenancy": s. 38(1).

[19] Although the arbitrator is entitled under s. 13(2) to have regard to all relevant factors including tenancy terms he is directed to disregard the criteria by reference to which the parties may have expressed new rents to be determined.

[20] The difference is expressed in *Woodfall, Landlord and Tenant*, Volume 1, para. 7.034 as follows: "For instance, if a lease is made of several houses, rendering the annual rent of £5,000, *viz.* for one house £3,000, for another £1,500, and £500 for a third house, with a clause of re-entry into all the houses for non-payment of any parcel of the rent; this is but one reservation of one entire rent, and the '*viz.*' afterwards does not alter the nature of the reservation, but only declares the value of each house. But if the lease had been of three houses, rendering for one house £3,000, for another £1,500, and for the third £500, with a condition to re-enter into all for the non-payment of any parcel; these are three several reservations and in the nature of three distinct demises; and each house in this case is only chargeable with its own rent".

[21] *e.g.* turnover rent.

[22] For example the situation might arise if part of the property were designated as a commercial enterprise or farm shop generating its own separate and separately reserved rent based on a turnover, with the remainder of the property being a farm with a statutory rent review in prospect.

[23] It is not suggested that matters can be safely dealt with by keeping one lease even where all elements of the rent fall into different parts of the exemptions within s. 9. This is because it is thought that on balance the exemptions are separate rather than cumulative: see para. 2.8 below.

particular a party dissatisfied with the outcome of a rent review, if he has the contractual right to terminate the tenancy, is perfectly entitled to exercise it. This state of affairs represents a clear policy decision in favour of allowing the landlord access to the vacant possession premium (subject to his contract) as against holding that landlord to a statutory rent review. It contrasts markedly with the evolution of protection afforded to tenancies within the Agricultural Holdings Act 1986 whereby[24] elaborate restrictions on the operation of notices to quit were imposed, thereby effectively binding a landlord to the rent as reviewed under the statute except in the most extreme circumstances.[25]

2.5 Exemption from statutory rent review: written agreements stipulating for no rent review

Where the tenancy is created by an instrument[26] expressly stating that the rent is not to be reviewed during the tenancy, the rent review provisions of Part II of the 1995 Act do not apply at all.[27] It has already been noted[28] that the taking of a fine or premium is not prohibited by the 1995 Act. Accordingly, and consistent with this lack of prohibition, a landlord who chooses to grant a lease with no rent reviews can be held to such a bargain. There are many commercial circumstances in which such an arrangement might be considered desirable: the obvious one is where the tenant intends to put significant capital investment of his own into the property in one form or another. The erection of new buildings is one possibility as is the development of some enterprise which requires heavy tenant's investment in an as yet unproven venture of a non-agricultural kind. Another situation would be where a listed or important building was in a condition of very serious disrepair which the tenant was willing to tackle and rectify during the course of the lease. In that situation it is perfectly possible that the tenant would not even be required to pay a fine or premium at the outset. This statutory exemption is one which must be embraced expressly and, it is submitted, it is not sufficient for parties simply to fail to say anything about a rent review, since otherwise the terms of section 10(6), initiating rent review on a fallback basis, will come into play so as to initiate a three-yearly rent review cycle. Secondly, it is clear that the statement as to the rent not being reviewed during the tenancy must appear in the instrument creating the tenancy and the likelihood is that subsequent variation of an original instrument will not satisfy section 9(a). This is because it is the time of creation of the tenancy which is important to establish the exemption which otherwise strikes down agreements to the contrary. Thirdly, although a fine or premium may be paid, in the absence of a rent review, and although the timing of the payment may be staged if necessary over a number of years, it is submitted that attempts to "inflate" or adjust the capital payment on the date of subsequent staged payments could easily result in the arrangement as a whole being regarded as one for the payment of a true rent.[29]

---

[24] Under the 1948 Act.
[25] See generally Chapter 12 below.
[26] *i.e.* a written tenancy agreement, not necessarily a deed.
[27] s. 9(a).
[28] See para. 2.2 above.
[29] See para. 2.2 above.

Exemption from statutory rent review: written agreements providing a timetable and stipulating the amount

2.6

Similarly exempt from the provisions of Part II rent review under the 1995 Act is any tenancy agreement created by an instrument[30] which stipulates that the rent is to be varied at a specified time or times during the tenancy by or to a specified amount but is otherwise to remain fixed.[31] The minimum variation within the terms of section 9(b)(i) is a single variation in the rent during the term by or to a specified amount. It is submitted that, unless this is contained within the tenancy agreement at the date of creation, there is no opportunity to rely in the section 9(b)(i) exemption. Conversely, however, provided there is at least one such alteration in the rent it would seem legitimate subsequently to vary the agreement to provide additional dates of variation.[32] This provision obviously allows the parties to organise one or more variations in the rental and to do so in such a way that the actual amount of the rent is stated. This would allow the creation of a programme of increasing rent identifiable from the outset. It obviously would allow identification of the amount in sterling whether the parties choose to identify the varied rent in terms of an exact figure or in terms of the stated sterling amount in addition to the current rent at the outset. It is unclear whether it is permissible to identify the varied rent by reference to a percentage of the current rent (this, of course, would allow the actual increase to be ascertainable at any time by simple mathematical calculation). It is unclear whether that type of wording would be allowable as a variation "by ... a specified amount" or whether a percentage should be regarded as a "specified formula" so as to fall within section 9(b)(ii). If the latter is the true case then a stipulated percentage increase would fall foul of the requirement in section 9(b)(ii) that a reduction in the rent should not be precluded. Stipulation by percentage increase would appear to have been omitted from consideration by the terms of section 9 and prudent advisers will accordingly avoid it, preferring to calculate the actual amount and fall clearly within section 9(b)(i) where that is intended. Since the statute provides no definition of "amount" or "formula", readers should perhaps consider standard dictionary definitions before attempting to draft these critical lease terms. The New Shorter Oxford English Dictionary, 1993 Edition, offers the following:

> "**amount**   The total to which anything amounts; the total quantity or number ... A quantity or sum viewed as the total reached."

> "**formula**   ... A general rule, principle, or relationship expressed in symbols, often as an equation ... In general scientific use, a group of symbols or figures condensing a set of facts."[33]

Perhaps the conundrum will only satisfactorily be resolved by litigation. If one looked at the problem from the opposite perspective and attempted to define what a

---

[30] *i.e.* a written agreement, not necessarily a deed.
[31] s. 9(b)(i).
[32] *i.e.* at all times it could be said that the tenancy was created by an instrument which provided for variation at a specified time.
[33] Meanings fairly obviously irrelevant have been omitted.

percentage was by use of the same dictionary, it may be possible to categorise it rather under "amount" than "formula". Thus:

> "**percentage** ... A rate or proportion per cent; a quantity or amount reckoned as so many hundredth parts of another, esp of the whole of which it is a part; a part considered in its quantitative relation to the whole, a proportion (of something) ..."

It is submitted that the use of the word "specified" in both section 9(b)(i) and (ii) throws no light on the problem raised by percentage rent increases. Other types of percentage calculation[34] cannot be ascertained at the grant of the lease and therefore have been classified under section 9(b)(ii).

Rent free periods are best accommodated, provided parties are able to ascertain at the outset the amount of rent desired throughout the term, by providing for a very nominal rental for a stipulated time and thereafter using section 9(b)(i) to provide a timetable for rent due for the remainder of the tenancy. Many commercial circumstances may dictate the usefulness of this particular choice including, as with section 9(a), the consideration of fairness to a tenant who intends to put in substantial investment of his own.

2.7 Exemption from statutory rent review: written agreements providing a timetable and stipulating a formula

The statutory rent review provisions in Part II of the 1995 Act do not apply where the tenancy is created by an instrument[35] which provides that the rent is to be varied at a specified time or times during the tenancy in accordance with a specified formula which does not preclude a reduction and which does not require or permit the exercise by any person of any judgment or discretion in relation to the determination of the rent of the holding, but otherwise is to remain fixed.[36] It is sufficient that there is at least one time for review specified by the tenancy agreement at the date of the creation of the tenancy.[37] The meaning of "formula" is suitably vague. A dictionary definition is provided above[38] and it is submitted that the following are included namely:

(i) rents linked to the turnover of a particular business, usually a business conducted on the property;

(ii) rents increased so as to reflect a profit percentage as at a particular time, the precise basis of the profit calculation being specified and objectively ascertainable;

(iii) rent expressed as a percentage of gross proceeds of sale of a particular crop;

---

[34] *e.g.* those in para. 2.7(ii)-(vi) below.
[35] *i.e.* a written agreement, not necessarily a deed.
[36] s. 9(b)(ii).
[37] If subsequently the tenancy agreement is varied so as to add other occasions falling within section 9(b)(ii) this would appear still to satisfy the strict wording.
[38] The preceding paragraph.

(iv) rent expressed as or linked to a percentage of sub-rents actually achieved (but not "achievable" since this involves the exercise of judgment[39]);

(v) rent which is index linked to an objectively ascertainable statistical measure such as published price indexes, inflation indexes, commodity prices or baskets of commodity prices;

(vi) rents which track the movement of sterling against other currencies including the ECU;

(vii) rents which track the minimum lending rate or the actual lending rate of a named institution as at a particular time.

Whichever measure is chosen must be "specified" and must be so specified at the outset when the tenancy is created by the instrument, *i.e.* it is not acceptable to stipulate that a third party at some future date (even by fallback) should nominate the particular formula. Any chosen formula must display two characteristics. The first is that it does not "preclude a reduction". Perhaps with some regret these authors conclude that this means only that the relevant formula might produce, at least in theory, a reduction in the rent. It is very doubtful whether English statutory construction should be regarded as being liberal enough to look into the historic performance of the chosen formula to see whether there was ever any real likelihood, armed with that information, that the parties could have contemplated an actual rent reduction occurring.[40] What is definitely disallowed is a formula which must be either upwards only or fluctuating on subsequent reviews but at all times guaranteeing as a minimum the initial rent. The second characteristic which the chosen formula must display is that it does not "require or permit the exercise by any person of any judgment or discretion in relation to the determination of the holding". This is designed to exclude the normal type of commercial rent review where very considerable judgment is exercised in fixing the rent, usually by an arbitrator or an expert in accordance with a contractual formula chosen by the parties. Sometimes provisions contained in complex "royalty" payment agreements will fall foul of this provision since there will be stipulations as to "fair" or "reasonable" amounts or percentages.

There is a clear conceptual distinction between matters which are capable of legal ascertainment and therefore valid because capable of being made certain on the one hand and, on the other, a specified formula within section 9(b)(ii). Persons drafting with the intention of falling within this sub-paragraph will have to scrutinise carefully the relevant wording to ensure that they are not drawn into the trap of thinking that that which is legally ascertainable will necessarily fall within the sub-paragraph. Further, care must be taken to ensure that in the application of

---

[39] Draftsmen should diligently study ***Ashworth Frazer Ltd v. Gloucester City Council*** [1997] 1 E.G.L.R. 104 where the CA divided over the use in context of the word "receivable".

[40] There is a contrast with the approach taken in European law, for example, in relation to Art. 119 of the Treaty of Rome regarding the principle that men and women should receive equal pay for equal work: covert discrimination may be found where job descriptions or categories are drawn deliberately in order to achieve the result that, for example, women receive less money for doing effectively the same job as men.

the formula itself there is no "hidden" element of the exercise of judgment: this is a particular problem where parties choose to link the rent to reflect a percentage of gross crop sale proceeds. It is only the price achieved, not the price achievable (which is a matter of judgment), which may be used. There may be some inconsistency in the statute barring for these purposes the exercise of judgment in the application of the specified formula when many very traditional formulae (*e.g.* retail price index or minimum lending rate) themselves are no more than the compilation of the result of the exercise of many individual judgments. The explanation, presumably, is that the more generalised published statistical information is so wide in its base as to be a true reflection of general economic conditions. Section 9(b)(ii) would allow the rent of a farm business tenancy to be linked to the increase or decrease of the rent on another identified rented farm since any judgment in fixing the rent of that farm is not a judgment exercised in relation to the farm business tenancy.[41] It should be pointed out that there is considerable commercial experience of indexed and particularly turnover linked rental arrangements and they are not arrangements necessarily embraced with enthusiasm in all sectors. Farm tenants should be cautious when considering them and landlords also should ascertain with care the long term effect of the indexation being contemplated. Often, for example, turnover rents are over-influenced by the personality or trade of the original tenant and fail to take account of the very different economics which might apply in the event of an assignment, the assignee running a less successful or a different type of business.[42] No landlord should consider a turnover rent without also considering his proposed assignment and user clauses. Further, when any individual assignment with change of user is being applied for, sufficient information should be requested so that a view can be taken as to what impact there will be on the rental.[43] Persons drafting turnover leases are advised to consider the American experience on this subject.[44] Finally it appears

---

[41] There are clearly possible problems with such a choice of rent formula ranging from the linkage itself influencing the rent levels on the farm targeted by the index to the possibility that the target farm may not remain in the rented sector throughout the entire duration of the farm business tenancy.

[42] The classic problem is one generated by a lease granted to a supermarket where, though margins are small, volume is enormous and the rental looks reasonable: a subsequent assignment to a low volume assignee in the same trade has a devastating effect on rental. Likewise leases which permit a change of use within a broad planning category may result in an original business structure being replaced by a totally different trading pattern and one which produces a very much lower rental.

[43] For drafting of turnover rental agreements it is sometimes helpful to stipulate what shall or shall not be regarded as reasonable in the context of landlord's refusal to allow a change of use. Under the Landlord and Tenant Act 1988, s. 1(5) withholding consent to assignment is only reasonable if completion of the transaction would put the tenant in breach of covenant, *e.g.* user. Quite apart from the statute, it does not follow as a matter of logic that a landlord is acting unreasonably if he refuses consent to a particular assignment only because it will involve a drop in the rent: it must be arguable that this was predictable from the outset and that rent levels are only one aspect of the assignment. This is precisely the sort of argument which landlords should not allow space for in their initial lease drafting.

[44] See, for example Milton R. Friedman, *Friedman on Leases*, (Practising Law Institute, New York City). Chapter 6 in the 2nd ed. (1983) deals extensively with the pitfalls of "percentage leases".

necessary to state the obvious, namely it is not possible to bring within section 9(b)(ii) a rent formula which is one which reflects in whole or in part the choice of the rent level that might have been determined in respect of the holding had the Agricultural Holdings Act 1986 applied to it. The rent formula under that Act clearly involves the exercise of judgment.

Are sections 9(a), (b)(i) and (ii) cumulatively available? 2.8

This is a difficult question and on balance it is concluded that they are not. What this means is that parties must choose which of these three exemptions they wish to apply to the tenancy and not attempt to combine elements of each. This conclusion is reached because, in order to decide the issue, the word "or" which appears in sub-sections 9(a) and (b) ought to be construed consistently. If one considers the content of each of the three options for compliance with section 9 it is apparent that each is a true alternative. Even within section 9(b) this is true, the more so if the possibility discussed[45] above is correct, that a percentage increase based on the initial rent would fail within section 9(b)(i). On this footing the word "or" is in each instance probably used disjunctively and therefore combinations of elements each of which falls within one of the alternatives is not a permissible cumulative position. The danger of inadvertently falling into this particular problem of construction arises where:

(i) there is a rent free period followed by an arrangement which falls somewhere within section 9;

(ii) there is a "dead rent" (*i.e.* a fixed element) combined with a royalty or turnover element (*i.e.* the traditional form of rent calculation for mining leases[46]);

(iii) parties choose to apply different rent provisions to different enterprises on the same farm.[47]

Determination of initial rent 2.9

The initial rent may be fixed at whatever rate the parties consider appropriate. Equally the fixing of the initial rent is not within the scope of Part II of the 1995 Act since the "review date" definition in section 10(6) would not be satisfied. Where the parties cannot agree the initial rent between themselves, determination by a third party will be recognised by the general law as valid.[48] Even if the determination of the third party is not made until after the tenant becomes entitled to possession[49] there appears to be no danger of this initial determination being overridden by a section 10 review.[50] There is no regulation of the level of the initial

---

[45] Para. 2.6 above.
[46] See *Woodfall, Landlord and Tenant*, Vol. 1, para. 7.043.
[47] See para. 2.3 above.
[48] ***Sudbrook Trading Estate v. Eggleton*** [1983] 1 A.C. 444.
[49] *i.e.* after the tenancy "begins": see s. 38(4).
[50] Section 10(4) deals with variation of rent; s. 10(6)(b) prescribes a minimum period of three years between specified dates before the statutory right can be exercised.

rent, which will no doubt reflect whether or not a premium has been given by the tenant in capital form.[51]

2.10 Enforceable contractual timetable for reviews: sections 10(4) and (5)

Sections 10(4) and (5) make available to the parties the opportunity to agree, if they do so in writing, the dates and frequency of rent review. Section 10(4) provides:

> "If the parties have agreed in writing that the rent is to be, or may be, varied as from a specified date or dates, or at specified intervals, the review date must be a date as from which the rent could be varied under the agreement."

Section 10(5) provides:

> "If the parties have agreed in writing that the review date for the purposes of this Part of this Act is to be a specified date or dates, the review date must be that date or one of those dates."

The agreement referred to in each of these sub-sections must be in writing but there is no stipulation that it should form part of the tenancy agreement itself. Parties may reach agreement for the purposes of section 10(4) or (5) after the tenancy agreement has been entered into and, perhaps, when an actual rent review is in contemplation some years later. The need for agreement in writing for these purposes applies even where the tenancy itself is an oral one. Each sub-section operates slightly differently. Sub-section (4) validates an agreement as to rent review "at specified intervals" (*e.g.* seven yearly); in addition it validates agreements where the rent must or may be varied as from a specified date or dates. This, for example, covers the situation where the parties agree that rent may be reviewed but only "as from" an identified date. A landlord, for example, with the opportunity to seek an increase in the rent as from a particular time but with no requirement for him to act thereafter may have the opportunity to choose the rent review date as he wishes provided the tenant is guaranteed a minimum period at the old rent. In such a circumstance section 10(4) operates to protect the tenant in his minimum period of fixed rent since the statute provides that the review date must be a date "as from which" rent could be varied under the agreement. In other words, it is not only the exact stipulation of a review date which is authorised but also the protection of a minimum period at the old rent. Sub-section (5) allows the parties to choose the review date for the purposes of Part II on an almost completely open basis. They can, if they wish, specify a sequence of particular dates for classification as review dates or, where appropriate, select as the review date a date other than the commencement of the tenancy.[52] It follows from the above that the parties may, if they wish, choose almost any frequency of rent review and are not limited to the three-yearly pattern contemplated by section 10(6). They are able to choose a repeating pattern of rent reviews (*e.g.* regularly two yearly, five yearly or seven yearly) or, if they prefer, a broken pattern (*e.g.* after two years then after three years then after five years). The only restriction in their choice arises by

---

[51] See para. 2.2 above.
[52] An agreement as to that being enforced by s. 10(6)(a).

implication in that section 10(3) stipulates that the review date must be at least 12 months but less than 24 months after the day on which the statutory review notice is given. Accordingly, it is submitted, parties cannot agree a rent review to take effect at nine monthly intervals.

Time of the essence 2.10.1

Where section 10(5) applies, that is to say the identification of the review date is expressly "for the purposes of this Part of this Act", that sub-section makes time of the essence in relation to that particular date or dates. That is the essential difference between sub-sections (5) and (4). Whether time is of the essence in relation to section 10(4) will depend on the terms of the contract and the section contemplates that the agreement as to the dates or intervals of the rent review relates to dates where the rent "is to be, or may be" varied.[53] Ascertainment of the date will be straightforward if the parties expressly stipulate that time is to be of the essence in relation to the review dates. In the case of a commercial contract it will normally be assumed in the absence of express provisions or contra-indications, that time will not be of the essence in relation to a rent review timetable.[54] Sometimes it is implied that time is of the essence in relation to the rent review timetable because of other features of the lease, in particular the timing of the exercise of a break clause.[55] Under a commercial contract where a rent review timetable is stipulated in respect of which time is not of the essence but which can only be triggered by one party taking steps, the other party is entitled to make time of the essence by serving a notice requiring the relevant step to be taken within a reasonable time.[56]

Rent trigger notice only available to landlord 2.10.2

There would seem to be a hidden problem in relation to the choice of contractual timetable offered by sections 10(4) and (5). Is the contractual timetable or choice

---

[53] *i.e.* recognises the possibility both of time being of the essence and of time not being of the essence under the contract.

[54] *United Scientific Holdings v. Burnley Borough Council* [1978] A.C. 904.

[55] For a comprehensive general discussion see *Woodfall, Landlord and Tenant*, Vol. 1, Chapter 8; for a convenient source of summaries of rent review cases and, more particularly, the precise terms of their contentious leases see the looseleaf Bernstein and Reynolds, *Handbook of Rent Review* (Sweet & Maxwell). The clearest cases where, by implication, time is of the essence in the rent review timetable are those where one or other party has the option to determine the lease being an option in respect of which time is of the essence (*C. Richards and Son v. Karenita* [1972] 221 E.G. 25; *United Scientific Holdings v. Burnley Borough Council* (above), Lord Simon at 946; *Al Saloom v. Shirley James Travel Service* (1981) 42 P. & C.R. 181; *Legal and General Assurance (Pension Management) v. Cheshire County Council* (1983) 46 P. & C.R. 160) and see the comprehensive assessment of these cases in *Central Estates Ltd v. Secretary of State for the Environment* [1997] 1 E.G.L.R. 239 by the CA).

[56] *United Scientific Holdings v. Burnley Borough Council* (above); *London and Manchester Assurance Co. v. Dunn and Co (GA)* [1983] 1 E.G.L.R. 111; *Amherst v. Walker (James) Goldsmith and Silversmith* [1983] Ch. 305; *Trustees of Henry Smith's Charity v. AWADA Trading and Promotion Service* (1984) 47 P. & C.R. 607; *Mecca Leisure v. Renown Investments (Holdings)* (1985) 49 P. & C.R. 12. However, *Woodfall*, Vol. 1 in respect of these cases observes that the opinions expressed in them are "for the most part *obiter*" (para. 8.013).

of review date only valid in circumstances where the rent review itself could be triggered by either party or is it sufficient if the rent review could be triggered only by one of them? On the face of it the wording of section 10(4) makes no requirement that both parties should have the opportunity to trigger the rent review dates but "the review date" is one which must be specified in a notice which itself may be given by either party under section 10(1). A timetable stipulated by contract and amounting to an agreement in writing should be something capable of appearing in a section 10(1) notice.[57] Finally there are further problems in assimilating to the statutory scheme fairly common types of commercial rent review clause which happen to include a specified rent review timetable but which can only be triggered by the landlord and may produce a "deemed" rent agreement.[58] Where the clauses operate so as to block or pre-empt any statutory review, those contractual provisions will be regarded as invalid to the extent that application of them would override the mechanism of a section 10 review by implementing or purporting to implement an alternative rent review procedure. It is submitted that section 10 contemplates the validity of contracts in regard to rent review timetable only in so far as they facilitate identification of an agreed date.[59]

---

[57] This poses difficulties of an important practical kind. Where either party may trigger a rent review, the tenant has the opportunity under s. 10(1) to serve his own notice. If only the landlord can serve a trigger notice but fails to, the tenant can serve notice making time of the essence but by this point it may be too late to operate a backdated review provision since s. 10(3) could no longer be complied with. Therefore it is submitted that where the timetable associated with a "landlord only" trigger notice deprives the tenant of the opportunity to serve a s. 10(1) notice, there are three possibilities. The first is that the entire attempt to provide a timetable fails because it produces a result inconsistent with statutory policy. The second possibility is that the date, if ascertainable, should be regarded as one in its original specified form as being fixed and time being of the essence in relation to it. If the latter assessment were not correct the parties' attempt to specify a rent review date would be frustrated by the choice of an inappropriate machinery. It is therefore suggested that parties are better to identify time as being of the essence in relation to a specific choice of dates than leave matters to fall perhaps into this lack of certainty. The third possibility is that the landlord only trigger is mere machinery of a type, which, if the landlord fails to initiate a review, the tenant may obtain a substituted machinery through the Courts (compare the analysis in *Addin v. Secretary of State for the Environment* [1997] 1 E.G.L.R. 99 and the substituted machinery in *Royal Bank of Scotland plc v. Jennings* [1997] 1 E.G.L.R. 101).

[58] For example the landlord may, in reference to particular dates, specify that he wishes a review to take place and suggest a rental which may only be challenged by a tenant's counter-notice in respect of which time is frequently of the essence. Where the tenant fails to respond within that time the rent review is by the contract "deemed" to have taken place to the increased rental (a result which is unavoidable on a true reading of two cases in the Court of Appeal namely *Henry Smith's Charity Trustees v. AWADA Trading and Promotion Services Ltd* (above) and *Mecca Leisure Ltd v. Renown Investments (Holdings) Ltd* (above)).

[59] It is submitted further that this somewhat draconian approach to construction is justified by the extremely limited opportunity under s. 12(b) to "opt out" of the statutory rent review after the review notice has been given. The opportunity is limited to determination

Scope for a purely contractual rent review clause 2.11

Once the statutory rent review procedure has been commenced by the giving of a rent review notice[60] and before any arbitrator has been appointed or applied for, the parties may appoint an expert to determine the rent on a basis agreed by them.[61] As a matter of general observation this authorises the survival of contractual rent reviews which contemplate a basis of assessment of the rent which differs from that provided in section 13. How widely it will be used remains to be seen but where parties are able to agree, and may well continue to prefer a rent review basis other than the statutory one, they have the opportunity, for so long as that consensus prevails, to opt jointly for assessment by an expert on the contractual basis. The section 12(b) window of opportunity is subject to some constraints. First, the opportunity itself does not stop the statutory review machinery and either party continues to be able in the six months ending with the review date to apply to the President of the RICS for the appointment of an arbitrator.[62] What if the expert is appointed after one of the parties has applied for an arbitrator to be appointed? What if the arbitrator has already been appointed but both parties then decide they wish the matter to be resolved by an expert? Rent review arbitrations take place under the Arbitration Act 1996 but there is no compulsory reference of the determination of the rent to arbitration.[63] Section 10(1) gives each party the opportunity to require that the rent be referred to arbitration and once the reference is constituted section 13 obliges the arbitrator to make his determination in accordance with the basis stated in that section.

Section 12(b) apparently contemplates that the parties retain the right to appoint an expert to determine the rent on a basis agreed by them. If that is the case the joint appointment of the expert will be valid even if one party has applied to the President for the appointment of an arbitrator. Where the arbitrator has already been appointed but the parties by joint action decide instead to proceed by expert determination, the matter is more difficult.[64] Section 10(6) (timing of the rent review cycle) contemplates on equal terms the rent review cycle being triggered three years, not more frequently, after an arbitration award or expert determination. It is inconceivable that there should be both an expert award and an arbitration award in respect of the very same rent review. As to the appointment of the expert, this must be under an agreement made since the notice was given.[65] That expert is

---

by a third party on an agreed basis and it is suggested that the statute does not contemplate the parties concluding the rent review by a "deemed" agreement as to rent levels purely by a failure to serve an appropriate counternotice in the fashion discussed.

[60] s. 10(1).
[61] s. 12(b).
[62] s. 12 generally.
[63] Rent reviews are exempt from compulsory reference to arbitration by s. 28(5)(a).
[64] Where the arbitrator is appointed by contract the parties will be in breach of that contract. Where the arbitrator is appointed by the President it is unclear whether that appointment impugns the parties' abilities thereafter to opt for expert determination, since the arbitrator is then seized with a statutory duty to make an award.
[65] Section 12(b) refers to "such an agreement", itself a reference back to the circumstance of an arbitrator who under s. 12(a) must be appointed "under an agreement made since the notice was given".

accordingly not a person to whom section 29[66] applies and specifically it is not necessary for the tenancy agreement itself to stipulate that an expert might be appointed to deal with the rent review. What section 12(b) contemplates is not only an opportunity for parties to opt out of the procedure provided by section 10 but also a general opportunity for them to couple this with opting out of the basis of determination under section 13. These are wide freedoms but they require consensus between the parties,[67] without which the statutory mechanisms remain effective. Once an arbitrator or an expert has been appointed by agreement, the opportunity to apply to the President for an arbitral appointment no longer arises.[68] Where the expert is appointed after the section 10 notice was given, it is not necessary that his appointment or the terms of it should be in writing, although it is clearly preferable that they should. As to the "basis agreed by the parties" this is a matter for them and they may choose, for instance, to ignore a pre-existing rent review clause and basis already included in the tenancy agreement, preferring to substitute another. The powers and duties of experts generally are dealt with elsewhere.[69] For convenience in this discussion the person appointed under section 12(b) is referred to as an expert and it is submitted that such a person could not be a mediator since his determination will be contractually binding on the parties.[70] Where the original tenancy agreement contains a rent review formula but a party persists in his choice of the statutory rent review basis and refuses to participate in the appointment of an expert at all, it is submitted that the other party has no remedy at all.[71]

---

[66] See para. 6.5 below.
[67] Where the identity but not the capacity of the parties changes, steps taken by the original party will bind his successor, *e.g.* the purchaser of a reversion will be bound by an arbitral appointment or an expert appointment made by his predecessor in title. Equally a tenant by assignment will be bound by similar steps taken by his predecessor in title. This is the case in all litigation and there is no statutory exception in Part II. *cf.* **Morris Marks v. British Waterways Board** [1963] 1 W.L.R. 1008 under the Landlord and Tenant Act 1954.
[68] s. 12.
[69] paras 6.83–6.87 below.
[70] Compare s. 29(2).
[71] These authors respectfully disagree with the suggestion in Scammell and Densham, *Law of Agricultural Holdings*, (8th Ed.) p. 959–960, that the aggrieved party might be able to claim damages for breach of contract, misrepresentation or rely on any equitable doctrine of estoppel. Although under a different code **Keen v. Holland** [1984] 1 W.L.R. 251 illustrates that estoppel cannot effect what a statute prohibits as a matter of contract. It is submitted that the statute quite clearly intends to disable contractual clauses designed to make a different provision from that which the statute itself does, except in very limited circumstances. This being so it would be wrong to reactivate the disabled clauses: if they cannot be relied upon directly to produce a particular result there is no reason to think that they survive for any purpose at all. The undesirability of allowing oblique enforcement of a supposedly disabled rent review provision is highlighted by the fact that any claim for damages must inevitably be based on the Court estimating the damages on the very calculation which the parties themselves have been prohibited from making. The wording in section 9 is to apply the statutory rent review "notwithstanding any agreement to the contrary" and the benefit of the rent review would be taken from a person relying on the statute if a damages claim was effected. This surely must be contrary to Parliamentary purpose.

Implementing the statutory rent review: general 2.12

All farm business tenancies other than those falling within section 9 and despite any agreement to the contrary[72] include the opportunity for landlord or tenant under section 10 to demand a rent review which, failing agreement, will be determined by arbitration.[73] The ascertainment of the appropriate review date will respect the parties' chosen timetable[74] but, unless an expert is appointed,[75] the arbitrator will determine the rent according to the criteria set out in section 13.[76]

Implementing the statutory rent review: requirements of a valid statutory review notice 2.13

Section 10(1) authorises the service by landlord or tenant of a notice in writing to be given to the other requiring that the rent to be payable, in respect of the holding, as from the review date shall be referred to arbitration in accordance with the Act. There is no prescribed form for such a notice.[77] "Holding" means the aggregate of the land comprised in the tenancy[78] and includes the agricultural land and any enterprise on the demised property.[79] "The review date" must be specified in the statutory review notice and must further comply with sub-sections (3) to (6) of section 10.[80] It is preferable to calculate the review date and identify it precisely by day month and year in the notice.[81] The review date must be at least 12 months but less than 24 months after the date on which the statutory review notice is given.[82] On the face of the statute, therefore, it is not possible to implement a rent review in

---

[72] s. 9.
[73] s. 10(1).
[74] See para. 2.10 above.
[75] s. 12(b) and para. 2.11 above.
[76] See paras 2.15–2.24 below. In particular the rent may be reviewed upwards or downwards but essentially to an open market level.
[77] For a precedent see Form 116 in Part V of this work.
[78] s. 38(1).
[79] Statutory rent review is not available in respect of part only of the land demised and the problems this may cause are discussed at para. 2.3 above.
[80] s. 10(2).
[81] The status of precedents which do not in terms specify the actual date may sometimes be questioned: whilst a circumlocution comprising a series of instructions to the recipient of a rent review notice was acceptable given the different wording of s. 12 of the Agricultural Holdings Act 1986, there is a clear instruction in s. 10(2)(a) actually to specify the date and further to ensure compliance with s. 10(3)–(6). In relation to an assured shorthold tenancy it was held by the CA in *Lower Street Properties Limited v. Jones* [1996] 28 H.L.R. 877 that in the case of a periodic tenancy the requirement to specify a date in a notice was satisfied where the actual date was not given but the notice was stated to expire "at the end of the period of your tenancy which will end after the expiry of two months from the service upon you of this notice". The issue is dealt with by Kennedy L.J. at 882 on the basis that "specified" means "made clear" and the form of words was acceptable because "the tenant knows or can easily ascertain the date referred to". It is not difficult to imagine circumstances where a notice fails this basic test where the date is not actually specified. Secondly there is a difference between the relevant statutory codes in that there is already an express statutory requirement that there be compliance with s. 10(3)–(6) and in context it may be that the need for a "specified" date must be separately and additionally satisfied, beyond a mere recitation that the date be one complying with those subsections.
[82] s. 10(3).

reference to a historic review date.[83] The review date is both the date of valuation and the date with effect from which any change in the rent will be valid.[84] The choice of review date is further limited by any agreement in writing between the parties which falls within sections 10(4) or (5).[85] Where there is no agreement falling within section 10(4) or (5), section 10(6) operates as a fallback to establish the review date. The first requirement is compliance with section 10(6) namely that the date:

> "must be an anniversary of the beginning of the tenancy or, where the landlord and the tenant have agreed in writing that the review date for the purposes of this Act is to be some other day of the year, that day of the year."

There may be some hidden pitfalls in this particular provision. First of all the anniversary of "the beginning of the tenancy" must be construed in accordance with section 38(4)[86] and this date may not be the same as the expressed commencement of the tenancy. Further, where there is an expressed commencement date the parties may not have gone so far as to agree in writing that the review date is specifically identified overtly for the purposes of the Act.[87] The agreement in writing for the purposes of section 10(6)(a) does not have to form part of the original tenancy agreement or have been entered into at the outset of the tenancy. The review date must satisfy the further condition in section 10(6)(b) that it does not fall before the end of a three-year period beginning with the last of any dates falling within that sub-section.[88] The orderly implementation of the three years bar is facilitated, where there is a new tenancy following severance of part of the reversion, by section 11.[89]

2.14 **Implementing the statutory rent review: appointment of the arbitrator**
A statutory rent review will normally, failing agreement,[90] result in the appointment of an arbitrator. There is an opportunity for the parties to choose expert determination, where both of them agree this.[91] The arbitrator may be appointed by the parties after the notice under section 10 has been given.[92]

---

[83] Contrary to much commercial practice, as sanctioned by the HL in *United Scientific Holdings v. Burnley Borough Council* (above).
[84] s. 13(1).
[85] See paras 2.10–2.10.2 above.
[86] See the discussion at para. 1.6 above.
[87] Care must be taken to distinguish an agreement in writing as to the review date for the purposes of the Act from a simple agreement as to what the review date should be. This distinction is one which also operates as between ss 10(4) and (5): see para. 2.10.1 above.
[88] Namely the beginning of the tenancy (as to which see the discussion above), the date of any previous rent review whether by arbitration or following expert determination or following agreement in writing between the parties.
[89] Not every severance of the reversion results in the creation of a new tenancy (see para. 12.20 below) but where this occurs with the agreement of the tenant and/or his participation in the deed of severance and consequent apportionment of the rent, section 11 will come into play.
[90] Form 117 in Part V of this work provides a precedent for a rent agreement.
[91] See para. 2.11 above.
[92] s. 12(a).

Alternatively following the statutory rent review notice and in the absence of any contractual arbitral appointment or appointment of an expert to determine the rent, each party has the opportunity during the period of six months, ending with the review date, to apply to the President of the RICS for him to appoint an arbitrator.[93] This means that time is of the essence for any application to the President and no valid application may be made after the review date.[94] An application to the President of the RICS for appointment of an arbitrator must be made in writing and be accompanied by such reasonable fee as the President determines in respect of the costs of making the appointment.[95] Where an appointed arbitrator dies or is incapable of acting and no new arbitrator is appointed by agreement either party may apply to the President of the RICS for a new arbitral appointment.[96] The arbitrator will act pursuant to the Arbitration Act 1996.[97]

Basis of valuation on statutory rent review: section 13   2.15

The valuation date for the purposes of a statutory rent review is "the review date".[98] Statutory rent reviews must be to an open market level and accordingly of necessity the possibility exists of a drop in the rent levels over a period of time. Section 13(1) directs the arbitrator with effect from the review date to increase or reduce the rent or direct that it should continue unchanged. It has already been seen that the statute bars the exemption of any chosen contractual formula which would preclude a reduction in the rent level[99] and it is submitted that any contractual term which provides for a statutory rent review but thereafter contractually for it to be enforceable on any upwards only basis is void.[1] For the same reason it is submitted that whereas a landlord may waive from time to time the collection of part of the rent, if the lease provides for the statutorily reviewed rent to be collectable in part only this is also void. The valuation formula itself is set out in sub-sections (2)–(5) being a direction to value on the open market but subject to a series of specific disregards. These are dealt with in sequence below.

---

[93] s. 12.

[94] The period of six months "ending with" the review date probably includes that date within the six month period: see *Halsbury's Laws of England*, Vol. 45 (4th ed.), para. 1127. The choice of wording appears quite deliberately to contrast with the terms of s. 12(3) of the 1986 Act which required the application for appointment of the arbitrator to be made "before" the review date.

[95] s. 30(2). This section is drafted in such a way as to apply even though strictly speaking rent is not required to be determined by arbitration.

[96] s. 30(3). The power to apply under s. 30(3) is not restricted to the period of six months ending with the review date.

[97] See generally paras 6.10–6.81 below.

[98] s. 13(1) and see para. 2.13 above. This contrasts with the statutory rent review under section 12 of the Agricultural Holdings Act 1986 where the determination date of the rental is the date of the reference (section 12(2) of the 1986 Act and Chapter 11). The 1995 Act does not allow the amount of rent to be influenced by the delays which may be inherent in the arbitration process.

[99] See s. 9(b)(ii) and para. 2.7 above.

[1] Such a provision would in substance represent a form of fundamental interference with the operation of the statutory rent review such as to frustrate its application.

2.16 Meaning of section 13(2)
This crucial section provides:

> "For the purposes of sub-section (1) above, the rent properly payable in respect of the holding[2] is the rent at which the holding might reasonably be expected to be let on the open market by a willing landlord to a willing tenant, taking into account (subject to sub-sections (3)[3] and (4)[4] below) all relevant factors, including (in every case) the terms of the tenancy (including those which are relevant for the purposes of section 10(4) to (6)[5] of this Act, but not those relating to the criteria by reference to which any new rent is to be determined)."

The single most important observation about the valuation formula is that it is overtly geared to open market.[6] This means that there should be no exercise to strip out scarcity value from rents agreed under the statute or observable in comparables on the open market. The meaning of the phrase "open market" has been considered in the context of commercial rent review on numerous occasions, by application to slightly different forms of words. The open market is a measure of value which means the same as a number of other similar phrases.[7] It is important to appreciate that the reference to the open market has identity with these other ways of expressing reference to that open market because this may well enable comparison between leases employing different formulations to be made. Whilst such an exercise would not be traditional for the purpose of comparing one farm rent with another it might be very useful in terms of a farm business tenancy since non-agricultural enterprises are likely to be part of the valuation exercise for which the arbitrator may have a non-agricultural comparable. It has been held that there is no difference between "open market rent" and "market rent".[8] The direction is to assess what the reasonable expectation would be as to open market letting and it would seem that a "reasonable" expectation would preclude reference to freak circumstances or rent offers.[9] It is submitted that a reasonable expectation would include the assumption that the landlord had taken all reasonable steps to advertise the property in the usual way and that the parties bidding in the open market would have taken steps to inform themselves of all the matters which would be of interest to a reasonably prudent and cautious bidder. Although the word "prudent" is not applied to the willing landlord or the willing tenant later in the valuation, it is

---

[2] See s. 38(1) and discussion in para. 2.3 above.
[3] See paras 2.17–2.22 below.
[4] See paras 2.23–2.24 below.
[5] Sub-paras 10(4) and (5) are considered at paras 2.10–2.10.2 above. Sub-s. (6) is considered at para. 2.13 above.
[6] These words, omitted from the valuation formula in s. 12 of the Agricultural Holdings Act 1986, have been reinstated in the 1995 Act (compare s. 8 of the Agricultural Holdings Act 1948).
[7] *e.g.* "market rent" or "rack rent".
[8] ***Sterling Land Office Developments v. Lloyds Bank plc*** [1984] 2 E.G.L.R. 135.
[9] Although possibly that type of element should be excluded from an open market valuation in any case: see ***Ponsford v. HMS Aerosols*** [1979] A.C. 63 and ***Cuff v. J and F Stone Property Company*** [1979] A.C. 87.

submitted that nothing is lost since the expectation as to what such parties might bid or be willing to accept is limited to what one would reasonably expect them to do in the open market.

The open market is contrasted with values established by non-arms length purchasers or markets from which particular bidders (who might otherwise be expected to participate) are excluded. Valuers are well versed in assessing farm rents where there may be very little comparable material, in which case budgets play an important part. However agricultural valuers may not have significant experience of properties for which there is effectively only one possible tenant namely the very tenant who is occupying. Where it is necessary to establish an "open market" rent for a property which is in effect only available to one purchaser it will be assumed that a bargain will be concluded.[10] A monopoly position either on the part of the landlord, who has a unique property, or on the part of the tenant, who may be the only possible bidder, does not render a hypothetical agreement impossible.[11] In a commercial lease drawn to the open market value as between willing lessor and willing lessee but in respect of a property where there was only one possible tenant, the characteristics of the willing lessor and the willing lessee were considered in detail, a consideration which should be regarded as highly instructive since the statutory wording in section 13 is almost identical.[12] The

---

[10] *F.R. Evans (Leeds) Limited v. English Electric Co Limited* (1978) 36 P. & C.R. 185 at 193.

[11] *Tomlinson v. Plymouth Argyle Football Co Limited* [1960] 6 RRC 173; *Inland Revenue Commissioners v. Clay* [1914] 3 KB 466.

[12] *F.R. Evans (Leeds) Limited v. English Electric Co Limited* (above) Donaldson J. at 189:

> "The first, and perhaps the most important, conflict between the parties is whether, in the application of the clause, the willing lessor is to be identified with the landlords and the willing lessee with the tenants. In a sense, the willing lessor must be the landlords because only they can dispose of the premises, but for the purposes of the clause the landlord is an abstraction— a hypothetical person with the right to dispose of the premises on an 18-year lease. As such, he is not afflicted by personal ills such as cash flow crisis or importunate mortgagees. Nor is he in the happy position of someone to whom it is largely a matter of indifference whether he lets in October 1976 or waits for the market to improve. He is, in short, a willing lessor. He wants to let the premises at a rent which is appropriate to all the factors which affect the marketability of these premises as industrial premises— for example, geographical location, the extent of the local labour market, the level of local rates and the market of competitive premises, that is to say, premises which are directly comparable or which, if not directly comparable, would be considered as viable alternatives by a potential tenant. ... Similarly, in my judgment, the willing lessee is an abstraction— a hypothetical person actively seeking premises to fulfil needs which these premises could fulfil. He will take account of similar factors, but he too will be unaffected by liquidity problems, governmental or other pressures to boost or maintain employment in the area and so on. In a word, his profile may or may not fit that of the English Electric Co. Ltd, but he is not that company. ... (at 190). The fact that it is very likely that the English Electric Co. Ltd would have been the only potential lessee is relevant, but its relevance is indirect. It does not matter whether the only potential lessee was this company or the XYZ Co. Ltd. What matters is that in the state of the market there was not likely to be more than one willing lessee. The effect of this fact is not, however, decisive because this single potential lessee is assumed to be a willing lessee— neither reluctant nor importunate, but willing. Just as the hypothetical lessor cannot rely over much on the fact that no

statute does not direct the arbitrator expressly as to what assumption he must make for the length of term which will be offered on the open market. It is submitted that there is now clear authority deriving from the commercial context to the effect that the arbitrator will be required to value the actual residue of the actual term and that he is not to assume that the full term of the original letting is available on the hypothetical market.[13] The arbitrator is to take into account all relevant factors, some of which are specifically highlighted by the valuation instruction. It is assumed that the arbitrator would in any event take into account all relevant factors.

In a normal open market valuation it will be expected that a valuer will consider and assess all manner of evidence in so far as he considers it useful and is not limited to one particular type of evidence such as comparables or budgeting.[14] The arbitrator is entitled to have regard to transactions agreed after the rent review date or before that date though in either case he will have to adjust or assess the relevance of the information to the actual review date.[15] The terms of the tenancy must always be considered. The arbitrator is specifically directed to have regard to the provisions which stipulate the frequency and timing of the rent review pattern but is directed to disregard any criteria by way of valuation formula to be found in the tenancy. Thus, where the parties have included in the lease a contractual rent review at, say, five-yearly intervals, the arbitrator will disregard the substantive content of the valuation or rent review procedure terms but will have regard to the general pattern of review (*i.e.* five yearly). He will disregard any instruction in the lease which requires the rental to be, for example, upwards only since he is bound to fix a rent without such a restriction.[16] The arbitrator will be aware of the passing rent and if he considers it persuasive in terms of his valuation he will have to assess it under the heading "all relevant factors" since "the terms of the tenancy" must, it is apprehended, be a reference to the terms of the tenancy available for letting on the hypothetical market which of necessity would not contain the current rental level. No doubt the arbitrator will take care to ensure that it is only the terms of the tenancy which he considers and not the effect of any personal arrangement peculiar to the particular tenant, such as the landlord waiving collection of rent. More difficult is the situation of a tenant operating with the benefit of a personal waiver or variation of a user covenant in his favour but expressly done by way of side letter or licence, possibly even on a gratuitous basis. It is suggested that the arbitrator is concerned only with the strict legal position and the one which is enforceable

---

property similar to the Walton Works is available on the market, so the hypothetical lessee cannot rely too much upon the fact that he has no competitors— he is, and is known to be, a willing lessee. Furthermore, it is known that he will remain a willing lessee so long as the willing lessor does not press his demand for rent beyond the point at which he is ceasing to act as a willing lessor and at which the willing lessee would cease to be such."

[13] ***Ponsford v. HMS Aerosols Ltd*** (above), Viscount Dilhorne at 76H; ***Pearl Assurance plc v. Shaw*** [1984] 274 E.G. 490, Vinelott J.; ***Norwich Union Life Insurance Society v. Trustee Savings Banks Central Board*** [1986] 1 E.G.L.R. 136, Hoffmann J; ***Ritz Hotel (London) Ltd v. Ritz Casino Ltd*** [1989] 2 E.G.L.R. 135, Vinelott J.

[14] ***Ritz Hotel (London) Ltd v. Ritz Casino Ltd*** (above) at 137.

[15] ***Segama NV v. Penny le Roy Ltd*** [1983] 269 E.G. 322.

[16] See s. 13(1).

between the parties: if a personal concession would not be available hypothetically on the open market to any other person then it should be disregarded as an actual concession. In so far as the landlord may have made a gratuitous concession relaxing the user but on the footing that he could on short or reasonable notice reverse the decision, it is submitted that no regard should be had to the effect of the relaxation. Although in one sense this is harsh for the landlord since he sees the tenant realising an uncovenanted and possibly valuable benefit, if he wishes to take rent for it then he should make a variation of the tenancy terms rather than allow the tenant to proceed on an arrangement dependent on his own goodwill.[17] The statute does not expressly require the arbitrator to assume that the holding is available with vacant possession although the occupation of the current tenant is to be disregarded.[18] In a commercial letting one would usually assume that the valuation would proceed on a vacant possession basis[19] but where there are sub-tenancies at the date of grant of the original head lease probably those sub-leases would be assumed.[20] If the head lease expressly contemplates sub-letting there is authority to suggest that the rent review of the head lease may take account of the existence of the sub-leases.[21] This conclusion is the more likely to be reached where the head lease imposes on the tenant a positive covenant to underlet[22] and the likelihood of this case law being applied is relatively strong since, as discussed below,[23] without special provisions in the head lease, it appears that the statute contemplates the head tenant paying rent on the sub-tenant's improvements.

Disregard of increase in rental value due to tenant's improvements falling within section 15 2.17

Section 13(3) and (5) requires all "tenant's improvements", as defined by section 15, to be disregarded in so far as they result in an increase in the rental value of the holding. There are three specific exceptions to this general disregard.[24] The definition in section 15 of a "tenant's improvement"[25] is extremely wide and is expressed to include both physical improvements and any intangible advantage obtained for the holding which becomes attached to it. In either case the element of tenant's improvement is limited to that which was obtained by the tenant by his own effort or wholly or partly at his own expense. Therefore, although "tenant" is defined so as to include a sub-tenant[26] it is only where the tenant's "own" effort or

---

[17] It is the terms of the tenancy which determine the use assumed on the rent review: see the reasoning (in the context of rent fixing on a renewal under the Landlord and Tenant Act 1954) of Potter L.J. in ***Northern Electric plc v. Addison*** [1997] 39 E.G. 175 at 177.
[18] s. 13(4)(a).
[19] ***Scottish and Newcastle Breweries plc v. Sir Richard Sutton's Settled Estates*** [1985] 2 E.G.L.R. 130; ***Hill Samuel Life Assurance v. Preston Borough Council*** [1990] 2 E.G.L.R. 127.
[20] ***Oscroft v. Benabo*** [1967] 1 W.L.R. 1087; ***Forte and Co. v. General Accident Life Assurance*** [1986] 2 E.G.L.R. 115.
[21] ***Scottish and Newcastle Breweries plc v. Sir Richard Sutton's Settled Estates*** (above).
[22] ***Laura Investment Co. v. Havering London Borough Council (No.2)*** [1993] 1 E.G.L.R. 124.
[23] See para. 2.17 below.
[24] See paras 2.19–2.21 below.
[25] See para. 5.4 below.
[26] s. 38(1).

expense is made that the item falls within the disregard. Further it is submitted that the wording of section 15(a) and (b) is directed to an improvement only to the extent that it is paid for by the tenant. Compensatable improvements, and therefore ones which by implication fall within section 15, will include the benefit of planning permission[27] and, probably, both fixed equipment[28] and "routine improvements".[29] It is not necessary for the purposes of rent review that the tenant should, on the determination of the tenancy, be entitled to compensation in respect of the particular improvement in order for that improvement to be considered a "tenant's improvement" so as to fall within the disregard. Section 15 establishes general categories and the subsequent sections in Part III set up conditions which not all tenant's improvements satisfy and therefore some of these improvements will not be eligible for compensation. It is to be noted that milk quota should be regarded as a tenant's improvement and therefore in general terms within the disregard. The statutory draftsman has embraced the threefold classification in *Woodfall* distinguishing chattels from fixtures so as to include within "improvements" both items which are fixtures and also items which are part and parcel of the land itself.[30]

2.18 Tenant's fixed equipment

"Fixed equipment" is defined by section 19(10)[31] but only for the purposes of compensation. There is no corresponding definition provided in relation to rent and section 13(3) expressly refers only to "tenant's improvements". Although fixed equipment has become part of the land in legal theory it is something which the tenant has rights to remove and, it is submitted, therefore falls to be dealt with in terms of section 13(4)(a).[32] In the normal way, aside from Part III of the Act, improvements do not include tenant's fixtures[33] and do not extend to the erection of buildings for the tenant's benefit even where the latter pays for specific features required only by him.[34]

---

[27] Compare s. 18.
[28] See definition in s. 19(10), and discussion at para. 5.6 below.
[29] See s. 19(10).
[30] "An object which is brought onto land may be classified under one of three broad heads. It may be (a) a chattel; (b) a fixture; or (c) part and parcel of the land itself. Objects in categories (b) and (c) are treated as being part of the land." This passage from *Woodfall* is endorsed in ***Elitestone Limited v. Morris*** (1997) 27 E.G. 116 by Lord Lloyd at 117. The case provides elaborate consideration of the distinction between chattels and the other two elements identified. In the context of a 1995 Act statutory rent review it should also be noted that chattels are disregarded because it is assumed that the present tenant is no longer on the property (see s. 13(4)(a)).
[31] "'Fixed equipment' includes any building or structure affixed to land and any works constructed on, in, over or under land, and also includes any thing grown on land for a purpose other than use after severance from the land, consumption of the thing grown or its produce, or amenity".
[32] See para. 2.23 below.
[33] ***New Zealand Government Property Corp v. H. M. and S.*** [1982] Q.B. 1145.
[34] ***Scottish and Newcastle Breweries plc v. Sir Richard Sutton's Settled Estates*** (above).

The arbitrator to have regard to increase in rental value attributable to any tenant's improvement provided under an obligation: section 13(3)(a) 2.19

The arbitrator is directed to have regard to increases in the rental value of the holding due to:

> "any tenant's improvement provided under an obligation which was imposed on the tenant by the terms of his tenancy or any previous tenancy and which arose on or before the beginning of the tenancy in question."

Normally "improvements" do not include works done before the tenancy is entered into,[35] so that the inclusion of works done under a previous tenancy or before the commencement of the present tenancy is of particular significance. It should be noted that the wording of licences should not be confused with the wording by way of establishing an obligation which would be necessary for works to fall within this paragraph. The wording of many licences might easily be construed, wrongly, as establishing an obligation because, for instance, the obligation exists to complete the works in accordance with planning permission, etc. The case of *Godbold v. Martin (the Newsagents)*[36] repays study in that the form of words there is one commonly encountered and was held to amount to no more than a licence to do works, at the tenant's desire, but in the event that the works were done the tenant was obliged to do them to a particular standard.[37] In order to fall within this paragraph the relevant obligation must be one which arises on or before the beginning of the tenancy in question[38] and, therefore, in effect this form of statutory wording is more generous to the tenant since obligations imposed on him subsequent to the commencement of the current tenancy do not fall within this paragraph and works done pursuant to that type of obligation will be disregarded by the arbitrator. A tenant's adviser should take care to check what obligations there are in the tenancy agreement which might ultimately require expenditure on improvements. Sometimes a clause will be relevant for this purpose which is not one primarily drawn with improvements in mind: thus, for example, a general covenant to comply with statutes might oblige a tenant to carry out works in accordance with bylaws, health regulations, etc., and works done, even if amounting to improvements, would be rentalised.[39]

---

[35] *Brett v. Brett Essex Golf Club* [1986] 1 E.G.L.R. 154; *Panther Shop Investments v. Keith Pople* [1987] 1 E.G.L.R. 131.

[36] [1983] 2 E.G.L.R. 128.

[37] See also *Historic House Hotels v. Cadogan Estates* [1993] 2 E.G.L.R. 151, affirmed at [1995] 1 E.G.L.R. 117.

[38] There remains doubt as to whether the position is the same under the Agricultural Holdings Act 1986, Schedule 2, para. 2(1)(a), where the equivalent provision is contained.

[39] *e.g.* compliance with fire precaution works was rentalised in a case where the tenant had entered into a general obligation to comply with statutes, no doubt much to the tenant's dismay: *Forte and Co. v. General Accident Life Assurance* [1986] 2 E.G.L.R. 115. The most expensive type of improvement at real risk of falling within this type of general covenant is the provision of slurry systems which stop pollution of the watercourses. Where a tenant is at risk of spending perhaps up to £100,000 in order to comply with various pollution control requirements it would be most unfortunate if his tenancy agreement contained a general covenant capable of being construed to oblige him to do

2.20 The arbitrator to have regard to any increase in the rental value of the holding reflecting landlord's contribution towards improvements: section 13(3)(b)

Section 13(3)(b) requires the arbitrator to have regard to any increase in the rental value of the holding due to:

> "any tenant's improvement to the extent that any allowance or benefit has been made or given by the landlord in consideration of its provision."

It is often the case that a landlord has a retained workforce or an ability to obtain discounted rates with contractors which therefore make it attractive for works to be done in the landlord's name but with the tenant meeting all bills. In these circumstances, it is apprehended, the landlord is acting as the agent of the tenant and is not himself providing the works. Where the tenant is in substance the person providing the works and pays for them they will be regarded as works by way of tenant's improvement, not landlord's improvement.[40] Where the landlord contributes directly either by providing materials or money towards the improvement the tenant is only entitled to have the improvement disregarded to the extent that he himself has paid for it.[41]

2.21 The arbitrator to have regard to tenant's improvements already compensated for by landlord: section 13(3)(c)

The arbitrator is required to have regard to any increase in the rental value of the holding due to:

> "any tenant's improvement to the extent that the tenant has received any compensation from the landlord in respect of it."

This provision appears designed to supplement section 23[42] which deals with compensation rights where the tenant remains in occupation during two or more successive tenancies. In short the parties may decide to "roll forwards" the statutory compensation but may equally choose for the landlord to recompense the tenant on the termination of an intervening tenancy and, where this happens, compensation claims are to that extent spent by the conclusion of the final tenancy. The word "compensation" contrasts with "allowance or benefit" in section 13(3)(b). Accordingly section 13(3)(c) is directed to statutory compensation or contractual compensation paid on a voluntary accelerated basis in respect of improvements already executed under a prior tenancy. There is an interesting problem in relation to the commonly encountered situation of a landlord "buying" an improvement which the tenant has already executed. On the face of it such a situation does not easily fall within either section 13(3)(b)[43] or sub-section (c).[44]

---

those works and therefore pay rent on them.
[40] *Scottish and Newcastle Breweries plc v. Sir Richard Sutton's Settled Estates* (above).
[41] See s. 13(3)(b).
[42] See para. 5.23 below.
[43] Because the allowance or benefit is not made in consideration of the **provision** of the improvement.
[44] The purchase price is not likely to be true compensation.

Perhaps a contractual compensation scheme can be voluntarily "accelerated" to bring the relevant improvement within sub-section (c) but it is doubtful whether an acceleration of statutory compensation could bring this particular type of deal into sub-section (c).[45]

Valuation difficulties under section 13(3)(b) and (c) 2.22

In both sections 13(3)(b) and (c) improvements will be rentalised "to the extent" of allowances, benefit or compensation from the landlord. As a matter of observation it is clear that the contribution made by any grant from outsiders is not reflected in these sub-paragraphs. In other words the grant element redounds to the benefit of the tenant. Secondly it is not easy to see quite how the valuation technique should be applied to these two sub-paragraphs. Given that sub-paragraph (b) is directed to the time of provision of the improvement it would seem logical to assess the allowance or benefit made by the landlord as a contribution to cost at the outset. For the purposes of the comparison there may well be difficulties in establishing the figures or value in money's worth of the tenant's contribution in circumstances where he chooses to use his own labour. Just as it would be wrong to allow the landlord to compute the value of any allowance or benefit except in terms of cost to himself,[46] so, it is submitted, it would be wrong to allow the tenant to value his own labour at the rate which would have been charged by outside contractors. Where materials are used which have not been "bought in" the same problem of valuation is encountered. All of this serves to emphasise the need for the landlord to establish at the time the cost to the tenant of making an improvement and, particularly where "secondhand" materials are being used, the cost of those materials.

Section 13(3)(c) must by necessary inference be directed not towards the cost of provision but towards the enduring value of the improvement as at the time when the compensation is assessed. Thus records should be kept of the basis on which the compensation was agreed and if, for instance, the landlord voluntarily pays half the compensation due at a historic point he should be able from his records to demonstrate that this was indeed what he did. Necessarily under sub-paragraph (c) the higher initial cost will have been carried by the tenant and the landlord may obtain a disproportionately large benefit by paying out the reduced value at a later date. However there seems to be very little unfairness in this since the tenant is not obliged to accept accelerated compensation payments and in any case presumably the payment he receives reflects the continuing value of the improvement on what is then a current basis. Tenants who agree "writing down" schemes should beware of the effect of sub-paragraph (c).

The arbitrator to disregard the tenant's occupation: section 13(4)(a) 2.23

The arbitrator is directed to disregard:

> "any effect on the rent of the fact that the tenant who is a party to the arbitration is in occupation of the holding."

---

[45] Section 26(1) entitles the compensation claim to be made in accordance with Part III (*i.e.* on termination) "notwithstanding any agreement to the contrary".

[46] *e.g.* if he obtains discounted prices he can only charge the discounted price and not the full amount into the computation.

This is a disregard which does not include the occupation of sub-tenants, nor the goodwill which may be generated by those sub-tenants. The purpose of this disregard is to remove from the bidding exercise the effect of any bid over the market which the sitting tenant might make in order to stay there and thereby prevent disruption to his business. It also results in the arbitrator ignoring any deleterious effect on the rent where the current tenant does not perform his obligations satisfactorily.[47] However the arbitrator is not required to pretend that the tenant has never been in occupation but simply to disregard the effect on rental caused by it.[48] The tenant's goodwill[49] will be disregarded in that it is caused by the tenant's conduct of his business.[50] Whereas in more traditional farming leases this particular provision was of limited interest, it may well be more important for farm business tenancies where there is an expected increase in diversification. To ignore the occupation of the tenant involves, it is submitted, ignoring the tenant together with his chattels and tenant's fixtures.[51]

Section 13(4)(a) does not require the arbitrator to ignore the fact that the tenant may be farming in close proximity to the holding and might for that reason make a bid in relation to the holding itself. This element of special bid generated by the tenant owning or enjoying other land is not the subject of a disregard and the arbitrator is entitled to assume that the tenant may participate in bidding for the subject holding if he believes this to be the true position.[52]

2.24 The arbitrator to disregard tenant's breach of covenant or default: section 13(4)(b)

The arbitrator is instructed that he:

> "shall not fix the rent at a lower amount by reason of any dilapidation or deterioration of, or damage to, buildings or land caused or permitted by the tenant."

The tenant cannot by creating or permitting a breach of covenant or waste succeed in reducing the rent that would be awarded at arbitration. That is the purpose of section 13(4)(b) and it establishes in statutory form the rule that a tenant cannot take advantage of his own wrong.[53] There is no case law which establishes whether or not a landlord's breach of covenant should be disregarded for the purposes of the rent being fixed. On the one hand it might be said that the property

---

[47] *Scottish and Newcastle Breweries plc v. Sir Richard Sutton's Settled Estates* (above).
[48] *Cornwall Coast Country Club v. Cardgrange* [1987] 1 E.G.L.R. 146.
[49] As distinct from any goodwill which attaches to the premises as such.
[50] *Prudential Assurance Co. v. Grand Metropolitan Estates* [1993] 2 E.G.L.R. 153.
[51] There is no other disregard available in relation to tenant's fixtures: contrast Schedule 2, paragraph 2(1)(a) of the Agricultural Holdings Act 1986. And see *New Zealand Government Property Corp v. H.M. and S.* (above); *Young v. Dalgety plc* [1987] 1 E.G.L.R. 116; *Ocean Accident and Guarantee Corporation v. Next plc* [1996] 2 E.G.L.R. 84.
[52] See *J.W. Childers v. Anker* (1996) 1 E.G.L.R. 1 and see para. 11.17 below.
[53] Referred to in *Expert Clothing Service and Sales v. Hillgate House* [1986] Ch. 340 and *Harmsworth Pension Funds Trustees Ltd v. Charringtons Industrial Holdings Ltd* (1985) 49 P. & C.R. 297, as illustrations of a more general rule.

should be valued in the condition in which it is found without investigating any history[154]; on the other, the tenant has a remedy in damages where the landlord fails to repair and in addition to that has the right to compel specific performance of the landlord's covenants and may do so within the three-year cycle of any rent review. This latter line of argument is preferred by the text of *Woodfall*, Volume 1.[155] These authors consider the argument to be very finely balanced in a statutory context where dilapidation or deterioration by the tenant is singled out for special treatment and nothing at all is said about the landlord's activities.[156]

Evidence in relation to rent reviews 2.25

The observations below[157] as to arbitrations under the Arbitration Act 1996 generally apply in relation to rent arbitrations. The only special feature of the evidential rules in relation to rent review is the treatment of awards made by an arbitrator. In ***Land Securities v. Westminster City Council***[158] rent determined by an arbitrator was held not to be admissible evidence on a subsequent rent review so as to establish the rent levels on the later occasion. The reasoning in that case, based only in part on the hearsay rule in civil proceedings, would extend to any determination by an expert. The decision survives the abolition of the hearsay rule in civil proceedings[159] since it was only partly related to the rule against hearsay evidence. It is an extremely inconvenient case not only[160] because its exact parameters are not as yet investigated by litigation.[161] It is suggested that where the rules of evidence apply but both parties agree that the arbitrator shall be entitled and required to take into account all expert or arbitral determinations the difficulty will be avoided in such a way that neither party can later challenge it. Subject to any agreement between the parties, an arbitrator under the 1996 Act may decide to admit and consider expert and arbitral determinations, even though neither are admissible in a Court.[162] The tenant's accounts/records of profits achieved are usually discoverable even where the strict rules of evidence apply[163]: it is likely that under the Arbitration Act regime arbitrators will rule that such material may be brought directly into evidence so as to enable the arbitrator better to assess whether

---

[154] See ***Ponsford v. HMS Aerosols*** (above); ***Sheerness Steel Co. plc v. Medway Ports Authority*** [1992] 1 E.G.L.R. 133.

[155] See para. 8.021 and attention is there drawn to ***Fawke v. Viscount Chelsea*** [1980] Q.B. 441.

[156] It is interesting to speculate what would happen if the landlord, in breach of the tenancy, entered on the property and improved it to the tenant's advantage: would the tenant be liable for rent? Using this hypothetical example there is no obvious answer from the lines of argument set out in this paragraph.

[157] See para. 6.53.

[158] [1993] 1 W.L.R. 286.

[159] The Civil Evidence Act 1995.

[160] Agricultural arbitrators are well used to considering other arbitral awards under s. 12 and Sched. 2, para. 1(3) of the Agricultural Holdings Act 1986.

[161] *Woodfall*, for instance, attempts to circumscribe the application of the case so as to rely on arbitral awards either as authority for a valuation principle or, in so far as it influences the market, by setting a market level in practice: para. 8.032 note 84.

[162] He would be entitled to make a direction to that effect pursuant to s. 34(2)(f) of the Arbitration Act.

[163] See ***Urban Small Space Ltd v. Burford Investment Co. Ltd*** [1990] 2 E.G.L.R. 120.

a particular level of rent is likely to be supportable by a tenant running a similar type of business to the actual one.

CHAPTER 3

REMOVAL OF FIXTURES AND BUILDINGS

3.1 Removal of fixtures and buildings: general

3.2 Mandatory nature of section 8

3.3 Section 8 exhaustive as regards fixtures: section 8(7)

3.4 No landlord's right to purchase items within section 8

3.5 Exclusions from section 8: works done in pursuance of obligation: section 8(2)(a)

3.6 Exclusions from section 8: replacement of a fixture or building belonging to the landlord: section 8(2)(b)

3.7 Exclusions from section 8: fixture or building already compensated for: section 8(2)(c)

3.8 Exclusions from section 8: fixtures or buildings with landlord's consent under section 17 conditional on tenant's agreement not to remove: section 8(2)(d)

3.9 Content of rights under section 8: general

3.10 Fixtures within section 8: section 8(1)(a)

3.11 Buildings within section 8: section 8(1)(b)

3.12 Meaning of fixtures or buildings acquired: section 8(5)

3.13 Manner of exercise of rights under section 8: section 8(3) and (4)

3.14 Forfeiture clauses and section 8

Removal of fixtures and buildings: general 3.1

The Agricultural Tenancies Act 1995 provides a new code to deal with a tenant's right to remove fixtures and buildings, and does so in one section namely section 8. The general position at common law in relation to fixtures is considered in the discussion relative to section 10 of the Agricultural Holdings Act 1986.[1] The terms of section 8 of the 1995 Act are very different from the terms of the equivalent section in the 1986 Act namely section 10.[2] Since any given tenancy will fall either under the 1986 Act or under the 1995 Act there appears little point in making direct comparison between the two codes. The new section 8 is, subject to one exception

---
[1] At para. 10.34 below.
[2] Considered at para. 10.34–10.43.

only,[3] both mandatory[4] and exhaustive as regards fixtures.[5] In short, section 8(1) provides that fixtures affixed or buildings erected by the tenant may be removed by him during the tenancy or thereafter during his continuance in possession as tenant, these items remaining "his property". There is a series of specific exemptions from the rights granted by section 8(1).[6] Whilst the items may be removable, the tenant must not cause avoidable damage to the holding[7] and must make good.[8] Items purchased are treated on an equivalent basis to items affixed or erected by the tenant.[9]

3.2 Mandatory nature of section 8

Section 8(6) provides in general terms that section 8 is to have effect notwithstanding any agreement or custom to the contrary. The only exception is that provided by section 8(2)(d).[10] The combination of the general rule in section 8(6) and the exception in section 8(2)(d) means that a tenant will always have the opportunity to choose whether to take compensation for his improvements or take them away unless the landlord's consent to the making of the improvement was expressly linked to the tenant's agreement not to take it away. This general proposition obviously presupposes that the tenant is entitled under Part III of the 1995 Act to appropriate compensation. It is submitted that in circumstances where the statute strikes down any agreement to a contrary effect, the parties cannot by conduct be estopped to the same effect as an express agreement. Arrangements which may be particularly vulnerable to this section are those where the landlord, for example, "matches" the tenant's expenditure on a building by providing an equivalent for use by the tenant, on the understanding that the tenant would not in fact remove his own building. Thus, where a landlord provides part of an expensive complex on this kind of basis he may well find that the tenant is nevertheless entitled to rely on section 8 unless the landlord has gone so far as to ensure that the tenant's building was erected under obligation.[11]

3.3 Section 8 exhaustive as regards fixtures: section 8(7)

Section 8(7) provides that no right to remove fixtures that subsists otherwise than by virtue of the section is to be exercisable by the tenant under a farm business tenancy. In other words if, for example, the contract, custom or the common law would otherwise have afforded the tenant an opportunity to remove fixtures, such rights are not exercisable. This aspect of section 8 is to be welcomed since it considerably simplifies what the position might otherwise be. All rights in relation to fixtures are now reduced to a uniform basis.

3.4 No landlord's right to purchase items within section 8

Although there is no part of section 8 which expressly prohibits a landlord from

---

[3] See s. 8(2)(d) and para. 3.8 below.
[4] See s. 8(6) and para. 3.2 below.
[5] See s. 8(7) and para. 3.3 below.
[6] See s. 8(2) and paras 3.5–3.8 below.
[7] s. 8(3) and para. 3.13 below.
[8] s. 8(4) and para. 3.13 below.
[9] s. 8(5) and para. 3.12 below.
[10] See para. 3.8 below.
[11] Therefore falling within s. 8(2)(a).

reserving to himself the right to purchase the tenant's fixtures and buildings, it is submitted that such an arrangement would clearly fall foul of section 8(6). It would, further, appear to be a clear statutory policy not to reproduce this type of right in the landlord's favour, in marked contrast to section 10 of the 1986 Act. However there may be circumstances in which a landlord may in fact achieve the equivalent result, provided the tenant wishes to co-operate. Section 8(6) operates to protect section 8 rights for so long as they subsist, and no more. If a landlord, for example, respects the tenant's right to remove fixtures but nevertheless agrees to purchase them in the event of the tenant leaving them at the end of the tenancy there appears to be nothing in section 8 to prevent that bargain being enforceable once the landlord takes the benefit of the fixtures in question.

Exclusions from section 8: works done in pursuance of obligation: section 8(2)(a) 3.5

The exclusion relates to any fixture affixed or building erected "in pursuant of some obligation". Such an obligation might be contained in the tenancy agreement or in a subsequent deed. There is no restriction that the obligation should be one owed to the landlord and, for example, it might equally be owed to the landlord's mortgagee. It is common form in many tenancy agreements to require the tenant to comply with statutes or bylaws, without specifying what they might be. If the contractual covenant is wide enough it is likely that the tenant will not be allowed to remove the fixtures or buildings in question even though neither party had given any thought to the particular type of fixtures or buildings at the time when the general covenant was entered into.[12] It would also seem that the language of the sub-section is wide enough to include within the exemption fixtures affixed and buildings erected as a result of the tenant complying with statutory duty or obligations imposed by bylaws or statutory instruments.[13] However there may be scope for a small doubt about this because the result will be to deprive the tenant of the right to remove buildings or special features required by legislation which may be not only very valuable but also absolutely essential to the trade being pursued. The word "obligation" might perhaps be confined to contractual matters on the footing that the exemption should be narrowly construed since section 8 is an enabling measure. Given the increasing tide of regulation as to the conditions in which food and animals may be handled it may produce anomalous results if the very wide construction of the word "obligation" is adopted. It should be noted that, for the exemption to apply, the obligation in question must have been in existence at the time when the relevant fixtures were affixed or buildings erected. Subsequent imposition of terms governing the works and purporting to impose a "backdated" obligation will fall foul of section 8(6). It is difficult to see how the exemption would work if section 8(5) were being relied on where the tenant acquires a fixture or building. Section 8(2)(a) does not specify who it is that must have been under the relevant obligation. As always, care must be taken in distinguishing an obligation,

---

[12] A useful and close parallel is provided by *Forte and Co. v. General Accident Life Assurance* [1986] 2 E.G.L.R. 115 where a general obligation to comply with statutes was held to cover the tenant's compliance with a need for fire precaution works, with the result that the tenant had to pay rent on those works.

[13] *i.e.* without any direct contractual liability to comply.

for example, to erect a building from an obligation to erect it to a certain standard, should the tenant choose to erect it at all.[14]

3.6 Exclusions from section 8: replacement of a fixture or building belonging to the landlord: section 8(2)(b)

Section 8(2)(b) provides that section 8 shall not apply to a fixture affixed or a building erected instead of some fixture or building belonging to the landlord. On the face of it this appears designed to cover mere replacements. These replacements must be ones made by the tenant on a voluntary basis (otherwise section 8(2)(a) would adequately cover the situation). However the precise scope of this exemption is not necessarily easy to ascertain. Certainly it applies if the tenant replaces a landlord's cow building with one of his own, but what if the tenant replaces the landlord's cow building with a different type of building or one which is very much better than the landlord's original building? It is doubtful whether much assistance can be drawn from the tenant's concurrent right, if he chooses, to take compensation for the relevant building since section 8 simply establishes an alternative option of removal. The language of this particular exemption suggests replacement but not necessarily mere replacement of like for like. However, on balance, it is suggested that the correct approach is to construe the exemption narrowly so as to give the full effect to the enabling content of section 8 and therefore to regard replacement as indicating like for like replacement only.[15]

3.7 Exclusions from section 8: fixture or building already compensated for: section 8(2)(c)

Section 8(2)(c) disapplies section 8 in the case of a fixture or building in respect of which the tenant has obtained compensation under section 16[16] "or otherwise".[17] "Compensation" appears limited to compensation on termination since that is the only time at which it would be claimable under section 16 and it is suggested "or

---

[14] This is the problem highlighted by ***Godbold v. Martin (The Newsagents)*** [1983] 2 E.G.L.R. 128 and ***Historic Houses Hotels v. Cadogan Estates*** [1993] 2 E.G.L.R. 151, affirmed at [1995] 1 E.G.L.R. 117 discussed at para. 2.19 above.

[15] ***Sunderland v. Newton*** (1830) 3 Sim. 450 concerned the assignees of a bankrupt tenant removing machinery and buildings. The items in question had been provided by the original tenant replacing equipment and a building of the landlord in circumstances where the new equipment and building were very considerably superior to the original ones. The landlord was successful in restraining the assignees from removing the machinery and building: in the case of the machinery it was held that the replacement machinery had been provided as part of the tenant's fulfilment of his repairing obligation; with regard to the new building it was held that it "must be protected by the same covenant as protected the old one". There was a covenant to repair and deliver up on termination of the lease consistent with that repairing covenant. The action took place during the currency of the lease. It is a case sometimes considered to establish a common law exemption relating to the removal of fixtures parallel in its terms to s. 8(2)(b). However it is suggested that the reasoning is closer to that underlying the terms of s. 8(2)(a) and therefore that it does not answer the question as to whether the exemption in s. 8(2)(b) should be construed narrowly or widely.

[16] See para. 5.7 below.

[17] See para. 5.3 below.

EXCLUSIONS FROM SECTION 8: FIXTURE OR BUILDING ALREADY COMPENSATED

otherwise" is intended similarly to be confined. Consequently the scope of this exemption appears to be restricted to the situation where either the landlord pays the tenant's compensation due on termination or alternatively the landlord and tenant have agreed for the purposes of section 23 that, in the case of successive tenancies, payment shall be made under section 16 at the conclusion of the earlier tenancy.

Although section 16 compensation is an entitlement arising on quitting the holding,[18] the claims procedure only requires that the compensation should be the subject of a claims notice "before the end of the period of two months beginning with the date of the termination of the tenancy". If the tenant gives early notice prior to termination and the parties then settled a claim by agreement in writing[19] the tenant will be entitled to compensation under section 16. It is submitted that in those circumstances the tenant "has obtained compensation" for the purposes of the exemption within section 8(2)(c) since he has an enforceable claim for the compensation which is quantified whether or not payment has actually been made.[20]

Exclusions from section 8: fixtures or buildings with landlord's consent under section 17 conditional on tenant's agreement not to remove: section 8(2)(d)   3.8

Section 8 does not apply to a fixture or building in respect of which the landlord has given his consent under section 17[21] on condition that the tenant agrees not to remove it and which the tenant has agreed not to remove. This particular exemption is clear. However it should be noted that it is limited to a condition as to non-removal which the tenant has chosen to accept under section 17 or which is a condition approved by an arbitrator following the tenant invoking section 19.[22]

Content of rights under section 8: general   3.9

In relation to fixtures and buildings[23] section 8(1) provides that they may be removed by the tenant during the continuance of the tenancy or at any time after the termination of the tenancy when he remains in possession as tenant (whether or not under a new tenancy). Whilst there is a right to remove these items, they "remain his property".[24] The phrase "during the continuance of the tenancy" covers any contractual period and in addition any period of continuance effected by section 5.[25] Whilst a notice to quit is running the tenancy itself, of course, continues. If the

---

[18] s. 16(1).
[19] See s. 22(3)(a).
[20] The only alternative view of this particular state of affairs would be that the section 8 rights override the agreement as to compensation and strike it down, if the tenant removes the relevant improvement, on a retrospective basis pursuant to s. 16(2).
[21] See para. 5.10 below.
[22] Where the arbitrator gives his approval that approval "shall have effect for the purposes of this Part of this Act ... as if it were the consent of the landlord". If the tenant, following the making of the arbitrator's award, proceeds to take advantage of the conditional consent it is submitted that he has thereby agreed not to remove the relevant fixture or building.
[23] See further paras 3.10–3.11 below.
[24] s. 8(1).
[25] See para. 4.5 below.

tenant intends to surrender the tenancy, he must take care to remove the fixtures prior to execution of the deed of surrender, since the tenancy itself determines at that point. At any time after the termination of the tenancy, the tenant is only entitled to remove fixtures/buildings if "he remains in possession as tenant (whether or not under a new tenancy)". This provision appears primarily designed to provide in relation to section 8 a safeguard equivalent to section 23.[26] In addition it will cover any tenant whose tenancy has been forfeited but in whose favour the Court has granted relief from forfeiture. It is of the essence of a right to forfeit that, when it is exercised, the tenancy determines.[27] Forfeiture of a head lease will determine all sub-leases[28] and such sub-tenants will continue in possession "as tenant" if they obtain relief from forfeiture from the Court. In the case of a remediable breach giving rise to the right to forfeit, the landlord must serve a notice under section 146 of the Law of Property Act 1925 which requires him to give reasonable notice. In the case of an irremediable breach a period of notice is not necessary.[29] The refusal of relief from forfeiture is rare, and the Court has the widest possible discretion to consider the conduct of the parties and all the circumstances of the case on an application for relief from forfeiture.[30] Undoubtedly a tenant or sub-tenant would be entitled to draw to the Court's attention in the context of relief the consequences of any inability to satisfy the requirements of section 8(1) if there was a risk of valuable fixtures/buildings no longer being removable. It should be noted that the definition of "tenancy" excludes a tenancy at will[31] and it may therefore be questionable whether a "tenant" could be said to include a mere tenant at will.[32] Section 8(1) states that fixtures or buildings within the section remain the property of the tenant so long as they may be removed: this allows such items to be charged under the Agricultural Credits Act 1928.

---

[26] Supplementary provisions with respect to compensation in relation to successive tenancies.

[27] *Clays Lane Co-operative v. Patrick* (1984) 49 P.&C.R. 72. This is the case whether the forfeiture is by physical re-entry or by Court proceedings.

[28] *Great Western Railway v. Smith* [1876] 2 Ch. D. 235.

[29] As to the contents of a good s. 146 notice see *Woodfall, Landlord and Tenant*, Vol. 1, para. 17.130 and following.

[30] See *Woodfall* (above), paras 17.165–17.166.

[31] s. 38(1).

[32] To include such a person appears to produce divergent definitions for "tenant" and "tenancy" in the terms of s. 38. It is not necessary to produce this divergence in order to make sense of the words in s. 8(1) "or at any time ... (new tenancy)" since successive tenancies and the grant of relief from forfeiture in combination may explain the drafting. On the other hand unless this divergence is accepted, the tenant holding over after expiry of a notice to quit, which is itself contested, will, if he loses the proceedings, also lose his right to remove fixtures and buildings. Such a risk seems a curious importation given that there is a special definition in s. 38(5) preserving the designations of landlord and tenant for the benefit of the parties until the conclusion of any proceedings taken under the Act in respect of compensation. The explanation may be that the divergent construction of "tenant" and "tenancy" in s. 8(1) is not to be accepted and that a person who unsuccessfully contests a notice to quit will lose his right to remove fixtures and buildings if the proceedings are not determined before the tenancy itself determines; in that circumstance the tenant would be thrown back onto his statutory compensation rights, the entitlement for which can be triggered by service of an appropriate claims notice at any time up to two months after the determination of the tenancy (s. 22(2)).

Presumably for the purposes of taxation and/or capital allowances these items would also be regarded as belonging to the tenant.[33]

Fixtures within section 8: section 8(1)(a) 3.10
The section applies to:

> "Any fixture (of whatever description) affixed, whether for the purposes of agriculture or not, to the holding by the tenant under a farm business tenancy."

These provisions expressly apply to fixtures whether for the purposes of agriculture or not and it is clear from the bracketed words that there is an intention to include not only business fixtures but any type of fixtures.[34] Although fixtures within the terms of section 8(1)(a) must be "affixed ... to the holding by the tenant", the definition of "tenant"[35] is wide enough to include a sub-tenant and an assignee. It is convenient to regard the definitions of "tenancy" and "tenant" in section 38 as being convergent since "tenancy" expressly includes an agreement for a tenancy or a sub-tenancy. Therefore if the fixture is affixed by the tenant or sub-tenant under an agreement for lease but prior to execution of the lease he will be entitled to rights under section 8. It would appear that the tenant, as against the head landlord, is entitled to rights of removal under section 8, whereas he would not be entitled to make a claim under section 15 for compensation.[36] The intermediate landlord (*i.e.* the head tenant) will nevertheless, despite having rights under section 8, be constrained by the fact that his own sub-tenant will, as against him, in all likelihood also have section 8 rights of removal.[37] However it will be noted that relevant fixtures are only those affixed by a tenant (or sub-tenant) under a farm business tenancy. This means that fixtures affixed by a sub-tenant who occupies under the provisions of the Landlord and Tenant Act 1954 do not fall within section 8. Finally, and to state the obvious, a chattel cannot fall within section 8(1)(a) and it may on occasions be necessary to discern whether a particular item is truly a fixture or a chattel.[38]

---

[33] Contrast *Melluish v. B.M.I. (No.3) Ltd* [1996] A.C. 454.
[34] *e.g.* decorative and ornamental or intended for use in the home.
[35] s. 38(1).
[36] Contrast the wording of s. 8 with that of s. 15 referring (in sub-paras (a) and (b)) to the tenant's "own" effort or expense.
[37] It is difficult to see who, should any third party choose to intervene, should ultimately be regarded as the owner of such fixtures where more than one person has the right to remove.
[38] As to which see *Elitestone Ltd v. Morris* (1997) 27 E.G. 116 and it should be noted that parts of a fixture continue to be treated as fixtures even though they may be removable when not in use: see *The Sheffield and South Yorkshire Permanent Benefit Building Society v. Harrison* (1884) 15 Q.B.D. 358, CA. Where a machine is connected only indirectly to the property (*e.g.* through a fixed motor), this connection will not alter the character of the main equipment as a chattel: *Hulme v. Brigham* [1943] 1 K.B. 152; *Northern Press and Engineering Co. v. Shepherd* (1908) 52 S.J. 715. These decisions may assist in relation to equipment with compressors, independent electrical generators and/or separate humidity controls.

3.11 Buildings within section 8: section 8(1)(b)

Section 8(1) applies to any building erected by the tenant under a farm business tenancy.[39] "Building" is defined to include any part of a building[40] but is not otherwise defined. Commentary in the preceding paragraph as to who for these purposes may be a tenant under a farm business tenancy applies also in relation to sub-paragraph (b). Although the words "whether for the purposes of agriculture or not" are not specifically given in relation to a building, it is submitted that this is likely to have been the intention and there is no visible restriction in the phrase "any building" to buildings erected for agricultural purposes. If this be correct, there is parity in the treatment of fixtures and buildings and it would seem no longer to matter whether a particular building is or is not a fixture. There are, however, two inter-related questions which remain to be considered. They are:

(i) What is a building? and

(ii) Is a building within section 8 even though it may be a chattel?

In the absence of a specific full definition, it is submitted that what amounts to a building is a question of fact and degree. Although this may be regarded as in one sense unsatisfactory, the conclusion appears to be sanctioned by authority.[41] A chattel will not normally be capable of being described as a building,[42] but sometimes structures which, in ordinary language, would be "buildings" are

---

[39] s. 8(1)(b).

[40] s. 38(1).

[41] It has been said that what is ordinarily called a building is "an inclosure of brick or stonework covered in by a roof" (Lord Esher M.R. in *Moir v. Williams* [1892] 1 Q.B. 264 at 270) but the case involved premises which in fact matched that description. In some contexts "building" may include the fabric and the ground on which that building stands (judgment of the Privy Council delivered by Lord Atkinson at 390 in *Corporation of the City of Victoria v. Bishop of Vancouver Island* [1921] 2 A.C. 384) but it is questionable whether such an interpretation would be appropriate for section 8 unless an issue arose as to whether the tenant was entitled to remove the foundations of the building and, on the strength of this case, it would appear that he is. There are many cases quoted in both *Stroud's Judicial Dictionary*, (5th ed., Sweet and Maxwell, 1986), Volume 1 under "Building" and in *Words and Phrases legally defined*, (3rd Ed., Butterworths, 1988). It is submitted that the appropriate range of choice is best encapsulated in two quotes from older authority to be found in *Words and Phrases legally defined* (above) namely: "The imperfection of human language renders it not only difficult, but absolutely impossible, to define the word 'building' with any approach to accuracy. One may say of this or that structure, this or that is not a building; but no general definition can be given; and our lexicographers do not attempt it. Without, therefore, presuming to do what others have failed to do, I may venture to suggest, that, by a 'building' is usually understood a structure of considerable size, and intended to be permanent, or at least to endure for a considerable time" (Byles J. in *Stevens v. Gourley* [1859] 7 C.B.N.S. 99 at 112/113). "A small kennel for a lap dog could not be called a building. But it is a question of degree, and in this case we come to a structure 9 feet long, 7 feet high, 3 feet wide, erected some 30 feet in front of the line of street, and roofed in and fastened securely to the ground, intended to be used by a person inside, and not easily carried away ... A structure like that may properly be called a building" (Pollock B. in *Brown v. Leicester Corp.* [1892] 57 J.P. 70 at 71).

[42] See *Cheshire County Council v. Woodward* [1962] 2 Q.B. 126 (under the town and country planning legislation) and in particular Lord Parker C.J. at 134 and 135.

chattels.[43] It is unclear whether a building which remains in its nature a chattel should be regarded as a building for the purposes of section 8.[44] It is submitted that probably chattels ought to be excluded from the category of buildings within section 8 since section 8 appears to be granting rights of removal in circumstances where there would otherwise be no such rights: in the case of chattels, they will normally always be removable by the tenant. On this basis, a narrow view of "buildings" limited to property which has become part of the land or a fixture is preferred, applying the approach in *Deen v. Andrews*.

It should also be noted that a building acquired by a tenant is to be treated in the same way as one erected by him.[45]

Meaning of fixtures or buildings acquired: section 8(5)   3.12

By section 8(5) rights under section 8 are available in relation to a fixture or building acquired by a tenant as they are in relation to a fixture or building affixed or erected by him. No special definition of "acquired" is provided. However it is submitted that this would include not only purchase and inheritance but also any transfer of an item, no matter how received.[46]

Manner of exercise of rights under section 8: section 8(3) and (4)   3.13

The tenant must not do any avoidable damage to the holding in the course of removing a fixture or building under section 8.[47] If he does cause damage which could or should have been avoided he is in breach of statutory duty and, presumably, the landlord would be entitled to an injunction to prevent the damage or, in lieu, to damages. There is no express right of action conferred. Where the tenant removes a fixture or building he must immediately make good all damage (presumably whether or not avoidable) caused by that removal.[48] It would seem unlikely that the Court would grant an order requiring the tenant to comply with section 8(4), although no express right of action is conferred on the landlord. It is

---

[43] *Woodfall, Landlord and Tenant* Vol. 1, para. 13.137 gives as examples Nissen huts, and free standing greenhouses.

[44] In *Deen v. Andrews* (1986) 52 P.&C.R. 17, decision of Hirst J., it was held that a large greenhouse standing on its own weight on a concrete base and remaining a chattel in its nature did not constitute a "building" for the purposes of a conveyance because in that conveyance the word was to be given the same meaning as in s. 62 of the Law of Property Act 1925 and, applying *H.E. Dibble Limited v. Moore* [1970] 2 Q.B. 181, s. 62 did not operate to convey chattels at all. Although *Deen v. Andrews* might be criticised on the basis that s. 62 only applies in default of agreement by the parties and, in the contractual context, the parties may have intended the language to cover the relevant greenhouse whether or not it enjoyed chattel status, the case highlights the particular problem of construction.

[45] s. 8(5).

[46] "We agree with the Judge in the Court below that the taxpayers' argument derives no support from the use of the word 'acquired' in connection with the words 'by means of' in sub-section (1) since, as he points out, 'as used by lawyers the word 'acquired' has long covered transactions of a purely passive nature and means little more than receiving'. Indeed, that is the second ordinary meaning given in the *Shorter Oxford English Dictionary* ...": Cohen L.J. in *Congreve v. Inland Revenue Commrs* [1947] 1 All E.R. 168 at 173 quoted in *Words and Phrases legally defined* (above).

[47] s. 8(3).

[48] s. 8(4).

submitted that a damages claim is the only likely outcome.[49] If and in so far as the landlord chooses to sue for damages after the tenancy has come to an end there is no procedure specified for the service of notices of claim.[50] At common law removal of a fixture which should not have been removed at all constitutes waste[51] and it is likely that the wrongful removal of items not authorised to be taken under section 8 is likewise waste.

3.14 Forfeiture clauses and section 8

It is considered that there are no difficulties in constructing a valid forfeiture clause being a clause which does not provide for a period of notice before that clause is capable of exercise.[52] The suggestion has been made that *Parry v. Million Pigs Limited*[53] may give rise to problems.[54] This suggestion is not considered to be correct, for the reasons given in paragraph 1.46 above.

---

[49] There is not only a historic reluctance to order tenants to effect repairing works but it will be appreciated that most claims will arise on termination of the tenancy and the tenant will have no independent rights to go on the property thereafter.
[50] Contrast the elaborate procedures under s. 83 of the Agricultural Holdings Act 1986 considered in paras 13.116–13.119 below.
[51] See *Woodfall, Landlord and Tenant*, Vol. 1, para. 13.166.
[52] Not to be confused with satisfactory compliance with s. 146 of the Law of Property Act 1925.
[53] [1980] 260 E.G. 281.
[54] See Scammell and Densham, *Law of Agricultural Holdings*, (8th ed.) pp. 1020–1021.

Chapter 4

TERMINATION OF TENANCY BY NOTICE

4.1 General

4.2 Termination of fixed term farm business tenancies of two years or less

4.3 Termination of weekly, monthly or quarterly periodic tenancies

4.4 Break clauses in fixed term agreements of two years or less or weekly periodic or quarterly tenancies

4.5 Tenancies for more than two years continue from year to year unless terminated by notice: section 5

4.6 Who may give notice under section 5: jointly held estates

4.7 Mandatory nature of section 5

4.8 Fixed terms of more than two years—break clauses: section 7

4.9 Exclusion from section 7: tenant's counternotice under section 140 of the Law of Property Act 1925

4.10 Exclusion from section 7(1): terms within section 149(6) of the Law of Property Act 1925

4.11 Grounds on which break clauses may be exercised

4.12 Who may give notice under section 7: jointly held estates

4.13 Notice to quit annual tenancies

4.14 Requirements of a valid notice to quit: section 6(1)

4.15 Exclusion from section 6: tenant's counter-notice under section 140(2) of the Law of Property Act 1925

4.16 Ascertainment of the length of a fixed term

4.17 No security of tenure

4.18 Compliance with the Protection from Eviction Act 1977

4.19 Who may give notice under section 6: jointly held estates

4.20 Disputes: jurisdiction of the Courts

4.1 General

By three short sections the 1995 Act disposes of the subject of termination of a farm business tenancy by notice. The rules are, in contrast to the Agricultural Holdings Act,[1] straightforward. The overriding feature of all the statutory provisions is, where the appropriate rules regarding notices are obeyed, the inevitable termination of the tenancy and any right to occupy. There is no question of serving counternotice or otherwise prolonging the tenancy and there is no jurisdiction in the Court to intervene so as to grant relief. Nor is it necessary, under the statute, to have any reason for terminating the tenancy. It appears, for example, perfectly lawful to terminate a yearly tenancy in circumstances where the landlord is simply dissatisfied with the rent fixed under Part II of the Act. This ability to bring a tenancy to an end is one which, it is hoped, the Courts will respect and not strive to frustrate. It is the essential guarantee of a farm business tenancy, and therefore the key to unlocking the availability of land for farming tenancies, that the tenant must leave when the tenancy is appropriately terminated. There has clearly been a choice by Parliament not to follow the model of the Landlord and Tenant Act 1954 allowing the tenant an opportunity to claim a new tenancy and the contrast with the scheme of protection under the Agricultural Holdings Act 1986 could not be more stark. The strength of these termination provisions[2] simply underline the need for the tenant at the bargaining stage when the terms of his tenancy are being considered to understand fully the implications of the tenancy he is granted.

4.2 Termination of fixed term farm business tenancies of two years or less

Fixed term farm business tenancies for terms of two years or less are entirely outside the scope of the notice provisions in sections 5–7 of the 1995 Act. There is, accordingly, no need to serve notice under the 1995 Act to bring such an agreement to an end since it will expire by effluxion of time. The most frequently encountered type of agreement falling within this category will be a grazing tenancy for part of a year. This type of agreement previously fell within an exception to the Agricultural Holdings Act 1986 contained within section 2.

4.3 Termination of weekly, monthly or quarterly periodic tenancies

Agreements which amount to weekly, monthly or quarterly periodic tenancies are not the subject of control as regards termination by notice under the 1995 Act. In order to terminate such interests it is only necessary to comply with the general law. At common law weekly tenancies are determinable by one week's notice, monthly tenancies by one month's notice and quarterly tenancies by one quarter's notice. This basic position may be overridden by the terms of the contract and where applicable, custom or other statutes.[3] Although in all probability farm business tenancies of these types will be rare they are likely to be encountered in the context of grazing land for horses where the business involves teaching riders or training horses and the demand for this particular service is not constant.

---

[1] See Chapter 12.
[2] ss. 5, 6 and 7.
[3] See generally *Woodfall, Landlord and Tenant*, Vol. 1, para. 17.208 *et seq.*

Break clauses in fixed term agreements of two years or less or weekly periodic or quarterly tenancies 4.4

There is no control at all and no need to comply with requirements of the 1995 Act in relation to break clauses contained in leases or tenancy agreements which themselves do not on termination fall within sections 5–7 of the 1995 Act. Thus the ability to bring to an end a two year tenancy by serving a contractual break notice 28 days in length will be valid and there is no provision in the 1995 statute which affects it.[4]

Tenancies for more than two years continue from year to year unless terminated by notice: section 5 4.5

Any fixed term farm business tenancy for a term of more than two years continues after the term date as a yearly tenancy unless an appropriate termination notice has been given. Without such a notice the term continues as from the term date[5] but otherwise on the terms of the original tenancy so far as applicable. It is therefore clear that the continuation tenancy is contractual in its nature and there is no parallel with the statutory tenancy familiar from the Rent Act 1977. The termination notice is not required to be in prescribed form but it must be a written notice given at least 12 months but less than 24 months before the term date and informing the other party of the giver's intention to termination the tenancy.[6] A suggested form of notice is contained in the Precedents in Part VI.[7] The essential test of validity will be the clarity with which the notice is drawn and the case law as to the construction of notices to quit is likely to be relevant.[8] Where the reversion has been severed each reversioner has the right to serve notice to quit in relation to his own part of the reversion[9] and this includes the right to serve a notice of termination under section 5.[10] A section 5 termination notice may be given by either the landlord or the tenant in order to bring the tenancy to an end. What if, before the expiry of the fixed term the tenant has actually vacated? Is any notice of termination necessary to bring the tenancy to an end? This is a very difficult question and it is cautiously suggested that in those circumstances no notice is required.[11]

---

[4] This contrasts with the need for notices under the Agricultural Holdings Act 1986 to comply with the terms of s. 25 which affect virtually all notices including break notices.
[5] *i.e.* the date fixed for the expiry of the term (s. 5(2)).
[6] s. 5(1).
[7] Form 103 (Fixed term: termination notice at expiry).
[8] See paras 12.25 and 12.29–12.30 below.
[9] s. 140 of the Law of Property Act 1925.
[10] s. 5(3).
[11] The tenant would have ceased to satisfy the business conditions before the expiry of the tenancy, therefore taking it outside the scope of the Act before s. 5 bites. This has the merit of logic and follows the parallel line of argument eventually adopted in relation to the Landlord and Tenant Act 1954 in ***Esselte AB v. Pearl Assurance plc*** [1997] 1 E.G.L.R. 73. However this may raise, if correct, a severe problem in relation to compensation: does the tenant who vacates early lose his compensation rights unless he has before leaving served claims notice so as to take advantage of s. 38(5)?

TERMINATION OF TENANCY BY NOTICE

4.6 Who may give notice under section 5: jointly held estates

This is a strangely difficult question. The reasoning underlying the ability of one joint landlord or tenant to serve notice to quit is that all periodic tenancies come to an end at the end of each period unless the parties by silence are taken to have agreed to a continuation. The purpose of giving the notice to quit is to demonstrate that this implicit agreement does not exist.[12] In the case of agreements prolonged by section 5 the continuation is statutory and the tenancy does not end unless a notice is served. Although by no means entirely clear it is submitted that probably a notice under section 5 designed to bring the tenancy to an end on the expressed expiry date is one which must be served by all of the joint landlords or tenants (as the case may be).[13]

4.7 Mandatory nature of section 5

The provisions contained within section 5 are mandatory and the section has effect notwithstanding any agreement to the contrary.[14] This clearly prevents parties from avoiding the notice provisions and the essential continuation until appropriate notice is given. However it is submitted that section 5(4) should not be construed so as to bar the parties from reaching agreement as to variation of the terms and conditions of the tenancy after the term date has been reached. There would appear to be no need to construe section 5(1) as requiring the parties to continue for ever on the terms of the original tenancy. Rather, it is submitted, the essential aim of the section is to indicate to parties on what basis the continuation will take place it being no part of the statutory policy to prevent the parties from, for example, varying the assignment clauses thereafter.[15] The wording of section 5(4) is considerably wider in its terms than the bracketed words in sections 6(1) and 7(1) which refer only to notices being invalid "notwithstanding any provision to the contrary in the tenancy".

4.8 Fixed terms of more than two years—break clauses: section 7

Where there is a contractual provision section 7 must be complied with otherwise any notice to quit will be invalid. There is no prescribed form for the statutory notice and it is only necessary that the notice be in writing and be given at least 12 months but less than 24 months before the date on which it is to take effect.[16] Section 7 applies whether the notice to quit intended to be given relates to the entire holding or to only part of it.[17] Section 7 is mandatory in that it invalidates any non-complying notice notwithstanding any provision to the contrary in the

---

[12] See ***Hammersmith and Fulham LBC v. Monk*** [1992] 1 A.C. 478 and para. 12.24 below.

[13] This may seem to be a curious conclusion since a notice given in respect of the first anniversary of that date appears to be treated as a notice to quit by s. 6(2) (*i.e.* could be given by one only of the joint landlords or tenants) even though at common law it is not possible to give a notice to quit before the tenancy begins.

[14] s. 5(4).

[15] Even under the Agricultural Holdings Act 1986 a statutory conversion under s. 2 simply establishes the terms of tenancy but has never been used so as to prevent the parties from varying the tenancy agreement thereafter.

[16] s. 7(1).

[17] Consequently a variety of precedents are suggested in Part VI of this work namely Form

tenancy.[18] But the section does not strike down a contractual clause which imposes restrictions consistent with the statutory requirements. Any notice to quit must comply with contractual requirements as well as (in so far as not inconsistent with) the statutory requirements. In other words where the contract requires the break notice to be served only in specific circumstances or only where particular reasons can be justified then these requirements remain and are unaffected by the terms of section 7. If a contractual break clause is being relied on it should be referred to on the face of the section 7 notice and if the contract imposes requirements as to the form of the notice, they also must be complied with before the notice will be valid. In substance the statute operates to provide a uniform period of notice but does not establish other conditions and leaves untouched conditions dealing with other matters which the parties themselves have chosen to impose. The statute[19] clearly contemplates not that a notice to quit must necessarily expire on the anniversary date but rather that the expiry date bears a certain relationship to the date on which the notice is given. If a break notice may only be given so as to expire on a stipulated date (whether or not it is the anniversary date) it is submitted that the clause will be valid but the opportunity for exercise is only available in accordance with the statute. Break clauses which are drawn so as to exclude all possibility of compliance with section 7 are therefore ineffective.[20] Resumptions of part of the property (*e.g.* for building purposes) exercisable on the traditional three or six months notice will therefore not allow the giver of the notice to comply with section 7 and such clauses will not be effective. Where the contractual clause provides for notice to be given which is "not less than" a stipulated length this allows the giver of the notice to comply with section 7 and such a clause will be effective.

Exclusion from section 7: tenant's counter-notice under section 140 of the Law of Property Act 1925   4.9

Where a tenant serves counter-notice under section 140(2) of the Law of Property Act 1925 his notice does not have to comply with section 7(1). The provisions of the 1925 Act are not in this aspect drawn with any special reference to agricultural property and the exclusion from section 7(1)[21] assimilates farm business tenancies to other types of tenancy.

Exclusion from section 7(1): terms within section 149(6) of the Law of Property Act 1925   4.10

A lease for life or lives or for a term determinable with life or lives or on the marriage of the lessee is governed by section 149(6) of the Law of Property Act 1925 and any notice required to bring such a term to an end is not affected by

---

104 (fixed term: tenant's break notice), Form 105 (fixed term: landlord's break notice), Form 106 (fixed term: tenant's notice to quit part), Form 107 (fixed term: landlord's notice to quit part).
[18] s. 7(1).
[19] s. 7(1).
[20] *e.g.* break clauses exercisable on six months notice.
[21] Contained in s. 7(2).

section 7(1) even where it is a farm business tenancy.[22] Part VI of this work provides a precedent for a notice of termination on the tenant's death.[23]

4.11 Grounds on which break clauses may be exercised

There is no control by the statute as to the use to which a break clause may be put and there is no requirement that any particular grounds be available or stated before a break clause may be given. This is a matter regulated entirely by the contract between the parties. It is a matter of construction of the contract as to what grounds have to be satisfied and in what circumstances. The statute imposes no requirement that contractual break clauses be exercised only reasonably.

4.12 Who may give notice under section 7: jointly held estates

A notice under section 7 is a true break clause and can only be exercised by all the joint landlords or all the joint tenants.[24]

4.13 Notice to quit annual tenancies

Section 6 governs notices to quit any annual farm business tenancy. This covers both tenancies which were yearly tenancies from the outset and also tenancies which become yearly tenancies pursuant to the operation of section 5 on the expiry of the fixed term. Section 6 applies whether the notice to quit relates to the whole or to part of the holding and any notice to quit which fails to comply with section 6(1) is invalid.

4.14 Requirements of a valid notice to quit: section 6(1)

The notice to quit must be in writing, expressed to take effect at the end of a year of the tenancy and must be given at least 12 months but less than 24 months before the date on which it is to take effect. There is no prescribed form for such a notice to quit. Various suggested precedents are contained within Part VI.[25] In the case of an annual tenancy arising after the expiry of a fixed term[26] the tenancy may be brought to an end on the first anniversary of the original term date (*i.e* 12 months after the date originally fixed for the expiry of the term) provided a notice complying with section 6 has been served. The notice is not invalidated because it is given before the original term date.[27] The ascertainment of the end of a year of the tenancy is a task familiar from the drawing of notices to quit in many contexts.[28] Section 6 takes effect "notwithstanding any provision to the contrary in the tenancy"[29] which

---

[22] s. 7(3).
[23] Form 112.
[24] *Leek and Moorlands Building Society v. Clark* [1952] 2 Q.B. 788 and see discussion at para. 12.24 below.
[25] Form 108 (tenant's notice to quit), Form 109 (landlord's notice to quit), Form 110 (tenant's notice to quit part), Form 111 (landlord's notice to quit part).
[26] *i.e.* pursuant to s. 5(1).
[27] s. 6(2). This provision is logical given the ability under s. 5 to bring a fixed term agreement to an end on the date expressed for its expiry, which necessarily involves the giving of a notice during the term.
[28] See discussion in relation to notices to quit under the Agricultural Holdings Act 1986 in para. 12.14 below.
[29] The same wording being applicable in the case of s. 7.

appears not to preclude acceptance by the recipient party of an invalid notice to quit and the making of a subsequent agreement to that effect.[30]

Exclusion from section 6: tenant's counter-notice under section 140(2) of the Law of Property Act 1925   4.15

Where a tenant serves counternotice under section 140(2) of the Law of Property Act 1925 his counternotice is governed entirely by that section and the requirements of section 6(1) do not apply even though the tenancy itself is a farm business tenancy. The section applies where there is a severed reversion.

Ascertainment of the length of a fixed term   4.16

Sections 5 and 7 refer to tenancies "for a term of more than two years" without making reference to the grant or beginning of the tenancy.[31] What is required is to ascertain on ordinary principles when the agreement was entered into and what, from that time, the length of the term was. This problem arises most frequently where the parties express the agreement to commence at a date prior to the date on which it was entered into. The subject has been comprehensively examined under the Agricultural Holdings Act in order to determine the true term and it is submitted that those cases will be followed.[32] Thus if a term is expressed to be a three-year term but is not in fact entered into until the last 18 months of the term are outstanding, the arrangement as a whole will be a term of 18 months and section 5 will not apply to it. In the same way, any contractual break clause will take effect according to its own terms since section 7 will not be applicable either.

No security of tenure   4.17

The net result of sections 5–7 is not to create a system of security of tenure but simply to allow the tenant a prescribed period of notice at the end of which he must quit the property. There are no special provisions in relation to sub-tenancies which, in the absence of some other code[33] applying, will fall with the head tenancy.

Compliance with the Protection from Eviction Act 1977   4.18

The Protection from Eviction Act 1977 applies, in certain circumstances, where premises are let as a dwelling. In particular where this is the case section 5 requires prescribed information to be contained on any notice to quit. It is submitted that there is no need to comply with section 5 of the 1977 Act because a farm business tenancy does not comprise premises "let as a dwelling" even if there is a dwelling on the holding. There is a close analogy with the case of *National Trust for Places of Historic Interest or Natural Beauty v. Knipe*[34] in which the Court of Appeal declined to apply section 5 of the 1977 Act to a notice to quit served under the

---

[30] Compare *Elsden v. Pick* [1980] 1 W.L.R. 898 and discussion at para. 12.4 below.
[31] It is submitted that the special definitions contained in s. 38(3) and (4) are therefore irrelevant.
[32] See *Keen v. Holland* [1984] 1 All E.R. 75 and *Pahl v. Trevor* [1992] 1 E.G.L.R. 22 explaining earlier case law. See paras 9.3 and 9.30–9.21 below.
[33] *e.g.* the Landlord and Tenant Act 1954.
[34] (1997) 40 E.G. 151.

Agricultural Holdings Act 1986 because premises let as an agricultural holding were not premises let as a dwelling.

4.19 Who may give notice under section 6: jointly held estates
A notice under section 6 is in nature a notice to quit and may be given by all or by any one of joint landlords or joint tenants.[35]

4.20 Disputes: jurisdiction of the Courts
A dispute as to the operation of sections 5–7[36] falls within the jurisdiction of the Courts: the wording of the compulsory arbitration provisions in section 28 does not seem appropriate to this type of dispute.[37]

---

[35] *Hammersmith and Fulham LBC v. Monk* [1992] 1 A.C. 478 and see the discussion at paragraph 12.24 below.
[36] *e.g.* as to whether a notice to quit was valid.
[37] See para. 6.2 below.

CHAPTER 5

COMPENSATION ON TERMINATION OF FARM BUSINESS TENANCY

5.1 Compensation on termination: general

5.2 Mandatory nature of Part III: section 26

5.3 Cases where only contractual compensation will be available

5.4 Meaning of "tenant's improvement"

5.5 Compensation in relation to sub-tenancies

5.6 Tenant's fixed equipment?

5.7 The right to compensation

5.9 Compensation for planning permission

5.10 Improvements other than planning permission

5.11 Reference to arbitration where no satisfactory landlord's consent: section 19

5.12 Non-routine improvements

5.13 Routine improvements

5.14 Acclimatisation or hefting of sheep

5.15 Section 19 arbitration

5.17 Compensation for planning permission

5.18 Compensation for other improvements

5.20 Making and determination of compensation claim

5.23 Supplemental provisions: successive tenancies, resumption of possession of part, severed reversions

Compensation on termination: general
Part III of the Agricultural Tenancies Act 1995 contains all the statutory provisions relating to compensation on termination of a farm business tenancy. For these purposes compensation means compensation to the tenant and there are no express provisions at all which allow for compensation to the landlord. Section 15[1] defines

---

[1] See para. 5.4 below.

a "tenant's improvement" and section 16[2] contains the terms of the tenant's entitlement. Sections 17–19 set out the conditions of eligibility for compensation which, in broad terms, relate to the need for the consent of either the landlord or (by way of substitution) an arbitrator. All tenant's improvements other than planning permission require a landlord's written consent[3]; compensation for planning permission requires additional conditions to be satisfied.[4] Where the landlord's consent is not available the tenant may proceed to arbitration to obtain a substituted consent.[5] The amount of compensation for all improvements apart from planning permission is as stipulated by section 20.[6] Section 21 deals with the amount of compensation for planning permission.[7] There is a special claims and disputes procedure,[8] and supplementary provisions are available for successive tenancies,[9] the resumption of possession of part of a holding[10] and where a reversionary estate is severed.[11] The compensation provisions are mandatory.[12]

5.2 Mandatory nature of Part III: section 26

Where Part III provides for compensation, the tenant is entitled only to compensation in accordance with those provisions and his entitlement stands "notwithstanding any agreement to the contrary".[13] It is clear that section 26(1) will override any contractual provision which directly prevents a compensation claim from being made and it is extremely likely that the sub-section operates to render invalid any contractual provision which indirectly results in the tenant being deprived of his otherwise rights under Part III.[14] Where a contract provides for compensation in circumstances where the Act does not, those contractual provisions are unaffected by section 26(1).[15] It will be recollected that section 19 of the Landlord and Tenant Act 1927 does not apply to a farm business tenancy[16]: there is nothing unlawful in a landlord providing an absolute bar on a change in use and, since section 19(3) does not apply, if the lease contains a covenant against change in use without consent, the landlord is entitled to stipulate that he shall be paid for the granting of his consent. Whilst the tenant may apply for an arbitrator's consent under sections 17 and 19 in the case of a physical improvement, the

---

[2] See para. 5.7 below.
[3] s. 17 and para. 5.10 below.
[4] s. 18 and para. 5.9 below.
[5] s. 19 and para. 5.11 below.
[6] See paras 5.18–5.19 below.
[7] See paras 5.17–5.19 below.
[8] s. 22 and paras 5.20–5.22 below.
[9] s. 23 and para. 5.23 below.
[10] s. 24 and para. 5.24 below.
[11] s. 25 and para. 5.25 below.
[12] See s. 26 and para. 5.2 below.
[13] s. 26(1).
[14] The language of s. 26(1) is mandatory and there are good parallels with the drafting and effect of corresponding parts of the Agricultural Holdings Act 1986 (see in particular para. 13.2 below).
[15] s. 26(2).
[16] See para. 1.29 above.

arbitrator must[17] consider the terms of tenancy and decide whether it is reasonable for the tenant to provide the improvement. In such a case the tenant has rights which override the contract and, if the arbitrator gives his consent it operates contractually, as well for the purposes of the Act, as though it were the landlord's consent directly to the making of the improvement[18] and indirectly to the change of use. However, if the tenant intends to do no more than apply for planning permission, his landlord's refusal to grant consent in particular to a change of use, is final.[19] If the landlord voluntarily agrees to compensate the tenant for obtaining a planning permission for change of use, despite the fact that implementation of such a planning permission would constitute a breach of the tenancy terms, the compensation provisions under the contract are saved by section 26(2). If subsequently the tenant decides, instead of claiming the contractual compensation on termination, to attempt to take advantage of the permission himself and chooses to do physical works and secures the landlord's or the arbitrator's consent to the doing of those works, the tenant on termination will be entitled to compensation for the physical improvements under the statute: whether or not he is also then entitled to the contractual compensation will depend on the terms of its drafting.[20]

It is not always easy to see exactly what is struck down by section 26(1). If the tenancy prohibits the making of any improvements, such a clause may subsequently be partly overridden (at least in relation to improvements for which actual consent of an arbitrator has been obtained under section 19(5)). At least from the time of the grant of the arbitrator's consent the contract must be regarded as modified and works done thereafter are lawful. This may mean that works which are not "routine improvements"[21] are unlawful if done before any arbitrator's consent is obtained and a forfeiture in respect of those works may be valid.[22] The landlord's contractual bar on the making of non-routine improvements is probably partially effective.[23] The situation in regard to "routine improvements" is totally different since these are defined by section 19(10) as relating only to lawful

---

[17] s. 19(5).
[18] s. 19(7).
[19] s. 18.
[20] Draftsmen are warned that there may be a problem of double compensation.
[21] s. 19(10).
[22] See s. 19(2) which then excludes such works from the compensation scheme under the statute.
[23] If the landlord attempted to forfeit before the tenant had had the opportunity to refer the matter to arbitration, it is submitted that the court would be unlikely to deal with the issue of relief from forfeiture unless and until the arbitrator had made his award, the effect of which might well be to vary the contract in the tenant's favour and accordingly provide a new basis for the court on which to grant relief from forfeiture. The interim status of the tenancy is interesting since forfeiture destroys its common law existence until it revests on the grant of relief. However, the definition of "tenancy" in s. 38(1), it is submitted, should be wide enough to cover the equitable rights remaining in the tenant in that interim period so as to found the arbitrator's jurisdiction.

improvements. A contractual bar on the making of an application for planning permission is likely to be unaffected by section 26(1).[24]

5.3 Cases where only contractual compensation will be available

Because of the drafting of Part III of the Act, and the underlying philosophy that the Act is to provide the essentials but still leaves scope for the parties to contract with relative freedom, there are a number of situations where on negotiating his farm business tenancy a tenant would be advised to make express provision for compensation on termination of his tenancy, depending on the circumstances he anticipates. These situations are:

(i) compensation to the head tenant for improvements provided by a sub-tenant[25];

(ii) compensation for an assignee where he has purchased improvements provided by the original tenant[26];

(iii) compensation in respect of sheep/beef quota left in the landlord's control[27];

(iv) compensation to the tenant in circumstances where expenditure or effort towards an improvement is provided by a company controlled by the tenant[28];

(v) acclimatisation or hefting of sheep.[29]

In circumstances where a tenant moves from one part of a landlord's estate to another and wishes to agree with the landlord that Agriculture Act compensation for milk quota on termination of the first tenancy[30] should be paid only on expiration of the second tenancy as at values current at that time, care must be taken to address the issue as to who will be responsible for payment in the event that either the land comprising the original tenancy or the reversion over the subsequent tenancy is sold on. In the normal way a deferred obligation of the type

---

[24] Section 18 leaves the matter of consent to the making of planning permission entirely to the landlord's discretion. If the tenant makes an application for planning permission in breach of the tenancy he has no right to compensation and it is likely that a landlord's forfeiture based on that breach would be successful. If, before the application for relief from forfeiture is disposed of, the tenant decides he wishes actually to go ahead and do an improvement which required planning permission then the contract may be varied by the arbitrator on an application under s. 19. If the planning permission in question relates to change of use and/or the tenant does not intend to proceed to the arbitrator for consent under s. 19, s. 26(1) does not appear to provide an impediment to the landlord's enforcement of his contractual rights at all.
[25] See para. 5.5 below.
[26] See para. 5.4 below.
[27] See para. 5.4 below.
[28] See para. 5.4 below.
[29] See para. 5.14 below.
[30] See Chapter 19.

described would fall upon the owner of the land comprised within the original tenancy as a personal obligation to pay but at a deferred date.[31]

Compensation under Part III is only claimable as at the termination of the tenancy on quitting: if the tenant wishes and the landlord is willing to pay an accelerated amount of money in respect of a tenant's improvement any ultimate compensation payable on termination will be reduced by a figure reflecting the advance payment.[32] Such arrangements are not made under Part III but are recognised by it.

It is also worth noting that there are cases where statutory compensation will be available but it will be extremely difficult to comply with section 19(2)[33] and it may be prudent to include in the contract of tenancy from the outset a consent to the making of the improvement.

Attention is drawn to the terms of sections 23 (successive tenancies),[34] 24 (resumption of possession of part of holding)[35] and 25 (compensation where the reversion is severed).[36] These are special applications provided by Part III exclusively in relation to statutory compensation. Where contractual compensation is being dealt with under a farm business tenancy it may be desirable to provide an approximate contractual equivalent.

Meaning of "tenant's improvement": section 15 5.4
There are two categories of "tenant's improvement" namely:

(a) any physical improvement which is made on the holding by the tenant by his own effort or wholly or partly at his own expense, or

(b) any intangible advantage which -

   (i) is obtained for the holding by the tenant by his own effort or wholly or partly at his own expense, and

   (ii) becomes attached to the holding.

Category (a)
What amounts to a physical "improvement" will always be judged from the perspective of the tenant, not the landlord and it is well established that works may be an "improvement" even if they damage the value of the property.[37] Physical improvements within this category are limited to those made by the tenant's "own" effort or expenditure and accordingly a tenant cannot claim where works were done and paid for by a sub-tenant. It appears that the extended definition of

---

[31] This is believed to be a scheme commonly entered into by a number of landlords. It will be recollected that a personal obligation of this type is contractual in its nature and does not run with the land.
[32] See s. 20(3) as regards improvements not consisting of planning permission and s. 21(3) where the improvement is the obtaining of planning permission.
[33] *e.g.* the provision of milk quota as an improvement.
[34] See para. 5.23 below.
[35] See para. 5.24 below.
[36] See para. 5.25 below.
[37] Luxmoore J. in **Bowles Brothers Ltd v. Sinclair** [1931] 2 Ch.325; Rowlatt J. in **Lilley and Skinner Ltd v. Crump** [1929] 73 S.J. 366; **Lambert v. F.W. Woolworth and Co.** [1938] 1 Ch. 883, CA.

"tenancy"[38] would enable the procedures in Part III to be implemented in relation to an agreement for a tenancy where the person taking the benefit of it had entered into possession. It would also appear that the extended definition of "tenant"[39] is displaced by the word "own" so as to exclude not only sub-tenants but also a claim made in respect of works effected by a predecessor in title. In other words an assignee cannot make a claim where the work was done by the original tenant.[40] Where there is an assignment of a farm business tenancy it is accordingly important that, if the assignee wishes to claim compensation from the landlord, an express contractual compensation scheme is established for his benefit. Such a scheme will be protected by section 26(2). The improvement must be provided by the tenant's "own effort or wholly or partly at his own expense" and there might appear to be a contrast between effort as sole contribution to the improvement and expense as partial contribution to the improvement. However, it is submitted, this would be an unnecessarily pedantic reading and it is considered that the tenant will be entitled to make a claim in respect of a physical improvement where he has contributed his own effort even though other parties may also have contributed whether in terms of effort or expense.[41] It is as yet unresolved whether expenditure by a partnership of which the tenant is a member or a company which the tenant controls will be regarded as the tenant's "own" expenditure. There is probably a line of division between these two cases: where the tenant is part of a partnership, partnership expenditure is undoubtedly that of the individual tenant as well as of his partners[42]; in the case of a company it would seem tolerably clear that the expenditure of the company is not the expenditure of the tenant.[43] Where the tenant is paid a salary for putting in work on a relevant physical improvement it is submitted that the effort in question should be regarded as that of any company paying his salary, since the company must act through servants or agents.[44] In the case of a corporate tenant work done by sub-contractors, whether or not paid for by the company, is likely to be regarded as the effort of the company.[45] "Routine improvements" are a sub-category within the overall description "physical improvement" and they are separately identified only because special rules apply to them when the tenant wishes to obtain an arbitrator's consent for the purposes of section 19.[46]

---

[38] s. 38(1).
[39] s. 38(1).
[40] Perhaps rather surprising but apparently intended: contrast s. 8(5) applying the right to remove fixtures. The assignee will be entitled to remove any fixture or building falling within s. 8. There are no special provisions in Part III to deal with assignees, although there are special provisions in s. 23 to deal with successive tenancies.
[41] This view is apparently shared by the authors of *Scammell and Densham, Law of Agricultural Holdings*, (8th ed.), p. 1026.
[42] There is nothing in the statute to indicate that "own" expenditure means that it must be several as distinct from joint and several expenditure.
[43] Compare on the issue of occupation by a company controlled by the tenant cases under the Landlord and Tenant Act 1954: *Cristina v. Seear* [1985] 2 E.G.L.R. 128, *Nozari-Zadeh v. Pearl Assurance plc* [1987] 2 E.G.L.R. 91.
[44] Compare Webster J. in *Trinity College Cambridge v. Caines* [1984] 2 E.G.L.R. 17 at 18M (quoted at para. 14.42 above) and *Wallace v. C. Brian Barratt & Son Ltd* [1997] 31 E.G. 97.
[45] See *Wallace v. C. Brian Barratt & Son Ltd* (above).
[46] See para. 5.13 below.

Category (b)

As to "intangible advantages", it is not known whether the test as to what may amount to an advantage will be viewed from the perspective of the landlord or of the tenant. It does, however, appear likely that improvements and intangible advantages in this respect ought to be treated in the same way, that is to say from the tenant's perspective. This leaves open the possibility that an "intangible advantage" may be no advantage at all, from the landlord's point of view, and this problem may be particularly evident in relation to planning permission for something which the landlord would not wish to see implemented. Within this category and sub-paragraph (i), the same observations are made in relation to the words "by the tenant by his own effort or wholly or partly at his own expense" as are made in relation to category (a) improvements above. What is meant by "obtained for the holding" and "becomes attached to the holding" is obscure. These do not appear to be legal terms of art. Planning permission is clearly intended to be an intangible advantage[47] and there is every prospect that milk quota and goodwill[48] are very probably included. Although, in loose parlance one may speak of milk quota or goodwill being "attached to" a holding, it is difficult to see how these kinds of advantages were obtained for the holding as distinct from being obtained by the tenant for himself. In all probability "obtained for the holding" is intended to be a vague umbrella term rather than a term of art.[49] Sheep and beef quotas may in one sense be regarded as attaching to the holding but, on termination of the tenancy, they do not remain on the holding[50] and accordingly no compensation claim can be made in respect of them.[51] If compensation is to be made available for a tenant who in fact wishes to "leave" sheep or beef quota to his landlord, great care will be required in the drawing of any provisions and any such compensation will not be under Part III of the 1995 Act.[52] On the face of it, it is difficult to see why entering into set aside or an SSSI management scheme should be regarded as an intangible advantage within these provisions but, if no over-precise legal meaning is attached to section 15(b), effect may be given to the reluctance by the Court to treat this type of arrangement as purely personal to the tenant.[53]

---

[47] See s. 17(5).

[48] Meaning goodwill which remains for the benefit of the holding after the tenant's own business use has come to an end.

[49] It can surely hardly be the case that Parliament intended the tenant to have a compensation claim for milk quota which he transferred on to the holding directly but not to have such a claim where the milk quota was transferred into a "holding" within the meaning of the Dairy Produce Quotas Regulations 1997 of which the farm business tenancy was only a part, if by the termination of the farm business tenancy all or part of that milk quota originally attaching to the larger area has become attached only to the area of the farm business tenancy. (In order to understand this point readers may find it helpful to consult Chapter 18.)

[50] Contrast milk quota.

[51] s. 16(2)(b).

[52] Although any such compensation will be preserved by s. 26(2). Persons attempting such an arrangement will need to consider the terms of the relevant Regulations giving rise to the quota and ought to bear in mind the impact on rent review of any terms they come to.

[53] See *J.W. Childers v. Anker* [1996] 1 E.G.L.R. 1 as quoted at para. 11.7 below.

5.5 Compensation in relation to sub-tenancies

A compensation claim may be made by a sub-tenant in relation to his own improvements and such a claim will, naturally, be made against the head tenant. The sub-tenant, for so long as the intermediate tenancy continues, has no direct claim against the head landlord. The head landlord cannot describe the sub-tenant's improvements as his "own" and accordingly has no claim in respect of those improvements against his own landlord. Thus the head tenant may findhimself in the position of having to pay out the sub-tenant but not being able to reclaim any part of that payment against his own landlord: in such a situation, if the head tenant wishes to be able to make such a claim against his own landlord, he must provide for this contingency in his contract from the outset. There are no special provisions which deal with sub-tenancies and if sub-letting during the tenant's term is anticipated provision of this type would be prudent: any contractual compensation provision is lawful by reason of section 26(2).

5.6 What is the status of tenant's fixed equipment?

The only point in the statute where "fixed equipment" is defined is section 19(10) in relation to compensation.[54] The purpose of providing the definition in section 19(10) is to exclude fixed equipment from the definition of "routine improvement".[55] What is not answered expressly by Part III is the treatment of fixed equipment in general terms. The definition itself is extremely wide[56] and appears to be drawn so as to include both fixtures affixed by the tenant and growing crops apart from where those crops are intended to be used after being severed or are intended to be consumed or were grown for amenity. Fixed equipment and buildings are the subject of extensive rights of removal under section 8.[57] Although outside the context of Part III of the Act improvements would not normally include tenant's fixtures,[58] the drafting of Part III appears to be somewhat wider than the traditional understanding. Section 15 bears a number of marks indicating that it is drafted in a relatively non-technical way[59] and it would appear logical to deduce from the wording of section 19(10) that "fixed equipment" would normally feature as a "routine improvement" had it not been expressly excluded from the definition. The following propositions, from the drafting of section 19(10) appear to be correct:

(i) fixed equipment falls within the description of physical improvement;

(ii) the improvement may be the provision of fixed equipment or of an improvement to fixed equipment;

---

[54] *i.e.* this definition does not feature in relation to rent review.

[55] As to which see para. 5.13 below.

[56] "'Fixed equipment' includes any building or structure affixed to land and any works constructed on, in, over or under land, and also includes anything grown on land for a purpose other than use after severance from the land, consumption of the thing grown or its produce, or amenity."

[57] See Chapter 3 above.

[58] See *New Zealand Government Property Corp v. H.M. & S.* [1982] Q.B. 1145 and see discussion in relation to rent at paras 2.17–2.18 above.

[59] See the discussion at para. 5.4 above.

(iii) the improvement is recognised by Part III even though the provision of that improvement is prohibited by the terms of the tenancy.[60]

Compensation for fixed equipment will only be available where the landlord gives his consent in writing as required by section 17 and it is of particular interest to note that the right of removal under section 8 does not apply where the landlord has consented under section 17 on terms that the tenant agrees not to remove the equipment in question.[61]

The essential right to compensation: section 16 — 5.7

The farm business tenant is entitled on termination of the tenancy, on quitting the holding, to obtain from his landlord compensation in respect of any tenant's improvement.[62] It follows that the tenant is not entitled during the term to any compensation except as agreed by a separate contract with the landlord.[63] The distinction between termination of the tenancy on the one hand and quitting the holding on the other should be observed.[64] It should be noted that the designation of landlord or tenant continues to apply until the conclusion of any proceedings taken under the Act in respect of compensation.[65] It is unclear what is to happen in circumstances where the tenant quits and the tenancy ends before any steps or proceedings are taken in respect of compensation under the Act.[66] Furthermore it should be noted that these special provisions do not apply in relation to purely contractual compensation.[67] No compensation is available in respect of any physical improvement removed from the holding[68] nor is the tenant entitled to compensation for an intangible advantage which does not remain attached to the holding.[69] Thus where the tenant is entitled to milk quota but manages his affairs so that the quota is removed from the holding by whatever means or is apportioned away from it there will be no compensation in respect of that milk quota. There may be a problem of timing in relation to ascertainment of that element of milk quota remaining on the tenanted holding as against other parts of a tenant's holding

---

[60] Since this rule is expressly reversed in relation to "routine improvements".
[61] s. 8(2)(d) and see para. 3.8 above.
[62] s. 16(1).
[63] See para. 5.3 above.
[64] See the observations at para. 8.22 below in relation to the 1986 Act. In addition s. 22(5) makes special provision for circumstances where the tenant lawfully remains in occupation of part of the holding after termination of a farm business tenancy.
[65] s. 38(5).
[66] See the point raised at para. 4.5 in relation to a tenant who quits before the expiry of a fixed term.
[67] The draftsman of contractual arrangements will no doubt take note.
[68] s. 16(2)(a): the rights of removal would include those arising under s. 8, as to which see Chapter 3 above.
[69] s. 16(2)(b).

as defined by the Dairy Produce Quotas Regulations 1997.[70] By contrast section 22(2) requires notice in writing to the landlord of the claim and the nature of the claim.[71] Other intangible advantages unlikely to remain attached to the holding include certain types of goodwill which are peculiar to the tenant's own business and which depart with him when that business ceases or removes itself.[72] The compensation provisions in relation to milk quota contained in Schedule 1 of the Agriculture Act 1986[73] do not apply in relation to a farm business tenancy,[74] quite obviously because this type of compensation would overlap with the terms of section 15(b).

5.8   Conditions of eligibility for compensation claim: general

For the purpose of establishing satisfaction of the conditions of eligibility in making a claim for compensation for his improvement, the tenant has two quite different regimes to consider. In relation to any claim for compensation in respect of the provision of planning permission the tenant must satisfy section 18[75] and, if the landlord does not give the consent required, there is no recourse to a substituted consent of an arbitrator. In the case of all other types of tenant's improvement the consent of the landlord will be required under section 17 but if such consent is not forthcoming the tenant may, subject to the terms of section 19, acquire a substituted consent from an arbitrator.[76] Whether or not a tenant may be able to establish a claim in relation to compensation for planning permission, he will not be debarred from proceeding under sections 17–19 in the hope of establishing the alternative claim for a completed improvement. The section 18 claim is only available for so long as the improvement is not completed or the change of use has not been effected.[77] There are no forms prescribed by statute for any of the steps or consents referred to in Part III.[78]

5.9   Conditions in relation to compensation for planning permission: section 18

Where the tenant's improvement consists of planning permission the tenant, in

---

[70] Where quota is required to be apportioned as between different parts of the holding for milk quota purposes there may be a delay of over two months before the tenant is able to identify what element of the quota will remain apportioned to his formerly tenanted land.

[71] It is submitted that delays inherent in the arbitration process dealing with apportionment ought not to deprive a tenant of his milk quota compensation under Part III, provided he has served a claims notice within the period stipulated by s. 22(2). It would seem proper to regard the arbitration award made in reference to the termination of the tenancy as having effect for all purposes as from that time and, in so far as a tenant's compensation claim under Part III requires to be amended with the benefit of hindsight it is suggested that an amendment of the figures should be regarded as allowable provided the nature of the claim, that is to say that it refers to milk quota, has already been identified within the statutory period.

[72] This is a point unlikely to be important in relation to a traditional agricultural business but may be of significance in relation to certain types of diversification.

[73] See Chapter 19 below.

[74] s. 16(3).

[75] See para. 5.9 below.

[76] See para. 5.11 and following below.

[77] s. 18(1)(c).

[78] Although a number of suggested forms are referred to in this narrative as being precedents provided in Part V of this work.

order to establish his claim, must satisfy three cumulative conditions.[79] First, the landlord must have given his consent in writing to the making of the application for planning permission.[80] It follows from this that no planning application should be made at all until the tenant has first requested the landlord for the consent he seeks in order to satisfy section 18(1)(a).[81] There is no statutory obligation on a landlord to consent or only to withhold consent on reasonable grounds: his position is governed entirely by the terms of the contract and it will be noted that section 19 of the Landlord and Tenant Act 1927 does not apply to farm business tenancies.[82] If the landlord does choose to give his consent, section 18(2) provides that the consent may be given either unconditionally or on condition that the tenant agrees to a specified variation in the terms of the tenancy.[83] The second requirement of section 18(1) is that the landlord's consent is expressly given for one of two purposes set out in section 18(1)(b) namely:

(i) of enabling a specified physical improvement falling within paragraph (a) of section 15 of this Act lawfully to be provided by the tenant, or

(ii) of enabling a tenant lawfully to effect a specified change of use.

Quite what the word "lawfully" is doing in these quoted words may be the subject of some speculation: its presence suggests that sub-paragraphs (i) and (ii) are only applicable to the provision of physical improvements or the effecting of a change of use in circumstances where these activities are prohibited by the existing terms of the tenancy. If this were not so, the word "lawfully" would be completely unnecessary. However the cumulative drafting of section 18(1) rather suggests that satisfaction of sub-paragraph (b) is necessary whether or not the tenant is already entitled under the terms of his contract to do acts in implementation of a planning permission which he has not yet obtained.[84] What if the landlord is willing to give written consent to the making of the application for planning permission but is not willing to go further in his consent so as to satisfy section 18(1)(b)? Since section 18 is apparently drafted so as to provide three cumulative conditions it is suggested that a failure to satisfy the second of them disables the tenant from making a claim under section 18 whether or not his tenancy agreement already contemplates and authorises the provision of the relevant improvements or the tenant making the change of use in question.[85] Accordingly there are three forms of general landlord's

---

[79] s. 18(1).
[80] s. 18(1)(a).
[81] See Form 119: Tenant's application for consent to the making of an application for planning permission.
[82] See para. 1.29 above.
[83] s. 18(3) further qualifies that the variation in question must be related to the physical improvement or the change of use in question. In other words the landlord may not impose conditions which have no bearing on the specific subject matter of the application made to him. Although the tenant is entitled to challenge any variation in tenancy terms required by the landlord (pursuant to s. 19(1)(c): see para. 5.11 below) it would appear that conditions quite obviously falling foul of the requirement in s. 18(3) are invalid.
[84] It is suggested that it would be a bizarre reading of s. 18 which would limit its availability to tenants whose tenancies did not contemplate or allow implementation of a planning permission.
[85] Where this situation arises the tenant will be debarred from s. 18 compensation but will be entitled to proceed to make the improvement or the change of use and then to claim under

consent in relation to section 18 which may be adapted for use by practitioners depending on the ambit and purpose of the landlord's consent:

(i) landlord's consent to tenant applying for planning permission but not to tenant making physical improvement[86];

(ii) landlord's consent to the tenant applying for planning permission for a physical improvement and making that physical improvement[87]; and

(iii) landlord's consent to the tenant applying for planning permission for change of use so as to enable the tenant to effect the change of use.[88]

Persons conducting negotiations with the tenant about the grant of a consent for the purposes of section 18 will no doubt take care that they do not correspond "subject to licence" believing that this form of words has the same protective effect as "subject to contract" or "subject to lease".[89] The third condition required to be satisfied by section 18(1) is that on the termination of the tenancy the specified physical improvement has not been completed or the specific change of use has not been effected.[90] It is suggested that substantial completion of the specific physical improvement will not debar the claim for compensation for planning permission even though those substantial works might be the subject of a separate claim under section 17.[91] Finally it is observed that the word "or" between section 18(1)(b)(i) and (ii) is without weight.[92]

5.10 **Conditions in relation to compensation for tenant's improvement not being a planning permission: sections 17 and 19**

Possible items of claim within the overall category of tenant's improvement covered by section 17 exclude:

---

section 17.

[86] Form 127 in Part V of this work.

[87] Form 125: this form comprises a consent for the purposes of s. 17 as well as 18.

[88] Form 126 in Part V of this work.

[89] Where consent is given "subject to licence" that licence had been held to be immediately effective: *Prudential Assurance Co Limited v. Mount Eden Land Limited* [1997] 1 E.G.L.R. 37, CA.

[90] s. 18(1)(c).

[91] Unless the shortfall is *de minimis* it would seem unfortunate to regard completion of the specific physical improvement as being effected when substantial works towards it have been done. After all, the landlord will take the benefit of the planning permission and the tenant by definition has not yet had the opportunity of exploiting the works which he has undertaken. This is quite separate from the issue as to whether the works actually done towards the main improvement have an independent value *e.g.* the tenant may have planning permission to erect a new farmhouse and may have set about it but if he has not yet put the roof on or installed the doors and windows the work that he has done still has value and could still be the subject of a s. 17 claim. There appears to be no reason for depriving the tenant of the benefit of his compensation for the planning permission itself particularly in circumstances where the house may be used without any restriction to agriculture.

[92] In so far as the landlord issues a consent falling within the first sub-paragraph an additional permissive element allowing the tenant not only to do the work but also to effect a change of use would be most unlikely to remove the consent from the terms of s. 18(1)(b)(i): indeed such a result would be most peculiar.

(i) improvements which consist of planning permission[93]; and

(ii) a change of use, whether or not this is advantageous to the holding.[94]

A tenant cannot make a claim for compensation in respect of any tenant's improvement unless the tenant has first obtained his landlord's consent in writing.[95] Section 15 determines what may amount to a tenant's improvement[96] and it would appear that tenant's fixed equipment may fall within this description.[97] Also included are "routine improvements" as defined by section 19(10).[98] Section 17 itself provides that the landlord's consent may be given either in the tenancy agreement "or elsewhere".[99] The landlord's consent may be unconditional or on condition that the tenant agrees to a specified variation in the terms of the tenancy.[1] Attention is drawn to the ineffective nature of "subject to licence" as a label where correspondence about the grant of a consent is being conducted.[2] Section 19 provides for an arbitrator's consent to be substituted for that of a landlord.[3] There is no requirement that an improvement within section 17 must be a lawful improvement.[4] Any rights available under Part III override the terms of the contract[5] and accordingly if the arbitrator gives his approval this has effect both for the purposes of Part III[6] and also for the purposes of the contract "as if it were the consent of the landlord".[7] This would end the unlawful status of any proposed improvements. It follows from this that (except in the case of routine im-

---

[93] s. 17(5): see s. 18 and para. 5.9 above.

[94] A change of use is not itself an improvement of any type although the planning permission which may give rise to it has a separate regime under s. 18. There is a clear contrast in the drafting of ss. 17(5) and 18(3) which supports the proposition that a change of use does not generate a compensation claim.

[95] s. 17(1).

[96] See para. 5.4 above.

[97] See para. 5.6 above.

[98] Although their treatment differs where the tenant seeks a substituted consent from an arbitrator. See para. 5.13 below.

[99] s. 17(2): in context this clearly means elsewhere in another document (*i.e.* an oral consent will not suffice since s. 17(1) stipulates writing).

[1] s. 17(3). Sub s. (4) further stipulates that the variation in question must be related to the tenant's improvement. Although a tenant may refer "any variation" required by the landlord to an arbitrator under s. 19(1)(c) (see para. 5.11 below), it is submitted that any condition imposed which falls foul of s. 17(4) is invalid.

[2] See **Prudential Assurance Co Limited v. Mount Eden Land Limited** [1997] 1 E.G.L.R. 37 discussed at para. 5.9 above.

[3] See para. 5.11 below.

[4] This may be deduced from the definition of "routine improvement" in s. 19(10) which expressly excludes from the category of "routine improvement" any improvement "whose provision is prohibited by the terms of the tenancy". Since the consent regime is relaxed in relation to routine improvements in that they may be commenced before a notice demanding arbitration is served it would be logical to offer that relaxed regime only to lawful routine improvements. Obviously if the tenant secures his landlord's agreement to the making of an otherwise unlawful improvement, it ceases to be unlawful. If the landlord does not give consent and the tenant applies to an arbitrator the arbitrator must under s. 19(5) consider the terms of the tenancy and whether, in the light of them, it is reasonable for the improvement to be provided.

[5] s. 26(1).

[6] *i.e.* for the purpose of claiming compensation.

[7] s. 19(7).

provements) for so long as the tenant has not begun work on an unlawful improvement the Court ought not to grant an injunction preventing a tenant from doing the work.[8] A routine improvement by definition is a lawful improvement[9] and it is difficult to imagine circumstances in which it would be appropriate to restrain the provision of them.

The following Forms are provided in Part V of this work in connection with section 17:

(i) the tenant's request for consent to an improvement[10];

(ii) the tenant's application for consent to implement a planning permission[11];

(iii) the landlord's consent to improvements.[12]

5.11 Reference to arbitration where no or no satisfactory consent from landlord: section 19

Where a satisfactory consent is not forthcoming from the landlord pursuant to section 17 the tenant has the opportunity by notice in writing given to the landlord to demand that there be a reference to arbitration.[13] This opportunity is subject to sub-sections (2) and (3) of section 19 and the opportunity only arises in three specific instances namely:

(i) the refusal of the landlord to give his consent under section 17(1).[14] A suggested form of tenant's reference to arbitration on improvements after such a refusal from the landlord is provided in Part V of this work.[15] A notice by the tenant in this case may not be given after the end of two months beginning with the day on which the notice of the refusal was given to the tenant;[16]

(ii) the failure of the landlord to give consent under section 17 within two months of a written request by the tenant for such consent.[17] It is not necessary for the tenant's request to make any reference to the two-month deadline even though this is an absolute statutory deadline giving rise to the tenant's right to call for arbitration. A suggested form for the tenant's reference to arbitration on improvements where the landlord fails to respond is provided in Part V of this work.[18] In a case within this provision no notice under section 19(1) may be given

---

[8] Once he begins the work he loses the opportunity under s. 19 to secure effective authorisation of those works and may thereafter in an appropriate case be restrained from proceeding to do the works.
[9] s. 19(10).
[10] Form 118.
[11] Form 120.
[12] Form 124.
[13] s. 19(1).
[14] s. 19(1)(a).
[15] Form 121.
[16] s. 19(3)(a).
[17] s. 19(1)(b).
[18] Form 122.

by the tenant after the end of the period of four months beginning with the day on which the written request referred to was given to the landlord;[19]

(iii) where the landlord requires a variation in the terms of the tenancy as a condition of giving his consent under section 17.[20] The tenant, it is submitted, may refer "any variation" to the arbitrator although variations clearly falling outside section 17(4) are bad.[21] This alternative contemplates that the landlord had identified a variation of tenancy related to the tenant's improvement which he wishes to see and which the tenant does not. For example, the landlord may be quite willing to have the improvement provided but may wish himself not to be involved in the process even though the terms of tenancy stipulate that he must provide materials. In a case within this provision no notice under section 19(1) may be given after the end of the period of two months beginning with the day on which notice of the variation referred to was given to the tenant.[22]

A form is provided for the tenant's reference to arbitration on improvements after the landlord has required conditions.[23]

Where any of these three situations arise and the tenant is aggrieved, he may proceed to arbitration. Where the landlord would be content to give his consent but only on the tenant agreeing to a variation in the terms of tenancy which does not conform with section 17(4), it is a difficult issue as to whether this amounts to a "refusal" or a "failure" or whether this should be treated as falling within section 19(1)(c).[24] It is difficult to see what the point of section 19(3) is unless it be to bring matters to a head finally once and for all. If the tenant fails to observe the time-limit in section 19(3), does this preclude him from serving a new request under section 17 in relation to the particular improvement? The answer to this question is not as clear as might be hoped.[25]

---

[19] s. 19(3)(b).
[20] s. 19(1)(c).
[21] Ignoring a bad condition should not necessarily result in construing a document as though the landlord had consented: rather the reverse since the landlord is refusing (on a ground not permitted by the statute) to give his consent.
[22] s. 19(3)(a).
[23] Form 123.
[24] A tenant would be well advised to treat this circumstance as amounting to a "refusal" if only because that is the sub-paragraph. with the shortest time-limit for the purposes of s. 19(3). Obviously where a demand for arbitration is served in this state of uncertainty suggested forms may have to be adapted so that any reference is valid and capable of falling in the alternative in any of the sub-paragraphs within s. 19(1).
[25] Suppose the tenant serves a subsequent request for the purposes of s. 17 and the landlord gives his consent: does this consent have no effect for the purposes of Part III because the previous notice fall foul of s. 19(3)? Is the tenant entitled to re-submit an application under s. 17 if he makes his scheme more elaborate than it had been under the first request, or is it only the elaboration which may be the subject of a valid s. 17 request and a consequent reference to s. 19? If the latter, is the arbitrator able to approve the provision of part only of a scheme which the landlord is otherwise able to prohibit? Or is this simply a factor for the arbitrator to consider when such a reference is made to him?

5.12 Non-routine improvements—beginning the works stops the reference: sections 19(2) and (9)

A tenant may not demand arbitration, except in the case of "routine improvements"[26] where he has already provided or begun to provide the improvement in question.[27] Similarly if he does demand arbitration under section 19 but then begins to provide the non-routine improvement, this operates effectively to stop the arbitration procedure. Thus neither party can thereafter apply for the appointment of an arbitrator[28]; any application not yet acted on by the President of the RICS becomes ineffective[29]; and, where the arbitrator has been appointed, he is not able to make an award on the substance of the application (*i.e.* under section 19(6)) and he may only make an award as to the costs of the reference.[30] In the last of these events it is difficult to imagine circumstances in which the arbitrator would do anything other than award the costs against the tenant.

5.13 Effect of providing "routine improvements": sections 19(2) and (10)

Where an improvement falls within the definition of "routine improvement" the fact that the tenant has already provided it or begins to provide it has no impact on either the tenant's ability to demand arbitration under section 19(1) or the subsequent conduct of the arbitration.[31] The definition of "routine improvement" in section 19(10) involves consideration of "fixed equipment"[32] since fixed equipment is excluded from the category of routine improvements. Fixed equipment is considered elsewhere[33] and "routine improvements" effectively are limited to lawfully provided physical improvements. This ties the tenant to whatever type of farming is permitted by the tenancy agreement and it will be recollected that the tenant has no right to freedom of cropping and disposal of produce which would override the terms of his tenancy. One may make a comparison with individual items selected for inclusion in Schedules 7 and 8 of the Agricultural Holdings Act 1986, whilst being aware that the 1995 Act does not descend to particularity and simply establishes an overall general category.[34] If the

---

[26] Defined by s. 19(10) and see para. 5.13 below.

[27] This poses a really serious question in relation to the provision of milk quota as an intangible improvement. Although the tenant may wish to occupy for milk production, as soon as he does there is a likelihood that quota will become attached to the land within the farm business tenancy and accordingly disable the tenant from pursuing an arbitration under s. 19. However it will be noted that s. 19(2) relates only to the procedural aspects of the tenant's claim and it would therefore overcome the problem if at the grant of the tenancy that document itself provided the requisite consent for milk quota to be brought onto the land.

[28] s. 19(9)(a).

[29] s. 19(9)(b).

[30] s. 19(9)(c).

[31] Although in the terms of s. 19(5) the arbitrator will be required to consider whether it is reasonable for the tenant to "have provided" the relevant improvement: contrast the use of language in s. 19(1).

[32] Also defined in that sub-section.

[33] See para. 5.6 above.

[34] However not all improvements within Scheds 7 and 8 will be routine improvements, in particular since a number of them relate to the provision of fixed equipment (*e.g.* provision of silos, making or removal of permanent fences). Depending on the permitted

EFFECT OF PROVIDING "ROUTINE IMPROVEMENTS": SECTIONS 19(2) AND (10)

parties in the tenancy agreement prohibit something which might otherwise be a "routine improvement" it will simply fall to be treated as all other improvements under section 19(2) and therefore works must not be done if section 19 rights are to be maintained. However no doubt the landlord will bear in mind that such a provision is likely to be inconvenient to the tenant and therefore will reduce the rent on a rent review.

Acclimatisation or hefting of sheep   5.14

This matter is the subject of special provisions in Schedule 8 of the Agricultural Holdings Act but does not fall, apparently, into the definition of "tenant's improvement" under section 15. Although many farmers regard this type of improvement as a "routine" improvement in that it has traditionally been included under "tenant-right matters" in Part II of Schedule 8 this is something which in terms of a farm business tenancy must be the subject of a contractual compensation regime.

Machinery of arbitration under section 19   5.15

Once the tenant has given notice under section 19(1) the parties may proceed to appoint an arbitrator. Where they have not done so either the tenant or the landlord may apply to the President of the RICS for an arbitrator to be appointed by him.[35] The arbitration itself falls within section 30.[36] The arbitrator appointed will proceed under the terms of the Arbitration Act 1996[37] but the terms of the Agricultural Tenancies Act 1995 will govern and override any inconsistent provisions of the Arbitration Act.[38]

The arbitrator's task: section 19(5)   5.16

Where the tenant wishes to make an improvement, the arbitrator is entitled to consider the matter in the widest possible terms:

> "The arbitrator shall consider whether, having regard to the terms of the tenancy and any other relevant circumstances (including the circumstances of the tenant and the landlord), it is reasonable for the tenant to provide the tenant's improvement."

---

system of farming, the various items in Part I of Sched. 7 of the 1986 Act excluding only item 8 appear to be routine improvements. Item 8 (provision of underground tanks) involves fixed equipment. Sched. 8, Part I appears to relate to routine improvements. Anything grown for use after severance from the land, consumption of the thing grown or its produce or amenity would be capable of falling within the definition of "routine improvement" and to some extent corresponds with items 7, 8 and 9 of Part II of Sched. 8. Sched. 8, para. 11 appears to be a routine improvement although item 10 does not. The contents of Sched. 7, Part II mostly relate to fixed equipment or an improvement to it but some items (*e.g.* item 22) may be routine improvements. Land drainage may be a routine improvement but, depending on the type of work done, may involve the provision of fixed equipment.

[35] s. 19(4).
[36] See para. 6.3 below.
[37] Statutory arbitrations are not excluded from the scope of the Arbitration Act 1996: contrast s. 84 of the Agricultural Holdings Act 1986.
[38] See generally paras 6.10–6.81 below.

The arbitrator is required to consider the terms of the tenancy but it will be recalled that (apart from routine improvements) the improvements in question may be lawful or unlawful at the time when the matters becomes before the arbitrator. It is clear that the arbitrator is entitled to consider the personal circumstances of the tenant and the landlord and therefore is not restricted to matters such as good husbandry or sound estate management but the overriding and decisive consideration is whether or not it is "reasonable" for the tenant to provide the improvement in question. It is suggested that an arbitrator should not be shy in permitting an unlawful improvement where, having regard to the overall circumstances, he regards it as reasonable for the improvement to be provided: otherwise it would be far too easy for the landlord to avoid paying compensation by the simple expedient of a contractual bar at the outset. Where the tenant would be in breach of statutory duty by failing to provide the improvement in question it is suggested that this must be very influential in the tenant's favour. Less clear is how the arbitrator should weigh the request of a tenant to provide improvements which meet super-high standards of particular (usually supermarket) customers. If high investment is rewarded by high profits the arbitrator may take the view that a section 8 right to remove is enough for the tenant if a compensation claim would be burdensome for a landlord unlikely ever to secure a full rental because of those improvements. In the case of an intangible advantage the arbitrator will need to satisfy himself as to exactly what it is the tenant is proposing to attach to the holding and, for example in relation to a management scheme, it will be necessary for the precise terms to be available for consideration.

The arbitrator is specifically authorised either to approve the provision of the tenant's improvement or to withhold his approval.[39] He is expressly disabled from subjecting his consent to any condition nor may he vary any condition required by the landlord under section 17(3). Thus if the arbitrator considers that the landlord's conditions for the purposes of section 17(3) are justifiable, it is likely that the arbitrator will withhold his consent altogether. In those circumstances section 19(8) provides that the withholding of the arbitrator's approval shall not affect the validity of the landlord's consent or the conditions to which it may have been subject. From the tenant's point of view he may be subject to the risk that the arbitrator withholds his approval but the landlord thereafter withdraws his consent.[40] Where the arbitrator gives his approval the approval has effect for the purposes of both the statute and the contract as though it were the consent of the landlord.[41] This has the direct effect of not only authorising the tenant's ultimate compensation claim but also of varying the tenancy agreement in circumstances where the improvement itself would otherwise have been unlawful. Indirectly this may cause a change of use to be lawful where that change of use is bound up with the use of the improvement itself.[42]

---

[39] s. 19(6).
[40] No doubt the well-advised tenant will consider carefully his prospects before the arbitrator and will, if he senses defeat, conclude with the landlord a variation of the tenancy agreement thereby converting the consent into a contractual form.
[41] s. 19(7).
[42] *e.g.* if a landlord had consented to milk quota being attached to a farm whose tenancy prohibits milk production this would by implication authorise subsequent use of the farm

Amount of compensation for planning permission: section 21   5.17

By section 21(1) compensation for planning permission will be:

> "an amount equal to the increase attributable to the fact that the relevant development[43] is authorised by the planning permission in the value of the holding at the termination of the tenancy as land comprised in a tenancy."

The compensation allowable relates to matters authorised by the planning permission whether or not the actual tenant has ever had an intention to implement it. Obviously the valuation takes place as at the termination of the current tenancy but it does not assume the terms of the current tenancy, rather the terms of a hypothetical tenancy which might then be entered into.[44] Presumably what the tenant will get in the form of his compensation is a figure calculated by reference to the increased letting value of the property with the benefit of the planning permission. The assessment of that figure will obviously involve an assessment as to what the terms of this hypothetical tenancy would be were such a letting to take place in the real world. In some circumstances this may be a rather difficult exercise to attempt since there is no other assumption as to what the terms of such a tenancy may be. It is suggested, albeit with diffidence, that the correct approach is to consider the market in the real world and attempt to assess the rental value of a new tenancy to be granted without a fine or premium and otherwise at arm's length with vacant possession as at the termination of the existing tenancy. What the tenant gets in the form of compensation is not simply the difference between the rent at termination of his own tenancy and the rent which would be payable under the hypothetical tenancy in a single year but rather the benefit of that difference in so far as it reflects "the value of the holding" to the landlord.[45] If the parties by contract have already provided for the tenant in consideration of the obtaining of planning permission to have any benefit, section 21(3) reduces the amount of compensation payable on termination. In those circumstances the reduction is "by the proportion which the value of the benefit bears to the amount of the total cost of obtaining the permission". Landlords who do not, at the time of entering into any contractual agreement of the type referred to in section 21(3), stipulate that the tenant identify the total cost of obtaining the permission will find it difficult to secure the benefit intended by section 21(3). This is particularly so if a number of years elapse between the agreement and the date when the compensation has to be paid. "The amount of the total cost" refers to an actual amount of expenditure incurred by the tenant but is otherwise unspecific as to what is here included.[46]

---

    for milk production. It is submitted that the arbitrator's award in similar circumstances produces the same effect.

[43] Defined by s. 21(2) as, essentially, the physical improvement or change of use consented to by the landlord under s. 18.

[44] Contrast in s. 21(1) "the tenancy as land comprised in a tenancy".

[45] Presumably valued by choosing an appropriate years' purchase.

[46] The fees of planning consultants/lawyers would obviously be included, but what of the management time of the tenant? Probably the latter should be regarded as a notional cost rather than a real one and should accordingly be disallowed.

5.18 Amount of compensation for tenant's improvement not consisting of planning permission: section 20

Section 20(1) stipulates that for tenant's improvements not consisting of planning permission the compensation shall be:

> "an amount equal to the increase attributable to the improvement in the value of the holding at the termination of the tenancy as land comprised in a tenancy."

For the most part the difficulties of assessment discussed in the preceding paragraph apply here also. Section 20(2) reduces the compensation in circumstances where the parties have contracted in writing for the tenant to have had a benefit in consideration of providing the improvement. This is a provision parallel to that contained in section 21(3) which is discussed in the preceding paragraph. There is a further proportionate reduction in the amount of compensation where a grant is provided to the tenant out of public money in respect of the tenant's improvement.[47] A landlord would be wise in the terms of his farm business tenancy to require the tenant to serve him with copies of all documents relating to grants: otherwise it may be difficult to take the benefit of section 20(3).[48] It is not necessary for the purposes of the valuation under section 20 to strip out value attributable to the fact that a physical improvement or change of use is authorised by planning permission.[49] Improvements consisting of planning permission are exclusively dealt with under section 21.[50]

5.19 Meaning of "benefit" in sections 20(2) and 21(3)

In each of these valuation provisions the issue will arise as to what "benefit" may have been allowed by the landlord in consideration of the provision of a tenant's improvement. The benefit in question must be found in the written agreement and furthermore must be directly linked in that agreement to the provision of the tenant's improvement. Subject thereto it is entirely open as to what "benefit" the landlord may allow whether by varying the rent, providing materials, meeting professional fees, or otherwise varying the tenancy agreement. In respect of the "benefit" the valuation exercise may be straightforward[51] or complex.[52] The risk here falls on the tenant, who may be advised to provide in the written agreement an exact quantification of what benefit the landlord is making available.

---

[47] s. 20(3).
[48] It is no use for a landlord to establish that the tenant ought to have had a grant as opposed to actually having a grant.
[49] s. 20(4).
[50] s. 20(5).
[51] Ascertaining, for example, the amount of any fees and VAT.
[52] The long term impact of changes in use or reduction in the rent.

Making and settling claims for compensation: section 22

5.20

Compensation claims are compulsorily referable to arbitration[53] and fall to be dealt with under section 30.[54] These arbitrations are governed by the Arbitration Act 1996 and are not exempted from that regime by the 1995 Act.[55]

Service of notice under section 22: section 22(2)

5.21

A compensation claim is not enforceable unless before the end of the period of two months beginning with the date of the termination of the tenancy the tenant has given notice in writing to his landlord of his intention to make the claim and of the nature of the claim.[56] It is submitted that the notice must be in terms which are sufficiently clear to bring home to the ordinary landlord that the tenant intends to make a claim for compensation under section 16 and furthermore what the nature of that claim is.[57] Owing to the similarity of drafting between this provision and the terms of section 83(2) of the Agricultural Holdings Act, commentary under that section may be of interest.[58] Where the tenant lawfully remains in occupation of part of the holding after termination of the farm business tenancy, the reference to termination is construed as a reference to the termination of the occupation of the part.[59] The main definition of "termination" of the tenancy is contained in section 38(1).[60]

Appointment of the arbitrator in relation to compensation

5.22

Once the claim has been made under section 22(2), the parties may at any time settle that claim by agreement in writing. Equally they may contractually appoint an arbitrator at any time once the claims notice has been served. If the claim is not settled or the subject of a contractual arbitration appointment, the first four months following termination of the tenancy is a period during which neither party may apply to the President of the RICS for the appointment of an arbitrator by him.[61] Thereafter either party may apply to the President.[62] Where either party applies under section 22(3) to the President for an appointment and the compensation

---

[53] s. 22(1).
[54] See para. 6.3 below.
[55] It should be noted that claims for compensation do not fall within s. 28 (s. 28(5)(c)) and the parties may not refer a compensation dispute to the determination of an expert: nor may they resolve a compensation dispute by using alternative dispute resolution or mediation. See generally paras 6.10–6.81.
[56] s. 22(2). A precedent is provided by Form 128 in Part V of this work.
[57] A test along these lines has been adopted in various contexts and originates with the Court of Appeal in *Amalgamated Estates Limited v. Joystretch Manufacturing Limited* (1980) 257 E.G. 489. See also **BSC Pension Fund Trustees Limited v. Downing** [1990] 1 E.G.L.R. 4 and **Lees v. Tatchell** [1990] 1 E.G.L.R. 10.
[58] See para. 13.117 below.
[59] s. 22(5).
[60] In terms identical to equivalent provisions in s. 96(1) of the Agricultural Holdings Act 1986, commented on at para. 8.22 below.
[61] If the tenant remains in occupation lawfully of part of the holding after termination the point at which he quits any part of the holding is the point regarded as the termination in reference to that part: s. 22(5).
[62] s. 22(3).

being claimed relates wholly or partly to a routine improvement[63] and at the same time an application is made under section 19(4) for consent to the making of a routine improvement, the President must appoint the same arbitrator on both applications.[64] The words "at the same time" are perhaps unfortunate.[65] If both applications are made by the same person only one fee is payable under section 30(2).[66]

5.23 Successive tenancies: supplementary provisions regarding compensation: section 23

Section 23(1) allows compensation due in respect of one farm business tenancy to be "rolled over" so as to be claimable at the end of a further farm business tenancy subsequently granted to the same tenant. This "roll over" will be available on more than one occasion but it must be demonstrated that the tenant "has remained in the holding" throughout. Section 23(2) authorises an agreement[67] between the parties that the tenant is to be paid out at the conclusion of the first farm business tenancy whether or not he remains in occupation under a subsequent tenancy. There is no requirement in section 23 for such an agreement to be in writing, but unless it is in writing an agreement will not preclude the arbitration process.[68] Where such an agreement has been made, the tenant is not entitled to claim compensation at the end of the subsequent tenancy in respect of any tenant's improvement covered by the agreement.[69] What section 23 does not do is to allow a "roll over" from a tenancy outside the farm business tenancy regime to a farm business tenancy. Moreover there may be difficulties in applying this section in circumstances where the personality of the tenant has changed from joint tenants to a sole tenant or vice versa. In those circumstances it will almost always be more prudent to make the claim at the conclusion of each tenancy rather than attempting to rely on the "roll over" provisions.[70] However, once the claim has been quantified it becomes a personal claim against the actual landlord and this claim will not run with the land.

5.24 Resumption of possession of part of holding: supplementary provisions regarding compensation: section 24

Section 24(1) applies the compensation provisions to the termination of the tenancy over part of the holding where the termination in question is caused by a

---

[63] See s. 19(10) and para. 5.13 above.
[64] s. 22(4).
[65] Taken literally this could never be capable of implementation unless it could be shown that two applications were physically posted in the same instant. It is suggested that perhaps this is intended to identify applications referable to the same time, that is to say the termination of the tenancy, which would allow the landlord to apply under s. 22 and the tenant to apply under s. 19(4) and to be treated as though the applications were made at the same time if they were actually sent or received within a few days of each other. Obviously s. 22(4) in the main body contemplates that different persons may make these applications.
[66] s. 22(4).
[67] A precedent is provided by Form 129 in Part V of this work.
[68] See s. 22(3).
[69] s. 23(3).
[70] After all, once the claim has been made and quantified it is not necessary that the tenant insist on immediate payment if he is prepared to accept payment at some later point.

landlord's notice to quit part[71] or by a notice in respect of a severed reversion.[72] Compensation in respect of planning permission relating to the relevant part will be an amount "equal to the increase attributable to the fact that the relevant development is authorised by the planning permission in the value of the original holding on the termination date as land comprised in a tenancy".[73] Corresponding provisions exist in relation to other types of improvement than planning permission.[74] Special definitions are given in section 24(5) for "the original holding", "the relevant development" and "the termination date". The quantification of compensation under section 24(2) and (3) is somewhat obscurely drafted. There is a marked contrast with the terms of section 74 of the Agricultural Holdings Act 1986 which, in effect, require each part of the holding to be valued separately when parts are taken back. Here a valuation takes place by reference to the increase in the value of the original holding generated by the works or planning permissions on the part taken back.[75] Because of the definition of "original holding" it is likely that the valuation must take account of the fact that this may vary from time to time depending on what was comprised within the tenancy at the point when each consent or arbitration award was given. Because of the way in which the valuation formula under section 24 has been drawn it may be the case that sometimes there is duplication between what is paid out when the part is dealt with and what is paid out when the tenancy as a whole comes to an end.[76]

Termination of entire tenancy where reversion severed: supplementary provisions regarding compensation: section 25　　5.25

Section 25 deals with the situation of the tenant quitting an entire holding where the reversion is severed (*i.e.* held by more than one landlord).[77] The tenant is entitled on quitting the entire holding to require that any compensation payable to him under section 16 should be determined "as if the reversionary estate were not so severed".[78] This requires the arbitrator to determine the compensation by simple application of sections 20 and 21 without the need to consider the separate ownerships of the reversion.[79] This provision offers an alternative to section 24 where that section would otherwise apply.[80] Section 25 is available at the tenant's

---

[71] s. 24(1)(a): all such rights are now contractual.
[72] s. 24(1)(b), the power to give the notice being under s. 140 of the Law of Property Act 1925.
[73] s. 24(3).
[74] s. 24(2). Although this sub-section refers to any tenant's improvement "provided for" the relevant part it is questionable whether this would permit a compensation claim to reflect work done off the holding (*e.g.* drainage work). The definition of "improvement" in s. 15 refers to an improvement "which is made on the holding".
[75] These are described as "anti-distortion provisions" by Scammell and Densham, *Law of Agricultural Holdings*, (8th ed.), page 1051. The useful example is given of a large grain store on the part taken back when the bulk of the land is retained.
[76] There is no obvious way round this difficulty: ss. 20(2) and 21(3) are directed to the time of the initial provision of the relevant improvement and the difficulty appears not to be dealt with elsewhere.
[77] See generally as to severance of the reversion para. 12.20 below.
[78] s. 25(1).
[79] Similar provisions exist in s. 75 of the Agricultural Holdings Act 1986.
[80] See the preceding paragraph.

choice and, if the tenant makes an election under the section, the arbitrator will apportion the amount awarded as between the persons who collectively constitute the landlord.[81] It appears that section 25 affects only the quantification of the compensation claim and not any other formal requirement of Part III.[82]

---

[81] s. 25(2). The arbitrator is also able to deal with costs in the same way.
[82] For example claims notices. It is suggested that the tenant should address any claims notice to all persons who together collectively constitute the landlord since the tenancy remains entire even though the reversion has been severed.

CHAPTER 6

DISPUTE RESOLUTION

6.1 General

6.2 Section 28 of the 1995 Act

6.3 Section 30 of the 1995 Act

6.5 Section 29 of the 1995 Act

6.8 The Arbitration Act 1996

6.9 Application of the Arbitration Act to arbitrations under section 29 of the 1995 Act

6.10 Application of the Arbitration Act to statutory arbitrations under the 1995 Act

6.11 Modifications of the Arbitration Act for statutory arbitrations

6.12 Court's concurrent jurisdiction regarding section 28 arbitrations

6.13 "Domestic arbitration agreements": sections 85–88 of the Arbitration Act

6.14 Summary of legislation applicable to 1995 Act arbitrations

6.15 Procedure and powers under arbitrations governed by the Arbitration Act

6.17 Mandatory sections in statutory arbitrations

6.37 Applications under Order 73

6.38 Non-mandatory sections in the case of statutory arbitrations under the 1995 Act

6.82 Appointment of arbitrator

6.83 Determination by an expert

6.88 Alternative dispute resolution

Resolution of disputes: general 6.1
Part IV of the 1995 Act contains a bare three sections dealing with dispute resolution. The paucity of the materials should not disguise the complexity of what is contained in that Part.[1] Section 28 contains general provisions for arbitration and appointment procedures.[2] Excluded from its terms are three specific situations contained within section 28(5) namely:

---

[1] s. 28(4) referring to the Arbitration Act 1950 has now been repealed: see now s. 9 of the Arbitration Act 1996.
[2] See paras 6.2 and 6.12 below.

DISPUTE RESOLUTION

(i) the determination of rent in pursuance of a statutory review notice.[3] This covers both determination by an expert[4] and also rent arbitrations[5];

(ii) cases within section 19(1).[6] These are arbitrations initiated by the tenant in the hope of securing an arbitrator's approval to an improvement being made[7];

(iii) any claim for compensation under Part III of the 1995 Act.[8] These are compulsorily referred to arbitration.[9]

Section 29 permits the general arbitration provisions in section 28 to be overridden by other binding procedures agreed by the parties.[10] Section 30[11] gives general procedures applicable to all arbitrations under the 1995 Act.[12] All these statutory arbitrations will proceed under the Arbitration Act 1996[13]; in relation to section 28 arbitrations the position as to concurrent jurisdiction of the Courts (if any) is not straightforward.[14] Finally, the Courts retain an independent jurisdiction in relation to forfeiture.[15]

6.2 Dispute resolution by arbitration under section 28

An apparently compulsory arbitration procedure prescribed by section 28 nevertheless is subject to the parties' ability to contract out in the terms of section 29.[16] It is also subject to the exceptions identified by the preceding paragraph. The section 28 procedure relates to any "dispute between the landlord and the tenant under a farm business tenancy, being a dispute concerning their rights and obligations under this Act, under the terms of the tenancy or under any custom".[17] In order to implement the arbitration provision it is necessary for either the landlord or the tenant to give notice in writing to the other in accordance with section 28(2)[18] specifying the dispute and warning the other party that he will apply to the President of the RICS for the appointment of an arbitrator unless within two months the parties have appointed the arbitrator by agreement. It will be

---

[3] s. 28(5)(a).
[4] s. 12(b) and para. 2.11 above.
[5] See para. 2.14 above.
[6] s. 28(5)(b).
[7] See para. 5.15 above.
[8] s. 28(5)(c).
[9] See para. 5.20–5.22 above.
[10] See paras 6.5 and 6.9 below.
[11] See para. 6.3 below.
[12] See para. 6.4 below.
[13] See paras 6.10–6.11 below.
[14] See para. 6.12 below.
[15] Forfeiture actions and any application for relief from forfeiture will be made by Court proceedings.
[16] See para. 6.5 below.
[17] s. 28(1).
[18] See Form 134 in Part V of this work.

appreciated that it is necessary not only to make the recipient aware that the notice is given under and for the purposes of section 28(2) but also to consider very carefully the terms describing "the dispute". It is these terms which, in due course, will establish the arbitrator's jurisdiction and there must be every incentive for parties who are in dispute to co-operate at least in terms of framing the specification of what it is they are in dispute about.[19] It would appear that it is not open to the parties under section 28 to appoint more than one arbitrator since section 30(1) requires determination by a sole arbitrator.[20] Appointment by agreement is considered elsewhere.[21] Once the two-month period in the notice under section 28(2) has expired either party may apply to the President of the RICS for the appointment of an arbitrator by him.[22] Section 30 governs the application.

Scope and terms of section 30 6.3
Section 30(1) provides that:

> "Any matter which is required to be determined by arbitration under this Act shall be determined by the arbitration of a sole arbitrator."

This section covers arbitrations which are the subject of a compulsory statutory reference for example in respect of sections 10, 19 and any claims for compensation under Part III. Equally it extends to arbitrations within section 28, whether or not any concurrent jurisdiction survives in the Court. However it would not extend to an arbitration established under section 29: this means that the supplementary provisions of section 30(2)/(3) are not available for those particular arbitrations. Section 30(2) requires an application under the Act to the President of the RICS to be made in writing and to be accompanied by a fee determined by the President.[23] The President is entitled to determine a "reasonable fee".[24] Section 30(3) authorises the President of the RICS on the application of either party to appoint a new arbitrator where "an arbitrator appointed for the purposes of this Act" dies or is incapable of acting and has not been replaced by appointment by the parties. It is submitted that the President on such an application is once again entitled to be paid his reasonable fee pursuant to section 30(2).[25] What is meant by "incapable of acting" is not further defined. Although, it is submitted, this probably covers matters other than illness, it is likely that in most cases illness will be the

---

[19] Chartered surveyors intending subsequently to hand litigation on to solicitors ought to consider carefully whether they or the solicitors ultimately to be instructed should draw the terms of this particular notice.

[20] If it is desired to establish a three person arbitration Tribunal this would have to be done under s. 29.

[21] See para. 6.82 below.

[22] s. 28(3).

[23] The Regulations governing the corresponding power to appoint under the Agricultural Holdings Act 1986 (The Agricultural Holdings (Fee) Regulations 1996, S.I. 1996 No.337) do not apply.

[24] Since this fee may vary from time to time advisers should check what it is since it may, theoretically, differ from the £115 authorised under the 1986 Act.

[25] It is further submitted that s. 30(2) will govern any request for a new arbitrator to be appointed notwithstanding s. 30(3) making no reference to an application to the President "in writing".

cause of this provision being relied on.[26] It has been suggested here that section 30 does not extend to arbitrations under section 29 and accordingly that an arbitrator "appointed for the purposes of this Act" does not include a section 20 arbitrator.[27]

6.4 Status of arbitrations within section 30

All these arbitrations are clearly statutory arbitrations and they are not excluded from the ambit of the Arbitration Act 1996. There is accordingly a contrast with arbitrations falling within section 29 which are in truth contractual arbitrations. These are also governed by the Arbitration Act 1996 but there are differences in the way in which that statute has to be modified so as to apply.[28]

6.5 Scope of section 29

Section 29 is drafted so as to cover various types of dispute resolution procedure. It is, however, only applicable to written tenancy agreements and only where there has been a joint reference to a third party or one party has referred and the other has failed to start the arbitration procedures under section 28(2). The preconditions for the operation of section 29 are clearly set out in section 29(1)(a) and (b). Sub-section (a) refers to a tenancy created by an instrument which includes provision for dispute resolution: the wording suggests that subsequent variation of the tenancy agreement to include such a matter is not sufficient to bring section 29(1)(a) into play. The sub-section is entirely unspecific as to what type of provision for dispute resolution may or may not be included and it is submitted that the following comply:

(i) determination or valuation by an expert

(ii) arbitration whether by one or more arbitrators

(iii) mediation provided that the recommendation of the mediator is binding in law on both parties.

What is more, section 29 does not necessarily contemplate that the resolution of the dispute will be in accordance with the parties' strict legal rights, although it is likely that, for example, most arbitration or expert determinations will be drawn to that effect.[29] Section 29(1)(b) applies only where the person to resolve the dispute is neither one of the parties nor appointed by one of them without the consent or concurrence of the other.[30] This means, for example, that the landlord's valuer may

---

[26] See Bernstein & Others, *Handbook of Arbitration Practice*, (3rd ed., Sweet & Maxwell, 1998), coolly observes "While it is an intrusion on his privacy, an arbitrator in a particularly costly and lengthy case should be prepared to give the parties access to his medical advisers or if it is desired to insure him against failure to perform his duties through illness or death, submit to medical examination by a Doctor of the Insurers' choice" (para. 2–208).

[27] The arbitrator's appointment is recognised under s. 29 but his appointment is for the purposes of the tenancy agreement not the statute.

[28] See paras 6.9 (s. 29 arbitrations), 6.10–6.11 (s. 30 arbitrations) and 6.14 (the contrast) below.

[29] Contrast arbitrators authorised to resolve matters *ex aequo et bono* and mediation.

[30] s. 29(1)(a)(i)/(ii).

determine a dispute under section 29 even if he is appointed by the landlord provided that the tenant consents or concurs in that appointment. It must be doubtful whether consent or concurrence extends any further than compliance with section 29(1)(b)(i), that is to say a joint reference by landlord and by tenant. Conversely it must be questionable whether, in the absence of consent, the tenant will have "concurred" in the appointment of the landlord's valuer by the landlord if he has simply failed to serve a notice under section 28(2) within the time limit specified by section 29(1)(b)(ii). Finally, in connection with section 29(1)(a) it is suggested that the sub-section should not be read as though it required the contractual provision to follow the wording of the sub-section and expressly exclude the parties mentioned in the inset paragraphs (i) and (ii). Rather, it is suggested, the sub-section should be construed to save a general disputes resolution provision in circumstances where persons within sub-sections (a)(i)/(ii) are not in fact the persons to resolve the dispute.[31]

Section 29(1)(b) requires that in addition one or other of the following should have happened namely a joint appointment by landlord and tenant of the third party[32]; alternatively either landlord or tenant may refer the dispute to the third party under the contractual provision[33] and that party has notified the other in writing of the making of the reference.[34] Time is of the essence in relation to this statutory period and the opportunity to override the contract and substitute an arbitration under section 28 will be permanently lost if the notice under section 28(2) is not served in time. It is an interesting question as to what a notice under section 28(2) ought to contain in order to nullify the procedure under section 29.[35]

If the tenancy contains a provision of the type identified by section 29(1)(a), must a party wishing to go to a section 28 arbitration wait until served with a notice of reference within section 29(1)(b)(ii) before initiating arbitration under section 28? We suggest not. Even though section 29 overrides section 28, access to section 28 would be unduly restrictive if any other answer were given to this question. For instance, section 29 arbitrations or dispute procedures are not necessarily capable of being triggered by either party. Unless section 28 simply overrode the contract, the effect of a tenancy provision falling within section 29(1)(a) but not implemented would be to deny the party not authorised to trigger the reference to any access to dispute resolution at all. Rather, it is suggested, section 29 operates in

---

[31] Form 130 gives a precedent for a tenancy clause for third party dispute resolution.
[32] Form 131 contains a precedent for the joint reference of a dispute by landlord and tenant to a third party.
[33] Form 132 provides a precedent for a reference of dispute by landlord or tenant to the third party. The statute does not require that the reference itself must be in writing although the contract may very well do so.
[34] Form 133 contains a precedent for a notice by landlord or tenant to the other party of his unilateral reference of dispute to the third party and the stipulated period of four weeks beginning with the date on which the other party was so notified has expired without that other party giving a notice under s. 28(2). Subs. 29(1)(b)(ii).
[35] It is submitted that the notice must, in order to displace the s. 29 procedure, specify the dispute which would otherwise have gone on to be resolved by the third party. It would not appear that the notice under s. 28(2) is invalidated by containing material relating to disputes in addition to the dispute falling within s. 29.

limited circumstances to save provisions which would otherwise simply be overridden by section 28, which after all is couched in mandatory terms.

6.6 Non-binding mediation not within section 29
Section 29(2) restricts its scope to the activities of a person, whether arbitrator or not, who is able to give a decision "binding in law" on both parties. In context this effectively means binding in contract.

6.7 Status of section 29 reference
An arbitrator acting under section 29 is acting under a contractual, not a statutory, reference and must be treated accordingly for the purposes of the Arbitration Act 1996.[36] Experts are obviously altogether outside the scope of the Arbitration Act and are considered separately below.[37] The activities of a mediator whose recommendation is contractually binding on the parties will be exclusively governed by the terms of the contract under which he is appointed.[38] Where a section 29 arbitration contains procedures relating to the appointment of the arbitrator they are valid for so long as not overridden by either party activating section 28 by service of a notice under section 28(2).

6.8 The Arbitration Act 1996
This Act is printed in full in Part VII of this work since so many of its provisions will be of interest to agricultural practitioners, both in terms of litigation and also in terms of drafting farm business tenancy agreements. The Arbitration Act generated, pursuant to section 109, the Arbitration Act 1996 (Commencement No.1) Order 1996[39] bringing the Act into force in stages.[40] So far there have been no orders relevant to this text made pursuant to section 98.[41]

---

[36] See para. 6.9 below.

[37] See paras 6.83–6.87.

[38] The difficulties of anticipating the dispute and sufficiently precisely providing for its resolution by this means are likely to be so great that we would not expect it to be used at all widely as a means of dispute resolution.

[39] S.I.1996 No.3146.

[40] December 17, 1996 is the commencement date for ss. 91 (relating to the power to make orders), 105, 108–110, Sched. 3, para. 36 (and s. 107(1) so far as it relates thereto), and so far as it relates to provision in the County Court rules, Sched. 4 (and s. 107(2) relating thereto), again relating to the County Court rules. The remainder excluding ss. 85–87 (subject to transitional provisions) came into force on January 31, 1997. The transitional provisions in Sched. 2 of the Order apply the statutes specified in s. 107 (the old law) to arbitrations commenced before January 31, 1997, arbitration applications commenced before that date and arbitration applications commenced on or after that date relating to arbitration proceedings commenced before that date. In relation to s. 46(1)(b) (provision for disputes to be decided in accordance with provisions other than law) where the arbitration agreement was made before January 31, 1997 the agreement is to have effect in accordance with the rules of law (including any conflict of laws rules) as they were prior to that date.

[41] That section contains a power to make further provision by regulations dealing with statutory arbitrations.

Application of the Arbitration Act to arbitrations under section 29 of the Agricultural Tenancies Act 1995
6.9

Assuming that the position described in paragraph 6.5 above is correct, namely that arbitrations falling within section 29 are true contractual arbitrations and not statutory arbitrations, the position in regard to the Arbitration Act is as follows. Section 4 of the Arbitration Act separates out two different categories of provision within the statute. Section 4(1) identifies the provisions listed in Schedule 1 as "mandatory" and as having effect notwithstanding any agreement to the contrary. These are:

sections 9–11 (stay of legal proceedings);
section 12 (power of court to extend agreed time limits)[42];
section 13 (application of Limitation Acts);
section 24 (power of court to remove arbitrator);
section 26(1) (effect of death of arbitrator);
section 28 (liability of parties for fees and expenses of arbitrators);
section 29 (immunity of arbitrator);
section 31 (objection to substantive jurisdiction of tribunal);
section 32 (determination of preliminary point of jurisdiction);
section 33 (general duty of tribunal);
section 37(2) (items to be treated as expenses of arbitrators);
section 40 (general duty of parties);
section 43 (securing the attendance of witnesses);
section 56 (power to withhold award in case of non-payment);
section 60 (effectiveness of agreement for payment of costs in any event);
section 66 (enforcement of award);
sections 67 and 68 (challenging the award: substantive jurisdiction and serious irregularity), and **sections 70 and 71** (supplementary provisions; effect of order of court) so far as relating to those sections;
section 72 (saving for rights of person who takes no part in proceedings);
section 73 (loss of right to object);
section 74 (immunity of arbitral institutions, etc.)
section 75 (charge to secure payment of solicitors' costs)

The remaining provisions of the statute are designated by section 4(2) as applicable on a fallback basis where the parties have not made their own arrangements by agreement. Comparison of the Arrangement of Sections in Part VII with the list above of mandatory matters reveals immediately how much freedom is left to the parties to govern the conduct of the arbitration in that sections 34 (procedural and evidential matters), 35 (consolidation of proceedings and concurrent hearings) and 36 (legal or other representation) are in the non-mandatory category.

Application of the Arbitration Act to statutory arbitrations under the Agricultural Tenancies Act 1995
6.10

Sections 94–98 of the Arbitration Act apply so as to modify the Arbitration Act for the purposes of any statutory arbitration but the position is not the same as that

---

[42] As to which see ***Fox and Widley v. Guram*** [1998] 3 E.G. 142, a very restrictive view of

which appertains to contractual arbitrations. Therefore statutory arbitrations proper under the 1995 Act, whether in pursuance of a notice under section 10, an arbitration under section 19, a compensation dispute under Part III or a dispute falling within section 28, or one which becomes subject to section 28 because a notice under section 28(2) is served, the dispute originally having been within section 29, will all be treated differently from arbitrations falling under section 29. The process of adaptation applies to every statutory arbitration whether the statute was made before or after the commencement of the Arbitration Act.[43] A statutory arbitration is defined as one which is "arbitration under an enactment".[44] The Agricultural Tenancies Act 1995 does not exclude the application of the Arbitration Act[45] but the 1995 Act overrides the terms of the Arbitration Act in so far as the 1995 Act is inconsistent with the 1996 Act.[46] Subject thereto, the provisions of Part I[47] of the Arbitration Act apply. This means that the procedural and other matters contained in sections 28 and 30 of the Agricultural Tenancies Act 1995 supplant any inconsistent provisions in sections 1–84 of the Arbitration Act.[48] Section 95(2) states that every statutory arbitration is taken to have its seat in England and Wales[49] and sections 1–84 of the Arbitration Act are to be construed as though a statutory arbitration were pursuant to an arbitration agreement and as if the enactment were the agreement, with the parties subject to the arbitration treated as though they were parties to the agreement.[50]

6.11 **Modifications of the Arbitration Act so far as applicable to statutory arbitrations: sections 96–98 of the Arbitration Act**

Section 96 deals with modifications in relation to three non-mandatory provisions namely sections 30(1) (competence of tribunal to rule on its own jurisdiction), section 35 (consolidation of proceedings and concurrent hearings) and 46 (rules applicable to substance of dispute). Section 97 provides that specific sections of the Arbitration Act do not apply in relation to a statutory arbitration. They are:

(a) Section 8 (whether agreement discharged by death of a party);

(b) Section 12 (power of Court to extend agreed time limits);

(c) Sections 9(5), 10(2) and 71(4) (restrictions on effect of provision that award condition precedent to right to bring legal proceedings).

In the absence of these provisions it is submitted that statutory arbitrations under

---

s. 12 being taken.

[43] s. 94(1).

[44] For these purposes subordinate legislation such as a statutory instrument is counted as an "enactment": s. 94(3) of the Arbitration Act.

[45] Accordingly s. 94(2)(b) of the Arbitration Act does not apply.

[46] s. 94(2)(a) of the Arbitration Act.

[47] ss. 1 to 84 inclusive.

[48] For example the notice and appointment procedures in s. 28(2)/(3) and the requirement of a sole arbitrator in s. 30 override the more liberal provisions of the Arbitration Act.

[49] As relevant for present purposes. This is of importance to s. 2 (scope of application of provisions) and s. 85 (domestic arbitration agreements) [not yet in force].

[50] s. 95(1).

the 1995 Act are not discharged by the death of the litigant since both in relation to the definition of "landlord" and "tenant" in section 38 of the 1995 Act there is an express statement that these designations include "any person deriving title" from the original landlord or tenant. As to section 12 of the Arbitration Act not being available, it is submitted that this makes virtually no difference to statutory arbitrations under the 1995 Act since all the relevant time-limits are either as provided by sections 28/30 and are accordingly strict or there are no time-limits applicable at all. It would appear that it is only in the case of a section 29 arbitration that complicated contractual time-limits will survive the impact of Part IV of the 1995 Act. If there are difficulties in relation to a possible section 10 arbitration as to whether time is or should be made of the essence in relation to a contractual rent review, it is submitted that any jurisdiction exercised by the Court would not be one deriving from the Arbitration Act and is accordingly unaffected by the non-availability of section 12.

Concurrent jurisdiction of the Court in relation to arbitrations within section 28 of the Agricultural Tenancies Act 1995   6.12

Where the 1995 Act creates a statutory right only capable of being crystallised or exercised through the compulsory arbitration procedures identified by section 28(5) it is submitted that the Court has no concurrent jurisdiction. The remaining general arbitration provisions contained in and governed by section 28 are, however, ones where the Court perhaps does have a concurrent jurisdiction.[51] As modified by section 97(c) of the Arbitration Act, section 9 consists only of sub-sections (1)-(4) in relation to statutory arbitrations. Section 1 of the Arbitration Act establishes general principles by which the Arbitration Act is to be construed,[52] including in particular:

(c) In matters governed by this Part[53] the court should not intervene except as provided by this Part.

Where a party applies under section 9 of the Arbitration Act the Court is required to grant a stay "unless satisfied that the arbitration agreement is null and void, inoperative, or incapable of being performed". It is suggested that this formulation is one which will necessarily result in virtually all arbitrations proceeding in preference to the exercise by the Court of its jurisdiction. Furthermore the formulation appears so strong that even matters involving fraud will be dealt with by the arbitrator, not the Court. However this does not mean that an arbitration award obtained by default will be enforceable if it perpetuates a fraud.[54] So far no

---

[51] As the section was originally drafted there was an express preservation of the jurisdiction of the courts in s. 28(4): however that section has now been repealed in its entirety and section 9 of the Arbitration Act governs matters.
[52] One might have expected s. 1 to deter the court from going behind the statute to the Report on the Arbitration Bill (prepared by Saville L.J. prior to the passage of the Act through Parliament), but there is no sign of this: see *Fox & Widley v. Guram* [1998] 3 E.G. 142 at 145.
[53] *i.e.* ss. 1–84 of the Arbitration Act.
[54] See the discussion in para. 12.47 below.

6.13 Further possible modification of Part I of the Arbitration Act in relation to domestic arbitration agreements, sections 85–88 of the Arbitration Act

Sections 85–87 of the Arbitration Act are not yet in force.[55] Although section 95(1) applies Part I of the Arbitration Act to statutory arbitrations as if they were pursuant to an arbitration agreement it is likely that statutory arbitrations are not intended to be the subject of the modifications set out in Part II of the Arbitration Act, sections 85–88. However those sections, when implemented, would apply in relation to any arbitration under section 29 of the Agricultural Tenancies Act 1995 in so far as the agreement in question is a "domestic arbitration agreement" for the purposes of section 85(2). That section repays study[56] and would mean, amongst other things, that where, for example, the landlord is a company incorporated outside the United Kingdom there is not a "domestic arbitration agreement". One of the most important differences between domestic and non-domestic agreements in the application of Part I of the Arbitration Act is in relation to the staying of legal proceedings. In relation to a "domestic arbitration agreement" the Court is required to grant a stay unless satisfied[57]:

(a) that the arbitration agreement is null and void, inoperative, or incapable of being performed or

(b) that there are other sufficient grounds for not requiring the parties to abide by the arbitration agreement.

An example of this is given by section 86(6). Whether an arbitration agreement is a domestic arbitration agreement is determined by reference to the facts at the time that the legal proceedings are commenced.[58] There are also special provisions relating to the effectiveness of an agreement to exclude the Court's jurisdiction.[59] The statement above that statutory arbitrations are not included in relation to these provisions is because it is only in the application of Part I of the Arbitration Act that the statutory arbitration is treated "as if" pursuant to an arbitration agreement[60]: sections 85–88 are to be found in Part II of the Arbitration Act.

---

[55] These sections are a serious embarrassment and in all probability a breach of the U.K.'s obligations under Art. 6 of the Treaty of Rome in so far as they would operate against the citizens of Member States. It is not anticipated that the Government will bring these provisions into force in the immediate future: the difficulty was apparently addressed by the Second Reading debate in the HL (see further Lord and Salzedo, *Guide to the Arbitration Act 1996*, (Cavendish Publishing Limited, 1996), p. xi).
[56] Printed in full in Part VII.
[57] s. 86(2):
[58] s. 86(4).
[59] s. 87.
[60] s. 95(1).

Summary of legislation applicable to 1995 Act arbitrations 6.14

For convenience, and applying the above discussion, matters may be summarised in relation to each different type of arbitration under the 1995 Act as follows but ignoring the possible application of sections 85–8 of the Arbitration Act.

Rent review arbitration under section 10 of the 1995 Act This is governed by sections 10–14 and 30 of the 1995 Act and subject thereto to sections 1–84 of the Arbitration Act as modified by section 96 of that Act but excluding sections 8, 12, 9(5), 10(2) and 71(4) of the 1996 Act. Schedule 1 of the Arbitration Act contains mandatory matters and any other applicable sections of the Arbitration Act may be modified by contract.

Arbitrations under section 19 of the 1995 Act These arbitrations are primarily subject to Part III of the 1995 Act and section 30 of that Act. Subject to those provisions sections 1–84 of the Arbitration Act apply as modified by section 96 but excluding sections 8, 12, 9(5), 10(2) and 71(4). Schedule 1 of the Arbitration Act contains mandatory matters and any other applicable sections can be modified by contract.

Compensation disputes under Part III of the 1995 Act These arbitrations are primarily governed by Part III of the 1995 Act and section 30 of that Act. Subject to those provisions sections 1–84 of the Arbitration Act apply as modified by section 96 but excluding sections 8, 12, 9(5), 10(2) and 71(4). Schedule 1 of the Arbitration Act contains mandatory matters and any other applicable sections can be modified by contract.

General arbitrations under section 28 of the 1995 Act These arbitrations are primarily governed by sections 28 and 30 of the 1995 Act and subject to those sections, sections 1–84 of the Arbitration Act apply as modified by section 96 but excluding sections 8, 12, 9(5), 10(2) and 71(4). Schedule 1 of the Arbitration Act contains mandatory matters and any other applicable sections can be modified by contract.

Arbitrations falling within section 29 of the 1995 Act It will obviously first be necessary to ascertain that section 29 does indeed apply to the particular arbitration. Subject to that, the arbitration is governed by, in this order:

(i) the mandatory sections in the Arbitration Act identified by Schedule 1 of that Act;

(ii) subject thereto, the contract;

(iii) subject to the above, sections 1–84 of the Arbitration Act.

Requirement for writing under the Arbitration Act 6.15

Attention is drawn to the terms of sections 5 and 6 of the Arbitration Act which are general provisions dealing with, respectively, the need for agreements to be "in writing" and the definition of "arbitration agreement". In so far as non-mandatory terms of Part I of the Arbitration Act may be modified by the parties' agreement, such agreement must be in writing in accordance with section 5.[61]

6.16 Procedure and powers under arbitration governed by the Arbitration Act 1996

It will be obvious from the above that any arbitration contemplated by the Agricultural Tenancies Act 1995, whether under that Act or not, presents to the arbitrator a precise but complex inter-relationship with the Arbitration Act. The first task of the parties and the arbitrator is likely to be identification of what procedures and powers are applicable to the particular arbitration having regard to the above. In many arbitrations it is likely that the ascertainment of procedure/ powers is straightforward but time-consuming. It will involve, preferably by agreement of all concerned, identification of statutory materials. It will be apparent from the above that there is considerable scope for difference between different types of arbitration and/or different contracts. In most cases it is suspected that the exercise is unlikely to give rise to problems: the enormous saving grace of the Arbitration Act (despite the need to modify in relation to statutory arbitrations) is its clarity of drafting. For this reason it is not necessary and probably not desirable to summarise the terms of the Arbitration Act. Because it is anticipated that arbitrations under section 29 of the Agricultural Tenancies Act 1995 may be relatively few whereas statutory arbitrations under that Act are likely to be relatively frequent, this chapter proceeds to comment on those mandatory provisions affecting the statutory arbitrations as modified by the Arbitration Act for that purpose. This work is not a specialised work in terms of its commentary on arbitration and those wishing to pursue more detailed research will need to consult a specialist literature.[62]

---

[61] It is clear that "in writing" is given a specific but very wide definition by s. 5: readers are referred to the full terms of that section in Part VII below.

[62] Lord and Salzedo, *Guide to the Arbitration Act 1996*, (Cavendish Publishing Limited, 1996) is a well organised and critical commentary section by section which at the front provides a Destination Table correlating new sections with either sections replaced or those which partly reflected the content of the new section. This table enables larger works dealing with the historic position to be usefully employed. Of these the most impressive is Mustill & Boyd, *The Law and Practice of Commercial Arbitration in England* (2nd ed., Butterworths, 1989). It is to be regretted that there is no new edition of that work. A most useful practical handbook is the Handbook of Arbitration Practice by Bernstein and Others, (3rd ed., Sweet & Maxwell, 1998). This includes amongst its contributions a section dealing with Agricultural Property Arbitrations by Derek Wood Q.C. the latter at para. 7–106 cross refers discussion of the sections into the text of the more general part. Russell on Arbitration is now in a new edition, (21st ed., Sweet & Maxwell, 1997) which is written to the text of the new Act. Much of that text is too geared to the commercial sector to be of interest to agricultural practitioners but the Appendices are helpful and include Ord. 73 of the RSC.

Mandatory sections in statutory arbitrations: sections 9–11 (stay of legal proceedings)   6.17

Sections 9(5) and 10(2) are excluded.[63] On January 31, 1997 the Rules of the Supreme Court Order 73 was substituted by an entirely new Order 73 designed to facilitate the operation of the Arbitration Act. In this work reference to Order 73 is to that new order. Order 73 now deals with applications under section 9(3) of the Arbitration Act. Under the old law, missing time-limits did not result in the arbitration agreement being inoperative[64] and a lack of cash to finance either the proceedings or payment of an award did not amount to the award being incapable of performance.[65] Where an impecunious plaintiff would be entitled to legal aid in the courts, this is not of itself a reason to refuse a stay to defendants wishing to pursue an arbitration claim. The correct question to ask is: if the plaintiff was not legally aided, would it be proper or improper to grant a stay of the arbitration?[66]

Mandatory sections in statutory arbitrations: section 13 (application of Limitation Acts)   6.18

This section applies without modification. "Legal proceedings" is defined by section 82(1) and "the court" is defined by section 105.

Mandatory sections in statutory arbitrations: section 24 (power of court to remove arbitrator)   6.19

Order 73 of the Rules of the Supreme Court provides a procedure for implementing this section. This is the means by which parties may complain if the arbitrator is in breach of his duties under section 33. Section 24(2) is not appropriate to cover the limited duty of appointment carried by the President of the RICS under section 30.

Mandatory sections in statutory arbitrations: section 26(1) (effect of death of arbitrator)   6.20

This section applies and is consistent with the powers of the President of the RICS under section 30(3) to appoint a new arbitrator in the event of the death of the original arbitrator.

Mandatory sections in statutory arbitrations: section 28 (liability of parties for fees and expenses of arbitrators)   6.21

This section applies in its entirety. "The court" is defined by section 105 and "upon notice" is a reference on to section 80. Any exercise under sub-section (2) should be cross-referred to section 64.

Mandatory sections in statutory arbitrations: section 29 (immunity of arbitrator)   6.22

This section applies in full. This is the first statutory recognition of an arbitrator's

---

[63] s. 97.
[64] *Radio Publicity v. Cie Luxembourgeoise* [1936] 2 All E.R. 721.
[65] *Paczy v. Haendler* [1981] 1 Lloyd's Rep. 302; *The Rena K* [1979] Q.B. 377.
[66] See *Edwin Jones v. Thyssen (Great Britain) Limited* (1991) 57 B.L.R. 116, CA.

immunity. As to "bad faith" see **Melton Medes v. Securities & Investments Board**.[67]

6.23 Mandatory sections in statutory arbitrations: section 31 (objection to substantive jurisdiction of tribunal)

A definition of "substantive jurisdiction" is provided by non-mandatory section 30(1), but that section has itself been modified by section 96 in relation to statutory arbitrations. Accordingly the reference in section 30(1)(a) to whether there is a valid arbitration agreement is to be construed as a reference to whether the enactment applies to the dispute or difference in question. "The court" is defined by section 105. No procedure is prescribed for the making of an objection but an objection of this type must be made "forthwith".[68] The reference in sub-section (1) to "the first step in the proceedings" includes any step such as applying for discovery, appearing on a directions summons, etc., and means a step indicating an election to treat the proceedings as valid.[69]

6.24 Mandatory sections in statutory arbitrations: section 32 (determination of preliminary point of jurisdiction)

New Order 73 in the Rules of the Supreme Court provides a procedure for this. This section applies in its entirety. As to "substantive jurisdiction", see the notes under the preceding paragraph.

6.25 Mandatory sections in statutory arbitrations: section 33 (general duty of tribunal)

This section applies in its entirety and is enforceable by means of section 24. It replaces the Court's previous ability to deal with misconduct in terms of removing

---

[67] [1995] Ch. 137 at 147:

> "The term 'bad faith' has a variety of meanings in different contexts. Thus in the field of administrative law, where the validity of a decision or act is challenged on this ground, it is sufficient that the power to decide or act has been exercised for purposes otherwise than those for which the power was conferred or without regard to the relevant, or only the relevant, considerations. There is no necessary moral connotation. But in the context of the tort of misfeasance in public office, or, as it is sometimes called, deliberate abuse of power, the term has a far more restricted meaning. A moral element is an essential ingredient. Lack of good faith connotes either (a) malice in the sense of personal spite or a desire to injure for improper reasons or (b) knowledge of absence of power to make the decision in question: see Wade & Forsyth, *Administrative Law*, (7th ed., 1994), p. 795, citing **Bourgoin SA v. Ministry of Agriculture Fisheries & Food** [1986] Q.B. 716. In my view, in the context of section 187 [of the Financial Services Act 1986], this more restricted meaning is to be adopted ... This hurdle in the way of a claimant is substantial, for the allegation of bad faith is, like that of fraud, one to be made only where there exists prima facie evidence justifying the allegation. If there is no reasonable evidence or grounds to support the allegation, a statement of claim making such an allegation will be struck out as an abuse of process." (Lightman J.)

[68] See s. 73. Section 73 may in normal circumstances simply mean "as soon as possible" as stipulated by s. 31(2). If there is a difference, s. 73 may be confined to challenges under s. 67 (direct challenges to an award on jurisdictional grounds).

[69] See **Eagle Star Insurance Co. v. Yuval Insurance Co.** [1978] 1 Lloyd's Rep. 357 at 361

the arbitrator or setting aside an award. Section 34 assists with the definition of "procedural and evidential matters". See also section 46 as to the law to be applied.[70]

Mandatory sections in statutory arbitrations: section 37(2) (items to be treated as expenses of arbitrators) 6.26
This sub-section applies without modification. The expenses of the arbitrators are considered by sections 59–65.

Mandatory sections in statutory arbitrations: section 40 (general duty of parties) 6.27
This section applies without modification and is enforceable by means of section 41, the Court's powers being contained in section 42. Order 73 of the Rules of the Supreme Court provides for section 42 applications.

Mandatory sections in statutory arbitrations: section 43 (securing the attendance of witnesses) 6.28
This section applies without modification. "Legal proceedings" is defined by section 82(1).

Mandatory sections in statutory arbitrations: section 56 (power to withhold award in case of non-payment) 6.29
This section applies without modification. New Order 73 of the Rules of the Supreme Court provides for applications under this section. As to "upon notice", see section 80. As to "the Court", see section 105. As to section 56(4) and "available arbitral process" see section 82(1).

Mandatory sections in statutory arbitrations: section 60 (effectiveness of agreement for payment of costs in any event) 6.30
This section applies without modification. It is to be noted that a contractual right to recover indemnity costs has been held sufficient to influence the Court in awarding indemnity costs in subsequent court proceedings[71]: presumably where the parties make a contract sufficient for section 60 a contractual provision relating to indemnity costs would have the same effect.

Mandatory sections in statutory arbitrations: section 66 (enforcement of award) 6.31
This section applies without modification. This section does not identify the grounds on which the court might refuse leave. However it is submitted that such refusals will be rare.

(Lord Denning M.R.).
[70] But in regard to statutory arbitrations section 46 applies with the omission of s. 46(1)(b) and is in any case subject to the transitional provisions noted at para. 6.8 above.
[71] *Church Commissioners for England v. Ibrahim* [1997] 1 E.G.L.R. 13, CA.

6.32 Mandatory sections in statutory arbitrations: sections 67 and 68 (challenging the award: substantive jurisdiction and serious irregularity) and sections 70 and 71 in aid of those sections

Section 71(4) does not apply.[72] A procedure in relation to section 70 is provided by new Order 73 in the Rules of the Supreme Court. Applications under section 67 are time limited by section 70(3). Section 68 establishes a new test designed to reduce technical objections which do not produce substantial injustice to the complainant. It should be noted that section 69 (appeal on point of law) is not a mandatory provision.

6.33 Mandatory sections in statutory arbitrations: section 72 (saving for rights of person who takes no part in proceedings)

This section applies in its entirety. Given the wide definitions of "landlord" and "tenant" in section 38(1) of the Agricultural Tenancies Act some modification of section 72, in practice, is required. For example, successors in title, will be bound by the award since they take under one of the original parties.

6.34 Mandatory sections in statutory arbitrations: section 73 (loss of right to object)

This section applies in its entirety. As to "substantive jurisdiction", see section 30(1) but subject to the remarks above in discussion of section 31.

6.35 Mandatory sections in statutory arbitrations: section 74 (immunity of arbitral institutions, etc.)

This section applies in its entirety and is consistent with the terms of section 30 of the Agricultural Tenancies Act 1975.

6.36 Mandatory sections in statutory arbitrations: section 75 (charge to secure payment of solicitors' costs)

This section applies in its entirety. For a definition of "the court", see section 105.

6.37 Applications under Order 73

New Order 73[73] provides in Part I for applications under the following sections of the Arbitration Act[74]:

> Sections 9(3), 12(2) [not applicable to statutory arbitrations], 18(2) [not applicable to statutory arbitrations since overridden by section 30 of the Agricultural Tenancies Act], 21(5) [not applicable to statutory arbitrations since overridden by section 30 of the 1995 Act], 24(2), 32(3), 42(3), 44(4)/(5), 45(3), 50(2), 56(4), 69(2)(4), 70(2)/(3) and 77(3) [but attention is drawn to the supplementary provisions of section 36 (service of notices) of the Agricultural Tenancies Act 1995.[75]]

---

[72] s. 97.
[73] Effective as of January 31, 1997.
[74] Those which are mandatory have been dealt with above: this list is complete.
[75] See paras 7.8–7.14 below.

Adaptation of non-mandatory sections in the case of statutory arbitrations 6.38

These take place as set out in paragraph 6.14 above and contractual modification of the non-mandatory sections of the Arbitration Act must be written.[76] Additionally there are the three specific adaptations of the non-mandatory provisions stipulated by section 96:

> **Section 30(1)** (Competence of tribunal to rule on its own jurisdiction).[77]
>
> **Section 35** (Consolidation of proceedings and concurrent hearings). This applies only so as to authorise the consolidation of proceedings, or concurrent hearings in proceedings, under the same enactment. Therefore where the same arbitrator is appointed in respect of a dispute under the statutory jurisdiction of section 30 of the Agricultural Tenancies Act 1995 and also a contractual dispute under section 29 of that Act, those proceedings cannot be consolidated under section 35 of the Arbitration Act.
>
> **Section 46** (Rules applicable to substance of dispute). This applies with the omission of sub-section (1)(b). The deletion of that sub-section means that statutory arbitrations must be resolved in accordance with the terms of the relevant statute (*i.e.* the Agricultural Tenancies Act 1995). However, since sub-section (1)(b) is available in relation to contractual disputes under section 29 of the 1995 Act, it will be appreciated that it can be used so as to permit the parties to proceed to an arbitration where their dispute is resolved by an arbitrator not in accordance with the strict legal rights of the parties (*e.g.* where the contract gives him a free discretion or where he is on one or more issues able to take into account or required to follow the report of a mediator)."

The above is relatively straightforward: the difficulty in relation to non-mandatory sections where statutory arbitrations are concerned is the question as to what parts of the Arbitration Act may be inconsistent with the provisions of the Agricultural Tenancies Act or with any rules or procedure authorised by it or recognised by it.[78] The type of adaptation required will not only constrain what the parties themselves can agree but will constrain the arbitrator in the exercise of powers apparently available to him under the Arbitration Act.[79] It is this particular problem of adaptation which is highlighted by further commentary in relation to the non-mandatory sections in the following paragraphs.

---

[76] See para. 6.15 above.
[77] See para. 6.23 above.
[78] s. 94(2)(a) of the Arbitration Act.
[79] For example under s. 48 of the Arbitration Act. It is obvious that the parties cannot enforce any agreement they may make for the purposes of s. 48(2) so as to prevent the arbitrator making an award in accordance with the 1995 Act, for instance under s. 19 of that Act. Equally clearly the arbitrator cannot use powers ostensibly available under s. 48(3)-(5) to enlarge his ability to deal with a dispute where his powers are already severely restricted by the 1995 Act: for instance, under s. 19(6) the arbitrator is given the ability to approve or withhold his consent and it is submitted that he cannot rely on s. 48 of the Arbitration Act so as to enable himself to grant the parties any remedy beyond that, not even for the purposes of enforcing his award. Enforcement is a matter for the Courts (see s. 66 of the Arbitration Act).

6.39 Non-mandatory sections in statutory arbitrations: section 4 (mandatory and non-mandatory provisions)

It is submitted that it is quite clear the parties cannot choose a foreign substantive law to replace that contained in the Agricultural Tenancies Act 1995, but theoretically procedural law of another jurisdiction (*e.g.* Scotland) could be used where the 1995 Act does not make any provision inconsistent with this. Therefore if the parties agree, for example, that pleadings are to be drawn in the form normal in Scotland but not in England or Wales this is permissible under section 4.

6.40 Non-mandatory sections in statutory arbitrations: section 5 (agreements to be in writing)

It is anticipated that the main scope for this section will be in relation to arbitrations under section 28. Additionally, in relation to arbitrations dealing with rent review, consent under section 19 and compensation generally under Part III there is some scope for the parties to agree procedural aspects but in these instances there will already be substantive legal rules in the 1995 Act.

6.41 Non-mandatory sections in statutory arbitrations: sections 6 (definition of arbitration agreement) and 7 (separability of arbitration agreement)

Section 6 will have application in relation to agreements under section 28 of the 1995 Act as will section 7. Neither will be relevant to any other kind of statutory arbitration under the 1995 Act.

6.42 Non-mandatory sections in statutory arbitrations: section 14 (commencement of arbitral proceedings)

This section appears consistent with the application of the 1995 Act.

6.43 Non-mandatory sections in statutory arbitrations: section 15 (the arbitral tribunal)

This section is not consistent with the operation of section 30 of the 1995 Act and should be regarded as not available.

6.44 Non-mandatory sections in statutory arbitrations: section 16 (procedure for appointment of arbitrators)

This is a very difficult section to adapt for the purposes of the 1995 Act. For the most part the 1995 Act contemplates that the parties may appoint an arbitrator but, if they do not do so, either party may apply to the President of the RICS for the appointment of an arbitrator by him and specific time-limits are provided for doing this.[80] Section 30 requires that the tribunal be a sole arbitrator and, if section 16(3) of the Arbitration Act applies by default the landlord and the tenant would be jointly required to appoint the arbitrator not later than 28 days after service of a request in writing by either party to do so. Section 18 is then available for one party to apply to the Court if necessary to make appointments itself. Section 19 is a provision in aid of this. It will be recalled that section 12 of the Arbitration Act is excluded in relation to statutory arbitrations.[81] This run of sections appears to

---

[80] *e.g.* s. 12, s. 19(4), s. 19(9), s. 22(4), s. 28(3).
[81] By s. 97(b).

produce a situation which will ultimately override those provisions in the 1995 Act designed to allow the President of the RICS, in default, to appoint. Therefore it is submitted that sections 16, 18 and 19 have no application to the 1995 Act and are inconsistent with it.

Non-mandatory sections in statutory arbitrations: section 17 (power in case of default to appoint sole arbitrator)   6.45

This section pre-supposes that both parties are to appoint an arbitrator and sub-section (1) provides that in default one party may appoint his arbitrator to act as sole arbitrator. It is submitted that section 17 is overridden by section 30 of the 1995 Act and has no application at all since the procedural contemplation is inappropriate to 1995 Act arbitrations altogether.

Non-mandatory sections in statutory arbitrations: sections 18 (failure of appointment procedure) and 19 (court to have regard to agreed qualifications)   6.46

Both these provisions are considered inapplicable to arbitrations under the 1995 Act as a result of the discussion in relation to section 16 of the Arbitration Act.

Non-mandatory sections in statutory arbitrations: section 20–22 (Chairman, Umpire, Decision-making where no chairman or umpire)   6.47

These are inapplicable in the case of a sole arbitrator as required by section 30 of the 1995 Act.

Non-mandatory sections in statutory arbitrations: section 23 (revocation of arbitrator's authority)   6.48

In so far as parties actually themselves appoint an arbitrator or choose another institution or person to appoint the arbitrator it would seem that section 23 has some scope for application. However the parties are not able, as a result of the revocation, to change the consequences of that revocation. For example, the power of the President of the RICS is only available under section 12 where "no arbitrator has been appointed"[82] and it is not correct to regard a revoked arbitration appointment as never having taken place at all.

Non-mandatory sections in statutory arbitrations: section 25 (resignation of arbitrator)   6.49

Section 25(1), establishing the parties' freedom to agree with the arbitrator as to the consequences of his resignation would appear to apply. However resignation by agreement will not in all probability result in the President being able to appoint a new arbitrator unless that resignation is by reason of the arbitrator's being incapable of acting further.[83] Section 25(3) permits an arbitrator who resigns to apply to the Court which will then decide whether it was reasonable for the arbitrator to resign. It is difficult to see how this part of section 25 is to be squared with the statutory duty imposed on arbitrators by the 1995 Act by, for example, section 13(1), 19 and Part III. Moreover those types of arbitrations involve strict

---

[82] s. 12(a).
[83] See s. 30(3).

time limits which the Court could not re-start. It appears the 1995 Act contemplates the parties being unaffected by a change of arbitrator only where the original arbitrator dies or becomes incapable and is then replaced.

6.50 **Non-mandatory sections in statutory arbitrations: section 26(2) (death of arbitrator or person appointing him)**
The words "unless otherwise agreed by the parties" appear to be inconsistent with any orderly functioning of the arbitration process and, given the extended definitions of "landlord" and "tenant" in section 38(1) of the 1995 Act, these words are not appropriate to cover the needs of landlord and tenant disputes under the 1995 Act.

6.51 **Non-mandatory sections in statutory arbitrations: section 27 (filling of vacancy, etc.)**
This section appears difficult to reconcile with section 30 and furthermore the fallback provisions in sub-sections (3)-(5) are inapplicable for the reasons discussed above in relation to section 16 of the Arbitration Act.

6.52 **Non-mandatory sections in statutory arbitrations: section 30 (competence of tribunal to rule on its own jurisdiction)**
Although section 96 of the Arbitration Act contemplates that statutory arbitrations may usefully be modified so as to include the terms of section 30,[84] not all statutory arbitrations under the 1995 Act appear in the same light. Whereas there may well be a useful function in section 28 arbitrations in allowing the parties to debar the arbitral tribunal from ruling on its own substantive jurisdiction, it is difficult to see how this can have been intended in relation to any of the other statutory arbitrations under the 1995 Act. This is a very difficult area and it may be that in the case of, for example, compensation arbitrations or arbitrations under section 19 in particular the Court would regard the arbitrator as necessarily having the power to rule on his own substantive jurisdiction, notwithstanding agreement by the parties to the contrary.

6.53 **Non-mandatory sections in statutory arbitrations: section 34 (procedural and evidential matters)**
These sections operate subject to any evidential or procedural constraints imposed directly or indirectly by the Agricultural Tenancies Act 1995. For example in relation to rent review section 13(2) requires the arbitrator to take into account various matters and in particular "all relevant factors" (*i.e.* such factors as the arbitrator may consider relevant[85]). Section 34(1), though constrained by the right of the parties to agree any matter, authorises the arbitrator to make his own choices about all procedural and evidential matters, some of which are specified by section 34(2). Therefore parties who do not wish the arbitrator, for example, to choose the inquiry procedure and decide himself the facts and the law[86] would be best advised

---

[84] For the modification see para. 6.38 above.
[85] Accordingly it is not possible for the parties under s. 34(1) to decide and agree what is to be regarded as relevant.
[86] s. 34(2)(g).

to debar him by their own written agreement to that effect. Amongst other things, where the parties do not agree what language regime is to apply, it is entirely open to the arbitrator if he wishes to allow parts of the proceedings to be conducted in Welsh and if necessary authorise translations to be made.[87] The arbitrator is entitled if he wishes to proceed on a documents-only basis and to provide for pleadings and amendment of those pleadings. What, however, he may not do is to by-pass any constraints set out in the 1995 Act, for example in relation to the content of notices.[88]

Litigants should no longer expect that full disclosure or discovery will necessarily be required in arbitration proceedings and the arbitrator is absolutely entitled to decide whether and how disclosure is to be done.[89] The arbitrator also has[90] the ability to contain questioning at any oral hearing,[91] subject to the dictates of fairness.[92] It is obvious that the purpose of section 34 is to encourage the parties to agree as much as possible as to the conduct of the hearing. Failing such agreement the arbitrator has such wide-ranging powers that they are almost entirely at the mercy of his rulings. Section 34 is supported by the mandatory sections 33 and 40.[93] What constraints there may be on the arbitrator's powers by the operation of the general law, as distinct from the application of the 1995 Act or the agreement of the parties, will undoubtedly develop in the form of case law under section 33.[94]

Non-mandatory sections in statutory arbitrations: section 35 (consolidation of proceedings and concurrent hearings)   6.54

This provision has been specifically adapted to statutory arbitrations.[95]

---

[87] See s. 34(2)(b).
[88] *e.g.* s. 22(2).
[89] See s. 34(2)(d).
[90] Perhaps somewhat refreshingly.
[91] See s. 34(2)(e).
[92] And reason: an arbitrator who only allows a party to ask questions of the other party about the other party's own case whilst refusing the questioning party to put any part of his own case is likely to be acting irrationally.
[93] See paras 6.25 and 6.27 above.
[94] Although Bernstein and Others, *Handbook of Arbitration Practice*, (3rd ed., Sweet & Maxwell, 1988) contains considerable discussion from p. 81 onwards as to "The Principles of Natural Justice", it remains to be seen whether the technical rules developed in that connection by English law in the adversarial context will be applied. The discussion in that text makes no mention of the difficulties of adaptation in circumstances where the arbitrator has the power to act, if he wishes, in an inquisitorial fashion. It is already clear, in the context of general public inquiries that the old certitudes as to the operation of the rules of natural justice, developed in the adversarial context, are gone (see criticism of the *Salmon Report* by Sir Richard Scott in "Procedures at Inquiries, The Duty to be Fair" printed in the *Journal of the Chartered Institute of Arbitrators*, Vol. 64, Supplement p. 60).
[95] See para. 6.38 above.

6.55 **Non-mandatory sections in statutory arbitrations: section 36 (legal or other representation)**

This provision is consistent with the 1995 Act. Section 82(2) provides a definition of a party to an arbitration agreement. It would be open to parties, for example, to agree that no lawyers should be used to represent either party.[96]

6.56 **Non-mandatory sections in statutory arbitrations: section 37(1) (powers to appoint experts, legal advisers or assessors)**

Section 37(2) is mandatory[97] but section 37(1) will apply on a default basis. The terms of section 37(1)(b) should be particularly noted since it has not hitherto been the practice of agricultural arbitrators necessarily to disclose let alone allow the parties to comment on legal advice offered by the arbitrator's legal adviser.

6.57 **Non-mandatory sections in statutory arbitrations: section 38 (general powers exercisable by the tribunal)**

The default provisions in section 38 (*i.e.* failing agreement by the parties) cannot displace the restrictions in the 1995 Act on the scope of the award to be made by the arbitrator. These are general powers designed to support and enhance the arbitration not to enlarge its scope.

6.58 **Non-mandatory sections in statutory arbitrations: section 39 (power to make provisional awards)**

This is a power to make a provisional award, the terms of which may not appear in any final award. This is not about the making of an interim award.[98] The powers under section 39 are not available unless the parties agree that the tribunal should have them: it is difficult to see why in any arbitration under the 1995 Act there would be any cause for agreeing this power.

6.59 **Non-mandatory sections in statutory arbitrations: section 41 (powers of tribunal in case of parties' default)**

These powers are technically subject to the parties' ability to agree that they should not apply but in practice it is unlikely that any party would feel confident enough of the co-operation of the other to make an agreement for the purposes of section 41(1). It is likely that any powers of the arbitrator to be exercised under this section

---

[96] "Represented in the proceedings" means generally but it would be equally open to parties, if they wished, to debar themselves from using lawyers or particular types of lawyers (*e.g.* Q.C.s) at the oral hearing stage or throughout. No doubt chartered surveyors will check with their insurers whether their activities are covered by insurance when they undertake what are normally regarded as legal tasks and no doubt they will take care not to contravene the Solicitors Act 1974. A bar on lawyers generally will cause serious problems if there is any attempt to apply to the Court and s. 20 of the Solicitors Act prohibits any person from acting as a solicitor in court proceedings. Furthermore, limiting oneself and the other party to using the services of solicitors, as distinct from that of the Bar, does not guarantee unrestricted access to the courts as there are limits on rights of audience: see section 19 of the Solicitors Act.

[97] See para. 6.26 above.

[98] See now non-mandatory s. 47.

ought to be exercised in the same way in which the parallel jurisdiction of the Court will be exercised.[99]

Non-mandatory sections in statutory arbitrations: section 42 (enforcement of peremptory orders of tribunal) 6.60

Although the parties may agree that these powers should not apply, it is unlikely in practice that they will do so. The procedure contemplated by section 42 is available under new Order 73 of the Rules of the Supreme Court. Neither this section nor the preceding one appear to conflict with the 1995 Act.

Non-mandatory sections in statutory arbitrations: section 44 (Court powers exercisable in support of arbitral proceedings) 6.61

Section 44 powers are exercisable on an application under new Order 73. It may be questioned whether the parties would be wise to allow the Court these powers by default and, in relation to statutory arbitrations apart from those under the general power in section 28 of the 1995 Act, it may be questionable whether these powers are consistent with the exclusive arbitral jurisdiction notwithstanding section 44 of the Arbitration Act purports to be "in support of" arbitration proceedings. The interference is so extreme that the jurisdiction may not be available at all. This is particularly evident from the terms of section 44(6) since it is only if the Court so orders that the arbitrator can countermand the court order.

Non-mandatory sections in statutory arbitrations: section 45 (determination of a preliminary point of law) 6.62

New Order 73 of the Rules of the Supreme Court deal with any applications to the Court under this section. Although this appears to be a wide jurisdiction the restricted circumstances in which it is exercisable[1] in fact make it a somewhat limited jurisdiction. It is submitted that the arbitrator should be extremely cautious in giving his permission for the purposes of section 45(2)(b) since he has the opportunity under section 37(1)[2] to appoint a legal adviser.

Non-mandatory sections in statutory arbitrations: section 46 (rules applicable to substance of dispute) 6.63

Sub-section (1)(b) has been deleted for the purposes of statutory arbitrations.[3] All statutory arbitrations under the 1995 Act, with the exception of disputes under section 28 in relation to a contract, will be decided according to the law of England and Wales.

Non-mandatory sections in statutory arbitrations: section 47 (awards on different issues) 6.64

These powers are in principle consistent with the 1995 Act.

---

[99] The best source of case law in this connection is the Rules of the Supreme Court and the commentary available under those rules in the *Supreme Court Practice* currently in a 1997 edition, (Sweet & Maxwell).
[1] s. 45(2).
[2] Unless otherwise agreed by the parties.
[3] See s. 96(4).

6.65 Non-mandatory sections in statutory arbitrations: section 48 (remedies)
In relation to statutory arbitrations under the 1995 Act these powers appear consistent only with arbitrations under section 28: they are clearly inconsistent with the task set to the arbitrator by the other compulsory arbitration provisions under the Act.

6.66 Non-mandatory sections in statutory arbitrations: section 49 (interest)
These powers are not consistent with the task of the arbitrator under the rent review provisions of the 1995 Act. There the arbitrator is making a determination not awarding an amount and if parties are to receive interest where the award post-dates the rent review date then they must provide for it in their contract. Clearly this power is not appropriate in the case of section 19 arbitrations but it may be useful to the arbitrator in terms of general compensation arbitrations under Part III of the 1995 Act and will be available for arbitrations under section 28 where appropriate.

6.67 Non-mandatory sections in statutory arbitrations: section 50 (extension of time for making award)
New Order 73 of the Rules of the Supreme Court provides for applications under this section. There is probably no scope for this section in connection with arbitrations required under the rent review provisions, section 19 or compensation claims under Part III of the 1995 Act: in all those cases the timing of the award is left entirely at large by the statute and, it is submitted, the parties cannot by contract restrict the arbitrator's time for the making of the award. However where the dispute arises under the contract and falls to be dealt with under section 28 there would seem scope for section 50 to apply.

6.68 Non-mandatory sections in statutory arbitrations: section 51 (settlement)
This would appear to be consistent with all statutory arbitrations under the 1995 Act.

6.69 Non-mandatory sections in statutory arbitrations: section 52 (form of award)
The wide terms of this section are not necessarily consistent with the arbitrator's duties where he has a very specific statutory task (*e.g.* determining rent or giving or withholding consent). Sub-section (5) will recite that the seat of the arbitration is England and Wales.[4] Even if the parties are free to agree that the award may be oral, an arbitrator would be well advised not to accept appointment if he was debarred from making an award in writing.

6.70 Non-mandatory sections in statutory arbitrations: sections 53, 54, 55 (Place where award treated as made, Date of award, Notification of award)
These sections are not adversely affected by the 1995 Act.

---

[4] See s. 95(2).

Non-mandatory sections in statutory arbitrations: section 57 (correction of award or additional award) — 6.71

In so far as consistent with other applicable provisions of the Arbitration Act[5] this section applies.

Non-mandatory sections in statutory arbitrations: section 58 (effect of award) — 6.72

Where the 1995 Act will not allow the parties to avoid its terms by express agreement, the prohibited result cannot be brought about by the parties agreeing for the purposes of section 58(1) that the arbitrator's award is not to be final and binding.[6]

Non-mandatory sections in statutory arbitrations: section 59 (costs of the award) — 6.73

As to "the recoverable costs of the arbitration", see section 63. Parties cannot contract out of this section: it is purely for the purposes of interpreting Part I of the Arbitration Act.

Non-mandatory sections in statutory arbitrations: sections 61 and 62 (Award of costs, Effect of agreement or award about costs) — 6.74

These sections are consistent with all statutory arbitrations under the 1995 Act.

Non-mandatory sections in statutory arbitrations: section 63 (the recoverable costs of the arbitration) — 6.75

This provision is consistent with all statutory arbitrations under the 1995 Act. Sub-section (5) will be recognised as setting out the normal standard basis of taxation in the High Court. The arbitrator is not, however, required to do a taxation in the way in which the High Court would do. In an appropriate case the arbitrator may consider the scales used by the County Court.

Non-mandatory sections in statutory arbitrations: section 64 (recoverable fees and expenses of arbitrators) — 6.76

This provision is consistent with all statutory arbitrations under the 1995 Act. Where parties are considering a general embargo on access to the courts, they should direct their attention to the terms of section 64 if they wish to preserve a power to control the matters within this section.

Non-mandatory sections in statutory arbitrations: section 65 (power to limit recoverable costs) — 6.77

This section is consistent with all statutory arbitrations under the 1995 Act. This may prove to be a very popular power if it is felt that expenditure by one party has or will exceed any reasonable level.

---

[5] *i.e.* in the light of the necessary adaptations for the purposes of the 1995 Act.
[6] See s. 26 of the 1995 Act.

6.78 **Non-mandatory sections in statutory arbitrations: section 69 (appeal on point of law)**
This section is consistent with all statutory arbitrations under the 1995 Act. New Order 73 of the Rules of the Supreme Court provides a procedure for section 69 purposes. It also provides for any supplementary use of section 70. The opportunity of appeal under section 69 is very constrained. It is based on the now repealed terms of section 1 of the Arbitration Act 1979. It is likely that, in so far as European law is the subject of a possible appeal, leave should be given.[7]

6.79 **Non-mandatory sections in statutory arbitrations: section 76 (service of notices)**
This section is available only subject to section 36 of the 1995 Act which applies to any notice or other document required or authorised to be given under the 1995 Act.[8]

6.80 **Non-mandatory sections in statutory arbitrations: section 77 (powers of court in relation to service of documents)**
The applicability of this section is limited. It takes effect subject to section 36 of the 1995 Act. The limitations on the availability of section 76 (see the preceding paragraph) should be noted. New Order 73 of the Rules of the Supreme Court prescribes a procedure for application to the Court.

6.81 **Non-mandatory sections in statutory arbitrations: sections 78–84 (Reckoning periods of time, Power of court to extend time limits relating to arbitral proceedings,[9] Notice and other requirements in connection with legal proceedings, Saving for certain matters governed by common law, Minor definitions, Index of defined expressions: Part I, Transitional provisions)**
These sections are not ones which call for any separate comment. They are all consistent with statutory arbitrations under the 1995 Act. For the most part they are in implementation of other provisions of the Act already commented on.

6.82 **Appointment of an arbitrator**
In the context of the Arbitration Act and the 1995 Act, it is likely that the only two methods of appointing an arbitrator will be either by agreement between the parties or by the President of the RICS. The precise timing of the appointment is, in most circumstances, not likely to be critical. However, particularly where for the purposes of section 12 of the 1995 Act it is necessary to ascertain whether or not an arbitrator has been appointed, it may occasionally be necessary to identify the precise time of appointment. Readers are reminded of the extreme difficulty of adaptation of the non-mandatory sections of the Arbitration Act to the requirements of arbitral appointment under the 1995 Act.[10] If those sections do not apply it would seem that the general position as regards appointment by agreement

---

[7] See under the old law *Bulk Oil (Zug) v. Sun International* [1983] 2 Lloyd's Rep. 587.
[8] See paras 7.9–7.14 below.
[9] Where the time-limit is agreed by the parties or specified by the Arbitration Act.
[10] See paras 6.44–6.47 above.

between the parties is identical to the situation under the Agricultural Holdings Act 1986 discussed in full below.[11] If, conversely, the Arbitration Act has some impact on the situation it is likely that it is limited to a requirement that all steps in the appointment are in writing.[12] The process of appointment by the President is considered above.[13] It is likely that much of the discussion in relation to an appointment in the context of the 1986 Act will be of interest under the 1995 Act also.[14] In particular it would appear that the appointment is made when the President executes the instrument of appointment, notice to the parties not being necessary to complete it.[15]

Resolution of disputes by an independent expert: general 6.83

Determination or valuation by an expert is contemplated by section 29 of the Agricultural Tenancies Act 1995[16] and in addition is a procedure which may be chosen by the parties for the purposes of their rent review under the 1995 Act.[17] For disputes relating to pure valuation there is much to be said for determination by an expert[18] but it should not be thought that only valuation, as distinct from legal, issues are suitable for determination by an expert. There is nothing to stop the parties in a suitable case from appointing a legal expert and there is much to be said for this given the highly specialised character of much agricultural litigation. The expert will be either appointed by the parties or, pursuant to the contract, appointed by a third party under a power conferred by the contract. In each case the relationship of the expert to the parties is purely contractual and he has no judicial function. The consequence is:

(i) the task of the expert is determined by the contract;

(ii) the expert is not bound to adopt any particular procedure unless so required by the contract;

(iii) the determination is not required to state reasons unless stipulated by the contract;

(iv) the expert has no power to award costs unless the contract so stipulates.

There is no statutory code governing any matter related to expert determination and the case law is in a state of continuous[19] evolution. What is clear is that the expert owes a duty of care to the parties and will be liable on a negligence suit if he

---

[11] paras 16.22.
[12] Owing to the impact of s. 5 of the Arbitration Act.
[13] para. 6.3.
[14] See para. 16.23 below.
[15] *University College, Oxford v. Durdy* [1982] Ch. 413. Under the 1995 Act, in so far as the arbitrator subsequently issues directions, it is possible that the "benevolent construction" expressly subsequently overturned by Sched. 11, para. 31 of the Agricultural Holdings Act 1986 is still available.
[16] See para. 6.5 above.
[17] See Chapter 2.
[18] *e.g.* rent, game damage, assessment of contractual compensation, contractual compensation for milk quota.
[19] Somewhat chaotic.

breaches it.[20] Ambiguity in the drafting of any aspect of an expert reference is particularly troublesome.[21]

6.84 Production of the expert determination
In this the expert is constrained by his contract but, unlike an arbitrator, is perfectly entitled to use his own skill and knowledge and is not required to give the parties any opportunity to comment on his materials or thought processes. It is this essential freedom from any requirement to act on the evidence and submissions of the parties which distinguishes the expert from the arbitrator.[22] So great is the expert's freedom that he is not obliged to make any findings accepting or rejecting the material or contentions put before him and furthermore he is not bound by any matters on which the parties themselves have agreed. His appointment is to give his own independent judgment on the task submitted and he is entitled to give whatever weight to the materials provided by the parties as he considers fit.[23] In circumstances where the valuer has had the benefit of detailed submission and evidence from the parties, he is not required to make his own inquiries as to further comparables.[24] However it has been stated in general terms that the expert's duty is to adopt the procedure and practices accepted as standard in his profession and was required to obtain detailed information about comparable transactions, failing which he will be liable in negligence.[25] In so far as he needs it, it is submitted that the expert is entitled to take legal advice and is not required to disclose it to the parties for comment or otherwise. Issues of law arising in relation to the matter he is required to determine are ones which he will determine without assistance from the Courts.[26] Even if both parties agree it is submitted that they cannot impose on the expert, once he has been appointed, any specific procedure or terms. Even if the expert comes to a figure which another expert might not have done, this does not of itself found an action in negligence.[27]

---

[20] *Arenson v. Casson Beckman Rutley & Co.* [1977] A.C. 405, HL; in contrast to the position of an arbitrator, who is immune from suit both at common law and now by s. 29 of the Arbitration Act: see *Sutcliffe v. Thackrah* [1974] A.C. 727, HL and *Campbell v. Edwards* [1976] 1 W.L.R. 403 (Lord Denning M.R. at 408B-C), CA, and para. 6.22 above. Whether an appointment should properly be classified as that of an expert or an arbitrator is not a matter of labelling but of substance (*Palacath Ltd v. Flanagan* [1985] 1 E.G.L.R. 86).

[21] For a form to avoid see *North Eastern Co-operative Society Ltd v. Newcastle upon Tyne City Council* [1987] 1 E.G.L.R. 142. See also *Langham House Developments Ltd v. Brompton Securities Ltd* [1980] 2 E.G.L.R. 117.

[22] *Palacath Ltd v. Flanagan* (above).

[23] *Palacath Ltd v. Flanagan*. Although where the valuer in fact determines a figure between the figures actually put forward by a landlord and a tenant this may well be taken by the Court to indicate that he has not been negligent: *Belvedere Motors Ltd v. King* [1981] 260 E.G. 813.

[24] *Wallshire Ltd v. Aarons* (1989) 260 E.G. 81.

[25] *CIL Securities Ltd v. Briant Champion Long* [1993] 2 E.G.L.R. 164, although this case may state too rigid a position.

[26] It is an uneasy relationship: see paras 6.86–6.87 below.

[27] *Zubaida v. Hargreaves* [1995] 1 E.G.L.R. 127.

Can one party frustrate the appointment process? 6.85

The short answer is: no. In a case where an option was activated by the tenant and the price was to be agreed by two valuers, one nominated by the tenant and the other by the landlord or, in default of agreement, by an umpire appointed by those two valuers, it was held that the landlord could not frustrate the entire process by refusing to nominate a valuer.[28]

Can an honest award be upset? 6.86

At the very highest level there is an extreme reluctance to find any error of law at all.[29] In *Campbell v. Edwards*[30] it was held that parties were bound by an honest valuation fixed by the agreed valuer in circumstances where both parties had acted on that valuation. Other valuers producing subsequent lower valuations did not give rise to any equitable remedy to the parties. Conversely if the expert was never validly appointed in the first place and the party seeking to upset the award has not validated the appointment, the award is not binding on him.[31] Whether or not the parties must be bound by an expert award which contains an error of law will depend on what their contract provides. If parties agree to be bound by the report of an expert and the expert does what he is asked to do that report cannot be challenged in the Courts "unless it could be shown that the expert had departed from the instructions given to him in a material respect".[32] Should an expert who makes a mistake of the law which is fundamental to his determination be regarded as addressing the tasks which the parties set him or not? Knox J. in *Nikko Hotels (U.K.) Limited v. MEPC Plc*[33] observed of an expert:

> "If he has answered the right question in the wrong way, his decision will be binding. If he has answered the wrong question, his decision will be a nullity."[34]

Although *Jones v. Sherwood Computer Services Plc* is regarded as good law, its application may produce difficulties, for example where the expert's decision

---

[28] *Sudbrook Trading Estate Ltd v. Eggleton* [1983] 1 E.G.L.R. 47, HL, overruling a long line of previous authorities.

[29] See *A. Hudson Pty Ltd v. Legal & General Life of Australia Ltd* [1986] 2 E.G.L.R. 130, PC: "In general their lordships consider that it would be a disservice to the law and to litigants to encourage forensic attacks on valuations by experts where those attacks are based on textual criticisms more appropriate to the measured analysis of fiscal legislation".

[30] (1976) 1 W.L.R. 403, CA.

[31] *Darlington Borough Council v. Waring & Gillow (Holdings) Ltd* [1988] 2 E.G.L.R. 159.

[32] *Jones v. Sherwood Computer Services Plc* [1992] 1 W.L.R. 277, CA as explained by Lord Slynn in *Mercury Communications Ltd v. DG of Telecommunications* [1996] 1 W.L.R. 48 at 58F. This is taken as endorsement of *Jones v. Sherwood Computer Services Plc* which expressly disapproved *Burgess v. Purchase & Sons (Farms) Ltd* [1983] Ch. 216.

[33] [1991] 2 E.G.L.R. 103 at 108B.

[34] The immediately preceding passage is weakened by the opinion of Lord Slynn quoted

involves the solution of a question of construction of documents.[35] The problem is in applying *Jones v. Sherwood Computer Services Plc* to any particular contract.[36]

6.87 Experts and the intervention of the Court

It is theoretically possible for the Court to grant an injunction to restrain an expert from proceeding with the determination of a dispute pending the Court's decision on an issue of construction, but it would seem unlikely that this relief would be granted in the normal way.[37] Where one party seeks to rely on the determination and the other wishes to challenge it as being based on a fundamental legal error, judgment under Order 14 will not be available to the first party.[38] Where both parties wish the Court to determine a question of law as to whether the Tribunal must act as experts or as arbitrators the Court may, unusually, decide the issue.[39] It would appear unlikely that an originating summons as to an issue of construction within the expert's remit would be struck out on a preliminary basis.[40] But even if the award of the expert is set aside for legal error, the Court will not itself substitute a new award.[41]

---

below.

[35] In *Mercury Communications Ltd v. DG of Communications* (above) Lord Slynn at 58H stated: "In my view when the parties agreed in clause 29.5 that the Director's determination should be Ltd to such matters as the Director would have power to determine under condition 13 of the BT licence and the principles to be applied by him should be 'those set out in those conditions' they intended him to deal with such matters and such principles as correctly interpreted. They did not intend him simply to apply such meaning as he himself thought they should bear. His interpretation could therefore be reviewed by the court. There is no provision expressly or impliedly that these matters were remitted exclusively to the Director, even though in order to carry out his task he must be obliged to interpret them in the first place for himself. Nor is there any provision excluding altogether the intervention of the court ... the issues of construction are ones which are not removed from the court's jurisdiction by the agreement of the parties."

[36] It appears that in *Pontsarn Investments Ltd v. Kansallis-Osake-Pankki* [1992] 1 E.G.L.R. 148 the words "his determination shall be final and binding" were sufficient to fix the parties with any legal error made in the course of the assessment.

[37] In *Norwich Union Life Insurance Society v. P&O Property Holdings Ltd* [1993] 1 E.G.L.R. 164 the CA considered that the particular dispute was so heavily involved with matters of fact that the court should not consider a legal issue in anticipation of his determination. It would seem likely, in the light of *Mercury Communications Ltd v. DG of Telecommunications* (above) that the rejection by Dillon L.J. at 169E of any jurisdiction in principle, contrary to the view of Hoffmann J. in *Royal Trust International Ltd v. Nordbanken* [summarised at 169E] is incorrect. The same conclusion appears to have been reached by Lightman J. in *British Shipbuilders v. VSEL Consortium Plc* February 2, 1996, unreported (the case being briefly reported mainly on another issue at (1996) T.L.R. 79 as at February 14, 1996).

[38] *Heyes v. Earl of Derby* [1984] 2 E.G.L.R. 87, CA.

[39] As "an indulgence and contrary to the usual practice of the court": Goulding J. at 117M in *Safeway Food Stores Ltd v. Banderway Ltd* [1983] 2 E.G.L.R. 116.

[40] *Postel Properties Ltd and Daichi Lire (London) Ltd v. Greenwell* (1992) 65 P.&C.R. 244.

[41] At any rate where the review provisions are still capable of being operated: see *JT Sydenham & Co. Ltd v. Enichem Elastomers Ltd* [1989] 1 E.G.L.R. 257 applying *Dean v. Prince* [1953] Ch. 590, Harman J. at 600.

Alternative Dispute Resolution 6.88

As stated above,[42] there is scope within the terms of section 29 to establish a contractual arrangement whereby the parties agree to be bound by the recommendation of a mediator. Such an agreement is, of course, subject to the possibility of being overridden by either party activating a section 28 reference.[43] Where the parties have opted for this possibility and actually implemented it, short of bad faith or fraud by the mediator, it would seem extremely unlikely that the Court would intervene if the parties were dissatisfied with the award. Unlike the appointment of an expert, mediation does not carry with it any necessary assumption that the determination or recommendation will be made in accordance with the parties' strict legal rights.[44]

---

[42] paras 6.5 and 6.7.
[43] See para. 6.7 above.
[44] It would seem quite possible that if a stipulation is made that matters must be dealt with in accordance with parties' strict legal rights, the procedure is that of an expert determination not of true mediation. If there is a non-contractual mediation voluntarily entered onto by the parties, this is outside s. 29 altogether and the parties are free to disregard the recommendation of the mediator if they wish to. There is no developed practice of mediation in relation to farming disputes of which the authors are aware, whether contractual or otherwise.

CHAPTER 7

MISCELLANEOUS

7.1 General

7.2 Mortgages of agricultural land: section 31

7.3 Powers of limited owners: sections 32–34

7.7 Preparation of documents by valuers and surveyors: section 35

7.8 Service of notices: section 36

7.15 Crown land: section 37

7.16 Miscellaneous forms

Miscellaneous provisions: general 7.1
This Chapter contains discussion of a number of matters which do not logically or conveniently fall within the preceding Chapters. It is also the case that in a number of instances the relevant legal provisions in the Agricultural Tenancies Act 1995 have in substance been discussed in the context of older legislation and in particular the Agricultural Holdings Act 1986, and we try to avoid duplication.

Section 31: mortgages of agricultural land 7.2
Section 31 amends section 99 of the Law of Property Act 1925 and, in relation to mortgages of agricultural land made on or after September 1, 1995 provides that Schedule 14 paragraph 12 of the Agricultural Holdings Act 1986 shall cease to have effect. The impetus for this particular reform is thought to have come from banks which were becoming increasingly sensitive to the risk that milk quota would be removed from the cover of their mortgage security by the simple expedient of creating sub-leases over the agricultural land, which could not be prohibited by contract under the terms of section 99 of the Law of Property Act 1925. Because of this link, the substantive discussion of section 31 is contained in the Chapter dealing with milk quota generally, Chapter 18, of this work. The critical date is the date of the mortgage being created and readers are referred on accordingly.[1]

Power of limited owners to give consents: general 7.3
Since January 1, 1997, when the Trusts of Land and Appointment of Trustees Act 1996 came into force,[2] no new strict settlements under the Settled Land Act 1925

---
[1] For mortgages created after March 1, 1948 but before September 1, 1995 see para. 18.31; for mortgages created on or after September 1, 1995 see para. 18.32 below.
[2] S.I. 1996 No.2974.

can be created. All existing trusts for sale and all new trusts relating to land (whether these trusts are express, implied, resulting, constructive or bare) are henceforth known as "trusts of land" under the 1996 Act. The only general category of land outside its terms is that of land within the Universities and College Estates Act 1925. Section 6(1) of the 1996 Act gives trustees of land in relation to the land subject to the trust all the powers of an absolute owner. Prior to that time the provisions of sections 32–34 of the Agricultural Tenancies Act 1995 were of importance both for Settled Land Act tenants for life and for trustees of a trust for sale, whose powers were effectively assimilated to those of the tenant for life. Those parts of section 33 which were of particular application to trustees of a trust for sale were repealed by the 1996 Act, as no longer required, and accordingly the terms of sections 32–34 are now limited to the powers of a Settled Land Act tenant for life and trustees holding land under the Universities and College Estates Act. In large parts the 1995 Act replicated corresponding provisions of the Agricultural Holdings Act 1986 but, in one particular respect, improved them.

7.4 Power of limited owners to give consents: section 32
These provisions replicate exactly the terms of section 88 of the Agricultural Holdings Act 1986.[3]

7.5 Power to apply and raise capital money: section 33
Section 33 is an improvement on the equivalent provisions under section 89 of the Agricultural Holdings Act 1986.[4] The difficulties of construction attaching to section 89 have been avoided and it is clear that section 33 allows the tenant for life to require reimbursement from capital money where section 16 compensation (and associated costs charges and expenses) have been met by the tenant for life. It should be noted, however, that section 33 does not authorise any recoupment from capital in circumstances where the tenant for life meets contractual compensation claims as distinct from those provided by section 16 of the 1995 Act.

7.6 Estimation of best rent for purposes of Acts and other instruments: section 34
This section replicates in substance the terms of section 90 of the Agricultural Holdings Act 1986.[5]

7.7 Preparation of documents, etc., by valuers and surveyors: section 35
This provision has been fully discussed in Chapter 1 above.[6]

7.8 Service of notices: section 36: general
Section 36(1) restricts the application of that section to the service of any notice or other document required or authorised to be given under the 1995 Act. This means, accordingly, that purely contractual notices which do not fulfil those conditions do not take the benefit of these service provisions. Parties must ensure that, in relation

---

[3] See para. 17.9 below.
[4] See discussion at paras 17.10–17.15 below.
[5] See paras 17.16 below.
[6] See para. 1.24.

SERVICE OF NOTICES: SECTION 36: GENERAL

to contractual notices, service terms within the contract are satisfactory. Section 36 equally does not apply to the service of legal proceedings or to the service of notices required by statutes other than the Agricultural Tenancies Act 1995.[7]

Due service: delivery to the recipient: section 36(2)(a)   7.9
Any notice or other document required or authorised to be given under the 1995 Act is duly given to a person if it is delivered to him.[8] This means delivery to the intended recipient personally.[9] As to the use of the ordinary post, see the discussion in Chapter 17.[10]

Due service: leaving the document at the recipient's proper address: section 36(2)(b)   7.10
Any notice or other document required or authorised to be given under the 1995 Act is duly given to a person if it is left at his proper address.[11] The proper address is[12] defined to mean:

(a) in the case of the secretary or clerk of a body corporate, the registered or principal office of that body, and

(b) in any other case, the last known address of the person in question.

Where a document is left at the proper address, it must be left in a manner which a reasonable person would adopt in order to bring the document to the notice of the addressee. On similar wording under the Agricultural Holdings Act 1986[13] it was held that notices slipped under the side door normally used[14] and a notice put through the letter box in a door in the back porch of the farmhouse[15] were properly served although in neither case did the tenant actually receive the document in question.

Due service: as authorised by the contract: section 36(2)(c)   7.11
Any notice or other document required or authorised to be given under the 1995 Act is duly given to a person if it is given to him in a manner authorised by a written agreement made, at any time before the giving of the notice, between him and the person giving the notice.[16] It should be noted that the written agreement in question need not necessarily be the tenancy agreement although it is unclear whether a simple letter expressing a willingness to be served in a particular way constitutes an "agreement" for these purposes since it is unlikely that any contract would in that way come about.[17] Where the written agreement permits service by fax or

---

[7] e.g. a notice under ss. 47 and 48 of the Landlord and Tenant Act 1987.
[8] s. 36(2)(a).
[9] See RSC., Ord. 65 and para. 17.18 below.
[10] At para. 17.21 below.
[11] s. 36(2)(b).
[12] s. 36(6).
[13] s. 93(1).
[14] *Newborough (Lord) v. Jones* [1975] Ch. 90, CA.
[15] *Datnow v. Jones* [1985] 2 E.G.L.R. 1, CA.
[16] s. 36(2)(c).
[17] For one thing consideration will not normally be present.

e-mail or even by direct computer link, it is the existence of the written agreement which allows this type of service to take place. In all other circumstances service by fax or other electronic means will not suffice, even if it is in fact received by the addressee.[18] Statutory notices are important documents and it would seem that section 36(3) places the risk of electronic failure or corruption on the giver of the notice except in those circumstances where the intended recipient has himself expressly undertaken that method of transfer.

7.12 Due service: service on a body corporate

Where a notice or other document required or authorised to be given under the 1995 Act is to be given to a body corporate the document is duly given if it is given to the secretary or clerk of that body.[19] That person may be served by personal delivery, by the document being left at the registered or principal office of the corporate body or in any other way authorised by a written agreement within the terms of section 36(2)(c).[20]

7.13 Due service: agent or servant managing, holding or carrying on business there: section 36(5)

Any notice or other document required or authorised to be given under the 1995 Act is duly given if it is given to an agent or servant in the limited circumstances identified by section 36(5). Sub-section (a), where service is to be effected on a landlord under a farm business tenancy, authorises service upon any agent or servant of the landlord who is responsible for the control of the management of the holding. There is no ancillary definition of the meaning of "control of the management of the holding": this may or may not extend beyond rent collection. However in circumstances where litigation is being conducted by solicitors temporarily authorised to collect the rent, it is submitted that those solicitors are not sufficiently responsible for the control of the management of the holding for this sub-section to apply. It is drafted, rather, so as to cover the normal activities of an estate office or retained surveyors who collect rent and deal generally with the tenant. Sub-section (b), where the document is to be given to a tenant under a farm business tenancy, authorises service upon an agent or servant of the tenant responsible for the carrying on of a business on the holding. This, where more than one business is being conducted, would authorise service on any agent or servant in respect of any of those businesses. Clearly this does not authorise service on a sub-tenant or upon any agent or servant of the tenant who happens to be on the holding but not conducting a business there. There is a particular usefulness in these provisions where the tenant dies and there is doubt as to the vesting of the tenancy.[21]

---

[18] s. 36(3).
[19] s. 36(4).
[20] *i.e.* generally by any method authorised by s. 36(2).
[21] Under corresponding provisions in s. 93(3) of the Agricultural Holdings Act service on the tenant's relatives who were in occupation and farming the land was effective as they were regarded as in the position of agents of the President of the Family Division (the person in whom at that time under s. 9 of the Administration of Estates Act 1925 the tenancy vested on intestacy): *Egerton v. Rutter* [1951] 1 K.B. 472. See also the discussion

It is assumed that service on a duly authorised agent, although not responsible for the control of the management or farming, will be valid.

Due service: change of landlord: section 36(7)   7.14

Where there is a change of landlord, any notice or other document required or authorised to be given under the 1995 Act by the tenant to the landlord is deemed to be given to the actual landlord in circumstances where the tenant serves the original landlord without having received a notice satisfying section 36(7)(a) and (b). Such a notice[22] must actually be received by the tenant and must constitute:

(a) notice that the person who before that time was entitled to receive the rents and profits of the holding has ceased to be so entitled and

(b) notice of the name and address of the person who has become entitled to receive the rents and profits.

It is an open question as to whether or not such a notice may be served before the actual transfer of the entitlement to receive the rents and profits has taken place.[23]

Application of the Act to Crown land: section 37   7.15

The 1995 Act applies to Crown land, as further defined by section 37(2). Argument as to who is to be treated as the owner of a Crown interest is referred, not to the Courts, but to the Treasury whose decision is final.[24] There are management provisions relating to treatment of compensation payments under section 16 where the tenancy forms part of the Duchy of Lancaster or Cornwall.[25]

Miscellaneous Forms   7.16

Forms which are not exclusively or directly generated by a need to comply with a provision of the 1995 Act but which nevertheless may be useful for farm business tenancies are provided as follows:

Form 113: Landlord's notice of severance of the reversion;
Form 114: Landlord's notice of change of landlord and giving landlord's address in England and Wales (sections 47 and 48 of the Landlord and Tenant Act 1987 and section 36(7) of the Agricultural Tenancies Act 1995);
Form 115: Notice giving landlord's address in England and Wales (sections 47 and 48 of the Landlord and Tenant Act 1987).[26]

---

under s. 93(3) at para. 17.23 below.

[22] A precedent is to be found as Form 114: Landlord's Notice of Change of Landlord and giving landlord's address in England and Wales sufficient for the purposes of s. 36(7) is to be found in Part V of this work.

[23] In *Railtrack plc v. Gojra* [1998] 8 E.G. 158 the CA (*obiter*) expressly refused to sanction the argument that no such notice (on almost identical provisions under s. 23(2) of the Landlord and Tenant Act 1927) could be given until after the change of landlord had occurred: see Wilson J. and Evans L.J. at 160, second column.

[24] s. 37(3).

[25] s. 37(5) or (6).

[26] All printed in Part V of this work.

MISCELLANEOUS

It is presumed that where the farm business tenancy includes one or more dwelling houses, sections 47 and 48 of the Landlord and Tenant Act 1987 will apply.[27]

---

[27] Those sections were applied to the Agricultural Holdings Act 1986 by the CA in ***Dallhold Estates (U.K.) Pty Ltd v. Lindsey Trading Properties Inc.*** [1994] 1 E.G.L.R. 93 and the reasoning would bring farm business tenancies under the 1987 Act likewise where the letting consists of or includes a dwelling. As to the effect of failure to comply with ss. 47 and 48 of the 1987 Act, see para. 12.55 below.

SECTION TWO

TENANCIES GOVERNED BY THE AGRICULTURAL HOLDINGS ACT 1986

CHAPTER 8

GENERAL PRINCIPLES AND DEFINITIONS

8.1 Introduction to the Agricultural Holdings Act 1986

8.2 1986 Act in relation to consolidation

8.3 Relationship of the 1986 Act to other statutory codes

8.13 No minimum size of holding: buildings

8.15 Abandonment of agricultural use

8.16 Definitions in section 1 of the 1986 Act: Agricultural holding, contract of tenancy, agricultural land, contract for an agricultural tenancy

8.20 Change in use during the tenancy

8.21 Application of the 1986 Act to old tenancies

8.22 Definition of "termination": section 96(1)

LIST OF STATUTORY DEFINITIONS
At the end of this Chapter is a complete list of all statutory definitions and their location within the Act

Introduction to the Agricultural Holdings Act 1986   8.1

Whether or not the Agricultural Holdings Act 1986 applies to a particular agreement will primarily depend on the date on which the agreement was entered into. If the agreement begins before September 1, 1995 it will be covered by the 1986 Act. In addition a limited category of agreements including in particular succession tenancies granted after that time are also covered by the 1986 Act.[1] The Act will apply not only to agreements which from the outset were tenancies or leases but, additionally, to certain licences which become converted into yearly tenancies.[2] The 1986 Act applies to all tenancies granted before it was passed and there are very limited opportunities for parties to fall within exceptions to the general scheme of statutory control.[3] There is no requirement for the service of notices prior to a 1986 Act tenancy being entered into nor is there any requirement that the agreement should be in writing. Because many informal arrangements have been converted into yearly tenancies under section 2 the statute provides for extensive control over the terms of the tenancy during its life.[4] The most important

---
[1] See generally paras 1.7–1.13 above.
[2] See paras 9.4–9.5 below.
[3] See Chapter 9.
[4] See Chapter 10.

149

provision, from a landlord's point of view, is the opportunity to call for a statutory rent review under section 12.[5] Although a 1986 Act tenancy may be terminated by all the usual methods of termination[6] the most important method of termination, and one which is the subject of detailed control by statute and statutory instrument, is the service of notice to quit.[7]

Disputes are sometimes referred under the Act to arbitration[8] and sometimes referred to determination by the Agricultural Land Tribunal.[9] When the tenancy comes to an end mandatory compensation claims are available which do not, except in the case of compensation for disturbance,[10] depend on the method of termination of the tenancy.[11] Special provisions deal with sub-tenancies, with market gardens and with smallholdings held by local authorities for that purpose.[12] Where a tenant dies there is frequently the opportunity for a close relative to claim a tenancy by succession and, if the tenant wishes to retire, he may nominate his chosen successor who may then apply to the Agricultural Land Tribunal for a direction in his favour so that he may take a succession tenancy.[13] These succession tenancies are new tenancies granted pursuant to a direction by the Agricultural Land Tribunal although certain termination claims which would otherwise be paid out at the end of the previous tenancy are "rolled forward" under the new tenancy. The complexity of the code as it stood in 1986 was the result of almost a century of gradual change, improvement and consolidation of its various aspects.

8.2 Status of the Agricultural Holdings Act 1986 in relation to consolidation

The principal Acts consolidated in the Agricultural Holdings Act 1986 are the Agricultural Holdings Act 1948, Part II of the Agriculture (Miscellaneous Provisions) Act 1976, the Agricultural Holdings (Notices to Quit) Act 1977 and the Agricultural Holdings Act 1984. Small areas of other Acts are also consolidated, in particular parts of the Agriculture Act 1958 and the Agriculture (Miscellaneous Provisions) Act 1968. In so far as the history of a particular provision is relevant it is discussed in relation to individual topics in Part I of this work. If the need arises to trace a statutory section, the tracing can take place either from the 1986 Act or from the previous statutory material by use of the Tables of Derivations and Destinations printed at the back of this work. The Agriculture Act 1986[14] was independently introduced to deal with problems generated by the presence of milk quotas. Since 1986 there has been only one major change namely the replacement of the original Case B in Schedule 3 by the Agricultural Holdings (Amendment) Act 1990. In so far as the Agricultural Holdings Act 1986 represented a consolidation, it did not include the Rent (Agriculture) Act 1976, the

---

[5] See Chapter 11.
[6] e.g. forfeiture, surrender, merger.
[7] See Chapter 12.
[8] e.g. under s. 12.
[9] e.g. succession claims under Part IV.
[10] This is only available to the tenant where the tenancy terminates by landlord's notice to quit.
[11] See generally Chapter 13.
[12] See Chapter 15.
[13] See Chapter 14.
[14] Dealt with in Chapter 19.

affinity of which is with the Rent Act code rather than the Agricultural Holdings code. In addition to pure consolidation, the Agricultural Holdings Act 1986 includes a small permitted amount of amendment, authorised by Parliament in the interests of more satisfactory consolidation. These permitted amendments were explained in the Law Commission's Report on the Bill[15] and in the minutes of the Joint Committee on Consolidation Bills.[16] For the variations from the ordinary legislative procedure reference should be made to the Consolidation of Enactments (Procedure) Act 1949. In Section 2 of Part I of this work (*i.e.* Chapters 8–17 dealing with the 1986 Act) the references which are not expressly linked to any statute are all references to the Agricultural Holdings Act 1986 and it is only occasionally that reference to a different statute will be necessary. On those occasions references to the Agriculture Act 1986 are by full title and references to other, earlier, statutes are usually simply a reference to the year, it being assumed that the reader will check the year against the contents of this paragraph so as to ascertain the full title of the statute.

Application of the Agricultural Holdings Act generally exclusive of other codes   8.3

In general terms the application of the Agricultural Holdings Act 1986 excludes the operation of any other landlord and tenant code.[17] It is convenient to verify this in relation to each of the major codes.[18]

Exclusion of tied "holdings"   8.4

Section 1(1) of the Agricultural Holdings Act 1986 excludes from the protection of the Act tied farm tenancies, such as those tenancies held by forest workers under the Forestry Commission by virtue of, and during the continuance of, their employment. It will be noted that this provision applies to tenancies which would be tenancies of agricultural holdings but for the employment tie. "Tied Cottages", *i.e.* dwelling-houses, with or without a piece of land cultivated for the domestic needs of the occupier, occupied by persons who are or have been employed in agriculture (and by protected successors) are governed by the different code of the Rent (Agriculture) Act 1976 or the Housing Act 1988.

Agricultural holdings and Part II of the Landlord and Tenant Act 1954   8.5

Section 43(1)(a) of the 1954 Act excluded from the protection given to business tenancies by that Act the tenancy of an agricultural holding. As originally worded, this did not exclude from protection as business tenancies those agricultural tenancies which, by virtue of section 2 of the 1948 Act,[19] were not technically "tenancies of agricultural holdings", *i.e.* tenancies for less than from year to year to which the Minister had given his prior approval, or tenancies made in

---

[15] Law Com: No. 153, December 1985.
[16] H.L. 56–11, H.C. 178–11, January 1986.
[17] The only limited qualifications are the operation of the Opencast Coal Act 1958 (dealt with at para. 8.6 below) and the allotments and smallholdings legislation dealt with in Chapter 15.
[18] See paras 8.5–8.12 below.
[19] Now s. 2 of the 1986 Act.

contemplation of the use of the land only for grazing or mowing during some specified period of the year.[20] The 1958 Act, however, amended section 43(1)(a) of the 1954 Act with retrospective effect so as to exclude from the definition of business tenancies those agricultural tenancies mentioned above which are not tenancies of agricultural holdings.[21] Thus the possibility that a tenant who did not qualify for security of tenure under the 1948 Act might acquire such security in respect of these particular tenancies under the 1954 Act was removed. There had previously been some uncertainty as to the exact status of fixed term tenancies granted for more than one year but less than two years.[22] This debate has now been settled and such tenancies fall within the Agricultural Holdings Act 1986 although they do not enjoy security of tenure.[23]

8.6 Effect of Opencast Coal Act 1958
The occupation or use of land for authorised opencast coal operations or restoration work does not prevent it from being an agricultural holding, or part of a holding, as the case may be, although it is not for the time being used for agriculture, if it is otherwise within the definition of an agricultural holding.[24]

8.7 Leasehold Reform Act 1967: exclusion
The provisions of Part I of the Leasehold Reform Act 1967, which confer on occupying tenants of leasehold houses rights to enfranchisement or an extended lease, do not apply to a tenant of a house comprised in an agricultural holding.[25]

8.8 Rent (Agriculture) Act 1976: "relevant licences/tenancies": exclusion
A tenancy protected by the Agricultural Holdings Act 1986 is expressly excluded from the definition of "relevant tenancy" for the purposes of the Rent (Agriculture) Act 1976 by Schedule 2, paragraph 2 of that Act.[26]

8.9 Rent Act 1977: "protected tenancies": exclusion
Sections 6 and 26 of the Rent Act 1977 operate to exclude automatically dwelling-houses let with more than two acres of agricultural land. In addition section 10 bars a tenancy from being a protected tenancy under the 1977 Act if the dwelling house is comprised in an agricultural holding within the meaning of the

---

[20] See commentary on s. 2(3)(a) in paras 9.7–9.11 below.
[21] 1958 Act, s. 8 and para. 29 of Sched. 1. Section 43(1)(a) of the 1954 Act was amended by the 1986 Act, Sched. 14, para. 21, to make changes in the wording consequential on the 1986 Act.
[22] Known as *Gladstone v. Bower* tenancies.
[23] See para. 9.20 below.
[24] Opencast Coal Act 1958, s. 14(2).
[25] Leasehold Reform Act 1967, s. 1(3)(b).
[26] The definition of "relevant licence" does not expressly refer to the 1986 Act and the modifications to para. 3 to the application of the Rent Act 1977 (the 1977 Act) omit s. 10 of the 1977 Act and ss. 6 or 26 of that Act. However a tenancy protected by the 1986 Act cannot in any circumstances be a "licence" since the conversion by s. 2 of the 1986 Act takes place immediately on the grant of the relevant licence. There is accordingly no need to make an express reference to the 1986 Act in relation to licences by the terms of Sched. 2 to the 1976 Act.

Agricultural Holdings Act 1986 and is occupied by the person responsible for the control (whether as tenant or as servant or agent of the tenant) of the farming of the holding.

Housing Act 1985: "secure tenancies": exclusion 8.10
Parts IV and V of the Housing Act 1985 confer on "secure tenants" of dwelling-houses let by local authorities and certain other bodies the right to buy their homes, security of tenure and other rights. A tenancy is, however, excluded from the category of "secure tenancy" if it is comprised in an agricultural holding and is occupied by a person responsible for the control (whether as tenant or as servant or agent of the tenant) of the farming of the holding.[27] Dwellings with more than two acres of appurtenant agricultural land are excluded from the 1985 Act in any case.[28]

Landlord and Tenant Act 1985, section 11: exclusion 8.11
The provisions of section 11 of the Landlord and Tenant Act 1985, formerly section 32 of the Housing Act 1961, under which important repairing obligations on the part of the landlord are implied in tenancies for less than seven years (which include tenancies from year to year) of a dwelling-house, do not apply to tenancies of agricultural holdings.[29]

Housing Act 1988: "Assured tenancies": exclusion 8.12
Assured tenancies are created by the Housing Act 1988. By Schedule 1, paragraph 6 there is an exclusion where a dwelling-house is let with more than two acres of agricultural land. In addition Schedule 1, paragraph 7 excludes dwelling houses comprised in an agricultural holding governed by the Agricultural Holdings Act 1986 where the dwelling-house is occupied by the person responsible for the control (whether as tenant or as servant or agent of the tenant) of the farming of the holding.

No minimum size of holding: holdings and allotments 8.13
There is no minimum size for an agricultural holding. An allotment of half an acre may be an agricultural holding if the produce is sold and not used for home consumption, and the fact that it may also be subject to the code of the Allotment Acts 1908 to 1950 does not prevent if from being subject to the 1986 Act.[30] An "allotment garden", however, can never be an agricultural holding, since by

---

[27] Housing Act 1985, Sched. 1, para. 8.
[28] Housing Act 1985, s. 112.
[29] Landlord and Tenant Act 1985, s. 14(3). But see the Agriculture (Maintenance, Repair and Insurance of Fixed Equipment) Regulations 1973 (S.I. 1973 No. 1473) for repairing obligations incorporated in every contract of tenancy of an agricultural holding except in so far as they would impose on one of the parties to an agreement in writing a liability which under the agreement is imposed on the other. These "model clauses" are discussed in Chapter 10.
[30] *Stevens v. Sedgeman* [1951] 2 K.B. 434, apparently misinterpreted by the county court judge in *Adsetts v. Heath* (1951) 95 S.J. 620, CC. See also *Look v. Davies* (1952) 160 E.G. 147, CC, a cottage let with one third of an acre. For a case relating to compensation under the Small Holdings and Allotments Act 1908, see *Earl of Plymouth v. Glamorgan County Council* (1974) 232 E.G. 1235, CC.

definition it is cultivated by the occupier for the purpose of consumption by himself and his family.[31]

8.14 A building may be an agricultural holding
A building without land other than its own site may constitute an agricultural holding, *e.g.* a cowshed rented from landlord A to use with land rented from landlord B, or a boiler-house, and in ***Blackmore v. Butler***[32] a cottage with garden let to a farm tenant (under a different tenancy from the farm), and occupied by the tenant's farm work, was held to be an agricultural holding.[33] A letting of a building which is separate from a letting of agricultural land, although simultaneous and connected with it, may not qualify for protection.[34]

8.15 Abandonment of agricultural use
An agricultural holding may cease to be such a holding if the use of the land for agriculture wholly or substantially ceases during the tenancy.[35] The landlord's consent to such an abandonment is not a necessary condition of the change taking place, although it may well be that the reverse change (from land which was not originally an agricultural holding to land which is such a holding) cannot take place without the landlord's consent.[36] The relevant time for the court to consider, in respect of evidence of abandonment, is the time leading up to a notice to quit in cases where a notice to quit has been served. In practice clear evidence of two years' cessation of agricultural activities would probably be sufficient to establish loss of the character of an agricultural holding, although a court might in some circumstances be satisfied with something less.[37] A unilateral abandonment of agricultural use which results in land ceasing to be an agricultural holding does not necessarily result in the tenancy becoming protected under the Rent Act 1977 even if the rateable value limits and other conditions for such protection are present. Evidence would be required from which could be inferred a new contract to let the premises "as a separate dwelling-house" within the Rent Acts.[38] It is likely that Courts will seek cogent evidence of abandonment:

---

[31] See s. 22(1) of the Allotments Act 1922 as amended by the Allotments Act 1950 and s. 109(3) of the 1947 Act. There are special rules as to notices to quit, etc., applicable to allotment gardens: see ***Wombwell UDC v. Burke*** [1966] 2 Q.B. 149. And see Chapter 15 below.
[32] [1954] 2 Q.B. 171; See also ***Lester v. Ridd*** [1990] 2 Q.B. 430; *cf.* ***Hasell v. McAulay*** [1952] 2 All E.R. 825.
[33] In this case, however, there was the special fact that the cottage was situated in the midst of farm land and had at all material times been used for housing agricultural workers. It is clear from ***Godfrey v. Waite*** (1951) 157 E.G. 582, referred to in a note at [1954] 2 Q.B. 175, that the mere fact that a cottage is used as a residence for an agricultural worker will not make it agricultural land.
[34] ***Darby v. Williams*** (1974) 232 E.G. 579.
[35] ***Hickson & Welch Ltd v. Cann*** (1977) 40 P. & C.R. 218, ***Wetherall v. Smith*** (1980) 256 E.G. 163, ***Russell v. Booker*** (1982) 263 E.G. 513.
[36] ***Wetherall v. Smith*** (above).
[37] ***Hickson & Welch v. Cann*** (above).
[38] ***Russell v. Booker*** (above). For a useful formulation of rules relating to change of user, see judgment of Slade L.J. in this case.

"The court is not lightly to treat a tenancy as having ceased to be within the protection of the Agricultural Holdings Act."[39]

Definition of "agricultural holding": section 1(1) 8.16

Only an "agricultural holding" is protected by the Agricultural Holdings Act 1986. The definition of an "agricultural holding" is set out in section 1(1), in turn incorporating the remainder of section 1. It should be noted at the outset that the Court of Appeal has held that, although the wording of section 1 of the 1986 Act differs from section 1 of the 1948 Act, there was no real difference in substance.[40] Accordingly light is thrown on the current section by the earlier case law. Section 1(1) provides:

> "In this Act 'agricultural holding' means the aggregate of the land (whether agricultural land[41] or not) comprised in a contract of tenancy[42] which is a contract for an agricultural tenancy,[43] not being a contract under which the land is let to the tenant during his continuance in any office, appointment[44] or employment held under the landlord."

The words "(whether agricultural land or not)" may seem a little odd in juxtaposition with "agricultural tenancy", but the intention seems to be to give statutory effect to the case law which developed around section 1 of the 1948 Act and which established that if the tenancy was in substance[45] an agricultural tenancy it could comprise some land which was non-agricultural. A mixed tenancy which contains some agricultural and some non-agricultural land cannot be severed so as to enable the agricultural holdings code to be applied to the former and not to the latter. the possibility of such severance, adumbrated by Tucker L.J. in *Dunn v. Fidoe* was decisively rejected in *Howkins v. Jardine*. It is also essential that the aggregate of the agricultural land is comprised in a single contract of tenancy.[46] As to the definition of "tenant", for the purposes of section 1 the definition contained in section 96(1) applies.[47] Licences converted by the operation of section 2 into tenancies[48] are able to satisfy this definition. The definition of "landlord" is to be found in section 96(1)[49] but it is important to note that the meaning of "landlord"

---

[39] Dillon L.J. in *Short v. Greeves* [1988] 1 E.G.L.R. 1 at 3D.
[40] Dillon L.J. in *Short v. Greeves* [1988] 1 E.G.L.R. 1 at 2B.
[41] See s. 1(4) and para. 8.18 below.
[42] See s. 1(5) and para. 8.17 below.
[43] See s. 1(2) and para. 8.19 below.
[44] For an arrangement held not to be an "appointment" see *Verrall v. Farnes* [1966] 1 W.L.R. 1254.
[45] In particular the judgment of Jenkins L.J. in *Howkins v. Jardine* [1951] 1 K.B. 614, and see also *Dunn v. Fidoe* [1950] 2 All E.R. 685.
[46] *Darby v. Williams* (1974) 232 E.G. 579: but see *Blackmore v. Butler* [1954] 2 Q.B. 171 for a supplemental agreement.
[47] It should be noted from consulting the list of statutory definitions at the end of this chapter that "tenant" receives special definitions for particular purposes and is so used elsewhere in the Act.
[48] See generally Chapter 9 below.
[49] Once again there are various extensions of this definition for particular purposes as stated in the list of statutory definitions at the end of this chapter.

has been the subject of considerable case law.[50] A sub-tenancy will be able to satisfy the terms of section 1.[51]

8.17 Definition of "contract of tenancy": section 1(5)

This is defined to mean a letting of land or an agreement for letting land for a term of years or from year to year. There is a special deeming in relation to leases within section 149(6) of the Law of Property Act 1925.[52] The phrase "term of years" is now known to include a lease for more than one but less than two years.[53] The contract in question need not be in writing but it must be one where the parties intend to create the legally binding relationship of landlord and tenant or such a legally binding licence as is capable of conversion under section 2: a "gentlemen's agreement", which is not contractual, does not fall within the sub-section.[54] In circumstances where a deed of partition of the tenancy was made without the landlord's consent and despite a prohibition in the lease, it has been held that the entirety of the original demise remained one single agricultural holding despite that partition.[55]

8.18 Definition of "agricultural land": section 1(4)

This is defined to mean:

(a) land used for agriculture which is so used for the purposes of a trade or business, and

(b) any other land which, by virtue of a designation under section 109(1) of the Agriculture Act 1947, is agricultural land within the meaning of that Act.

The Minister under section 109(1) of the 1947 Act can designate land which would not otherwise be within the definition of agricultural land (*e.g.* land used non-commercially, as for research, or derelict land), with certain kinds of land excluded from his powers.[56] It would appear that this provision is very rarely used, if used at all, and no case is known where an attempt has been made to include set

---

[50] Noted at para. 13.12 below.
[51] For the treatment of sub-tenancies, see paras 15.1–15.17 below.
[52] Leases or underleases at a rent or in consideration of a fine for life or lives or any term of years determinable with life or lives or on the marriage of the lessee. Such interests are converted into a term of 90 years determinable after the death or marriage, as the case may be, of the original lessee (or survivor of them) by notice as provided by that section.
[53] See para. 9.20 below.
[54] See *Goldsack v. Shore* [1950] 1 K.B. 708; *Steyning and Littlehampton Building Society v. Wilson* [1951] Ch. 1018; *Bahamas International Trust Co. Ltd v. Threadgold* [1974] 1 W.L.R. 1514; *Avon County Council v. Clothier* (1977) 242 E.G. 1048.
[55] *Lester v. Ridd* [1990] 2 Q.B. 430 in which *Howkins v. Jardine* [1951] 1 K.B. 614 was applied.
[56] "In this Act the expression 'agricultural land' means land used for agriculture which is so used for the purposes of a trade or business, or which is designated by the Minister for the purposes of this sub-section, and includes any land so designated as land which in the opinion of the Minister ought to be brought into use for agriculture: Provided that no designation under this sub-section shall extend–(a) to land used as pleasure grounds, private gardens or allotment gardens."

aside land within such a designation. Whether or not set aside land qualifies to be described as "agricultural land" without such a designation will probably depend on what activities (if any) the occupier conducts on such land. As a matter of law, land includes buildings.[57] Section 96(1) provides the key definition namely that of "agriculture" as follows:

> "'Agriculture' includes horticulture, fruit growing, seed growing, dairy farming and livestock[58] breeding and keeping, the use of land as grazing land, meadow land, osier land, market gardens and nursery grounds, and the use of land for woodlands where that use is ancillary to the farming of land for other agricultural purposes, and 'agricultural' shall be construed accordingly."

The definition of "agriculture" is inclusive and it has correctly been pointed out that the definition does not in terms include "the commonest form of agriculture, namely, the growing of corn".[59] An ultimate agricultural use does not make a tenancy agricultural if the immediate use is non-agricultural.[60] What is required is current agricultural use: a number of the uses identified in section 96(1) are, in effect, deliberate expansions of what the term "agriculture" would normally comprise. The use of the word "other" before "agricultural purposes" may be technically superfluous.[61] The definition of "livestock" is also an inclusive one. In *Minister of Agriculture v. Appleton*,[62] under similar definitions in a different statute, it was held that the breeding of cats and dogs for research was not within the words "livestock breeding and keeping", although the definitions of both "agriculture" and "livestock" are extensive. "Livestock breeding and keeping" must be confined to activities which can be brought within the general meaning of "agriculture". It is now well established that, although the keeping of horses used for recreation does not come within the definition of "agriculture", the use of land as grazing land for such "non-agricultural" horses does satisfy the definition.[63] The grazing must, however, be the predominant or substantial use[64] and, although the grazing of stud horses is within the definition, the running of the stud farm itself is not[65]; nor is the use of land for gallops, *i.e.* for the exercise of racehorses over it.[66] The keeping of pheasants for sport is not "agriculture".[67] Fish farming has given

---

[57] *Mann v. Gardner* (1990) 61 P.&C.R. 1, [1991] 1 E.G.L.R. 9. As pointed out above, an agricultural holding may involve only a building: see para. 8.14.

[58] Defined in s. 96(1) as follows: "'Livestock' includes any creature kept for the production of food, wool, skins, or fur or for the purpose of its use in the farming of land or the carrying on in relation to land of any agricultural activity."

[59] Stamp L.J. in *McClinton v. McFall* [1974] 232 E.G. 707, second column.

[60] *Dow Agrochemicals v. E.A. Lane (North Lynn) Ltd* (1965) 115 L.J. 76, CC.

[61] See *Secretary of State for Wales v. Pugh* [1970] 120 L.J. 357, CC.

[62] [1970] 1 Q.B. 221.

[63] *Rutherford v. Maurer* [1962] 1 Q.B. 16; *McClinton v. McFall* (above).

[64] cf. *Sykes v. Secretary of State for the Environment* [1981] 257 E.G. 821 (*incidental grazing in paddocks used for schooling horses, training young riders, or awaiting gymkhana events was not sufficient*).

[65] *McClinton v. McFall* (above), *Re Joel's Lease, Berwick v. Baird* [1930] 2 Ch. 359.

[66] *Bracey v. Read* [1963] Ch. 88; cf. *University of Reading v. Johnson-Houghton* [1985] 276 E.G. 1353.

[67] *Glendyne (Lord) v. Rapley* [1978] 1 W.L.R. 601; *Reeve v. Atterby* [1978] C.L.Y. 73;

rise to divergent views according to whether the subject matter is the law of rating or the law of agricultural holdings. So far as agricultural holdings are concerned the better view is that fish are "livestock".[68] Mink may also be "livestock" within this definition.[69] For the general purposes of the 1986 Act there are special applications of the definition of agriculture contained in section 96(1).[70] In the rating context the word "keeping" in terms of keeping livestock has been considered to mean "some element of holding as an end in itself and means more than a mere halting in the course of transit".[71] The operation of breeding and rearing thoroughbred horses for the purposes of recreation is not an agricultural operation.[72] "Pasture" is separately defined by section 96(1) to include meadow.[73] As to what may be a use "in connection with agriculture", see *Blackmore v. Butler*.[74]

It has been established, despite a dictum by Jenkins L.J. which suggested the contrary,[75] that the expression "trade or business" is not confined to agricultural trade or business, with the perhaps unexpected result that land used for grazing horses belonging to a riding school constituted an agricultural holding.[76] The phrase "trade or business" appears to give rise to little difficulty in the context of the 1986 Act although it would seem logical to suppose that the trade or business purposes in question must be more than an incidental part of the total activity.[77] Keeping animals for consumption, as opposed to sale, does not bring the relevant tenancy within the 1986 Act.[78]

Normanton (Earl) v. Giles [1980] 1 W.L.R. 28.

[68] Dicta by Lord Parker C.J. in *Belmont Farm Ltd v. Minister of Housing and Local Government* (1962) 13 P.&C.R. 417; *Minister of Agriculture, Fisheries & Food v. Appleton* (above). Contrast for rating purposes, whether in England and Wales or Scotland, fish were not regarded as livestock, a divergence from Scottish law having been removed by the decision of the CA in *Cresswell (Valuation Officer) v. British Oxygen Co. Ltd* [1980] 1 W.L.R. 1556.

[69] Although not so for rating purposes: *Jones (Valuation Officer) v. Davies* (1977) 244 E.G. 897 (LT).

[70] Section 96(4) provides that in the Act, references to the farming of land include references to the carrying on in relation to the land of any agricultural activity; s. 96(5) provides that in the Act, references to the use of land for agriculture include, in relation to land forming part of an agricultural unit, references to any use of the land in connection with the farming of the unit.

[71] *Gunter (Valuation Officer) v. Newtown Oyster Fishery Co. Ltd* (1977) 244 E.G. 140, Mr Emlyn Jones at 181H.

[72] *Whitsbury Farm and Stud Ltd v. Hemens (Valuation Officer)* [1988] 1 E.G.L.R. 159, HL, affirming the CA decision at [1987] 1 E.G.L.R., but on a different ground. The CA reports are worth referring to for the copious citation of authorities: but it must be remembered that this is primarily a rating case.

[73] The meaning of "permanent pasture" is considered at para. 10.55.

[74] See para. 8.14 above.

[75] *Howkins v. Jardine* [1951] 1 K.B. 614 at para. 629.

[76] *Rutherford v. Maurer* [1962] 1 Q.B. 16; see also *McClinton v. McFall* (1974) 232 E.G. 707.

[77] There is considerable case law in relation to that issue under s. 23 of the Landlord and Tenant Act 1954: see Hill & Redman, *Law of Landlord and Tenant*, Division B, commentary on section 23.

[78] By extension from the observation of Denning L.J. in *Stevens v. Sedgeman* [1951] 2 K.B. 434 at 440 observing that growing vegetables or fruit for home consumption amounted to

Definition of "contract for an agricultural tenancy": section 1(2) 8.19

A contract of tenancy for the purposes of section 1 is a contract for an agricultural tenancy:

> "If, having regard to-
>
> (a) the terms of the tenancy,
>
> (b) the actual or contemplated use of the land at the time of the conclusion of the contract and subsequently, and
>
> (c) any other relevant circumstances,
>
> the whole of the land comprised in the contract, subject to such exceptions only as do not substantially affect the character of the tenancy, is let for use as agricultural land."

It seems difficult to resist the conclusion that this is a prolix way of saying that the tenancy must be in substance a tenancy of agricultural land. If the "exceptions" did "substantially affect" the character of the tenancy it would not be in substance such a tenancy.[79] As pointed out above,[80] the terms of section 1 do not differ in essence from the previous formulation of the test as to whether or not a tenancy, regarded in a broad common sense way, is in substance a tenancy of agricultural land. The terms of the present definition direct attention not only to the use at the commencement of the tenancy but also to the parties' contemplated use of the land, which may or may not have commenced at the time when the letting is granted. For these purposes it is submitted that the contemplation must be a joint contemplation of both parties, not simply the contemplation of one of them.[81] Thus land which the tenant is to reclaim for agricultural use but which cannot be put to agricultural use from the outset may nevertheless fall within section 1 if there is the appropriate contemplation. A tenancy must be either wholly within or wholly outside the 1986 Act: a notice to quit an agricultural holding must be good or bad as a whole. Thus premises may be in substance a retail shop although they comprise a stock garden which supplies a small part of the produce sold in the shop, as in ***Monson v. Bound***[82] or in substance a riding school, although there are incidental agricultural activities, as in ***Deith v. Brown***,[83] or an establishment for keeping or schooling horses, with grazing merely incidental, as in ***Sykes v. Secretary of State for the Environment***.[84] On the other hand, a tenancy may be in substance a tenancy of agricultural land although it includes some cottages sublet to persons not engaged in agriculture,[85] or an inn partly used for the licensed trade and partly for the

---

no more than an allotment garden.

[79] See *e.g.* ***Monson v. Bound*** [1954] 1 W.L.R. 1321.

[80] para. 8.16.

[81] Compare the terms of s. 2(3)(a) where "contemplation" for the purposes of that section is discussed at para. 9.8. The relevant contemplation will be ascertained from words and conduct, rather than the subjective actual intention of a party.

[82] [1954] 1 W.L.R. 1321.

[83] [1956] J.P.L. 736.

[84] (1981) 257 E.G. 821 (actually a planning decision but relevant on this point).

[85] ***Howkins v. Jardine*** [1951] 1 K.B. 614.

agricultural business.[86] The "character" of a tenancy will be a question of fact in every case. The arithmetical proportion of home grown as opposed to imported produce in the turnover of the business is not a conclusive test of substantiality. In *Short v. Greeves*[87] a garden centre was held to be an agricultural holding although the home-grown agricultural content of the business represented only 40 per cent of total turnover and the bought-in produce represented 60 per cent. It is submitted that the Court will be assisted by photographs and a view of the holding so as to ascertain its "character". Turnover may sometimes be a misleading indicator, since the conduct of the non-agricultural business may not significantly interfere with the overall impression created of an agricultural holding.[88] Retailing and food processing[89] do not constitute agricultural use: it is the impact of any permitted retailing or food processing use which will have to be assessed as against the overall character of the tenancy. The character in question is the character of the tenancy as a letting of agricultural land as distinct from a letting with a "rural" feel. But even if the subject-matter of the tenancy is agricultural land, it will not constitute an agricultural holding if the object of the tenancy, as was the case of an attornment clause of a mortgage, is incidental to the security of a loan[90] or is for some other purpose than to enable the land to be farmed.

8.20 Change in use during the tenancy: section 1(3)

A new provision introduced by the 1984 Act and now embodied in section 1(3) of the 1986 Act gives statutory effect to what was probably the correct view[91] at common law, namely, that the use of land for agriculture contrary to the terms of a contract of tenancy would not make the land an agricultural holding so as to attract the benefits of the 1986 Act, unless the breach was effected with the landlord's permission, consent or acquiescence. The section refers to the permission consent or acquiescence of "the landlord", which, it is submitted, means the landlord from time to time as distinct from only the current landlord.[92] There is an interesting

---

[86] *Dunn v. Fidoe* [1950] 2 All E.R. 685 (perhaps more doubtful on the facts).
[87] [1988] 1 E.G.L.R. 1.
[88] A farm shop which uses exclusively bought in produce may be of an unobtrusive appearance even though it may generate a very high turnover.
[89] Even of home-grown produce.
[90] *Steyning and Littlehampton Building Society v. Wilson* [1951] Ch. 1018.
[91] See per Evershed M.R. in *Godfrey v. Waite* (1951) 157 E.G. 582 (referred to at [1954] 2 Q.B. 175) and the judgment of Somervell L.J. in *Iredell v. Brocklehurst* (1950) 155 E.G. 268, also the county court decision in *Kempe v. Dillon-Trenchard* (1951) 101 L.J. 417.
[92] See the definition in s. 96(1) and contrast the terms of s. 23(4) of the Landlord and Tenant Act 1954 where business use in breach of the tenancy is not effective to bring the tenancy within the 1954 Act "unless the immediate landlord or his predecessor in title has consented to the breach or the immediate landlord has acquiesced therein". Case law under the 1954 Act, however, may afford some useful guidance: thus in *Bell v. Alfred Franks & Bartlett Co. Ltd* [1980] 1 All E.R. 356 acquiescence was considered to involve simply a passive standing by without objecting to a breach of covenant whereas by contrast "consent" required a positive affirmative act accepting the breach whether by written or oral acceptance or even (in appropriate circumstances) an implied acceptance by conduct: see Shaw L.J. at 360. See also cases cited in Hill & Redman, *Law of Landlord and Tenant*, Division B, commentary under s. 23(4).

contrast between the terms of this provision and equivalent provisions in section 1(7) of the Agricultural Tenancies Act 1995.[93]

Application of the 1986 Act to old tenancies: section 98

8.21

The general rule is that the Act applies in relation to tenancies of agricultural holdings irrespective of the date of their creation and applies in relation to acts, regardless of when they were done. There are a few exceptions set out in section 98 where time is of importance.[94] Therefore, although a tenancy granted in 1932 over a farm did not at the date of its grant enjoy the full panoply of rights visible in the Agricultural Holdings Act 1986, such a tenancy is, subject to the exceptions set out in section 98, generally governed by the terms of the 1986 Act. Early tenancies often contain rudimentary terms and benefit particularly from the application of sections 6 and 7. Two specific sections of the Act refer to particular dates and the effect of those provisions is preserved.[95]

Definition of "termination": section 96(1).

8.22

Section 96(1) provides that:

> "'Termination', in relation to a tenancy, means the cesser of the contract of tenancy by reason of effluxion of time or from any other cause."

The termination of a tenancy is the date of key importance, principally in relation to compensation for improvements and tenant-right matters. The termination of the tenancy should not be confused with the tenant quitting: there may be a termination without a quitting or a quitting without a termination.[96] The tenant may assign his tenancy and thus quit without the tenancy terminating. Where a contract of tenancy fixes different dates at which different parts of the holding are to be quitted (*e.g.* the arable land at one date and the farmlands, buildings, and pasture at another), the termination of the tenancy will usually be the last of such dates.[97] It has been held that a tenant holding under a 21-year lease determinable at the end of the first seven or 14 years will be entitled to compensation if he quits at the end of 14 years, although the lease expressly provides for compensation to be paid "at the end of the term".[98] For the position where a tenant lawfully remains in occupation of part of a holding after the termination of the tenancy, see section 83(6).[99] Under the 1923 Act, the meaning of "termination" has been considered in the County Court.[1] It would appear that

---

[93] See the discussion at para. 1.19 above.
[94] The most significant being in relation to Sched. 12, compensation before various dates, the latest of which is December 31, 1951.
[95] ss. 4 and 34.
[96] See s. 69 and (for old improvements) Sched. 9, para. 5; *Ware v. Davies* (1931) 101 L.J.K.B. 1 for the position where the tenant remains in possession during a series of tenancies. In that case the earlier tenancies terminate without his quitting the holding.
[97] See *Swinburne v. Andrews* [1923] 2 K.B. 483; *Re Arden and Rutter* [1923] 2 K.B. 865; *Re Paul, ex p. Portarlington (Earl)* (1889) 24 Q.B.D. 247; *cf. Strang v. Stewart* [1887] 14 R. 637. But see *Black v. Clay* [1894] A.C. 368 and *Morley v. Carter* [1898] 1 Q.B. 8.
[98] *Bevan v. Chambers* [1896] 12 T.L.R. 417.
[99] And *Swinburn v. Andrews* (above), Bankes L.J. at 489 and *Re Arden and Rutter* (above).
[1] *Street v. Cottey* [1947] E.G.D. 136.

GENERAL PRINCIPLES AND DEFINITIONS

any means by which the tenancy is terminated falls within this wide definition and it is not possible to construct a convincing *genus* so as to construe the words "or from any other cause" in the definition according to the *ejusdem generis* rule. For the purposes of section 74 there is a special definition of "termination".[2]

8.23 **List of statutory definitions**

The authors have been able to trace no less than 106 definitions provided by the Act, many of these being defined in more than one section. Rather than repeat these definitions wherever they appear in reference to a particular section, we have assembled the definitions in an alphabetical list so that readers may, as they read a particular section, more easily check whether there is a definition applicable.

---

[2] See s. 74(4).

LIST OF STATUTORY DEFINITIONS

Words defined in or used for the purposes of the Agricultural Holdings Act 1986. All references are to that Act, unless otherwise stated.

Accepted proportion	Schedule 8, Part II, paragraph 11(3)
Additional compensation	Section 60(2) and (4)
Aftercare condition (for Schedule 3, paragraph 8)	Schedule 3, paragraph 8
Agisted livestock (for section 18)	Section 18(5)
Agreed	Section 96(1)
Agreement	Section 96(1)
Agricultural	Section 96(1)
Agricultural holding	Section 1(1) Section 96(1)
Agricultural land	Section 1(4) Section 96(1)
Agricultural unit	Section 96(1) Section 109 to the Agriculture Act 1947
Agriculture	Section 96(1)
Amalgamation (Case H)	Section 26(1) of Agriculture Act 1967
Amount of the tenant's actual loss	Section 60(5)
Arable land (for section 15)	Section 15(7)
Basic compensation	Section 60(2) and (3)
Board	Schedule 12, paragraph 4(3)
Body corporate controlled by a close relative	Schedule 6, paragraph 1(2)
Building	Section 96(1)
Case	Section 96(1) Section 26(2)

163

LIST OF STATUTORY DEFINITIONS

Close relative (of the retiring tenant)	Section 35(2) Section 49(3)
Commercial unit of agricultural land	Schedule 6, paragraphs 3 and 4
Connected person	Schedule 6, paragraph 10(3)
Contract for an agricultural tenancy	Section 1(2)
Contract of tenancy	Section 1(5) Section 96(1)
County Court	Section 96(1)
Date of death	Section 35(2)
Date of the insolvency (for section 80(4))	Section 80(9)
Deceased	Section 35(2)
District	Schedule 3, paragraph 7(1)
Dwelling-house (for Schedule 3, paragraphs 4 & 5)	Schedule 3, paragraph 7(2)
Eligible person (retirement succession)	Section 36(3) and Schedule 6 Section 50(2)
Date of any relevant notice (for Case G)	Schedule 3, paragraph 12(b)
Evesham custom	Section 80(3)-(5) Section 81(2)
Excess qualifying leys	Schedule 8, Part II, paragraph 11(3)
Excluded matters	Schedule 12, paragraph 8(2)
Farming of land	Section 96(4)
Fixed equipment	Section 96(1)
Holding (for succession on death of tenant) (succession on retirement)	Section 35(2) Section 49(3)

LIST OF STATUTORY DEFINITIONS

Housing authority	Schedule 3, paragraph 7(1)
Hill land	Schedule 8, Part II, paragraph 10(2)
Hill sheep	Schedule 8, Part II, paragraph 10(2)
Insolvent	Section 96(2)
(for the purposes of section 80(3))	Section 80(9)
Landlord	Section 96(1)
(death succession)	Section 48(2)
(retirement succession)	Section 56(4)
(compensation)	Section 96(6)
Landlord's improvements	Schedule 2, paragraph 2(2)(c)
(for Schedule 2, paragraph 2)	
Leys	Schedule 8, Part II, paragraph 11(3)
Livelihood condition	Schedule 6, paragraph 1
Livestock	Section 96(1)
(for section 18)	Section 18(5)
(for section 19)	Section 19(3)
Local Government Funds	Section 96(1)
Long term improvements	Section 95(7)
(for section 95)	
Minister	Section 96(1)
Model clauses	Section 7(1)
	Section 96(1)
Modifications	Section 84(5)
(for section 84)	
New holding	Schedule 2, paragraph 5(1)
Nominated successor	Section 49(3)
Notice to do work	Section 28(6)
(for section 28)	
Occupancy condition	Schedule 6, paragraph 1
Old improvements	Schedule 9, paragraph 1(2)
Original holding	Schedule 2, paragraph 5(1)(a)

LIST OF STATUTORY DEFINITIONS

Original landlord	Section 93(5)(a)
Pasture	Section 96(1)
Period of residence protection	Schedule 5, paragraph 1
Person validly designated by the deceased in his will	Section 40(1)
Prescribed	Section 96(1)
Prescribed period	
(death succession)	Section 48(2)
(retirement succession)	Section 56(4)
(for section 67(5))	Section 67(7)
President	Section 22(2)
(for section 22)	Schedule 11, paragraph 1(1)
Prisoner	Schedule 11, paragraph 12(1)
(for Schedule 11, paragraph 12)	
Productive capacity	Schedule 2, paragraph 1(2)(a)
Qualifying leys	Schedule 8, Part II, paragraph 11(3)
Question (a)	Section 48(4)
Question (b)	Section 48(4)
Reasonable cost of work	Section 11(8)
(for section 11)	
Related earning capacity	Schedule 2, paragraph 1(2)(b)
Related holding	Section 35(2)
(retirement succession)	Section 49(3)
Relevant compensation	Section 9(2)
Relevant improvement	Section 64(1)/(2)
	Section 96(1)
Relevant land	Schedule 12, paragraph 4(5)
Relevant notice	Section 61(6)
(disturbance compensation)	
Relevant period	Section 53(2)
	Section 54(2)

LIST OF STATUTORY DEFINITIONS

Relevant previous notice (disturbance compensation)	Section 63(4)
Relevant service	Schedule 5, paragraph 1
Relevant time (deferment of relevant time) (death succession) (retirement succession)	Section 46 Section 46 Section 48(2) Section 51(6) Section 55(8)
Rent (for Schedule 2 paragraphs 4(1)(b)/(c))	Schedule 2, paragraph 5(2)(b)
Rent properly payable (succession)	Section 48(9)
Restoration condition (for Schedule 2, paragraph 8)	Schedule 3, paragraph 8(2)
Retirement date	Section 49(3)
Retirement notice	Section 49(3)
Retiring tenant	Section 49(3)
Roots (for section 15)	Section 15(7)
Rules of good estate management	Section 96(3) Section 10 of the Agriculture Act 1947
Rules of good husbandry	Section 96(3) Section 11 of the Agriculture Act 1947
Service man	Schedule 5, paragraph 1
Short period of training	Schedule 5, paragraph 1
Short term improvements (for section 95)	Section 95(7)
Tenancy (death succession) (retirement succession)	Section 35(2) Section 49(3)

LIST OF STATUTORY DEFINITIONS

Tenant   Section 96(1)
  (exclusions)   Section 34(2)
      Section 37(9)
  (succession)   Section 48(2)
  (retirement succession)   Section 49(2)
      Section 56(4)
  (compensation)   Section 96(6)
  (for Case G)   Schedule 3, paragraph 12(a)

Tenant right matters   Section 95(7)
  (for section 95)

Tenant's fixed equipment   Schedule 2, paragraph 2(2)(b)
  (for Schedule 2, paragraph 2)   Schedule 2, paragraph 2(3)(b)

Tenant's improvements   Schedule 2, paragraph 2(2)(a)
  (for Schedule 2 paragraph 2)   Schedule 2, paragraph 2(3)(a)

Tenant's pasture   Section 76(2)
  (for section 76)

Term date
  (for section 3)   Section 3(4)
  (for section 4)   Section 4(4)

Termination   Section 96(1)
  (for section 74)   Section 74(4)

Termination date   Section 12(4)
  (following the date of the demand)

Tribunal   Section 96(1)

Use of land for agriculture   Section 96(5)

Year   Section 20(3)(b)
  (for section 20(2))

1951 Act   Schedule 5, paragraph 1

CHAPTER 9

STATUTORY CONTROL OVER INTERESTS GRANTED

9.1 Nature of and mechanisms for security of tenure

9.2 Conversion by section 2 of interests for less than a tenancy from year to year

9.6 Exemptions from the operation of section 2: Ministerial approval

9.7 Grazing agreements

9.13 Grantor's interest less than a tenancy from year to year

9.14 Pre-March 1, 1948 agreements

9.19 Mandatory nature of conversion

9.20 *Gladstone v. Bower* agreements

9.21 Tenancies for two years or more: operation of section 3

9.25 Operation of section 4

9.28 Contracting out under section 5

9.1

The nature of and mechanisms for security of tenure

This chapter deals with a number of provisions, to be found in sections 2 to 5 of the 1986 Act, which impose statutory restrictions on the letting of agricultural land for interests less than from year to year and which, subject to exceptions, provide that a fixed term of two years or more shall continue as a tenancy from year to year instead of expiring on the term date. In very general terms section 2 operates to convert lettings or exclusive licences into annual tenancies.[1] There are certain exceptions to this process which are contemplated by section 2 itself[2] and there are other transactions which are not captured by section 2 for reasons extraneous to the terms of that section.[3] *Gladstone v. Bower*[4] agreements, that is to say agreements for more than one but less than two years, are not prolonged on the termination of the letting.[5] Section 3 continues a fixed term tenancy of two years or more on an annual basis,[6] but section 3 does not cover agreements made before the January 1, 1921.[7]

---

[1] See paras 9.2–9.5 below.
[2] See prior approval by the Minister, para. 9.6 below; grazing agreements, paras 9.7–9.12 below; grantors with interests less than a tenancy from year to year, para. 9.13 below.
[3] See agreements made before March 1, 1948, para. 9.13 below; agreements of a non-contractual character or which for other reasons cannot be modified to fall within s. 2, paras 9.5 and 9.17–9.18.
[4] [1960] 1 Q.B. 170 (Diplock J.); [1960] 2 Q.B. 384, CA.
[5] See para. 9.20 below.
[6] See paras 9.21–9.22.
[7] See para. 9.23 below.

Section 4 deals with the death of the tenant, in certain cases, where the tenancy is within section 3.[8] It has historically been possible to contract out of the effect of section 3 subject to the restrictions in section 5 including the grant of Ministerial approval.[9] The net result of these sections is that ultimately all protected interests will be annual tenancies. This in turn brings into play the restrictions on the operation of notices to quit discussed in Chapter 12. The severity of these restrictions combined with the extensive controls over interests granted by contract form the foundation of the scheme of security of tenure under the Agricultural Holdings Act 1986.

9.2 General object of section 2

The wording of section 2 of the 1986 Act reproduces in substance section 2 of the 1948 Act, but the arrangement of the parts of the section is different. The large body of case law which accumulated on the old section 2 remains applicable, although references in these cases to section 2(1) must now be read as references to section 2(1) and (2) and references to the proviso to section 2(1) must now be interpreted as referring to section 2(3).[10]

The definition of a contract of tenancy[11] as a letting of land for a term of years or from year to year would, if it stood by itself without qualification, mean that tenancies could be excluded from all the rights and obligations of the agricultural holdings code by the simple device of ensuring that they were granted for interests less than from year to year, even if they were periods of 364 days. This was held to be the case under the 1923 Act in *Land Settlement Association Ltd v. Carr*.[12] The object of section 2 of the 1986 Act is to close this loophole by bringing within the Act, subject to certain defined exceptions, agreements under which land is let for use as agricultural land for an interest less than a tenancy from year to year or under which a licence is granted (for whatever length of time) to occupy land for use as agricultural land, provided that in either case if the interest had been created instead as a tenancy from year to year the land would have been an agricultural holding. A tenancy for one year certain is an interest less than a tenancy from year to year,[13] and is thus protected by section 2(2)(a), but a tenancy for a fixed period of more than one year but less than two years is a greater interest than a tenancy from year to year, and is thus not protected.[14] These two propositions were settled only after some doubt and controversy.

9.3 Scope of section 2

Section 2(2) covers lettings for less than from year to year and licences of any duration. Cases show that numbers of informal arrangements which were never intended by the parties to create tenancies of agricultural holdings, with all the

---

[8] See paras 9.23–9.25 below.

[9] See paras 9.26–9.31 below.

[10] The division of the section into four instead of two subsections probably on the whole makes for clarity, but it is not certain that the redrafting was worthwhile.

[11] s. 1(5). It may be noted here that s. 2 does not apply at all to agreements made before March 1, 1948: see Sched. 12, para. 1.

[12] [1944] K.B. 657.

[13] *Bernays v. Prosser* [1963] 2 Q.B. 592; *Rutherford v. Maurer* [1962] 1 Q.B. 16; *Lower v. Sorrell* [1963] 1 Q.B. 959.

[14] *Gladstone v. Bower* [1960] 2 Q.B. 384, CA. See para. 9.20 below.

consequent obligations and security of tenure, have been caught by what is now section 2(2) and undergone a "sea-change".[15] Most of the cases where section 2 has operated to transform a lesser interest into a tenancy from year to year have been cases where the agreement has been held to create a licence.[16] Tenancies for less than from year to year, apart from the grazing or mowing tenancies which are covered by section 2(3)(a), are occasionally created either by accident or to accommodate the grower of a specialist crop. In one case landlords who intended to create a *Gladstone v. Bower*[17] tenancy for more than one year but less than two years overlooked the principle that a grant cannot operate retrospectively so as to confer an interest in land on the grantee before the execution of the grant.[18] They granted the tenant retrospectively a *Gladstone v. Bower* tenancy, but at the date of execution the tenancy had only a few days left to run.[19] The result was to create a tenancy for a few days, which fell squarely within section 2(2)(a) and was converted into a tenancy from year to year. A tenancy for one year certain is a tenancy for less than from year to year and is, therefore, caught by section 2(2)(a) and converted accordingly.[20] A tenancy for a fixed term of 364 days, unless it falls within section 2(3)(a)[21] will be converted, as will the periodic 364 day tenancy which under the old law[22] did not qualify as a contract of tenancy.

Conversion of licences by section 2 9.4

Section 2(2) covers, in addition to lettings for less than from year to year, agreements under which a person is granted a licence to occupy land for use as agricultural land. It is necessary to consider the law that has developed in regard to such licences, which, when the subsection applies, take effect as agreements for a tenancy from year to year. The effect of the decision in *Street v. Mountford*[23] on the type of licence which is converted into a yearly tenancy by section 2(2)(b) is in a sense academic, since the *Street v. Mountford* hallmarks of a tenancy, a grant for a term (either fixed or periodic), at a rent, with exclusive possession, are precisely those required by section 2(2)(b) and the associated case law in order to bring about such a conversion. It is true that the decision in *Street v. Mountford* related to

---

[15] See generally para. 9.4 below. The transformation is of sufficient substance to merit this description: The interest "doth suffer a seachange into something rich and strange" (*The Tempest*, Act 1, scene 2).

[16] Sometimes it is doubtful whether the interest is a licence or a tenancy: see *Collier v. Hollinshead* (1984) 272 E.G. 941 at 945 ("indicia" rather pointing to a tenancy) where there was the additional complication as to whether an arrangement made by one or two joint lands was binding on the other. *Street v. Mountford* [1985] A.C. 809 has also to be considered, since it clarifies the concept of tenancy and correspondingly reduces the scope for construing an arrangement to be a licence.

[17] [1960] 2 Q.B. 384.

[18] See *Roberts v. Church Commissioners for England* [1972] 1 Q.B. 278.

[19] *Keen v. Holland* [1984] 1 W.L.R. 251; (1983) 269 E.G. 1043.

[20] *Bernays v. Prosser* [1963] 2 Q.B. 592; see also *Lampard v. Barker* (1984) 272 E.G. 783. It should be noted that an agreement from April 1 to March 31 is an agreement for 365 days, *i.e.* for a year certain: *Cox v. Hurst* (1976) 239 E.G. 123.

[21] See *Reid v. Dawson* [1955] 1 Q.B. 214.

[22] *Land Settlement Association Ltd v. Carr* [1944] K.B. 657.

[23] [1985] A.C. 809, a "succinct" decision: *Brooker Settled Estates v. Ayer* [1987] 1 E.G.L.R. 50, CA.

residential accommodation, but the ratio was based on landlord and tenant principles which are of general application. The licence for the purpose of section 2(2), in contrast with the tenancy under that subsection, can be of any duration. It will be converted into a yearly tenancy, if the other conditions are present, however long its term.[24] But it should not be forgotten that in *Street v. Mountford* itself it was recognised that the grant of exclusive occupation did not automatically result in the grant of a tenancy.[25]

Section 2(2)(b) will apply to the licence only if it is enforceable at law, *i.e.* is a licence for valuable consideration, not a gratuitous licence.[26] The consideration may take various forms other than a payment of money, *e.g.* an undertaking to clean the land[27] or an agreement to break a farming partnership with a third party.[28] These cases show that sometimes informal and provisional arrangements (provided that consideration is present) will attract section 2(2).[29] But a licence which is purely gratuitous remains revocable. However, circumstances which did not operate on the mind of either party to a licence are unlikely to be held to amount to valuable consideration so as to effect a conversion within section 2.[30] The licence must be a licence conferring exclusive occupation of the land on the licensee.[31] Thus it cannot be a licence to the licensee jointly with the licensor, nor can it be a licence to the licensor's manager or agent.[32] *A fortiori* it cannot be a

---

[24] *Snell v. Snell* (1964) 191 E.G. 361. See also generally *Finbow v. Air Ministry* [1963] 1 W.L.R. 697.

[25] See Lord Templeman in *Street v. Mountford*, above at 821: "In *Errington v. Errington and Woods* [1952] 1 K.B. 290 and in the cases cited by Denning L.J. at p.297 there were exceptional circumstances which negatived the *prima facie* intention to create a tenancy, notwithstanding that the occupier enjoyed exclusive occupation. The intention to create a tenancy was negatived if the parties did not intend to enter into legal relationships at all, or where the relationship between the parties was that of vendor and purchaser, master and service occupier, or where the owner, a requisitioning authority, had no power to grant a tenancy". This was cited and applied by Ferris J. in *Colchester Borough Council v. Smith* [1991] Ch. 448 at 485.

[26] See *Goldsack v. Shore* [1950] 1 K.B. 708; *King v. Turner* [1954] E.G.D. 7; *Harrison–Broadley v. Smith* [1964] 1 W.L.R. 456; *Verrall v. Farnes* [1966] 1 W.L.R. 1254; *Holder v. Holder* [1968] Ch. 353, Cross J. affirmed by CA, (in relation to an arrangement not intended to create legal relations at all); *Epps v. Ledger* (1972) 225 E.G. 1373; *Mitton v. Farrow* (1980) 255 E.G. 449 (consideration being agreement to reclaim land); *Collier v. Hollinshead* (1984) 272 E.G. 941 (where the rent, although more than nominal, was far below a market rent).

[27] *Mitton v. Farrow*, above.

[28] *Epps v. Ledger*, above.

[29] See also *Collier v. Hollinshead*, above. In *Gold v. Jacques Amand Ltd* [1992] 2 E.G.L.R. 1 a contract was implied for the creation of a licence capable of conversion even though the original licence arrangement was non-contractual before building works had commenced. The facts are unusual.

[30] The allegation that the previous surrender of a valuable tenancy might amount to such consideration, when neither party regarded the surrender as such consideration, was rejected by Ferris J. in *Colchester Borough Council v. Smith*, above at 489.

[31] See *Harrison-Broadley v. Smith*, above; *Epps v. Ledger*, above; *Bahamas International Trust Co. Ltd. v. Threadgold* [1974] 1 W.L.R. 1514; *James v. Lock* (1978) 246 E.G. 395. In *Midgley v. Stott* (1977) 244 E.G. 883 the point that the licence was non-exclusive could not be taken in the Court of Appeal because it was not put forward in the County Court.

[32] *Harrison-Broadley v. Smith*, above, applied in *Padbury v. York* [1990] 2 E.G.L.R. 3.

licence merely to take the produce of the land[33] or merely to go on the land in pursuance of a farming partnership with the occupier.[34] A retention of a right of access is not inconsistent with a grant of exclusive occupation.[35]

The question of "the necessary modifications" mentioned in section 2(1) is dealt with separately in paragraph 9.5. It appears unnecessary, at the point of agreeing to the terms of a licence, to specify a precise date for the commencement of the licence[36] but it is necessary to be able to render the subject matter of the licence certain by some means.[37] What is unclear from the wording of section 2 itself is the point at which the conversion takes place.[38] The conversion has now been held to be immediate in its effect so as to result in an anniversary date coinciding with the commencement, not the expiry of, the licence.[39] Where a tenancy is not created because there is a failure to specify the commencement date, a licence capable of conversion will ensue.[40]

"Necessary modifications": scope and effect of words in section 2(1)　　9.5
Section 2(1) provides that if the conditions mentioned in the section are satisfied, the agreement shall then take effect "with the necessary modifications" as if it were an agreement for the letting of the land for a tenancy from year to year. The meaning of "the necessary modifications" has given rise to some discussion. In *Goldsack v. Shore*[41] Lord Evershed M.R. said that, for section 2(1) to apply, the interest in question "must be capable of being so modified (and that must mean modified consistently with its own terms) as to become enlarged into a tenancy from year to year". This principle was expressed in greater detail by Pearson L.J. in *Harrison-Broadley v. Smith*,[42] where he considered that the transformation of the defendant's licence as a partner to go on the land into a protected tenancy from year to year was a change into something radically different. He said:

> "That which is to take effect is the original agreement, with the necessary modifications. It is not permissible to substitute for the original agreement a radically different agreement and make that take effect instead of the original agreement."[43]

---

[33] *Wyatt v. King* (1951) 157 E.G. 124 (a puzzling case; see [1963] 1 W.L.R. 1262 at 1270; and (1955) 99 S.J. 402).
[34] *Harrison-Broadley v. Smith*, above.
[35] *Harrison-Broadley v. Smith* and *Bahamas* case, above; *Secretary of State for Social Services v. Beavington* (1981) 262 E.G. 551. See also *Lampard v. Barker* (1984) 272 E.G. 783 and, for an exercise of construction limited to the face of the agreement, *Evans v. Tompkins* [1993] 2 E.G.L.R. 6.
[36] Contrast the position with leases: see *Secretary of State for Social Services v. Beavington* [1982] 1 E.G.L.R. 13.
[37] *e.g.* by reference to a growing season.
[38] *i.e.* whether at the commencement of the relevant licence or at its termination.
[39] *Calcott v. J.S. Bloor (Measham) Ltd* [1998] E.G.C.S. 25, CA (judgment February 17, 1998).
[40] *James v. Lock* [1978] 1 E.G.L.R. 1.
[41] [1950] 1 K.B. 708, CA, at 713.
[42] [1964] 1 W.L.R. 456 at 467.
[43] He elaborates his reasons at 467–469, *ibid.*

In *Verrall v. Farnes*,[44] however, where a surprising result was achieved,[45] Cross J. sounded a note of caution. He said:

> "I cannot read his [Pearson L.J.'s] words as meaning that a Court has a general discretion to exclude from the operation of the section cases where the application of it produces surprising results which Parliament may not have contemplated."[46]

A curious situation arose in *Bahamas International Trust Co. Ltd v. Threadgold*.[47] The Court of Appeal, accepting a concession by the owners' counsel that the licensee had an exclusive licence, nevertheless decided that section 2(1) did not confer upon him a tenancy from year to year because this would have involved modifications which would have given him a radically different agreement. The House of Lords held that, despite counsel's concession, the licence was non-exclusive, so that section 2(1) did not apply at all; the licensee did not obtain a tenancy from year to year, but for a different reason. The Court of Appeal's application of the "necessary modifications" doctrine was not discussed, Lord Diplock saying "[T]he instant appeal does not provide an appropriate occasion for considering it".[48] It may be that Lord Diplock's studious avoidance of comment indicated less than full approval of the doctrine, but in another case, *Walters v. Roberts*, it was applied by Nourse J. without question.[49] In view of Lord Diplock's reservation, there may remain a slight doubt as to the scope of the doctrine unless or until it is resolved by the House of Lords.[50] It is therefore still possible that the "bold construction"[51] mentioned (but not considered) by Megaw

---

[44] [1966] 1 W.L.R. 1254.

[45] A licence to occupy land was held to be transformed into a protected tenancy from year to year, even though no rent was payable under the yearly tenancy until either the tenant offered to pay it or the landlord succeeded in getting a rent fixed by arbitration. Neither of the parties in this case intended that an immediate tenancy should be created; indeed they intended to enter into a probationary arrangement for the precise purposes of deciding whether a tenancy should be created.

[46] [1966] 1 W.L.R. 1254 at 1268.

[47] [1974] 1 W.L.R. 1514, CA and HL.

[48] *ibid.*, at 1528.

[49] (1980) 258 E.G. 965. The point arose rather incidentally, in regard to a submission that a purchaser in occupation under a conditional contract of sale was granted a licence which became transformed into a tenancy from year to year by section 2(1). Nourse J. had no difficulty in deciding that this, so far from being a "necessary modification", was a radical transformation. The licence here was only granted as an adjunct to the purchaser's equitable interest in the land and in the expectation that that interest would in due course mature into full legal ownership. The point might have been decided without reference to the "necessary modifications" doctrine.

[50] The Court of Appeal's reliance on it in the *Bahamas* case is reduced to the status of dicta by the House of Lords decision.

[51] "We do not have to consider the possible bold construction of section 2(1), which would, in any event, be inconsistent with what was said in *Goldsack v. Shore*, that once it is found that an agreement complies with the opening provisions of section 2(1) it must be within the subsection, and it must be turned into a tenancy from year to year, however drastic, surprising, unjust or absurd the effect might be in relation to the agreement made between the parties." [1974] 1 W.L.R. 1514 at 1521. This would give minimal effect to the words "with the necessary modifications" in section 2(1).

L.J. in the *Bahamas* case may be found to be correct. Some disputes as to necessary modifications would be suitable for arbitration, but others might raise difficult questions of law for the Courts.[52]

Exemption from conversion by section 2: prior approval by the Minister: **9.6**
section 2(1)
Section 2 does not affect cases where the Minister has given approval under subsection (1) to the letting or grant before the agreement for it has been entered into. This may be a "blanket" approval of all lettings or grants of particular types or by particular landlords or grantors, but not of all lettings or grants whatsoever.[53] It is essential that the approval should have been given before the agreement is made.[54] It is also essential that the approval has not expired before the agreement is made.[55] Provided that there is in existence a current Minister's approval, a tenancy arising by implication may be covered by it, although it is desirable, to avoid doubt, that the Minister's approval should be followed by an express written agreement.[56] Under this provision the Minister may approve a tenancy of not more than one year or a licence of any duration.[57] Although now only of historical interest, a statement was issued in July 1984 setting out the criteria which the appropriate Minster was to follow in giving approval under section 2(1).[58]

Exemption from conversion by section 2: grazing agreements: section 2(3)   **9.7**
(a)
There is no conversion into an annual tenancy in circumstances where either a letting or licence is granted which is made (whether or not it expressly so provides) in contemplation of the use of the land only for grazing or mowing (or both) during some specified period of a year.[59] The kinds of agreements which are within section 2(3)(a) are described in different ways in different parts of the country. Sales of grass keep or sales of mowing grass are exempt from conversion provided that they cover a specified period of the year. They are to be distinguished from contracts of agistment, which consist of taking in another person's cattle to feed

---

[52] See generally para. 9.16 below.
[53] *Finbow v. Air Ministry* [1963] 1 W.L.R. 697.
[54] *Bedfordshire County Council v. Clarke* (1974) 230 E.G. 1587. See also as to precise timing of Minister's approval.
[55] *Secretary of State for Social Services v. Beavington* (1981) 262 E.G. 551, where, because no one thought of securing a renewal of the approval, a licence was converted by section 2(1) into a fully protected tenancy.
[56] *Epsom and Ewell Borough Council v. Bell (C.) (Tadworth) Ltd* (1982) 266 E.G. 808. The Minister gives his approval to the letting; it is not his function to approve the terms of the agreement.
[57] s. 2(1). The letting must under this dispensing power be for an interest less than a tenancy from year to year, and the largest interest which comes effectively within the description is an interest for one year certain. No limit is placed on the duration of a licence. But these provisions must now be read in conjunction with s. 5 and the Minister's policy statement: see para. 9.33 below. Although under s. 2(1) the Minister may in theory approve a licence of any duration, there are difficulties about drafting very long licences which the Courts are not going to construe as tenancies.
[58] Reproduced in full at pp. 343–345 of the 13th edition of this work.
[59] s. 2(3)(a).

and confer no interest in land on the stock owner, who is not allotted any specific part of the land.[60] The words "or both" in section 2(3)(a) were added on consolidation on the recommendation of the Law Commission to resolve any possible doubt that "or"[61] should be understood conjunctively.[62] Although the precise terms of typical "grass keep" agreements may differ, their essential features are for these purposes identified by the statute.[63] It should be also noted that, because of their unprotected status, lettings which are grass keep agreements have been popular vehicles for the transfer of quota.[64]

9.8 **"Contemplation" for the purposes of section 2(3)(a)**

In *Scene Estate Ltd v. Amos*[65] there was a large number of successive three months agreements extending over several years. Both parties expected the arrangement to continue, but each three months agreement was self-complete, a new arrangement being made each time. There was no power for the tenant to stay more than the three months and no obligation on the landlord to allow him to do so. It was held that all that was "in contemplation" of the agreement was three months, so that each period fell within the provision in section 2(3)(a). The agreement has to be scrutinised to see what it contemplates. Thus in one case[66] the agreement referred to "grazing for six months' periods", which implied a letting for at least a year and therefore not in contemplation only of a specified period of the year.[67]

In another case[68] there was a succession of six months agreements which, taken by themselves, would have each been within section 2(3)(a), but the parties at the outset contemplated the arrangements lasting "for several years", so that the tenant became a tenant from year to year. In a difficult decision[69] the Court of Appeal has

---

[60] See *Richards v. Davies* [1921] 1 Ch. 90 and *Masters v. Green* (1888) 20 Q.B.D. 807. Contrast *Fawcett (Thomas) & Sons Ltd v. Thompson* [1954] E.G.D. 5.

[61] In s. 2 of the 1948 Act.

[62] See Law Com. No.153 on the Agricultural Holdings Bill, Cmnd. 9665 (December 1985) p.4.

[63] For example in *Luton v. Tinsey* [1979] 1 E.G.L.R. 1, Megaw L.J. at 1K summarised the material features as follows:

> "A 'grass keep' agreement was an agreement under which the landlord gave permission—a licence, to put it in legal jargon—to the licensee to pasture his beasts on the land, and to mow the grass if he wished, and to take away the mown grass or hay. Apart from that, the licensee has no other rights in respect of the land by virtue of the licence. The other feature of a 'grass keep agreement' which is of vital importance is that it is for less than one year."

[64] See paras 18.21–18.22 below.

[65] [1957] 2 Q.B. 205.

[66] *Rutherford v. Maurer* [1962] 1 Q.B. 16.

[67] One year is, of course, less than from year to year and is thus caught by the main provision on section 2(2): *Bernays v. Prosser* [1963] 2 Q.B. 592.

[68] *Short Bros. (Plant) Ltd v. Edwards* (1978) 249 E.G. 539. "Several years" was held to mean at least three. The individual six monthly agreements were regarded by the Court as a sham.

[69] *Stone v. Whitcombe* (1980) 257 E.G. 929. The rights outside the grazing season could not have been exclusive rights of occupation, as these would have attracted section 2(2). Perhaps they were non-exclusive rights to go on the land, as is suggested at the end of Waller L.J.'s judgment, to stop others from using or doing things on the land.

held that, although the expressed duration of an agreement was for a year certain, the licence to occupy under the agreement was made in contemplation only of its use for grazing and mowing during the grazing season. The difficulty here is to know what kind of rights were conferred on the grazier by the agreement during the part of the year other than the grazing season. The agreement in this case, although it scraped through the test, is not one to be recommended. If a person so conducts himself that he must be taken to be entering into a grazing agreement for a specified period, he will be assumed to have contemplated such an agreement even if in fact he did not.[70] Although the "contemplation" is to be gathered essentially from the terms of the agreement, it may sometimes be permissible to consider extrinsic evidence.[71]

Meaning of "some specified period of a year" for the purposes of section 2(3)(a)   9.9

"Specified period of the year" means merely "specified part of the year" and any part less than a full year may be specified, even 364 days.[72] The period need have no agricultural significance.[73] The word "only" in the paragraph refers both to the period and the use.[74] As already mentioned, a letting for a full year is the creation of an interest less than from year to year and falls within section 2(2)(a).[75] A series of grazing or mowing agreements, each for a period of less than a year, may be within this provision as long as there is nothing to indicate that the real intention was to grant an enduring interest of a year or more.[76] Anything which would create a power to extend an interest beyond a specified part of the year, such as an option to renew, would risk taking the interest out of the paragraph.[77]

As to specification of the period, it must be clear what period is intended by the parties, but it is not essential that actual dates should be mentioned. Such phrases as the "grazing season", "the summer grasskeeping", even (in Scotland) "the growing season" have been accepted.[78]

---

[70] *Chaloner v. Bower* (1983) 269 E.G. 725, applying the objective view of consensus expressed in the classic statement by Blackburn J. in *Smith v. Hughes* (1871) L.R. 6 Q.B. 597 at 607.

[71] See *Scene Estate Ltd v. Amos* [1957] 2 Q.B. 205 at 213 (*per* Parker L.J.) and see para. 9.15 below.

[72] *Reid v. Dawson* [1955] 1 Q.B. 214; *Scene Estate Ltd v. Amos* [1957] 2 Q.B. 205.

[73] *Reid v. Dawson*, above.

[74] *Scene Estate Ltd v. Amos*, (above). Thus the grazing must not be incidental, but must be the predominant use: *cf. Sykes v. Secretary of State for the Environment* (1981) 257 E.G. 821.

[75] *Bernays v. Prosser* [1963] 2 Q.B. 592; *Lampard v. Barker* (1984) 272 E.G. 783.

[76] *Scene Estate Ltd v. Amos* [1957] 2 Q.B. 205.

[77] See (1955) 99 S.J. 357—too risky to rely on this. But words of mere reassurance as to probability of continued occupation should not be construed as having contractual force: *South West Water Authority v. Palmer* (1983) 268 E.G. 357, CA.

[78] See *Goldsack v. Shore* [1950] 1 K.B. 708 at 712–713; *Mackenzie v. Laird* 1959 S.C. 266 and the English County Court case of *Butterfield v. Burniston* (1961) 180 E.G. 597; *Luton v. Tinsey* (1978) 249 E.G. 239; *Stone v. Whitcombe* (1980) 257 E.G. 929; *Chaloner v. Bower* (1983) 269 E.G. 725; *Boyce v. Rendells* (1983) 268 E.G. 268; *Gairneybridge Farm Ltd. and King* 1974 S.L.T. (Land Ct.) 8; *Watts v. Yeend* [1987] 1 W.L.R. 323; [1987] 1 E.G.L.R. 4.

9.10 Use of land within section 2(3)(a) for grazing or mowing

The exclusion states clearly that the use of the land is only for grazing or mowing. It must first of all be noted that the exclusion does not cover the seasonal use of land for some other kind of specialised agricultural activity, even if it could be carried out during part of the year. However, purely ancillary or subsidiary activities, such as maintaining fences or drains, cutting weeds, or providing shelter for the grazing cattle, would not prevent the land from being used "only" for grazing. An example would be the use of outbuildings for the stabling of ponies grazing on the land.[79] In *Lory v. London Borough of Brent*[80] a grazing agreement for 364 days required the farmer "to keep the said land as grassland only and not to plough the same except in the interests of good husbandry on a crop rotation basis". The farmer stayed in occupation after the 364 days and in fact ploughed and harrowed the land for three successive years and laid it down each year to a cereal crop. It was held that the ploughing and crop rotation, although they might be regarded as subsidiary to the use of the land for grazing, could not be regarded as subsidiary to use for a period of less than a year; they were directed to improvement over a longer period. It is clear from *Boyce v. Rendells*[81] that acts such as ploughing or sowing during the continuance of a grazing agreement are not *ipso facto* fatal to the application of the exception, but their occurrence is somewhat dangerous from the point of view of the grantor, as they may provide some evidence from which a fully protected agricultural tenancy may be inferred. It would be safer not to include ploughed land in the grazing agreement and not to allow the grazier to plough any part of the land.

9.11 Break between successive specified periods for the purposes of section 2(3)(a)

It is a counsel of perfection that there should be a break between successive periods of, say, 364 days to avoid the risk of creating a tenancy form year to year, and indeed some agreements have provided for stock to be removed from the land and possession give up at the end of a period. The Courts do not appear, however, to take a strict view on this point. In *Scene Estate Ltd v. Amos*[82] the successive three months agreements spread over several years and, although it appears that each agreement contained a requirement that at the end of the period "all stock shall be removed from the said land, and possession of the land given up",[83] there is no indication that this was in fact done.[84]

---

[79] *Avon County Council v. Clothier* (1977) 242 E.G. 1048. The grazing can be of non-agricultural animals, *e.g.* horses or ponies kept for recreational riding: *Rutherford v. Maurer* [1962] 1 Q.B. 16; *McClinton v. McFall* (1974) 232 E.G. 707. But the land must be used only for such grazing: *cf. Sykes v. Secretary of State for the Environment* (1981) 257 E.G. 821 (a planning case, where "substantial" or "predominant" use for grazing was sufficient, which is not as strong as "only").

[80] [1971] 1 All E.R. 1042.

[81] (1983) 268 E.G. 268.

[82] [1957] 2 Q.B. 205.

[83] *ibid.*, at 209.

[84] Consider also *Cox v. Hurst* (1976) 239 E.G. 123; *Luton v. Tinsey* (1978) 249 E.G. 239; in *South West Water Authority v. Palmer* [1983] 2 E.G.L.R. 5, CA, a first instance judge

Grazing agreement following tenancy from year to year: effect 9.12

It is clear from the Rent Act case of *Foster v. Robinson*[85] that it is possible for a protected tenancy to be surrendered by operation of law in a case where the tenant is granted a licence. The same result occurs where the tenant co-operates in the substitution of his tenancy with a licence granted in favour of another person.[86] Despite the fact that a protected interest is being replaced by an unprotected one the Court must apply the ordinary principles as to surrender.[87] The surrender must, of course, be unequivocal and genuine.[88] Thus an agricultural tenancy from year to year may be surrendered by operation of law where the tenant accepts the grant of a grazing licence. Clearly such a transaction needs to be carefully examined.[89]

Exemption from conversion by section 2: grantor with interest less than a tenancy from year to year: section 2(3)(b) 9.13

Where a letting or a licence to occupy land is granted by a person whose interest in the land is less than a tenancy from year to year and has not taken effect as such a tenancy by virtue of section 2, conversion under section 2 does not take place of the sub-interest.[90] Presumably the general dearth of litigation over this provision reflects the fact that it is relatively easy to identify grantors within the terms of section 2(3)(b).[91] It is submitted that section 2(3)(b) also prevents the conversion of any interest granted by a beneficiary, not being a person vested with statutory leasing powers.[92]

---

was criticised for attaching importance to a failure to break continuity of occupation because this overlooked *Scene Estate Limited v. Amos* (above) and *Reid v. Dawson* [1955] 1 Q.B. 214 (see Oliver L.J. at 11L-M); *Epsom and Ewell Borough Council v. Bell (C.) (Tadworth) Ltd* (1982) 266 E.G. 808.

[85] [1951] 1 K.B. 149, and its subsequent application: see *Bungalows (Maidenhead) v. Mason* [1954] 1 W.L.R. 769 and *Scrimgeour v. Waller* (1980) 257 E.G. 61, all three cases in the Court of Appeal.

[86] See, also in the context of the Rent Acts, *Collins v. Claughton* [1959] 1 W.L.R. 145 where the husband, who was a statutory tenant, agreed with the landlord that his wife should become the new tenant instead of himself. When his wife terminated the tenancy the husband thereafter had no right to remain on the property as against the landlord.

[87] *ibid.*, at 159.

[88] See *Short Bros (Plant) Ltd v. Edwards* (1978) 249 E.G. 539.

[89] In a County Court case, *Somerset County Council v. Pearse* [1977] C.L.Y. 53, CC, the judge refused to infer the surrender of an old tenancy from year to year which had been succeeded by 15 grazing licences, holding that definite proof was needed to show that a major asset like a protected agricultural tenancy had been surrendered and that a mere implication would not suffice. There were special features in this case. If the judge intended to go so far as to say that an express instrument of surrender was essential he would have been in error.

[90] s. 2(3)(b).

[91] As to which see generally paras 9.2–9.12 above.

[92] For these purposes it is unlikely that there is any distinction to be drawn between beneficiaries entitled to occupy under s. 12 of the Trusts of Land and Appointment of

9.14 Exclusion from section 2: agreements made before March 1, 1948: Schedule 12, paragraph 1

Agreements made before the March 1, 1948 are entirely outside the scope of section 2 of the 1986 Act.[93]

9.15 Problems in construing agreements

The correct application of sections 2–5 of the Act requires great care to be taken in construing any agreement between the parties. Some guidance on the problems which can be generated is to be found not only in the general law but also specifically in the case law arising in the context of section 2. The first question will always be as to whether any written agreement genuinely represents the agreement between the parties or whether a particular written agreement is a "sham".[94] Where the oral agreement is deliberately "papered up" with misleading documentation, no regard will be had to that documentation[95]: but any underlying oral agreement is dealt with in the normal way, including for the purposes of surrender.[96] Where the doctrine of "sham" is not an issue the Court will confine itself to examining the terms of any agreement and concentrate on the issue of construction.[97] Where a written agreement is ambiguous it is permissible to look at the surrounding circumstances to see whether one can deduce from them more clearly what the agreement actually was.[98] In the absence of ambiguity and any question of sham the Court will confine itself to the terms of the agreement whatever the parties may, subjectively, have intended.[99] In contractual terms what a party intends is judged

---

Trustees Act 1996 (set out at para. 14.62 below) and any other beneficiary.
[93] Sched. 12, para. 1.
[94] See Diplock L.J. in *Snook v. London and West Riding Investments* [1967] 2 Q.B. 786:

"As regards the contention of the plaintiff that the transactions between himself, Auto Finance and the defendants were a 'sham', it is, I think, necessary to consider what, if any, legal concept is involved in the use of this popular and pejorative word. I appreciate that, if it has any meaning in law, it means acts done or documents executed by the parties to the 'sham' which are intended by them to give to third parties or the Court the appearance of creating between the parties legal rights and obligations different from the actual legal rights and obligations (if any) which the parties intend to create. But one thing, I think, is clear in legal principle, morality and the authorities ... for Acts or documents to be a 'sham', with whatever legal consequences follow from this, all the parties thereto must have a common intention that the Acts or documents are not to create the legal rights and obligations which they give the appearance of creating. No unexpressed intentions of a 'shammer' affect the rights of the party whom he deceived ...".

[95] See *Short Bros (Plant) Limited v. Edwards* [1979] 1 E.G.L.R. 5.
[96] But of course the person surrendering in the context of surrender and re-grant must reasonably be able to conclude that this will be the effect of the new agreement: see *Short Bros (Plant) Limited v. Edwards* (above) at 9A.
[97] "It follows, therefore, that the first task, in my judgment, the Court has to perform is to construe these three agreements ... those circumstances, unless there was evidence that the agreements were shams, there is no reason why the Court should look beyond those agreements": Lawton L.J. in *Boyce v. Rendells* [1983] 2 E.G.L.R. 146 at 148L-M.
[98] See *Evans v. Tompkins* [1993] 2 E.G.L.R. 6 at 8D but, of course, conduct will not override the clear terms of a written agreement.
[99] "If the agreement is express on the subject, then I do not think that one is entitled to look

objectively.¹ In so far as, judged objectively, the parties never reached a consensus there is no agreement at all and accordingly nothing capable of conversion by section 2 into a tenancy.² The operation of section 2 does not exclude the parties from relying, where appropriate, on the doctrine of rectification even in circumstances where, if a document was re-written, the resulting agreement would not any longer be a protected tenancy.³ Therefore, in the light of the above, assertions by occupiers of agricultural land that they have occupied continuously and paid for their occupation must be scrutinised very carefully. Sometimes what they have been doing is in fact completely irrelevant to the legal position; sometimes it is admissible. Sometimes, if admissible, it is inconclusive in assisting as to the terms of the agreement, that is to say what the rights of the parties were on an objective determination of intention. After all, a person's activities may indicate the terms of a tenancy but equally may be evidence of waiver of rights by the other party.

A great deal of the extensive litigation to which section 2 has given rise has been due to vague and loose informal arrangements which have turned out to mean something quite different from what the parties, or one of them, intended.⁴ The lesson is to have clear written agreements, drafted in the light of the case law.

Jurisdiction of Court and Arbitrator: section 2(4)   9.16

Section 2(4) states that any dispute arising as to the operation of section 2 shall be referred to arbitration under the Act. Arbitration under section 2(4) is curiously under-used and recourse to the court is quite normal. On the face of it there is a mandatory reference to arbitration, and any arbitration will be governed by the terms of section 84 and Schedule 11.⁵ Certainly there are some issues which may conveniently be dealt with by the courts since they will be issues of law not caught in the arbitration provision such as determination as to whether or not section 2

---

beyond it unless it is for the purpose of showing that the agreement is a complete sham. In other words, in the case of a genuine agreement which expressly says that the lease is for grazing or mowing only, and expressly says that the period is a period of less than a year, there is no right, in my view, to look beyond the agreement itself": Parker L.J. in *Scene Estate Limited v. Amos* [1967] 2 Q.B. 205 at 213.

¹ "If, whatever a man's real intention may be, he so conducts himself that a reasonable man would believe that he was assenting to the terms proposed by the other party, and that other party upon that belief enters into the contract with him, the man thus conducting himself would be equally bound as if he had intended to agree to the other party's terms": *Smith v. Hughes* [1871] L.R. 6 Q.B. 597, Blackburn J. at 607 quoted and applied in *Chaloner v. Bower* [1984] 1 E.G.L.R. 4 at 6A-B.

² *Obiter dicta* of Eveleigh L.J. in *Chaloner v. Bower* (above) at 6F where in the alternative he was prepared to endorse the approach of the first instance Judge to that effect.

³ See *Ashdale Land and Property Co Ltd v. Manners* [1992] 2 E.G.L.R. 5, Maddocks J. sitting as a Judge of the High Court and *obiter*, Griffiths J. in *Cox v. Husk* [1976] 2 E.G.L.R. 1 at 4E.

⁴ See *Midgley v. Stott* (1977) 244 E.G. 883; *James v. Lock* (1977) 246 E.G. 395; *Luton v. Tinsey* (1978) 249 E.G. 239; *Short Bros (Plant) Ltd v. Edwards* (1978) 249 E.G. 539; *Stone v. Whitcombe* (1980) 40 P. & C.R. 296; *South West Water Authority v. Palmer* (1983) 268 E.G. 357, CA; *Chaloner v. Bower* (1983) 269 E.G. 725; *Lampard v. Barker* (1984) 272 E.G. 783; *Collier v. Hollinshead* (1984) 272 E.G. 941; *Watts v. Yeend* [1987] 1 W.L.R. 323; [1987] 1 E.G.L.R. 4.

⁵ Including the case stated procedure. See generally paras 16.61–16.65.

operates a conversion at all.[6] By contrast there may well be situations where there is a need to modify the agreement and this must be dealt with by arbitration.[7] In terms of arbitration, the difference between an arbitrator appointed under section 2(4) and section 6[8] is that an arbitrator acting under section 2(4) is able to determine the tenancy terms on a wider basis. He is not limited to the matters in Schedule 1 but is required to modify all contractual terms where necessary. The onus of proof is on the landlord or licensor to show that subsection (3) of section 2 applies so as to exclude the protection given by the section.[9] In most cases the issue as to the application of the subsection will be found when the occupier defends proceedings by the owner for possession, but in *Lory v. London Borough of Brent*[10] the form of legal proceedings was an action by the plaintiff occupier in the Chancery Division for a declaration as to his rights.

9.17 Transactions not caught by section 2(1): general

Section 2(1) does not cover land not let for use as "agricultural land" within the meaning of the Act, *e.g.* an allotment garden, or a licence which is not a licence to occupy the land for use as agricultural land.[11] It does not cover land which would not be an "agricultural holding" even if the tenancy were converted into a yearly tenancy, *e.g.* tied holdings.[12] Arrangements not intended by the parties to create legal rights at all are obviously not covered[13] and the section cannot apply to a mortgagor who has attorned tenant, since the substance there is to provide security for a loan, not to create a relationship of agricultural landlord and tenant.[14]

9.18 Transactions not caught by section 2(1): relationship to Landlord and Tenant Act 1954

The relationship between the Agricultural Holdings Act 1986 and the Landlord and Tenant Act 1954 is established by section 43 of the latter. If a tenancy falls within the 1986 Act, the 1954 Act does not apply. The risk (from the landlord's point of view) that tenancies which, by virtue of section 2, did not take effect as tenancies of agricultural holdings might be business tenancies which would qualify for security of tenure under Part II of the Landlord and Tenant Act 1954

---

[6] See *Goldsack v. Shore* [1950] 1 K.B. 708.
[7] For example determination of the term date of a yearly tenancy in the circumstances described by the last part of paragraph 9.4 above. The county court decision in *Powell v. Stevens* (1951) 101 L.J. 109 (that disputes as to the terms of a tenancy are referable to arbitration) is only briefly reported and there is no higher authority on the point. For a form of demand for arbitration see Form 1 in Part V of this work.
[8] As to s. 6, see paras 10.2–10.7.
[9] See *Scene Estate Ltd v. Amos* [1957] 2 Q.B. 205, CA at 212; *Lory v. London Borough of Brent* [1971] 1 All E.R. 1042; *Midgley v. Stott* (1977) 244 E.G. 883; *James v. Lock* (1977) 246 E.G. 395; *Watts v. Yeend* [1987] 1 W.L.R. 323; (1986) 281 E.G. 912.
[10] See above.
[11] See 1947 Act, s. 109(1), (2); *cf. Harrison-Broadley v. Smith* [1964] 1 W.L.R. 456.
[12] See s. 1(1). But parties cannot take an interest out of s. 2(1) by disguising its nature: *Keen v. Holland* [1984] 1 W.L.R. 251 at 259.
[13] *Holder v. Holder* [1966] 2 All E.R. 116 at 125 (not in [1968] Ch.353).
[14] *Steyning and Littlehampton Building Society v. Wilson* [1951] Ch. 1018: and to the same effect *Walters v. Roberts* (1980) 41 P. & C.R. 210 dealing with the situation of vendor and purchaser.

was removed by an amendment to section 43(1)(a) of the latter by the Agriculture Act 1958, section 8 and paragraph 29 of Schedule 1.[15]

Mandatory nature of conversion 9.19

It is not possible to contract out of security of tenure since this is fundamental to the nature of protection available to tenancies within the Agricultural Holdings Act 1986. This issue is discussed elsewhere.[16] It is suggested that a corollary of this is that the conversion procedure is intended necessarily to operate on the reality of transactions. Thus it is not possible by estoppel to avoid the impact of conversion.[17] Similarly there is no scope for the operation of other procedural or evidential doctrines the effect of which would be to estop a tenant either in or out of the protection of the 1986 Act.[18]

Gladstone v. Bower agreements 9.20

The apparent anomaly of *Gladstone v. Bower*[19] tenancies has been known since 1964, but Parliament has chosen to do nothing about them despite manifold legislative opportunities. These are tenancies, for terms of more than one year but less than two years, which are not within either section 2 or section 3 of the 1986 Act. Are they tenancies of agricultural holdings at all? The alternative possibilities were that such tenancies are tenancies of agricultural holdings which, although not attracting security of tenure, would enable the tenant to claim compensation for improvements and tenant-right (if appropriate) and the landlord to claim compensation for dilapidations, or that they are not tenancies of agricultural holdings at all, but are in all probability within Part II of the Landlord and Tenant Act 1954. Arguments had been advanced for each of these views.[20] The controversy has now been ended by the Court of Appeal in *EWP Limited v. Moore*[21] in which it was held that a tenancy of agricultural land for a term of more than one year but less than two years created a tenancy of an agricultural holding within the 1986 Act but without having available to it the security of tenure

---

[15] Section 43(1)(a) of the 1954 Act has been further amended by the substitution of a reference to the 1986 Act for the reference to the 1948 Act: see 1986 Act, Sched. 14, para. 21.

[16] See para. 12.3.

[17] This possibility was rejected by the Court of Appeal in *Keen v. Holland* [1984] 1 E.G.L.R. 9. At 12E Oliver L.J., delivering the judgment of the Court, held: "Once there is in fact an actual tenancy to which the Act applies, the protection of the Act follows and we do not see how, consistently with *Johnson v. Moreton*, the parties can effectively oust the protective provisions of the Act by agreeing that they shall be treated as inapplicable. If an express agreement to this effect would be avoided, as it plainly would, then it seems to us to follow that the statutory inability to contract out cannot be avoided by appealing to an estoppel."

[18] For example in *Padbury v. York* [1990] 2 E.G.L.R. 3 at 6F a submission was rejected in the High Court for that reason. An attempt was made in effect to raise an estoppel by relying on the principle that the Court will not permit a party to advance a contention of fact which results in that party admitting that he has been guilty of some breach of the law or unconscionable dealing, to which, as a matter of public policy, the Court will not turn a blind eye.

[19] [1960] 1 Q.B. 170 (Diplock J.); [1960] 2 Q.B. 384, CA.

[20] See the summary on pp. 21–22 of the 13th edition of this work.

[21] [1991] 2 E.G.L.R. 4.

provisions. It was necessary to the decision to look at the more general question as to what a "term of years" involved where less than two full years had been granted: in general conveyancing the phrase could include a term for any fixed period, including one of less than a year and it was held that the draftsman of the Act should not be taken as intending that the statute should be wholly inapplicable to fixed terms of between one and two years. The result, therefore, is that the compensation provisions available in respect of agricultural tenancies[22] are available except in so far as a disturbance compensation claim presupposes that a notice to quit has been served in order to bring the tenancy to an end.[23]

Once the fixed period, therefore, of the *Gladstone v. Bower* agreement has come to an end no notice to quit is required in order to secure possession and there is no security of tenure available either under the 1986 Act or the Landlord and Tenant Act 1954.[24] Backdated agreements should be checked to ensure that an actual term of the requisite length was created.[25]

9.21 Termination of tenancies for two years or more: scope of section 3

Section 3 applies to fixed terms of two years or more. A term of less than a year and a term for a year certain fall within section 2 of the Act, subject to the provisions already discussed. A term for more than a year but less than two years expires by effluxion of time.[26] Section 3 does not apply in the case of a long lease with an option to break at intervals: these break dates are not the "term date", although a notice exercising the option is a notice to quit[27] which will attract section 25 and section 26(1) as well as section 60 of the 1986 Act. Section 3 does not prevent the forfeiture of the term in a suitable case.[28] It must also be remembered that the common law rule that a term of years cannot be limited to commence before the date of grant applies.[29]

9.22 Termination of tenancies for two years or more: operation of section 3

Section 3, which derives its origin from the Agriculture Act 1920,[30] lays down the general rule that a tenancy for a term of two years or more is not to terminate automatically by effluxion of time on the date fixed for the expiry of the term, but will continue as a tenancy from year to year (on the terms of the original tenancy so far as applicable) unless, not less than one year nor more than two years before the

---

[22] See generally Chapter 13.
[23] It follows, therefore, that claims for disturbance compensation cannot be made.
[24] See s. 43 of the 1954 Act.
[25] See para. 9.3 above.
[26] *Gladstone v. Bower* [1960] 2 Q.B. 384.
[27] *Edell v. Dulieu* [1923] 2 K.B. 247, CA; [1924] A.C. 38, HL.
[28] *Parry v. Million Pigs Ltd.* (1980) 260 E.G. 281.
[29] *Roberts v. Church Commissioners for England* [1972] 1 Q.B. 278, CA: *Bradshaw v. Pawley* [1980] 1 W.L.R. 10; contrast *Keen v. Holland* (1983) 269 E.G. 1043. But, as is clear from *Bradshaw v. Pawley*, a lease may create obligations in respect of a period prior to execution, *e.g.* payment of rent from an anterior date. These "backdating" cases are explained in *Pahl v. Trevor* [1992] 1 E.G.L.R. 22.
[30] Agriculture Act 1920, s. 13. Section 3 of the 1986 Act does not apply to a tenancy granted or agreed to be granted before January 1, 1921, the date when the 1920 Act came into force: see Sched. 12, para. 1 of the 1986 Act.

term date,[31] a written notice has been given by either party to the other of his intention to terminate the tenancy.[32] This general rule is, however, subject to the provisions of section 4 as to the death of the tenant before the term date and the provisions of section 5 as to a form of officially approved contracting out. It is expressly declared that the notice to terminate mentioned above is to be deemed for the purposes of the 1986 Act to be a notice to quit.[33] This ensures that the tenant will gain the normal entitlement of an annual tenant to compensation for disturbance. A lease for a life or lives, converted into a determinable term of 90 years by section 149(6) of the Law of Property Act 1925, would be a bizarre intruder into the world of agricultural tenures, but in case it happens Parliament has carefully excluded such an interest from the present section 3.[34]

Exclusion from section 3: agreements made before January 1, 1921: Schedule 12, paragraph 2 9.23

In relation to any tenancy granted or agreed to be granted before January 1, 1921 section 3 of the 1986 Act is inapplicable.[35] This provision is now almost certainly spent.

Restricted ability to contract out of section 3: section 5 9.24

There is a specific prohibition of contracting out of section 3 except as permitted by section 5.[36]

Tenant's death before term date: section 4 9.25

Section 4, a provision introduced in 1984[37] and applicable only to tenancies granted on or after September 12, 1984, provides that one class of tenancies for fixed terms of two years or more shall not continue as mentioned in section 3 but shall determine by effluxion of time without attracting security of tenure. This applies (except as mentioned in section 4(1)(c)) where the tenant (or the survivor of joint tenants) dies before the term date.[38] It must be noted that the tenant in this context means the person (or the survivor of the persons) to whom the tenancy was granted, *i.e.* the original tenant or joint tenants to whom the actual grant was made.[39] The date of termination is discussed below.[40] In the cases identified by

---

[31] Defined in s. 3(4) as the date fixed for the expiry of the term.
[32] s. 3(1).
[33] s. 3(2).
[34] s. 3(3). Section 149(6) of the 1925 Act actually covers a lease at a rent or fine "for life or lives or for any term of years determinable with life or lives or on the marriage of the lessee". For a non-agricultural case, see **Bass Holdings Ltd v. Lewis** [1986] 2 E.G.L.R. 40.
[35] Sched. 12, para. 2.
[36] s. 5(1). One of the few cases where a specific prohibition of contracting out is enacted. Other cases are ss 15(1), 25(1) and 78(1). But sections which contain no express prohibition of contracting out may nevertheless be subject to an implied prohibition on grounds of public policy: see **Johnson v. Moreton** [1980] A.C. 37.
[37] 1984 Act, Sched. 3, para. 2.
[38] *i.e.* before the date fixed for the expiry of the term: s. 4(4) and s. 3(4).
[39] See wording of s. 4(1)(a) and (b); *cf.* the phrase in the original s. 24(2)(g) of the 1948 Act, as interpreted in **Clarke v. Hall** [1961] 2 Q.B. 331.
[40] See para. 9.26.

paragraph 9.26(b) below, the tenancy "shall terminate" on the term date or its first anniversary, as the case may be. No security of tenure is attracted, but compensation for any improvements or tenant-right, if appropriate, will be available. Also, by a specific provision,[41] compensation for disturbance, basic and additional, is safeguarded. Unless the tenancy has been assigned, it will vest according to normal procedure in the tenant's personal representatives during the interval between the tenant's death and the term date.

9.26 Date of termination: section 4

The date of termination will either be the term date or the first anniversary of the term date. The position is as follows:

(a) if the tenant had before his death given notice under section 3(1) to terminate the tenancy, *i.e.* a notice given not less than one year nor more than two years before the term date, the tenancy will continue after the term date from year to year[42]; but

(b) if no such notice has been given, then,

(i) if the death takes place one year or more before the term date, the tenancy will terminate on the term date[43];

(ii) if the death takes place less than a year before the term date, the tenancy will terminate on the first anniversary of the term date.[44] During this 12 months' extension the other terms of the tenancy will continue to apply.[45]

9.27 Position of assignees: operation of section 4

It is conceivable that the original grantee of the fixed term may assign his interest before his death to a third person. The position of such an assignee needs a little consideration. Assuming that the original tenant dies before the term date, it seems clear that as a result of his death the provisions of section 4(2) will come into operation, so that the tenancy will terminate on the term date or its first anniversary without attracting any security of tenure. In these circumstances the assignee's interest will altogether cease on the term date; he will be unable to invoke the continuation rights of section 3. If, on the other hand, the original tenant, having assigned his interest, survives the term date, the assignee will be able to rely on section 3 and enjoy the continuation rights thereby given.

---

[41] s. 4(3).
[42] s. 4(1)(c). The normal rule under section 3, attracting security of tenure.
[43] s. 4(2)(a).
[44] s. 4(2)(b).
[45] *ibid.*, "so far as applicable".

Approved contracting out of section 3: section 5   9.28

Although as a general rule private arrangements to contract out of section 3 are forbidden,[46] an exception is made for a procedure to contract out with the express approval of the Minister.[47] The procedure applies to the grant of a tenancy of not less than two and not more than five years. The main consequence, if the procedure is carried out, is that the term will in fact expire on the expiry date. There will be no continuation of the tenancy and there will be no compensation for disturbance,[48] but there is nothing to exclude compensation for improvements or tenant-right except the practical limitation of the shortness of the term. If the tenant dies during the currency of the term the tenancy will vest in the normal way in his personal representatives.

Procedural requirements in section 5(2)   9.29

There is a series of cumulative requirements as to procedure set out in section 5(2). They are:

(a) Before the grant of the tenancy the persons who will be the landlord and tenant must agree that section 3 shall not apply to the tenancy.[49]

(b) Before the grant those persons must make a joint application in writing to the Minister for his approval of that agreement.[50]

(c) Before the grant the Minister must notify the parties of his approval of the agreement.[51]

Where the statute requires something to be done before the tenancy is granted, it is a question of fact as to what order the events took.[52] Where the statute stipulates the making of a joint application, such an application may be made by a suitably instructed agent.[53] The key issue is to ensure that the parties do indeed have the approval of the Minister to the proposed agreement. It is submitted that the agreement for these purposes means an agreement the essential features of which are that it relates to agricultural land and will be for a fixed term of not less than two and more than five years. In other words, the concern is not with the full terms of the individual agreement, since these features are inessential for the purposes of section 5.[54]

---

[46] s. 5(1).
[47] ss 5(2) and (3). For "the Minister", see s. 96(1) (in relation to England, the Minister of Agriculture, Fisheries and Food; in relation to Wales, the Secretary of State).
[48] It will be noted that s. 5 does not contain anything corresponding to s. 4(3).
[49] s. 5(2)(a).
[50] s. 5(2)(b).
[51] s. 5(2)(c). Presumably this means that the notification must be received by the parties before the grant of the tenancy. Contrast *Bedfordshire County Council v. Clarke* (1974) 230 E.G. 1587.
[52] See *Bedding v. McCarthy* (1994) 41 E.G. 151.
[53] There appears to be reason of principle why the parties should have to instruct separate agents for this purpose.
[54] See *Epsom and Ewell Borough Council v. C. Bell (Tadworth) Limited* [1983] 1 E.G.L.R. 7 where in relation to a ministerial approval for the grant of a tenancy pursuant to s. 2 of the 1948 Act, His Honour Judge Rubin sitting as a Judge of the Chancery

9.30 Construing the Minister's approval

The Minister's approval is not a statute and it must be construed on an objective basis but so as to ascertain what the Minister intended. This simple statement is, it is submitted, the correct reconciliation of the two reported cases which deal with a construction of the Minister's approval which though ostensibly issued in identical terms was construed differently in each case. In *Pahl v. Trevor*[55] the Court of Appeal construed the word "period" in an approval as not meaning "term". It is important to note that in that case it was expressly stated that there was no reason why the Minister should have wished to grant a consent to a tenancy which would commence on a precise date.[56] In *Jones v. Owen*[57] the High Court[58] applied *Pahl v. Trevor* but concluded that the relevant approval was intended to establish a period within which the relevant agreement could be operative rather than requiring a precise commencement date. What one may reasonably deduce from this is that Courts are not unduly sympathetic to tenants obtaining tenancies apparently under section 5 and thereafter attempting to rely on technicalities so as to bring themselves within the scope of section 3. In so far as relevant to the issue of construction it should be noted that approvals are granted in exercise of the policy contained in the statement of July 19, 1984.[59]

9.31 Requirement of writing: section 5(3)

There are strict requirements in relation to writing which, it is submitted, cannot be waived in that there would seem to be a public policy interest in establishing in written form any application of the contracting out provisions in section 5. The specific requirements are:

(a) The contract of tenancy must be in writing.[60]

(b) The contract itself, or a statement endorsed on it, must indicate, in whatever terms, that section 3 does not apply to the tenancy.[61]

It may be, on the analogy of a case under section 38(4) of the 1954 Act,[62] that a lack of formality in the execution of the lease could be cured by the application of

---

Division held at 9D: "... I agree with the learned Judge when he decided that the minister was not concerned with the particular terms of the agreement to be entered into ... There is nothing there which requires the minister to approve of the terms of the agreement which, *ex hypothesi*, had not then been entered into and, indeed, may not by then have been finally settled. That seems to me, again, to be consistent with the general policy of the Act, and in particular this section which was dealing with security of tenure in respect of particular land, and the minister was concerned with that aspect of the matter only".

[55] [1992] 1 E.G.L.R. 22.
[56] Contrast the dissent by Dillon L.J.
[57] (1997) 32 E.G. 85.
[58] His Honour Judge Weeks Q.C. sitting in the High Court.
[59] See para. 9.33 below.
[60] s. 5(3).
[61] *ibid.*
[62] *Tottenham Hotspur Football & Athletic Co. Ltd v. Princegrove Publishers Ltd* [1974] 1 W.L.R. 113.

the doctrine of ***Walsh v. Lonsdale***,[63] so that section 3 would be effectively excluded. No forms are prescribed for any part of the procedure.

Effect of failure to satisfy conditions in section 5: section 5(1) 9.32

Any failure to comply with any of the necessary conditions set out in section 5(2) or (3) will result in section 3 of the Act applying to the relevant agreement. In other words, full security of tenure will attach to the tenancy.

Exercise of Minister's discretion under sections 2 and 5: historic policy 9.33

In July 1984 a policy statement was issued by the relevant Ministers explaining the basis on which the discretion under sections 2 and 5 was to be exercised.[64] In the normal way short term interests were to be permitted (whether in the form of licences or tenancies) in the case of land over which development was pending, reorganisation and transitional arrangements, specialist cropping agreements, allotment land temporarily surplus to requirements and operational requirements on Government and other land (*e.g.* in particular land over which the Ministry of Defence have training or firing ranges). Prior to this statement being issued there were no published guidelines, but the Northfield Committee's Report contained a statement, obtained from the Ministry of Agriculture, of ministerial policy.[65]

---

[63] (1882) 21 Ch.D. 9.
[64] Reproduced in full at pp. 343–345 of the 13th edition of this work.
[65] See Report Cmnd. 7599 (July 1979), para. 245.

CHAPTER 10

PROVISIONS AFFECTING TENANCY DURING ITS CONTINUANCE

10.1 Introduction

10.2 Machinery of section 6: right to written tenancy agreement; arbitration

10.8 Provisions concerning fixed equipment: section 7

10.25 Arbitration where terms of written agreement inconsistent with model clauses: section 8

10.27 Transitional arrangements where liability in respect of fixed equipment is transferred: section 9

10.28 Construction of repairing obligations

10.29 Leasehold Property (Repairs) Act 1938 not applicable

10.30 Landlord and Tenant Act 1985, sections 11–16 applicable to sub-let dwelling-houses

10.31 Remedies generally

10.34 Right to remove fixtures: section 10

10.44 Direction to landlord to provide alter or repair fixed equipment: section 11

10.50 Right to increase rent for landlord's improvements: section 13

10.55 Variation of tenancy terms as to permanent pasture: section 14

10.59 Disposal of produce and cropping: section 15

10.68 No distress for rent due more than a year previously: section 16

10.70 Compensation to be set off against rent for purposes of distress: section 17

10.71 Restrictions on distraining third party property: section 18

10.72 Settlement of disputes as to distress: Section 19

10.74 Game damage: section 20

10.78 Extension of tenancies in lieu of claims to emblements: section 21

10.79 Rights to require records to be made: section 22

10.86 Landlord's power of entry: section 23

10.87 Restriction of landlord's contractual damages: section 24

Introduction 10.1
This chapter covers an assortment of matters, dealt with in sections 6 to 24 of the Agricultural Holdings Acts, which essentially arise during the life of the tenancy.

Rent, and more particularly a statutory rent review under section 12, is dealt with in Chapter 11 of this work. Claims arising on termination of the tenancy are covered by Chapter 13. For convenience the contents of this chapter reflect the order of the statute as follows: rights to a written tenancy agreement (section 6)[1]; the model repairing clauses and the Regulations made under section 7[2]; arbitration where the terms of a written agreement are inconsistent with the model clauses (section 8)[3]; transitional arrangements where liability for fixed equipment is transferred (section 9)[4]; tenant's right to remove fixtures and buildings (section 10)[5]; provision of fixed equipment necessary to comply with statutory requirements (section 11)[6]; variation of tenancy terms in regard to permanent pasture (section 14)[7]; disposal of produce and cropping (section 15)[8]; distress (sections 16–19)[9]; compensation for game damage (section 20)[10]; extension of tenancies in lieu of claims to emblements (section 21)[11]; right to require certain records to be made (section 22)[12]; landlord's power of entry (section 22)[13]; and restriction of landlord's remedies for breach of contract of tenancy (section 24).[14]

10.2 Right to written tenancy agreement: section 6

The object of section 6 is the promotion of written tenancy agreements for agricultural holdings. Although it is legally possible to have created an oral tenancy of a holding, and although there are throughout the country a number of oral tenancy agreements in existence granted many years ago and not yet committed to paper, it is desirable that agreements should be recorded in writing.[15]

10.3 Machinery provided by section 6: reference to arbitration

The machinery is that either party may require the tenancy to be put into writing. This procedure covers cases where there is no written agreement at all,[16] cases where there is a written agreement but it does not embody all the terms of the tenancy (including the "model clauses" incorporated by virtue of section 7[17]) and

---

[1] Paras 10.2–10.7 below.
[2] Paras 10.8.-10.24 below.
[3] Paras 10.25–10.26 below.
[4] Para. 10.27 below.
[5] Paras 10.34–10.43 below.
[6] Paras 10.44–10.54 below.
[7] Paras 10.55–10.58 below.
[8] Paras 10.59–10.67 below.
[9] Paras 10.68–10.73 below.
[10] Paras 10.74–10.77 below.
[11] Para. 10.78 below.
[12] Paras 10.79–10.85 below.
[13] Para. 10.86 below.
[14] Para. 10.87 below.
[15] It has been seen earlier in Chapter 9 that some fully protected tenancies of agricultural holdings have arisen out of informal arrangements which were never intended to create such tenancies.
[16] For an example of an oral agreement causing difficulty, see *Epps v. Ledger* (1972) 225 E.G. 1373. An agreement may consist of letters provided they set out the terms: *Grieve & Sons v. Barr* 1954 S.C. 414.
[17] The 1986 Act reverts to the expression "model clauses" used in the early days of the 1948 Act as a popular name for the terms as to the maintenance, repair and insurance of fixed

cases where the written agreement does not provide for one or more of the matters specified in Schedule 1 to the 1986 Act. The first step is for either party to request the other to enter into an agreement embodying all the terms of the tenancy and including provision for all the Schedule 1 matters. Such a request,[18] and the failure to conclude such an agreement as a result, are a condition precedent to a reference to arbitration. No time is laid down for compliance with the request, but presumably the requesting party should allow a reasonable time to elapse before setting the arbitration procedure in motion.[19] One of the most frequently encountered disputes is as to the identity of the tenant. Sometimes, for example, this arises because over a period of time the rent has been paid on an account other than that of the individual with whom discussions may have originally taken place. At any rate, where there is uncertainty as to the identity of the tenant it is suggested that a prudent course for a landlord to adopt is to address any section 6 notice to "the tenant" and to serve it upon all persons who may be the tenant; where this step is taken an explanatory open letter should accompany the section 6 notice stating that the notice is given without any admission as to the identity of the tenant. Failing agreement between the parties, the arbitrator will in due course establish the identity of the tenant as part of the matters covered by his award.

Matters within Schedule 1 10.4

Schedule 1 to the 1986 Act contains a number of basic provisions which Parliament has considered to be essential, but a well-drawn tenancy agreement will, of course, contain many more. Schedule 1, paragraph 5 prescribes that, but not how, the "incidence" of rates should be dealt with. It will also be noted that there is no specific reference in the Schedule to the incidence of liability for repairs. The obligations of both parties in this respect are contained in the "model clauses".[20]

Schedule 1, paragraph 1: The names of the parties.

This enables the arbitrator to identify specifically the parties to an agreement. Usually the difficulty will be the identity of the tenant but, occasionally, this provision will enable trustees to be identified by name, as distinct from by the description of a settlement.

Schedule 1, paragraph 2: Particulars of the holding.

This authorises an exact description to be made where necessary by reference to plans of the land comprised within the holding.

---

equipment incorporated in contracts of tenancy by virtue now of section 7 of the 1986 Act and the Agriculture (Maintenance, Repair and Insurance of Fixed Equipment) Regulations 1973 (S.I. 1973 No. 1473).

[18] It is not laid down as necessary, but it is desirable, that such a request should be made in writing. For a form see Part V Form 2.

[19] The request for arbitration should be made to the other party (see Part V, Form 3). Schedule 11 governs the arbitration itself and in particular contains provision for appointment of the arbitrator.

[20] *i.e.* in the Agriculture (Maintenance, Repair and Insurance of Fixed Equipment) Regulations 1973 (S.I. 1973 No. 1473). In its original form in the 1948 Act, Schedule 1 did include a reference to the incidence of liability for repairs and a covenant by the landlord to reinstate and insure buildings, both of which are covered by the above

Schedule 1, paragraph 3: The term.

This enables the arbitrator to identify the duration and commencement of the term. This is of particular importance in circumstances where there is dispute as to the commencement day and consequently difficulty in identifying the term date for the purposes of a notice to quit.

Schedule 1, paragraph 4: The rent and the dates on which it is payable.

This enables the arbitrator to identify the current rent. It is not a provision authorising a rent review to take place. However it should be noted that section 6(3) allows the arbitrator, if he feels it equitable, to vary the rent in limited circumstances.

Schedule 1, paragraph 5: Rates including drainage rates.

This is a provision which has never been changed to reflect the fortunes of changes to the general rating system.

Schedule 1, paragraph 6: Covenant by the tenants in the event of destruction by fire of harvested crops grown on the holding for consumption on it to return to the holding the full equivalent manurial value of the crops destroyed, in so far as the return of that value is required for fulfilment of the tenant's responsibilities to farm in accordance with the rules of good husbandry.

As a result of the decision in *Re: Hull and Meux (Lady)*,[21] it became a common practice to require a tenant to covenant to insure his hay and straw against fire and to replace the manurial value of any hay or straw destroyed by fire. In that case the tenant had covenanted to stack and consume on the holding all hay and straw produced thereon, and to carry out and spread on the fields the manure arising therefrom. Some stacks were accidentally destroyed by fire during the tenancy and it was held that the landlord was not entitled to compensation for the resulting loss of manurial value, the covenant applying only to things in existence and there being no breach on the tenant's part.[22]

Schedule 1, paragraph 7: A covenant by the tenant (except where the interest of the tenant is held for the purposes of a government department or where the tenant has made provision approved by the Minister in lieu of such insurance) to insure against damage by fire all deadstock on the holding and all harvested crops grown on the holding for consumption on it.

This provision is relatively limited in that the only risk insured against is fire and there is no corresponding requirement that the tenant lay out any insurance money on replacement of items lost.

---

regulations. This caused some confusion. See paragraph 10.19 below.

[21] [1905] 1 K.B. 588.

[22] See, however, Regulation 4(2) of the Agriculture (Calculation of Value for Compensation) Regulations 1978 (S.I. 1978 No. 809) which requires a deduction to be made from the tenant's compensation when hay, fodder, crops, straw, roots, manure or compost are, amongst other things, destroyed by fire.

Schedule 1, paragraph 8: A power for the landlord to re-enter on the holding in the event of the tenant not performing his obligations under the agreement.

This, again, is a very narrow provision. It does not purport to be an actual draft since any power of re-entry, in order to be valid, would have to provide for the power of re-entry to be exercisable only on sufficient notice to enable the tenant to claim any compensation on termination.[23] The power of re-entry under Schedule 1 does not extend to the bankruptcy or receivership of the tenant.[24]

Schedule 1, paragraph 9: A covenant by the tenant not to assign, sub-let or part with possession of the holding or any part of it without the landlord's consent in writing.

This important matter was for a long time lacking from Schedule 1 but was added first by section 17 of the Agriculture (Miscellaneous Provisions) Act 1976. The reader is referred on to commentary on section 6(5) of the present Act for the machinery designed to prevent an assignment from taking place pending the outcome of an arbitration under section 6.[25] There is no implication that the landlord's consent may only be withheld on reasonable grounds.

Duty of arbitrator under section 6　　　　　　　　　　　　　　　　　　　　10.5

The arbitrator is directed to specify in his award the existing terms of the tenancy subject to any agreed variations. He must then consider whether the terms so specified (including any agreed variations) cover all the matters mentioned in Schedule 1, whether in a manner consistent or inconsistent with the Schedule. The arbitrator is not empowered to override an inconsistent term.[26] If the arbitrator finds that any of the matters itemised in the Schedule is not covered in that sense by the existing agreement, he should then ascertain whether the parties can agree on terms to fill the gaps. If so, he must specify the agreed material. If not, he must[27] fill the gaps himself by including in his award such provisions in regard to these matters as are reasonable and just. Further, if the parties agree, the arbitrator may include in his award matters entirely outside the Schedule provided that they "relate" to the tenancy.[28] He has, however, no power to go outside his remit under section 6 and rewrite the parties' contract.

Effect of award under section 6　　　　　　　　　　　　　　　　　　　　　10.6

The award has effect as if the terms and conditions contained in it were contained in an agreement in writing made by the landlord and tenant.[29] This does not,

---

[23] See generally the decision in *Parry v. Million Pigs Limited* [1980] 260 E.G. 281 and para. 13.2 below.
[24] Matters which in commercial drafting normally are included as triggers for the landlord's power to re-enter.
[25] See para. 10.7 below.
[26] s. 6(2)(b).
[27] The wording is mandatory, "shall make provision". He has no discretion to omit any item and, in any case, it seems unlikely that it would be "reasonable and just" to do so.
[28] s. 6(2)(c).
[29] s. 6(4). In view of the terms of s. 6(4) it seems unnecessary, and is not the practice, for a formal agreement to be executed embodying the terms of the award. The award itself has effect as if it were an agreement.

however, operate as a new agreement between the parties but as a variation of the agreement previously in force.[30] The variation takes effect as from the making of the award or from such later (but not earlier) date as is specified in it.[31] The arbitrator is given a limited power to vary the rent of the holding if he considers it equitable to do so by reason of any provision which he is required to include in the award.[32] He is not, however, at liberty to alter the rent for any reason other than, or to a greater extent than is justified by, the inclusion of any such provision.[33] Where the effect of the award is to transfer from one party to the other a pre-existing liability for the maintenance or repair of an item of fixed equipment, there are special compensation provisions.[34]

10.7 Assignment, etc., pending outcome of arbitration under section 6

The special provision contained in section 6(5) and (6) is intended to close a loophole which could otherwise nullify the steps taken by a landlord in accordance with section 6 to have included in the tenancy agreement the covenant preventing assignment, etc., without the landlord's consent, set out in Schedule 1, paragraph 9. The danger was that an assignment might take place pending the outcome of the arbitration proceedings and vest the tenancy in the assignee. It was therefore necessary not merely to prohibit such an assignment, etc., during this period but to declare void any transaction in contravention of the prohibition.[35] The provision applies not only to assignments but also to sublettings or parting with possession of the whole holding or any part of it. The period covered by this special provision is the period beginning with the date of service of the landlord's request to the tenant to enter into an agreement covering the matters specified in Schedule 1 and ending with the date of the conclusion of the agreement or the date when the award takes effect, as the case may be.[36]

10.8 Provisions concerning fixed equipment: general

Sections 7 to 11 deal with a number of matters relating to fixed equipment. Fixed equipment is defined as including[37] "any building or structure affixed to land and

---

[30] s. 6(4). This provision reverses the effect of an old decision under the 1948 Act, ***Hollings v. Swindell*** (1950) 155 E.G. 269 (Vaisey J.), to the effect that a subsisting notice to quit was rendered ineffective, by an award under the section corresponding to section 6, on the ground that the award operated as a new agreement.

[31] s. 6(4). Presumably the discretion given to postpone the effect of the award is intended to mitigate hardship.

[32] s. 6(3).

[33] It should be noted that any variation under s. 6(3) is to be disregarded for the purpose of the frequency of general rent arbitrations under s. 12: see Sched. 2, para. 4(2)(a).

[34] See s. 9 (para. 10.27 below), and Chapter 11.

[35] It has been established that an assignment contrary to a covenant in a lease prohibiting assignment was nevertheless an effective assignment of the interest: ***Old Grovebury Manor Farm Ltd v. W. Seymour Plant Sales and Hire Ltd (No.2)*** (1979) 1 W.L.R. 1397, ***Governors of Peabody Donation Fund v. Higgins*** [1983] 1 W.L.R. 1091, ***Pazgate Ltd v. McGrath*** (1984) 272 E.G. 1069, and ***Fuller v. Judy Properties Ltd*** (1991) 2 E.G.L.R. 41.

[36] s. 6(6).

[37] s. 96(1). "Includes" indicates an extensive definition, giving the expression defined its ordinary meaning and then also the other meanings specified which might not be within the ordinary meaning.

any works on, in, over or under land, and also includes anything grown on land for a purpose other than use after severance from the land, consumption of the thing grown or of its produce, or amenity, and any reference to fixed equipment on land shall be construed accordingly."

Terms for maintenance, repair and insurance of fixed equipment: incorporation of "model clauses"

10.9

The object of sections 7 and 8 is to introduce some uniformity into tenancy agreements in relation to provisions for the maintenance, repair and insurance of fixed equipment, to define clearly the respective obligations of landlord and tenant, and to ensure that one or other party is responsible for the repair of each item, or at any rate that there is some provision (which could be a provision expressly relieving a party from liability) covering each item.[38] Section 7 gives the Minister[39] power to provide by regulations a set of statutory model clauses, prescribing terms as to the maintenance, repair and insurance of fixed equipment, which are deemed to be incorporated in every contract of tenancy of an agricultural holding, subject to one important exception. They are deemed to be incorporated "except in so far as they would impose on one of the parties to an agreement in writing a liability which under the agreement is imposed on the other".[40] The first set of regulations were issued in 1948.[41] The second set of regulations are the Agriculture (Maintenance, Repair and Insurance of Fixed Equipment) Regulations 1973.[42]

Condition of incorporation: effect of *Burden v. Hannaford*

10.10

It is clear from the words quoted above that it is a condition precedent to the incorporation of a provision in the model clauses that there should be no written contractual provision actually imposing on one of the parties a positive liability which a model clause provision would impose on the other. Before the decision of the Court of Appeal in ***Burden v. Hannaford***[43] it was generally considered that once this condition was satisfied the model clause provision would override an inconsistent contractual provision provided that the latter did not impose liability, *e.g.* would override a provision relieving a party in whole or in part from liability, such as a wear and tear exception or a limitation of liability to repair by reference to the state of the premises on entry. ***Burden v. Hannaford***, however, decided that where the model provision is incorporated (the condition precedent having been

---

[38] See ***Burden v. Hannaford*** [1956] 1 Q.B. 142,CA discussed later. For terms implied by the common law, see ***Wedd v. Porter*** [1916] 2 K.B. 91; ***Warren v. Keen*** [1954] 1 Q.B. 15. The implied obligations in section 11 of the Landlord and Tenant Act 1985 do not apply to agricultural holdings.

[39] See s. 96(1). The Minister has to consult bodies representing the interests of agricultural landlords and tenants in drafting the regulations: s. 7(1). The regulations include provision for arbitration in regard to questions arising under them: s. 7(2).

[40] s. 7(3).

[41] The Agriculture (Maintenance, Repair and Insurance of Fixed Equipment) Regulations 1948 (S.I. 1948 No.184).

[42] S.I. 1973 No.1473, now amended by the Agriculture (Maintenance, Repair and Insurance of Fixed Equipment) (Amendment) Regulations 1988 (S.I. 1988 No.281). And see the Agriculture (Time Limits) Regulations 1988 (S.I. 1988 No.282).

[43] [1956] 1 Q.B. 142,CA.

fulfilled) it has still to be read together with the contract, and if there is inconsistency the contract prevails.[44] Thus it was held that a contractual provision expressly relieving the tenant from a liability to repair hedges prevailed over the model clause. On the same reasoning, a fair wear and tear exception and a "condition as on entry" clause would prevail. Logically, the decision on *Burden v. Hannaford* would operate to give such prevailing force to oral as well as to written terms of this kind, but there are difficulties about extending it to oral terms and it may well be that a court would interpret it as confined to written ones. It may be mentioned here that the ordinary rules of construction applicable to covenants in a lease apply to the model clauses.[45]

10.11   Contract of tenancy and regulations: problems revealed by decided cases

It is not unusual for a contract of tenancy to include a clause expressly incorporating the regulations, perhaps combined with separate covenants by landlord and tenant to carry out such repairs, etc., as are specified as their respective liabilities in the regulations. The contract will necessarily refer, for identification, to the statutory instrument containing the regulations which are operative at the date of the contract. The question will then arise as to whether the parties' obligations should be attached to amended or substituted regulations introduced in the future. Unless it is clear from the contract that a substituted version is intended to replace the version of the regulations referred to by the contract then the original version is the contractual version and ought to be treated as such for all purposes. In other words, where this version differs from the current version of the regulations the current regulations will be incorporated in the normal way.

There is a certain amount of case law dealing with the relationship between rights and remedies provided under the regulations and rights and remedies available under the law of contract: these cases are not necessarily easy to reconcile with one another. There are three specific areas of difficulty. First there is the need to construe carefully the meaning of "repair" under the Regulations.[46] Secondly, there is the problem as to whether arbitration under paragraph 15 of the Schedule operates so as to allow parties to stay any simultaneous court action.[47] Thirdly, and perhaps most worryingly, it is now unclear what "incorporation" under the Regulations means in terms of remedies as compared with remedies available under the express terms of a contract. *Grayless v. Watkinson*[48] appears to suggest that in the case of obligations deriving purely from the Regulations there is no corresponding right to common law damages unaffected by any steps which the tenant may have taken to crystallise the landlord's liability such as availing himself of the notice procedure under the Regulations. The result of the notice procedure is

---

[44] This was applied in *Roper v. Prudential Assurance Co. Limited* (1992) 1 E.G.L.R. 5, noted at para. 10.19 below.
[45] See *Evans v. Jones* [1955] 2 Q.B. 58. See also *Barrow Green Estate Co. v. Walker (Executors of)* [1954] 1 W.L.R. 231 and the county court case of *Robertson-Ackerman v. George* (1953) 103 L.J. 496. But see further para. 10.19 below.
[46] See para. 10.19 below.
[47] See para. 10.24 below.
[48] [1990] 1 E.G.L.R. 6.

to establish the extent of the landlord's default and the reasonable cost of remedying it. But it would appear that steps taken under the notice procedure bar subsequent action by way of straightforward damages for failure to repair. The alternative analysis of this case is that it demonstrates that there simply is no opportunity to claim damages where the Regulations offer a possible avenue of redress. The full range of relief in the case of breach of a contract would include not only damages but also actions for specific performance. The suggestion that these more traditional avenues of redress might not be available under the Regulations was vigorously rejected by Owen J. in *Hammond v. Allen*.[49] He also held that the landlords, who had failed to serve a counter-notice in time could not therefore rely on paragraph 15 of the Schedule to require arbitration as there was not considered to be any "claim question or difference". Where the regulations provide an opportunity for a step to be taken but do not require that that step be taken it is unclear whether specific performance or damages are available in addition to the remedy prescribed by the Regulations. Even if these remedies were available it would still appear to be the case that where there is a dispute the provisions of paragraph 15 must be implemented first.[50]

Landlord's rights and liabilities under the 1973 Regulations 10.12

Paragraphs 1–4 of the Schedule of the 1973 Regulations impose on the landlord a series of liabilities which inter-lock with liabilities imposed on the tenant by paragraphs 5–11. This text does not set out the entire contents of the Regulations, which are to be found printed in full in Part III, but summarises the overall picture. Readers are advised to check the full list of detailed items direct from the Regulations. In general terms the landlord is obliged to do the following:

Schedule, paragraph 1(1) Execute all "repairs and replacements" to specific parts of the farmhouse cottages and farm buildings. These are identified individually, the principal items being roofs, with chimney stacks, pots, gutterings and downpipes, main walls[51] and exterior walls. The obligation covers interior repair or decoration consequent on structural defects. Although curiously drafted it would appear that the Regulation intends to include floors floor joists ceiling joists and timbers exterior and interior staircases and fixed ladders doors windows and skylights[52] in the landlord's main obligation covering repair and replacement.

---

[49] [1994] 1 All E.R. 307.

[50] See Knox J. in *Tustian v. Johnston* [1993] 2 All E.R. 673, and see para. 10.24 below.

[51] "Main" seems to mean taking part of the weight of the superstructure or having something to do with the stability of the building; a mere dividing wall would not be included: *cf. Holiday Fellowship v. Hereford* [1959] 1 W.L.R. 211; see also *Blundell v. Obsdale Ltd* [1958] E.G.D. 144. Main walls in this sub-paragraph are distinguished from exterior walls and must mean those main walls which are not exterior walls. If it stood by itself "main walls" would include exterior walls. Although in some contexts "exterior walls" might include doors and windows in the walls and their frames with sills, they do not in the present case as doors and windows are mentioned later as a sepraate category. In *Holiday Fellowship v. Hereford*, it was decided that windows and their frames were not part of the "main walls" of a house, distinguishing *Boswell v. Crucible Steel Co. of America* [1925] 1 K.B. 119.

[52] The specific reference to skylights removes an old doubt as to whether they were parts of the roof or are windows. It is also made clear that the fixed frames of doors, windows and

Whilst this is not a straightforward grammatical reading of the first part of paragraph 1(1), from the recoupment provisions which enable the landlord to recover half the reasonable cost from the tenant in respect of these items it may be deduced that they are intended to be included. The recoupment provision itself relates to recovery of half the reasonable cost, *i.e.* not to a demand based on an estimate in advance of the work being done by the landlord.[53]

Schedule, paragraph 1(2) To execute all "repairs and replacements" to underground water supply pipes water and sewage installations (excluding the covers and tops of cess pools).

Schedule, paragraph 1(3) To "replace" anything mentioned by the Schedule paragraph 5(1) as a tenant's liability which has "worn out or otherwise become incapable of further repair". To this there are two exclusions only being (a) the tenant's liability to spend up to £100 annually replacing damaged tiles or slates[54] and (b) replacement or repair necessary because of wilful acts or negligence by the tenant or members of his household or employees and replacements necessary because of the tenant's own failure to repair (Schedule, paragraph 6).

Schedule, paragraph 2 To insure the farmhouse cottages and buildings to full value against fire damage, to do all "repair or replacement" consequent on fire damage and to lay out insurance monies in doing those works. Where insurance money is provided, the ability to recover half the reasonable cost from the tenant under the Schedule, paragraph 1(1) is not available.

Schedule, paragraph 3 At least five yearly to do all outside painting[55] creosoting or treatment of the farmhouse cottages and buildings. There are special provisions relating to the doors and windows and to the interior structural steelwork of open sided farm buildings. In the case of doors windows eaves—guttering and downpipes half the reasonable cost of the work can be recouped from the tenant with a complicated restriction on the amount that can be claimed where the work is done before the beginning of the fifth year of the tenancy.

---

skylights are included in the landlord's liability (subject to the exceptions for glass, glass substitute, sashcords, locks and fastenings).

[53] See *Robertson-Ackerman v. George* (1953) 103 L.J. 496,CC.

[54] The limit was, up to March 24, 1988, £25. See now the Sched., para. 8.

[55] The landlord's liability to paint "as often as may be necessary in order to prevent deterioration" appears to leave no room for any implication of liability on the tenant for external decoration under his residual general repairing covenant "to keep and leave ... in good tenantable repair". It has been held that such a general repairing covenant involves the amount of painting that is necessary for the prevention of decay: see *e.g.* **Monk v. Noyes** (1824) 1 C. & P. 265 and *Proudfoot v. Hart* (1890) 25 Q.B.D. 42. Paragraph 3, when read with the opening words of Part II of the Sched., seems to exclude any such implication. Paragraphs 7 and 11 impose specific inside painting obligations on the tenant. If it is desired to make the tenant liable for any outside painting it is essential to do so in clear express terms.

Schedule, paragraph 4 The landlord has no liability to execute repairs or replacements or to insure buildings or fixtures which are the property of the tenant nor (subject to the insurance monies being laid out) to execute repairs or replacements necessary by reason of a wilful act or the negligence of the tenant or his household or employees.

Tenant's rights and liabilities under the 1973 Regulations 10.13
This text summarises the tenant's rights and liabilities in general terms leaving the reader to check the detailed wording against the actual Regulations.[56] The tenant is obliged:

Schedule, paragraph 5(1) To "repair and to keep and leave clean and in good tenantable repair order and condition" the farmhouse cottages and farm buildings together with[57] all fixtures and fittings above ground[58] and expressly included are all fences hedges field walls gates and posts ponds ditches and yards. The obligation extends to all fixtures, regardless of who provided them, and to items whether they were available at the commencement of the tenancy or whether they were erected or provided thereafter.

Schedule, paragraph 5(2) To "repair or replace" removable covers to manholes, inspection chambers and sewage disposal systems.

Schedule, paragraph 5(3) To "keep clean and in good working order" all roof valleys, eaves-guttering, downpipes, wells, septic tanks, cess pools and sewage disposal systems.

Schedule, paragraph 5(4) To use carefully and protect from wilful, reckless or careless damage items where the landlord is responsible for repair or replacement under paragraph 1 and to report in writing immediately any damage where the landlord is responsible for repair or replacement.

Schedule, paragraph 6 To "replace or repair" and thereafter paint, etc., where fixed equipment is damaged by wilful act or the negligence of the tenant or members of his household or employees and further to replace anything which is

---

[56] Printed in Part III below.
[57] The list of individual items covered by the tenant's liability to repair, apart from those covered by "all fixtures and fittings" was increased in 1973 and is now fairly comprehensive. It will be noted that the tenant is made specifically liable for repairs to "electrical supply systems and fittings". Before 1973 there was doubt about electricity supply systems. As regards water supply, again a doubtful area at one time, the wording of the landlord's liability set out in para. 1(2) should be compared carefully with the tenant's liability under para. 5. The distinciton between the landlord's liability for underground pipes and installations and the tenant's liability for systems and fittings situated above ground is crucial. There is no satisfying legal distinction between drains and sewers. The nature of the effluent is not decisive: *cf Falconar v. South Shields Corporation* (1895) 11 T.L.R. 223. In normal usage a drain refers to a channel for carrying drainage from a single building, while a sewer refers to a larger system. The division of liability between landlord and tenant as set out in paras 1(2) and 5(2) should be noted.
[58] In the case of hydraulic rams the obligation extends to them whether situated above or below the ground.

the subject of the tenant's repairing obligation under paragraph 5(1) where the need for replacement is generated by the tenant's failure to repair. Both these responsibilities are subject to the landlord's responsibility to reinstate after fire damage.[59]

Schedule, paragraph 7 At least once in seven years to clean paint and decorate the interior of the farmhouse cottages and farm buildings and in the last year of the tenancy to limewash the inside of all buildings previously treated by that process.

Schedule, paragraph 8 To replace damaged tiles and slates but only to the extent of £100 annually.[60]

Schedule, paragraphs 9 and 10 To maintain the hedges by an appropriate programme of cutting or laying and to maintain wide and clear the ponds ditches and watercourses.

10.14 Landlord's ability under the Regulations to demand money based on estimates: Schedule, paragraph 11

By the Schedule, paragraph 11 there are specific limited opportunities provided for the landlord to demand from the tenant the payment of a sum of money based on an estimate, as distinct from recovery of cost actually met. These opportunties relate to the last year of the tenancy: first allowing the landlord to estimate and claim a percentage of cleaning and decorating costs which would otherwise be carried by the tenant under the seven-yearly cycle in the Schedule, paragraph 7; secondly allowing him to claim part of the estimated cost of painting, etc., doors windows eaves guttering and downpipes of buildings.[61] In either case on a dilapidations claim being made against the tenant on termination of the tenancy, accrued liabilities under paragraph 11 are taken into account.[62]

10.15 Default by the tenant in relation to repairs or replacement: Schedule paragraph 4(2)

The Schedule, paragraph 4(2) provides a remedy in circumstances where the tenant does not start work on repairs or replacements which are his liability by reason of paragraphs 5, 6, 7 and 8. Where two months elapse and no work is done or if the works are begun but not completed within three months of receiving from the landlord a written notice given for that purpose,[63] the landlord may enter and execute the repairs or replacements and recover the reasonable cost from the tenant forthwith. The landlord's notice may be challenged by a tenant's counter-notice in writing[64] in which the tenant must specify the grounds on which, and the items of repair or replacement in respect of which, he denies liability and he must require the

---

[59] Whether or not he has received insurance monies.
[60] The limit up to March 24, 1988 being £25 annually.
[61] If he were to do these works under para. 3 he would be entitled to a part recoupment (see above).
[62] Para. 11(3).
[63] *i.e.* not a notice to remedy in prescribed form, given as a preliminary to Sched. 3, Case D notice to quit.
[64] Given under the Sched., para. 4(3)(a).

question of liability to be determined by arbitration under the 1986 Act. There is no prescribed form for this. The counter-notice suspends operation of the landlord's notice until the conclusion of the arbitration by the arbitrator's award being delivered to the tenant.[65]

Landlord's failure to execute repairs other than to an underground water pipe: Schedule, paragraph 12 (1)

10.16

If the tenant serves written notice specifying necessary repairs other than repairs to an underground water pipe upon the landlord and calls on the landlord to execute those repairs and he fails to do so within three months of receiving that notice the tenant is entitled to execute the repairs himself.[66] If the landlord wishes to contest his liability to do those repairs he has one month in which to serve counter-notice in writing[67] specifying the grounds on which and the items of repair in respect of which he denies liability and may require the question of liability to be determined by arbitration under the 1986 Act. There is no prescribed form for this. On service of this counter-notice a tenant's notice under paragraph 12(1) is suspended until termination of the arbitration meaning in this case the date on which the arbitrator's award is delivered to the landlord.[68] Where the tenant's paragraph 12(1) notice is unchallenged or where the award is delivered to the landlord but not complied with within the three-month period, the tenant may do the work himself and may seek to rely on paragraph 12(1) for recoupment of the reasonable cost. He cannot recoup any cost which he would himself otherwise have had to carry by complying with his own obligations under the Schedule but is otherwise entitled to be paid forthwith.

Landlord's failure to execute repairs to an underground water pipe: Schedule, paragraph 12(2)

10.17

The tenant may serve on the landlord a written notice specifying necessary repairs to an underground water pipe which the landlord is obliged to repair and may demand that the landlord execute the specified repairs. If the landlord fails to do so within a week of receipt of this notice the tenant may execute those repairs himself. He has a right to recover the reasonable cost from the landlord except to the extent that he the tenant would otherwise have been required to pay for the works pursuant to his own responsibilities under the Schedule. The right to reclaim the reasonable cost from the landlord does not arise until a month has expired following the execution of the repairs. This delay accommodates the landlord's opportunity to serve a counter-notice under the Schedule, paragraph 12(5)(a) being a counter-notice in writing specifying grounds on which, and the items of repair in respect of which, the landlord denies liability and requiring the question of liability to be determined by arbitration under the 1986 Act. The service of the counter-notice does not operate to suspend the tenant's right to do the relevant

---

[65] This derives from the Sched., para. 4(3)(c) and means that where the landlord pays the arbitrator's fees in order to have access to the award, the arbitration is not regarded as terminated until the tenant himself has a copy of the award.
[66] Sched., para. 12(1).
[67] Sched., para. 12(5)(a).
[68] Para. 12(5)(d).

works one week after the landlord has received the tenant's notice. What it does do is suspend the tenant's opportunity to recoup the cost until the issue of liability is determined in his favour by arbitration.[69]

10.18 Landlord's failure to execute replacements: Schedule, paragraph 12(3)
The tenant may serve on the landlord a written notice specifying necessary replacements which the landlord has failed to execute and calling on a landlord to execute them. If the landlord fails to do those works within three months the tenant is entitled himself to execute the replacements and recover the reasonable cost from the landlord. The right to recover excludes any element of the cost which the tenant himself would have to bear in order to comply with his obligations under the Schedule. On receipt of the tenant's notice the landlord has one month in which to serve counter-notice in writing on the tenant[70] specifying the grounds on which, and the items of replacement in respect of which, he denies liability and requiring the question of liability to be determined by arbitration under the 1986 Act. There is no prescribed form for the counter-notice. The service of such a counter-notice suspends the notice itself until termination of the arbitration[71] meaning in this case delivery of the arbitrator's award to the landlord.[72] In the case of replacements there is a further restriction on the tenant's opportunity to claim reimbursement. In relation to replacement executed in any year of the tenancy terminating after March 24, 1988 the ceiling on the recoupment claim is either (whichever is the smaller) the amount of the annual rent or £2000.[73] It has been held[74] that the tenant cannot evade this restriction by launching a damages claim for the full amount expended. The net result would seem to be that where the tenancy comes to an end before the tenant has fully recouped the amount of his expenditure on the annual basis he has no recourse against the landlord for the amount outstanding. The attractiveness of the paragraph 12 remedy in the tenant's hands must therefore be very considerably reduced as against the prospect of suing the landlord for specific performance of the liability to replace. But there is general uncertainty as to the availability of specific performance directly through the Courts as opposed to by way of enforcing an arbitration award which has been made establishing the other party's responsibility under the Schedule, paragraph 15.[75] This uncertainty is discussed in relation to paragraph 15.

10.19 Meaning of "repair" and "replacement" under the Regulations
In the general way contractual repairing covenants will include (subject to any special wording) any replacements necessary to achieve a repair.[76] This general view has been adopted in relation to agricultural tenancies in the knowledge that the Regulations treat differently "repairs" and "replacements".[77] The drafting of

---

[69] Sched., para. 12(5)(c).
[70] Sched., para. 12(5)(a).
[71] Sched., para. 12(5)(b).
[72] Sched., para. 12(5)(d).
[73] Sched., para. 12(4).
[74] *Grayless v. Watkinson* [1990] 1 E.G.L.R. 6.
[75] See para. 10.24 below.
[76] See para. 10.28 below.
[77] *Roper v. Prudential Assurance Co. Limited* [1992] 1 E.G.L.R. 5. Evans-Lombe Q.C.

the Regulations appears to differ to some extent from the normal general understanding as to what is comprised within "repair". Schedule paragraph 1(3) requires the landlord to provide replacements to items mentioned in paragraph 5(1) (tenant's general liability in relation to buildings and fixtures) where the item in question has "worn out or otherwise become incapable of further repair". This suggests that the tenant's responsibility to repair does not include total replacement. Partial replacement (*e.g.* new nails or other materials) is nearly always necessary under the general heading of repair and it must therefore be a question of fact or degree as to the point at which the tenant's ability to "patch up" is exhausted and gives rise to the landlord's obligation to replace. The exact relationship between improvement by way of the provision of new fixed equipment under section 11 and the landlord's obligation to replace under the Schedule paragraph 1(3) may in individual cases be difficult to define. This is particularly the case where complex schemes for dealing with sewage or waste disposal are required which incorporate features of an original but now exhausted or unsatisfactory system.[78] It is noticeable that throughout the Schedule repairs and replacements are mentioned as distinct and separate matters including in relation to the procedures for challenging a request for a landlord to execute specific repairs or replacements.[79] The net position appears to be that where the landlord's obligation to repair particular parts of the buildings is involved it is coupled with an additional requirement that he replace where necessary those parts. The general repairing covenant imposed on the tenant falls short of total replacement and therefore perhaps short of what would be required in a commercial contract but some element of replacement must be included in the word "repair". There is, perhaps confusingly, a further express requirement in the Schedule, paragraph 6(2) requiring the tenant to replace items where the need for replacement is caused by a failure to repair.

What all this means is that a person investigating which paragraph of the Regulations to use in relation to a particular item of work will need to know not only what is required by way of replacement or straightforward repair by way of reinstatement but also something about the history of the item and the cause of the item being worn out or damaged or otherwise in need of replacement.

Disputes as to redundancy of fixed equipment: Schedule, paragraph 13   10.20

If landlord or tenant considers that fixed equipment is redundant or, before being damaged by fire, was redundant to the farming of the holding that party may give the other two months notice in writing requiring that the question whether such item of fixed equipment is or was redundant shall be determined in default of agreement by arbitration under the 1986 Act. There is no prescribed form for such a demand.[80] If the arbitrator awards that the item is or was redundant the Schedule

---

sitting as a Deputy Judge of the Queen's Bench Division refused to construe a contractual obligation on the tenant to "repair" so as to exclude replacements.

[78] Surveyors will no doubt take care to ensure that there is no confusion as to how individual items are being dealt with and what procedures they wish to invoke in relation to different elements of an overall scheme.

[79] See paras 10.16–10.18 above.

[80] For a precedent see Form 8 in Part V of this work.

paragraph 14 applies to it and neither party has any liability thereafter in respect of any antecedent breach of any obligation to maintain repair or replace that item. The landlord is entitled to demolish and remove the item and to go on the holding for those purposes.[81] The test as to what redundancy amounts to is set out in paragraph 13(2) and the arbitrator must be satisfied that the repair or replacement of the item is not reasonably required having regard to:

(a) (i) The landlord's responsibilities to manage the holding in accordance with the rules of good estate management[82]; and

(ii) the period for which the holding may reasonably be expected to remain a separate holding; and

(b) the character and situation of the holding and the average requirements of a tenant reasonably skilled in husbandry.[83]

This formulation gives the arbitrator very considerable scope for exercising his professional opinion on the evidence presented to him. It should be noted that there is no general ability at common law, in the absence of an express contractual term, simply to disregard fixed equipment as redundant. Items continue to be subject to the various repairing responsibilities and it is only on termination that a claim as to dilapidations will be tested. Understandably parties may not wish to take the risk that, if they allow a building to fall into disrepair, they will be faced either with a heavy dilapidations claim on termination or, in the case of a landlord, with an ongoing risk of being required to put a building into repair when it is believed to be redundant. The paragraph 13 provision enables matters to be brought to a head at an early stage. Where an item is awarded as redundant neither party has any responsibility to maintain repair replace or insure in relation to it.

10.21 **Time of the essence for service of counter-notices**
All counter-notices required to be served under paragraph 12 of the Regulations must be served within the period stipulated and time is of the essence.[84]

10.22 **Obsolete fixed equipment**
There is no provision in relation to obsolete equipment which corresponds to the right to demand arbitration in relation to redundant equipment. Should the parties agree in writing that a particular item of equipment is in fact obsolete the Schedule paragraph 14(1) relieves both parties of any responsibility to maintain repair replace or insure that item.

---

[81] Sched., para. 13(1).
[82] See s. 10 of the Agriculture Act 1947.
[83] Sched., para. 13(2).
[84] *Hammond v. Allen* [1994] 1 All E.R. 307. For a counter-notice precedent see Form 6 in Part V of this work.

Subsidence relieving the obligation to execute work: Schedule 14, paragraph (2)   10.23

Where the execution of work is rendered impossible except at prohibitive or unreasonable expense because of subsidence of land or the blocking of outfalls which are not under the control of either landlord tenant then the Regulations do not create any liability on either landlord or tenant.[85]

Disputes under the Regulations: Schedule, paragraph 15   10.24

The Schedule, paragraph 15 provides that all claims questions or differences arising "under the foregoing provisions" which are not otherwise referred to compulsory arbitration under the Act "shall be determined, in default of agreement, by arbitration under the Act". This would appear to be a general mandatory reference to arbitration in the event of any "claim question or difference". Some light on the meaning of this paragraph is thrown by the *Tustian v. Johston* cycle of litigation.[86] At first instance Knox J. held that paragraph 15 referred to compulsory arbitration under the 1986 Act any dispute as to the extent of repairing obligations of landlord or tenant under Parts I and II of the Schedule and as to the extent to which either party was in breach of those obligations. He considered that those questions had to be answered before a claim to either damages or specific performance was available. Because the arbitrator has no power to award specific performance, a claimant who desired it would have to establish the extent of the breach by an arbitration award and then seek enforcement by specific performance through the courts. On that basis he stayed the tenant's actions for damages for breach of covenant and specific performance of repairing obligations under the Regulations. The Court of Appeal lifted the stay to allow the tenant to apply for summary judgment under Order 14 but not for any other purpose and without determining the merits of the appeal. The Court of Appeal considered that[87] the question which arises on Order 14 applications (*i.e.* whether a triable issue exists) is essentially the same as that which arises on an application for a stay pursuant to an arbitration clause (*i.e.* whether there is a dispute or difference which is capable of being and is required to be referred to arbitration). What this seems to suggest is that parties wishing to insist on the arbitration procedure ought prudently to put forward the basis of their claim question or differences so as to establish the right to rely on paragraph 15 and exclude the jurisdiction of the Court. It would appear that, where the element of dispute is so minimal that an Order 14 application for summary judgment would succeed against that party, there is in substance no sufficient claim question or difference so as to bring into play paragraph 15. This at least is the negative side of

---

[85] As to the correct construction of para. 14(2) it is submitted that the land which is the subject of the relevant subsidence may be under the control of either landlord or tenant and it is only in relation to the blocking of outfalls that those outfalls should not be under the control of either party. The last sub-clause of the paragraph contains a verb referring back to a plural subject, "outfalls" not referring back to "land". Accordingly it is submitted that "or" in that sub-paragraph is used disjunctively.

[86] At first instance, Knox J. reported at [1993] 2 All E.R. 673 and on appeal noted at [1993] 3 All E.R. 534. The litigation settled following the Court of Appeal hearing.

[87] On the basis of the review of authorities by Saville J. in *Hayter v. Nelson* [1990] 2 Lloyd's Rep. 265 at 269–271.

the equation that is to say where there appears to be no or virtually no dispute. What however remains unanswered is whether or not Knox J. was correct in his analysis as to the exclusive jurisdiction of the arbitrator. It is submitted that he was.[88]

Where a landlord fails to serve a counter-notice in response to a tenant's notice under paragraph 12 of the Regulations it is likely that the Court would regard there as being no "claim, question or difference" within the meaning of paragraph 15.[89]

10.25 Contracting out of the Regulations: control by resort to arbitration

It is possible to contract out of the model clauses by providing in the contract of tenancy for a different allocation of obligations covering the same ground, by shifting the burden of liability more to the shoulders of the landlord or of the tenant. If, however, the contract fails to cover a point, either by imposing an obligation on one or other of the parties or by expressly relieving from it,[90] the statutory liability under the Regulations will be let in. Further, freedom of contracting out is controlled by a provision which enables either party to take to arbitration the terms of a written tenancy agreement which departs substantially[91] from the statutory model, provided that (and this is a condition precedent which must be fulfilled before the arbitrator assumes jurisdiction) the party has tried and failed to persuade the other party to vary the agreement to bring it into conformity with the model.[92] The arbitrator must consider whether the substantial departure from the model is justifiable when regard is had to the circumstances of the holding and of the landlord and tenant.[93] He must disregard the rent, as the question is not whether the contractual repairing provisions are appropriate in view of the rent, but whether they are appropriate in view of the holding and the parties' circumstances.[94] The arbitrator may then vary the contractual terms as seems to him reasonable and just,[95] and may make such consequential adjustment in the rent as appears equitable.[96]

---

[88] This obviously establishes a difference between parties relying on the Regulations and parties relying on the express terms of the contract for enforcement of repairing obligations, the latter being entitled to apply direct for specific performance to the court. However this appears to be the contemplation of the statutory instrument which is drafted as a fallback where parties have failed to deal with particular responsibilities. It must be remembered that the Regulations operate to fill out the terms of agreements which may have begun as oral short term licences and been converted by section 2 into long term arrangements.

[89] See *Hammond v. Allen* [1994] 1 All E.R. 307. But see in relation to a commercial arbitration *Halki Shipping Corp. v. Sopex Oils Ltd* [1998] 2 All E.R. 23,CA.

[90] *Burden v. Hannaford* (above).

[91] s. 8(1): "effects substantial modifications". For a precedent for the initial request see Form 4 in Part V of this work: for a subsequent reference to arbitration see Form 5.

[92] s. 8(2).

[93] s. 8(3).

[94] *ibid*. "Circumstances" seem to include personal circumstances: contrast "relevant circumstances" in ss 10 and 11 of the 1947 Act (applied by s. 96(3) of the 1986 Act) defined to exclude personal circumstances by s. 109(3) of the 1947 Act. The arbitrator may therefore take into account, *e.g.* the landlord's residence abroad, his possession of an estate yard for repairs, the expensiveness of the equipment, such as bridges or water meadow equipment.

[95] s. 8(3).

[96] s. 8(4).

Award under section 8 10.26

The award of an arbitrator under section 8 has effect as if the terms and conditions in it were contained in a written agreement made by the landlord and the tenant.[97] This does not, however, operate as a new agreement but as a variation of the agreement previously in force.[98] The variation takes effect as from the making of the award or such later date as the award specifies.[99] It must be noted that, although the first reference to arbitration under these provisions may be made at any time after the tenancy begins, a second or subsequent reference must be at an interval of at least three years from the coming into effect of a previous award.[1] It should also be noted that an increase or reduction of rent under section 8(4) is to be disregarded for the purpose of the frequency of rent arbitrations under section 12.[2]

Transitional arrangements where liability in respect of fixed equipment is transferred: section 9 10.27

Section 9 deals with cases where, by virtue of any of the previous three sections, liability for the maintenance, repair or insurance of fixed equipment is transferred from one party to the contract of tenancy to the other during the currency of the tenancy.[3] Section 9 enables compensation for a failure to repair by the tenant or the landlord which exists at the date of transfer of liability to be determined by arbitration and paid to the other party without waiting until the termination of the tenancy on quitting the holding. A claim to such compensation must be made within a prescribed period beginning with the date when the transfer of liability takes effect.[4] Section 9(4) deals with a different point. Its object, which is not entirely self-evident,[5] appears to be to enable an arbitrator under section 6 (provision of written tenancy agreements) to specify, as an existing term of the tenancy which is to be reduced into writing, an oral term which would otherwise be overridden by new model clauses.

Construction of repairing obligations 10.28

It has been decided that the liability placed on the tenant by the "model clauses" to repair and keep and leave clean and in good tenantable repair, order and condition is not merely to keep and leave in as good repair and condition as at the beginning

---

[97] s. 8(5).
[98] *ibid.*, *cf.* s. 6(4).
[99] s. 8(5).
[1] s. 8(6).
[2] Sched. 2, para. 4(2)(a).
[3] s. 9(1), (2) and (3). s. 9(1) and (2) deal with the case where the liability is transferred to the landlord, s. 9(3) with the case where it is transferred to the tenant. The transfer may result from an award under s. 6 which varies contractual terms or from the impact of the model clauses or an award under ss 7 or 8.
[4] s. 9(1) and (3). The prescribed time is one month from the date on which the transfer takes effect as laid down in the Agriculture (Miscellaneous Time-Limits) Regulations 1959 (S.I. 1959 No.171). For a form of notice requiring arbitration under s. 9 see Form 7 in Part V of this work.
[5] Not to mention some difficulty in reconciling the subsection with the decision in ***Burden v. Hannaford*** [1956] 1 Q.B. 142,CA. For an explanation of and discussion of the difficulties of this subsection see (1956) J.P.L. 15–17.

of the tenancy, but on the other hand cannot be said without qualification to be "to put" in repair. The true test is whether as a matter of good husbandry and common sense, and having regard to the age and character of any particular item, its condition at the beginning of the tenancy, and the length of the tenancy, the tenant did in fact perform the obligations set out in the clauses as an agricultural tenant to keep and leave the fixed equipment in question in good tenantable repair, order and condition.[6] This is helpful in general, but it must always be remembered that a covenantor's obligation depends primarily on the words of his covenant, although construction of it will be affected by various matters including the nature of the property, the length of the term and other relevant circumstances.[7] It would be difficult for a tenant who had been in for, say, 15 or 20 years to seek to answer on termination of his tenancy a claim for infestation by pleading that there was a trace of eelworm at the commencement of the tenancy. The general principles which have been developed in regard to the construction of express covenants to repair apply to the interpretation of the model clauses.[8]

10.29 Leasehold Property (Repairs) Act 1938 not applicable
The Leasehold Property (Repairs) Act 1938, which restricts the enforcement of repairing covenants during the currency of certain leases by requiring the landlord to obtain the leave of the court, and the scope of which was considerably extended by section 51 of the Landlord and Tenant Act 1954, does not apply where the property comprised in the tenancy is an agricultural holding.[9]

10.30 Landlord and Tenant Act 1985, sections 11–16 applicable to sublet dwelling-houses
The obligations placed on lessors of dwelling-houses by sections 11–16 of the Landlord and Tenant Act 1985 (formerly sections 32 and 33 of the Housing Act 1961) where the "lease" is for a term of less than seven years do not apply "to a lease of a dwelling-house which is a tenancy of an agricultural holding within the

---

[6] Evershed M.R. in *Evans v. Jones* [1955] 2 Q.B. 58 at 66.

[7] The main works on dilapidations, with detailed commentary on the construction of this type of covenant, are N. Dowding and K. Reynolds, *Dilapidations the modern law and practice* (Sweet and Maxwell, 1995) and *Woodfall, Landlord and Tenant*, Vol.I, Chapter 13.

[8] Among the main relevant cases are the following: *Brown v. Trumper* (1858) 26 Beav. 11; *Proudfoot v. Hart* (1890) 25 Q.B.D. 42; *Lister v. Lane* [1893] 2 Q.B. 212; *Lurcott v. Wakeley* [1911] 1 K.B. 905; *Calthorpe v. McOscar* [1924] 1 K.B. 716; *Pembery v. Lamdin* [1940] 2 All E.R. 434; *Wates v. Rowland* [1952] 2 Q.B. 12; *Jaquin v. Holland* [1960] 1 W.L.R. 258; *Collins v. Flynn* [1963] 2 All E.R. 1068; *Brew Bros Ltd, v. Snax (Ross) Ltd* [1970] 1 Q.B. 612; *Ravenseft Properties Ltd v. Davstone (Holdings) Ltd* [1980] 1 Q.B. 12; *Elmcroft Developments Ltd v. Tankersley-Sawyer* (1984) 270 E.G. 140; *Post Office v. Aquarius Properties Ltd* [1987] 1 E.G.L.R. 40, (1987) 281 E.G. 798; *Elite Investments Ltd v. T.I. Bainbridge Silencers Ltd* [1986] 2 E.G.L.R. 43; *Stent v. Monmouth District Council* [1987] 1 E.G.L.R. 59, (1987) 282 E.G. 705; *Holding & Management v. Property Holding & Investment Trust* [1990] 1 E.G.L.R. 65. These cases, and others, are summarised and synthesised in *Woodfall, Landlord and Tenant*, Vol.I, Chapter 13.

[9] See 1938 Act, s. 7; 1954 Act, s. 51(1)(c); 1986 Act, Sched. 14, para. 17.

meaning of the Agricultural Holdings Act 1986".[10] These provisions which impose on the landlord obligations to repair the structure and exterior of the dwelling-house and various installations in the dwelling-house (and avoid[11] any covenant which would place any of these obligations on the tenant), do not therefore apply to the farmhouse which is let as part of the holding. They could, however, apply to sublet cottages on the holding where the subletting is not itself the tenancy of a holding.

Tort of waste 10.31

Although rarely invoked in practice, it should not be entirely forgotten that a landlord still has a remedy against a tenant based on the contract of tenancy, but on tort, the tort of waste. Unfortunately the case law is old and to some extent uncertain. It would seem that all tenants are liable for voluntary waste and that tenants for a term of years may be liable also for permissive waste.[12] Whether tenants from year to year are liable for permissive waste is somewhat doubtful, but they are probably under a duty (which would place upon them a rather similar but technically lesser liability) to use the premises in a tenant-like manner.[13] It is highly unlikely that an agricultural landlord would be advised at the present day to bring an action for permissive waste against a tenant, but there might be cases where an application for an injunction to stop voluntary waste (cutting down timber,[14] destruction of buildings or other serious acts[15] in contravention of the tenancy which would do lasting damage to the landlord's estate) would still be appropriate. However use of the property for a reasonable purpose contemplated by the tenancy will not give rise to a complaint in waste, even if damage is caused.[16] Waste necessarily involves a permanent change to the character of the property.[17]

Landlord's remedies for dilapidations 10.32

The landlord has at his disposal a number of possible remedies which his advisers should consider in the light of the particular circumstances. He may:

(1) apply for a certificate of bad husbandry and follow it up with the appropriate notice to quit[18];

---

[10] Landlord and Tenant Act 1985, s.14(3), as amended by para. 64 of Sched. 14 to the 1986 Act.
[11] Unless the County Court has authorised its conclusion; *ibid.*, s. 12.
[12] "May" because such liability depends on whether the case of ***Yellowly v. Gower*** (1855) 11 Ex. 274 was correctly decided. It is, however, still possible to argue even today that this decision was erroneous because founded on a misrepresentation by Lord Coke in 1641 (The Second Institute) of statutes passed in 1267 (Marlebridge) and 1278 (Gloucester)!
[13] ***Regis Property Ltd v. Dudley*** [1959] A.C. 370 at 407 (Lord Denning). See also ***Warren v. Keen*** [1954] 1 Q.B. 15.
[14] ***Phillips v. Smith*** (1845) 14 M.&W. 589; ***Channon v. Patch*** (1826) 5 B.&C. 897.
[15] ***Boswell v. Crucible Steel*** [1925] 1 K.B. 119.
[16] ***Manchester Bonded Warehouse v. Carr*** (1880) 5 C.P.D. 507; ***Saner v. Bilton*** (1878) 7 Ch.D. 815.
[17] ***West Ham Central Charity Board v. East London Waterworks Co.*** [1900] 1 Ch. 624.
[18] s. 26(2), Sched. 3, Case C; see para. 12.51 below.

(2) serve a notice to do work on the correct statutory form and follow it up with the appropriate notice to quit[19];

(3) apply to the Agricultural Land Tribunal for consent to a notice to quit on one of the grounds specified in section 27 of the 1986 Act;

(4) enter the holding under the procedure set out in paragraph 4(2) of the Schedule to the Agriculture (Maintenance, Repair and Insurance of Fixed Equipment) Regulations 1973[20];

(5) bring an action for damages in the courts during the currency of the tenancy under the rule in *Kent v. Conniff*[21];

(6) apply to the courts for an injunction against the commission of voluntary waste or under section 15(5)(a) of the 1986 Act to restrain the tenant from exercising his statutory rights of disposal of produce and freedom of cropping in such a way as to injure or deteriorate the holding;

(7) apply to the courts for the forfeiture of the tenancy;

(8) claim compensation under section 71(1) at the termination of the tenancy;

(9) claim compensation under section 71(3) at the termination of the tenancy;

(10) claim compensation under section 72 at such termination.

10.33 Orders for specific performance: repairs

An order for specific performance may be granted by the Court in the form of a direction to achieve a particular result. Such a remedy is discretionary and in theory is reserved for circumstances where damages would provide an inadequate remedy. In the case of building contracts[22] and repairing covenants[23] the need for precision in the order is stressed.[24] What is required is clarity, the issue of precision being a question of degree.[25] There appears to be no difficulty, in an appropriate case, in the tenant securing against his landlord an order for specific performance of a repairing covenant.[26] Conversely, based on dicta of Lord Eldon in *Hill v. Barclay*,[27] it has been historically thought unlikely that specific

---

[19] Case D in Sched. 3; see paras 12.53–12.75 below.
[20] S.I. 1973 No.1473.
[21] [1953] 1 Q.B. 361.
[22] *Wolverhampton Corp. v. Emmons* [1901] 1 K.B. 515.
[23] *Jeune v. Queens Cross Properties Limited* [1973] 3 All E.R. 97, [1974] Ch.97.
[24] See also Lord Upjohn in *Morris v. Redland Bricks Limited* [1970] A.C. 652 at 666: "The court must be careful to see that the defendant knows exactly in fact what it has to do and this means not as a matter of law but as a matter of fact, so that in carrying out an order he can give his contractors the proper instructions."
[25] See Lord Hoffmann in *Co-op Insurance Society Limited v. Argyll Stores (Holdings) Limited* [1997] 3 All E.R. 297 at 304.
[26] *Jeune v. Queens Cross Properties Limited* (above).
[27] [1810] 1 6 Ves. Jun. 402.

performance could be obtained of a tenant's repairing covenant,[28] but in appropriate circumstances specific performance may be ordered against a tenant, provided the result desired is sufficiently specified.[29]

Tenant's right to remove fixtures and buildings: section 10

10.34

Section 10, which deals with the tenant's right to remove fixtures and buildings, reproduces section 13 of the 1948 Act as amended by the 1984 Act[30] and improved in some drafting respects. In construing section 10 it is important to bear in mind that it is a statutory modification of the common law rule that anything annexed to the freehold by the tenant becomes the absolute property of the owner of the freehold. In so far, therefore, as the conditions laid down for the operation of this statutory modification are not satisfied, the owner's common law rights are restored. The common law established exceptions to its own rule in the case of articles affixed for ornament and convenience,[31] and for trade purposes,[32] but the common law exception for trade was not extended by the courts to general agriculture.[33] It was allowed in the case of such things as greenhouses and hothouses erected by market gardeners and nurserymen, as these were regarded as trades, although with an agricultural flavour, but not in the case of non-specialised agriculture.[34] The ordinary agriculturist may be able to rely on the common law exception for articles of ornament and convenience so far as various articles affixed to the farmhouse are concerned, and he may, in some cases, be able to claim that an article is not a fixture at all but a mere chattel,[35] but his rights in respect of agricultural fixtures as such are derived from statute. Attention is drawn to the important House of Lords decision in *Elitestone Limited v. Morris*[36] in which the modern law as to how to identify a chattel or a fixture is restated.

Rights under section 10: general rule

10.35

Subject to the exceptions and conditions mentioned below, a tenant may remove, either during the tenancy or within two months from its termination, any engine, machinery, fencing or other fixtures (of whatever description)[37] affixed, whether for the purposes of agriculture or not, and any building erected by him on the

---

[28] See *Regional Properties v. City of London Real Property Company* (1980) 257 E.G. 65.
[29] See *Rainbow Estates Ltd v. Tokenhold Ltd* (1988) 24 E.G. 123, Lawrence Collins Q.C. sitting as a deputy judge of the Chancery Division, and for general discussion see also *Woodfall, Landlord and Tenant*, Vol.I, Chapter 13 in particular paras 13.099–13.100.
[30] 1984 Act, s. 10(1) and Sched. 3, para. 6. See also annotations to present section in Part II.
[31] *Spyer v. Phillipson* [1931] 2 Ch. 183,CA; and see older cases cited in *Woodfall op. cit.*, paras 13.144–13.145.
[32] *Penton v. Robart* (1801) 2 East 88; *Webb v. Bevis* [1940] 1 All E.R. 247; and see Woodfall, *op.cit.*, paras 13.142–3.
[33] *Elwes v. Maw* (1802) 3 East 38; *New Zealand Government Property Corporation v. H.M. & S. Ltd* [1982] Q.B. 1145.
[34] See the interesting Digest of Evidence, before the House of Commons Committee on agricultural customs, compiled by Shaw and Corbet (1849) at pp.188 *et seq.*
[35] *e.g.* some types of dutch barns, granaries and sheds, but not, of course, all: see *Webb v. Bevis* [1940] 1 All E.R. 247; *Penton v. Robart supra*; *Mears v. Callender* [1901] 2 Ch.388. For recent cases on the general law, see the *New Zealand* case, *supra*, and *Young v. Dalgety plc* [1987] 1 E.G.L.R. 116.
[36] (1997) 27 E.G. 116.
[37] This negatives the application of the *ejusdem generis* rule.

holding.³⁸ It is expressly stated that the fixture or building shall remain the tenant's property so long as he may remove it by virtue of the above rule.³⁹ These provisions apply to a fixture or building acquired by a tenant as they apply to a fixture or building affixed or erected by him.⁴⁰ The special privileges given to agricultural tenants do not prejudice any right of removal subsisting otherwise, *e.g.* the common law rights to remove trade fixtures and those affixed for ornament or convenience.⁴¹

10.36 Exceptions to tenant's rights under section 10
The general rule does not apply to the following cases:⁴²

(a) a fixture affixed or a building erected in pursuance of some obligation, *e.g.* in the contract of tenancy.⁴³

(b) a fixture affixed or a building erected instead of a fixture or building belonging to the landlord, *i.e.* mere replacements.⁴⁴

(c) a building for which the tenant is entitled to claim compensation, whether under the 1986 Act or otherwise.⁴⁵ Thus, in the case of a building, if the tenant can claim compensation for it as an improvement, because he has erected it with the landlord's consent in writing, he is restricted to the compensation claim, but in the case of a fixture other than a building, *e.g.*, a bridge, he can elect either to remove it or to claim compensation. It would seem that a tenant could remove a building for which he was not "entitled" to compensation because its value, calculated on the "years" principle in accordance with an agreement under section 67 had become exhausted.

(d) a fixture affixed or a building erected before January 1, 1884.⁴⁶

(e) a fixture or building acquired by the tenant before January 1, 1901.⁴⁷

---

³⁸ s. 10(1)(a) and (b).
³⁹ *ibid.* On the effect of a surrender and regrant, see **Leschallas v. Woolf** [1908] 1 Ch. 641, but consider comments in *New Zealand Government Property Corporation v. H.M.& S. Ltd* [1982] Q.B. 1145.
⁴⁰ s. 10(7), but a tenant is not entitled by virtue of s. 10(1) to remove a fixture or building acquired by him on or before December 31, 1900: Sched. 12, para. 3.
⁴¹ s. 10(8).
⁴² Owing to the similarity of language, some usefulness may be found in considering the discussion of the exceptions to s. 8 of the 1995 Act, paras 3.5–3.8 above.
⁴³ s. 10(2)(a).
⁴⁴ s. 10(2)(b).
⁴⁵ s. 10(2)(c). The only definition of a "building" in the 1986 Act is the not very helpful extensive one in s. 96(1), "building" includes any part of a building.
⁴⁶ s. 10(2)(d). This was the date of commencement of the Agricultural Holdings (England) Act 1883, which for the first time gave tenants a right of removal of fixtures and buildings without the consent of the landlord, which had been required under the Agricultural Holdings (England) Act 1875.
⁴⁷ Sched. 12, para. 3. The application to fixtures in buildings acquired by a tenant was made by the Agricultural Holdings Act 1900, s. 4. That Act came into operation on January 1, 1901.

Conditions for the exercise of the right under section 10 10.37
The exercise of the right of removal is subject to certain conditions:

(a) The tenant must have paid all rent owing by him and performed or satisfied all his other obligations to the landlord in respect of the holding.[48] This is a formidable requirement, involving literally (subject presumably to the de minimis rule) the full discharge of all repairing obligations, including those incorporated in the tenancy by the model clauses.[49] A tenant who loses his right of removal because of failure to repair remains, of course, liable for the dilapidations which caused the loss.

(b) The tenant must have given his landlord at least one month's previous written notice of his intention to remove the fixture or building, and this must have been given at least one month before the termination of the tenancy.[50] The landlord can, while the tenant's notice is current, elect by a counternotice in writing to purchase the fixture or building, and, if he does, the tenant loses his right of removal, but the landlord becomes liable to pay him the fair value to an incoming tenant.[51] Any dispute as to such value is determinable by arbitration under the 1986 Act.[52]

(c) In removing the fixture or building the tenant must not do any avoidable damage and must, immediately after the removal, make good any damage actually done.[53]

Property in the fixture or building: effect of non-compliance with the conditions 10.38
So long as the tenant is legally entitled to remove the fixture or building by reason of section 10(1) it remains his property, but it ceases to be his property if he has not removed it within two months from the termination of the tenancy. Further, if he

---

[48] s. 10(3)(a): *cf. West Country Cleaners (Falmouth) Ltd v. Saly* [1966] 1 W.L.R. 1485. In the county court case of *Roberts v. Magor* (1953) 103 L.J. 703 a tenant in arrears with his rent at the time he sent his notice of intention to remove fixtures was held not thereby to lose his rights; the tenant could comply with is obligations subsequently and then exercise his rights.

[49] s. 7. See for comparison *Bass Holdings Ltd v. Morton Music Ltd* (1988) Ch. 493,CA, on fulfilment of conditions precedent, and more recently *Bairstow Eves v. Ripley* (1993) 65 P.&C.R. 220; *West Middlesex Golf Club v. Ealing LBC* (1994) 68 P.&C.R. 461 and *Trane v. Provident Mutual Life* (1995) 1 E.G.L.R. 33.

[50] s. 10(3)(b). For effect of failure to give notice on disturbance compensation, see *Re Harvey and Mann's Arbitration* (1920) 89 L.J.K.B. 687; 123 L.T. 242 (the better report). For effect of a tenant being in arrears at the time he gives notice, see *Roberts v. Magor*, (above). On the period of one month, see *Dodds v. Walker* [1981] 1 W.L.R. 1027, HL. For a form of notice see Form 9 in Part V of this work.

[51] s. 10(4). For a form of landlord's counternotice see Form 10 in Part V of this work.

[52] s. 10(6). It would seem that the valuation would have to be based on the difference between the value of the holding with the fixture or building upon it and the value without such fixture or building. The 1984 Act (Sched. 3, para. 6(3)) removed a previous doubt as to whether arbitration under the agricultural holdings code applied.

[53] s. 10(5).

removes it during the tenancy or within two months from its termination, but without complying with either condition (a) or (b) above, it is submitted that he forfeits the statutory privilege conferred by section 10, he is divested of the ownership, and the landlord is restored to his full common law right as owner, so that he can sue the tenant, or a third party if appropriate, for conversion. Failure to comply with condition (c) above, however, which is not a condition precedent, does not appear to affect the vesting of ownership, but to give the landlord a right to compensation. The landlord's rights of ownership are, of course, restored to him if he gives the counternotice mentioned in section 10(4).

10.39 Contracting out and custom as regards section 10

It has been assumed as correct since *Premier Dairies Ltd v. Garlick*[54] that the parties were at liberty to contract out of the provisions now to be found in section 10,[55] either by enlarging the tenant's statutory rights or by restricting them, *e.g.* by confining the right of removal to certain scheduled figures only. However, in *Johnson v. Moreton*[56] Lord Hailsham expressed some doubt as to *Mears v. Callender* and, apparently, *Premier Dairies v. Garlick*.

A customary right of removal free from the statutory restrictions would, if established, be good,[57] but such a custom seems rare.

10.40 Position of incoming tenant as regards section 10

Only the landlord is given a right to purchase by section 10, not the incoming tenant. It is, however, not uncommon for the incoming tenant to be allowed, with the landlord's approval, to purchase fixtures from the outgoer. In such a case the incomer acquires the same right of removal as if he had himself affixed or erected the fixture or building in question.[58]

---

[54] [1920] 2 Ch.17.

[55] The right of removal without landlord's consent goes back to the Agricultural Holdings (England) Act 1883, s. 34. It was held in *Mears v. Callender* [1901] 2 Ch. 388 that s. 34 could be contracted out of. Similarly in *Premier Dairies Ltd v. Garlick*, *supra*, the view was taken that s. 21 of the Agricultural Holdings Act 1908 could be contracted out of. The same view has been generally held in regard to s. 22 of the Agricultural Holdings Act 1923 and s. 13 of the 1948 Act.

[56] [1980] A.C. 37 at 58, where, referring to the rule that a person may renounce a purely private right, Lord Hailsham said: "See also *Mears v. Callender* ... as to which, however, I have some doubt ... and *Premier Dairies Ltd v. Garlick* where, as counsel for the respondent pointed out, the statutory scheme was different in some important respects." It is suggested that Lord Hailsham's doubt may not be strong enough to overturn the traditional interpretation.

[57] s. 97, "under any custom of the country". This must be distinguished from a customary right to compensation, which is abolished, section 77.

[58] s. 10(7).

Opencast coal operations

10.41 In certain cases a tenant who suffers loss through the forced sale (due to impending opencast coal operations) of a fixture or building,[59] which he has a right under section 10 to remove, is entitled to compensation from the mining corporation.[60]

Market garden tenants

10.42 Market garden tenants have certain special privileges in regard to removal.[61]

Record under section 22 of fixtures or buildings

10.43 By section 22 of the Act the tenant is entitled at any time during the tenancy to require the making of a record of any fixtures or buildings which he has a right under section 10 to remove.[62]

Direction to landlord to carry out work for the provision, alteration or repair of fixed equipment: section 11

10.44 Section 11 of the 1986 Act gives the tenant a right to apply to the Agricultural Land Tribunal for a direction to the landlord to provide, alter or repair fixed equipment in order to enable the tenant to comply with statutory requirements.[63] The tenant's livelihood might depend on such compliance. If the landlord fails to carry out the direction the tenant has, among other remedies, the right to carry out the necessary work himself and recover the cost.[64] Section 11 gives the tenant power to get certain work done without delay at the landlord's expense and thus supplements the tenant's right under the 1986 Act to receive compensation for the unexhausted value of improvements at the end of the tenancy, and his right under paragraph 12 of the Agriculture (Maintenance, Repair and Insurance of Fixed Equipment) Regulations 1973[65] to execute repairs to fixed equipment which are the landlord's responsibility, if the landlord fails to do so, and recover the reasonable cost from him forthwith.

Procedure under section 11

10.45 The tenant's application to the Tribunal under section 11 must specify the agricultural activity which the tenant proposes to carry on. A statutory form is provided for the purpose of the application, and the application should be made substantially in accordance with the form. There is also a form for the landlord's

---

[59] See s. 27(1) and s. 28(4) of the Opencast Coal Act 1958, as amended by 1986 Act, Sched. 14, para. 29.
[60] Note the changes to the Opencast Coal Act by the Coal Industry Acts 1987 and 1994.
[61] s. 79(3). See Chapter 15 below.
[62] The cost of such a record will be borne in equal shares by landlord and tenant unless they agree otherwise: s. 22(3).
[63] It is submitted that "requirements imposed under any enactment" is wide enough to cover E.C. Regulations enforceable by virtue of the European Communities Act 1972.
[64] s. 11(6).
[65] S.I. 1973 No.1473.

reply.[66] The general procedure when a case is stated by a Tribunal on a question of law to the High Court is dealt with elsewhere.[67] It may be noted here that where the question of law arises from an application to the Tribunal under section 11 of the 1986 Act any notice of motion to the court for an order directing the Tribunal to state a case, as well as any notice of the motion by which application is made to the court to determine the question of law, must be served on the authority having power to enforce the statutory requirement (in addition to all parties to the proceedings and the secretary of the Tribunal).[68] The authority is entitled to appear and be heard in the proceedings on the motion.[69]

10.46 Conditions of a successful application under section 11
In order to succeed in an application to the Tribunal under section 11 the tenant must satisfy the Tribunal (and the onus is on him) that the following conditions are fulfilled.

(1) It must be reasonable, having regard to the tenant's responsibilities to farm the holding in accordance with the rules of good husbandry, that he should carry on on the holding the agricultural activity specified on his application to the extent and in the manner so specified.[70]

(2) Either (a) the tenant will contravene statutory requirements in doing so unless fixed equipment is provided on the holding, or (b) it is reasonable to use fixed equipment already on the holding for purposes connected with the activity, but, unless such equipment is altered or repaired, the tenant will in so using it contravene statutory requirements.[71]

(3) If it appears to the Tribunal that the specified activity has not been carried on on the holding continuously for a period of at least three years immediately preceding the application, the Tribunal must be satisfied that the starting of the activity did not or (if not yet started) will not constitute or form part of a substantial alteration of the type of farming carried on.[72] An obvious example of a substantial alteration would be a change from arable to dairy farming; a mere extension or improvement of the present farming enterprise requiring more equipment would not be

---

[66] See rule 6 of the Agricultural Land Tribunals Rules 1978 in Sched. to the Agricultural Land Tribunals (Rules) Order 1978 (S.I.1978 No.259). This work in Part V supplies two forms of precedent, one short (Form 11) and one long (Form 12). The Application by the tenant to the ALT is Form 13 and the landlord's reply Form 13A in Part V. Forms 13 and 13A are prescribed.
[67] See paras 16.61–16.65 below.
[68] RSC, Ord. 94, r. 7(2).
[69] ibid., r. 7(3).
[70] s. 11(1).
[71] ibid.
[72] s. 11(2). The original wording of this provision in s. 4 of the Agriculture Act 1958 contained an ambiguity, which is now removed by the insertion of the word "continuously" before "for". The word "for" by itself might have meant either "continuously throughout" or "at any time within", although in a previous edition of this work the former was taken to be the correct meaning. See 12th edition of this work, p.162.

CONDITIONS OF A SUCCESSFUL APPLICATION UNDER SECTION 11

such an alteration. A tenant who wants to change to a substantially different type of enterprise may be able to obtain the landlord's consent or the Tribunal's approval to improvements which will attract compensation at the end of the tenancy, so far as they have an unexhausted value then, but he will have to pay for them himself when they are executed.[73]

(4) It must be reasonable to give the direction, having regard to the landlord's responsibilities to manage the land comprised in the holding in accordance with the rules of good estate management and also to the period for which the holding may be expected to remain a separate holding and to any other material consideration.[74] It is clear that this condition affords considerable scope to the landlord to resist the application.

(5) It is a condition that the tenant should have requested the landlord in writing to carry out the work which is the subject of the application and the landlord has either refused to do so or has not agreed to do so within a reasonable time of the request.[75]

Cases where a direction under section 11 is excluded 10.47

In two cases the Tribunals' power to give a direction is specifically excluded.

(1) The first is where the landlord is already under a duty to carry out the work to comply with a requirement imposed on him by or under a statute.[76]

(2) The second is where provision is made by the contract of tenancy, or by any other agreement between the landlord and tenant, for the carrying out of the work by either of them.[77] "Agreement" here presumably means an enforceable contract, since the idea behind this exclusion is that if the parties already have rights and obligations enforceable at law covering the work in question they should be left to pursue their normal remedies. The contract of tenancy will include the "model clauses" contained in the 1973 regulations,[78] so far as incorporated. Thus the Tribunal have no jurisdiction to direct a landlord to carry out work of repair which he is under a liability to carry out by virtue of these regulations. Nor, of course, have they jurisdiction to direct the landlord to carry out work which is the tenant's liability under the regulations as incorporated in the contract.[79]

---

[73] Subject to the landlord's right under s. 67(5) of the Act.
[74] s. 11(3)(a).
[75] s. 11(3)(b). For a form see Part VI Forms 11 and 12.
[76] s. 11(4).
[77] ibid.
[78] Agriculture (Maintenance, Repair and Insurance of Fixed Equipment) Regulations 1973 (S.I. 1973 No.1473).
[79] s. 11(4).

10.48 Nature of direction under section 11 and power to grant extensions of time

If the necessary conditions are fulfilled, the Tribunal may direct the landlord to carry out, within a period specified in the direction, such work for the provision, or, as the case may be, the alteration or repair, of the fixed equipment in question as will enable the tenant to comply with the statutory requirements.[80] The Tribunal is given power, on an application by the landlord, to extend the specified period, and to grant further extensions, if satisfied that there will not be enough time both to complete preliminary arrangements in connection with the required work (including in appropriate cases the obtaining of a decision on an application by the landlord for a grant) and actually to carry out the work.[81] Many grants require prior approval and the right to claim them is lost if work is begun before they are approved. The power to extend time would enable the landlord to avoid the loss which would occur if he had to begin the work, in order to comply with the direction, before receiving such approval.

10.49 Tenant's remedies where landlord fails to comply with direction under section 11

If the landlord fails to comply with a direction under section 11 the tenant is given the same remedies as if the contract of tenancy had contained an undertaking by the landlord to carry out the work required by the direction within the period allowed by the Tribunal.[82] Thus the tenant can sue the landlord as for a breach of contract and recover damages for any loss caused by the landlord's default, subject to the ordinary rules in regard to remoteness. It is expressly provided that the tenant's remedies are to include the right to carry out the work himself and recover the reasonable cost thereof from the landlord notwithstanding any term in the contract restricting the carrying out by the tenant of alterations to the holding.[83] "Reasonable cost" in cases where the tenant has received an Exchequer grant means the reasonable cost less the grant.[84]

10.50 Right to increase rent under section 13

If the landlord carries out an improvement in compliance with a direction under section 11 he will be entitled to increase the rent of the holding under section 13.[85] The provisions of section 13 generally will apply including the provision for a reduction in the rent increase where the landlord has received a grant. Where the tenant has carried out the work himself on the landlord's default in complying with the direction, and has recovered the reasonable cost from the landlord (reduced by any grant received by the tenant) the provisions of section 13 will apply as if the improvement had been carried out by the landlord (and as if any such grant had

---

[80] s. 11(1).
[81] s. 11(7).
[82] s. 11(5).
[83] s. 11(6).
[84] s. 11(8). In the event of a dispute as to what was "reasonable" this would have to be determined by the Courts as there is no provision for arbitration under the 1986 Act.
[85] s. 13(2)(b). See for a precedent Form 15 in Part V of this work.

been made to him).[86] The provisions of section 13 generally are considered elsewhere.[87]

Direction under section 11 to intermediate tenant: rights against his landlord   10.51

Where, on the application of a sub-tenant, the sub-tenant's immediate landlord is directed to carry out work under section 11 which constitutes an improvement under Schedule 7, the immediate landlord is given protection against loss if he quits the holding on the termination of his tenancy while the improvement still possesses an unexhausted value. He will, of course, have been able to increase the sub-tenant's rent under section 13(2)(b), but it would be inequitable if he had to leave at the end of his own tenancy without being compensated for the unexhausted value of his expenditure. It is therefore provided that he will be able to claim compensation by virtue of section 64 and Schedule 7 from his superior landlord without having to fulfil the requirement of section 67 in regard to obtaining his landlord's consent to the improvement.[88] It is also provided that the immediate landlord will be able to claim against his superior landlord even if the work was actually carried out by the sub-tenant (on the immediate landlord's default), since in that case the sub-tenant will have had an enforceable right to recover from the immediate landlord the reasonable cost of the work.[89] It should be mentioned here that where a sub-tenant applies to the Tribunal for a direction to be given to his immediate landlord, the superior landlord will be a party to the proceedings[90] and entitled to be heard by the Tribunal.

Good estate management and good husbandry responsibilities   10.52

Section 11 refers (in subsection (1)) to the tenant's responsibilities to farm the holding in accordance with the rules of good husbandry, and (in subsection (3)) to the landlord's responsibilities to manage the land comprised in the holding in accordance with the rules of good estate management. It is provided in section

---

[86] s. 13(5), *i.e.* any Exchequer grant made to the tenant will be treated as if made to the landlord for the purpose of reducing the rent increase proportionately in accordance with s. 13(4)(a).

[87] See paras 11.40–11.44 below.

[88] s. 68(2)(a).

[89] s. 68(2)(b). The immediate landlord will be able to claim under s. 64 of the Act. It may be noted that s. 68(2)(b) has been drafted in accordance with a Law Commission recommendation that where an immediate landlord claims compensation from the superior landlord in respect of work carried out by the sub-tenant, s. 66(5) will have effect as if any grant made to the tenant in respect of the work out of moneys provided by Parliament has been made to the immediate landlord. (Otherwise the anomalous result would be produced that the immediate landlord who fails to comply with a direction of the Tribunal under s. 11 could pay to the tenant the cost of carrying out the work after deducting the amount of any grant out of public money which has been received by the tenant, but would then be entitled, on the termination of the tenancy, to claim compensation from his superior landlord without taking such a grant into account under s. 66(5)). See Law Com. No. 153 and Minutes and Report of Joint Committee on Consolidation Bills, H.L. 56–1 and H.C. 178–1.

[90] See r. 12 of the Agricultural Land Tribunals Rules 1978 in the Sched. to the Agricultural Land Tribunals (Rules) Order 1978 (S.I. 1978 No.259).

96(3) that sections 10 and 11 of the Agriculture Act 1947 (which define the circumstances in which an owner and occupier are deemed to fulfil these responsibilities) apply for the purposes of the 1986 Act. Although since the repeal of the 1947 Act, except for sections 10 and 11, these responsibilities are not enforced by state-administered sanctions, they constitute a code of estate management and husbandry behaviour which, applied in different contexts, can have a number of legal consequences. Although for many years section 11 was virtually unused, it has in recent times come into more frequent use owing to the need of dairy tenants to comply with requirements imposed as to the quality of control over farm effluent. Section 11 provides an opportunity for the landlord to be called upon to contribute towards the cost of statutory compliance where, without it, there is a very real risk that enforcement agencies will act to draconian effect. The capital cost of compliance may be very heavy.[91] It is submitted that, whilst the Tribunal may consider the gross capital cost under "any other material consideration"[92] a probable closure of the dairy enterprise as an alternative to re-equipping the farm is likely to outweigh the landlord's complaints as to the expenditure involved.

10.53 **Contracting out of section 11: not permissible**
Although section 11 does not include an express prohibition of contracting out of the rights given by the section, it is thought that as a matter of public policy it would not be permitted.[93]

10.54 **Limited owners and section 11**
A tenant for life has power to settle claims under section 11 in the same way as if he were owner in fee simple.[94]

10.55 **Variation of terms as to permanent pasture: section 14**
The object of section 14[95] is to provide a means by which clauses in tenancy agreements which require certain fields, or a certain proportion of the holding, to be maintained as permanent pasture may be modified if this is expedient for securing the full and efficient farming of the holding.[96]

Farming practice may favour the plough up of permanent pasture[97] in many

---

[91] And s. 11 may provide a bargaining tool for the tenant to encourage the landlord voluntarily, but over a long planned period, to contribute towards compliance.
[92] s. 11(3)(b).
[93] For the general principle, see per Farwell J. in *Soho Square Syndicate Ltd v. E. Pollard & Co.* [1940] Ch. 638 at 644 and for the general considerations which are relevant, see *Johnson v. Moreton* [1980] A.C. 37.
[94] s. 88.
[95] s. 14 reproduces, with drafting improvements, s. 10 of the 1948 Act. The jurisdiction had been transferred to arbitrators from the Minister by the 1958 Act, Sched. 1, para 6.
[96] s. 14(1),(2).
[97] On the meaning of "permanent pasture", it must be said that the precise legal definition is not too clear and most of the cases are old. The criterion seems sometimes to be mere age (pasture laid down 20 or more years ago), sometimes the character of the seeds mixture (showing the intention to produce permanent grass and not a temporary ley), sometimes contractual (an obligation to maintain in the same condition throughout the tenancy); *cf.* s. 15(7). The last is the most clear cut from a legal standpoint but does not always fit. For

VARIATION OF TERMS AS TO PERMANENT PASTURE: SECTION 14

cases where it would formerly have been regarded not only as "waste" in law, but irresponsible.[98]

Procedure under section 14 10.56

The procedure is for the landlord or tenant, as the case may be, to serve on the other party a notice in writing[99] demanding a reference to arbitration of the question whether it is expedient to secure the full and efficient farming of the holding that the area of land required to be maintained as permanent pasture should be reduced.[1] Section 14 does not make arbitration conditional on a previous unsuccessful attempt to agree, but no doubt in practice the parties will try to reach agreement before resorting to arbitration.

Nature of award under section 14 10.57

The arbitrator may direct in his award that the contract of tenancy is to have effect subject to such modifications as he specifies in regard to land which the contract requires to be maintained as permanent pasture or to be treated as arable; and he may give incidental directions modifying the cropping clause.[2] The contract is presumably modified from the date of the award or from such later date as the award specifies. The contract will be read as varied by the award, which should be preserved as a document of title. It seems clear that the jurisdiction of the arbitrator is confined to determining whether the area of permanent pasture is to be reduced or to remain unchanged, and that he has no jurisdiction to increase it.

The arbitrator may give an order the effect of which will be to ensure that when the tenant quits on the termination of the tenancy the land under pasture will be an

---

example, the 1923 Act regarded permanent pasture as an improvement which the tenant could make and for which, if laid down with the landlord's consent, he could obtain compensation. The essence of the meaning in the present section is contractual, but there is a physical flavour; otherwise the word "permanent" is really otiose. Among the old cases the following may be referred to: ***Atkins v. Temple*** (1625) 1 Rep. Ch. 13; ***Fermier v. Maund*** (1638) 1 Rep. Ch. 116; ***Drury v. Molins*** (1801) 6 Ves. 328; ***Birch v. Stephenson*** (1811) 3 Taunt. 469; ***Morris v. Morris*** (1825) 1 Hog. 238; ***Martin v. Coggan*** (1824) 1 Hog. 120; ***Simmons v. Norton*** (1831) 7 Bing. 640. At common law ploughing up "ancient meadow" was prima facie waste and could be restrained in equity by injunciton, even in the absence of an express covenant not to plough up. Normally a tenant was not restrained from ploughing up pasture which he had laid down himself on land which was arable at the commencement of the tenancy: ***Rush v. Lucas*** [1910] 1 Ch. 437, but in the exceptional case of ***Clarke-Jervoise v. Scutt*** [1920] 1 Ch. 382, where the tenant had covenanted not to plough up "any" grassland, and there were other special circumstances, an injunction was granted to prevent him from ploughing up permanent grass over 20 years old laid down by himself during the tenancy. Today, apart from the machinery of s. 14, ploughing up, if regarded as waste at all, would be more readily regarded as ameliorative or meliorating waste. Sched. 8 refers simply to "pasture" in Part II, para. 9, grass being treated as a crop and not as an improvement, in accordance with the modern outlook.

[98] Section 14 deals with the case where the contract requires land to be maintained as permanent pasture. If the contract is silent the tenant may plough up, subject to the law as to waste. Even on the old authorities such action, if waste at all, might be "ameliorative waste": see ***Simmons v. Norton*** (1831) 7 Bing 640.

[99] For form, see Form 16 in Part V of this work.

[1] s. 14(2). See s. 14(4) for the affected area.

[2] s. 14(3).

area not exceeding what the contract before modification required, and, if temporary pasture is to be sown for this purpose, may specify the seeds mixture in the order, thus influencing the length of the ley.[3]

10.58 Compensation in regard to permanent pasture: provisions for averaging

The tenant will not be entitled to compensation when he quits on the termination of the tenancy for pasture laid down under the above provisions to restore the pasture area.[4] Further, the Act inhibits an interesting piece of suggested chicanery by preventing the tenant from treating his inferior pieces of pasture as laid down in compliance with the order, and claiming pieces of pasture as laid down in compliance with the order, and claiming compensation on his superior pieces, by a provision[5] that the value per hectare for compensation purposes is to be averaged over the whole of the tenant's pasture,[6] including that laid down under the order. If the parties without resort to arbitration reach agreement with regard to the modification of a pasture clause, section 78(2) enables the contract to exclude compensation for resowing, notwithstanding the general ban in section 78(1) on contracting out of statutory compensation.

10.59 Disposal of produce and cropping: object of section 15

Section 15 deals with provisions in the contract of tenancy concerning the disposal of produce[7] and the control of cropping. It ensures a large measure of freedom for the tenant from unreasonable restriction while safeguarding the health of the holding and regulating the position as the tenancy approaches its end. The section opens by relieving the tenant from the full rigour of contractual[8] or customary[9] obligations in regard to cropping and the disposal of produce, subject to certain conditions and exceptions.[10] It necessarily applies, therefore, only where such a contractual or customary obligation exists. Thus the exclusion of manure[11] from the relief in respect of disposal does not mean that manure can never be sold off; it

---

[3] s. 14(4) and (5), expressing the point in more exact but more complicated language.
[4] s. 76(1)(a).
[5] s. 76(1)(b).
[6] "Tenant's pasture" means pasture laid down at the tenant's expense or paid for by him on entering on the holding: s. 76(2).
[7] This includes hay from permanent pasture, although the freedom of cropping does not apply to the latter: see s. 15(1)(b) and (7).
[8] For examples of covenants in the contract of tenancy restricting selling-off and cropping, see *Legh v. Lillie* (1860) 6 H.& N. 165; *Willson v. Love* [1896] 1 Q.B. 626; *Chapman v. Smith* [1907] 2 Ch. 97; *Bowers v. Nixon* (1848) 12 Q.B. 558; *Fleming v. Snook* (1842) 5 Beav. 250; *Doe d. Winnall v. Broad* (1841) 10 L.J.C.P. 80. Covenants prohibiting selling-off in the last year of the tenancy cover the produce of previous years as well as the produce of the last year; *Gale v. Bates* (1864) 33 L.J.Ex. 235; *Meggeson v. Groves* [1917] 1 Ch. 158. For the effect on a covenant to conserve hay and straw of their destruciton by fire, see *Re Hull and Meux (Lady)* [1905] 1 K.B. 588.
[9] This need not be immemorial or universal, but must be more than an individual or estate practice and must be reasonable: *Tucker v. Linger* (1883) 8 App.Cas. 508; *Womersley v. Dally* (1857) 26 L.J.Ex. 219; *Bradburn v. Foley* (1878) 3 C.P.D. 129 and as to custom generally see paragraph 13.107–13.114 below.
[10] s. 15(1), (4), (5).
[11] This removed a doubt which existed under s. 30 of the 1923 Act.

means that if there is (as indeed is usual)[12] a contractual or customary restriction on the disposal of manure, such a restriction remains fully operative and is not modified by section 15. Where the liberty given by section 15(1) applies it enables the tenant to disregard any restriction on selling-off, except for manure, and any cropping restriction affecting arable[13] land. Thus, the freedom of selling applies to hay from permanent pasture, but such pasture may not be ploughed up under the provision.[14] Section 15(1) does not relieve a tenant from a covenant or term restricting the type of farming on the holding, *e.g.* restricting it to dairy farming.

Exclusions from section 15 10.60

The freedom given by section 15(1) is excluded in the last stage of the tenancy. It does not apply[15]:

(a) In the case of a tenancy from year to year, as respects the year before the tenant quits the holding or any period after he has given or received notice to quit which results in his quitting the holding. This appears to mean that if more than 12 months' notice is given, say, 22 months, the freedom is excluded (*i.e.* the contractual or customary restrictions apply) during the whole of that period. But if less than 12 months' notice is given (as it can be in some cases under section 25) the freedom is excluded for the whole year before the tenant quits, and not merely the period of the notice. If there is a contractual or customary provision against selling off, this will be effective in the last year of the tenancy, not only in respect of produce actually grown in that year, but also in respect of produce, such as hay, grown in any previous year.[16]

(b) In the case of a tenancy other than a yearly tenancy, such as a lease for a fixed term, as respects the year before its termination.

---

[12] See **Gough v. Howard** (1801) Peake Add. Cas. 197.
[13] "Arable land" does not include land in grass which, by the terms of a contract of tenancy, is to be retained in the same condition throughout the tenancy: s. 15(7). This distinction between arable land and permanent pasture, based on a contractual provision seems to be the only firm distinction in law: see notes as to "permanent pasture" under s. 14 above.
[14] But see s. 14 for machinery to vary terms as to permanent pasture.
[15] s. 15(2). Although the meaning of subs. (2) has caused doubts in the past, it seems to be accepted that s. 15(1) is excluded in any case during the last year of the tenancy even if a shorter notice than 12 months is legitimately given, but that if a longer notice than 12 months is in fact given section 15(1) is excluded during that longer period. It may seem odd that a tenant's freedom should be withdrawn for a period which antedates the notice, but *cf.* **Wilmot v. Rose** (1854) 23 L.J.Q.B. 281 and **Eldon (Lord) v. Hedley Bros.** [1935] 2 K.B. 1. Clearly in order to restore the prescribed rotation in the last year earlier action may well be essential. This may put the tenant in a difficulty where the landlord gives a bare 12 months' notice and in an almost impossible position where less than 12 months' notice is properly given under s. 25(2). But parties may agree specially as to cropping in the last year.
[16] **Gale v. Bates** (1864) 33 L.J. Ex. 235; **Meggeson v. Groves** [1917] 1 Ch. 158. Contrast wording of s. 15(3).

10.61 Position under section 15 in regard to manure

It was noted above that if there is a contractual or customary restriction (as there usually is) on the disposal of manure produced on the holding, such a restriction remains in operation and is not modified by section 15(1). Section 15, however, contains a further provision applicable (*inter alia*)[17] to manure,[18] which provides that, subject to any agreement in writing to the contrary,[19] the tenant shall not at any time after he has given or received notice to quit sell or remove from the holding any manure unless the landlord's written consent has first been obtained. The position is therefore that any contractual or customary restriction will apply to manure produced on the holding either during the whole period of the tenancy or, according to the terms of the restriction, for some lesser period. In addition, unless there is an agreement in writing giving the tenant liberty to dispose of manure, he must not, after giving or receiving notice to quit, sell or remove from the holding any manure[20] without the landlord's prior consent in writing. So far as manure produced on the holding is concerned, there might be an overlap between the contractual or customary restriction and the statutory prohibition in section 15(3).

10.62 Prohibition under section 15 of sale or removal of other material

The prohibition in section 15(3) applies to compost as well as to manure and also to "any hay or straw or roots grown in the last year of the tenancy".[21] "Roots" means "the produce of any root crop of a kind normally grown for consumption on the holding",[22] not "cash crops", like potatoes or sugar beet.

10.63 Conditions in section 15 for the protection of the holding

Before, or as soon as possible after, he exercises his rights[23] of disposal of produce or cropping the tenant must make suitable and adequate provision to protect the holding. The provision which he must make is the following[24]:

(a) in the case of an exercise of the right to dispose of produce, to return to the holding the full equivalent manurial value of all crops sold off or

---

[17] It applies also to compost and to hay, straw and roots grown in the last year of the tenancy: s. 15(3).

[18] "Manure", as used in s. 15 and distinguished from "compost," means dung or manure produced by the excrement of animals; "compost" means decayed organic matter used as fertiliser.

[19] This means an agreement (in writing) enabling a tenant to sell or remove the produce mentioned after the giving or receipt of a notice to quit. Most agreements, however, are restrictive of disposal of the manure and other produce in question. It would appear that the effective field of operation of subs. (3) is where there is no agreement or custom restricting disposal and no "contrary" written agreement permitting it.

[20] "Any manure" would, technically, cover manure not produced on the holding, although it might be unlikely that the tenant would wish to sell or remove manure which had been imported.

[21] "Grown in the last year of the tenancy" applies only to hay, straw or roots. Manure and compost are not "grown" (apart from the grammatical indication).

[22] s. 15(7).

[23] *i.e.* the rights conferred by s. 15(1).

[24] s. 15(4).

removed from the holding in contravention of the custom, contract or agreement, and

(b) in the case of an exercise of the right to practise any system of cropping, to protect the holding from injury or deterioration.

If the tenant fails to make such suitable and adequate provision he renders himself liable to the pursuit by the landlord of the remedies mentioned in section 15(5) and (6) discussed below.

Landlord's remedies for tenant's wrongful exercise of section 15 rights 10.64

If the tenant exercises the rights given to him by section 15(1) in such manner as to, or to be likely to, injure or deteriorate the holding, the landlord will be entitled to obtain an injunction,[25] if the case so requires, to restrain the tenant from exercising those rights in that manner. He will also have the right in any case, on the tenant's quitting the holding on the termination of the tenancy, to recover damages[26] for any injury to or deterioration of the holding attributable to the exercise by the tenant of those rights.[27] These are the landlord's only remedies.[28] In order to support a claim for an injunction the landlord must obtain an arbitrator's award determining that the tenant is exercising, or has exercised, his rights under section 15(1) in such a manner as to, or to be likely to, injure or deteriorate the holding.[29] It is also provided that the arbitrator's award, for the purposes of the proceedings for an injunction, and also for the purposes of an arbitration to recover "damages" on the tenant's quitting the holding at the termination of the tenancy, shall be conclusive proof of the facts stated in the award.

Application of section 15(1) to smallholdings 10.65

The freedom of cropping and disposal of produce given by section 15(1) does not apply to a tenancy of land let by a smallholdings authority or by the Minister as a smallholding in pursuance of a scheme, approved by the Minister for the purposes of section 82, which (a) provides for the farming of such holdings on a co-operative basis, (b) provides for the disposal of the produce of such holdings, or (c) provides other centralised services for the use of the tenants of such holdings.[30] The Minister may, however, withdraw his approval if it appears to him that the scheme is not being satisfactorily carried out, in which case the freedom of cropping and

---

[25] For a case where an injunction was granted under a corresponding earlier provision, see **Heap v. Wilkes** (1910), reported only in *The Times*, October 29, 1910.

[26] "Damages" suggests an action for damages in the courts, but s. 15(6) refers to "an arbitration under paragraph (b)", *i.e.* under s. 15(5)(b), which includes the word "damages". In view of s. 83(1) one would expect that any claim arising on the termination of the tenancy would be determined by arbitration. There is a slight unresolved doubt because of the dictum by Singleton L.J. in **Kent v. Conniff** [1953] 1 Q.B. 361 at p.370.

[27] s. 15(5).

[28] *ibid.*: "the following remedies, but no other".

[29] s. 15(6). This refers to an arbitration during the tenancy in aid of an injunction, as distinct from an arbitration to determine compensation at the end of the tenancy. For a form of demand for arbitration for these purposes see Form 17 in Part V of this work.

[30] s. 82(1): see **Williams v. Minister of Agriculture**, *The Times*, October 17, 1986; and see (1985) 275 E.G. 1082 (note).

disposal will be restored.[31] The Minister must give due notice to the managers of the scheme and allow them an opportunity of making representations.[32]

10.66 Section 15 and mineral workings
The freedom given by section 15(1) did not apply to anything done in contravention of arrangements, or provisions included in leases, under section 20 of the Mineral Workings Act 1951 in relation to worked ironstone land, for the purpose of bringing it to a good state of cultivation and fertility. The whole of the 1951 Act has now been repealed, but there are transitional arrangements in regard to section 20 contained in section 4 of the Mineral Workings Act 1985.[33]

10.67 Sale of Farming Stock Act 1816
Where the freedom given by section 15(1) does not apply, as in the last year of the tenancy, not only will the tenant be liable for any breach of covenant restricting selling-off, but he and every purchaser from him will be bound by section 11 of the Sale of Farming Stock Act 1816, which prohibits a purchaser from using or disposing of produce in a manner contrary to the tenant's obligations. A landowner will, for example, be entitled to recover damages from the purchaser of hay or straw sold by the tenant in breach of covenant.[34]

10.68 Distress: general
The general law of distress for rent, a complicated and technical subject, is beyond the scope of this book. Full accounts will be found in the standard general text-books on landlord and tenant.[35] Only the special provisions in regard to distress in the case of agricultural holdings are dealt with here. These date back to the Agricultural Holdings Act 1883 and are now to be found in sections 16 to 19 of the 1986 Act. They concern respectively the period of arrears of rent for which distress may be levied, the extent to which the tenant may set off compensation due to him against the rent owing by him, certain limitations as to the things which may be the subject of distress, and provisions for the settlement of disputes.

10.69 No distress for rent due more than a year previously: section 16
The ordinary rule is that distress may be levied to recover arrears of rent up to six years from the date on which the arrears become due.[36] In the case of an agricultural holding, however, the landlord may not distrain for rent which became due more than one year before the making of the distress.[37] This, however, is subject to the qualification that where, according to the ordinary course of dealing between the

---

[31] s. 82(2).
[32] s. 82(3).
[33] There are few such arrangements now in existence and they are being phased out. For repeals, see Mineral Workings Act 1985, ss 1 and 10 and Sched. 2.
[34] *Eldon (Lord) v. Hedley Bros.* [1935] 2 K.B. 1.
[35] See, *e.g.* Woodfall, *Landlord and Tenant*, Vol. I, Chapter 9.
[36] Limitation Act 1980, section 19. Rent is due on the morning of the day appointed for payment, but is not in arrears until after midnight: *Cutting v. Derby* (1776) 2 W.Bl 1075; *Dibble v. Bowater* (1853) 2 E. & B. 564; *Re Aspinall, Aspinall v. Aspinall* [1961] Ch. 526.
[37] s. 16(1).

landlord and the tenant, the payment of rent has been deferred until the expiry of a quarter or half-year after the date on which the rent legally became due, then for the purposes of distress the rent is deemed to have become due at the expiry of that quarter or half-year, and not at the date at which it became legally due.[38] It is the practice on some estates not to require payment of the rent until a quarter or half-year after it becomes due. The effect of this provision may be to allow more than one year's rent to be distrained for. Thus in a case where rent is legally due on Lady Day (March 25) and Michaelmas (September 29) but by the custom of the estate the Lady Day rent is payable on June 24 and the Michaelmas rent on Christmas Day, the landlord would be entitled in any half year to distrain for anything up to three half-years' arrears of rent.[39]

Where the tenant becomes bankrupt, the landlord may, after the commencement of the bankruptcy, distrain only for six months' rent accrued due prior to the order for adjudication.[40]

The balance of the arrears of rent which the landlord is prevented from recovering by distress, as a result of the restrictions of section 16(1), may be recovered in an action at law, subject to the maximum of six years' arrears.[41]

Compensation to be set off against rent for purposes of distress: section 17 10.70
The tenant may set off against the rent the amount of any compensation[42] due to him under the Act or under custom or agreement, provided that it is ascertained before the landlord distrains. The right of distress is then restricted to any balance after the set-off.[43] Compensation will normally be "ascertained" as a result of agreement or arbitration.

Restrictions on distraining on property of third party: section 18 10.71
Certain property on the holding belonging to third parties is absolutely privileged from distress. This privilege is given to agricultural and other machinery on the holding under an agreement with the tenant for its hire or use in the conduct of his business and to livestock on the holding for breeding purposes.[44] A qualified privilege from distress is given in the case of agisted livestock[45]; *i.e.* livestock

---

[38] s. 16(2).
[39] See *Re Bew, ex p. Bull* (1887) 18 Q.B.D. 642, decided on s. 44 of the 1883 Act, which is reproduced in s. 16 of the 1986 Act.
[40] Insolvency Act 1985, s. 80.
[41] Limitation Act 1980, s. 19.
[42] Although this provision applies to any compensation due to the tenant of a holding, it would be unlikely to apply to compensation for disturbance or improvements. It could apply, say, to game damage compensation (s. 20). At common law set off is not allowed: *Absolem v. Knight* (1742) Bull.N.P. 181; *Willson v. Davenport* (1833) 5 C.& P.531; *Pratt v. Keith* (1864) 33 L.J. Ch.528.
[43] s. 17.
[44] s. 18(1)(a) and (b).
[45] s. 18(2) and (5). Sub-section (5) defines "agisted livestock" to mean livestock belonging to another person which has been taken in by the tenant of an agricultural holding to be fed at a fair price. Contrast arrangements, whether lettings or licences, which give exclusive possession of land for feeding: *Masters v. Green* (1888) 20 Q.B.D. 807. Making an agistment contract is not a breach of a covenant against assignment and subletting: *cf. Richards v. Davies* [1921] 1 Ch. 90. Agisted sheep were probably

belonging to another person which has been taken in by the tenant of the holding to be fed at a fair price.[46] The contract of agistment, which confers no interest in land on the owner of the stock, and is legally in the nature of a bailment,[47] must be distinguished from arrangements which create an interest in land, however temporary, such as a contract by which a tenant, in consideration of a fixed sum, allows the stock owner the exclusive right to feed the grass in certain fields for four weeks.[48] At common law agisted cattle could be distrained for rent, subject to a doubt in respect of a person who carried on a trade of agisting.[49] By section 18, however, agisted livestock are not to be distrained if other sufficient distress[50] can be found; and if distrained because other sufficient distress cannot be found the amount recoverable by distress is limited to the amount agreed to be paid for the agistment or the unpaid balance.[51] The owner of the agisted stock may, at any time before it is sold under the distress, redeem it by paying to the distrainer such amount, which is to be in full discharge against the tenant of the equivalent amount due under the agistment.[52] Any portion of the agisted livestock which remains on the holding is liable to be distrained for the full amount for which the whole of the livestock is distrainable.[53] The "fair price"[54] need not be in cash, but would cover "milk for meat" arrangements.[55] Gratuitous arrangements are not covered.

10.72 Settlement of disputes as to distress: section 19
Section 19 makes special provisions for the settlement of disputes in regard to distress on an agricultural holding which are in addition to the ordinary remedies by action of trespass or replevin. Section 19 provides for disputes (a) in respect of distress having been levied on an agricultural holding contrary to the above provisions of the 1986 Act, (b) as to the ownership of any livestock distrained or the price to be paid for the feeding of that stock, (c) as to any other matter or thing relating to a distress on an agricultural holding. Such disputes may be determined[56]

---

conditionally privileged apart from this section: **Keen v. Priest** (1859) 28 L.J. Ex. 157. For an agister's liability for safe custody, see **Coldman v. Hill** [1919] 1 K.B. 443. Note that the contract of agistment is not normally such as to enable the bailee of the stock to claim either a general or a particular lien against the stock owner: see **Re Southern Livestock Producers Ltd** [1964] 1 W.L.R. 24, where it was held that a contract to care for pigs did not involve the element of "improvement" which the cases have established as a necessary ingredient of entitlement to a particular lien.

[46] s. 18(5), "livestock" is defined in the same paragraph as including any animal capable of being distrained.
[47] As to whether the bailee has a lien, see **Re Southern Livestock Producers Ltd** [1964] 1 W.L.R. 24.
[48] **Masters v. Green** (1888) 20 Q.B.D. 807.
[49] **Miles v. Furber** (1873) L.R. 8 Q.B. 77.
[50] Presumably not itself conditionally privileged. An owner of stock will be able to recover their value from the distrainer if he sells them contrary to this section: see, e.g. **Keen v. Priest**, (above).
[51] s. 18(2).
[52] s. 18(3). This means the price agreed without the addition of costs.
[53] s. 18(4).
[54] s. 18(5).
[55] **London and Yorkshire Bank v. Belton** (1885) 15 Q.B.D. 457.
[56] This provides a summary procedure, but does not take away any existing remedy.

by the country court or, on complaint, by a magistrates' court. The court in either case may make an order for restoration of any livestock or things unlawfully distrained, may declare the price to be paid for feeding, or may make any other order that justice requires.[57] "Livestock" in this context includes any animal capable of being distrained.[58] An appeal lies to the Crown Court by any person aggrieved by a decision of a magistrates' court.[59] An appeal on a point of law lies from a county court to the Court of Appeal.[60]

Contracting out of sections 16–19: not permissible 10.73

Although not specifically excluded, it is thought that on general grounds contracting out of sections 16 to 19 would not be allowable.

Compensation for damage by game: position at common law 10.74

At common law the tenant had the exclusive right to the game,[61] including hares and rabbits, on land in his occupation, unless, as is in fact commonly the case, such right is reserved to the landlord. Under the Ground Game Act 1880,[62] however, the tenant in occupation has an inalienable right to take and kill ground game (hares and rabbits) so that a reservation of such game to the landlord will give him only a concurrent right with the tenant. At common law "game" has no very precise meaning and it is a defined in different ways for various statutory purposes, including section 20 of the 1986 Act.[63] It is quite usual for the landlord, having reserved rights to game, to let them to a third person, the sporting tenant.[64] The common law gives a right to compensation for damage from game in certain circumstances. There is normally no liability for damage from the natural increase of game already on the land, but if game is brought on to the land to an unreasonable amount, or caused to increase to an unreasonable extent, and damage is thereby caused to neighbouring land, liability arises. Thus in ***Farrer v. Nelson***,[65] where land was let with a reservation of sporting rights to the landlord, who had let them to a sporting tenant, the agricultural tenant recovered damages from the

---

[57] s. 19(1). Despite their width, it is doubtful whether these words confer on a magistrates' court a power to award damages for illegal distress: ***Lowe v. Dorling*** [1905] 2 K.B. 501 at 504.
[58] s. 19(3).
[59] s. 19(2).
[60] County Courts Act 1984, s 77. See ***Hanmer v. King*** (1887) 57 L.T. 367.
[61] See generally *Woodfall, Landlord and Tenant*, Volume I, Chapter 14, section 2. For the common law position, see ***Moore v. Plymouth (Lord)*** (1819) 3 B. & Ald. 66; ***Pochin v. Smith*** (1887) 52 J.P. 4; ***Farrer v. Nelson*** (1885) 15 Q.B.D. 258; ***Hilton v. Green*** (1862) 2 F. & F. 821; ***Birbeck v. Paget*** (1862) 31 Beav. 403; ***Seligman v. Docker*** [1949] Ch. 53. On the position of the sporting tenant, see ***Cope v. Sharpe*** (No.2) [1912] 1 K.B. 496; ***Mason v. Clarke*** [1955] A.C. 778. See also the Game Act 1831, for protection for express reservations of game, and the Ground Game (Amendment) Act 1906, for tenant's concurrent right to kill ground game (hares and rabbits).
[62] Amended in certain respects by the Ground Game (Amendment) Act 1906.
[63] See text below.
[64] See ***Mason v. Clarke*** [1955] A.C. 778. Strictly the "reservation" to the lessor will probably be a grant to him by the lessee of a *profit a prendre*.
[65] (1885) 15 Q.B.D. 258. See A.L. Goodhart's discussion in *Essays in Jurisprudence and the Common Law*, p.159. For other cases see also the next paragraph.

sporting tenant for injury to crops due to pheasants coming from a wood (reserved to the landlord) in excessive numbers. A landlord may, of course, assume a contractual obligation to keep down game, and will be liable for breach of it.[66]

10.75 Statutory compensation for damage by game: section 20 generally

Section 20 of the 1986 Act gives the tenant a right to compensation against his landlord for damage[67] to his crops from any wild animals or birds,[68] the right to kill and take which is vested in the landlord or anyone (other than the tenant himself) claiming under the landlord.[69] It will be convenient to continue to use the word "game" for the purpose of the 1986 Act, provided that it is understood to mean "any wild animals or birds". Hares and rabbits are not covered by the definition because at least a concurrent right to take them must be vested in the tenant. Section 20 does not deprive the tenant of any rights to compensation he may have at common law or by contract, but his statutory right cannot be curtailed by contract.[70] The landlord is liable to the tenant although the sporting rights have been vested in a sporting tenant.[71] The tenant has no direct right against the sporting[72] tenant under this section, but the landlord has a right of indemnity against the latter.[73] The landlord is liable under the section not only for damage for game from his own coverts but also for damages caused by game from a neighbouring estate, and even during the close season.[74] He has probably a

---

[66] *Erskine v. Adeane* (1873) 8 Ch.App. 756; *Barrow v. Ashburnham (Lord)* (1835) 4 L.J.K.B. 146.

[67] It was held (on a corresponding Scottish provision) that this includes damage by game from a neighbouring estate, as well as from the landlord's own coverts, and even during the close season: *Thomson v. Galloway (Earl)*, 1919 S.C. 611.

[68] This wording is substituted for "game" in s. 20(1) instead of "game" being defined later in the section as meaning "any wild animals or birds". The previous restrictive and selective definition of "game" in s. 14 of the 1948 Act (as "deer, pheasants, partridges, grouse and black game") has thus been superseded. It will be convenient to continue to use the word "game" for the purpose of the 1986 Act, bearing in mind its new simplified meaning. For protection of "wild animals and birds" and definitions, see the Wildlife and Countryside Act 1981, Part I, and Scheds 1–7. At common law "game" was a word of undefined meaning: *per* Erle J. in *Jeffryes v. Evans* (1865) 19 C.B. (N.S.) 246 at 264 and it has been used in statutes in a variety of meanings.

[69] This replaces the previous awkward form "anyone claiming under him other than the landlord" in s. 14(1) of the 1948 Act (1984 Act, Sched. 3, paragraph 7). The 1948 form was intended to prevent the tenant's right to compensation from being defeated by the device of not reserving sporting rights in the tenancy agreement, but arranging for them to be sublet by the tenant to the landlord. The new form avoids this difficulty.

[70] s. 78.

[71] Provided that the sporting tenant does not derive his rights from the agricultural tenant.

[72] In *Inglewood Investment Ltd v. Forestry Commission* [1988] 1 W.L.R. 959 it was held that a reservation of sporting rights in the form "all game, woodcocks, snipe and other wild fowl, hares, rabbits and fish" did not include deer. Harman J.'s decision contains an interesting review of authorities by a judge with a countryman's knowledge. As a result of the different wording now used in s. 20 as compared with previous Acts the above decision is of less direct relevance; but it should be studied by draftsmen of agricultural tenancy agreements, and those granting sporting rights.

[73] s. 20(5).

[74] *Thomson v. Galloway (Earl)* 1919 S.C. 611.

common law right of indemnity against such a neighbouring owner.[75] Although section 78 would prevent a landlord from contracting out of his liability to compensate the tenant, there is nothing to prevent a sporting tenant from contracting out of his liability to indemnify the landlord.

Conditions of right to compensation under section 20 for damage by game 10.76
The tenant's statutory right under section 20 is subject to a number of conditions

(a) The right is only in respect of damage by "wild animals or birds"[76] the right to kill and take which is vested in the landlord or anyone (other than the tenant himself) claiming under the landlord. Thus it would not appear to cover damage by rooks, pigeons or small birds and it does not, for the reason mentioned above, cover damage by hares or rabbits.

(b) If, although the sporting rights are reserved to the landlord, he gives the tenant a written licence to kill any or all of the categories comprised under "wild animals or birds", the tenant's right to compensation is excluded in respect of the category or categories mentioned in the licence.[77] In other words, the landlord can confine his licence to a particular species of game, in which case the tenant would be entitled to claim compensation for damage caused by other species.

(c) There is no longer any condition that entitlement to compensation depends on the damage exceeding a particular amount per acre or hectare, as under the 1948 Act,[78] but the good sense of tenants is likely to restrain *de minimis* claims.

(d) Notice in writing of the occurrence of the damage must have been given to the landlord within one month after the tenant first became, or ought reasonably to have become, aware of the occurrence.[79]

(e) The landlord must be given a reasonable opportunity to inspect the damage. This means in the case of a growing crop,[80] before it is begun to be reaped, raised or consumed; in the case of a crop which has been reaped or raised, before it is begun to be removed from the land.[81] It would seem wise to interpret this as meaning "before any of the crops", and not merely the damaged portion, is dealt with in the manner mentioned. What is a "reasonable opportunity" will depend on the

---

[75] *Farrer v. Nelson* (1885) 15 Q.B.D. 258.
[76] s. 20(1).
[77] *ibid.*, and see *Ross v. Watson* 1943 S.C. 406, decided under corresponding Scottish provisions.
[78] Originally an amount exceeding 1s. per acre, later (by S.I. 1975 No.447) amended to exceeding 12p. per hectare.
[79] s. 20(2)(a). Distinguish this from notice of the claim, with full particulars, under s. 20(2)(b). For forms, see Forms 18 and 19 in Part V of this work.
[80] Seed once sown is to be treated as a growing crop whether or not it has germinated: s. 20(3)(a). This removes a doubt previously raised. The amendment was made by the 1984 Act Sched. 3, para. 7.
[81] s. 20(2)(b).

circumstances. If harvesting is imminent the tenant cannot be expected to wait too long, but it would be wise to warn the landlord of the situation.[82]

(f) Notice in writing of the actual claim, with particulars, must be given within one month after the expiry of the year in respect of which the claim is made. "Year" for this purpose means any period of 12 months ending in any year with September 29, or with such other date as may by agreement between the parties be substituted for that date.[83] The reference to one month after the expiry of the year does not mean that the notice must be delayed until that month has begun; it may be given during the year in question.[84] It is essential to observe that the notice under this heading and the preliminary notice under (d) above are both required as conditions of entitlement.

10.77 Arbitration under section 20

The amount of compensation under section 20 is, in default of agreement made after the damage has been suffered, to be determined by arbitration under the Act.[85] Where the sporting rights are vested in a sporting tenant the tenant's claim is against the landlord, but the latter is entitled to be indemnified by the sporting tenant; any questions as to this right of indemnity are also determinable by arbitration under the Act.[86] This enables the sporting tenant to be brought in as a third party in the proceedings. The measure of compensation appears to be the full amount of the damage.

10.78 Extension of tenancies in lieu of claims to emblements: section 21

Ever since the Landlord and Tenant Act 1851 an agricultural tenant whose tenancy was liable to sudden termination as a result of the cesser of the landlord's interest

---

[82] See *Dale v. Hatfield Chase Corporation* [1922] 2 K.B. 282; *Barbour v. M'Douall* 1914 S.C. 844.

[83] s. 20(3)(b). The parties might for example agree on February 1, as the end of the pheasant and partridge shooting season.

[84] *Morton's (Earl) Trustees v. Macdougall* 1944 S.C. 410.

[85] s. 20(4).

[86] s. 20(5). The sporting tenant can probably contract out of this liability to indemnify. A landlord has no statutory right of indemnity against a neighbouring owner, although game from the latter's property may cause damage for which the agricultural tenant can claim against the landlord under this section; but there may be a common law right of indemnity: *Thomson v. Galloway (Earl)* 1919 S.C. 611; *Farrer v. Nelson* (1885) 15 Q.B.D. 258. The agricultural tenant has no direct remedy under the Act against the sporting tenant; *cf. Inglis v. Moir's Tutors* (1871) 10 M. 204. For the sporting tenant's power to protect his rights against interference by the agricultural tenant, see *Mason v. Clarke* [1955] A.C. 778.

EXTENSION OF TENANCIES IN LIEU OF CLAIMS TO EMBLEMENTS: SECTION 21

(where the landlord was entitled for life[87] or some other uncertain duration)[88] has possessed a better right than the ancient right of emblements, which meant a right physically to re-enter and take and carry away the crops which he had sown, provided that the latter were those vegetable productions of the soil[89] which matured or returned a profit within the year in which labour and expense had been devoted to them. Section 21 of the 1986 Act, reproducing earlier provisions, provides that a tenant holding at a rackrent[90] whose tenancy is terminated by the death or cesser of the interest of a landlord entitled for his life or other uncertain interest is to continue in occupation until the occupation is determined by a 12 months' notice to quit, expiring at the end of a year of the tenancy.[91] It seems that, despite the apparently mandatory words "and shall then quit", such a notice will have the same effect under the Act as any other notice to quit, *i.e.* will enable the tenant to claim compensation for disturbance if he quits, and will enable him in appropriate cases to serve a counter-notice and claim security of tenure under section 26(1). The succeeding landlord becomes entitled to an apportioned part of the rent from the date of death or cesser until the date of quitting.[92] Also, the conditions of the original tenancy apply during the continued occupation and on the termination of that occupation.[93] There is no recent authority on this section; any relevant cases are mentioned in the annotations to section 21.

---

[87] When a tenant for life of settled land grants tenancies under his Settled Land Act powers, the farm tenant will not be affected by the death of the tenant for life or the cesser of his beneficial interest. In practice, therefore, the present section may not be of much importance. It is not clear whether a tenancy granted by a landlord entitled for his life is necessarily a tenancy "for life or lives or for any term of years determinable with life or lives" so as to bring into play section 149(6) of the Law of Property Act 1925. Is it an estate *pur autre vie*? See Challis, *Law of Real Property* (3rd ed.), page 357.

[88] It was considered by Judge Carey Evans in *Stephens v. Balls* (1957) 107 L.J. 764,CC, (see also [1957] E.G.D. 237) that section 21 would apply to a tenancy granted to an incumbent.

[89] As to the kinds of produce covered, the word "emblements" includes not only corn sown, but also roots, potatoes, hemp, flax, hops and other "growing crops of those vegetable productions of the soil which are annually produced by the labour of the cultivator". It does not include such things as fruit trees, or oak, elm, ash or other trees or crops such as clover which remain productive beyond the first year. As the rights given by section 21 are "instead of claims to emblements", they can only be exercised by persons who would have been entitled to emblements at common law; *Stradbrooke v. Mulcahy* (1852) 2 Ir. C.L.R. 406. But to claim under section 21 a tenant must also be a tenant of an agricultural holding under s. 1(1): contrast *Haines v. Welch* (1868) L.R. 4 C.P. 91. See also *Evans v. Roberts* (1826) 5 B.&C. 829 and *Latham v. Atwood* (1638) Cro.Car. 515 but contrast *Graves v. Weld* (1833) 3 B.&Ad. 105.

[90] The means a rent of the full annual value or near it: *Re Sawyer and Withall* [1919] 2 Ch. 333 at 338.

[91] s. 21(1). This provision applies only to those tenants who before the statutory right would have been entitled at common law to emblements: *Stradbrooke (Lord) v. Mulcahy* (1852) 2 Ir.C.L.R. 406. There seems now little justification for retaining this relic of s. 14 of the Agriculture Act 1920.

[92] s. 21(2). Presumably, the apportioned amount ascertained under the Apportionment Act 1870.

[93] s. 21(3).

10.79 Record of the holding under section 22: general
Section 22, incorporating some amendments made by the 1984 Act,[94] enables a landlord or tenant to require a record to be made of the condition of the fixed equipment[95] on the holding and of the general condition of the holding itself (including any parts not under cultivation).[96] In addition it enables the tenant to require a record of any fixtures or buildings which under section 10 he is entitled to remove and of any existing improvements executed by him or for which he paid the outgoing tenant.[97]

10.80 Machinery for making record under section 22
The record is to be made by a person appointed by agreement between the landlord and tenant, or, in default of agreement, by the President of the Royal Institution of Chartered Surveyors.[98] The application for an appointment by the President must be accompanied by such fee as is prescribed by the Minister for such application.[99] Any instrument of appointment purporting to be made by the President by virtue of section 22(2) and to be signed by him or on his behalf is to be taken to be such an instrument or document unless the contrary is shown.[1]

10.81 Entry on holding under section 22
An appointed person (whether appointed by agreement or by the President) may, on production of evidence of his appointment, enter the holding at all reasonable times for the purpose of making any record authorised by section 22.[2]

10.82 Costs and disputes under section 22
In the absence of agreement the cost of such a record is borne by the landlord and tenant in equal shares. It is, however, not unusual to provide in the contract of tenancy that the cost of the record should be borne by the party requiring it. It seems that the cost could only be recovered by action at law; it is not a matter referred to arbitration under the Act.

10.83 Function and effect of record under section 22
A record made under section 22 is a condition precedent to a claim by a tenant for compensation for high farming under section 70,[3] but this is the only statutory

---

[94] 1984 Act, Sched. 3, para. 8.
[95] s. 16 of the 1948 Act specified certain types of fixed equipment only (buildings, fences, gates, road, drains and ditches) not fixed equipment generally.
[96] s. 16 of the 1948 Act referred to "the cultivation" of the holding, thus excluding the uncultivated parts, instead of "the general condition."
[97] s. 22(1)(a) and (b). For form of request, see Form 20 in Part V of this work.
[98] s. 22(2).
[99] s. 22(4). For "prescribed," see s. 96(1). The present fee is £115: see the Agricultural Holdings (Fee) Regulations 1996 (S.I. 1996 No.337).
[1] s. 22(5).
[2] s. 22(2). The 1984 Act, which added this provision (Sched. 3, para.8) abolished the more general power of entry by a person authorised by the Minister conferred by s. 91 of that Act. The present provision gives a power of entry as of right (at reasonable times) but no doubt in practice the tenant will be approached to agree a convenient time, and the landlord informed.
[3] s. 70(2)(b).

effect given to it. Apart from being a condition of a claim under section 70, it is only evidence. It is not deemed to be part of the contract of tenancy, it does not by itself create any rights or liabilities, and it cannot override anything in the contract. The fact that the record proves that, say, the condition of certain fixed equipment was poor on entry does not mean that the tenant is excused from keeping it and leaving it in a better state of repair if that is what his contractual or statutory obligations required.[4] To fulfil its function in providing evidence the record should be compiled with clarity and precision and include any necessary structural details of buildings and correct schedules of cropping and pastures. Accompanying plans are desirable and photographs may be of crucial value. The record and any accompanying plans, photographs and other documents should be authenticated by the signatures of both parties and dated. It is perhaps surprising that greater use is not made of the record procedure.

Record-maker not an arbitrator 10.84
Although the person appointed, whether by agreement or by the President of the RICS, may well by drawn from the panel of arbitrators,[5] the appointee is not for the purpose of section 22 an arbitrator. In making a record he is not acting as an arbitrator or subject to the provisions of Schedule 11 as to time or otherwise.

Form of record under section 22 10.85
There is no prescribed form for a record.

Landlord's power of entry: section 23 10.86
The landlord has no legal right to enter on the holding during the tenancy without the tenant's permission unless he is authorised to do so by contract, express or implied, or by statute. A landlord who enters without authority is a mere trespasser.[6] Section 23 of the 1986 Act gives a statutory right for the landlord to enter for three purposes, (a) viewing the state of the holding, (b) fulfilling his responsibilities to manage the holding in accordance with the rules of good estate management,[7] and (c) providing or improving fixed equipment on the holding otherwise than in fulfilment of those responsibilities.[8] It should also be noted that the "model clauses"[9] contain a power for the landlord to enter and carry out the repairs if the tenant is in default.[10] Tenancy agreements often specify other

---

[4] *Proudfoot v. Hart* (1890) 25 Q.B.D.42. But the obligations may take some account of the condition on entry: *Evans v. Jones* [1955] 2 Q.B. 58.
[5] Sched. 11, para. 1(5).
[6] For a strong case showing that the landlord commits a trespass if he enters his tenant's premises without contractual or statutory authority, see *Stocker v. Planet Building Society* (1879) 27 W.R. 877. The contractual authority may be implied: *Saner v. Bilton* (1878) 7 Ch.D. 815; *Mint v. Good* [1951] 1 K.B. 517; *McGreal v. Wake* (1984) 269 E.G. 1254.
[7] See s. 96(3).
[8] The purposes mentioned in paras (b) and (c) were added to (a) (which was in section 28 of the 1923 Act) by s.43 of the 1947 Act.
[9] s. 7 and the Agriculture (Maintenance, Repair and Insurance of Fixed Equipment) Regulations 1973 (S.I. 1973 No.1473).
[10] See para. 4(2) of the Sched. to the above Regulations.

purposes for which the landlord may enter, *e.g.* taking game, felling timber, working mines, and sometimes add "and all other reasonable purposes".

10.87 Restriction of landlord's remedies for breach: penal rents and liquidated damages excluded by section 24

It was formerly common to include in agricultural tenancy agreements clauses fixing penal or increased rents or a stipulated sum as damages for a very wide variety of breaches of covenant, such as selling off produce, breaking up permanent pasture, departing from a particular system of cultivation, grubbing underwoods, burning heather, and so on. There were numerous decisions which distinguished a penalty proper, against which the tenant could obtain relief, from liquidated damages, which were enforceable.[11] Even the 1923 Act, which abolished penal rents generally, made an exception for terms or conditions against the breaking up of permanent pasture, the grubbing of underwoods, the felling, cutting, lopping or injuring trees, or regulating the burning of heather.[12] The 1947 Act[13] removed certain exceptions to the restriction which had remained since section 6 of the 1900 Act, namely, the breaking up of permanent pasture, the grubbing of underwoods, the felling, cutting, lopping or injuring of trees, or regulating the burning of heather. The 1948 Act in turn abolished these exceptions and the 1986 Act, reproducing section 15 of the 1948 Act, provides that, notwithstanding anything in a contract of tenancy of an agricultural holding making a tenant liable to pay a higher rent or other liquidated damages in the event of a breach, the landlord shall not recover more than the damage actually suffered by him.[14]

---

[11] Thus only the amount of actual damage can now be recovered in any case, and clauses providing for increased rents if, say, permanent pasture is broken up, are no longer included in tenancy agreements. Formerly, a liquidated sum was recoverable provided that it was not in substance a penalty, and the general rule was that if the stipulated amount was proportioned to the extent of the breach of covenant it was treated as liquidated damages, but if the same amount was payable on the breach of any one of various stipulations of different degrees of importance it was a penalty. For cases, see p. 268 of the 12th edition of this work.

[12] 1923 Act, s. 29.

[13] Sched. 7, para 7.

[14] s. 24. In some cases the landlord will not even recover that; see s. 71 and *cf.* s. 18(1) of the Landlord and Tenant Act 1927.

Chapter 11

RENT REVIEW

11.1 Introduction

11.2 Procedural matters including time-limits

11.4 Analysis of rent review basis

11.7 Omission of reference to open market and general

11.10 Comparable lettings and scarcity

11.15 Scarcity and the subject holding

11.16 Marriage value

11.18 Valuations in conditions of no scarcity

11.19 Premiums and comparable lettings

11.20 Disregards generally

11.21 Tenant's improvements and fixed equipment

11.23 Grants

11.24 Tenant's own occupation

11.25 Dilapidation by tenant

11.26 Quotas

11.28 Rates

11.29 Frequency of rent reviews

11.33 Miscellaneous

11.40 Landlord's right to increase rent for his improvements: section 13

11.44 Tenant's agreement to pay interest on landlord's capital outlay

Procedural Table Relating To Rent Review

Part VI of this work contains Procedural Tables. Table 12: Variation of Rent by Arbitration sets out the times limited for taking steps in connection with a rent arbitration and refers to any forms in Part V of this work. The Table is intended to supplement a reading of Chapter 11 and provide a convenient reference point so that it is not necessary to duplicate information.

Statutory rent reviews: introduction 11.1

The provisions for the variation of rent of agricultural holdings by arbitration are contained in section 12 and Schedule 2.[1] Section 12 gives each party the right to

---

[1] The original provisions of the 1948 Act, amended by the 1958 Act, were further amended by the Act of 1984. Although irrelevant for statutory interpretation, it is of some historical

demand[2] arbitration as to the rent payable in respect of the holding and lays upon the arbitrator the duty of determining the rent properly payable. It makes provision to ensure that an arbitrator is appointed, either by agreement or as a result of an application to the President of the RICS, without undue delay after a demand for arbitration has been made. Schedule 2 contains the details of the formula to be applied by the arbitrator in the assessment of the rent properly payable and detailed provisions governing the frequency of arbitrations.

The right given by section 12 is for the landlord or tenant of an agricultural holding by a notice in writing[3] served on the other to demand that the rent to be payable in respect of the holding as from "the next termination date" shall be referred to arbitration under the Act.[4] The next termination date following the date of the demand is the next day following the date of the demand on which the tenancy of the holding could have been determined by notice to quit given at the date of the demand.[5] The machinery of section 12 will normally be invoked in the case of tenancies from year to year, but it appears to follow from *Edell v. Dulieu*[6] that it could be used to fix the rent payable from the date when a lease for a fixed term of years is "broken" under an option to determine it before the expiration of the full term. Apart from this possible case, section 12 has no application during the currency of a fixed term. Such a term could, however, contain a rent review clause on the lines of clauses familiar in leases of business properties.[7]

The arbitrator's duty on a reference to him under section 12 is expressed to be to "determine what rent should be properly payable in respect of the holding at the date of the reference".[8] Having done so, he must, with effect from the next

---

interest to note that the 1984 amendments, consolidated in the 1986 Act, were partly the result of a "package agreement" reached between the County Landowners' Association (CLA) and the National Farmers' Union (NFU) in 1981 by which, *inter alia*, the CLA agreed to support a reform of the rent provisions desired by the NFU in return for the latter's acceptance of the modification, desired by the CLA, of the scheme of statutory tenancy succession.

[2] Can such a demand be withdrawn by the party making it without the consent of the other? There is at present no superior court authority, but Judge Barr in a persuasive county court judgment, in *Buckinghamshire County Council v. Gordon* [1986] 2 E.G.L.R. 8; (1986) 279 E.G. 853, held that such a notice cannot be unilaterally withdrawn. He likened the procedure to that under the Landlord and Tenant Act 1954 rather than to an ordinary action where a party may discontinue proceedings.

[3] For an advisory form see Form 14 in Part V of this work.

[4] s. 12(1).

[5] s. 12(4).

[6] [1924] A.C. 38.

[7] For an example in an agricultural lease, see *Million Pigs Ltd v. Parry (No.2)* (1983) 268 E.G. 809.

[8] s. 12(2). "The date of the reference" is the date when the arbitrator is effectively appointed. This is the valuation date and it precedes the date when the rent thus determined becomes payable, which is the "next termination date", defined in s. 12(4). "The date of the reference" is the same wording as in the old s. 8 of the 1948 Act, not a self explanatory phrase. The meaning of the effective appointment of the arbitrator is discussed later in the text. In providing for a valuation date different from the date as from which any varied rent becomes payable, s. 12 diverges from the usual practice in commercial rent review clauses.

termination date following the date of the demand for arbitration, increase or reduce the rent previously payable or direct that it shall continue unchanged.[9]

Time limited for appointment of or application for appointment of arbitrator   11.2

An important condition affecting the validity of a demand for arbitration with respect to the rent under section 12 is that it will cease to be effective on the next termination date following the demand unless before that date one of two things has happened, either (a) an arbitrator has been appointed by agreement between the parties, or (b) an application has been made to the President of the RICS for the appointment of an arbitrator by him.[10] This condition, the fulfilment of which is essential for the arbitrator's jurisdiction, must be kept in mind.

Time-limits and procedural points affecting a rent arbitration   11.3

It is necessary to consider certain rules governing the time for proceeding with a rent arbitration. Readers are referred to **Procedural Table 12: Variation of Rent by Arbitration** in Part VI. The rules as formulated in *Sclater v. Horton*[11] and *University College, Oxford v. Durdy*[12] were modified by the Act of 1984.[13] The present position may be set out as follows:

Date of demand for arbitration The demand for a reference to arbitration as to rent must be made as long before the term day on which it is proposed that the variation of rent should take effect as a notice to quit would have to be given to terminate the tenancy on that day.[14] That day, called "the next termination date",[15] has the same meaning as "the next ensuing day" in the old section 8(1) of the 1948 Act. Thus, in the case of a Michaelmas tenancy, if the proposed rent change was to take effect on September 29, 1989, the demand for arbitration would have to be made before September 29, 1988.[16]   11.3.1

"Date of the reference": valuation date The "date of the reference" (for the meaning of this expression, see below) is the date as at which the rental value has to be determined, *i.e.* the valuation date.[17] The rent which the arbitrator has to determine is the rent which is properly payable at that date.   11.3.2

Demand for arbitration: condition of effectiveness The rule in *Sclater v. Horton*[18] was that the date of the reference must precede the next termination date,   11.3.3

---

[9] *ibid.*
[10] s. 12(3). For application forms, see Form 67A in Part V of this work.
[11] [1954] 2 Q.B. 1 CA.
[12] [1982] Ch. 413, CA.
[13] In the new ss 8 and 8A, substituted for the old s. 8 of the 1948 Act, and now consolidated in the 1986 Act, s. 12 and Sched. 2.
[14] s. 12(1), (4). "The next termination date" has precisely the same meaning as, but is more expressive than, "the next ensuing day" in the old s. 8 of the 1948 Act. The words "could have been determined" refer to the timing, not to the validity, of the notice to quit; the fact that after serving a notice to arbitrate on rent the landlord serves a notice to quit to which the tribunal refuse consent, so that in fact the tenancy could not have been effectively terminated, is immaterial: see **Wallingford Estates Ltd v. Tench** [1951] E.G.D 22, CC.
[15] s. 12(1), (4).
[16] Chapter 12 deals with the termination dates of yearly tenancies.
[17] s. 12(2).

i.e. the date from which the proposed variation of rent is to take place. This meansthat if an arbitrator had not been effectively appointed before the next termination date the demand for arbitration ceased to be effective.[19] This rule was modified by the 1984 Act,[20] with the result that an application to the President of the RICS for the appointment of an arbitrator will have the same effect as an appointment by agreement in preserving the effectiveness of the demand. In other words, a demand ceases to be effective on the next following termination date unless before that date either an arbitrator has been appointed by agreement or an application has been made to the President of the RICS for an appointment.

11.3.4 **"Date of the reference": meaning** The "date of the reference" means, not the date of the actual arbitration hearing, but the date of the effective appointment of the arbitrator.[21] The arbitrator is not effectively appointed until he has accepted the appointment, but he can, of course, signify his willingness in advance of the actual appointment. The court in *University College, Oxford v Durdy* rejected the submission that, in the case of an appointment by the minister,[22] receipt of notice of the appointment by the parties was necessary in order to perfect it. The Court's view was given statutory effect[23] and it is now provided that an arbitrator appointed by the President of the RICS shall be taken to have been so appointed at the time when the President executed the instrument of appointment.[24] The "benevolent construction" suggested by the court in *Durdy's* case, that time should not begin to run against parties until they received notices, is ruled out by statute.[25] The position in regard to the appointment of an arbitrator by agreement of the parties is different; the appointment in that case cannot be regarded as complete until the arbitrator's appointment is contractually binding.

11.3.5 **Arbitrator to determine rent: not to be appointed too early** As the rent has to be determined as at the date when the arbitrator is appointed, it is obviously desirable that there should not be a long gap between this valuation date and the date from which the resulting rent starts to operate, *i.e.* the "next termination date". To meet this point there is a special provision in the case of appointments by the President of the RICS for rent arbitrations; "any such appointment shall in any event not be made by him earlier than four months before the next termination date

---

[18] [1954] 2 Q.B. 1, CA.

[19] *Sclater v. Horton* [1954] 2 Q.B. 1, CA and *University College, Oxford v. Durdy* [1982] Ch. 413, CA. See especially per Evershed M.R. and Denning L.J. [1954] 2 Q.B. 13.

[20] 1984 Act, s. 1 (s. 8(13) of the 1948 Act as amended); now consolidated in s. 12(3) of the 1986 Act.

[21] *Sclater v. Horton* and *University College, Oxford v. Durdy*, above. The interesting judgment of Kerr L.J. in *Durdy's* case showed that the court in *Sclater v. Horton* could have given a more flexible meaning to the expression, but Eveleigh and Griffiths L.J.J. were clear that the fixed meaning was part of the *ratio* of the decision in *Sclater*.

[22] As from January 1, 1986 the President of the RICS.

[23] 1984 Act, Sched. 3, para. 28(10).

[24] 1986 Act, Sched. 11, para. 31.

[25] *ibid*, reproducing 1984 Act, Sched. 3, para. 28(10). The County Court decision in *Richards v. Allinson* (1978) 249 E.G. 59 must now be regarded as overruled.

following the date of the demand".[26] There is no such rule in the case of appointments made by agreement of the parties.

Invalid appointments It follows from what has been said in paragraph (3) above that the demand for arbitration ceases to be valid if there has been neither a completed appointment of the arbitrator (by the parties or President of the RICS), nor an application to the president for an appointment, before the next termination date. An appointment of an arbitrator (on or) after that date is *ipso facto* invalid unless it is made in pursuance of an application to the President made before that date (or unless the arbitrator has been appointed in place of another as mentioned in the next paragraph).   **11.3.6**

Replacement of arbitrator: deemed time of appointment In cases where an arbitrator dies, or is incapable of acting, or for seven days after notice from either party requiring him to act fails to act, a new arbitrator may be appointed as if no arbitrator had been appointed.[27] Where a new arbitrator is appointed in place of another under this provision (or otherwise) "the date of the reference" in section 12(2) of the 1986 Act is to be construed as the date when the original arbitrator was appointed.[28] Thus the new arbitrator is deemed to have been appointed when the original arbitrator was appointed and it follows that he will have the same powers as the original arbitrator would have had and that any adjustment of rent will take effect from what was the next termination date after the date of the demand for arbitration.[29] The replacement of an arbitrator may be on the grounds, *inter alia*, of death, incapacity to act, or removal by court order.   **11.3.7**

Invalid appointment: costs An arbitrator whose appointment is not made in accordance with the above rules as to time will not have jurisdiction to make a rental award, but will have jurisdiction to make an award as to costs.[30]   **11.3.8**

Rent properly payable: definition generally   **11.4**
The definition of the "rent properly payable" is set out in general terms in paragraph 1(1) of Schedule 2 and is expanded in later paragraphs of the Schedule. In view of its importance the wording is quoted for convenience below:

> "For the purposes of section 12 of this Act, the rent properly payable in respect of a holding shall be the rent at which the holding might reasonably be expected to be let by a prudent and willing landlord to a prudent and willing tenant, taking into account (subject to sub-paragraph (3) and paragraphs 2 and 3 below) all relevant factors, including (in every case) the terms of the

---

[26] Sched. 11, para. 1(3). The appointment is to be made as soon as possible after receipt of the application as a general rule, but in this particular case not earlier than the time mentioned.
[27] Sched. 11, para. 2.
[28] Sched. 11, para. 3.
[29] This embodies in statutory form the principle of the Scottish decision in **Dundee Corporation v. Guthrie** [1969] S.L.T. 93, where the replacement arbitrator was not in fact appointed until about a year-and-a-half after the term date from which the variation of rent was to take effect. It was uncertain whether this ruling applied in England and Wales until given statutory effect by the 1984 Act (Sched. 3, para. 28(3)).
[30] Sched. 11, para. 30.

tenancy (including those relating to rent), the character and situation of the holding (including the locality in which it is situated), the productive capacity of the holding and its related earning capacity, and the current level of rents for comparable lettings, as determined in accordance with sub-paragraph (3) below."

Two expressions mentioned in the above passage are defined as follows[31]:

(a) "productive capacity" means the productive capacity of the holding (taking into account fixed equipment and any other available facilities on the holding) on the assumption that it is in the occupation of a competent tenant practising a system of farming suitable to the holding, and

(b) "related earning capacity" means the extent to which, in the light of that productive capacity, a competent tenant practising such a system of farming could reasonably be expected to profit from farming the holding.

11.5 Rent properly payable: analysis

It will be seen that this central part of the rent arbitration formula combines hypothesis and facts. The tenant envisaged as the determinant of the rent is a model tenant in a factual situation. The rent sought is that which might reasonably be expected[32] to be paid by a hypothetical tenant who is at once willing, prudent and competent and who is assumed to be carrying on a system of farming suitable to the holding. The actual tenant may more or less nearly approach this model, but it is the model that decides what is the rent properly payable. The hypothetical tenant, however, is assumed to be using the fixed equipment and other facilities which are *de facto* available, to be bound by the subsisting terms of the tenancy agreement, and to be farming the holding in its actual geographical situation, surrounded by its real physical locality.[33] In other words the tenant and his standard of farming are hypothetical, but the external circumstances with which he has to contend are factual.

11.6 "Prudent" and "willing"

As a result of an amendment made by the 1984 Act,[34] the word "prudent" was added to "willing", so that the phrase is now "let by a prudent and willing landlord to a prudent and willing tenant".[35] It seems doubtful what, if anything, of substance

---

[31] Sched. 2, para. 1(2).

[32] "Might reasonably be expected" refers to the reasonable expectations of properly qualified persons who have taken pains to inform themselves properly. It is the expectation, not the rent, which is to be reasonable. The "prudent and willing landlord" (see text below) may reasonably be expected to think of the permanent well being of the holding, and the security for future payments of rent, and may well reject "freak" or "fancy" offers, although financially attractive. A landlord is in a different position from a vendor who may reasonably be expected to accept the highest bid from a financially sound bidder without worrying too anxiously about what will happen to the land when he has parted with his interest in it.

[33] Sched. 2, para. 1(1), (2).

[34] 1984 Act, s. 1 (substituting an amended s. 8 for the old 1948 Act section).

[35] 1986 Act, Sched. 2, para. 1(1).

is added to "willing" by "prudent". It was probably presumed in any case that the "willingness" was in fact prudent rather than reckless, that the tenant would not be willing to pay a ruinously high rent and that the landlord would not be willing to accept an unreasonably low one. A willing landlord, on the other hand, was probably not thought likely to be led astray by very high bids of a freakish or fancy nature, giving warning of the risk of an irresponsible and wasteful tenant; and a willing tenant would not expect to obtain a farm with high amenity by offering a rent nowhere near a sensible level.[36]

Omission of any reference to the "open market" 11.7
The most obvious change in the rent formula made by the 1984 Act,[37] and incorporated in the 1986 Act, is the omission of any reference to the open market. On the face of it, this omission seems a most significant difference, suggesting a belief by Parliament that the omission would have an effect on arbitrated rent levels. It is submitted, however, that, despite the absence of a reference to it, the concept of the open market is probably implicit in the present formulation. There seem to be three reasons why this is so.

(i) "The rent at which the holding might reasonably be expected to be let" involves the idea of reasonable people exercising an informed judgment in regard to the probable rent level. It is suggested that this can be nothing other than an invocation of the conception of a market in the minds of the prudent and willing landlord and tenant.

(ii) The use of rents of comparable holdings as a means to settlement or determination involves the principle of a hypothetical market; comparison of rents implies an appeal to a standard of values which is unintelligible without resort to the unifying idea of a market.

(iii) The instruction to disregard scarcity in the rents of comparable holdings assumes a capacity to visualise an actual market in which the rents passing are enlarged or "distorted" by scarcity and then an ability to make an appropriate deduction therefrom in order to arrive at the correct scarcity-less rent.

---

[36] *cf.* discussions of "willing" in cases on valuation of land for compulsory acquisition, such as ***Vyricherla Narayana Gajapatiraju v. Revenue Divisional Officer, Vizagapatam*** [1939] A.C. 302 and ***Glass v. Inland Revenue*** [1915] S.C. 449. The words "willing" excluded any element either of reluctance or over-anxiety. In particular it excluded the old "sympathetic hypothesis" of the unwilling seller, whose unwillingness had to be overcome by the payment of an extra 10 per cent: see per Scott L.J. in ***Horn v. Sunderland Corporation*** [1941] 2 K.B. 26 at 40. Despite the view expressed in the text, however, no doubt advocates will seek to extract from the word "prudent" some flavour of additional meaning to support their arguments. An interesting recent discussion of the willing landlord and the willing tenant (in the context of commercial rent review clauses) by Donaldson J. (as he then was) will be found in ***F.R. Evans (Leeds) Ltd v. English Electric Co. Ltd*** (1977) 245 E.G. 657; 36 P.&C.R. 185 quoted at paragraph 2.16 above. His comments on the implication of a market should be noted. See also ***Law Land Co. Ltd v. Consumers' Association Ltd*** (1980) 255 E.G. 617, CA and ***Dennis & Robinson Ltd v. Kiossos Establishment*** [1987] 1 E.G.R. 133 CA, for further discussion.

[37] 1984 Act, s. 1.

It must be said, however, that the deafening silence in the formula as to the open market, compared with the wording of the old section 8, causes difficulty. The question of the treatment of the open market was raised in *J.W. Childers Trustees v. Anker*.[38] It is submitted that a careful reading of that case does not result in the debate as to the effect of the omission of any reference to "open market" in the statutory formula being answered. In *J.W. Childers Trustees v. Anker* the Court of Appeal, amongst other things, had to consider whether or not an arbitrator on a statutory rent review was entitled to have regard to a management agreement entered into between the tenant and the Nature Conservancy Council and his entitlement to compensation following designation of the area including the tenancy as a Site of Special Scientific Interest. The Court also had to decide whether or not the arbitrator was entitled to have regard to "marriage value" generated by the tenant occupying other nearby property.[39] In relation to each of these items, and as a preliminary to the discussion, the tenant attempted to use the concept of the "open market" so as to displace the relevance of any actions by the actual tenant in the real world: in this he was unsuccessful in his argument and the Court had regard both to the management agreement and to the potential uplift where the tenant himself occupied other land and might perhaps be expected to bid more for the nearby subject holding the rent of which was being reviewed. For the purposes advanced by the tenant the expression "open market valuation" was not adopted so as to deflect the Court from application of the widest construction of the arbitrator's ability to have regard to what he took to be relevant matters.[40] The

---

[38] [1996] 1 E.G.L.R. 1.

[39] See para. 11.17 below.

[40] The relevant reasoning is that of Morritt L.J. at page 5C–6A: "As a preliminary to the second and third questions counsel for the tenant advanced arguments before the judge and this court as to the nature of the arbitration required by s. 12 and Sched. 2 to the Agricultural Holdings Act 1986. His submission is that the letting assumed for the purpose of ascertaining the rent payable is an open market letting with vacant possession. This was rejected by the judge. At 16E of the transcript he said:

'In my judgment, the legislative intention was by s. 12(2) and Sched. 2 to provide a complete statutory code to fixed (sic) rent and that code should be applied without addition, or, I add, subtraction.'

Later, at 17 he said:

'What is relevant in this particular case is this particular statutory formula, and that requires an objective approach to the fixing of the rent. It is a barren exercise to compare that with the open market; such a comparison is not relevant and it takes the arbitrator's eye and the court's eye off the ball.'

The judge's approach was criticised by counsel for the tenant on the basis that it could permit the arbitrator to produce any figure he liked provided that he took only relevant matters into account. It was submitted that the requirement that the rent 'shall be the rent at which the holding might reasonably be expected to be let by a prudent and willing landlord to a prudent and willing tenant' necessarily required an open market approach to be varied if at all by the subsequent provisions of the Schedule.

Counsel for the landlord accepted that those words pointed to a market and required the arbitrator to use his knowledge of the market. But he did not accept that the Schedule required what is known as an open market valuation.

For my part I think that the judge's approach was right. The predecessor of Sched. 2, para. 1, was s. 8 of the Agricultural Holdings Act 1948. Originally it contained no reference to open market. It was amended by s. 2 of the Agriculture Act 1958 so as to require the rent to be that at which 'having regard to the terms of the tenancy (other than those relating to rent) the holding might be reasonably expected to be let in the open market by a willing landlord to a willing tenant, there being disregarded ...'. That formula was amended in turn by the Agricultural Holdings Act 1984, s. 1, so as to exclude the reference to the open market and subsequently consolidated into the Agricultural Holdings Act 1986, Sched. 2. There is no reason to suppose that such exclusion was not intended to have effect.

But in any event the use of the expression 'open market valuation' is only convenient shorthand for the various assumptions to be made in carrying out such a valuation. If those assumptions are different to those required by Sched. 2 then to describe that valuation as an open market valuation is likely to lead to the adoption of the wrong assumptions. If the assumptions are the same then the description adds nothing. I suspect the problem has arisen because those required to operate the Schedule have taken the judge too literally. In stating that the code should be applied without addition or subtraction he did not mean assumptions could not be implied on the basis of well known principles of statutory construction; rather that the question of whether that assumption should be implied must be answered directly from a consideration of the words used in the Schedule not indirectly by attaching a label to the Schedule as a whole.

I turn then to the second question which asks to what extent, if at all, the management agreement is relevant to the determination of the rent. The judge considered that the arbitrator was entitled to have regard to it and that the extent to which he paid regard to it was a matter for him. His conclusion was on the basis that non-farming income was a relevant factor included in the statutory formula in addition to the farming income referred to in para. 1(2).

Counsel for the tenant submits that the judge was wrong. He claims that an agreement entered into by the individual tenant cannot be relevant when the formula, in para. 1(1) requires consideration of a hypothetical prudent and willing tenant and, in para. 3(a) requires the occupation of that tenant to be disregarded when the agreement is personal to the tenant and will terminate with his tenancy. He submits, in the alternative, that if its consideration is required by the statutory formula the arbitrator may not consider it unless it would be known to the hypothetical prudent and willing tenant. For this purpose he relies on *Electricity Supply Nominees Ltd v. London Clubs Ltd* [1988] 2 E.G.L.R. 152 for the proposition that if the arbitrator is concerned with how the market would have assessed earning capacity then the arbitrator may only take account of information which would have been available to the market.

I do not accept these submissions. In my view, the answer given by the judge was right though I would add to it a reference to the principles stated in the judgment of this court. The designation of the land as an "SSSI" Site of Special Scientific Interest has the effect of restricting or delaying to the point of restriction the agricultural operations which may be carried out on it. The designation is a local land charge and therefore known to all those concerned in the market. The market also knows that those disadvantages and restrictions, which may well affect the productive capacity of the land and its related earning capacity, may be offset by compensation payments made to a tenant of the holding as part of a management agreement. It seems to me that the existence of such offset and its likely amount must be relevant factors for the purposes of the statutory formula. Were it otherwise one side of the equation would be considered, but not the other. Given that the ability to restrict normal agricultural operations and the existence of compensation payments are relevant factors, then this management agreement may be the best evidence of the stringency of the restrictions likely to face the hypothetical tenant and the amount of the offset available to compensate for them. Thus it must be a relevant document for the arbitrator to consider on that basis. No doubt one or other of the parties will submit to him that it should not be followed because of other aspects of the case, as no doubt they will do with rent comparables. It will be a matter for the arbitrator to determine the weight (if any) to be attached to the management agreement. As the matter to be determined is the equivalent of actual earning capacity, not how the market would have seen it, the fact if it be one that the management agreement, and the details it contains are normally confidential, is immaterial.

underlying concept of the open market, suggested above, is, of course, subject to the various disregards and qualifications set out in detail in Schedule 2.

11.8 "All relevant factors": specific factors enumerated

The arbitrator is directed, in determining the rent properly payable, to take into account all relevant factors. Certain specific factors are then stated to be included, namely[41]:

> "the terms of the tenancy (including those relating to rent), the character and situation of the holding (including the locality in which it is situated), the productive capacity of the holding and its related earning capacity, and the current level of rents for comparable lettings."

Thus "all relevant factors" has its ordinary meaning and, without detracting from that, covers also the specific matters mentioned above. In general it may be said that the matters mentioned, such as the terms of the tenancy and the character and situation of the holding, are those which a competent arbitrator would in any case be expected to take into account without being expressly directed to do so. There is one point which may, however, he noted. The present formula refers to the terms of the tenancy "(including those relating to rent)" in contrast with the old section 8 of the 1948 Act which said "other than those relating to rent".[42] The latter formula was probably based on the consideration that, as the very matter in issue was the amount of the rent to be determined, it was the other terms, and not the existing rent, which had to be considered.[43] A term relating to rent, as distinct from the amount of the rent, may, however, be relevant. The former wording, in the old section 8, might, for example, have had the effect of nullifying a provision, say, for the abatement of rent in consideration of improvements carried out by the tenant; the present wording avoids this anomaly. As stated above, the existence of a management agreement and of an SSSI designation in relation to the tenanted land are relevant factors for the purposes of rent review.[44]

11.9 "Productive capacity" and "related earning capacity"

Those factors are among those specifically enumerated as relevant factors to be taken into account in determining the rent properly payable.[45] Their definitions direct attention not to the actual tenant practising his actual system of farming, but to a hypothetical competent tenant practising a system suitable to the holding,[46]

I would dismiss the appeal in so far as it challenges the answer of the judge to the second question."

[41] 1986 Act, Sched. 2, para. 1(1). The fact that a particular tenancy still had succession rights attached to it, as compared with another which had not, might be a relevant circumstance in determining the rental value.

[42] As does s. 34(1) of the Landlord and Tenant Act 1954 in relation to business tenancies.

[43] See also, in relation to business tenancies, *O'May v. City of London Real Property Co. Ltd* [1983] 2 A.C. 726 and *Cardshops Ltd v. Davies* [1971] 1 W.L.R. 591.

[44] See *J.W. Childers Trustees v. Anker* (commented on and quoted above).

[45] Sched. 2, para. 1(1).

[46] Para. 1(2).

although not necessarily the most suitable system possible. If the actual tenant is not competent or not practising a suitable system he will not be allowed a lower rent on that account. "Productive capacity" by itself does not indicate profitability, but "related earning capacity" introduces the conception of the profits which a competent tenant, practising a suitable system, could reasonably be expected to make. This competent tenant is a hypothetical person although the activities of the actual tenant may furnish useful evidence of what may be achievable. External factors, such as changes in government assistance, EEC directives, quotas, and marketing policies generally, could affect earning capacity without necessarily affecting productive capacity. Earnings from non-agricultural activities, such as income from caravan sites or catering for tourists, do not come within "related earning capacity", but are certainly "relevant factors" which may be taken into account. Having arrived at the profits from all sources, having used farm budgets, gross margin analyses, and all other methods, the question remains as to how profits are to be divided between landlord and tenant after any necessary charges have been made. The fact that they have been divided in the past in a certain ratio does not indicate the basis on which the distribution has been made. In the last resort it seems to depend on the interaction of the judgments of the two parties as to the rent at which the holding might reasonably be expected to be let. This is, in however shadowy a form, the mechanism of the market.

In ***Enfield London Borough Council v. Pott***[47] an arbitrator's award was set aside for error on the face of the award for various reasons. One was the failure of the arbitrator to distinguish properly between "productive capacity" and "related earning capacity". A further reason was that although the arbitrator was entitled to have regard to the passing rent as a "relevant factor" he appears to have totally disregarded it because it contained an element of scarcity value: this degree of confusion was regarded as unsatisfactory. The third mistake made by the arbitrator was to produce figures for related earning capacity of the holding and then straightforwardly split it between landlord and tenant without taking account of the value of a farm shop which ought to have been regarded as a "relevant factor". The vice of the award was failing to deal clearly with the farm shop and essentially ignoring it by proceeding to split an income derived exclusively from farming activities.[48] This case illustrates the fact that arbitrators giving reasons must think clearly and express themselves clearly and take care to include under the proper heading each matter which they consider to be relevant and helpful. It is not that the valuer must necessarily rely on any one of the relevant factors but simply that he explain clearly how he has dealt with them and to what extent he considers they should be reflected in the rent which he fixes.[49]

---

[47] [1990] 2 E.G.L.R. 7, Judge Bridges Adams in the Edmonton County Court.

[48] In other words, it was not the application of a 50:50 split in itself which caused the difficulty but simply using that split in circumstances where the underlying income did not incorporate the farm shop.

[49] Courts will not be anxious to intervene so as to correct the figures in an arbitrator's award, the court being concerned only to establish that the arbitrator has proceeded to use the correct criteria and has coherently explained the way in which he dealt with the evidence properly before him. Matters of the arbitrator's assessment as to strength of the evidence before him are, effectively, unchallengeable, subject only perhaps to obvious mathematical error on the face of the award.

11.10 **"Current level of rents for comparable lettings": evidence**

The reference to the level of rents for comparable lettings[50] is developed in a provision[51] which deals both with the evidence of which the arbitrator is to take account and with certain matters which he is required to disregard. "Disregards", which are (at least in form) divided into two classes,[52] are considered later. The arbitrator is directed to take into account "any available evidence" with respect to the following:

> "the rents (whether fixed by agreement between the parties or by arbitration under this Act) which are, or (in view of rent currently being tendered) are likely to become, payable in respect of tenancies of comparable agricultural holdings on terms (other than terms fixing the rent payable) similar to those of the tenancy under consideration."

The lettings to be used for comparison must be on terms broadly similar to those affecting the subject holding. It would make nonsense of the formula if "similar" were to be interpreted as practically identical. It is an essential part of the valuer's art to make the adjustments necessary to allow true comparability to be perceived, just as it is to discard an alleged comparable which has basic dissimilarities rendering it useless. "Terms fixing the rent payable" are excluded because they may depend on peculiarities of the particular contract.[53] If it is proposed to cite lettings of alleged comparable holdings before an arbitrator, it is essential that full information as to the properties cited and as to the terms of the relevant tenancies should be available, with satisfactory evidence in support.[54] It will be noted that evidence as to rents currently being tendered[55] is recognised as material which an arbitrator may take into account. The facts as to the tender would, of course, have to be clearly proved by suitable evidence and all necessary information as to the holding which was the subject of the tender made available. In the end the arbitrator will have to decide what weight, if any, should be given to evidence of tenders. There is a clear statutory direction to have regard to rents produced following an arbitration, therefore authorising the arbitrator to consider evidence which he would not be able to consider on a straightforward commercial rent review.[56] It is suggested that in considering the current level of rents for comparable lettings the arbitrator is probably concerned here exclusively with tenancies protected by the Agricultural Holdings Act 1986. It is difficult to see how lettings entered into governed by the Agricultural Tenancies Act 1995 could be regarded as falling within this provision.[57] This does not, however, mean that

---

[50] 1986 Act, Sched. 2, para. 1(1).

[51] Para. 1(3).

[52] Those specifically in relation to determining the rents of comparable lettings and those "on a reference under s. 12".

[53] See, *e.g.* the arrangement in ***Plumb Brothers v. Dolmac (Agriculture) Ltd*** (1984) 271 E.G. 373.

[54] For practical notes, see RICS Guidance Notes for Valuers.

[55] In Sched. 2, para. 1(3).

[56] Contrast ***Land Securities v. Westminster City Council*** [1993] 1 W.L.R. 286, a decision not reversed by the Civil Evidence Act 1995 abolishing the hearsay rule in civil proceedings.

consideration of rents achieved on farm business tenancies should be wholly disregarded by the arbitrator under the 1986 Act. He may regard these lettings as producing relevant and helpful evidence but he must not introduce them under Schedule 2, paragraph 1(3) as distinct from under the rubric "all relevant factors".[58] In relation to comparable lettings falling within Schedule 2, paragraph 1(3) there are specific directions for three matters to be disregarded.[59]

Matters to be disregarded: general 11.11

Paragraphs 1, 2 and 3 of Schedule 2 contain three separate sets of directions to the arbitrator in regard to matters to be disregarded in determining the rent properly payable and, as will be seen, there is an important question as to the precise effect of one of the directions. The three relate respectively to (1) rents for comparable lettings, (2) tenant's and landlord's improvements, and (3) the effect of the tenant's occupation and of dilapidation caused or permitted by the tenant.

Matters to be disregarded in determining rents for comparable lettings 11.12

The object of disregarding specified matters in determining the rents for comparable holdings must be to improve comparability by eliminating features which would detract from the value of the comparison. It will, however, be submitted that the disregard of the element of scarcity in comparable rents has an impact beyond its immediate effect on the comparable rents. The direction to the arbitrator under this heading is to disregard scarcity, "marriage value" and allowances made in consideration of premiums.

Scarcity disregarded in relation to comparable lettings 11.13

"Any element of the rents in question which is due to an appreciable scarcity of comparable holdings available for letting on such terms compared with the number of persons seeking to become tenants of such holdings on such terms" is to be disregarded.[60] This is an instruction to the arbitrator to disregard the element of scarcity in the rents of comparable holdings and the point which immediately becomes apparent is that there is no instruction to disregard scarcity in the rent of the subject holding itself.

"Scarcity value" must be distinguished from special amenity value appertaining to the particular holding.[61] Parliament did not intend to exclude that element of value which is due to the superior advantages of a particular farm as distinct from that which is created by the general shortage of farms to let. The latter should also

---

[57] Sched. 2, para. 1(1) refers to comparable lettings as determined in accordance with sub-para. (3). The wording quoted above limits consideration to comparable agricultural holdings (*i.e.* lettings under the 1986 Act) on terms similar to those of the holding under review. It is difficult to see how a farm business tenancy, with the different provision for security, could fall within this paragraph. It is also the case that sub-para. (3) expressly refers to arbitration under the 1986 Act and, where there is reference to agreement between the parties, this occurs at a time when the farm business tenancy legislation did not exist.
[58] See para. 11.18 below.
[59] See paras 11.11–11.19 below.
[60] Sched. 2, para. 1(3)(a). *cf.* Rent Act 1977, s. 70(2) in relation to rents of dwelling-houses.
[61] *cf.* **Metropolitan Property Holdings v. Finegold** [1975] 1 W.L.R. 349 at 352.

be distinguished from universal inflation affecting the price level of all goods and services, owing to an excess of money supply in the economy rather than shortages of things to buy.

11.14 Techniques in ascertaining "scarcity" value

Where the value of scarcity is to be taken out of a comparable letting it is not always easy to see quite how the valuation itself should be done. This problem is effectively the same whether the valuation proceeds under the Agricultural Holdings Act 1986 or under the Rent Act 1977 section 70(2)[62] and accordingly case law under the latter section may afford some guidance. Traditionally the adjustment will be made by a simple deduction to reflect scarcity[63] and such a deduction may be extremely high where circumstances warrant it.[64] The amount of any discount actually applied ought to be explained by the arbitrator in his award but it is unlikely that he would be required to demonstrate the actual mathematical adjustment as between individual comparables.[65] It would appear unlikely that valuing scarcity out by reference to a landlord's fair return on capital would be acceptable.[66] There is no restriction on the way in which an arbitrator must approach this task and it is submitted that any method may be adopted, provided it is supported by the evidence, which is not unlawful or unreasonable.[67]

11.15 Should scarcity be disregarded in relation to the subject holding?

Does this mean that, as a literal construction would suggest, Parliament intended that scarcity in the rent of the subject holding should not be disregarded, that it should, on the contrary, be accepted as an element of the rental value?[68] In that case the purpose of the direction to disregard scarcity in the rents of comparables was merely to produce some uniformity of valuation basis *inter se* and not to affect the assessment of the rent of the subject holding itself. This would be a somewhat

---

[62] "70(1) in determining, for the purposes of this Part of this Act, what rent is or would be a fair rent under a regulated tenancy of a dwelling-house, regard shall be had to all the circumstances (other than personal circumstances) and in particular to —; (a) the age, character, locality and state of repair of the dwelling-house; (b) if any furniture is provided for use under the tenancy, the quantity, quality and condition of the furniture ... (2) For the purposes of the determination it shall be assumed that the number of persons seeking to become tenants of similar dwelling-houses in the locality on the terms (other than those relating to rent) of the regulated tenancy is not substantially greater than the number of such dwelling-houses in the locality which are available for letting on such terms ...".

[63] *Batt v. London City and Westcliff Properties Limited* (1967) 111 S. J. 684.

[64] e.g. *Western Heritable Investment Co. Limited v. Husband* [1983] 2 A.C. 849 at 40%.

[65] *Spath Holme Limited v. Greater Manchester and Lancashire Rent Assessment Committee* [1995] 2 E.G.L.R. 80; *Northumberland and Durham Property Trust v. London Rent Assessment Committee* [1997] 1 E.G.L.R. 236.

[66] This type of yardstick was heavily criticised as "a notoriously unreliable method of valuation, normally used only as a last resort" by Lord Keith in *Western Heritable Investment v. Husband* (above) at 857.

[67] This is the standard which constrains valuation in the Rent Act context: *Mason v. Skilling* [1974] 1 W.L.R. 1437.

[68] Giving an answer to this question was something which was carefully avoided both in *J.W. Childers Trustees v. Anker* (above) and also in *Enfield London Borough Council v. Pott* [1990] 2 E.G.L.R. 7, CC.

surprising result, but if it is the correct construction it must be accepted, however contrary it might be to the actual intentions of the promoters of the Act.[69] It is, however, submitted that the literal construction is not in this case correct, but must yield to the "golden rule".[70] The following points are put forward in support of this view.

(1) If the literal construction were applied to section 70(2) of the Rent Act 1977, which is in principle the same as the present direction,[71] although perhaps more scientifically expressed, it would mean that scarcity should be disregarded in relation to the "similar dwelling-houses in the locality", but not in relation to the subject dwelling. This, however, would be directly contrary to the decision and reasoning of the House of Lords in *Western Heritable Investment Co. Ltd v. Husband*.[72]

(2) The objection, on a literal reading, that the direction does not instruct the arbitrator to disregard scarcity in the case of the subject holding itself is based on a failure to grasp the essential nature of scarcity. Scarcity is not an attribute inherent in the scarce object as a thing in itself, like the number of its hectares or the character of its soil, but something which exists only in a relationship. The truth is that scarcity with reference to a particular object can only be defined in terms of the demand for and supply of similar objects. This explains why the present provision[73] defines the scarcity element in respect of the subject holding in terms of the disequilibrium between demand and supply of comparable holdings.[74]

(3) It might be objected that in a particular case there could be no comparable. Does that mean that the formula is inoperative and that a rent inflated by scarcity must simply be accepted? First of all, the complete absence of any comparable, even an imperfect one which could be used with necessary adjustments, is perhaps not very common.

---

[69] Views expressed by Government spokesmen during the parliamentary progress of the Bill are of purely historical interest and of not the slightest probative value, but it is clear that they considered that what is now Schedule 2, para. 1(3)(a) merely gave statutory approval to the arbitrators' practice of excluding scarcity value in their rent determinations (see *e.g.*, per Lord Belstead, Hansard, H.L. Vol. 447, col. 1009 and the Minister of Agriculture, Hansard, H.C. Vol. 55, col. 859). The Court of Appeal in *J.W. Childers v. Anker*, above at 6F refused to look at Hansard on the grounds that the legislation was "neither ambiguous, obscure nor productive of absurdity" (Morritt L.J.).
[70] See *Nokes v. Doncaster Amalgamated Collieries Ltd* [1940] A.C. 1014 at 1022; see also *Luke v. I.R.C.* [1963] A.C. 557, at 577, *per* Lord Reid.
[71] Sched. 2, para. 1(3)(a).
[72] [1983] 2 A.C. 849. "In my opinion it is clear that on a proper construction the sub-section. requires fair rents to be determined on the hypothetical basis that the house-letting market in the locality is in a state of equilibrium in respect that the number of comparable dwelling-houses available for letting does not substantially exceed the number of persons seeking to become tenants", per Lord Keith of Kinkel at 856.
[73] In Sched. 2, para. 1(3)(a).
[74] The point comes out more clearly in s. 70(2) of the Rent Act 1977, technically a better formulation of the concept.

Secondly, if it is accepted that the intention of the formula is to eliminate scarcity from the subject holding, it is not too difficult to infer that even in the absence of an actual comparable an attempt should be made to do so.

(4) Is there really any reason why scarcity should be eliminated from comparables unless the object is to enable the arbitrator to arrive at the correct answer for the rent of the subject holding? The reasoning here is analogous to that which Lloyd J. (as he then was) found "irresistible" in *No.99 Bishopsgate Ltd v. Prudential Assurance Co. Ltd*,[75] namely, that there could be no conceivable point in a lease directing that the arbitrator should have regard to comparable lettings with vacant possession unless it was to indicate that he was to determine the rent on that basis.

A possible criticism that this interpretation of the direction to disregard scarcity is inconsistent with that given below to the direction in regard to marriage value is discussed later.

It is any "appreciable" scarcity which has to be eliminated, not, as in the Rent Act 1977, a "substantial" scarcity.[76] "Appreciable" is clearly greater than minimal, but seems to be less than "substantial". In other words, the present provisions go further than the Rent Act towards eliminating scarcity. It is dangerous to play with synonyms, but perhaps it may be said that the arbitrator should aim at a total exclusion of scarcity value, but will not be in error if only an insignificant residue of such value is left.

11.16   Marriage value disregarded in relation to comparable lettings
The arbitrator is directed to disregard "any element of those rents[77] which is due to the fact that the tenant of, or a person tendering for, any comparable holding is in occupation of other land in the vicinity of that holding that may conveniently be occupied together with that holding".[78] The object here is to eliminate one kind of "marriage value", namely, the enhancement of the rent of a comparable holding due to the fact that the tenant thereof occupies other land in the vicinity which might conveniently be occupied with that holding. (The direction also covers a person tendering for the comparable holding, but it is perhaps doubtful whether much evidence of this kind with be forthcoming).

11.17   Arbitrator to have regard to marriage value in relation to the subject holding
It will again be immediately apparent that there is no direction to disregard marriage value appertaining to the subject holding itself, whether such enhancement of value is derived from the existence of other land in the vicinity belonging to the tenant of the subject holding or from the attraction which the holding has for neighbouring farms whose bids could raise its value. On a literal interpretation,

---

[75] (1984) 270 E.G. 950 at 952. Lloyd J.'s decision was affirmed by the Court of Appeal at [1985] 1 E.G.R. 72; (1985) 273 E.G. 984.
[76] Rent Act 1977, s. 70(2).
[77] *i.e.* rents for comparable lettings.
[78] Sched. 2, para. 1(3)(b).

marriage value should be disregarded in determining the rents of comparable holdings, but should not be disregarded, *i.e.* should be taken into account as an element of value, in determining the rent of the subject holding. Is this literal interpretation, which has been rejected above in the case of scarcity, to be accepted in the case of marriage value? Would this be an unjustifiable inconsistency, or are there grounds to support a different construction in the two cases? It is suggested that, despite a formal or apparent inconsistency, there are in fact such grounds. In the case of marriage value there are no compelling reasons for departing from the literal interpretation, which produces a sensible result. The position in regard to scarcity is entirely different. As has been shown, scarcity as a factor affecting the subject holding can be defined only in terms of the relation between the demand for and supply of comparable holdings. Therefore a literal reading, restricting the effect of the disregard provision to the comparable holdings, in abstraction from the subject holding, is an artificial construction which makes no sense. On the other hand a literal interpretation of the direction in regard to marriage value in comparables makes perfectly good sense. Without it the wide diversity of the circumstances of particular "marriages", with the consequent haphazard and heterogeneous effect on value, could lead to confusion and could obscure true comparability. The object of this direction on this view is to ensure that comparables are truly comparable.

In ***J.W. Childers Trustees v. Anker***[79] the Court of Appeal concluded that marriage value in relation to the subject of the rent review was a relevant factor which the arbitrator was entitled to investigate and give such weight to as he considered fit and that he should do so irrespective of whether the additional land generating the "marriage value" is farmed by the actual tenant or by a third party. The tenant made two arguments in favour of excluding marriage value in relation to the subject holding, and each argument was rejected. First the tenant relied on the terms of Schedule 2, paragraph 3(a) requiring a disregard of the occupation of the subject holding by the tenant. Secondly the tenant relied on Schedule 2, paragraph 1(3)(b), the exclusion of marriage value in relation to comparables. Having been apprised of the possible different inferences to be drawn in relation to the disregard of scarcity/marriage value in treatment of comparables, the Court expressly limited its judgment to marriage value and did so in terms which leave open the analysis above in relation to the treatment of scarcity on the subject holding.[80]

---

[79] [1996] 1 E.G.L.R. 1.

[80] Thus Morritt L.J. at 6C-E: "This case is not concerned with whether scarcity (whether of demand or supply) is to be considered or excluded in the assessment of the rent for the subject holding, that question must await determination in a case in which it is raised. So far as marriage value is concerned I do not think that the provisions of para. 1(3)(b), which in terms relate to the exclusion of marriage value from a comparable, can be used to exclude such value from the assessment of the rent for the subject holding. That subparagraph does not in terms apply; and there is every reason to exclude marriage value from the former and not the latter so as to avoid potential double counting.

Thus one is thrown back to the terms of para. 1(1). The "character and situation of the holding (including the locality in which it is situated)" plainly bring in consideration of the fact that the subject holdings are bare land less in area than what might be considered as an economic unit yet potentially attractive on that account to a farmer seeking to

11.18 **Valuation in conditions where there is no scarcity**

Economic conditions may change such that, although there is no scarcity in the market, very high rents may be paid. This is a position which in relatively recent times has been seen in the residential market and it is possible that it may surface in relation to agricultural land, given the greater availability of land following the farm business tenancy legislation under the Agricultural Tenancies Act 1995. Under the Rent Act the subject holding must be valued without including any element of scarcity but in making such a valuation it is not proper for evidence of recent market lettings to be disregarded in favour of the evidence of rents registered, even in conditions where some tenants may regard the market rent as being far too high.[81] If as a result of greater availability of land an arbitrator concludes that scarcity is no longer a factor in high rents it is submitted that the rents achieved under farm business tenancies may prove to be helpful evidence as to what ought properly to be paid on a statutory rent review under the Agricultural Holdings Act 1986. Clearly this type of evidence cannot fall within Schedule 2, paragraph 1(3)[82] but this is hardly surprising since when the 1986 legislation was drafted farm business tenancies were not in contemplation. There is no reason in principle why an arbitrator should close his eyes to rents achieved under farm business tenancy arrangements and they may prove to be a "relevant factor". However one would expect the arbitrator to exercise great care in his assessments of the farm business tenancy transactions. In particular it is suggested that although farm business tenancy rents may be in relation to insecure tenancies it would not necessarily be appropriate to think that the prudent or willing parties in the statutory rent review under the 1986 Act would necessarily achieve a higher rental simply because the 1986 Act tenancy enjoyed greater protection.

It is submitted that where farm business tenancy evidence is presented to an arbitrator he may have regard to it and ought to consider what explanation there may be for the rents achieved under the farm business tenancies. For example, if rent levels really reflect high agricultural prices and a strong green pound it would seem logical to suppose that those conditions would appertain for the hypothetical tenant bidding in relation to the 1986 Act rent review. Conversely if there is some other explanatory factor which would not normally be expected to influence the hypothetical bidding in relation to the statutory rent review then the evidence of the farm business tenancies may be relatively limited in its usefulness to the arbitrator. Particularly given the treatment of the same problem in relation to the residential

---

expand. Such a farmer is a hypothetical figure in the range of prudent and willing tenants that the arbitrator is required to consider. In my view, it is plain that marriage value is a relevant factor for the consideration of the arbitrator. As with all the relevant factors the weight (if any) to be attached to it is a matter for him. I would dismiss the appeal against the judge's conclusion on the third question also and affirm the form of the answer he has given."

[81] ***BTE Limited v. Merseyside and Cheshire RAC*** [1992] 1 E.G.L.R. 116; ***Spath Holme Limited v. Greater Manchester and Lancashire Rent Assessment Committee*** [1995] 2 E.G.L.R. 80. Indeed, in the Rent Act valuation the Courts in those conditions consider that the assessment should commence with the market evidence and only thereafter consider evidence of other registered rents: ***Northumberland and Durham Property Trust v. London Rent Assessment Committee*** [1997] 1 E.G.L.R. 236.

[82] For the reasons identified above in para. 11.10.

Premiums disregarded in relation to comparable lettings 11.19

The arbitrator is directed to disregard any effect on the rents of comparable holdings which is due to any allowances or reductions made in consideration of the charging of premiums.[83] This direction does not give rise to much difficulty. Its object is clearly to arrive for purposes of comparison at the true rents of these comparable holdings. "Premium" in this context is, of course, used in the narrow sense of some pecuniary consideration in addition to rent, not in the broad sense sometimes employed, *e.g.* "the vacant possession premium" or "bids including key money or premium".

Matters to be disregarded "on a reference under section 12" 11.20

A number of matters are directed by paragraphs 2 and 3 of Schedule 2 to be disregarded by the arbitrator, not in determining the current level of rents for comparable lettings, but "on a reference under section 12 of this Act". In addition, section 15 of the Agriculture Act 1986 requires the arbitrator to disregard certain increases of rental value due to milk quotas. These "disregards" are free from some of the problems which have been discussed above. They comprise, in addition to the special case of milk quotas, certain tenant's improvements or fixed equipment, certain landlord's improvements, the effect of the tenant's occupation, and dilapidation, etc., caused or permitted by the tenant.

Tenant's improvements or fixed equipment disregarded 11.21

The arbitrator is directed to disregard any increase in the rental value of the holding due to tenant's improvements or fixed equipment other than improvements executed or equipment provided under an obligation imposed on the tenant by the terms of his contract of tenancy.[84] The question as to what an "improvement" may amount to is judged from the viewpoint of the tenant, not the landlord.[85] Specifically works may amount to an improvement although they may produce damage or diminution in the value of the premises or do not add to the letting value of the holding.[86] Hence the disregard in Schedule 2 relates to the increase in rental value due to improvements. "Tenants improvements" means "any improvements which have been executed on the holding, in so far as they were executed wholly or

---

[83] Sched. 2, para. 1(3)(c). See para. 2.2 above and in relation to the Rent Acts see *Woodfall, Landlord and Tenant*, Vol. 3, para. 23.150 for the collected cases distinguishing rent from a premium.

[84] Sched. 2, para. 2(1)(a). "Fixed equipment" was not mentioned in the old s. 8 of the 1948 Act in association with improvements. "Fixed equipment" is defined in s. 96(1) of the 1986 Act and "tenant's fixed equipment" is defined in Sched. 2, para. 2(2)(b), as "fixed equipment provided by the tenant". This presumably refers to chattels provided by the tenant which have become part of the demised premises and have lost their character as chattels. See also the discussion on similar provisions under the Agricultural Tenancies Act 1995 at paras. 2.17–2.23 above.

[85] Luxmoore J. in *Bowles Brothers Limited v. Sinclair* [1931] 2 Ch. 325; Rowlatt J. in *Lilley and Skinner Limited v. Crump* [1929] 73 S. J. 366; *Lambert v. F.W. Woolworth and Co.* [1938] 1 Ch. 883, CA.

[86] Slesser L.J. in *Lambert v. Woolworth* (above) at 901.

partly at the expense of the tenant (whether or not that expense has been or will be reimbursed by a grant out of money provided by Parliament or local government funds) without any equivalent allowance or benefit made or given by the landlord in consideration of their execution".[87] "Tenants's improvements" and "tenant's fixed equipment" extend to improvements executed and equipment provided during a previous tenancy of the holding unless the tenant received any compensation on the termination of that (or any other) tenancy.[88] It is not the tenant's improvements as such which must be disregarded, but "any increase in the rental value of the holding which is due" to them. This is not a mere matter of words. The direction to disregard extends not only to the annual equivalent of the cost of the improvement but also to the increased value of the holding, being latent value actually released or realised by the improvement; not, however, to value attached to the holding with the as yet unrealised potential for the improvements.[89] The improvements for this purpose need not, it is submitted, be agricultural improvements.[90]

11.22 **"High farming" a tenant's improvement**
The continuous adoption by the tenant of a system of "high farming", which is an independent head of compensation under section 70, is also treated as an improvement executed at the tenant's expense for the purpose of the direction to the arbitrator to disregard increases in the rental value of the holding due to tenant's improvements.[91]

11.23 **Landlord's improvements: grant aided element disregarded**
An increase in the rental value of the holding due to the landlord's improvements would normally be regarded. But it is to be disregarded if, and in so far as he has received, or will receive grants out of money provided by Parliament or local government funds in respect of the execution of the improvements.[92]

---

[87] Sched. 2, para. 2(2)(a). The explanation of the words in brackets is that a tenant should not pay a higher rent because of his own expenditure even if it is reimbursed from an outside source. "Allowance or benefit" was discussed in a number of Scottish cases later superseded by s. 44 of the Agricultural Holdings (Scotland) Act 1949. See *McQuater v. Ferguson* [1911] S.C. 640; *Galloway (Earl) v. McClelland* [1915] S.C. 1062; *Buchanan v. Taylor* [1916] S.C. 129; *Findlay v. Munro* [1917] S.C. 419; *Mackenzie v. Macgillivray* [1921] S.C. 722.

[88] Sched. 2, para. 2(3), a belated measure of justice to tenants given by the 1984 Act, s. 1 (s. 8A(4) of the 1948 Act as amended). Before this the principle of *East Coast Amusement Co. Ltd v. British Transport Board* [1965] A.C. 58 probably applied (although corrected for business tenants by s. 1 of the Law of Property Act 1969). For the position of a person not yet a tenant allowed into occupation to carry out improvements with a view to the grant of a tenancy, see *Hambros Bank Executor and Trustee Co. Ltd v. Superdrug Stores Ltd* [1985] 1 E.G.L.R. 99; (1985) 274 E.G. 590.

[89] See County Court decision of *Tummon v. Barclay's Bank Trust Co. Ltd* (1979) 250 E.G. 980.

[90] See *Tummon v. Barclay's Bank Trust Co. Ltd*, above (caravan site improvements on holding). For some abstruse valuation issues in regard to the effect on rental values of commercial improvements, see decisions of Forbes J. in *GREA Real Property Investments Ltd v. Williams* (1979) 250 E.G. 651 and *Estates Projects Ltd v. Greenwich London Borough* (1979) 251 E.G. 851.

[91] Sched. 2, para. 2(4).

Tenant's own occupation of the holding disregarded 11.24

The arbitrator is required to disregard any effect on the rent of the fact that the tenant who is a party to the arbitration is in occupation of the holding.[93] This may be said to be intended to prevent a sitting tenant from being either unfairly prejudiced or unmeritoriously advantaged. The distinction is similar to that in section 34 of the Landlord and Tenant Act 1954, which was considered in *Harewood Hotels Ltd v. Harris*,[94] where Lord Evershed M.R. approved a comment in Woodfall that "this seems to dispose equally of any accretion to the rent attributable to such occupation (the premises have to be envisaged as empty premises in the market) and of the 'sitting tenant' concession". The position of subtenants remained obscure.[95]

Dilapidation, etc., by tenant 11.25

Although not technically a "disregard", it is appropriate to include here the direction that the arbitrator must not fix the rent at a lower amount by reason of any dilapidation or deterioration of, or damage to, buildings or land caused or permitted by the tenant.[96] In other words, the arbitrator should treat the holding as if the dilapidation, deterioration or damage did not exist.[97] It is, of course, assumed that the dilapidation, etc., is due to the tenant's failure to discharge obligations which fall upon him.

Disregard of certain rent increases due to milk quotas 11.26

The subject of milk quotas, so far as it is relevant to agricultural holdings, is considered at length in Chapter 19. Certain increases in rental value attributable to milk quotas are required by the Agriculture Act 1986[98] to be disregarded in a rent arbitration. These are increases in rental value due to "transferred quota".[99] It has been decided to discuss this particular disregard separately because the subject is best considered within the general context of the milk quota legislation. It may, however, be mentioned here that the possession of milk quota by the sitting tenant

---

[92] Sched. 2, para. 2(1)(b). For definition of landlord's improvements, see *ibid.*, para. 2(2)(c). Contrast position as to grants in aid of tenant's improvements. A landlord should not be able to increase the rent when the improvement has been paid for out of public money, but a tenant should not be required to pay a higher rent because of his own expenditure, even if subsidised by a third party.
[93] Sched. 2, para. 3(a). See also the discussion at para. 2.24 above.
[94] [1958] 1 W.L.R. 108 at 111.
[95] See discussion in relation to the Agricultural Tenancies Act 1995 at para. 2.16 above.
[96] 1986 Act, Sched. 2, para. 3(b). See as to disrepair by landlord, *Strathclyde Regional Council v. Arnell* 1987 S.L.C.R 44.
[97] *cf.* Lord Parker C.J. in *Metropolitan Properties Limited v. Wooldridge* (1968) 20 P.&C.R. 64 at 66: "There is only one course open under the statute: that is, to value the premises as they are, assuming that the tenant had performed the covenants, whatever they are and however severe they are". Paragraph 3(b) would in fact cover dilapidations caused by the tenant's tort *e.g.* waste but such would probably also be a breach of contract. See also in relation to corresponding provisions under the Agricultural Tenancies Act 1995 at para. 2.25 above.
[98] Agriculture Act 1986, s. 15(1).
[99] *ibid.*, Sched. 1 para. 1(2).

is in general a matter to be regarded in a rental arbitration. The disregard provision in the Agriculture Act 1986 is thus a specific statutory exception to the general rule.

11.27 Treatment of other types of quotas
Milk quota is unique in being, for the most part, transferred with land.[1] There are other types of EC quota which in substance amount to the right to claim subsidy for certain animals under certain conditions.[2] These other types of quota are not attached to land and the question is as to whether or not an arbitrator may have regard to them in fixing the rent. On the face of it these types of quota should not be assumed to be available to the tenant hypothetically bidding at the statutory rent review; however, it would appear from *J.W. Childers Trustees v. Anker*[3] that a management agreement, undoubtedly personal to the actual tenant, was something that the arbitrator should have or might have regard to.[4] It is unclear whether the reasoning applicable to management agreements, namely that they are the best evidence of the stringency of restrictions likely to face the hypothetical tenant and the amount of offset available by way of compensation, could be applicable in relation to other types of quota. On balance it would seem unlikely that this is a satisfactory explanation for inclusion of, for example, sheep quota in what is being offered to the hypothetical tenant on the valuation. The arbitrator probably cannot include, for instance, sheep/beef quota in his consideration as something being offered. But it would seem logical that, if the bidding tenants are all sheep farmers with their own quota or are persons likely to bring quota with them, the issue of quota may not significantly affect the valuation.

11.28 No provision in regard to rates
The provision contained in the old section 8(2)(b) of the 1948 Act (requiring that account should not be taken of the relief from payment of rates) was abolished by the Act of 1984.[5] Thus, fortunately, vanished from the statute book a perplexing direction, never tested by a superior court in England and Wales, although interpreted alarmingly in Scotland[6] and by a bold County Court judge in Cornwall,[7] but probably in practice honoured more in the breach than in the observance.

11.29 Frequency of applications: general rules
The general principle is that the variation of rent under section 12 may not take place more frequently than at three-year intervals; and the rent cannot be varied within three years from the commencement of the tenancy.[8] Subject to various provisions mentioned later, the main rule is that a demand for arbitration shall not

---

[1] In the manner discussed in Chapter 18.
[2] *e.g.* sheep, beef and suckler cows.
[3] [1996] 1 E.G.L.R. 1, discussed above.
[4] Passage quoted at para. 11.7 above.
[5] The ss 8 and 8A substituted by s. 1 of the 1984 Act for the old s. 8 of the 1948 Act did not reproduce the old s. 8(2)(b).
[6] *Guthe v. Broatch* [1956] S.C. 132.
[7] *Tummon v. Barclay's Bank Trust Co. Ltd* (1979) 250 E.G. 980.
[8] *ibid.*, Sched. 2, para. 4(1)(a). Contrast s. 8(2) and (6), which permit a first reference at any time after the tenancy begins, but subsequently impose a three-year interval.

be effective if the next termination date falls earlier than the end of three years from any of the following dates:

(a) the commencement of the tenancy:

(b) the date as from which there took effect a previous increase or reduction of rent[9] (whether made under this section or otherwise); or

(c) the date as from which there took effect a previous direction of an arbitrator under section 12 that the rent should continue unchanged.[10]

Thus the three-year ban operates from the previous increase or reduction, whether made under section 12 or by negotiated agreement. The "no change" result must, however, result from an award, in order to activate the bar, not from a negotiated standstill. These rules are subject to provisions that certain increases and reductions in rent are to be disregarded for the purpose of the three-year bar; to a special application where a new tenancy has been created by a contract between a person entitled to a severed part of the reversionary estate and the tenant of the entirety; and to an exclusion where there has been an adjustment of boundaries or some other variations in the tenancy.

Matters not affecting frequency of applications 11.30
The following are to be disregarded for the purposes of paragraph 4(1)(b)[11]:

(a) an increase or reduction of rent under section 6(3) (variation consequential on award specifying terms of a written tenancy agreement) or section 8(4) (variation consequential on an award where terms of tenancy are inconsistent with the "model clauses");

(b) (i) an increase of rent for a landlord's improvements under section 13(1);

---

[9] An agreed reduction of rent following the compulsory acquisition of part of the holding thus sets off the three-year bar and does not come within one of the exceptions: it is unlikely that it could be regarded as "an adjustment of boundaries" within para. 6, as this seems to be aimed at comparatively small alterations. In cases where part of a holding is resumed, or taken by compulsory acquisition, and no reduction of rent is made, there is in fact an increase of rent per hectare, but it is submitted that this is not an increase within the meaning of para. 4(1)(b), which must refer to the actual amount of rent for the holding as a whole. It was held by a County Court judge in *Bolesworth Estate Co Ltd v. Cook* (1966) 116 New L.J. 1318 (note in (1996) 116 L.J. 739) that a "built-in" formula for the calculation of rent (*e.g.* by reference to the gallonage of milk sold) which in fact produces a variable money rent does not result in an "increase or reduction" within (what is now) para. 4(1)(b), so as to create a continuing bar to arbitration. There is much to be said for this view in principle, as the basis of rent agreed by the parties has remained unchanged, but the point is open to doubt in the absence of a superior Court decision. Is an increase pursuant to a progressive rent formula in the agreement an "increase" within the provision? It is difficult to argue that it is not. It is not entirely clear why para. 4(2) refers only to the present sub-para. (b) of para. 4(1) and not to sub-paras (a) and (c) also.
[10] Sched. 2, para. 4(1).
[11] Para. 4(2).

(ii) an increase agreed between landlord and tenant under section 12(3);

(iii) a reduction of rent agreed in consequence of any change in the fixed equipment provided by the landlord;[12]

(c) a reduction of rent under section 33[13] of the Act, where the landlord resumes possession of part of the holding either by virtue of section 31(1) or in pursuance of a provision in the contract of tenancy.

It would have been unreasonable to allow the above variations to set in motion a new three-year cycle.

11.31 Contract with persons entitled to severed part of reversion[14]
This provision prevents a new three-year cycle from starting to run when all that has happened is the creation of a new contract of tenancy at a proportionate rent between a person entitled to a severed part of the reversionary estate and the tenant of the whole holding. Although the mere severance of the reversion does not automatically result in the emergence of separate new tenancies,[15] an express contract between a person entitled to a severed part of the reversion and the tenant of the entirety can create a separate tenancy of the part of the holding whereon the severed part is reversionary.[16] The three-year cycle is only prevented from running, however, if the rent of the new holding is the "appropriate portion" of the rent previously payable for the entirety.[17] Future changes[18] in the rent of the new tenancy will, of course, set the three-year cycle running.[19] Whether the rent of the new holding is "merely the appropriate portion" may constitute a valuation exercise for the arbitrator. As to severance of the reversion generally see paragraph 12.20. It should be noted that simple severance of the reversion, where the tenancy remains entire, does not give the owner of the severed part the right to serve a section 12 notice on his own.[20]

11.32 Adjustment of boundaries or variation of terms
Certain tenancy variations of a more or less minor character, and consequential adjustments of rent, are not to be taken as resulting in a new contract of tenancy or otherwise triggering off a new three-year cycle. This covers the adjustment of the boundaries of the holding and a variation of the terms of the tenancy exclusive of

---

[12] A surrender of part of a holding, whether or not it includes or consists of a building or other fixed equipment, is not a "change in the fixed equipment" but a change in the holding itself and accordingly the occasion of such a surrender will trigger the three yearly rent cycle: *Mann v. Gardner* [1991] 1 E.G.L.R. 9.
[13] See Chapter 12 below for discussion of this section.
[14] Sched. 2, para. 5.
[15] *Jelley v. Buckman* [1974] Q.B. 488.
[16] As the judgment of Stamp L.J. in *Jelley v. Buckman* makes clear.
[17] *i.e.*, there is no real change which calls for a review.
[18] Or the arbitrator's decision that the rent should remain unchanged.
[19] Sched. 2, para. 5(2).
[20] Section 140 of the Law of Property Act 1925 enables notices to quit to be served without the concurrence of the owner of the other severed part(s) but not a rent review notice.

those relating to rent,[21] *e.g.* the addition to the tenancy of a conservation covenant.[22] The common law as to the kind of variations which result in a new tenancy was examined in ***Jenkin R. Lewis & Son Ltd v. Kerman*.**[23]

Use of arbitrator's expertise in determining rent 11.33

Questions have been raised as to the use by the arbitrator of his own expertise in determining rent. The matter is somewhat complex and not entirely free from difficulty. Clearly the arbitrator must consider and give due weight to any evidence tendered and make full use of all his equipment of expert knowledge to assess it. He must not use specific evidential material known to him, but not to the parties, without putting it to the parties and affording them an opportunity to comment on it.[24] But what is the position if no evidence, or no acceptable evidence, of rental value is put to the arbitrator? Can he, like a judge to whom no evidence is presented, decline to determine the rent and dismiss the proceedings? Evidently not: "On a reference under this section the arbitrator shall determine what rent should be properly payable in respect of the holding".[25] An agricultural arbitrator appears in this respect probably to be in the same position as a rent assessment committee, concerning which Widgery J. made the following observation:

> "A judge in civil litigation, who finds all the evidence unacceptable, can retire behind the onus of proof and dismiss the plaintiff's claim; but the rent assessment committee, once they embark on their inquiry, must produce a fair rent at the end of it all, and if the evidence tendered to them proves unacceptable or unreliable what else can they do but draw on their wisdom, experience and judgment and do the best that they can in the circumstances.[26]"

It would seem that in this limiting case the agricultural arbitrator has a residual valuation function which he cannot escape, where, unassisted by the parties, he must perforce use his accumulated knowledge and experience to arrive at the proper rent. Can the arbitrator go outside the figures stated by the parties and award more than the landlord's too modest demand or less than the tenant's over-generous offer? Subject to two specific considerations, it is submitted that the answer is no. It is a sound general principle that courts and Tribunals should not give parties more than they ask for; otherwise litigation would become a sheer gamble.[27] If, however, first, an arbitrator felt serious doubts as to whether a figure put forward was within the sphere of the reasonable, his correct course would be to

---

[21] Sched. 2, para. 6.
[22] Sched. 3, Part II, para. 9(2).
[23] [1971] Ch. 477. As to surrender and re-grant generally see paras 1.13 and 14.8.
[24] *cf. Fox v. P.G. Wellfair Ltd* [1981] 2 Lloyd's Rep. 514; (1981) 263 E.G. 589 and 657; *Top Shop Estates Ltd v. C. Danino* (1984) 273 E.G. 197.
[25] s. 12(2).
[26] *Metropolitan Properties Co. (FGC) Ltd v. Lannon* [1968] 1 W.L.R. 815 at 861.
[27] See *Thomson v. Anderson* (1870) L.R. 9 Eq. 523; *Fletcher v. Robertson* [1919] 56 S.L.R. 305; *Ellerby v. March* [1954] 2 Q.B. 357; *Morecambe and Heysham Corporation v. Robinson* [1961] 1 W.L.R. 373; and *Societe Franco-Tunisienne d'Armement Tunis v. Government of Ceylon* [1959] 1 W.L.R. 787.

put the matter to the parties for discussion: he should not fix a figure outside the parties' range without warning. Secondly, there may well arise circumstances where parties have put forward material and invited the arbitrator to make mathematical calculations or adjustments based on that material. It is perfectly possible that an arbitrator may adopt a method canvassed by the parties on a body of evidence put forward by them but ultimately reject a particular adjustment or an adjustment in a particular amount. The result of that may well produce a higher or lower rent figure but it is submitted in those circumstances the arbitrator cannot be criticised if he finds a figure which happens to be higher than, for example, the landlord is asking for.[28]

11.34 Rent awards do not normally create a new tenancy
The decision of the Court of Appeal in *Jenkin R. Lewis & Son Ltd v. Kerman*[29] made it clear that:

(1) an agreement to increase the rent of a holding which remains the same in size does not necessarily result in the creation of a new contract of tenancy, although if the parties indicate their intention to create a new contract the law will give effect to that intention;

(2) an arbitration award of an increased rent does not of itself result in a new contract of tenancy;

(3) conversely if the parties wish to extend an existing fixed term lease for a further number of years, not by the grant of a reversionary lease to take effect on the expiry of the present term, but by the immediate substitution of the longer term, a new contract will necessarily be created. Again, if it is desired to add new land to the holding, not by means of a separate tenancy at a separate rent, but so that there is a single tenancy of all the land at a new enlarged rent issuing out of every part of it, a new letting is implied.

---

[28] For example in a rent arbitration where the tenant expends his energy in attacking the landlord's farm budget but fails to deal with a comparable transaction produced by the landlord, the arbitrator may well decide that the landlord's adjustment of the comparable as required by Sched. 2, para 1(3)(a)–(c) is miscalculated or too great having regard to the explanation for such adjustment put forward by the landlord. The arbitrator's adjustment to the comparables may turn out to be more generous towards the landlord than the landlord's own figures and if this is translated through into the final award because the comparable is extremely persuasive then it is submitted the arbitrator should not be criticised for basing himself on the evidence which both parties have had the opportunity to discuss and it is presumed that the arbitrator will raise the issue of the adjustment with the parties before making his award. The problems which will otherwise result are illustrated by *Amego Litho Ltd v. Scanway Ltd* [1994] 1 E.G.L.R. 15.

[29] [1971] Ch. 477. Buckley J. whose own decision in this case was reversed by the CA, explained that his decision in the earlier case of *Sellar v. Reid* (1965) 193 E.G. 19 (which appeared to be authority for the view that a rent award under s. 8 created a new contract of tenancy) did not depend on an award but on a number of factors which together justified the inference of a new tenancy.

Jurisdiction of an arbitrator 11.35

The arbitrator in a rental arbitration, like many other tribunals, has jurisdiction to decide matters which are incidental, ancillary or collateral to the main issue which he has to determine. Thus he may have to decide who is the landlord, whether the subject-matter is an agricultural holding, or whether the tenancy is a tenancy from year to year or for a fixed term, but he will naturally consider whether to state a case if his jurisdiction depends on a difficult point of law.[30]

Opencast Coal Act 1958 11.36

The Opencast Coal Act 1958 directs[31] an arbitrator in a rental arbitration not to take into account any increase or diminution in the rental value of the holding which is attributable to the occupation of it, or part of it, by a person with the benefit of the opencast planning permission usually the Coal Authority[32] for "permitted activities" in connection with opencast coal production. The explanation is that the Act contains elaborate compensation provisions for the benefit of the owner and occupier. The rent continues to be payable by the tenant to his landlord despite the opencast occupation.[33]

Landlord's promises not to increase the rent 11.37

The effect of a landlord's promise not to seek an increase of rent, or to ask for a limited increase only, sometimes gives rise to questions. An undertaking by the landlord not to refer the amount of rent to arbitration under section 12 may be consideration for a promise by the tenant to pay some increase of rent, although such a promise without consideration would not be enforceable unless made under seal.[34] A question may also arise as to whether an undertaking by the landlord not to increase rent for a fixed period is given on condition of some specific *quid pro quo* from the tenant (on the failure of which the favourable level of rent would cease to operate) or whether the true consideration for the landlord's promise is to be found in the whole of the tenant's obligations under the lease.[35] This depends on the correct construction of the lease in the light of the surrounding circumstances.[36]

---

[30] *Kirby v. Robinson* (1965) 195 E.G. 363.

[31] Opencast Coal Act 1958, s. 14 as substituted by Sched. 8, para. 5, to the Housing and Planning Act 1986, and further amended in part by Coal Industry Act 1987, s. 1(2) and Sched. 1, para. 7(c) and the Coal Industry Act 1994, s. 52 and Sched. 8, Part I, para 5.

[32] The Coal Authority is the successor body to British Coal Corporation having available to it under the Coal Industry Act 1994, s. 52, Sched. 8 a special regime which after December 31, 1999 comes to an end. Pre-existing orders and directions made under the 1958 Act will survive December 31, 1999 without adverse effect (1994 Act, s. 52(1) and (3)).

[33] It should also be noted that para. 4 of Sched. 7 to the 1958 Act as amended confers a special jurisdiction on arbitrators to vary the terms of the tenancy, including rent, in consequence of opencast operations.

[34] See comments in *Chatwood Safe and Engineering Co. Ltd v. Frank* [1952] C.P.L. 532.

[35] *Plumb Bros v. Dolman (Agriculture) Ltd* (1984) 271 E.G. 373.

[36] May L.J., *ibid*, at 374 and Purchas L.J. at 376 depreciated the use of the phrase "factual matrix" as possibly suggesting an appeal to the subjective intentions of the parties.

11.38 Change of landlord
If after the notice demanding arbitration has been served the reversion is assigned, the new landlord can, it is submitted, continue the proceedings.[37]

11.39 Acceptance of rent pending arbitration
The acceptance of rent on the existing basis by the landlord pending the result of the reference does not operate as a waiver of the demand for arbitration because, in the absence of agreement, he cannot demand more.

11.40 Landlord's right to increase rent for his improvements: section 13
The landlord is given a statutory right[38] in certain cases to increase the rent where he has carried out an improvement which increases the rental value of the holding. In order to exercise this right he must serve on the tenant a notice in writing[39] within six months from the completion of the improvement. The rent may then be increased as from the date of completion by an amount equal to the increase in the rental value attributable to the improvement.[40] There is no need to go to arbitration to secure this increase, but arbitration under the Act is available in case of disputes.[41] The improvement need not be one which attracts compensation under Part V or Part VI of the 1986 Act, but it must fall within one of the categories set out below.[42] An increase of rent under this provision is disregarded for the purpose of the three-year interval between rent arbitrations under section 12 of the Act.[43] In order to secure the benefit of the rent increase being disregarded for the purpose of the three-yearly cycle it is not necessary to serve statutory notices under section 13: the disregard includes "any reduction of rent agreed between the landlord and the tenant of the holding in consequence of any change in the fixed equipment provided on the holding by the landlord".[44]

11.41 Improvements to which the right applies: section 13(2)
Section 13 applies to the following categories of improvements carried out by the landlord:

>   (a) an improvement carried out at the request of, or in agreement with, the tenant;

---

[37] *cf. Morris Marks v. British Waterways Board* [1963] 1 W.L.R. 1008 (a case under the Landlord and Tenant Act 1954).
[38] s. 13.
[39] See for a form, Part V Form 15.
[40] s. 13(1). In the case of land affected by opencast coal working ("the permitted activities") the increased rental value due to an improvement is to be assessed as if the opencast operations had not been carried out; the position is adjusted by the compensation provisions of the Opencast Coal Act 1958, s.14 as substituted by Sched. 8, para. 5, to the Housing and Planning Act 1986. For a form of notice of claim by the landlord under s. 13(1) see Part V Form 15.
[41] s. 13(7).
[42] s. 13(2).
[43] Sched. 2, para. 4(2)(b).
[44] See para. 11.30 above.

IMPROVEMENTS TO WHICH THE RIGHT APPLIES: SECTION 13(2)

(b) an improvement carried out in compliance with a direction by the Tribunal under section 11 to provide, alter or repair fixed equipment, or carried out by the tenant and the reasonable cost recovered from the landlord on the latter's failure to comply with the Tribunal's direction;[45]

(c) an improvement carried out in pursuant of a notice served by the landlord under section 67(5) of the Act (where the landlord has elected to carry out himself a long-term improvement approved by the Tribunal);

(d) an improvement carried out in compliance with a statutory direction given to the landlord by the Minister;

(e) works to comply with a notice under section 3 of the Agriculture (Safety, Health and Welfare Provisions) Act 1956 in regard to the provision of sanitary conveniences and washing facilities;

(f) an improvement carried out in compliance with an improvement notice within the meaning of Part VII of the Housing Act 1985 or the undertaking accepted under that part, or in compliance with similar provisions in Part VIII of the Housing Act 1974.[46]

Agreement between landlord and tenant: section 13(3) 11.42

No increase shall be made under the statutory right given by section 13(1) in respect of an improvement within paragraphs (a), (b) or (f) above if, within six months from its completion, the landlord and tenant agree on an increase of rent or other benefit in respect of it.[47] The reference to "other benefit" is undoubtedly wide enough to cover the commonly encountered situation where the landlord agrees with the tenant that the latter shall pay interest on the landlord's capital expenditure on the improvement as distinct from an increase in the rental.

Reduction of increases for contributions: section 13(4) 11.43

Where the landlord has received an Exchequer (or where appropriate a local government) grant in respect of the improvement, or in the case within paragraph (f) above if the tenant has contributed to the landlord's cost, the increase of rent is to be reduced proportionately.[48]

Tenant's agreement to pay interest on landlord's capital outlay 11.44

This has already been considered in relation to section 13(3).[49] In theory at the next rent review arrangements for the payment of interest should be subsumed into the section 12 review. In the interval the interest payment is not rent and should not

---

[45] s. 13(5) and (6). The reasonable cost will be reduced by any Exchequer grant received by the landlord: see s. 11(6) and (8).
[46] Both those provisions are now spent. The 1974 Act, in so far as relevant, was repealed by the Housing (Consequential Provisions) Act 1985, s. 3 and Sched. 1; the relevant parts of the 1985 Act were repealed by the Local Government and Housing Act 1989, ss. 165(2) and 194(4) and Sched. 12, Part II subject to limited savings in S.I. 1990 No.431, Sched. 1, para. 12.
[47] s. 13(3).
[48] s. 13(4).
[49] See above, para. 11.42.

be treated as rent for any purpose. Where money is due to be paid and is not paid the landlord has no opportunity, accordingly, to serve notice to pay rent as a preliminary to a Case D notice to quit.[50] In practice many agreements to pay interest on landlord's capital outlay are never in fact ultimately subsumed into the normal rent review cycle but continue for years under supplemental agreements. These supplemental agreements give rise to the issue as to whether or not it is permitted to "contract out" of section 12 at all. Clearly the problem does not arise in relation to section 13, which contemplates that agreements may be reached as to benefit without variation of the rent but the difficulty remains in relation to section 12 which, on the face of it, is mandatory in its language. The status of an agreement as to the payment of interest when no section 12 review takes place is not impeached: the problem arises where the parties go through a section 12 rent review whether concluding the exercise by agreement or by arbitral award. It seems unlikely that in principle contracting out of section 12 is permissible[51] but there appears to be a limited tolerance of agreements whereby statutory rights are foregone, provided those rights were available at the time when the agreement to forego them was made.[52] It is suggested, but cautiously, that following the section 12 rent review the contractual agreement to pay interest is probably closer in its nature to the exception represented by *Elsden v. Pick* than the cases dealing with full "contracting out".[53]

11.45 Opencast coal activities
Where improvements have been affected by anything done for the purpose of carrying out "permitted activities" in connection with opencast coal mining, the increase in rental value attributable to the improvements is to be assessed as if it had not been done.[54]

---

[50] By contrast, however, he may serve notice in Form 3 of S.I. 1987 No.711 (Form 25 in Part V of this work) being notice to remedy not being a notice to do work: see generally para. 12.60.
[51] *Johnson v. Moreton* [1980] A.C. 37.
[52] *Elsden v. Pick* [1980] 1 W.L.R. 898 and see discussion at paras 12.3–12.4 below.
[53] A similar problem is encountered in relation "turnover rent" (*e.g.* payment of so many pence per litre of milk produced) but that type of contract has not been examined by the higher Courts in terms of considering the issue of validity/contracting out. See further the discussion noted at para. 11.29 above in relation to *Bolesworth Estate Co. Limited v. Cook* [1966] 116 New L.J. 1318 (note in [1966] 116 L.J. 729).
[54] See s. 14(7) of the Opencast Coal Act 1958 as substituted by para. 5 of Sched. 8 to the Housing and Planning Act 1986.

Chapter 12

TERMINATION OF TENANCY: NOTICES TO QUIT

- 12.1 Scheme of security of tenure
- 12.5 Length of notice to quit
- 12.17 Notices to quit part of holding
- 12.23 Drafting and construction of notices to quit
- 12.31 Procedure in relation to notices to quit capable of reference to the Agricultural Land Tribunal
- 12.34 Consent by Agricultural Land Tribunal to operation of notice to quit
- 12.44 Cases where consent of Agricultural Land Tribunal not required
- 12.46 Jurisdiction of the Courts
- 12.49 Case A: Small holdings
- 12.50 Case B: Non-agricultural use
- 12.51 Case C: Certificate of Bad Husbandry
- 12.52 Case D: Non-payment of rent and remediable breach
- 12.55 Notice to pay rent
- 12.61 Notices to remedy involving the doing of work
- 12.75 Notices to remedy other than notices to do work
- 12.76 Case E: Non-remediable breach
- 12.78 Case F: Insolvency
- 12.79 Case G: Death of tenant
- 12.82 Case H: Amalgamation or reshaping of agricultural unit
- 12.83 Arbitration
- 12.92 Members of the Reserve and Auxiliary Forces

PROCEDURAL TABLES RELATING TO NOTICES TO QUIT

Part VI of this work contains procedural tables dealing separately with each different type of notice to quit. In order to save a huge amount of duplication the details regarding procedure and Forms are not fully set out again in the text of this chapter. Readers are referred to the following Tables which are intended to be the primary guide through procedural matters. Comment in the text is designed as a supplement to assist progress through the more complex areas. The following tables are provided:

1. Notices to quit capable of reference to the Agricultural Land Tribunal.
2. Notices to quit: Cases A, B and E.
3. Notice to quit: Case C.
4. Notices to quit under Case D following notice to pay rent.
5. Notice to quit: Case D and notice to do work of repair, maintenance or replacement.
6. Notice to quit under Case D following notice to remedy not including work of repair maintenance or replacement.

In so far as there may be a notice to quit given under Case G reference may be useful to Procedural Tables designed for the succession chapter, Chapter 14, and an introduction to those tables is to be found at the beginning of that chapter.

12.1 Scheme of security of tenure: origins

One of the more important benefits conferred on tenants by the law of agricultural holdings is the system of security of tenure introduced by the Agriculture Act 1947 and then embodied, to stand for the future with little significant alteration in the consolidating Agricultural Holdings Act 1948. This aspect ranks in importance with the statutory right to compensation for improvements which was first placed on a secure footing by the Agricultural Holdings Act 1883. Since 1948 statutory additions and case law accretions have increased the complexity in detail of the system. The statutory framework was consolidated in the Agricultural Holdings Act 1986 which is, together with its associated case law, considered in this Chapter.

12.2 Scheme of security of tenure: general

The 1986 Act works quite straightforwardly by offering tenants considerable protection in relation to the giving of and operation of notices to quit by the landlord. It is because of this fact that the majority of fixed term leases will be converted into periodic tenancies on the expiry of the fixed term, and for the same reason informal agreements are turned by section 2 into periodic tenancies. The result is, in each case, to assimilate those arrangements to a periodic annual tenancy which between 1948 and 1986 was the contractual norm. The 1986 Act makes general provision for a minimum 12 months' notice to quit to be given whether in relation to the whole or part of a tenancy,[1] which rule is itself subject to a number of important exceptions.[2] Notices to quit part of a holding deserve special treatment[3] not least because the statute creates an opportunity under section 31 for the landlord to serve notice to quit part for particular purposes. The tenant has also a special statutory right in certain circumstances to treat a notice to quit part as a

---

[1] See paras 12.5 below.
[2] See paras 12.6–12.13 below.
[3] See paras 12.18–12.22 below.

notice to quit the entirety pursuant to section 32.[4] However the single most important feature of security is the extremely limited opportunity for the landlord to obtain possession following the service of notice to quit. In very general terms, the tenant has the opportunity within the fixed period of one month from the giving of the notice to quit to serve a counter-notice requiring that section 26(1) should apply to the notice to quit. Obviously if no such notice is served the notice to quit takes effect but where the counter-notice is served the landlord will only be able to take possession in circumstances where the Tribunal consent to the operation of the notice. That matter is governed by section 27 which establishes various specific grounds[5], one of which must be proved by the landlord. In addition the Tribunal is required to withhold consent to the landlord's request if in all the circumstances it appears to them that a fair and reasonable landlord would not insist on possession.[6]

In combination sections 26 and 27 represent a formidable barrier to the landlord obtaining possession.[7] The landlord is entitled to apply to the Tribunal for consent to the operation of the notice to quit whether or not one of the grounds he must establish under section 27(3) is stated on the face of the notice to quit.[8] By way of exception from the above provisions there are eight special Cases[9] where the tenant cannot serve a general counter-notice under section 26(1). Each of the Cases will be immediately recognisable since the terms of each Case require that the reason for the notice to quit should be stated in it. These Cases are dealt with below one by one.[10] The response to a notice to quit served under each of the special Cases is different. If the tenant does nothing the notice to quit takes effect. If, however, the tenant is not content simply to let the notice to quit take effect, in some but not in all Cases steps can be taken which may have the effect of defeating the notice to quit if the landlord is unable to prove the ground alleged. The reader in dealing with any special Case is advised to consult carefully the Procedural Tables appearing in Part VI of this work. This Chapter deals with the substantive law and the relevant procedure for each Case together for convenience. In particular it should be noted that the provisions of Case D are, procedurally, fiendishly complicated and have therefore been set out at some considerable length. Readers must also be aware that there are prescribed forms for many purposes ranging from pleadings before the Agricultural Land Tribunal to the form of the notice to pay rent preliminary to a notice to quit under Case D. Once again, these are referred to in the Procedural Tables. Finally, and very much a matter of minority interest, there are special

---

[4] See para. 12.21 below.
[5] In s. 27(3).
[6] s. 27(2).
[7] For the specific grounds see paras 12.35–12.40 below; for commentary on the "fair and reasonable landlord" proviso see para. 12.41 below.
[8] The importance of stating the ground relates to the amount of compensation which may be payable and not to the issue of possession.
[9] See s. 26(2) and Sched. 3.
[10] Case A: smallholdings at para. 12.49 below; Case B: non-agricultural use at para. 12.50 below; Case C: certificate of bad husbandry at para. 12.51 below; Case D: non-payment of rent and remediable breach at paras 12.52–12.75 below; Case E: irremediable breach at paras 12.76–12.77 below; Case F: insolvency at para. 12.78 below; Case G: death of tenant at paras 12.79–12.81 below; Case H: amalgamation or re-shaping of agricultural unit at para. 12.82 below.

provisions which adapt the security of tenure machinery so as to protect members of the reserve and auxiliary forces.[11]

12.3 Mandatory nature of protection

Apart from the statutory exceptions parties cannot agree in advance that a notice to quit of less than 12 months shall be valid. In contrast to the provisions of section 70 (in relation to compensation) there is no express anti-contracting out term in the 1986 Act. However it has now been settled once and for all by the House of Lords in *Johnson v. Moreton*[12] that contracting out is not permitted precisely because of the importance of the statutory scheme of security of tenure, this importance being a matter of public interest and not simply private right. In that case the parties created a contractual framework whereby the giving of a counter-notice in reliance on section 26(1) would become a breach of contract so as to trigger the opportunity to rely on Case E (irremediable breach) and thereby give the landlord the opportunity to take possession. It is now clear that contracting out, whether direct or indirect is prohibited. This prohibition is distinct from the long established prohibition on a party waiving in advance by contract his right to receive sufficient notice to enable him to give the month's notice required by sections 60(6)(a), 70(2)(a) or 72(4).[13] It would appear, however, that the general prohibition does not preclude a party who has in fact received a defective notice to quit from treating it as valid.[14]

12.4 Waiver of defect in notice to quit

After *Johnson v. Moreton*[15] the Court of Appeal in *Elsden v. Pick*[16] held that a party to a tenancy agreement was not prevented by the statute from waiving his strict right to insist on a full twelve months notice and was entitled to accept termination of the tenancy before expiry of that period. In that case the tenant gave notice to quit to the landlord which would have been invalid because too short: but the landlord accepted the notice as valid since the tenant wished to quit. When later the tenant changed his mind and requested that the notice be disregarded, the landlord refused and sued successfully for possession. Although one might experience some slight unease in reading the judgment of Shaw L.J. which appears to limit the element of public interest in the termination of the tenancy,[17] the reasoning of Brightman and Buckley L.J.J. appears more securely based on the distinction between the creation of a tenancy agreement shorn of some aspect of security of tenure (which is prohibited) on the one hand and, on the other, enforcement of a subsequent decision by a party who is fully protected to forego

---

[11] Sched. 5 and see paras 12.92–12.94 below.
[12] [1980] A.C. 37.
[13] As to which generally see para. 13.2 below.
[14] See para. 12.4 below.
[15] Above.
[16] [1980] 1 W.L.R. 898.
[17] "A contractual provision which inures for the benefit of a party can be waived by that party albeit that his right to that benefit is reinforced by statute. There may be circumstances which might qualify this situation, as where an element of public interest is involved, but in such a case one would expect the statutory provision to speak in terms of illegality (thus: 'it shall be unlawful') rather than of mere invalidity." (906B.)

some aspect of the protection as part of a contract.[18] There is an obvious difference between creating a tenancy which is not fully protected and allowing a party to make a binding decision after he has received notice to quit that he will accept it. It must also be said, in support of *Elsden v. Pick* that there is a huge practical importance in the parties having the opportunity to make binding arrangements in the last year of the tenancy and to plan in advance on a secure footing for possession to be given at a particular time. Because of the need for the farming of land to be planned in advance and arrangements made it is infinitely less satisfactory that a landlord should have to wait and see whether his tenant chooses to quit or not at the expiry of the notice to quit. In so far as good management of land is a matter of public policy, that consideration would in relation to the last year of the tenancy rather tend to support the Court of Appeal's approach in *Elsden v. Pick*.[19]

Minimum 12 months notice to quit: section 25(1)   12.5

Section 25(1) requires that a notice to quit an agricultural holding is invalid if it expires before the expiry of 12 months from the end of the current year of tenancy. This rule applies to notices to quit the whole or part of an agricultural holding and despite any contrary contractual provisions. It applies equally to notices by tenants

---

[18] See Brightman L.J. at 907G–908B: "a tenant is not bound to accept less than the statutory 12 months notice to quit served by his landlord (nor vice versa) even if the tenancy agreement so provides. If the tenant chooses to do so, he can simply ignore a short notice served on him and resist any attempt by the landlord to recover possession on the strength of it. But if the tenant wishes to do so, he can bind himself to accept it. The parties are entitled to agree that the notice shall be treated in all respects as if it were a notice of the statutory length. If the parties so agree the tenancy will come to an end on the agreed date by virtue of the defective notice to quit which it is agreed shall be treated as valid. Such an agreement could not effectively be made before a notice to quit is served, because the parties cannot agree that the tenancy shall be capable of being terminated by a short notice. Neither the landlord nor the tenant can bind himself in advance to accept a short notice from the other of them. That would be a "provision to the contrary" in, or supplemental to, the contract of tenancy and would not be effective. But once an invalid notice has been served, which the recipient is entitled to ignore, I see nothing in s. 23 [of the 1948 Act, now consolidated] to prohibit an agreement between landlord and tenant that the notice shall be followed by the same consequences as if it were valid". And Buckley L.J. at 909F-H: "a contract to render an existing defective notice to quit effective by waiving the defect is not, in my view, a contract to vary the tenancy agreement. An agricultural tenancy could not, consistently with s. 23 [of the 1948 Act], be modified by agreement between the parties in such a way that either party to it could terminate it by a notice to quit which did not accord with the terms of the section. Such an agreement would conflict with the words of the section which are within brackets. But it does not follow from this that, when a notice to quit has been given which fails to satisfy the requirements of the section, the parties cannot effectually agree that, notwithstanding the defect in the notice, it shall take effect as though it were a valid notice. Such an agreement would not, in my opinion, conflict with any part of the section. It would not alter any of the terms of the tenancy agreement. Its effect is that the parties agree to the tenancy coming to an end on the date specified in the notice, subject to which the tenancy remains in full force and effect".

[19] Acceptance of a bad notice to quit as valid will not disentitle a tenant from compensation, including compensation for disturbance: see *Westlake v. Page* [1926] 1 K.B. 298 and *Kestell v. Langmaid* [1950] 1 K.B. 233 noted at paragraph 13.22 below.

as well as notices by landlords.[20] The rule applies not only to fixed terms where a break clause is to be exercised,[21] but also to leases for two years or more which continue as yearly tenancies after the expiration of the fixed term.[22] The effect of the rule is not to alter the nature of the tenant's interest but to fetter the landlord's right to give a valid notice to quit.[23] In a case where the landlord serves a break notice to determine the fixed term, the service by the tenant of a counter-notice under section 26(1) appears to preserve the tenant's security as a tenant from year to year.[24] A notice to quit of the correct length is nevertheless invalid if it is served before the commencement of the tenancy.[25] There is nothing invalid in a provision in the contract of tenancy requiring a notice to quit of more than the statutory length or a provision by which the landlord accepts an additional fetter on his normal right to give notice.[26]

Despite the mandatory nature of protection[27] it appears that a landlord at least may be estopped from serving a notice to quit at all in appropriate circumstances.[28]

Apart from the statutory restriction imposed by section 25 as to length, the general common law principles in relation to notices to quit apply.[29]

There are a limited number of statutory exceptions from the scope of section 25(1). They are:

(i) the insolvency of the tenant: section 25(2)(a)[30]

(ii) non-agricultural use where part only of the tenancy is resumed: section 25(2)(b)[31]

(iii) notice from the tenant to the sub-tenant: section 25(2)(c)[32]

(iv) section 149(6) of the Law of Property Act 1925: section 25(2)(d)[33]

(v) tenant's notice to quit after statutory rent review: section 25(3)[34]

---

[20] *Flather v. Hood* (1928) 44 T.L.R. 698 (a decision on s. 25 of the 1923 Act).
[21] *Edell v. Dulieu* [1924] A.C. 38 a decision of the House of Lords on the Agriculture Act 1920 containing almost identical provisions; and see *Gladstone v. Bower* [1960] 1 Q.B. 170 at p. 177 (Diplock J.).
[22] Under s. 3.
[23] See Pearce L.J. in *Gladstone v. Bower* [1960] 2 Q.B. 384 CA, at 394.
[24] This appears correct as a matter of logic and was so held in an unreported County Court case in 1968 *Young v. Hopkins*, Judge Bulger in the Cheltenham County Court.
[25] *Lower v. Sorrell* [1963] 1 Q.B. 959, especially the judgment of Pearson L.J.
[26] See *Re Midland Railway Company's Agreement, Charles Clay and Sons Ltd v. British Railways Board* [1971] Ch. 725 (a non-agricultural tenancy of the railway land with a proviso that the tenancy was not to be terminated until the landlord's required the land for purposes of their undertaking).
[27] See para. 12.3 above.
[28] See *Datnow v. Jones* [1985] 2 E.G.L.R. 1 at 2f-h, and *John v. George* [1996] 1 E.G.L.R. 7.
[29] See as to the date of expiry para. 12.14 below and as to construction paragraphs 12.29 and 30 below.
[30] See para. 12.6 below.
[31] See para. 12.7 below.
[32] See para. 12.8 below.
[33] See para. 12.9 below.
[34] See para. 12.10 below.

(vi) bad husbandry certificate: section 25(4)[35]

(vii) historic agreements: public purposes: Schedule 12, paragraph 4[36]

(viii) tenant's failure to do work within an extended time: the Agricultural Holdings (Arbitration on Notices) Order 1987 (S.I. 1987 No.710) Article 7(4) and 15(4)[37].

Section 25 applies only to agricultural holdings, not to every tenancy affecting agricultural land.[38]

Less than 12 months' notice to quit: insolvency of tenant: section 25(2)(a)   12.6

The minimum period for notice to quit prescribed by section 25(1) is excluded where the tenant is insolvent.[39] For these purposes a tenant is insolvent where section 96(2) is satisfied. If the tenancy is held jointly by two persons only one of whom becomes insolvent it is submitted that the exception in section 25(2)(a) cannot apply as a matter of ordinary grammar (since in those circumstances "a" tenant has become insolvent but not "the" tenant). In any case if the purpose of the exception is to protect the landlord where his tenant can no longer meet the rent such a landlord is adequately protected by the existence of the other tenant who is solvent.

Less than 12 months' notice to quit: non-agricultural use: resumption of part (section 25(2)(b))   12.7

The minimum period of notice prescribed by section 25(1) is not required in the case of a notice to quit given pursuant to a contractual clause authorising the resumption of possession for some specified purpose other than the use of the land for agriculture. The exemption is available whether the notice to quit in question relates to the whole or part only of the holding.[40]

It is now established that a clause authorising resumption "for any non-agricultural purpose" is within the exception.[41] Although such a clause may provide for less than 12 months' notice, it must not, on pain of invalidity,[42] provide for a notice too short to enable the tenant, if he wishes, to give notice not less than one month before the termination of the tenancy of his intention to claim more than the minimum disturbance compensation[43] or to claim compensation (rare as such a claim may be) for "high farming".[44] Otherwise, the clause would offend against

---

[35] See para. 12.11 below.
[36] See para. 12.12 below.
[37] See para. 12.13 below.
[38] cf. *Steyning and Littlehampton Building Society v. Wilson* [1951] Ch. 1018.
[39] s. 25(2)(a).
[40] See s. 25(2)(b).
[41] *Paddock Investments Ltd v. Lory* (1975) 236 E.G. 803, CA, approving county court decision in *Dow Agrochemicals Ltd v. E.A. Lane (North Lynn) Ltd* (1965) 192 E.G. 737. There is a difference between specified and specific: see in another context *McMorran v. A.E. Marrison (Contractors) Ltd* [1944] 2 All E.R. 448.
[42] *Re Disraeli Agreement* [1939] Ch. 382; *Coates v. Diment* [1951] 1 All E.R. 890; *Parry v. Million Pigs Ltd* (1980) 260 E.G. 281, and see para. 13.2 below.
[43] s. 60(3)(b) and (6)(a).
[44] s. 70(2)(a).

section 78(1). For safety, the clause should provide for, say, two months' notice. A clause sometimes found authorising resumption "for the purposes specified in section 31 of the Agricultural Holdings Act 1948"[45] is inadvisable as not all such purposes are non-agricultural. A power merely to enter on a holding to carry out works, *e.g.*, to work gravel deposits, is not the same thing as to resume possession of part of the holding. Care is needed in the drafting of an early resumption clause. For example, if the landlord is not going to carry out the non-agricultural purpose personally the applicability of the clause may depend on its precise wording.[46] A special statutory provision may be noted here which protects a tenant against the possible adverse effect on his compensation of the operation of an early resumption clause.[47]

12.8 Less than 12 months notice to quit: notice from tenant to sub-tenant: section 25(2)(c)

The minimum period of notice provided for by section 25(1)[48] does not apply where the notice to quit is given by a tenant to a sub-tenant.[49]

This exception is not confined to (although clearly appropriate to) the case where the tenant has been given notice to quit by his own landlord. It therefore gives carte blanche to determine sub-tenancies by less than 12 months' notice, but subject to common law rules as to notices, any contractual arrangements, and the security of tenure provisions of the Act.[50]

12.9 Less than 12 months' notice to quit: section 149(6) of the Law of Property Act 1925: section 25(2)(d)

The minimum period of notice to quit prescribed by section 25(1)[51] does not apply where the tenancy is one which by virtue of section 149(6) of the Law of Property Act 1925 has taken effect as such a term of years as is mentioned in that sub-section.[52]

This exception relates to leases for a life or lives, or for a term of years determinable with life or lives or on the marriage of the lessee, which were converted by section 149(6) into a term of 90 years determinable after the death or marriage by at least one months' notice in writing expiring on the appropriate quarter day. Tenancies of this kind are also excepted from section 3 of the 1986

---

[45] Now s. 31 of the 1986 Act.
[46] ***Rugby Joint Water Board v. Foottit*** [1973] A.C. 202, where the House of Lords construed the words "which the landlords may from time to time require" as restricting resumption to purposes carried out by or by order of the landlords and not by a third party, such as an acquiring authority. The decision is still authoritative on this particular point, but so far as compensation for compulsory acquisition is concerned it was reversed in one respect by s. 48 of the Land Compensation Act 1973.
[47] Section 62, which entitles the tenant, in addition to any other compensation payable, to an amount equal to the additional benefit which he would have received if the tenancy had been terminated on the expiration of 12 months from the end of the tenancy year current when the notice was given. See para. 13.32 below.
[48] See para. 12.5 above.
[49] s. 25(2)(c). This exception does not extend to a notice given by a sub-tenant to a tenant.
[50] For position of sub-tenants generally, see paras 15.2–15.18 below.
[51] See para. 12.5 above.
[52] s. 25(2)(d).

Act, so that, if not determined before, they will terminate by effluxion of time at the end of the 90 years. In the case of present day agricultural tenants these are matters of academic interest only.[53]

Although relieved of the statutory twelve months requirement, the common law rules apply as to length and otherwise.

Less than 12 months' notice to quit: tenant's notice to quit after statutory rent review: section 25(3)

12.10

The minimum period of notice required by section 25(1)[54] does not apply in a case where an arbitrator, in a rent arbitration under section 12, has increased the rent and the tenant has as a result given a notice to quit of at least six months, provided that the notice to quit is framed to terminate the tenancy at the end of the tenancy year beginning with the date as from which the increase of rent is effective.[55] Such a notice is valid notwithstanding any term in the contract of tenancy requiring a longer period of notice.[56]

Less than 12 months' notice to quit: bad husbandry certificate: section 25(4)

12.11

In a case where an Agricultural Land Tribunal grant a certificate of bad husbandry under paragraph 9 of Part II of Schedule 3,[57] the Tribunal may specify in the certificate a minimum period of notice to quit, not being less than two months, and direct that this period shall apply instead of the period required by section 25(1). If they do, and if the landlord serves such a notice, stating in it that the Tribunal has given a direction under section 25(4), the notice will not be invalid for non compliance with section 25(1).[58] It will also be immune from challenge on the ground that the contract of tenancy requires a longer period of notice or because the notice expires on a date other than the end of a year of the tenancy.[59] As the holding may be deteriorating rapidly through bad husbandry this relaxation of restrictions on the notice to quit is essential.

Less than 12 months' notice to quit: historic agreements: public purposes: Schedule 12, paragraph 4

12.12

Section 25(1) does not apply where a tenancy subsists under an agreement made before March 25, 1947, and the notice to quit is given by the Secretary of State under the agreement because the land is required for naval, military or air force purposes, or the notice is given by statutory undertakers, or a government department or local authority for a non-agricultural purpose for which the land was acquired or appropriated.[60]

---

[53] But they have cropped up in the context of the Rent Acts; *Kingswood Estate Co. Ltd v. Anderson* [1963] 2 Q.B. 169. See also [1986] 2 E.G.L.R. 40.
[54] See para. 12.5 above.
[55] Section 25(3), derived from an amendment made by s. 5 of the 1984 Act.
[56] s. 25(5).
[57] See para. 12.51 below.
[58] s. 25(4). this provision was also derived from an amendment made by s. 5 of the 1984 Act.
[59] s. 25(5).
[60] Sched. 12, para. 4. This summarises briefly provisions which are somewhat complicated in detail, but as they relate to agreements made before March 25, 1947 it is not thought necessary to examine the details here.

12.13 Less than 12 months' notice to quit: tenant's failure to do work within an extended time: 1987 Order Articles 7(4) and 15(4)

Notices to quit on dates specified by an arbitrator under articles 7(4) and 15(4) of the Agricultural Holdings (Arbitration on Notices) Order 1987,[61] in the event of a tenant's failure to do work within an extended time, are valid notwithstanding that the notices are served less than 12 months before the date of termination (and notwithstanding that that date is not the end of a year of the tenancy).

12.14 Less than 12 months' notice to quit: length of notice and date of expiry

The length of notice required in the excepted cases will, unless otherwise expressly provided,[62] depend on the contract or the established common law rules. For example, if the contract is silent the rule that half a years notice is required to terminate a yearly tenancy will apply. Again, unless otherwise expressly provided, the normal rule in regard to the date of expiry will apply, *i.e.* that the notice should expire at the midnight separating the last day of the tenancy from the anniversary of its commencement.[63] The general proposition is that where a term is expressed to commence "from" a specified day, that day is in strictness not included at the beginning of the term. However this rule does not apply where the rent is payable in advance, the date "from" which the term is expressed to run being the first date in respect of which rent is payable. In those circumstances the date "from" which the term runs is in fact the first day of the term.[64]

12.15 Entry on parts at different dates

Where different parts of the holding were entered at different times the notice to quit may be expressed to expire on the day appropriate for the principal or substantial part, but the tenant should actually quit on the various dates corresponding to the dates of entry. It is a question of fact which part is principal or substantial and which parts are accessorial.[65]

12.16 Effect of second notice to quit

It sometimes happens that a second notice to quit is served, purporting to terminate the tenancy at a later date. What is the effect? It is now established that the effect is not to withdraw, cancel or waive the first notice, which will operate in the normal manner, but to provide some evidence which, together with other evidence such as significant actions by the tenant, might provide material for an inference of

---

[61] S.I. 1987 No.710.
[62] *e.g.* in the unlikely event of (d) operating, the statutory rule would apply. In the cases mentioned in (h), the length (and date of expiry) are governed by the articles.
[63] A notice specifying either day will normally be accepted as referring to that midnight: see **Poole v. Warren** [1838] 8 A. & E. 582 at 588; **Ackland v. Lutley** [1839] 9 A. & E. 879; **Sidebotham v. Holland** [1895] 1 Q.B. 378; **Crate v. Miller** [1947] K.B. 946; **Bathavon RDC v. Carlile** [1958] 1 Q.B. 461; **Schnabel v. Allard** [1967] 1 Q.B. 627. **Sidebotham v. Holland** and **Crate v. Miller** were applied by the Court of Appeal in **Yeandle v. Reigate and Banstead Borough Council** [1996] 1 E.G.L.R. 20 to save a notice to quit expressed to expire on September 28, when the first day of the tenancy was September 29.
[64] See for discussion of the rule and its qualification **Whelton Sinclair (A Firm) v. Hyland** [1992] 2 E.G.L.R. 158 and **Ladyman v. Wirral Estates Limited** [1968] 2 All E.R. 197.
[65] **Doe d. Heapy v. Howard** [1809] 11 East 498; and see *Woodfall, Landlord and Tenant*, Volume 1, para. 17.259.

agreement to create a new tenancy.[66] A second notice to quit, given to expire before the first, will, if it allows the proper length of notice required by law, and is otherwise free from defects, be valid and effective, superseding the first.[67] In *Land v. Sykes*[68] Scott L.J. at 4J stated:

> "I do not see any reason why the approach to formation of contract in landlord and tenant cases should be any different from the approach to formation of contracts generally. The Judge cited an observation of Lord Mansfield in *Doe d. Cheny v. Batten* (1775) 1 Cowp. 243 at page 245 that:
>
>> "The question therefore is, *quo animo* the rent was received, and what the real intention of both parties was?"
>
> This observation does not deal with the manner in which the intention is to be ascertained and, for my part, I think it should be ascertained by an objective approach to what has been said and done."[69]

Notice to quit part of an agricultural holding 12.17

At common law a notice to quit part of the land comprised in a tenancy is bad in the absence of a clause in the tenancy agreement allowing such notice to be given.[70] This rule has, however, been modified by statute, with the result that in the case of agricultural holdings a valid notice to quit part of the holding may be given in three cases:

(1) under section 31 of the 1986 Act;

(2) under a clause in the contract of tenancy;

(3) under section 140 of the Law of Property Act 1925 when a reversion has been severed.

A notice to quit part, although valid under one or other of these three headings, will be subject to the security of tenure provisions of sections 26–28 of the 1986 Act and to the 12 months length of notice to quit requirement of section 25 unless it comes within a statutory exception, *e.g.* section 25(2)(c).

---

[66] *Lower v. Sorrell* [1963] 1 Q.B. 959, following *Tayleur v. Wildin* [1868] L.R. 3 Exch. 303 and *Freeman v. Evans* [1922] 1 Ch. 36, and rejecting the Irish Court of Appeal case of *Inchiquin v. Lyons* [1887] 20 L.R. Ir. 474. See also *Lowenthal v. Vanhoute* [1947] K.B. 342. Only the House of Lords can now reach a different conclusion.

[67] *Thompson v. McCullough* [1947] K.B. 447.

[68] [1992] 1 E.G.L.R. 1.

[69] In that case although a first notice to quit was valid the Court refused to spell the grant of a new tenancy from subsequent notice to pay rent by the landlord followed by acceptance of the cheque sent as a result: the requisite intention was not found.

[70] See *Re Bebington's Tenancy, Bebington v. Wildman* [1921] 1 Ch. 559; *Woodward v. Dudley* [1954] Ch. 283. And for older cases to the same effect see *Right d. Fisher v. Cuthell* (1804) 5 East 491; *Doe d. Rodd v. Archer* (1811) 14 East 244; *Price v. Evans* (1872) 29 LT 835.

12.18 Notice to quit part of holding: section 31

Section 31, which applies only to a notice to quit part of an agricultural holding held on a tenancy from year to year[71] given by the landlord of the holding, specifies one "purpose" and eight "objects" for which a valid notice to quit[72] may be given.

The "purpose" is "adjusting the boundaries between agricultural units or amalgamating agricultural units or parts of such units".[73]

The "objects"[74] are as follows:

(a) the erection of cottages and other houses for farm labourers, whether with or without gardens[75];

(b) the provision of gardens for cottages or other houses for farm labourers"[76];

(c) the provision of allotments;

(d) the letting of land (with or without other land) as a smallholding under Part III of the Agriculture Act 1970[77];

(e) the planting of trees[78];

(f) the opening or working of a deposit of coal, ironstone, limestone, brick-earth or other mineral, or a stone quarry or a clay, sand or gravel pit, or the construction of any works or buildings to be used in connection therewith;

(g) the making of a watercourse or reservoir;

(h) the making of a road, railway, tramroad, siding, canal or basin, or a wharf, pier, or other work connected therewith.[79]

---

[71] And thus cannot be invoked in the case of a notice in respect of a "break" clause.

[72] By implication a notice in writing: "the notice states that it is given", s. 31(1). For a precedent see Form 34 in Part V of this work.

[73] This was added to the traditional list of "objects" by the 1947 Act, Sched. 7, para. 6, which inserted it in s. 27 of the 1923 Act. For "agricultural unit", see s. 96(1) and 1947 Act, s. 109(2); and see commentary (for a different purpose) in para. 14.42 (succession).

[74] The "objects" have a respectable antiquity, dating from s. 52 of the Agricultural Holdings (England) Act 1875, from which they have been handed down without much change to the present day.

[75] This wording, amended by the 1984 Act, Sched. 3, para. 39, replaced the ambiguous phrase previously used, "farm labourers' cottages or other houses", thus giving statutory effect to what had been considered the better view: see *Paddock Investments Ltd v. Lory* (1975) 236 E.G. 803.

[76] A similar replacement for "gardens for farm labourers' cottages or other houses": see last note.

[77] This wording was substituted by the Agriculture Act 1970, s. 64(2) and Sched. 4, consequentially on changes in the smallholdings code by Part III of the 1970 Act.

[78] For a county court case, see *Secretary of State for Wales v. Pugh* (1970) 120 L.J. 357 (timber trees divorced from any agricultural activity).

[79] This is in practice an extremely important head since it allows the taking back of land to provide infrastructure in the form of roads, roundabouts and pavements where the main development is covered by a contractual clause but these works are not.

The tenant's power to treat a notice to quit part under this section as if it were a notice to quit the whole holding[80] is mentioned below.

Notice to quit part of holding: contractual clause 12.19

The contract of tenancy may contain an express provision enabling the landlord to resume possession of part of the holding for specified purposes, *e.g.* building. If the purpose specified is a non-agricultural purpose under section 25(2)(b) the contract of tenancy may provide for a notice to quit of less than 12 months.[81] It is, however, important to remember that a clause of this kind is void, by reason of section 78 of the Act, if it purports to enable the landlord to resume possession without notice, or with insufficient notice to allow the tenant, if he so desires, to claim more than the minimum compensation for disturbance by giving notice under section 60(6)(a), or to make a claim for "high farming" under section 70(2)(a).[82] Both of these provisions require the tenant to give notice of intention to make a claim not less than one month before the termination of the tenancy. It is suggested that the resumption clause should provide for two or three months' notice by the landlord. The tenant has no power to "enlarge" a notice to quit part given under a clause in the contract of tenancy into a notice to quit the whole holding: section 32 does not apply in this case. It may be mentioned here that if both section 25(2)(b) and Case B in Schedule 3 apply the landlord will be able to resume possession of part at short notice and avoid any claim for security of tenure, but he will not avoid a claim for disturbance compensation, either the "basic compensation" or the "additional compensation".[83]

Notice to quit part of holding: severance of the reversion 12.20

The old law was that on the severance of the reversion, as by the sale of the reversionary interest in part of the holding, the owner of a severed part could not give the tenant a valid notice to quit the corresponding part of the holding unless the severance had been recognised by the apportionment of the rent. This rule was altered by legislation, now enacted in section 140 of the Law of Property Act 1925, but subject to a special right of the tenant to enlarge the notice to quit part into a notice to quit the entire holding. As originally drafted, however, section 140(2) deprived a tenant of an agricultural holding of compensation for disturbance when he elected to quit the entire holding in this way. Legislation had to be passed to correct this anomaly[84] and the matter is now dealt with by section 32 and sections 60(1) and 63(3) and (4) of the 1986 Act.

---

[80] See s. 32, and para. 12.21 below.

[81] See para. 12.7 above. A clause simply authorising resumption "for any non-agricultural purpose" or words to that effect is within s. 25(2)(b): ***Paddock Investments Ltd v. Lory*** (1975). 236 E.G. 803. A clause authorising resumption "for any of the objects mentioned in s. 31(2)" would not be within s. 25(2)(b) as some of those are agricultural. If the purpose is agricultural the normal 12 months length of notice must be given. For a precedent of such a notice to quit to be given under Sched. 3, Case B see Form 35 in Part V of this work.

[82] See generally para. 13.2 below.

[83] See s. 60(2) and s. 61(1) and (2), and paras 13.18.-13.19 below.

[84] Initially the Law of Property (Amendment) Act 1926, s. 2, and later s. 32 and 34(1)(b) of

The view was at one time held that severance of the reversion coupled with the legal apportionment of the rent resulted in the creation of separate tenancies of the severed parts,[85] and that payment by the tenant without protest of the rents apportioned by agreement among the reversioners constituted a sufficient legal apportionment for this purpose.[86] This view was decisively rejected by the Court of Appeal in **Jelley v. Buckman**,[87] where Stamp L.J., giving the judgment of the court, said: "We can find nothing in the section[88] to suggest for a moment that the legislature intended that following a severance to which the lessee was not a party he should find himself holding part of his land under one tenancy and part under another".[89] Section 140(1) of the 1925 Act gives each reversioner remedies, such as the right to serve a notice to quit, "in like manner as if" there were separate tenancies, but this does not make them separate tenancies. The words "to which the lessee was not a party" in the above quotation from Stamp L.J.'s judgment are, however, important. If the tenant is a party to the deed or instrument which apportions the rent and it is made quite clear that the intention is to create separate tenancies (not merely to record agreement to the apportionment figures) then it is submitted that separate tenancies will result. **Jelley v. Buckman** has important consequences for agricultural holdings compensation and arbitration.[90] It has been held by the Court of Appeal that the conveyance of the reversionary interest in part of a farm to "bare trustees" did not constitute a severance to which section 140 applies. It was said that section 140 was intended to deal with the situation where there was a real transfer of interest by the reversioner, not a transfer to a bare trustee, who could be required to reconvey it at any time.[91] However **Persey v. Bazley** has not so far been used successfully to challenge the common practice of

---

the 1948 Act, then s. 9 of the 1977 Act replacing s. 32 of the 1948 Act.

[85] *e.g.* A.J. Spencer in the last edition (8th) of his *Agricultural Holdings Act 1923*, p.84.

[86] County court decision in **Paul v. Caldwell** (1960) 176 E.G. 743 overruled as a result of **Jelley v. Buckman** [1974] Q.B. 488.

[87] **Jelley v. Buckman**, *supra*, at p. 498. Cases in which *Jelley v. Buckman* was subsequently cited include **Dodson Bull Carpet Co. Ltd v. City of London Corporation** [1975] 1 W.L.R. 781; **William Skelton & Son Ltd v. Harrison & Pinder Ltd.** [1975] Q.B. 361 and **Nevill Long & Co. (Boards) Ltd v. Firmenich & Co.** (1981) 261 E.G. 461 (affirmed (1983) 268 E.G. 572), but these were cases in which features of Part II of the Landlord and Tenant Act 1954 were relevant and they are not of much assistance for agricultural holdings.

[88] Section 140 of the Law of Property Act 1925.

[89] Severance of the term is unlikely to change the nature of the tenancy: **Lester v. Ridd** (1989) 3 W.L.R. 1793, where the tenancy of a dwellinghouse continued to be governed by the 1986 Act after severance and did not fall within the Leasehold Reform Act 1967. Severance of the reversion is even less likely to have an impact on the nature of the tenancy.

[90] It was followed in the county court case of **Stiles v. Farrow** (1976) 241 E.G. 623, where separate notices by reversioners requiring rent arbitration were held to be invalid. But see now s. 74(3) of 1986 Act as to compensation.

[91] **Persey v. Bazley** (1984) 47 P.&C.R. 37; (1983) 267 E.G. 519. There seems no authority for this ruling and it creates difficulties in principle. Surely the tenant is concerned only with the holder of the legal estate? The decision seems to run counter to the basis of the 1925 property legislation.

freeholds being severed as between "friendly" parties whether or not the same be done in order to create the opportunity or power to serve a notice to quit part.[92]

The impact of severance of the reversion upon the construction of a notice to quit served by the owner of the retained part was considered by the Court of Appeal in *Land v. Sykes*[93] in the commonly encountered circumstances that the entire rent was still paid to the original owner without apportionment. The tenant was aware of the conveyance away of a small part of the farm and ultimately was served notice to quit which in the heading referred to the entire holding by description but in the body requested possession of land held from the giver of the notice as tenant. The powers of the original landlord are summarised as limited, in terms of a notice to quit, to the area retained.[94] The notice to quit was upheld on the basis that in context it was clear and that any possible ambiguity was cured by the knowledge of the tenant that the landlord's interest was limited to the areas actually retained.[95]

Notice to quit part of holding: tenant's right to treat it as notice to quit the entirety: section 32   12.21

If a tenant is given a notice to quit part of a holding by virtue of section 31 of the 1986 Act, or by a person entitled to a severed part of the reversionary estate in the holding (by virtue of section 140 of the Law of Property Act 1925), but not where the notice to quit part is given by virtue of a clause in the contract of tenancy,[96] he is given an important right by section 32 of the 1986 Act. He may, if he so wishes "enlarge" the notice into a notice to quit the entire holding. To do this he must serve a counter-notice in writing on the landlord or (as the case may be) on the persons severally entitled to the severed parts of the reversion, within 28 days of the giving of the notice to quit,[97] to the effect that he accepts the notice to quit as a notice to quit the entire holding given by the landlord or by the several reversioners.[98] The tenant could elect to serve this counter-notice even if the notice to quit related to a

---

[92] In *John v. George* [1996] 1 E.G.L.R. 7 the landlords conveyed part of the reversion to trustees on trust for their infant daughter whereon the trustees served notice to quit in relation to that part upon the tenant. At first instance the severance was attacked as insufficient for the purposes of s. 140(1) of the Law of Property Act 1925 in the light of *Persey v. Bazley* but the submission was rejected at first instance by Judge Moseley Q.C. sitting as a Judge of the High Court (reported at [1995] 1 E.G.L.R. 9) and the issue was not appealed. The Court of Appeal therefore proceeded on the footing that the landlord had the right to serve notice to quit part.

[93] [1992] 1 E.G.L.R. 1.

[94] Parker L.J. at 3K.

[95] Parker L.J. at 4A-C and Farquharson L.J. at 5D.

[96] The tenant having by contract accepted that he was content to receive notice as to a part.

[97] If the effectiveness of the notice to quit depends on the outcome of arbitration or ALT proceedings, the tenant has 28 days to serve the counter-notice from the time when it is determined that the notice to quit is effective: s. 32(2)(b). For a form, see Form 37 in Part V of this work electing to accept the notice to quit in relation to the entirety.

[98] s. 32(2). The words "given by the landlord", etc., are important as showing that the "enlarged" notice to quit is deemed to be a notice given by the landlord, thus attracting compensation for disturbance, etc. (This was what was lacking in the original s. 140(2) of the Law of Property Act 1925 before amendment.) It may also be noted that for the purpose of art. 16 of the Arbitration on Notices Order 1987 (S.I. 1987 No.710) the notice to quit part is deemed to be a notice to quit the whole: this relates to the position of sub-tenants where the tenant has himself been given notice to quit by his own landlord.

small and unimportant part of the holding, but the size of the part and its importance in the farming of the holding are material facts in assessing the compensation for disturbance.[99]

12.22 Notice to quit part of holding: reduction of rent

Section 33(1) of the 1986 Act provides for a "proportionate" reduction of rent where the landlord "resumes possession" of part of the holding either by virtue of section 31(1) or in pursuance of a provision in the contract of tenancy. "Resumes possession" must mean resumes in pursuance of a notice to quit of the requisite length.[1] A "proportionate" reduction of rent is a matter of valuation rather than arithmetic based on acreage. Also, the tenant is entitled to have taken into account in the reduction "any depreciation of the value to him of the residue of the holding caused by the severance or by the use to be made of the part severed".[2] Again, where, as sometimes happens, the contract of tenancy provides that the tenant is to be entitled to some benefit or relief if the landlord exercises his contractual right to resume possession of a part, the arbitrator, if there is a dispute referred to arbitration, is to take this into account in assessing the amount of the reduction.[3] The amount of the reduction under section 33 may be settled by agreement between the parties after the landlord resumes possession of the part, but in default of agreement it is to be determined by arbitration under the 1986 Act.[4]

It will be noted that section 33 contains no reference to the apportionment of rent on a severance of the reversion. This is not a purely landlord and tenant matter, but involves the rights *inter se* of two or more reversioners and the rights of the tenant. The procedure of arbitration under the 1986 Act does not apply. Legal apportionment of rent on the severance of the reversion requires the consent of all parties concerned or judicial process unless it is done under a statutory provision such as section 20 of the Landlord and Tenant Act 1927.[5] It may be noted that section 74 of the 1986 Act contains provisions dealing with compensation parallel to those in section 33 dealing with rent where the landlord resumes possession of part of the holding under section 31(1) or under the contract of tenancy.[6]

---

[99] s. 63(3), and see para. 13.34 below.
[1] See below para. 13.2 as to the rule exemplified in *Re Disraeli Agreement, Coates v. Diment* and *Parry v. Million Pigs Ltd*.
[2] s. 33(1): *cf.*, wording of s. 7 of the Compulsory Purchase Act 1965.
[3] s. 33(3).
[4] s. 33(2).
[5] See *Bliss v. Collins* (1822) 6 B. & Ald. 876; *Swansea Corporation v. Thomas* (1882) 10 Q.B.D. 48; and *Burgoyne v. Ainsworth* (1885) 79 L.T.J. 377, CC, for apportionment by a jury. It has been done by a judge sitting without a jury. The function of apportioning rent under s. 20 of the Landlord and Tenant Act 1927 is now vested in the Secretary of State for the Environment: see Secretary of State for the Environment Order 1970 (S.I. 1970 No.1681). As to apportionment of rent not *ipso facto* creating separate tenancies, see above para. 12.20.
[6] Section 74 deals also with other cases including resumption of part by a person entitled to a severed part of the reversionary estate.

Notice to quit: no requirement for inclusion of material prescribed under the Protection from Eviction Act 1977   12.23

Where an agricultural holding includes one or more dwellings a notice to quit the agricultural holding itself is not required to include information prescribed under section 5 of the Protection from Eviction Act 1977. The Court of Appeal in *National Trust v. Knipe*[7] held that an agricultural holding which happened to include dwelling houses was not "premises let as a dwelling" within section 5 of the 1977 Act.[8]

Notices to quit: jointly held estates   12.24

The leading case in this area of law is now ***Hammersmith and Fulham London Borough Council v. Monk***[9] in which the House of Lords reviewed the main body of case law pre-1925 and thereafter and concluded that a periodic joint tenancy held by two or more joints tenants could be determined at common law by a notice to quit given by one only of those joint tenants without the agreement of any other joint tenant (unless the tenancy terms provided otherwise). In reaching this conclusion it is clear that previous inconsistencies in the case law are swept aside and the position of notices given by landlords and by tenants is assimilated.[10] It should be of particular interest to landlord and tenant lawyers that this case is one of a number which expressly refuse to recognise any difference in principle between contracts of tenancy and any other contracts when it comes to the ordinary application of contractual principles and issues of construction.[11] It should be noted however that certain positive dealings with a joint tenancy still require the concurrence of all the joint tenants if they are to be effective.[12] These actions include the exercise of a break clause in a lease, the surrender of the term,[13] the making of a disclaimer, the exercise of an option to renew the term and an application for relief from forfeiture. The submission that the interposition of a statutory trust for sale involving trustees should therefore require those trustees to act unanimously was rejected.[14] The modern rule therefore now reflects precisely the law as stated in ***Doe d. Aslin v. Summersett*** and is equally applicable to both landlords and tenants.[15]

---

[7] [1997] 40 E.G. 151.

[8] The relationship of agricultural holdings to the housing statutes is not always predictable. Contrast *Maunsell v. Olins* [1975] A.C. 373, HL, and *Dallhold Estates (U.K.) Pty Ltd v. Lindsey Trading Properties Inc* [1994] 1 E.G.L.R. 93, CA.

[9] [1992] 1 All E.R. 1.

[10] See Lord Bridge at page 4h–5c and Lord Browne-Wilkinson at 11e-j.

[11] In *Hammersmith and Fulham LBC v. Monk* see in particular Lord Bridge at 3c-g and see also *Mannai Investment Co. Limited v. Eagle Star Life Assurance Co. Ltd* [1997] 3 All E.R. 352, HL, noted at para. 12.29 below.

[12] Lord Bridge in *Hammersmith and Fulham LBC v. Monk* at 9g-h.

[13] *Leek and Moorlands Building Society v. Clark* [1952] 2 All E.R. 492, [1952] 2 Q.B. 788.

[14] See Lord Browne-Wilkinson at 11g - 12b "it may be that, as between the lessees, the giving of the notice to quit was a breach of trust, theoretically giving rise to a claim by Mr Monk against Mrs Powell for breach of trust. Even this seems to me very dubious since the overreaching statutory trust for sale imposed by the Law of Property Act 1925 do not normally alter the beneficial rights *inter se* of the concurrent owners".

[15] Lord Bridge at 4h–5c encapsulated the reasoning in the case as follows: "In ***Doe d Aslin***

12.25 Drafting the notice to quit

Although at common law an oral notice to quit would be sufficient and sections 25 and 26 do not prohibit the giving of an oral notice, in practice such notices are never used.[16] Virtually all tenancy agreements provide for written notice to quit and in any case the giving of a written notice to quit meets the otherwise difficult issue of proof. Although there are many prescribed forms in this area of the law, there is no prescribed form for a notice to quit. Practice forms are provided in this work which will need to be adapted so as to make it clear to the recipient exactly what is required.[17] Where one of the special Cases referred to in section 26(2) and Schedule 3 is to be used, then the notice to quit must in any case be in writing since the relevant Case must be referred to on the face of the notice. The required length of the notice to quit is dealt with elsewhere in this Chapter.[18] Notices to quit part of a holding need particular care since it may be necessary to include references to statutory or contractual provisions.[19] Considerable importance is attached to the

---

v. Summersett [1830] 1 B.&A.D. 135, 109 E.R. 738 the freehold interest in land let on a yearly tenancy was vested jointly in four executors of a will to whom the land had been jointly devised. Three only of the executors gave notice to the tenant to quit. It was held by the Court of King's Bench that the notice was effective to determine the tenancy. Delivering the judgment, Lord Tenterden C.J. said (1 B. & Ad. 135 at 140–141, 109 E.R. 738 at 739–740), 'Upon a joint demise by joint tenants upon a tenancy from year to year, the true character of the tenancy is this, not that the tenant holds of each the share of each so long as he and each shall please, but that he holds the *whole* of *all* so long as he *and all* shall please; and as soon as any one of the joint tenants gives a notice to quit, he effectually puts and end to *that* tenancy; the tenant has a right upon such a notice to quit to give up *the whole*, and unless he comes to a new arrangement with the other joint tenants as to their shares, he is compellable so to do. The hardship upon the tenant, if he were not entitled to treat a notice from one as putting an end to the tenancy as to the whole, is obvious; for however willing a man might be to be sole tenant of an estate, it is not very likely he should be willing to hold the undivided shares of it; and if upon such a notice the tenant is entitled to treat it as putting an end to the tenancy as to the whole, the other joint tenants must have the same right. It cannot be optional on one side, and on one side only'. (My emphasis). Now it was rightly pointed out in argument that part of the reasoning in this passage was dictated by considerations derived from the incidents of joint land tenure at law which were swept away by the reforming legislation of 1925. But this can in no way detract from the validity of the proposition emphasised in the judgment that the yearly tenant of a property let to him by joint freeholders 'holds the *whole* of *all* so long as he *and all* shall please.' This by itself is a sufficient and independent ground for the conclusion of the court that notice to quit by any one joint freeholder was effective to determine the tenancy. Precisely the same reasoning would apply to the operation of a notice to quit by one of two or more joint yearly tenants."

[16] The drafting of s. 26 lends some faint support to the idea that an oral notice to quit would be satisfactory because of the contrast in subss. (a) and (b), the latter (the tenant's counter-notice) being required to be in writing and stated to be "served".

[17] See precedents in Part V as follows: notice to quit by the tenant to his landlord (Form 38), notice to quit by the tenant to the sub-tenant (Form 39), notice to quit by the landlord ending a fixed term tenancy at the contractual expiration date (Form 27), notice to quit by the landlord without reasons given (Form 28), notice to quit by the landlord giving reasons for the purposes of s. 61(3) (Form 29), notice to quit by the landlord relying on one or more of the special Cases in Sched. 3, a form which requires careful adaptation, (Form 30), notice to quit under Case G (Form 31).

[18] Paras 12.5–12.14 above.

[19] See paras 12.17–12.20 above.

clear identification of the land within a notice to quit[20]; where part only of the holding is the subject of the notice to quit it is helpful to use Ordnance Survey numbers for identification and/or a plan.[21]

The identity of the landlord or the tenant may be obscure or contested[22] and in such circumstances there seems to be nothing wrong with addressing the notice to "the landlord" or, as the case may be, "the tenant" and serving it upon all persons who may satisfy that description. In addition there are special provisions in section 93 designed to assist.[23] Particularly useful is the power under section 93(3) where there is an agent or servant responsible for the control or management or the farming of the holding to give the notice to that person.[24] Where there is a change of landlord which has not been notified to the tenant in terms of name and address of the new landlord, notices served on or delivered to the original landlord are deemed to be served on or delivered to the actual landlord.[25] Where the expiry date of the notice is uncertain it is appropriate to use the general rubric for termination.[26] Where a mistake occurs or there is uncertainty, the true construction of the notice to quit may well be a contested matter. The approach to construction in these circumstances is dealt with below.[27]

Drafting the notice to quit: use of the general rubric 12.26

The validity of a notice to quit may be saved by apt general words, such as "or at the expiration of the year of your tenancy which shall expire next after the end of 12 months from the service upon you of this notice". Such a formulation is not too vague.[28] The rubric was decisively approved by the Court of Appeal in *Addis v. Burrows* in circumstances where the ascertainment of the correct termination date was itself a difficult question of law.[29]

---

[20] See paras 12.20 (severance of the reversion).
[21] Although in the latter case where the boundary of the notice to quit does not coincide with a field boundary there may be difficulty on steeply inclined land of identifying the areas included or excluded. However on marginal questions of area see para. 12.30 below.
[22] *e.g.* under s. 6.
[23] See separate discussion at para. 12.29 below.
[24] By this it is submitted that the statute intends the notice to be addressed to the recipient since there appears to be a distinction between the giving and the serving of the notice.
[25] s. 93(5).
[26] See the next following paragraph.
[27] Paras 12.29–12.30 below.
[28] c.f. *P. Phipps and Son (Northampton and Towcester Breweries) Ltd v. Rogers* [1925] 1 K.B. 14 which was distinguished by the CA in *Addis v. Burrows* [1948] 1 K.B. 444.
[29] Evershed L.J. at 454 stated "... [T]he whole object of this formula, as pointed out in the authorities, is to get over the difficulty a landlord might find himself in if he, the landlord, wrongly interpreted the agreement or gave a wrong date. It is intended to cast the duty on the tenant to satisfy himself, by looking at the instrument, what is the correct date upon which he ought to go out. That fact that he is involved in that problem is no objection of itself to the form of words which has been used". Lord Green M.R. expressly disapproved the suggestion in the leading textbook Foa that *Phipps v. Rogers* (above) invalidated a notice to quit where the recipient was in doubt when possession would be demanded because he had to solve difficult questions of law.

12.27 Rule in *Budge v. Hicks*[30]: requirement of clarity in choice of Case

The landlord must make it quite clear in his notice to quit under which Case in Schedule 3 he is proceeding, and the nature of the facts on which he is relying or the reason for the notice, as appropriate. For example, he must make it clear whether he is relying on Case D or Case E. Ambiguity may deprive him of the benefit of section 26(2) and, as a result of the next rule, may render his notice to quit entirely invalid. Because of the extreme importance to the recipient of the notice to quit in knowing which procedure is applicable it is suggested that, notwithstanding the slightly more liberal basis of construction of notices to quit discussed below,[31] there may still be very limited scope, if any, for curing or ignoring an error on the face of a notice to quit which might leave the recipient in doubt as to the procedure employed.[32]

12.28 Rule in *Cowan v. Wrayford*[33] and *Mills v. Edwards*[34]: requirement of clarity as to whether notice to quit is given alternatively under a Case and as an ordinary notice to quit

This rule, originally formulated in *Cowan v. Wrayford* and emphatically reaffirmed in *Mills v. Edwards*, is that if the landlord wishes to rely on the notice to quit taking effect as an ordinary unqualified notice to which section 26(1) applies, if he should fail to substantiate a Case in Schedule 3, he must make this abundantly clear either by framing the notice to quit expressly and unambiguously in the alternative or by serving two notices.[35] If he does not, if he relies solely on a Schedule 3 Case and fails to substantiate it, he cannot, according to this rule, fall back on the contention that the notice to quit should take effect as a simple unqualified notice without reasons to which a counter-notice might be given by the tenant under section 26(1); the reasons given being simply disregarded as redundant. Since *Mills v. Edwards* there is less justification for the tenant to serve a precautionary counter-notice when served with a notice to quit in pursuance of one

---

[30] [1951] 2 K.B. 335.
[31] See paras 12.29–12.30.
[32] Conversely, of course, the Court might regard the recipient as burdened by alternative responses to a notice, each without prejudice to the other. But it is suggested that this degree of sophistication may be going one step too far if that is what is required to save an otherwise bad notice.
[33] [1953] 1 W.L.R. 1340.
[34] [1971] 1 Q.B. 379.
[35] See on this question Somervell L.J. in *Cowan v. Wrayford*, above, at 1344. On two notices, see also *French v. Elliott* [1960] 1 W.L.R. 40. On two notices generally, see *Lowenthal v. Vanhoute* [1947] K.B. 342. From the landlord's point of view the advantages of two notices are (1) the tenant's ability to freeze a notice to quit by requiring arbitration (art. 12 of the Arbitration on Notices Order 1987 (S.I. 1987 No.710)) would apply only to a notice under certain Cases in Sched. 3; and (2) if one of the notices is bad for any reason the other is unaffected. The Court of Appeal's criticisms in *Mills v. Edwards*, above, led to the revision of the original art. 10 of S.I. 1964 No.706 and its replacement by the wording now found in art. 11 of the Arbitration on Notices Order 1987 (S.I. 1987 No.710), which meets the criticisms. The CA in *Mills v. Edwards* doubted the correctness of *Hammon v. Fairbrother* [1956] 1 W.L.R. 490 and considered *Harley v. Moss* [1962] E.G.D. 403 wrongly decided. (For a note on somewhat misleading statements made by Salmon and Cross L.JJ. see S.J. for Oct. 8, 1971, p.750).

of the Cases in Schedule 3. As regards reasons, the simple dichotomy formulated in *Cowan v. Wrayford*[36] between notices to quit which do not require reasons and notices to quit which do is no longer valid.[37] It may be vital for a landlord to state reasons in order to avoid the possibly crippling additional compensation for disturbance equal to four times the rent of the holding.[38] Finally the remarks at the conclusion of the preceding paragraph are equally applicable to this rule.

Construction of notices to quit 12.29

The long and difficult debate as to how strictly a notice to quit will be construed has now finally been resolved by the House of Lords with, for agricultural lawyers, dramatic results. In *Mannai Investment Co. Limited v. Eagle Star Life Assurance Co. Limited*[39] leases relating to offices and a car park contained a single opportunity in favour of the tenant to break the term. When the tenant did serve notice, instead of expiring on January 13, 1995 as they ought to have done, the notices were expressed to expire on January 12, 1995.[40] Break notices in leases have traditionally been construed in a very strict way and it is some mark of the strength of the strict construction tradition that two members[41] of the House of Lords dissented on the main issue, namely whether the two notices which gave the wrong date could be taken as valid. The majority said they could. The majority overruled the main strict construction case *Hankey v. Clavering*[42] thereby ending over forty years of uneasy tension between liberal and strict construction approaches.[43] The decision in *Hankey v. Clavering* forms an important strand in the reasoning of many agricultural cases and will taint the survival and usefulness of those decisions. *Carradine Properties Limited v. Aslam*[44] was applied in the same tradition as *Frankland v. Capstick*[45] through to the more recent cases such as *Crawford v. Elliott*[46] and *Land v. Sykes*[47] so as to save the notices. Because for agricultural lawyers there is interest not only in relation to notices to quit but also the approach to construction of statutory notices under Case D[48] it is important to look at the reasoning of each speech in the majority in some detail.

Lord Steyn based his conclusion on five numbered propositions[49] namely (1) the

---

[36] [1953] 1 W.L.R. 1340.
[37] It was not perhaps correct without qualification even in 1953; *Hammon v. Fairbrother* and *Harley v. Moss*, above, were criticised in *Mills v. Edwards*.
[38] See ss 61(3), (4), 60(4). For a precedent regarding compensation see Form 29 in Part V of this work: for a general 'alternative' form of notice to quit see Form 32 in Part V.
[39] [1997] 3 All E.R. 352
[40] Attempts to save the notices based on *Sidebotham v. Holland* [1895] 1 Q.B. 378 failed: Lord Goff at 354g-j; Lord Jauncey at 367e; Lord Steyn at 368e-g; Lord Clyde at 384b-c (although the integrity of that decision was not impugned).
[41] Lord Goff and Lord Jauncey.
[42] [1942] 2 All E.R. 311, [1942] 2 K.B. 326, CA.
[43] Evident in the agricultural world from the text of Scammell and Densham's *Law of Agricultural Holdings* (8th ed., 1997) p. 156–159.
[44] [1976] 1 All E.R. 573.
[45] [1959] 1 W.L.R. 204, CA.
[46] [1991] 1 E.G.L.R. 13, CA.
[47] [1992] 1 E.G.L.R. 1, CA.
[48] See para. 12.54 below.
[49] At 368h–370c.

contracts did not prescribe that the notices must contain specific information; (2) the construction of the notices is objective not subjective[50]; (3) the purpose of the notice, to inform the landlord of the tenant's decision to terminate the lease, is important; (4) break clauses are part of a general category of unilateral notices served under contractual rights reserved *e.g.* notices to quit, notices to determine licences and notices to complete and may be valid if they are "sufficiently clear and unambiguous to leave a reasonable recipient in no reasonable doubt as to how and when they are intended to operate"; (5) on the facts it is obvious that the reasonable recipient would have appreciated that the tenant wished to determine the leases on the third anniversary date but wrongly described it as January 12, instead of January 13. The reasonable recipient would not have been perplexed by a minor error in the notices. In dismissing an argument that one date should not be substituted for another, he summarised: "The real question is a different one: Does the notice construed against its contextual setting unambiguously inform a reasonable recipient how and when the notice is to operate *under the right reserved*? As Lord Hoffmann has observed we no longer confuse the meaning of words with the question of what meaning in a particular setting the use of words was intended to convey".[51]

Lord Hoffmann approached the question of construction by first considering the way in which language is used to convey meaning and, in particular, the wrong language being used to convey without difficulty the meaning of the speaker.[52] He examines at some length the explanation for the result in **Hankey v. Clavering** which he concludes is a rule of evidence,[53] and records that **Hankey v. Clavering**

---

[50] "The construction of the notices must be approached objectively. The issue is how a reasonable recipient would have understood the notices. And in considering this question the notices must be construed taking into account the relevant objective contextual scene. The approach in *Reardon Smith Line Ltd v. Hansen-Tangen* ... [1976] 3 All E.R. 570 ... which deals with the construction of commercial contracts, is by analogy of assistance in respect of unilateral notices such as those under consideration in the present case. Relying on the reasoning in Lord Wilberforce's speech in the *Reardon Smith* case ..... at 574–575, three propositions can be formulated. First, in respect of contracts and contractual notices the contextual scene is always relevant. Secondly, what is *admissible* as a matter of the rules of evidence under this heading is what is arguably relevant. But admissibility is not the decisive matter. The real question is what evidence of surrounding circumstances may ultimately be allowed to influence the question of interpretation. That depends on what meanings the language read against the objective contextual scene will let in. Thirdly, the inquiry is objective: the question is what reasonable persons, circumstanced as the actual parties were, would have had in mind. It follows that one cannot ignore that a reasonable recipient of the notices would have had in the forefront of his mind the terms of the leases. Given that the reasonable recipient must be credited with knowledge of the critical date and the terms of clause 7(13) the question is simply how the reasonable recipient would have understood such a notice. This proposition may in other cases require qualification ...".

[51] At 373j–374a.

[52] At 375e–376a "... no one, for example, has any difficulty in understanding Mrs Malaprop. When she says 'She is as obstinate as an allegory on the banks of the Nile', we reject the conventional or literal meaning of allegory as making nonsense of the sentence and substitute "alligator" by using our background knowledge of the things likely to be found on the banks of the Nile and choosing one which sounds rather like 'allegory'."

[53] 376b–379g.

had been applied not only to break clauses but also to notices to terminate periodic tenancies.[54] He describes the rules for construction of notices as not having yet caught up with the move to common sense interpretation of contracts and that there appeared to be no reason for not bringing the rules for notices up to date.[55] He therefore endorsed the approach of Goulding J. in *Carradine Properties Limited v. Aslam* (above): "is the notice quite clear to a reasonable tenant reading it? Is it plain that he cannot be misled by it?", on the basis that the reasonable tenant must be taken to know the terms of the lease.[56]

Lord Clyde also endorsed the formulation of Goulding J.[57] and concluded that the standard of reference was that of the reasonable man exercising his common sense in the context and in the circumstances of the particular case such that the evident intention of a notice should not be rejected in preference for a technical precision.[58]

The impact of the decision can hardly be overstated. Henceforth whenever there appears to be a technical defect or ambiguity on a notice to quit the decision as to whether the notice is good or bad will be made by reference to the *Mannai Investment v. Eagle Star* case. It remains, of course, to see whether the Courts would find that there was some special quality in section 25 which prevented the full scope of the rules of construction in the *Mannai Investment v. Eagle Star* case. It is suggested that this must be very doubtful. Section 25 does not require a notice to contain specific information[59] nor is a notice to quit by virtue of section 25 classifiable with "documents in which the need for certainty is paramount" which

---

[54] 379j: reference to *Doe d. Spicer v. Lea* (1809) 11 East 312.
[55] 380f–381a: "In the case of commercial contracts, the restriction on the use of background has been quietly dropped. There are certain special kinds of evidence, such as previous negotiations and express declarations of intent, which for practical reasons which it is unnecessary to analyse, are inadmissible in aid of construction. They can be used only in an action for rectification. But apart from these exceptions, commercial contracts are construed in the light of all the background which could reasonably have been expected to have been available to the parties in order to ascertain what would objectively have been understood to be their intention: see *Prenn v. Simmonds* [1971] 3 All E.R. 237 at 239, [1971] 1 W.L.R. 1381 at 1383. The fact that the words are capable of a literal application is no obstacle to evidence which demonstrates what a reasonable person with knowledge of the background would have understood the parties to mean, even if this compels one to say that they used the wrong words. In this area, we no longer confuse the meaning of words with the question of what meaning the use of the words was intended to convey. Why, therefore, should the rules for the construction of notices be different from those for the construction of contracts? There seems to me to be no answer to this question. All that can be said is that the rules for the construction of notices, like those for the construction of wills, have not yet caught up with the move to common sense interpretation of contracts which is marked by the speeches of Lord Wilberforce in *Prenn v. Simmonds* and *Reardon Smith Line Limited v. Hansen-Tangen* ... [1976] 3 All E.R. 570; [1976] 1 W.L.R. 989. The question is therefore whether there is any reason not to bring the rules for notices up to date by overruling the old cases."
[56] At 381d. This test had already been approved by the CA in *Germax Securities Limited v. Spiegal* (1978) 37 P.&C.R. 204 at 206.
[57] At 382h.
[58] At 383c.
[59] See the first reason given by Lord Steyn.

should not be construed so as to mean different things to different people.[60] It is suggested that the better view is that section 25 is designed to safeguard, to the recipient of a notice to quit, a minimum period and whether or not, as a matter of construction, the minimum should be regarded as given pursuant to the notice brings the issue squarely within the corners of the *Mannai Investment v. Eagle Star* decision.

The second point which deserves specific thought is the fate of notices to quit where the wrong person has been named as the landlord. In principle it must be inescapable that the *Mannai Investment v. Eagle Star* case will cure many defects but there is still scope for such notices to be saved by the application of other considerations. In particular there is scope for a notice to be saved by section 93(3)[61] or by a general agency.[62] The final point to be noted is that there is every likelihood that the actual decision in *Divall v. Harrison*, could not now be supported and should not be followed.[63]

12.30 **Construction of notices to quit: use of the de minimis rule**

The maxim *de minimis non curat lex*[64] can be used to disregard marginal errors or small failures to comply with notices. There is surprisingly little use of this maxim in the agricultural context although traces of it can be found.[65] No doubt this historical lack of popularity has been due to the "strict construction" school of thought.[66]

12.31 **Procedure in relation to notices to quit capable of reference to the Agricultural Land Tribunal**

Procedural Table 1: Notices to quit capable of reference to the Agricultural Land Tribunal.

---

[60] Lord Hoffmann at 380c separates out this category and gives as an example bankers' commercial credits.

[61] See also discussion at para. 12.25 above.

[62] See the argument as to the position of the general agent in *Divall v. Harrison* [1992] 2 E.G.L.R. 64 at 66D and *Combey v. Gumbrill* [1990] 2 E.G.L.R. 7, decision of Mr J.A.D. Gilliland Q.C., sitting in the Stockport County Court, at 7K. In fact in that case the Assistant Recorder held that on the true construction of the orders in the matrimonial proceedings a wife had full and complete authority to conduct the farming business and under the agricultural holdings legislation (section 93 presumably) had sufficient authority to serve a notice demanding arbitration under Article 9 of the 1987 Order (S.I. 1987 No.710).

[63] The Court of Appeal held that a notice to quit was invalid because it was served by a firm of solicitors on behalf of the plaintiff who was not at the time the landlord; it was served by the solicitors as speciality agents and failed to identify the correct landlord notwithstanding that two of the partners in the firm were the landlord at the time. The decision is essentially based on *Hankey v. Clavering*.

[64] The law does not care for the smallest things.

[65] See *Land v. Sykes* [1992] 1 E.G.L.R. 1 at 4C (Court of Appeal) in reference to a strip 9 foot by 200 foot out of a 291 acre farm; and *Luttenberger v. North Thoresby Farms Limited* [1993] 1 E.G.L.R. 3 at 9m (Ferris J.) where a failure to pay £8.40 on a demand of £15,264 was described as subject to the *de minimis* rule.

[66] See *Pickard v. Bishop* (para. 12.53 below) and *Hankey v. Clavering*, now overruled (para. 12.29 above).

Tenant's right to serve counter-notice: section 26(1)

The mechanism used to enforce the tenant's security of tenure is to enable him to challenge the landlord's notice to quit within one month of receiving it and thus compel the landlord to seek the consent of the Agricultural Land Tribunal if he wishes to preserve its effectiveness.[67] There are, however, a number of important circumstances where this procedure for challenging the landlord's notice is excluded.[68] It has sometimes been said that in these instances the notice to quit is "incontestable", but this is misleading; they are only immune from challenge by the counter-notice and consent of Tribunal procedure.[69] Before serving a counter-notice a tenant should be quite sure that this is in all the circumstances the appropriate rejoinder to make to the landlord's notice to quit. Prima facie it would not be appropriate if one of the Cases in Schedule 3 applies.[70]

A counter-notice must be served on the landlord not later than one month[71] from the giving of the notice to quit; there is no provision for the extension of the time-limit in section 26(1)(b).[72] There is no prescribed form of counter-notice.[73] A valid counter-notice must indicate unambiguously an intention to invoke section 26(1),[74] although it will not be invalidated by a mere technicality.[75] In general there is a marked trend towards a more common sense and less technical construction of unilateral notices.[76] The true test, it is submitted, is that the counter-notice should be in terms which are sufficiently clear to bring home to the ordinary landlord that the tenant is purporting to exercise his right under section 26(1).[77] It is contrary to public policy to contract out of the service of a counter-notice.[78] In the case of joint tenants all must join in the service of a counter-notice since this preserves the rights and obligations created by the tenancy agreement[79]; where, however, the need

12.32

---

[67] s. 26(1).
[68] s. 26(2) and Sched. 3; see para. 12.2 above.
[69] In some cases they can be challenged by arbitration proceedings, in others by legal proceedings and even, in one case, by both arbitration and counter-notice procedures (s. 28).
[70] But in some circumstances it might be wise to serve both a counter-notice and a notice requiring arbitration. And there is one case where both (at different times) are expressly allowed: s. 28.
[71] Calculated in accordance with the corresponding date rule: *Dodds v. Walker* [1981] 2 All E.R. 609.
[72] But in certain cases the one month runs from the termination of an arbitration which the tenant has resorted to unsuccessfully: see 1986 Act, s. 28(4)(b) and art. 11 of the Arbitration on Notices Order 1987 (S.I. 1987 No.710).
[73] For suggested form, see Form 36 in Part V of this work.
[74] See *Mountford v. Hodkinson* [1956] 1 W.L.R. 442.
[75] See *Ward v. Scott* [1950] W.N. 76.
[76] See *Mannai Investment Company v. Eagle Star Assurance Company* [1997] 3 All E.R. 352 and see para. 12.29 above.
[77] Test applied by the Court of Appeal in *Amalgamated Estates Limited v. Joystretch Manufacturing Limited* [1980] 257 E.G. 489 adopted in relation to a "relevant notice" served by executors for the purposes of Case G in *BSC Pension Fund Trustees Limited v. Downing* [1990] 1 E.G.L.R. 4, A. Blackett-Ord sitting as a deputy High Court judge, and *Lees v. Tatchell* [1990] 1 E.G.L.R. 10, CA, in which the *Joystretch* case is expressly followed and *BSC Pension Fund v. Downing* is approved.
[78] See *Johnson v. Moreton* [1980] A.C. 37 and see para. 12.3 above.
[79] See *Featherstone v. Staples* [1986] 1 W.L.R. 861, CA, a decision which, it is submitted,

for all tenants to join in the service of a counter-notice is used as a device by a landowner to engineer possession by means of an associated partnership agreement, that device will fail as contrary to public policy.[80] There are special provisions for the service of a counter-notice on behalf of a serviceman tenant.[81] In so far as a tenancy is held on trust there is the possibility of an application to the Court requiring any reluctant trustee to serve counter-notice and preserve the tenancy: the grant of any order is discretionary.[82]

12.33 **Landlord's application to Tribunal: sections 26(1) and 27: general**
Following the tenant's counter-notice the landlord must apply to the Tribunal for their consent if he wishes to save his notice to quit. His application must be made within one month of the service of the counter-notice[83] and the application must be made on the prescribed form,[84] which requires a statement of the grounds on which the landlord relies and the main relevant facts. The application must relate to a notice to quit the whole holding except in cases where the Act allows or recognises a notice to quit part. A plea of *res judicata* by the tenant based on a previous decision of the Tribunal will seldom succeed; the agricultural situation is not static, but has constant potential for change.[85] The onus is, however, on the applicant landlord to prove his case. Where the Tribunal consent they have power to postpone the termination of the tenancy for any period not exceeding 12 months if the notice to quit would otherwise operate on, or within six months after, the giving of consent.[86]

There are six separate grounds for the Tribunal's consent set out in section 27 of the 1986 Act.[87] The Tribunal are given no power to consent if none of these grounds is present.[88] Section 27(1) provides that the Tribunal shall consent to a

---

survives unaffected *Hammersmith and Fulham LBC v. Monk* [1992] 1 All E.R. 1, discussed at paragraph 12.29 above.

[80] *Featherstone v. Staples* (above).

[81] See Sched. 5, para. 6 and the Reserve and Auxiliary Forces (Agricultural Tenants) Regulations 1959 (S.I. 1959 No.84).

[82] See *Harris v. Black* (1983) 46 P.&C.R. 366; *Sykes v. Land* [1984] 2 E.G.L.R. 8; *Cork v. Cork* (1997) 16 E.G. 130.

[83] Rule 2 in Sched. 1 to the Agricultural Land Tribunals (Rules) Order 1978 (S.I. 1978 No.259). This rule applies also to applications for consent under s. 28.

[84] Form 1 in the appendix to the above rules: see Form 40 in Part V of this work. Failure to comply with the form is not necessarily fatal: r. 38. There is also a prescribed form for the tenant's reply, printed as Form 40A in Part V of this work.

[85] *Wickington v. Bonney* (1983) 266 E.G. 434, but there is a "risk of alienating the ear of the tribunal" if the applicant puts substantially the same case as on a previous occasion; at 439.

[86] Agricultural Holdings (Arbitration on Notices) Order 1987 (S.I. 1987 No.710), art. 13. This power is exercisable on the Tribunal's own motion or on the tenant's application made not later than 14 days after the giving of consent. For form of application, see r. 3 in Sched. 1 to the Agricultural Land Tribunals (Rules) Order 1978 (S.I. 1978 No.259) and Form 2 in appendix to rules; this is printed as Form 42 in Part V of this work with the tenant's reply shown as Form 42A.

[87] s. 27(3)(a) to (f).

[88] *cf.* decisions on earlier form of the legislation: *R. v. ALT for the Wales and Monmouth Area, ex p. Davies* [1953] 1 W.L.R. 722 and *R. v. ALT for the Eastern Province, ex p.*

notice to quit a holding (or a part of a holding if appropriate and permissible) if, but only if, they are satisfied as to one or more of these six grounds. And section 27(2) goes on to provide that even if they are so satisfied they shall withhold consent "if in all the circumstances it appears to them that a fair and reasonable landlord would not insist on possession". Proof of one of the six grounds is therefore a necessary, but not a sufficient, condition for the giving of consent. It will be noted that the "fair and reasonable landlord" principle is expressed in mandatory, not discretionary, terms. The Tribunal's procedure should be to decide first whether at least one of the six grounds has been established by the landlord and then consider, as a separate issue, whether the fair and reasonable landlord direction applies. A failure to distinguish clearly and apply their minds to these two issues may lead to their decision being quashed on judicial review,[89] or, if a case is stated, justify the court in sending the case back to the Tribunal for reconsideration.[90] Tribunals are subject to a two-fold obligation to give reasons for decision, an obligation conditional on request under the Tribunals and Inquiries Act 1971[91] and an absolute obligation, not dependent on request, under the Agricultural Land Tribunals Rules 1978.[92] Reasons, of course, not only explain the decision but facilitate an attack on it by judicial review or case stated.[93]

Tribunal's consent to notice to quit: grounds for consent 12.34

The Act provides that the Tribunal shall consent[94] to the operation of the notice to quit in accordance with the landlord's application if satisfied[95] as to one or more of the six grounds discussed below. The further condition as to the "fair and reasonable landlord" is considered later.[96] It will be noted that the ground or grounds must be specified by the landlord in his application to the Tribunal, but the grounds do not necessarily have to be stated on the notice to quit (a matter for the landlord to consider[97]). References to Scottish case law have been cut back in this edition.[98] What must be recollected in relation to the operation of section 27(2)

Grant [1956] 1 W.L.R. 1240.
[89] *cf.* the two stages in *R. v. ALT for the Eastern Province, ex p. Grant* [1956] 1 W.L.R. 1240, which appears still applicable in principle.
[90] *Evans v. Roper* [1960] 1 W.L.R. 814 (under s. 6 of Agriculture (Miscellaneous Provisions) Act 1954).
[91] See s. 12 and Sched. 1, item 1(a).
[92] See r. 31(1). The rules are in Sched. 1 to the Agricultural Land Tribunals (Rules) Order 1978 (S.I. 1978 No.259).
[93] Cases on the extent of the duty to give reasons, which applies to a wide range of Tribunals, are extremely numerous, but the classic statement is still that of Megaw J. in *Re Poyser and Mills' Arbitration* [1964] 2 Q.B. 467 at 478.
[94] s. 27(1).
[95] The subjective expressions "if satisfied" (s.27(1)) and "if it appears to them" (s. 27(2)) confer a discretion which is difficult to challenge effectively: *cf.* **Ross-Clunis v. Papadopoullos** [1958] 1 W.L.R. 546 at 560. But its exercise may be reviewed if it could be shown that no reasonable Tribunal could have been so satisfied, or, possibly, if the Tribunal applied a wrong legal test or misunderstood the nature of the matter in respect of which they had to be satisfied.
[96] See below para. 12.41 below.
[97] Against the consequences for compensation: see Chapter 13.
[98] Virtually identical provisions in s. 24 of the Agricultural Holdings (Scotland) Act 1991 to those in s. 27 of the 1986 Act are the subject of extensive and excellent treatment in

and (3) is the overwhelming sympathy with the tenant which in practice most Agricultural Land Tribunals will have: a landlord is unlikely to succeed in an application to the Tribunal unless his case is very strong indeed. The grounds of application are as follows.[99]

12.35 Good husbandry: section 27(3)(a)

"[T]hat the carrying out of the purpose for which the landlord proposes to terminate the tenancy is desirable in the interests of good husbandry as respects the land to which the notice relates, treated as a separate unit."[1]

The words "treated as a separate unit" make it clear that it would not be permissible under this head to show that the land would be better farmed if amalgamated with other land.[2] The advantages of amalgamation may be canvassed under the next heading (sound management). The present paragraph envisages a comparison between the regime under the existing tenant and the proposed new regime with reference to the subject holding.[3] The replacement of a poor farmer by a good farmer would come under this head.[4] It would therefore be legitimate to offer evidence as to the standard of husbandry of the landlord (if he proposed to take the land in hand) or of a proposed replacement tenant, to show the likelihood of better utilisation and/or greater productivity. But it would not be legitimate to show that these desirable improvements would result from a union of the holding within the landlord's, or the proposed replacement's, own land. A landlord cannot establish this ground for consent merely by showing that the tenant is a bad farmer, but he can do so by presenting a satisfactory scheme for amelioration.[5] Although there is a clear logical distinction[6] between this head and the next (sound management) it may in practice be difficult, especially where the subject land constitutes an estate by itself, to disentangle good husbandry from sound management considerations; the same facts may have an aspect of both.[7] While a pedantic distinction may be impracticable, a total obliteration of the classification could constitute an error of law.

It will not be easy to persuade a Tribunal that this ground applies and there is a considerable sympathy for the existing tenant in most cases.

Chapter 18 of Gill, *The Law of Agricultural Holdings in Scotland* (3rd ed., W. Green) which now sets out the effect of Scottish case law as to the implementation of the section. It is no longer necessary to pursue the parallel in this work.

[99] See paras 12.35–12.40 below.

[1] s. 27(3)(a). For the rules of good husbandry, see s. 96(3), and s. 11 of the Agriculture Act 1947. See also paras 10.52 and 13.82.

[2] This is more restrictive than the decisions in *Ex p. Davies* [1953] 1 W.L.R. 722 and *Ex p. Grant* [1956] 1 W.L.R. 1240, cases under the old para. (a), under which it was permissible to show that the amalgamation would result in more efficient farming of the subject land, but not that it would have this effect on the other land.

[3] cf. *Davies v. Price* [1958] 1 W.L.R. 434.

[4] But not merely the replacement of an efficient but selfish farmer by one more considerate to his neighbours.

[5] cf. *Lewis v. Moss* (1962) 181 E.G. 685, (ALT).

[6] Which must be maintained.

[7] *Greaves v. Mitchell* (1971) 222 E.G. 1395.

Sound management: section 27(3)(b) 12.36

"that the carrying out of the purpose is desirable in the interests of sound management of the estate of which the land to which the notice relates forms part or which that land constitutes."[8]

Here again a comparison is involved between the present and the proposed regime, but in this case the Tribunal may look beyond the land to which the notice to quit relates and consider, *e.g.*, whether the amalgamation of that land with other land belonging to the landlord would produce a more economic unit of production.[9] It is not necessary under this head to show that the land to which the notice relates is itself being badly farmed. Paragraph (b) assumes that the landlord has a concrete scheme of management to put to the Tribunal; a vague suggestion that the holding is uneconomic will not do.[10] In one case a Tribunal decided that it was not desirable in the interests of sound management to dispossess a tenant who was absent serving a 21 months' prison sentence, the farm having been well managed during this period.[11] Although this paragraph is likely to be most frequently invoked for a scheme of amalgamation with other land, it can apply where the landlord is able to show, for estate management rather than husbandry reasons, that his proposed regime is desirable for the holding considered by itself.[12] But this ground cannot be used to justify a notice to quit given merely to enable the landlord to renegotiate the letting on terms more favourable to himself.[13] The purpose must relate to the physical management of the land, not merely to the landlord's financial benefit, but it might involve an actual reduction in the physical size of the holding if the sale of parts was desirable to finance a scheme beneficial to the remainder.[14] The personal financial position of the landlord is not a relevant consideration under this head, although it may be under paragraph (e) (greater hardship).[15] It has already been noted that where the land to which the notice relates constitutes an estate by itself it may be difficult to disentangle husbandry and management considerations.[16] The "estate", however, must be land owned by the landlord and the subject-matter of the notice to quit must be part of, or the whole of, that land. If at some time the reversion on the land held by the tenant has been severed, the landlord having transferred part of it to, say, an estate company, he could not by himself alone serve a valid notice to quit the entire holding and invoke the present paragraph.

"Sound management" is a deliberately different expression from "good estate

---

[8] s. 27(3)(b).
[9] This makes it clear that the Tribunal may do what under the original legislation they were not entitled to do in *R. v. ALT for the Wales and Monmouth Area, ex p. Davies* [1953] 1 W.L.R. 722 and *R. v. ALT for the Eastern Province, ex p. Grant* [1956] 1 W.L.R. 1240.
[10] *cf. Lewis v. Moss* (1962) 181 E.G. 685, (ALT).
[11] *Merstham Manor Ltd v. Maiklem* [1967], reported only in the journal of the Chartered Land Agents' Society for that year, at 362.
[12] *Greaves v. Mitchell* [1971] 222 E.G. 1395.
[13] *National Coal Board v. Naylor* [1972] 1 W.L.R. 908.
[14] *Lewis v. Moss* (1962) 181 E.G. 685, (ALT).
[15] See *Purser v. Bailey* [1967] 2 Q.B. 500, and para. 12.39 below.
[16] *Greaves v. Mitchell, supra.* (an estate of only twenty-five-and-a-half acres).

management" and does not attract the definition of the latter in section 10 of the 1947 Act,[17] although there is clearly some identity of content. "Sound management" has no exact definition, but it seems to suggest the idea of sensible, well-informed and well-judged action. Lord Widgery C.J. said in *National Coal Board v. Naylor*[18] that the phrase refers to the obligations of a landlord as one of the producers in a partnership which produces food from the land. "The obligation of the tenant is to observe the rules of good husbandry; the obligation of the landlord is to manage the estate properly." Ashworth J. in the same case said that sound management "related to the management of the farm in the physical sense of the word and is something quite distinct from the financial result to the landlord himself".[19] It might even be sound "management" to sell one farm in order to raise capital for the rest of the estate. Sound management involves looking at the whole estate and every part of it, including the effect of the proposed scheme on the land to which the notice relates. The effect on the personal farming fortunes of the tenant is, however, irrelevant under this paragraph, although relevant under the "fair and reasonable landlord" provision.[20]

An applicant who presents a substantially identical case after too short an interval risks "alienating the ear of the Tribunal" and being penalised in costs,[21] although the application cannot be defeated by a plea of issue estoppel since management changes over time.

12.37 Agricultural research, education, experiment or demonstration or the enactments relating to smallholdings: section 27(3)(c)

"[T]hat the carrying out of the purpose is desirable for the purposes of agricultural research, education, experiment or demonstration, or for the purposes of the enactments relating to smallholdings.[22]"

There is no superior court authority on the construction or application of the first limb of this paragraph, which appears to be rarely used in practice. It seems clear, however, that "agricultural" qualifies not only research[23] but also "education, experiment or demonstration".[24] "Research" could cover private research. It will be noted that there has been a slight change from the 1977 Act in this paragraph,

---

[17] Incorporated in the 1986 Act by s. 96(3).
[18] [1972] 1 W.L.R. 908; *sub nom. Naylor v. National Coal Board* (1972) 221 E.G. 1285.
[19] [1972] 1 W.L.R. 908. The omission of "estate" and the substituting of "sound" for "good" gives "sound management" a wider connotation than "good estate management", which has a more technical, more professional flavour, suggesting the kind of management which a good land agent might exercise. "Management" might concern itself with wider financial considerations than "estate management".
[20] *Evans v. Roper* [1960] 1 W.L.R. 814. They may also be relevant under s. 27(3)(e) (greater hardship). See para. 12.39 below.
[21] *Wickington v. Bonney* (1983) 266 E.G. 434.
[22] s. 27(3)(c).
[23] For old cases on agricultural research see *Wilts County Council v. Habershon* (1952) 159 EG 157 and *Wood v. East Sussex County Council* (1954) 164 EG 402.
[24] *cf. Paddock Investments Ltd v. Lory* (1975) 236 E.G. 803 on s. 8(2)(a) and (b) of 1977 Act (amended by 1984 Act to remove ambiguity and now in s. 31(2)(a) and (b) of the 1986 Act in the amended form).

allotments having been separated from smallholdings and given a new paragraph of their own.²⁵ This paragraph would cover a case where it is desirable to terminate the smallholder's tenancy, not for inefficiency, but because he has taken on too much land and in reality has ceased to be a smallholder, and the landlord wishes to relet to a beginner.

Allotments: section 27(3)(d)

12.38

"[T]hat the carrying out of the purpose is desirable for the purposes of the enactments relating to allotments."²⁶

Greater hardship: section 27(3)(e)

12.39

"[T]hat greater hardship would be caused by withholding than by giving consent to the operation of the notice."²⁷

As in all the paragraphs of section 27(3) the onus is on the landlord to establish the ground for consent. The wording is reminiscent of that used in the Rent Act 1977, with the difference that the onus there is on the tenant to show that greater hardship would be caused by granting the landlord possession than by refusing it.²⁸

Hardship is not easy to define or to apply consistently in practice. Moreover it is extremely difficult to persuade a Tribunal that the balance of hardship is as perceived by the landlord. It was established in *Purser v. Bailey*²⁹ that hardship in this context is not restricted to hardship in the possession or use of the holding or to hardship to the landlord as a particular individual. It is at large and, on the analogy of the Rent Act rule as stated by Asquith L.J. in *Harte v. Frampton*,³⁰ the question is whether there would be greater hardship to anyone "on the landlord's side" as compared with the tenant's, weight being given to the closeness or remoteness of the relationship. Thus hardship to relatives interested in the deceased landlord's estate, who would be in difficulties if the farm could not be sold with vacant possession, would be relevant.³¹ But a strong case must be made by a landlord relying on *Purser v. Bailey* to persuade the Tribunal to deprive the tenant of his livelihood. Obvious cases of possible relevant hardship are, on the landlord's side,

---

[25] s. 27(3)(d). Section 3(3)(c) of the 1977 Act said "smallholdings or allotments".

[26] s. 27(3)(d). The enactments are known collectively as the Allotments Acts 1908 to 1950. An allotment (not being an "allotment garden") which is let to a tenant and is used for the purposes of trade or business may be an agricultural holding: *Stevens v. Sedgeman* [1951] 2 K.B. 434. Distinguish an "allotment garden", which is cultivated by the occupier for the purpose of consumption by himself and his family: Allotments Act 1922, s. 22(1).

[27] s. 27(3)(e).

[28] Rent Act 1977, s. 98 and Sched. 15, Case G and para. 1 in Part III of Sched.; and see *Piper v. Harvey* [1958] 1 Q.B. 439.

[29] [1967] 2 Q.B. 500.

[30] [1948] 1 K.B. 73 at 79.

[31] See *Purser v. Bailey*, above, where the circumstances of the widow and son were regarded: *cf. Addington v. Sims* [1952] E.G.D. 1, (ALT).

the prevention of a son from taking up farming, and on the tenant's side the disturbance of an aged relative living in the farmhouse, but comparative weight of hardship and proximity of relationship or connection are material. The loss to the tenant of all the effort and expenditure in building up a diary herd is a clear example of hardship.[32] The fact that the tenant has another farm and so is not wholly dependent on the holding under notice will in some cases be a relevant factor. Hardship frequently raises financial issues, but is not confined to them. The frustration of a landlord's son prevented from starting on his own account may rank as hardship, although the mere interruption of a family tradition is not itself hardship.[33] Hardship to a sub-tenant in principle would fall within the wording of the section; however it is not unknown for a Tribunal to decline to include such a matter in its consideration.[34] Evidence that a tenant has previously negotiated to surrender his tenancy may count against him on the issue of hardship.[35] It appears from a line of Scottish Land Court decisions that the tenant's security of tenure should not in itself be regarded as a hardship to the landlord; this is surely correct in principle.[36] The tenant's quality as a farmer, the level of husbandry attained judged by the condition of the land, may in some circumstances be relevant under the head of greater hardship.[37] A landlord is not estopped from raising the issue of greater hardship within a year of a previous unsuccessful attempt to do so. The principle of *res judicata* does not apply to the agricultural situation, which is not static. Further, the landlord is not confined to adducing evidence showing a material change in circumstances; once the issue of greater hardship is raised, the matter is entirely at large.[38] It is an error of law for a Tribunal, in considering relative hardship, to take into account the history of previous proceedings in which one of the parties has suffered frustration and disappointment. The Tribunal are concerned only with the issue of relative hardship in relation to the present notice to quit.[39]

A Tribunal should keep the issue of greater hardship distinct from the application of the "fair and reasonable landlord" provision, although the facts may be relevant to both.[40] A Tribunal could take account of hardship in applying that provision; but it is possible for a landlord to succeed in establishing greater

---

[32] *Kinson Brothers v. Swinnerton* (1961) 179 EG 691, (ALT)
[33] See the Scottish decision in *Crawford v. McKinlay* [1954] S.L.C.R. 39.
[34] *Blizzard v. Kennett*, an unreported case before the S.E. Tribunal, ref. S.E. 87/1960; *sed quaere*.
[35] *R. v. ALT for the S.E. Area, ex p. Bracey* [1960] 1 W.L.R. 911 (a hard case for the tenant as the negotiations were "without prejudice", but this did not appear on the face of the record).
[36] See "The Law of Agricultural Holdings in Scotland" by Gill (3rd ed.) para. 18.21; although the Court of Session in *Graham v. Lamont* [1971] S.C. 170 went rather near it.
[37] *R. v. ALT for the S.E. Area, ex p. Parslow* (1979) 251 E.G. 667.
[38] *Wickington v. Bonney* (1983) 266 E.G. 434.
[39] *Cooke v. Talbot* (1977) 243 E.G. 831. Lord Widgery C.J. said at 835 that the Tribunal must prepare a "balance sheet of hardship".
[40] The issues are not always kept distinct: see *Chetwynd (Viscountess) v. Edwards* (1967) 204 E.G. 822.

hardship and nevertheless to be refused consent because in the circumstances a fair and reasonable landlord would not insist on possession.[41]

Non-agricultural use not within Case B: section 27(3)(f)

12.40

"[T]hat the landlord proposes to terminate the tenancy for the purpose of the land's being used for a use, other than for agriculture, not falling within Case B.[42]"

This provision is somewhat unspecific being designed to catch all non-agricultural uses which do not fall within the current Case B.[43] The main use to which this head is put is in order to secure land for private forestry or for landscaping where such is a pre-condition, of but not part of, a planning permission being granted.[44] If a notice to quit is given by virtue of this paragraph no statement in the notice will exclude the tenant's security of tenure or compensation for disturbance, whether "basic" or "additional".[45]

The condition specified in this paragraph is not to be treated as satisfied if the use proposed is used for the "permitted activities" in relation to opencast coal production.[46]

"Fair and reasonable landlord" provision: section 27(2)

12.41

Even if they are satisfied as mentioned in subsection (1) above, the Tribunal shall withhold consent under section 26 above to the operation of the notice to quit if in all the circumstances it appears to them that a fair and reasonable landlord would not "insist on possession".[47] Although this direction proposes an objective standard, "a fair and reasonable landlord", there is necessarily a subjective element in its application or administration, as it has to "appear to them", *i.e.* to the Tribunal, that such a landlord would not insist on possession. Does this make the

---

[41] *Jones v. Burgoyne* [1963] E.G.D. 435.

[42] s. 27(3)(f). This use is defined by contrast with Case B, as to which see para. 12.50 below.

[43] For changes in the drafting of Case B see paragraph 12.50 below. In the case of *Stevenage Development Corporation v. Ivory* [(1960), unfortunately unreported; information given by development corporation] the Tribunal for the Eastern Area held that an application by the development corporation for consent to a notice to quit land proposed to be developed as part of the new town of Stevenage was properly made under section 25(1)(e) of the 1948 Act (corresponding to the present section 27(3)(f)) and that the circumstances were not such as to support a notice to quit under section 24(2)(b) (Case B in Schedule 3 to the present Act). Planning permission derived from a special development order is not permission granted on an "application" within the meaning of Case B. In the *Ivory* case, however, the Tribunal withheld consent by applying the "fair and reasonable landlord" provision.

[44] Many development schemes require the development in question to be hidden and for the "screening" to be in place some considerable time before the main application for outline planning permission which is the purpose of the screening, is granted.

[45] For these, see s. 60, and paras 13.22–13.31 below.

[46] Opencast Coal Act 1958, s. 14(6), as substituted by Housing and Planning Act 1986, Sched. 8, para. 5 (new s. 14(5)).

[47] s. 27(2). Although this direction (it is not merely a power) is now in a substantive subsection and not in a proviso, as in the 1948 Act (s. 25(1), proviso), the effect does not seem to be altered.

Tribunal's determinations under the direction wholly unreviewable by the courts? In view of the tendency of modern administrative law, the answer is probably not. If it could be shown that a Tribunal have misdirected themselves by applying the wrong legal test, or if there were no grounds on which any reasonable Tribunal could have reached the conclusion reached by the Tribunal, their conclusion could be attacked by judicial review.[48]

In applying the direction the Tribunal are required to look at all relevant circumstances.[49] They may invoke it to refuse to disturb a good, sound farmer even where a case can be made for the achievement of greater efficiency under paragraph (a) or (b) of section 27(3).[50] The Tribunal may take account of hardship to the tenant although the landlord has not himself made hardship an issue under section 27(3)(e).[51] Even if the landlord has raised the issue of hardship and can show that the balance is in his favour, the Tribunal may properly hold that a fair and reasonable landlord would not insist on possession, as the productivity of the holding, brought by the tenant to a high level, might suffer in the landlord's less experienced hands.[52] A fair and reasonable landlord would not insist on ending a successful agricultural enterprise in order to establish an experimental undertaking the commercial success of which was problematical.[53] Even where the tenant's holding is not viable by itself, and the landlord can make out a case for dispossession in favour of an amalgamation, the Tribunal may prefer an arrangement which allows the tenant to continue to farm the holding as a viable unit with other land. It can be a mistake for a Tribunal to invite the parties themselves to discuss the application of the fair and reasonable landlord provision.[54] However where the landlord maintains an open commitment to provide either land or money in the event of securing possession this may be an important factor for the Tribunal in assessing the impact of the notice to quit: it is not necessary for the tenant actually to accept the offer but the landlord must undertake to make it available despite the fact that the tenant may currently not be interested in accepting it. This, for example, would allow the landlord to make residential accommodation available for an elderly tenant or to provide a lump sum to buy an annuity. Should one of the parties successfully challenge the implementation by the Tribunal of the "fair and reasonable landlord" provision, it would seem likely that in many cases remission to the Tribunal for reconsideration

---

[48] For the principles, see, *e.g.*, **Ashbridge Investments Ltd v. Minister of Housing and Local Government** (1965) 1 W.L.R. 1320 and, generally, **Anisminic Ltd v. Foreign Compensation Commission** [1969] 2 A.C. 147.

[49] **Cooke v. Talbot** (1977) 243 E.G. 831 at 835, *per* Lord Widgery C.J.

[50] **Evans v. Roper** [1960] 1 W.L.R. 814.

[51] **Evans v. Roper** [1960] 1 W.L.R. 814.

[52] **Jones v. Burgoyne** [1963] E.G.D. 435; (1963) 188 E.G. 497.

[53] For example in the Scottish decision **Carnegie v. Davidson** [1966] S.L.C.R. App. 147.

[54] **Collins v. Spurway** (1967) 204 E.G. 801. The landlord had satisfied the Tribunal about his proposal to use the land for forestry, but the Tribunal were concerned about the possible application of the provision and adjourned the hearing to allow the parties to discuss the position, including the compensation payable to the tenant and a "sweetener" which had been mentioned. The parties could not agree, the Tribunal gave consent to the notice to quit, and the matter ended up in the Divisional Court on an application by the tenant for a mandamus, which was refused.

is the correct course.[55] The conception of the fair and reasonable landlord appears again, in a different context, in section 28(5).[56] Finally, it may be noted that the model landlord envisaged by section 27(2) must be both fair and reasonable, even to the extent of not automatically insisting on possession although bearing the greater weight of hardship. This seems to envisage a standard in some cases not far short of magnanimity.

Conditions on consent to notices to quit: section 27(4) and (5) 12.42

The Tribunal are empowered, when giving consent to a notice to quit, to impose such conditions as appear to them requisite for securing that the land to which the notice relates will be used for the purpose for which the landlord proposes to terminate the tenancy.[57] The Tribunal are also enabled, on the landlord's application, to vary or revoke any such condition, if they are satisfied, by reason of a change of circumstances or otherwise, that this should be done.[58] The condition must relate to the land which is the subject of the notice to quit and to the purpose for which the landlord proposes to terminate the tenancy.[59] The Tribunal may, for example, require the holding to be let to an approved tenant or the landlord to reside in the farmhouse and farm the holding himself, but they have no jurisdiction to require the landlord to grant a lease of other land to the outgoing tenant.[60]

The only sanction for disobedience to a condition is for the Crown to apply to the Tribunal to impose a penalty on the landlord not exceeding two years' rent at the rate payable immediately before the termination of the tenancy (or a proportion of such rent is the notice related to part of the holding).[61] The penalty is paid to the Exchequer,[62] not to the tenant, and the landlord's default does not affect the operation of the notice to quit or justify the tenant in refusing to give up possession.[63] No form is now prescribed for the application for a penalty. The

---

[55] *e.g.* ***Cooke v. Talbot*** (1977) 243 E.G. 831 where the Tribunal had decided that there was an overwhelming case for giving consent to the notice to quit on the ground of greater hardship to the landlords and that a fair and reasonable landlord would insist on possession. Unfortunately the Tribunal erred in law in allowing their judgment to be influenced in deciding the issue of hardship by their knowledge of disappointments suffered by the landlords in previous, quite distinct, proceedings between the same parties. While the court found no fault with the Tribunal's treatment of the fair and reasonable landlord provision, they were obliged to send the case back for reconsideration as a result of the Tribunal's error in their treatment of hardship.

[56] See para. 12.74 below and ***Clegg v. Fraser*** (1982) 264 E.G. 144.

[57] s. 27(4). On a literal interpretation, this would not enable the Tribunal to impose a condition in a case under paragraph (e) (greater hardship) since no "purpose" is mentioned in that paragraph: It is thought, however, that this is too narrow. The landlord applying under paragraph (e) must disclose his "intention" on his application, *e.g.* "to farm it myself" or "to let it to another tenant." Is this not sufficient indication of a "purpose"?

[58] s. 27(5). For prescribed form of application, see Form 41 in Part V of this work. For an unsuccessful attempt to vary, see ***Jones v. West Midlands ALT*** (1962) 184 E.G. 78.

[59] See *per* Ashworth J. in ***National Coal Board v. Naylor*** [1972] 1 W.L.R. 908 at 913.

[60] *cf.* ***R.v. ALT (S.E. Area), ex p. Boucher*** (1952) 159 E.G. 191 (decision quashed on *certiorari*).

[61] s. 27(6).

[62] s. 27(8).

[63] *cf.* ***Martin-Smith v. Smale*** [1954] 1 W.L.R. 247.

Tribunal may order any party to pay what the Tribunal consider a reasonable contribution to the costs of the proceedings.[64] The Tribunal's order imposing the penalty is enforceable in the same manner as a county court order.[65]

The conditions provided for by section 27(4) relate to a need to ensure that the land will be used for the purpose for which the landlord proposes to terminate the tenancy. There may be land or money provided for the benefit of the tenant on a voluntary basis as discussed in the previous paragraph. Section 27(4) is not appropriately drafted to cover that type of offer by the landlord nor does the Tribunal have a power to make a conditional order granting the landlord consent to the operation of the notice to quit. What if the landlord secures consent on the basis that for example money or accommodation will be available to the tenant but once an order has been made refuses to make any such provision?[66] If the tenant has not vacated the property it seems reasonably clear that when sued for possession he could rely on the fact as a defence[67] that the Tribunal's consent was obtained by fraud. The position if the tenant has actually vacated is less clear since innocent third parties may have become involved. But it is possible that the courts might order the reinstatement of the original tenancy as a form of setting aside the effect of the Tribunal's consent.[68]

12.43 Postponement of termination of tenancy: 1987 Order, Article 13

Where a Tribunal has consented to a notice to quit they have power to postpone the termination of the tenancy if it would otherwise take effect on or within six months after the giving of the consent.[69] The exercise of this power will avoid hardship where the interval is too short to allow for the necessary changes to be made. The Tribunal may direct the postponement either of their own motion or on the tenant's application. Such application has to be made not later than 14 days after the giving of the consent. The tenant must give written notice of his application to the landlord at the same time as he applies to the Tribunal (except, of course, where the application is made at the hearing). The landlord is entitled to be heard on the application.

---

[64] s. 27(7).
[65] s. 27(9).
[66] In practice this problem is largely to be regarded as theoretical since the Tribunal is likely to give a clear indication during the course of the hearing as to how they are evaluating matters and the well advised tenant, if about to lose, will no doubt secure a contractual commitment from the landlord and then agree to the order being made.
[67] See *Lazarus Estates Limited v. Beasley* [1956] 1 Q.B. 702, Denning L.J. at 712 and Parker L.J. at 721.
[68] See by comparison in relation to undue influence: *Goldsworthy v. Brickell* (1987) Ch. 378 where an agricultural tenancy agreement was set aside. Any setting aside is likely to be limited to a transaction directly procured by fraud as distinct from a transaction related to and dependent upon the original transaction: see *Sanctuary Housing Association v. Baker* (1998) 9 E.G. 150 where a fraudulently procured consent to an assignment was set aside but the assignment made in consequence was not (even though the assignee knew of the fraud), CA.
[69] Sched. 4, para. 5 (for the order-making power) and the Arbitration on Notices Order 1987 (S.I 1987 No.710), art. 13, for the Tribunal's power to postpone the termination of the tenancy for a period not exceeding 12 months.

Cases where consent of Tribunal to operation of the notice to quit is not required 12.44

As already mentioned,[70] there are a number of circumstances where security of tenure, in the form of the tenant's right to serve a counter-notice in reply to a notice to quit (thereby making the operation of the notice to quit dependent on the consent of the Agricultural Land Tribunal), is excluded. Eight specific Cases where the Tribunal's consent is not required[71] are set out in Schedule 3 to the 1986 Act, Cases A to H. The fact that in these Cases the right to serve a counter-notice is excluded does not, of course, mean that tenants in the circumstances described have no defence to, or means of contesting, a notice to quit. Before dealing with the eight specific Cases[72] certain general principles must be noted.

Notices to quit may take effect although founded on a defective notice to pay rent or to remedy breaches 12.45

It is not too early in the study of security of tenure to warn of a trap into which tenants could fall. A tenant or his advisers may see that a notice to pay rent or a notice to remedy is defective and is thus not a valid foundation for a notice to quit based on non-compliance. Unfortunately, if the tenant fails to challenge the reason stated in the notice to quit by initiating arbitration proceedings within a month of receiving the notice to quit he will be precluded from contesting the reason. For this purpose the arbitration procedure is mandatory and the time-limit of one month is inflexible.[73] The Court simply has no jurisdiction to grant relief to the tenant.

Jurisdiction of the Courts: common law invalidity of notice to quit 12.46

It is correct to state in general terms that where there is a defect in the notice to quit such that it would not be enforceable at common law then the Courts retain

---

[70] See para. 12.2 above.

[71] It is not true without qualification that consent is not required in all theses Cases. There is a right to serve a counter-notice where under Case D a notice to quit states that it is given by reason of the tenant's failure to comply with a notice to do work; the tenant here has a twofold remedy, to demand arbitration and to serve a counter-notice; see below paras 12.64 and 12.72. There are also special rules for members of the reserve and auxiliary forces: see below paras 12.92–12.94 and following. Provided that these qualifications are borne in mind, it is convenient to refer to the Cases as relating to circumstances where security of tenure is excluded. Apart from the eight Cases security of tenure is excluded in certain circumstances where a notice to quit is given to a sub-tenant.

[72] The correspondence between the lettering of the Cases in the 1977 and 1986 Acts is as follows:

    1977 A B C D E F G H I
    1986 - B C D E F G H A

(The 1977 Case A was abolished by the 1984 Act, s. 10(2) and Sched. 4, and there is now no Case corresponding to it. Case I was added to the 1977 Act by s. 6 of the 1984 Act and is now Case A in the 1986 Act.)

[73] See art. 9 of the Arbitration on Notices Order 1987 (S.I. 1987 No.710) and *Magdalen College, Oxford v. Heritage* [1974] 1 W.L.R. 411, where the notice to quit took effect despite the landlord's previous statutory notice being void. See also *Harding v. Marshall* (1983) 267 E.G. 161, CA; *Parrish v. Kinsey* (1983) 268 E.G. 1113, CA; *Crown Estate Commissioners v. Allingham* (1973) 226 E.G. 2153; *Ladds Radio and Television Limited v. Docker* (1973) 226 E.G. 1565; *A-G (Duchy of Lancaster v. Simcock* (1966)

jurisdiction. This is true in relation to notices to quit over which the Agricultural Land Tribunal has jurisdiction and also in relation to those notices which fall within the special Cases.[74] The type of point which could be taken by the Court would be, for example, those arising on a construction of the notice if the tenant wished to allege that the notice had not been served, was addressed to the wrong person or was in respect of the wrong land or the wrong expiry date. This type of challenge is, in respect of certain Cases, the only challenge available.[75] In respect of the Cases where arbitration is available under Article 9 of the Agricultural Holdings (Arbitration on Notices) Order 1987 (S.I.1987 No.710)[76] the common law ground of challenge is not one within the mandatory scope of the reference to arbitration. Arbitration is available where the tenant wishes to contest a reason stated on the notice to quit.[77] Thus, if the tenant fails in arbitration to rebut the reasons stated on the face of such a notice[78] or if the tenant fails to call for arbitration at all then he may defend himself in the courts when enforcement is taken of the notice to quit or alternatively he may commence declaratory proceedings attacking the validity of the notice to quit.[79]

12.47 **Jurisdiction of the Courts: fraud**
The Courts retain jurisdiction to deal with allegations of fraud and this jurisdiction is not excluded even where Article 9 of the Agricultural Holdings (Arbitration on Notices to Quit) Order[80] applies.[81] This jurisdiction would appear not only to survive a failure to challenge the reasons stated on the face of a notice to quit where one of the Cases in Schedule 3 applies and arbitration is available[82] but also to provide a concurrent jurisdiction where allegations of fraud can and perhaps should be made. The availability of this jurisdiction was highlighted in ***Rous v. Mitchell***[83] where the first instance judgment of Aldous J.[84] was upheld. The basis of the judgment was a passage in ***Derry v. Peek***[85] in the context of common law fraud involving dishonesty.[86] The landlord's case for possession based on an

---

Ch. 1.
[74] Although in ***Cawley v. Pratt*** [1988] 2 E.G.L.R. 6 the Court felt it unnecessary to decide the point, the case being disposed of on another ground.
[75] *e.g.* under Case G.
[76] Cases A, B, D and E.
[77] *i.e.* the underlying ground upon which the landlord uses to rely on the procedure.
[78] *i.e.* fails in the arbitration.
[79] ***Magdalen College, Oxford v. Heritage*** [1974] 1 W.L.R. 411 and the cases following it referred to in the last paragraph are distinguishable.
[80] S.I. 1987 No.710.
[81] ***Magdalen College, Oxford v. Heritage*** [1974] 1 W.L.R. 441, Megaw L.J. at 446 and ***Rous v. Mitchell*** [1991] 1 All E.R. 676 (CA).
[82] *e.g.* ***Rous v. Mitchell*** (above).
[83] (1991) 1 W.L.R. 469, also reported as ***Stradbroke v. Mitchell*** [1991] 1 E.G.L.R. 1.
[84] [1989] 2 E.G.L.R. 5.
[85] [1889] 14 A. C. 337.
[86] Lord Herschell at 374: "Secondly, fraud is proved when it is shown that a false representation has been made (1) knowingly, or (2) without belief in its truth, or (3) recklessly, careless whether it be true or false. Although I have treated the second and third as distinct cases, I think the third is but an instance of the second, for one who makes

allegedly fraudulent statement in the notice to quit claiming that the tenant was in breach of his tenancy was refused on the basis that the statement was made recklessly, without an honest belief in its truth and therefore fraudulently.[87] If common law fraud is to be alleged it must be in the clearest possible terms and the use of equivocal language will not suffice.[88] Finally, a litigant who alleges fraud and fails will probably have to pay indemnity costs.[89]

Exclusion of security of tenure: Cases in Schedule 3   12.48

The tenant's right to serve a counter-notice under section 26(1) of the 1986 Act, in response to the landlord's notice to quit, and thus to require the Tribunal's consent to its effectiveness, is excluded in the following eight Cases set out in Schedule 3. It is an essential requisite of each of the Cases that the relevant fact or reason mentioned in the Case is stated in the notice to quit. Failure to do so will prevent the notice from having effect for the purposes of the Case and may, as a result of other rules[90] prevent it from taking effect altogether. It is certainly advisable, and in practice should be treated as essential, that the required statement is contained literally in the notice to quit. A statement in an accompanying letter may not be regarded in England and Wales with the same benevolence as in Scotland.[91] The statement should be unequivocal, should identify the relevant Case and follow its wording.[92]

---

the statement under such circumstances can have no real belief in the truth of what he states. To prevent false statements being fraudulent, there must, I think, always be an honest belief in its truth. And this probably covers the whole ground, for one who knowingly alleges that which is false, has obviously no such honest belief."

[87] In certain respects ***Rous v. Mitchell*** itself is an unfortunate case and there appears to have been no consideration given to the difference between actual fraud involving dishonesty that is to say an intention to deceive and equitable fraud for which dishonesty is not a necessary factor but which might include cases of gross and culpable negligence (***Nocton v. Lord Ashburton*** [1914] A.C. 932, HL, as explained in ***Armitage v. Nurse*** [1997] 2 All E.R. 705, Millett L.J. at 710). As to what may be fraudulent and dishonest behaviour see ***Agip (Africa) Ltd v. Jackson*** (1992) 4 All E.R. 385, Millett J.; the contrast between conscious impropriety and carelessness is highlighted in ***Royal Brunei Airlines v. Tan*** (1995) 3 W.L.R. 64, PC.

[88] See ***Belmont Finance Corp Limited v. Williams Furniture Limited*** [1979] 1 All E.R. 118, Buckley L.J. at 130–131.

[89] This was the order made by Ferris J. in ***Luttenberger v. North Thoresby Farms Limited*** [1993] 1 E.G.L.R. 3 at 11d where the solicitor who drafted the relevant notice was found to have had a reasonable ground to believe that a statement concerning non-payment of rent which was contained in the notice to quit was a true statement at the time when that notice was served.

[90] e.g. ***Cowan v. Wrayford***; ***Mills v. Edwards*** (see para. 12.28 above).

[91] ***Turton v. Turnbull*** [1934] 2 K.B. 197 is a decision which could be quoted in favour of the letter being treated benevolently, but it would be better not to rely on it (unless *ex post facto* one has to!). The Scottish cases of ***Graham v. Lamont*** 1971 S.C. 170 and ***Copeland v. McQuaker*** 1973 S.L.T. 186, both cases on "reorganisation payments" under the 1968 Act (*cf.* now 1986 Act, s. 61(3)) went further in liberal construction than English courts may be prepared to go. And see generally commentary in relation to notices in para. 12.32 above.

[92] For precedents see Part V of this work Forms 30, 31 and 32.

12.49 Case A: Smallholdings[93]

"[T]he holding is let as a smallholding by a smallholdings authority or the Minister in pursuance of Part III of the Agriculture Act 1970 and was so let on or after 12th September 1984, and

(a) the tenant has attained the age of sixty-five, and

(b) if the result of the notice to quit taking effect would be to deprive the tenant of living accommodation occupied by him under the tenancy, suitable alternative accommodation is available for him, or will be available for him when the notice takes effect, and

(c) the instrument under which the tenancy was granted contains an acknowledgement signed by the tenant that the tenancy is subject to the provisions of this Case (or to those of Case I in section 2(3) of the Agricultural Holdings (Notices to Quit) Act 1977), and it is stated in the notice to quit that it is given by reason of the said matter."

Procedural Table 2: Notices to quit: Case A. Absolute time-limits apply.[94] Supplemental provisions are contained in Schedule 3 paragraphs 1–7.

This Case was added by the 1984 Act.[95] It enables a smallholdings authority or the Minister to give a notice to quit excluding section 26(1) of the 1986 Act to tenants who have attained the age of 65, subject to safeguards as to the availability of suitable alternative accommodation. It applies to lettings on or after September 12, 1984, and the instrument of letting must contain an acknowledgment signed by the tenant that the tenancy is subject to the provisions of this Case.[96] It will be noted that the right to serve such a notice to quit is vested only in the smallholdings authority or the Minister. If the land is sold (unless to another smallholdings authority) the new owner cannot serve such a notice and so oblige the tenant to retire. The attitude of Parliament appears to be that smallholdings still have a modest value, although the extent to which they have provided a ladder for progress to larger holdings has been disappointing; that there should be no power to veto sales of smallholdings and that authorities should remain free to sell parts of their estates; that, to provide for movement and the release of holdings to younger people, retirement at age 65 should be facilitated; but that the compulsory loss of the holding should not also involve loss of living accommodation. The succession provisions (Part IV of the 1986 Act) do not apply to smallholdings.[97] The

---

[93] Sched. 3, Part I.
[94] Part V of this work contains precedents: Form 30 for the notice to quit and Form 33 for the tenant's demand for arbitration.
[95] 1984 Act, s. 6(6), then called "Case I". Case A is, therefore, a provision for the compulsory retirement of smallholders, as recommended by the Northfield Committee: Report of the Committee of Inquiry into the Acquisition and Occupancy of Agricultural Land, Cmnd. 7599, July 1979, paras 559 to 563.
[96] 1986 Act, Sched. 3, Part I, Case A.
[97] The decision to the contrary in *Saul v. Norfolk County Council* [1984] Q.B. 559, CA, was annulled by the 1984 Act (Sched. 1, para. 2(6), amending s. 18(4)(f) of the 1976

CASE A: SMALLHOLDINGS

provisions in paragraphs 1 to 7 of Part II of Schedule 3 to the 1986 Act constitute a code of rules about suitable alternative accommodation for smallholders modelled closely on Part IV of Schedule 15 to the Rent Act 1977. Cases decided on that Part IV will often be relevant in determining questions arising on the Case A provisions.

Arbitration is provided in relation to reasons stated in notices to quit under Case A.[98] Basic compensation for disturbance, but not additional compensation, is payable in respect of notices to quit under Case A.[99]

Case B: Non-agricultural use[1]

12.50

"[T]he notice to quit is given on the ground that the land is required for a use, other than for agriculture—

(a) for which permission[2] has been granted on an application made under the enactments relating to town and country planning,[3]

(b) for which permission under those enactments is granted by a general development order[4] by reason only of the fact that the use is authorised by—

   (i) a private or local Act,

   (ii) an order approved by both Houses of Parliament, or

   (iii) an order made under section 14 or 16 of the Harbours Act 1964,

(c) for which any provision that —

   (i) is contained in an Act, but

   (ii) does not form part of the enactments relating to town and country planning,
   deems permission under those enactments to have been granted,

(d) which any such provision deems not to constitute development for the purposes of those enactments, or

---

Act). See s. 38(4) of present Act.

[98] See art. 9 of the Agricultural Holdings (Arbitration on Notices) Order 1987 (S.I. 1987 No.710).

[99] s. 61(2).

[1] Sched. 3, Part I.

[2] No account is to be taken of any permission relating to the working of coal by opencast operations granted subject to a restoration condition and to an aftercare condition in which the use specified is use for agriculture or forestry (see Sched. 3, para. 8).

[3] "The enactments relating to town and country planning" means the planning Acts (as defined in section 336(1) of the Town and Country Planning Act 1990) and any enactment amending or replacing any of those Acts (Sched. 3, para. 8A). In relation to any time before the commencement of the 1990 Act previous statutes are identified by Sched. 3, para. 8A(2).

[4] An order under section 59 of the Town and Country Planning Act 1990 which is made as a general order (see Sched. 3, para. 8A).

(e) for which permission is not required under the enactments relating to town and country planning by reason only of Crown immunity, and that fact is stated in the notice."

Procedural Table 2: Notice to quit: Case B. Absolute time limits apply. Supplemental provisions are contained in Schedule 3, paragraphs 8–8A.

The current provisions of Case B were inserted into the 1986 Act by the Agricultural Holdings (Amendment) Act 1990.[5] The current Case applies to any notice to quit served on or after July 29, 1990.[6] To a large extent case law decided under the previous wording[7] is helpful in dealing with Case B in the new form. Essentially Case B authorises land to be taken back for a non-agricultural use where planning permission has been granted or is not necessary because of one of the reasons stated in sub-paragraphs (b)–(e) and the ground of the notice is stated on the face of it. There is no prescribed form of notice to quit.[8] A tenant receiving notice to quit may call for arbitration in which circumstance the arbitrator will verify that the landlord has demonstrated the ground stated on the notice.[9] No statement as to the landlord's grounds will exclude either the basic or the additional compensation for disturbance.[10] It is not necessary for the landlord to demonstrate that he reasonably requires the land, only that he actually requires it and has a bona fide intention to carry out development and a reasonable prospect that it will be carried out.[11] The requirement is not necessarily only that of the landlord but may

---

[5] The new wording has the effect of reversing the decision in *Bell v. McCubbin* [1990] 1 Q.B. 976, [1989] 2 E.G.L.R. 3, CA, where the landlord successfully took back a dwelling house on the holding within the terms of Case B because there was an established residential use in respect of it.

[6] For notices served prior to that time the original wording of the 1986 Act, Case B applies.

[7] The old Case B read:

"the notice to quit is given on the ground that the land is required for a use, other than for agriculture–

(a) for which permission has been granted on an application made under the enactments relating to town and country planning, or

(b) for which, other than by virtue of any provision of those enactments, such permission is not required,

and that fact is stated in the notice."

[8] See below precedent Forms 30/35 in Part V of this work and also Form 33 for the tenant's demand for arbitration.

[9] See art. 9 of the Agricultural Holdings (Arbitration on Notices) Order 1987 (S.I. 1987 No.710), Part II below.

[10] Contrast Cases C, D, E, F and G where the relevant ground being stated will exclude basic and additional compensation: see s. 61(1); and para. 13.18 below.

[11] *Paddock Investments Ltd v. Lory* [1975] 236 E.G. 803, approving *Jones v. Gates* [1954] 1 W.L.R. 222 on this point. Compare in relation to section 30(1)(f) of the Landlord and Tenant Act 1954 the intention which a landlord must demonstrate: *DAF Motoring Centre (Gosport) v. Hatfield & Wheeler* [1982] 2 E.G.L.R. 59, CA; *London Hilton Jewellers v. Hilton International Hotels* [1990] 1 E.G.L.R. 112, CA. A reasonable prospect means one which is strong enough that a reasonable landlord would act upon it:

be the requirement of any person who is entitled to take advantage of the planning permission or, as the case may be, the opportunity to use the land for a non-agricultural purpose.[12] In so far as the Case refers to "permission", it has been held that an outline permission will suffice.[13] Care should be taken to ensure that the correct sub-paragraph within Case B is selected if the notice to quit makes reference to it.[14] In relation to sub-paragraph (e) (Crown immunity), the Crown is entitled to change the use of land from agriculture to afforestation because the Crown is not bound by statute except by express words or necessary implication.[15] A use may be non-agricultural for the purposes of Case B although that use is related to an ultimate purpose which is itself agricultural.[16] In order to be successful in gaining possession pursuant to Case B it is submitted that the landlord must be able to demonstrate a relevant requirement for all of the land within the notice to quit, *i.e.* he should avoid inclusion within the notice to quit of areas of land which are not the subject of the non-agricultural use.[17] In *John v. George*[18] the Court of Appeal held that landlords were estopped from serving a notice to quit under Case B as a result of assumptions made and negotiations entered into prior to the grant of the relevant planning permission.

Practical problems:

Stage development It is quite common for a landlord to want to take back part only of the land within the tenancy in circumstances where he has planning permission for a large development which itself will be completed in stages, there being a substantial gap in time between the projected stages. Clearly the landlord will have to be satisfied that he has the power either by contract, statute or severance of the reversion[19] to serve an effective notice to quit part and it should be noted that for this purpose it may be necessary for the notice to quit to carry additional information related to the power to give it at all.[20] Where the work is to be done in stages, subject to checking that areas required for access are included, it

12.50.1

See under the 1954 Act *Cadogan v. McCarthy & Stone Developments* (1996) E.G.C.S. 94, N.P.C. 77.
[12] See in relation to planning permission *Rugby Joint Water Board v. Foottit* [1973] A.C. 202.
[13] See *Dow Agrochemicals v. EA Lane (North Lynn) Ltd* (1965) 115 L.J. 76, (1965) 192 E.G. 737, CC; *Paddock Investments Ltd v. Lory* (above).
[14] Under the original wording of Case B it was held that where permission is required to have been granted on an application made under the enactments relating to town and country planning a general permission under a General Development Order would not suffice: *Minister of Agriculture v. Jenkins* [1963] 2 Q.B. 317 at 324.
[15] *Minister of Agriculture v. Jenkins* (above); *Secretary of State for Wales v. Pugh* (1970) 120 L.J. 357, CC, (planting of trees grown for timber, not for a use ancillary to farming).
[16] For example the manufacture of agricultural chemicals or agricultural implements, or other products ancillary to agriculture: see *Dow Agrochemicals v. EA Lane (North Lynn) Ltd* (above).
[17] The argument was made at some length in *Cawley v. Pratt* [1988] 2 E.G.L.R. 6, CA but it was not necessary in order to dispose of the case to deal with it.
[18] [1996] 1 E.G.L.R. 7.
[19] See para. 12.18–12.22 above.
[20] For example a reference to a contractual clause.

may be preferable to take only the first stage required so that the tenant is not able to mount any challenge on the ground that the land "is" not required, although it may be required at a date in the future. The language of Case B suggests that the land must be required at the date of the giving of the notice to quit and it is suggested that the requirement must be for use on the expiry of the notice to quit or a relatively short time thereafter.

12.50.2 **Landscaping: grazing** Landscaping, depending on what it consists of, will not normally be an agricultural use; however care should be taken to ensure that the mistake is not made of thinking of unprofitable agricultural use as though it were a non-agricultural use altogether. Thus if parkland will be grazed by a flock of sheep which is kept for that purpose or open land will be let off to a grazier whilst building takes place on the remainder of the land, the grazing areas will in truth be used for an agricultural purpose and are likely to be fatal to a Case B notice to quit if included within it.

12.50.3 **Landscaping: trees** The relationship between Case B and section 27(2)(f) should not be forgotten. It may occasionally be necessary first to take land for private forestry by application to the Tribunal in order to comply with requirements imposed by a planning authority which would not otherwise authorise yet further land to be the subject of permission. Although it is usually quite difficult to persuade a Tribunal that a fair and reasonable landlord would insist on possession, the likelihood is that the application to the Tribunal is enormously strengthened if it is intended to precede or supplement a development which would undoubtedly fall within Case B being a development which landlord intended to start imminently or had already started. Ideally some thought to timetabling the taking back of possession should be given at the point before which applications are made for planning permission so that any screening or landscaping requirements of the local authority can be considered.

12.50.4 **Timetable for possession** Despite the availability of Case B, it should not be thought that possession will necessarily be available in a very short time. Although the arbitrator is required to issue his award within 56 days of his appointment,[21] the President of the RICS may enlarge that time period whether it has expired or not.[22] If the case involves a point of law a case stated to the County Court may involve considerable delay.[23] Even if the landlord is successful under Case B possession will still have to be obtained by court proceedings if the tenant refuses to go. Cumulatively it can be seen that the tenant has some opportunity for creating delay within the legitimate workings of the procedures available to him but this can prove expensive to a landlord who, if contemplating work, may be paying

---

[21] Sched. 11 para. 14(1).
[22] Para. 14(2).
[23] See Sched. 11, para. 26.

contractors to sit idle or paying interest on a bank loan with no income in sight generated by the development.

Case C: Certificate of bad husbandry 12.51

"[N]ot more than six months before the giving of the notice to quit, the Tribunal granted a certificate under paragraph 9 of Part II of this Schedule that the tenant of the holding was not fulfilling his responsibilities to farm in accordance with the rules of good husbandry, and that fact is stated in the notice."

Procedural Table 3: Notice to quit: Case C.

Supplemental provisions are contained in Schedule 3, paragraph 9.

Case C applies where, not more than six months before the giving of the notice to quit, the Tribunal has granted[24] the landlord a certificate that the tenant was not fulfilling his responsibilities to farm in accordance with the rules of good husbandry[25]; and that fact is stated in the notice to quit[26]. The onus is on the landlord to satisfy the Tribunal as to the tenant's default; if so satisfied the Tribunal are required to grant the certificate.[27] There are statutory forms for the landlord's application and the tenant's reply.[28]

Arbitration procedure is not provided for contesting the landlord's application: the matter is to be settled by the Tribunal. The Tribunal is empowered, when granting a certificate of bad husbandry, to specify in the certificate a minimum period of notice to quit, not being less than two months.[29] This means *any* period of two months, not restricted to a period ending at the end of a year of the tenancy.[30] The provision is so worded as to protect a notice of such short length against any plea of invalidity under section 25(1) or under contract or at common law as the holding may be deteriorating rapidly through bad husbandry, this relaxation is essential. A tenant is not to be taken to have failed to fulfil his responsibilities under the rules of good husbandry by permitting occupation for authorised opencast coal working or facilitating the use of land for such purposes.[31] The Tribunal are in effect directed, in considering whether to grant a certificate of bad husbandry, not

---

[24] In the older version of Case C in the 1948 Act there was until 1984 the odd provision that the notice to quit had to be given within six months from the *application* for the certificate (which was amended by s. 6(3) of the 1984 Act). The old provision could give rise to difficulties: see **Cooke v. Talbot** (1977) 243 E.G. 831.

[25] See s. 96(3) for the application of these rules for the purposes of the 1986 Act.

[26] For a precedent see Form 30 in Part V of this work.

[27] Sched. 3, Part II, para. 9(1). There is clearly no discretion involved once the landlord has proved his case.

[28] See Forms Part V. The application must be made on a form substantially to the like effect as the statutory form: see Forms 3 and 3R in the appendix to the Rules in the Schedule to the Agricultural Land Tribunals (Rules) Order 1978 (S.I. 1978 No.259), printed as Forms 26 and 26A in Part V of this work. But failure to comply may not necessarily be fatal: r. 38.

[29] Section 25(4), an exception to s. 25(1).

[30] s. 25(5).

[31] Opencast Coal Act 1958, s. 14(3) substituted by the Housing and Planning Act 1986, Sched. 8, para. 5.

to treat as bad husbandry any practice adopted by the tenant in pursuance of any conservation provisions in the tenancy or other agreement (*e.g.* a management agreement) with the landlord.[32] Neither basic compensation nor additional compensation for disturbance is payable where section 26(1) is excluded by virtue of Case C.[33]

The only comment which requires to be made, as a practical matter, is that Tribunals appear willing to tolerate extraordinarily low levels of farming without issuing a certificate of bad husbandry. Perhaps the explanation is the machinery of Case D and notices to do work which, in the long run, ought to give the tenant considerable opportunity to mend his ways before he is required to leave the holding. One potential problem relates to the neglect of land which has been set aside pursuant to E.C. Regulations whereby, in short, the tenant is paid for not farming the land. Although potentially a serious problem, the availability of modern pesticides and chemicals to restore land after the set aside period may well have persuaded landlords that it is worthwhile to tolerate the tenant's entry into set aside because, at the end of the day, it will be reflected in the rent. There appears to be very little evidence of litigation in terms of reliance on Case C in order to reverse the effect of set aside. Whether or not the Tribunal would grant a Case C certificate where the problem was generated by the tenant's E.C. set aside remains an open question because the Tribunal is not administering an E.C. scheme when it exercises its statutory functions under Case C.[34]

12.52 Case D: Non-payment of rent and remediable breach[35]

"[A]t the date of the giving of the notice to quit the tenant had failed to comply with a notice in writing served on him by the landlord, being either—

(a) notice requiring him within two months from the service of the notice to pay any rent due in respect of the agricultural holding to which the notice to quit relates, or

(b) a notice requiring him within a reasonable period specified in the notice to remedy any breach by the tenant that was capable of being remedied of any term or condition of his tenancy which was

---

[32] Sched. 3, Part II, para. 9(2). The conservation purposes specified cover flora or fauna, geological or physiographical features of special interest, buildings or other objects of archaeological, architectural or historic interest, and, more generally, conservation or enhancement of the natural beauty or amenity of the countryside or the promotion of its enjoyment by the public. (Such conservation provisions are also to be regarded for the purposes of Cases D and E as terms or conditions not inconsistent with the rules of good husbandry: Sched. 3, Part II, paras 10(1)(d) and 11(2).

[33] s. 61(1).

[34] It may well be that Case C ought to be amended to provide specifically for this problem as it does in the terms of Sched. 3, para. 9 in respect of other matters. If the U.K. is at fault in failing to make appropriate allowance the tenant's remedy, if ejected, may lie against the U.K. but not his landlord (see ***Francovich v. Italy*** [1991] E.C.R. I-5357 where damages were successfully claimed against the Italian Republic for failing to transpose a directive into national law as a result of which the plaintiff suffered loss). It is perhaps arguable that the wide discretion afforded to the Tribunal would permit them to make allowance.

[35] Sched. 3, Part I.

CASE D: NON-PAYMENT OF RENT AND REMEDIABLE BREACH

> not inconsistent with his responsibilities to farm in accordance with the rules of good husbandry,
>
> and it is stated in the notice to quit that it is given by reason of the said matter."

Procedural Table 4: Notices to quit under Case D following notice to pay rent; Table 5: Notice to quit: Case D and notice to do work of repair, maintenance or replacement; Table 6: Notice to quit under Case D following notice to remedy not including work of repair, maintenance or replacement. Supplemental provisions are contained in Schedule 3, paragraph 10. Absolute time-limits apply.

Case D: general   12.53

Case D has occasioned more litigation and has become more complex than any of the other Cases. A preliminary written notice in a prescribed form is a requirement of each limb of Case D.[36] The courts have historically taken a very strict view of preliminary notices generally, whether notices to pay rent or notices to remedy, and they did so before the notice to pay rent had to be in a prescribed form.[37] As has been noted elsewhere, however, a tenant might not be able to take advantage of defects in a preliminary notice if he neglects to safeguard his rights by requiring arbitration on the notice to quit.[38] The landlord was until recently under no duty to warn the tenant of his restricted rights to contest the reason stated in the notice to quit, and the serious danger that he might lose both his livelihood and his home if he failed to take the correct procedural steps, a fact which was deplored by the Court of Appeal.[39] However, in 1984 it was decided to incorporate in the prescribed forms of notice to pay rent and to remedy a warning note drawing the tenant's attention to his twofold vulnerability.[40] The twofold risk is (a) failing to serve notice requiring arbitration within one month of the service on him of a notice to quit, and (b) failing within three months after the service of the notice requiring arbitration to agree on the appointment of an arbitrator or to apply to the President of the RICS for the appointment of an arbitrator.[41] Questions relating to

---

[36] See Sched. 3, para. 10(1)(*a*) of the 1986 Act and see the Agricultural Holdings (Forms of Notice to Pay Rent or to Remedy) Regulations 1987 (S.I. 1987 No.711) and Part V of this work Forms 22, 23 and 25. For an arbitration demand following receipt of Form 23, see Form 24. For a general demand for arbitration on receipt of notice to quit see Form 33. For landlord's notice to quit see Form 30.

[37] See ***Pickard v. Bishop*** (1975) 31 P. & C.R. 108; 235 E.G. 133; ***Jones v. Lewis*** (1973) 25 P. & C.R. 375; ***Dickinson v. Boucher*** (1983) 269 E.G. 1159; ***Magdalen College, Oxford v. Heritage*** [1974] 1 W.L.R. 441; (1974) 230 E.G. 219. For the general principle, see *Macnab of **Macnab v. Anderson*** 1957 S.C. 213, 1958 S.L.T. 8.

[38] See para. 12.45 above. ***Parrish v. Kinsey*** (1983) 268 E.G. 1113.

[39] See ***Harding v. Marshall***, *supra*, per Ackner L.J. at 161 and 162. There is no equity to relieve a tenant who neglects to require arbitration, even if he is of extreme old age, is handicapped and totally ignorant of these technicalities: see ***Parrish v. Kinsey*** (1983) 268 E.G. 1113 (a hard case).

[40] See now the notes to the forms in the Agricultural Holdings (Forms of Notice to Pay Rent or to Remedy) Regulations 1987 (S.I. 1987 No.711).

[41] See articles 9 and 10 of the Agricultural Holdings (Arbitration on Notices) Order 1987 (S.I. 1987 No.710).

possible remedy by the landlord where the tenant has removed milk quota from the holding are dealt with elsewhere.[42]

12.54 Construction of statutory notices to pay rent or to remedy

The courts had historically adopted a fairly hard line on the need for correctness and on the absence of any misleading matter, whether in a notice to pay rent due or in a notice to remedy breaches. Thus a notice to pay rent was held to be bad because it named the wrong landlord, even though the person named had been the landlord until recently, when he transferred the ownership to the trustees of his own settlement, and the notice was signed by the agents who had acted for the settlor when he was the landlord and who had received the rents from the tenant throughout the tenancy.[43] In another case the notice was held bad because it contained the name and address of one only of the joint tenants.[44] In *Magdalen College, Oxford v. Heritage*[45] the notice to pay rent was held to be defective because it omitted to specify the time-limit of two months, but this is now an essential part of the statutory form.[46] In *Dickinson v. Boucher*[47] the rent was due but the amount was incorrectly stated. The situation in relation to notices to pay rent was regarded as analogous to forfeiture,[48] hence the severity.

It is not, however, correct to suppose, even adopting a hard line of construction where accuracy in the notice is concerned, that all mistakes would necessarily be fatal to a statutory notice. In *Official Solicitor v. Thomas*[49] the notice to pay rent erroneously referred to "supplemental agreement" in the singular, whereas in strictness the reference ought to have been plural since there were two such agreements. The tenant's allegation that this mistake invalidated the notice to pay rent was rejected because the wording sufficiently achieved its statutory purpose namely to inform the tenant of the source of the relevant obligation and the tenant could not reasonably have been misled.[50] Subsequently in *Dallhold Estates (U.K.)*

---

[42] See Chapter 18 and para. 13.105 below.
[43] *Pickard v. Bishop* (1975) 31 P. & C.R. 108; 235 E.G. 133,CA, a hard case. Browne L.J. dissented in a powerful judgment.
[44] *Jones v. Lewis* (1973) 25 P. & C.R. 375. It must be understood that the defect here was in the *form* of notice. The point must not be confused with the *service* of a notice which is served in the proper form on one joint tenant only, as to which see such cases as *Doe d. Bradford v. Watkins* (1806) 7 East 551; *Doe d. Macartney v. Crick* (1805) 5 Esp. 196 (marginal note incorrect); and a modern case, *Greenwich London Borough v. McGrady* (1982) 267 E.G. 515. (For a criticism of these decisions, see article in [1983] Conv. 194). On the question of notices to quit and jointly held estates see generally para. 12.24 above.
[45] [1974] 1 W.L.R. 441; (1974) 230 E.G. 219.
[46] See Form 22 in Part V of this work.
[47] (1983) 269 E.G. 1159.
[48] *Pickard v. Bishop* (above).
[49] [1986] 2 E.G.L.R. 1, CA.
[50] Nicholls L.J. at 6K-M: "[Counsel for the tenant] submitted that the particulars given in this notice failed to pass the strict test applied in *Pickard v. Bishop* and *Dickinson v. Boucher*. I cannot accept this submission. The area of complaint is limited to the sufficiency and accuracy of the description of the term of the tenancy which the landlord is notifying the tenant has been broken. The intended purpose of that part of the notice is that the tenant should have drawn to his attention what is the source of the obligation which the landlord is saying the tenant has failed to fulfil in the respects particularised in the right hand column. The achievement of that purpose requires the identification of the

Pty Limited v. Lindsey Trading Properties Inc.[51] the Court of Appeal applied the approach displayed in *Official Solicitor v. Thomas* in circumstances where rent was described as being "due" by reference to the dates in respect of which it was reserved even though strictly speaking the rent did not become "due" at all until later when a notice under section 48 of the Landlord and Tenant Act 1987 was served.[52] These two cases show that where a very strict line of construction is taken in relation to a notice there is nevertheless an opportunity for a notice to be good even if it contains an error. In fact the test propounded in *Official Solicitor v. Thomas* and *Dallhold Estates (U.K.) Pty. Limited v. Lindsay Trading Properties Inc.* is stated in terms which compare closely with the approach of the House of Lords in *Mannai Investments v. Eagle Star Assurance*, discussed at some length above.[53] Even if the strict perspective of *Pickard v. Bishop* and the earlier cases survive, the real question now, where there is a mistake, is as to whether the circumstances are such that the error could not reasonably have misled the tenant. It is submitted that the treatment of errors now establishes a suitable "common sense" approach in relation to statutory notices to pay and notices to remedy closely paralleling the approach in relation to notices to quit. It may be nowadays that the essential difference in the approach of the Court between, on the one hand a notice of a statutory character, and on the other hand a notice to quit will manifest itself largely in the degree of caution with which a Court would find in relation to the statutory notices that the tenant could not reasonably have been misled.

---

source with reasonable particularity. Normally the source will be a specific clause, readily identifiable, in a written tenancy agreement. In other instances, as here, it will not be. In either case the adequacy of the description is a question of degree, to be answered in the light of all the circumstances. ... I cannot accept the tenant's submission to the effect that any inaccuracy in this description, however trivial or immaterial or however obviously a slip, and regardless of whether the tenant may be misled by it or not, is necessarily fatal. So to decide, with regard to the part of the notice with which this appeal is concerned, would be to carry the need for strict compliance with the statutory requirements to an absurd length, and for no apparent purpose. In the present case the description was terse, but it did identify the source as a supplemental agreement (which, plainly, was being contrasted with the tenancy agreement itself) and the essential subject-matter of that agreement (payment of interest on the landlord's improvements). The only inaccuracy relied on is the omission of the letter 's' after the phrase 'supplemental agreement'. Given that it is accepted for the tenant that, despite the inaccuracy and the terseness, this tenant could not reasonably have been misled, in my view the particulars given were good enough."

[51] [1994] 1 E.G.L.R. 93

[52] See Ralph Gibson L.J. at 98H-K: "... In so far as the notice inaccurately asserted that the rent 'otherwise due' had been due on and from the quarter days listed, it did not mislead and could not reasonably have misled the tenant in any way. Furthermore, it did not and could not affect the clarity of the notice as to what the tenant was required to do or what the effect would be if the tenant did not comply with it. To treat this notice as invalid, therefore, would be to carry the need for strict compliance with the statutory requirement to a length beyond any useful purpose. The statutory purpose of the notice was fully satisfied." Peter Gibson L.J. at 99J welcomed the approach in *Official Solicitor v. Thomas* which he summarised as one "whereby errors in completing a statutory notice which could not reasonably have misled the tenant to whom it was addressed may be held in appropriate cases not to invalidate the notice".

[53] See para. 12.29.

12.55 **Notice to pay rent: requirements of a sufficient notice**

The rent must actually be *due* at the date when the notice to pay rent is served.[54] Now that the notice to pay rent has to be in the statutory form some of the older cases which considered informal documents are no longer relevant.[55] A question might arise as to when rent is "due", if, for example, an estate practice has developed and appears settled of accepting rent at intervals different from those specified in the contract of tenancy, say, at half-yearly instead of quarterly intervals. Can a landlord then suddenly take the tenant by surprise and choose to treat the rent as due on a strict quarter day?[56] In so far as there may be one or more dwelling houses on the holding it will be necessary to have satisfied section 48 of the Landlord and Tenant Act 1987[57] before the rent can properly be described as "due".[58] Non-compliance with section 48 does not extinguish the rent liability but simply suspends it until such point as notices are actually served.[59] Rent is not paid simply by the tenant getting a cheque into the landlord's possession; although doing this may amount to the defence of "tender" so as to avoid interest if sued in debt, the rent nevertheless remains "due" so as to found a notice to pay rent.[60] It is an unresolved question whether the notice to pay procedure is available only where the obligation to pay the rent derives from the contract of tenancy: this work suggests not.[61]

---

[54] *Magdalen College, Oxford v. Heritage*, (above), *Pickard v. Bishop*, (above). For an earlier case, see *Urwick v. Taylor* [1969] E.G.D. 1106 (one day before rent became due).

[55] e.g., *Sharpley v. Manby* [1942] 1 K.B. 217.

[56] This question was not actually decided in *Crown Estate Commissioners v. Allingham* (1972) 226 E.G. 2153, owing to the nature of the proceedings. It is thought, however, that a court would not allow a tenant to be prejudiced in these circumstances. There is a close analogy with withdrawal of acceptance of substituted performance of the obligation to pay in cash, the ability to make that withdrawal being limited to the giving of "timely notice" (see the *Tankexpress* case, referred to in para. 12.56 below).

[57] Section 48 provides: (1) A landlord of premises to which this Part applies shall by notice furnish the tenant with an address in England and Wales at which notices (including notices in proceedings) may be served on him by the tenant. (2) Where a landlord of any such premises fails to comply with sub-section (1), any rent or service charge otherwise due from the tenant to the landlord shall (... be treated for all purposes as not being due from the tenant to the landlord at any time before the landlord does comply with that sub-section.

[58] *Dallhold Estates (UK) Pty Limited v. Lindsey Trading Properties Inc.* [1994] 1 E.G.L.R. 93.

[59] See *Dallhold v. Lindsey* (above).

[60] *Official Solicitor v. Thomas* (above), at 3–4.

[61] It has been known for a landlord to secure a judgment of the Court for rent outstanding before then serving a notice to pay under Case D. In those circumstances the question arises as to whether the notice to pay in referring to "any rent due" can refer to the amount contained within the judgment or must be restricted to an amount arising out of a contractual debt. After obtaining the judgment, the landlord has merged the debt in the judgment. The cause of action in debt is destroyed (*Kendall v. Hamilton* [1879] 4 App Cas 504 and *Re European Central Railway* [1876] 4 Ch.D. 33). There is, however, a more liberal line of construction which could well be applied to the present problem. It is illustrated by *Aman v. Southern Railway Company* [1926] 1 K.B. 59 in which a judgment for arrears of interest due on stock was regarded as a claim under an absorption scheme even though the original debt had been merged in the judgment. It is suggested that the technical doctrine of merger with judgment has no real place in the functioning of

Notice to pay rent: compliance by the tenant 12.56

In principle the landlord is entitled to payment of the rent in cash by the due date. The landlord may expressly or by implication, particularly by a course of dealings, have demonstrated that he is content to accept payment by cheque instead.[62] But a substituted method of payment which has been accepted between the parties will apply, in appropriate circumstances, to cover the ongoing dealings between the parties.[63] Some care may be required to discern exactly what a course of dealing may amount to and in particular the extent to which the landlord may be regarded as having accepted the tenant's arrangements for payment.[64] Payment by cheque is a conditional payment only and not a satisfaction of the obligation to pay unless the parties agree to treat it in that way. A conditional payment will be defeated on non-payment of the cheque on presentation.[65] Action by the creditor, once the conditional payment has been made, is suspended[66] and if the cheque is met, the date of payment is regarded as the time when it was given.[67] Hence in some circumstances receipt of the cheque within the relevant two-month period will constitute good payment.[68] Where the cheque is received within the relevant two months but not met on presentation there is a failure to comply with the notice to pay in time.[69] There is no obligation on the landlord to re-present the cheque immediately or at all.[70] If there is a defect on the rent cheque which causes it not to be met on first presentation, any subsequent presentation will only "relate back" to the time after the defect was corrected and the cheque given in payment.[71] Questions have also arisen as to when precisely tenants have complied with the two month time-limit for payments. It has been held that a cheque posted before the expiry date but not received until two days later was within time, the accepted mode of payment over the years being by means of a cheque posted by the tenant.[72] A post-dated cheque received before, but not payable until after, the two months is not a compliance.[73] Where money is owing, the debtor is entitled subject

---

Case D. The description "rent" is still an accurate description of the monies unpaid even though the source of the liability has been transferred from the contract into the judgment. On this basis it is suggested that the landlord's right to serve a notice to pay ought to survive the making of a judgment in respect of rent where that judgment has not been met.

[62] *Beevers v. Mason* (1978) 37 P.&C.R. 452, Shaw L.J. at 458.
[63] *Tankexpress A/S v. Compagnie Financiere Belge des Petroles SA* [1949] A.C. 76, Lord du Parcq at 103; *The Brimnes* [1975] Q.B. 99.
[64] But by contrast a tenant who always pays late cannot thereby deprive the landlord of his opportunity to serve notice to pay and thereby force the tenant to pay his rent on time, or take the consequences.
[65] *Re Romer & Haslam* [1893] 2 Q.B. 286, Lord Esher M.R. at 296.
[66] *Cohen v. Hale* (1878) 3 Q.B.D. 371, Cockburn C.J. at 373.
[67] *Felix Hadley & Co. v. Hadley* [1898] 2 Ch. 680, Byrne J. at 682.
[68] *Beevers v. Mason* (above) explained in *Official Solicitor v. Thomas* (above).
[69] *Hannaford v. Smallacombe* [1994] 1 E.G.L.R. 9, CA.
[70] Although it is standard practice with banks to present the cheque three times, it is understood, before returning it to the payee.
[71] See *Luttenberger v. North Thoresby Farms Ltd* [1993] 1 E.G.L.R. 3, Ferris J. approved in *Hannaford v. Smallacombe* (above) at 12.
[72] *Beevers v. Mason* (1978) 248 E.G. 781; there were other problems in this case and it must not be taken as deciding generally that posting *per se* is service.
[73] *Att.-Gen. (Duchy of Lancaster) v. Simcock* [1966] Ch.1.

to any agreement with the creditor to appropriate any payment he makes as he wishes and the creditor must apply it accordingly.[74] In the absence of such an appropriation the right passes to the creditor to appropriate the money paid.[75] Appropriation by the debtor must be communicated to the creditor.[76] The law relating to appropriation becomes important where the tenant may wish to argue that he has already in fact paid the very rent included within the landlord's notice to pay.[77] The payment must be made in full—payment of a substantial amount, like substantial compliance with a notice to remedy, is not good enough.[78] However, where the failure to comply is *de minimis* the notice is regarded as complied with.[79] Payment must be made in a proper manner: merely to leave a rent cheque at the shared dairy of the farmhouse has been held insufficient.[80]

12.57 **Notice to pay rent: consequent notice to quit**
Here, as in the case of a notice to remedy breaches,[81] the words "at the date of the giving of the notice to quit the tenant had failed to comply" do not imply a *locus poenitentiae* between the expiry of the time-limit and the service of the notice to quit. Where the landlord actually receives payment following the expiry of the two month period but prior to serving his notice to quit, the notice to quit is not thereby invalidated.[82] The notice to quit must not be served prematurely, before the time-limit of two months has elapsed. In one case where the time-limit expired at midnight a notice to quit posted before, but not delivered until after, that midnight was held not to be premature.[83]

12.58 **Notice to pay rent: the availability of set-off**
There is no reported case in which a tenant has been allowed the defence of set-off, whether equitable or otherwise,[84] so as to defeat a landlord's Case D notice to pay rent where the rent has admittedly not been paid. In *Sloan Stanley Estate Trustees v. Barribal*[85] the issue was whether the terms of the Land Drainage Act 1976, section 72(5)(d)[86] gave the tenant the right to deduct from the rent due an amount

---

[74] *Milverton Group v. Warner World* (1995) 2 E.G.L.R. 28 at 31H.
[75] *Cory Brothers & Co. Ltd v. Owners of the Turkish Steamship "Mecca"* [1897] A.C. 286, Lord MacNaughten at 293.
[76] *Leeson v. Leeson* [1936] 2 K.B. 156.
[77] Such an argument was made, unsuccessfully, in *Official Solicitor v. Thomas* (above).
[78] *Price v. Romilly* (1960) 1 W.L.R. 1360.
[79] *Luttenberger v. North Thorseby Farms Ltd* (above), Ferris J. and see further in relation to the *de minimis* principle paragraph 12.30 above.
[80] *Flint v. Fox* (1956) 106 L.J. 828.
[81] *Price v. Romilly* (above).
[82] *Stoneman v. Brown* [1973] 1 W.L.R. 459, CA; followed in *Hannaford v. Smallacombe* [1994] 1 E.G.L.R. 9, at 13, CA.
[83] *French v. Elliott* [1960] 1 W.L.R. 40. See also *Macnab v. A. & J. Anderson* [1955] S.C. 38.
[84] As to set off generally see *Hanak v. Green* [1958] 2 Q.B. 9, CA and *British Anzani (Felixstowe) Limited v. International Marine Management (U.K.) Ltd* [1980] Q.B. 637.
[85] [1994] 2 E.G.L.R. 8.
[86] "(d) The occupier of any hereditament may (subject to any agreement to the contrary) recover from the owner thereof any amount paid by him on account of an owner's drainage rate and may deduct that amount from any rent payable by him to the owner".

in respect of the owner's drainage rate in circumstances where the tenant had not in fact paid that rate. The Court held that on the plain words of the statute, in the circumstances, there was no right of set-off under the statute. However, *obiter*, one member of the Court observed that they would have been prepared to accept the possibility of set-off against rent perhaps going so far as to accept equitable set-off including in relation to unliquidated damages.[87] The 1948 Act, Case D does not differ materially from the wording of the modern Case D. By contrast with the notice to remedy procedure it can be seen that the agricultural legislation provides, apparently deliberately, a most draconian penalty if the rent is not paid. This might suggest that landlords were intended to be protected in relation to rent whilst being expected to put up with very serious restrictions otherwise on the right to serve notice to quit. These considerations may indicate that set-off of a liquidated debt is in a different and more acceptable category for these purposes than set-off in the form of unascertained unliquidated damages. Finally one must recall the strictness with which notices to pay rent have been construed[88]; if any element of over-demand in the Case D notice to pay rent is sufficient to vitiate it and unliquidated damages can be set off the availability of Case D may be restricted almost to vanishing point.[89]

Notice to pay rent: procedure 12.59
Once the rent is due, the landlord may at any time serve notice to pay rent in prescribed form requiring payment within two months. If the tenant pays that is the end of the matter; if he does not the landlord may choose to serve notice to quit, at which point the tenant may within one month of receipt of the notice to quit demand arbitration on the ground stated in the notice to pay rent. The full procedure, its time limits and forms should be checked from Table 4 (notices to quit under Case D following notice to pay rent) in Part VI.

Notices to remedy: statutory forms and procedure 12.60
Two different forms of notices to remedy are prescribed.[90] A notice to remedy which requires the doing of any work of repair, maintenance[91] or replacement must be in Form 2 and any other notice to remedy in Form 3. A notice to remedy which is not in the prescribed form or in a form substantially to the same effect (and it must be remembered that the notes to the forms, which include important

---

[87] Balcombe L.J. at 11J.
[88] See *Pickard v. Bishop* and generally para. 12.54 above.
[89] There must be hardly a farm in England or Wales where no landlord's disrepair is to be found.
[90] By the Agricultural Holdings (Forms of Notice to Pay Rent or to Remedy) Regulations 1987 (S.I. 1987 No.711), Forms 2 and 3 (Form 1 is the notice to pay rent due). See Sched. 3, para. 10(2) for authority. The notice to remedy forms are respectively Forms 23 and 25 in Part V of this work.
[91] It is not yet clear whether "maintenance" is confined to fixed equipment or would cover such agricultural maintenance as the eradication of weeds like couch. There is a very slight indication in *Wykes v. Davis* [1975] Q.B. 843; (1974) 233 E.G. 265,CA, that it would cover the latter, as the court assumed that the then Form 1 did cover it, but the point was not in issue. For comments in another context which might be helpful, see *Hereford and Worcester C.C. v. Newman* [1975] 1 W.L.R. 901.

warnings, are an essential part of what is prescribed) will be invalid for the purpose of Case D, *i.e.* will not provide a foundation for a notice to quit operating under the Case.[92] It will be seen later that in the case of "notices to do work"[93] provision is made[94] for certain material questions to be determined by arbitration after the service of the notice to do work, thus enabling decisions to be made on these matters without waiting for the crucial stage of the notice to quit. This very important arbitration procedure, as well as the arbitration procedure following the notice to quit, are discussed fully later.[95] There is no place for intermediate arbitration in the case of a notice to remedy other than a notice to do work; arbitration is possible only at the notice to quit stage. In the case of a notice to do work the question whether it is in the prescribed form is one of the questions which can be raised at the intermediate stage and it *must* be raised if the tenant is also contesting his liability to do work.[96] If the tenant is not contesting his liability to do work (or seeking the deletion of items of work or the substitution of a different method or material)[97] he can raise a question as to the prescribed form either at this intermediate stage or in an arbitration following the notice to quit.[98] In the case of a notice to remedy other than a notice to do work, the question whether it is in the prescribed form can only be raised in an arbitration on the notice to quit (or possibly in court proceedings).

Any notice to remedy breaches must specify a definite time for compliance, which must be a reasonable period.[0] Further, where the notice is a notice to do work a period of less than six months shall not be treated as a reasonable period within which to do any such work.[1] In order to prevent persecution, it is additionally provided that where a notice to do work is served in the prescribed form, any further notice requiring the doing of any such work[2] which is served on the tenant less than 12 months after the earlier notice is to be disregarded unless the

---

[92] See reg. 2(2) of the above Regulations (S.I. 1987 No.711). As to the status of the notes, *cf. Boltons (House Furnishers) v. Oppenheim* [1959] 1 W.L.R. 913 at 920.

[93] A convenient abbreviation for a notice to remedy which requires the doing of any work of repair, maintenance or replacement: s. 28(6).

[94] By the Agricultural Holdings (Arbitration on Notices) Order 1987 (S.I. 1987 No.710) Part II.

[95] See below paras 12.62–12.66 in relation to arbitration on receipt of a notice to do work: paras 12.64 and 12.83–12.87 in relation to arbitration following receipt of a notice to quit.

[96] See the 1987 Order, art. 4(1).

[97] *ibid.*, art. 3(1) (b) and art. 4(1).

[98] *ibid.*, art. 4(2).

[99] Sched. 3, Case D(b).

[1] Sched. 3, Part II, para. 10(1)(c).

[2] *e.g.* presumably any work of maintenance, repair or replacement, although different in its detailed items from the previous notice.

earlier notice was withdrawn with the tenant's agreement in writing.³ It is sufficient if the earlier notice to do work is withdrawn by the date of the "notice to quit"⁴; also, a tenant can waive the need to comply with the 12 months' provision.⁵

A notice to remedy which complies with the statutory form so far as its layout is concerned might nevertheless be bad if it is obscure or ambiguous in its reference to the breaches alleged and the remedial action required.⁶ The alternative procedures, time limits and forms are set out for reference in Table 5 (notice to quit under Case D and notice to do work of repair maintenance or replacement) and Table 6 (notice to quit under Case D following notice to remedy not including work of repair maintenance or replacement) in Part VI.

Notices to remedy: general   12.61

A change of landlord, *e.g.* as a result of a sale of the reversion, between the service of the notice to remedy (the same would apply to a notice to pay rent due) and the service of the notice to quit will not invalidate the latter.⁷   12.61.1

Failure to remedy *any* of the breaches specified in a notice to remedy will, subject to the rule *de minimis non curat lex*,⁸ be sufficient foundation for a notice to quit under Case D. As already mentioned, substantial compliance is not enough.⁹ A tenant has, however, in respect of notices to do work (but not in respect of other kinds of notices to remedy) the opportunity of testing the ground in advance by arbitration on that notice. He does not then have to choose between complying *in toto* with a schedule which he partly disputes and risking the loss of his holding (farm, home and livelihood) by ignoring the items which he contests.¹⁰   12.61.2

The statutory forms of notices to remedy have greatly reduced, but not entirely destroyed, the importance of earlier cases which laid it down that the preliminary notice must be peremptory and unambiguous.¹¹ It is, however, still important that the notices to pay rent and to remedy should, in addition to complying with the statutory form, be clear and that the notice to quit, apart from exhibiting the same virtues, should refer unequivocally¹² to the preliminary notice on which it is based.   12.61.3

A notice to remedy which relates to several breaches must specify a time for compliance which is *ab initio* reasonable for *all* the breaches included in the notice. If it is reasonable for some but not all it is wholly bad.¹³ The period specified might   12.61.4

---

³ Sched. 3, Part II, para. 10(1)(b).
⁴ ***Mercantile and General Reinsurance Co. Ltd v. Groves*** [1974] Q.B. 43. It does not have to be withdrawn before the further notice to do work is served.
⁵ Compare ***Elsden v. Pick*** [1980] 1 W.L.R. 898: see generally paragraph 12.4 above.
⁶ ***Morris v. Muirhead*** 1969 S.L.T. 70 (it is insufficient merely to allege failure "to manage and cultivate the lands in accordance with the rules of good husbandry").
⁷ See para. 13.12 below.
⁸ See para. 12.30 above.
⁹ ***Price v. Romilly*** [1960] 1 W.L.R. 1360.
¹⁰ See paras 12.62–12.66 below.
¹¹ Cases such as ***Waller v. Legh*** (1955) E.G. 201, CC, and ***Macnab of Macnab v. Anderson*** 1968 S.L.T. 8, and see generally para. 12.54 above.
¹² See para. 12.54 above.
¹³ ***Wykes v. Davis*** [1975] Q.B. 843; (1974) 233 E.G. 265,CA. In ***Price v. Romilly***, *supra* which appears to support a contrary view, the point was not fully considered. ***Shepherd v. Lomas*** [1963] 1 W.L.R. 962 is distinguishable: see text below.

be *ab initio* unreasonable (a) because it was insufficient to enable one of the breaches to be remedied, although sufficient for the others, or (b) because, although each breach taken separately could be remedied within the time, the period was insufficient for all the breaches taken together.

12.61.5 The Court of Appeal has considered the question of reasonableness of the time to be specified in the context of a notice to remedy which did not involve the doing of work, but the relevant observations are of assistance in relation to assessing what would be a reasonable period also under notices to do work.[14]

12.61.6 If the time specified is *ab initio* reasonable for all the items, the fact that it subsequently *becomes* unreasonable for some does not render the notice to remedy invalid as respects those for which the time remains reasonable; the tenant will neglect the latter at his peril. In **Shepherd v. Lomas**,[15] the period of six months specified for the whole of the work was *ab initio* reasonable, but because of the landlord's failure to supply materials it became unreasonable for those items for which materials were needed; the notice to remedy was not void *ab initio*.

12.61.7 The Court of Appeal in **Wykes v. Davis**[16] specifically reserved the question whether the danger of a notice to remedy being pronounced void *ab initio* could be avoided either by specifying in one notice different time-limits for remedying different breaches or by serving at the same time a number of separate notices to remedy, each specifying a particular time limit for remedying a particular breach.

12.61.8 As in the cases based on non-compliance with a notice to pay rent due, the notice to quit must not be served prematurely, *i.e.* before the period set for compliance has elapsed.[17]

12.61.9 A tenant does not "comply" by remedying a breach after the date set for completion but before the service of the notice to quit.[18] Previously it was thought that the landlord should, however, in such a case be careful to consider any step he takes before serving the notice to quit in case such step might be construed as waiving his right to proceed under Case D.[19] However in **Hannaford v. Smallacombe** the Court of Appeal rejected the suggestion that acceptance of the rent referred to in the notice to pay, after that notice had expired, operated to destroy the landlord's right to serve notice to quit.

---

[14] See **Sumnall v. Statt** [1984] 2 E.G.L.R. 4, relevant extracts summarised in para. 12.75 below (notices to remedy other than notices to do work).

[15] Above.

[16] Above.

[17] **Cowan v. Wrayford** [1953] 1 W.L.R. 1340 at 1343,CA; **Hughes v. Taylor** (1950) 156 E.G. 141,CC; and see **French v. Elliott** [1960] 1 W.L.R. 40 (when the notice to quit, based on failure to pay rent, just escaped being premature), and para. 12.57 above.

[18] **Price v. Romilly** [1960] 1 W.L.R. 1360, curiously not mentioned in **Att.-Gen. (Duchy of Lancaster) v. Simcock** [1966] Ch.1, where, however, the point did not require decision owing to the jurisdiction issue. The view expressed in **Price v. Romilly** was confirmed in **Stoneman v. Brown** [1973] 1 W.L.R. 459, **Luttenberger v. North Thoresby Farms Ltd** (1993) 1 E.G.L.R. 3 and **Hannaford v. Smallacombe** (1994) 1 E.G.L.R. 9. See in relation to notice to pay rent para. 12.57 above.

[19] A point which appears not have been overlooked by Pennycuick J. in his *obiter* remarks in **Att.-Gen. (Duchy of Lancaster) v. Simcock**, above, at 7.

A notice to quit should make it abundantly clear that it is intended to rely on Case D and not Case E.[20] A "calculated obscurity" might be fatal.[21]

12.61.10

If a notice to quit under Case D is based *both* on the tenant's alleged failure (a) to comply with a notice to pay rent and (b) to comply with a notice to remedy breaches, the notice to quit may be effective if (a) is established even if the notice is inoperative so far as it is based on (b) because arbitration proceedings are in process.[22] It is also possible, and may be preferable, for two independent notices to quit to be served under Case D, one based on failure to pay rent and the other based on breach of covenants, and for one of these to take effect although the other fails, or is suspended pending the termination of arbitration proceedings.[23]

12.61.11

Although there is a clear analogy between notices to remedy under Case D and notices under section 146 of the Law of Property Act 1925, there is a warning in *Wykes v. Davis*[24] against treating decisions under section 146 as necessarily applicable to Case D. For example, a notice given under section 146 in respect of a number of breaches is capable of operating as a separate notice in respect of each breach.[25] The section 146 cases must therefore be treated with some caution.[26]

12.61.12

The fact that the landlord is himself in breach of a tenancy obligation does not *ipso facto* disentitle him from invoking the procedure under Case D, but it is otherwise if the performance of some act of the landlord, *e.g.* the provision of materials, is a *condition precedent* to the tenant's liability.[27]

12.61.13

A provision in a tenancy agreement enabling a landlord, on the failure of the tenant to carry out repairs for which he is responsible, to enter and carry out such repairs at the tenant's expense does not exclude the landlord's remedy under Case D.[28]

12.61.14

A tenant must carry out items of work which he is not contesting in the notice to do work. The fact that he is contesting other items does not excuse him from the

12.61.15

---

[20] ***Budge v. Hicks*** [1951] 2 K.B. 335,CA; see para. 12.27 above. For a precedent of notice to quit see Form 30 in Part V of this work.
[21] ***Macnab of Macnab v. Anderson*** 1958 S.L.T. 8 (words then actually used of the preliminary notice, not the notice to quit).
[22] ***French v. Elliott*** [1960] 1 W.L.R. 40.
[23] *ibid*. It is nowadays routine for notices to quit to be served with an open covering letter stating that each notice is given without prejudice to any other notice.
[24] [1975] Q.B. 843; (1974) 233 E.G. 265,CA. But see Purchas L.J. in ***Troop v. Gibson*** [1986] 1 E.G.L.R. 1; (1985) 277 E.G. 1134.
[25] Contrary to the reservation in ***Wykes v. Davis*** mentioned in para. 12.61.7 above.
[26] For s. 146 cases, see generally *Woodfall, Landlord and Tenant*, Vol. 1 (28th ed.) Chapter 17, s. 5. And see ***Pannell v. City of London Brewery Co.*** [1900] 1 Ch. 496; ***Fox v. Jolly*** [1916] 1 A.C. 1; ***Silvester v. Ostrowska*** [1959] 1 W.L.R. 1060 (s. 14 of the Conveyancing Act 1881 was the predecessor of s. 146 of the Law of Property Act 1925). See also ***Expert Clothing Service & Sales Ltd v. Hillgate House Ltd*** (1985) 275 E.G. 1011 and 1129 and ***British Petroleum Pension Trust Ltd v. Behrendt*** (1985) 276 E.G. 199.
[27] ***Shepherd v. Lomas*** [1963] 1 W.L.R. 962, especially Pearson L.J. at 974.
[28] This hardly needs authority, but see ***Halliday v. Fergusson (William) & Sons*** 1961 S.L.T. 176, overruling the decision of the Scottish Land Court in ***Forbes-Sempill's Trustees v. Brown*** [1964] S.L.C.R. 36. A provision of the kind referred to is in the "model clauses": see S.I. 1973 No.1473, para. 4(2) of the Schedule.

12.61.16 performance of the former.[29] It will be seen that the "contest"[30] has been very widely interpreted, applying to form or contents, legal grounds or matters of fact.[31]

"Capable of being remedied" is itself incapable of very precise definition. It cannot mean capable if time and expense are no object or if the consent of third parties who are under no obligation to give consent is obtained; and there is no actual authority for a working rule of 12 months sometimes invoked. It has been held that a breach of covenant personally to reside in a farmhouse is remediable in this sense.[32] At one time it was thought that the breach of a covenant not to sublet was remediable,[33] but this view is no longer held.[34] An assignment contrary to a covenant against assignment is irremediable, as it vests the tenancy in the assignee despite the breach.[35] Breaches consisting of failure to repair or to farm in accordance with the rules of good husbandry would in the normal way be remediable, as possibly would the breach of a covenant to insure.[36] It is arguable that there may be drastic cases where the breach has too serious consequences or would require much too long a time to be treated as reasonably capable of remedy. And the cutting of timber contrary to an obligation of the tenancy might in some cases be irremediable. But in general terms the distinction between breaches which are remediable and irremediable remains very problematic.[37]

12.61.17 Certain actions subsequent to the service of a notice to remedy may indicate an intention by the landlord to waive the notice, *e.g.* if he agrees with the tenant to submit matters to arbitration under section 8 or section 12.[38] But in all cases it is a question of evidence of the parties' intentions, not of fixed rules based on chronology of events.[39]

12.61.18 For the purpose of Case D, provisions in a conservation covenant, whether in the contract of tenancy or in a separate agreement, are to be regarded (if they would not otherwise be so regarded) as not inconsistent with the tenant's responsibilities to farm in accordance with the rules of good husbandry.[40]

---

[29] *Ladds Radio and Television Ltd v. Docker* (1973) 226 E.G. 1565.
[30] See Agricultural Holdings (Arbitration on Notices) Order 1987 (S.I. 1987 No.710), art. 9, and generally, paragraphs 12.62–12.66 below.
[31] *Magdalen College, Oxford v. Heritage* [1974] 1 W.L.R. 441.
[32] *Lloyd's Bank Ltd v. Jones* [1955] 2 Q.B. 298; and see para. 12.75 above.
[33] *Thomas Fawcett & Sons Ltd v. Thompson* [1954] E.G.D. 5 (letting of grazing).
[34] *cf. Scala House and District Property Co. Ltd v. Forbes* [1974] Q.B. 575 (not relating to agricultural property, but to premises in Soho); and see *Troop v. Gibson* [1986] 1 E.G.L.R. 1 at 5(D); (1985) 277 E.G. 1134 at 1139.
[35] *Old Grovebury Manor Farm Ltd v. W. Seymour Plant Sales and Hire Ltd (No.2)* [1979] 1 W.L.R. 1397,CA; *Governors of Peabody Donation Fund v. Higgins* (1983) 10 H.L.R. 85,CA; *Sanctuary Housing Association v. Baker* (1998) 9 E.G. 150, CA.
[36] Consider *Farimani v. Gates* (1984) 271 E.G. 887,CA although not directly in point.
[37] See for fuller discussion para. 12.76.1 below in the context of Case E.
[38] See *Shepton Mallet Transport Co. Ltd v. Clarke* [1953] C.P.L. 343, CA.
[39] See also under 12.61.9 and para. 12.16 above.
[40] Sched. 3, Part II, para. 10(1)(d). Conservation covers protection of flora or fauna, geological or physiographical features of special interest, buildings or other objects of archaeological, architectural or historic interest and, generally, the conservation or enhancement of the natural beauty or amenity of the countryside or the promotion of its enjoyment by the public: paragraph 9(2).

Neither basic compensation nor additional compensation for disturbance is payable where section 26(1) is excluded by virtue of Case D.[41]   12.61.19

Arbitration on notices to do work   12.62
The provisions for arbitration in regard to notices to do work are contained in articles 3 to 8 of the Agricultural Holdings (Arbitration on Notices) Order 1987.[42] The order draws an important distinction between questions for which the arbitration procedure is available *only* at the notice to do work stage and questions where in certain circumstances the tenant has an *option* of seeking arbitration at the notice to do work stage or of requiring arbitration under article 9 of the order *after* receiving a notice to quit.

Where arbitration is available only at the notice to do work[43] stage   12.63
If the tenant wishes to have any of the following questions determined by arbitration under the 1986 Act, he *must*[44] do so by requiring arbitration within one month of the service on him of the notice to do work:

(a) his liability under the terms or conditions of his tenancy to do any of the work specified in the notice;

(b) the deletion from the notice of any item or part of an item of work on the ground that it is unnecessary or unjustified; or

(c) the substitution, in the case of any item or part of an item of work, of a different method or material for the method or material which the notice would otherwise require to be followed or used.[45]

The tenant's notice requiring arbitration under this provision must be in writing, must be served on the landlord within one month after the service on the tenant of the notice to do work and must specify, as the case may be:

(a) any items in respect of which the tenant denies liability;

(b) any items or parts of items which the tenant claims to be unnecessary or unjustified; and

(c) any method or material in respect of which the tenant desires a substitution to be made.[46]

---

[41] s. 61(1).
[42] S.I. 1987 No.710. The order-making powers are contained in the 1986 Act, s. 29 and Sched. 4, paras 8–13.
[43] "Notice to do work" means "a notice served on a tenant of an agricultural holding for the purposes of paragraph (b) of Case D, being a notice requiring the doing of any work of repair, maintenance or replacement": s. 28(6).
[44] The tenant cannot raise these issues at a different stage or in a different form of proceedings.
[45] S.I. 1987 No.710, art. 3(1).
[46] *ibid.*, art. 3(2) and (3). No form is prescribed for the tenant's notice. For a precedent see Form 24 in Part V of this work.

If the tenant is raising any of the above questions, then any *other* questions arising under the notice to do work must be raised at the same time, *i.e.* within a month of the service of the notice to do work.[47] Thus the tenant has no option as to the time for raising these other questions *if* he is raising issues as to his liability to do the work or seeking deletion of items or substitution of different methods or materials. What such "other" questions might be is discussed below.

12.64 **Where tenant has an option as to arbitration on other questions at the notice to do work stage or at the notice to quit stage**
If the tenant does not require arbitration as to questions of liability to do the work or as to the deletion of items or substitution of methods or materials,[48] but wishes to raise other matters, he has an option. He may either raise these other matters within a month of receiving the notice to do work or wait until after he receives a notice to quit and raise them then in an arbitration under article 9 of the order.[49] It will be seen later that a tenant may also require arbitration under article 9 if supervening events have interrupted his timetable to an unreasonable extent.[50] It would seem wise for the tenant to raise all relevant matters of which he is aware at the notice to do work stage.

12.65 **Distinction between questions as to liability, etc., and other questions**
There could be queries as to the dividing line between questions as to the tenant's "liability under the terms or conditions of his tenancy to do any of the work specified in the notice"[51] and other questions. It is suggested that questions as to liability include the following:

(a) pure questions of construction, *e.g.* whether on the true construction of the contract of tenancy (including where relevant the "model clauses"[52]) the liability to repair a particular item of fixed equipment falls on the landlord or tenant;

(b) a mixed question of construction and fact, *e.g.* whether, having regard to the contract of tenancy and the physical condition of a wall, the interior covering of which is affected by a structural defect, the landlord or tenant is liable for repairs. A similar mixed question might be where the tenant contends that his liability to repair fixed equipment is subject to the provision of materials by the landlord and that these have not been supplied;

(c) a pure question of fact, such as whether an item of fixed equipment, the repair of which is admittedly the tenant's liability, is in fact out of repair.

---

[47] *ibid.*, art. 4(1) and (2).
[48] *i.e.* the matters mentioned in *ibid.*, art. 3(1).
[49] *ibid.*, art. 4(2).
[50] *ibid.*, art. 4(3). See para. 12.67 below.
[51] *ibid.*, art. 3(1)(a).
[52] Agriculture (Maintenance, Repair and Insurance of Fixed Equipment) 1973 (S.I. 1973 No.1473).

It is suggested that other questions[53] might include the following:

(a) the question whether the time specified in the notice to do work is a reasonable period in which to carry out the work;

(b) the question whether the breach alleged in the notice to do work is in fact one which is capable of being remedied at all (perhaps a desperate defence for a tenant, but conceivable);

(c) the question whether the term or condition which the tenant is alleged to have broken is inconsistent with the fulfilment of the tenant's responsibilities to farm in accordance with the rules of good husbandry (this point could arguably be regarded as one of liability);

(d) the question whether the notice to do work was invalid because it was not in the prescribed form or was not properly served on the tenant or was for some other reason ineffective.

As the matters which affect the tenant's liability or the deletion of items or the substitution of methods or materials can only be raised at the notice to do work stage, the practical answer, if there is the slightest doubt, is to raise matters at that stage.

Undisputed work must be done without delay 12.66

If there is any work specified in the notice to do work which the tenant does not dispute, he should do such work in compliance without waiting for the outcome of the arbitration as to the other work which he disputes. If he does not, he will put himself in the wrong and enable the landlord to serve a notice for non-compliance.[54] There are provisions for the recovery of the cost of work which the tenant has carried out although under no obligation to do so.[55]

Subsequent events making time unreasonable 12.67

If a tenant who has required arbitration and has been found liable to comply with a notice to do work discovers that some supervening circumstances make it unreasonable to require him to do the work within the time as extended by article 6 (see below), he may raise the matter in an arbitration under article 9 after receiving the notice to quit. He may have raised the reasonableness of the time in an arbitration at the notice to do work stage and the arbitrator, having found the time allowed to be reasonable,[56] may have extended it to compensate for the time consumed by the arbitration. Nevertheless, if *supervening* events make the time as extended unreasonable, the tenant may raise the matter again in an arbitration

---

[53] *i.e.* which fall within art. 4(1), as distinct from art. 3(1) of the S.I. 1987 No.710.
[54] See ***Ladds Radio & Television Service Ltd v. Docker*** (1973) 226 E.G. 1565. See also n. 3 to Form 2 in the Schedule to the Agricultural Holdings (Forms of Notice to Pay, Rent or to Remedy) Regulations 1987 (S.I.1987 No.711).
[55] S.I.1987 No.710, art. 8.
[56] The arbitration cannot extend a time which was *ab initio* unreasonable: see further text in para 12.67.

under article 9 at the notice to quit stage.[57] It must be emphasized that the tenant can only rely on the time having become reasonable through some supervening occurrence. A time which was *ab initio* unreasonable cannot be adjusted by the arbitrator so as to make it reasonable either at the notice to do work stage or at the notice to quit stage. And it should be remembered that the time specified in a notice to do work must be reasonable for *all* the items included in the notice.[58]

12.68 Extension of time for doing work
Article 6(1) of the Arbitration on Notices Order provides that where a tenant requires any question to be determined by arbitration under articles 3 or 4, the time specified for doing the work shall be extended until the termination of the arbitration. This is merely an automatic safeguard to prevent the time specified from running out before the termination of the arbitration. Article 6(2), however, goes further and provides that where the tenant is liable to comply with a notice to do work, or with any part of it, the arbitrator shall extend the time for doing that work by such further period as he thinks fit. It is most important to understand that the arbitrator's power (and duty) under article 6(2) to extend the time arises only if he finds that "the tenant is *liable to comply*." This involves a finding not only that the tenant is liable as a matter of legal obligation under the tenancy to do the work specified, but also that the time originally set by the landlord for the doing of the work was reasonable and that the notice to do work was valid in point of form. If the time had been *ab initio* unreasonable, or if the form had been invalid, the tenant would not have been "liable to comply" with the notice and no question of an extension of time could have arisen. The power to extend time which was *ab initio* reasonable is to offset the loss of time used up in the arbitration proceedings.

12.69 Date of termination of tenancy on failure to do work
Where the arbitrator has, under article 6(2), extended the time specified for doing any work he may, either of his own motion or on the application of the landlord, made not later than 14 days after the termination of the arbitration, specify a date for the termination of the tenancy by notice to quit in the event of the tenant's failure to do the work within the extended time.[59] The date so specified, however, must not be earlier than the later of the following two dates. These are (a) the date on which the tenancy could have been terminated by notice to quit served on the expiration of the time originally specified in the notice to do work, or (b) six months after the expiration of the extended time.[60] The notice to quit must be served on the tenant within one month after the expiration of the extended time.[61] The specified date need not be the end of a year of the tenancy and the notice to quit may be less than a 12 months notice, thus dispensing with both common law and statutory rules.[62]

---

[57] S.I. 1987 No.710, art. 4(3).
[58] ***Wykes v. Davis*** [1975] Q.B. 843.
[59] S.I. 1987 No.710, art. 7(1).
[60] *ibid.*, art. 7(2).
[61] *ibid.*, art. 7(4).
[62] *ibid*. This is fair to the landlord, who should not be penalised for tenant's failure to comply with an extended time.

If the landlord applies for a date to be specified, then, unless the application is made "at the arbitration", he must at the same time give written notice of the application to the tenant; and the tenant is entitled to be heard on the application.[63] There may, therefore, be a "hearing" on this point after the termination of the arbitration, *i.e.* after the delivery of the award to the tenant,[64] which constitutes a statutory modification of the *functus officio* rule.[65] Such a hearing may involve additional costs, which will fall to be dealt with under Schedule 11 to the 1986 Act.[66]

Recovery of cost of work 12.70

It has already been mentioned that a tenant who does work required by a notice to do work which he is under no obligation to do may recover the cost of such work.[67] It is the duty of the arbitrator to determine the reasonable cost of such work, and the amount is recoverable by the tenant in the county court under the provisions of section 85(1) of the 1986 Act. A possible case where a tenant might wish to carry out disputed work before the arbitration is where such work would most conveniently and economically be carried out in conjunction with work which was undisputed.

Special provisions regarding notices to do work 12.71

Special provisions are applied by article 15 to subsequent notices to quit when the time specified for doing any work in a notice to do work is extended under the provisions above considered of article 14. These provisions are as follows:

(1) in extending the time the arbitrator may specify a date for termination of the tenancy by a subsequent notice to quit in the event of the tenant's failure to do the work within the extended time[68];

(2) the date so specified must not be earlier than the date on which the tenancy could have been terminated by the original notice to quit or six months after the expiration of the extended time, whichever of these is the later[69];

(3) the subsequent notice to quit shall be valid notwithstanding that it is served less than 12 months before the specified date or that that date is not the end of a year of the tenancy, there thus being a dispensation from section 25(1) and from common law requirements[70];

---

[63] *ibid.*, art. 7(3).
[64] *ibid.*, art. 2(1).
[65] Other examples of such modification are the "slip rule" in the 1986 Act, Sched. 11 para. 20, and the provision for "reasons" for awards in Sched. 11, para. 21.
[66] *ibid.*, para. 23.
[67] S.I. 1987 No.710, art. 8.
[68] *ibid,.* art. 15(1).
[69] *ibid,.* art. 15(2).
[70] See paras 12.5 and 12.13 above and *ibid* art. 15(4).

(4) the notice to quit so authorised to take effect on a date specified by the arbitrator must be served on the tenant within one month after the expiration of the extended time[71];

(5) the arbitrator may specify the date either of his own motion or on the application of the landlord made at the arbitration or not later than 14 days after its termination. The wording there is similar to the wording in the parallel case under article 7(1). Unless the application is made at the arbitration the landlord must at the same time as he applies give written notice of the application to the tenant, who is entitled to be heard on the application.[72]

Paragraphs (5) and (6) of article 15 of the 1987 Order are best considered after examination of the provisions of section 28 of the 1986 Act to which these paragraphs are subsidiary.

12.72 Additional remedy for tenants served with a notice stated to be given by reason of non-compliance with notice to do work: section 28

General effect of section 28 The broad effect of section 28 is to widen and strengthen the remedies available to a tenant faced with a notice to quit given by reason of non-compliance with a notice to remedy which is a notice to do work.[73] Apart from section 28 the tenant's remedy would normally be to require arbitration to contest the reason stated in the notice to quit; he would not be entitled to serve a counter-notice with a view to forcing the landlord to apply to the Agricultural Land Tribunal for consent to the notice.[74] As a result of section 28 the tenant is given a choice of remedies. He may simply serve a counter-notice requiring that section 28(2) shall apply to the notice to quit, in which case that notice will not have effect unless, on the application by the landlord, the Tribunal consent to its operation. He may, instead, require the validity of the reason stated in the notice to be determined by arbitration. He may, having served a counter-notice, change his mind and require arbitration, in which case that particular counter-notice lapses. If he has required arbitration and fails, he can then, being given a *locus poenitentiae*, fall back on a counter-notice (even if he has already served one which has lapsed) and seek the consent of the Tribunal. The only thing he cannot do is first to complete the proceedings before the Tribunal and, having failed there, require arbitration.

---

[71] *ibid*,. art. 15(4).
[72] Arbitration on Notices Order 1987, art. 15(3). See comment, above paragraph 12.61 on the costs and a "hearing" after the arbitrator would otherwise be *functus officio*.
[73] A "notice to do work" means a notice served on the tenant of an agricultural holding for the purposes of para. (b) of Case D, being a notice requiring the doing of any work of repair, maintenance or replacement: 1986 Act, s. 28(6).
[74] Before the 1976 Act there was a practical dichotomy between notices to quit to which the correct response was a notice requiring arbitration and notices to quit to which the correct response was a counter-notice which placed the onus on the landlord of seeking the consent of the Agricultural Land Tribunal to the operation of the notice to quit. Section 12 of the 1976 Act introduced the scheme, now enshrined in s. 28 of the 1986 Act, by which the tenant has the choice of either remedy and can, indeed, avail himself of both.

Procedure under section 28 12.73
Section 28 applies where the notice to quit given to the tenant includes a "statement in accordance with Case D to the effect that it is given by reason of the tenant's failure to comply with a notice to do work".[75] It will be seen that the time-limit for serving a counter-notice (except in the circumstances mentioned in section 28(4)(b)) or a notice requiring arbitration is not later than one month from the giving of the notice to quit; and that in the section 28(4)(b) case the counter-notice may be served not later than one month from the date when the arbitrator's award is delivered to the tenant.[76] If, having first of all served a counter-notice, the tenant changes course and decides on arbitration, the notice requiring arbitration (which nullifies the counter-notice) must also be served not later than one month from the giving of the notice to quit.[77]

Tribunal's consent: under section 28: "fair and reasonable landlord" 12.74
It is provided that, on the application of the landlord under section 28(2) for the Tribunal's consent to the notice to quit, the Tribunal *shall* consent *unless* it appears to them, having regard:

(a) to the extent to which the tenant has failed to comply with the notice to do work,

(b) to the consequences of his failure to comply with it in any respect, and

(c) to the circumstances surrounding any such failure,

that a fair and reasonable landlord would not insist on possession.[78]

The matters to which the Tribunal can have regard are *confined* to those mentioned in (a), (b) and (c) above and the onus seems clearly to be on the tenant to establish that, in the light of these limited considerations, a fair and reasonable landlord would not insist on possession. The case of ***Clegg v. Fraser***,[79] decided on the former wording,[80] in which it was held that the Tribunal could take into account every relevant circumstance, including the specific matters now set out in section 27(3) of the 1986 Act, is thus overruled. The original wide discretion was probably cut down to prevent the tenant from raising issues which he had already raised (or ought to have raised) at the earlier stage of arbitration on the notice to do work. As the issue of liability will have been settled at that stage (and in some cases there will also have been an arbitration on the reason stated in the notice to quit)

---

[75] s. 28(1)(b).
[76] s. 28(3), (4) and (4)(b).
[77] See precedents in Part V of this work: for counter-notice under s. 28(2), Form 36, for general demand for arbitration, Form 33.
[78] s. 28(5). The present wording is much more restrictive than in section 4(4) of the 1977 Act (and its predecessor, s. 12(4) of the 1976 Act) which referred to "all the circumstances". The previous very wide discretion was cut down by s. 7 of the 1984 Act.
[79] (1982) 264 E.G. 144.
[80] The contrast between s. 27(2) and (3) and s. 28(5) should be noted. It is clear, for example, that general issues of hardship should not be canvassed under s. 28(5), but it would no doubt be permissible to establish that there were adverse circumstances surrounding the tenant's failure to comply which should be taken into account.

there does not seem to be much for the landlord to prove on the present application to the Tribunal. It will be for the tenant to discharge the burden of proof by enlarging on the specific circumstances above mentioned.

12.75 Notices to remedy other than notices to do work

In the case of notices to remedy other than notices to do work there is no provision for an intermediate stage of arbitration to resolve questions on receipt of the notice to remedy. If the tenant thinks that the notice to remedy is open to challenge because, say, it is not in the prescribed form or that the time specified for remedying the breach is unreasonable, or on some other ground, he will in practice have to decide whether to take the risk of not complying, in reliance on success in an arbitration following the notice to quit, when he will be able to challenge the notice. What might be a reasonable time for remedy, what factors should be taken into account in assessing it, the extent to which the personal circumstances of the tenant are relevant and what knowledge should be assumed on the part of the landlord have all been considered by the Court of Appeal in *Sumnall v. Statt*.[81]

An example of a notice to remedy other than a notice to do work is a notice requiring the tenant to reside personally in the farmhouse in accordance with a term

---

[81] [1984] 2 E.G.L.R. 4. The case concerned a notice where the landlord complained the tenant was in breach of a covenant to reside constantly at the farmhouse in circumstances where the tenant was due to be detained at Her Majesty's pleasure for four years. In giving the judgment of the Court Cumming-Bruce L.J. said: "... the arbitrator, in considering the length of notice specified in the notice, must look at the covenant and its discharge in the light of the object of the covenant as described by Singleton L.J. in the case that I have cited. [*Lloyds Bank Limited v. Jones* [1955] 2 Q.B. 298.] It would give an example of a situation personal to the tenant which could, in my view, be relevant to the length of the notice. If the remediable covenant was a failure to do works and the tenant had been unable to do the works for a period of seven months by reason of shortage of liquid money or borrowing ability but would be able, as the landlord knew, to do the work in eight months' time when his temporary financial difficulty would be relieved, being a financial difficulty arising from the operations of the farm during a difficult farming season, it might be that to give the tenant notice to do the works in seven months would be an unreasonable period when the landlord knew that in eight months the tenant would be able to do the works. It would be relevant to consider all the circumstances, the nature of the works of repair, the way in which the landlord's interest was affected by the failure to do the works, and the arbitrator would have to consider whether it was reasonable or unreasonable in all the circumstances to deprive the tenant of the opportunity to do the works in eight months instead of seven (6F-7G) ... it is reasonable to take into account not only what the landlord actually knew about the probable release date but also what he could reasonably have discovered about the release date if he had made reasonable inquiries (7H) ... The question whether a notice requiring a breach of covenant to be remedied within a specified time is reasonable must, in my opinion, depend on the circumstances of the particular case. In my judgment the extent to which the landlord is likely to be prejudiced by a prolonged breach of the covenant and the degree of likelihood that the tenant will be likely, as a practical matter, to be able to remedy the breach within the time specified in the notice, are both matters which may be relevant to the arbitrator's consideration of what he considers to be reasonable in any particular case. Indeed, any matter which appears to the arbitrator to bear upon the question whether the landlord has stipulated a reasonable period within which the tenant must remedy the breach of covenant should, in my judgment, be taken into consideration by the arbitrator. The view which he forms will depend upon the balancing of all such considerations. (8E)."

in the contract of tenancy.[82] The reader is referred to Procedural Table 6 (notice to quit under Case D following notice to remedy not including work of repair maintenance or replacement).[83]

Case E: Non-remediable breach 12.76

"At the date of the giving of the notice to quit the interest of the landlord in the agricultural holding had been materially prejudiced by the commission by the tenant of a breach, which was not capable of being remedied, of any term or condition of the tenancy that was not inconsistent with the tenant's responsibilities to farm in accordance with the rules of good husbandry, and it is stated in the notice that it is given by reason of the said matter.[84]"

Procedural Table 2: Notices to Quit: Case E Supplemental provisions are contained in Schedule 3, paragraph 11. Absolute time-limits apply.

Case E applies where at the date of the giving of the notice to quit the interest of the landlord in the agricultural holding had been materially prejudiced by the commission by the tenant of a breach, which was not capable of being remedied, of any term or condition of the tenancy which was not inconsistent with his responsibilities to farm in accordance with the rules of good husbandry,[85] and it is stated in the notice that it is given by reason of this matter.[86]

The notice to quit under Case E should make it absolutely clear that the landlord is proceeding under this Case and not under Case D.[87] No preliminary notice is required under Case E and in fact any such notice might cause doubt as to which Case was being invoked. The notice should not, by a "calculated obscurity" refer to both Cases in the hope that one will apply.[88] Case E is one of the four Cases (A,B,D and E) where resort to arbitration is provided for the purpose of contesting any reasons stated in the notice to quit, and is the only procedure for this purpose.[89] It is one of the five Cases (C,D,E,F and G) where both basic and additional compensation for disturbance are excluded.[90]

There is a special provision applicable where the landlord is a smallholdings authority or where the landlord is the Minister and the holding is on land held by him for the purposes of smallholdings. In these circumstances, in considering whether the interest of the landlord has been materially prejudiced, regard is to be

---

[82] See generally para. 12.61.16 as to this covenant.
[83] See Part VI.
[84] Sched. 3, Part I.
[85] See s. 96(3).
[86] Sched. 3, Part I, Case E.
[87] *Budge v. Hicks* [1951] 2 K.B. 335, and see para. 12.27 above.
[88] The phrase was actually used in connection with a preliminary notice to pay rent in *Macnab of Macnab v. Anderson* 1958 S.L.T. 8.
[89] Agricultural Holdings (Arbitration on Notices) Order 1987 (S.I. 1987 No.710), art. 9, and see Procedural Table 2: Notices to quit: Case E. In Part V of this work precedents are available: Form 30 for the landlord's notice to quit and Form 33 for the tenant's demand for arbitration in response.
[90] s. 61(1). (Where Cases A or H apply basic compensation for disturbance is not excluded, but additional compensation is excluded.)

had to the effect of the breach not only on the holding itself but also on the carrying out of the arrangements made by the authority or the Minister for the letting and conduct of smallholdings.[91] There is, in relation to Case E, a provision in the same terms as that already mentioned in relation to Case D for the purpose of safeguarding the effectiveness of conservation covenants in the tenancy or other relevant agreement.[92]

Case E cannot be used as part of an artificial mechanism to create a tenancy shorn of full security of tenure[93] since to do so would be contrary to public policy.

12.76.1 Case E: meaning of non-remediable breach

It is critical to decide at the outset whether the breach complained of is remediable, in which case Case D applies, or irremediable in which case Case E applies. The difference between the two is neatly summarised:

> "In my view the draftsman of Case D and Case E was contemplating different kinds of breaches, as compared to breaches of a particular kind which the tenant might or might not at any time be capable immediately of remedying.[94]"

As already mentioned in discussing Case D, the correct view is that assignment or sub-letting in breach of covenant is a non-remediable breach.[95] Other possible examples given in the last edition of this work of a failure to farm in accordance with the rules of good husbandry causing severe and lasting deterioration, allowing buildings to fall down through continued neglect of repair, cutting of valuable timber, perhaps using a mechanical hedge-cutter on mature quickthorn or holly hedges of possible irremediable breaches probably cannot survive.[96] Breaches of negative user covenants were once thought more likely to be non-remediable than breaches of continuing positive covenants but this may no longer be true.[97] "Not capable of being remedied" in Case E must be construed in a common-sense way; it does not mean incapable of remedy under any possible combination of

---

[91] Sched. 3, Part II, para. 11(1).
[92] See *ibid.*, para. 11(2) and para. 12.61.18 above.
[93] *Johnson v. Moreton* (see para. 12.3 above).
[94] (Cumming-Bruce L.J. in *Sumnall v. Statt.*) [1984] 2 E.G.L.R. 4 at 7C.
[95] See para. 12.61.16 above and *Scala House and District Property Co. Ltd v. Forbes* [1974] Q.B. 575 and *Troop v. Gibson* [1986] 1 E.G.L.R. 1; (1985) 277 E.G. 1134; the landlords failed in this case because the principle of estoppel by convention applied, as explained in *Amalgamated Investment and Property Co. Ltd v. Texas Commerce International Bank Ltd.* [1982] Q.B. 84. It may be noted that assignment of the whole is a breach of a covenant against parting with possession of a part; *Troop v. Gibson, supra*; *Field v. Barkworth* [1986] 1 E.G.L.R. 46. (The converse does not, of course, apply).
[96] See *Savva v. Hussein*, discussed in footnote below.
[97] For a discussion (in the context of s. 146 of the Law of Property Act 1925) see *Expert Clothing Service and Sales Ltd v. Hillgate House Ltd* [1986] Ch. 340,CA, where breach of an obligation to reconstruct by a specified date was held to be remediable, although a once for all breach. See also *Bass Holdings Ltd v. Morton Music Ltd* [1987] 2 W.L.R. 397. But the situation has been overtaken by *Savva v. Hussein* (see next footnote).

circumstances.⁹⁸ In reality the main use of Case E is in relation to the creation of legal estates which constitute a breach of the tenancy agreement.⁹⁹ Questions relating to the removal of milk quota from a holding are considered elsewhere.¹

Case E: meaning of material prejudice 12.76.2

The landlord must demonstrate that his interest in the holding as a landlord had sustained prejudice in a fashion which was "material". This seems to mean appreciable² rather than substantial. Clearly if the prejudice is of a type unlikely to demonstrate any significant impact on the interest of the landlord it must be questionable whether an arbitrator, if the notice to quit is challenged, would find that there was any prejudice. For this reason, litigation in the context of Case E will

---

[98] *Troop v. Gibson* (1985) 277 E.G. 1134; [1986] 1 E.G.L.R. 1. Purchas L.J. in this case rejected an argument that the construction differed from that under s. 146 of the 1925 Act. As a result there is serious question over the subsequent decision of the Court of Appeal in *Savva v. Hussein* (1997) 73 P.&C.R. 150 which establishes a classification for the purposes of s.146 which is rather different from that quoted above in the body of this paragraph deriving from Cumming–Bruce L.J. in *Sumnal v. Statt* (above). In *Savva v. Hussein* it was necessary to establish the difference between remediable and irremediable breach but citation of authority appears to have been thin. Staughton L.J. at 154 stated: "In my judgment, except in a case of breach of a covenant not to assign without consent, the question is: whether the remedy referred to is the process of restoring the situation to what it would have been if the covenant had never been broken, or whether it is sufficient that the mischief resulting from a breach of the covenant can be removed. When something has been done without consent, it is not possible to restore the matter wholly to the situation which it was in before the breach. The moving finger writes and cannot be recalled. That is not to my mind what is meant by a remedy, it is a remedy if the mischief caused by the breach can be removed. In the case of a covenant not to make alterations without consent or not to display signs without consent, if there is a breach of that, the mischief can be removed by removing the signs or restoring the property to the state it was in before the alterations." Aldous L.J. (at 156–7) stated: "In one sense a breach can never be remedied because there must have been non-compliance with the covenant for there to be a breach. That cannot be the solution. Thus, the fact there has been a breach does not determine whether it can be remedied in the way contemplated by the Law of Property Act, s. 146 ... There is in my view nothing in the statute, nor in logic, which requires different considerations between a positive and negative covenant, although it may be right to differentiate between particular covenants. The test is one of effect. If a breach has been remedied then it must have been capable of being remedied." He also disapproved the statement of law of Mummery J. in *Billson v. Residential Apartments Ltd* (1990) 60 P.&C.R. 392 [at first instance] at 406: "I reject the defendant's arguments on the ground that the breach of covenant committed by making the alterations in the property without the plaintiff's consent "first had and obtained" was not capable of remedy by the defendants. It was a breach of the covenant for the defendants to embark on alterations to the property without first applying for and seeking to obtain the plaintiffs' consent. Now that the alterations have been made without consent it is impossible for the defendants to comply with the covenant which required them first to apply for consent so that they could either obtain it or, if they did not obtain it, be in a position to contend that they were entitled to make improvements because the plaintiffs had unreasonably withheld consent ... In those circumstances I hold that the breach was not capable of remedy." That statement had already been expressly neither approved nor disapproved when the *Billson* case reached the Court of Appeal.

[99] But see the constraint within Case E discussed in the next paragraph.

[1] See chapter 18, and para. 13.105 below.

[2] Perhaps quantifiable.

normally arise only where the landlord apprehends he may succeed on the issue of material prejudice. The obvious way to establish "material prejudice" would be to show a substantial reduction in the value of the landlord's reversion resulting from the breach, although there may be cases where material prejudice can be demonstrated without such proof. Although breach of the covenants against assignment and sub-letting are the most frequent causes of Case E notices being served, in the case of sub-lettings it now appears that there is no material prejudice in the abstract to the landlord by the creation of a sub-letting. In *Pennell v. Payne*[3] the Court of Appeal held that there was no prejudice to the freeholder where the tenant sub-let because the sub-tenant had no security of tenure as against the freeholder[4] and without the freeholder's co-operation the head tenant could not serve an upwards notice to quit so as to fix the freeholder with the sub-lease. The decision does not, however, operate to render all sub-leases safe from complaint under Case E if, for example, the sub-tenant, though not in breach of the terms of his own lease, was carrying on activities which were prejudicial to the interest of the freeholder.

12.77 Case E: an assignor's dilemma

It quite often happens that a tenant may believe himself entitled to assign his tenancy in circumstances where he is unable to prove categorically the terms of that tenancy. Usually this is because the agreement was oral or because the arrangement was a licence converted into a tenancy or, occasionally, because the tenancy agreement is very old, struck through in parts or has been lost. The way out of the uncertainty is, of course, to acquire a written agreement if necessary through section 6 proceedings[5] but once a demand has been served under section 6 the ability to assign is lost.[6] It is usually to the tenant's advantage (*i.e.* provided not a breach of covenant) to assign the tenancy to a company controlled by himself or his family and thereby avoid the possibility of the tenancy coming to an end by a landlord's notice served on the tenant's death.[7] Obviously if the tenant assigns to the company, believing he is entitled to do so, but it is subsequently discovered that he was not entitled to do so the landlord would be entitled to serve a Case E notice to quit and would indeed have suffered material prejudice in that he would no longer be able to terminate the tenancy on the death of the tenant. Where there is

---

[3] [1995] 2 All E.R. 592. Overruling *Brown v. Wilson* and various other cases suggesting that a tenant might serve upwards notice to quit and, because he should not be permitted to derogate from his own grant to the sub-tenant, should accordingly be treated as fixing the landlord with the interest of the sub-tenant.
[4] *Sherwood v. Moody* [1952] 1 All E.R. 389.
[5] See paras 10.2–10.7 above. It will be recollected that where an assignment takes place following service of a s. 6 notice, the assignment is void: contrast an assignment effected in breach of the tenancy agreement which is perfectly valid in itself although it gives rise to possible opportunities for the landlord to terminate the tenancy (see *Old Grovebury Manor Farm v. Seymour Plant Sales and Hire* [1979] 1 W.L.R. 263, *Governors of Peabody Donation Fund v. Higgins* (1983) 10 H.L.R. 85 and *Sanctuary Housing Association v. Baker* (1998) 9 E.G. 150).
[6] See para. 10.7 above.
[7] Under Case G.

doubt in this fashion as to the ability to assign, the assignment will often take place at the same time as other arrangements designed to put the landlord back in his previous position should there be an arbitration award or court decision in the landlord's favour establishing that the assignment was a breach. Sometimes this is done by a re-assignment in escrow, the escrow being triggered by the relevant arbitration or court finding and it is usually considered necessary to make provision for the landlord's costs to be met so that he does not suffer financially as a result of the litigation.[8] There would appear to be no other way for the tenant to use his valuable right to assign without staking the survival of the tenancy on the assignment being lawful.[9]

Case F: Insolvency   12.78

> "At the date of the giving of the notice to quit the tenant was a person who had become insolvent, and it is stated in the notice that it is given by reason of the said matter.[10]"

For this purpose a tenant is insolvent if:

(a) he has been adjudged bankrupt or has made a composition or arrangement with his creditors, or

(b) where the tenant is a body corporate, a winding-up order has been made with respect to it or a resolution for voluntary winding-up has been passed with respect to it (other than a resolution passed solely for the purposes of its reconstruction or of its amalgamation with another body corporate).[11]

Arbitration is not provided to resolve any dispute as to a tenant's insolvency. This is a matter for the courts. Neither basic compensation nor additional compensation for disturbance is payable where section 26(1) is excluded by virtue of Case F.[12] It will be recalled that the requirement of a 12 months' length of notice does not apply where the tenant is insolvent.[13] Where there has been an assignment of the tenancy, the bankruptcy of the original tenant does not afford the opportunity to rely on Case F. The tenant is considered to mean the tenant for the time being.[14] The tenant whose insolvency is contemplated by this provision is not simply one of two joint tenants, it is submitted, but, in the case of joint tenants, all of those

---

[8] The more cautious will provide for indemnity costs.
[9] Of course the dilemma does not arise where the tenant wishes to sub-let, even in breach of his agreement, because of the decision in ***Pennell v. Payne*** [1995] 2 All E.R. 592, discussed above.
[10] Sched. 3, Part I.
[11] s. 96(2).
[12] s. 61(1).
[13] s. 25(2)(a).
[14] An analogy is offered in relation to forfeiture clauses. Where a forfeiture clause was exercisable on the bankruptcy of the tenant, the bankruptcy of the original lessee rather than the current tenant (who had taken by assignment) was not sufficient to found a forfeiture: ***Smith v. Gronow*** [1891] 2 Q.B. 394.

persons.[15] The lease, properly drawn, will be likely to contain a forfeiture clause,[16] including a proviso for re-entry in case of bankruptcy or company insolvency, so that the landlord may have a choice between Case F and forfeiture proceedings. Since there is no opportunity for relief in relation to Case F its use will inevitably be preferred to that of a forfeiture clause.

12.79 Case G: Death of tenant[17]

> "The notice to quit is given—
>
> (a) following the death of the person who immediately before his death was the sole (or sole surviving) tenant under the contract of tenancy, and
>
> (b) not later than the end of the period of three months beginning with the date of any relevant notice,
>
> and it is stated in the notice to quit that it is given by reason of that person's death."

Procedural Table 7: Succession on death where Case G notice to quit has been served. Supplemental provisions are contained in Schedule 3, paragraph 12. The three months time-limit stated in Case G is absolute.

For the purposes of Case G "tenant" does not include an executor, administrator, trustee in bankruptcy or other person deriving title from a tenant by operation of law.[18] "The date of any relevant notice" means either the date on which a notice in writing was served on the landlord by or on behalf of the executor or administrator of the deceased tenant's estate informing the landlord of the tenant's death, *or* the date on which the landlord was given notice by virtue of section 40(5) of any application with respect to the holding under section 39 or 41, whichever of these two events (if both occurred) was the first.[19]

12.80 Case G: historical background

Case G has undergone changes both in nomenclature and substance since it appeared as section 24(2)(g) of the 1948 Act. In 1961 it was interpreted in ***Clarke v. Hall***[20] to produce the literally correct, but anomalous, result that the landlord could serve a notice to quit on an assignee of the tenancy who was in actual possession

---

[15] There seems no reason to suppose that Parliament intended the landlord to by-pass the full security of tenure provisions where he had recourse to one solvent tenant. Therefore, at this point in the legislation it is submitted that "the tenant" should be given its grammatical meaning. See ***Featherstone v. Staples*** [1986] 1 W.L.R. 861, CA.

[16] The special provisions of s. 146(9) and (10) of the Law of Property Act 1925 should be noted in relation to forfeiture of leases of agricultural land and bankruptcy respectively.

[17] Sched. 3, Part I.

[18] Sched. 3, Part II, para. 12(a). Thus a notice to quit cannot be served under Case G in respect of the death of a personal representative who has had the tenancy vested in him following the death of the tenant: see ***Costagliola v. Bunting*** [1958] 1 All E.R. 846 (in some respects a better report than that at [1958] 1 W.L.R. 580).

[19] 1986 Act, Sched. 3, Part II, para. 12(b), and see para. 12.81.1 below.

[20] [1961] 2 Q.B. 331.

within three months of the death of the person with whom the contract of tenancy was made, *i.e.* the original grantee of the tenancy, although he might have assigned the tenancy many years before and there might, indeed, have been intermediate assignments.[21] The rule in ***Clarke v. Hall*** lasted from 1961 to 1976, when it was abolished by the 1976 Act and amended wording substituted,[22] which was reproduced in the 1977 Act.[23] Case G was amended in some respects by the 1984 Act[24] and, as so amended, embodied in Schedule 3 to the 1986 Act. The substance of the landlord's position following the death of a tenant was, however, wholly changed by the family succession scheme introduced by the 1976 Act, as a result of which close relatives of the deceased tenant could lay claim to a tenancy.[25] Although this was ended by the 1984 Act in relation to the death of a tenant whose tenancy was granted on or after July 12, 1984,[26] the abolition of the scheme was made subject to extraordinarily careful provisions for the avoidance of retrospective action. The consequence is that the scheme will continue to operate into the twenty-first century.[27]

Case G: the modern position 12.81

The important point to be understood in the present context is that the effectiveness of a notice to quit under Case G is severely restricted as a result of the succession scheme[28] and is now in certain events defeasible. The landlord should not, however, regard his position as hopeless. Apart from his right to challenge the eligibility and suitability of an applicant[29] for a tenancy under the succession scheme, a notice to quit based on Case G may still be effective if (1) no application to become the tenant of the holding is made, or (2) none of the applicants are regarded as suitable by the Tribunal, or (3) the Tribunal consents to the operation of the notice to quit in relation to the whole or a part of the holding.[30] The Tribunal must, before giving a direction entitling an applicant to a tenancy, afford the

---

[21] The wording in s. 24(2)(g) of the 1948 Act which gave rise to this decision was "the tenant with whom the contract of tenancy was made". The effect of ***Clarke v. Hall*** was anomalous because it placed the security of the sitting tenant (his farm, home and livelihood) at the mercy of a purely fortuitous occurrence, the death of a stranger, totally unconnected with his personal circumstances or his farming.

[22] By s. 16 of the 1976 Act.

[23] s. 2(3), Case G, of the 1977 Act. The amended wording now embodied in Sched. 3, Part I, Case G, in the 1986 Act, "a person who immediately before his death was the sole (or sole surviving) tenant under the contract of tenancy" was clearly intended to abolish the rule in ***Clarke v. Hall***, but a purist might still question its efficacy. Is "tenant under the contract of tenancy" wholly apt to describe an assignee with whom the landlord's relationship is based on privity of estate only, not privity of contract? However, the assignee is a tenant "under the contract of tenancy" in the sense that the rights and responsibilities in the contract have devolved upon him, although not in the sense that the contract was *made* with him.

[24] 1984 Act, s. 6(5).

[25] Provisions now contained in Part IV of the 1986 Act: see Chapter 14 below.

[26] It should also be noted that there are a number of cases excluded from succession scheme: sections 36 to 38.

[27] See s. 34.

[28] See generally Chapter 14 below.

[29] s. 39(7).

[30] ss. 39(7), 43 and 44.

landlord an opportunity to apply for its consent to the operation of his notice to quit.[31] It is therefore in the interests of a landlord to serve a notice to quit under Case G even where there is the possibility of a successful claim to a tenancy by a surviving close relative of the deceased tenant.[32] The following general points are to be noted.

12.81.1   **Case G: notice from the executors.** Although Case G incorporates the amendment made by the 1984 Act,[33] to meet the criticism that the landlord does not always receive timely notification of the deceased tenant's death, there is still something to be said for a clause in the contract of tenancy binding the personal representatives of the tenant, or other persons in whom the tenancy is vested at law or in equity immediately after his death, to give notice of the death and the date thereof within, say, one month of its occurrence. An action for damages would lie for loss caused by the breach of this undertaking and the breach would be likely to qualify as a non-remediable breach under Case E. What may amount to a "relevant notice" for the purposes of Case G is a notice in writing served on the landlord by or on behalf of an executor or administrator which is in terms which are sufficiently clear to bring home to the ordinary landlord that he was indeed being given a notice within Schedule 3, paragraph 12.[34] Unless and until a relevant notice is served, notwithstanding the landlord's knowledge of the tenant's death, the three month period is not running against the landlord and his right to serve a Case G notice to quit remains. Once the three months after service of the notice has ended the right to serve a Case G notice to quit is irrevocably lost.[35]

12.81.2   **Case G: serving the notice to quit** A notice to quit under Case G addressed to the late tenant's "executors" has been held to be effective although he died intestate; the person or persons who are in actual possession of the holding and

---

[31] s. 44.
[32] For a precedent of a notice to quit see Form 31 in Part V of this work.
[33] 1984 Act, s. 6(5). See now 1986 Act, Sched. 3, Part I, Case G and Part II, para. 12(3).
[34] This is the test in *Amalgamated Estates Ltd v. Joystretch Manufacturing Ltd* (1980) 257 E.G. 489 as applied at first instance in *BSC Pension Fund Trustees Ltd v. Downing* [1990] 1 E.G.L.R. 4 as subsequently approved by the CA in *Lees v. Tatchell* [1990] 1 E.G.L.R. 10. Those cases illustrate graphically that the issue is not whether the landlord knew the tenant had died but whether he had been served a relevant notice. Knowledge of the tenant's death, a rent demand sent direct to one of the executors, a rent payment made on the personal account of one of the executors, an obituary notice in the local paper, a small news item and a letter to the landlord's managing agents from a firm of solicitors saying they did not act in connection with the estate of the tenant have all been held not to amount to a relevant notice for the purposes of Case G. This is because "[t]he landlord could not possibly reasonably, let alone necessarily, have concluded from those documents that the clock had started to tick against him". (Parker L.J. in *Lees v. Tatchell* at 12C).
[35] Where the tenant died before the introduction of the modern Case G by the amendments made to the 1984 Act and the three months following the tenant's death expired under the old regime it is submitted that the effect of the post-1984 provisions is not to revive the landlord's opportunity to serve a notice to quit despite the absence of a "relevant notice" within the meaning of the current Case G. It is submitted that the better view is that such a revival was not intended by Parliament and that under the pre-1984 law, once the tenant died and the landlord failed within three months to serve a notice to quit, the opportunity

carrying on the farming will be regarded as the agent or agents of the person or persons in whom the tenancy is legally vested for the purpose of service.[36] A person who leaves a will, but appoints no executors, probably dies intestate for this purpose.[37] The best course, if it is doubtful whether the tenant died intestate or not, is to serve notice on the Public Trustee[38] and on the person actually in control of the holding and managing the farming; the notice to the latter should be addressed as to the personal representatives of the deceased tenant. The notice addressed to the Public Trustee should not describe him as a personal representative; although the tenancy vests in him on intestacy, he does not actually *become* a personal representative. It is important in cases of doubt not to serve notice *only* on the President as this would be completely ineffective if the tenancy had vested in executors.[39]

Joint tenancies and succession If there has been a joint tenancy of the holding Case G and the succession scheme apply on the death of the surviving joint tenant.[40]   **12.81.3**

Response to Case G notice to quit Arbitration is not available to resolve disputes in regard to the application of Case G.[41] Executors or administrators receiving a Case G notice to quit must therefore check the notice to see whether it is valid at common law and, if it is not, they may challenge it through the Courts. If however it appears to be valid there is no opportunity for challenge and they will no doubt direct their minds to the service of appropriate claims notices for compensation including in relation to fixtures and milk quota.[42] If following the tenant's death there is no notice to quit and none is received within the three months following a relevant notice from the executors, the executors' tenancy may yet be brought to an end by a successful succession application.[43] Where a Case G notice to quit has been served and there is an application by way of succession the procedure has been dealt with separately for convenience.[44]   **12.81.4**

---

to rely on Case G was extinguished so as to be incapable of subsequent revival in the absence of express words to that effect. It is impossible to see why Parliament should have intended otherwise and submitted that the Courts should not so find.

[36] See *Egerton v. Rutter* [1951] 1 K.B. 472; *Harrowby v. Snelson* [1951] 1 All E.R. 140; *Wilbraham v. Colclough* [1952] 1 All E.R. 979. See also 1986 Act, s. 93(3) and *Sweeny v. Sweeney* (1876) I.R. 10 C.L. 375 at 379.

[37] *Harper v. Taylor* (1950) 100 L.J. 108,CC. An unsuspected assent could be awkward.

[38] Formerly service was directed to be upon the President of the Family Division. See now Practice Direction [1995] 3 All E.R. 192. The address is P.O. Box 3010, London WC2B 6JS, Telephone 0171–664-7196.

[39] See the unfortunate case of *Thorlby v. Olivant* [1960] E.G.D. 257.

[40] Sched. 3, Part I, Case G; s. 35(1)(3). It is probably not essential for a notice to quit to state expressly that it is being served on the death of the survivor of joint tenants (see *per* Buckley J. in *Jenkin R. Lewis Ltd v. Kerman* [1971] Ch. 477 at 487) but it is desirable to do so. The wording of Case G (reproducing earlier legislation) avoids the necessity for all the joint tenants to die in the three months before the giving of the notice to quit; see *Woodward v. Earl of Dudley* [1954] Ch. 283.

[41] It is not one of the four cases to which arbitration applies (A, B, D and E).

[42] See generally Chapter 13 and in relation to milk quota, Chapter 19.

[43] See Chapter 14 and Procedural Table 8: Succession on death where no Case G notice to quit is served.

[44] See Table 7: Succession on death where Case G notice to quit has been served.

12.81.5 Case G: disturbance compensation Neither basic nor additional compensation for disturbance is payable where section 26(1) is excluded by virtue of Case G.[45]

12.82 Case H: Amalgamation or reshaping of agricultural unit[46]

"The notice to quit is given by the Minister and—

(a) the Minister certifies in writing that the notice to quit is given in order to enable him to use or dispose of the land for the purpose of effecting any amalgamation (within the meaning of section 26(1) of the Agriculture Act 1967) or the reshaping of any agricultural unit, and

(b) the instrument under which the tenancy was granted contains an acknowledgment signed by the tenant that the tenancy is subject to the provisions of this Case (or to those of Case H in section 2(3) of the Agricultural Holdings (Notices to Quit) Act 1977 or of section 29 of the Agriculture Act 1967)."

This Case enables the Minister to recover possession of land let temporarily pending its use for the effecting of amalgamations or the reshaping of an agricultural unit. Historically the same provisions applied to notices given by a rural development board, but only one such board was established (the Northern Pennines Rural Development Board) and this was later abolished.[47] Case H in section 2(3) of the 1977 Act was the predecessor of the present Case H. The original provisions were in section 29(4) of the Agriculture Act 1967. If the Minister's certificate is given in writing and the instrument granting the tenancy has contained the acknowledgment mentioned in Case H(b), the notice to quit will be excluded from section 26(1) of the Act. It is not provided that the certificate is to be contained in the notice to quit; it appears to be effective whether contained in the notice to quit or in a separate document, provided that the latter clearly refers to and identifies the notice. It should be noted that "agricultural unit" means land which is an agricultural unit for the purposes of the Agriculture Act 1947.[48]

Arbitration is not provided for any disputes relating to this Case. Basic compensation for disturbance is payable, but additional compensation is excluded.[49]

12.83 Scope of arbitration machinery: restriction to Cases A, B, D, E.
Where a tenant wishes to contest the reason stated in a notice to quit given for one or more of the reasons stated in Cases A, B, D and E he is entitled to demand arbitration which is the only available means of challenge to those reasons.[50]

---

[45] s. 61(1).
[46] Sched. 3, Part I.
[47] By the Northern Pennines Rural Development Board (Dissolution) Order 1971 (S.I. 1971 No.224).
[48] s. 96(1). For discussion as to the meaning of "agricultural unit" in connection with succession see s. 36(3)(a) and para. 14.42 below.
[49] s. 61(2).
[50] See art. 9 of the Agricultural Holdings (Arbitration on Notices) Order 1987 (S.I. 1987

Limited types of general challenge can be pursued in the Courts.[51] Reference is made to the following Procedural Tables:

Table 2: Notices to Quit: Cases A, B and E;
Table 4: Notices to Quit under Case D following notice to pay rent;
Table 5: Notice to Quit: Case D and Notice to do work of repair, maintenance or replacement;
Table 6: Notice to Quit under Case D following notice to remedy not including work of repair maintenance or replacement.

Each of these Cases has been discussed above[52]. The original regulation governing arbitration on notices to quit, the Agriculture (Control of Notices to Quit) Regulations 1948,[53] regulation 4, was not mandatory but permissive as was shown in *Budge v. Hicks*,[54] and in *Jones v. Gates*.[55] It is interesting, in view of the mandatory character of article 9, to note that in *Paddock Investments Ltd v. Lory*.[56] Goulding J. and the Court of Appeal appeared to accept that there was jurisdiction to grant declaratory relief by originating summons.

Arbitration on notice to quit: when applicable 12.84

The arbitration procedure following the service of a notice to quit applies[57] where it is stated in the notice that it is given for one or more of the reasons specified in Cases A, B, D or E and the tenant wishes to contest any of the reasons so stated. It is provided that he *shall* then within one month after the service of the notice to quit serve on the landlord notice in writing requiring the question to be determined by arbitration under the 1986 Act. There is no prescribed form for the tenant's notice requiring arbitration, but it should obviously follow closely the wording of the relevant article.[58] If necessary, it should expressly reserve any rights which the tenant does not wish to prejudice by requiring arbitration, *e.g.* a contention that the notice is bad at common law.

Time-limit for appointment of arbitrator: 1987 Order, Article 10 12.85

A time-limit for the appointment of an arbitrator to determine questions under Article 9 was introduced in 1984 and amended in 1987. It is now provided that a notice under article 9 requiring arbitration under the 1986 Act shall cease to be effective three months after the date of service of that notice unless, before the expiry of those three months, either an arbitrator has been appointed by agreement between the parties or, in default of such an agreement, an application has been made by the tenant or the landlord under paragraph 1 of Schedule 11 to the 1986

No.710).
[51] See paras 12.46 and 12.47 above.
[52] Case A at para. 12.49; Case B at paras 12.50–12.50.4; Case D at paras 12.52 to 12.75 and Case E at paras 12.76 to 12.77.
[53] S.I. 1948 No.190.
[54] [1951] 2 K.B. 335 at 340, 342, 343.
[55] [1954] 1 W.L.R. 222 at 226.
[56] (1975) 236 E.G. 803.
[57] See art. 9 of the Agricultural Holdings (Arbitration on Notices) Order 1987 (S.I. 1987 No.710).
[58] For a suggested form, see below Form 33 in Part V of this work.

Act for the appointment of an arbitrator.[59] Thus unless the tenant secures agreement to the appointment of an arbitrator or himself applies for an appointment within the time-limit he will lose his right to contest any reason stated in the notice to quit. As to when precisely the arbitrator is appointed, there is now a considerable body of case law.[60]

12.86 **Service of counter-notice under section 26(1) by tenant: 1987 Order, Article 11**

Article 11 of the Arbitration on Notices Order provides that where there has been an arbitration under article 9 in respect of a notice to quit which is capable of taking effect either as a notice to quit to which section 26(2) of the 1986 Act applies or in the alternative as a notice to quit to which section 26(1) of that Act applies, and, in consequence of the arbitration, the notice to quit takes effect as a notice to quit to which section 26(1) applies, the time within which a counter-notice may be served by the tenant on the landlord under section 26(1) of the 1986 Act shall be one month from the termination of the arbitration. The present wording, embodying in a clearer form an amendment first made in 1972[61] fully meets criticisms[62] of earlier versions of the order,[63] which implied that a landlord who had failed to establish his contention in arbitration proceedings could automatically in all circumstances rely on his notice to quit taking effect as an ordinary unqualified notice unless the tenant served counter-notice under section 26(1). The better opinion before the 1972 amendment was that, in the light of the views expressed in *Cowan v. Wrayford*,[64] the landlord could rely on this happy result only if he had made it quite clear by serving a notice to quit expressed to be in the alternative (or by serving two notices) that, if he failed under what was then section 24(2)[65] of the 1948 Act, he would rely on the notice to quit as an unqualified notice to which the then section 24(1)[66] applied. The present article 11 refers clearly to cases where (the landlord having failed in the arbitration but having taken the precaution of serving a notice to quit in the alternative[67]) the tenant needs to protect himself against the landlord's second shot by serving a counter-notice under section 26(1) of the 1986 Act within one month of the receipt of the arbitration award.[68] The landlord may, instead, serve two separate notices, to each of which the tenant would need to respond in the appropriate way.

---

[59] Agricultural Holdings (Arbitration on Notices) Order 1987 (S.I. 1987 No.710), art. 10.
[60] See paras 16.21–16.23 below.
[61] By the Agriculture (Notices to Quit) (Miscellaneous Provisions) Order 1972 (S.I. 1972 No.1207), art. 5(2).
[62] See *Mills v. Edwards* [1971] 1 Q.B. 379,CA. The wording had been previously criticised by text books: see the 12th edition of the present work, p.75.
[63] See art. 10 of the Agriculture (Notices to Remedy and Notices to Quit) Order 1964 (S.I. 1964 No.706) and, earlier, art. 7 of the Agricultural Land Tribunals and Notices to Quit Order 1959 (S.I. 1959 No.81).
[64] [1953] 1 W.L.R. 1340,CA.
[65] Subsequently s. 2(2) of the 1977 Act and now s. 26(2) of the 1986 Act.
[66] Subsequently s. 2(1) of the 1977 Act and now s. 26(1) of the 1986 Act.
[67] *i.e.* under the appropriate Case and, in the alternative, as a notice to which s. 26(1) applies.
[68] A counter-notice under s. 26(1) has normally to be served within one month of the giving of the notice to quit. Article 11 allows it to be served within one month from the

Arbitration on notice to quit: suspension of notice to quit during proceedings: 1987 Order, Article 12

12.87

There is an *automatic* suspension of the operation of the landlord's notice to quit during the period of three months allowed[69] for the appointment of an arbitrator by agreement or for making an application under paragraph 1 of Schedule 11 for an appointment in default of agreement; and if such an appointment or application is duly made the automatic suspension continues until the termination of the arbitration,[70] *i.e.* until the date when the arbitrator's award is delivered to the tenant.[71] This means that if no such appointment or application is made within that time-limit the automatic suspension of the operation of the notice to quit ceases and the tenancy is no longer preserved from termination. This somewhat drastic result of laxity in proceeding with the arrangements for arbitration should be appreciated by the tenant and his advisers. On the other hand, if the appointment or application is duly made, the tenancy is automatically preserved (without any order by the arbitrator) if it would otherwise perish before delivery of the award.

Postponement of operation of notice to quit after termination of arbitration: 1987 Order, Article 13

12.88

Article 13 of the Arbitration on Notices Order deals both with the postponement of a notice to quit by order of an arbitrator and postponement by order of an Agricultural Land Tribunal, although it is in a group of articles concerned otherwise only with arbitration. Article 13 complements article 12 and assumes that the arbitration has taken place and that the landlord has succeeded in establishing his ground under the appropriate Case, so that the notice to quit has effect in consequence of the arbitration. The arbitrator is empowered, where the notice to quit would, but for article 13, come into operation on or within six months after the termination of the arbitration, to postpone the termination of the tenancy for a period not exceeding 12 months.[72] The postponement may be directed by the arbitrator either of his own motion or on the application of the tenant made not later than 14 days after the termination of the arbitration. The tenant's application may be made at the arbitration, which is the sensible time to make it. If it is made afterwards a separate hearing may be required and additional costs incurred. The tenant must then give written notice to the landlord of the application and the landlord is entitled to be heard.[73]

Extension of time under notice to remedy after notice to quit: general power to extend: 1987 Order, Article 14

12.89

Article 14 confers on the arbitrator a general power of extension where a notice to quit is stated to be given by reason of the tenant's failure to remedy a breach of any

---

termination of the arbitration, *i.e.* from the delivery of the arbitrator's award to the tenant: Arbitration on Notices Order, art. 2(1).

[69] *i.e.* allowed by art. 10 of S.I. 1987 No.710.
[70] Art. 12 of S.I. 1987 No.710.
[71] *ibid.*, art. 2.
[72] S.I. 1987 No.710, art. 13(1). There is no prescribed or other suggested form: as long as the request is clear it suffices.
[73] S.I. 1987 No.710, art. 13(2).

term or condition of his tenancy within the time specified in the notice to remedy or within that time as extended by the landlord or by an extension of time already given by the arbitrator under article 6[74] or under article 14 itself.[75] The following points should be noted in regard to this power.

12.89.1 It applies to a notice to quit given for failure to remedy any breach of the terms and conditions of the tenancy, in contrast with article 15, which contains provisions applicable to a notice given for failure to comply with a notice to do work.

12.89.2 The time as originally specified or extended must have been reasonable—there is no power to transform an originally unreasonable time-limit into a reasonable one.

12.89.3 It must appear to the arbitrator that, notwithstanding that the time as originally specified or as extended was reasonable, it would, in consequence of anything happening before the expiration of that time, have been unreasonable to require the tenant to remedy the breach within that time.

12.89.4 The arbitrator may (a) treat the time as having been extended, or further extended, and may make his award as if the time had not expired, (b) where the breach has not been remedied at the date of the award, extend the time by such period as he considers reasonable, having regard to the length of time which has elapsed since the service of the notice to remedy.

12.89.5 Whether the arbitrator treats the time as having been extended or whether he actually extends the time, the notice to quit which is the subject of this present arbitration must necessarily fail to take effect in so far as the landlord is relying on Case D.[76] (If the arbitrator has treated the time as extended this will be because the tenant has remedied the breach before the date of the award and is to be deemed to have done so before the time-limit has expired, so that the notice to quit for failure to remedy cannot succeed. If the time is actually extended, this means that there has not as yet been a failure to comply with the notice to remedy, so that the present notice to quit cannot take effect. There may, however, be a subsequent failure which can provide the foundation for another notice to quit).

12.89.6 Where the arbitrator makes an order extending the time the award has a twofold effect. In addition to determining that the notice to quit which is the subject of the instant reference is ineffective for the purpose of Case D, the award preserves the validity of the notice to remedy already given by modifying the specified time-limit so that it can function as a foundation for a subsequent notice to quit under Case D in the event of non-compliance.

12.89.7 It should be observed that in the case of a notice to remedy other than a notice to do work there are no provisions (such as those to be mentioned below in connection with article 15)[77] by which the tenancy can be terminated by the

---

[74] See above para. 12.68.

[75] *i.e.* in a previous arbitration under art. 9 on a previous notice to quit.

[76] One must not overlook the possibility that it might still take effect as a simple unqualified notice to quit to which s. 26(1) applies, if, but only if, the landlord makes it clear that he intends to rely, in the alternative, on its so taking effect: see art. 11 of the Arbitration on Notices Order 1987 and para. 12.70 above.

[77] See Arbitration on Notices Order 1987, art. 15(4).

subsequent notice to quit on a date other than the end of a year of the tenancy or on less than 12 months' notice.

Other matters: 1987 Order, Article 15(5) and (6); section 28(2) 12.90

Article 15(5) and (6) safeguard in another respect the remedies of a tenant who has been served with a notice to quit stated to have been given by reason of failure to comply with a notice to do work. In cases where the arbitrator extends the time for remedying breaches, the notice to do work remains alive to provide a foundation for a subsequent notice to quit, although the notice to quit which was the subject of the arbitration has failed. Such a subsequent notice might not contain the essential statement[78] required by section 28(1)(b) of the 1986 Act and thus might fail to satisfy a condition of the tenant's right to serve a counter-notice requiring the Tribunal's consent to the notice to quit. Article 15(5) prevents the tenant's additional remedy from being frustrated because of such a technical oversight. The counter-notice must be served on the landlord within one month of the giving of the subsequent notice to quit (or, if the date specified in that notice for the termination of the tenancy is earlier, before that date). Article 15(6) applies to the proceedings for consent to the subsequent notice to quit the same restrictive provisions about the circumstances which the Tribunal may take into account, in applying the fair and reasonable landlord principle, as are contained in section 28(5).[79]

The words in parenthesis in section 28(2) ("whether as a notice to which section 26(1) above does or does not apply") may at first seem obscure. They have in fact been inserted to avoid a possible trap for the tenant. The landlord may have served a notice to quit framed under Case D and in the alternative as a simple unqualified notice to which section 26(1) applies. In the absence of the words in parentheses it might have been claimed that a counter-notice given under section 28(3) or (4) related only to the notice to quit in so far as it was framed under Case D and that, accordingly, no counter-notice had been served in response to the "simple" notice, so that the latter took effect.

Abolition of rule that notice to quit is invalidated by subsequent contract of sale 12.91

The 1984 Act abolished the provision, dating back to 1919, by which a notice to a tenant to quit an agricultural holding, or land comprised in it, was rendered void if during its currency a contract was made for the sale of the landlord's interest in the land affected by the notice or any part of it. The provision, of which judges professed themselves unable to discover the true object or the mischief it was intended to remedy, originated in the Agricultural Land Sales (Restriction of Notices to Quit) Act 1919 and was reproduced in a succession of Acts ending with section 7 of the 1977 Act. It had become a trap and an embarrassment and its disappearance occasioned no regret.[80]

---

[78] That it was "given by reason of the tenant's failure to comply with a notice to do work".
[79] See para. 12.74 above.
[80] For abolition, see 1984 Act, s. 10(2) and Sched. 4. For the old learning, see the 12th edition of this work, pp.93–96 and 287–289.

12.92 Protection of members of reserve and auxiliary forces
The security of tenure provisions and machinery of the 1986 Act are modified in certain respects in the interests of persons serving in the reserve and auxiliary forces, *i.e.* in most kinds of service in HM Forces other than regular service.[81] The modifications are to be found in Schedule 5 to the 1986 Act and the relevant statutory instruments.[82]

12.93 Protection of members of reserve and auxiliary forces: conditions
These concessions in favour of the servicemen apply where:

(1) the serviceman tenant is the tenant of an agricultural holding which comprises such a dwelling-house as is mentioned in section 10 of the Rent Act 1977, that is to say, a dwelling-house occupied by the person responsible for the control (whether as a tenant or as servant or agent of the tenant) of the farming of the holding[83];

(2) the tenant is performing a period of relevant service other than a short period of training[84];

(3) during his "period of residence protection" he is given a notice to quit the holding or a part to which Schedule 5 applies.[85]

12.94 Protection of members of reserve and auxiliary forces: concessions

12.94.1 The tenant who receives a notice to quit when the above conditions are satisfied may serve a counter-notice under section 26(1) of the 1986 Act requiring the consent of the Agricultural Land Tribunal notwithstanding the existence of any such circumstances as are mentioned in Cases B to G in Schedule 3. If the Tribunal are satisfied that such circumstances exist, however, they may, subject to the next sub-paragraph, consent to the operation of the notice to quit although they are not satisfied that the landlord has established any of the grounds in section 27(3)(a) to (f) of the 1986 Act.[86]

12.94.2 In deciding whether to give or withhold consent to the notice to quit the Tribunal are required to consider (a) to what extent (if at all) the existence of the circumstances mentioned in Cases B to G or in section 27(3) is directly or indirectly attributable to the serviceman's performing or having performed the period of service in question, and (b) to what extent (if at all) the giving of such consent during the period of protection would cause special hardship in view of the circumstances directly or indirectly attributable to the serviceman's performing or

---

[81] For "relevant service", see Sched. 5, para. 1 and the Reserve and Auxiliary Forces (Protection of Civil Interests) Act 1951, s. 64(1) and Sched. 1.
[82] See the Agricultural Holdings (Arbitration on Notices) Order 1987, art. 17 and the Reserve and Auxiliary Forces (Agricultural Tenants) Regulations 1959 (S.I. 1959 No.84).
[83] Sched. 5, para. 2(2).
[84] Para. 1 and para. 2(1)(a).
[85] Para. 2(1)(b), Sched. 5 applies to a part which consists or comprises a dwelling-house occupied by the person responsible for the control (whether as tenant or as servant or agent of the provision) of the farming of the holding: *ibid*, para. 2(2)(a) and (b).
[86] *ibid.*, para. 3(1), and see as to those grounds paras 12.35–40 above.

having performed that period of service. Having given such consideration to these matters, it is provided that the Tribunal shall withhold their consent unless in all the circumstances they consider it reasonable to give it.[87]

12.94.3 The provisions in the last sub-paragraph apply even if the notice to quit has been given before the beginning of the tenant's period of residence protection, provided that the Tribunal have not made their decision before that date.[88]

12.94.4 If it appears to the Tribunal, on the landlord's application for consent, that the notice to quit was given for one or more of the reasons specified in Case B, D or E and it is expedient that any question arising out of these reasons should be determined by arbitration between the landlord and the tenant before the Tribunal decide whether to grant or withhold consent, they may require that the question be determined accordingly.[89]

12.94.5 The chairman of the appropriate Tribunal is empowered to direct that a fit person may be authorised to serve a counter-notice under section 26(1) of the 1986 Act on behalf of a serviceman who is serving abroad. The chairman is also empowered to direct that such a person should be deemed to be authorised to perform any necessary act or conduct any necessary proceedings consequential on the service of the counter-notice on behalf of the absent serviceman. "Abroad" means outside the United Kingdom.[90]

---

[87] 1986 Act, para. 3(2).
[88] *ibid.*, para. 4. The provisions in question are to apply "with the necessary modifications".
[89] Art. 17(2) of the Agricultural Holdings (Arbitration on Notices) Order 1987. Art. 17(3) modifies art. 9 to conform with the concessions to servicemen and art. 17(4) provides that art. 11 shall not apply but that the tenant may serve a counter-notice one month from the termination of the arbitration.
[90] Reserve and Auxiliary Forces (Agricultural Tenants) Regulations 1959 (S.I. 1959 No.84).

CHAPTER 13

COMPENSATION AND CUSTOM

13.1   General introduction

13.2   Mandatory nature of compensation

13.5   Termination of tenancy of part of holding

13.11 Compensation for disturbance

13.41 Compensation for improvements and tenant-right matters

13.43 Old improvements

13.51 Tenant-right

13.57 New improvements

13.75 High farming claims

13.80 Landlord's compensation for dilapidations and general deterioration

13.107 Custom

13.115 Settlement of claims on termination of tenancy

13.123 Writing down schemes

PROCEDURAL TABLES RELATING TO COMPENSATION

Part VI of this work, Table 11, sets out the timetable which relates to the making of the various compensation claims. In fact Table 11 also includes the timetabling for fixtures, which are dealt with in Chapter 10 and compensation for milk quotas which is dealt with in Chapter 19. Table 11 is designed to allow the practitioner a cross-check to make sure that the relevant notices are served in time since some must be served before the tenancy terminates and others may be served after that point.

General Introduction

Part V of the Agricultural Holdings Act 1986 sets out the main types of compensation available on termination of a protected tenancy, being compensation to the tenant or to the landlord as the case may be. This Chapter deals with statutory compensation and also the relationship between custom and statutory compensation. That relationship has historically been somewhat complex but it is unlikely that nowadays many of those complexities raise live problems. This Chapter also deals with what survives of customary rights. It is convenient to deal with surviving custom here partly because of the interrelationship with the statutory provisions and partly because some of the more important customs relate **13.1**

COMPENSATION AND CUSTOM

to termination of the tenancy and quitting the land. The intention is to cover in sequence not only the types of statutory claim and custom but also the means by which termination claims can be resolved. Various provisions described by the statute as supplemental are dealt with first on the basis that they apply more or less generally. The reader is referred to the contents summary for this Chapter.

Compensation in relation to milk quotas and the Agriculture Act 1986 is dealt with separately in Chapter 19. The procedural timetable concerning compensation claims should be consulted in relation to the service of claims notices, in respect of which the periods differ depending on the type of claim.

Old improvements continue to feature in this edition even though the number of tenancies to which the relevant rules apply must now be few. The law makes provision for these items and the authors did not feel able simply to ignore those parts of the statute.

13.2 Mandatory nature of compensation: section 78

Save as mentioned below,[1] where the 1986 Act provides for compensation a landlord or tenant is entitled to compensation in accordance with those provisions and not otherwise, and is so entitled notwithstanding any agreement to the contrary.[2] This very important rule, which invalidates any agreement varying, subtracting from, postponing, frustrating the enforcement of, or otherwise impairing the statutory rights to compensation, is subject only to the cases where the Act itself expressly permits some variation in the statutory provisions. The rule must otherwise be strictly applied. Thus a clause which purports to cut down any relevant time-limit for claiming compensation would be void.[3] A clause which purports to enable a landlord to resume possession of part of a holding without notice, or subject to a length of notice too short to permit the tenant to give notice of intention to claim under section 60(6)(a) or section 70(2)(a) is void as an attempt to curtail the tenant's rights.[4] On the same principle, a forfeiture clause is void if it

---

[1] See para. 13.3.
[2] s. 78(1).
[3] *Cathcart v. Chalmers* [1911] A.C. 246. Here the HL in a Scottish appeal unanimously declared void a contractual clause which required the tenant to make his compensation claim before the last month of the tenancy whereas the Agricultural Holdings Act 1900 provided that the tenant "shall" be entitled to compensation and the Agricultural Holdings (Scotland) Act 1883 provided that no claim shall be made after determination of the tenancy.
[4] In *Re Disraeli Agreement* (1939) 1 Ch. D. 382, Crossman J., was adopted and applied by Streatfield J. in *Coates v. Diment* (1951) 1 All E.R. 890 the former case being decided under the Agricultural Holdings Act 1923 and the latter under the 1948 Act. Sometimes an agreement will provide that a tenancy may be determined on "not less than" a stipulated period of time, usually by way of a notice to be served prior to the exercise of a right to forfeit. In these circumstances it is submitted that the clause may be valid provided that it would authorise the service of a prior notice sufficiently long to permit the tenant to serve his own claims notice one month before the termination/exercise of the forfeiture. Sometimes such a notice to be served by the landlord is described as a notice "in writing prior to" the exercise of the right to forfeit. On this form of words it is possible that any individual notice given may or may not, whilst complying with the contract, also allow the tenant the requisite period within which to make his own claim. It is submitted that with this form of words the clause itself will not be struck down at the outset but that the individual service of notices by the landlord may be struck down if in fact an insufficient

does not provide for a notice of re-entry of sufficient length to enable the tenant to give notice of intention to make such claims.[5] Although an agreement which cuts down or frustrates the statutory right to compensation is void, it may sometimes be legitimate to arrange matters so that the right to compensation never arises, *e.g.* to provide that a holding is not to be treated as a market garden, with the object of excluding any possible claim for fruit trees and bushes.[6] But this proposition probably cannot be pressed too far.[7]

It is unclear how far the courts would uphold an agreement by the tenant to make no improvements on his holding. It may be argued that such an agreement by the tenant did not cut down rights to compensation, but merely prevented rights from coming into existence. Conversely it could equally well be argued that such a clause falls foul of the very general terms of section 78(1) which has already struck down in their entirety clauses having adverse impact on a tenant's possible claim, although the clause itself was designed for completely different purposes. It may perhaps be that the resolution of this problem hinges on the precise improvement in question and that in certain circumstances the general clause may be unenforceable but that it is not wholly void. Thus there are improvements for which landlord's consent is required and without it no compensation is available.[8] If the landlord, by refusing consent, is entitled to stop any compensation accruing, why should he not be entitled to stipulate that the improvement in question should not be done at all? Clearly, by contrast, there are other circumstances where either no consent is required from the landlord[9] or, if the landlord refuses his consent, the consent of the Tribunal may be substituted.[10] In these two latter instances it is suggested that the bar on making improvements be treated as unenforceable: Schedule 8, Part 1 states that no consent is required and section 64(1) states that in relation to those matters compensation shall be payable; in relation to long term improvements section 67(6) states that the approval of the Tribunal shall have effect "as if it were the consent of the landlord, and any terms subject to which the approval was given shall have effect as if they were contained in an agreement in writing between the landlord and the tenant". The difficulties of a contractual prohibition being enforceable in some circumstances but not in others are appreciated but may be said to be justified by the different treatments of different types of improvement.[11]

Section 78(1) only limits the rights of landlords and tenants where other

---

period is allowed to the tenant before the right to forfeit is exercised.
[5] *Parry v. Million Pigs Ltd* (1980) 260 EG 281. Ewbank J. applying *Coates v. Diment* (above) to a forfeiture clause.
[6] *Re Masters and Duveen* [1923] 2 K.B. 729, where the CA held that before clauses restricting compensation were to be struck down the condition precedent that the letting was agreed to be a market garden had to be satisfied.
[7] See discussion in Lely and Aggs, *Agricultural Holdings* (5th ed.) pp. 164–166.
[8] See para. 13.61.
[9] Short term improvements: see para. 13.63.
[10] See in relation to long term improvements para. 13.62.
[11] In other words the distinction between one set of circumstances and another arises from the difference in the way in which the statute treats different types of improvement and not simply from the facts in the individual case. In that sense there is a real difference between the discussion in relation to improvements and the invalidity affecting a forfeiture clause expressed to be exercisable on three weeks' notice, which will be a bad clause even

provisions of the Act provide a specific remedy and does not, therefore, prevent a landlord from bringing an action for damages for breaches of covenant during the currency of the tenancy.[12] It is sometimes overlooked that an agreement for the surrender of a tenancy may be in conflict with section 78(1) if, in addition to recording the agreement to surrender, it purports to modify the statutory rights to compensation which will arise on the termination of the tenancy.[13]

13.3 Permitted exclusion of compensation: sections 78(2), 66(4), 67(2), 71(3) and 81(1)

Section 78(2) Section 78(2) expressly provides that where the landlord and the tenant agree in writing on such a variation of the terms of the tenancy in regard to permanent pasture as can be made by an arbitrator under section 14, the agreement may exclude compensation in the same way as section 76(1)(a) excludes it where the variation is made by order of the arbitrator.[14]

Section 66(4) Substituted compensation for matters within Schedule 8 Part II.[15]

Section 67(2) Conditions as to compensation where the landlord consents to long term improvements are validated by section 67(2).[16]

Section 71(3) Section 71(3) gives the landlord the opportunity to opt for contractual compensation for deterioration of particular parts of the holding.[17]

Section 81(1) Fair and reasonable compensation agreed by contract in writing for an improvement in relation to market gardens overrides statutory compensation.[18]

13.4 Non-statutory compensation unenforceable without an agreement in writing: section 78(3)

Section 78(3) makes it clear that it is perfectly legitimate for the landlord and tenant to provide, by means of an agreement in writing, for compensation in cases where the Act does not provide for compensation. The requirement that such additional compensation must be provided for by an agreement in writing does not apply to a claim by a tenant in respect of a tenant-right matter where the tenant has not elected for the appropriate statutory basis of compensation as regards the tenant-right matters in Schedule 8, Part II.[19] In such a case the tenant may be entitled

---

though in the particular case the landlord may actually give six weeks' notice.

[12] *Kent v. Conniff* [1953] 1 Q.B. 361 at 371 (Singleton L.J.), 374 (Birkett L.J.). Where the landlord's claim for forfeiture during the term was refused the CA allowed a claim for damages despite the continuance of the tenancy, rejecting the suggestion that Parliament had limited the landlord's opportunity of claiming his loss to the time when the tenant actually quits.

[13] See para. 13.120 below.

[14] Under s. 14(4).

[15] See para. 13.68.

[16] See in relation to Sched. 7, Part I para. 13.61 below.

[17] See paras 13.83–13.87.

[18] See para. 15.27.

[19] s. 78(3) and Sched. 12, para. 9.

by virtue of custom to compensation; his customary right is preserved from abolition by the saving reference in section 77 to Schedule 12, paragraph 8(c) of which dispenses with the need for an agreement in writing. In cases where the customary basis of compensation is not thus preserved it is open to the parties, if they wish, to embody in a written agreement compensation provisions of the kind which formerly derived their force from custom, in so far as they are not covered by the matters specified in Schedule 8, Part II.[20]

Termination of tenancy of part of holding: section 74 13.5
Section 74 provides for the position in regard to compensation generally when the landlord lawfully resumes possession of part of the holding. This covers compensation for improvements and tenant-right as well as disturbance.[21] By section 74(4) references in the 1986 Act to the termination of the tenancy of, or of a part of, a holding include references to the resumption of possession of a part of a holding in the circumstances mentioned in the four cases set out below.

(1) Resumption under section 31
Although section 74(1) uses the expression "resumes possession"[22] and does not mention a notice to quit by the landlord, in fact section 74(1) operates only where a notice to quit is given by the landlord, and as a result of a well-established principle,[23] possession of part cannot be resumed by the landlord without notice to the tenant, and, indeed, without such a length of notice as will enable him in his turn, if he so desires, to serve on the landlord the notice of not less than a month required to assert rights under section 60(6)(a) or section 70(2)(a), as the case may be. Where a part of a holding is resumed by virtue of section 31(1) the provisions of the Act in regard to compensation apply to that part as if it were a separate holding which the tenant had quitted in consequence of a notice to quit.[24] A notice to quit under section 31 alone does not dispense with a full 12 months' notice, but it may do so if the notice is also under a clause in the contract of tenancy.

(2) Resumption by virtue of section 43
In this case, although the notice to quit given to the tenant under Case G, following the death of the tenant, was a notice to quit the entire holding, the Tribunal, on an application by a person wishing to become tenant, has consented to the operation of the notice to quit in relation to a part of the holding only. The resulting notice to quit part, which would be invalid at common law, is given

---

[20] *e.g.* a provision for an offgoing or away-going crop of winter wheat, in effect a cash payment based on the estimated value of the crop in accordance with rules laid down by the local agricultural valuers' association.

[21] In relation to compensation for disturbance see also para. 13.16 below.

[22] Section 27(2) of the 1923 Act, from which s. 60 of the 1948 Act and s. 74 of the 1986 Act are derived, was defectively drafted. It said in effect that the tenant was to get compensation if the landlord wrote him a letter of intention to resume possession. The defect was corrected in the 1948 Act.

[23] See **Re Disraeli Agreement** [1939] Ch. 382, **Coates v. Diment** [1951] 1 All E.R. 890, and **Parry v. Million Pigs Ltd** (1980) 260 E.G. 281: see para. 13.2 above.

[24] s. 74(1). It is assumed that the tenant in this case has given no counter-notice under s. 32 of the Act.

validity by statute[25] and the provisions of the Act as to compensation apply to the part as if it were a separate holding.[26]

(3) Resumption under clause in contract of tenancy

Here again, the compensation provisions of the Act apply to the part as if it were a separate holding, but a direction is added that the arbitrator must, in assessing the compensation, take into consideration any benefit or relief allowed to the tenant under the contract of tenancy in respect of the resumed land. This direction is, however, qualified; it is not to apply to the amount of "additional compensation" under section 60(2)(b).[27]

(4) Resumption of part by a person entitled to a severed part of reversion: section 140 of the Law of Property Act 1925

Until the anomaly was rectified by the Agricultural Holdings Act 1984,[28] a person served with a notice to quit part of the holding by a person entitled to a severed part of the reversionary estate in the holding[29] was not entitled to any compensation if he quitted that part.[30] He could qualify for compensation by "enlarging" the notice to quit the part into a notice to quit the entire holding, by serving counter-notices under section 32(b) of the 1948 Act[31] on all the persons severally entitled to the severed parts of the reversion. In that case he could claim against them in respect of the entirety as together constituting the landlord. If, however, he decided to quit the part only, he forfeited compensation. The amendment made by the 1984 Act is now embodied in section 74(3) of the 1986 Act, which provides that, in the circumstances mentioned, the provisions of the Act with respect to compensation shall apply as if the part in question were a separate holding which the tenant had quitted in consequence of the notice to quit, and as if the person resuming possession were the landlord of that holding.[32]

13.6 Compensation where reversionary estate in the holding is severed: section 75

Section 75 is concerned with the severance of the reversion,[33] but, in contrast with the material under paragraph 13.5, it deals with compensation payable to the quitting tenant in respect of the entire holding in a case where the tenancy of the entirety is vested in the tenant but the reversion has been severed and is split

---

[25] s. 43(2).
[26] s. 74(1). There is, of course, no question in this case of any counter-notice under s. 32.
[27] s. 74(2)(a) and (b). It seems fair that a benefit provided for by the contract should be taken into account in assessing the normal compensation. The "additional compensation" for disturbance (s. 60(2)(b)) is in a different category; presumably it is a matter of policy that this sum should not be tampered with in any way. The cases mentioned in para. 13.54 above should be borne in mind under this head also.
[28] 1984 Act, Sched. 3, para. 14.
[29] A notice made valid by s. 140 of the Law of Property Act 1925.
[30] It would have been different if separate tenancies of the separate parts of the holding had been created, but the mere severance of the reversion did not result in the emergence of separate tenancies: see para. 12.20 above.
[31] Now s. 32(1)(b) of the 1986 Act.
[32] s. 74(3).
[33] As to which generally see para. 12.20.

between more than one reversioner. All that section 75 does is to enable the tenant to require, if he so wishes, that any compensation payable to him under the Act in respect of the entirety shall be determined as if the reversionary estate were not so severed.[34] Where the tenant does so require, the arbitrator must, where necessary, apportion the amount awarded between the persons who together constitute the landlord of the holding. Any additional costs of the award caused by the apportionment are to be paid by those persons in such proportions as the arbitrator determines.[35] This provision, of which the drafting was improved by the 1984 Act,[36] is derived from section 17 of the Agriculture Act 1920. It appears that before January 1, 1921, when section 17 of the 1920 Act came into operation, the tenant had to pursue separate claims against the several reversioners in order to recover the total compensation to which he was entitled on quitting the whole holding.[37] The position today seems to be that a tenant of the entirety, on quitting the holding, could pursue the several reversioners under section 74(3) as if they were landlords of separate holdings or could require the total compensation to be determined under section 75 as if the reversionary estate had not been severed. There is an absence of superior court authority on the interpretation of the provision now embodied in section 75,[38] the implications of which are to some extent obscure. Judge Moore Cann in the County Court case of *Weston v. Devonshire (Duke)*[39] held (1) that the liability of the reversioners for the sums apportioned to them is several, not joint and several, and (2) that there is no provision in the section for dealing with counterclaims for dilapidations by some but not all the reversioners, or, even if they all joined in making a counterclaim, for apportioning any amount awarded between them. If section 75 is invoked by a tenant, he should serve all notices in connection with his claims to compensation on all the reversioners concerned.

Restrictions on compensation for things done in compliance with the Act: 13.7
section 76

Although grouped together with other general supplementary provisions in the scheme of Part V of the Act ("Compensation on Termination of Tenancy"), section 76 more logically falls to be mentioned under those parts of this work dealing with compensation for improvements and tenant-right matters. The reader is accordingly referred to paragraph 13.74 below.

---

[34] s. 75(1).
[35] s. 75(2).
[36] 1984 Act, Sched. 3, para. 15. The content was also improved by the omission of the confusing references to the rent not having been apportioned by the tenant's consent or under any statute. The significance of this was obscure; if the implication was that such apportionment *ipso facto* resulted in separate tenancies, it was incorrect.
[37] *Eaton v. Swetenham* [1912] E.G.D. 98, His Honour Judge Moss delivering judgment on a case stated by an arbitrator. The Judge appears to have accepted the submission that the statute intended a compensation claim to be effective on termination only against the person then entitled to the rent and profits, and accordingly he rejected such a claim brought against the original landlord of the entirety who had conveyed away the relevant part of the land.
[38] Its predecessors were s. 17 of the 1920 Act, s. 18 of the 1923 Act and s. 61 of the 1948 Act.
[39] (1923) 12 L.J.C.C.R. 74.

COMPENSATION AND CUSTOM

13.8 No compensation under custom for improvement or tenant right matters: section 77

Section 77 provides for the abolition of customary compensation. This is a matter of some, although diminishing, importance. It is treated separately below.[40]

13.9 Compensation where a tenancy is not binding on a mortgagee

The obscurely drafted and rarely applicable provisions under the above head, which were contained in section 66 of the 1948 Act, were repealed by the 1984 Act.[41]

13.10 Scope for custom

Despite the terms of section 77 abolishing compensation under custom,[42] custom still has a part to play in relation to other matters. This is discussed below.[43] Attention should also be drawn to the terms of section 97, which subject to express contrary provisions of the statute, generally preserves the rights and remedies available under any custom of the country.

COMPENSATION FOR DISTURBANCE

13.11 An overview

The 1986 Act divides compensation for disturbance into basic compensation and additional compensation.[44] "Basic compensation" is the traditional compensation for disturbance which dates from section 4 of the Agricultural Holding Act 1906.[45] "Additional compensation" is the name now given to the "sum to assist in the reorganisation of the tenant's affairs" which was provided by section 9 of the 1968 Act and which was payable only if compensation for disturbance was payable.[46] The principle of compensation for disturbance, which antedates the more modern principle of security of tenure, is that a tenant who quits the holding in consequence of a notice to quit given by his landlord is entitled,[47] subject to certain exceptions,[48] to compensation for his dispossession. The rules relating to basic compensation will be considered first,[49] then the provisions affecting additional compensation.[50]

13.12 Circumstances when disturbance compensation may be available: notice to quit the entirety: section 60

Compensation under section 60 may be available where the tenancy of an agricultural holding terminates by reason of a notice to quit the entirety given by

---

[40] See paras 13.107 and 13.111–13.113.
[41] 1984 Act, s. 10(2) and Sched. 4.
[42] See para. 13.8 above.
[43] See paras 13.107–13.110 and 13.114.
[44] s. 60(2), (3), (4).
[45] This Act never came independently into force. The disturbance provisions were repeated in s. 11 of the 1908 Act, s. 12 of the 1923 Act and s. 34 of the 1948 Act.
[46] In some cases not payable even if compensation for disturbance was payable: see paras 13.18–13.20 below.
[47] See paras 13.12–13.16 and 13.22.
[48] See paras 13.18–13.20 below.
[49] See paras 13.22–13.29 below.
[50] See para. 13.30 below.

the landlord and in consequence the tenant quits.[51] This covers not only periodic tenancies but in addition those tenancies terminated by a landlord's notice under section 3 (fixed term for two years or more) because such a notice is deemed to be a notice to quit.[52] Where a lease ends by the landlord exercising a break clause, his notice given to effect the break is a notice to quit.[53]

As to quitting the holding "in consequence" of the notice to quit see paragraph 13.22 below.

Landlord The landlord when the notice to quit is given may not be the same as when the compensation is payable.[54] An equitable owner, such as a purchaser under an uncompleted contract of sale, may be "landlord" within the definition in section 96(1) but only a legal owner can give a valid notice to quit.[55]

Circumstances when disturbance compensation may be available: term of two years or more terminating under section 4 prior to the term date by reason of the tenant's death: section 4(3)   13.13

In the case of a tenancy granted on or after September 12, 1984 being a fixed term tenancy for two years or more terminated under section 4 by the tenant's death,

---

[51] s. 60(1)(a).
[52] s. 3(2).
[53] *Edell v. Dulieu* [1923] 2 K.B. 247, CA, affirmed at [1924] A.C. 38.
[54] See *Dale v. Hatfield Chase Corporation* [1922] 2 K.B. 282, *Bradshaw v. Bird* [1920] 3 K.B. 144, *Tombs v. Turvey* [1923] 93 L.J.K.B. 785, *Waddell v. Howat* [1925] S.C. 484, *Richards v. Pryse* [1927] 2 K.B. 76, *Farrow v. Orttewell* [1933] Ch. 480. In *Bradshaw v. Bird* landowners let to tenants and thereafter sold the freehold to a purchaser. The tenants gave the purchaser, who was then entitled to the rents and profits, notice of intention to claim compensation. The CA held that the purchaser was "the landlord" within the meaning of the relevant Acts. In *Dale v. Hatfield Chase Corporation* the tenant had given notice to the landlord of his intention to claim compensation for disturbance. Before the appointment of an arbitrator to adjudicate that claim the landlord assigned the reversion. The CA held that the original notice of intention to claim was binding upon the subsequent landlord. In *Tombs v. Turvey* the agricultural tenancy expired on September 29, 1922. In the previous May the landlord had agreed to complete a sale of the reversion on that very date but in fact completion took place subsequently on November 2. By the terms of the contract the rent due on September 29, did not belong to the purchaser. Accordingly the Court of Appeal held that the purchaser was not at the date of the termination of the tenancy the "landlord" within the meaning of the legislation. In *Richards v. Pryse* a tenancy expired on September 29, that being the date named as the date for completion in a prior sale of the reversion with an express provision that the rent be apportioned up to the date of completion. The CA held that "completion" in terms of the apportionment meant the date of actual completion and not the date stipulated by the contract. Accordingly the vendor not the purchaser was the "person entitled to receive the rents and profits" at the expiry of the tenancy and therefore the person required to pay compensation to the tenants. In *Farrow v. Orttewell* the person who had agreed to buy the reversion expectant on the tenancy gave notice to quit before completion had taken place. When the tenant duly gave up possession and then claimed compensation against the person giving the notice the purchaser of the reversion claimed that he was not required to pay. The CA, affirming Bennett J. held first, that before completion the purchaser of the reversion had no right to give notice to quit but that on the facts, secondly, the purchaser was estopped by his conduct from denying the validity of the notice to quit with the result that the tenant was entitled to his compensation.
[55] *Bradshaw v. Bird, Farrow v. Orttewell* (above).

section 4(3) expressly deems the tenancy to terminate by reason of a notice to quit given by the landlord of the holding. Consequently such a case falls within the general principles applicable to a tenancy terminated by landlord's notice to quit.[56]

13.14 **Circumstances when disturbance compensation may be available: tenant's counternotice: section 60**

Where the tenancy of an agricultural holding terminates by reason of a counter-notice given by the tenant under section 32 and the tenant quits in consequence of the counter-notice compensation may be available. The tenant's counter-notice under section 32 is given in response to a landlord's notice to quit part only of the holding.[57] As to the meaning of landlord, see paragraph 13.12 above. As to quitting "in consequence" of the counter-notice see paragraph 13.22 below. In the normal way a tenant faced with a landlord's notice to quit part may consider either a counter-notice to quit the entirety or simply in response quitting that part included within the notice to quit. Each of these situations is dealt with separately below.[58]

13.15 **Landlord's notice to quit part followed by tenant's counternotice to quit the entirety**

Special compensation for disturbance provisions apply where the tenant quits the whole holding in consequence of a counter-notice given by him under section 32, after having been given notice to quit part under section 31 or by a person entitled to a severed part of the reversionary estate in the holding.[59] The tenant will, if the normal conditions are fulfilled, be entitled to compensation for disturbance in respect of the whole holding. If, however, two conditions are present he will receive compensation only in respect of the part of the holding to which the notice to quit actually related. These two conditions are (a) that the part of the holding affected by the notice to quit, together with any part affected by a "relevant previous notice" rendered valid by section 31, is less than one-fourth of the original holding, and (b) that the holding as proposed to be diminished is reasonably capable of being farmed as a separate holding.[60] Where there is no severance of the reversion a "relevant previous notice" means a notice given by the same person who gave the current notice to quit. Where the current notice to quit is given by a person entitled to a severed part of the reversion the "relevant previous notice" means a notice given either by that person or by any other person so entitled.[61]

13.16 **Landlord's notice to quit part followed by tenant quitting part only**

A tenant may be given notice to quit part of the holding in the following cases:

(1) under section 31(1) and (2)[62];

---

[56] See para. 13.12 above.
[57] As to s. 32 see para. 12.21 above.
[58] Paras 13.15–13.16 below.
[59] s. 60(1)(b) and 63(3).
[60] s. 63(3). See paras 13.26 and 13.27 below.
[61] s. 63(4): see para. 13.35 below.
[62] See above para. 12.18 above.

(2) under section 43[63];

(3) under a clause in the contract of tenancy; and

(4) by the owner of a severed part of the reversion.[64]

In cases (1) and (4) the tenant may, if he wishes, cause the notice to quit part to be "enlarged" by virtue of section 32 into a notice to quit the entire holding. In case (2) he cannot, as he is not empowered to alter the determination of the Tribunal, and in case (3) he cannot, as he is bound by the term of his own contract. In cases (2) and (3), therefore, the tenant must, and in cases (1) and (4) he may, treat the notice as being, what on its face it is, a notice to quit part only. If in fact he quits the part only, what is his position in regard to compensation? In cases (1) and (2) the provisions of the 1986 Act in regard to compensation, including compensation for disturbance, apply to the part of the holding as if it were a separate holding which the tenant had quitted in consequence of a notice to quit.[65] In case (3) the provisions as to compensation apply in the same way as in case (1) and (2), but the arbitrator is directed in this case in assessing compensation (except the "additional compensation" for disturbance[66]) to take into consideration any benefit or relief allowed to the tenant under the contract of tenancy[67] in respect of the land resumed by the landlord.[68] In case (4) the provision of the 1986 Act in respect of compensation apply to the part of the holding as if it were a separate holding which the tenant had quitted in consequence of the notice to quit and the person resuming possession were the landlord of that separate holding.[69] Consistently with these provisions it is provided that reference in the 1986 Act to the termination of the tenancy of, or (as the case may be) of part of, a holding includes reference to the resumption of possession of part of a holding in the circumstances described in the above cases.[70]

Circumstances when disturbance compensation not available: surrender, notice to quit by tenant, *Gladstone v. Bower* agreements, forfeiture   13.17

Because of the procedures specified by section 60 as being preconditions for disturbance compensation namely termination in consequence of a landlord's notice to quit or a tenant's counter-notice under section 32 it follows that tenancies which terminate for some other reason or as a result of some other process are not

---

[63] This applies where the Tribunal, in the case of a notice to quit within Case G given by reason of the death of the tenant, give consent in relation to part only of the holding: see para. 14.94 below.
[64] By virtue of s. 140 of the Law of Property Act 1925.
[65] s. 74(1).
[66] s. 60(2)(b).
[67] The early resumption compensation under s. 62 is a statutory, not a contractual, benefit.
[68] s. 74(2)(a) and (b).
[69] s. 74(3). This reproduces an important amendment made by the 1984 Act, Sched. 3, para. 14. Before that amendment the tenant of the entirety served with a notice to quit under s. 140 of the Law of Property Act 1925 could only obtain compensation if he gave a counter-notice to all the persons severally entitled to the severed parts of the reversion, stating that he accepted the notice to quit as a notice to quit the entire holding. If he wished to quit the part only he was not entitled to any compensation. See the 12th edition of this work, pp. 106–107.
[70] s. 74(4).

ones following which disturbance compensation may be claimed. Destruction of the tenancy by surrender, which is a consensual process, disentitles the tenant from claiming disturbance compensation. If the tenant wishes, he may of course negotiate for a capital sum to be paid on surrender, whether or not this capital sum equates to what might otherwise have been claimable following a landlord's notice to quit. In so far as surrender itself appears to be compellable where the parties have agreed it[71] there appears to be no reason why the payment of a capital sum at the time of surrender should not also be enforceable. Where the tenancy terminates by reason of a tenant's notice to quit, no compensation for disturbance is payable since presumably the tenant could choose his time of quitting so as to mitigate or avoid loss. *Gladstone v. Bower* agreements are in truth tenancies falling within the general terms of the 1986 Act as tenancies of an agricultural holding but, because of a loophole, the full scheme of security of tenure is not available.[72] Although other types of compensation may be available, compensation for disturbance is not available because the tenancy terminates not by a landlord's notice but as a result of the effluxion of time and there is no special provision "deeming" a notice to quit to have been served by the landlord.[73] Similarly termination of the tenancy consequent on forfeiture by the landlord falls entirely outside the circumstances giving rise to disturbance compensation under section 60. This result is not, however, draconian, because of the possibility of relief from forfeiture and also the fact that a successful forfeiture will have been brought about by the tenant's own breach of covenant, alternatively a condition as to the tenant's insolvency, in the normal way.

13.18 Exclusion of disturbance compensation in Cases C, D, E, F and G: section 61(1)

Section 61(1) provides that no disturbance compensation at all, neither basic nor additional, is to be payable where the landlord's notice is given under Case C (certificate of bad husbandry),[74] D (remediable breach),[75] E (irremediable breach),[76] F (insolvency of tenant),[77] or G (death of the tenant).[78]

13.19 Exclusion of additional compensation in Cases A and H: section 61(2)

Basic compensation is available but additional compensation is excluded where the relevant notice to quit falls within Case A (smallholdings tenant reaching the age of 65)[79] or H (notice to quit by the Minister for the purpose of amalgamations or the reshaping of agricultural units).[80]

---

[71] *Elsden v. Pick* [1980] 1 WLR 898, discussed at para. 12.4 above.
[72] See para. 9.20 above.
[73] Contrast for other fixed term tenancies ss 3(2) and 4(3) discussed in paras 13.12 and 13.13 respectively above.
[74] See para. 12.51 above.
[75] See para. 12.52–12.75 above.
[76] See paras 12.76–12.77 above.
[77] See para. 12.78 above.
[78] See paras 12.79–12.81.5 above.
[79] See para. 12.49 above.
[80] See para. 12.82 above.

Exclusion of additional compensation depending on landlord's grounds for termination: section 61(3)   13.20

Additional (but not basic) compensation is excluded if the relevant notice to quit contains a statement either that the carrying out of the purpose for which the landlord proposes to terminate the tenancy is desirable on any of the grounds mentioned in paragraphs (a) to (c) of section 27(3) (good husbandry, sound management, agricultural research, etc.) or that the landlord will suffer hardship unless the notice has effect.[81] If the landlord makes an application to the Tribunal for consent to the notice to quit, it is a further condition of the exclusion that the Tribunal should consent to the operation of the notice and state in the reasons for their decision that they are satisfied as to any of the matters mentioned in paragraphs (a), (b), (c) and (e), (e) being that greater hardship would be caused by withholding than by giving consent to the operation of the notice.[82] It will be noted that the additional payment is not excluded where the Tribunal has consented to the notice on the ground mentioned in paragraph (d), namely, for the purpose of allotment. If by any chance the tenant does not serve a counter-notice under section 26(1)(b), the mere statement by the landlord in his notice to quit invoking one of the grounds mentioned above will itself suffice to exclude liability for additional compensation.[83] It is to be noted, however, that there are two sets of circumstances where the prima facie exclusion of additional compensation under the present provision is overridden and the right to such compensation restored.[84]

There are two Scottish decisions raising the question a to whether the statement which is required as a condition of excluding additional compensation can be in a covering letter accompanying the notice to quit although not in the notice itself. It was accepted in both cases that the covering letter could be read with the notice to quit, but in one case the Court of Session was able (by very liberal interpretation) to spell out of the letter a statement as to hardship, whereas in the other case they could not.[85] In a much older English decision the court was prepared to treat a notice to quit as contained in two documents.[86]

---

[81] s. 61(3)(a).

[82] s. 61(3)(b). The difference between the allegation of *hardship* in the notice to quit and the decision as to *greater hardship* by the Tribunal is simply that the determination that the hardship is "greater" is a matter for the Tribunal's judgment.

[83] A tenant who receives a notice to quit which by inadvertence omits the essential statement, on the other hand, must decide whether it would be in his interests to refrain deliberately from serving a counter-notice, and, instead, to quit the holding with the entitlement to basic and additional compensation for disturbance plus any other compensation due to him.

[84] See para. 13.21 below.

[85] *Barns Graham v. Lamont* 1971 S.L.T. 341 (where the court could discern the required statement) and *Copeland v. McQuaker* 1973 S.L.T. 186 (where they felt unable to do so). See also as regards reorganisation payments an article by A.G.M. Duncan in [1973] S.L.T. 141.

[86] *Turton v. Turnbull* [1934] 2 K.B. 197, where the Court of Appeal held that no compensation was payable by the landlord where the reason for giving the notice to quit was set out in an accompanying letter. As to this liberal approach: Scrutton L.J. in *Turton v. Turnbull* at 202 "I am not going to lay down any precise and general rule as to the terms of a notice to quit; it is enough to say that it must make it reasonably clear to the tenant that it is being given for one or more of the reasons mentioned in s. 12. Further, if there are two

13.21 Saving for additional compensation where Tribunal gives certain reasons: section 61(4) and (5)

In the cases described above additional compensation is not payable. Parliament has, however, provided that in certain circumstances a case which prima facie comes within the exclusion is to be excepted from it and will attract such compensation. There are two sets of circumstances where this applies.

The first is where the Tribunal gives more than one reason for consenting to the notice to quit and the reason includes both one which would negate the landlord's liability and also the matter mentioned in section 27(3)(f) (*i.e.* non-agricultural use not falling within Case B). A possible example would be where consent is given on the dual ground of (a) hardship to the landlord and (b) proposed use of private forestry.[87]

The second is where the reason given by the Tribunal consists of or includes that mentioned in section 27(3)(b) (sound management) but the Tribunal would have been satisfied also as to the matter mentioned in section 27(3)(f) if it had been specified in the landlord's application for consent (which it was not). In a case where the Tribunal would have been so satisfied, it is directed to include a statement to that effect in its decision.[88] An example might be a case where the reason given was the interest of sound management, but the Tribunal would have been satisfied that the landlord proposed to use the land for forestry if he had specified this use in his application. This remarkable provision demonstrates the length to which Parliament wished to go to safeguard the tenant where the landlord's reason includes a non-agricultural use (even if unexpressed).

13.22 The right to basic compensation: section 60

The principle is that where the tenancy of an agricultural holding terminates by reason of a notice to quit the whole holding given by the landlord, and in consequence of the notice the tenant quits the holding, the tenant is entitled to compensation for disturbance in accordance with section 60. "In consequence" means that there must be no break in the causal sequence between the giving of the notice and the quitting, and it is a question of fact in any case whether it is unbroken. It may be unbroken despite an interval of time between the notice taking effect and the tenant's departure, and may subsist even if the proximate cause of the departure is the order of a court to give up possession.[89] It has also been held that a tenant who quits in consequence of a notice which is in fact bad but which he accepts as good is entitled to compensation for disturbance.[90]

---

documents they must be connected internally with each other; in this case it is sufficient that they were sent in the same envelope and one of them refers to and is to be read with the other; it is not necessary that each should refer to the other".

[87] s. 61(4).
[88] s. 61(5).
[89] See *Preston v. Norfolk County Council* [1947] K.B. 775, CA, following *Mills v. Rose* (1923) 68 S.J. 420, CA, distinguishing *Cave v. Page* (1923) 67 S.J. 659, and dissenting from *Hendry v. Walker* 1927 S.L.T. 333. See also *Gulliver v. Catt* [1952] 2 Q.B. 308 where the CA applied *Preston v. Norfolk County Council* to the 1948 Act.
[90] See *Westlake v. Page* [1926] 1 K.B. 298 at 304 (Bankes L.J.); *Kestell v. Langmaid* [1950] 1 K.B. 233 acceptance of a bad notice to quit as valid was held by the Court of Appeal to entitle the tenant to compensation. See also *Farrow v. Orttewell* [1933] Ch. 480 where the

Meaning of basic compensation: section 60(2) and (3) 13.23

Basic compensation for disturbance is defined by section 60(3) in an alternative format. The minimum amount of basic compensation, payable without proof of any actual loss, is as specified by sub-paragraph (a)[91] as equivalent to one year's rent of the holding. That sum may be inflated, with proof, to a greater amount as identified by sub-paragraph (b).[92] Subject to compliance with the requirements of section 60(6)[93] sub-paragraph (b) of section 60(3) enables the tenant to claim a maximum of the tenant's actual loss[94] or two years' rent of the holding (whichever is the smaller).

Basic compensation: an amount equal to one year's rent: section 60(3)(a) 13.24

Section 60(3)(a) refers to "an amount equal to one year's rent of the holding at the rate at which rent was payable immediately before the termination of the tenancy". "Rent" is not defined, but it clearly means the total actual amount of rent at the rate payable just before the tenancy ends, including such part as may be attributable to interest on improvements, and probably means the rent that the tenant is legally liable to pay[95] as distinct from a lower rent accepted temporarily on compassionate grounds.[96] Clearly the landlord who, shortly before termination of the tenancy, secures an increase in the level of rental does himself no service as in most cases this will operate to inflate the amount of compensation due on termination, this being to dramatic effect if additional compensation based on four times the current rent is also payable.

Basic compensation: the amount of the tenant's actual loss: section 60(3)(b) 13.25

Section 60(3)(b) contains a somewhat complex formulation for a claim. First, the tenant must comply with the requirements of sub-section (6)[97] and then must demonstrate the amount of his actual loss, the ceiling for the claim being the equivalent of two years rent of the holding. To this maximum basic disturbance compensation, however, may be added any "additional" disturbance compensation to which he may be entitled[98] and any compensation due to him under any other head (*e.g.* compensation for improvement/tenant right).[99]

---

equitable owner served notice to quit and was estopped from denying its validity or the consequent liability to compensation (CA); ***Streat v. Cottey*** [1947] E.G.D. 136, a straightforward application of ***Westlake v. Page*** in the County Court, *cf.* ***Johnston v. Malcolm*** 1923 S.L.T. (Sh.Ct.) 81 and ***Thomas v. NFU Mutual Insurance Society Ltd*** [1961] 1 W.L.R. 386, where Diplock J held that once a tenant had left a holding on termination of the tenancy all rights in the crops were at an end and he had only a compensation claim.

[91] See para. 13.24 below.
[92] See para. 13.25 below.
[93] See paras 13.28–13.29 below.
[94] See paras 13.25–13.27 below.
[95] *i.e.* is compellable to pay: ***Re Howell's Application*** [1972] Ch. 509.
[96] But where there is a binding estoppel preventing the landlord from ever claiming the relevant rent there may be no rent payable so as to found a compensation claim.
[97] See paras 13.28–13.29. For a precedent of the tenant's notice to claim the higher level of basic compensation for disturbance see Form 51 in Part V of this work.
[98] See para. 13.30 below.
[99] s. 60(7).

13.26 Basic compensation: meaning of "the amount of the tenant's actual loss": section 60(5)

"The amount of the tenant's actual loss" is defined by section 60(5) to mean the amount of the loss or expense directly attributable to the quitting of the holding which is unavoidably incurred by the tenant upon or in connection with the sale or removal of his household goods, implements of husbandry, fixtures, farm produce or farm stock on or used in connection with the holding and this is stated to include "any expenses reasonably incurred by him in the preparation of his claim for basic compensation" excluding the costs of any arbitration to determine questions arising under sections 60 or 61. The costs of the arbitration, which are expressly excluded from the calculation by the section, will be dealt with in the arbitrator's award.

13.27 Commentary on loss or expense

Some of the old cases dealing with the item of loss or expense are still applicable, although their importance was diminished when it was enacted that proof of loss was unnecessary unless more than the minimum amount was claimed.[1] Where proof is necessary, the loss or expense must be shown to be caused by the quitting. Where loss is avoidable, indirect or too remote[2] (such as loss from the sale of stock which would have been sold in any case, damage suffered by furniture in transit,[3] or a loss due to an error in valuation[4]) it will be disallowed. Although the fees paid by a tenant for the valuation of his stock before sale was disallowed in a 1912 case,[5] the present words[6] "any expense reasonably incurred by him in the preparation of his claim for basic compensation" seems to cover the normal employment of a professional adviser in connection with the claim.[7] The words "claim for basic compensation" make it clear that the expense of other claims under the Act is not covered.[8] Loss on a forced sale of stock by auction, as compared with a sale in normal circumstances, and even the costs of supplying customary refreshment to those attending the auction, have been held to be covered.[9] Loss due to deterioration of stock on a sale[10] and loss attributable to sheep not tied to the

---

[1] Under the 1923 Act it was necessary to prove *some* loss or expense as a condition of claiming even the minimum compensation: see ***Minister of Agriculture and Fisheries v. Dean*** [1924] 1 K.B. 851 (where the holding was occupied by subtenants); ***Re O'Conner and Brewin's Arbitration*** [1933] 1 K.B. 20 (where the claim failed for insufficiency of the particulars delivered); ***Spreckley v. Leicestershire C.C.*** [1934] 1 K.B. 366; ***McLaren v. Turnbull*** 1942 S.C. 179 (on Scottish 1923 Act). This condition was removed by the 1947 Act and the change was embodied in the 1948 Act.

[2] See ***Re Evans and Glamorgan C.C.*** (1912) 76 J.P. 468 (Joyce J. gives examples of expenses directly attributable to a sale); ***Barbour v. McDouall*** 1914 S.C. 844; ***Keswick v. Wright*** 1924 S.C. 766.

[3] ***Evans v. Lloyd*** [1912] E.G.D. 392.

[4] ***Macgregor v. Board of Agriculture for Scotland*** 1925 S.C. 613.

[5] ***Re Evans and Glamorgan County Council*** (above).

[6] Not in the 1908 Act.

[7] *cf.* ***Dunstan v. Benney*** [1938] 2 K.B. 1, where the CA held that the valuer's fee was a claimable expense.

[8] Thus disposing of an old query: see Lely and Aggs, *Agricultural Holdings* (5th ed.), p.84.

[9] ***Re Evans and Glamorgan County Council*** (above).

[10] ***Barbour v. McDouall*** 1914 S.C. 844.

holding being sold at "break-up" instead of "going concern" value have been allowed.[11] Where the "sale or removal" is unlawful between the landlord and tenant, as where fixtures are removed without compliance with the statutory conditions, consequent loss claimed is not allowable.[12] It has been held in the county court that a tenant who has sublet all the holding except the farmhouse can nevertheless claim on the usual basis for loss in the removal of his household goods from the farmhouse.[13]

Basic compensation: the requirements of section 60(6) as to notice of claim 13.28

By section 60(6)(a) the tenant is required to demonstrate that he has not less than one month before the termination of the tenancy given to the landlord notice in writing of his intention to make a claim for an amount under section 60(3)(b). It was held under earlier provisions that a notice by one only of joint tenants, being the one who in fact suffered loss, was a sufficient notice for this purpose.[14] This view appears now to be accepted.[15] A resumption clause in a contract of tenancy is void if it purports to resume possession without giving sufficient notice to the tenant to enable him, in response, to give the one months' notice required by the present provision.[16] As to the question whether one notice would satisfy both this section and section 83(2) see paragraph 13.37 below. As to what amounts to "not less than one month" some guidance is to be obtained from the case law.[17]

Basic compensation: the requirements of section 60(6) as to an opportunity 13.29
of making a valuation

The tenant must further demonstrate by section 60(6)(b) that he has, before their sale, given to the landlord a reasonable opportunity of making a valuation of any such goods, implements, fixtures, produce or stock as are mentioned as part of his actual claim for loss or expense.[18] It is a question of fact for the arbitrator whether

---

[11] *Keswick v. Wright* 1924 S.C. 766.
[12] *Re Harvey and Mann's Arbitration* (1920) 89 L.J.K.B. 687.
[13] See *Re Sampson and Horsfall* (1921) 10 L.J.C.C.R. 90.
[14] *Howson v. Buxton* (1928) 97 L.J.K.B. 749. Two judges (Scrutton and Sankey L.JJ) found in the claimant tenant's favour relying on the mischief rule of construction. One Greer L.J., agreed in the result but on the basis that the tenant who gave the notice on behalf of the joint tenants had actual authority to do so.
[15] See para. 13.36 below.
[16] See para. 13.2 above.
[17] *Dodds v. Walker* [1981] 1 W.L.R. 1027. This case is the authoritative statement as to the corresponding date rule whereby in calculating a period which had elapsed after the giving of the landlord's notice and excluding that day, the relevant period was the specified number of months thereafter which ended on the corresponding day of the appropriate subsequent month (HL); *E.J. Riley Investments Ltd v Eurostyle Holdings Ltd* [1985] 1 W.L.R. 1139 (a straightforward application of *Dodds v. Walker* by the CA in the context of the Landlord and Tenant Act 1954); *Manorlike Limited v. Le Vitas Travel Agency and Consultancy Services Ltd* (1986) 278 E.G. 412 (the CA held that a notice requiring the tenant to vacate "within a period of three months" was equivalent to a notice, as required by the lease, requiring the tenant to vacate "not less than three months" after the notice being given). There are very many cases dealing with the calculation of time periods, best researched from the notes in *The Supreme Court Practice* (Sweet & Maxwell, 1997) Vol. 1 under Order 3.
[18] As defined by s. 60(5): see paras 13.25–13.27 above.

a "reasonable opportunity" has been given. The giving of a notice of intention to claim compensation is not necessarily sufficient, nor is the failure to give a notice of sale necessarily fatal.[19] The tenant should clearly ensure that the reasonableness of the opportunity is put beyond doubt.

13.30 **Meaning of additional compensation: section 60(2) and (4)**

Additional compensation is defined to be an amount equal to four years rent of the holding at the rate at which rent was payable immediately before the termination of the tenancy of the holding.[20] This obviously means the actual rent of the holding and not a hypothetical "rent properly payable".[21] In the case of part of the holding, the amount of the additional compensation will be four times the appropriate portion of the actual rent.[22] Thus the maximum total compensation for disturbance which a tenant could obtain would equal six years rent of the holding.[23] The basic provision for additional compensation in substance reproduces section 9(2) of the Agriculture (Miscellaneous Provisions) Act 1968.[24] Expressed for the moment in a broad and general way, the object is to enable the tenant to obtain the additional compensation when the land is to be used otherwise than for agriculture. Forestry would be such a non-agricultural use. It is not intended that the tenant should qualify for this additional payment if he is dispossessed for a valid agricultural reason. However, owing to the manner in which the Act places on the landlord the onus of stating the reason, it is possible for the tenant to obtain the additional compensation, despite the existence of a good agricultural reason for his displacement, if the landlord has omitted to include the appropriate wording on his notice to quit. Thus a landlord may have to pay a very large sum, in some case running into many thousands, not because he lacks a good reason for getting rid of his tenant, but merely because he has failed to inert certain words on to a piece of paper.[25] Contracting out of liability to make the additional compensation payment is prohibited.[26]

---

[19] *Dale v. Hatfield Chase Corporation* [1922] 2 K.B. 282 (the CA held that the mere lapse of an interval of several months between notice of intention to claim compensation and the sale or removal of items does not of itself satisfy the requirement that the landlord be given a reasonable opportunity to make a valuation); *Barbour v. McDouall* [1914] S.C. 844.
[20] See para. 13.24 above.
[21] Contrast the exercise under s. 12.
[22] See s. 74.
[23] Maximum two years under basic compensation plus four years under additional compensation.
[24] Under s. 9 of the 1968 Act the "sum to assist in the reorganisation of the tenant's affairs" was payable only if compensation for disturbance in the traditional sense was payable (but was not always payable then).
[25] Thus the advice of Cross L.J. in *Mills v. Edwards* [1971] 1 Q.B. 379 at 395 should not be followed: "A landlord who means to give a notice to quit under s. 24(1) of the Act of 1948 will, if he is wise, refrain from giving any reasons for doing so".
[26] s. 78(1).

Availability of disturbance compensation in addition to other compensation: section 60(7)   13.31

Compensation for disturbance is in addition to other compensation which the tenant may be entitled to apart from section 60.[27] For example the tenant is entitled to any other statutory payments[28] and any matters agreed additionally by contract.[29]

Extra compensation for operation of early resumption clause: section 62   13.32

A tenant is not to be placed at a financial disadvantage through the operation of a clause in his tenancy agreement allowing possession of the land to be resumed for non-agricultural purposes at less than 12 months' notice.[30] Where the tenant quits in consequence of such a notice compensation is payable by the landlord (in addition to any other compensation payable) of an amount equal to the value of the additional benefit which would have accrued to the tenant if the tenancy had been terminated by the notice on the expiration of 12 months from the end of the year of tenancy current when the notice was given.[31] The early resumption clause is not invalidated or transformed into a clause actually requiring 12 months' notice to be given. This provision merely nullifies the disadvantageous effect on compensation. There is a special provision for the purpose of defining the meaning of the current year of the tenancy in the case of a term of two years or upward. The current year for this purpose is the year beginning with such day in the period of 12 months ending with the date on which the notice is served as corresponds to the day on which the term would expire by effluxion of time.[32] An example will make this clear. If the term was due to expire by effluxion of time on September 29, 1990, and the landlord gave a notice on March 10, 1986 to resume possession on May 10, 1986, the tenant could claim compensation for the additional benefit which he might have expected to receive if he had been left undisturbed until September 29, 1987.

Disturbance compensation: special provisions relating to sub-letting: section 63(1) and (2)   13.33

Although not entitled to security of tenure against a landlord superior to his own landlord[33] the sub-tenant is nevertheless entitled when his tenancy comes to an end to claim compensation for disturbance. The main provisions discussed above in relation to the tenant will normally avail the sub-tenant in circumstances where his own tenancy terminates by notice to quit served by his own landlord or where his tenancy terminates following his own service of a section 32 counter-notice.[34] In essence the normal provisions apply as between the tenant and the sub-tenant just

---

[27] s. 60(7).
[28] Such as improvements/tenant right.
[29] For example special payments for milk quota beyond the terms of the Agriculture Act 1986.
[30] s. 62(1).
[31] s. 62(2).
[32] s. 62(3).
[33] *Sherwood v. Moody* [1952] 1 All E.R. 389, [1952] 1 T.L.R. 450. For subtenancies generally see paras 15.2–15.18 below.
[34] See generally paras 13.12–13.16 above.

as they do between the tenant and his own landlord. However there is one special difficulty which arises where the interest of the tenant is terminated in circumstances where no notice to quit is served on the sub-tenant whose interest however is destroyed by operation of law. To cover this situation there are special provisions in section 63(1) and (2).

If a sub-tenant in occupation quits the holding because his interest has perished at common law by reason of the tenant's superior interest having terminated by notice to quit, there would, in the absence of a special provision, be a problem about the sub-tenant's entitlement to compensation. Compensation for disturbance is dependent on the receipt of a notice to quit and in the case under consideration the sub-tenant's interest has come to an end by operation of law, not by a notice to quit. However, it is now provided that in such a case the sub-tenant shall be entitled to compensation as if he quitted the holding in consequence of a notice to quit (or a counter-notice given under section 32).[35] There is a complementary provision enabling a tenant to recover compensation for disturbance, notwithstanding the technical difficulty that (not being in occupation) he did not "quit" the holding, if in consequence of a notice to quit given by his own landlord he becomes liable to pay compensation to the subtenant.[36]

13.34 Disturbance compensation: reduced compensation where notice to quit less than one quarter of the original holding: section 63(3) and (4)

The operational context of these provisions is discussed in paragraph 13.15 above. The reference in section 63(3)(a) to the part of the holding affected by the notice to quit being less than one-fourth of the original holding is a reference to a simply mathematical acreage. The essential fairness of the statutory provision is preserved by the terms of section 63(3)(b) in that compensation for disturbance is only barred in circumstances where what is left is reasonably capable of being farmed as a separate holding. This presumably means farmed economically as a viable separate holding and clearly this means that what is viable in terms of size will vary according to soil types, climate and the nature of whatever enterprise it would be reasonable to assume. The section is not, however, limited to the actual farming of the particular tenant if, for example, his enterprise is unsuitable for his particular farm. This provision as a whole is designed to allow compensation only, in one sense, where the tenant's action in serving the counter-notice was "reasonable": it would be curious if an idiosyncrasy of the tenant's own farming enterprise should be assumed for the purposes of construing section 63(3)(b).

---

[35] s. 63(1). This is the result of an amendment made by the 1984 Act, Sched. 3, para. 9(2). Before this amendment there had been a mystery about s. 34(3) of the 1948 Act (now s. 63(2) of the 1986 Act), as it implied that the sub-tenant was entitled to compensation for disturbance although there was no mention of a requirement for the tenant to give a notice to quit to the sub-tenant.

[36] s. 63(2). See last note. Note the words "in consequence of a notice to quit given by his landlord", not in consequence of a notice to quit given by the tenant himself, although the technical difficulty about the tenant not "quitting" exists whether the subtenant's interest is terminated by operation of law or by a notice given by the tenant. It should be noted that the compensation which the tenant may become liable to pay to the subtenant includes compensation under s.62 (early resumption clause) as well as under s. 60.

Meaning of "relevant previous notice": section 63(4)   13.35

The special definition contained in section 63(4) is ancillary to the provisions of section 63(3) discussed in the immediately preceding paragraph. The operational context of section 63(3) is discussed elsewhere.[37] Sub-section (4) is the result of redrafting by the 1984 Act of section 34(4) of the 1948 Act, which appeared to use the word "landlord" to mean two different things in the same sentence (see 1984 Act Sched. III, para. 9(3)). The redrafted provisions cover notices given by persons entitled to severed parts of the reversion as well as by the landlord of the entirety.

Disturbance compensation: how and when to make a claim   13.36

A claim for basic compensation amounting to one year's rent equivalent under section 60(3)(a) and a claim for additional compensation amounting to four years rent equivalent under section 60(4) must be claimed by satisfying the requirements of section 83(2). That section provides that termination claims whether under the Act, custom or agreement are not to be enforceable unless before the expiry of two months from termination of the tenancy the claimant has served notice in writing on his landlord.[38] The relevant notice may therefore be served in the two months following termination of the tenancy.

In relation to the enhanced level of basic compensation available under section 60(3)(b) (a maximum equivalent to two years rent of the holding) there is a separate and earlier deadline. Claims must be the subject of a notice satisfying section 60(6)(a) that is to say a notice in writing given not less than one month before the termination of the tenancy.

There is no prescribed form for the making of any of these claims. It is submitted that the only essential feature of any such written claim is that it must be clear in general terms what it is that the tenant is claiming[39] and in relation to a notice under section 60(6)(a) it is probably also important to refer in terms to a claim being made "for an amount under section 60(3)(b)". Suggested draft forms are provided in Part V of this work.[40]

There is a special problem in relation to whether a further claims notice is required in circumstances where a claims notice under section 60(6)(a) has already been served.[41]

Who should serve the notice where there are joint tenants has been the subject of some discussion in the case law. Clearly in the normal way joint tenants ought to serve claims notices jointly; but there are circumstances where the joint tenants cannot or will not co-operate. For example it is not uncommon for a joint tenant who has retired from the partnership to play no active part whatever including in relation to a tenancy which he still strictly speaking holds jointly. Sometimes such a person cannot be contacted during the relevant time limit, or does not wish to become involved. In these unsatisfactory circumstances the case law on balance suggests that a notice served by one of the joint tenants, he being a person with some and perhaps the entire beneficial interest will probably suffice. The decision

---

[37] Para. 13.15 above.
[38] See the general discussion in para. 13.117 below.
[39] See also para. 13.119 below.
[40] Cross-referenced into sections dealing with the substantive law.
[41] See para. 13.37 below.

in ***Howson v. Buxton***[42] that notice by one only of joint tenants, being the one who in fact suffered loss, was sufficient is probably correct.[43]

13.37 **Notice of intention to claim: two notices or one?**
The requirement referred to above in paragraph 13.36 that a notice under section 60(6)(a) be served not less than one month before the termination of the tenancy has given rise to the question as to whether or not a further notice of intention to make a claim is also necessary under section 83(2).[44] Clearly the correct and cautious advice in every case is to serve two notices: one under section 60(6)(a) and a separate notice under section 83(2). However there are circumstances in which mention of the claim under section 60(3)(b) is forgotten by the person drawing up the section 83(2) notice. In these circumstances it becomes critical to decide whether or not two notices are actually required. There is no High Court authority directly on this point which must therefore be resolved by the application of logic.

The almost identical parallel arises in relation to "high farming"[45] claims where once again a notice must be served at least one month prior to termination of the holding.[46] The requirement for a notice at least one month prior to termination of the tenancy also arises in relation to claims for general deterioration of the holding made by the landlord. In relation to that type of claim there is a highly persuasive County Court decision[47] to the effect that where the pre-termination notice gives all the necessary particulars both for the pre-termination notice and the requirements of (the equivalent of) section 83(2) there is no need to serve a further notice under the latter section. The validity of a pre-termination notice satisfying the requirements of a notice which might be given post-termination was founded upon ***R v. Preston Borough Council, ex parte Quietlynn Ltd.***[48]

13.38 **Disturbance compensation: how the claim is dealt with**
In general terms the reader is referred to paragraphs 13.115–13.112 and 13.124 below dealing with settlement of claims. It will of course be appreciated that whereas full details of the claim are not required either by section 60(6)(a) or section 83(2) to be inserted into the claims notices, those details must be available for insertion into the Statement of Case to be delivered to the arbitrator appointed under Schedule 11.[49] Proof in relation to basic compensation under section

---

[42] (1928) 97 L.J.K.B. 749

[43] It was regarded with doubt in view of the remarks of Greer L.J. in that case and comments in ***Jacobs v. Chaudhuri*** [1968] 2 Q.B. 470. ***Howson v. Buxton*** was distinguished in ***Newman v. Keedwell*** (1977) 244 E.G. 469, where a strict view was taken on an analogous point. Subsequent decisions in other contexts which have taken a more flexible view of joint proprietorship have somewhat restored the authority of ***Howson v. Buxton***: see ***Lloyd v. Sadler*** [1978] Q.B. 774, ***Tilling v. Whiteman*** [1980] A.C. 1 and ***Featherstone v. Staples*** [1986] 1 W.L.R. 861, CA.

[44] See the general provision discussed at para. 13.117 below.

[45] See para. 13.77 below.

[46] See s. 70(2)(a).

[47] ***Hallinan (Lady) v. Jones*** (1984) 272 E.G. 1087: the Judge, Mr Peter Langdon-Davies, sitting as an Assistant Recorder being very experienced in agricultural matters.

[48] *The Times*, March 22, 1984, CA.

[49] The usual 35 day time-limit from the arbitrator's appointment applies to this document.

60(3)(a) and additional compensation under section 60(4) is fairly straightforward: it is necessary to prove the amount of the rent at the termination of the tenancy and the claim can be computed as a matter of mathematics. If there is to be a claim at the higher level of basic compensation brought under section 60(3)(b) it will in addition be necessary to prove (1) the service of an appropriate claims notice under section 60(6)(a) and (2) the amount of the loss or expense for items within the body of the loss claim for the purposes of section 60(5) and (3) the reasonable opportunity given to the landlord to make a valuation of any items mentioned in the claim.

A note as to Case B

13.39 A notice to quit based on Case B (non-agricultural use)[50] will automatically attract basic and additional compensation for disturbance if the notice takes effect. Such liability cannot be excluded. However, of course, the notice to quit must contain the normal statement required to exclude the right to serve a counter-notice under section 26(1), *i.e.* must clearly on its face be a Case B notice to quit. For a variety of reasons, notices under Case B may be preceded or accompanied by a separate and different notice under section 27(3)(f).[51] Notices to quit based on section 27(3)(f) always attract basic compensation and additional compensation for disturbance.

Tenant wishing to quit with full compensation: a procedural problem

13.40 Even where a tenant wishes to give up his tenancy, having been served with a notice to quit, he will no doubt still wish to ensure that he obtains the maximum basic and additional compensation for disturbance. The question arises as to whether or not he would be in difficulty if (in response to a notice to quit following which a counter-notice might be served) he fails to serve a counter-notice referring the matter to the Agricultural Land Tribunal but instead simply serves notice of his intention to make a compensation claim. The answer seems to be that he would indeed be in some difficulty. That is because the drafting of section 61(3) (4) and (5) presuppose that the notice to quit has been referred to the Tribunal for adjudication. The advice therefore to a tenant must in these circumstances be to serve a protective counternotice in response to the landlord's notice to quit; if the tenant did not do so, the landlord's mere statement under section 61(3)(a) would exclude additional compensation. Clearly if the matter is referred to the Tribunal there is a risk that the Tribunal will refuse consent to the landlord's notice to quit. However it would seem correct that the Tribunal would realise, if the tenant chose to put in no evidence, that opposition was somewhat token.

COMPENSATION FOR IMPROVEMENTS AND TENANT-RIGHT MATTERS

General: Improvements and tenant-right compensation

13.41 Paragraphs 13.41–13.74 deal with the tenant's rights to compensation for improvements and tenant-right matters when he quits the holding on the termination of the tenancy. The common law recognised no such rights unless

---

See generally in relation to arbitration paras 16.14–16.77 below.
[50] See paras 12.50–12.50.4 above.
[51] Use, other than for agriculture, not falling within Case B.

secured by contract or by local custom.[52] Before the Agricultural Holdings Acts, compensation for improvements was to some extent provided for by the custom of the country, notably in Lincolnshire, Leicestershire and Glamorganshire, but this was exceptional. Customary compensation for what would now be called "tenant-right matters" had, indeed, become fairly common by about the middle of the nineteenth century, but, apart from the customs of a few special areas, it was not usually payable for improvements.[53] Eventually statutory compensation was provided for improvements and, ultimately, for tenant-right matters. Today compensation is mainly governed by statute, but written agreements are allowed to regulate it within certain limits, and custom as an independent general source of rights to compensation for tenant right is preserved (in certain circumstances) only for tenants in occupation before March 1, 1948.[54] One important point may be made here. Compensation for improvements and tenant-right depends on the tenant quitting the holding on the termination of the tenancy, but, unlike compensation for disturbance, it does not depend on the tenant quitting in consequence of a notice to quit.

13.42 **Distinction between improvements begun before and those begun on or after March 1, 1948**

It is still possible, although after nearly 50 years it cannot now be a frequent occurrence, for tenants to claim compensation in respect of improvements begun before March 1, 1948. Those "old improvements", which are broadly speaking the 1923 Act improvements,[55] are set out in Part II of Schedule 9 to the 1986 Act. The improvements carried out on or after March 1, 1948 are, for obvious reasons, no longer described as "new improvements". The expression "relevant improvement" is now used to describe an improvement specified in Schedule 7 or Part I of Schedule 8 to the 1986 Act begun on or after March 1, 1948.[56] So far as these "relevant improvements" are concerned it is immaterial that the tenant entered into occupation before March 1, 1948 provided that the improvement was begun on or after that date.[57] There still exist accordingly two different sets of rules[58] for similar improvements dependent on the date on which the improvement was begun.

---

[52] ***Wigglesworth v. Dallison*** (1779) 1 Dougl. 201; ***Caldecott v. Smythies*** (1837) 7 C.& P. 808 (Parke B.).

[53] See, for very interesting information, the *Digest of Evidence* (1849) given to the House of Commons Committee appointed to inquire into agricultural customs in respect of tenant-right, compiled by Shaw and Corbet.

[54] Sched. 12, para. 6, also paras 2–9. See para. 13.51 below.

[55] "Broadly speaking" because there are some differences in items compared with those in Sched. 1 to the 1923 Act.

[56] s. 64(1) and (2). Part II of Sched. 8 covers tenant-right matters.

[57] s. 64(3).

[58] By an amendment made by the 1984 Act, Sched. 3, para. 10, however, the measure of compensation for old improvements was assimilated to that for long-term new

Rules governing compensation for old improvements 13.43

Paragraphs 13.44–13.49 contain a summary of the compensation rules for old improvements,[59] being in essence a restatement of the 1923 Act law.

Old improvements: right to compensation 13.44

The tenant is entitled to compensation from the landlord for an old improvement on quitting the holding on the termination of the tenancy, whether or not he was under an obligation to carry it out by the terms of his tenancy (except where the contract was made before January 1, 1921, when such an obligation disentitles him.)[60] Instead of claiming this statutory compensation the tenant may claim any compensation to which he may be entitled under custom, agreement or otherwise.[61] The meaning of "termination" in relation to a contract of tenancy is defined by section 96(1). In order to entitle the tenant to compensation for an old improvement, the land must have been a "holding" within the meaning of the 1923 Act when the improvement was begun or must then have fallen to be treated as a holding by virtue of section 33 of that Act.[62] A case might arise, therefore where it would be necessary to investigate the history of the land, and to consider both the definition of a holding in section 57(1) of the 1923 Act and the effect of section 33. The latter section (reproducing the effect of section 20 of the Agriculture Act 1920) amended the meaning of "holding" to meet such a case as *Re Lancaster and Macnamara*[63] (where agricultural and non-agricultural land were included in one letting and the whole was held not to be a "holding") by applying the provisions as to compensation for improvements and disturbance to the part exclusive of the "non-statutory" land.

Old improvements: measure of compensation 13.45

Somewhat surprisingly, the 1984 Act altered the measure of compensation for old improvements from the value to an incoming tenant[64] to the increase in the value of an agricultural holding as a holding, having regard to the character and situation of the holding as a holding and the average requirements of tenants reasonably skilled in husbandry.[65] In practice this change is not likely to have a marked effect. In assessing the amount of compensation payable to a tenant in respect of an old improvement, account must be taken of (*i.e.* a deduction must be made in respect of) any benefit given or allowed by the landlord in consideration of the tenant's executing the improvement, whether it is expressly stated in the contract of tenancy that is so given or allowed or not.[66] The benefit, which should for safety

---

improvements in the 1948 Act. See now Sched. 9, Part I, para. 2, and para. 13.39 below.
[59] See para. 13.49 below as to what constitutes an "old improvement".
[60] Sched. 9, Part I, para. 1(1), (2), (3).
[61] Para. 1(4).
[62] Sched. 9, Part I, para. 1(5).
[63] [1918] 2 K.B. 472.
[64] See 1948 Act, s. 37. The amendment was made by the 1984 Act, Sched. 3, para. 10.
[65] Sched. 9, Part I, para. 2(1). This was the measure for long-term new improvements under the 1948 Act (s.48) and is the measure for relevant improvements" in Sched. 7 to the 1986 Act. In principle this basis, which is in essence the value to a landlord, should be higher than value to an incoming tenant.
[66] Sched. 9, Part I, para. 2(2). These words were no doubt inserted (originally by the 1920

have been expressly stated to be such, would often be a reduction of rent, but could have been something provided by the landlord, *e.g.* timber, drainpipes, or other materials, or even temporary pasture handed over to the tenant free of charge on entry, but not the mere non-termination of a tenancy. The benefit must have been given or allowed in consideration of the improvement; a benefit which had no such nexus is not taken into account under this provision.

13.46   Old improvements: consents

The written consent of the landlord, given prior to the execution of the improvement, is a condition of compensation for the old improvements (except drainage)[67] specified in Part II of Schedule 9 to the 1986 Act.[68] The consent may be signified in the contract of tenancy itself, but a clause providing merely that if the tenant should plant fruit trees and should wish at the end of the tenancy to remove them he should be allowed to do so was held not to be a consent in the required sense.[69] The landlord's consent may be unconditional or "upon terms as to compensation or otherwise" agreed between him and the tenant.[70] The better view is that a landlord could impose a condition that no compensation should be paid.[71] Where consent was given upon agreed terms as to compensation such

---

Act) to meet ***McQuater v. Fergusson*** 1911 S.C. 640. In that case the Court of Session in relation to the 1908 Act found that (in the words of the Lord President): "I think any benefit must be a benefit specially mentioned and allowed, and that it cannot mean the mere consideration that, if the stipulations had not been exactly as they are, the landlord would have asked for more rent".

[67] As to drainage, see below.

[68] The items in Part II of Sched. 9 correspond, with a few omissions, to those in Part I of Sched. 2 to the 1948 Act. Part II of Sched. 2 consisted of the one item, "Drainage", which is reproduced as item 16 in Part II of Sched. 9 to the 1986 Act. Part III of the 1948 Act Sched. 2 has disappeared, having been declared non-effective by para. 27 of Sched. 3 to the 1984 Act; all the improvements contained in it, begun before March 1, 1948, have long since been incapable of producing claims.

[69] ***Re Morse and Dixon*** (1917) 87 L.J.K.B. 1, CA; ***Mears v. Callender*** [1901] 2 Ch. 388 (Cozens-Hardy J. held that at common law fruit trees were not removable but that the terms of the lease could represent consent in writing to planting an orchard for the purposes of the legislation (at 398)); ***Gardner v. Beck*** [1947] E.G.D. 169 (the Divisional Court applied ***Mears v. Callender*** on the point that the lease itself can constitute a consent and found to be null and void an express proviso stipulating that no terms of the lease should be taken as being consent to the making of an improvement or planting of orchards within the meaning of the legislation).

[70] Sched. 9, Part I, para. 3(1).

[71] This is contrary to the opinion of Cozens-Hardy J. in ***Mears v. Callender*** [1901] 2 Ch. 388 at 399, but in accordance with that of the Scottish Court of Session in ***Turnbull v. Millar*** 1942 S.C. 521 (Lord Jamieson dissenting). In reference to the opportunity of the landlord to give his consent "upon such terms as to compensation or otherwise as may be agreed upon" Lord Mackay in ***Turnbull v. Millar*** stated: "I think it is again clear that if the Act had meant merely that, as an alternative to *conditional* consent the landlord and the tenant might validly agree on a substituted scale of compensation and nothing else it would have been so expressed. It seems to me absolutely necessary on the general principles I have adverted to that the words 'or otherwise' must be afforded a suitable meaning. They are alternative to compensation. It is not to compensation 'and otherwise'. It is to compensation 'or otherwise'." (at 544) This view is reinforced by the observations of Lord Hailsham L.C. in ***Johnson v. Moreton*** [1980] A.C. 37 at 58.

compensation is substituted for that payable under the Act.[72] In the case of drainage[73] (this is now past history, but could be relevant to a present right) the tenant must have given not more than three and not less than two months' notice in writing to his landlord, before beginning to execute the improvement, of his intention to execute it and of the manner in which he proposed to do so. Further, the landlord and tenant must have agreed on the terms on which the improvement was to be executed, or, in a case where no agreement was reached and the tenant did not withdraw the notice, the landlord must have failed to exercise within a reasonable time the right given to him by section 3 of the 1923 Act to carry out the improvement himself.[74] The requirement in regard to prior notice of intention could have been dispensed with by agreement, whether in the contract of tenancy or otherwise.[75] If the parties agreed (whether after notice was given or by an agreement to dispense with notice) on the terms of compensation for the improvement, such compensation is payable in substitution for compensation under Schedule 9 to the 1986 Act.[76]

Old improvements: changes of tenancy during one occupation 13.47

A tenant will, on quitting the holding, be entitled to compensation for old improvements made during his occupation of the holding notwithstanding the fact that they were made during a tenancy which was not the actual tenancy at the end of which he quitted.[77] This may be so for a number of reasons, such as some agreed change of substance in the terms or conditions of the original tenancy which in law created a new tenancy, or an express or implied surrender and regrant. There must not, however, if this provision is to apply, be a material change in the identity of the holding, *e.g.* a substantial alteration of size. The loss of a part will not necessarily affect identity, but the tenant should, on quitting the part which is relinquished, claim compensation in respect of it.

Old improvements: subrogation of incoming tenant to rights of outgoer 13.48

If an incoming tenant has, with the written consent of his landlord, paid the outgoer any compensation payable under or in pursuance of Schedule 9 in respect of the whole or part of an old improvement, he will stand in the place of such outgoer when he himself quits the holding.[78] The result is that when the tenant quits he claims compensation as if he had been tenant not only during his own term but also that of his predecessor.

It may be noted here that an alleged custom that the outgoing tenant should look to the incomer instead of the landlord for his compensation was held bad in *Bradburn v. Foley*.[79] It is upon the landlord that the legal obligation to pay compensation to the outgoer rests, but the incomer may, of course, assume the

---

[72] Sched. 9, Part I, para. 3(2).
[73] Now shown as item 16 in Part II of Sched. 9. (It was item 19 in Sched. 1 to the 1923 Act).
[74] Sched. 9, Part I, para. 4(1).
[75] Para. 4(2).
[76] Para. 4(3).
[77] Para. 5(1).
[78] Sched. 9, Part I, para. 5(2).
[79] (1878) 3 C.P.D. 129.

obligation by express or implied agreement.[80] An agreement between the outgoer and the incomer to which the landlord is not a party does not affect the landlord's rights.[81] If the incomer agrees to pay such a sum on entry as is found due in respect of compensation from the landlord, the liability to pay arises at, and the period of limitation runs from, the date when the amount due is ascertained.[82] Although an agreement between the landlord and the incomer, placing on the latter the liability for the outgoer's compensation, is perfectly valid between the parties to it, an agreement by the outgoer with the landlord that the former will look only to the incomer for compensation would offend against section 78 and thus be void.[83]

13.49 List of old improvements for which compensation may still be payable: Schedule 9, Part II

The list of old improvements which could still give rise to compensation claims, consisting of 16 items, is set out in Part II of Schedule 9 to the 1986 Act.[84]

13.50 Compensation to tenant for relevant improvements and tenant-right matters

"**Relevant improvements**" "Relevant improvements" are the category which in the 1948 Act were called "new improvements".[85] They are the improvements specified in Schedule 7 or Part I of Schedule 8 to the 1986 Act carried out on the holding by the tenant, being improvements begun on or after March 1, 1948.[86] Provided that the improvement was begun on or after that date it is immaterial that the tenant was in occupation before that date.[87]

---

[80] *Codd v. Brown* (1867) 15 L.T. 536 demonstrates that it is a question of fact in each case as to who has assumed the legal responsibility which otherwise falls on the landlord; *Stafford v. Gardner* (1872) L.R. 7 C.P. 242 is a case where the Court inferred that the implied contract between incomer and outgoer was subject to the right of the landlord to be paid rent arrears out of the valuation.

[81] *Petrie v. Daniel* (1804) 1 Smith K.B. 199.

[82] *Cheshire C.C. v. Hopley* (1913) 130 L.T. 123, Divisional Court.

[83] *cf. Greenshields v. Roger* 1922 S.C. (HL) 140.

[84] It is in the main the same as Parts I and II of Sched. 1 to the 1923 Act and of Sched. 2 to the 1948 Act, with three omissions, laying down of permanent pasture, protecting young fruit trees. and removal of bracken, gorse, tree roots, boulders, or other like obstructions to cultivation.

[85] After the best part of 50 years they could hardly any longer be called "new".

[86] s. 64(1), (2). The improvements in Sched. 7 and Part I of Sched. 8 are basically the same as in Sched. 3 and Part I of Sched. 4 to the 1948 Act. A few changes are due to amendments made by the 1984 Act, Sched. 3, para. 25. "Works of irrigation" (not normally a tenant's improvement) were deleted. A modern improvement, "Provision of underground tanks" is added to Part I of Sched. 7. The erection or construction of loading platforms, etc., (item 11) is required by modern needs. Item 16 (water courses, etc.) is amplified to provide for, *e.g.* equipment for spray irrigation. "Sewage disposal" is extended to cover farm waste (item 25). The growing of herbage crops for commercial seed production is now in Part II of Sched. 8 as a tenant-right matter. Two new items are found at the end of Sched. 7, the grubbing up of orchards or fruit bushes and planting trees otherwise than as an orchard and bushes other than fruit bushes.

[87] s. 64(3).

Tenant-right matters 13.51

It was the 1947 Act which gave tenants for the first time a statutory right to compensation for the main tenant-right matters. Before then an outgoing tenant's claim in respect of "tenant-right" was based either on custom or on the contract of tenancy.[88] The statutory right is now based on section 65(1) of the 1986 Act and Part II of Schedule 8. The expression "tenant-right" came to be used to describe the right of the tenant to take or receive after the end of his tenancy the benefit of money and labour expended by him on cleaning, tilling and sowing the land during the tenancy, which he would otherwise lose on its determination. The word did not normally cover permanent improvements, which were not as a rule the subject of customary compensation.[89] It included such things as growing or severed crops or produce left on the farm by the outgoing tenant, *e.g.* hay, straw, sometimes farmyard manure, and seeds sown, tillages, cultivations or acts of husbandry carried out by the outgoer, the benefit of which would be reaped, not by him, but by his successor. The agricultural year has no clear beginning or end. It is most important that a tenant who is going to quit should not on that account cease to carry on the normal round of agricultural operations upon which the cycle of production depends, and in order to ensure that he does so fair compensation is essential. The customs of tenant-right which evolved in the course of time, and which created in favour of the tenant a species of property capable of assignment,[90] and binding the land,[91] helped in this way to increase agricultural production, but they had some defects.

The 1947 Act abolished customary compensation[92] in respect of tenant-right matters (subject to a qualified saving for the claims of sitting tenants in occupation on March 1, 1948) and substituted a statutory right of compensation for the main items. Among the reasons which led to the decision to abolish customary compensation were the wide variations in the customs (*e.g.* "consuming value" for the crops in some areas, "market value" in others, "seeds and labour" basis for acts

---

[88] The common law did not confer such a right: *Caldecott v. Smythies* (1837) 7 C. & P. 808, Parke B.
[89] The custom in Lincolnshire was an exception.
[90] *Petch v. Tutin* (1846) 15 M. & W. 110; *Cary v. Cary* (1862) 10 W.R. 669.
[91] *Wormersley v. Dally* (1857) 26 L.J. Ex. 219; *Faviell v. Gaskoin* (1852) 7 Exch. 273; *Mansel v. Norton* (1883) 22 Ch.D. 769 (the CA expressly found that the liability to pay the outgoing tenant was a liability attaching to the land and that the landlord for the time being was, in this case, the person entitled for life to the rents and profits); *Bennett v. Stone* [1902] 1 Ch. 226 where Buckley J., as a matter consequential on his ruling that vendors of a tenanted farm be ordered to give specific performance of the sale contract but not on the basis of wilful default, held that in the account of rents and profits the vendors were entitled to be allowed what they had paid for the outgoing tenant's valuation together with the expenses of realising the crops; *Re Derby (Earl) and Fergusson's Contract* [1912] 1 Ch. 479 where Joyce J. on a vendor and purchaser summons held that a written consent under the terms of the lease by the landlord to the tenant making improvements (which as a result the tenant was entitled to be paid compensation for) is a term of the tenancy which the purchaser took with notice in the sale contract and accordingly any claim subsequently for such compensation must be carried by the purchaser; *Dale v. Hatfield Chase Corporation* [1922] 2 K.B. 282 (noted under para. 13.12 above).
[92] 1947 Act, s. 27; 1986 Act, s. 77. See also paras 13.8 and 13.107 below.

of husbandry in some areas, the expensive "away-going crop" basis in the north); the uncertainty which in some cases existed in regard to the precise nature of the customary rights; and the fact that in some districts the customary basis of valuation compelled an incoming tenant to lock up an undue amount of capital in the holding, leaving insufficient working capital for efficient farming. Although customary compensation has been abolished (subject to the saving mentioned) it is, of course, still possible to claim tenant-right compensation under contract, and so the parties may, if they wish, embody in the contract of tenancy features of the old customary basis of compensation in their district which they want to preserve, with the result that some variations in tenant-right may still be encountered on occasion despite the hope of complete standardisation which lay behind the 1947 Act provisions. The uniform statutory basis does not override such contractual variations.[93] It must be appreciated that it is only customary compensation which is abolished. Agricultural customs not related to compensation are unaffected.[94]

13.52 General entitlement to compensation for relevant improvements and tenant-right matters

The statutory right to compensation for relevant improvements and tenant-right matters is given by sections 64(1) and 65(1),[95] the right arising on the termination of the tenancy and on the tenant's quitting the holding. In the case of improvements the material question is the date when the improvement was begun; it must have been begun on or after March 1, 1948 to qualify as a relevant improvement. In the case of tenant-right matters the material question is the date when the tenant entered into occupation of the holding, although as the year 1948 recedes into history this question arises less frequently. If the tenant entered into occupation on or after March 1, 1948, he will (apart from the complication in the special case of compensation for the acclimatisation value of hill sheep)[96] be entitled automatically to claim compensation for the tenant-right matters specified in Part II of Schedule 8 on the statutory basis, subject to any provisions on a written contract of tenancy varying the statutory measure of compensation or method of calculation.[97] If, however, the tenant entered into occupation before March 1, 1948, the statutory provisions apply only if the tenant gives notice in writing to his landlord before the termination of the tenancy electing that they shall apply.[98]

13.53 Election on tenant-right matters: variations related to tenant's dates of occupation

This is a procedure which has become more complex over the years. There are two different cases, (1) tenant-right matters generally, (2) acclimatisation, hefting or

---

[93] But they must be in writing: see s. 66(4) and s. 78(3).
[94] s. 97; and see para. 13.107 below.
[95] Section 65(1) applies on whatever date the tenant entered into occupation of the holding: s. 65(3). But this is subject to the special provisions for election in Sched. 12, paras 6 to 8, where dates of entry into occupation are relevant in respect of the tenant-right matters mentioned in these paragraphs.
[96] See para. 13.55 below.
[97] s. 66(4).
[98] Sched. 12, para. 6.

settlement of hill sheep.⁹⁹ In the case of sod fertility claims it was decided, after initial hesitation, not to require elections.

(1) Election on tenant-right matters generally: pre-March 1, 1948 occupiers 13.54
In the case of a tenant who was in occupation before March 1, 1948,¹ the statutory basis of compensation for tenant-right does not apply unless he takes positive steps before the termination of his tenancy to declare his election. He must give notice in writing to his landlord stating his election that the statutory basis contained in section 65(1) and Part II of Schedule 8 is to apply to him.² The Act does not provide for the tenant's notice of election to be given by a specified date before the termination of the tenancy, but in cases where the tenancy terminates by notice to quit the landlord is empowered to force the tenant to declare his election by giving him a notice in writing³ to that effect while the notice to quit is current. The tenant must then give notice of his election within one month from the giving of the landlord's notice, or, where the operation of the notice to quit depends on any proceedings under section 26 or 27 or Schedule 3 to the 1986 Act, one month from the termination of these proceedings.⁴ If the tenant does not do so, he will be debarred from electing for the statutory basis. It should be noted under this heading that the tenant must elect for the whole of the matters in Part II of Schedule 8; he is not entitled to choose one or some only.⁵ It is a case of all or nothing. If he does not elect for the statutory basis he will be entitled, when the time comes, to claim compensation for tenant-right (a) under his contract of tenancy, or (b) under custom, but in the case of custom, only in respect of matters of the kind specified in Part II of Schedule 8.⁶

(2) Acclimatisation, hefting or settlement of hill sheep: pre-December 30, 1951 occupiers 13.55
Special provisions for election apply to the tenant-right matter now set out in paragraph 10 of Schedule 8 to the 1986 Act, the "acclimatisation, hefting or settlement of hill sheep on hill land". This item was added to the list of tenant-right matters in 1951.⁷ The explanation of this item, perhaps more familiar in the north

---

⁹⁹ These matters are dealt with in paras 6, 7, 8 and 9 of Sched. 12. As to sod fertility, see para. 13.56 below.
¹ No doubt a diminishing number of tenants, but the law must continue to provide for them.
² Sched. 12, para. 6(1). For a precedent for the tenant's notice of election see Form 52 in Part VI of this work.
³ For a precedent for the landlord's notice see Form 53 in Part V of this work.
⁴ Para. 6(2).
⁵ This has been recognised under the 1948 Act and it is confirmed by the wording of the 1986 Act, Sched. 12, para. 6(2). For a problem which this rule created in regard to a claim for temporary pasture laid down after March 1, 1948, see the 12th edition of this book, p. 118. There are, of course, special provisions in regard to items 10 and 11 in Sched. 8, dealt with in the text below, where the tenant entered into occupation on dates later than March 1, 1948.
⁶ See s. 77(1) and Sched. 12, para. 8. The 1947 Act resulted in the loss of some customary rights to compensation.
⁷ By an Agricultural Holdings Act (Variation of Fourth Schedule) Order 1951 (S.I. 1951 No.2168), revoked by 1986 Act, Sched. 15, Part II. The omission of this matter was pointed out in 1948 by James Muir Watt in *A Guide to the Agricultural Holdings Act*

of England and in Wales than to readers in the South, is that a hill flock of sheep develops in time, under proper management, an immunity to tickborne diseases and the habit of remaining within the limits of its proper hill grazing, although this is often unfenced. It thus becomes more valuable than a flock not so habituated, which would require long and laborious training to bring it to the same standard. It is this additional value which is recognised as a proper subject for tenant-right compensation.[8] An outgoing tenant is entitled to be paid, not merely the ordinary market value of the animals in the hill bound flock, but this additional sum also.[9] As to terminology, "acclimatisation" is self-explanatory; "hefting" means the careful herding of a flock until it becomes familiar with and settles on its "heft", *i.e.* the hill or area of hill on which it grazes and from which it does not stray; "settlement" is the equivalent term used in Wales.[10] It should be noted that the tenancy agreement ought to "bind the flock to the hill", *i.e.* to provide that the tenant is to leave the acclimatised hill flock behind on quitting. In the absence of such a provision the tenant would not be obliged to do so, although it might in fact be more profitable to do it, and thus obtain the added value, than to sell the flock away from the holding. The rules as to election are as follows. A tenant in occupation before March 1, 1948, who had already made an election under section 47(1)(c) of the 1948 Act (*i.e.* the normal election in regard to tenant-right matters generally) before December 31, 1951 has to make another, specific, election in regard to the new item of acclimatisation in order to be able to claim in respect of it. A tenant who entered into occupation on or after March 1, 1948, but before December 1, 1951, has to make an election in regard to acclimatisation for the same reason.[11] The provisions explained under (1) above, as to the landlord's right to serve a notice putting the tenant to his election apply, *mutatis mutandis*, to election in regard to acclimatisation.[12] Where a tenant entered into occupation on or after December 31, 1951 there is no question of election: the statutory basis for acclimatisation applies automatically.

1948, pp.59–60. The point was taken up by the Committee on Agricultural Valuation in their second report and the 1951 order was made on their recommendation. For calculation of compensation, see the Agriculture (Calculation of Value for Compensation) Regulations 1978 (S.I. 1978 No.809). Sched. 1, para. 11, as amended by the Agriculture (Calculation of Value for Compensation) (Amendment) Regulations 1980 (S.I. 1980 No.751), reg. 3(2)(a) and the Agriculture (Calculation of Value for Compensation) (Amendment) Regulations 1983 (S.I. 1983 No.1475), reg. 3(2).

[8] At the time of writing, this addition, which is a matter of valuation in the circumstances of each case, must not exceed £8 per sheep plus 10%. of the market value of each sheep: see S.I. 1983 No.1475 above.

[9] The flock may, of course, belong to the landlord and merely be let to the tenant, in which case this question does not arise. The tenant may pay an annual "Sheep rent" for the stock of acclimatised sheep. This would not be a "rent" subject to s. 12, although the value of the sheep stock and the terms of the letting or agreement might be material in assessing the true rent of the holding.

[10] See pp.28–29 and 87–89 of the Report of the Committee on Hill Sheep Farming in England and Wales (Cmd.6498, 1944).

[11] Sched. 12, para. 7(1), (2). These rules have been expressed in the present tense to apply to tenancies not yet terminated, but in fact the majority of elections will have already been made under the 1948 Act and are now past history.

[12] Para. 7(3).

(3) Sod fertility value: extended to pre-July 1, 1978 occupiers 13.56

A new tenant-right claim in respect of sod fertility, based on the residual value of leys, was introduced in 1978[13] as a result of a recommendation in the Fourth Report of the Committee on Agricultural Valuation.[14] The committee had concluded that an outgoing tenant should be credited with the benefit to the soil attributable to laying down leys in excess of the normally accepted proportion of the total arable area of the holding, in those parts of the country where the farming practice is to grow a succession of arable crops. A period under grass can enhance the yield of subsequent arable crops, especially in areas of moderate rainfall where there is more arable farming.[15] The introduction of this new tenant-right matter required a variation in the relevant schedule to the Act and new provisions for compensation.[16] It was originally intended that the tenants who entered into occupation on or after March 1, 1948 but before July 1, 1978[17] should be required to elect in favour of the statutory basis,[18] but it was subsequently decided that the "sod fertility" head of claims should be available to such tenants automatically.[19] This was a sound decision as there was no customary basis on which such a claim could be founded.[20] The claim is additional to the ordinary tenant's pasture claim.[21]

Meaning of "improvement" 13.57

The general meaning of "improvement"[22] is probably far wider than is relevant to the right to claim compensation on termination of the tenancy considered in this Chapter. The entitlement on termination relates very specifically to matters included in Schedules 7 and 8. These range from specific items such as erection of wirework for hop gardens[23] to broad general categories such as the erection alteration or enlargement of buildings.[24]

---

[13] See the Agricultural Holdings Act 1948 (Variation of Fourth Schedule) Order 1978 (S.I. 1978 No.742). But see also the Agricultural Holdings Act 1948 (Variation of Fourth Schedule) Order 1985 (S.I. 1985 No.1947). Both of these were revoked by the 1986 Act. Sched. 15, Part II.

[14] Published in 1977.

[15] See pp.11–12 of the Report.

[16] See Agriculture (Calculation of Value for Compensation) Regulations 1978 (S.I. 1978 No.809), Sched. 1, para. 12, as amended by the Agriculture (Calculation of Value for Compensation) (Amendment) Regulations 1980 (S.I. 1980 No.751) and the similarly named regulations of 1983 (S.I. 1983 No.1475), reg.3. See particularly the substitution in reg. 3(2)(d) for the somewhat vague and ambiguous reference to a district where "the growing of a succession of tillage crops on the same arable land is normal farming practice" of the clearer proposition "areas of the country where arable crops can be grown in an unbroken series of not less than six years", etc.

[17] See the Agricultural Holdings Act 1948 (Variation of Fourth Schedule) Order 1978 (S.I. 1978 No.742), art. 4 (this article was revoked by S.I. 1985 No.1947). Both of these were revoked by the 1986 Act, Sched. 15, Part II.

[18] The revoked art. 4 (see last note) dealing with election extended to no less than four subparagraphs.

[19] See art. 4(2)(a) and (b) of S.I. 1985 No. 1947.

[20] See para. 13.112 below.

[21] Sched. 8, para. 9.

[22] See para. 11.21 above.

[23] Sched. 7, Part II, item 20.

13.58 Classification of improvements

In order to understand which procedures are applicable to any particular work which is planned, it is first necessary to identify where in relation to Schedules 7 and 8 it is classified. Essentially for these purposes there are three groups of improvements.

Schedule 7 Part I: improvements to which consent of the landlord is required.

Schedule 7 Part II: improvements to which consent of the landlord or the approval of the Tribunal is required.

Schedule 8 Part I: improvements (to which no consent is required).

The contents of Schedule 7 replaces Schedule 3 to the 1948 Act with a few amendments made by the 1984 Act (Schedule 3, paragraph 25).[24]

Schedule 8 includes amendments to its predecessor (Schedule 4 to the 1948 Act) as a result of recommendations of the Committee on Agricultural Valuation in their Third and Fourth Reports (1969 and 1977). The amendments to Schedule 4 to the 1948 Act were made by the Agricultural Holdings Act 1948 (Variation of Fourth Schedule) Orders of 1978 and 1985 (S.I. 1978 No.742 and S.I. 1985 No.1947). Both of these orders were revoked by the present Act (Schedule 15, Part II).

13.59 Assembling a scheme of works

In the normal way it is not too difficult to establish which part of the relevant Schedules is applicable to any particular scheme of work intended. However there are some rather complex schemes now made necessary by the requirement to minimise agricultural pollution, particularly in the case of intensive livestock enterprises. Many such enterprises were installed some years before the National Rivers' Authority policy of strict policing of pollution. Consequently where complex schemes are drawn up in order to comply it may sometimes be difficult to disentangle the various aspects of the work unless some thought is given to this in advance. Thus, the provision of underground tanks falls within Schedule 7, Part I[25] but a number of other highly relevant items fall within Schedule 7, Part II and do in fact require the landlord's consent which, if not given, may be applied for to the Tribunal. This includes erection alteration or enlargement of buildings, and making or improvement of permanent yards,[26] the making or improvement of water courses, culverts, ponds, wells or reservoirs or of works for the application of water power for agricultural or domestic purposes or of works for the supply distribution or use of water for such purposes (including the erection or installation

---

[24] The changes are: Part I, item 2: omission of "works of irrigation". Neither this nor the "making of water meadows", which remains, is normally a tenant's improvement; item 8: "provision of underground tanks", a modern improvement, is added; Part II, item 10: these are derived from s. 98(3) of the Housing Act 1974 and s. 231(2) of the Housing Act 1985; item 11: this, another essential modern improvement, was added by the 1984 Act; item 16: this item is the old number 13 replaced a more elaborate formula for water installations including, *e.g.* equipment for spray irrigation; item 25: this is extended from "provision of means of sewage disposal".
[25] Item 8.
[26] Item 9.

of any structures or equipment which form part of or are to be used for or in connection with operating any such works),[27] the provision of facilities for the storage or disposal of sewage or farm waste.[28] As to the validity of writing down schemes see paragraph 13.123 below.

Planning permission 13.60

The obtaining of planning permission by the tenant does not constitute an improvement and no compensation of any kind is available for it. It is only the physical work itself which may, if the appropriate procedures are followed, give rise to a claim.

Consents and notices required: Schedule 7, Part I 13.61

The landlord's consent in writing is an absolute condition of compensation for improvements specified in Schedule 7, Part I,[29] and such consent may be given unconditionally or upon such terms as to compensation or otherwise as may be agreed upon in writing between the landlord and tenant. The provisions as to any such agreement as to compensation will override the statutory measure of compensation laid down in section 66(1).[30] The consent may be given in the contract of tenancy itself.[31] As already mentioned, when considering old improvements, the better view is that a landlord can make it a condition of consent that no compensation should be paid.[32] The improvements in Part I may be said to be of a kind to alter the character of a holding or to be otherwise of such a special type as to make it reasonable to require the landlord's consent without giving the tenant the right to resort to the Agricultural Land Tribunal, as he can in the case of Part II improvements below. In contrast with old improvements[33] it is not stated that the landlord's consent must be obtained before the execution of the improvement, but it would be wise for the tenant to assume that this is the position. Where the landlord does give consent it must be clear, not hypothetical or ambiguous.[34] Probably a land agent charged with the general management of an estate can give it.[35] It is advisable for a tenant to obtain the landlord's personal consent and preserve it like a document of title. As to the position of the purchaser from the landlord, see *Re Derby (Earl) and Fergusson's Contract* [1912] 1 Ch. 479.

Consents and notices required: Schedule 7, Part II 13.62

In the case of the improvements enumerated in Schedule, 7 Part II, the main body of long term improvements encountered in practice, if the landlord refuses his

---

[27] Item 15.
[28] Item 25.
[29] s. 67(1).
[30] For the statutory measure of compensation, see para. 13.66 below.
[31] See *Gardner v. Beck* [1947] E.G.D. 169 Divisional Court where a positive obligation to do work was construed (perhaps inevitably) as a consent, and *Mears v. Callender* was cited with approval; cf. *Mears v. Callender* (1901) 2 Ch. 388 at 398.
[32] See paras 13.46 for reference to authorities.
[33] See Sched. 9, para. 3(1).
[34] See *Re Morse and Dixon* (1917) 87 L.J.K.B. 1. Perhaps a surprising decision on the facts but authority for the proposition that activities explicable on more than one basis will not necessarily be sufficient to found a consent.
[35] *Re Pearson and l'Anson* [1899] 2 Q.B. 618, CA.

consent or seeks to impose conditions which the tenant finds unacceptable, the tenant may apply to the Tribunal for approval to the carrying out of the improvement.[36] The Tribunal may give its approval unconditionally or conditionally or may withhold it; it may make it a condition that the compensation shall be less than would otherwise be payable, but cannot increase it.[37] It should be noted that the tenant must first seek the landlord's consent; he is not given the right of applying at once to the Tribunal without having approached the landlord. If the Tribunal grants approval, the landlord may, within the prescribed period[38] from receiving notification of their decision, give notice in writing to the Tribunal and the tenant that he proposes to carry out the improvement himself.[39] If the landlord serves no such notice or if he serves it but the Tribunal determines, on the tenant's application,[40] that the landlord has failed to carry out the improvements within a reasonable time, the Tribunal's approval has the same effect for compensation purposes as if it were the landlord's consent.[41] If, however, the landlord does carry out the improvement, he will be entitled to claim an increase of rent in accordance with section 13.[42]

It is worth mentioning that landlords sometimes give consent to an improvement on condition that its value is written off over a period corresponding to its estimated life. It may be desirable for a tenant to seek professional advice as to the period of write-off; 10–15 years, say, may be much too low for a well-built structure. However, a tenant may be entitled to remove a building for such he is not entitled to compensation because, on the "years principle", its value has become exhausted.

13.63 Consents and notices required: Schedule 8

No consent or approval is necessary as a condition of obtaining compensation for the short term improvements specified in Schedule 8 of Part I or for the tenant-right matters in Part II. In the case of mole drainage, however, but not in other cases, it is a condition of obtaining compensation that the tenant should have given the landlord notice in writing of his intention to carry it out not later than one month before the drainage works were begun.[43] Failure to do so is an absolute bar to the tenant's claim.

---

[36] s. 67(3). The tenant must be "aggrieved" before applying. For form of application see Form 6 in the Appendix to the Rules in the Agricultural Land Tribunal (Rules) Order 1978 No.259) and Form 57 in Part V of this work. See also r. 7. For the landlord's reply see Form 57A in Part V of this work.

[37] s. 67(4). The words "*reduction* of the compensation" imply that the Tribunal cannot go so far as to substitute *no* compensation for some compensation.

[38] One month from receiving the notification in writing: see r. 7 in the schedule to the Agricultural Land Tribunals (Rules) Order 1978 (S.I. 1978 No.259). See s. 67(7) for power. For a precedent for the landlord's notice see Form 58 in Part V of this work.

[39] s. 67(5).

[40] See r. 7(3) of S.I. 1978 No.259 on application to the Tribunal and Form 7 in the Appendix to the Rules: Form 59 in Part V of this work. For the landlord's reply see Form 59A in Part V of this work.

[41] s. 67(6).

[42] s. 13(2)(c).

[43] s. 68(1). For a precedent of the tenant's notice see Form 60 in Part V of this work.

Consents not required for improvement works under Housing Act 13.64

The landlord's consent is not required in the case of works carried out in pursuance of an improvement notice or an accepted undertaking under Part VII of the Housing Act 1985. If a person other than the tenant has contributed to the cost of carrying out the works, compensation as assessed under section 66 of the 1986 Act must be reduced proportionately.[44]

Works directed under section 11 13.65

The position where on the application of a sub-tenant of an agricultural holding the Tribunal have directed the immediate landlord to carry out work under section 11 of the 1986 Act has already been discussed.[45]

Measure of compensation: Schedule 7, section 66(1) 13.66

The measure of compensation for the relevant improvements specified in Schedule 7 to the 1986 Act is "an amount equal to the increase attributable to the improvement in the value of the agricultural holding as a holding, having regard to the character and situation of the holding and the average requirements of tenants reasonably skilled in husbandry".[46] This is the same formula as now for old improvements, the latter having been amended by the 1984 Act.[47] It will be noted that the test is the average requirements of a tenant reasonably skilled is husbandry, not necessarily the requirements of the actual tenant. The words "as a holding" imply that the land is let land. The improvement must be suitable to the holding, and is usually valued by capitalising the increase in rental value of the holding attributable to it. The skill of the valuer is shown in assessing this increase and in determining an appropriate rate of interest and judging the estimated life of the improvement. The method of calculating compensation is not prescribed by regulations, in contrast with the improvements in Schedule 8, Part I.

Measure of compensation: short term improvements and tenant-right matters: section 66(2) 13.67

The measure of compensation for the less durable improvements specified in Part I of Schedule 8 and for the tenant-right matters in Part II of the Schedule is the value to an incoming tenant calculated in accordance with such method, if any, as may be prescribed.[48] The method of calculation has in fact been prescribed in regulations which have been drawn up and revised at frequent intervals in accordance with the advice given to the minister by an expert committee, the Committee on Agricultural Valuation, whose reports are documents of great interest to all concerned with the principles of law and valuation relating to agricultural holdings.[49] The current principal regulations are the Agriculture

---

[44] s. 68(5). See also Housing Act 1985, s. 231 for various provisions which affect agricultural holdings. Works carried out in compliance with an improvement notice or undertaking under the Housing Act are included among the improvements specified in para. 9 of Sched. 7 of the 1986 Act.
[45] s. 68(2). See paras 10.44–10.49 and 10.51–10.54 above.
[46] s. 66(1).
[47] Para. 13.45 above.
[48] s. 66(2).
[49] The committee now derives its authority from s. 92 of the 1986 Act (originally s. 25(2) of

(Calculation of Value for Compensation) Regulations 1978,[50] which have been amended several times since they were introduced.[51] The 1978 regulations set out the method of calculating the new tenant-right claim for residual sod fertility value, applicable in certain districts. There are differences between the Part I improvements and the Part II tenant-right matters in regard to the freedom of the parties to substitute their own measure of value and method of calculation.

13.68 Substituted compensation and additional compensation

(i) **Schedule 7: section 67(2).** In the case of improvements included in Schedule 7, the landlord and tenant may agree in writing to substitute a different measure of compensation for that laid down in section 66(1).[52] The better view, contrary to the opinion of Cozens-Hardy J. in *Mears v. Callender*[53], is that the landlord may stipulate that there should be no compensation at all.[54]

(ii) **Schedule 8, Part I: section 66(2) and (3).** The Act does not allow the parties to vary by agreement the statutory measure of compensation in the case of the short-term improvements specified in Part I of Schedule 8.[55] These improvements, which include such matters as liming or chalking, application of fertilisers and consumption of feeding-stuffs by animals, are the subject of frequently changing compensation regulations. Since no power to vary the statutory measure is given in this case, any agreement which purports to do so will be invalid by virtue of section 78. If, however, the parties have entered into an agreement in writing whereby any benefit is given or allowed to the tenant in consideration of his carrying out a relevant improvement specified in Part I, such benefit is to be taken into account in assessing the compensation.[56]

---

the 1947 Act and later s. 79 of the 1948 Act). So far the committee has issued four reports.
[50] S.I. 1978 No.809.
[51] Effectively, at the date of writing, by the Agriculture (Calculation of Value for Compensation) (Amendment) Regulations 1981 (S.I. 1981 No.822) and the Agriculture (Calculation of Value for Compensation) (Amendment) Regulations 1983 (S.I. 1983 No.1475). The Agriculture (Calculation of Value for Compensation) (Amendment) Regulations 1980 (S.I. 1980 No.751) appear to have been superseded by the later two.
[52] s. 67(2).
[53] [1901] 2 Ch. 388 at 399.
[54] See *Turnbull v. Millar* [1942] S.C. 521 (although Lord Jamieson dissented), a view strengthened by the observations of Lord Hailsham L.C. in *Johnson v. Moreton* [1980] A.C. 37 at 58. These cases are further noted at para. 13.46 above.
[55] s. 66(2): "shall be" the value, etc.
[56] s. 66(3). As to benefit there are some useful Scottish decisions on corresponding provisions: see *McQuater v. Fergusson* (1911) S.C. 640 (noted at para. 13.45 above); *Galloway (Earl) v. McClelland* (1915) S.C. 1062 (on this point the majority in the Court of Session limited *McQuater v. Fergusson* to cases similar to it and in the instant case held that if a tenant were able to claim compensation in respect of temporary pasture the benefit to be set against it is the temporary pasture handed over to the tenant free of charge on his entry, this being a "benefit" although not referred to as such in the lease); *Buchanan v. Taylor* (1916) S.C. 129 where a payment by the landlord to the outgoing

(iii) **Schedule 8, Part II: section 66(2).** In the case of the tenant-right matters specified in Part II of Schedule 8, although there are regulations laying down a statutory measure of compensation, it is open to the parties, in a written contract of tenancy, to substitute such measure of compensation, to be calculated in accordance with such method, as they may specify, instead of the statutory measure and method.[57] Thus the parties may contract out of the current regulations so far as Part II of Schedule 8 is concerned. By this method some old customary bases of compensation may be preserved in written agreements if the parties so desire. In some cases contracts of tenancy will preserve a high scale of valuations in order to recoup tenants for substantial payments made on ingoing.

(iv) **Other cases: section 78(3).** The landlord and tenant are at liberty to agree in writing for compensation to be paid in cases not covered by the Act.[58]

Limitations on compensation

13.69

(i) **Tenancies before 1921: contractual requirements.** In the case of a contract of tenancy made before January 1, 1921, the tenant is not entitled to compensation for an improvement specified in Schedule 7 or Part I of Schedule 8 to the 1986 Act which he was required to carry out by the terms of his tenancy.[59]

(ii) **Section 14(4) of the 1986 Act.** No compensation is payable to a tenant under statute, custom or agreement in respect of anything done under section 14(4) of the Act (*i.e.* no compensation for pasture laid down to restore the pasture area in pursuance of an arbitrator's order after a direction reducing the area to be maintained as permanent pasture).[60]

(iii) **Acts in breach of tenancy: section 65(2).** The tenant is not entitled to compensation for crops or produce grown, seeds sown, fallows or acts of

---

tenant was held to be a legitimate deduction against the ultimate compensation payment to the subsequent tenant, not being struck down as an agreement depriving the subsequent tenant of his right to claim compensation; *MacKenzie v. Macgillivray* (1921) S.C. 722 where a tenant successfully claimed an improvement without any countervailing benefit from the landlord where the landlord's only contribution was to abstain from terminating the tenancy at a time when he knew the tenant was making improvements by way of laying down pasture; *Findlay v. Munro* (1917) S.C. 419 following *Galloway (Earl) v. McClelland* (above) since in laying down temporary pasture the tenant was only fulfilling a contractual obligation under the lease.

[57] s. 66(4).
[58] s. 78(3).
[59] Sched. 12, para. 5 (and see to the same effect *Galloway v. McClelland* (above)). In the case of contracts made on or after January 1, 1921, the tenant could not be debarred from claiming compensation by the insertion of express terms in his tenancy agreement requiring him to carry out the scheduled improvements: for the history of this matter, not now of enthralling interest, see Lely & Aggs, *Agricultural Holdings*, (5th ed.) pp.34–35.
[60] s. 76(1); and see paras 10.55–10.58 above.

husbandry performed, or pasture laid down, in contravention of the terms of a written contract of tenancy, unless (a) what he did was reasonably necessary in consequence of a direction under the 1947 Act,[61] or (b) the tenant can show that the term of the contract contravened was inconsistent with the fulfilment of his good husbandry responsibilities.[62]

(iv) **Tenant's grants: section 66(5).** The tenant's compensation is to be reduced if he has received or will receive an Exchequer grant or a grant out of local government funds in respect of a relevant improvement specified in Schedule 7 or Part I of Schedule 8.[63] There seems, however, to be no provision for the relief of the landlord if the tenant, being eligible to receive a grant, fails to apply for it.

13.70 Improvements: successive tenancies during one occupation: section 69(1)

A tenant who has remained in occupation of the holding during two or more tenancies, *e.g.* where his original tenancy has been surrendered and replaced by one with some differences in its terms, is not deprived of compensation in respect of relevant improvements by reason of the fact that they were made during a tenancy other than the one which terminates when he quits.[64] It is implicit in section 69(1) that both the tenant and the holding maintain their identities during the successive tenancies. Any significant change in the identity of either could invalidate a claim made under this provision.[65] Such a change of tenancy could result from an express or implied surrender and re-grant and might therefore occur without the tenant realising. It is also to be noted that the successive tenancies referred to in section 69(1) are two tenancies each of which was protected by the 1986 Act. If a tenant takes a new tenancy under the Agricultural Tenancies Act 1995 he does not fall within section 69(1) at the termination of the farm business tenancy. Nor does the 1995 Act deal with this situation.[66]

13.71 Subrogation of incoming tenant to rights of outgoer and taking over of improvements from landlord: section 69(2) and (3)

If an incoming tenant has, with the written consent of the landlord[67] paid the outgoer any compensation payable to him by the landlord under or in pursuance of the Act in respect of the whole or part of a relevant improvement, or has paid the

---

[61] Ministerial power under s. 95 of the 1947 Act to give special directions to secure production. This is probably now obsolete in practice.

[62] s. 65(2). For the rules of good husbandry see s. 11 of the 1947 Act (applied by s. 96(3) of the 1986 Act).

[63] s. 66(5). The extension to local government funds (defined by s. 96(1)) was introduced by the 1984 Act (Sched. 3, para. 11).

[64] s. 69(1). A similar provision applies to old improvements: Sched. 9, para. 5(1). *cf.* the analogous provision in regard to rent: Sched. 2, para. 2(3).

[65] There is no application of the concept of a "related holding" as there is in Part IV of the Act for the purposes of succession.

[66] Section 23(1) of the 1995 Act ensures continuity of the compensation claim between two successive tenancies each of which was a farm business tenancy.

[67] For precedents for the tenant's application for consent and the landlord's consent see Forms 55 and 56 respectively in Part V of this work.

landlord any such compensation payable to an outgoer, he will stand in the place of such outgoer as regards such compensation when he himself quits the holding.[68] Under the section the tenant has such rights only as his predecessor would have had if he had remained tenant. The value of the improvement may have become exhausted by the time the incomer quits. He is thus not entitled as of right to claim the amount he paid to his predecessor, but he should keep receipts and vouchers to show that he did pay. As to the enforcement of an agreement by the incomer to pay compensation to the outgoer and the application of the Statutes of Limitation see ***Cheshire County Council v. Hopley***.[69] Section 69(2) is applicable where there is an actual outgoer to whom compensation is due. There is, however, an additional provision applicable where there is no outgoing tenant but where the incomer when entering into occupation pays the landlord any amount in respect of the whole or part of a relevant improvement. In that case the tenant can claim, subject to any agreement in writing with the landlord, compensation when he quits as if he had executed the improvement while he was a tenant.[70] The same comments apply to this section regarding the possibility of exhaustion of the improvement as are made above in relation to section 69(2).

It will be noted that the statutory rights under this heading are limited to "relevant improvements" and do not extend to tenant-right matters. They do not, therefore, apply to pasture, which is classified as a tenant-right matter in Part II of Schedule 8 and not as an improvement. Paragraph 9 of Schedule 8, however, gives the tenant a right to compensation for pasture which he paid for on entering on the holding.

Sub-tenancies and work subject to a direction under section 11: section 68(2)   13.72
The provisions of section 11 enabling a tenant to apply to the Tribunal for a direction requiring his landlord to carry out work for the provision, alteration or repair of fixed equipment can apply as between a sub-tenant and his immediate landlord. This can in turn result in certain events in complications between the immediate and the superior landlords which are reflected in paragraph 68(2)(a) and (b). As to sub-paragraph (a), section 67 is stated not to apply as respects a claim by the immediate landlord. If on the application of the sub-tenant the immediate landlord has carried out the works required, the immediate landlord will have a claim for compensation against his superior landlord at the termination of the tenancy if the required works constituted a relevant improvement within Schedule 7. The present sub-section provides that section 67 will not apply in respect of such a claim: in other words, the actual consent of the superior landlord to the works will not be a condition of compensation. This is clearly necessary. As to sub-paragraph (b), the immediate landlord may not carry out the work as required by the direction, in which case the sub-tenant under the general powers of section 11 is entitled to carry out the work himself and recover the reasonable cost of it from the immediate landlord. If the sub-tenant has received a grant he will be able to recover only the

---

[68] s. 69(2). An alleged custom that the outgoer should look to the incomer rather than his landlord has been held bad: ***Bradburn v. Foley*** (1878) 3 C.P.D. 129.
[69] (1923) 130 L.T. 123.
[70] s. 69(3). Clearly the tenant should take care to preserve evidence of the payment and of the precise reason for it, identifying the improvement beyond dispute.

reasonable cost reduced by the amount of the grant.[71] At the termination of the immediate landlord's tenancy he will be entitled to compensation from his superior landlord in respect of the work, in so far as it constitutes a relevant improvement. It would, however, be anomalous if the immediate landlord, who has repaid to the sub-tenant the costs less the grant, should be able to recover from the superior landlord compensation which did not take the grant into account: this would be an undeserved windfall for the immediate landlord.[72]

13.73 **Schemes approved under section 1 of the Hill Farming Act 1946: section 68(3) and (4)**
Section 68(3) and (4) are intended to safeguard accrued rights under previous enactments but these schemes are obsolete and are not further discussed.

13.74 **Restrictions on compensation for things done in compliance with Act: section 76**
Section 76 deals with two matters which have been mentioned elsewhere, and they are merely mentioned here for completeness in the context of supplementary provisions with respect to compensation. Section 76(1) and (2) excludes compensation for compliance by a tenant with an arbitrator's order under section 14 in regard to the pasture to be left, and provides against a possibly unfair practice by the tenant in claiming compensation for other pasture.[73] Section 76(3) excludes compensation for action taken by a tenant to secure his rights under section 15(4), *i.e.* the making of suitable and adequate provision to return the manurial equivalent of produce sold off or to protect the holding from injury or deterioration.[74]

"HIGH FARMING" CLAIMS

13.75 **Compensation for continuous adoption of special system of farming: section 70**
Section 70 of the 1986 Act, reproducing with certain amendments a provision which originated in the Agriculture Act 1920,[75] gives the tenant a right to claim compensation, on quitting the holding on the termination of the tenancy, for what is sometimes called "high farming",[76] but which the Act defines as "the continuous adoption of a system of farming" which has been more beneficial to the holding than the system required by the contract of tenancy, or, if no system is so required, than the system normally practised on comparable holdings.[77] The value of the

---

[71] s. 11(8).
[72] In fact such a windfall arose under s. 4(6)(b) of the 1958 Act, but is eliminated by the draftsman of the present Act by virtue of the words "and as if any grant made to the sub-tenant in respect of the work out of money provided by Parliament had been made to the immediate landlord". See also Law Com: No. 153 and Minutes and Report of Joint Committee on Consolidation Bills H.L. 56–1 and H.C. 178–1, where the point is discussed.
[73] See para. 10.58 above.
[74] See para. 10.63 above.
[75] 1920 Act, s. 16, and carried forward in s. 9 of the 1923 Act and s. 56 of the 1948 Act.
[76] "High farming," although a stylish, is not a statutory, expression and it should be avoided in a formal notice of claim.
[77] s. 70(1).

holding must have been increased by this means "during the tenancy", which means the tenancy at the end of which compensation is claimed, since section 70 includes no provision similar to that in section 69(1) (in the case of specific improvements) enabling a series of tenancies of one occupier to be treated as one.

Measure of compensation 13.76

The measure of compensation, in the rare case where a valuation is required, is the same as for specific long-term improvements,[78] namely, the increase in the value of the holding as a holding having regard to the character and situation of the holding and the average requirements of tenants reasonably skilled in husbandry.[79] This is the objective standard of a let farm, excluding the requirements of a specialist as well as those of a freakish or eccentric farmer.

Conditions of claim: section 70(2) 13.77

There are two conditions precedent to the making of a claim under section 70, the absence of either of which is fatal to its success. They are as follows:[80]

(a) **Tenant's notice in writing.** The tenant must have given the landlord notice in writing, not later than one month before the termination of the tenancy, of his intention to claim compensation under section 70.[81] It was pointed out in a number of cases that one reason why a resumption clause in a contract of tenancy would be void if it provides for the taking of possession by a landlord without notice, or on notice of one month or less, is that it would not permit a tenant to serve a notice under the provision which is now section 70(2)(a), if he should wish to do so, and would thus contravene the rule now embodied in section 78(1).[82]

(b) **Record of condition.** A record must have been made under section 22 of the 1986 Act of the condition of the fixed equipment on the holding and of the general condition of the holding.[83] Compensation under section 70 is not recoverable in respect of any matter arising before the making of this record, or if more than one, the first of them.[84]

Allowances and exclusions: section 70(4) and (5) 13.78

In assessing the value of an agricultural holding for the purposes of compensation under section 70, due allowance must be made for any compensation agreed or awarded to be paid to the tenant for a relevant improvement[85] or an old

---

[78] s. 66(1); and see para. 13.66 above.
[79] s. 70(1). The value to an incoming tenant, is the basis in England and Wales for the short term improvements or tenant-right matters in Sched. 8 to the 1986 Act: see s.66(2).
[80] s. 70(2).
[81] s. 70(2)(a). For a precedent of the tenant's notice see Form 61 in Part V of this work.
[82] See para. 13.2 above. As to whether, in the event of a claim a further notice under s. 83(2) may be required see para. 13.37 above.
[83] s. 70(2)(b). The 1984 Act, Sched. 3, para. 12 substituted "the fixed equipment on the holding and the general condition of the holding" for "the condition of the buildings, fences, gates, roads, drains and ditches on, and the cultivation of, the holding".
[84] s. 70(3).
[85] "Relevant improvement" covers the items specified in Sched. 7 and Part I of Sched. 8

improvement[86] or, where the tenant is entitled to statutory compensation for tenant-right matters, to any such matter in Part II of Schedule 8[87] which has caused or contributed to the benefit.[88] The object of this provision is simply to prevent the tenant from recovering compensation twice for the same thing. Further, a tenant cannot recover, under the guise of compensation for high farming, compensation for a relevant improvement, an old improvement, a market garden improvement or (where the tenant is entitled to statutory compensation for tenant-right matters) for any such matter as is specified in Part II of Schedule 8.[89] For example, a tenant cannot make use of section 70 to obtain what is in effect compensation for an improvement specified in Part I of Schedule 7 without having first obtained his landlord's consent.

13.79 Difficulties in the way of a section 70 claim

There are formidable difficulties in the way of a successful claim under section 70 of the 1986 Act, as under section 56 of the 1948 Act and section 23 of the 1923 Act. The provision is in fact largely a dead letter. A system of cropping different from that prescribed by the contract of tenancy might have to be abandoned in the last year, in view of section 15(2) of the 1986 Act, with the possible loss of its benefit to the holding. Further, there are obvious practical difficulties in disentangling the effects of specific improvements, which are the subject of separate claims, in causing or contributing to the benefit. And there would not be much point in making a claim under section 70 in lieu of claims for specific long term improvements as the measure of compensation is the same. Finally modern concepts of "enhancement value" and "residual sod fertility" tend, in respect of tenant-right, to go some way towards preserving for the tenant in a more realistic and scientific way the benefit of good husbandry.

LANDLORD'S COMPENSATION FOR DILAPIDATIONS AND GENERAL DETERIORATION

13.80 General: sections 71 - 73

The main statutory provisions relating to the landlord's claim for dilapidations to, or deterioration of, the holding are to be found in sections 71 to 73 of the 1986 Act. These three sections deal respectively with specific dilapidations (or, as the marginal note puts it, deterioration of particular parts of the holding), general deterioration of the holding and the position when the tenant has remained on the holding during two or more successive tenancies.

---

begun after March 1, 1948: see s. 64(2) and s. 70(4).

[86] Sched. 8, Part II.

[87] The tenant may not have elected for the statutory basis in one of the cases where he was required to elect by a certain date: see Sched. 12, paras 6–8. In that event s. 70(4) has effect omitting any reference to the statutory matters in Part II of Sched. 8 for which he did not elect: Sched. 12, para. 8(a).

[88] s. 70(4).

[89] s. 70(5). See above as to election, and Sched. 12, para. 9(a), which applies also to s. 70(5).

The statutory claim for specific dilapidations to, or deterioration of particular parts of, the holding under section 71(1)   13.81

Section 71(1) gives the landlord a statutory right to recover compensation from the tenant, when the latter quits the holding on the termination of the tenancy, in respect of the dilapidation or deterioration of, or damage to, any part of the holding or anything in or on the holding caused by non-fulfilment by the tenant of his responsibilities to farm in accordance with the rules of good husbandry.[90] This covers such specific failures by the tenant as the failure to apply sufficient fertilisers to land from which successive hay crops have been taken, or allowing pasture land to develop into rough herbage, with an abundance of weeds and moss.[91] It also covers damage done by such neglect as failure to maintain and repair specified buildings, fences, hedges and ditches.[92] It covers such well known heads of claim as produce sold off, cropping irregularities, shortage of seeds, excessive cropping (whether of white straw crops, potatoes or roots) and foul land. Although the claim under section 71(1) is statutory, and not contractual, it has been held by the Court of Appeal[93] that in determining such a claim the arbitrator is bound to take into account (1) the terms of the contract of tenancy, (2) the terms of any other agreement affecting the holding, so far as material, and (3) the provisions of the Agriculture (Maintenance, Repair and Insurance of Fixed Equipment) Regulations,[94] in so far as they are incorporated in the contract of tenancy.[95] The court rejected the landlord's submission that, as the claim was statutory, no regard should be paid to any contractual arrangement, such as a provision in the contract of tenancy that the landlord would repair the fixed equipment before the tenant entered on the holding.[96] It was clear from sections 10(3) and 11(3) of the 1947 Act that the tenant's good husbandry responsibilities in relation to maintenance and repair may be affected by contract and the terms of the contract may in turn be affected by the regulations.[97] The measure of compensation under section 71(1) is the cost of making good the dilapidation, deterioration or damage, but, as discussed in more detail below, this is subject to a ceiling, applicable to both the

---

[90] See s. 96(3), and para. 13.82 below.
[91] *e.g. Evans v. Jones* [1955] 2 Q.B. 58 (item 9, at 63). A claim for specific deterioration under s.71 must be distinguished from a claim for general deterioration under s. 72.
[92] See also *Barrow Green Estate Co. v. Exors of Walker decd.* [1954] 1 W.L.R. 231.
[93] In *Barrow Green Estate Co. v. Exors of Walker decd.* (above).
[94] Then S.I. 1948 No.184, now S.I. 1973 No.1473.
[95] On incorporation, see *Burden v. Hannaford* [1956] 1 Q.B. 142 and paras 10.10–10.11 above.
[96] The court found a difficulty in the absence of any reference to an *agreement* in s.11(3) of the 1947 Act. But s. 10(3) and s.11(3) have to be read together, and, so read, they dovetail. If they both referred to an agreement the position where neither party is liable under the agreement would have been left in doubt. As it is, the owner remains liable (under the rules of good estate management) for any repair and maintenance not shifted to the tenant by a written tenancy agreement or S.I. 1973 No.1473. See [1954] J.P.L. 401 at 404 on this point.
[97] Questions as to the interaction of the contract and the regulations may arise, as can be seen from *Burden v. Hannaford*, above and see paras 10.8–10.24. See also [1956] J.P.L. 8 at 15.

statutory and the contractual claim, of the amount (if any) by which the value of the landlord's reversion is diminished by the dilapidation, deterioration or damage.[98]

13.82 Meaning of the rules of good husbandry
Section 96(3) applies for the purposes of the 1986 Act the rules of good husbandry set out in section 11 of the Agriculture Act 1947. The reader is referred to the text of that Act in Part II of this work. The focus of the rules of good husbandry is the extent to which the occupier is maintaining efficient production "while keeping the unit in a condition to enable such a standard to be maintained in the future". The specific matters to which section 11(2) refers all contemplate agricultural efficiency, proper stocking levels and the good condition of fields used for grazing or arable farming. It is hardly surprising that these rules applicable to the immediate post-war period should concentrate on standards of efficiency and, by inference, the ability of the country to maintain itself by producing food.[99] However by the close of the twentieth century, in face of agricultural overproduction on a European scale, the 1947 rules of good husbandry, and a failure to observe them, frequently do not match the modern complaints of landlords and the modern activities of tenants. This is particularly evident in relation to continuing encouragement from the Community Agricultural Policy to farmers essentially either not to farm or to farm to an "extensive" standard. In the former case land may be put into set aside[1] and in the latter case organic or low-tech farming methods may be favoured. Equally the introduction of additional value into freehold or tenanted ownership of farm land by milk quotas can be the subject of bitter complaint if the tenant by one means or another reduces or sells quota which had been enjoyed with a tenanted farm.[2] The sanctions by which the original 1947 Rules were enforced have long since disappeared but the definition in section 11 is given statutory effect in the present section 71(1) and is frequently given contractual effect by being incorporated into tenancy agreements direct.[3] The rules are incorporated elsewhere into statutes.[4]

13.83 The contractual claim under section 71(3) and its relation to a common law action for damages
Section 71(3) provides that, notwithstanding anything in the Act, the landlord may, in lieu of claiming compensation under section 71(1), claim compensation "in respect of matters specified in that subsection" under and in accordance with a written contract of tenancy. Morris L.J. in ***Kent v. Conniff***[5] expressed the view

---

[98] s. 71(5). This limitation was due to an amendment made by the 1984 Act, Sched. 3, para. 13.
[99] See the observations of Lord Hailsham on this subject in ***Johnson v. Moreton*** [1980] 1 A.C. 37.
[1] See also paras 10.52 and 12.35 above.
[2] See para. 13.105 below.
[3] See para. 10.52 above.
[4] ss 11(1), 27(3)(a) and (b), 51(3)(a), 65(2)(b), 72(1), Sched. 1, para. 6, Sched. 3, Part I, Cases C, D and E, Part II, paras 9(1), 1(d) and 11(2) and also s. 14(3) of the Opencast Coal Act 1958.
[5] [1953] 1 Q.B. 361 at 377.

obiter that the words "matters specified therein"[6] meant simply the dilapidation, deterioration of, or damage to, any part of the holding or anything in or on the holding, and are not restricted to such dilapidation, deterioration or damage as is caused by non-fulfilment of the tenant's good husbandry responsibilities. A claim framed under section 71(3) is subject to certain restrictions referred to later.

The correct interpretation of what is now section 71(3) originally gave rise to difficulty, one view being that as a result of the joint operation of the provision now in sections 71(3), 78(1) and 83(1) any claim by the landlord based on contract which fell within the wording in section 71(3) was necessarily postponed until the tenant quitted the holding on the termination of the tenancy and that the landlord's remedy was then arbitration, not an action in the courts. According to this view the landlord could not bring an action for damages in the courts during the currency of the tenancy for breaches of contract covered by section 71(3). This view was, however, challenged by dicta of Singleton L.J. in ***Gulliver v. Catt***[7] and rejected by Slade J.[8] and the Court of Appeal in ***Kent v. Conniff***.[9] It is now established that the landlord may bring an action for damages in the courts during the currency of the tenancy for breaches of contract, and that such an action may include both claims for dilapidations for buildings or other fixed equipment and claims for breaches affecting the farm land itself. In coming to this conclusion the Court of Appeal was influenced mainly by the consideration that the provisions now in section 71(3) and (4) were not worded in clear or strong enough terms to deprive a landlord of his common law access to the courts during the tenancy.[10] They merely give the landlord an option when the tenant quits the holding on the termination of the tenancy to claim a contractual, instead of a statutory, basis in respect of the condition of the holding at that time.[11]

Conditions of the contractual claim under section 71(3) 13.84

If the landlord elects to pursue his claim on the contractual basis under section 71(3), certain conditions and restrictions have to be borne in mind. They are as follows.

Written contract of tenancy 13.85

There must be a written[12] contract of tenancy. If, however, there is a written contract, the landlord is entitled to rely on repairing obligations which are not actually set out in the contract itself but which are incorporated in it by virtue of

---

[6] There is a slight, but immaterial, difference in the wording between the phrase in the 1948 and 1986 Acts.
[7] [1952] 2 Q.B. 308 at 312 and 313.
[8] [1952] W.N. 342; 2 T.L.R. 209 (***Kent v. Conniff*** at first instance).
[9] [1953] 1 Q.B. 361.
[10] See Scrutton L.J.'s statement of the principle on ***Re Arden and Rutter*** [1923] 1 K.B. 865 at 878.
[11] ***Kent v. Conniff*** [1953] 1 Q.B. 361 at 371, 374 and 378.
[12] s. 71(3). If the tenancy is purely oral, the landlord can in effect achieve the same result by relying on s. 71(1), as the joint effect of ss 10(3) and 11(3) of the 1947 Act (see s. 96(3) of the 1986 Act) and s. 7 of the 1986 Act is that the tenant's responsibilities under the regulations become part of his responsibilities under the rules of good husbandry. The tenancy in ***Evans v. Jones*** [1955] 2 Q.B. 58 was oral.

section 7(3) of the 1986 Act and the Agriculture (Maintenance, Repair and Insurance of Fixed Equipment) Regulations 1973.[13]

13.86 **Time of making a claim**
A contractual claim under section 71(3), like the statutory claim under section 71(1), may be pursued only on the tenant's quitting the holding on the termination of the tenancy.[14] This is subject to one exception, mentioned in section 9(1) and (2) of the Act, where the landlord is allowed during the tenancy to bring a claim for accrued dilapidations on the transfer of liability for the repair of fixed equipment to him from the tenant by virtue of sections 6, 7 or 8.

13.87 **Election**
Compensation cannot be claimed in respect of any one agricultural holding both on the contractual basis of section 71(3) and the statutory basis of section 71(1).[15] The object is to prevent the landlord from having the best of both worlds, by relying on section 71(3) so far as it suits him, and then falling back on the statutory claim for the balance.[16] The landlord must make up his mind which basis to select, although he may frame his notice of intention to claim in the alternative and defer his choice until the arbitration.[17] The point is that "no one is to have an effective or enforceable claim to compensation in respect of any holding both under a contract of tenancy and under subsection (1)".[18] This, again, is subject to the exception of a section 9 claim, which, as mentioned above, may be brought during the tenancy.[19] It would be unreasonable to prevent a landlord who had brought such a claim on a contractual basis during the tenancy from electing to rely on the statutory basis at the end of the tenancy.

13.88 **Arbitration**
The landlord's contractual claim, if pursued under section 71(3), must be determined by arbitration under the 1986 Act, and not by action in the courts. This is the result of section 83(1). ***Kent v. Conniff***,[20] however, established, as mentioned above, that if a landlord has a cause of action at common law during the tenancy he may pursue it in the courts and need not wait for arbitration proceedings under section 71(3) at the end of the tenancy. Indeed, there might be cases where a cause of action which arose during the tenancy was no longer in existence on the tenant's quitting the holding at the end of the tenancy.[21]

---

[13] S.I. 1973 No.1473. See paras 10.8–10.24 above.
[14] 1986 Act, s. 71(4)(a). See above as to a common law action *during* tenancy.
[15] s. 71(4)(b).
[16] The new uniform ceiling on compensation in s. 71(5) (introduced by 1984 Act, Sched. 3, para. 13) would probably in any case reduce the attraction of such a manoeuvre.
[17] *Boyd v. Wilton* [1957] 2 Q.B. 277, CA.
[18] *ibid*, per Jenkins L.J. at 286.
[19] s. 71(4).
[20] [1953] 1 Q.B. 361, CA, and see para. 13.83 above.
[21] *ibid*, per Morris L.J. at 378.

"Matters specified" 13.89

A contractual claim under section 71(3) can be made only "in respect of matters specified" in section 71(1). If the interpretation of Morris L.J. is correct,[22] this covers any dilapidation, deterioration or damage to parts of the holding or anything in or on it, but a narrower interpretation is that the dilapidation, deterioration or damage in question must be caused by bad husbandry. This point seems to have little practical importance, however, as a contractual claim arising on or out of the termination of the tenancy in respect of matters not specified in section 71(1) would, in any case, have to be determined by arbitration as a result of section 83(1). Section 71(3) seems to be intended only to meet the difficulty that a contractual claim covering the same ground as section 71(1) would otherwise be invalidated by section 78(1).

Common law proceedings: action for damages and forfeiture 13.90

The principle, which might be called the rule in *Kent v. Conniff*, that a landlord may bring an action for damages in the courts during the tenancy for breaches of contract affecting the holding, appears to be subject to one exception, which results from section 15(5) of the 1986 Act. If his contractual claim is in effect for breach of the tenant's obligation not to exercise his rights under section 15 in such a way as to injure or deteriorate the holding, section 15(5)(b) provides that his remedy in "damages"[23] is postponed until the tenant quits the holding on the termination of the tenancy, and it seems clear that his sole remedy then is by arbitration, and that he cannot at this stage bring an action.[24] A landlord is at liberty to bring proceedings at any time for the forfeiture of the tenancy, if he fulfils the statutory conditions, but forfeiture is, of course, a discretionary remedy and the landlord would need a strong, and procedurally correct, case for success.[25] It should also be mentioned that a forfeiture clause in an agricultural tenancy agreement is void under section 78(1) of the 1986 Act if it does not provide for a notice of re-entry of sufficient length to enable a tenant to exercise a possible right under section 60(6)(a) or section 70(2)(a) of the Act.[26] It is the service of the writ claiming possession, not the mere issue of the writ, which constitutes the notional re-entry in proceedings for forfeiture.[27] The need to serve a notice under section 146 of the

---

[22] *ibid*, at 377–378.
[23] "Damages" suggests an action at law, but, despite this word, which dates from s. 3 of the Agricultural Holdings Act 1906 (an Act which never came independently into force but was consolidated in the Agricultural Holdings Act 1908) it is submitted that arbitration is the only remedy. The explanation of the use of the word "damages" is probably that nomenclature was not so settled at that date: the provision for a single arbitrator was only introduced in 1906.
[24] But see Singleton L.J. in *Kent v. Conniff* [1953] 1 Q.B. 361 at 370, suggesting a postponed "right to recover damages". However, a postponed right to a common law action for damages seems contrary to the scheme of the Act.
[25] The landlord failed (but on facts, not law) to secure a forfeiture in *Kent v. Conniff*, *supra*. See the remarks on forfeiture by Morris L.J. at 375.
[26] See *Parry v. Million Pigs Ltd* (1980) 260 E.G. 281, and para. 13.2 above.
[27] *Canas Property Co Ltd v. K.L. Television Services Ltd* [1970] 2 Q.B. 433, CA.

Law of Property Act 1925 must not be overlooked; a landlord cannot avoid this requirement by purporting to enforce a forfeiture in the guise of a surrender.[28]

13.91 **Relevance of "model clauses" to both statutory and contractual claims**
The repairing liabilities set out in the Agriculture (Maintenance, Repair and Insurance of Fixed Equipment) Regulations 1973[29] are relevant to claims under section 71(1), claims under section 71(3) and to actions at common law. As these repairing, etc., terms are, when the qualifying condition is fulfilled, deemed to be incorporated in the contract of tenancy, their relevance to claims under section 71(3) and to actions based on contract is obvious. Their relevance to section 71(1) claims is due to their bearing (as part of the contract of tenancy) on the tenant's good husbandry responsibilities through the interaction of sections 10(3) and 11(3) of the 1947 Act.[30] In considering the effect of the incorporation of the model clauses where there are existing contractual provisions dealing in some manner with a liability, the decision in *Burden v. Hannaford*[31] must be borne in mind.

13.92 **Standard of repair: construction of repairing obligations**
There is no rule that a tenant is either bound or entitled to leave the land as he found it; he must leave it in the condition required to discharge his good husbandry responsibilities.[32] In relation to contractual obligations the reader is referred to discussion elsewhere.[33]

13.93 **Measure of compensation**
The measure of compensation under section 71(1) is the cost, as at the date of the tenant's quitting the holding, of making good the dilapidation, deterioration or damage,[34] but, as a result of an amendment made in 1984,[35] there is a ceiling to the amount of such compensation. It must in no case exceed the amount (if any) by which the value of the landlord's reversion in the holding is diminished owing to the dilapidation, deterioration or damage in question.[36] Before the 1984 Act

---

[28] *Plymouth Corporation v. Harvey* [1971] 1 W.L.R. 549, Plowman, J.
[29] S.I. 1973 No.1473.
[30] See s. 96(3) of the 1986 Act for the application of these 1947 Act provisions for the purposes of the 1986 Act.
[31] [1956] 1 Q.B. 142, and see paras 10.10–10.11 above.
[32] See *Williams v. Lewis* [1915] 3 K.B. 493 where Bray J. held that although the common law required a tenant to cultivate the land in a good and husbandlike manner according to the custom of the country he was not further required to deliver the land at the end of the tenancy in a clean and proper condition, properly tilled and manured; *Evans v. Jones* [1955] 2 Q.B. 58; compare *Proudfoot v. Hart* (1890) 25 Q.B.D. 42 where in relation to a house the CA held that a covenant to keep it in "good tenantable repair" and so leave it at the end of the term required the tenant to put and keep the premises in such repair as having regard to the age character and locality of the house would make it reasonably fit for the occupation of a tenant of the class who would be likely to take it (Lord Esher, M.R. at 50 and 52–53).
[33] See para. 10.28 above.
[34] s. 71(2).
[35] 1984 Act, Sched. 3, para. 13.
[36] s. 71(5). The same ceiling (apart from s. 18 of the Landlord and Tenant Act 1927) applies to the contractual claim under s. 71(3). For the text of s. 18 of the 1927 Act see para. 1.29 above.

amendment it was possible for a landlord, by framing his claim under section 57(1) of the 1948 Act, instead of under section 57(3), to obtain a higher level of compensation, based on cost.

The measure of damages for the contractual claim under section 71(3) is governed by the ordinary rules applicable to breaches of contract. At common law the measure of damages for failure to repair was the amount by which the reversion was depreciated in marketable value by the property being out of repair, but the cost of putting the property into the state in which it should have been put by the tenant afforded prima facie evidence of the damage to the reversion.[37]

Limit to amount of damages: section 71(5) 13.94

Section 71(3) claims are, however, subject to two ceilings limiting the amount of damages. The first is the general ceiling, to which claims under section 71(1) are also subject, namely, that the amount of compensation must in no case exceed the diminution, if any, in the value of the reversion.[38] If the scope of the contractual claim is as wide as Morris L.J. suggested,[39] this limitation on the level of compensation is comprehensive. The second ceiling is derived from section 18(1) of the Landlord and Tenant Act 1927 and is in respect of damages for breach of covenant "to keep or put premises in repair". As the latter part of section 18(1) speaks of the "premises" as being pulled down or structurally altered, it seems clear that the word has the narrow meaning of a building or fixed equipment. The ceiling here is expressed in much the same terms as in section 71(3) of the 1986 Act, namely, "the amount (if any) by which the value of the reversion (whether immediate or not) in the premises is diminished". There may be some kinds of injury to the holding which are not within the ambit of the ceiling in section 18(1) of the 1927 Act but are within that of section 71(5) of the 1986 Act. It should be noted that in cases where section 18(1) applies, and the landlord is proposing at the end of the tenancy to convert the land to a non-agricultural use which will involve the demolition of the farmhouse and other buildings, he may be prevented from recovering compensation for the tenant's failure to repair them, owing to the provision in the second part of section 18(1).[40]

---

[37] *Joyner v. Weeks* [1891] 2 Q.B. 31 where the CA held that additionally the measure of damages is not affected by the landlord subsequently having let the property and being no worse off than he would have been if the tenant's covenant had been performed; *Jones v. Herxheimer* [1950] 2 K.B. 106 where the CA also held that although the normal ceiling on damages was the difference between the value of the reversion repaired and the reversion unrepaired, it was not necessary to calculate both figures in the simple case where the landlord's expenditure was no more than was reasonably necessary to make the building fit for reoccupation or reletting and would be regarded as on the face of it the diminution in the value of the reversion due to the tenant's breach of covenant (the property in question was a dwelling house). In the case of a claim at common law under the **Kent v. Conniff** rule the length of time a lease has to run is relevant, but most agricultural tenancies are from year to year.

[38] s. 71(5).

[39] See para. 13.89 above.

[40] See *Salisbury v. Gilmore* [1942] 2 K.B. 38 where the CA disallowed the landlord's claim where at the moment when the covenant to leave the premises in repair fell to be performed the building was going to be pulled down at or shortly after the termination of the tenancy; *Cunliffe v. Goodman* [1950] 2 K.B. 237 where the CA, in the context of the

13.95 Limit to amount of damages: section 24

Section 24 of the 1986 Act, which prevents a landlord from recovering more than the amount of the actual damage suffered by him, in consequence of the tenant's breach of contract, notwithstanding a provision for a penal rent or other liquidated damages, is also relevant to contractual claims.

13.96 Impact of high-tech farming methods

The landlord must prove damage. Departure from a rigid rotation laid down in the tenancy agreement, especially if it is the old four-course shift, does not necessarily involve injury to the holding. It must also be borne in mind that available modern cultivation methods, highly concentrated fertilisers and powerful weed and pest killers, make it possible to remedy dilapidations more quickly than in the past.

13.97 Dilapidations: effect of assignment of the reversion

It was established by the Court of Appeal in *Re King, decd.*[41] that after the assignment of the reversion the assignee alone is entitled to sue the tenant for breaches of covenant to repair, whether such breaches occurred before or after the assignment of the reversion. In this respect there is no difference in principle between a common law action, a contractual claim based on section 71(3) and a section 71(1) claim. It was subsequently held in *London and County Ltd v. W. Sportsman Ltd*[42] that an assignee of the reversion may sue and re-enter for rent in arrears at the date of the assignment, the opinion expressed by Lord Denning M.R. in *Re King, decd.*, above,[43] on the effect of section 141 of the Law of Property Act 1925 not being followed.[44]

13.98 Effect on dilapidations claims of severance of the reversion

Before the law was altered by the 1984 Act[45] a tenant who quitted part of the holding in consequence of a notice to quit given by a person entitled to a severed part of the reversionary estate in the holding (a notice given legal validity by section 140 of the Law of Property Act 1925) was not liable to a dilapidations claim in respect of the part quitted. There was neither a quitting of the entire holding nor a termination of the tenancy.[46] The amendment made by the 1984 Act is now

---

landlord allegedly having decided to demolish the building and allegedly having a continuing intention at termination of the lease to that effect, considered in some detail how firm such an intention must be and the extent to which the intention must be achievable; *Family Management v. Gray* (1979) 253 E.G. 369 where the CA reversed the Official Referee in the calculation of damages under s. 18(1) of the 1927 Act in so far as he had assumed the loss of rental value without taking account of new full repairing leases with the existing sub-tenants which had been entered into after the end of the lease. Other cases under section 18 are listed in Woodfall on "Landlord and Tenant" Vol. 1, para. 13.082.

[41] [1963] Ch. 459. See also *Arlesford Trading Co. Ltd v. Servansingh* [1971] 1 W.L.R. 1080, applying *London and County Ltd v. W. Sportsman Ltd*.
[42] [1971] Ch. 764, CA.
[43] [1963] Ch. 459 at 481.
[44] On this point the decision in *Rickett v. Green* [1910] 1 K.B. 253 was correct and that in *Flight v. Bentley* (1835) 7 Sim. 149 incorrect.
[45] 1984 Act, Sched. 3, para. 14.
[46] Equally the tenant was not able to obtain compensation in respect of the part.

embodied in section 74(3) of the 1986 Act, whereby the provisions of the Act with respect to compensation apply in the circumstances mentioned above as if the part of the holding were a separate holding which the tenant had quitted in consequence of the notice to quit and as if the person resuming possession were the landlord of that separate holding. On this basis the person entitled to a severed part of the reversion can claim compensation for dilapidations and the tenant can claim any compensation to which he would have been entitled if there had been a separate tenancy of the part in question.[47]

Claim for general deterioration of the holding: section 72 13.99

Section 72 provides that, in so far as the compensation payable for specific dilapidations to parts of the holding, or anything in or on it, under section 71(1) or (3) does not compensate the landlord for the reduction in the value of the holding, due either to these specific matters or otherwise by non-fulfilment by the tenant of his responsibilities under the rules of good husbandry, the landlord may recover compensation for such reduction under the heading of "compensation for general deterioration of the holding".[48] The amount thus recoverable under section 72 is equal to the amount (so far as not recoverable under section 71(1) or (3)) of the decrease in the value of the holding as a holding, having regard to the character and situation of the holding and the average requirements of tenants reasonably skilled in husbandry.[49] This would cover a case, for example, where compensation under section 71 might be limited to the cost of re-seeding but the farm would have to be let for some years at a reduced rent while a mismanaged pasture was being re-established. Other possible examples might be a neglect of ditches leading to injury to field drainage, or practices leading to a heavy build-up of crop diseases or deterioration of soil structure (although the latter might not be easy to prove).[50] The predecessor of section 72 (section 58 of the 1948 Act) was judicially considered in *Evans v. Jones*,[51] where Evershed M.R. said:

> "As I understand it, section 58 covers, among others, the case where, as a result of the specific failures by the tenant (which failures are the subject of claims made under section 57), the landlord can also prove a general depreciation of his farm as a whole; that claim being, however, subject to the limitation that he must always, in the kind of case where there is also a claim under section 57, bring into account anything he recovers under section 57, so that he does not in any case recover twice over."

---

[47] But note the option given by s. 75 to the tenant, on quitting the *entire* holding, to have the compensation assessed as if the reversion had not been severed.

[48] 1986 Act, s. 72(1) and (2). The words "compensation for general deterioration of the holding" in the marginal note to s. 72 are not actually in the section, but they are an accurate concise description of its content. A record under s. 22 of the condition of the holding at the critical dates could be helpful.

[49] s. 72(3). This formula for a decrease in value is the exact obverse of the formula for an increase in s. 66(1) and s. 70(1).

[50] *cf.* the facts (although not a dilapidations claim) in *Hotchkin v. Leggott* (1966) 197 E.G. 669, a case dealing with the cause of flooding on bulb growing land.

[51] [1955] 2 Q.B. 58 at 64.

It is clear from Evershed M.R.'s interpretation that a section 72 claim may either be made in conjunction with a section 71 claim (in which case account must be taken of the section 71 compensation in order to avoid duplication) or as an independent claim.

13.100 Section 72 claims: requirement of preliminary notice

It is most important to notice that it is a condition precedent to a section 72 claim that the landlord must, not later than one month before the termination of the tenancy, give notice in writing to the tenant of his intention to claim compensation under the section.[52] Failure to do so is fatal. The question has been raised as to whether, if such a notice of intention has been given, it is necessary in addition to serve a notice of intention to claim in respect of the same subject-matter under section 83(2).[53] There is no High Court authority but there is a persuasive county court decision which held that a second notice under section 83(2) was not required.[54] The prudent course is to serve two notices in order to be on the safe side.[55] No preliminary notice need be given for a section 71 claim, but, of course, the section 83(2) notice will be required.

13.101 Application of statutes

The reader is referred to paragraphs 10.29 (Leasehold Property (Repairs) Act 1938 not applicable) and 10.30 (Landlord and Tenant Act 1985, ss. 11–16 applicable to sub-let dwelling-houses).

13.102 Section 25 of the Opencast Coal Act 1958

Section 25 of the Opencast Coal Act 1958[56] represents one of the rare occasions where a statutory dilapidations claim can be considered during the course of the tenancy. This is in the context of compensation in respect of agricultural land where there is a compulsory rights order under the 1958 Act.[57]

---

[52] s. 72(4). For a precedent of the landlord's notice see Form 62 in Part V of this work.

[53] The same point arises in relation to the one month's notice required by s.60(6)(a) and s. 70(2)(a).

[54] *Hallinan (Lady) v. Jones* (1984) 272 E.G. 1081. See para. 13.37 above.

[55] In any case there will probably have to be a notice under s. 83(2) covering other claims.

[56] As amended by the 1986 Act, Sched. 14 para. 27.

[57] "25. Deductions from tenant's compensation

(1) Where a tenant of an agricultural holding is entitled to compensation under section 24 of this Act in respect of land constituting or forming part of that holding, there shall be deducted from the amount of that compensation, calculated apart from this sub-section, the amount of any compensation which would have been recoverable from the tenant by the landlord—

(a) under section 71 of the Act of 1986 (which relates to compensation for dilapidation, deterioration or damage for which the tenant is responsible), or

(b) under section 72 of that Act (which relates to compensation for general reduction in the value of the holding due to the tenant's failure to fulfil his responsibilities),

if the tenancy under which that land was held immediately before the date of entry had terminated immediately before that date and the tenant thereunder had then quitted

Record of holding under section 22   13.103
The 1986 Act does not make the existence of a record a condition precedent to a section 71 or 72 claim, but such a record could obviously provide useful evidence of deterioration.

Successive tenancies: protection for landlord: section 73   13.104
Section 73, which is the landlord's counterpart of the provision in section 69(1) in favour of the tenant, prevents the landlord's claim from being defeated on the technical ground that is made on the termination of a tenancy subsequent to that during which the default occurred, in a case where the tenant remains in occupation during two or more consecutive tenancies. This meets the difficulty which could arise on a surrender and regrant or where the parties have agreed on variations which might be held to result in a new tenancy.

Damages for loss of milk quota   13.105
The situation as regards loss of milk quota is extremely complicated being dependent not only on the presence or absence of specific tenancy clauses dealing with milk quota but also partly dependent on the method by which the quota may have been transferred away. The general content of Chapter 18 is essential to understanding the background to milk quotas and the strengths and weaknesses of any contractual clauses.[58] The landlord's position where there is no contractual provision dealing with milk quota is considered separately.[59]

Litigation designations   13.106
Section 96(6) provides that the designations of landlord and tenant should continue to apply to parties until the conclusion of proceedings taken under or in pursuance of the Act in respect of compensation.

Custom

Recognition of custom: scope of section 77   13.107
Although section 77 of the 1986 Act repeats[60] the abolition (subject to certain savings) of customary rights to compensation, it does not affect customs other than

---

    the holding on the termination of his tenancy:
      Provided, that for the purposes of this subsection, no account shall be taken of any dilapidation or deterioration of, or damage to, any part of the holding which was not comprised in the compulsory rights order, or of any reduction in the value of any such part of the holding.

(2) For the purposes of the last preceding subsection, any provision of the Act of 1986, whereby any right to compensation is conditional upon the making of a claim, or the giving of notice of intention to make a claim, shall be disregarded.

(2A) In this section references to the Act of 1986 and to sections 71 and 72 of that Act include respectively references to the Act of 1948 and to sections 57 and 58 of that Act.

(3) (Applicable to Scotland)".

[58] As to which see paras 18.23–18.24 below.
[59] See para. 18.27 below.
[60] See s. 64 of the 1948 Act and (the original abolition provision) s. 27 of the 1947 Act.

those relating to compensation. There are, as will be seen below, important agricultural customs not concerned with rights to compensation, and the application of these is in no way affected by section 77. Once such a custom is established it is incorporated in every agricultural tenancy in the district where it is found, unless excluded expressly or impliedly by the terms of the agreement.[61] The draftsman of an agricultural tenancy agreement should always inquire what customs prevail in the district where the holding is situated, ascertain the wishes of those instructing him, and mention in express and unambiguous language any customs which it is desired to exclude. Even if it is proposed that certain recognised customs should apply it is a matter for consideration whether it is not better to exclude custom generally and to set out in precise terms in the agreement the nature of the desired rights which would otherwise derive their force from custom.

13.108 **General rules in regard to custom**
Agricultural customs need not be immemorial or universal, need not even cover a whole county, but must be more than the usages of one particular estate or the property of one individual, however extensive it may be. Such estate or particular usages will not be imported into the terms of a tenancy unless it is shown that the tenant was aware of them.[62] Customs, on the other hand, are the usages which have achieved general recognition and acceptance in the district where they have prevailed for a reasonable length of time and which, if valid, are binding on the parties.[63] A custom must be proved as a fact by the party setting it up,[64] and must be reasonable in order to be valid, the reasonableness being a question of law for the court, not a question of fact.[65] An alleged custom, for example, that the outgoing tenant should look to the incomer for the payment of tenant-right to the exclusion of the landlord was held in a famous case to be unreasonable.[66] There are a number of reported cases in which the courts have pronounced on the reasonableness or otherwise of alleged customs.[67]

13.109 **Customs not relating to compensation**
Customs not relating to compensation, and consequently unaffected by section 77 of the 1986 Act, are generally concerned with rights at the beginning and end of the

---

[61] *Webb v. Plummer* (1819) 2 B. & Ald. 746; *Roberts v. Barker* (1833) 1 C. & M. 808; *Hutton v. Warren* (1836) 5 L.J. Ex. 234; *Wilkins v. Wood* (1848) 17 L.J.K.B. 319; *Re Constable* (1899) 80 L.T. 164; *Richards v. Davies* [1921] 1 Ch. 90. Among earlier cases, see *Wigglesworth v. Dallison* (1779) 1 Doug. K.B. 201 (Lord Mansfield C.J.).
[62] *Womersley v. Dally* (1857) 26 L.J. Ex. 219.
[63] *Williams v. Lewis* [1915] 3 K.B. 493 at 494 (noted at para. 13.92); *Legh v. Hewitt* (1803) 4 East 154; *Dalby v. Hirst* (1819) 1 Brod. & Bing. 224; *Tucker v. Linger* (1883) 8 A.C. 508; *Dashwood v. Magniac* [1891] 3 Ch. 306 at 324; *Womersley v. Dally* (above).
[64] *Caldecott v. Smythies* (1837) 7 C. & P. 808 (Parke B.).
[65] *Bradburn v. Foley* (1878) 3 C.P.D. 129; *Tyson v. Smith* (1838) 9 A. & E. 406 at 421. For examples, see *Wigglesworth v. Dallison* (1779) 1 Doug. K.B. 201; *Griffiths v. Tombs* (1833) 7 C. & P. 810; *Doe d. Dagget v. Snowdon* (1779) 2 Wm. Bl. 1224; *Tucker v. Linger* (1833) 8 A. C. 508.
[66] *Bradburn v. Foley* (above), noted at para. 13.71.
[67] See also *Dixon's Law of the Farm* (6th ed.), by Aubrey J. Spencer, a scholarly editor. This work is a repository of much old learning.

tenancy. Pre-entry is the custom by which an ingoer is permitted to enter the land, or part of it, before his term day to prepare the soil or to sow, *e.g.* before a spring term day to sow spring corn or small seeds, or before an autumn term day to break leys and stubbles and to sow winter corn. Holdover is the custom by which an outgoer remains in possession of part of the buildings and land, *e.g.* a boosey pasture,[68] for the purpose of harvesting, threshing and marketing crops. For example, in the case of spring changes of tenancy, the outgoer sometimes has a customary right to remain in possession of the farmhouse, buildings and cottages (or part of them) and part of the pasture land, in order to complete the consumption on the holding by his livestock of crops grown in the previous season, and sometimes for lambing. In the case of autumn changes (usually Michaelmas) the outgoer sometimes has a customary right to remain in possession of part of the land, and possibly part of the buildings, in order to harvest, thresh and market or consume corn, root crops or fruit. Other customary rights are to have corn threshed or straw stacked by a landlord or an incoming tenant, or the right to an away-going crop which arises in the case of Lady Day tenancies and need not necessarily (although it may) involve holdover, since the outgoer's right may not be to remain in possession of land or buildings but to re-enter at harvest time and to harvest, thresh and market the corn crops sown, sometimes with the use of part of the buildings at the time. The right to an away-going crop in this literal sense, *i.e.* in the primitive sense of an actual right of physical possession or entry for harvesting, must be distinguished from the right into which it may be commuted of receiving enlarged monetary compensation on the basis of the value of the mature crop at harvest. In the former sense the right to an away-going crop is not affected by the abolition of customary rights to compensation. In the latter sense it had become converted into a right to customary compensation and is consequently abolished by section 77, subject to certain savings to be mentioned later. The custom of holdover does not apply to some cash crops of modern origin, such as sugar-beet, potatoes and similar cash crops, and there is much to be said for making express provision for it in the agreement and excluding custom, which would not in any case cover all the crops for which holdover is needed and may (where it does apply) leave some matters unregulated.

Customary rights of the kind mentioned above, involving the taking and retention of physical possession or entry, as distinct from rights to compensation, still exist in some districts. In other districts, however, they had in course of time before 1948 been commuted for cash and had given rise to the types of customary compensation to which section 77 refers. For example, in the case of the customs of pre-entry the outgoer came to act as the incomer's agent and prepared and sowed the land for him, thus making actual physical pre-entry unnecessary but giving rise to compensation to the outgoer on the seeds and labour basis. Similarly, in the case of the customs of holdover, the incomer came to act as the outgoer's agent and harvested the crops for him, thus making actual physical holdover unnecessary but

---

[68] The spelling, like the content, seems to vary. In Shropshire it was a "boozy pasture", being an inclosure of grass land appointed by the landlord to enable the outgoing tenant to consume thereon any hay or straw not consumed at the termination of the tenancy: see *Dixon*, p.734.

giving rise to compensation to the incomer on the market value basis. Again, as has been mentioned, the outgoer's right actually to harvest an away-going crop, whether coupled with a right of holdover or a right of re-entry, became in most districts (where the custom prevailed) converted into a right of compensation on the basis of the estimated value of the crop when harvested.

It must also be borne in mind that changes in arable farming, the development of specialised enterprises, labour changes, and other alterations in farming practice may mean that some customs once operative have fallen into disuse, so that proof of their existence might now be difficult.

13.110 Customary compensation: no uniformity pre-1948
Immediately before March 1, 1948, when customary compensation was abolished,[69] subject to the savings discussed below, England and Wales were covered by an elaborate pattern of compensation customs, varying in different areas and even in different parts of the same county.[70] The subject-matter of these customs included compensation for crops which the outgoer had left in the ground, hay, straw, roots, manure, tillages and acts of husbandry carried out by the outgoer, and in some districts such as Lincolnshire compensation for purchased feeding stuffs, artificial fertilisers and even drainage. There were numerous local variations of the general pattern.

13.111 Abolition of customary compensation: section 77
Parliament in 1947 considered that the wide variety of existing compensation customs was detrimental to the best interests of agriculture, not only because there was some uncertainty as to the exact position in certain districts, but also because the heavy expense of some of the customary bases, *e.g.* in the Yorkshire Ridings, compelled the incomer to lock up too much capital on entry, leaving him insufficient for the proper working of the farm. Accordingly the Agriculture Act 1947 established for the first time a statutory basis of compensation for the main tenant-right matters and abolished customary rights to compensation. This abolition, which is now repeated in section 77 of the 1986 Act, was subject to certain long-term savings designed to safeguard the rights of sitting tenants. As, however, the savings were not entirely co-extensive with the range of customary rights abolished, some difficulties arose.

13.112 Limitations on abolition of customary compensation
Section 77 abolishes customary compensation subject to the following limitations:

(1) **Pre 1948 improvements:** Compensation can continue to be claimed under custom for an improvement begun before March 1, 1948, provided that it is an improvement of a kind specified in Schedule 7 or

---

[69] It was abolished by the 1947 Act (see ss. 27 and 34(2)), reproduced in s.64 of the 1948 Act and again in s. 77 of the 1986 Act.

[70] See Dixon's *Law of the Farm* (6th ed.), Appendix II; A.J. Spencer's *Agricultural Holdings Act 1923* (8th ed.), 266 and following, *Jackson* (9th ed.) 309 and following. A schedule of customs was drawn up in 1945 by the Central Association of Agricultural Valuers for private circulation to their members.

Part I of Schedule 8[71] to the 1986 Act. If by any chance there existed customary rights to compensation for improvements of a type not so specified they are irretrievably lost.

(2) **Pre 1948 tenant right:** In cases where the tenant was a sitting tenant on March 1, 1948 and has not made an election in favour of the statutory basis of compensation for the tenant-right matters now set out in paragraphs 7–10 of Part II of Schedule 8 to the 1986 Act, he can claim compensation under custom in respect of tenant-right matters, but, and this is important, only if they are matters of a kind specified in Part II of Schedule 8.[72]

(3) **Pre 1952 occupiers: hill sheep:** In cases where the tenant was in occupation of the holding before December 31, 1951,[73] and immediately before that date the statutory basis of compensation applied to him in respect of the matters now specified in items 7 to 9 of Part II of Schedule 8, he will be able to claim compensation under custom in respect of item 10 (acclimatisation, hefting or settlement of hill sheep on hill land) unless before the termination of the tenancy he elects for the statutory basis in regard to this item.[74] It had already been noted in 1948[75] that, contrary to the intentions of Parliament, the drafting of the saving provisions for sitting tenants had caused one type of customary compensation to be inadvertently destroyed without providing an equivalent statutory right. This was the acclimatisation value of hill sheep. This point was considered by the Committee on Agricultural Valuation, and on their recommendation[76] the Minister made an order adding to Part II of Schedule 4 to the 1948 Act the lost item in question. The result was that tenants who entered before December 31, 1951 had preserved to them any customary rights in regard to acclimatisation unless they made a specific election for the statutory basis, while those who entered on or after that date have the benefit of that basis automatically.

---

[71] Probably not many of the improvements specified in Part I of Sched. 8 will have remained claimable.
[72] Sched. 12, para. 6 and para. 8.
[73] The date when the Agricultural Holdings Act (Variation of Fourth Schedule) Order 1951 (S.I.1951 No.2168) came into operation, adding to Sched. 4 to the 1948 Act the "acclimatization, hefting or settlement of hill sheep on hill land". This is now item 10 in Sched. 8 to 1986 Act.
[74] 1986 Act, Sched. 12, para. 7 and para. 8.
[75] See J. Muir Watt, "A Guide to the Agricultural Holdings Act 1948", *Current Law Guide No.5* (1948) pp.59–60.
[76] See their Second Report (1950), paras 10–16.

It may be noted that there is no similar saving for a claim under custom in respect of "sod fertility".[77] The reason is there was never any customary compensation for this tenant-right item. It is entirely a creation of statute.[78]

13.113 Rules in regard to customary compensation when saved

In those cases where rights to customary compensation are saved the rules established by legal decisions before the general abolition of compensation based on custom are still relevant. Some of these decisions are indeed applicable to liability under contract or statute. It is established, for example, that customary liability attaches to the landlord's interest, notwithstanding the assignment of the reversion or its devolution on death.[79] A vendor who after contract but before completion has paid the outgoing tenant for tenant-right is entitled, in the absence of contrary agreement, to be reimbursed by the purchaser,[80] and a purchaser who buys subject to a tenancy is deemed to have notice of the outgoer's claim.[81] The "outgoing tenant's valuation" in a contract of sale has been held to be the balance due after deducting what is due to the landlord for dilapidations.[82] As mentioned already, an alleged custom that the liability for payment of tenant-right to the outgoer rests on the incomer to the exclusion of the landlord is bad, but the incomer may, of course, assume liability to the outgoer by contract.[83] Such an agreement cannot affect the rights of the landlord without his consent, *e.g.* his right to be paid arrears of rent out of the amount of the valuation payable to the outgoing tenant.[84] It has been held that a custom (in Norfolk) for the landlord to deduct the amount of arrears of rent from the outgoing tenant's valuation is good and may operate even where the outgoing tenant is bankrupt.[85] If the outgoing tenant has been guilty of breaches of contract, or is otherwise in default, it is the landlord, not the incoming tenant who should pursue him.[86]

---

[77] This is clear from the Fourth report of the Committee on Agricultural Valuation (1977) paras. 32–34 and from inquiries made from different parts of England and Wales.

[78] See the Agricultural Holdings Act 1945 (Variation of Fourth Schedule) Order 1978 (S.I. 1978 No.742) as amended by the Agricultural Holdings Act (Variation of Fourth Schedule) Order 1985 (S.I. 1985 No.1947). See now para. 11 of Sched. 8 to 1986 Act. All three Variation of Fourth Schedule Orders were revoked by the 1986 Act, Sched. 15, Part II.

[79] *Mansel v. Norton* (1883) 22 Ch.D. 769 (noted at para. 13.51 above; *Faviell v. Gaskoin* (1852) 7 Exch. 273. In that case it was held first that the agreement did not exclude the custom of the country and secondly that the landlord was liable to pay to the outgoing tenant the expenses which an incoming tenant would have to pay, there being no incoming tenant since the tenancy came to an end; *Womersley v. Dally* (1857) 22 L.J. Ex. 219.

[80] *Bennett v. Stone* [1902] 1 Ch. 226 (noted at para. 13.51 above).

[81] *Re Derby (Earl) and Fergusson's Contract* [1912] 1 Ch. 479; *Dale v. Hatfield Chase Corporation* [1922] 2 K.B. 282. Both cases are noted at para. 13.51 above.

[82] *Oades v. Spafford* [1948] 2 K.B. 74, applying *Dalton v. Pickard* (1911), reported at [1926] 2 K.B. 545n.

[83] *Bradburn v. Foley* (1878) 3 C.P.D. 129; *Codd v. Brown* (1867) 15 L.T. 536 (noted at para. 13.48 above); *Stafford v. Gardner* (1872) L.R. 7 C.P. 242 (noted at para. 13.48 above); *Sucksmith v. Wilson* (1866) 4 F.& F. 1083.

[84] *Petrie v. Daniel* (1804) 1 Smith K.B. 199; *Stafford v. Gardner* (1872) L.R. 7 C.P. 242.

[85] *Re Wilson, ex p. Hastings* (1893) 62 L.J.Q.B. 628.

[86] *Davis v. Connop* (1814) 1 Price 53; *Holding v. Pigott* (1831) 7 Bing. 465. See also

A tenant may lose his customary rights to compensation if he abandons the holding during the tenancy,[87] and the trustee in bankruptcy who disclaims is not entitled to compensation for tenant-right.[88]

A customary obligation for tenant-right has been held to be a "contract, obligation or liability affecting land", so as to enable the court under Order 11 of the RSC to allow service out of the jurisdiction.[89]

Tenant-right, including prospective tenant-right, is assignable property,[90] and constitutes an "agricultural asset" for the purposes of the Agricultural Credits Acts.[91]

The present position in regard to the "Evesham Custom" is discussed elsewhere.[92]

Customary Term Days 13.114

For an interesting account of the number of term-days in customary use (no less than 30) and recommendations for the reduction of term-days to four, the reader is referred to the Second Report of the Committee on Agricultural Valuation, published in 1950.[93]

SETTLEMENT OF CLAIMS ON TERMINATION OF TENANCY

Method of settlement 13.115

Claims arising on the termination of the tenancy may be, and generally are, settled by agreement between the parties or their respective valuers, whose forms of appointment will give them authority to agree as well as to take various steps in default of agreement. If, however, disputes arise which cannot be settled by agreement, the Act provides that they shall be settled by arbitration.[94]

Scope of arbitration: section 83(1) 13.116

This important sub-section provides:

> (1) Without prejudice to any other provision of this Act,[95] any claim of whatever nature by the tenant or landlord of an agricultural holding against the other, being a claim which arises—

Strickland v. Maxwell (1834) 2 Cr. & M. 539.
[87] *Whittaker v. Barker* (1832) 1 Cr. & M. 113; *England v. Shearburn* (1884) 52 L.T. 22. See also *Breadalbane (Marquess) v. Stewart* [1904] A.C. 217.
[88] *Re Wadsley, Bettinson's Representative v. Trustee* (1925) 94 L.J. Ch. 215.
[89] *Kaye v. Sutherland* (1887) 20 Q.B.D. 147; approved in *Tassell v. Hallen* [1892] 1 Q.B. 321 at 325.
[90] *Petch v. Tutin* (1846) 15 M. & W. 110; *Cary v. Cary* (1862) 10 W.R. 669.
[91] Agricultural Credits Act 1928, s. 5(7).
[92] See paras 15.31–15.35.
[93] For a breakdown county by county of term dates as at the end of the 19th century see "The Law of Landed Estates" by Sidney Wright (London, Estates Gazette Ltd), Customs of the Country, pp. 295–315.
[94] Under s. 83(1).
[95] There are a number of other specific matters referred to arbitration under the Act in other sections *e.g.* ss. 2(4), 6(1), 8(2), 9(3), 10(6), 12(1), 13(7), 14(2), 15(6), 20(4), (5), 28(4), 29 and Sched. 4, s. 33(2), s. 48, s. 56(3). There are also some matters so referred under

(a) under this Act or any custom[96] or agreement,[97] and

(b) on or out of the termination of the tenancy[98] of the holding or part of it,

shall, subject to the provisions of this section, be determined by arbitration under this Act."

If the claim does fall within section 83(1) it is compulsorily referred to arbitration and the jurisdiction of the court is excluded. Such a claim cannot even be made the subject of a set-off or counterclaim in an action properly brought by the other party in the court, *e.g.* for rent or breaches of covenant.[99] However the compulsory reference of a claim to arbitration does not mean that more fundamental questions, upon which the existence of the claim, or the jurisdiction of the arbitrator, depends, are excluded from the consideration of the Courts.[1] In ***Paddock Investments Limited v. Lory*** (1975) 236 E.G. 803 the HC accepted jurisdiction to grant declaratory relief as to the validity of notices to quit; the Court of Appeal refused the declaration sought by the landlords, but did not question the

---

subordinate legislation, such as the Agricultural Holdings (Arbitration on Notices) Order 1987 (S.I. 1987 No.710).

[96] This has to be read subject to s. 77 which (with certain savings) abolishes customary compensation. See paras 13.107–13.114 above.

[97] Claims based on tort, such as trespass or nuisance, are clearly not within this formula. The 1923 Act (s. 16(1)) included the tort of waste, which overlaps with a breach of contract to repair, *etc.*, but the 1948 Act and the present Act make no reference to it except in the general saving for other rights or remedies (s. 97 of the present Act).

[98] Claims which do not so arise, and which are not otherwise specifically referred to arbitration under the Act, may be pursued in the courts. For example, a landlord may bring an action against a tenant during the tenancy for breach of contract: ***Kent v. Coniff*** [1953] 1 Q.B. 361, CA. Also tenants may bring actions against landlords during the tenancy for breaches of contract or to raise matters not within the jurisdiction of an arbitrator: compare ***R v. Powell, ex p. Camden (Marquis)*** [1925] 1 K.B. 641; ***Harrison v. Ridgeway*** (1925) 133 L.T. 238 in which the Divisional Court on appeal from the CC held that the termination of the tenancy was a condition precedent to the right to have a dispute under the Agricultural Holdings Act 1923 decided by arbitration and that where the tenancy had not been determined the CC had jurisdiction to try a damages claim against the landlord.

[99] ***Gaslight Coke Co. v. Holloway*** [1885] 52 L.T. 434; ***Schofield v. Hincks*** [1888] 58 L.J.Q.B. 147. In the earlier case a tenant attempted to set up an unquantified claim for improvements as a defence when his landlord sued him for rent. The tenant's counterclaim was struck out as not available since the statute had provided and required that quantification should take place by means of arbitration. The case was followed in ***Schofield v. Hincks***. Both cases were under similar wording in the Agricultural Holdings Act 1883 on appeal to the Divisional Court from the County Court.

[1] Compare ***Farrow v. Orttewell*** [1933] Ch. 480; ***R v. Powell, ex p. Camden (Marquis)*** (above); ***Simpson v. Batey*** [1924] 2 K.B. 666; ***Donaldson's Hospital Trustees v. Esslemont*** [1926] S.L.T. 526 in which it was conceded that the arbiter did not have an exclusive jurisdiction to determine whether the tenancy was terminated, and the HL then went on to construe the relevant lease; ***Goldsack v. Shore*** [1950] 1 K.B. 708 in which the court, as distinct from an arbitrator under s. 2 of the 1948 Act, was held to have jurisdiction to determine whether a transaction was an "agreement" within the meaning of s. 2.

legitimacy of the procedure, despite the arbitration machinery under the Act. It must also be remembered that the formidable administrative law remedy of judicial review may on occasion be available to a party to the contract. A tenant may defend an action for possession in the court on the ground that a notice to quit is bad at common law.

Section 83(1) refers only to claims between landlord and tenant. It does not therefore cover claims between incoming and outgoing tenants.[2] Nor does it cover a question between a landlord and a bank which has taken an assignment of farming stock and other assets.[3] It seems that certain matters preliminary to the determination of the claim, such as the question whether a tenancy has terminated, may be decided either as a separate issue by the courts or by an arbitrator[4] as incidental to the claim.

Enforcement of claim: section 83(2) 13.117

Section 83(2) restricts enforcement of the claims identified by section 83(1). Unless before the expiry of two months from termination of the tenancy the claimant has served[5] notice in writing on his landlord or tenant, as the case may be, of his intention to make the claim, it will not be enforceable at all. Calculation of the relevant two-month period ought not to give rise to any difficulty. Two months means two calendar months[6]; the termination of the tenancy will have to be calculated by reference to the termination procedure employed. In the case of a notice to quit the termination is at the point of midnight between two calendar dates and for these purposes it is submitted that the actual anniversary date of the tenancy (although it can be used to describe, by benevolent construction, the termination point of the tenancy) should not be counted as the date from which the period under section 83(2) is reckoned but rather as the first date within that period.[7] If the tenancy terminates by surrender that date will have to be identified by reference to the appropriate deed or, in the case of surrender by some other method, by close examination of the facts. Where there is termination by forfeiture the time of any peaceable re-entry or the issue of court proceedings (as the case may be) is the point of forfeiture and service of a claims notice under section 83 ought prudently to be served notwithstanding the possibility of relief from forfeiture.

---

[2] Compare ***Greenshields v. Roger*** [1922] S.C. (H.L.) 140 in this case the outgoing and incoming tenants entered into a contract whereby the outgoing tenant's claims for compensation for unexhausted manures and feeding stuffs were to be determined by a three-man valuation panel. The oversman (umpire) refused to deal with the claim on the grounds that s. 11(1) of the Agricultural Holdings (Scotland) Act 1908 required matters to be dealt with by a single arbiter (arbitrator): "All questions which under this Act or under the lease are referred to arbitration shall ... be determined, notwithstanding any agreement under the lease or otherwise providing for a different method of arbitration, by a single arbiter". The HL held that the statute affected relations only between the outgoing tenant and his landlord and did not affect the contract in issue; ***Cameron v. Nicol*** [1930] S.C. 1.

[3] ***Ecclesiastical Commissioners for England v. National Provincial Bank Ltd*** [1935] 1 K.B. 566.

[4] Subject to the possibility of a case being stated on a point of law.

[5] As to service of notices generally see paras 17.17–17.24 below.

[6] See the notes to para. 13.28 above.

[7] See as to the termination of the date of the tenancy para. 8.22 above.

Can a valid claims notice be served before termination of the tenancy? This question arises because there is a possible implication from the construction of section 83(1) and (2) together that no valid claims notice can be served before the termination of the tenancy: section 83(1) refers to a claim "which arises ... on or out of" termination of the tenancy. Use of the present tense might suggest that the section contemplates the claim crystallizing or arising only on or out of termination and not at any earlier point. However it must be said that such a construction serves no useful purpose and if anything the recipient of the notice is better informed as to what his position will be at termination of the tenancy. It may be possible to reconcile the tensing of section 83(1) by reading the present tense as adjectival or identificatory rather than being used to limit the period for service of a claims notice. One can see that section 83(2) is intended to provide a backstop date beyond which a stale claim cannot be brought; there seems to be no useful function in limiting the validity of a claims notice which is served during the last year of the tenancy when the parties presumably are preparing to assess possible claims, whether or not formal notice at that stage has been served.[8]

Finally there are some claims which are the subject of a requirement as to notice not less than one month prior to termination of the tenancy.[9] The question arises as to whether or not a further additional notice is necessary under section 83 in a case where the notice prior to termination has in fact been served. On balance this work considers that service of a second notice (though prudent) is not essential.[10]

13.118 Authority in relation to termination claims

The overwhelming majority of termination claims are dealt with by valuers rather than solicitors. Indeed one would not normally expect a solicitor to be able to draw up or understand the detail of certain types of claims without the assistance of a valuer. Care should be taken by valuers to ensure that the terms of their appointments expressly allow them to compromise doubtful claims either of their own client or of opposing parties. There is normally no implied authority empowering the valuer to concede a claim which is unenforceable against his client and this may give rise to difficulties in circumstances where the issue of enforceability is itself a complex issue of law. Clients ought to be given advice as to any areas of difficulty and should be asked to confirm in writing authority for settlement of doubtful or possibly unenforceable claims.

13.119 Notice of intention to claim: section 83(3)

This sub-section provides:

> "A notice under sub-section (2) above shall specify the nature of the claim; but it shall be sufficient if the notice refers to the statutory provision, custom or term of an agreement under which the claim is made."

---

[8] One wonders how far in advance of termination a valid claims notice may be served; but this issue is probably highly academic.

[9] Sections 60(6)(a) (enhanced level of basic compensation for disturbance), s. 70(2)(a) ("high farming") and s. 72(4) (landlord's compensation for general deterioration of the holding).

[10] See para. 13.37 above.

The object of the Act is to give the other party fair and reasonable notice of the claim he has to meet in order to enable him to decide whether to agree, compromise or resist,[11] but not at this stage to particularise the items of claim in minute detail.[12] Full "particulars" are not required at this preliminary stage.[13] However if the full particulars are indeed served under section 83(2) this would comply with the sub-section assuming that the relevant statutory provision, custom or tenancy agreement in question was referred to.[14] Although it is stated to be a sufficient specification to refer to the statutory provision custom or tenancy agreement, care should be taken to ensure that the relevant reference is as specific as it can be made. Thus a general reference to a Schedule to the Act is undesirable where particular items in relevant paragraphs can be given. Where there is a reference to "custom"

---

[11] *cf.* the reasoning under the 1923 Scottish Act in ***McLaren v. Turnbull*** 1942 S.C. 179 at 195; ***Simpson v. Henderson*** 1944 S.C. 365 at 379; ***Adam v. Smythe*** 1948 S.C. 445; ***Edinburgh Corporation v. Gray*** 1948 S.C. 538. *cf.* and contrast the requirement as to "particulars" in s.16(2) of the 1923 Act and the cases of ***Re O'Connor and Brewin's Arbitration*** [1933] 1 K.B. 20 and ***Spreckley v. Leicestershire C.C.*** [1934] 1 K.B. 366. In both of these cases the CA held that simple quantification of two years' rent did not amount to the specification of particulars of claim for compensation for disturbance, *i.e.* the detailed items had to be specified. Although the requirement is now different, some of the reasoning is helpful. For a case where a county court judge went to the limit in accepting a notice in very broad terms, see ***Re Hewetson and Pennington-Ramsden's Arbitration*** (1966) 116 New L.J. 1613 ("my claim will be for tenant-right improvements, painting and under clause quiet enjoyment"). See also ***Lord Newborough v. Davies*** (1966) 116 New L.J. 1291, in which (CC, Judge Meurig Evans) a notice under s. 70 of the 1948 Act was regarded as satisfactory because the recipient "would have no doubt as to what kind or what nature of claim was being put forward" once he had looked at the Schedule to the notice. Perhaps much of this case law can be synthesised by application of the test that what is required in the notice of intention to make a claim is that the notice should be in terms which are sufficiently clear to bring home to the ordinary landlord that the tenant is purporting to exercise his rights: ***Amalgamated Estates Ltd v. Joystretch Manufacturing Ltd*** (1980) 257 E.G. 489 which has been applied in relation to equivalent provisions regarding claims under the Sched., para. 11 of the Agriculture Act (see para. 19.19 below).

[12] For a discussion of the difference between the notice of intention to claim under s. 83(2) and the Statement of Case with necessary particulars and a comparison with the 1923 Act procedure, see ***E.A. and A.D. Cooke Bourne (Farms) Ltd v. Mellows*** [1983] Q.B. 104, [1981] 262 E.G. 229. For a precedent of the notice of intention to claim compensation on termination of the tenancy (including for milk quota) see Form 65 in Part V of this work.

[13] Contrast ***Spreckley v. Leicestershire CC*** [1934] 1 K.B. 366 and ***Re O'Connor and Brewin's Arbitration*** [1933] 1 K.B. 20 under the 1923 Act.

[14] Compare ***Jones v. Evans*** [1923] 1 K.B. 12 in which the CA held that, having regard to the severity of the penalty attached to non-compliance (namely, total extinguishment of the claim) the presumption was that the requirement of "particulars" was not intended to be construed strictly and that for the purpose of keeping the claim alive and enabling to get before the arbitrator a less degree of particularity was required to satisfy the section than would be required of particulars of a statement of claim in an action even if the arbitrator might ultimately order further and better particulars to be given [the section in question was s. 18(1) of the Agriculture Act 1920: "any such claim as is mentioned in this section shall cease to be enforceable after the expiration of two months from the termination of the tenancy unless particulars thereof have been given by the landlord to the tenant ... before the expiration of that period"].

there is a reference to "custom" the custom in question should be identified in general terms so that the recipient can understand what is being referred to. A reference to a term of an agreement should be checked: many agreements lump together a number of items in an individual clause. It should be clear which, in that situation, of various potential claims is to be made. A notice so vague and general as to give no real assistance to the other party in deciding his course of action is, it is submitted, insufficient. An indication of an intention to serve a notice of intention is not good enough.[15]

13.120 Mandatory nature of section 83
The language of section 83 is mandatory. Further it is likely that section 83 is covered in relation to statutory compensation by the mandatory terms of section 78.[16] A condition in a contract of tenancy which purports to reduce the time allowed by the Act to give notice of intention to claim is void.[17] It therefore follows that compromise of claims should always be made under cover of the relevant statutory notices having been served. Moreover such a course is recommended even where a surrender is contemplated and the parties may already have agreed the quantification of mutual claims. It is suggested that the parties must adopt a procedure which implements section 83 but does not seek to avoid it. Thus mutual service of claims notices (alternatively acknowledgment of claims coupled with waiver of a requirement to serve a notice) and a provision in a deed of surrender (subsequent to the actual clause of surrender) whereby the relevant claims are mutually off set, either to an agreed sum payable by one party to the other, or to mutual extinguishment is infinitely preferable to a bald statement of the type commonly encountered that "no compensation shall be payable by either party to the other".

13.121 Period allowed for settlement by agreement: determination by arbitration
The landlord and tenant are allowed a fixed period of eight months from the termination of the tenancy to settle by agreement in writing any such claims as are mentioned in section 83(1).[18] If, by the expiration of the period of eight months, any such claim has not been settled, it "shall" then be determined by arbitration.[19] It is submitted that the purpose of these specific provisions is to enable the parties to resort to arbitration by right after the relevant eight-month period has expired. It is extremely doubtful whether section 83(4) was intended to prevent the parties from appointing an arbitrator by agreement during the eight-month period.[20] However the unilateral right to claim arbitration only arises after the eight-month

---

[15] *Hallinan (Lady) v. Jones* (1984) 272 EG 1081, CC.
[16] See para. 13.2 above.
[17] Compare *Cathcart v. Chalmers* [1911] A.C. 246, and see para. 13.2 above.
[18] s. 83(4). The 1984 Act substituted this period of eight months for the previous period in s. 70 of the 1948 Act of four months with provisions for extension: 1984 Act, Sched. 3, para. 18. Where s. 83(6) applies, the eight months will run from the termination of occupation of the relevant part.
[19] s. 83(5).
[20] It is submitted on the analogy of the views expressed by the HL in *Kammins Ballroom Co. Ltd v. Zenith Investments (Torquay) Ltd* [1971] A.C. 850 that the parties could by agreement waive the eight months limitation.

period. Equally it is difficult to imagine that the statute in section 83(5) is intended to require an arbitration where in fact the parties have agreed the amount of any claims but outside the eight-month period and without an arbitrator having been appointed. It would be very curious if it were necessary to appoint an arbitrator only then to ask him to make an award by consent. Conversely, where an arbitrator has in fact been appointed then it will be necessary to terminate the arbitration by asking for a consent award.

Occupation of part after termination of tenancy: section 83(6) 13.122
Where a tenant lawfully remains in occupation of part of an agricultural holding after the termination of the tenancy, references in section 83 to the termination of the tenancy shall, in the case of a claim relating to that part of the holding, be construed as references to the termination of the occupation.[21] This provision does not refer to cases where, under the contract of tenancy itself, *e.g.* in an express holdover clause, possession of one part of the holding is to be given up at a different date from the rest, since in such a case the tenancy does not terminate until the later date, whereas section 83(6) deals with a continuation of occupation after the termination of the tenancy. Bankes L.J. in *Swinburne v. Andrews*[22] expressed the opinion that the provision applies to the case where, after the termination of the tenancy, the tenant is allowed to remain in possession of part for a time. A tenant's right to an away-going crop, if it involves only a right of re-entry and not a right of holdover, will neither prolong the original tenancy for the purpose of section 83(2) nor bring section 83(5) into operation. The time-limits in section 83, therefore, run in that case from the date provided for in the contract for termination, not the date of exercise of strictly limited rights in connection with the away-going crop.[23]

Writing down schemes 13.123
As will be evident from the need to secure consent for the improvements within Schedule 7[24] and the ability of parties to substitute a different measure of compensation from that laid down in section 66(1)[25] there is considerable scope for parties to agree a scheme whereby the value of particular improvements is written down year by year such that, depending on the date of termination of the tenancy, an agreed amount of compensation will be available at that time in respect of particular items. It also seems tolerably clear that a writing down scheme which ultimately concludes with a zero valuation will be valid for improvements falling within Schedule 7; equally the landlord, if he wishes, may insist on a covenant for reinstatement. This work considers that a condition that no compensation at all should be paid is a valid condition[26] and that such arrangements, do not fall foul of

---

[21] s. 83(6).
[22] [1923] 2 K.B. 483 at 489. See also *Re Arden and Rutter* [1923] 2 K.B. 865 following *Swinburne v. Andrews* and *Coutts v. Barclay-Harvey* 1956 S.L.T (Sh.Ct.) 54.
[23] *Coutts v. Barclay-Harvey*, above.
[24] See paras 13.61 and 13.62 above.
[25] s. 67(2) and para. 13.66.
[26] See para. 13.46 above (in relation to old improvements: consents and notices required)

section 78[27] because that section commences with the works "save as expressly provided in this Act"; it is submitted that these writing down schemes implement, and do not avoid, the express terms of the statute.

13.124 **Arbitration**

This is dealt with generally in Chapter 16. One special feature of the arbitration award in relation to termination claims is the provision of a prescribed form of award.[28]

---

but the reasoning is equally applicable to relevant improvements.

[27] See para. 13.2 above.

[28] The Agricultural Holdings (Form of Award in Arbitration Proceedings) Order 1990 (S.I. 1990 No.1472).

Chapter 14

SUCCESSION ON DEATH OR RETIREMENT

14.1 Introduction

Succession on death

14.2 General scheme of Part IV
14.3 Tenancies to which Part IV applies
14.9 Exclusions from statutory succession
14.24 Making the application
14.27 Landlord's response
14.30 Making the application to be treated as eligible
14.33 Conditions for eligibility
14.34 Eligible relatives
14.36 The livelihood condition
14.52 The occupancy condition
14.70 Application to be treated as eligible
14.72 Suitability
14.75 Priority of applications
14.78 The Agricultural Land Tribunal
14.83 Seeking consent to operation of the notice to quit
14.84 Effect of direction by Agricultural Land Tribunal
14.85 Agreement and/or arbitration as to tenancy terms and rent
14.92 Changeover and adjustment to new tenancy
14.97 Succession tenancies: relationship to Agricultural Tenancies Act 1995
14.98 Succession tenancies: "rollover" of milk quota compensation

Succession on retirement

14.100 General scheme of Part IV: on retirement of the tenant
14.101 Conditions for operation of the retirement scheme
14.105 Exclusions from the retirement scheme
14.106 Availability of retirement where the tenant is under 65 but infirm
14.107 Inter-relationship of retirement notice and notices to quit
14.109 Application by the nominated successor and requirements to be satisfied
14.112 Application by landlord requesting a refusal of direction based on greater hardship

14.113 Fate of application
14.116 Arbitration on terms of any new tenancy
14.117 Death of tenant after giving retirement notice but before vesting of new tenancy in nominated successor; meaning of "the relevant time"
14.119 Effect of Tribunal direction on nominated successor's succession to other holdings
14.120 Succession planning
14.121 Miscellaneous

PROCEDURAL TABLES RELATING TO SUCCESSION

Part VI of this work contains procedural tables relevant to the progress of applications under the succession on death and succession on retirement provisions. These tables are designed to assist the reader in collating forms and time limits and are also designed to remind the reader what will happen if a relevant step is taken or not taken. The tables are:

7. Succession on death where Case G notice to quit has been served.
8. Succession on death where no Case G notice to quit is served.
9. Succession on retirement.
10. Arbitration following succession direction.

These tables work together in the following way.

In the case of succession following the tenant's death the application must be made within three months of the death. The procedure will then follow either Table 7 or Table 8, depending on whether a Case G notice to quit, by reason of the tenant's death, has been served. In the event that the applicant is successful he will be entitled to a direction and in the event that the terms of the new tenancy are not agreed, there will be arbitration as set out in Table 10. In the case of succession on the tenant's retirement, the procedure is as stated in Table 9. Once a direction has been awarded by the Tribunal, the ensuing procedure in the case of arbitration as to the terms of the tenancy is as set out in Table 10. Therefore whether on death or retirement, once the Tribunal has awarded a direction the procedure is to be found in Table 10.

14.1 Introduction

The Agriculture (Miscellaneous Provisions) Act 1976 introduced a fundamental change in the law of agricultural holdings in England and Wales by providing for a statutory succession on death to agricultural holdings.[1] At that time Parliament considered that there was sufficient evidence of hardship, although in a minority of cases, to justify the conferment on close relatives of a qualified right of succession. The objection that the creation of such a new statutory right, denying to the landlord for perhaps 100 years the opportunity of repossession, might damage the

---

[1] The word "succession" is a little misleading, as in general (apart from certain cases by agreement) the successful applicant does not become a successor in title to the deceased tenant. He does not succeed to the deceased tenant's tenancy, but acquires an entirely new tenancy, although the terms will be in general the same.

landlord and tenant system, and consequently harm agricultural production, was rejected by the government of the day. Less than 10 years later, however, this rejected view prevailed.[2] The right to succession was abolished upon the death of a tenant whose tenancy was granted on or after July 12, 1984, but the arrangements for phasing out the succession scheme were marked by a meticulous avoidance of retrospection which Justinian would have admired.[3] The result is that the legacy of succession will endure well into the twenty-first century. Paradoxically, in the course of phasing out, the succession scheme acquired a new dimension; it was *extended* to succession *inter vivos* on retirement.[4]

SUCCESSION ON DEATH

General scheme of Part IV: on death of the tenant 14.2

Part IV of the 1986 Act together with Schedule 6 contains the relevant provisions for a statutory succession on the tenant's death. When the sole or sole surviving tenant of an agricultural holding dies certain close relatives have the opportunity to apply to the Agricultural Land Tribunal for the grant of a new tenancy. This opportunity exists whether or not the landlord serves a notice to quit by reason of the death under Case G. There is a strict three month time-limit after the death during which the application must be made. An applicant must prove not only that he is a close relative of the deceased but also that he is able to satisfy the livelihood and commercial unit conditions which together constitute his eligibility to apply. These latter requirements are extremely technical and in the case of the principal source of livelihood test, a person who strictly speaking fails the test is able to request the Tribunal to exercise a discretion in his favour to raise what would otherwise be a bar on eligibility. However this request for the exercise of the Tribunal's discretion must also be made during the three months following the deceased's death. A person who is ruled to be eligible must also demonstrate his suitability to be given a new tenancy of the holding. If successful, the Tribunal will make a direction in the applicant's favour unless the landlord has both served a notice to quit on the tenant's death and by reason of it and is further able to demonstrate one of the grounds of opposition set out in section 27(2) of the Act. Any new tenancy in favour of the applicant will take the place of the old tenancy and will be on terms which are agreed or directed by arbitration.

Tenancies to which Part IV applies 14.3

In essence the succession provisions are historic in nature and it can in general terms be said that section 34(1)(a) enacts the general principle that the succession provisions apply to a tenancy of an agricultural holding granted before July 12, 1984. Section 34(1)(b) sets out a range of tenancies granted on or after that date which nevertheless will qualify for succession rights.[5] Apart from tenancies

---

[2] Agricultural Holdings Act 1984, s.2.
[3] "*Nova constitutio futuris formam imponere debet, non praeteritis*": Justinian 2, Inst. 292.
[4] See 1986 Act, ss. 49–59. It should be noted that the retirement provisions, like the succession on death provisions, apply only to tenancies granted before July 12, 1984 (subject to the exceptions in s.34(1)(b) of the 1986 Act): see s.49(1)(a) and s.34(1)(a).
[5] See paras 14.5–14.8.

granted on or after July 12, 1984 and falling outside section 34(1)(b) there are circumstances where no succession is allowed.[6]

14.4 Tenancies granted on or after July 12, 1984

Tenancies granted on or after July 12, 1984 and carrying succession rights are those referred to in section 34(1)(b). The four cases in point are not simply transitional provisions but rather, in the case of (i) and (ii) of sub-paragraph (b) are directed to preserving rights established through the grant of a protected tenancy prior to July 12, 1984. Sub-paragraph (iii) gives parties a useful instrument for negotiation whilst sub-paragraph (iv) is designed to stop tenancies accidentally losing succession rights.

14.5 Tenancies obtained by virtue of a direction

A tenancy granted on or after July 1, 1984 will carry succession rights if that tenancy was obtained by virtue of a direction of the Tribunal under section 39 (succession on the tenant's death) or section 53 (retirement succession). The wording of the section on its face quite clearly covers a tenancy in question being obtained pursuant to the 1986 Act. In addition, as a matter of logic, it is also applicable to a tenancy obtained prior to the passage of the 1986 Act (*e.g.* after July 12, 1984 but before the passage of the 1986 Act) and for these purposes it is submitted that the transitional provisions in Schedule 13, paragraph 1(1) have effect. It is submitted that the result is the same whether the relevant Tribunal direction was before or after July 12, 1984.

14.6 Tenancies granted following a direction

The succession provisions apply to a tenancy granted or on after July 12, 1984 where the tenancy was granted following a direction under section 39 in circumstances within section 45(6). This covers the case of a tenant who has been granted a direction under section 39 but who, prior to any vesting by virtue of that direction, takes his tenancy by a direct grant from the landlord in accordance with section 45(6).[7] Such a tenant has the same qualifications as the tenant referred to in paragraph 14.5 above, the only difference being in the vesting machinery. It is submitted that where a direction was granted under the preceding legislation the reference to section 39 should be read as including any direction given under that previous legislation.[8]

14.7 "Contracting-in tenancies"

Succession is available in the case of a tenancy being granted by a written contract of tenancy indicating (in whatever terms) that Part IV of the 1986 Act is to apply.[9] This is a provision which specifically permits parties to contract into succession. It may be of value, for example, where there is a sale of the freehold and a lease back of the property to the vendor. There is no particular form of words to be used in order to "contract in" to the succession provisions and moreover the wording of the section makes it unclear whether it is even necessary to refer specifically to Part IV

---

[6] See paras 14.9–14.23 below.
[7] The corresponding provision under preceding legislation was s. 23(6) of the 1976 Act.
[8] See Sched. 13, para. 1(1) of the 1986 Act.
[9] s. 34(1)(b)(iii).

of the Act as distinct from indicating that the effect intended by the parties is the availability of statutory succession. It is, however, a curiosity that in order to fall within this provision the tenancy must be granted by a written contract of tenancy containing the relevant indication and an oral tenancy (notwithstanding a corresponding agreed intention) cannot fall within these terms. A written contract of tenancy indicating (in whatever terms) that section 2(1) of the 1984 Act is not to apply is to be taken to be within section 34(1)(b)(iii).[10]

Grant to the existing tenant: surrender and re-grant 14.8
A tenancy granted on or after July 12, 1984 to a person who immediately before that date was a tenant of the holding or of any agricultural holding which comprised the whole or a substantial part of the land comprised in the holding will carry succession rights.[11] This sub-section protects the position of a tenant whose tenancy was granted prior to July 12, 1984 but who becomes entitled after that date to what is in law a new tenancy as a result of a surrender and re-grant. There is a need for this provision because there is the possibility that a surrender and re-grant may take place by operation of law without the parties necessarily realising that this has occurred. Although changes of tenancy terms will not normally have that effect,[12] the addition of land to the tenancy does have that result.[13] Amalgamation of the rent of two separate holdings does not necessarily involve a surrender and regrant.[14] The net position is that a landlord offering one or two extra fields to the tenant of a large farm will not run the risk that the existing tenancy which carries succession rights is surrendered and the new tenancy with the extra fields is created without succession. What a substantial part of the land comprised in the holding may amount to is a question of fact in each case. It is worth noting in passing that this section is very wide and there is a difference between "a tenant" and "the tenant".[15]

Exclusions from statutory succession 14.9
There are a considerable number of exclusions from statutory succession, each discussed below, set out in the following sections: 34(2), 36(2)(a), 36(2)(b), 37(1)(a) and (b), 37(2), 37(6), 38(1), 38(2), 38(3), 38(4) and 38(5).

Tenant deriving title by operation of law: section 34(2) 14.10
For the purposes of section 34 "tenant" does not include an executor, administrator, trustee in bankruptcy or other person deriving title from a tenant by operation of law.[16] Although there is a general definition of "tenant" in section 96, the word is more closely defined for the purposes of Part IV. These provisions parallel the use of the word "tenant" for the purposes of Case G.[17] The provision is not well drafted since literally construed the word "tenant" is only seen in section

---

[10] Sched. 13, para. 1(2).
[11] s. 34(1)(b)(iv).
[12] See *Jenkin R. Lewis and Son Ltd v. Kerman* [1971] Ch. 477.
[13] See *Baker v. Merckel* [1960] 1 QB 657, *Re Savile Settled Estates* [1931] 2 Ch. 210.
[14] See *J.W. Childers v. Anker* [1996] 1 E.G.L.R. 1, CA.
[15] See under the previous legislation the debate in *Jackson v. Hall, Williamson v. Thompson* [1980] A.C. 854; see also *Featherstone v. Staples* [1986] 1 W.L.R. 861.
[16] s. 34(2).
[17] Sched. 3, para. 12.

34(1)(b)(iv), but limited to that sub-section the restricted definition seems rather meaningless. It is submitted that it was probably intended to cover the circumstance of any tenancy referred to in section 34(1) being held by a person in a trustee-like capacity.

14.11 **Fixed term with more than 27 months unexpired at the tenant's death: section 36(2)(a)**

No succession is possible where the deceased at his death held under a tenancy for a fixed term of years of which more than 27 months remained unexpired.[18] Section 4 of the 1986 Act[19] provides for the death of the tenant during the fixed term with the result that the tenancy will terminate (without any further security of tenure) either on the original expiry date or on the first anniversary of that date. There appears however to be a limited need for section 36(2)(a) in that section 4 applies only to tenancies granted on or after September 12, 1984[20] but section 36(2)(a) applies to tenancies granted on or after July 12, 1984. There remains the possibility that a tenancy within section 34(1)(b)(ii), (iii), or (iv) might be tenancies for fixed terms.

14.12 *Gladstone v. Bower* **tenancies: section 36(2)(b)**

The death of a tenant holding for a fixed term of more than one but less than two years will not give rise to the possibility of statutory succession. Tenancies falling within this description are recognised as being protected by the 1986 Act even though they do not carry full security of tenure.[21] Such a tenancy is in effect a short term interest and it would be inappropriate for the complex machinery of statutory succession to apply.

14.13 **Two previous successions having occurred: section 37**

Where two previous successions have occurred the death of the sole or sole surviving tenant will not give rise to the opportunity for further succession to take place: section 37 specifies five different occasions which count towards the two-succession rule.[22] For the purposes of section 37 "tenant" has the same meaning as in section 34.[23] Throughout section 37 the occasions in question are concerned with not only the holding but, in the alternative, a "related holding". This is defined to mean "in relation to the holding, any agricultural holding comprising the whole or a substantial part of the land comprised in the holding".[24]

14.14 **Where tenancy obtained by virtue of a direction: section 37(1)(a)**

One occasion counting as a statutory succession is the obtaining of a tenancy by virtue of a direction of the Tribunal under section 39. For a direction made and a consequent tenancy obtained prior to the enactment of section 39 it is submitted that a succession should be regarded as having occurred.[25] It is not necessary for the

---

[18] s. 36(2)(a).
[19] Reproducing s. 3A inserted in the 1948 Act by Sched. 3, para. 2(2) to the 1984 Act.
[20] s. 11(2) of the 1984 Act.
[21] See *EWP Ltd v. Moore* [1991] 45 E.G. 180.
[22] Discussed in paras 14.14–14.18 below.
[23] s. 37(9); see also para. 14.10 below.
[24] s. 49(3).
[25] See Sched. 13, para. 1(1).

entirety of the original tenant's tenancy to be within the new letting nor for all joint tenants to satisfy the relevant criteria, provided one of them does.[26] It is not necessary for the new tenancy to include the whole of the land held by the original tenant nor for more than one of joint tenants to satisfy the relevant criteria.[27]

Where tenancy granted by landlord following a direction: section 37(1)(a)   14.15
A succession is regarded as taking place where a tenancy was granted following a direction under section 39 in circumstances within section 46(6).[28] It is submitted that a grant following a direction under equivalent previous legislation has the same effect.[29] Section 45(6) applies where a successful applicant who is both eligible and suitable enters into a tenancy with the landlord before the statutory deemed grant takes place at the relevant time.[30] It is not necessary for any new tenancy to relate to the whole of the original tenant's holding nor for all joint tenants to satisfy the relevant criteria provided one of them does.[31]

Where tenancy granted by landlord to a close relative who was sole   14.16
remaining applicant: section 37(1)(b)
An occasion of statutory succession is regarded as taking place where the landlord grants a tenancy to a close relative of the deceased tenant who was or had become the sole or sole remaining applicant for a direction.[32] In this circumstance matters have not proceeded as far as a direction from the Tribunal and, in effect, the applicant's claim remains unadjudicated. It is only necessary that he be a close relative of the deceased tenant.[33] Although this kind of tenancy counts for two-succession rule, it is not a tenancy to which section 34(1)(b) applies.[34] It is not necessary for any new tenancy to comprise the whole of the land within the original tenancy nor for all joint tenants to satisfy the relevant criteria provided one of them does.[35]

Succession *inter vivos* by agreement: section 37(2)   14.17
A deemed succession is regarded as taking place if during the tenant's life as a result of an agreement between himself and the landlord a new letting or an assignment takes place in favour of a person who at that time would have been a close relative had the tenant died immediately before the relevant grant or assignment.[36] This provision is considerably wider than that discussed in paragraph 14.16. Here there is no age limit in relation to the tenant and no

---

[26] s. 37(4)(a) and (b).
[27] s. 37(4)(a)/(b). Sub-s. (4) does not apply to a tenancy granted before September 12, 1984 in the circumstances identified by sub-s. (8).
[28] s. 37(1)(a).
[29] Sched. 13, para. 1(1).
[30] See para. 14.96 below.
[31] s. 37(4)(a)/(b). Sub-s. (4) does not apply to a tenancy granted before September 12, 1984 in the circumstances identified by sub-s. (8).
[32] s. 37(1)(b).
[33] As defined by s. 35(2).
[34] But the parties may contract into succession under s. 34(1)(b)(iii).
[35] s. 37(4). Sub-s. (4) does not apply to a tenancy granted before September 12, 1984 in the circumstances identified by sub-section (8).
[36] Close relative for these purposes is defined by s. 35(2).

requirement for the close relative to demonstrate his general eligibility or suitability. It is a useful means by which an ageing tenant can secure the succession to his chosen relative with the landlord's agreement. The landlord's interests are safeguarded by the fact that the arrangement counts as one of the two statutory successions. Such an arrangement is not a transaction within section 34(1)(b). If the term commences after the date of grant the holding is not regarded as let until the commencement of the term.[37] It is sufficient to trigger the succession occasion that an assignment is made to joint tenants only one of whom satisfies the criteria in section 37(2).[38] However section 37(5) does not apply in the circumstances identified by section 37(8). This restriction is appropriate in order to preserve the historic position because between 1976 and September 12, 1984 statutory succession was only regarded as taking place in the event of the grant of a new tenancy as distinct from the wider current provisions which include an assignment. In relation to any time before September 12, 1984 section 37(2) has effect only as modified by section 37(7).[39] For tenancies granted on or after September 12, 1984[40] the liberal provisions of section 37(4) apply. On that basis (excluding the case of assignment) the tenancy need not involve the entirety of the original tenant's holding[41] and the occasion is regarded as taking place where only one of joint tenants satisfies section 37(1) or (2).[42] The case of *Saunders v. Ralph*[43] provides an illustration of the application of section 37 and conveniently sets out the statutory history of the equivalent provisions since 1976.[44]

---

[37] s. 37(3).
[38] s. 37(5).
[39] As substituted it reads "if on any occasion prior to the date of death the holding or a related holding became let under a new tenancy granted by the landlord, with the agreement of the outgoing tenant, to a person who, if the outgoing tenant had died immediately before the grant would have been his close relative, that occasion shall for the purposes of sub-section (1) above be deemed to be an occasion such as is mentioned in that sub-section on which a tenancy of the holding or a related holding was obtained by virtue of a direction of the Tribunal under section 39 below".
[40] And which therefore fall outside s. 37(8). It is submitted that in section 37(8)(a) the reference is directed to the original tenancy not to any subsequent tenancy. The matter can be tested most easily by reference to an original tenancy granted before the September 12, 1984 which is assigned: in such a case the reference must be to the original tenancy. It is accordingly suggested that, although it is more ambiguous, in the case of a new tenancy being granted following an original tenancy itself granted prior to September 12, 1984 s. 37(8)(a) should be read in the same way as referring to the original tenancy and, on that footing, the transitional provisions would operate in an identical fashion depending on the date of grant of the original tenancy rather than the date of the subsequent transaction.
[41] s. 37(4)(a).
[42] s. 37(4)(b).
[43] [1993] 2 E.G.L.R. 1.
[44] However the Court, Jowitt J., applied the analysis of statutory succession to occasions taking place prior to 1976. With great respect it is submitted that this is not an appropriate approach. In many parts of the country there are occupying tenants holding in direct succession from their fathers and grandfathers and sometimes great grandfathers; it is suggested that the legislation was intended not to put these people in a worse position than

Succession on retirement at age 65 or over (deemed occasion): section 37(6)   14.18

The grant of a tenancy by virtue of a direction of the Tribunal under section 53(7) on a retirement succession is one which counts as the occasion of a statutory succession.[45]

Ordinary notice to quit followed by tenant's death where no counter-notice under section 26(1) or Tribunal had consented to operation of the notice to quit: section 38(1)   14.19

Section 38(1) excludes from the succession provisions any tenancy where at the date of death there is a valid notice to quit to which section 26 applies and either no counter-notice has been served or the Tribunal has already consented before the death to the operation of the notice to quit. In either of these circumstances such a notice to quit cannot be challenged and the tenancy is doomed to extinction.

Notice to quit under Case C or F followed by tenant's death: section 38(2)   14.20

Section 38(2) excludes from the succession provisions any tenancy where at the date of the tenant's death there is a valid notice to quit given prior to it which falls within either Case C (bad husbandry) or Case F (insolvency).[46] A valid notice to quit under Case C or Case F cannot be challenged and the tenancy must come to an end on expiry of the notice to quit.

Notice to quit under Case B, D or E followed by tenant's death but no demand for arbitration; alternatively notice to quit has been upheld or can no longer be challenged: section 38(3)   14.21

Section 38(3) excludes from the succession provisions any tenancy where at the date of the death there is a valid notice to quit given before that date which had either been upheld or could no longer be challenged being a notice to quit under Case B (non-agricultural use), D (remediable breach) or E (irremediable breach).[47] Although the drafting of sub-section (3) is somewhat terse it would appear that the objective is to disapply the succession provisions where the notice to quit must take effect on its expiry had the tenant not in the meantime died.

Tenancy a smallholding: section 38(4)   14.22

Section 38(4) excludes from the succession provisions tenancies consisting of land held by a smallholding authority or the Minister of Agricultural Fisheries and Food for the purposes of smallholdings within the meaning of Part III of the Agriculture Act 1970, whether the tenancy was granted before or after commencement of that Part. This is a statutory reversal of the decision of the Court of Appeal in *Saul v. Norfolk County Council*.[48] However, smallholdings authorities are required,

---

that enjoyed by a tenant whose father had not previously occupied the property. The legislation by contrast was probably simply designed to ensure that *enforced* successions although given under the shadow of the 1976 legislation should not be expected on more than two occasions. This is not quite the same as a submission as to retrospectivity as rejected by the learned Judge.

[45] s. 37(6).
[46] These Cases are to be found within Sched. 3.
[47] These Cases are to found in Sched. 3.
[48] [1984] Q.B. 559. Section 38(4) is worded as amended by the 1984 Act (Sched. 1, para.

when they intend to re-let a holding following the death of a tenant, to give priority consideration to certain specified near relatives of the deceased.[49]

14.23 Charity trustees holding land to settle ex-servicemen in agriculture: section 38(5)

Section 38(5) excludes from the succession provisions any tenancy granted by trustees of charitable trusts the sole or principal object of which is the settlement or employment in agriculture of ex-service personnel. It would not be possible to carry out the object of those trusts if the succession scheme applied.

14.24 Making the application: time limits

Section 39(1) provides that an application by an eligible person is to be made within the period of three months beginning with the day after the date of death. This period is calculated by reference to the corresponding date rule in computing time.[50] The Tribunal is not able to extend this statutory period and a failure to comply with it renders the application invalid.[51] In rare circumstances it might be arguable that compliance with the statutory time limit had been waived.[52] The application should be made to the Agricultural Land Tribunal for the appropriate area.[53] The applicant must be eligible at the date of the tenant's death and cannot thereafter render himself eligible by engaging in appropriate transactions.[54] A person losing eligibility after the date of death and after the application has been made will be ineligible thereafter for all purposes and the originally valid application will become invalid.[55] By contrast the question of suitability is determined by the Tribunal and a person who at the deceased's death may not have been suitable may become suitable thereafter.

An application under section 39 which is withdrawn or abandoned is to be treated as though it had never been made.[56]

14.25 Making the application: form

The question as to what form to use for making an application is governed by the Agricultural Land Tribunals (Succession to the Agricultural Tenancies) Order

---

2(6)). It contrasts with the original wording of s. 18(4)(f) of the 1976 Act excluding from succession tenancies granted "in pursuance of the said Part III" of the Agriculture Act 1970, *i.e.* granted under and after the 1970 Act. In **Saul v. Norfolk County Council** the CA held that a tenancy granted in 1965 was not granted "in pursuance" of the 1970 Act and accordingly did enjoy the benefit of the succession provisions.

[49] Smallholdings (Selection of Tenants) (Amendment) Regulations 1976 (S.I. 1976 No.2001).
[50] See **Dodds v. Walker** [1981] 1 W.L.R. 1027.
[51] **Kellett v. Alexander** [1981] 1 E.G.L.R. 1 at 3C-E, Woolf J.
[52] There is scope perhaps for extension of the approach in **Kammins Ballrooms Co. Ltd v. Zenith Investments (Torquay) Ltd** [1971] A.C. 850, HL.
[53] Not under any circumstances to be confused with the Lands Tribunal.
[54] Section 39(2) enacting the majority view of the HL in **Jackson v. Hall** [1980] A.C. 854.
[55] s. 39(2). Contrast the minority opinion of Lord Russell in **Jackson v. Hall** (above) at 893B-C.
[56] s. 40(4).

1984.[57] Rule 3(1) requires that Form 1 of the Order is to be used.[58] However a cursory glance at that Form demonstrates that it is not helpful in that it refers to repealed legislation. Any applicant may apply on the prescribed form; however a number of Tribunals have modified the prescribed form to update the references to current legislation and have therefore in effect created forms "substantially to the like effect [to the prescribed form] with such variations as circumstances may require".[59] Since these updated forms are not contained in any statutory instrument, they can only be obtained by a request from each individual Tribunal. Where more than one tenancy is held by the deceased at his death a separate form should be used in respect of each holding.[60] If there is more than one applicant, each applicant should file a separate form.[61] Notice of the application, also in prescribed form,[62] must at the time of making the application[63] be served on the landlord and on any person who to the knowledge of the applicant had made or may be able to make an application.[64] Late service of the notice of application may be cured by the exercise of the Tribunal's discretion.[65]

Making the application: how to complete the form 14.26

The information provided on the application forms the basis for determination of the case and completion of the form is therefore an extremely important task. It will not be easy for a lawyer to complete this form without input from a land agent, particularly bearing in mind the information required by paragraphs 2 (description of the holding and its farming), 4 (description of the buildings) and 5 (statement as to agricultural unit). Particular care is required in completing paragraph 5. Even if the Tribunal allows an amendment to the material originally submitted under paragraph 5, some scepticism can be expected as to the accuracy of any amendment. Paragraph 10 (dealing with principal source of livelihood) is often a critical paragraph in terms of the litigation and, moreover, probably all the information relevant to it is exclusively in the possession of the applicant. Therefore, again, accurate completion of this paragraph at an early stage is highly desirable. The same can be said of paragraph 12 (commercial unit test). Neither paragraph gives sufficient space for what will normally be necessary for proper completion of the request. Where necessary the person completing the form will have to create a Rider on a separate piece of paper and cross-refer the form to it. Part C of the form requires identified documents to be attached. Copies of a map of the holding and other land referred to in paragraph 5 must be provided in duplicate.

---

[57] S.I. 1984 No.1301.
[58] See Form 43 in Part V of this work.
[59] Bringing the updated form within r. 1(3) of the Order.
[60] As to procedure generally see para. 14.77 below.
[61] As to procedure generally see para. 14.78 below.
[62] Form 3 in the Order. See Form 45 in Part V of this work.
[63] Construed to mean "promptly" having regard to the circumstances of the particular case: Woolf J. in *Kellett v. Alexander* [1981] 1 E.G.L.R. 1 at 2G.
[64] Rule 5 of the Order which also requires the applicant to inform the Tribunal of the name and address of each person notified and further to give that information in the application itself.
[65] *Kellett v. Alexander* (above) pursuant to r. 37 and/or 38 of the principal Agricultural Land Tribunals (Rules) Order 1978 (S.I. 1978 No.259). See also para. 14.29 below.

Similarly duplicate copies will be needed of any other document it is intended to produce. Usually it is helpful to produce at an early stage copies of the accounts of the applicant if they show his principal source of livelihood. Often the applicant and the deceased will have been partners in which case the joint trading accounts should be attached. If in addition the applicant was partner in another business (which is quite common) those accounts should also be attached. The Notes to the form are very helpful and indicate categories of documents to which thought should be given. For example it would be usual and helpful to attach (when available) the deceased's death certificate, the deceased's marriage certificate, the applicant's birth certificate and any statement of assets on which the applicant intends to rely. As to this last, it may be that it is not available until a later stage when the applicant and/or his adviser has completed his researches. A full description of the applicant's work on the holding or any relevant agricultural unit should be given on the form and any supporting documentation (such as a contract of employment or certificates of education) should be attached.

Where the applicant also wishes to make an application to be treated as eligible the same form is to be used.[66]

14.27 Landlord's response: form

By section 39(7) the Tribunal must afford the landlord in every case the opportunity to state his views on suitability of the applicant. In fact the prescribed form presupposes, as rule 6 of the 1984 Order provides,[67] that the landlord may wish to oppose the whole or any part of the application. He must within one month after a copy of the application has been served on him reply in Form 1R.[68] The time-limit prescribed appears only in the Rules not in the statute. Once again, as with the application itself,[69] the form normally used is one prepared by and available through each regional Tribunal and contains references to current legislation rather than the old legislation, as contained in the prescribed form. The form is obtainable on request to the Tribunal. If the landlord also wishes to obtain the Tribunal's consent to the operation of a notice to quit a separate form must also be completed.[70]

14.28 Landlord's response: how to complete the form

Completion of the landlord's Form 1R is relatively straightforward. It is customary to ask a land agent to check the contents of paragraphs 2 and 4 of the applicant's application. In the event of any dispute it is extremely helpful if appropriate maps can be attached to Form 1R (in duplicate as requested by paragraph 5 of the form). The burden of proving the claim on eligibility rests firmly with the applicant and a statement that no admissions are made generally will suffice to alert the applicant that he must prove all aspects of eligibility and fully prove any claim under section 41 to be treated as eligible. Paragraph 4 of the form allows the statutory opportunity to express the landlord's opinion on the applicant's suitability.

---

[66] See paras 14.30–14.32 below.
[67] SI 1984 No.1301.
[68] See Form 43A in Part V of this work.
[69] See para. 14.25 above.
[70] See generally para. 14.83 below.

Sometimes it is clear that suitability can be admitted immediately; on other occasions suitability may be either denied or not admitted. Although it is sufficient completion of the form simply to state that suitability is denied or not admitted, it is very helpful to the Tribunal to indicate precisely what is perceived to be the difficulty with the application. It is in the nature of a succession application that the landlord or his agent may very well already know the applicant and his or her work on the holding. Objections to suitability will clearly carry more weight if stated on the form immediately; there is in this respect a contrast with eligibility where virtually all of the relevant information will be exclusively in the applicant's possession and not that of the landlord. In so far as there is insufficient space it is permissible to append a separate piece of paper and create a Rider to an answer given under the appropriate paragraph.

Filing, serving and amending forms: what time-limits may be extended or amendments allowed by the Tribunal   **14.29**

Rule 3 provides that applications and applications to be treated as eligible must be made at the same time and in the same form. Each is an application "to the Tribunal" and service upon any other party is a subsequent procedural requirement, not constitutive of the application itself.[71] If no application is made in time to the Tribunal, failure to observe that time limit is fatal. Where a time limit derives from the statute, as does that, there is no opportunity for the Tribunal to exercise its discretion in favour of extending time. However there is a power where time limits are prescribed by statutory instrument, to extend the time limit and, where appropriate, permit amendment of a duly made application or duly filed document.[72] The chairman may extend time on such terms and conditions as appear to him just,[73] whilst a failure to comply with the Rules will not render proceedings or acts invalid unless the chairman or the Tribunal so direct.[74] In the case of the time limit, the chairman may therefore act on his own which enables matters to proceed without the full Tribunal being convened. Similarly the chairman has the power to act under rule 38 to determine that proceedings are invalid but it is submitted that he ought not to do so unless there are very special circumstances and in the normal way so serious a step ought to be taken only by the full Tribunal. Strictly speaking a request to amend a document filed is a failure to comply with the Rules because the Rules require the relevant application to be filed within a particular period; amendments prior to the expiry of that period would

---

[71] See *Kellett v. Alexander* [1981] 1 E.G.L.R. 1, Woolf J. Section 40(5) requires rules to be made, but does not itself specify any time-limits. The relevant rules are in S.I. 1984 No.1301.
[72] Agricultural Land Tribunals (Rules) Order 1978 (S.I. 1978 No.259), rr. 37 and 38.
[73] r. 37. In *Moss v. National Coal Board* (1982) 264 E.G. 52 the HC gave further guidance in regard to r. 37. An application under it for extension of time is not an "interlocutory" application under r. 18 of the succession Rules (S.I. 1984 No.1301), which relates to matters incidental to the preparation of the substantive case. The chairman is not bound to afford an oral hearing in the case of applications under r. 37 to extend time, but must, of course, consider any relevant written representations and exercise his discretion judicially. He can use it to extend the 28 day time-limit for requesting a reference to the HC of a question of law arising in the course of the proceedings.
[74] r. 38.

appear to be as of right. Ultimately should the Tribunal refuse to extend the time-limit for service of a Reply to any application (whether by landlord or by applicant), the effect is as provided by rule 15.[75]

14.30 Making the application to be treated as eligible: form
An application under section 41 to be treated as eligible must be made with the same time period and on the same form as the main application under section 39.[76] The form prescribed by the 1984 Order[77] is in practice replaced by many Tribunals making available an almost identical form with reference to current legislation.[78] Part B of the form is the relevant section of it for these purposes.

14.31 Making the application to be treated as eligible: completion of the form
The same general comments apply as to lack of space and the filing of riders as are made under paragraph 14.26 above. It is not any admission of a defect in the main section claim also to file a claim under section 41. It is perfectly routine for applicants to make claims under each heading, particularly in view of the extremely technical problems generated by the source of livelihood condition regarding eligibility.

14.32 Making the application to be treated as eligible: time-limits incapable of extension
Section 41(2) provides a statutory time-limit within which the application to be treated as eligible must be made. This is not a time-limit capable of extension.[79] As to the meaning and availability of any application to be treated as eligible and the exercise of the Tribunal's discretion see paragraphs 14.70–14.71 below.

14.33 Conditions for eligibility
"Eligible person" for the purposes of Part IV of the Act means any surviving close relative of the deceased tenant[80] who satisfies the livelihood test in section 36(3)(a) and the commercial unit test in section 36(3)(b). Each of these is dealt with separately below.[81]

14.34 Close relative of the deceased tenant
The deceased tenant must have been survived by at least one of a limited number of close relatives[82] and the applicant must be within this class.[83] The class consists of:

---

[75] See further under para. 14.78 below.
[76] Section 41(2) and r. 3(2) of the Agricultural Land Tribunals (Succession to Agricultural Tenancies) Order 1984 (S.I. 1984 No.1301).
[77] Form 1 (Succession on Death); see Form 43 in Part V of this work.
[78] As perhaps contemplated by r. 1(3)(b) of the 1984 Order.
[79] Although in rare circumstances it may possibly be the case that a time-limit is waived: see *Kammins Ballrooms Company Ltd v. Zenith Investments (Torquay) Ltd* [1971] A.C. 850, HL.
[80] Being a sole or sole surviving tenant: s. 35(1)(b).
[81] Relationship to the deceased at paras 14.34–14.35; the livelihood condition at paras 14.36–14.51; the occupancy condition at paras 14.52–14.69.
[82] s. 35(1)(b).
[83] s. 36(1) and (3).

(a) the wife or husband of the deceased,

(b) a brother or sister of the deceased.

(c) a child of the deceased,

(d) any person (not within (b) or (c) above) who, in the case of any marriage to which the deceased was at any time a party, was treated by the deceased as a child of the family in relation to that marriage.[84]

There seems no reason to exclude from the definition of wife or husband a separated spouse, whose status can be proved by simple production of a marriage certificate. A brother or sister of the deceased is not identified as being a full or half brother or sister and it would appear that both are included in this category. Proof of relationship may be demonstrated by appropriate birth/marriage certificates. A "child" must mean any person below the age of majority (*i.e.* 18) and may be an illegitimate or adopted child.[85] A "treated" child must be so treated in relation to a marriage to which the deceased was a party. It follows that if the deceased was a bachelor, widower or divorcee the child would not qualify. An orphan child brought up by grandparents would only qualify if it could be established that the child was treated by the grandparents as a child in relation to their own marriage. A step-child, foster child or child taken in without formal adoption would have to fall within the "treated" category in order to qualify.

Non-eligible family members 14.35

The restriction to a spouse of the deceased or a person treated as a child of the family in relation to a marriage of the deceased appears out of keeping with modern conditions where marriages may be shortlived and co-operative cohabitation long term and stable. It is doubtful whether the farming community is exempt from general sociological trends but it is likely that the heart of the present legislation derives from historic perceptions.[86] Consequently a mistress or cohabitee is excluded, as is any gay partner. Nephews, nieces and grandchildren are all quite clearly outside the definition in the normal way, as is a son-in-law or daughter-in-law of the deceased. Any of these persons might be materially dependent on the deceased and/or the holding but there is no opportunity for the Tribunal to extend the availability of succession.

The livelihood condition 14.36

The livelihood condition to be satisfied before an applicant may be considered eligible is contained in section 36(3)(a). The applicant must demonstrate that:

> "In the seven years ending with the date of death his only or principal source of livelihood throughout a continuous period of not less than five years, or two or more discontinuous periods amounting to not less than five years, derived from his agricultural work on the holding or on an agricultural unit of which the holding forms part."

---

[84] s. 35(2).
[85] See the Children Act 1975, Sched. 3, para. 3(5).
[86] 1976.

14.37 The livelihood condition: the relevant period

The satisfaction of the livelihood condition is often the most contentious aspect of any succession application. The first point to note in relation to this condition is that the applicant is entitled to choose which period of five years he wishes the Tribunal to consider.[87] Strictly speaking it would appear that the applicant is entitled to start with the date of death and cast his eye backwards for seven years in order to seek out a total of time amounting to five years within the seven in order to satisfy the test. In reality, of course, it is extremely difficult to assimilate financial information without first erecting a year by year framework for comparative purposes. Thus it may be convenient to divide the period of seven years into seven individual years so that the financial information may more easily be compared. For example, it is unlikely that the deceased will die on the last day of his accounting year; the likelihood is that profits from a business (and drawings from that business) will have to be apportioned so as to show what part of the profit or drawings derive from the period included within each of the seven years material to the test. To some extent it might be said this gives the applicant the ability to demonstrate a "creative" approach to the figures. There is, however, considerable convenience in adopting this approach, particularly in cases where more than one set of accounts has to be analysed and compared.

14.38 Meaning of livelihood

It is now tolerably clear that "livelihood" essentially relates to consumption rather than financial entitlement. In *Trinity College Cambridge v. Caines* [1984] 2 E.G.L.R. 17, Webster J. concluded:

> "That the expression 'source of livelihood' means what the applicant spends or consumes on her ordinary living expenses from time to time in money and/or kind and that it does not include money that she has available to spend but does not in fact spend for that purpose.[88]"

In a similar vein Stuart-Smith L.J. in *Welby v. Casswell* [1995] 2 E.G.L.R. 1 stated:

> "Livelihood can be defined as 'means of living' (see *Shorter Oxford Dictionary*), that is to say what is spent or consumed for the purpose of living. The source of one's livelihood in so far as it is money, is income; in so far as it is the use or consumption of goods, it is benefits in kind.[89]"

Since actual consumption or expenditure is the test, mere financial entitlement, if demonstrated, is not sufficient proof for the purposes of the test unless it can also be demonstrated how much of that income, where there is more than one source, has been spent. This has the curious result that the prudent applicant who reinvests farm profits in the business and chooses to live frugally from his savings will not be able to demonstrate that his means of living derives from the farm.

---

[87] *Bailey v. Sitwell* [1986] 2 E.G.L.R. 7, Hodgson J.
[88] At 19H.
[89] At 3D.

Source of livelihood
14.39

There has been a period of uncertainty as to whether the statute requires the Tribunal to consider not simply the ostensible source of livelihood but also any underlying finance giving rise to it. In *Bailey v. Sitwell* (above) the judge at first instance refused to take account of the fact that part of the capital employed in the business generating the livelihood came from the deceased tenant. He preferred instead to confine attention, in terms of derivation of livelihood, to the immediate fact that the applicant had worked on the farm and drawn from it the only money that he drew from anywhere. In *Welby v. Casswell* (above) this approach was specifically approved[90] and in that case the Court of Appeal declined to investigate where money to fund the partnership business itself had come from as distinct from having regard to the applicant's ability to draw on the business because of his work for it. Whether or not the business made a profit in a year when the applicant drew from it was not germane.[91] Millett L.J. summarised matters as follows:

> "... the section is not concerned with whether an applicant for a new tenancy was living beyond his means or with how the excess was funded. It requires him to establish his economic dependence on the holding by showing that his work on the holding provided his main means of livelihood."[92]

His agricultural work
14.40

The meaning of "agricultural work" is not defined by the statute. Clearly it would include manual labour whether skilled or unskilled. Equally clearly some element of supervision and management in relation to farming would be included. If there is to be a dispute it will normally centre upon the extent to which secretarial book-keeping or computer work can be classified as "agricultural" work. It would appear likely that the issue is not one of principle so much as a question of fact and degree. A person who simply calculates the wages bill for farm workers is probably the wrong side of the line; a person who keeps milk records or plans the cropping cycle is probably the right side of it. It is submitted that this is a matter primarily for the good sense of the Tribunal having regard to the circumstances of the individual farm. In relation to the deceased tenant's wife there is a special provision whereby his work counts as hers.[93]

Work on the holding
14.41

The applicant must demonstrate that his livelihood was derived from his agricultural work on the holding or on an agricultural unit of which the holding forms part.[94] On the face of it there does not appear to be any difficulty in identifying the holding or relevant agricultural unit; however on closer inspection there may well be a problem. Specifically in *Trinity College Cambridge v. Caines*[95] it was held at first instance by Webster J. that the expression the holding

---

[90] Stuart-Smith L.J. at 3L-M
[91] Stuart-Smith L.J. at 3A-M.
[92] *Welby v. Casswell* (above) at 4B-C.
[93] See para. 14.44 below.
[94] s. 36(3)(a).
[95] [1984] 2 E.G.L.R. 17 at 19L–20H.

or an agricultural unit of which it forms part could not properly be construed so as to include land which did not at the date of death form part of the holding or a relevant agricultural unit. Put more simply this means that the applicant must look through the relevant seven-year period focusing in on the block of land which at the deceased's death comprised the holding and the unit as it stood at that time. If there have been changes in the composition of the holding or the agricultural unit adjustments will have to be made to the financial calculations.[96]

The second point to note is that work counting in favour of the applicant is work "on" the holding or a relevant agricultural unit. It would therefore include an independent agricultural business taking place on the holding (*e.g.* a separate sheep enterprise) but would exclude money derived from agricultural work physically performed elsewhere. The difficult case, of course, is one such as that of a contracting business performed largely off the holding but where the machinery was stored on the holding and in addition the contracting was also performed for the deceased tenant.

14.42 **Agricultural unit of which the holding forms part**
The applicant's only or principal source of livelihood throughout the relevant five-year period must be derived from his agricultural work on the holding "or on an agricultural unit of which the holding forms part".[97] Section 96 defines "agricultural unit" to mean land which is an agricultural unit for the purposes of the Agriculture Act 1947. Section 109(2) of that Act states:

> "109(2) In this Act the expression "agricultural unit" means land[98] which is occupied as a unit for agricultural purposes, including—
>
> (a) any dwelling house or other building occupied by the same person for the purpose of farming the land, and
>
> (b) any other land falling within the definition in this Act of the expression "agricultural land" which is in the occupation of the same person, being land as to which the Minister is satisfied that having regard to the character and situation thereof and other relevant circumstances it ought in the interests of full and efficient production to be farmed in conjunction with the agricultural unit, and directs accordingly:
>
> Provided that the Minister shall not give a direction under this sub-section as respects any land unless it is for the time being not in use for any purpose which appears to him to be substantial having regard to the use to which it might be put for agriculture."

There are further definitions in section 109(3) of the 1947 Act including in particular "agriculture". Section 109(5) provides:

---

[96] See further the second problem discussed in para. 14.42 below.
[97] s. 36(3)(a).
[98] It has been held that the wording of the section excludes any useful reference to the definition of "land" in the then Interpretation Act: see ***Hasell v. McAulay*** [1952] 2 All E.R. 825, Lord Goddard C.J. at 826E.

"109(5) References in this Act to the farming of land include references to the carrying on in relation to the land of any agricultural activity; and in relation to any agricultural activity the person having the right to carry it on shall be deemed to be the occupier of the land."

The first question to be considered is whether, in order to find an agricultural unit it is necessary that the tenure of the unit or parts of it should be the same as that on which the holding itself was enjoyed (*i.e.* held solely in the name of the deceased whether on a tenanted or freehold basis). It is submitted that this is not the case and that section 109 and in particular section 109(5) directs attention not so much to formal tenure as a legally enforceable right under which particular parts of land are enjoyed or (in the case of land not actually occupied) are deemed to be enjoyed. A partnership confers upon non-land owning partners the right to enjoy land and to use it for farming purposes. It is submitted that the view expressed above is supported by observations of Webster J. in *Trinity College Cambridge v. Caines*.[99] It is submitted that where land is occupied by a partnership all areas farmed together by the partners should be considered as one agricultural unit. This may produce a problem in relation to periods prior to the date of death where the composition of the partnership was different or where some other farming arrangement appertained. In those circumstances it would appear that the correct figures to take for livelihood would be based only on drawings and/or benefits derived from the holding as distinct from any larger agricultural unit.

The second problem encountered is the question as to what land to include from time to time in the designation agricultural unit where the blocks of land farmed together have fluctuated over a period of time (even though occupied by the same persons). This difficulty was highlighted in the case of *Trinity College Cambridge v. Caines*.[1] The question referred to the Judge was whether the expression "the holding or on an agricultural unit of which the holding forms part" could properly be construed so as to include land which did not at the date of death of the deceased tenant form part of the holding or an agricultural unit of which the holding at that date formed part. The Judge replied in the negative stating that he regarded the use of the present tense in the statute as conclusive in relation to the date of death. He expressly rejected the view that the agricultural unit might include such blocks of land as from time to time over the historic period were occupied together with the holding. This is not a convenient conclusion in terms of presentation of the case for the Agricultural Land Tribunal since it will require advisers to assist in "breaking up" accounts to discern the relevant profitability of different parcels of land on the assumption that they were farmed separately as distinct from together which was the reality. Thus if block A forms part of the agricultural unit with the holding at death but during the relevant five-year period blocks A and B were farmed as part

---

[99] [1984] 2 E.G.L.R. 17 at 18M: "but even though Mrs Caines is managing the farm, that does not in my judgment constitute the carrying on by her of 'any agricultural activity'. It is the tenant or the partnership, or Richard himself, who carries on that activity and who has the right to carry on the activity of farming Stanbridge Farm and of employing Mrs Caines to manage, not to carry on, that activity—giving her no right to carry on that activity".
[1] [1984] 2 E.G.L.R. 17.

of a unit with the holding, in ascertaining how far the applicant may have been dependent on the holding farmed together with block A at any one time profits or figures relating to block B will have to be stripped out. In a case where both blocks A and B were occupied at the date of death with the holding but during the historic period only block A was occupied with the holding it is submitted that the *Trinity College Cambridge v. Caines* decision does not apply and the correct figure to take is the figure generated historically by the holding and block A (on the basis that the greater—blocks A and B—includes the less—block B), and subsequently the entire agricultural unit of the holding plus blocks A and B.

The third difficulty to be considered is how an agricultural unit may be proved. It is to be expected that the Tribunal will interest itself in the extent to which any alleged agricultural unit is farmed on an integrated basis with the holding. This could include crop rotation, shared equipment, shared staff, shared holding number for official purposes such as subsidy, common accounts and common purchasing policies. This type of detail can usually be demonstrated by looking at June census returns, IACS forms, stock movement books, ledgers or computer records and company or partnership accounts.

14.43 **What is the principal source of livelihood**
In practice Tribunals have approached the assessment of principal source of livelihood on the basis that livelihood relevantly derived (*i.e.* from the holding or an agricultural unit of which it forms part) must outweigh in terms of value all other sources of livelihood. In other words it is not a question of ascertaining which source of livelihood is the greatest, without lumping together all the non-relevant livelihood.[2] The meaning of livelihood,[3] and of source of livelihood[4] are discussed elsewhere as is the question of how to compare sources of livelihood.[5]

14.44 **Agricultural work by the deceased counting as work by his wife**
There is a special provision in section 36(4) whereby in the case of the deceased's wife the reference to an applicant's agricultural work is to be read as a reference to agricultural work carried out by either the wife or the deceased (or both of them). This provision avoids the difficulties of the farmer's wife whose working husband, although expecting her to help on the farm, did not pay her. It has the benefit of avoiding any argument as to "pooling" of entitlement.[6] There still remains the problem of periods of time during which the deceased and his wife may have been dependent on partnership income generated on the holding at a time when he was too old or too ill to work. A wife caring for an older husband in these circumstances takes no benefit from the special provision in section 36(4).

---

[2] This approach underlies the figures in *Wilson v. Earl Spencer's Settlement Trustees* [1985] 1 E.G.L.R. 3, Hodgson J.
[3] At para. 14.38 above.
[4] At para. 14.39 above.
[5] At para. 14.48 below.
[6] See para. 14.46 below.

Full time higher education: Schedule 6, paragraph 2   14.45

By Schedule 6, paragraph 2 a maximum of three years full-time education undergone by the applicant at a university college or other higher or further education establishment counts as a period throughout which his only or principal source of livelihood derived from his agricultural work on the holding. The applicant is entitled to choose the relevant three years for the purposes of this deemed satisfaction of the test[7] and if he has in fact enjoyed substantial outside income and his further education course lasted more than three years the ability to choose may be important to him. It is to be noted that there is no requirement at all that any aspect of the course should be connected with agriculture.

How applicant may demonstrate eligibility: livelihood   14.46

The applicant's objective must be to show not only each source of livelihood, both relevantly derived and derived from outside sources, but also to do this in a way which allows true comparison for the purposes of the statutory test.[8] Since livelihood means income consumed or benefits in kind[9] it is necessary in relation to benefits in kind to value or assess in a monetary fashion to allow the comparison to take place.[10] Reference is made to paragraph 14.48 below for the discussion as to how to make the comparison between sources of livelihood.

In relation to benefits in kind consumed or enjoyed by the applicant, normally a list of items enjoyed, an assessment of the quantity of them and a value of the retail cost of them is the fairest way of making the assessment. Quite often "benefits in kind" are shown either on partnership accounts or income tax returns, usually filled in by accountants without doing the full and detailed exercise and nearly always on the basis of what would be acceptable to the Inland Revenue rather than what precisely has actually been going on. It is submitted that these kind of figures drawn up for a different purpose should not be preferred to figures reached after a full and detailed retrospective assessment. In fact the value of items such as daily milk, eggs, meat, poultry and vegetables can be very considerable. Other benefits in kind are much easier to quantify since they are usually paid for in cash by the partnership, company or employer, *e.g.* telephone bills, petrol, the cost of a car, heating bills, electricity. As to the benefit of accommodation see paragraph 14.50 below.

How applicant may demonstrate eligibility: discovery   14.47

Because livelihood means income consumed, in many cases it is important to ascertain what items of consumption can be "counted in" in the applicant's favour. Clearly expenditure on food, bills for the household, items of household equipment, the provision of the family car and the cost of running it (including insurance) and holidays are in. Equally clearly items such as pension contributions

---

[7] See ***Bailey v. Sitwell*** [1986] 2 E.G.L.R. 7, Hodgson J. for the principle that the applicant may choose—although not in that case related specifically to Sched. 6, para. 2.
[8] See para. 14.43 above.
[9] See para. 14.38 above.
[10] See ***Wilson v. Earl Spencer's Settlement Trustees*** [1985] 2 E.G.L.R. 3, Hodgson J.: the failure by the tribunal to assess fringe benefits in financial terms led to the case being remitted.

and savings schemes do not constitute livelihood. School fees (frequently a very heavy item) fall more into an area for discussion and debate. On the one hand it might be argued that the statute is concerned only with expenditure to keep the applicant as distinct from other members of his family particularly bearing in mind the problems of "pooled" resources. Conversely, on the other hand, it would seem reasonable to assume that the applicant with a legal duty to maintain a wife and/or children or who is in fact maintaining a cohabitee and/or children ought to be regarded as in a sense himself enjoying the money spent in keeping them to whatever standard he deems appropriate. It would seem on that basis curious to allow the cost of the family washing machine but not the children's clothes or school fees.[11]

However unfair it may seem, where savings are made from an agricultural wage paid to the applicant rather than consumed, the value of those savings does not count as livelihood. Where the applicant is a partner it is not his partnership entitlement which represents his livelihood but rather the drawings he made and any salary he used in order to keep himself.

The problem of "pooled" resources arises where the applicant shares a household and more than one person contributes to it. This might be the situation with husband and wife or co-habitees whether homosexual or heterosexual. It is also likely to arise where the applicant and the deceased shared the household. In the latter case it has been held that the task of the Tribunal is "to identify what part of the total expenditure on the livelihood of the household was the applicant's and what was the father's".[12] Where the pool is created by the merged resources of husband and wife there is some suggestion that the other spouse may be beneficially entitled to half of the applicant's contribution to the pool by virtue of the marriage so as to cut down what one might otherwise view as the applicant's contribution.[13] However it is suggested that this approach is grossly unfair and is not sufficiently clear in the reported decision for a Tribunal to be able to ascertain its extent.[14]

14.48 How to compare sources of livelihood: Schedules
Discovery is not normally ordered by the Tribunal except as a last resort following a request from one party or the other. As stated above[15] it is customary to attach some documentation to the application when it is made. Generally speaking the applicant's advisers will be aware that the burden is on the applicant to prove his case and the applicant will volunteer some documentation and may respond to a "shopping list" from the landlord's advisers. It is normally necessary and proper for the applicant to provide records stretching back over seven years from the

---

[11] It appears to have been assumed by Webster J. in *Trinity College Cambridge v. Caines* [1984] 2 E.G.L.R. 17 at 19E that the cost of educating children would have been an item of family expenditure included within the general description of livelihood. But it is not clear whether in that case there was any argument over the Judge's observation.
[12] *Bailey v. Sitwell* [1986] 2 E.G.L.R. 7, Hodgson J. at 8C.
[13] *Wilson v. Earl Spencer Settlement Trustees* [1985] 1 E.G.L.R. 3 at 4.
[14] Apart from anything else it has the extraordinary result of discriminating against married couples compared to unmarried or gay couples, which appears illogical.
[15] para. 14.2 above.

deceased's death which will demonstrate the applicant's financial dependence on the holding. Any relevant contract of employment, the applicant's tax returns, the June census returns (usually showing him as an employee) and corresponding documentation for the applicant's wife will be provided. Any relevant partnership deed and partnership accounts will normally be provided. Disclosure must be made of any adverse items such as expenditure from savings or investments and it would be customary to request an accountant (frequently the partnership accountant) to assist in drawing up such a list. In some cases the applicant may be able to provide copies of bills paid or may obtain a statement from a utility supplier as to consumption: this is not normally necessary with a partnership since that expenditure is frequently shown in the partnership accounts. The applicant may have bank accounts which show weekly amounts being drawn for groceries or (increasingly nowadays) may have credit card accounts which list expenditure and therefore make it much easier for his advisers to reconstruct how he has been living. School fees[16] are usually an item easily ascertained by requesting the school to provide a statement. In so far as documents already exist the landlord might, if his reasonable requests are resisted, consider applying to the Tribunal for an order for discovery. In so far as documentation would have to be created for the purposes of the case he will not be entitled to demand discovery in advance of being given the material but if he is given it at a very late stage it would be reasonable for him to complain to the Tribunal and in some circumstances may cast doubt on the reliability of the evidence being given.

If an agricultural unit is being alleged for some part of the relevant seven years it is appropriate to ask for June census returns, IACS forms, the deceased's partnership deed and accounts, the stock movement books ledgers and where appropriate computer records of the person farming and such other documentation as a land agent may advise would assist in deciding whether or not there was in truth integrated farming.

Rule 30 of the Agricultural Land Tribunals (Succession to Agricultural Tenancies) Order 1984[17] applies rule 20 of the principal Agricultural Land Tribunals (Rules) Order 1978[18] to succession applications. Rule 20 requires that a party shall furnish to the secretary on his request any document or other information which the Tribunal may require and which it is in the power of the party to furnish, and shall afford to all other parties an opportunity to inspect such document or a copy of such document, and to take copies thereof. This however does not require the furnishing of any information which would be contrary to the public interest to disclose. Essentially therefore any application for discovery should be made to the chairman of the Tribunal under rule 19 of the principal Rules[19] in writing stating the grounds of the application. If the Tribunal decides to require documents in a party's power (therefore including documents held by the Ministry to the party's order), the other party to the litigation must have an opportunity to inspect the document or a copy of it and to take copies therefrom.[20]

---

[16] As to which see para. 14.47 above.
[17] S.I. 1984 No.1301.
[18] S.I.1978 No.259,
[19] As applied by r. 30 of the 1984 Order.
[20] There have been occasional instances where documents have been ordered to be made

SUCCESSION ON DEATH OR RETIREMENT

The Tribunal has a discretion as to what to require and it is submitted that a robust view should be taken: the applicant comes to the Tribunal and must prove his case—where a landlord has reason to suspect that there may be documents or information in what would be otherwise private bank accounts or credit card accounts which would damage the applicant's case it is not appropriate for the Tribunal to take an exaggerated view of an applicant's desire for privacy. The interests of justice ought to override such sensitivities.

14.49 **Effect on figures of complex land holdings: reconstructing from accounts**
Even in the simplest cases it is usual to encounter sources of livelihood which are relevant and count in the applicant's favour on the application and others which are not relevantly derived and count against him. The easiest (and increasingly the usual) way to compare the two[21] is to draw up comparative schedules of relevantly derived and non-relevantly derived livelihood for each of the years stretching back year by year from the deceased's death. The relevantly derived element might include, for example, the applicant's wages or partnership drawings, the value of his accommodation, the value of benefits in kind, the amount of any bills paid for the household. In the non-relevantly derived schedule, column by column, one might show for each material year income spent from savings or interest received, money from outside work, and benefits provided on a basis unconnected with farming on the holding. It is submitted that here is the appropriate place to show any wife's earnings or household contributions from another person rather than undertaking a separate "pooling" exercise.

Having drawn up the schedules at a relatively early stage the applicant's advisers ought to be able to form a clearer picture of whether or not the application is likely to succeed. Increasingly in recent years cases are settled without going to full hearing because expertise in making the relevant comparisons is increasing.

Not unusually different farming enterprises are shown in the same accounts. From an Inland Revenue point of view this is not a problem but it is a great problem for the Tribunal. If, for example, there is an agricultural unit but the profits from it are contained within accounts showing other elements as well or other blocks of land it will be necessary to "break" the accounts. A reconstruction will then have to take place so as to show what might reasonably be reflected in the accounts from the actual agricultural unit, whether this is by using gross margins or by calculating a separate budgetary exercise based on historic figures. Clearly this is a very skilled exercise and it will require a land agent rather than an accountant to do it.[22]

14.50 **How to reflect the benefit of accommodation in figures**
Where the applicant resides on the holding and does so by reason of his agricultural work this will nearly always be a very major component in his livelihood. It is

---

available to the other party on a "visit and see but do not take copies" basis. This is contrary to all litigation practice, unfair since the person visiting may not ultimately be responsible for giving the decisive advice and clearly contrary to r. 20 of the principal Rules.

[21] As required: see para. 14.43 above.

[22] Notwithstanding the fact that the accountant may initially have drawn up the accounts. He may be able to explain the basic figures to a land agent but where knowledge of

submitted that the valuation of this benefit should be not what was the cost to the provider of the accommodation but what was the value of it to the applicant. In other words what would the applicant from time to time have had to pay in order to enjoy the benefit of the accommodation? Expert evidence on this is nearly always required. If the applicant occupied accommodation on the basis that he owned it but by reason of his work mortgage payments were met, it is submitted that the true test here is the actual cost expended by the person meeting the payments (these being payments which would otherwise have to be met by the applicant himself).

It should be noted that the benefit of accommodation may count either in favour or against the applicant depending on the reason why he has it. Once reduced to figures those accommodation figures ought to be inserted in the appropriate place in the schedules. It is submitted that where the accommodation is provided or paid for by reason of the applicant's work it is not appropriate to take back part of that benefit into the non-relevantly derived figures to reflect any concurrent part-time work by the applicant's spouse or cohabitee.[23]

Principles for succession planning 14.51

Because of the value to a farmer of a tenanted holding it is quite normal for succession planning to take place once the decision has been taken for a family member to continue farming into the next generation. Just as retirement succession has made it increasingly attractive for elderly farmers to retire rather than holding the tenancy until they die, so also there are changes in the way farmers will live in order to achieve a successful succession. Gone are the days where the farmer's son will necessarily be kept working on the farm for long hours with virtually no pay, sustained if he is lucky by part-time earnings of his wife. Such a situation creates a potential succcession disaster. A legal adviser contemplating a succession planning arrangement must have clear and accurate information as to the way in which the existing business or businesses run, where they take place and what the accounting position is. It is usually a straightforward matter to ensure that the potential applicant does not run the danger of failing the occupancy condition[24]: the real problem is making sure that his source of livelihood is demonstrably from the holding or an agricultural unit of which it forms part. If the tenant's holding is large enough to support him it is better that the applicant should derive his livelihood exclusively from it rather than becoming involved with dependency on an agricultural unit. This then avoids the problem of the technical requirements of an agricultural unit failing in any one year.[25] Ideally the applicant will reside on the holding in a property made available to him rent free because he is working on the holding and he will live exclusively or mainly from his wage or partnership drawings derived from that work. Where it is not convenient to have a partnership which reflects only farming on the holding it is satisfactory to have a legal obligation confining the applicant's work to that holding so that all his income/drawings comes from that. If the business is limited to the holding as many

---

farming is required it is submitted that an accountant is not appropriately qualified.
[23] The cohabitee may enjoy the accommodation but its provision derives exclusively from the applicant's work.
[24] See paras 14.52 and following below.
[25] See para. 14.42 above.

benefits in kind as possible (documented as time goes by) are helpful; conversely if the farming enterprise includes other blocks of land beyond the holding or an agricultural unit of which it forms part, benefits in kind will partly count against the applicant and they should by preference be reduced or eliminated.

Where there is necessarily income which might count against the applicant he should be given the firmest advice to save it and put it undoubtedly beyond reach so that he is not tempted to spend it on his living expenditure or annual holidays. One delicate problem is the situation of partners where the father is the tenant but one of the sons wishes to succeed. The potential applicant may as a result of succession planning have to take inferior accommodation or less in the form of wages/drawings so as to tie in with demonstrable expenditure. It is suggested that the way round the problem is to ensure that his partnership capital is "topped up" from year to year but not spent on livelihood. The second main area where succession planning plays a part is in checking, in good time, that the applicant will have available to him sufficient capital to continue the enterprise in the event of the tenant's death. Sometimes this can be considered in advance by building up a partnership capital; sometimes a family decision will be taken to leave matters open until the run up to any Tribunal hearing at which point other potential partners will come in bringing their capital and making it contractually available to him.

14.52 **The occupancy condition**
In order to be eligible the applicant must demonstrate a negative condition namely that he is not the occupier of a commercial unit of agricultural land.[26] Schedule 6 provides most of the detailed legislation as to this condition. The original provisions on the subject in the 1976 Act were unsatisfactory and they were radically amended by the 1984 Act.[27]

14.53 **Material dates for fulfilment of occupancy condition: section 39(2)**
The applicant must be an eligible person at the date of death and must not in the meantime have ceased to be such a person.[28]

14.54 **Commercial unit of agricultural land: Schedule 6, paragraph 3**
A commercial unit of agricultural land is defined by Schedule 6, paragraph 3 to mean a unit of agricultural land which is capable, when farmed under competent management, of producing a net annual income of an amount not less than the aggregate of the average annual earnings of two full-time male agricultural workers aged 20 or over. Paragraphs 3(2), 4 and 5 of Schedule 6 combine to produce a mixture of subjective and objective elements in the application of this test.

14.55 **The subjective element: "farmed under competent management"**
The decision as to what system of farming would be undertaken on any particular land is essentially subjective in that there is considerable scope for argument in some cases over the choice between different enterprises. For present purposes the

---

[26] s. 36(3)(b).
[27] Now in the consolidated legislation; formerly 1984 Act, s. 3, Sched. 1; s. 4, Sched. 2.
[28] Section 39(2) embodying the opinion of the majority in *Jackson v. Hall* [1980] A.C. 854.

land is apparently considered as it stands with whatever buildings are there regardless of who paid for them.

The objective element: units of production 14.56
Once an appropriate system of farming has been selected the net annual income, if units of production have been prescribed by the Minister, must be assessed in accordance with those units.[29] These figures do not allow further deductions or allowances for matters such as the provision of working capital or the possibility of bank interest charges. The units of production may be changed from time to time.[30]

A mathematical test: aggregate of the average annual earnings, etc. 14.57
The threshold for a commercial unit is represented by the aggregate of the average annual earnings of two full-time male agricultural workers aged 20 or over.[31] This is by no means a scientific or definite threshold in that the Tribunal will have to resolve (i) whether to use national statistics for England and Wales or whether to use ones for the local region; (ii) whether or not the average includes overtime; (iii) whether the delay since the production of the figures requires the threshold to be inflated or deflated. As to the first of these it is submitted that national figures are preferable since that produces uniformity across the country. As to the second there appears to be no reason to exclude overtime. As to the third problem it is possible that the Tribunal might undertake such an exercise although it is doubtful whether they would feel competent to do it without expert help.

Ministerial statements as to net annual income: who may make the request 14.58
Schedule 6, paragraph 5 makes provision for the Minister to issue statements as to the net annual income of land pursuant to a request made to him. The request may be made by any close relative of the deceased (*i.e.* including the applicant), the landlord or the secretary of the Tribunal.[32] It is usual for the secretary of the Tribunal to make the request, having enquired of the parties to any litigation what if any request they would wish to be made. Sometimes it is helpful prior to any litigation and for the purposes of advice for the potential applicant to make his own request to the Minister.

Ministerial statements as to net annual income: making the request 14.59
Where a decision has been taken to make a request to the Minister, the person preparing the request will obviously have to identify very precisely by reference both to a plan and a schedule the land to be included in the assessment. "Relevant land" which might be included in such a request is defined by Schedule 6, paragraph 5(2). Essentially these are blocks of land occupied by the close relative with or without other persons and whether on a deemed or actual basis.[33] At the stage of making the request it is not, however, necessary to investigate the question of occupation.

---

[29] Sched. 6, paras 3(2) and 4.
[30] See the Agricultural Holdings (Units of Production) Orders printed in Part III.
[31] Sched. 6, para. 3(1).
[32] Sched. 6, para. 5(1)(a).
[33] See generally the provisions of Sched. 6, paras 6–10.

Because of the complexity of the occupation provisions in Schedule 6 and occasionally that of the close relative's landholdings it is necessary to make multiple requests to the Minister, one request for each combination of blocks of land.

14.60 Ministerial statements as to net annual income: extent to which binding

Any statement issued by the Minister is evidence of his view and a signature purporting to be on behalf of the Minister is taken to be such unless the contrary is shown.[34] Essentially the determination by the Minister as to what in his view the net annual income is that the land is capable of producing will be no more than a starting point for the Tribunal. It is customary for a surveyor engaged or employed by the Minister to inspect the relevant land for the purpose of selecting an appropriate enterprise; thereafter the units of production will be applied to that enterprise. The written statement provided by the Minister will contain the grounds for the view[35] and it is not likely that the Tribunal will be easily persuaded to depart from the Minister's view. It has the great merit of being issued by a person who is not party to the litigation. However the Minister's view is no longer conclusive, as it was under previous legislation.[36] Once the Minister's opinion has been issued, it may be amended by him if it appears to him that his original view is affected by any units of production subsequently issued by a statutory instrument in pursuance of paragraph 4 of Schedule 6.[37] It may be questioned whether the Minister may revise his opinion for any other reason.[38] One of the rare instances where the Tribunal may choose to call its own witness is where the Minister has expressed a view which appears to be unacceptable to both parties. In those circumstances it would be sensible for the Tribunal to call the witness and allow both parties to cross-examine.[39]

14.61 Occupation which counts for the purposes of the occupancy condition[40]

There is no relevant definition of "occupation" special to these purposes and no doubt the Tribunal will view the word in the widest possible sense, bearing in mind for these purposes the contents of Schedule 6. It is also relevant to consider in this context the need for consistency with the use of that word in relation to "agricultural unit"[41] but, of course, excluding the additional deemed element of

---

[34] Sched. 6, para. 5(4) and (5).
[35] In accordance with Sched. 6, para. 5(1)(b).
[36] Section 18(2)(c) of the 1976 Act applying s. 40(2)(a) of the Agriculture Act 1967 and see *R. v. Agricultural Land Tribunal (Wales), ex p. Hughes* (1980) 255 E.G. 703.
[37] Sched. 6, para. 5(3).
[38] On the one hand it may be said that he is *functus* having responded to the original request; on the other hand in the event of a dispute one would expect the Ministry surveyor to attend and give evidence, which suggests that what is intended is the up to date opinion of the Minister and to that extent the opportunity to revise a historic opinion by reference to updated units of production supports that view.
[39] The power to do this is available because r. 33 of the 1984 Agricultural Land Tribunals (Succession to Agricultural Tenancies) Order 1984 (S.I. 1984 No.1301) makes available the powers to the Tribunal under r. 29(2) of the Principal Rules (S.I. 1978 No.259).
[40] See para. 14.52 above.
[41] See para. 14.42 above.

occupation applied to "agricultural unit" by section 109(5). In particular it is submitted that the applicant does not occupy land in circumstances where he merely manages land for another person as an employee.[42] In the case of occupation by the potential applicant's spouse or controlled company, the occupation is deemed to be that of the potential applicant.[43] Where the statute deems the potential applicant to occupy via his spouse or controlled company but the spouse or controlled company was jointly occupying land with a third party the applicant will be fixed by apportionment with a part only of the net annual income of the relevant land by the application of the apportionment provisions in Schedule 6, paragraph 7.[44] Schedule 6 proceeds by requiring certain interests to be disregarded from the outset.[45] It then creates a series of deemed occupations or disapplications of the disregard in Schedule 6, paragraph 6[46] Without a special provision this would normally result in the entire net annual income from relevant land in being attributed to the potential applicant. That would clearly be unfair in circumstances where the occupation is joint with another party. For certain types of joint occupation[47] Schedule 6 applies apportionment provisions.[48] There are many difficulties in the construction of Schedule 6.

Occupation to be disregarded for the purposes of occupancy condition[49]: 14.62
Schedule 6, paragraph 6

Certain types of occupation by the potential applicant will be disregarded for the purposes of the occupancy condition and will not count against him. Schedule 6, paragraph 6 contains a list of seven categories of occupation which will be disregarded provided the potential applicant occupies by virtue of the specified interest only. If there is some other additional basis for occupation the disregard will fall away and the interest in question will count against the applicant. It should be noted that the disregard is extended so as to cover all the calculations and provisions of paragraphs 7, and following of, Schedule 6.[50]

The six types of disregarded occupation are (a) an agreement approved by the Minister before it was entered into as set out in section 2(1) and a tenancy for grazing use falling within section 2(3)[51]; (b) a *Gladstone v. Bower* tenancy for more than one but less than two years, *i.e.* an interest without long term security of tenure under the Act[52]; (c) any tenancy not within (a) or (b) which does not have effect as a contract of tenancy for the purposes of the Act, meaning presumably an interest within section 2(3)(b)[53]; (d) a tenancy falling within section 5 that is to say

---

[42] Compare Webster J. in *Trinity College Cambridge v. Caines* [1984] 2 E.G.L.R. 17 at 18M, quoted in para. 14.42 above.
[43] Sched. 6, para. 9(1).
[44] Sched. 6, para. 9(2).
[45] See para. 14.62 below.
[46] See paras 14.63, 14.64, 14.68 and 14.69 below.
[47] See paras 14.65 and 14.66 below.
[48] See para. 14.67 below.
[49] See para. 14.52 above.
[50] Sched. 6, para. 6(3).
[51] Sched. 6, para. 6(1)(a).
[52] Sched. 6, para. 6(1)(b).
[53] Sched. 6, para. 6(1)(c).

without the benefit of long term security and granted pursuant to Ministerial approval[54]; (dd) any farm business tenancy for less than 5 years and any periodic tenancy which is also a farm business tenancy[55]; (e) occupation only as a licensee, which covers therefore grazing licences and non-contractual licences and it is submitted occupation by a beneficiary purely by the permission[56] of the trustees[57]; (f) occupation of a non-beneficial character such as executor, administrator, trustee in bankruptcy or other capacity deriving by operation of law.[58]

Special care needs to be taken in distinguishing occupation as a licensee from occupation pursuant to a right under section 12 of the Trusts of Land and Appointment of Trustees Act 1996. Where a beneficiary occupies with the permission of trustees but does so without any right under section 12 (for example because he has only an interest in the fund not in the land) the occupation is disregarded for the purposes of Schedule 6 paragraph 6(1).[59] Section 12 of the 1996 Act provides:

"12(1) A beneficiary who is beneficially entitled to an interest in possession in land subject to a trust of land is entitled by reason of his interest to occupy the land at any time if at that time -

(a) the purposes of the trust include making the land available for his occupation (or for the occupation of beneficiaries of a class of which he is a member or of beneficiaries in general). or

(b) the land is held by the trustees so as to be so available.

(2) Sub-section (1) does not confer on a beneficiary a right to occupy land if it is either unavailable or unsuitable for occupation by him.

(3) This section is subject to section 13."

Section 13 deals with exclusion and restriction of the right to occupy. It will become necessary to enquire what if any "purpose" may be demonstrated in relation to any particular trust. It is possible the courts will build on similar types of

---

[54] Sched. 6, para. 6(1)(d).

[55] Sched. 6, para. 6(1)(dd), this is rather a curiously worded provision in relation to periodic tenancies but underlying the logic of the statute is presumably the assumption that the longest period of any periodic tenancy is likely to be 12 months.

[56] *i.e.* not a beneficiary with a right to occupy under s. 12 of the Trusts of Land and Appointment of Trustees Act 1996, as to which see para. 14.65 below.

[57] Sched. 6, para. 6(1)(e), to be contrasted with the wording of the previous statutory provisions in the notoriously vague "occupies it as a licensee only" of s. 18(2)(c) of the Agriculture (Miscellaneous Provisions) Act 1976. For commentary on the old form of wording (and some doubts on the new) see Michelle Slatter "Only: A Four-Letter Word? Statutory Succession and Agricultural Holdings" *Conveyancer and Property Lawyer*, Vol. 50, p. 320 (the otherwise unreported case of **Brooks v. Brown** (Forbes J.) is noted at 327 and criticised in the article).

[58] Sched. 6, para. 6(1)(f).

[59] Whereas many express trusts may give a beneficiary only an interest in income, virtually all implied trusts will give the beneficiary an interest in land.

OCCUPATION TO BE DISREGARDED FOR THE PURPOSES OF OCCUPANCY CONDITION

investigation under (now repealed) section 30 of the Law of Property Act 1925 or section 17 of the Married Women's Property Act 1882.[60]

Disapplication of disregard: grant by spouse or controlled body corporate: Schedule 6, paragraph 6(2) 14.63

Where the potential applicant holds one of the disregarded interests referred to in Schedule 6, paragraph 6(1) but following a grant by his spouse or a company controlled by him,[61] the disregarding provisions fall away and the Tribunal will in fact have regard to his occupancy of the area of land in question. This is an obvious anti-avoidance provision.

Deemed occupation in the case of licence or tenancy granted by close relative, spouse or controlled company: Schedule 6, paragraph 10(1) 14.64

In the case of certain of the interests which would normally be disregarded under Schedule 6, paragraph 6(1) there may be deemed occupation where the grantor is the potential applicant or a connected person or both and at that time the grantor had rights to occupy which themselves did not fall within paragraph 6(1)(a)–(f). Where such a grant is made to a person who then holds under one of the interests in Schedule 6, paragraph 6(1)(a)–(d) then normally the entire land will be treated as occupied by the close relative. This is clearly meant to apply where the potential applicant and/or a person connected to him divest themselves temporarily of occupancy in favour of someone else who takes what is in effect a short term interest. It would appear the grant to a third party of a farm business tenancy is not covered by these anti-avoidance provisions.[62] A "connected person" is defined[63] to mean the potential applicant's spouse or a company controlled by the potential applicant. Where occupation counts against the potential applicant by virtue of paragraph 10 the apportionment provisions will apply if non-connected parties were also amongst the grantors.[64]

Joint occupation: cases covered 14.65

In the case of joint occupation of agricultural land by the potential applicant and one or more other persons as

(a) beneficial joint tenants

(b) tenants in common

(c) joint tenants under a tenancy, or

(d) joint licensees

the potential applicant is treated as occupying the whole of the land but subject to his right to apply to the Tribunal for a determination that only part of the net

---

[60] *Jones v. Challenger* [1961] 1 Q.B. 176; *Re Evers' Trust, Papps v. Evers* [1980] 1 W.L.R. 1327; *Dennis v. McDonald* [1982] Fam. 63.
[61] Such a body corporate is defined by Sched. 6, para. 1(2).
[62] Perhaps an oversight.
[63] Para. 10(3).
[64] Sched. 6, para. 10(2) applying para. 7.

income should count against him.[65] Similar provisions apply in the case of a spouse or controlled company sharing occupation of land which in turn is deemed to be occupied by the potential applicant.[66] In such a case, once again, the opportunity exists for the potential applicant to request the Tribunal to ascertain that element of net income of the land which would count against him for succession purposes.[67] However paragraph 9 speaks simply of "joint occupation of land by [his] spouse or a body corporate and any other person or persons". It is not clear whether this is in fact a wider and different formulation from that contained in Schedule 6, paragraph 7(1).[68]

It is not clear whether the Trusts of Land and Appointment of Trustees Act 1996 has affected the application of the description "beneficial joint tenants". Schedule 6, paragraph 7 does not concern itself with whether a beneficiary might have an interest only in income as distinct from in land; "beneficial" joint tenancy appears to be a description wide enough to cover both.[69]

Clearly Schedule 6, paragraph 7 contemplates that the potential applicant as one of two joint licensees should be treated as occupying the entire area but should be entitled to apply under paragraph 7(3) for part only of the net income to count against him. This is only capable of reconciliation with the disregard in Schedule 6, paragraph 6(1)(e) if the reader assumes that the "licensee" status under paragraph 7 is something different from that under paragraph 6. Quite what that difference might consist of is not stated. If it had been intended that a licensee with a contractual right to remain was to have that occupation disregarded[70] it would have been helpful to spell it out. On balance it is suggested that occupation as a licensee on a contractual basis for a substantial period (*e.g.* a partnership) is outside the disregard but inside the joint occupation provisions. But essentially this is a matter for resolution by the Court. Nor is it easy to resolve this problem of construction by reference to any intrinsic merits.[71]

14.66 **Joint occupation: cases apparently not covered**

The great curiosity under Schedule 6, paragraph 7 is the apparent assumption that the potential applicant and the other persons will all occupy "as" persons within one of the identified alphabetical sub-paragraphs. Not only is the word "or" used to

---

[65] Sched. 6, para. 7(2) and see para. 14.67 below.
[66] See Sched. 6, para. 9.
[67] Application by Sched. 6, para. 9(2) of para. 7(2) and (3).
[68] See para. 14.66 below.
[69] Happily "beneficial joint tenant" is not as such a term of art although it can be understood by reference to the law prior to 1996. The distinction between on the one hand joint tenants and on the other tenants in common survives the 1996 Act as do the rules for severance: see ss 34 and 36 of the Law of Property Act 1925 as amended by the 1996 Act and in particular by Sched. 2.
[70] *e.g.* a partner during the currency of a fixed term partnership agreement where he himself is not one of the landowners.
[71] A licensee in partnership with his mistress may be much more secure than one in partnership with his neighbour (or vice versa!). Even the test of what is secure can be rather speculative: it might mean the ostensible duration of the partnership; it might mean the voting rights under it; or it might mean something referable to the shares in net assets where the interest in land is held as a partnership asset (although such test would be worthless in a case where the partnership was insolvent).

separate sub-paragraphs (c) and (d) (and by implication the other sub-paragraphs) but, more convincingly, one may point to the drafting of Schedule 6 paragraph 7(3). If this were thought to be the correct construction of paragraph 7(1) it throws up very serious problems where the shared occupation is mixed, with some occupiers enjoying one status and some another.

Commonly encountered examples of this are (i) where the applicant may only be a licensee but occupies as a partner with joint tenants or joint freeholders; (ii) where the potential applicant holds the freehold himself but occupies it together with two partners who are licensees; (iii) where the potential applicant is a tenant or a freeholder or a licensee and occupies land under a share farming arrangement where the other share farmer also occupies but as regards the land in a different capacity; (iv) where one of three or more joint tenants in equity has severed his or her interest in equity such that the trustees of the legal estate hold for a mixed group where as between the one who had severed and the others there is a tenancy in common but as between the others *inter se* there is a joint tenancy including the right of survivorship. This can happen when one of the erstwhile joint tenants makes a will. What this means is that Schedule 6, paragraph 7(1) is not nearly as conveniently drafted as the all inclusive paragraph 9(2) where there appears to be no assumption as to all occupiers occupying by virtue of the same status. However, exclusion of the cases of simultaneous occupation by a group of occupiers enjoying differing status appears pointless. It would seem preferable to ignore too close a construction of paragraph 7(1) and to take a purposive stance that paragraph 9 which is fairly obviously intended to assimilate the position for occupation by the spouse or controlled company can provide the guidance for a wide construction of paragraph 7. This would allow the mixed cases to fall within paragraph 7 and allows the application of paragraph 7(3).[72]

Limitation to the appropriate share: meaning 14.67
The applicant may apply to the Tribunal[73] for a determination of the net annual income capable of being produced by land which he is regarded as occupying and further for a determination as to the applicant's appropriate share of such net annual income. This is required to be ascertained in accordance with Schedule 6, paragraph 7(3). Where the applicant is "a beneficial or other joint tenant or a joint licensee" the total income is divided by the number of joint tenants or joint licensees.[74] Where the applicant is a tenant in common he will be faced with an amount "proportionate to the extent for the time being" of his undivided share in the land as against those of other tenants in common. These provisions are fairly straightforward in relation to the simple cases identified by paragraph 14.65 where all parties fall within the same categorisation (*i.e.* all are joint tenants alternatively tenants in common alternatively joint tenants under the tenancy alternatively joint licensees). But even in these circumstances the determination of the Tribunal in accordance with paragraph 7(3)(a) may well produce unexpected results. Thus if three partners occupy the property of a stranger all as licensees each will be fixed

---

[72] Although rather curiously.
[73] Sched. 6, para. 7(2). There is no form for doing this and a letter or even a verbal request at the hearing should suffice.
[74] Sub-para. (a).

with one third of the net annual income attributable to that land even though under the partnership arrangement, say, 80 per cent of the profit may go to one of the partners. There are clearly succession planning possibilities within these provisions.

If paragraph 7 is considered as including the cases of "mixed" occupation identified by paragraph 14.66 above the Tribunal appears able to make a determination provided at least one other person enjoys the same status as the potential applicant.[75] However this is apt to produce many curiosities.[76] So far there has been no litigation to clarify matters.

Finally it should be pointed out that there are succession planning opportunities in connection with the provisions relating to undivided shares in land. The Tribunal will determine the applicant's share of the net annual income by reference to his share in the land. He may choose to have only a small share in the land itself and instead take a very large share in the profits of the partnership exploiting it.

14.68 Deemed occupation in case of tenancy or licence granted by close relative, spouse, or controlled company: application of joint occupation provisions (Schedule 6, paragraph 10(2))

Where an outside party is jointly responsible for creating a tenancy or licence captured by Schedule 6, paragraph 10(1) the apportionment provisions apply as though the outside party jointly occupied the land which is deemed to be occupied by the potential applicant.[77] Schedule 6, paragraph 10(2) is not happily worded. However it is possible to see that the intention is to refer the application of paragraph 7 to the actual interest held by a third party and (one assumes) the actual interest held by the potential applicant, his spouse and/or controlled company (even though no mention is made of a "respective interest" in relation to the spouse or controlled company). This infelicity of drafting arises because the deeming in paragraph 10(1) relates not to a legal interest but to occupation by the potential applicant. Literally construed the provisions of Schedule 6, paragraph 7(3) also reproduce the problem. In other words the apportionment provisions do not on the face of it allow for apportionment in the case of the spouse or controlled company. However if one takes a purposive approach to paragraph 10(2) it is tolerably clear that the only fair and consistent application of the paragraph would be to treat apportionment as available not just where the applicant grants a tenancy or licence falling within paragraph 10(1) but also where his spouse or controlled company does the same thing.[78]

---

[75] For example there would need to be at least one other joint licensee where the applicant was a licensee.

[76] Including the apparent nonsense that where a landowner takes care to ensure his land is not a partnership asset then enters into partnership with the applicant and his brother the applicant would be fixed with one third of the net income of the land but contrast the position where the same landowner under the same circumstances enters into partnership only with the applicant who is a licensee. Because he is not a "joint licensee" the determination provisions in relation to appropriate share appear not to work at all.

[77] As to Sched. 6, para. 10(1) see para. 14.63 above.

[78] Sched. 6, para. 10(2) may allow of a "purposive" approach only because it begins with the words "where the tenancy or licence referred to in sub-paragraph (1) above was

Deemed occupation in case of Tribunal direction: Schedule 6, paragraph 8   14.69

Where the applicant already has the benefit of a Tribunal direction under section 39 in relation to the death of the same tenant but a different holding the applicant or potential applicant is treated as occupying the whole of that other holding. Where he is entitled to a direction in the same circumstances on part of another holding held by the deceased he is deemed to be in occupation of that part.[79] Where these deeming provisions apply and the relevant direction in fact created the right to a joint tenancy to vest in two different close relatives of the deceased, the apportionment provisions in Schedule 6, paragraph 7 are applied as though each close relative was jointly occupying with the other as joint tenants.[80] This particular provision stems from a recommendation of the Northfield Committee[81] that a successor should be restricted to one commercial unit from one landlord.

Application to be treated as eligible: meaning and availability   14.70

Section 41 offers the opportunity for a person who fails the livelihood condition[82] to apply to the Tribunal to be treated as though he were eligible. A succession application on death made under section 39 will in fact be made during the same statutory period of three months following the death as an application under section 41 and the two will be made on different parts of the same form.[83] The opportunity to make the request under section 41 is available to any surviving close relative of the deceased tenant[84] who for some part of the seven years ending with the date of death worked full-time or part-time in agricultural work on the holding.[85] Such a person must demonstrate that he is not the occupier of a commercial unit of agricultural land.[86] It is also necessary for the jurisdiction in section 41 to be available that the applicant demonstrates in relation to the livelihood condition[87] that though he does not fully satisfy it, that condition is satisfied to a material extent.[88]

The livelihood condition contained in section 36(3)(a) requires the applicant to show that for five out of the last seven years his principal source of livelihood was derived from his agricultural work on the holding or on an agricultural unit of which the holding forms part. The condition embodies, therefore, demonstration of a minimum commitment in terms of time and a quantum test in relation to the applicant's overall livelihood. In addition there are many technical difficulties in

---

granted by the person or persons ...".
[79] Sched. 6, para. 8(1).
[80] Sched. 6, para. 8(2).
[81] Cmnd. 7599, para. 630.
[82] See paras 14.36–14.51 above.
[83] See paras 14.30–14.32 above.
[84] See paras 14.34–14.35 above.
[85] As to "agricultural work" see para. 14.40 above; as to work on the holding see para. 14.41 above and note further that persons who have never worked on the holding but were students able to take advantage of Sched. 6, para. 2 cannot bring themselves within s. 41 since the special provisions of Sched. 6, para. 2 relate only to satisfaction of the livelihood test: see para. 14.45 above.
[86] s. 41(1)(a), and see paras 14.52–14.69 above.
[87] See paras 14.36–14.51 above.
[88] s. 41(1)(b).

understanding exactly what is required on the facts of any individual case to satisfy the livelihood condition.[89] What may amount to "material" satisfaction of the livelihood condition has been the subject of considerable speculation. After a period of divergent practice by the different Tribunals, a judicial consensus appears to have emerged to the effect that "material" means "substantial in terms of time and important in terms of value". This formulation was devised by the Tribunal for the Northern Area in *Dagg v. Lovett*[90] and was approved and adopted by the High Court in three subsequent cases.[91] It is now clear that section 41 is regarded as available in principle not simply in hard luck cases where there is "not quite" the ability to satisfy the livelihood test but as having a much wider availability.[92] There is in addition a specific statutory provision stipulating that cases where the livelihood condition is not fully satisfied include cases where the applicant's agricultural work on the holding fell short of providing him with his principal source of livelihood because the holding was too small.[93] In the formulation "important in terms of value" it should be noted that this refers not to whether a relevant contribution is an important contribution towards livelihood generally but whether it is an important satisfaction of the 51 per cent requirement.[94]

14.71 **Application to be treated as eligible: exercise of the Tribunal's discretion**
By section 41(3) if the Tribunal is satisfied that the applicant is a person to whom the section applies it must consider whether in all the circumstances it would be fair and reasonable for the applicant to be able to apply under section 39 for a direction entitling him to a tenancy of the holding.[95] The words "fair and reasonable" and "in all the circumstances" make available to the Tribunal the very widest consideration of the procedural bar. This aspect of the jurisdiction was described in

---

[89] These problems are highlighted by the discussion in paras 14.36–14.51 above.
[90] Reported at (1979) 251 E.G. 75; the subsequent reported history of this case relates to the suitability issue progressing through being quashed in the HC by Sir Douglas Frank Q.C. (1980) 254 E.G. 993 to reinstatement by the CA (1980) 256 E.G. 491.
[91] *Littlewood v. Rolfe* [1981] 2 All E.R. 51; *Wilson v. Earl Spencer's Settlement Trustees* [1985] 1 E.G.L.R. 3; *Trustees of James Raine (Senior) v. Raine* [1985] 275 E.G. 374.
[92] His Honour Judge Edgar Fay Q.C. sitting as a High Court Judge in *Littlewood v. Rolfe* (above) at 58 stated "I do, however, find some assistance in sub-section (2)(b) of section 21, the paragraph setting up the further hurdle to the successor tenant of whether the order is fair and reasonable. I think this points to a wide interpretation of the 'material extent'. If the 'not quite' view were right and the let out consisted of what may be called 'the hard luck cases' (where the applicant has 59 months instead of 60; or 49% in livelihood instead of the 51% which would make it the principal source) then it is difficult to see how any Tribunal could find that it was not fair and reasonable to make the order bearing in mind that the applicant still has the final hurdle of suitability to surmount. On the other hand if jurisdiction is given over a wide spectrum of facts by a beneficial interpretation of the word 'material' the Tribunal will have a real task in deciding where lies fairness and reasonableness". This was expressly followed in *Wilson v. Earl Spencer's Settlement Trustees* (above) by Hodgson J. at 6.
[93] s. 41(6). Illustrating a case where, in all likelihood, the applicant never actually satisfied the livelihood condition at any point.
[94] *Wilson v. Earl Spencer's Settlement Trustees* (above).
[95] s. 41(3)(b).

Littlewood v. Rolfe as a "further hurdle" for the applicant to surmount.[96] Its purpose was explained in ***Trustees of James Raine (Senior) v. Raine***.[97] It is directed to the question whether it is fair and reasonable for the applicant to qualify for the eligible class and is not concerned with the overall merits of the case or with a general enquiry into relative hardship as between the parties. A wide consideration of circumstances directed to this question might lead a Tribunal to conclude that it is not fair and reasonable to allow an applicant to qualify if, for example, he is really a person whose case on livelihood is of the most technical type and he has a vast outside income available to him on which he chooses not to live in order to attempt qualification for the purposes of section 39. If the Tribunal exercises the discretion in the applicant's favour then it must determine that he is to be treated as an eligible person[98] and on that basis any application made under section 39 will accordingly be treated as one made by an eligible person.[99] If the application to be treated as eligible fails, the application generally is dismissed.[1] Once the Tribunal's direction has been made in favour of the applicant sections 36 to 38 of the Act apply as though he had been eligible from the outset.[2]

Suitability: relevant matters 14.72

Where an application for a tenancy of a holding is made under section 39 by an eligible person the Tribunal must determine whether the applicant is in its opinion a suitable person to become the tenant of the holding.[3] If there are two or more eligible applicants and each is suitable the Tribunal may be required to decide which is the more or most suitable.[4] Before a determination as to suitability is made the applicant must afford the landlord an opportunity of stating his views on the suitability of each applicant.[5] If there is only one suitable applicant that person must be given a direction entitling him to a tenancy of the holding.[6] If there is more than one applicant the statute lays down a procedure to decide which is to take the tenancy.[7]

In deciding what is suitable the Tribunal is required to have regard to all relevant matters including those specifically referred to in section 39(8). They are: the extent to which an applicant has been trained in or has had practical experience of agriculture; the age, physical health and financial standing of the applicant; the views of the landlord on suitability. The opinion of the landlord on suitability will be stated on the landlord's filed Form 1R.[8] The Tribunal will no doubt view with

---

[96] [1981] 2 All E.R. 51 at 58.
[97] [1985] 2 E.G.L.R. 4 at 7 "it is concerned, in other words, not so much with the merits themselves as with the question of overcoming a procedural bar (if I can call it that)", Forbes J.
[98] s. 41(3).
[99] s. 41(5).
[1] s. 39(3).
[2] s. 41(4).
[3] s. 39(2)(b).
[4] s. 39(6).
[5] s. 39(7).
[6] s. 39(5).
[7] See para. 14.75 below.
[8] See para. 14.27 above.

caution the assertions of an applicant in his application that the landlord has never made any adverse comment as to the applicant's abilities; it is not to be expected that a landlord will gratuitously insult his tenant's close relatives when, prior to the tenant's death, there is no point in doing so. The landlord's candid opinion (or more usually that of his land agent) is likely to be formed after the tenant has died and usually after interviewing the applicant. In contrast to eligibility, suitability is judged at the date of the hearing before the Tribunal and it is to be expected that an applicant will acquire or enhance farming skills in order to make a convincing application.

14.73 Suitability: discovery
The general powers of the Tribunal to compel discovery are discussed in the final part of paragraph 14.48 above. There are certain documents which one would expect to be volunteered by the applicant. They include his birth certificate, any qualifications in agriculture, proof (if available) of his employment in agriculture, any letter of recommendation from any other landlord given for the purpose, a health certificate from his doctor and at some point a list of his capital assets which are said to enable him to finance the farming of the holding. In the case of the list of assets it is usual to request a land agent to advise as to how much money would be required and an accountant to verify that it would be available and if so from what sources.

14.74 Suitability: discussion
There is little judicial guidance on what suitability may amount to and by and large the matter is one for the Tribunal bearing in mind its skilled lay composition. One rare but helpful formulation from the courts is that of Ackner L.J. in ***Dagg v. Lovett***[9]:

> "As the Tribunal rightly pointed out, it was essential that the applicant for the tenancy should show the Tribunal that she was capable of taking over the farm and had sufficient ability to farm the land at a level where the landlord would receive a fair rent for the farm and the tenant would achieve a reasonable standard of living."

This is a rather different question from asking whether or not the applicant would succeed in being offered a tenancy on the open market. In the context of overall suitability one would expect the Tribunal to take an interest in the applicant's skill, knowledge and ability when it comes to practical farming. Section 39(8)(a) specifically draws attention to this matter. Where farming ability is in issue it would be possible and is perhaps expected that the applicant will draw up a budget indicating to the Tribunal how he intends to farm and why he has drawn it up the way he has. Frequently a budget of that type will be backed up by the evidence of a land agent not by offering to substitute his opinion for that of the Tribunal but rather by offering the Tribunal his opinion of the strengths and weaknesses of the budget and of the suitability issue generally thereby offering the Tribunal the opportunity to discuss matters with a professional witness who, if

---
[9] [1980] 2 E.G.L.R. 10 at 12M.

called by the applicant, will back the application with his professional support. There appears little doubt that in practice Tribunals are interested in the applicant's proposed handling of the farm and in particular the economics implied by it. Frequently a challenge to the applicant's skill will be coupled with a challenge to the adequacy of his financial standing. Every farm needs working capital and the question will be one as to how much and where it is to come from. How much is a matter for expert evidence whereas the source of the finance may variously be cash, the existing farming stock and/or bank borrowings.

In many instances the applicant will be able to tell the Tribunal that he has lined up, conditional on a favourable direction, potential farming partners who are contractually committed to assisting financially if the Tribunal make a direction in the applicant's favour. Classically this will happen where the applicant is the son of the deceased tenant and his mother is the major beneficiary under the deceased's will; the widow may enter into a contract conditional on the Tribunal granting her son a direction, being a contract under which her inherited share, and if she has one her own share in the farming stock, are made available to the applicant for the duration of a partnership for a fixed period. There is no age beyond which an applicant is debarred from making an application although it is submitted that it must be unlikely that a Tribunal would grant a direction to a person who was or was approaching the age of 65, this being the age of retirement under Part IV of the Act. As to physical health, this should not be confused with being free of disability. It is not unknown for persons with long-term disability of one type or another being able to farm successfully: the statute does not require that the applicant be healthy only that the Tribunal should consider his state of health and whether or not it would enable him to farm.

Procedure where more than one applicant: section 39(3)-(6)   14.75

If there is more than one applicant for a holding the Tribunal will have to determine in the case of each eligible applicant whether he is suitable.[10] But if one of the applicants is validly designated by the deceased tenant in his will as the person he wished to succeed him as tenant of the holding that person has absolute priority and the Tribunal must deal with his application first and will only proceed to the other applications if that applicant proves unsuitable.[11] Where only one applicant proves suitable, he must receive the tenancy.[12] If more than one person is suitable the more or most suitable will receive the tenancy.[13] However there will be no direction at all in circumstances where the landlord is successful under section 44 in requesting consent to the operation of a notice to quit.[14] The ALT Rules[15] deal with the procedure at the hearing in the case of a sole applicant.[16] Rules 17 and 18

---

[10] s. 39(3).
[11] s. 39(4). As to what is meant by a designation in the deceased's will for this purpose see para. 14.76 below.
[12] s. 39(5).
[13] s. 39(6).
[14] See para. 14.83 below.
[15] The Agricultural Land Tribunal (Succession to Agricultural Tenancies) Order 1984 (S.I. 1984 No.1301).
[16] r. 16 and see below at para. 14.79.

deal with the somewhat complex position where there are multiple applicants. Essentially the first question is to decide whether or not there is a designation in the deceased's will (which may itself be a contested issue).[17] If there is a designated person, his application is dealt with first under rule 16.[18] If the designated applicant is considered eligible and suitable other applications are dismissed and, subject to any adjournment under rule 13, any application by the landlord for consent to the operation of a notice to quit will be heard.[19] Where the designated applicant is not successful, his application is dismissed and all the other applications will be heard in the order stipulated by rule 18.[20] Rule 18 sets out at some length the order in which the specific issues will have to be determined in the case of multiple applicants where nobody claims a designation. This rule allows the Tribunal to choose the order in which the various applicants are to be heard.

14.76 Designation in the deceased's will: section 39(4) and section 40

The deceased tenant may in his will designate the person he wishes to succeed him as tenant of the holding.[21] Section 40 states that a will includes a codicil and that the will must be the subject of a grant of probate or administration. The designation may take the form of either an effective specific bequest of the tenancy[22] or a statement specifically mentioning the holding or the deceased's tenancy of it and exclusively designating that person as the one the deceased wished to succeed as tenant of it.[23] In the latter case the designation may be of a person "in whatever words, and whether by name or description". Furthermore where there is a designation within section 40(1)(b) it is permissible to designate different people in different circumstances provided "in the events which have happened" the designation operates to designate one person exclusively.[24] Provided the probate or administration giving the designation is valid at the time when the Tribunal make a direction, subsequent revocation or variation of the probate or administration will not affect matters.[25]

14.77 Procedure where deceased held more than one holding: section 42

In cases where the deceased tenant held more than one holding there is a statutory provision governing the orderly consideration of separate applications in respect of such holdings (whether these are applications made by the same person or by a number of persons). If at the expiry of the period of three months beginning with the day after the date of death there are pending before the Tribunal separate applications of this kind, they are, subject to the provisions of any relevant

---

[17] r. 17(1).
[18] r. 17(3).
[19] r. 17(4).
[20] r. 17(5).
[21] As to the procedural impact of such a designation see para. 14.75 above.
[22] s. 40(1)(a).
[23] s. 40(1)(b).
[24] s. 40(2).
[25] s. 40(3).

statutory instrument,[26] to be heard and determined in the following order[27]:

(a) where all the applications were made by the same person, in such order as he decides;

(b) where the applications were made by two or more persons, in such order as they agree, or, failing agreement, as decided by the chairman of the Tribunal.[28]

The chairman is not, however, at liberty to decide the sequence by any criterion he favours; he is obliged to list the applications in descending order of the size of the holdings.[29] Naturally, by contrast, the applicant will wish to maximise the advantage to him of being able to choose the order in which the holdings are dealt with. Normally, therefore, he will deal with the smallest holdings first, stopping short of a collective size which would amount to a commercial unit. Thereafter he will pick the holding which will take him over the commercial unit level but which is the most important holding to him. In this way he may be able to take over the largest holding held by the deceased together with a collection of smaller holdings which in aggregate are less than one commercial unit.

The Agricultural Land Tribunal: the succession rules 14.78

The Agricultural Land Tribunal[30] has in relation to succession applications a separate set of rules, the Agricultural Land Tribunals (Succession to Agricultural Tenancies) Order 1984[31] as supplemented by parts of the principal Rules.[32] The succession Rules append various prescribed forms[33] but a form "substantially to the like effect with such variations as the circumstances may require" is equally valid. In fact it appears that several Tribunals are operating with forms identical to the prescribed forms save only that references to legislation are to current legislation.[34] Rule 3 provides for the making of an application by an eligible person and/or one wishing to be treated as an eligible person.[35] The landlord's reply is regulated by rule 6 and must be made within one month.[36] The applicant is required to serve notice of his application in accordance with rule 5. The landlord may apply for consent to the operation of the notice to quit in accordance with rule 4 in Form 2;[37] the time-limit for making his application is four months after a copy of the applicant's succession application is served on him and in the case of multiple

---

[26] *i.e.* an order made under s. 40(5). The relevant order is at present the Agricultural Lands Tribunal (Succession to Agricultural Tenancies) Order 1984 (S.I. 1984 No.1301). There are no provisions in this Order affecting the rules laid down in s. 42.
[27] s. 42(1).
[28] s. 42(2).
[29] s. 42(3).
[30] As to which see generally paras 16.2–16.13 below.
[31] S.I. 1984 No.1301.
[32] The Agricultural Land Tribunals (Rules) Order 1978 (S.I. 1978 No.259).
[33] Printed in Part V of this work as Forms 43–49.
[34] See r. 1(3)(b).
[35] See paras 14.24 and 14.30–14.32 respectively.
[36] See paras 14.27–14.28 above.
[37] See Form 44 in Part V of this work.

applications it will be at least those four months or one month after the date on which the number of applications is reduced to one or, at the Tribunal's direction, one month.[38] The applicant may reply to the landlord's application in Form 2R[39] and must do so within one month after service on him of the landlord's application.[40] He may also reply to any other application and must do so within one month after the time for such an application to be made, the reply being filed in Form 4.[41] The Tribunal's secretary has general duties relating to service of documents.[42] It is possible to apply for an extension of time in the case of any time-limits stipulated solely by the Rules (as distinct from the statute).[43] If no reply from the landlord is received by the secretary within the time allowed, the landlord will not be allowed to dispute any matter alleged in the application,[44] but this prohibition does not affect the landlord's right to rely on his own application for consent to a notice to quit[45] and also does not affect his right under section 39(7) of the 1986 Act to state his views on the suitability of the applicant.[46] An applicant who wishes to oppose an application for a tenancy by any other person failing to reply in time to that application will not be entitled to dispute any matter alleged in that application, but he may still claim superior suitability.[47]

In relation to applications and replies rule 11 of the succession Rules applies various of the principal Rules. Rule 16 of the principal Rules (excluding rule 16(5) applies[48]; rule 18 applies excluding paragraph (2)[49]; in the case of an application by the landlord rule 15(2)[50] of the principal Rules applies; rule 18(2)[51] of the principal Rules applies to a reply under rule 7 of the succession rules once the relevant period has expired and, following the withdrawal of the reply, there is no other outstanding reply to the application by the landlord. Rule 14 of the succession rules applies the following provisions from the principal Rules in so far as they relate to preparation for hearing and to the hearing:

(i) Rule 19 interlocutory applications.

(ii) Rule 20 disclosure of documents.[52]

---

[38] Since it would be difficult for the landlord to calculate these periods himself, the secretary of the Tribunal is required to inform the landlord of the start of any relevant period by virtue of r. 4(5).
[39] See Form 44A in Part V of this work.
[40] r. 7.
[41] See r. 8 and Form 46 in Part V of this work.
[42] r. 10.
[43] See para. 14.29 above.
[44] r. 15(1).
[45] r. 15 and r. 4.
[46] r. 15(1).
[47] r. 15(3).
[48] Formal requirements of any application, reply and supporting documentation.
[49] Rule 18 deals with the withdrawal of an application or reply.
[50] In the absence of any reply within the time allowed the Tribunal may decide to make an order in the terms of the application without a formal hearing.
[51] Where a reply is withdrawn the Tribunal may decide to make an order in the terms of the application without a formal hearing.
[52] See para. 14.29 above.

THE AGRICULTURAL LAND TRIBUNAL: THE SUCCESSION RULES

(iii) Rule 23(2) and (4) notice of hearing.

(iv) Rule 24 Tribunal to sit in public.

(v) Rule 25 right of audience whereby a party may appear in person, by counsel, by a solicitor or by a representative appointed in writing.

(vi) Rule 26(2) and (3) procedure at the hearing.[53]

(vii) Rule 27 default of appearance.[54]

Rule 20 applies to succession proceedings following the tenant's death these additional provisions from the principal Rules:

(i) Rule 28 evidence.[55]

(ii) Rule 29 witnesses.[56]

(iii) Rule 30 inspection of land.[57]

(iv) Rule 31.[58]

(v) Rule 33 request for a reference to the High Court of a question of law under section 6 of the Agriculture (Miscellaneous Provisions) Act 1954.[59]

(vi) Rule 34 modification of Tribunal's decision following High Court proceedings.

(vii) Rule 35 mode of service.

(viii) Rule 36 substituted service.

(ix) Extension of time.[60]

---

[53] See para. 14.79 below.
[54] Powers to dismiss an application in default of appearance or to proceed to determine an application in the absence of the other party.
[55] Evidence may be admitted notwithstanding that it would not be admissible in a court of law and evidence may be given orally on oath or on affirmation or otherwise, by affidavit with the party's consent or by means of written statements produced by the maker when giving evidence or, if the Tribunal consents, by another witness. A deponent or maker of a written statement may be required to attend for the giving of live evidence.
[56] Parties may give evidence themselves, call their own witnesses and cross-examine other people's witnesses. The Tribunal may call a witness who may thereafter be cross-examined and the Tribunal may require any witness to give evidence on oath or affirmation. The County Court Rules (CCR) apply to the issue of witness summonses as they apply to arbitrations.
[57] Wide powers exercisable on 24 hours' notice but parties, representatives and expert witnesses may attend.
[58] Written reasoned decision if necessary by a majority with a power to correct clerical errors and a duty on the secretary to supply copies to the parties, copies to be duly certified.
[59] See paras 16.9–16.11 below.
[60] See para. 14.29 above.

SUCCESSION ON DEATH OR RETIREMENT

(x) Rule 38 failure to comply with rules.[61]

(xi) By sub-paragraph (2) of rule 20 of the succession rules any dismissal of an application counts as a decision and must be reasoned, to be given in a single document at the conclusion of the proceedings unless the chairman directs otherwise.

Rule 21 makes provision for postponement of the operation of a notice to quit or direction. Applications by tenants under section 44(6) to defer the operation of a notice to quit in cases where the Tribunal has consented to the notice must be made in writing to the secretary of the Tribunal before the hearing or made orally at the hearing.[62] Similarly any application under section 46(2) for a direction to have effect from a later time than the date defined in section 46(1) must be made in writing to the secretary before the hearing or orally at the hearing.[63]

14.79 The Agricultural Land Tribunal: conduct of hearing

Although a party may appear in person it is more usual for a solicitor, counsel or a chartered surveyor to conduct any advocacy.[64] The Tribunal has a general power to adjourn a hearing[65] but there is an understandable reluctance to adjourn a hearing once the parties and the Tribunal are assembled; this is hardly surprising given the occasional difficulties encountered in finding a day when the lay members of the Tribunal and the part time legal chairman will all be available at once. This reluctance to adjourn is often reinforced by the very limited powers of the Tribunal in relation to costs.[66] The best course is usually for the Chairman to be flexible about fixing the original hearing date taking into account at that stage what the parties have to say about readiness for trial coupled with an instruction to the parties to notify the Tribunal at once if for any reason the hearing date appears unrealistic. Subject to any special provisions in the various Rules the general rule is that the procedure at the hearing will be as the Tribunal may direct but subject to any direction given by the legal chairman.[67] It is usual, to take a simple model,[68] for the applicant's representative to open his case summarising the main points at issue and making any necessary legal submissions and then for him to call any relevant witnesses who may be then cross-examined and re-examined.[69] The applicant himself may give evidence and will usually do so. It is extremely unusual for the Tribunal ever to call a witness although there is a power to do it.[70] Witnesses may be sworn and usually will be expected to give evidence on oath or affirmation[71] and

---

[61] See para. 14.29 above.
[62] r. 21(1).
[63] r. 21(2).
[64] Rule 25 of the principal Rules requires a chartered surveyor to be appointed in writing and the Tribunal will customarily require to see the appointment.
[65] Rule 26(3) of the principal Rules.
[66] See para. 16.12 below.
[67] Rule 26(2) of the principal Rules.
[68] In contrast to the complex arrangements identified by para. 14.75 above.
[69] Rule 29 of the principal Rules.
[70] r. 29(2): there is no restriction to any particular time at which the Tribunal is to do this. See para. 14.60 above for the possible exercise by the Tribunal of this power.
[71] r. 29(3).

this expectation is extended to professional witnesses even where they have prepared a report in writing. Although it is possible for evidence to be given orally without the use of written statements, it is usual for the Tribunal to permit written statements to be used and this it may do whether or not there has previously been an order requiring disclosure of the written statement to the other party.

It had been the habit of Tribunals, long before the use of written statements by way of witness evidence in the courts, to use written statements for evidence in chief not only in order to save time but mainly in order that witnesses unused to court proceedings (and occasionally unused to handling documentation of any kind) should be able to give evidence coherently without feeling intimidated by the procedure generally. Technical objections as to the admissibility of evidence never troubled Tribunals[72] and as a result hearsay evidence will routinely be included where it is helpful. The normal curb on abuse of rule 28(1) is the hostility of the Tribunal to time wasting or what they regard as unseemly or dishonourable allegations. Given the large role of the Tribunal's discretion in relation to the substantive law at various points, it is normally regarded as critical by the advocate to ensure that the Tribunal is in general terms sympathetic to his client. Parties are expected to do the best they can with the material they are able to obtain. For this reason, if they have confidence in the material presented, the advocate may expect the Tribunal to take notice of Ministry statistics (even though not proved by the maker), gross margin calculations from standard textbooks, old photographs of the farm (not proved by the maker) and expressions of opinion about the weather, the state of land and the difficulties of farming it by any person actually farming a block of land (even though he is not a qualified expert). It is normal for the Tribunal to allow all witnesses to attend during the giving of evidence even though any person listening may subsequently give evidence on the same point. Indeed an attempt to exclude witnesses from the audience will be regarded in the normal way as oppressive behaviour. The only rare exception to this is where there may be an allegation of fraud and only then of a type where there is a real reason to suspect collusion between the witnesses appearing for one side (*i.e.* as distinct from anticipating that their evidence may at the end of the day differ). It is perceived as a slight for a witness to be excluded and Tribunals are anxious not to upset a witness unnecessarily bearing in mind that usually the witness will be a neighbouring farmer who has taken the time off from his own work and often made elaborate arrangements for his livestock to be fed by other people and his arable work to be delayed. Although there is a power to receive evidence by affidavit[73] a signed written statement by a party not attending may be admitted under rule 28(1). The maker of such a statement may be ordered to attend[74] but usually parties are left to present their evidence as they think fit and the Tribunal will attach whatever weight to it as is considered appropriate.

Once the applicant's evidence has been presented, the respondent will normally be invited to make his opening observations and then call his witnesses who will

---

[72] Rule 28(1) of the principal Rules allows the admission of evidence even if it would not be admissible in a court of law.
[73] r. 28(2)(b).
[74] r. 28(3).

then also be cross-examined and re-examined. The respondent, having put forward all the evidence on which he wishes to rely, will then make his closing speech on all points of law and all points of fact and evidence. The applicant will usually be permitted to have the final speech in reply but must not at this stage introduce new arguments or authorities unless the respondent is subsequently given the opportunity to comment on those new matters. To do otherwise would constitute risking a breach of the rules of natural justice.

In succession cases it is almost inescapable that the Tribunal will wish to inspect the holding and quite possibly other land within the agricultural unit and occasionally yet other land farmed by the witnesses in the case.[75] The precise point at which one or more inspections take place is for the Tribunal to decide although there is a predictable pattern in that the lay members of the Tribunal will usually drive along the nearest main road to "cast an eye" over the land before having a full detailed inspection after the hearing or during a break in the proceedings. Inspections have to be conducted circumspectly and occasionally difficulties may arise.[76] The making of the decision, any request for a reference to the High Court and any modification of the Tribunal's decision following such a reference are dealt with elsewhere.[77]

14.80 **The Agricultural Land Tribunal: direction to more than one applicant**

Direction in favour of up to four applicants. In circumstances where up to four applicants satisfy the Tribunal that they are eligible and suitable, it is available to the landlord to consent to the Tribunal granting a direction in favour of up to four of the applicants so that a joint tenancy will be granted ultimately.[78] This means that the Tribunal is then relieved of the task of selecting the more or most suitable from the group of suitable applicants. Four is, of course, the maximum number of persons permitted at law to hold a joint interest.

New tenancy granted by landlord. In some cases the person or persons entitled to a tenancy by the Tribunal's direction may, before the relevant time,[79] negotiate and agree the terms of a new tenancy with the landlord and accept a direct grant of a tenancy from him. In that case the tenancy is actually created by the grant and does not vest by the device of a deemed grant as it would otherwise have done. Where this actual grant takes place the direction ceases to have effect and it is expressly provided that the arbitration arrangements in section 48 have no application, the terms of the tenancy having been settled by negotiation between the parties.[80] A tenancy granted by the landlord in this way, following a direction, counts as one of the two "occasions" for the purpose of the "two occasions" rule governing the number of successions under the scheme.[81] It is also one of the categories of

---

[75] See the powers of inspection of land under r. 30 of the principal Rules.
[76] See para. 16.4, "Inspection", below.
[77] See paras 16.6. and 16.8–16.11 below
[78] s. 39(9).
[79] s. 46.
[80] s. 46(6). This new negotiated tenancy is not of course destroyed by s.45(5) as the title stems from the grant, not the direction.
[81] s. 37(1)(a).

succession rights safeguarded from abolition where the original tenancy was granted before July 12, 1984.[82]

Agricultural Land Tribunal: landlord and applicant in agreement 14.81

In general terms reference is made to paragraph 14.80 above "new tenancy granted by landlord". There is at present a divergence in practice as to how Tribunals handle a situation where the landlord and the applicant may be in agreement that a direction should be made in the applicant's favour. Essentially some Tribunals appear willing to accept a letter from the landlord agreeing with the direction being made; other Tribunals (and it is submitted more correctly) insist that the applicant should appear before them presenting uncontested evidence (*e.g.* in the form of an unsworn witness statement) upon which they can exercise their statutory function.

Restriction on operation of notice to quit given by reason of death of tenant: 14.82
section 43

Before the introduction by the 1976 Act of the succession scheme the death of the tenant provided landlords with one of the very few opportunities to regain possession of the holding and thus to decide whether to re-let it, to retain it for the landlord to farm it himself or to take part in one of the joint ventures which did not involve the creation of a tenancy. The succession scheme necessarily involved a restriction on the landlord's rights to obtain possession on death, but did not destroy those rights completely. The present position is that a notice to quit given by the landlord under Case G following the death of the tenant will be operative in certain circumstances, namely:

(1) if no application under section 39 to become tenant of the holding is made within the time-limit of three months beginning with the day after the date of death[83];

(2) if one or more applications have been made, but no applicant has been found to be suitable[84];

(3) if one or more applications have been made, but the Tribunal consents to the notice to quit in relation to the whole or part of the holding.[85]

If the Tribunal's consent is restricted to part only of the holding there is an express dispensation from the common law invalidity of a notice to quit part.[86]

It is therefore still important from the landlord's point of view to serve a notice to quit pursuant to Case G, in the proper form and within the time-limit laid down,[87] following the death of the tenant.

---

[82] s. 34(1)(b)(ii). In this respect it differs from the tenancy mentioned in s.37(1)(b), which does not qualify under s.34(1)(b).
[83] s. 43(1)(a).
[84] s. 43(1)(b)(i).
[85] s. 43(1)(b)(ii). See s. 44.
[86] s. 43(2). For common law rule, see **Re Bebington's Tenancy, Bebington v. Wildman** [1921] 1 Ch. 559.
[87] See above para. 12.46 and following.

14.83 Opportunity for landlord to obtain Tribunal's consent to operation of notice to quit: section 44

It is the duty of the Tribunal, before giving a direction entitling a successful applicant to a tenancy of the holding, to afford the landlord, in a case where a notice to quit falling within Case G has been given, an opportunity of applying for its consent to the operation of the notice.[88] The provisions of section 27 (grounds for consent such as good husbandry, sound management, etc.), including the fair and reasonable landlord provision, are applied to the application for, and the giving of, consent under the present section 44.[89] The landlord's application for consent to a notice to quit, which has to be made on Form 2,[90] may be made at any time after he receives notice under rule 3(1) of the application,[91] but must be made within time-limits which differ according to whether, at the expiry of the relevant three month period for the filing of applications by close relatives, only one application or more than one application was pending. In the former case the landlord's application must be made within four months after a copy of that single application in Form 1 is served on him. In the latter case the landlord's application must be made (a) within four months after a copy of the first of the applications is served on him, or (b) within one month after the date on which the number of the applications pending is reduced to one or within one month after such earlier date as the Tribunal may direct, whichever of those periods expires last.[92] Where the landlord is not entitled to dispute a matter alleged in the applicant's application he is still entitled to rely on his own application for consent to a notice to quit.[93] An applicant who intends to oppose the landlord's application for consent to a notice to quit under rule 4 must, within one month after a copy of the application has been served on him, reply to it on Form 2R.[94] The usual provisions for extension by the Tribunal of non-statutory time-limits apply.[95] A somewhat obscure subsection[96] provides that the Tribunal is not to entertain an application for their consent unless the application is made in pursuance of section 44(1). Reference should be made to the previous discussion of applications for consent under section 27.[97] If the Tribunal does give its consent to the operation of the notice to quit it must dismiss any applications for a tenancy of the holding under section 39.[98] The Tribunal may, however, with the agreement of the person or persons entitled to a tenancy of the holding, give a direction relating to a *part* of the holding only. In that case it *must* consent to the operation of the notice to quit in relation to the part of the holding excluded from that direction, without any further enquiries: the question of

---

[88] s. 44(1).
[89] s. 44(2). The penalty for breach of condition in s.27(6) also applies.
[90] See Form 44 in Part V of this work.
[91] r. 4(1) of the Agricultural Land Tribunals (Succession to Agricultural Tenancies) Order 1984 (S.I. 1984 No.1301).
[92] r. 4(3), (4).
[93] r. 15 and r. 4.
[94] r. 7; see Form 44A in Part V of this work.
[95] See para. 14.29 above.
[96] s. 44(3).
[97] See paras 12.13–12.19 above.
[98] s. 44(4).

grounds for consent, etc., under section 27 does not then arise.[99] It is possible that the Tribunal may not give its consent until within three months of the expiry date of the notice to quit, or, indeed, until after that date. In such cases the tenant may apply to the Tribunal for deferment. The Tribunal has a discretion to defer the operative date of the notice to a date not later than the end of three months beginning with the original expiry date or with the date on which the Tribunal gives its consent, whichever is the later.[1]

Effect of direction by Agricultural Land Tribunal: sections 45–46   14.84

Vesting of a new tenancy The machinery for vesting a tenancy is not by way of statutory assignment[2] of the deceased's tenancy from his personal representatives to the person or persons entitled, but a deemed grant from the landlord of an entirely *new* tenancy. Until the date of vesting of the new tenancy the deceased's tenancy will continue to be vested in his personal representatives. The date on which the deemed grant and acceptance of the new tenancy takes place, the date on which the title to it vests in the applicant, is described as "the relevant time".[3] "The relevant time" means the end of the 12 months immediately following the end of the year of the tenancy in which the deceased died. This is subject to the exception that, if a notice to quit within Case G had been given on the death of the deceased, and the notice would, apart from section 43, have terminated the tenancy at a date after the end of those 12 months, "the relevant time" means that date.[4] Normally this would allow sufficient time for all necessary arrangements to be made. There might, however, be occasions when the direction is not given until very near the relevant time, or even after it, *e.g.* if a point of law has been referred to the High Court before the Tribunal's decision. In such a case, if the direction is given within the period of three months ending with the original relevant time, the tenant may apply to the Tribunal, which *may* specify a new relevant time, such a time to fall within three months immediately following the original relevant time. If, however, the direction is not given until after the original relevant time, the Tribunal is *required* to specify a new relevant time in its direction; such a time must fall within the three months immediately following the giving of the direction but otherwise as the Tribunal thinks fit.[5]

Position when there has been a lease of the reversion A special provision has been necessary to deal with difficulties which have arisen, and could arise, through a grant by the deceased tenant's landlord of a tenancy of the reversion to a third person. A concurrent lessee becomes *pro tanto* an assignee of the reversion and

---

[99] s. 44(5).

[1] s. 44(6) and (7). For procedure, see r. 21 of the Agricultural Land Tribunals (Succession to Agricultural Tenancies) Order 1984 (S.I. 1984 No.1301) and para. 14.78 above.

[2] An assignment can, however, take place under s.37(2) on the occasion of an *inter vivos* agreement between the landlord, tenant and incomer.

[3] s. 45(1).

[4] s. 46(1).

[5] s. 46(2). Consequential provisions are made in s. 48. The definition of "the prescribed period" in s.48(2) is framed to ensure that the landlord or tenant will have at least three months from the time of the direction in which to serve a notice demanding arbitration on the terms of the tenancy or the rent.

consequently the "landlord" of the tenant so far as the payment of rent and the observance of covenants are concerned during the concurrence of the interests, the original tenant becoming a quasi-sub-tenant.[6] The interposition of a concurrent lessee does not fit well into the mechanism of the succession scheme, as Tribunals discovered before the provisions now in section 45(2) to (4) were introduced by the 1984 Act.[7] In the absence of these provisions the deemed grant and acceptance of the new tenancy, to which the successful applicant was entitled, might have been held to result in the creation of a vulnerable sub-tenancy of which the concurrent lessee was the immediate landlord. Section 45(2) removes the difficulty by providing that the deemed grant of a tenancy shall be taken to be made, not by the concurrent lessee, the *pro tanto* landlord, but by the person for the time being entitled to the interest from which the deceased's tenancy was derived.[8] The result will be as if the concurrent lessee's interest and any other supervening interest were not in existence at the relevant time.[9] Thus if A was the freeholder who granted the tenancy to the tenant now deceased, and A subsequently granted a lease of the reversion to B, A, not B, would be the person deemed to grant the new tenancy to the successful applicant. Although the effect *for this purpose* would be the same as if B's interest were non-existent, this convenient fiction would not affect B's ordinary rights and liabilities as the landlord during the subsistence of the concurrent lease.[10] During the subsistence of the concurrent lease the new tenancy deemed to be granted under section 45(1) would be a quasi-sub-tenancy; it would not perish like an ordinary sub-tenancy on the dropping of the concurrent lease, but would continue freed from the latter. Section 45(3) provides a safeguard against the device of a *series* of leases of the reversion.[11]

Death of successful applicant before the relevant time Section 45(8) empowers the Lord Chancellor to provide by regulations for the contingency of a person or any of the persons whom the direction entitles to a tenancy or joint tenancy of the holding dying before the tenancy had actually vested at the relevant time. The broad effect of the regulations[12] is that the succession provisions are in the case of the death of such a person applied with the necessary modifications. In the case of joint tenants the position is simply that the

---

[6] Megarry and Wade *The Law of Real Property*, (5th ed., Stevens & Sons Ltd, 1984), pp.664–665. A "quasi subtenant" because his position is not in all respects the same as an ordinary sub-tenant whose interest has been carved out of his immediate landlord's interest.

[7] 1984 Act, s.3(1), interposing subs. (1A) into s.23 of the 1976 Act. For an example of the difficulties experienced, see ***Cheshire v. Elwes and the Colesbourne Estate Co.*** (1979) Hamilton No.76 at 97–99, and S.W. Area ref. SW/ALT/TS/67. The Tribunal were in doubt as to who was the "landlord" for the purpose of the deemed grant and acceptance of the new tenancy following upon a direction. The Tribunal expressed a tentative view that the concurrent lessee was the landlord.

[8] s. 45(2).

[9] s. 45(2).

[10] s. 45(4).

[11] s. 45(3), "whether immediately or otherwise". It has been doubted whether this closes a possible loophole enabling the landlord to undermine the successor's security of tenure, but it is not clear that this criticism is valid.

[12] At present the Agriculture (Miscellaneous Provisions) Act 1976 (Application of Provisions) Regulations 1977 (S.I. 1977 No.1215).

direction continues to have effect in relation to the other joint tenant or tenants who survive.

Terms of new tenancy unless varied by arbitration: section 47   14.85
The terms of the new tenancy or joint tenancy to which a direction by the Tribunal entitles the person or persons concerned are in general the same as those on which the holding was let immediately before the contract of tenancy subsisting at the date of the deceased tenant's death comes to an end.[13] This general correspondence is subject to the following qualifications.

1. The terms may be varied as a result of the arbitration proceedings mentioned in section 48.[14]

2. If the deceased on the date of death held a tenancy of the holding for a fixed term of years it is to be treated as if before the death it had been converted into a tenancy from year to year, but otherwise on the same terms as the actual tenancy so far as applicable.[15]

3. If the terms would not otherwise have included a covenant by the tenant not to assign, sub-let or part with possession of the holding or any part of it without the landlord's consent in writing, the terms are to have effect as if they included such a covenant.[16] This qualified covenant is to be distinguished from the absolute prohibition of assignment of rights conferred by a direction. That absolute prohibition is contained in section 45(7).

Arbitration on terms of new tenancy: section 48   14.86
Section 48 provides for arbitration under the Act[17] on the terms of the new tenancy which results from the Tribunal's direction. As already mentioned,[18] these arbitration provisions do not apply if the Tribunal's direction has been superseded before the relevant time by the direct grant of a tenancy by the landlord. There is no need for arbitration where the terms of the tenancy have been freely negotiated between the parties, but where the new tenancy is the non-negotiated product of the deemed grant which is built into the direction there may be questions as to rent or terms which require arbitration.

Demand for arbitration: time-limit   14.87
The demand for arbitration may be made by either landlord or tenant under the new tenancy[19] and must be made within the "prescribed period" which means the period

---

[13] s. 47(1). It does not end with the deceased tenant's death, as it will normally vest in his personal representatives and continue until the deemed grant and acceptance of the new tenancy take place at the "relevant time" (s.45(1)) or an earlier direct grant under s.45(6).
[14] See para. 14.86 below.
[15] s. 47(2).
[16] s. 47(3).
[17] s. 84 and Sched. 11.
[18] s. 45(6). See also s.48(1), and para. 14.80.
[19] s. 48(2).

between the giving of the direction and either (a) the end of three months immediately following the "relevant time" or (b) the end of three months immediately following the date of the giving of the direction, whichever last occurs.[20]

14.88 Scope of arbitration

At any time within the above prescribed period the landlord or tenant may by notice in writing served on the other demand a reference to arbitration of one or both of the following questions,[21] described as "question (a)" and "question (b)":

(a) what variations in the terms of the tenancy which the tenant is entitled to or has obtained by virtue of the direction are justifiable having regard to the circumstances of the holding and the length of time since the holding was first let on those terms;

(b) what rent should be or should have been properly payable in respect of the holding at the relevant time.[22]

In fact, as will be seen, the arbitration provisions cover the variation in the terms of the tenancy in the light of the circumstances and history of the holding; the settlement of compensation appropriate to the termination of the deceased's tenancy and the commencement of the new tenancy; and either a restricted adjustment of rent consequential on the variation of terms or a complete review of the rent properly payable, according to the scope of the arbitration demanded.

14.89 Arbitration as to variation in the terms of tenancy

Alternative references to arbitration. The reference to arbitration may take one of three forms, which differ in scope.

---

[20] *ibid*. The result is somewhat complex. If one ignores the possible effect of a direction by the Tribunal fixing a later relevant time, the result is as follows:

The prescribed period =

(A) the period between the date of the giving of the direction and

(1) the end of 15 months immediately following the end of the year of the tenancy in which the deceased died, or, if later,

(2) three months after the date on which a notice to quit under Case G would (apart from s.43) have terminated the tenancy; or

(B) the period between the date of the giving of the direction and the end of three months immediately following the date of the giving of the direction, whichever of (A) or (B) is the later.

If a direction postponing the original relevant time is given by the Tribunal under s. 46(2), it would be necessary to substitute the later relevant time for (1) and (2) under (A) above.

[21] s. 48(3).
[22] s. 48(4).

Question (a) only. If "question (a)" only is referred, the subject-matter of the arbitration will be (1) what variations, if any, are justifiable in the terms of the tenancy, (2) whether any, and if so what, consequential rent adjustment is equitable in the light of any such variations, (3) what, if any, is the fair and reasonable amount of compensation payable by the tenant to the landlord and by the landlord to the tenant in respect of the termination of the deceased's tenancy of the holding, *i.e.* in short, an ingoing payment by the new tenant and a payment by the landlord related to the dilapidation moneys received by him.[23] The compensation question is also addressed separately below.[24]

Question (b) only. If "question (b)" only is referred, the reference is confined to a determination of the rent properly payable in respect of the holding at the relevant time. The definition of "rent properly payable" for this purpose is noted below.[25]

Question (a) and Question (b). If both "question (a)" and "question (b)" are referred, the reference will cover (1) variations which are justifiable in the terms of the tenancy, (2) a full review of the rent properly payable, not merely an adjustment of rent consequential on the variations, and (3) fair and reasonable compensation, as mentioned above.[26]

Arbitration as to rent   14.90
For the purpose of these arbitration proceedings "the rent properly payable" is defined in terms consistent with Schedule 2 to the Act, but necessarily omitting some of the detailed provisions in the Schedule not applicable to a statement of the rent at a particular point of time, *i.e.* at the "relevant time". The definition incorporates the central formula of Schedule 2 by providing that for the purposes of section 48 the rent properly payable shall be the rent at which the holding might reasonably be expected to be let by a prudent and willing landlord to a prudent and willing tenant, taking into account all relevant factors, including (in every case) the terms of the tenancy or prospective tenancy (including those relating to rent) and any such other matters as are specifically referred to in Schedule 2, paragraph 1(1), (2) and (3).[27] In any future rent arbitration between the parties in accordance with section 12, that section and Schedule 2 as a whole will, of course, apply in the normal way.

Arbitration Award   14.91
On any reference under the above provisions the arbitrator may include in his award, in addition to the directions required by his determinations of the matters referred to him under the Act, such further provisions relating to the tenancy as the landlord and tenant agree to be included.[28] If the arbitrator decides to vary the terms of the tenancy, the variation will take effect as from the relevant time, as will

---

[23] s. 48(5), (6) and (8).
[24] See para. 14.95 below.
[25] s. 48(7) and (9).
[26] s. 48(5), (7), (8) and (9).
[27] s. 48(9).
[28] s. 48(10).

any consequential adjustment of rent.[29] If there is a reference of the rent properly payable this will also take effect from the relevant time.[30] If the award is made before the relevant time, section 47(1) (new tenancy to be on same terms as deceased's contract of tenancy) will have effect subject to, and in accordance with, the award.[31] If the award is made after the relevant time it will have effect as if its terms were contained in a written agreement entered into by the landlord and tenant and having effect as from the relevant time.[32]

14.92 Cessation of inconsistent tenancy
When the new tenancy vests in the person or persons entitled under the direction, any previous tenancy of the holding inconsistent with the new tenancy, *e.g.* the tenancy held by the deceased tenant's personal representatives, automatically ceases. In case there should be any doubt as to the effect of the deemed grant of the new tenancy in supplanting the previous tenancy, it is provided that if the previous tenancy would not otherwise come to an end at the relevant time, it shall cease at that time as if terminated by a valid notice to quit given by the tenant.[33]

14.93 Prohibition of assignment of rights conferred by direction
There is an absolute prohibition of the assignment of the rights conferred by a direction during the interim period between the giving of the direction and the vesting of the new tenancy.[34] This must be distinguished from the qualified restriction on assignment, etc., which is written into the new tenancy when it has vested in the person entitled to it.[35] It would be inconsistent with the succession scheme if the rights given by the direction, after investigation of the claimant's eligibility and suitability, were to be freely transferable. Where the successful applicant(s) have a direction in their favour but die before the new tenancy vests, special provisions apply.[36]

14.94 Directions relating to part of deceased's holding
Where one or more applicants would, subject to section 44 (landlord's opportunity to request consent to the operation of a notice to quit) be entitled to a direction under section 39 then it is open to the applicant(s) to accept instead a tenancy of a part of the holding. There appears to be no opportunity for the Tribunal to participate in deciding what precise part of the holding should be the subject of the direction: any direction in fact given by the Tribunal will in those circumstances relate to the agreed part of the holding only.[37] It is expressly provided that references in section 45 (effect of a direction) and in section 48 (arbitration on terms of new tenancy) to the holding are to be read as references to part of the

---

[29] s. 48(5), (6). For "relevant time" see s. 46.
[30] s. 48(7).
[31] s. 48(11).
[32] s. 48(12).
[33] s. 45(5).
[34] s. 45(7).
[35] s. 47(3).
[36] The Agriculture (Miscellaneous Provisions) Act 1976 (Application of Provisions) Regulations 1977 (S.I. 1977 No.1215).
[37] s. 39(10).

holding where the direction relates to a part only and the context requires this meaning.[38]

Compensation as between landlord and successor tenant 14.95

As between the landlord and the deceased tenant's personal representatives the normal compensation arrangements on the termination of a tenancy, based on the contract of tenancy and the relevant statutory provisions, will apply. There is nothing in the 1986 Act which prevents claims in respect of improvements and tenant-right by the personal representatives, on the one side, and any landlord's claims in respect of dilapidations and breaches of contract, on the other side, from being settled or determined in the usual way. Special statutory arrangements, however, had to be made to define the position as between the landlord and the new tenant who comes in under the succession scheme. Normally the position between the landlord and an incoming tenant is regulated by the contract of tenancy. It is fairly common for the incomer to agree to pay the landlord the amount payable by the latter to the outgoing tenant in respect of improvements and tenant-right and for the landlord to agree to pay to the incomer the amount received from the outgoer in respect of dilapidations or breaches of contract. There are, of course, many variations in these arrangements according to the individual circumstances. However, except in the case mentioned in section 45(6) (where the person entitled under a direction to a tenancy accepts a direct grant by agreement with the landlord before the relevant time) there is no contract between the landlord and the successor under the statutory scheme. It was therefore necessary to regulate the matter by statute and this is done in the provisions of section 48 which direct the arbitrator to determine the respective sums payable. So far as payment by the incoming successor is concerned, the arbitrator is required to fix the compensation at so much as is in all the circumstances fair and reasonable of the compensation payable by the landlord under the 1986 Act, custom or agreement to the deceased tenant's estate in respect of the determination of the deceased's tenancy.[39] So far as payment by the landlord to the incomer is concerned, the arbitrator is required to fix the compensation at so much as is in all the circumstances fair and reasonable of the compensation payable to the landlord, whether under the 1986 Act or under the agreement, on the termination of the deceased's tenancy, in respect of those dilapidations which the incoming tenant is or will be liable to make good under the terms of his tenancy.[40] Thus the arbitrator is given a considerable measure of discretion, but within a framework which is familiar to him, to decide the amounts payable by the tenant and landlord respectively.

Grant of tenancy following direction but before the relevant time: section 45(6) 14.96

Where a person or persons entitled by virtue of a direction to take a tenancy as from the relevant time in fact become tenant before the relevant time, the direction no longer has effect and arbitration on the terms of tenancy is no longer available.[41]

---

[38] s. 46(3).
[39] s. 48(5)(a) and (8)(a).
[40] s. 48(5)(b) and (8)(b).
[41] s. 45(6).

As to a tenancy granted following direction but before the relevant time being a tenancy in relation to part only of the deceased's holding, see paragraph 14.80 above.

14.97 Succession tenancies: relationship to Agricultural Tenancies Act 1995

Section 4 of the 1995 Act provides that certain tenancies should be excluded from the application of that Act and should continue to be governed by the terms of the Agricultural Holdings Act 1986, notwithstanding their being tenancies beginning on or after September 1, 1995. Three of the categories specified by section 4(1) of the 1995 Act are quite obviously designed to cover most forms of succession tenancy. They are:

(i) A tenancy obtained by virtue of a direction of the Tribunal under section 39 (death) or 53 (retirement);[42]

(ii) A tenancy granted following a direction under section 39 (death) in circumstances falling within section 45(6) (grant voluntarily prior to the relevant time);[43]

(iii) A tenancy granted on an agreed succession by a written contract of tenancy indicating (in whatever terms) that the succession provisions in Part IV of the 1986 Act are to apply to the tenancy.[44] "Agreed succession" is defined by section 4(2).[45] For the purposes of section 4(2) certain definitions from the 1986 Act are imported.[46] It will be recalled that section 37(1), to which reference is made in the definition of "agreed succession" has been discussed above.[47]

The net effect of these statutory provisions is to create a significant group of

---

[42] s. 4(1)(b) of the 1995 Act.
[43] s. 4(1)(c) of the 1995 Act; as to s. 45(6) see para. 14.96 above.
[44] s. 4(1)(d) of the 1995 Act.
[45] For the purposes of sub-section (1)(d) above, a tenancy ("the current tenancy") is granted on an agreed succession if, and only if,—

(a) the previous tenancy of the holding or a related holding was a tenancy in relation to which Part IV of the 1986 Act applied, and

(b) the current tenancy is granted otherwise than as mentioned in paragraph (b) or (c) of sub-section (1) above but in such circumstances that if—

(i) Part IV of the 1986 Act applied in relation to the current tenancy, and

(ii) a sole (or sole surviving) tenant under the current tenancy were to die and be survived by a close relative of his,

the occasion on which the current tenancy is granted would be for purposes of sub-section (1) of section 37 of the 1986 Act be taken to be an occasion falling within paragraph (a) or (b) of that sub-section.

[46] "Agricultural holding", "contract of tenancy", "close relative" (s. 35(2)) and "related holding" (s. 35(2)).
[47] As to s. 37(1)(a) see para. 14.15; as to s. 37(1)(b) see para. 14.16.

tenancies to which the 1986 Act continues to apply despite its being overtaken by the 1995 Act for the vast majority of tenancies beginning on or after September 1, 1995. It will, however, be recalled that the grant of a tenancy to a person falling outside the technical definition of "close relative"[48] cannot fall within section 4(1)(b), (c) or (d). Where, for example, a grandchild or son-in-law is granted a new tenancy, unless by virtue of "Evesham custom"[49], that tenancy will be governed by the 1995 Act.

Succession tenancies: "roll over" of milk quota compensation 14.98

Schedule 1, paragraph 2 of the Agriculture Act 1986 "rolls over" milk quota compensation claims from the previous tenant to his successor (whether on death or retirement). The previous tenant or his estate are not able to make a claim for this type of compensation and instead, by appropriate "deemings" the benefit of the claim is effectively transferred to the incoming successor tenant. In the drafting of paragraph 2 of the Schedule the reference to April 2, 1984 is a reference to the first day in respect of which milk quota was available under the Dairy Produce Quotas Regulations 1984. Because of the value of milk quota these "roll over" provisions are very helpful to landlords: the net effect is to defer the need to meet a compensation claim to the time when vacant possession is likely to be available. Once again the warning must be given that the grant of a tenancy to a person such as a grandchild or son-in-law who is therefore not a "close relative" of the deceased or retiring tenant will not bring into play the "roll over" provisions in the Agriculture Act.[50]

A practical problem: the analysis of historical events 14.99

In crude terms succession is normally available twice in relation to a particular holding: this is the net result of the exclusions in section 37.[51] It has been the subject of some discussion as to whether succession voluntarily prior to 1976 (the introduction of any statutory succession) should count as one of the two instances of succession for the purposes of section 37. In one case, ***Saunders v. Ralph***[52] pre-1976 voluntary successions were held to count. This work is critical of that mechanical construction of section 37.[53] However for the practitioner there is a real problem here as to whether these pre-1976 events can satisfactorily be dealt with even if there may be an occasion potentially counting as one succession. There is no doubt that as time goes by documenting pre-1976 successions will become increasingly difficult; the difficulty since 1976 is nowhere near so great

---

[48] See para. 14.35 above.
[49] s. 4(1)(e) of the 1995 Act.
[50] The outgoing or deceased tenant is required by statute to have the opportunity to make any claim under Sched. 1 of the Agriculture Act 1986 and it is not possible to contract out of that right. However there appears to be nothing to stop the landlord and the new tenant making contractual provisions in relation to voluntary milk quota compensation conditional upon the circumstance becoming a reality that the previous tenant does not in fact make a claim within the two months following the termination of his tenancy as required by para. 11(1) of Sched. 1 of the Agriculture Act 1986.
[51] See para. 14.13 above and following.
[52] [1993] 2 E.G.L.R. 1.
[53] See para. 14.17 above.

because those operating in the shadow of the legislation or indeed under it realise that there is a need to keep records and ensure that the events can be correctly identified as falling within section 37 (or its predecessors). For pre-1976 occasions there may be difficulty in ascertaining not only who the tenant was but what his relationship was to any of the parties currently alive or even of obtaining reliable evidence as to what the holding from time to time consisted of. Although the Tribunal is not bound by the hearsay rules it must necessarily take a sceptical attitude towards pre-1976 materials designed for some other purpose. A landlord wishing to run the argument against his tenant that two successions have already taken place may well be advised to do some research before the tenant dies so that the relevant information is to hand in a reasonably authoritative form.[54]

14.100 SUCCESSION ON RETIREMENT

Introductory

It has been seen that in one case a succession *inter vivos* may take place by agreement between the landlord and the tenant whereby the latter retires in favour of a close relative who either obtains a grant of a new tenancy from the landlord or takes an assignment of the retiring tenant's existing tenancy.[55] Such an arrangement, although *inter vivos*, is deemed for the purpose of the "two-occasion" rule to be an occasion on which a tenancy was obtained on the death of a tenant by virtue of a direction of the Tribunal.[56]

In contrast with this, sections 49 to 58 introduce a scheme of *inter vivos* succession which is not dependent on the agreement of the landlord, but is, on the other hand, conditional on the retiring tenant's attaining the age of 65 or being incapable by reason of infirmity of continuing to farm to an acceptable standard. The retirement provisions consolidated in sections 49–50 are derived from Schedule 2 to the Agricultural Holdings Act 1984, which give legislative force to a recommendation of the Northfield Committee (Report of the Committee of Enquiry into the Acquisition and Occupancy of Agricultural Land, Cmnd 7599, 1979).[57] In accordance with the unanimous conclusion of the Northfield Committee, there is no provision for the compulsory retirement of the tenant: the arrangement require his voluntary co-operation.[58] In its details the retirement scheme follows *mutatis mutandis* the provisions of the scheme for succession on death.

---

[54] This may involve consulting the registry of births, marriages and deaths, parish records or old estate plans.
[55] s. 37(2).
[56] *ibid.*
[57] At para. 634 the Committee recommended "that there should be encouragement for transfer earlier than death. We are agreed that this could be achieved by providing that the tenant might, at or after age 65, with his nominated successor, apply for the transfer of the tenancy. The landlord could contest the application both to oppose the succession and to put his own case for possession (as though a notice to quit on death had been served). If the ALT... found for the landlord, or that the successor was not suitable, the existing tenancy would continue until the tenant's death again brought the 1976... Act into play".
[58] This contrasts with the retirement of tenants of statutory smallholdings: see Case A in

Conditions for operation of the retirement scheme 14.101

Provided the exclusions from the retirement scheme[59] do not apply there are conditions for the operation of the retirement scheme which conditions relate to the tenancy[60], to persons[61] or are as to notice.[62]

Conditions related to the tenancy 14.102

There are two conditions related to the tenancy. The first is that the tenancy of the tenant whose retirement is sought must be a tenancy granted before July 12, 1984 or a tenancy in one of the categories mentioned in section 34(1)(b).[63] Furthermore the tenancy must be a tenancy from year to year.[64]

Conditions related to persons 14.103

The retiring tenant must at the retirement date[65] be at least 65 years of age or incapable, by reason of bodily or mental infirmity, of conducting the farming of the holding so as to fulfil the responsibilities to farm in accordance with the rules of good husbandry.[66]

The nominated successor[67] must be a close relative of the retiring tenant, must be otherwise eligible within the meaning of the principal livelihood and the occupancy conditions,[68] and must be found suitable by the Tribunal.[69] These conditions are closely modelled on the conditions for succession on death and the commentary above will with minor modifications apply.

Conditions as to notice 14.104

The retiring tenant (or tenants in the case of a joint tenancy) must serve on the landlord a "retirement notice"[70] indicating clearly but not in any prescribed terms that he (or they) wish a single eligible person named in the notice to succeed him (or them) as tenant of the holding as from a date specified in the notice. The date specified must be a date on which the tenancy could have been determined by notice to quit given at the date of the notice and which falls not less than one year, but not more than two years, after the date of the notice.[71]

Exclusions from the retirement scheme 14.105

A number of the exclusions from the succession on retirement scheme correspond, with only the necessary modification required by the substitution of retirement for

---

Sched. 3 of the 1986 Act.
[59] See para. 14.105 below.
[60] para. 14.102 below.
[61] para. 14.103 below.
[62] para. 14.104 below.
[63] s. 49(1)(a).
[64] *ibid.*
[65] The date specified in the retirement notice as the date from which the proposed succession is to take place: ss 49(3) and 49(1).
[66] s. 51(3).
[67] s. 49(3).
[68] s. 50(2) and Sched. 6.
[69] s. 53(5), (6), (7).
[70] See Form 47 in Part V of this work.
[71] s. 49(1)(b).

death, with those in sections 37 and 38.[72] These include tenancies subject to a valid notice to quit given before the retirement date which, for one reason or another, cannot be effectively challenged,[73] exclusions where the "two succession" limitation applies, tenancies of smallholdings and tenancies granted by charitable trusts for ex-servicemen.

There are, however, certain exclusions from the retirement scheme which are peculiar to that scheme.

1. An application is excluded if some other person has duly made an application in relation to the holding (or a related holding) in respect of a previous retirement notice given by the retiring tenant naming that other person.[74] However it should be noted that if the person named in the earlier retirement notice has not acted upon it by applying, the person named in the later one may apply. Moreover by virtue of section 53(10) an application by the nominated successor which is withdrawn or abandoned is to be treated as if it had never been made. Finally, an application by the nominated successor which is invalidated by section 52(1) or (2) (notices to quit restricting operation of section 53) must be treated as if it had never been made.[75]

2. An application is excluded if at the retirement date[76] the retiring tenant will be under 65 years of age,[77] but this exclusion is subject to the important exception of physical or mental incapacity on the part of the retiring tenant.[78]

14.106 Availability of retirement where the tenant is under 65 but infirm

The phrase used is "incapable, by reason of bodily or mental infirmity, of conducting the farming of the holding in such a way as to secure the fulfilment of the responsibilities of the tenant to farm in accordance with the rules of good husbandry". The retirement notice must state this ground and that the incapacity is likely to be permanent.[79] In the case of joint tenants the exception applies only if they *all* meet this requirement, a perhaps unusual concurrence and synchronisation of infirmity. The Act does not provide the Tribunal with any specific guidance as to how they should satisfy themselves that this exception applies. No doubt they will

---

[72] s. 51(1) and s.49(3). See in relation to death paras 14.9–14.23 above.
[73] This covers also the cases mentioned in s. 51(4), the wording of which should be compared with s. 38(3). See also s. 51(5) and (6). The effect is that the retirement notice is held in suspense until the fate of the notice to quit has been settled one way or the other. If the notice to quit is upheld the retirement notice will lapse. If, on the other hand, the notice to quit fails to take effect, the retirement notice and the subsequent succession procedures will operate; and the "relevant period" will be calculated from the date of the event which has settled the fate of the notice to quit.
[74] s. 51(2).
[75] s. 52(5).
[76] See s. 49(3) and (1).
[77] s. 51(3). There is no reduction of age if the retiring tenant is a woman.
[78] s. 51(3)(a) and (b).
[79] s. 51(3)(b).

require medical evidence. If the Tribunal are not persuaded that the incapacity has been demonstrated, and they in consequence dismiss the application, the successor nominated in the unsuccessful attempt cannot try his luck again on the tenant's death.[80] It would, however, be open to a different applicant to apply on the death of the tenant.

Restriction on retirement notice by reference to certain notices to quit 14.107
Where a valid notice to quit is given on or after the date of the giving of the retirement notice, but before the Tribunal have begun to hear any application by the nominated successor, the effect in some cases is to nullify the retirement notice. There are two categories of Cases, in one of which the retirement notice is rendered ineffective immediately, in the other contingently on the outcome of further proceedings. If the notice to quit is given under Case F (insolvency) or Case C (where a certificate of bad husbandry had been given in response to an application made before the date of the giving of the retirement notice) the retirement notice is of no effect.[81] If the notice to quit is given under Case B (land required for a non-agricultural use) or Case D (founded on a notice to pay rent or a notice to remedy given before that date) the retirement notice is held in suspense until its fate is settled by the outcome of arbitration or Tribunal proceedings.[82] If the notice to quit is upheld, the retirement notice is of no effect. If the notice to quit fails, the retirement notice and the subsequent succession procedure operate; and, if necessary, the "relevant period" is extended.[83]

Restriction by retirement notice of certain notices to quit 14.108
This category of notices to quit covers any such notice (whether given to the tenant before or on or after the date of the giving of the retirement notice), not being a notice falling within the provisions, noted above, of section 38 (as applied by section 51(1)) or section 51 or 52. It is a residual category and the object is to ensure that notices to quit other than those of the kinds specifically dealt with earlier do not prevent an application for a tenancy being made by a nominated successor under section 53. The effect of the provisions in section 54[84] is to suspend the operation of the notice to quit pending the outcome of the application to the Tribunal by a nominated successor. If the Tribunal give a direction entitling the applicant to a tenancy, the notice to quit then lapses.[85]

Application by the nominated successor 14.109
Application The application by the nominated successor to the Tribunal for a direction entitling him to a tenancy of the holding must be made within the period of one month beginning with the day after the date of the giving of the retirement

---

[80] s. 57(4).
[81] s. 52(1)(b) and (a).
[82] s. 52(2)(b) and (a).
[83] s. 52(3) and (4). For "relevant period", see s. 53(2).
[84] The draftsman evidently thought it more logical to deal first with applications for a tenancy (s. 53) and then with a provision which ensures that notices to quit (other than those already dealt with) will not prevent an application for a tenancy from going ahead (s. 54).
[85] s. 54(2).

notice.[86] The application must be accompanied by a copy of the retirement notice and must be signed by both the nominated successor and the retiring tenant(s).[87] The time-limit of two months for making the application is inflexible, subject to the extension provided by sections 51(6) and 52(4). An application by a nominated successor for a direction entitling him to a tenancy must be made in Form 5[88] and will not be entertained unless made within the "relevant period", which in this context means the period of one month beginning with the day after the date of the giving of the retirement notice.[89] A landlord who intends to oppose the application, in whole or part, must reply on Form 5R within one month after a copy of the application has been served on him.[90] The nominated successor should have served notice of his application on the landlord, on Form 6.[91] The parties to the proceedings on an application by a nominated successor are the nominated successor, the landlord, and the retiring tenant or (in the case of a joint tenancy) all the retiring tenants. If no reply from the landlord to an application by the nominated successor is received by the secretary within the one month allowed,[92] then the landlord will not be entitled to dispute any matter alleged in that application; but this does not affect the landlord's right to express his views on the suitability of the nominated successor in accordance with section 53(6).[93] Amendments and applications for the extension of any time-limit prescribed by the Tribunal rules are discussed at paragraph 14.29 above.

Allegation of tenant's incapacity: retirement under age 65 If the retirement notice includes a statement that the retiring tenant is, or will at the retirement date be, incapable by reason of bodily or mental infirmity of conducting the farming of the holding in such a way as to secure the fulfilment of the responsibilities of the tenant to farm in accordance with the rules of good husbandry, and that such incapacity is likely to be permanent, then, before proceeding any further, the Tribunal must decide whether it is satisfied that such incapacity does or will exist.[94] This matter, which goes to the Tribunal's jurisdiction, must be determined as a preliminary issue. Section 53(11), which requires provision to be made by

---

[86] s. 53(1) and (2). For the "corresponding date" rule in calculating the expiry date of a period of months allowed for on application, see *Dodds v. Walker* [1981] 1 W.L.R. 1027, HL.
[87] s. 53(3).
[88] Rule 23(1) of the Agricultural Land Tribunals (Succession to Agricultural Tenancies) Order 1984 (S.I. 1984 No.1301). See Form 48 in Part V of this work. However, as discussed in para. 14.25 above, a modernised form substantially to the like effect may be supplied by the Tribunal. The commentary under para. 14.26 above in relation to completing the form on a succession on death will be helpful in completing the form on a retirement succession. Completion of the landlord's response is commented on at paras 14.27–14.28.
[89] s. 53(1), (2); r. 23(2).
[90] r. 25. See Form 48A in Part V of this work.
[91] r. 24. See Form 49 in Part V of this work.
[92] r. 25.
[93] r. 31.
[94] s. 53(4).

order under section 73(3) of the Agriculture Act 1947 for the application for a direction under section 53 to give notice to the landlord has been implemented.[95]

The formal requirements and general rules relating to documents to be filed and supporting documentation are contained in rule 16 of the principal Rules[96] excluding rule 16(5)[97] and rule 18 of the principal Rules, excluding rule 18(2) (withdrawal of application or reply) also apply.[98] The Tribunal secretary is obliged to serve a copy of each filed document on each party.[99]

Requirement for nominated successor to show his eligibility and suitability 14.110

The Tribunal must be satisfied that the nominated successor was an eligible person at the date of the giving of the retirement notice and that he has not subsequently ceased to be such a person.[1] If satisfied as to eligibility the Tribunal must then determine whether the applicant is suitable.[2] In making such a determination the Tribunal must have regard to all relevant matters, including:

(a) the extent to which the nominated successor has been trained in, or has had practical experience of, agriculture,

(b) his age, physical health and financial standing,

(c) the views (if any) stated by the landlord as to his suitability.[3]
(Before making a determination the Tribunal must afford the landlord an opportunity of stating his views on this point.)[4]

The reader is referred to the detailed discussion of eligibility and suitability in relation to succession on death, which *mutatis mutandis*, applies to succession on retirement.[5] There is, however, in the case of the latter no provision similar to that in section 41 for a person not fully eligible to be treated as eligible.

It should be noted that the complex provisions of Schedule 6, which have been discussed in relation to succession on death, are applied with a few necessary modifications to succession on retirement.[6] Thus all the provisions about disregard of certain types of occupation, about joint occupation, deemed occupation, occupation by spouse or controlled company, and so one, are incorporated.

The normal procedure is that the nominated successor shall begin and that the

---

[95] See the Agricultural Land Tribunals (Succession to Agricultural Tenancies) Order 1984 (S.I. 1984 No.1301), r. 24 and Form 6 in the Schedule to the Order.
[96] The Agricultural Land Tribunals (Rules) Order 1978 (S.I. 1978 No.259).
[97] Applied by r. 28 of S.I. 1984 No.1301.
[98] r. 28 of S.I. 1984 No.1301.
[99] r. 27.
[1] s. 53(5).
[2] s. 53(5).
[3] s. 53(6).
[4] *ibid*.
[5] Eligibility is discussed at paras 14.33–14.69, suitability at paragraphs 14.72–14.74 above.
[6] s. 50(4) and Part II of Sched. 6.

other parties shall be heard in such order as the Tribunal may determine.[7] There is a special provision that, where the retirement notice is given on the ground of the retiring tenant's incapacity, the Tribunal must first consider whether such incapacity exists and is likely to be permanent. If they are not satisfied on these points they must dismiss the nominated successor's application.[8]

14.111 No opportunity for the nominated successor to be treated as eligible (*cf.* section 41)

Where the nominated successor is unable to demonstrate that he is fully eligible his application will fail. There is no opportunity for a person who just fails the livelihood test to request the Tribunal to exercise a discretion in his favour. This is therefore a stark contrast with the provisions of section 41 (applicable following the tenant's death).[9] Because of the technical quality of the livelihood test, if there is the slightest doubt as to it being satisfied it will be more prudent to wait until after the tenant has died so that the Tribunal are able in the circumstances of section 41 to save the application.

14.112 Application by landlord requesting a refusal of direction based on greater hardship

If the Tribunal finds that the nominated successor is suitable as well as eligible, they must, subject to the greater hardship provision mentioned below, give a direction entitling him to a tenancy.[10]

The Tribunal must not give such a direction if, on an application made by the landlord, it appears to it that greater hardship would be caused by giving the direction than by refusing the nominated successor's application.[11] On the analogy of Case 9 in Schedule 15 to the Rent Act 1977 (para. 1 in Part III of Sched. 15) and the cases decided thereon the onus of proof would seem to be on the person alleging the hardship, *i.e.* in this case the landlord. This greater hardship provision may be compared in principle with the opportunity given to the landlord by section 44 of the 1986 Act, in the case of succession on death, to apply to the Tribunal for consent to a notice to quit. The present provision, however, limits the ground of the landlord's opposition to greater hardship, whereas under section 44 the landlord can rely on any of the grounds in section 27.[12]

14.113 Withdrawal or abandonment of the application: section 53(10)

An application under section 53 by a nominated successor which is withdrawn or abandoned (as distinct from being dismissed) is to be treated as if it had never been made.[13] The effect of this is that such an application having thus been made a

---

[7] r. 32(1) of the Agricultural Land Tribunals (Succession to Agricultural Tenancies) Order 1984 (S.I. 1984 No.1301).
[8] r. 32(2).
[9] As to which see paras 14.70–14.71 above.
[10] s. 53(7).
[11] s. 53(8).
[12] s. 44(2). As to which see para. 14.83 above.
[13] s. 53(10).

non-event, will not prevent another application being made under a different retirement notice.[14]

Rejection of the application by the Tribunal: section 53(9) 14.114
If the Tribunal reject the nominated successor's application, the tenancy remains vested in the retiring tenant (whose retirement is thus thwarted) and the retirement notice is of no effect.[15] This result is without prejudice to section 51(2), as a result of which this retirement notice, even though it has become abortive by dismissal of the application, will have excluded any other application in pursuance of a retirement notice given by the retiring tenant.[16]

Effect of a direction entitling the nominated successor to a tenancy 14.115
Section 55 of the 1986 Act is modelled closely on the provisions in section 45, which describe the effect of a direction in the case of succession on death.[17] The mechanism of succession is the same, a deemed grant and acceptance of a tenancy,[18] taking effect from the "relevant time", which is, however, necessarily defined in different terms from the definition in section 46. For the purpose of succession on retirement the "relevant time" means the "retirement date"[19] (*i.e.* the date specified in the retirement notice as the date from which the proposed succession is to take place)[20] unless the time is postponed by the Tribunal on account of delay in the giving of the direction.[21]

Section 55 contains a provision, similar to that in section 45, designed to overcome the difficulty of a concurrent lease or lease of the reversion, granted subsequently to the retiring tenant's tenancy and derived from the reversion interest from which that tenancy was derived.[22]

There are provisions similar to those in respect of succession on death as to the cessation of the old tenancy,[23] the absolute prohibition of the assignment of rights conferred by the direction as distinct from rights under the new tenancy once it has vested,[24] and as to regulations to provide for the case where the nominated successor dies before the relevant time.[25]

Arbitration on terms of new tenancy 14.116
Unless varied by the arbitration procedure mentioned below, the terms of the new tenancy to which the nominated successor is entitled by virtue of the direction will

---

[14] *i.e.* s. 51(2) will not apply.
[15] s. 53(9).
[16] s. 53(9).
[17] As to which see para. 14.84 above.
[18] It should be noted that there is no statutory assignment of the retiring tenant's tenancy to the successor. A new tenancy is deemed to be created.
[19] s. 55(8).
[20] s. 49(1) and (3). It must be a date on which the tenancy of the holding could have been determined by notice to quit given at the date of the notice and which falls not less than one year, but more than two years, after the date of the notice.
[21] s. 55(8)(a) and (b).
[22] s. 55(2), (3) and (4): *cf.* s.45(2), (3) and (4). And see para. 14.84 above.
[23] s. 55(5); *cf.* s. 45(5).
[24] s. 55(6); *cf.* s. 45(7).
[25] s. 55(7); *cf.* s. 45(8).

be the same as those on which the holding was let immediately before the giving of the retirement notice.[26] But if the terms would not otherwise have included a covenant by the tenant not to assign, sub-let or part with provision of the holding or any part of it without the landlord's consent in writing, the terms are to have effect as if they included such a covenant.[27]

The provisions for arbitration already discussed in relation to the terms of the new tenancy in the case of succession on death[28] are applied, subject to minor necessary modifications and new definitions, to the tenancy which vests in the nominated successor on retirement.[29]

14.117 Death of tenant after giving retirement notice but before vesting of new tenancy in nominated successor: section 57

Provision has to be made for the contingency of the death of the retiring tenant after he has given the retirement notice but before the new tenancy has vested in the nominated successor at the relevant time.[30] There are three different sets of circumstances.

(1) If the death occurs before an application by the nominated successor has been made to the Tribunal, or before any such application has been finally disposed of, the retirement notice becomes of no effect. In that event the normal succession provisions set out in sections 36 to 48 apply on the tenant's death.[31]

(2) If the death occurs after a direction has been given entitling the nominated successor to a tenancy, but before the relevant time,[32] the matter proceeds as an *inter vivos* succession despite the death and the succession on death provisions in sections 36 to 48 do not apply.[33]

(3) If the death occurs after the Tribunal has disposed of the nominated successor's application otherwise than by giving a direction, *i.e.* if his application has failed, the succession on death provisions in sections 36 to 48 come into operation. But, it should be noted, the nominated successor who has failed to obtain a direction is precluded from applying under section 39 or section 41 on the death.[34] The justification for this prohibition may be that the landlord could have been involved already in

---

[26] s. 56(1); *cf.* s.47(1). And see para. 14.85 above.
[27] s. 56(2); *cf.* s.47(3). Distinguish the absolute prohibition of assignment of the rights conferred by the direction during the interval before the new tenancy has vested in the nominated successor: s. 55(6).
[28] s. 48. As to which see paras 14.86–14.91 above. Form 50 in Part V of this work is a precedent for a demand for arbitration by a successful applicant on the tenant's retirement.
[29] s. 56(3) and (4). For the relevant definition of "the rent properly payable" for the purposes of this arbitration, see s. 48(9) and para. 14.90 above.
[30] s. 57(1).
[31] s. 57(2).
[32] See s. 55(8) for "the relevant time", and para. 14.118.
[33] s. 57(3).
[34] s. 57(4).

two contests with the same person, once when the latter approached the landlord for an agreement under section 37(2) and again when he appears as a nominated successor.

Meaning of "the relevant time": section 55(8)   14.118
The new tenancy will normally vest in the nominated successor at the retirement date as specified in the retirement notice, except where there has been delay in giving the direction and the "relevant time" is deferred as mentioned in section 55(8)(a) and (b). Where a direction is given within the period of three months ending with the retirement date the tenant may apply to the Tribunal for it to substitute as the retirement date a date falling within the period of three months immediately following the original retirement date. Where the direction is given after the original retirement date the Tribunal is required to specify in the direction as the relevant time a date falling within the period of three months following the giving of the direction.

Effect of Tribunal direction on nominated successor's succession to other holdings: section 58   14.119
This provision[35] deals with the question of multiple succession. It applies where the retiring tenant dies at a time when the nominated successor has become entitled, by virtue of a direction, to a tenancy of the holding, but the tenancy has not yet vested in him. In these circumstances it is provided that for the purpose of determining whether, in relation to any *other* holdings held by the retiring tenant at the time of his death, the nominated successor was disqualified as being the occupier of a commercial unit, he shall be deemed to be in occupation of "the holding". If the holding is a commercial unit he would thus fail the "occupancy condition"[36] in the event of his applying for a tenancy of any other holding held by the retiring tenant.

Succession planning   14.120
The best succession planning can only be achieved by means of a thorough acquaintance with the technicalities of the livelihood and occupancy conditions[37] coupled with a detailed factual review of the circumstances of the applicant. There are two main differences between succession on death and succession on retirement: the availability of a section 41[38] application to be treated as an eligible person in the event of the tenant's death and, by contrast, the availability of one limited ground for a landlord's positive case in the event of retirement (greater hardship).[39] As between these two differences there is no doubt that it is far more valuable to have available the Tribunal's discretion under section 41 if there is the slightest doubt about the strength of the applicant's application on livelihood.

---

[35] s. 58.
[36] See Sched. 6, para. 1(1) and s.36(3)(b). For other definitions relating to Part IV of the Act, see s.59. For discussion as to the occupancy condition see paras 14.52–14.69 above.
[37] See paras 14.36–14.51 (livelihood), 14.52–14.69 (occupancy) and in particular paras 14.51 and 14.67 above.
[38] See paras 14.70–14.71 above.
[39] See para 14.112 above.

Although in the case of succession on death the landlord has the opportunity to mount a case under all the substantive grounds contained within section 27 when asking the Tribunal for consent to the operation of the notice to quit[40] it is so difficult to secure that consent that the applicant should not be swayed towards a retirement application because of the availability then of a single ground in the form of greater hardship unless there are very exceptional circumstances.

14.121 Miscellaneous

The relationship of succession tenancies to the Agricultural Tenancies Act 1995 (whether the succession is by virtue of death or retirement) is dealt with at paragraph 14.97 above. The "roll over" of milk quota compensation from the retiring tenant to the incoming succession tenant is governed by the provisions referred to in paragraph 14.98 above. The difficulties of analysing historical events apply equally to both succession on death and succession on retirement.[41]

14.122 The Agricultural Land Tribunal and retirement succession

Part III of the Agricultural Land Tribunals (Succession to Agricultural Tenancies) Order 1984[42] deals with procedure in relation to succession *inter vivos* under sections 49–58 of the 1986 Act. Many of the principal Rules[43] apply to the general administrative machinery of applications, replies and hearings, and it may be noted that the valuable safety-net rules, 37 and 38 (extension of time and validation of procedural defects) apply.[44] Those Rules dealing with the making of an application and the filing of replies have already been referred to.[45] The chairman is obliged to fix a time and place for the hearing as soon as practicable.[46] In practice the venue will normally be fairly close to the holding so that an inspection may take place with relative convenience. Sometimes a purpose court building is available but more often where necessary government offices, chapels, public houses, or hotels will be convenient and are used. In relation to the preparation for hearing and the hearing rule 30 applies, with necessary modifications, various of the principal Rules:

(i) Rule 19 interlocutory applications.

(ii) Rule 20 disclosure of documents.[47]

(iii) Rule 23(2) and (4) notice of hearing.

(iv) Rule 24 Tribunal to sit in public.

(v) Rule 25 right of audience whereby a party may appear in person, by counsel, by a solicitor or by a representative appointed in writing.

---

[40] See para 14.83 above.
[41] See para. 14.99 above.
[42] S.I. 1984 No.1301.
[43] The Agricultural Land Tribunals (Rules) Order 1978 (S.I. 1978 No.259).
[44] See para. 14.29 above.
[45] para. 14.109 above.
[46] r. 29 of S.I. 1984 No.1301.
[47] See para. 14.29 above.

THE AGRICULTURAL LAND TRIBUNAL AND RETIREMENT SUCCESSION

(vi) Rule 26(2) and (3) procedure at the hearing.[48]

(vii) Rule 27 default of appearance.[49]

Rule 30 applies to retirement succession proceedings the following additional provisions from the principal Rules:

(i) Rule 28 evidence.[50]

(ii) Rule 29 witnesses.[51]

(iii) Rule 30 inspection of land.[52]

(iv) Rule 31.[53]

(v) Rule 33 request for a reference to the High Court of a question of law under section 6 of the Agriculture (Miscellaneous Provisions) Act 1954.[54]

(vi) Rule 34 modification of Tribunal's decision following High Court proceedings.

(vii) Rule 35 mode of service.

(viii) Rule 36 substituted service.

(ix) Extension of time.[55]

(x) Rule 38 failure to comply with rules.[56]

(xi) By sub-paragraph (2) of rule 33 any dismissal of an application counts as a decision and must be reasoned, to be given in a single document at the conclusion of the proceedings unless the chairman directs otherwise.

In cases where a direction is given within the period of three months ending with

---

[48] See para. 14.79 above.
[49] Powers to dismiss an application in default of appearance or to proceed to determine an application in the absence of the other party.
[50] Evidence may be admitted notwithstanding that it would not be admissible in a court of law and evidence may be given orally on oath or on affirmation or otherwise, by affidavit with the parties' consent or by means of written statements produced by the maker when giving evidence or, if the Tribunal consents, by another witness. A deponent or maker of a written statement may be required to attend for the giving of live evidence.
[51] Parties may give evidence themselves, call their own witnesses and cross-examine other people's witnesses. The Tribunal may call a witness who may thereafter be cross-examined and the Tribunal may require any witness to give evidence on oath or affirmation. The County Court Rules apply to the issue of witness summonses.
[52] Wide powers exercisable on 24 hours' notice but parties, representatives and expert witnesses may attend.
[53] Written reasoned decision if necessary by a majority with a power to correct clerical errors and a duty on the secretary to supply copies to the parties, copies to be duly certified.
[54] See paras 16.8–16.11 below.
[55] See para 14.29 above.
[56] See para 14.29 above.

the retirement date an application by the tenant for a postponement of the operation of the direction, under section 55(8)(a), must be made in writing to the Secretary before the hearing or orally at the hearing.[57] As to the conduct generally of a hearing, see paragraph 14.79 above.

---

[57] r. 34.

Chapter 15

SUB-TENANCIES, MARKET GARDENS, SMALLHOLDINGS

15.1 General

SUB-TENANCIES

15.2 Meaning of sub-tenancy

15.3 Sub-tenancy protected by the Agricultural Holdings Act 1986

15.4 Concurrent leases

15.6 Power to make special provisions for sub-tenants

15.7 Sub-tenancies and sections 25 and 26

15.9 Position of sub-tenants and notices to quit

15.15 Surrender or merger of head tenancy

15.16 Forfeiture of head tenancy

15.17 "Collusive" activity between head landlord and head tenant

15.18 Sub-tenancy schemes to avoid security of tenure

MARKET GARDENS

15.19 Meaning and treatment of market gardens

15.21 Special privileges relating to market gardens

15.26 Qualification for special privileges relating to market gardens

15.27 Agreements in writing

15.28 Pre- January 1, 1896 tenancies

15.29 Direction by Agricultural Land Tribunal

15.31 "Evesham custom"

SMALLHOLDINGS

15.36 General

15.37 Freedom of cropping and disposal of produce

15.38 Termination of schemes

15.39 Other matters

15.1 Sub-tenancies, market gardens, smallholdings

This chapter deals with three particular types of agricultural holding, each of which requires especial care. Sub-tenancies of agricultural holdings are true protected tenancies falling within the main regime of the Agricultural Holdings Act but they enjoy a more precarious existence and there are adaptations for sub-tenants.[1] Market gardens are given separate treatment, mainly because of the special compensation regime attached to them.[2] Smallholdings, although subject to considerable statutory control outside the scope of the 1986 Act, are also given distinct treatment by that statute.[3] Although aspects of the treatment relating to these special cases are discussed in this Chapter, where the main scheme applies but with minor modifications, the relevant detail is supplied in the mainstream discussion and this Chapter simply refers on to it.

SUB-TENANCIES

15.2 Meaning of sub-tenancy

A sub-tenancy is an interest carved out of a greater interest which is not itself a freehold. For example where the freeholder grants a term of years and the tenant grants a yearly tenancy, the sub-tenant holds directly of the intermediate tenant and in law, subject only to statutory exceptions, the expiry of the intermediate tenancy operates to destroy the sub-tenancy. A yearly tenant who sub-let from year to year at common law was thought to create a sub-demise only for so long as the original demise to the intermediate tenant lasted.[4] But where the intermediate tenancy is protected by the Agricultural Holdings Act 1986 and continues for that reason it is submitted that the status of the occupier remains that of a sub-tenant. Where a yearly tenant sub-lets on a yearly basis he has been held to be entitled to exercise the right of distress.[5] Where the tenant lets for the whole of his own term this amounts in law to an assignment.[6] Because a yearly tenancy is a "springing" interest which may continue for many years the yearly tenant may, conceptually, sub-let from year to year or for a fixed term.[7] Consequently a yearly agricultural tenant may, subject to the terms of his lease, sub-let on a yearly or fixed term basis and the sub-tenancy, depending on the circumstances of the sub-tenancy, may or may not be protected by the Agricultural Holdings Act 1986. It is perfectly possible that the sub-tenant may be protected by the Landlord and Tenant Act 1954 even though the head tenant is protected by the 1986 Act. In the latter case the rights of the sub-tenant and the security of tenure of the sub-tenant are governed by

---

[1] See paras 15.2–15.18 below.
[2] See paras 15.19–15.35 below.
[3] See paras 15.36–15.39 below.
[4] *Pike v. Eyre* [1829] 9 B.&C. 909.
[5] *Curtis v. Wheeler* [1830] Moo & M. 493.
[6] See *Woodfall, Landlord and Tenant*, Chapter 16, s. 7.
[7] *Oxley v. James* [1844] 13 M.&W. 209. Although much rarer, in theory the same situation

the 1954 Act.[8] It is anticipated that protection of the sub-tenant by the 1954 Act where the head tenant is protected by the 1986 Act is relatively unusual.[9]

Sub-tenancy protected by the Agricultural Holdings Act 1986   15.3
Where the sub-tenancy is protected by the 1986 Act the relations between the sub-tenant and the intermediate tenant are governed by the statute, subject to limited exceptions, in exactly the same way as they would be if the sub-tenant was a head tenant and his own landlord the freeholder. In particular it should be noted that the definition of "tenant" in section 96(1) is stated to mean "the holder of land under a contract of tenancy" including any "person deriving title from a tenant". This is subject to circumstances where the context may otherwise require. There are a very few examples of special treatment, detailed below. Therefore as between the sub-tenant and his immediate landlord there are rights of extensive security of tenure, rent review and compensation.[10]

Creation of sub-tenancy distinguished from creation of concurrent or overriding lease   15.4
The creation of a sub-tenancy should be carefully distinguished from the action of an existing landlord in carving a lease out of his own reversion which is itself expectant on an existing tenancy. The effect of this is to grant a lease of the reversion which takes effect immediately and therefore carries with it the right to take the rent. The legal effect of the transaction is to create a concurrent or overriding term which in substance is an assignment of the reversion.[11]

Effect of grant of a concurrent lease   15.5
The question is sometimes asked as to whether a landlord by granting a lease for a term of years of his reversion[12] can undermine the security of an existing yearly tenant by transforming him into a sub-tenant. It is submitted that he cannot. Although the lessee of the reversion becomes an assignee *pro tanto* of the reversion and therefore the landlord of the original tenant, with the power to claim the rent from him, enforce his covenants and give him notice to quit, the relationship between the two is not that of tenant and sub-tenant. The term of years and the yearly tenancy are *concurrent* tenancies. The true sub-tenancy is an interest carved out of a greater interest[13] and the latter must exist before the former, even if only for a moment. A true sub-tenancy ends, apart from statutory exceptions, on the expiry

---

appertains in relation to other periodic tenancies.

[8] And the reader is accordingly referred to standard works dealing with that statute, *e.g. Woodfall, Landlord and Tenant*, Vol. 2, Part 3 and Hill & Redman, *Law of Landlord and Tenant* Vol. I, Part B.

[9] Conversely it is anticipated that in relation to the farm business tenancies legislation occupation by business sub-tenants may be anticipated to become quite common.

[10] As to the special provisions required in connection with disturbance compensation see para. 13.33 referring to s. 63(1) and (2). There are also special provisions in relation to rights to milk quota compensation under the Agriculture Act 1986, considered at para. 19.12 referring to Sched. 1, para. 4 of that Act.

[11] See generally *Woodfall, Landlord and Tenant*, Chapter 6, s. 4 and Megarry & Wade, *The Law of Real Property* (5th ed.), pp. 664–665.

[12] *i.e.* a lease of the reversion taking effect immediately, not a reversionary lease.

[13] See para. 15.2 above.

of the term from which it is carved but the yearly tenancy, in the case being considered, would not be affected by the extinguishment of the concurrent term; the yearly tenancy would simply revert to being a direct tenancy held from the original landlord. If, on the other hand, the yearly tenancy comes to an end during the subsistence of the concurrent term, the lessee for the concurrent term becomes entitled to possession. It is possible, by one of the curiosities of English real estate law, for the concurrent lease to be of shorter duration than the tenancy of which it temporarily becomes the reversion.[14] The subject of a concurrent lease has arisen in connection with the succession scheme now embodied in Part IV of the Agricultural Holdings Act 1986 and there are provisions to obviate the difficulties which might otherwise arise for the machinery of succession if the deceased tenant's landlord had granted a lease of the reversion to a third person.[15]

15.6 Power to make special provisions for sub-tenants
Among the matters for which the Lord Chancellor may make provision by order under the powers given to him by the 1986 Act, section 29 and Schedule 4 are:

(i) to exclude the application of section 26(1) in relation to sub-tenancies in such cases as might be specified in the order; and

(ii) to make such provision as appears to the Lord Chancellor expedient for the purpose of safeguarding the interests of sub-tenants, including a provision enabling the Agricultural Land Tribunal, where the interest of a tenant is terminated by a notice to quit, to secure that a sub-tenant will hold from the landlord on like terms as he held from the tenant.

The first of those powers is presently exercised by article 16 of the Agricultural Holdings (Arbitration on Notices) Order 1987[16]. The second power which, if exercised would transform the current situation, has never in fact been exercised. Rule 13[17] in the Agricultural Land Tribunal (Rules) Order 1978[18] entitles a sub-tenant to be a party to proceedings before the Tribunal but, clearly, this right is of no assistance where the tenant has not served a counter-notice on the head landlord so that no such proceedings take place.

15.7 Sub-tenants and section 25
There are two specific provisions which adapt the operation of section 25 to the circumstances of a sub-tenancy. The first is section 25(2)(c) exempting from the minimal one year's notice a notice by the tenant to the sub-tenant.[19] A sub-tenant

---

[14] See *Re Moore & Hulm's Contract* [1912] 2 Ch. 105 and the Law of Property Act 1925, s. 149(5).
[15] See s. 45(2), (3) and (4) on the tenant's death and s. 55(2), (3) and (4) in the case of lifetime successions.
[16] S.I. 1987 No.710.
[17] "Where an application is made to the Tribunal in respect of an agricultural holding the whole or any part of which has been sub-let, every landlord, tenant and sub-tenant of that holding shall be a party to the proceedings on that application" (except in relation to drainage cases).
[18] S.I. 1978 No.259.
[19] See further para. 12.8 above.

will therefore be entitled to the ordinary notice period at common law, that is to say six months expiring on the term date, in circumstances where his own landlord serves notice to quit.

Sub-tenancies and section 26 — 15.8

The second adaptation to the position of sub-tenants relates to the ability to serve counter-notice under section 26. By article 16 of the Agricultural Holdings (Arbitration on Notices) Order 1987[20] it is provided:

> "16.(1) Section 26(1) of the 1986 Act shall not apply where notice to quit an agricultural holding or part thereof is given to a sub-tenant by a tenant who has himself been given notice to quit that holding or part thereof and the fact that the tenant has been given such notice is stated in the notice given to the sub-tenant.
>
> (2) Such a notice given to a sub-tenant shall have effect only if the notice to quit given to the tenant by the landlord itself has effect.
>
> (3) Where a tenant accepts notice to quit part of a holding as notice to quit the whole under section 32 of the 1986 Act, then, for the purpose of this article, the notice given by him shall be deemed to be a notice to quit the entire holding."

Position of sub-tenants and notices to quit — 15.9

The position of sub-tenants, as a result of the combination of common law rules and statutory modifications is now one of some complexity as well as vulnerability. For convenience the subject is broken down into five separate sub-headings, depending on who has served the relevant notice to quit.

Notice to quit given by tenant to sub-tenant: no action taken by head landlord — 15.10

The tenant and sub-tenant here are in the same position as any other landlord and tenant where the 1986 Act operates on the tenancy. The sub-tenant may, assuming section 26(2) does not apply, serve a counter-notice under section 26(1) on the tenant and the tenant will then have to apply to the Tribunal for consent if he wishes to preserve the effectiveness of his notice to quit.

Notice to quit by head landlord to tenant: no notice to quit given by tenant to sub-tenant — 15.11

In this case if the head landlord's notice to quit takes effect, the sub-tenancy simply perishes by operation of law with the tenancy. There is no machinery by which the tenant can prevent this from happening, but the sub-tenant's right to compensation for disturbance is safeguarded.[21]

---

[20] S.I. 1987 No.710.
[21] See para. 13.33 above.

15.12 Notice to quit given by head landlord to tenant: tenant giving notice to quit to sub-tenant with statement required so as to exclude the application of section 26(1) to sub-tenancies

Reference is made to article 16 of the Agricultural Holdings (Arbitration on Notices) Order 1987 quoted above which applies in the circumstance that the head landlord gives notice to quit and the tenant then gives notice to quit to the sub-tenant requiring section 26(1) to be excluded in relation to the sub-tenancy. The effect of such a notice by the tenant is provisional and it is conditional on the notice which the tenant himself received taking effect. Article 16 makes it clear that if for any reason the notice to quit given by the head landlord does not take effect the sub-tenant's interest is preserved. Where the head landlord's notice to quit is indeed effective the sub-tenancy perishes with the tenancy. There is nothing in article 16 to defeat the common law rule and the Lord Chancellor has not exercised his power to save the sub-tenancy. Once again the sub-tenant's compensation for disturbance is safeguarded.[22]

15.13 Notice to quit given by head landlord to tenant: tenant giving notice to quit to sub-tenant but failing to insert in that notice to quit a statement required to exclude the application of section 26(1) to the sub-tenancy

The tenant may, on receiving a notice to quit from the head landlord, serve a notice to quit on the sub-tenant but (for any or no reason) may omit the statement mentioned in article 16 of the Agricultural Holdings (Arbitration on Notices) Order 1987[23] that he himself has been given notice to quit by the head landlord. In that case the sub-tenant is not precluded from serving a counter-notice under section 26(1) on the tenant. This will not, however, avail the sub-tenant anything if the head landlord's notice to quit on the tenant is effective; again the sub-tenancy perishes with the tenancy, even if the sub-tenant has successfully invoked section 26(1) in procedures before the Agricultural Land Tribunal.[24] The common law rule is paramount that "every subordinate interest must perish with the superior interest on which it is dependent".[25] On the other hand, if the head landlord's notice to quit to the tenant is not effective the sub-tenant's counter-notice may enable him, by securing a favourable Tribunal decision, to preserve his sub-tenancy. In this case, unlike the circumstances in *Sherwood v. Moody*, a victory before the Tribunal will be real, not illusory. Thus, while the service of the sub-tenant's counter-notice can make no difference if the superior tenancy is extinguished, the failure to serve it may be fatal if that tenancy survives.

15.14 Tenant gives notice to quit to superior landlord: position of sub-tenant

After a long period of doubt and confusion it has now been settled by the Court of Appeal that a tenant cannot by serving notice to quit upon his landlord foist the sub-tenant on that landlord such that the two come into a direct relationship on

---

[22] See para. 13.33 above.
[23] Quoted above.
[24] *Sherwood v. Moody* [1952] 1 All E.R. 389.
[25] *Bendall v. McWhirter* [1952] 2 Q.B. 466, Romer L.J. at 487. There are, of course, statutory modifications of this rule in other contexts, *e.g.* s. 137 of the Rent Act 1977 in relation to protected or statutory tenancies of dwelling-houses.

termination of the tenancy.[26] The general rule operates that a sub-tenancy perishes with the tenancy which supports it even in circumstances where the tenant destroys his tenancy by service of an upwards notice to quit.[27]

Effect on sub-tenancy of surrender or merger of head tenant's interest   15.15

Both at common law[28] and by statute[29] the surrender of the head lease or the merger of the freehold with the head lease[30] results in the sub-tenant being promoted to the status of head tenant. The effect in the context of the 1986 Act is significantly to enhance the status of the sub-tenant's estate in terms of security.[31]

Forfeiture of the head tenancy   15.16

If the head tenant's interest is forfeited, the sub-tenant's interest will be destroyed unless the court in its discretion grants him relief under section 146(4) of the Law of Property Act 1925. The court may, on the sub-tenant's application, made either in proceedings by the head landlord to enforce the forfeiture or in an action brought by the sub-tenant himself, make an order vesting the land in the sub-tenant for the term of the latter's sub-tenancy or any less term.[32]

"Collusive" activity between head landlord and head tenant so as to destroy sub-tenancy   15.17

The above analysis describes the position where the head tenant and the head landlord do not act "collusively" that is to say in concert with the sole objective of destroying the sub-tenancy. There will be, no doubt, many circumstances where the freeholder is delighted if his head tenant chooses to serve notice to quit but this does not of itself invalidate the effect of that notice to quit. The courts have

---

[26] The argument that this might be the case was based upon the decision of Hilbery J. in *Brown v. Wilson* (1949) 156 E.G. 45 and the concession by counsel in *Mellor v. Watkins* [1874] L.R. 9 Q.B. 400, despite the doubts in Foa, *General Law of Landlord and Tenant* (8th ed. (the last) page 832, n.(g). *Mellor v. Watkins* is now overruled.

[27] *Pennell v. Payne* [1995] 1 E.G.L.R. 6, CA.

[28] *Fairweather v. St. Marylebone Property Company Ltd* [1963] A.C. 510, see Lord Denning at 546; *Webb v. Russell* [1789] 3 T.R. 393 (in relation to merger).

[29] Section 139 of the Law of Property Act 1925 re-enacting s. 9 of the Real Property Act 1845: "(1) where a reversion expectant on a lease of land is surrendered or merged, the estate or interest which as against the lessee for the time being confers the next vested right to the land, shall be deemed the reversion for the purpose of preserving the same incidents and obligations as would have affected the original reversion had there been no surrender or merger thereof".

[30] *i.e.* the tenant acquiring the freehold reversion so that the headlease is "drowned" in the superior interest.

[31] Contrast above where notice to quit is served by or on the intermediate tenant.

[32] In *Barclays Bank Plc v. Prudential Assurance Co. Ltd* (1998) 10 E.G. 159 it was held that the Court did have jurisdiction under s. 146(4) of the Law of Property Act 1925 to grant relief from forfeiture to a mortgagee, as an undertenant. Where the head lease had been disclaimed, the position of the undertenant was deemed to be as if the lease had not been disclaimed. The effect of the disclaimer being to interfere with the position of third parties as little as possible, the sub-tenant's right to relief from forfeiture is a right which does not require to be interfered with. In that case the applicant for relief from forfeiture, the bank, was required to take its relief not only on the terms of the actual lease but also on the terms of a supplemental lease.

developed an exception to the destruction of the sub-tenancy in circumstances where landlord and head landlord act together "collusively" in order to destroy the sub-tenancy.[33] There has, however, been no precise analysis of the circumstances which will amount to collusion but it is clear that a successful allegation of "collusion" does not necessarily involve one of dishonesty.[34] It would appear to be sufficient for an agreement to be collusive that it amounts to no more than an agreement between the head landlord and the head tenant that the head tenant should not serve counter-notice to a notice to quit.[35] In applying *Sparkes v. Smart* the High Court[36] has shown a willingness to treat circumstances of "collusion" as amounting in the alternative to the equivalent of a surrender in substance.[37] For the cautious practitioner it must be assumed that any agreement between the head landlord and the head tenant, whether or not the agreement is legally enforceable, that the two will co-operate so as to act together with a view to destroying the sub-tenancy will probably amount to a "collusive" situation and therefore one in which their joint actions will be ineffective.[38]

15.18 **Sub-tenancy schemes to avoid security of tenure**
Prior to the decision in *Gisbourne v. Burton*[39] it had been fairly common to encounter the creation of a head tenancy in circumstances where it was intended subsequently to create a sub-tenancy, whose status was accordingly relatively insecure in terms of the Agricultural Holdings Act 1986. Since that decision[40] all transactions of that type, although not "sham" are likely to be struck down as artificial transactions designed to disguise the real grant of agricultural tenancies lacking a crucial aspect of protection, namely security of tenure.[41]

---

[33] *Sparkes v. Smart* [1990] 2 E.G.L.R. 245 followed in *Barrett v. Morgan* [1997] 1 E.G.L.R. 1.
[34] See Purchas L.J. in *Sparkes v. Smart* at 252 D.
[35] Stuart-Smith L.J. in *Sparkes v. Smart* at 253H-K: ... "In my judgment, there was overwhelming evidence of collusion. The transaction made no sort of economic sense unless vacant possession could be obtained. On the basis of the advice then being given and the belief that the Plaintiff had that there was a sub-tenancy or s. 2 licence, it is inconceivable that he would have paid £92,000 for land subject to a sitting tenant at a rent which gave a return of less than 1%. It required the co-operation of William not to serve a counter-notice for there to be a prospect of obtaining vacant possession. That co-operation was forthcoming. In my judgment, the Judge was fully justified in holding that there was a collusive agreement."
[36] P. W. Smith Q.C. sitting as a Deputy Judge of the Chancery Division in *Barrett v. Morgan* (above).
[37] At 4J-K.
[38] A head landlord who suspects that his head tenant will not wish to serve counter-notice is probably best advised simply to serve notice to quit and not to enter into any discussions either before service or during the period within which the tenant may serve his counter-notice. Furthermore he should take care not to arrange, after the counter-notice period has run out but before expiry of the notice to quit, for any early surrender of the head tenancy: such an action would automatically promote the sub-tenant to head tenant and operate to destroy the effect of the notice to quit.
[39] (1989) Q.B. 390.
[40] Subject to a powerful dissenting judgment by Ralph Gibson L.J.
[41] Although the court gave leave to appeal to the HL regrettably this appeal was not proceeded with.

MARKET GARDENS

Treatment of market gardens 15.19

Market gardens, *i.e.* agricultural holdings which are cultivated as market gardens, attract certain additional privileges as a result of sections 79–81 of the 1986 Act, provided that the conditions laid down by these sections are satisfied. Apart from these additional privileges they are ordinary agricultural holdings and the general provisions of the Act, including the compensation provisions, apply to them.

Meaning of "market garden" 15.20

The 1986 Act does not define market gardens[42] but the basic requirement for a market garden to be an agricultural holding[43] makes it clear that the market gardens covered by the Act are those which are cultivated as such for the purpose of a trade or business, not supply for the purpose of supplying the needs of the occupier and his family for domestic consumption. In *Watters v. Hunter* [44] the Scottish Lord President said:

> "The trade or business of a market gardener is, in my opinion, the trade or business which produces the class of goods characteristic of a greengrocer's shop, and which in ordinary course reaches that shop via the early morning market where such goods are disposed of wholesale. It is, no doubt, the case that this class of goods includes small fruit, and, it may be, flowers. But this does not warrant the extension of "market garden" to the highly specialised industry in which the defender was engaged". [an experimental bulb growing establishment]."

Market gardening connotes the growing for sale of garden produce, whether fruit, flowers or culinary vegetables, and does not cover the activities of nursery grounds or specialised seed-producing stations. The occasional sale of a crop from a garden used mainly for domestic supply is not enough to constitute the business of market gardening.[45] Land practically covered with greenhouses,[46] land used for growing raspberries for jam-making[47] and land used as an orchard with rhubarb and other crops grown underneath the trees, the fruit and the crops being sold,[48] have been held to be market gardens. As will be seen below, however, mere *de facto* use of land as a market garden does not attract the special market garden

---

[42] Nor did its predecessors, the 1948 Act and the Agriculture Act 1947; the 1947 Act in fact repealed, without re-enacting, the definition of the expression previously found at s. 57(1) of the 1923 Act.
[43] Section 79(1) read in conjunction with s. 1(1) and (4).
[44] 1927 S.C. 310.
[45] *Re Hammond* (1844) 14 L.J.Q.B. 14; *Bickerdike v. Lucy* [1920] 1 K.B. 707; *Re Wallis* (1885) 14 Q.B.D. 950.
[46] *Purser v. Worthing Local Board* (1887) 18 Q.B.D. 818; but see *Smith v. Richmond* [1899] A.C. 448. As to apiary, see *Hood Barrs v. Howard* (1967) 210 E.G. 768 (rating).
[47] *Grewar v. Moncur's Curator Bonis* 1916 S.C. 764. See as to the law in Scotland on market gardens, Chapter 30 of Gill, W. Green The Law of Agricultural Holdings in Scotland (3rd ed., 1997).
[48] *Lowther v. Clifford* [1927] 1 K.B. 130.

privileges given by the Act; for that certain qualifying conditions have to be fulfilled.[49]

15.21 Special privileges relating to market gardens
Suitably qualified market gardens[50] attract four principal types of privilege. These are special entitlements in respect of tenant's improvements,[51] the removal of fixtures,[52] the removal of fruit trees and bushes[53] and improvements purchased by the tenant.[54] Certain conditions have to be fulfilled to qualify for these privileges.[55]

15.22 Special privileges relating to market gardens: tenant's improvements
By section 79(2), the tenant of a market garden is entitled to compensation for two categories of improvements. Improvements of the five kinds set out in Schedule 10 to the 1986 Act, and begun on or after March 1, 1948, attract compensation without the need to obtain the landlord's consent to, or to give him any notice of, their execution.[56] Of improvements begun before March 1, 1948, only those consisting of the erection or enlargement of buildings for the purpose of the trade or business of a market gardener attract compensation, and then only provided that any such improvement received the landlord's consent in writing.[57] The reason for the exception of *alteration* of buildings from the category of pre-1948 improvements attracting compensation[58] is that alteration was not added as a head of market garden compensation until provision was made for it by the 1947 Act, taking effect on March 1, 1948.

15.23 Special privileges relating to market gardens: removal of fixtures
The tenant of a market garden has rather wider rights than tenants of other holdings in regard to the removal of fixtures.[59] These are as follows:

(a) If a tenant is otherwise entitled under section 10 of the 1986 Act to remove a building, his right of removal is not excluded by the fact that he has a right to compensation in respect of the building. In the case of an

---

[49] See para. 15.26 below.
[50] See 15.26 below.
[51] See para. 15.22 below.
[52] See para. 15.23 below.
[53] See para. 15.24 below.
[54] See para. 15.25 below.
[55] See para. 15.26 below.
[56] Such improvements are treated as if they were included among the improvements specified in Part I of Sched. 8 to the Act; s. 79(2). See paras 13.63 and 13.68 above.
[57] These improvements are treated as if they were included within Part II of Sched. 9 to the Act; s. 79(2). See paras 13.44–13.48 above.
[58] In contrast to para. 5 of Sched. 10 of the 1986 Act.
[59] For the position in the case of an ordinary agricultural holding, see s. 10 and paras 10.34–10.42 above.

ordinary agricultural holding a right to compensation excludes removal as a result of section 10(2)(c).[60]

(b) The tenant's right to remove a building *acquired* by him[61] applies no matter when the building was erected.[62] In the case of an ordinary agricultural holding, this right is restricted to buildings erected on or after January 1, 1884, the commencement date of the Agricultural Holdings (England) Act 1883, which first gave a tenant a relatively unfettered right of removal.

Special privileges relating to market gardens: removal of fruit trees and bushes 15.24

The tenant of a market garden may remove fruit trees and fruit bushes planted by him on the holding and not permanently set out, provided that he does so before the termination of the tenancy.[63] If he does not, they remain the property of the landlord and the tenant is not entitled to any compensation in respect of them; if he removes them after the termination, he may make himself liable to the landlord for damages.[64] This right is to remove fruit trees and bushes not permanently set out, in contrast to the right of compensation given in respect of fruit trees and bushes which are permanently set out.[65] Fruit trees and bushes are permanently set out where they are in positions from which it is not intended to transplant them; trees and bushes which are in fact too aged for transplanting would probably be treated as being in this category whatever the intention. Trees and bushes which are "not permanently set out" (and which the tenant is therefore entitled to remove) thus seem to be those kept for sale or for filling up gaps in plantations and not too aged for the latter.[66]

Special privileges relating to market gardens: improvements purchased by tenant 15.25

The tenant of a market garden can claim compensation in respect of the whole or part of an improvement which he has purchased from a predecessor even if the landlord has not consented in writing to the purchase.[67] By contrast, a tenant of an ordinary agricultural holding must have obtained such consent.[68]

---

[60] ss. 79(3)(a) and 10(2)(c). Thus the tenant has a choice of remedies.
[61] The right to remove fixtures and buildings *acquired*, as distinct from affixed or erected, by the tenant was first given by the Agricultural Holdings Act 1900. Thus it is only buildings acquired since the date that this Act came into force—January 1, 1901—which a market garden tenant is entitled to remove: see ss. 4 and 13 of the 1900 Act, and Sched. 12, para. 3 of the 1986 Act.
[62] ss. 79(3)(b) and 10(2)(d).
[63] s. 79(4).
[64] *Barff v. Probyn* (1895) 64 L.J.Q.B. 557.
[65] s. 79(4) and Sched. 10, para. 1.
[66] This puts the market garden tenant in virtually the same position as a nursery man was at common law.
[67] s. 79(5).
[68] s. 69(2).

15.26 Special privileges relating to market gardens: qualification

An agricultural holding may qualify for market garden privileges in three ways: by agreement in writing,[69] under certain contracts current on January 1, 1896,[70] and following a direction by the Agricultural Land Tribunal[71].

15.27 Qualification for special privileges relating to market gardens: agreement in writing

The compensation provisions applicable to market gardens apply to an agricultural holding in respect of which it is agreed in writing (not necessarily in a contract of tenancy) that the holding shall be let or treated as a market garden.[72] Such an agreement may relate to part only of a holding, in which case the special market garden privileges will attach to that part as if it were a separate holding.[73] Mere use as a market garden is not sufficient. In a case where there was a lease to a tenant described as a market gardener, and the holding was in fact cultivated as a market garden, but there was a proviso that "nothing herein contained shall be deemed to be an agreement by the landlord that the premises hereby demised or any part thereof shall be let or treated as a market garden", it was held that this negatived any agreement of the kind in question.[74]

The onus of proving the necessary agreement rests on the tenant.[75] An agreement that the holding be let for the purpose of a market garden includes an agreement simply giving permission for such use, as inferred from a covenant not to use for any trade except that of a market gardener[76]; by contrast, a clause merely giving the tenant a right to remove fruit trees, bushes or plants will not of itself constitute an agreement to let or treat as a market garden.[77] An agent who has the normal management of an estate has, unless his authority has been limited, power to agree that the tenant should be allowed to convert agricultural land into a market garden.[78] Although the conversion of arable and pasture into a market garden without the landlord's consent will not entitle the tenant to compensation for market garden improvements or to other market garden privileges, it is not necessarily a breach of covenant to cultivate a farm "in a good and husbandlike manner according to the best rules of husbandry practised in the neighbourhood".[79]

---

[69] See para. 15.27 below.
[70] See para. 15.28 below.
[71] See para. 15.29 below.
[72] s. 79(1). Such agreement must have been made on or after January 1, 1896 (see Sched. 12, para. 10(1)) which was the date when the Market Gardeners Compensation Act 1895 came into operation.
[73] s. 79(1).
[74] *Re Masters and Duveen* [1923] K.B. 729.
[75] *Bickerdike v. Lucy* [1920] 1 K.B. 392.
[76] *Saunders-Jacobs v. Yates* [1933] 1 K.B. 392; [1933] 2 K.B. 240, CA.
[77] *Re Morse and Dixon* (1917) 87 L.J.K.B. 1.
[78] *Re Pearsons and I'Anson* [1899] 2 Q.B. 618.
[79] *Meux v. Cobley* [1892] 2 Ch. 253.

Qualification for special privileges relating to market gardens: certain contracts current on January 1, 1896   15.28

The second way in which a holding may qualify for market garden privileges is to have fulfilled certain conditions on, January 1, 1896[80]; this is clearly a diminishing category of holdings. Where under a contract of tenancy current on January 1, 1896 a holding was in actual use or cultivation as a market garden on that date, with the knowledge of the landlord, and the tenant had before that date,[81] without previous written notice of dissent from the landlord, executed any of the Schedule 10 improvements (with one exception) the tenant is in the same position as in a case where, after January 1, 1896, there is an agreement in writing to let or treat as a market garden.[82] The one exception was the 'alteration' (not being an enlargement) of a building.[83] These provisions may also apply to part of a holding as if it were a separate holding.[84] Where these qualifying conditions are established, the tenant's right to compensation for market garden improvements extends both to those executed before and to those executed after January 1, 1896.[85] Moreover, once the conditions are established, the better view is that the landlord's power to dissent from future improvements ceases, although contrary opinion has been expressed.[86]

Qualification for special privileges relating to market gardens: direction by the Agricultural Land Tribunal   15.29

Where the tenant of an agricultural holding wishes to make on the holding or part of it a Schedule 10 improvement, but is unable to obtain his landlord's agreement in writing that the holding, or that part of it, shall be treated as a market garden, the tenant may apply to the Agricultural Land Tribunal for a direction to that effect.[87] The Tribunal, if satisfied that the holding, or the part, is suitable for the purposes of market gardening,[88] may direct that the provisions of section 79 shall apply to the

---

[80] This is the date of the coming into force of the first market garden compensation statute, the Market Gardeners' Compensation Act 1895.

[81] "Had then" are the words used. In some of the earlier Acts the words were "has then", which were interpreted to mean "thereafter": see *Smith v. Callander* [1901] A.C. 297; *Mears v. Callander* [1901] 2 Ch. 388; *Taylor v. Steel-Maitland* 1913 S.C. 562.

[82] 1986 Act, Sched. 12, para. 10(2).

[83] For the explanation of this exception, see para. 15.21 above.

[84] 1986 Act, Sched. 12 para. 10(4). In addition, it has been held possible for the part in question to vary in accordance with the terms of the tenancy agreement. In *Taylor v. Steel-Maitland* 1913 S.C. 562, a Scottish case on a corresponding provision, where the same number of acres (part of a larger holding) but not always the same fields were cultivated annually as a market garden, the fluctuating content of the market garden did not prevent the privileges from attaching to the particular fields which were, in fact, under cultivation at the end of the tenancy.

[85] Sched. 12, para. 10(3).

[86] See G.A. Johnstone, *Agricultural Holdings Act 1908*, p.184.

[87] s. 80(1). See Part V, Forms 64 and 64A of this work for form of application and reply (Forms 8 and 8R of the Appendix to S.I. 1978 No.259). The tenant should first make a request to his landlord (see Part V, Form 63 of this work, not a prescribed form) and, on refusal, or on failure by landlord to agree within a reasonable time, apply to the Tribunal on the prescribed form.

[88] Owing to the rare use of these provisions, there is an absence of guidance as to the factors which Tribunals are likely to take into account in deciding whether the holding or part is suitable.

holding or the part; and the direction may relate to all of the improvements specified in Schedule 10 or to some only.[89] These provisions will then apply to any qualifying improvements executed after the direction.[90] A direction under section 80(2) of the Act may be given by the Tribunal although the contract of tenancy provides that the holding shall not be used as a market garden.

15.30 **Qualification for special privileges relating to market gardens: direction by Agricultural Land Tribunal: conditions of direction**

The Tribunal may give a direction under this section subject to such conditions, if any, for the protection of the landlord as the Tribunal think fit.[91] Where the direction relates to part of the holding only, the tribunal may, on the application of the landlord, impose a condition that the direction will only take effect if the tenant consents to the holding being split into two parts, one of which being that to which the direction relates and held at a rent apportioned, if necessary, by arbitration, but otherwise on the same terms and conditions (so far as applicable) as those on which the holding is held.[92] In so far as the "Evesham Custom" is incorporated by section 80 of the 1986 Act following a direction of the Tribunal, it is a statutory provision, and the custom as such, *i.e.* as one species of customary compensation, is abolished.[93] However, the content of the custom may be applied even in the absence of a direction of the Tribunal simply by the agreement in writing of the landlord and the tenant of a market garden holding.[94]

15.31 **Direction by Agricultural Land Tribunal: "Evesham Custom"**

Where the Tribunal makes a direction under section 80(2) of the Act that the holding is to be treated as a market garden, the 1986 Act applies the substance of the 'Evesham Custom', by sections 80(3) to (5) of the Act.[95] Where such a direction has been given, and where the tenancy is terminated by a notice to quit given by the tenant or by reason of the tenant's insolvency,[96] the tenant will not be entitled to any compensation in respect of the market garden improvements specified in the direction unless he introduces a successor in accordance with the conditions about to be described. This peculiar compensation provision has no application where the notice to quit is given by the landlord.

---

[89] s. 80(2).
[90] s. 80(2).
[91] s. 80(6).
[92] s. 80(7). The special compensation provisions in ss. 80(3), (4) and (5) will apply only to that part of the holding which the Tribunal designates as a market garden.
[93] It has been abolished since the 1947 Act.
[94] 1986 Act, s. 81(2). In these circumstances, the source of the compensation rights is neither statute nor custom, but written contract.
[95] This statutory embodiment of the custom has appeared in all Agricultural Holdings Acts since first introduced by the Agriculture Act 1920, s. 15(3).
[96] Insolvency for the purposes of s. 80(3) and (4) is defined in s. 80(9) by reference to s. 96(2).

"Evesham custom": conditions for compensation 15.32

The conditions are twofold[97]: (a) the introduction by the tenant of a successor to the tenancy, and (b) the failure of the landlord to accept the successor. The tenant must, not later than one month after the date on which the notice to quit is given or the date of the insolvency, as the case may be, (or such later date as may be agreed) produce to the landlord an offer in writing "by a substantial and otherwise suitable person" to accept a tenancy on the terms of the existing one and to pay to the outgoing tenant all the compensation due to him under the Act or the contract of tenancy.[98] The offer must be one which will hold good for a period of three months. There must be a failure by the landlord to accept the offer within three months after it has been produced.[99]

"Evesham custom": operation of custom 15.33

The results, according to the circumstances, will be as follows:

(a) If the tenant fails to produce such a substantial and suitable person who acts in accordance with the condition, he will not be entitled to compensation for the market garden improvements in question, but will be able to claim from the landlord for general compensation otherwise due to the outgoing tenant of an agricultural holding under the Act.

(b) If the tenant does produce such a person but the landlord fails to accept him, the landlord will himself have to pay to the tenant his market garden compensation (in addition to any other compensation to which he is entitled).[1]

(c) If the landlord does accept the person proffered the tenant will look to that person for his compensation generally (including his market garden compensation) in accordance with the arrangement, and the incomer will be liable to pay to the landlord any sums due from the outgoer in respect of rent or breach of contract or otherwise in respect of the holding (*e.g.* dilapidations) and may deduct this amount from the compensation payable to the outgoer, subject to any agreement between them.[2] A new tenancy created in this way is not a new tenancy for the purposes of Schedule 2 (arbitration on rent) of the 1986 Act, *i.e.* it does not trigger off a three-year stop on rent changes.[3]

The principle underlying these somewhat complex arrangements appears to be that if the tenant is allowed against the landlord's wishes to change the character of the holding, and he then by his own act or financial default brings the tenancy to an

---

[97] 1986 Act, s. 80(4).
[98] Presumably a dispute as to whether the proffered successor is "substantial" and "otherwise suitable" can be determined by an arbitrator as incidental to the claim for compensation at the end of the tenancy.
[99] s. 80(3) and (4).
[1] s. 80(3) and (4).
[2] s. 80(5).
[3] s. 80(8).

end, he should not be permitted to saddle the landlord with the (possibly heavy) market garden compensation involved.

15.34 **"Evesham custom": measure of compensation**
The measure of compensation for market garden improvements is the value of those improvements to an incoming tenant. This is implied by the provision in section 79(2) that the Act shall apply as if improvements in Schedule 10 were included among those in Part I of Schedule 8.[4]

15.35 **"Evesham custom": compensation substituted by agreement**
A landlord and a tenant of a holding to which sections 79 and 80 of the 1986 Act apply may, by an agreement in writing, substitute for the statutory compensation payable under these sections in respect of market garden improvements compensation which is "fair and reasonable" having regard to the circumstances existing when the agreement was made.[5] They may also substitute for the compensation provisions which would otherwise be applicable the compensation provisions known as the "Evesham Custom" and set out in sections 80(3) to (5), as applicable to the particular circumstances.[6]

SMALLHOLDINGS

15.36 **Smallholdings within the 1986 Act**
The 1986 Act deals with smallholdings only in a few limited respects. The general legislation affecting smallholdings is to be found in the Agriculture Act 1970 and the regulations made under it and is beyond the scope of this work.[7]

15.37 **Smallholdings: freedom of cropping and disposal of produce**
Section 15(1) of the 1986 Act, which, subject to certain conditions, confers on tenants of agricultural holdings freedom of cropping and disposal of produce, notwithstanding any custom or contract of tenancy,[8] does not apply to a tenancy of land let as a smallholding (a) by a smallholdings authority[9] or (b) by the Minister[10] in pursuance of a scheme approved by the Minister for the purposes of section 15. Such a scheme must be one which:

(a) provides for the farming of such holdings on a co-operative basis;

(b) provides for the disposal of the produce of such holdings; or

---

[4] s. 66(2). The measure would be the same whether the improvements were begun before March 1, 1948, or on or after that date.
[5] s. 81(1).
[6] s. 81(2). The parties may agree that these provisions will apply in all the circumstances, including where the notice to quit is given by the landlord.
[7] For a full explanation as to the working of the smallholdings legislation see *Halsbury's Laws of England*, 4th ed., Vol. 2, and for the relevant collected statutes see *Halsbury's Statutes*, 4th ed., Vol. 2.
[8] See paras 10.59–10.66 above.
[9] County Councils in England and Wales: Agriculture Act 1970, s. 38.
[10] As defined in s. 96(1) of the 1986 Act.

(c) provides for other centralised services for the use of the tenants of such holdings.[11]

Co-operative schemes for farming and centralised provisions for the disposal of produce are inconsistent with the freedom given by section 15(1).

Smallholdings: termination of schemes 15.38

If at any time it appears to the Minister that the provisions of a scheme approved by him for the purposes of section 82 are not being satisfactorily carried out, he may withdraw his approval of the scheme.[12] Before withdrawal he must give the persons responsible for the management of the scheme at least one month's warning of the date when the withdrawal will take effect and section 15(1) will become applicable; and he must give those persons an opportunity of making representations to him.[13] At the end of the month, unless the Minister has revoked his warning, section 15(1) will apply.[14]

In *Williams v. Minister of Agriculture*[15] the Minister terminated a marketing scheme and centralised services for tenants of Land Settlement Association Smallholdings in the Chawston Estate in Bedfordshire, not because the tenants had been at fault, but because the Minister no longer thought that it was necessary or expedient to maintain the arrangements. One of the tenants complained that this was a breach of his tenancy agreement, but as the agreement required the Minister to provide only such marketing arrangements and centralised services "as he may from time to time consider necessary or expedient", the Court of Appeal held that there was no breach.

Smallholdings: other matters 15.39

Special adjustments for smallholdings are to be found in the following parts of the 1986 Act:

(a) Schedule 3, Case A (notice to quit smallholding where tenant 65)[16];

(b) Schedule 3, Case E (extended scope of material prejudice)[17];

(c) Section 27(3)(c) (consent to notice to quit where purpose desirable under enactments relating to smallholdings)[18];

(d) Section 31(2)(d) (notice to quit part where object is letting as a smallholding)[19];

---

[11] s. 82(1).
[12] Thereby bringing the tenancy outside the application of s. 82 and reinstating the application of s. 15(1).
[13] s. 82(3)(a) and (b).
[14] s. 82(3).
[15] See report in *The Times*, July 11, 1985, and article in (1985) 275 E.G. 1076 at p. 1082.
[16] See para. 12.49 above.
[17] See para. 12.76 above.
[18] See para. 12.37 above.
[19] See para. 12.18 above.

(e) Section 38(4) (exclusion of smallholdings from succession scheme, overruling *Saul v. Norfolk County Council*.)[20]

In addition, the determination of the rent to be charged for a smallholdings tenancy is directly referable to the provisions of section 12 and Schedule 2 of the 1986 Act.[21]

---

[20] [1984] Q.B. 559,CA and see para. 14.22 above.
[21] See 1970 Act, s. 45.

CHAPTER 16

DISPUTE RESOLUTION

16.1 Dispute resolution: general

AGRICULTURAL LAND TRIBUNALS

16.2 Agricultural Land Tribunals: constitution

16.3 Agricultural Land Tribunals: how to find them

16.4 Agricultural Land Tribunals: procedure

16.5 Agricultural Land Tribunals: postponement by Tribunal of operation of notice to quit

16.6 Agricultural Land Tribunal: reasons for decisions

16.7 Agricultural Land Tribunals: judicial review

16.8 Agricultural Land Tribunals: case stated procedure

16.12 Agricultural Land Tribunals: costs

ARBITRATION UNDER THE AGRICULTURAL HOLDINGS ACT 1986

16.14 Arbitration under the Agricultural Holdings Act 1986: general

16.15 AHA arbitration: relationship to other procedures

16.19 AHA arbitration: formal powers of the Lord Chancellor

16.20 The application of Schedule 11

16.21 Appointment of an arbitrator

16.26 Remuneration of the arbitrator

16.27 Statements of Case

16.31 Arbitrator's communication with the parties

16.32 Challenge to the arbitrator's jurisdiction

16.33 Procedure and conduct of arbitration

16.48 Arbitrator's inspection of the holding

16.49 Legal assistance for the arbitrator

16.50 Arbitration hearing: time allocated for presentation

16.51 The arbitration award and the reasons for it

16.61 Judicial control of the reference

16.71 Supervision of arbitrators by the Council on Tribunals

16.72 Arbitration and costs

16.1 Dispute resolution: general

This Chapter sets out a certain amount of basic procedural information as to disputes affecting agricultural holdings. The substantive law, including the circumstances in which a particular forum is appropriate, is dealt with in the preceding Chapters. There are many disputes which will still remain within the jurisdiction of the public courts whereas there are other disputes which are compulsorily or by choice referred to hearings before the Agricultural Land Tribunals or arbitration. The purpose of this Chapter is mainly to indicate the constitution and proper functioning of the Agricultural Land Tribunals and arbitrations under the Agricultural Holdings Act 1986. The broader picture is, however, more complex and readers should not be left with the impression that all disputes are referable to one or the other of these. Aside from the public courts, the parties may, subject to the provisions of the Agricultural Holdings Act 1986, choose in their contract to refer specific matters to either arbitration or the determination of an expert. In the case of a contractual arbitration which is not by the 1986 Act referred to a statutory arbitrator, all appointments will now take place under the Arbitration Act 1996.[1] In the case of determination by an expert, this text has chosen to locate the commentary in Chapter 6[2] since it is likely that the majority of expert determinations will take place in connection with farm business tenancies. The Agricultural Land Tribunals administer the succession provisions and, because of the special adaptations necessary to the main Rules, the succession jurisdiction of the ALT is considered in Chapter 14 together with the substantive law.[3] Where there is a statutory reference under the 1986 Act to arbitration this will be governed by the terms of Schedule 11 together with any rules to be found in the specific section which requires the arbitration to take place.

It is not practicable or helpful to re-summarise these many occasions in this procedural Chapter: readers will find that the subject matter of the substantive law includes in every case a statement as to statutory arbitration to which the contents of this Chapter are supplemental. Two points require to be noted at the outset: first, it is not possible to contract into the statutory jurisdiction of the 1986 Act and any attempt to do so will simply result in an Arbitration Act reference with the terms of Schedule 11 (presumably) superimposed as the contractual element for the purposes of the Arbitration Act[4]; secondly, arbitrations under the Agricultural Holdings Act 1986 are excluded from the scope of the Arbitration Act by virtue of section 84 of the Agricultural Holdings Act[5] and therefore the case law as it stood prior to the enactment of the Arbitration Act 1996 will continue to apply to

---

[1] The commencement and transitional provisions of that statute are set out at para. 6.8 above and readers are referred to generally Chapter 6 which deals extensively with the Arbitration Act.

[2] paras 6.83–16.87.

[3] As to the succession Rules see paras 14.78–14.79 (succession on death of the tenant) and 14.122 (succession on retirement of the tenant).

[4] Accordingly those arbitrations fall within the general text of Chapter 6 above but, in so far as the parties may agree something by contract, adaptations of the non-mandatory provisions described in that Chapter will accordingly take place. Parties should be discouraged from undertaking this particular exercise since the result is fiendishly complicated.

[5] See para. 16.14 below.

arbitrations under the 1986 Act. For this reason it has been thought desirable to give a more extensive treatment to 1986 Act arbitrations as it is not anticipated that books dealing with the post Arbitration Act system will continue to maintain an appropriate up to date commentary for those limited sectors excluded from the Arbitration Act. The rules for arbitrators under the 1986 Act are considerably less liberal than they are under the Arbitration Act. Finally it is appropriate to point out that arbitrations under the Dairy Produce Quotas Regulations 1997[6] are under a separate code[7] to which the Arbitration Act 1996 does not apply.[8] The terms of Schedule 2 to the 1997 Regulations are essentially modelled on statutory arbitrations under the Agricultural Holdings Act 1986 and so the wider commentary in this Chapter on 1986 Act arbitrations may be of interest and application to arbitrations under the Dairy Produce Quotas Regulations 1997. The net result is that this Chapter deals first with Agricultural Land Tribunals[9] but does not repeat the material regarding succession to be found in Chapter 14 and, secondly, with arbitrations under the Agricultural Holdings Act.[10]

AGRICULTURAL LAND TRIBUNALS

Agricultural Land Tribunals: constitution 16.2

Agricultural Land Tribunals were established under the provisions of section 73 of the Agriculture Act 1947.[11] Amendments affecting them were made by the Agriculture (Miscellaneous Provisions) Act 1954[12] and by the Agriculture Act 1958.[13] Originally appellate bodies, they are now tribunals of first instance and they are subject to the supervisory jurisdiction of the Council on Tribunals by virtue of the Tribunals and Inquiries Act 1971.[14] England and Wales are divided into eight areas[15] for the purposes of the Tribunals, but Tribunals may sit in two or more divisions if necessary.[16] The power to constitute the Tribunal areas is vested in the Lord Chancellor.[17] Where a holding lies partly in the area of one Tribunal and partly in the area of another, the jurisdiction is vested in the Tribunal in whose area the greater part of the holding is situated.[18]

The chairman of each Tribunal, who must be a barrister or solicitor of not less than seven years standing, is appointed by the Lord Chancellor and holds office for

---

[6] See generally Chapter 18.
[7] Discussed at para. 18.17 below.
[8] See Sched. 2, para. 35 of the Dairy Produce Quotas Regulations 1997 (S.I. 1997 No.733).
[9] Paras 16.2–16.13 below.
[10] Para. 16.14 below.
[11] The details of their constitution were set out in Sched. 9 to the 1947 Act, paras 13–18 as amended by the 1958 Act, Sched. 1, para. 5.
[12] ss. 4–6 and Sched. 1, partly superseded by the 1958 Act.
[13] See s. 8 and paras 3–5 of Sched. 1, also s. 10 and Part I of Sched. 2.
[14] See Sched. 1, para. 1(a), to that Act.
[15] For these areas see the Agricultural Land Tribunals (Areas) Order 1982 (S.I. 1982 No.97).
[16] See s. 73(5) of the 1947 Act as amended by the 1958 Act, Sched. 1, para. 3(e).
[17] See s. 73(1) of the 1947 Act as amended by the 1958 Act, Sched. 1, para. 3(a).
[18] See s. 75 of the 1947 Act as amended by the 1958 Act, Sched. 1, para. 4. See also para. 1(2) of Sched. 1, to the Agricultural Land Tribunals (Rules) Order 1978 (S.I. 1978 No.259).

three years but is eligible for reappointment. He may resign by notice in writing to the Lord Chancellor and his appointment is revocable by the latter for incapacity or financial embarrassment. The Lord Chancellor is required to draw up for each Tribunal a panel of deputy chairmen who must be barristers or solicitors of not less than seven years standing, and whose functions are referred to later. He is also required to draw up for each Tribunal panels of persons appearing to him to represent farmers and landowners respectively, the persons in question to be selected from nominations made at his request by (at the time of writing) the National Farmers' Union and the Country Landowners' Association, subject to the Lord Chancellor's right to include other persons if not enough, or not enough suitable, nominations are made.[19]

The Tribunal is specifically constituted for each hearing[20] and consists of the permanent chairman or, in his absence, a person nominated by him to act as such either from the panel of deputy chairmen (whether for that or any other Tribunal) or from among other Tribunal chairmen, and one person nominated by the chairman from each of the farmers' and landowners' panels for that Tribunal, or from a corresponding panel from another Tribunal. The chairman may, if it appears to him expedient, nominate two assessors to assist the Tribunal at the hearing, but he is under no obligation to do so, and the use of assessors is in fact rare.[21] If the chairman of a Tribunal is prevented by sickness or any other reason from making these nominations, or otherwise discharging his duties, the duties may be discharged by a person appointed by the chairman (or if the chairman is unable to appoint, by the Lord Chancellor) from the panel of deputy chairmen for that Tribunal.[22] Membership of the House of Commons is a disqualification.[23]

A technical defect in the constitution of a Tribunal, or the disqualification of a person purporting to act as a member thereof, will not, if subsequently discovered, invalidate a decision.[24]

16.3 Agricultural Land Tribunals: how to find them

As stated in the previous paragraph, the Order setting out the formal details of the Agricultural Land Tribunals is to be found in S.I. 1982 No.97. However it would be unwise to rely on this in isolation. Not only has there been reorganisation of local authorities but in addition to that Government offices change location, telephones and fax numbers at regular intervals. Therefore readers, particularly if they have documents to file, are advised to locate the relevant Tribunal secretary and ensure that they have the correct location and dialling numbers. We provide

---

[19] See paras 13–15 of Sched. 9 to the 1947 Act, as substituted by para. 5(2) of Sched. 1 to the 1958 Act.

[20] para. 16(1) of Sched. 1, as substituted by the 1958 Act. It was held in the Scottish case of *McCallum v. Arthur* [1955] S.C. 188 that when a case was heard by the three members of the Land Court, but one died before judgment was delivered, a purported decision by the two survivors was invalid.

[21] para. 16(2), (3) of Sched. 9 above, as substituted. Such assessors would be selected by the chairman from a panel of professional men nominated by the President of the Royal Institution of Chartered Surveyors.

[22] para. 16A of Sched. 9 above as substituted.

[23] para. 19 of Sched. 9.

[24] para. 20, *ibid*.

here the best information available at the time of going to press and draw particular attention first to the re-amalgamation of the whole of Wales into one administrative centre in Cardiff and secondly to the fact that the Western Area ALT has relocated during 1998. If it is proving difficult to track down any particular ALT, the Ministry of Agriculture will often have the relevant information. **Do not confuse the Agricultural Land Tribunals with the Lands Tribunal.**[25] In so far as there may be some confusion as to whether Cleveland falls within the Northern or the Yorkshire and Humberside Area it would be prudent to make duplicate applications, one to each area.[26] It will be recalled that all these offices are in Government buildings and that normal office hours are likely to apply: if, therefore, a document is being filed at the last minute it would be wise in advance to establish what time the office closes. A decision has been taken in terms of this text to continue all references to local government areas as they stood in 1982, even though some of them now no longer exist.

Details of ALTs in England

Eastern Area ALT	Bedfordshire	Block B
	Cambridgeshire	Government Buildings
	Essex	Brooklands Avenue
	Hertfordshire	Cambridge
	Lincolnshire	CB2 2DR
	Norfolk	Tel: 01223 462727
	Northamptonshire	Fax: 01223 455652
	Suffolk	
	London Boroughs north of the River Thames except Richmond upon Thames	
Midlands Area ALT	Derbyshire	Block C
	Hereford and Worcester	Government Buildings
	Leicestershire	Whittington Road
	Nottinghamshire	Worcester
	Warwickshire	WR5 2LQ
	West Midlands	Tel: 01905 763355
		Fax: 01905 763180

---

[25] The Lands Tribunal has no jurisdiction of particular relevance to agricultural holdings although it has been known for persons enquiring after the Agricultural Land Tribunal wrongly to be referred to the Lands Tribunal. In terms of the service of documents and in particular the making of applications within a time-limit this can be catastrophic.
[26] Although the relevant Tribunals may not argue as to invalidity, doubtless the opponent party will.

Northern Area ALT	(?) Cleveland Cumbria Durham Northumberland Tyne & Wear	Eden Bridge House Lowther Street Carlisle CA3 8DX Tel: 01228 523400 Fax: 01228 592013
South Eastern Area ALT	Berkshire Buckinghamshire East Sussex Hampshire Isle of Wight Kent Oxfordshire Surrey West Sussex London Boroughs south of the River Thames including Richmond upon Thames	Block B Government Offices Coley Park Reading RG1 6DT Tel: 01189 581222 Fax: 01189 392263
South Western Area ALT	Avon Cornwall Devon Dorset Gloucestershire Somerset Wiltshire Isles of Scilly	Block III Government Buildings Burghill Road Westbury-on-Trym Bristol BS10 6NJ Tel: 01179 591000 Fax: 01179 505392
Western Area ALT	Cheshire Greater Manchester Lancashire Merseyside Shropshire Staffordshire	MAFF Building Electra Way Crewe Cheshire CW2 6PT Tel: 01270 754236 Fax: 01270 754260
Yorkshire and Humberside Area ALT	(?) Cleveland Humberside North Yorkshire South Yorkshire West Yorkshire	Government Buildings Crosby Road Northallerton Yorkshire DL6 1AD Tel: 01609 773751 Fax: 01609 780179

Agricultural Land Tribunals in Wales

Welsh Area ALT Whole of Wales Secretary to the ALT
(Wales)
Cathays Park
Cardiff
CF1 3NQ
Tel: 01222 823165
Fax: 01222 823562
General switchboard
Tel: 01222 825111

16.4

Agricultural Land Tribunals: procedure

The procedure of the Agricultural Land Tribunal is laid down by the Lord Chancellor under the powers given by the Agriculture Act 1947.[27] The current orders in force under these powers are the Agricultural Land Tribunals (Rules) Order 1978[28] and the Agricultural Land Tribunals (Succession to Agricultural Tenancies) Order 1984.[29] The former are "the principal rules" and the latter deal with procedure in relation both to applications for succession on the death of a tenant[30] and to applications by persons nominated by a retiring tenant.[31] These orders contain both the rules of procedure and the relevant prescribed forms. The full text of the orders, including the forms, is set out in Part III of this work. The procedural provisions governing succession cases are dealt with elsewhere.[32]

The principal Rules, since they appear in a single document can be conveniently read without significant need for commentary in this Chapter. Although written in relation to succession applications,[33] it may be helpful to consult the earlier text in relation to **conduct of hearing**.[34] The following simply highlights specific powers available to the Tribunal, to summarise the more important powers at a glance.

Consent to a notice to quit. An application for the Tribunal's consent to the operation of a notice to quit must be made within one month of the service of the tenant's counter-notice. The application is to be made on Form 1.[35]

Approval of improvements. The time within which the landlord must serve a notice under section 67(5) of the 1986 Act that he intends himself to carry out an improvement is one month from receipt of notice of the Tribunal's approval of the improvement.[36]

---

[27] Section 73(3) and (4) as amended by the 1958 Act, Sched. 1, para. 3. See minor amendment to s. 73(3) in para. 18 of Sched. 14 to the 1986 Act.
[28] S.I. 1978 No.259.
[29] S.I. 1984 No.1301.
[30] *ibid.*, Sched., Part II.
[31] *ibid.* Sched., Part III.
[32] In regard to succession on death of the tenant at paras 14.78–14.79 and in regard to succession following the retirement of the tenant at para. 14.122.
[33] Arguably the Tribunal's most active jurisdiction.
[34] See para. 14.79 above.
[35] r. 2(2), (3). In ***Purser v. Bailey*** [1967] 2 Q.B. 500 the landlord died after making an application to the Tribunal for consent to the notice to quit, but before the hearing took place. A grant of administration was made to his son, limited to the application to the Tribunal, "an unusual grant" in the words of Lord Denning M.R. (at 507).
[36] r. 7(2).

Parties. Apart from specific provisions, there is a general provision that any party against whom any relief is sought under rules 2 to 11 shall be a party to proceedings on the application. If the holding which is the subject of the application is sublet (in whole or in part) every landlord, tenant or sub-tenant will be parties.[37]

Replies. In general a party who intends to oppose an application must, within one month of a copy of the application being served on him, reply in the Form R appended to the application. If he fails to do so the Tribunal may decide to make an order in the terms of the application.[38]

Withdrawal of application or reply. A party is at liberty to withdraw an application or reply at any time before the hearing and where a reply is withdrawn the Tribunal may (except in a drainage case) decide to make an order in the terms of the application without a formal hearing. The withdrawal may give rise to an award of costs.[39]

Hearings. A party is under a duty to furnish the secretary on his request with any document or other information which the Tribunal may require and which it is in the party's power to furnish; and the secretary must give all other parties an opportunity of inspection or taking copies.[40] The Tribunal must sit in public unless it appears to it that there are exceptional reasons for the hearing to take place in private, but a member of the Council of Tribunals in his or her capacity as such has a right to attend a sitting in private as well as in public.[41] A party may appear and be heard in person or by counsel or solicitor or by any representative appointed in writing.[42] If a party fails to appear at the time fixed for the hearing the Tribunal may, if satisfied that the party has been afforded an adequate opportunity of attending, (a) dismiss the application if it is the applicant who fails to appear, (b) in any other case, proceed in the absence of that party.[43]

Evidence. A Tribunal, unlike an agricultural arbitrator, may admit evidence notwithstanding its inadmissibility in a court of law. Evidence may be given on oath or on affirmation or otherwise, by affidavit if the parties consent, or by means of written evidence produced by the maker when giving evidence (or produced, if the Tribunal consents, by another witness). But the Tribunal may, either on its own motion or on the application of any party, order the personal attendance of a deponent or maker of a written statement for examination and cross-examination, or admit any map, plan or other document in evidence.[44] The Tribunal may itself call a witness who may, after giving evidence, be cross-examined by any party.[45]

---

[37] r. 12.
[38] r. 15(2).
[39] r. 18.
[40] r. 20.
[41] r. 24.
[42] r. 25.
[43] r. 27.
[44] r. 28(2), (3).
[45] r. 29(2).

The Tribunal may require any witness to give evidence on oath or affirmation.[46] The provisions of the County Court Rules as to the issuing of witness summonses apply as they apply for arbitrations.[47]

Inspection. The Tribunal is empowered to enter on and inspect an agricultural holding owned or occupied by any party (whether the subject holding or not) and inspect any equipment, livestock or produce thereon. Notice of the Tribunal's intention to inspect must be given by the secretary to all parties and to any other occupier of the holding and must be given at least 24 hours before the intended entry unless given orally at the hearing. The parties, their representatives and expert witnesses and any other occupier of the holding may attend.[48] The conduct of the inspection is a particularly difficult aspect of any case from the point of the view of the chairman. Parties should be warned that they must not speak to the Tribunal unless in response to a direct question from the Tribunal and they should be asked in advance to warn their employees similarly not to say anything either to the Tribunal or in the presence of the Tribunal. There is plenty of potential for embarrassment as well as misconduct. At a practical level land agents or lawyers warning their clients as to behaviour on a Tribunal visit should also in advance request the occupier to have any guard dogs securely tied up and further to keep a respectful distance from the Tribunal members. If there are areas of the farm with limited access[49] it is only fair to warn the Tribunal of this in advance. Lawyers representing parties are likely to need substantial footwear and, when it is cold, very heavy clothing. If something untoward should occur, for example employees making prejudicial assertions in the presence of the Tribunal, considerations of fairness must prevail and, it is submitted, it will be the duty of the Tribunal to draw attention to the incident at the outset of any resumed hearing and allow the parties to comment or present evidence if they wish. Lay Tribunal members will, of course, be aware of the gravity of the situation and may have to restrain their natural first reactions to what they see.[50]

Decision. The decision of the Tribunal, which may be a majority decision, must be given in writing together with a statement of the Tribunal's reasons for its decision. There is a "slip" rule, by which the chairman may correct any "clerical mistake" in the written record of the decision.[51] Although it is customary to request the help of the parties in drawing up a first draft of a special case stated, this is something which is only possible once the Tribunal has produced its reasoned written decision. It would not be acceptable for the parties to become involved in writing the initial decision although to some extent the legal chairman may have in his note of evidence a list of items which are common ground between the parties. It is

---

[46] r. 29(3).
[47] r. 29(4). See CCR, Ord. 20, r. 12.
[48] r. 30.
[49] *e.g.* food processing areas where anyone entering must not be wearing boots and must have special clothing or hair nets.
[50] For example it is not unknown for lay Tribunal members to fall about with laughter at the standard of a building or the way in which crops have been sown.
[51] r. 31. No doubt this slip rule should be interpreted strictly, like that under RSC, Ord. 20, r. 11.

submitted that the Tribunal should not put pressure on the parties to agree anything once the hearing is concluded.[52]

Service. Every application, reply or other document required or authorised by these rules to be served on any person shall be deemed to have been duly served if it is delivered to him or left at his proper address, or sent to him by post in a registered letter or by recorded delivery.[53]

Extension of time. The time appointed by or under these rules (but not any time-limit laid down by the 1986 Act) for doing any act or taking any step in connection with any proceedings may be extended by the chairman on such terms and conditions, if any, as may appear to him just.[54]

Failure to comply with rules. Any failure to comply with the provisions of these rules does not render the proceedings, or anything done in pursuance thereof, invalid unless the chairman or the Tribunal so direct.[55]

16.5 Agricultural Land Tribunals: postponement by Tribunal of operation of notice to quit

When the Tribunal consents to the operation of a notice to quit it has power[56] either of its own motion or on the application of the tenant (made no later than 14 days after the giving of the consent) to postpone the termination of the tenancy for a period not exceeding 12 months if the notice to quit would otherwise become effective on[57] or within six months after the giving of the consent. It is not clear from a reading of Article 13 of the 1987 Order when the relevant 12 months commences (*i.e.* whether from the date of the ruling or from the point at which the notice to quit would otherwise expire).

---

[52] Post-hearing directions are unnecessary if the chairman is keeping an appropriate note and the issue of post-hearing requests for matters to be agreed generates not only further expense but in addition considerable anxiety and annoyance to the parties themselves. Virtually all hearings before the Agricultural Land Tribunal will be, since the parties have not settled, cases where there is some degree of animosity. It must be remembered that, whether or not an admission may have been made in cross-examination, it is quite another matter for the party making the admission to secure the agreement of his client that he had made it: post-hearing directions to agree anything put appalling pressure on expert witnesses in a quite unnecessary way.

[53] r. 35(1).

[54] r. 37. For an example of application, see *Purser v. Bailey* [1967] 2 Q.B. 500.

[55] r. 38.

[56] Not under the 1978 Rules Order, but under art. 13 of the Agricultural Holdings (Arbitration on Notices) Order 1987 (S.I. 1987 No.710), a rather unexpected place.

[57] The word "on" perhaps requires explanation. A notice to quit which, under s. 25(2) is quite legitimately of less than 12 months duration might in the normal course expire before the Tribunal has reached a decision, or even before the hearing. As a result of s. 26(1), however, the notice cannot take effect unless and until the Tribunal consents. Presumably, however, if the Tribunal does consent the notice would take effect at the moment when consent is given ("on ... the giving of the consent") unless the Tribunal exercises its power of postponement.

Agricultural Land Tribunal: reasons for decisions 16.6

As tribunals under the direct supervision of the Council on Tribunals,[58] Agricultural Land Tribunals are under a duty to furnish a statement, either written or oral of the reasons for decisions, if requested on or before the giving of the decisions.[59] Rule 31 of the 1978 Order[60] requires the decision of the Tribunal to be given in writing "together with a statement of the Tribunal's reasons for their decision". This requirement is independent of any request.

Agricultural Land Tribunals: control by the High Court through judicial review 16.7

Before the enactment of section 6 of the Agriculture (Miscellaneous Provisions) Act 1954 the only means by which the High Court could control Agricultural Land Tribunals was by the machinery of the prerogative orders of certiorari, prohibition and mandamus. As a result of section 6 of the 1954 Act it became possible to refer questions of law to the High Court by means of a case stated, and this procedure is discussed below. The prerogative orders are, however, still available as part of the more flexible and comprehensive system of judicial review introduced as a result of the Law Commission's recommendations in 1976[61] and now covered by section 31 of the Supreme Court Act 1981 and the revised Order 53 of the Rules of the Supreme Court.

Under the older prerogative order machinery which preceded the remodelled administrative law code of judicial review there were a number of instances where prerogative orders were issued to the Agricultural Land Tribunals and other cases where the applicability of the orders was discussed.[62]

Since the introduction of judicial review there have been a few cases where applications for it have been made in relation to Agricultural Land Tribunals.[63] It

---

[58] Tribunals and Inquiries Act 1971, Sched. 1, para. 1(a).
[59] *ibid.*, s. 12.
[60] Incorporated and applicable in relation to succession decisions: see para. 14.78 above.
[61] Report on Remedies in Administrative Law (Law Com. No.73; Cmnd. 6407 (1976)).
[62] See ***R. v. ALT for Wales and Monmouth Area, ex p. Davies*** [1953] 1 W.L.R. 722; ***R. v. ALT for Eastern Province, ex p. Grant*** [1956] 1 W.L.R. 1240; ***R. v. ALT (S.E. Province), ex p. Palmer*** [1954] J.P.L. 181; ***Davies v. Price*** [1958] 1 W.L.R. 434. On the more general questions on the meaning of "record" and "speaking order", see ***R. v. Northumberland Compensation Appeal Tribunal, ex p. Shaw*** [1952] 1 K.B. 338 at 352 (Denning L.J.) and ***Davies v. Price*** (above), at 441, 443. See also Lord Sumner in ***R. v. Nat Bell Liquors Ltd*** [1922] 2 A.C. 128 at 199 for the face of the record which does not speak, "the unscrutable face of a sphinx". In ***R. v. ALT for S.E. Area, ex p. Bracey*** [1960] 1 W.L.R. 911 certiorari was refused on incorrect grounds, but the decision is supportable on other grounds. See also ***R. v. ALT (S.E. Area), ex p. Boucher*** (1952) 159 E.G. 191 and ***R. v. ALT (S.E. Area), ex p. Hooker*** [1952] 1 K.B. 1.
[63] For example ***R. v. ALT for the S.E. Area, ex p. Parslow*** (1979) 251 E.G. 667 was an application for certiorari which probably just preceded the new procedure. It was an odd case where certiorari seemed unsuitable *ab initio* and was refused. In ***Moss v. National Coal Board*** (1982) 264 E.G. 52 a complaint that the refusal of the chairman of a Tribunal to extend time under what is now rule 37, and to afford to an oral hearing of the application to extend time, was a breach of natural justice was dismissed; the proceedings were brought by way of judicial review. ***R. v. ALT for the Eastern Area, ex p. Moses: Moses v. Hurst*** (1983) 269 E.G. 168, framed both as a case stated and as a judicial review, was the case where there were no satisfactory findings of facts or issues of law; the case stated was

is, however, clear that in suitable circumstances the remedies available by means of judicial review can be used. Judicial review would be appropriate where the challenge to a Tribunal's decision is on the ground of lack of jurisdiction, error of law on the face of the record, or breach of the rules of natural justice. An error of law not disclosed on the face of the record, such as the misconstruction of a statute, could not be corrected by judicial review. The remedy would be to request the Tribunal to state a case under section 6 of the 1954 Act and, if the request is refused, to apply to the Court for an order directing the Tribunal to do so. Errors of law not revealed on the record (and it must be remembered that it is an error of law to act on no evidence) may be rectified by the procedure of case stated, but there is no remedy for errors of fact. Affidavit evidence is not admissible to support an application for certiorari on the ground of error of law not manifest on the record, but the Court is entitled to look at affidavit evidence in support of an allegation of want of jurisdiction or of bias or other breach of the principles of natural justice, like receiving evidence from one party in the absence of the other.[64]

16.8 Agricultural Land Tribunals: reference of questions of law by case stated: general procedure

The procedure under section 6 of the Agriculture (Miscellaneous Provisions) Act 1954 for the control of Agricultural Land Tribunals on questions of law is to refer such questions, by means of a case stated by the Tribunal, for the decision of the High Court.[65] The case stated should set out the question or questions of law to be referred to the Court and the facts found by the Tribunal. It is signed by the chairman and delivered to the party requesting the reference within two months of the date of the request, or, as the case may be, within two months of the order of the High Court directing the reference.[66] The procedure provides, in effect, for an appeal on a point of law.[67] It should be noted that an Agricultural Land Tribunal cannot state a case of its own motion; there must first be a request by a party. The request may be made before or after the Tribunal has given its decision.[68] If the case is referred to the Court before the Tribunal have given its decision it becomes a consultative case, as distinct from an appeal, *i.e.* a case for an opinion to be applied by the Tribunal when it make its own decision. The proceedings in the High Court are begun by originating motion by the person to whom the case is delivered. Notice of such motion must be served on the secretary of the Tribunal and on any other party or parties to the proceedings, and a copy of the case must be served with any such notice.[69] The notice of motion must set out the applicant's contentions on the question of law to which the case stated relates.[70] The Court has power to

---

remitted and the application for judicial review dismissed.
[64] *R. v. ALT for S.E. Area, ex p. Bracey* [1960] 1 W.L.R. 911 (Lord Parker C.J.).
[65] This will normally be a single judge: see RSC, Ords 56 and 57 and Ord. 94, r. 7.
[66] Agricultural Land Tribunals (Rules) Order 1978 (S.I. 1978 No.259), r. 33(3). See below as to case stated by direction of the High Court.
[67] Parker L.J. in *Davies v. Price* [1958] 1 W.L.R 434 at 442 described it as "an appeal by way of case stated".
[68] Agriculture (Miscellaneous Provisions) Act 1954, s. 6(1).
[69] RSC, Ord. 56, r. 10.
[70] RSC, Ord. 56, r. 10(3).

amend a case or order it to be returned to the Tribunal for amendment and may draw inferences of fact from the facts stated in the case.[71]

Agricultural Land Tribunals: reference of questions of law by case stated: case stated at the request of a party 16.9

A party may request a Tribunal to state a case and the Tribunal may do so in response at any time during the proceedings and before the Tribunal gives its decision.[72] Alternatively, such a request may be made after the decision has been given, but in that case it must be made in writing to the secretary of the Tribunal not later than 14 days from the date on which a copy of the Tribunal's decision was sent to the party making the request, and must be accompanied by as many copies of the request as there are parties; the secretary must then serve a copy on every party.[73] If the Tribunal propose to comply with the request it must do so, as mentioned above, within two months after the date of the request. When a case is served on the party requesting it notice must be given to every other party to the proceedings that the case has been served on the party named, and on the date specified, in the notice.[74] The originating motion for the determination of the case must be entered for hearing and the notice thereof served on the other party or parties and the secretary of the Tribunal within 14 days after the case stated was served on the applicant.[75] The motion is entered for hearing in the Crown Office (*i.e.* the Crown Office and Associates' Department of the Central Office) and the entry is formally made when a copy of the notice of motion, and any other documents required to be lodged before entry (including a copy of the case stated) have been lodged in that office.[76] The party entering the motion for hearing must also lodge copies of the proceedings for the use of the judges.[77] Where the Tribunal proceedings arose on an application under section 11 of the 1986 Act (provision of fixed equipment necessary to comply with statutory requirements) the notice of motion must be served on the authority having power to enforce the relevant statutory requirement as well as on the other party or parties and the secretary of the Tribunal.[78]

Agricultural Land Tribunals: reference of questions of law by case stated: case stated by direction of the High Court 16.10

If a Tribunal, after giving its decision, refuses a party's request to refer a question of law to the High Court, provision is made for the party aggrieved by the refusal to apply to the High Court for an order directing it to do so.[79] It will be noted that there is no machinery to direct a Tribunal to state a case on a consultative basis before it

---

[71] *ibid.*, r. 11.
[72] This is the consultative case. If the Tribunal refuses to state a case at this stage it cannot be ordered to do so, as the power to direct it arises only if it refuses "after giving [its] decision": 1954 Act, s. 6(2).
[73] S.I. 1978 No. 259, r. 33(1). Form 76 in Part V of this work contains a precedent for the request itself.
[74] RSC, Ord. 56, r. 9(3).
[75] *ibid*, r. 10(4).
[76] *ibid.*, Ord. 57, r. 2. The Crown Office List is noted at 57/2/1.
[77] *ibid.*, r. 2(2).
[78] RSC, Ord. 94, r. 7(2). The authority has the right to appear and be heard.
[79] 1954 Act, s. 6(2).

has given its decision, although, of course, it may agree a request to do so. If the Tribunal refuses the request the secretary must, not later than 14 days from the date of his receipt of the request, notify all parties of the refusal. If the party making the request, and being aggrieved by the refusal, intends to apply to the High Court for a direction he must, within seven days after receiving notice of the refusal, serve on the secretary notice in writing of the intended application, accompanied by copies of the notice, which the secretary will serve on the other parties.[80] The application is made by originating motion to the Court.[81] Notice of the motion must be served on the secretary of the Tribunal and all other parties to the proceedings; and if the proceedings arose on an application under section 11 of the 1986 Act, the notice of motion must be served also on the authority having power to enforce the relevant requirements.[82] The notice of motion must state the grounds of the application, the question of law on which it is sought to have the case stated and any reasons given by the Tribunal for refusing to state a case. The motion must be entered for hearing, and the notice thereof served, within 14 days after receipt by the applicant of notice of the refusal of his request to state a case.[83] If the Court directs the Tribunal to state a case, the case must be sent to the party who made the request within two months after the Court's direction.[84] The subsequent procedure is the same as when a case is stated on request without a direction.[85]

16.11 Agricultural Land Tribunals: reference of questions of law by case stated: consequential proceedings

If the Tribunal at the request of a party refers a question of law to the High Court before giving its own decision, the Tribunal proceedings will be adjourned pending the High Court's decision, which the Tribunal will apply in due course when it gives its decision. The position is slightly more complicated where the Tribunal has given its decision before the reference and the procedure is in the nature of an appeal. It is provided that where, after a Tribunal has given its decision, it refers a question to the Court, or receives notice of an intended application for an order directing it to do so, effect shall not be given to its decision unless and until it otherwise orders after the High Court proceedings arising therefrom, have been concluded or have lapsed.[86] The High Court's decision may necessitate a modification of the Tribunal's original decision and this will need to be embodied in an order. In suitable cases the order may postpone (or further postpone) the date at which a tenancy is to terminate by notice to quit if the notice is held to be effective.[87] In some cases it may be necessary to have a further Tribunal hearing to decide what modifications or other directions are required, but if the chairman does not consider that this is necessary he is empowered to make the

---

[80] See 1954 Act, s. 6(4) and r. 33(2) of S.I. 1978 No.259. Form 77 in Part V of this work is a precedent for notice to the ALT of an intention to apply to the High Court.
[81] RSC, Ord. 56, r. 8.
[82] RSC, Ord. 94, r. 7; the authority has the right to appear and be heard.
[83] RSC, Ord. 56, r. 8.
[84] r. 33(3) of S.I. 1978 No.259.
[85] RSC, Ord. 56, r. 9 and 10.
[86] 1954 Act, s. 6(5).
[87] 1954 Act, s. 6(5).

required order himself.[88] Where the chairman does consider that a further hearing is required he is to fix the date, time and place of the hearing, and if the further hearing cannot take place before the Tribunal as originally constituted he is empowered, and required, to cause a fresh Tribunal to be constituted for that purpose.[89] The High Court may remit a case to the Tribunal for reconsideration with directions as to which matters should be taken into account and what excluded.[90]

Agricultural Land Tribunals: nature of jurisdiction as to costs 16.12

Until the Agriculture (Miscellaneous Provisions) Act 1954 Tribunals had no power to award costs, but they were given a limited power by section 5 of that Act. The power is restricted to a case where it appears to the Tribunal that any person concerned in a reference or application (including any minister or government department) has acted frivolously, vexatiously or oppressively in applying for or in connection with the reference or application. The Tribunal may order such a person to pay to any other person either a specified sum in respect of the costs incurred by him at or with a view to the hearing or the taxed amount of those costs, and an order can be made whether or not the matter proceeds to a hearing.[91] It is clearly not Parliament's intention that Tribunals should award costs automatically against the loser. The reason why the 1947 Act had made no provision as to costs was that it was feared that the risk of incurring costs might deter people from seeking the Tribunal's protection. The power given by the 1954 Act was deliberately narrow, the object being to check the unjustifiable invocation of the Tribunal's machinery, *e.g.* to prevent a landlord from abusing the procedure by serving notice to quit year after year, without regard to the merits of his case, in an effort to persecute and harass the tenant into quitting. It also enables a Tribunal to penalise last-minute withdrawals which put opponents to unnecessary trouble and expense.

It should be noted that there is an additional and separate power to deal with costs which is conferred by section 27(7) of the Agricultural Holdings Act 1986 in proceedings under section 27.[92]

Agricultural Land Tribunals: taxation of costs and recovery 16.13

If the Tribunal orders costs to be taxed, they are taxable in the County Court according to the County Court scale directed by the order, or, if the order gives no direction, by the Court.[93] Sums payable under the Tribunal's orders for costs are recoverable, if the Court so orders, as if payable under an order of the Court and an application may be made *ex parte* by affidavit for an order as to recovery.[94] Such an

---

[88] 1854 Act, s. 6(6): r. 34(1) of S.I. 1978 No.259.
[89] 1954 Act, s. 6(6): r. 34(1) and (2) of S.I. 1978 No.259.
[90] ***Evans v. Roper*** [1960] 1 W.L.R. 814. In ***Wilson v. Earl Spencer's Settlement Trustees*** [1985] 2 E.G.L.R. 3 a case was remitted to the Tribunal for the fringe benefits enjoyed by a claimant in succession proceedings to be calculated in precise financial terms.
[91] 1954 Act, s. 5(1) as amended by the 1958 Act, s. 8 and para. 26 of Sched. 1.
[92] The Tribunal is entitled by order to provide "for the payment by any party of such sum as the Tribunal consider a reasonable contribution towards costs".
[93] 1954 Act, s. 5(2). See CCR, Ord. 38, r. 22.
[94] 1954 Act, s. 5(3) and CCR, Ord. 25, r. 12.

DISPUTE RESOLUTION

order will enable advantage to be taken of the County Court process of execution. The powers of the County Court under section 5 of the 1954 Act are exercisable by the registrar.[95] An application for the taxation of costs is made by originating application.[96] The proof of the Tribunal's order for the purpose of County Court applications is facilitated by the provision that a document purporting to be a document duly executed or issued on behalf of a Tribunal shall, until the contrary is proved, be deemed to be a document so executed or issued.[97]

ARBITRATION UNDER THE AGRICULTURAL HOLDINGS ACT 1986

16.14 Scope of arbitration under the Agricultural Holdings Act 1986
Arbitration under the 1986 Act is a special code of statutory arbitration the object of which is to provide agricultural landlords and tenants with a simple and efficient method of settling disputes. The Arbitration Acts 1950, 1979 and (now) 1996 have never applied to this type of arbitration.[98] The agricultural code was amended and modernised by the 1984 Act[99] and is now set out in the 1986 Act, section 84 and Schedule 11. There are many matters which, on a compulsory basis, are referred to arbitration to be conducted under Schedule 11.[1] Form 66 in Part V of this work is a form of appointment of a valuer with full powers to secure the appointment of an arbitrator.

16.15 Compulsory arbitration and the continuing jurisdiction of the Courts
Although the arbitration provisions of the 1986 Act are comprehensive, the following actions fall within the jurisdiction of the Courts:

(a) actions in tort generally;

(b) actions during the tenancy for non-payment of rent;

(c) actions for recovery of possession of the holding[2];

(d) actions by a tenant for illegal distress;

(e) action for rectification of a tenancy agreement;

(f) action by a landlord against a tenant during the tenancy on a covenant to pay outgoings[3];

---

[95] 1954 Act, s. 5(4).
[96] See CCR, Ord. 38, r. 22.
[97] 1947 Act, Sched. 9, para. 24.
[98] See s. 84 of the 1986 Act.
[99] s. 10(1) and Sched. 3, paras 19 and 28 of the 1984 Act.
[1] Of these the most frequently encountered is probably the settlement of claims on termination of the tenancy but see also the commentary at para. 13.116 below.
[2] The position in Scotland appears to be different: see wide scope of s. 74 of the Agricultural Holdings (Scotland) Act 1949 and *Houison-Craufurd's Trustees v. Davies* [1951] S.C. 1 and *Brodie v. Kerr*; *McCallum v. McNair* [1952] S.C. 216.
[3] *Lowther v. Clifford* [1927] 1 K.B. 130.

(g) action by a landlord during the tenancy for breach of tenant's covenant to repair[4];

(h) action by a tenant during the tenancy for breach of a landlord's covenant to repair;

(i) action for a declaration that a notice to quit is invalid. This is a question which is logically prior to a decision on a claim arising "on or out of the termination of the tenancy"[5];

(j) proceedings to obtain a decision on the construction of a contract of tenancy[6];

(k) relief by way of injunction and proceedings for forfeiture.[7]

As a matter of general principle, if there is any doubt whether the jurisdiction of the Court is ousted by a statutory provision, it will be interpreted as not having this effect, since clear and definite indications are required of the intention of the legislature to deprive a citizen of his common law right of access to the courts.[8] But where it is clear that a matter is compulsorily referred to arbitration under the 1986 Act, and the jurisdiction of the courts is ousted, the matter cannot even be made the subject of a counterclaim in an action properly brought by the other party.[9]

Nature of arbitration 16.16

Arbitration is a species of private[10] judicial proceeding for the determination of disputes, and an arbitrator exercises a judicial function. He is a judge and his

---

[4] *Kent v. Conniff* [1953] 1 Q.B. 361.
[5] See *Paddock Investments Ltd v. Lory* (1975) 236 E.G. 803 (summonses in Ch.D. for declarations as to validity of notices to quit) see also *Farrow v. Orttewell* [1933] Ch. 480; cf. *R v. Powell, ex p. Camden* [1925] 1 K.B. 641; *Simpson v. Batey* [1924] 2 K.B. 666.
[6] *Re Disraeli Agreement* [1939] Ch. 382 (construction summonses in Ch.D.).
[7] See remarks of Mocatta J. in *Ward v. Space Design Ltd* (1969) 213 E.G. 893. And see *Parry v. Million Pigs Ltd* (1980) 260 E.G. 281.
[8] See *Kent v. Conniff* [1953] 1 Q.B. 361; *Re Arden and Rutter* [1923] 2 K.B. 865 at 878. cf. *Goldsack v. Shore* [1950] 1 K.B. 708. For general saving, see s. 97 of the 1986 Act.
[9] See *Gaslight & Coke v. Holloway* (1885) 52 L.T. 434; *Schofield v. Hincks* (1888) 58 L.J.Q.B. 147. cf. also the cases where a tenant who fails to safeguard his rights by requiring arbitration in regard to the notice to quit, when arbitration is mandatory, cannot obtain relief from the courts: see *Magdalen College, Oxford v. Heritage* [1974] 1 W.L.R. 441; and further paras 12.45 and 10.24 above.
[10] It is entirely a matter for the agreement of the parties whether any publicity should be given to the award. In so far as the European Convention on Human Rights may shortly be incorporated directly into U.K. law there is considerable scope for an argument that compulsory arbitration breaches the terms of Art. 6.1 of the Convention in that there is no public hearing and further judgment is not pronounced publicly. There is a clear distinction for these purposes between compulsory and voluntary arbitrations where the guarantee of the Convention is satisfied by the element of choice available to the parties: see "Arbitration and Article 6 of The European Convention on Human Rights" by Wedam-Lukic in the *Journal of the Chartered Institute of Arbitrators*, Vol. 63, Supplement, p. 16. The official Guide to the Convention produced by the Council of Europe (Strasbourg, 1991), p. 44 suggests (but not on a binding basis) that if the parties

conduct at all stages of the arbitration must be judicial. An arbitrator who keeps constantly in mind that he is a judge will instinctively observe many of the rules, and avoid the worst pitfalls, mentioned in the following pages. Arbitration as a judicial process must be distinguished not only from a simple valuation, but also from a more complex procedure superficially resembling arbitration, namely, the arrangement by which two lawyers acting for the landlord and tenant respectively are empowered in certain events to appoint a third valuer to act as an umpire.[11] The basic difference is that the umpire is not appointed to judge but to substitute his expertise for that of the other two valuers in order to reach a settlement. He is acting purely as a valuer whose skill and judgment are, by agreement, to be binding, and the outcome of his efforts is not an award (which is a species of judgment), but a valuation (which is the conclusion of an expert). The difference is important because the rules regulating arbitrations do not apply to his procedure and the position of an arbitrator in regard to personal liability differs from that of a valuer or expert.[12] An arbitrator carries out not a valuation but a judicial inquiry involving the hearing and weighing of evidence and argument. This does not mean, however, that the arbitrator, who is usually an experienced valuer, must divest himself of his expert knowledge. On the contrary, he should use it to the full, and it will help him to decide expeditiously and efficiently, but he must in the main use it in aid of his judicial function, to help him to appreciate the issues, grasp the technical details quickly, sift the evidence (and, indeed, supplement it by what he sees with his own expert eyes or apprehends with his own expert mind), and distinguish good points from bad.

16.17 **Simultaneous disputes under the 1986 Act and under the Arbitration Act**
Compulsory arbitration under the 1986 Act means arbitration by a single arbitrator under section 84 and Schedule 11, the parties being unable to refer such matters by preference to the procedures available under the Arbitration Act.[13] In circumstances where there are simultaneous disputes one of which must be determined under the 1986 Act and the other which must be determined under the Arbitration Act, it is not possible to consolidate[14] the two arbitrations and there ought therefore to be two separate arbitral appointments, one under each code even if the same person is in fact appointed. The appointee will certainly have to produce two separate arbitration awards but no doubt the parties may give him great assistance in agreeing convenient procedures which will shorten his task.[15]

---

consent the hearing may be private but that in all circumstances judgments must be pronounced publicly. No doubt this is unwelcome news to litigants in agricultural arbitrations.

[11] This arrangement must also be distinguished from a procedure under the Arbitration Act by which two arbitrators appoint a third arbitrator who is called an umpire. The umpire in that case is a true arbitrator. It is not a procedure possible in agricultural arbitrations. The arrangement by which two valuers appoint a third valuer to act as an umpire is not now often used in England and Wales, although there is no legal objection to it.

[12] See paras 6.83–6.87 above.

[13] See Chapter 6 above.

[14] It is quite impossible to match the mandatory sections of the Arbitration Act (see para. 6.9 above) to the terms of Sched. 11 of the 1986 Act.

[15] *e.g.* agreeing that evidence in one arbitration should stand as evidence in another where

Simultaneous arbitrations under the 1986 Act and the Dairy Produce Quotas Regulations

16.18

The Agriculture Act 1986, in relation to a tenant's claim for compensation for milk quota on termination of the tenancy, provides that any claim under that Act is to be determined by arbitration under the Agricultural Holdings Act 1986.[16] This type of arbitration requires the arbitrator, amongst other things, to ascertain how much quota will be left on the tenanted holding on the termination of the tenancy. If the tenant farmed other land in addition, the termination of the tenancy operates to trigger an apportionment of a type which is likely to result in apportionment by arbitration under the Dairy Produce Quotas Regulations 1997.[17] The terms of an arbitration under the 1997 Regulations, Sched. 2 are not such as to allow consolidation with an arbitration under the 1986 Act.[18] Accordingly it is suggested that though it may be convenient for the same person to be appointed as the arbitrator in the case of simultaneous disputes, one under the 1986 Act and the other under the 1997 Regulations, he must produce separate awards. If the parties to the 1986 Act arbitration are willing to be bound by relevant evidence in the 1997 Regulations arbitration this will somewhat shorten the proceedings under the 1986 Act.[19]

1986 Act arbitration: formal powers of the Lord Chancellor

16.19

As a result of amendments made by the 1984 Act, the former limited rule-making power under the 1948 Act[20] has been superseded by enlarged powers over procedure conferred on the Lord Chancellor and now embodied in section 84 of the 1986 Act.[21] The Lord Chancellor is empowered to modify by order the statutory provisions in Schedule 11 (subject to the limitations mentioned below). He may prescribe forms for proceedings (*e.g.* proper pleadings in certain cases) and forms of awards.[22] The "modifications" he may make in Schedule 11 include additions, omissions and amendments.[23] The limitations on his power to modify Schedule 11 are that he must not make provisions inconsistent with paragraphs 1 to 6, 11 to 13, 14(2), 17, 19, 21, 22, 26 to 29 and 32.[24] The new powers substitute a more flexible machinery for the rigidity of the old Schedule 6 of the 1948 Act, which could be

---

appropriate.

[16] Sched. 1, para. 11(1) of the Agriculture Act 1986.
[17] See in particular para. 18.18 below.
[18] As to an arbitration under the Regulations see para. 18.17 below.
[19] It would be wrong to ask the parties to the 1997 Regulations arbitration to be bound by the evidence in the other arbitration since not all of the parties will be parties to that other arbitration and therefore cannot participate in it.
[20] The Minister's powers were transferred to the Lord Chancellor by the 1977 Act (Sched. 1, para. 1(6), but the changes in the content of the powers were made by the 1984 Act (Sched. 3, para. 19).
[21] s. 84(2) to (4).
[22] s. 84(3).
[23] s. 84(5).
[24] s. 84(4). The matters with which the Lord Chancellor must not tamper cover provisions for the appointment and remuneration of arbitrators, witnesses, enlargement of time for award, award of compensation in accordance with valid agreement, binding nature of award, duty to give reasons, interest, and provisions as to special case, setting award aside, and remission.

amended only by legislation. It may be that the limitations on the Lord Chancellor's powers to modify Schedule 11 go somewhat too far; there might, for example, have been some merit in enabling him to substitute a simple appeal on a point of law for the case stated procedure (paragraph 26). At the time of writing the Lord Chancellor has not yet exercised his new powers as to forms for proceedings.

16.20 The application of Schedule 11

Arbitrations taking place under Schedule 11 are subject to the express terms of that Schedule and, in addition, must be conducted impartially and fairly. The arbitrator is not entitled to disregard either the law as to what the parties' rights are or, without the express consent of all the parties, the formal rules as to evidence which apply in a Court of law.[25] The terms of Schedule 11 are fully set out in Part II of this work and the paragraphs are grouped as follows:

Paragraphs 1–6	Appointment and remuneration of arbitrator.
Paragraphs 7–13	Conduct of proceedings and witnesses.
Paragraphs 14–20	Award.
Paragraph 21	Reasons for award.
Paragraph 22	Interest on awards.
Paragraphs 23–25	Costs.
Paragraphs 26–28	Special case, setting aside award and remission.
Paragraphs 29–32	Miscellaneous (recoupment of arbitrator's fees from the other party; costs awards where the arbitrator has no jurisdiction on the substance; date of appointment by the President of the RICS; presumption as to due execution).

Much of the remainder of this Chapter is designed to set the terms of Schedule 11 in the context of the wider law applicable.[26]

---

[25] He is, however, permitted to take advantage of the various Civil Evidence Acts.

[26] Readers wishing to research any particular aspect must take careful note that the changes to commercial arbitration effected by the Arbitration Act 1996 are so dramatic that it is questionable how far the modern law of arbitration now offers a parallel to statutory arbitrations under Sched. 11. In the less liberal climate of the Arbitration Acts 1950–1979 (now repealed) the commercial case law was more often applicable and continues to be referred to in this Chapter. The best source of discussion on the pre-1996 Arbitration Acts is Mustill & Boyd, *Commercial Arbitration* (2nd ed., Butterworths, 1989). This text incorporates a certain amount of case law after that edition but before the introduction of the Arbitration Act 1996.

Appointment of an arbitrator: general   16.21

An arbitrator is appointed by agreement between the parties, or, in default of agreement, by the President of the RICS.[27]

The words "in default of agreement" merely mean that the parties have not in fact agreed. It is not a condition precedent to appointment by the President that they should first have attempted to reach agreement, so that such appointment is perfectly valid if made on the application of a party who has made no effort to agree or, indeed, has given no prior notification to the other.[28]

Where, however, a notice requiring arbitration within a time-limit is laid down as a precondition (as by Article 3 or 4 or Article 9 of the Agricultural Holdings (Arbitration on Notices) Order 1987)[29] an appointment is void if such a precondition is not fulfilled.[30]

Appointment of an arbitrator: by agreement between the parties   16.22

An appointment by agreement must be made in writing.[31] Provided that there is no doubt about the fact of appointment, it does not appear to be essential that the document appointing the arbitrator should be signed by each party in the presence of the other.[32] An agreement that an arbitrator should be appointed in the future, however, is not the same thing as the actual appointment of an arbitrator, a point which may be important where time-limits are in question.[33] An appointment of an arbitrator is not as such a document which requires to be stamped, but it may in some cases be made under seal and for that reason require stamping. The appointment of an arbitrator by agreement, as distinct from an appointment by the President, requires co-operation and communication between the parties.[34] The modern law as to appointment by the parties under Schedule 11 is virtually encapsulated in two Court of Appeal cases namely ***Hannaford v. Smallacombe***[35] and ***Robinson v. Moody***.[36] Where the parties make a joint offer of an appointment to the arbitrator, and he accepts it, this results in separate contractual relations between the arbitrator and each of the appointing parties.[37] What amounts to an

---

[27] Sched. 11, para. 1(1). The transfer of the function of appointing arbitrators from the Minister of Agriculture, Fisheries and Food to the President of the RICS was made by s. 8 of the 1984 Act and the Agricultural Holdings Act 1984 (Commencement) Order 1985 (S.I. 1985 No.1644). The transfer took effect on January 1, 1986. The statutory authority is now Sched. 11, para. 1, to the 1986 Act. Copies of the forms of application to the President of the RICS for appointment of an arbitrator are reproduced in Part V by permission of the Institution. Form 67A relates to appointment in a s. 12 rent review: 67B is the form of application for appointment in all other 1986 Act arbitrations.

[28] ***F.R. Evans (Leeds) Ltd v. Webster*** (1962) 112 L.J. 703; 184 E.G. 269,CC.

[29] S.I. 1987 No.710.

[30] ***French v. Elliott*** [1960] 1 W.L.R. 40.

[31] Sched. 11, para. 5.

[32] *cf*. ***Lord v. Lord*** (1857) 26 L.J.Q.B. 34 and ***Re Hopper*** (1867) L.R. 2 Q.B. 367.

[33] ***Chalmers Property Investment Co. v. MacColl*** [1951] S.C. 24.

[34] See ***Tew v. Harris*** (1847) 11 Q.B. 7 and ***Tradax Export SA v. Volkswagenwerk AG*** [1970] 1 Q.B. 537 and see ***University College, Oxford v. Durdy*** [1982] Ch. 413 for discussion of these two cases.

[35] [1994] 1 E.G.L.R. 9.

[36] [1994] 2 E.G.L.R. 16.

[37] Evans L.J. in ***Robinson v. Moody*** (above) at 19J.

appointment will depend primarily on the facts of each case and the parties are entitled to stipulate in their agreement, if they wish, that the appointment will take effect from the moment that both sides know of the arbitrator's willingness to act. In the absence of such a provision, where there is an agreement on the identity of the arbitrator and an irrevocable agreement to appoint him subject only to his willingness to act, the appointment is complete when the arbitrator actually accepts it.[38] It is still not entirely clear whether the issue of appointment is to be regarded as exclusively one of status or of contract. The completion of the appointment would appear not to require, in the absence of an express stipulation, any contact with the parties. Thus:

> "In my judgment, what are required to complete an appointment of an arbitrator by agreement of the parties are two matters: first, that the person appointed has accepted to act as arbitrator; and, second, that there is clear evidence of this acceptance and of the date on which it occurred.[39]"

It is desirable that the arbitrator should accept his appointment in writing, although this is not prescribed by the Act, and the appointment will be effective if he does in fact proceed under it without the formality of writing.[40]

16.23 Appointment of arbitrator by the President of the RICS

If the parties are unable to agree, or do not in fact agree, on an arbitrator, either party or both should apply to the President for an appointment. The President makes his appointment from among the members of the Lord Chancellor's panel of arbitrators.[41] It is provided that no application may be made to the President for an appointment unless the application is accompanied by the prescribed fee[42] for an

---

[38] Kennedy L.J. in *Robinson v. Moody* (above) at 18M–19C. The previous edition of this work at page 278 suggested that in all cases the arbitrator's acceptance being notified to the parties was an essential ingredient in the completion of the appointment. Although that passage was approved *obiter* in *Hannaford v. Smallacombe* by Henry L.J. at 11L it was expressly not applied in *Robinson v. Moody*.

[39] Roch L.J. in *Robinson v. Moody* (above) at 20D expressly on the basis that the question is one of status, he then continued with an alternative suggestion as to the appointment being concluded at a different point if the matter rested on contract. (The actual alternative chosen must be viewed with caution as it appears to ignore the established contractual postal rule.)

[40] See *Itez Shipping Pte Ltd v. China Ocean Shipping Co. (The "Jing Hong Hai")* [1989] 2 Lloyd's Rep. 522 where consent to an appointment was inferred from the arbitrators beginning to act in terms of the appointment.

[41] Sched. 11, para. 1(5).

[42] The fee is prescribed, not by the President but by the Minister; see s. 96(1) ("prescribed") and s. 94(1). As the payment of the fee is a statutory condition of the application (Sched. 11, para. 1(2)) an application, although delivered in time, would be invalid if not accompanied by the fee: contrast *Staines Warehousing Co. Ltd v. Montagu Executor & Trustee Co. Ltd* [1986] 1 E.G.L.R. 101, where, although the RICS Guidance Notes required a fee on the application for the appointment of an expert, the lease itself (in contrast with the present statutory provision) did not. The statutory instrument prescribing the fee requires a draft approved by an affirmative resolution of each House of Parliament: s. 94(3). Note that an application is not "made" until it is received. The

application.[43] Such a fee covers any subsequent application for the exercise of the President's functions under Schedule 11 in relation to the arbitration in question (including an application for the appointment in an appropriate case of a new arbitrator).[44] The President must make an appointment as soon as possible after he receives the application, but there is a special provision that, where the application relates to a rent arbitration under section 12 of the 1986 Act, the appointment must not be made earlier than four months before the "next termination date" following the date of the demand for arbitration.[45] The object is to ensure that the circumstances at the date of valuation (which is the "date of the reference", *i.e.* the date when the arbitrator's appointment is completed) do not differ too much from those when the new rent begins to be payable. It may be noted here that a notice under article 9 of the Agricultural Holdings (Arbitration on Notice) Order 1987 requiring arbitration will not be effective three months after the date of that notice unless before the expiry of the three months an arbitrator has been appointed by agreement or an application has been made to the President for an appointment.[46] The President will select an arbitrator from the Lord Chancellor's panel.[47] Where the arbitration relates to a holding in Wales the arbitrator appointed must possess a knowledge of Welsh agricultural conditions and, if either party so requires, a knowledge of the Welsh language.[48] An arbitrator appointed by the President is appointed at the time when the President executed the instrument of appointment: notice to the parties is not necessary to complete the appointment.[49] Any instrument of appointment purporting to be made in the exercise of the President's appointing function and to be signed by or on behalf of the President shall be taken to be such an instrument unless the contrary is shown.[50]

Before making the appointment the President will do his best to make sure that the proposed appointee had no interest in, or connection with, the dispute or the parties which would raise even a suspicion of bias, it being of the greatest importance that justice should not only be done but should be manifestly and undoubtedly seen to be done.[51] In making the appointment, however, the President is acting in an administrative, not in a judicial or even quasi-judicial, capacity.[52] It is not for the President to attempt to decide whether there is a proper claim or not.

---

current Regulations are the Agricultural Holdings (Fee) Regulations (S.I. 1996 No.337) prescribing a fee of £115. The previous Regulations (S.I. 1985 No.1967) prescribed £70.

[43] Sched. 11, para. 1(2).
[44] *ibid.*
[45] Sched. 11, para. 1(3). See note above as to when an application is "made".
[46] S.I. 1987 No.710.
[47] Sched. 11, para. 1(5).
[48] para. 1(4). The forum in which a challenge to the arbitrator's jurisdiction under this head must be made is the County Court, not the High Court: **Jones v. Pembrokeshire CC** [1967] 1 Q.B. 181.
[49] Sched. 11, para. 31; and see **University College, Oxford v. Durdy** [1982] Ch. 413. Para. 31 also makes clear that the periods mentioned in paras 7 and 14 shall start to run from the time of execution, thus rejecting the "benevolent construction" suggested in that case.
[50] para. 32.
[51] *cf.* **R. v. Sussex Justices, ex p. McCarthy** [1924] 1 K.B. 256 at 259, Lord Hewart C.J.; **Metropolitan Properties Co. (FGC) Ltd v. Lannon** [1969] 1 Q.B. 577.
[52] **Ramsay v. McLaren** [1936] S.L.T. 35: *cf.* **University College, Oxford v. Durdy** [1982] Ch. 413.

He will appoint if on the face of it there appears to be a bona fide claim in dispute.[53] The matter must, of course, be one which falls within the arbitrator's jurisdiction. If an arbitrator is appointed by the President to decide upon a dispute which he has no jurisdiction to determine, an application for judicial review could be made, seeking an order of prohibition to restrain him from acting, and, in a proper case, costs may be awarded against the party who asked for the appointment, in the absence of special circumstances.[54] Arbitrators are empowered to take the opinion of the County Court as to whether they have jurisdiction and may make an award as to costs and recover their own remuneration although it is held that they have no jurisdiction.[55] It should be mentioned that, in the case of a rent arbitration under section 12 of the 1986 Act, a demand for arbitration ceases to be effective on the "next termination date" unless before that either an arbitrator has been appointed by agreement between the parties or an application has been made to the President for the appointment of an arbitrator.[56] An arbitrator should not accept an appointment if this time-limit has already expired and the President should not make an appointment in such circumstances.[57]

16.24 **Appointment of arbitrator: new appointment**
If an arbitrator dies, or is incapable of acting, or fails to act for seven days after a written notice from either party requiring him to act, a new arbitrator may be appointed as if no arbitrator had been appointed.[58] Where an arbitrator has been appointed in the place of another arbitrator (whether under this provision or otherwise) the reference in section 12(2) to the date of the reference is to be construed as relating to the date when the original arbitrator was appointed.[59]

16.25 **Revocation of arbitrator's appointment**
An arbitrator's appointment cannot be revoked by one of the parties only but may be revoked by the consent in writing of both.[60] The arbitrator's appointment is not

---

[53] See *Christisons Trustees v. Callender Brodie* (1906) 8 F. 928. *cf. United Co-operative Ltd v. Sun Alliance & London Assurance Co. Ltd* (1986) 282 E.G. 91 (appointment of expert by President) as to limits of President's responsibilities to enquire.
[54] *R. v. Powell* [1925] 1 K.B. 641; *Westwood v. Barnett* 1925 S.C. 624; *R. v. LCC* [1894] 1 Q.B. 453; *R. v. Liverpool JJ, ex p. Roberts* [1960] 1 W.L.R. 585.
[55] Sched. 11, paras 26 and 30.
[56] s. 12(3). The "next termination date" is defined in s. 12(4). It is, in short, the date from which any change in the rent will take effect. See generally Chapter 11.
[57] The President should preferably obtain the necessary information on this point from the applicant. An application is not "made" to the President until it has been received at the offices of the RICS.
[58] Sched. 11, para. 2. Note County Court decision in *Pennington-Ramsden v. McWilliam* [1982] C.L.Y. 28, CC. Form 68 in Part V of this work is a precedent of a notice requiring the arbitrator to act.
[59] Sched. 11, para. 3. This results from an amendment made by the 1984 Act Sched. 3, para. 28(2). It embodies the principle of the Scottish decision in *Dundee Corporation v. Guthrie* 1969 SLT 93; it had not been clear whether this decision would have been followed in England and Wales. It will be noted that para. 3 is a saving provision only in relation to this specific rent arbitration point; but see *Pennington-Ramsden v. McWilliam* [1982] C.L.Y. 28, CC.
[60] Sched. 11, paras 4 and 5. It is submitted that the power of the parties together to revoke the arbitrator's appointment applies to arbitrators appointed by the President as well as

revoked by the death of a party.[61] If the parties manage to settle their differences before the hearing, so that the arbitrator is not required to act, they should revoke his appointment and thus leave matters in a tidy state, unless they wish him to make a consent award. There is no provision enabling an arbitrator to resign once he has taken on the burden of a reference. In case of illness or other disabling circumstance he may get the parties to consent to the revocation of his appointment, or he may become *functus officio* if he fails to act for seven days after a notice from either party requesting him to do so.

Remuneration of the arbitrator 16.26

The arbitrator's remuneration is dealt with in Schedule 11, paragraph 6. Where the arbitrator is appointed by agreement between the parties it is provided that his remuneration will be such amount as may be agreed upon him and by the parties, or, in default of agreement, fixed by the registrar of the County Court (subject to an appeal to the judge) on an application by the arbitrator or either of the parties.[62] An arbitrator would be wise, if considering accepting a contractual appointment, to secure agreement of the parties to his fees or hourly rate and reimbursement of disbursements in advance of accepting the appointment.[63] Nevertheless it is still often the case that an arbitrator is appointed by agreement but simply fixes his own charges and states the amount of fees due when he notifies the parties that his award is ready. The arbitrator does not as a rule part with his award until his charges are paid.[64] There is in practice rarely any difficulty about the acceptance of the arbitrator's charges, but the procedure authorised in paragraph 6 is available if a difficulty should arise.[65] Schedule 11, paragraph 29 safeguards the position of a party who pays to the arbitrator, on taking up the award, more than the award directs him to pay. The award may, for example, direct the other party to pay the costs of the award or part of them. In that event the party taking up the award can recover the appropriate amount from the other party. There is no prescribed scale of remuneration for an arbitrator. Arbitrators have sometimes based their charges on the analogy of the valuation fees, but a time basis is probably more usual and more appropriate. The position where an arbitrator has no jurisdiction is covered by Schedule 11, paragraph 30. When the arbitrator is appointed by the President his remuneration will be such amount as may be agreed upon by the arbitrator and the

---

those appointed by agreement; this appears to have been the opinion of Kerr L.J. in *University College, Oxford v. Durdy* [1982] 3 W.L.R. 94 at 104. Form 69 in Part V of this work is a precedent for this.

[61] Sched. 11, para. 4. There was a doubt about this until it was set at rest by the 1984 Act, Sched. 3, para. 28(4).

[62] Sched. 11, para. 6(a).

[63] There is nothing to stop the parties agreeing a commitment fee for the arbitrator where it is appropriate to the particular case. Once appointed, the arbitrator, in any further discussions about fees, must take extreme care to ensure that any proposal he makes is made openly to both parties otherwise he runs the risk of misconduct: see *K/S Norjarl A/S v. Hyundai Heavy Industries Co. Ltd* [1991] 1 Ll.Rep. 524, CA and *Turner v. Stevenage Borough Council* [1997] 3 W.L.R. 309, CA.

[64] This has been a general practice but (now see s. 56 of the Arbitration Act). As to arbitrator's lien, see *Re Coombes* (1850) 4 Ex. 839; *Ponsford v. Swaine* (1861) J.& H. 433; *R. v. S. Devon Ry* (1850) 15 Q.B. 1043.

[65] For details of procedure, see CCR, Ord. 38, r. 22, and Ord. 25, r. 12.

parties or, in default of agreement, fixed by the President.[66] It has been the practice in fixing the arbitrator's remuneration to include his travelling expenses and the hire of rooms, but not legal expenses incurred by him, *e.g.* in preparing a case for the County Court. The latter expenses should be covered by the arbitrator in his award as to costs and will be taxable as such. Whether the arbitrator is appointed by agreement or by the President, his proper remuneration is recoverable by the arbitrator as a debt due from either of the parties.[67]

16.27 **Statement of Case: 35 day deadline**
It is provided that the parties to the arbitration shall, within 35 days from the appointment of the arbitrator, deliver to him a statement of their respective cases with all necessary particulars.[68] It is further provided that no amendment or addition to the statement or particulars shall be allowed after the expiration of the 35 days except with the consent of the arbitrator, and that a party to the arbitration shall be confined at the hearing to the matters alleged in the statement and particulars delivered to him and any amendment or addition duly made.[69] Arbitrators should not adopt too restrictive an attitude to an application for consent to an amendment or addition. Amendments should be freely allowed if they will enable the other side to know sufficiently the case which they will have to meet; the test is whether the other side will be any worse off than they would have been if the statement of case had been properly drafted in the first instance. Arbitrators should be liberal in consenting so long as injustice is not caused to the opposite party.[70] If, of course, no Statement of Case (or nothing which could reasonably be regarded as a Statement of Case) is delivered within the statutory time-limit, no amendment or addition is then possible.[71] The express power given to allow amendments or additions after the expiry of the 35 days seems clearly to negate the existence of any implied power for the arbitrator to extend time for the delivery of the statement of case itself.[72] The Scottish Land Court, however, on a similar provision, has allowed a late statement to be received with the consent of the other party.[73]

Where the arbitrator is requested to allow leave to amend, and that is a contested application, he should ensure that, before making his decision, he has seen the exact proposed amendments.[74] It is to be expected that the party requesting the amendment, if successful, will be ordered to pay costs occasioned by the

---

[66] Sched. 11, para. 6(b).
[67] Sched. 11, para. 6.
[68] Sched. 11, para. 7. The Scottish Sheriff Court decision in **Robertson's Trustees v. Cunningham** 1951 S.L.T. 89 (Sh. Ct.) as to the need to deliver two documents, a "statement of claim" and "particulars" is incorrect: see (1965) 115 L.J. 135.
[69] para. 7(a) and (b).
[70] **E.D. and A.D. Cooke-Bourne (Farms) Ltd v. Mellows** [1983] Q.B. 104; see particularly remarks by Cumming-Bruce L.J. [1983] Q.B. 104 at 110 and Templeman L.J. at 124. In that case the arbitrator should have followed a "supplemental statement of case".
[71] See County Court case of **Church Commissioners for England v. Matthews** (1979) 251 E.G. 1074, CC.
[72] There is a series of County Court decisions to this effect. The older ones are referred to in a previous edition of this work: see 12th ed., p. 179, note 57. More recent ones are the **Church Commissioners** case (above) and **Richards v. Allinson** (1978) 249 E.G. 59, CC.
[73] **Suggett v. Shaw** (1985) Sutherland R.N. 392.
[74] This is the practice of the Courts: see notes to the RSC, Ord. 20, r. 5.

amendment itself. However if the application is contested, and the party opposing the amendment is unsuccessful, the costs of any contested hearing should be ordered to be paid by the unsuccessful party. This still leaves the person seeking the amendment to pay the other costs occasioned by it. Where the amendment is allowed on the day of the hearing, the other party should be given an opportunity to consider the amendment and if necessary amend his own case and adduce additional evidence: in particular the arbitrator should listen favourably to any necessary request in consequence of the amendment for an adjournment in order to obtain additional evidence.[75]

Drafting the Statement of Case 16.28

The purpose of the Statement of Case is to allow each party the opportunity to put forward his own case and this primary document is not necessarily to be drawn with the elaborateness of a pleading intended for use by a Court. Nor is it the appropriate place to set out by anticipation a defence to or a rebuttal of the other party's case.[76] For the most part the Statement of Case may be expected to be a simple document setting out the main facts and issues and identifying what if any remedy is requested of the arbitrator. It is not necessary to request costs nor to reserve the right to call evidence (though some precedents do this).[77]

It is not laid down how detailed the particulars must be, but clearly something considerably more detailed than information given in the notice under section 83(2) is required in the case of claims arising on the termination of the tenancy.[78] The particulars should set out all the individual improvements and tenant-right matters, or, on the other side, all the individual items of dilapidations for which claims are being made. A copy of the contract of tenancy should be annexed. Supporting evidence, *e.g.* vouchers, receipted accounts and so forth, is not required at this pleading stage, but it would assist the arbitrator to know in advance of the hearing what matters are agreed. The statement should make it clear whether claims are based on terms of the contract of tenancy or on statutory provisions. A conditional statement is not valid nor can particulars delivered by one party be relied on in support of the other party's case.[79]

Obtaining a copy of the other party's Statement of Case 16.29

There is at present no statutory requirement that each party should supply the other with a copy of his Statement of Case, but the arbitrator should remedy this

---

[75] *J. Leavey and Co. v. Hirst* [1944] K.B. 24, CA illustrates the practice of the Courts.
[76] *Earl of Plymouth v. Glamorgan County Council* (1974) 232 E.G. 1235, CC.
[77] Form 70 in Part V of this work is given as an example, as is Form 71 (in relation to a milk quota claim).
[78] It was pointed out in *Cooke-Bourne (Farms) Ltd v. Mellows*, (above), at 116 of Q.B. report, that the old 1923 Act cases, under the "one-stage" procedure, *Re O'Connor and Brewin's Arbitration* [1933] 1 K.B. 20 and *Spreckley v. Leicestershire CC* [1934] 1 K.B. 366, can still give useful guidance as to "particulars". This is "provided that the arbitrator focuses his attention on the sufficiency of the particulars given by the claimant, not only in his original statement of case but also in the statement of case which has been amended or been the subject of addition on supplemental statements" (Cumming-Bruce L.J.).
[79] See *Church Commissioners for England v. Matthews*, (above).

omission by asking each party to furnish him with an additional copy for transmissions to the other and, when he has received both statements in duplicate, send to each party a copy of his opponent's statement.

16.30 Consequence of not delivering a Statement of Case within the 35 day deadline

If a party fails to deliver a Statement of Case within the 35 days allowed, he is precluded by paragraph 7(b) of Schedule 11 from putting forward any positive case at the hearing. This provision may be compared with the rules of pleading that failure to serve a statement of claim or defence may result in the dismissal of the action or the entry of judgment against the defendant, as the case may be, but it is extremely inflexible. The arbitrator is given no discretion. The party in default may cross-examine his opponent and the latter's witnesses, with a view to demolishing or reducing the opponent's claims, but he cannot advance his own.[80]

The statutory inhibition cannot be circumvented by giving effect to his claim as a "set-off".[81]

16.31 Communication with the parties

The golden rule is that an arbitrator should have no correspondence or dealing with one party without the knowledge of the other. It is a safe practice, which should be invariably followed, to see that when one party sends a communication to the arbitrator, even on some trivial or innocuous matter, the other party should receive a copy, and to send copies to both parties of any communication from the arbitrator, however routine or trivial. The arbitrator should go to any lengths to avoid the slightest suspicion that he is acting unjudicially. He is a judge and his conduct must be, in a judicial sense, immaculate. Communication with the parties by telephone should be avoided.

16.32 Challenge to the arbitrator's jurisdiction

The arbitrator may be faced before or at the outset of the hearing with a contention by one of the parties that his appointment is invalid or that for some other reason he has no jurisdiction. In order to resolve this matter the arbitrator may state in the form of a special case for the opinion of the County Court any question as to his jurisdiction; and he must do so if so directed by the judge on an application made by either party.[82] An arbitrator is not, however, bound to state a case (unless directed to do so) every time his jurisdiction is challenged, although, particularly when the issue of jurisdiction turns upon abstruse legal points, it may in some circumstances be the wise course to take. Arbitrators, like other Tribunals of limited jurisdiction, are entitled to inquire into their own jurisdiction, with a view to deciding whether to continue with the arbitration, but they can never give themselves jurisdiction by deciding that they have it if in fact they have not.[83]

---

[80] *Collett v. Deeley* (1950) 100 L.J. 108, CC; *Stewart v. Brims* 1969 S.L.T. 2 (Sh. Ct.).

[81] *Re Bennion and National Provincial Bank's Arbitration* (1965) 115 L.J. 302. It is possible that the Lord Chancellor under the powers given him by s. 84 of the Act may rationalise these provisions.

[82] Sched. 11, para. 26. See *F.R. Evans (Leeds) Ltd v. Webster* (1962) 184 E.G. 269, CC.

[83] *Christopher Brown Ltd v. Genossenschaft Oesterreichischer Waldbesitzer R GmbH*

Their decision as to jurisdiction, if erroneous, can have no effect on the parties' rights. An arbitrator, faced with a doubt or challenge as to his jurisdiction, must use his judgment about the appropriate action in the light of all the circumstances. He must make up his mind either:

(a) to state a case for the opinion of the County Court on jurisdiction;

(b) to decide that he has no jurisdiction and make an order as to costs only; or

(c) to make an award on the assumption that he has jurisdiction, leaving it to be determined, if necessary, in court proceedings whether his assumption was correct.[84]

An arbitrator has a clear jurisdiction to decide matters which are incidental, ancillary or collateral to the main issue before him, *e.g.* to determine in a rental arbitration who is the landlord and whether the tenancy is a lease for a fixed term or a tenancy from year to year.[85] The High Court does not have jurisdiction to decide questions relating to the arbitrator's jurisdiction, this being a matter, like misconduct and error of law, which Parliament has entrusted to the County Court.[86]

Fixing the hearing 16.33
The arbitrator should pay reasonable regard to the convenience of the parties in making arrangements for the time and place of the hearing. If he were to exercise his discretion in a wholly unreasonable way, so as in effect to deny one party the opportunity of being heard, the award would be liable to be set aside.

There may arise the need to postpone or to adjourn the hearing and the arbitrator should be extremely careful to deal with any requests relating to this in a patient and reasonable way. In particular, great care should be taken to deal properly with any request for an adjournment so as to enable a party to secure legal representation. A request for this purpose was made, in one case by the tenant in person, as the parties were assembling and out of earshot of the landlord's solicitor.

[1954] 1 Q.B. 8 at 12–13 (Devlin J.); ***R. v. Pugh (Judge), ex p. Graham*** [1951] K.B. 623 at 629; and for the general principles the classic judgment of Devlin J. in ***R. v. Fulham, Hammersmith & Kensington Rent Tribunal, ex p. Zerek*** [1951] 2 K.B. 1; *cf.* ***Re Purkiss' Application*** [1962] 1 W.L.R. 902 at 914. See also ***Horton v. Kurzke*** [1971] 1 W.L.R. 769, where the arbitrator's decision that he had no jurisdiction meant that he found that there was no agricultural tenancy.

[84] *e.g.*, in a possession action if the question of jurisdiction turned on the validity of a notice to quit.

[85] ***Kirby v. Robinson*** (1965) 195 E.G. 363. He could decide this issue as a preliminary point: ***Cormack v. McIldowie's Executors*** 1972 S.L.T. (Notes) 40. Naturally, if difficult points of law are involved he will consider whether to state a case.

[86] 1986 Act, Sched. 11, paras 26 and 27. And see ***Jones v. Pembrokeshire County Council*** [1967] 1 Q.B. 181, following ***Re Jones and Carter*** [1922] 2 Ch. 599. High Court control

The arbitrator's refusal[87] resulted in the arbitrator's award being set aside for misconduct.[88]

16.34 The arbitrator's power to proceed *ex parte*

It is, of course, one of the most fundamental rules, not only of arbitrations but of all judicial proceedings, that both sides must be fairly heard, and each in the presence of the other: *audi alteram partem*.[89] A party is not, however, at liberty to frustrate the proceedings by obstruction, and all arbitrators have an inherent power and a duty, in a proper case and after taking proper steps, to proceed *ex parte*, *i.e.* in the absence of the obstructive party.[90] The arbitrator must judge for himself when it is right to take this somewhat drastic action.[91] It should not be taken lightly, but it is justifiable where the arbitrator is convinced that a party is deliberately setting out to defeat the object of the reference. The *ex parte* hearing should not take place without due warning. If, for example, one of the parties fails to attend a duly arranged hearing, properly notified, and the arbitrator is satisfied of his obstructive intention, the arbitrator should adjourn the proceedings and give the absent party clear notice that the hearing will proceed at a specified time and place whether that party is present or not.[92] A reasonable length of notice must be given and the arbitrator should do his best to ensure that the time and place fixed are such as to give both parties a reasonable opportunity of attending. Where the arbitrator does have to proceed *ex parte*, after taking all these reasonable steps, he has the difficult task of being scrupulously fair, and appearing to be so, towards both parties. He must neither accept with a less rigorous scrutiny than normal the case of the party

---

was impliedly removed by the express conferment of jurisdiction on the County Court.

[87] "Well we are all here, so let's carry on and see how we get on" (***Thomas v. Official Solicitor*** [1983] 1 E.G.L.R. 1 at 4C).

[88] The CA in that case applied the words in ***Rotheray and Sons Ltd v. Carlo Bedarida and Co.*** [1961] 1 Lloyd's Rep. 220 of McNair J. at 224: "The more difficult question, however, is whether the extent of that irregularity is such as to justify interference by this court either by way of setting aside the award or remitting the award. The determination of that issue, as it seems to me, depends upon whether the court is satisfied that there may have been—not must have been—or that this irregularity may have caused—not must have caused—a substantial miscarriage of justice that would be sufficient to justify the setting aside or remitting of the award, unless those resisting the setting aside or remission could show that no other award could properly have been made than that which was in fact made, notwithstanding the irregularity".

[89] Authority is hardly required, but *cf.* ***Harvey v. Shelton*** (1844) 7 Beav. 455 at 462; ***Oswald v. Earl Grey*** (1855) 24 L.J.Q.B. 69; ***Re Gregson and Armstrong*** (1894) 70 L.T. 106; ***Bache v. Billingham*** [1894] 1 Q.B. 107 at 110, 112, 113; ***Re Brien and Brien*** [1910] 2 Ir.R 84; ***R. v. Birkenhead J. ex p. Fisher*** [1962] 1 W.L.R. 1410; ***R. v. Gravesend J., ex p. Sheldon*** [1968] 1 W.L.R. 1699; ***R. v. Kingston-upon-Hull Rent Tribunal, ex p. Black*** (1949) 65 T.L.R. 209; ***Malloch v. Aberdeen Corp.*** 1971 1 W.L.R. 1578; ***The Myron*** [1970] 1 Q.B. 527.

[90] ***Wood v. Leake*** (1806) 12 Ves. 412; ***Wenlock v. River Dee Co.*** (1883) 53 L.J.Q.B. 208. There is an inherent power to proceed *ex parte* in a proper case in all arbitrations; of course, after most careful consideration.

[91] In ***Beckett v. South Devon Homes (Teignmouth) Ltd*** (1971) 220 E.G. 33 awards made *ex parte* were set aside because items were included which had been specifically reserved for determination at a later date. There was no misconduct in the decision to hear *ex parte*.

[92] ***Gladwin v. Chilcote*** (1841) 9 Dowl. 550.

present nor go out of his way to act as an advocate for the case of the absent party. "His function was to hold the scales as evenly as he could and to act fairly and judicially in the conduct of the hearing."[93]

Arbitrator's correct approach 16.35

An arbitrator is not likely to go far astray in the control of the hearing if he remembers that he is a judge and that, although he is dealing with a specialised and limited subject-matter, his adjudicatory function is identical in substance to that of a judge of the High Court.[94] He must always act fairly and in a wholly judicial spirit. If, for example, one party appears by counsel without having given the other party due notice of his intention to do so, the arbitrator should be ready to grant that other party an adjournment in order to instruct counsel.[95] He should in general be ready to grant an adjournment where one party is genuinely taken by surprise and would be at a serious disadvantage if not given extra time; but an arbitrator should be wary of tactical applications for adjournments made for purposes of delay.[96] Arbitrations may be conducted in a more or less formal manner. There is certainly no need to reproduce the formal atmosphere of a trial in the courts, but informality should not be allowed to go so far as to imperil the judicial character of the proceedings. The arbitrator should scrupulously avoid any indiscretion, such as

---

[93] Dunn L.J. in *Fox v. P.G. Wallfair Ltd* [1981] 2 Lloyd's Rep. 514 at 528. The arbitrator in this case, with the best of intentions and conceiving it to be his duty, acted as the unacknowledged advocate of the absent party. The award was set aside and he was removed. This is an instructive case for arbitrators especially when one side is not represented. *cf.* observations of Leggatt J. in *Top Shop Estates Ltd v. C. Danino* (1984) 273 E.G. 197.

[94] Although it is written for commercial arbitrators there is still helpful guidance to be found in the 2nd edition of the Bernstein and Wood, *Handbook of Arbitration Practice*, (Sweet and Maxwell, 1993). The third edition, referred to in Chapter 6, is written under the shadow of the Arbitration Act 1996 and is therefore less easy to use for the arbitrator under the Agricultural Holdings Act 1986.

[95] *cf. Whatley v. Morland* (1834) 2 Dowl. 249.

[96] *Eastham v. Tyler* (1847) 2 Saund. & C. 136; *cf. Societe Franco-Tunisienne d'Armement-Tunis v. Government of Ceylon* [1959] 1 W.L.R. 787 (In this case the CA remitted a case to arbitrators for reconsideration as there had been a breach of the rules of natural justice where the arbitrators failed to give one party a sufficient opportunity to reframe their case in the light of an unexpected development). See also *Ostreicher v. Secretary of State for the Environment* [1978] 1 W.L.R. 610, CA; *London Supplementary Benefits Appeal Tribunal, ex p. Bullen* (1976) 120 S.J. 437, DC; *R. v. Thames Magistrates, ex p. Polemis* [1974] 1 W.L.R. 1371. (In this case a conviction was quashed as being made in breach of the rules of natural justice where the defence had not been given sufficient time to prepare their case. Lord Widgery C.J. at A-C stated: "... of the versions of breach of the rules of natural justice with which in this court we are dealing constantly, perhaps the most common today is the allegation that the defence were prejudiced because they were not given a fair and reasonable opportunity to present their case to the court, and of course the opportunity to present a case to the court is not confined to being given an opportunity to stand up and say what you want to say; it necessarily extends to a reasonable opportunity to prepare your case before you are called upon to present it. A mere allocation of court time is of no value if the party in question is deprived of the opportunity of getting his tackle in order and being able to present his case in the fullest sense".); *R. v. Rent Assessment Committee for London, ex p. Ellis-Rees* (1982) 262 E.G. 1298.

having luncheon with one of the parties during the hearing, even if the indiscretion is not as gross as in **Re Hopper**.[97] The arbitrator should either avoid all social contact with the parties during the proceedings or make sure that both parties are present. Even if they are both present the arbitrator should avoid accepting hospitality from one of them. The arbitrator should particularly be aware that if the parties are using the same facilities as the arbitrator at lunchtime there is a risk that informal contact with them will take place: this should be avoided.[98] It goes without saying that the arbitrator must be free from any interest which might tend to bias his judgment or which might even give rise to a reasonable suspicion of bias, although unfounded. *Nemo iudex in causa sua*.[99] An interest arising after appointment might render him unfit.[1]

16.36 Procedure at the hearing: general points

Arbitrations are private judicial proceedings; either party or the arbitrator may object to the presence of strangers. The parties themselves, persons claiming through them, professional advisers and persons assisting the parties (*e.g.* a son who helps his father with his accounts) and, of course, witnesses are entitled to be present in the normal case.[2] The order of the procedure normally follows that of a

---

[97] (1867) L.R. 2 Q.B. 367 (Umpire becoming intoxicated at dinner given by one of the parties, the other not being present. The subject of the reference was mentioned but in a jocular manner. Surprisingly, the award (in favour of the host) was not set aside on that ground). See also **Re Maunder** (1883) 49 L.T. 535; **Moseley v. Simpson** (1873) L.R. 16 Eq. 226.

[98] The arbitrator should not be shy of enquiring where the parties intend to have lunch, so that he may make his own different arrangements.

[99] *cf.* **Metropolitan Properties Co. (FGC) Ltd v. Lannon** [1969] 1 Q.B. 577. (In this case, although there was no allegation of actual bias, the circumstances of the legal chairman and his connection with tenants on rent reviews of another block of flats owned by the same group of companies as the landlord in the rent assessment application before him was such that it created a reasonable impression that he was biased and accordingly afford a ground for the decision to be quashed and remitted to another assessment committee). Of course if both parties are fully aware of an interest and accepted the position before appointment there is no ground for complaint; but the acceptance should be made or recorded in writing. See also **Sellar v. Highland Ry** (1919) 56 S.L.R. 216, HL; **Malmesbury Ry v. Budd** (1876) 2 Ch. D. 113.

[1] **Blanchard v. Sun Fire Office** (1890) 6 T.L.R. 365; **Edinburgh Magistrates v. Lowine** (1903) 5 F. 711. The test is objective, *i.e.* what a reasonable man would have inferred from the arbitrator's conduct: *cf.* **Tracomin SA v. Gibbs Nathaniel (Canada) Ltd** [1985] 1 Ll. Rep. 586.

[2] See **Haigh v. Haigh** (1861) 31 L.J. Ch. 420. In fact any person, whether he is a professional man or not, may attend the hearing as a friend of either party, may take notes, may quietly make suggestions and give advice: **Collier v. Hicks** (1831) 2 B.&A. 663 at 669, Lord Tenterden C.J.; **McKenzie v. McKenzie** [1971] P. 33, CA (hence the expression "McKenzie man"). It is entirely a matter for the arbitrator's discretion whether witnesses should remain outside the arbitration room until required to give their evidence or should be allowed to be present while other witnesses are being examined; *cf.* **Moore v. Lambeth County Court Registrar** [1969] 1 W.L.R. 141. (In this case the CA rejected a complaint that natural justice was violated by witnesses being allowed to remain in court and in the sight and hearing of other witnesses as they gave their evidence. Edmund Davies L.J. at 142D-G stated: "No rule of law requires that in a trial the witnesses to be called by one side must all remain out of court until their turn to give testimony arises. This is purely a matter within the discretion of the court. Indeed, if the court rules that witnesses should be out of

court action. The claimant or his advocate opens his case and produces his evidence. When his case is closed the opposite party, if he adduces evidence, proceeds by himself or his advocate to open his case and to comment on his opponent's. He then produces his evidence and sums up his case. The claimant has a right of reply. The procedure in regard to examination, cross-examination and re-examination is the same as in the Court. If the respondent offers no evidence the claimant or his advocate sums up his case after his evidence has been given, and the respondent replies. If there is a counterclaim it should be dealt with as a claim according to the above procedure after the main claim has been dealt with. It is one of the duties of an arbitrator to take proper notes of the hearing. He has no authority to employ a shorthand writer at the expense of the parties unless they have consented. He should give a specific direction in his award in regard to the payment of these costs for the purpose of taxation. The parties' consent to the employment of a shorthand writer should be recorded in writing.

Long hours of hearing should be avoided. No doubt from the best of motives and in an endeavour to save the parties coming back on another day, agricultural arbitrators will frequently sit for hours far longer than they should do. There are good reasons why the Courts commence proceedings in the late morning and it is simply not acceptable to do, as some agricultural arbitrators will, a day's sitting which runs from 9a.m. to 7 or 7.30 in the evening. It is not generally helpful at all to start at 9a.m., particularly on the first morning of a hearing and it is never acceptable to put pressure on parties to start early as though they were somehow otherwise wasting time. Not only is there is a need frequently for parties to travel to the hearing or, in the case of a farmer, to execute his essential tasks before the hearing begins but in addition to that there are frequently matters which need to be discussed when everyone is together and there is no convenient time for this discussion to take place except immediately prior to the hearing. It is not appropriate for parties to have to explain why they need the time since this will invariably involve matters of detail which the arbitrator should not be hearing. A convenient time to begin is usually 10a.m. and, if both parties are volunteering to start at 9.30, that time may be adopted. If the hearing begins before 10a.m. and the arbitrator intends to sit until 1p.m. then there should be at least a 15 minute break

---

court and a witness nevertheless remains inside, while the trial judge may well express his grave displeasure over such disobedience, he has no right to refuse to hear the evidence of such a witness ... whether or not witnesses are to remain in court being solely a matter of discretion, judges vary upon that as upon many other matters. If I may be purely personal for one moment, my own preference in cases which, if not actually arising under the criminal jurisdiction, yet, like contempt proceedings, are certainly on the fringe or savour of a criminal prosecution, is for the witness to be out of court. But I know other judges who take exactly the opposite view; they prefer the witnesses to remain in court so that they may observe their reaction when they hear the evidence of other witnesses. It cannot rightly be said that, if witnesses are allowed to remain in court, justice cannot be done ..."); and see ***R. v. Smith (Joan)*** [1968] 1 W.L.R. 636, CA. (In criminal proceedings the normal rule and practice is that the defendant must be called before other defence witnesses and a conviction was not overturned when defending counsel was not allowed to call the other witnesses before his own client).

during which refreshments should be made available. Equally the arbitrator should not pressure the parties to have less than one hour at lunchtime: again, this is not time wasted and the parties and their representatives invariably make progress during this time. Arbitrators sometimes forget that the need to take instructions during the breaks allows the arbitration itself to be conducted expeditiously. The arbitrator should normally bring proceedings to a close at 5.30p.m. There is really no excuse for going on beyond this time and, if the arbitrator absolutely must do it, it is essential that there is a late afternoon break with refreshments. After 5.30 it is almost invariably the case that non-lawyers, including the arbitrator, are suffering from exhaustion and lack of concentration, frequently coupled with low blood sugar. It is no real saving of time since cross-examination becomes bad tempered, witnesses go to pieces and the arbitrator's note is likely to deteriorate. The hearing should not be an ordeal for the parties themselves and the arbitrator should never press on if legal representatives indicate that a witness may be too exhausted to go on beyond 5.30p.m.[3] If, whether through long hours or from any other cause, a witness appears to be physically distressed, the arbitrator must intervene and impose a short adjournment during which the witness can have a glass of water and a break. Justice is not served by inducing the kind of physical stress which the Courts, by their practices, have banished. If the conclusion of a case requires no more than an additional half hour's sitting up to 6p.m. then it would seem, unless there has been a very early start, sensible to sit until 6p.m.

16.37 **Rules of evidence**
The rules of evidence in an arbitration are the same as in an action at law and should, subject to any agreement between the parties, be strictly enforced by the arbitrator.[4] There is no general relaxation of the rules, as there is in the case of Agricultural Land Tribunals,[5] but there is nothing to prevent parties from agreeing to dispense with strict proof in regard to particular matters. The acceptance of inadmissible evidence or the rejection of relevant admissible evidence could in some circumstances constitute misconduct on the part of the arbitrator and result in the award being set aside. It is, therefore, essential that arbitrators should be familiar with the laws of evidence. It is not, however, proposed to try to summarise the rules here. Attention is drawn to the Civil Evidence Acts 1968, 1972 and 1995. The last of these made provision for the admissibility of hearsay evidence and it

---

[3] This is usually because the witness will have risen extremely early, possibly at 5a.m., to do his farming work and in addition to that may be elderly. Often, not wishing to disoblige the arbitrator, such a person will insist that he is capable of carrying on, when it is quite clear that he is not.

[4] *Re Enoch and Zaretsky, Bock & Co.* [1910] 1 K.B. 327 ("It is plain that the courts do allow considerable latitude, in practice at any rate, to the reception of evidence by umpires, but to say as a general proposition that they are not bound by the rules of evidence appears to me to be entirely misleading and likely to produce very great injustice": Farwell L.J. at 336); cf. *A.G. v. Davison* (1825) Mc.Cl.&Y. 160; *Williams v. Wallis & Cox* [1914] 2 K.B. 478. (In this case an arbitrator was found guilty of misconduct in that he excluded (wrongly) relevant evidence).

[5] See r. 28 of the Agricultural Land Tribunals Rules 1978 in Sched. 1 to the Agricultural Land Tribunals (Rules) Order 1978 (S.I. 1978 No.259).

applies to arbitration.⁶ The 1995 Act is now in force.⁷ Attention is drawn to the provision in Order 38, rule 20 of the Rules of the Supreme Court for hearsay notices to be served.⁸

Parties to the arbitration 16.38

The parties to the arbitration and all persons claiming through them respectively are required, subject to any legal objection, to submit to being examined by the arbitrator, on oath or affirmation, in relation to the matters in dispute. Subject, again, to any legal objection, the parties and such persons must produce all samples and documents within their profession or power which may be required, or called for, and do all other things which during the proceedings the arbitrator may require.⁹ Although this wording, when contrasted with that applicable to witnesses generally,¹⁰ suggests that the arbitrator is bound to examine the parties and persons claiming through them on oath or affirmation, it has been held (it is submitted, correctly) in a Scottish Sheriff Court that he has a discretion to do so or not.¹¹ "Documents" will include accounts and vouchers, and the arbitrator may require the latter to be verified as well as produced.¹² The word "power" in the expression "possession or power" refers to evidence which is not in a party's actual possession but which he is legally able to compel a third person to produce. Under words almost the same as those in Schedule 11, paragraph 8 ("do all other things", etc.) it has been held that an arbitrator has power to order discovery either by the making of affidavits of documents or by the answering of interrogatories on oath.¹³ The reference in paragraph 8 to "all persons claiming through them" indicates that assignees of one or other of the parties to the arbitration may be present and take part in it. Thus, if before the hearing a tenant assigned his tenancy (assuming that he is not precluded from doing to) the assignee would be entitled to take part in the arbitration (and bound under this paragraph to co-operate in it) although the assignor would remain a party. The award would have to be made as between the original parties, but the tenant's assignee would be bound by it.¹⁴

Witnesses at the arbitration 16.39

The arbitrator may, if he thinks fit, examine witnesses on oath or affirmation, and he is given a general power to administer oaths and take affirmations.¹⁵ A person

---

⁶ s. 11 of the 1995 Act.
⁷ All sections other than 10 and 16(5) came into force on January 31, 1997 (S.I. 1996 No.3217).
⁸ Changes to Ord. 38, which are relevant to the 1995 Act are to be found in the Second Cumulative Supplement to the 1997 edition of the *Supreme Court Practice*.
⁹ Sched. 11, para. 8. Form 73 in Part V of this work is a precedent for a notice by the arbitrator to produce documents.
¹⁰ para. 9 ("shall, if the arbitrator thinks fit").
¹¹ *MacLean v. Chalmers Property Investment Co. Ltd* 1951 S.L.T. (Sh. Ct.) 71, the wording is similar in the Scottish Act.
¹² *cf. Atkyns v. Baldwyn* (1816) 1 Stark, 209.
¹³ *Kursell v. Timber Operators and Contractors Ltd* [1923] 2 K.B. 202. In this case both the making of affidavits and the power to call for interrogatories on oath were held within the powers of an arbitrator acting under the Arbitration Act 1889.
¹⁴ Sched. 11, para. 19 to the 1986 Act and s. 96(6).
¹⁵ Sched. 11, para. 9. Form 72 in Part V of this work contains forms of oath or affirmation

who wilfully gives false evidence on oath or affirmation is liable to be prosecuted for perjury. There are provisions for compelling the attendance of witnesses.[16] The provisions of County Court Rules in regard to the issuing of witness summonses apply, subject to any modifications prescribed by such rules, for the purposes of the arbitration as if it were an action or matter in the County Court.[17] The application for a witness summons is made to the appropriate County Court offices. The arbitrator himself cannot issue a witness summons. Any person who is summoned under these rules as a witness and who refuses or neglects, without sufficient cause, to appear or produce any documents required by the summons, or who refuses to be sworn or give evidence, is liable to such fine as the County Court judge may direct.[18] This is subject to the condition that at that time of service of the summons he was paid or tendered his expenses, including (where prescribed by County Court Rules) compensation for loss of time.[19] Any person present (although not summoned) at an arbitration who, being required to give evidence, refuses to be sworn or give evidence is liable to a similar fine.[20] The County Court judge may direct that the fine or some part of it shall, after deducting costs, be used to indemnify the party injured by the refusal or neglect.[21] There are special provisions, which need not be set out here, for securing the evidence of prisoners, whether serving a sentence or committed for trial, or confined under civil process.[22] An arbitrator may properly take the evidence of a sick or infirm person at that person's residence.[23] It should be noted that the arbitrator has no power himself to call a witness without the consent of the parties. It is for the parties alone to decide what witnesses to call, the arbitrator's role being judicial, not inquisitorial.[24]

16.40 Valuer-advocate

The arbitrator should ensure that valuer-advocates distinguish clearly and sharply between their functions as advocates and as witnesses. If they give evidence they

---

for a witness in an arbitration.

[16] There are interesting restrictions in the High Court on the use of a *subpoena duces tecum* in arbitrations. Such a subpoena will only be issued for a legitimate purpose and is subject to the same restriction as discovery in an action is namely that the documents in question must be necessary for fairly disposing of the matter and to the extent that it would be oppressive to order production (**Sunderland Steamship P. & I. Association v. Gatoil International Inc.** [1988] 1 Lloyd's Rep. 180). However where a witness expresses himself in a materially different sense when acting for different sides objections of privacy and confidentiality will be overridden in the public interest, but a general "fishing expedition" will not be allowed (**London and Leeds Estates Ltd v. Paribus Ltd (No.2)** [1995] 1 E.G.L.R. 102).

[17] para. 10 and CCR, Ord. 20, r. 12.
[18] para. 11(1).
[19] para. 11(3).
[20] para. 11(3)(b).
[21] para. 11(4).
[22] paras 12 and 13.
[23] *Tillam v. Copp* (1847) 5 C.B. 211.
[24] *Re Enoch and Zaretsky, Bock & Co.* [1910] 1 K.B. 327; *Fallon v. Calvert* [1960] 2 Q.B. 201 at 204. (But in this case it was also held that where a witness had given evidence the judge could recall him without thereby adopting an inquisitorial role).

should take the oath and move to the seat reserved for witnesses, at which point they will be liable to cross-examination. Any views on value which they may express while acting as advocates are not evidence and must not be allowed to slip through as such. It might seem somewhat formal to require a valuer-advocate to demonstrate physically in the manner suggested the distinction between his two roles, but otherwise muddle is only too likely to result. The combination of the roles in a successful and unobjectionable manner requires a degree of maturity and skill in all but simple cases.

Evidence at arbitrations: "without prejudice" correspondence 16.41

Correspondence properly marked "without prejudice" should not be read at the arbitration unless both parties agree. If one party improperly attempts to read such correspondence the other party should immediately object, with "a bold and unequivocal protest",[25] and the arbitrator should order the offending party to stop. The arbitrator should pay no regard to any part which he has heard. The failure of the arbitrator to exclude such correspondence in these circumstances would be misconduct which might lead to the award being set aside.[26] There is a very large amount of case law dealing with this subject and this book intends only to highlight the problem. A helpful summary of certain rules is to be found in *South Shropshire District Council v. Amos*.[27] The rule against the reception in evidence of "without prejudice" offers does not prevent such an offer being put in evidence if it has in fact been accepted and resulted in a binding contract. The rule is intended to protect negotiations, not to suppress evidence of a concluded contract.[28] Although the "without prejudice" restriction would normally cover communications relating to costs, it is possible by an express reservation, in the original "without prejudice" marking, to exclude such communications from the restriction (the "Calderbank exception").[29]

Evidence at arbitrations: past condition of holding or buildings 16.42

The physical condition of the holding or buildings thereon at some date prior to the hearing, *e.g.* when the outgoing tenant quitted, may be a material fact but may not

---

[25] *Shield Properties & Investments Ltd v. Anglo-Overseas Transport Co. Ltd* (1984) 273 E.G. 69, Bingham J. at 73.
[26] *cf. Walker v. Wilsher* (1889) 23 Q.B.D. 335; *Stotesbury v. Turner* [1943] K.B. 370.
[27] [1986] 2 E.G.L.R. 194 and in particular Parker L.J. at 195/6: "In order to avoid any possibility of future unnecessary disputes about such matters we conclude by stating that we agree with the learned judge (a) that the heading 'without prejudice' does not conclusively or automatically render a document so marked privileged; (b) that, if privilege is claimed but challenged, the court can look at a document so headed in order to determine its nature; and (c) that privilege can attach to a document headed 'without prejudice' even if it is an opening shot. The rule is, however, not limited to documents which are offers. It attaches to all documents which are marked 'without prejudice' and form part of negotiations, whether or not they are themselves offers, unless the privilege is defeated on some other ground as was the case in *Re Daintrey*". The latter case is reported at [1893] 2 Q.B. 116 and refers to a document which was held to be a clear act of bankruptcy which could be put in evidence on the hearing of the bankruptcy petition.
[28] *Tomlin v. Standard Telephones and Cables* [1969] 1 W.L.R. 1378, CA.
[29] See *Cutts v. Head* [1984] Ch. 290, CA. The "Calderbank exception" comes from *Calderbank v. Calderbank* [1976] Fam. 93,CA, but is now of general application:

be ascertainable by inspection at the date of the hearing owing to repairs or improvements carried out subsequently. In such a case the arbitrator is not merely entitled but bound to hear any relevant evidence tendered in regard to such past condition.[30] It is, of course, entirely a matter for him to decide what weight is to be given to the evidence in question.[31]

16.43 **Evidence at arbitrations: stamping of documents**

Attention is drawn to the terms of section 14 of the Stamp Act 1891.[32] Very few leases will escape stamp duty.[33] It is the arbitrator's responsibility to see that documents which are put in as evidence are properly stamped if they attract stamp duty. If the document is not stamped, or is insufficiently stamped, the arbitrator must not receive it in evidence unless it is one which may be stamped after execution.[34] In the latter case it may be received in evidence if the proper stamp duty and appropriate penalty are paid. The safe course is for the arbitrator to require a deposit forthwith to cover the total amount due, as he is liable to account for it to the Commissioners of Inland Revenue. It is usual in court actions to accept an undertaking from the solicitor for the party tendering the document to pay the amount as soon as it is ascertained, and as the solicitor is an officer of the court and the court has permanent machinery for ensuring that the undertaking is observed,

---

Megarry V.-C. in *Computer Machinery Co. Ltd v. Drescher* [1983] 1 W.L.R. 1379 at 1383.

[30] *cf. Williams v. Wallis and Cox* [1914] 2 K.B. 478.

[31] A record duly made under s. 22 could be valuable.

[32] **14. Terms upon which instruments not duly stamped may be received in evidence.**
(1) Upon the production of an instrument chargeable with any duty as evidence in any court of civil judicature in any part of the U.K., or before any arbitrator or referee, notice shall be taken by the judge arbitrator, or referee of any omission or insufficiency of the stamp thereon, and if the instrument is one which may legally be stamped after the execution thereof, it may, on payment to the officer of the court whose duty it is to read the instrument, or to the arbitrator or referee, of the amount of the unpaid duty, and the penalty payable on stamping the same, and of a further sum of one pound, be received in evidence, saving all just exceptions on other grounds. (2) The officer, or arbitrator, or referee receiving the duty and penalty shall give a receipt for the same, and make an entry in a book kept for that purpose of the payment and of the amount thereof, and shall communicate to the Commissioners the name or title of the proceedings in which, and of the party from whom, he received the duty and penalty, and the date and description of the instrument, and shall pay over to such person as the Commissioners may appoint the money received by him for the duty and penalty. (3) On production to the Commissioners of any instrument in respect of which any duty or penalty has been paid, together with the receipt, the payment of the duty and penalty shall be denoted on the instrument. (4) Save as aforesaid, an instrument executed in any part of the U.K., or relating, wheresoever executed, to any property situate, or to any matter or thing done or to be done, in any part of the U.K., shall not, except in criminal proceedings, be given in evidence, or be available for any purpose whatever, unless it is duly stamped in accordance with the law in force at the time when it was first executed.

[33] Leases where the term does not exceed seven years or is indefinite and the rent does not exceed £500 annually, no premium having been paid, do not result in a liability for payment: all other rates are to be found under Sched. 1 of the Stamp Act 1891 in Butterworth's *Orange Tax Handbook*, Revised 1997–98, at p. 2039.

[34] Stamp Act 1891, s. 14(1), (4).

no difficulty arises. Presumably an undertaking by a party's solicitor would be accepted in arbitration, and perhaps that of a valuer, surveyor or land agent whose professional society could take disciplinary action if the undertaking was not honoured. A practical difficulty is that an arbitrator, unlike a court, has no permanent machinery to ensure that such undertakings are carried out. The arbitrator must himself be on the alert to take notice of the stamping as neither counsel nor solicitor will draw his attention to the absence or the insufficiency of the stamp, it being an invariable professional convention that they will not take the "stamp objection". It is sometimes thought that, if both parties agree, the arbitrator can look at an unstamped document without regard to the rules about stamping. This is a misapprehension. The arbitrator must not look at it, whatever the parties agree, until the proper payment is made. In view of the peremptory wording of section 14 of the Stamp Act 1891, the acceptance in evidence of an unstamped or insufficiently stamped document in breach of the Act would appear to be misconduct which would endanger the award. So rigorous in fact is the rule preventing unstamped documents from being received in evidence that it has been held that the Court cannot look at its own order if unstamped, being "an instrument executed", and operating to transfer property, within the meaning of section 14(4) of the Act.[35]

Evidence at arbitrations: arbitrator's own expertise 16.44

The question of the extent to which agricultural arbitrators may properly use their own expertise in determining the matters before them has given rise to some discussion. Although the arbitrator functions as a judge, he is chosen for his special knowledge and experience as a professional man serving the agricultural industry, with skills in such subjects as estate and farm management, including financial advice, and valuation. There is no doubt that in sifting and appraising the evidence before him the arbitrator may use, to the utmost of his ability, his own expert knowledge. In so far as he is using his general store of accumulated knowledge and experience there is no need for him to disclose it (and it would in fact be a difficult thing to do) to the parties. It is an accepted portion of his professional equipment.[36] The arbitrator must conscientiously consider all the evidence, expert and factual, presented to him before he reaches his decision.[37] In weighing this evidence he may (indeed he is in duty bound to) employ all his own expertise. Using the touchstone of his own general knowledge and experience, he is entitled to reject, accept in part, or adopt with modifications, the evidence presented, including, *e.g.*

---

[35] *Sun Alliance Insurance Ltd v. Inland Revenue Commissioners* [1972] Ch. 133.
[36] The underlying principles have been discussed more in the USA than in the U.K. *cf. National Labour Relations Board v. Seven-Up Bottling Co. of Miami Inc.* 344 U.S. 343 (1953) at 348–9, where the U.S. Supreme Court said that the Board was entitled to bring to bear on a back-pay problem "its cumulative experience that begat understanding and insight". Holmes J. recognised that the determination of an administrative tribunal "may express an intuition of experience which outruns analysis and sums up many unnamed and tangled impressions": *Chicago, Burlington and Quincy Ry Co. v. Babcock* 204 U.S. 585, 598 (1907).
[37] *cf. London Export Corporation Ltd v. Jubilee Coffee Roasting Co. Ltd* [1958] 1 W.L.R. 271 at 280; *Mediterranean and Eastern Export Co. Ltd v. Fortress Fabrics (Manchester) Ltd* [1948] 2 All E.R. 186 at 187.

expert evidence as to values.[38] The use of his general knowledge and experience, his accumulated wisdom, must be distinguished from private knowledge of special facts relevant to the particular case before him, *e.g.* knowledge of an individual comparable upon which reliance might be placed to determine the issue. This kind of information must be disclosed and put to the parties for their observations. The arbitrator must not, in effect, give himself secret evidence.[39] There may be cases where the evidence presented to the arbitrator is so scanty or inconclusive that he is called upon to use his general knowledge and experience not merely to appraise the evidence but also to supplement it.[40] In this residual case the arbitrator is *pro tanto* acting as an expert, but he is still subject to all the obligations which attach to his judicial function. He cannot depart from his general knowledge and experience and rely on particular private information without disclosing it.[41] It is submitted that, as a matter of caution, the arbitrator should, when in doubt, always give the parties an opportunity to comment on his approach if it differs from that of the parties.[42]

16.45 No permissible departure from construction agreed by parties without further reference to them

In circumstances where the parties are agreed as to the meaning or construction of a particular document, an arbitrator must not, without further reference to the parties, depart from what they have agreed.[43] Although it has been stated that the arbitrator may resolve matters by inviting the parties to address him on the issues

---

[38] See Lord Denning M.R. in ***Fox v. P.G. Wellfair Ltd*** [1981] 2 Lloyd's Rep. 514 at 522; *cf.* Lord Wigery C.J. in ***Metropolitan Property Holdings Ltd v. Laufer*** (1974) 29 P.&C.R. 172 at 176–177.

[39] See especially Dunn L.J. in ***Fox v. P.G. Wellfair Ltd*** (above) at 528–529, *e.g.* his illustration in regard to the valuation of a bull; see also ***Top Shop Estates Ltd v. Danino*** (1984) 273 E.G. 197, and *cf.* ***Zermalt Holdings SA v. Nu-Life Upholstery Repairs Ltd*** [1985] 2 E.G.L.R. 14.

[40] See generally para. 11.33 above.

[41] *cf.* ***Owen v. Nicholl*** [1948] 1 All E.R. 707 (information obtained by an arbitration in other proceedings).

[42] It is not always easy to predict whether or not the court will remit an award where the arbitrator in such circumstances does not give the parties an opportunity of comment: contrast ***Secretary of State for the Environment v. Reed International plc*** [1994] 1 E.G.L.R. 22 (where the High Court did not remit, Evans-Lombe J. at 25: "... I have finally concluded that I should not remit this award. It seems to me that what the arbitrator was here doing was the exercise of pure valuation experience on his part. The point with which he was dealing was a pure valuation point, and what the arbitrator was doing was really partially accepting the submission of Reed that there should be an uplift, but not accepting it in full. It also seems to me that to remit the award for reconsideration at this point to this arbitrator would be highly unlikely to serve any useful purpose. The arbitrator has come to this conclusion. It is hard to see how the parties can, on the basis of the current evidence, submit other than that his approach was technically wrong, which is likely to be a submission that the arbitrator will reject. ...") and ***Unit 4 Cinemas Ltd v. Tosara Investment Ltd*** [1993] 2 E.G.L.R. 11 where the High Court remitted an award where the arbitrator used an estimated maintainable profit which had not been the subject of evidence although closely related material had been.

[43] ***Techno Ltd v. Allied Dunbar Assurance plc*** [1993] 1 E.G.L.R. 29.

which trouble him,[44] a disagreement of this type is likely, in the context of an agricultural dispute, to justify a consultative case stated.

Arbitrator bound by his own procedural directions 16.46

Where the arbitrator issues procedural directions on the basis of which the arbitration is to be conducted, it is misconduct on his part to ignore or fail to implement those directions. Although one might have thought that this was obvious, three cases illustrate that this is not so and in each case the award was set aside or remitted.[45]

Conduct of arbitration: overriding requirement of fairness 16.47

The requirement that the arbitrator act at all times fairly is one which cannot be over stressed. There are many, regrettable, instances where awards are set aside because something has been done by the arbitrator which either is unfair or appears to be unfair.[46] An arbitrator is not entitled to adopt a procedure which deprives a party of the services of a solicitor or counsel if he wished to have them.

It is fundamental to arbitration that the system is adversarial and each party is entitled to put forward his own evidence and to cross-examine the other party. There are special difficulties where one party is represented and in these circumstances the arbitrator must endeavour to make good any disadvantage which the unrepresented party sustains by being unrepresented. This does not mean that the arbitrator must "fight the case" for the unrepresented litigant but he must take special care to consider all the arguments which might possibly be made in favour of the unrepresented party's position. He cannot, however, go so far as to stop the lawyer instructed from cross-examining the unrepresented litigant. All these problems, which are very difficult to deal with in practice, are discussed at length in *Chilton v. Saga Holidays plc*.[47] Where the arbitrator takes a very technical line as to whether there was an omission in the evidence and the omission is easily capable of remedy, it is misconduct to proceed without allowing the parties (or one of them) to rectify the omission.[48] Where evidence is obtained after the conclusion of the hearing, the arbitrator should not receive or act on this evidence without first giving the parties an opportunity to address him on it unless they have a clear agreement that they do not wish to do so.[49] It is a breach of the

---

[44] *ibid.*, at 32.
[45] In *Control Securities plc v. Spencer* [1989] 1 E.G.L.R. 136 the award was set aside because the arbitrator had failed to deal with comparables in accordance with his own directions; in *Mount Charlotte Investments plc v. Prudential Assurance* [1995] 1 E.G.L.R. 15 the award was set aside where the arbitrator considered inadmissible evidence contrary to his directions and went to inspect unidentified hotels; in *Oakstead Garages Ltd v. Leach Pension Scheme (Trustees) Ltd* [1996] 1 E.G.L.R. 26 the award was remitted to the arbitrator, having been successfully attacked because the arbitrator failed to visit the comparables when all along he had said that he would.
[46] See the discussion below at para. 16.66 dealing with "misconduct".
[47] [1986] 1 All E.R. 841, CA.
[48] *Fairclough Building Ltd v. Vale of Belvoir Superstore Ltd* [1990] 56 B.L.R. 74 applying *Fox v. Wellfair Ltd* [1981] 2 Ll. Rep. 514.
[49] *Soceidad Iberica de Molturacion SA v. Nidera Handelscompagnie BV* [1990] 2 Lloyd's Rep. 240.

rules of natural justice, in certain cases, to refuse a request for a hearing.[50] It is essential not just that the parties should receive a fair trial but also that a fair minded person should not be able to entertain a reasonable suspicion that a fair hearing was impossible.[51] However where the arbitrator has previously acted as an independent expert determining one of the comparables in a rent review, it is not misconduct for the arbitrator to proceed with the arbitration and the situation does not raise any question as to bias.[52] Although it would not be subject to the accusation of unfairness, the practice of issuing post-hearing directions for parties to agree the effect of evidence is to be discouraged.[53]

16.48 Arbitrator's inspection of the holding

The arbitrator has the power, and in a great many cases it will clearly be essential, to inspect the holding. What he himself sees during the inspection, provided that it is relevant to the issues he has to decide, is just as much evidence as the evidence put before him by the parties. He should inspect either accompanied by both parties or their representatives or on his own, never in the company of one party only.[54] There are some advantages from the arbitrator's point of view in making the inspection on his own, but two possible dangers should be noted. First, the arbitrator must studiously avoid receiving statements or information from persons he meets on the holding and he must be careful not to take with him on the inspection a colleague from whom it may appear that he is receiving evidence behind the backs of the parties.[55] Secondly, the inspection might reveal some matter of importance likely to influence his decision which had not been raised before him and reliance on which would take the parties by surprise; natural justice would require this matter to be put to the parties and their observations sought.[56] The same might apply to elaborate tests or experiments, going beyond the normal acceptance of inspection, carried out by the arbitrator, possibly with the aid of an assistant, in the absence of the parties.[57] If possible the inspection should take place before lapse of time has caused the condition of the holding to differ from

---

[50] *Town and City Properties (Development) Ltd v. Wiltshier Southern Ltd* (1988) 44 B.L.R. 109. This does not mean that in all cases a full hearing is necessary but in this particular case the arbitrator had led the parties to believe that there would be a hearing and that he was visiting the property simply to form a "preliminary view" whereas in fact he used the visit as an opportunity of drafting his award.

[51] See *Turner (East Asia) Pte v. Builders Federal (Hong Kong) Ltd* (1988) 42 B.L.R. 122 (High Court of the Republic of Singapore) reviewing and considering the various English authorities.

[52] *Moore Stephens and Co. v. Local Authorities' Mutual Investment Trust* [1992] 1 E.G.L.R. 33. Cross-examination on expert opinion in these circumstances may be addressed to the opposing party's valuer and the arbitrator himself may supply information as to any question of fact as to that particular comparable.

[53] See the commentary above at para. 16.4 under "Decision".

[54] See *Hegarty v. Winters* (1953) 162 E.G. 89.

[55] *Ellis v. Lewin* (1963) 107 S.J. 851.

[56] cf. *R. v. Paddington and St Marylebone Rent Tribunal, ex p. Bell London and Provincial Properties Ltd* [1949] 1 K.B. 666 at 682; also *Fairmount Investments Ltd v. Secretary of State for the Environment* [1976] 1 W.L.R. 1255.

[57] cf. *Top Shop Estates Ltd v. Danino* (1984) 273 E.G. 197; *Hickmott v. Dorset County Council* (1977) 35 P.&C.R. 195.

that at the material time. In the case of rental arbitrations where evidence of rent paid on comparable holdings is proffered it may become necessary to inspect the latter if such evidence is of reduced value without inspection.

Legal assistance for the arbitrator 16.49

The rules which govern the obtaining of legal assistance by the arbitrator appear to be as follows:[58]

(a) If the arbitrator obtains the consent of both parties, then no difficulty can arise. Despite what is said below, therefore, an arbitrator who wishes to have his legal adviser sitting with him, for example, may feel that it is wise to secure the parties' agreement before the hearing begins.

(b) An arbitrator may, without the parties' consent, obtain legal assistance in the drawing up of his award.[59] The need for such assistance has become greater since, as a result of section 12 of the Tribunals and Inquiries Act 1971, an otherwise perfectly sound award may be set aside because inadequate reasons are given for it. An arbitrator is also entitled to obtain legal assistance in the preparation of a special case.

(c) It seems that an arbitrator is entitled, without the parties' consent, to seek legal assistance about the procedure to be followed in the conduct of the arbitration and the general rules of evidence.[60]

(d) It seems also that an arbitrator may, without the parties' consent, obtain legal advice about the general principles of law which are relevant to the case, as distinct from the actual issues of law which arise in it[61]; in practice a distinction not always easy to draw.

(e) The next rule is really implicit in the last. An arbitrator should not, without the parties' consent, obtain legal assistance in regard to the actual issues of law in the arbitration.[62] Such assistance should be sought by stating a special case for the opinion of the court. If, with the parties' consent, an issue of law arising in the arbitration is submitted to counsel (instead of being stated in a case for the court's opinion) it is important that the proposed submission should be shown to the parties

---

[58] See generally *Russell on Arbitration* (20th ed.), pp. 231–233. (This is the old edition.)
[59] *Threlfall v. Fanshawe* (1851) 1 L.M.&P. 340; *Galloway v. Keyworth* (1854) 15 C.B. 228; *Re Underwood and the Bedford and Cambridge Ry* (1861) 11 C.B. (N.S.) 442; *Re Collyer-Bristow & Co.* [1901] 2 K.B. 839. In this case the costs of the arbitrator's solicitor was allowed on a taxation: "The bill of costs is not the bill of the solicitor to one of the two parties to the reference, but of the umpire's solicitor. It seems to me that it is a bill of costs which ought to be taxed as between solicitor and client ..." (Vaughan Williams L.J. at 841).
[60] See *Threlfall v. Fanshawe* (above) and authorities cited in the next note.
[61] *Louis Dreyfus & Co. v. Arunachala Ayya* (1931) L.R. 58 IA 381; see also *Dobson v. Groves* (1844) 14 L.J. Q.B. 17 at 21 and *Ellison v. Bray* (1864) 9 L.T. 730.
[62] *Louis Dreyfus & Co. v. Arunachala Ayya* (above) and cases in the previous footnote.

because if the arbitrator obtains an opinion based on an erroneous statement of facts, and acts upon it, the award may be set aside.[63]

(f) The old view was that an arbitrator had to obtain the parties' consent before arranging for his legal advisor to sit with him at the hearing.[64] A different view has been taken more recently in a trade arbitration.[65] Despite this, it is strongly recommended that the consent of the parties should be obtained before making this arrangement.

(g) An arbitrator should at all costs avoid going to the solicitor of one of the parties for advice, as this would be an act of impropriety which would jeopardise the award, even if it might not in all cases vitiate it.[66]

(h) It must always be remembered that giving due consideration to advice is one thing: delegation of the arbitrator's judicial function to a third party is quite another.

(i) Where an arbitrator properly obtains legal assistance he is, of course, entitled to charge the proper costs of such assistance as part of the costs of his award.

16.50 Arbitration hearing: time allocated for presentation

Obviously whatever procedure the arbitrator adopts, the hearing must be conducted both fairly and in such a way that the parties are not taken by surprise so as to be unable to deal with any matter which the arbitrator will take into consideration.

Although it is correct that parties should have the opportunity to address the arbitrator on all material matters it is not the case that they should expect to do so without any constraint whatsoever as to time. In this regard the practice of the courts provides a helpful model. It is quite usual to direct that the parties should provide their witness statements in writing in advance of the evidence being given and, at the hearing, for the relevant witness simply to confirm the contents of that statement under oath by way of evidence in chief. If there are additional matters which are usefully dealt with in examination in chief, and which do not generate a need for further evidence in rebuttal, the courts allow this to be done "live" in the witness box. It is suggested that an arbitrator adopting this practice could not be criticised and will make significant savings in time. In farming cases it is to be expected that some things are very helpfully dealt with "live", such as correlating photographs and buildings and/or commenting on documents or materials which have become available since the statement was provided. Parties might usefully be asked in advance of the hearing how long is likely to be required for witness

---

[63] *Re Hare* (1839) 6 Bing. N.C. 158 at 162.
[64] *Proctor v. Williamson* (1860) 8 C.B. (N.S.) 386.
[65] See *per* McNair J. in *Giacomo Costa Fu Andrea v. British Italian Trading Co.* [1961] 2 Ll. Rep. 392 at 402. The case went to the CA, [1963] 1 Q.B. 201, where there was no indication that there was any disagreement with McNair J. on this point.
[66] *Re Underwood and Bedford, etc., Ry* (1861) 11 C.B. (N.S.) 442; and see *Behren v. Bremer* (1854) 3 C.L.R. 40.

evidence, as distinct from submissions on the footing that the statements will be the bulk of the evidence in chief. Restricting cross-examination by time is not a practicable exercise, since witnesses are likely to "spin out" their answers if they feel that this will disadvantage the questioner. The better course, in terms of managing cross-examination, is to let the questioner ask his/her questions and, if necessary, request the witness to listen to the question carefully and direct his answer to it rather than making a speech. Some arbitrators sit totally silent through the evidence: this is not very helpful to the advocates and in particular if there are matters which at the close of the evidence the arbitrator would like to confirm with the witness as to whether or not he has correctly understood the position, the arbitrator should ask his questions when the particular witness has completed his re-examination.

As to speeches by the parties, it is now quite clearly the practice of the higher courts to make a reasonable allowance and to hold counsel to that allowance, unless there is a very good reason why it should be extended. Although arbitrators do not have the experience of the courts as to what may appear reasonable in the circumstances of the case, there is no reason why an arbitrator should not invite counsel to make an estimate and to discuss it before him. The estimate will no doubt be influenced by whether or not the arbitrator is prepared to read "behind the scenes" in advance of the legal submissions and/or during a break in the submissions themselves. It used to be the practice of the courts never to do any supplementary reading but only ever to read out loud during the case and in full. This state of affairs has in recent years changed radically and it is submitted that the arbitrator ought to be willing to read a full case in advance of a presentation and should indicate to the lawyers that they should pick out the parts on which they particularly rely but that the arbitrator will re-read the entire case in the light of the submissions being made. The arbitrator will undoubtedly find it helpful if some legal submissions are made in writing in advance or at the close of the hearing whereas submissions on the facts are nearly always better dealt with orally. The closing submissions made by advocates are not evidence in the case and, although the arbitrator will wish to keep a note of what is said, the extent of the note is a matter for his own discretion (*i.e.* it does not have to be a total and complete record of every word that was said).

The arbitrator must keep a careful eye on the conduct of the advocates and should restrain one party interrupting another party's cross-examination unless there is a stated objection to a particular question upon which the arbitrator may immediately rule. Where the person asking questions in cross-examination is not so much asking a question as making a speech, the arbitrator should intervene so as to restrict matters to questions. Where a question is asked the questioner must always be restrained from interrupting the witness before the witness has fully given his answer. It is not acceptable for the questioner to interrupt the answer before it is completed. If the witness abuses this position it is easy enough for the arbitrator to bring him to book. Where the party who opens the case brings in new points or legal materials during his closing speech the arbitrator must give the other party the opportunity to deal with the new materials. This must be done even though it may produce inconvenience in terms of the timing or the length of the hearing: the fault is that of the party who introduced the new material, not that of the party who must deal with it. If the arbitrator fails to respond appropriately to this particular challenge he will undoubtedly find that his award is subject to attack.

16.51 Arbitration: time for making the award
The arbitrator is required to make and sign his award within 56 days of his appointment, subject to the power of the President of the RICS to enlarge the time whether that time has expired or not.[67] The practice of the Minister of Agriculture, before the function of appointment was transferred to the President, was to grant extensions freely; this practice has continued. It has been held in Scotland that an award made after the permitted time (including any extension) may be set aside for misconduct.[68]

16.52 Arbitration: interim awards
The arbitrator may, if he thinks fit, make an interim award for the payment of any sum on account of the sum to be finally awarded.[69] If this power is exercised it should be made clear on the face of the award that it is an interim award, lest any question should arise as to the arbitrator's power to re-open it. An interim award should be exact within its defined limits, not a provisional estimate to be corrected later. Apart from the exception of interim awards, the award should be a complete instrument in itself.[70] It is, however, competent for the parties to agree that separate awards should be given on different matters referred to the arbitrator.[71]

16.53 Arbitration: form of award
A form of award is specified in the Agricultural Holding (Form of Award in Arbitration Proceedings) Order 1990[72] and the use of this form, or a form to the like effect, with such modifications as the circumstances may require, is mandatory. A radical departure from the statutory form will make the award invalid, the "modifications" permitted by the Order being intended only to enable the form to fit the facts, not to allow a different species of award.[73] The current form replaced its predecessor.[74]

A conditional award is not permitted, so that when an arbitrator expressed his award to be conditional on a special case (which was set out in the same document) not being set down for hearing, or, if set down, being withdrawn, it was held that he had not made any award.[75] An award in the form of a special case is not allowed by

---

[67] Sched. 11, para. 14(1), (2).
[68] *Halliday v. Semple* 1960 S.L.T. (Sh. Ct.) 11.
[69] Sched. 11, para. 15. In the case of commercial arbitration awards an interim award could be final in all respects excepts costs, reserving the costs until later. It would be sensible if the same procedure could be adopted under para. 15, but it is likely that "on account of the sum" means the sum excluding costs.
[70] *Gould v. Staffordshire Potteries Waterworks Co.* (1850) 5 Ex. 214; *Public Trustee v. Randag* [1966] Ch. 649.
[71] *Dowse v. Coxe* (1825) 3 Bing. 20; *Wrightson v. Bywater* (1838) 3 M.&W. 199.
[72] S.I. 1990 No.1472, printed in Part III of this work. The content also appears at Form 75 in Part V of this work.
[73] *Public Trustee v. Randag* (above).
[74] Printed at pp. 545–547 of the last edition of this work.
[75] *Public Trustee v. Randag* (above). The object may have been to avoid the need to apply for a further extension of time or to avoid the delay involved in adjourning the arbitration.

the agricultural arbitration code.[76] An oral award, it is submitted, would be void. The official form provides for the award to be witnessed as well as signed. The signing and attestation of the award constitute its execution, and this is an important point in time. The acts of publishing the award to the parties (*i.e.* notifying them that it has been made and may be taken up on payment of expenses)[77] and delivering it (*i.e.* sending it to the party who takes it up by paying the costs)[78] are of less importance, at any rate so far as the time-table of Schedule 11 is concerned.[79]

Arbitration: consent award 16.54

There is no objection to an award by consent, *i.e.* an award embodying an agreement reached between the parties, thus avoiding the need for a hearing and the decision of the arbitrator on contested questions. Such an award should follow the statutory form with minor modifications to indicate that it is an award by consent and not made after the hearing and examining witnesses and other evidence. In some cases parties may settle their disputes by agreement without requiring the preparation of a consent award and it is, of course, essential for the arbitrator to make sure that such an award is desired.

Contents of arbitration awards: statutory requirements 16.55

The arbitrator must state separately in his award the amounts awarded in respect of the several "claims" referred to him, and, on the application of either party (made before the award), he must specify the amount awarded in respect of any particular improvement or any particular matter the subject of the award.[80] The statutory duty, in the absence of an application by a party, is to state separately the amounts awarded in respect of each separate claim, *e.g.* the disturbance claim, the improvements claim, the tenant-right matters claim, the "high farming" claim, and the landlord's dilapidations claim, but these amounts need not be itemised to show the amounts for specific improvements, tenant-right matters or dilapidations unless an application for such itemisation is made. If such an application is made before the award, however, the arbitrator must accede to it. If he did not, he would be guilty of misconduct, just as he would if he failed, without any application, to state separately the amounts of the separate claims.[81]

Where the compensation payable under an agreement is by the Act substituted for the statutory compensation for improvements or tenant-right matters, the arbitrator must award compensation in accordance with the agreement instead of in accordance with the Act.[82] The award must fix a day not later than one month after

---

[76] Since the Arbitration Act 1979 (s. 1) the procedure by special case, including awards in the form of a special case, has been abolished for commercial arbitrations. They do not feature in the Arbitration Act 1996.
[77] *MacArthur v. Campbell* (1833) 5 B. & Ad. 518.
[78] *Hicks v. Richardson* (1797) 1 Bos. & P. 93.
[79] The 21 days "after the date of the award" allowed by CCR, Ord. 44, r. 3 for an application to set aside seem also to run from execution.
[80] Sched. 11, para. 16(a) and (b).
[81] See *Hamilton v. Peeke* (1926) L.J. C.C.R. 54, CC.
[82] Sched. 11, para. 17.

the delivery of the award for the payment of the money awarded as compensation, costs or otherwise.[83]

The obligation imposed on arbitrators to give reasons for their decisions, in accordance with section 12 of the Tribunals and Inquiries Act 1971, is of such importance that it is dealt with separately.

16.56 **Arbitration awards: reasons**

Agricultural arbitrators, whether appointed by agreement or by the President of the RICS,[84] are required to furnish a statement of reasons for their decision if requested to do so under section 12 of the Tribunals and Inquiries Act 1971. The request must be made "on or before the giving of notification of the decision" and may be written or oral. Normally the request will be made before the end of the hearing, but may be given "on" receipt of the award. Clearly a lengthy delay would invalidate such a request, but there is no definite authority as to when it would be reasonable to refuse it.[85] Arbitrators should give "on" a fairly liberal interpretation and respond to the request even if in some cases it may be desirable to point out that they are no longer under an obligation to do so. The arbitrator is entitled to refuse to furnish a statement to "a person not primarily concerned" with the decision if of opinion that to furnish it would be contrary to the interests of any person primarily concerned.[86] In practice a request for reasons is likely to be made only by a party, but it is conceivable that an assignee of one of the parties might wish to request a statement. As an award is binding on assignees,[87] he would normally be entitled to it. It would clearly be misconduct for an arbitrator to refuse to state any reasons at all in a case where a request has been properly made. Failure to give adequate reasons, however, is not a matter of misconduct but a possible ground for an application to set the award aside for error of law.[88]

This jurisdiction is considered in more detail later.[89] Since the classic decision of Megaw J. in *Re Poyser and Mills' Arbitration*[90] a large amount of case law has developed in relation to reasons given by a variety of Tribunals. It would be inappropriate to discuss it here at length, but a few points may be made. Megaw J.'s formulation is still constantly quoted as the guiding principle:

"Parliament provided that reasons shall be given, and in my view that must be

---

[83] Sched. 11, para. 18.

[84] Sched. 11, para. 21. From 1959 until 1984 this requirement applied only to arbitrators appointed "otherwise than by agreement". See 1984 Act, Sched. 3, para. 28(7) for the change.

[85] There is a little indirect authority that "on" may extend to a reasonable time thereafter: *Scott v. Scott* [1921] P. 107, CA (by analogy from a very different context). The Lord Chancellor's Department has expressed the view that a liberal meaning was intended: see Annual Report of Council of Tribunals for 1969–70, para. 58.

[86] Tribunals and Inquiries Act 1971, s. 12(2).

[87] Sched. 11, para. 19.

[88] Sched. 11, para. 27(2). Misconduct and error of law on the face of the award are now both matters for the County Court, the latter having been brought within the County Court jurisdiction by s. 15(1) of the Agriculture (Miscellaneous Provisions) Act 1972. Before that a motion in the High Court was necessary.

[89] See para. 16.68 below.

[90] [1964] 2 Q.B. 467.

read as meaning that proper, adequate reasons must be given which will not only be intelligible, but which deal with the substantial points that have been raised."[91]

Courts are naturally pre-disposed to be favourable to upholding rather than destroying an arbitration award.[92] The arbitrator must explain in his award how he reached his conclusions and, where figures are given as the award, he should explain how he arrived at those figures.[93] It is submitted that reasons must be intelligible, cover the substantial points and be sufficiently clear and detailed that the parties can understand how the final award is made up. This general statement is perhaps more helpful to an arbitrator than a detailed study as to whether or not the Scottish doctrine that reasons should be given to explain the details of valuations applies in England.[94] Where in the course of the proceedings a special case has been stated for the opinion of the County Court, it may be desirable to attach to the award not only the statement of reasons, but also, as appendices, copies of the special case and the County Court judge's order thereon, since all these documents may be necessary to show fully the reasons for the award. As a

---

[91] *ibid.*, at 479. *cf.* Megaw J. again in ***Givaudan & Co. Ltd v. Minister of Housing and Local Government*** [1967] 1 W.L.R. 250. Other early cases are ***Hughes v. Homewood*** [1963] E.G.D. 670 and ***Price v. Romilly*** [1960] 1 W.L.R. 1360. Megaw J.'s formulation was elaborated by Sir Douglas Frank Q.C. (sitting as a deputy judge) in ***Guppys Properties Ltd v. Knott (No.3)*** (1981) 258 E.G. 1083, in which he withdrew some observations he had made in ***Guppys Properties Ltd v. Knott (No.2)*** (1979) 253 E.G. 907, commending the very strict and almost unworkable doctrine of the Scottish Court of Session in ***Albyn Properties Ltd v. Knox*** 1977 S.L.T. 41; ***Glasgow Heritable Trust Ltd*** 1977 S.L.T. 44.

[92] See the authorities quoted and applied in ***Learmonth Property Investment Co. Ltd v. Amos Hinton & Sons plc*** [1985] 1 E.G.L.R. 13 by Walton J. at 15, 2nd column.

[93] Some guidance is to be found in ***Thomas v. Countryside Council for Wales*** [1994] 1 E.G.L.R. 17 at 21G from Rougier J.: "Finally, I come to the third issue raised in the appeal, namely the contention that the matter should be remitted to the arbitrator for him to make further findings of fact and to give his reasons for arriving at the award which he did. I can deal with this fairly shortly. It should be said at once that, since the arbitrator was specifically asked to state his reasons, sadly, it is apparent that he has not done so. Apart from the bare statement that he has considered this, that or the other factor, he has merely given figures for the three years in question. It has been quite impossible for either party to determine just how the arbitrator has arrived at those three figures. While accepting Mr Bush's submission that an arbitrator cannot be expected to make every single minute finding of fact involved in a fairly complex award, yet where the whole purpose of the arbitration is to calculate and arrive at a specific sum or sums of money payable by way of compensation, then the steps and calculations by which those sums are arrived at, in my judgment, must amount either to primary findings of fact or at least to reasons. In the present award virtually no reasons have been given; Mr Bush himself, when asked point blank how one could determine the method whereby the arbitrator had arrived at the three figures referred to, was unable to supply an answer, nor could anyone else."

[94] This debate is covered by pp. 300–301 of the previous edition of this work. The arbitrator must use his common sense as to how much of his workings should be provided before the parties can understand how and why he reached the conclusions and figures that he did.

general guide it is helpful to consider the following informal rules which have been evolved by case law over the years:

(a) The award must comply with any directions contained in the reference, unless they are of an immaterial nature.[95]

(b) The making of the award must not be delegated by the arbitrator to another person, but the arbitrator may take disinterested legal advice about its preparation.[96]

(c) The award must deal finally with all matters referred, unless it is expressed to be an interim award.[97]

(d) The award must determine the actual matters submitted for decision and not suggest some general equitable arrangement.[98]

(e) The award must be certain, not open to doubt or ambiguity, *e.g.* in regard to whether a matter has been dealt with, how it has been decided, or the amount involved.[99]

Reasons for costs. It is not clear that the requirement to give reasons on request under the Tribunals and Inquiries Act 1971 extends to giving reasons for the exercise of the arbitrator's discretion as to costs.[1] But if the arbitrator has not adopted the normal rule that "costs that follow the event", and has deprived the successful party of his costs or has otherwise exercised his discretion in an unusual manner, he should give reasons for an exceptional order.

16.57 Arbitration awards: interest on award
Unless the award otherwise directs, any sum directed to be paid by the award carries interest as from the date of the award, and at the same rate as a judgment debt.[2] There is no provision as to interest for a period before the date of the award. The present provision gives the arbitrator a discretion (which must be exercised judicially) as to whether interest shall be payable as from the date of the award, but he has no discretion as to the rate of interest. Normally the arbitrator will give no direction, allowing the statutory provision to apply automatically.

16.58 Arbitration awards: finality of award
Subject to the power to make an interim award for the payment of a sum on account,[3] the award is final and binding on the parties and the persons claiming

---

[95] *Gatliffe v. Dunn* (1738) Barnes 55.
[96] *Johnson v. Latham* (1850) 19 L.J. Q.B. 329; *Re Underwood and Bedford Ry* (1861) 31 L.J. C.P. 10; *Louis Dreyfus & Co. v. Arunachala Ayya* (1931) L.R. 58 Ind. App. 381.
[97] *Nickels v. Hancock* (1855) 7 De. G.M. & G. 300; *Public Trustee v. Randag* [1966] Ch. 649.
[98] *Ross v. Boards* (1838) 8 A.&E. 290; *Jager v. Tolme* [1916] 1 K.B. 939.
[99] *Re Tidswell* (1863) 33 Beav. 213.
[1] *cf. Perry v. Stopher* [1959] 1 W.L.R. 415.
[2] Sched. 11, para. 22. This provision was introduced by the 1984 Act, Sched. 3, para. 28(7). Before that the arbitrator had no power to award interest.
[3] Sched. 11, para. 15.

under them respectively.[4] Once the award is made the arbitrator is, subject to very limited express statutory exceptions, *functus officio*. At common law he could not even correct a clerical error in it,[5] but he is given a limited statutory power "to correct in the award any clerical mistake or error arising from any accidental slip or omission".[6] This "slip rule", the wording of which is based on the similar rule for judgments or court orders, must be interpreted in accordance with the narrow meaning given to it by the authorities.[7] It is restricted to correcting a failure of the award to carry out the manifest intention of the arbitrator, not to correct a mistake of fact or law under which the arbitrator was labouring when he made the award or to introduce new matter which later occurred to him. Other minor exceptions to the *functus officio* rule are contained in articles 7 and 15 of the Agricultural Holdings (Arbitration on Notices) Order 1987,[8] which enable an arbitrator to specify a date for the termination of a tenancy for certain purposes if an application is made to him not later than 14 days after the termination of the arbitration. Another statutory exception, not so minor, is the arbitrator's power and duty to give reasons if properly requested to do so when the award has been notified to the parties. An arbitrator cannot reopen his own award,[9] but the County Court may remit an award, or any part of the award, to the arbitrator for reconsideration.[10] The finality of an award is, of course, also subject to the provisions mentioned below for the setting aside of an award by the court.[11]

Arbitration awards: stamping of award 16.59

At one time an award had to be stamped, but the need for stamping was abolished by the Finance Act 1949. The abolition was unqualified, so that an award does not have to be stamped even where, as a result of section 6(4) of the 1986 Act, it takes effect as if it were an agreement.

Arbitration awards: enforcement of award 16.60

If a sum awarded to be paid for compensation, costs or otherwise by a landlord or tenant is not paid within 14 days after its due date, it is recoverable, if the County Court so orders, as if it were payable under an order of that court.[12] The award may be enforced by application *ex parte* by filing an affidavit verifying the amount

---

[4] Sched. 11, para. 19: *cf. Caledonian Railway v. Turcan* [1898] A.C. 256; *Martin v. Boulanger* (1883) 8 App. Cas. 296. But it is not binding on strangers to the reference. *cf, Tunbridge Wells Local Board v. Ackroyd* (1880) 5 Ex. D. 199; *Evans v. Rees* (1839) 10 Ad. & El. 151 at 155.
[5] *Irvine v. Elnon* (1806) 8 East. 54; *Mordue v. Palmer* (1870) L.R. 6 Ch. 22.
[6] Sched. 11, para. 20.
[7] See RSC, Ord. 20, r. 11 and the authorities there cited. In particular see *R. v. Cripps, ex p. Muldoon* [1984] Q.B. 686, CA. *cf.* also *Pedler v. Hardy* (1902) 18 T.L.R. 591; *Sutherland v. Hannevig* [1921] 1 K.B. 336.
[8] S.I. 1987 No.710.
[9] It seems doubtful whether the *MacFarlane* ruling, whereby a tribunal can reopen and rehear a case on limited grounds of natural justice, can be applied to arbitration: see *R. v. Kensington and Chelsea Rent Tribunal, ex p. MacFarlane* [1974] 1 W.L.R. 1486.
[10] Sched. 11, para. 28(1); see also court's alternative power to vary the award: Sched. 11, para. 28(2) (changes made by 1984 Act, Sched. 3, para. 28(9)).
[11] paras 16.66–16.68 below.
[12] s. 85(1) of the 1986 Act.

remaining due to the applicant and by producing the award or a duplicate thereof and filing a copy. The application may be heard and determined by the registrar. The procedure by filing an affidavit has superseded the previous procedure by an originating application.[13]

16.61 Judicial control of the reference: nature of statement of case to the Court
The arbitrator may on his own initiative at any stage of the proceedings before he makes his award, and must if so directed by the County Court on the application of either party, state in the form of a special case for the opinion of the County Court (1) any question of law arising in the course of the arbitration and (2) any question as to the jurisdiction of the arbitrator.[14] The special case is a consultative case and is an interlocutory matter arising in the course of the arbitration. There can be more than one such consultative case.[15] It is not permissible to state the award in the form of a special case.[16] The procedure for stating a case, and for applying for an order directing the arbitrator to state a case, is to be found in the County Court Rules.[17] As the proceedings commence when the arbitrator is effectively appointed, he can state a case immediately after he is appointed and before he hears evidence.[18] This may sometimes be convenient, and of course a case as to the arbitrator's jurisdiction should be stated as soon as possible. It seems clear that an arbitrator can neither state a case of his own volition nor be directed to state a case after he has made his award, since the proceedings terminate with the award.[19]

Only questions of law can be the subject of a special case stated. It must, however, be remembered that the question whether there is any evidence to support a finding of fact is itself a question of law and can be posed in the form of, or as part of, a special case.[20]

---

[13] See CCR, Ord. 25, r. 12.
[14] Sched. 11, para. 26.
[15] *Public Trustee v. Randag* [1966] Ch. 649.
[16] This has never been possible in the case of a agricultural award. It was possible in commercial award under the Arbitration Act of 1950 until the 1979 Arbitration Act abolished the procedure.
[17] CCR, Ord. 44, rr. 1, 2. The case should include a concise statement of the question of law and such facts and reference to such documents as may be necessary to enable the judge to decide the question of law. An application for an order directing an arbitrator to state a case should be made by originating application in accordance with Ord. 3, r. 4.
[18] *Dale v. Hatfield Chase Corporation* [1922] 2 K.B. 282.
[19] See Lord Halsbury L.C. in *Tabernacle Permanent Building Society v. Knight* [1892] A.C. 298, 302; *Mordue v. Palmer* (1870) L.R. 6 Ch. 22; *Re Palmer & Co. and Hosken & Co.* [1898] 1 Q.B. 131, 138; *Re Mongomery Jones & Co. and Liebenthal* (1898) 78 L.T. 406.
[20] *Tersons Ltd v. Stevenage Development Corp.* [1965] 1 Q.B. 37 (CA: see in particular Upjohn J. at 51–52). See also *Hemns v. Wheeler* [1948] 2 K.B. 61. (In this appeal from the County Court to the CA it was held that whether there was evidence to support the judge's findings of fact and whether the inferences which he had drawn were possible inferences from the facts were questions of law for the appeal). And see *British Launderers Research Association v. Hendon Borough Rating Authority* [1949] 1 K.B. 462 (CA: see Denning L.J. at 471–472 as to the distinction between primary facts, which are a matter for the tribunal of fact, and conclusions derived from them). See further *Edwards v. Bairstow* [1956] A.C. 14. (In this tax case an award of the General

Judicial control of the reference: direction to state a case   16.62

If the arbitrator feels that the application to him by a party to state a case is frivolous and made merely for the purposes of delay or is otherwise unjustifiable, he may refuse to do so, but it may be misconduct for him, having refused to state a case, to make his award without giving time for an application to be made to the court for an order directing him to state a case.[21] If the arbitrator does not agree to state a case, however, the party requesting it should lose no time in applying to the court for a direction.[22] The court has no jurisdiction to order a case to be stated on a point of law not raised in the reference to arbitration or arising out of it.[23]

If an order is made directing the arbitrator to state a special case he must adjourn the reference until the case has been dealt with. If necessary, he should apply for an extension of time for making his award. The "opinion" of the court on a case stated is binding on the arbitrator and must be applied by him. If he were to disregard it he would be guilty of misconduct.[24]

Judicial control of the reference: appeals   16.63

An appeal lies to the Court of Appeal from the opinion of the County Court on a case stated, and from a direction to state a case.[25] There is a further right of appeal to the House of Lords by leave of the Court of Appeal or of the House.[26] An arbitrator, it is submitted, should not issue his award if he knows that an appeal is pending.

Commissioners was set aside and an inference of fact was overturned on the basis that no person acting judicially or properly instructed as to the relevant law could have come to the determination reached, even though there was no apparent error of law on the face of the determination, HL). See also *Bracegirdle v. Oxley* [1947] 1 K.B. 349. (In this criminal case the Divisional Court asserted its right to review the decisions of justices both where there was no evidence on which they could have reached their decision and also where their decision was perverse *i.e.* where it was impossible to say that a reasonably minded bench of justices having the relevant facts before them could have come to the decision to which they did: see Lord Goddard C.J. at 356). See also *Ashbridge Investments Ltd v. Minister of Housing and Local Government* [1965] 1 W.L.R. 1320. (In this case the same basis of intervention was applied to a Ministerial determination as was applied to interference by the higher courts with findings by lower courts: see in particular Lord Denning M.R.).

[21] *Re Palmer & Co. v. Hosken & Co.*, (above).
[22] *Slade v. Lord Manton's Exors* (1923) L.J. C.C.R. 83,CC; *Re Spiller's and Baker's Arbitration* [1897] 1 Q.B. 312. See also *Halfdan Greig v. Sterling Coal Corp* [1973] Q.B. 843 as to the principles for exercising the court's discretion to direct a special case to be stated.
[23] *Stevens v. Feoffees of the Poor Lands in the Parish of Downham* [1926] W.N. 168. In this case the Divisional Court, having first found that it had jurisdiction, held that the County Court Judge had wrongly ordered the arbitrator to state a case on a point of law which was not raised by the arbitration being a point which therefore could not be litigated).
[24] *Mitchell-Gill v. Buchan* (1921) S.C. 390.
[25] See s. 77 of County Courts Act 1984 and RSC, Ord. 59, r. 19. See also *Lloyds Bank Ltd v. Jones* [1955] 2 Q.B. 298; *Stevens v. Feoffees of the Poor Lands in the Parish of Downham*, (above).
[26] Administration of Justice (Appeals) Act 1934.

16.64 Judicial control of the reference: drafting the special case

The arbitrator is entitled to employ legal assistance in drafting the special case and to charge for it in the costs of the arbitration. If possible the special case should be agreed by both parties before it is filed. The statement of the special case is, however, the arbitrator's responsibility, and the parties cannot dictate either the findings of fact or the questions of law.[27] They can only influence the form of the case by persuading the arbitrator to adjust it or by persuading the County Court judge to remit it to the arbitrator for a restatement or further statement.[28] An ordinary action in the court to compel the arbitrator to state questions of law in accordance with the wishes of one of the parties would be incompetent.[29]

The case should be divided into numbered paragraphs and should contain a clear statement of the facts found proved or admitted, the contentions of both parties, and the question or questions of law involved. It should be signed by the arbitrator. The material parts of the tenancy agreement or other strictly relevant document should be mentioned, and it may be desirable to annex a copy of the agreement to the case. The case should be concise, not discursive. It should not, for example, discuss the evidence on which the findings of fact have been reached. Even where the point of law is the question whether there is any evidence to support a finding of fact, a transcript of the evidence should not be appended to the special case; the case should state the effect of the evidence so far as relevant. It is not correct to set out the evidence "in its raw, unprocessed state".[30]

16.65 Judicial control of the reference: proceedings in the County Court

When the case is agreed by the parties and signed by the arbitrator it is usual for one of the parties to file it with the registrar of the County Court, with a copy for the judge, and the arbitrator need not then trouble himself further about the details of the procedure. He is not a respondent to the case or a party to the court proceedings, and will not as a rule attend the hearing, but will await the receipt of the sealed copy of the judge's order and must act upon it. If there is difficulty about agreeing the case, and it is left to the arbitrator to settle and file it, he should instruct an experienced solicitor, who will see that all the procedural formalities are complied with.[31]

On the hearing of the special case the judge is at liberty to draw any inference of fact from the case and the documents referred to therein. He may, if he thinks it necessary, remit the case to the arbitrator for a restatement or a further statement.[32] The court cannot, however, draw an inference of fact which is in conflict with a fact found, whether by inference or not, by the arbitrator. If there is a doubt about what an arbitrator would find, or what inference he would draw, the power to remit the case should be used.[33]

---

[27] A precedent is offered as Form 74 in Part V of this work.
[28] CCR, Ord. 44, r. 2(5).
[29] *Forsyth-Grant v. Salmon* 1961 S.L.T. 262.
[30] *Tersons Ltd v. Stevenage Development Corporation* [1965] 1 Q.B. 37, Pearson L.J. at 56.
[31] For procedure generally, see CCR, Ord. 44, r. 2.
[32] CCR, Ord. 44, r. 2(5).
[33] See *Re Bonnett and Fowler* [1913] 2 K.B. 537. (In this case the CA, considering an

Judicial control of the reference: misconduct and setting aside the award 16.66

It is provided by Schedule 11, paragraph 27 that where the arbitrator has misconducted himself, the County Court may remove him.[34] It is also provided that where the arbitrator has misconducted himself, or an arbitration or award has been improperly procured, or there is an error of law on the face of the award, the County Court may set aside the award.[35] It will be seen that jurisdiction in respect of misconduct and jurisdiction in respect of error of law on the face of the award are both vested in the County Court.

"Misconduct" is a misleading term, since it covers act and omissions ranging from corruption or dishonesty, conduct which is morally blameworthy, to technical or procedural irregularities which do not involve the slightest suggestion of moral blame.[36] It will be noted that misconduct may result in the removal of an arbitrator or, without any such removal, in his award being set aside.[37] The power to remove an arbitrator, which would have to be exercised before he became *functus officio* by making his award, is one which "would no doubt be sparingly exercised in cases where the misconduct was of a technical nature not affecting his competence or the propriety of allowing him to continue in office".[38] Presumably the court would exercise the power of removal in cases where an arbitrator had shown by words or conduct such evidence of bias as to indicate his unfitness to discharge his judicial duties in a proper manner.[39] As might be expected, the removal of an arbitrator during the arbitration for misconduct has been reported much less frequently than the setting aside of an award. Examples of misconduct for which the court might set aside an award are the following:

(a) Proceeding *ex parte* without sufficient justification or sufficient warning.[40]

---

agricultural award under the County Court (Agricultural Holdings) Rules 1909 doubted whether the CA was entitled to draw inferences of law and fact where there was "a clear finding of an absence of the necessary fact" (Kennedy L.J. at 548)), and *cf*. ***Universal Cargo Carriers Corporation v. Citati (No.2)*** [1958] 2 Q.B. 254. In this case the judgment below was overturned where, on hearing a special case stated under the Arbitration Act 1950, the judge had failed to draw an irresistible inference from the facts found. Parker L.J. at 264–5 stated that the power to draw inferences must not be used as "a convenient method of avoiding the necessity of remitting to an arbitrator". If there was "any conceivable doubt as to what the arbitrator would find or what inference he would draw", the matter must be remitted.

[34] Sched. 11, para. 27(1).
[35] Sched. 11, para. 27(2).
[36] See comments in ***Moran v. Lloyd's*** [1983] Q.B. 542, at 548–9. *cf*. Diplock J. in ***Heaven and Kesterton Ltd v. Sven Widaeus A/B*** [1958] 1 W.L.R. 248 at 255. See also Bingham J.'s comments in ***Zermalt Holdings SA v. Nu-life Upholstery Repairs Ltd*** [1985] 2 E.G.L.R. 14
[37] Sched. 11, para. 27(1) and (2).
[38] *Russell on Arbitration* (20th ed.) p. 157. In ***Fox v. P.G. Wellfair Ltd*** [1981] 2 Ll. Rep. 514 (a commercial, not agricultural, case) the arbitrator was removed although his integrity was not questioned; there were fundamental breaches of natural justice in his handling of the arbitration.
[39] *cf*. ***"Catalina" v. "Norma"*** (1938) 61 Ll.L.R. 360; ***Re Enoch and Zarestsky Bock & Co.*** [1910] 1 K.B. 327.
[40] ***Sharpe v. Bickerdyke*** (1815) 3 Dowl. H.L. 102; ***The Myron*** [1970] 1 Q.B. 527.

(b) Excluding from hearing persons entitled to be present.[41]

(c) Improper rejection or acceptance of evidence. Receipt of inadmissible evidence which goes to the root of an issue before the arbitrator will be regarded as misconduct.[42]

(d) Improper delegation of duties.[43]

(e) Unfair refusal of an adjournment, *e.g.* to enable a party to instruct counsel where his opponent had done so, or to enable a party to consider fresh evidence produced by his opponent or a fresh issue of importance raised, possibly by the arbitrator; or to evaluate a development which would take him unfairly by surprise unless he had a reasonable opportunity to consider its implications.[44]

(f) Disregard of elementary rules of natural justice, such as *nemo debet esse judex in propria causa*; allowing a fair hearing to both parties; ensuring that each party is aware of the case made against him.[45]

(g) Failure to "expose for the comments and submissions of the parties" matters which are likely to form the subject of the decision. A decision should not be based on specific points which the parties have never had the chance to deal with.[46]

(h) Examining a witness in the absence of one or both parties; obtaining evidence himself instead of letting the parties adduce it; giving himself "secret evidence"; using, without disclosure, particular knowledge as distinct from the general knowledge and experience which an expert arbitrator is entitled to use; inspecting the property accompanied by a person not a party to the arbitration.[47]

---

[41] *Haigh v. Haigh* (1861) 31 L.J. Ch. 420.

[42] *Walford, Baker & Co. v. Macfie* (1915) 84 L.J. K.B. 2221; *Williams v. Wallis and Cox* [1914] 2 K.B. 478. See also *Faure Fairclough Ltd v. Premier Oil and Cake Mills Ltd* [1968] 1 Lloyd's Rep. 237 and *Garton v. Hunter* [1969] 2 Q.B. 37 at 44, CA.

[43] *Re Eastern Counties Ry and Eastern Union Ry* (1863) 3 De G.J.&S. 610.

[44] *Whatley v. Morland* (1834) 2 Dowl 249; *cf. Societe Franco-Tunisienne d'Armement-Tunis v. Government of Ceylon* [1959] 1 W.L.R. 787 (a 1950 Act arbitration, where the award was remitted, not set aside); *Thomas v. Official Solicitor* (1982) 265 E.G. 601,CA; *cf.* also *R. v. Rent Assessment Committee for London, ex p. Ellis-Rees* (1982) 262 E.G. 1298.

[45] *cf. Metropolitan Properties Co. (FGC) v. Lannon* [1969] 1 Q.B. 577; *Tracomin SA v. Gibbs Nathaniel (Canada) Ltd* [1985] 1 Lloyds Rep. 586; *Phipps v. Ingram* (1835) 3 Dowl. 669.

[46] *Zermalt Holdings SA v. Nu-Life Upholstery Repairs Ltd* [1985] 2 E.G.L.R. 14; *Top Shop Estates Ltd v. C. Danino* [1985] 1 E.G.L.R. 9.

[47] *Harvey v. Shelton* (1844) 7 Beav. 455; *Re Plews and Middleton* (1845) 6 Q.B. 845; *Re O'Connor and Whitlaw's Arbitration* (1919) 88 L.J. K.B. 1242; *Ellis v. Lewin* (1963) 107 S.J. 851; 188 E.G. 493. *cf.* also *Fox v. P.G. Wellfair Ltd* [1981] 2 Ll. Rep. 514; *Top Shop Estates Ltd v. Danino* (1984) 273 E.G. 197.

(i) After refusing to state a case, proceeding to make the award without allowing time for an application to the court to direct him to state a case.[48]

(j) Acceptance of hospitality from one of the parties; provided that it is not a mere indiscretion but there is some indication of an intention to corrupt or actual corruption.[49] A flagrant disregard of the appearance of impartiality might now be sufficient.

(k) Mistake about the scope of the reference, resulting in a refusal to hear evidence on a proper claim.[50]

(l) Failure to state separately the amounts awarded in respect of the several claims, or, on application made at the proper time, in respect of particular improvements or matters.[51]

(m) Failure to make his award within the time laid down by the 1986 Act, including any extension granted by the President.[52]

(n) Failure to apply the opinion given by the court on a case stated.[53]

(o) Exceeding his jurisdiction, *e.g.* by including in an award under the 1986 Act matters not referred to arbitration under that Act, or by adjudicating on a matter not submitted to him, as by awarding to a party something not claimed, or otherwise by making an order or giving a direction not within his powers, as in favour of or against someone not a party to the arbitration.[54]

(p) Fixing his own remuneration on a basis which is wholly extravagant or indicates a serious misunderstanding of his duty.[55]

(q) Failure to deal with costs in the award or exercising the discretion as to costs in an unjudicial manner.[56]

---

[48] *Re Palmer & Co. and Hosken & Co* [1898] 1 Q.B. 131.
[49] See *Re Hopper* (1867) L.R. 2 Q.B. 367; *Moseley v. Simpson* (1873) L.R. 6 Eq. 226. (In neither case was the award set aside on this ground). To accept such hospitality would, however, be extremely unwise. If the circumstances were such as to convey an impression of bias, the courts might take a different view.
[50] *Samuel v. Cooper* (1835) 2 A.&E. 752.
[51] Sched. 11, para. 16. *Hamilton v. Peeke* (1926) L.J. C.C.R. 54,CC (on old provisions).
[52] Sched. 11, para. 14(1) and (2); *Halliday v. Semple* 1960 S.L.T. (Sh. Ct.) 11.
[53] *Mitchell-Gill v. Buchan* 1921 S.C. 390.
[54] *Hassall v. Cholmondeley* (1935) 79 S.J. 522; *cf. Societe Franco-Tunisienne d'Armement-Tunis v. Government of Ceylon* [1959] 1 W.L.R. 787; *Price v. Popkin* (1839) 10 A.&E. 139; *Croft v. Brocklesby* (1972) 224 E.G. 1405.
[55] *cf. Government of Ceylon v. Chandris* [1963] 2 Q.B. 327. But it is not misconduct to seek in open negotiations with both parties agreement to a change in the basis or payment of the arbitrator's fees: see *K/S Norjarl A/S v. Hyundai Heavy Industries Co. Ltd* (1991) 1 Lloyd's Rep. 524, CA and *Turner v. Stevenage Borough Council* [1997] 3 W.L.R. 309, CA.
[56] *cf. Re Becker, Shillan & Co. and Barry Bros* [1921] 1 K.B. 391; *Heaven and Kesterton Ltd v. Sven Widaeus A/B* [1958] 1 W.L.R. 248 at 255; *Smeaton Hanscombe & Co. Ltd v. Sassoon I. Setty, Son & Co. (No.2)* [1953] 1 W.L.R. 1481; *Lewis v. Haverfordwest RDC* [1953] 1 W.L.R. 1486; *Pepys v. London Transport Executive* [1975] 1 W.L.R.

It is possible that in some of the cases where formerly an award would have been set aside the court will now use the power first given by the 1984 Act[57] to remit the award to the arbitrator for reconsideration. An award may be set aside not only for misconduct or error of law on its face but also if "an arbitration or award has been improperly procured".[58] This would cover a case where there was no misconduct by the arbitrator but the award cannot stand because one party had fraudulently concealed a matter which he ought to have disclosed, or wilfully misled or deceived the arbitrator. "Improperly procured" has a flavour of fraud. It does not include a case where an arbitration has taken place and an award has been made as a result of an incorrect but innocent claim by one of the parties that he was the landlord of the other. Indeed in such case there is in strictness no award to set aside since the whole arbitration is a nullity.[59] An arbitrator is not guilty of misconduct, even in the technical sense, by making a mistake of fact or law. As the present Master of the Rolls has said, "To err in fact or law is not only human but an occupational hazard" on the part of an arbitrator or a judge.[60]

An arbitrator must be made a party to an application to the County Court to set the award aside,[61] and if he appears and takes part in the proceedings he makes himself an active party and costs may be given against him.[62] Further, if the arbitrator has been guilty of such collusion that one of the parties would be entitled to bring an action against him, and his award is set aside on that ground, costs may be given against him even if he does not appear.[63] An appeal lay on a question of law from a County Court judge's decision to set aside an award under the 1908 Act,[64] and it would appear that the position is the same under the 1986 Act. The appeal would be to the Court of Appeal.

Although, if the proper steps are taken, an award may be set aside for the arbitrator's misconduct, the party against whom it is sought to enforce the award cannot plead the arbitrator's misconduct as a defence to an action by the other party.[65] It would appear that if an award is set aside, or if the court removes an arbitrator, the arbitration is at an end and a new arbitrator may be appointed. This is, of course, a serious and costly matter for the parties. If, on the other hand, an award is remitted the arbitrator retains his jurisdiction but must proceed in accordance with the court's order.

234; *The Erich Schroeder* [1974] 1 Lloyd's Rep. 192

[57] 1984 Act, Sched. 3, para. 28(9). See now 1986 Act, Sched. 11, para. 28.

[58] Sched. 11, para. 27(2).

[59] *South Sea Co. v. Bumstead* [1734] 2 Eq. Cas. Ab. 80; *Metcalfe v. Ives* (1737) 1 Atk. 63; *Gartside v. Gartside* (1796) 3 Anst. 735; *Schofield v. Allen* (1904) 116 L.T. 239; *Wood v. Durose* (1958) 172 E.G. 295.

[60] *Port Sudan Cotton Co. Ltd v. Govindaswamy Chettiar & Sons* [1977] 1 Ll. Rep. 166 at 178, Donaldson J.

[61] CCR, Ord. 44, r. 3.

[62] *Lendon v. Keen* [1916] 1 K.B. 994. In *Ellis v. Lewin* (1963) 107 S.J. 851 the arbitrator was a party and represented by counsel, but does not appear to have taken an active part. The costs were awarded against the landlord.

[63] *ibid.*

[64] *Williams v. Wallis and Cox* [1914] 1 K.B. 478.

[65] *Birtley & District Co-operative Society Ltd v. Windy Nook and District Industrial Co-operative Society* [1959] 1 W.L.R. 142 (under 1950 Act but in principle applicable to agricultural arbitrations).

Judicial control of the reference: remission of award for reconsideration 16.67
A valuable new power given for the first time by the 1984 Act[66] is for the County Court to remit the award, or any part of the award, to the reconsideration of the arbitrator.[67] Remission, rather than the setting of the award aside, is appropriate where there have been "procedural mishaps"[68] short of misconduct, or misconduct of the less serious kind. Examples are refusal to grant a postponement of the hearing which ought to have been granted, determining an issue on reliance of matters which had not been put to the parties, or "giving himself evidence" without allowing the parties an opportunity of commenting on it.[69]

Where remission is ordered the arbitrator must, unless the order otherwise directs, make and sign his award within 30 days after the date of the order.[70] The court may, however, extend, or further extend, that time for such period as it thinks proper if it is satisfied that the time-limit is for any good reason insufficient.[71] Where it appears to the County Court that there is an error of law on the face of the award the court may, instead of remitting the award, vary it by substituting a corrected version of the erroneous part; and the award will then have effect as so varied.[72]

Judicial control of the reference: error of law on the face of the award 16.68
The County Court may set the award aside for an error of law on its face.[73] This means some erroneous legal proposition which is stated in the award itself, or in a document incorporated therewith, and which is the basis of the award.[74] The award then becomes a "speaking award" and the court may consider it. The doctrine that the court can look at a document "incorporated" with the award has,

---

[66] 1984 Act, Sched. 3, para. 28(9).
[67] Sched. 11, para. 28(1).
[68] This phrase is intended to describe a miscellany of cases where remission had been ordered and not to delimit the extent of jurisdiction under this head. If in principle it was right to order remission, it does not matter that this label is not appropriate (Lord Donaldson M.R. in *King v. Thomas McKenna Ltd* [1991] 2 Q.B. 480 at 496F).
[69] Unless, as in *Fox v. P.G. Wellfair Ltd* [1981] 2 Lloyd's Rep. 514, there was such a complete mishandling of the arbitration as to justify setting the award aside and removing the arbitrator.
[70] Sched. 11, para. 28(3).
[71] Sched. 11, para. 28(4). It does not say whether the application must be made before the expiry of the current time-limit and, by contrast with the explicit restriction in s. 70(3) of the 1948 Act, it would seem that it need not; but *ex abundanti cautela* it would be as well to apply before the current time-limit expires.
[72] Sched. 11, para. 28(2).
[73] Sched. 11, para. 27(2). Before 1972 this jurisdiction was vested in the High Court, but by s. 15(1) of the 1972 Act the County Court was given exclusive jurisdiction under this head.
[74] *Re Jones and Carter* [1922] 2 Ch. 599; *Champsey Bhara & Co. v. Jivaj Balloo Spinning and Weaving Co. Ltd* [1923] A.C. 480; *Racecourse Betting Control Board v. Secretary of State for Air* [1944] Ch. 114. See also *Heaven and Kesterton Ltd v. Sven Widaeus A/B* [1958] 1 W.L.R. 248 at 255, and *cf. L.E. Cattan Ltd v. A. Michaelides & Co.* [1958] 1 W.L.R. 717 at 719 ("a speaking award"). See also *Lloyd's Bank Ltd v. Jones* [1955] 2 Q.B. 298 at 310. Not every document referred to in an award is "incorporated": see *Giacomo Costa Fu Andrea v. British Trading Co. Ltd* [1963] 1 Q.B. 201.

however, to be applied critically and strictly. Pleadings do not fall within a special category which can always be looked at—they can only be looked at if the arbitrator has incorporated them. Statements of case in an agricultural arbitration would be subject to the same rule.[75] The court will not look at affidavit evidence proffered to show that the arbitrator failed to take a material factor into account, there being no indication of error on the face of the award.[76] An award may be set aside under this head if it appeared on its face to be based on an erroneous interpretation of the contract of tenancy[77] or of the statutory provisions or disclosed an error as to the law of evidence.[78]

The effect of giving an inadequate statement of reasons in response to a request under section 12 of the Tribunals and Inquiries Act 1971 has not been entirely clear on the authorities. According to one view it constitutes an error of law entitling a court to set the decision or award aside[79]; on this view the addition of legally irrelevant reasons could amount to an excess of jurisdiction.[80] The other view has been that the failure to give adequate reasons is not itself an error of law and that if a mixture of good and bad reasons is given the decision or award stands as valid provided that the reasons are independent and severable.[81] A useful synopsis of these conflicting authorities is provided in *Crake v. Supplementary Benefits Commission*.[82] This difficulty should not be confused with the allegation that there has been a finding of fact which was made without evidence.[83] The power now given to courts to remit an award to the arbitrator for reconsideration[84] relieves them in some cases of a difficult decision as to whether the award should be set aside for inadequacy of reasons. In many cases sufficiency of reasons is due to poor drafting rather than error; and this can be corrected on reconsideration.

County Courts will no doubt exercise this jurisdiction on the same strict principles as guided the High Court when the jurisdiction was vested in it.[85] Extraneous

---

[75] See *Belsfield Court Construction Co. Ltd v. Pywell* [1970] 2 Q.B. 47, where it was held that the pleadings were not incorporated and hence no error on the face of the award.
[76] *Re Allen and Matthews' Arbitration* [1971] 2 Q.B. 518.
[77] For an example, see *Maxwell-Lefroy v. Bracey* [1956] E.G.D. 305; see also (1956) 100 S.J. 201.
[78] cf. *R. v. Nat Bell Liquors Ltd* [1922] 2 A.C. 128 at 144. For a recent example of an error of law consisting of an incorrect construction of the tenancy agreement, see *Burton v. Timmis* (1986) 281 E.G. 795, CA; independent obligations misconstrued as interdependent.
[79] *Re Poyser and Mills' Arbitration* [1964] 2 Q.B. 467; *Givaudan & Co. Ltd v. Minister of Housing and Local Government* [1967] 1 W.L.R. 250. *Hughes v. Homewood* (1963) 188 E.G. 875.
[80] *Anisminic Ltd v. Foreign Compensation Commission* [1969] 2 A.C. 147 (because taking irrelevant factors into account).
[81] *Re Allen and Matthews' Arbitration* [1971] 2 Q.B. 518; *Mountview Court Properties Ltd v. Devlin* (1970) 21 P.&C.R. 689, 693; *Paultons Square Properties Ltd v. LCC* (1965) 63 L.G.R. 158.
[82] [1982] 1 All E.R. 498, Woolf J.
[83] An undoubted jurisdiction but one which the court will often treat with distaste: see generally Mustill & Boyd, *Commercial Arbitration* (2nd ed., Butterworths, 1989) p. 596 and n. 12.
[84] Sched. 11, para. 28(1).
[85] There is no High Court jurisdiction at first instance for complaints based on misconduct or error of law on the face of the record, the jurisdiction under these heads being

considerations not appearing on the face of the award, must be excluded.[86] It is a question of construction whether the arbitrator intended to invite those reading the award to read also the document which is alleged to be incorporated.[87]

Judicial control of the reference: no remedy for mistakes of fact or law except as above 16.69

Apart from the County Court's jurisdiction in regard to misconduct and error of law on the face of the record, including the power of remission, there is no remedy where the arbitrator in good faith makes a mistake of law or fact in his decision. He may be prevented from making a mistake of law by being compelled to state a special case, but if this machinery is not used and he makes a mistake of law which is not apparent on the face of the award or any document incorporated therewith there is no jurisdiction in the court to correct it. There is no appeal in the ordinary sense from his decision.[88] Even if the exercise of the arbitrator's discretion as to costs is based on an erroneous view taken by him of the law, the court cannot interfere unless the award is a "speaking award" which discloses its own error.[89]

Judicial control of the reference: judicial review theoretically available 16.70

An application for judicial review may be made in respect of awards made by a statutory arbitrator, *i.e.* an arbitrator given compulsory jurisdiction by a statute, such as arbitrators under the 1986 Act, whether their actual appointment is by virtue of an agreement or by the President.[90] This means that the prerogative orders of certiorari, mandamus, prohibition and remedies by way of injunction and declaration are available to an applicant for judicial review who can satisfy the court that the remedy in question is appropriate in the circumstances. Judicial review will not be available where the arbitrator's jurisdiction derives from contract, not statute.[91] But although in theory judicial review might be competent in cases where an agricultural arbitrator exceeded his jurisdiction or was guilty of a breach of fundamental rules of natural justice, it seems that, in view of the other

---

exclusively in the County Court. For cases on the previous law where the error in law jurisdiction was still vested in the High Court, see *Re Jones and Carter* [1922] 2 Ch. 599 and *Jones v. Pembrokeshire County Council* [1967] 1 Q.B. 181; *Price v. Williams* (1967) 201 E.G. 863. It was "unfortunate dichotomy", *per* Megaw J. in *Re Poyser and Mills' Arbitration* [1964] 2 Q.B. 467 at 475. Although the High Court has now no first instance jurisdiction, the CA has appellate jurisdiction from the County Court. For example, see *Burton v. Timmis* (1986) 281 E.G. 795.

[86] *Re Jones and Carter* [1922] 2 Ch. 599; *Price v. Romilly* [1960] 1 W.L.R. 1360.
[87] *Giacomo Costa fu Andrea v. British Italian Trading Co. Ltd* [1963] 1 Q.B. 201 at 216, 217, 219.
[88] See *Tersons Ltd v. Stevenage Development Corp.* [1965] 1 Q.B. 37 at 47 and 51.
[89] *Heaven and Kesterton Ltd v. Sven Widaeus A/B* [1958] 1 W.L.R. 248.
[90] See Supreme Court Act 1982, s. 31 and RSC, Ord. 53, r. 1. See also *R. v. National Joint Council for the Craft of Dental Technicians, ex p. Neate* [1953] 1 Q.B. 704; *Port Arthur Shipbuilding Co. Ltd v. Arthurs* [1969] S.C.R. 85; *Imperial Metal Industries (Kynoch) Ltd v. AUEW* [1979] I.C.R. 23, 33.
[91] *cf. R. v. Powell, ex p. Camden* [1925] 1 K.B. 641, *R. v. National Joint Council for the Craft of Dental Technicians (Disputes Committee), ex p. Neate* (above); *R. v. Agricultural Land Tribunal for S.E. Area, ex p. Bracey* [1960] 1 W.L.R. 911. See generally *O'Reilly v. Mackman* [1983] 2 A.C. 237 and *Law v. National Greyhound Racing Club Ltd* [1983] 1 W.L.R. 1302.

remedies open to an applicant, successful applications will be very rare. An application based on complaint of the alleged inadequacy of reasons would be likely to fail.[92]

16.71 Supervision of arbitrators by the Council on Tribunals
Arbitrators appointed otherwise than by agreement are among the categories of Tribunals which are under the direct supervision of the Council on Tribunals.[93]

16.72 Arbitration and costs generally
The costs of, and incidental to,[94] the arbitration and award (*i.e.* the whole costs of the reference) are in the discretion of the arbitrator, who may direct to and by whom, and in what manner, the costs, or any part of the costs, are to be paid.[95] In awarding costs the arbitrator is directed to take into consideration (a) the reasonableness or unreasonableness of the claim of either party, whether in respect of amount or otherwise, (b) any unreasonable demand for particulars or refusal to supply particulars, and (c) generally all the circumstances of the case. The arbitrator may disallow the costs of any witness whom he considers to have been called unnecessarily and any other costs which he considers to have been unnecessarily incurred.[96] On the application of either party, the costs awarded shall be taxable in the County Court according to such of the County Court scales as may be directed by the arbitrator, or, in the absence of any such direction, by the County Court.[97]

The arbitrator's discretion is not fettered by the rules and practice of the judges of the High Court in awarding costs,[98] but he must exercise his discretion by making some order as to costs[99] and must exercise it in a proper judicial, not in a capricious or irresponsible, manner.[1] The parties may, however, before the arbitration make an agreement as to costs, which, if otherwise valid, is enforceable notwithstanding the arbitrator's discretion.[2]

The general working principle which should be followed, other things being

---

[92] See *R. v. Secretary of State for the Environment, ex p. GLC*, *The Times*, December 30, 1985.
[93] Tribunals and Inquiries Act 1971, Part I of Sched. I, para. 1(b), as amended by the 1986 Act, Sched. 14, para. 49. Thus arbitrators appointed by the President are subject to the Council's supervision.
[94] "Costs of, and incidental to": *cf.* as to this expression *Re Fahy's Will Trust* [1962] 1 W.L.R. 17.
[95] Sched. 11, para. 23.
[96] Sched. 11, para. 25.
[97] Sched. 11, para. 24.
[98] *Gray v. (Lord) Ashburton* [1917] A.C. 26, a remarkable position; contrast *Foster v. Great Western Ry* (1882) 8 Q.B.D. 515.
[99] *Richardson v. Worsley* (1859) 5 Ex. 613; *Re Becker, Shillan & Co. and Barry Bros* [1921] 1 K.B. 391.
[1] *cf. Stotesbury v. Turner* [1943] K.B. 370; *Rosen & Co. v. Dowley and Selby* [1943] 2 All E.R. 172; *Smeaton Hanscomb & Co. Ltd v. Sassoon I Setty, Son & Co. (No.2)* [1953] 1 W.L.R. 1481; *Lewis v. Haverfordwest RDC* [1953] 1 W.L.R. 1486; *Heaven and Kesterton Ltd v. Sven Widaeus A/B* [1958] 1 W.L.R. 248; *Fenceline Ltd v. W.J. Simms Sons & Cooke Ltd* (1972) 224 E.G. 1041.
[2] *Mansfield v. Robinson* [1928] 2 K.B. 353.

equal, is that adopted by the courts—costs should follow the event. The arbitrator may simply award that the costs of and incidental to the arbitration and award shall be paid by the named party. Any such costs are taxable in the County Court, whether or not the arbitrator gives a direction to that effect.[3] If in a proper case the arbitrator decides that there is no reason to give preference to either party, the sensible course is to direct that each party should bear his own costs and pay half the costs of the award, as this will avoid the need for the inquiry into the costs of the parties which would be required by an order that each party should bear half the total costs of the reference. The type of order is appropriate not only where, for example, the sum awarded falls exactly midway between the two parties' figures (which will seldom happen) but also where it is not substantially or significantly nearer the one than the other. Mathematical exactness in awarding costs is seldom possible. There may, however, be cases where the winner has clearly failed on one identifiable issue; in such a case the order might be that the winner should receive his costs except in so far as they had been increased by the issue on which he had failed.

An agricultural arbitrator appears to have no power, unless the parties have given it to him, to award costs on the basis of solicitor and client, and if he does so the award may be set aside.[4] An agricultural arbitrator is not given power to "tax or settle" the amount of the costs, taxation being the function of the County Court registrar, with a right of appeal to the judge.[5] In practice agricultural arbitrators do sometimes settle the costs, but this is done with the parties' consent, since either may require taxation.

Although in a proper case the arbitrator may correctly exercise his judicial discretion by depriving the successful party of his costs, and although he is not fettered by the rules which have been laid down to guide the courts,[6] he should consider all the circumstances most carefully before making such an order. He should consider the situation even more earnestly since such an order is clearly in danger of being challenged as an unjudicial exercise of discretion, although one cannot say that it is never justifiable.[7]

In exercising his discretion an arbitrator will naturally take into account "open" offers (but must not take into account "without prejudice" offers) made before the arbitration.

Where a "sealed" offer is made, it is analogous to a payment into court or alternatively a written offer without prejudice save as to costs and is subject to the same principles as those applicable in the High Court.[8] Where money claims only are at issue for consideration by the arbitrator, in deciding whether a claimant has

---

[3] Sched. 11, para. 24. When the arbitrator fixes the scale the registrar should not fix a different scale: *Perkins (H.G.) Ltd v. Brent-Shaw* [1973] 1 W.L.R. 975.

[4] *Griffiths v. Morris* [1895] 1 Q.B. 866; *Seccombe v. Babb* (1840) 6 M.&W. 129.

[5] Sched. 11, para. 24.

[6] *Gray v. Lord Ashburton* [1917] A.C. 26.

[7] For a 1950 Act case, see *Heaven and Kesterton Ltd v. Sven Widaeus A/B* [1958] 1 W.L.R. 248. The award of costs involves the exercise of a judicial discretion not the recognition of a legal right: see *President of India v. Jadranska Slobodna Plovidba* (1922) 2 Ll. Rep. 274.

[8] *Everglade Maritime Inc. v. Schiffahrtsgesellschaft Detlef von Appen m.b.H.* [1993] Q.B. 780 CA.

achieved more by rejecting an offer and continuing with the arbitration than by accepting it, the arbitrator should take no account of the incidence of costs in the reference but should only have regard to the claim for principal and interest.[9]

16.73 Costs and arbitration: the special case
There is no doubt that, as a result of Schedule 11, paragraph 23, the costs of the special case (not merely the costs of its preparation,[10] but also the costs of the hearing) can be dealt with by the arbitrator. It has been suggested that the County Court has no power to deal with the costs of the special case on the ground that the court's general discretion in CCR, Ord. 38, r. 1 is "subject to the provisions of any Act or rule" and therefore subject to Schedule 11, paragraph 23. It is, however, submitted that the County Court has power to deal with the costs of a special case if it thinks fit; in practice some County Court judges have made orders as to such costs while others have left them to the arbitrator. Similarly, where there is an appeal to the Court of Appeal, that court may itself make an order as to costs or leave it to the arbitrator to include them in his award.

16.74 Costs and arbitration: costs where award is set aside
If an award is set aside on the ground of misconduct or error of law on the face of the award, or because the award has been improperly procured, the party to whom the arbitrator has awarded costs cannot recover them.[11] The award is a nullity and, therefore, any order as to costs contained in it is inoperative. Further, the court cannot substitute a new order for costs so far as the arbitration proceedings are concerned. The costs of the County Court proceedings to set aside the award are in the discretion of the judge and will usually, in the absence of special circumstances, follow the event. The arbitrator will not in the normal case be condemned in costs if he takes no part in the proceedings.[12] The question arises as to what happens if one party has already paid to the other party costs under an award which is later set aside, whether for misconduct or error of law, or where the parties have made a payment to the arbitrator in respect of his own charges. It would seem that payments so made are not in general recoverable. If, however, there has been something in the nature of a conspiracy between one of the parties and the arbitrator, it is submitted that the party who has had the award set aside will be able to recover, by action, damages including his costs of the arbitration.

---

[9] *Everglade Maritime Inc.* (above).
[10] *McQuater v. Fergusson* 1911 S.C. 640.
[11] cf. *Davis v. Witney UDC* (1899) 15 T.L.R. 275.
[12] The principles applied by the courts, as explained in *Lendon v. Keen* [1916] 1 K.B. 994, are as follows: (1) if the arbitrator himself appears and takes part in the proceedings he may be ordered to pay the costs; (2) if he has been guilty of such collusion as to entitle one of the parties to bring an action against him, and his award is set aside on that ground, he may be ordered to pay the costs whether he appears and takes part in the proceedings or not; (3) if he has been guilty of a technical act of misconduct only, without any dishonesty or lack of good faith, and has taken no part in the proceedings, he cannot be ordered to pay the costs.

Costs and arbitration: costs where the arbitrator has no jurisdiction The provisions of Schedule 11 relating to the fixing and recovery of the remuneration of an arbitrator and the making and enforcement of an award as to costs, together with the ancillary provisions in the Schedule, apply where the arbitrator has no jurisdiction to decide the question referred to him in the same way as where he has jurisdiction.[13] The costs of a special case to determine his jurisdiction will be included in the costs which may properly be dealt with under this provision. 16.75

Costs and arbitration: additional costs of apportionment under section 75 of the 1986 Act 16.76
Where the arbitrator has to apportion the tenant's compensation under section 75 in a case where the reversionary interest in the holding is severed, the arbitrator is required to direct in what proportions any additional costs of the award caused by the apportionment are to be paid by the persons who together constitute the landlord.[14]

Costs and arbitration: date for payment of costs 16.77
The award must fix a day not later than one month after the delivery thereof for the payment of any costs awarded.[15]

---

[13] Sched. 11, para. 30. Before the 1958 Act (Sched. 1, para. 21(1)) an arbitrator who had no jurisdiction could neither make an award as to the costs of the arbitration nor enforce the payment of his own remuneration or expenses.
[14] s. 75(1), (2).
[15] Sched. 11, para. 18.

CHAPTER 17

MISCELLANEOUS

17.1 Miscellaneous provisions: general

17.2 Recovery and charging of sums due

17.8 Limited owners

17.17 Service of notices

17.25 Crown land

Miscellaneous provisions: general 17.1
This chapter brings together a number of matters which do not fall conveniently or logically into the discussion in the other Chapters of this work. The main areas covered are: recovery and charging of sums due[1]; limited owners[2] and service of notices[3].

RECOVERY AND CHARGING OF SUMS DUE

Recovery by order of the County Court 17.2
Subject to the provisions excluding personal liability in the case of a landlord entitled otherwise than for his own benefit,[4] where a sum agreed or awarded under the Act to be paid for compensation, costs or otherwise by a landlord or tenant is not paid within 14 days after the time when the payment becomes due, it is recoverable, if the County Court so orders, as if payable under an ordinary order of that court.[5] In the case of an award the 14 days will run from the date fixed by the award for payment, which must not be later than one month after the delivery of the award.[6]

Charges on the holding: tenant's charges 17.3
In certain cases the tenant is given the right to apply to the Minister for an order charging the holding with payment of the amount due in respect of compensation from the landlord. Where the landlord is personally liable the tenant may obtain such a charge if the landlord fails to pay the amount within one month from the date when it becomes due.[7] Where the landlord is entitled to receive the rents and profits

---

[1] ss. 85–87, see paras 17.2–17.7 below.
[2] ss. 89–90, see paras 17.8–17.16 below.
[3] s. 93, see paras 17.17–17.24 below.
[4] s. 85(3).
[5] s. 85(1). See *Grundy v. Hewson* [1933] 1 K.B. 787.
[6] Sched. 11, para. 18.
[7] s. 85(2).

of the holding otherwise than for his own benefit, *e.g.* as a trustee, he is not personally liable for any sum agreed or awarded under the Act to be paid to the tenant, or awarded to be paid by the landlord, but if he does not pay it for one month after it becomes due the tenant may obtain a charging order.[8]

17.4 Section 85: enforcement: commentary

It will occasionally be necessary to trace the history of this section.[9] The very general words "a sum agreed or awarded under this Act" in sub-section (1) would cover, amongst other things, additional compensation payable under section 60(2) and early resumption compensation under section 62 as well as ordinary compensation for improvements and tenant right. It covers, it is submitted, the sums payable following death or retirement under section 48(5)(b) and section 56(3). The reference to "compensation, costs or otherwise" includes rent increased as a result of a rent arbitration and the *ejusdem generis* rule does not apply.[10] Where a sum of money is payable, it becomes due on the date specified in the agreement or, if no date is specified, on the date of the agreement itself. In the case of an award the arbitrator must[11] fix a day not later than one month after delivery of the award as the date for payment. The sub-section gives the County Court jurisdiction, regardless of the amount, although there is some question as to whether or not the High Court also has jurisdiction.[12]

The reference in sub-section (2) to compensation is a far narrower expression than, for example "compensation costs or otherwise" in the preceding sub-section, as are the words "any sum agreed or awarded under this Act" in sub-section (3).

In sub-section (3), the words "otherwise than for his own benefit" will cover ordinary trustees but there is some doubt whether a tenant for life of settled land can be regarded as entitled to receive the rents and profits "otherwise than for his own benefit".[13] Although sub-section (3)(a) provides that the landlord shall not be under any liability, that landlord may in fact pay and obtain a charge under section 86(1). A personal action cannot be brought by the tenant against the personal representatives of a deceased landlord who is within the words of section 85(3), since the tenant is restricted to the charge.[14] Any charging order falling within sub-section (3)(b) will be dealt with in terms of priority as required by section 87(6).

---

[8] s. 85(3). Section 85 covers sums agreed or awarded under the Act generally.
[9] See Law Com: No. 153, p. 6 and Minutes and Report of Joint Committee on Consolidation Bills (H.L. 56, H.C. 178).
[10] See *Grundy v. Hewson* (above).
[11] Sched. 11, para. 18.
[12] The view taken by Talbot J. in *Horrell v. St John of Bletso (Lord)* [1928] 2 K.B. 616 that the jurisdiction of the High Court was not ousted was doubted by Megaw J. in *Jones v. Pembrokeshire County Council* [1967] 1 Q.B. 181 as inconsistent with the principle of *Re Jones & Carter* [1922] 2 Ch. 599 that where the County Court is expressly given jurisdiction the jurisdiction of the High Court is *pro tanto* abrogated.
[13] See an article by E.H. Scamell on "The Special Position of Limited Owners of Agricultural Land" in (1951) 15 Conv. (N.S.) 415, pp. 418–419.
[14] *Edwardson v. Townend* (1929) 73 S.J. 109.

Charges on the holding: landlord's charge for repayment 17.5

A landlord is entitled to obtain from the Minister an order charging the holding with a sum paid or payable in any of the following circumstances: (1) where he has paid to the outgoing tenant compensation for an improvement, a tenant-right matter, or disturbance;[15] (2) where he has exercised his rights under section 67(5) to carry out himself an improvement approved by the Tribunal;[16] or (3) where, being entitled to receive the rents and profits of the holding otherwise than for his own benefit (*e.g.* as trustee), he has paid or is going to pay the tenant any sum agreed or awarded under the Act for compensation or to be paid by the landlord.[17] A charge can be obtained under the third category above before any money is actually paid to the tenant. This enables money to be provided by a land improvement company or other lender without the landlord having to find the cash first. A landlord is entitled (at his own cost) to request an arbitrator who is determining the outgoing tenant's claim for compensation in respect of improvements or tenant-right matters to certify the amount of the compensation and the term for which a charge may properly be made, having regard to the time at which the improvements or tenant-right matters in question are to be deemed to be exhausted.[18] These provisions enabling a landlord to obtain a charge are particularly useful to limited owners, but they may be useful even to owners beneficially entitled in fee simple in cases where it is desirable to place transactions affecting real estate on a separate footing from others. A charge created by a limited owner under section 86 will enure for the benefit of his estate after his death, subject to any directions by the Minister in regard to the time at which an improvement is to be taken to be exhausted, so that his personal representatives will be able to enforce it. It should be noted that the rights conferred by section 86 on a landlord to obtain a charging order must not be exercised by trustees for ecclesiastical or charitable purposes except with the approval in writing of the Charity Commissioners.[19]

Section 86: Power of landlord to obtain charge on holding: commentary 17.6

The reference to the landlord, in sub-section (1) includes the executors of a deceased landlord.[20] There is a contrast between the words "has paid" in sub-section (1)(a) and sub-section (3) where the charge is obtainable before payment. Compensation paid in respect of damage from game does not fall within section 86(1)(a). In regard to sub-section (2) it should be noted that tenant-right does not fall within the sub-section. In regard to sub-section (3) there arises the same problem in relation to the tenant for life of settled land as mentioned above in relation to section 85.[21] The bracketed words in section 86(3) will apply where the land is already agreed to be sold.[22]

---

[15] s. 86(1)(a).
[16] s. 86(1)(b).
[17] s. 86(3).
[18] s. 86(2).
[19] s. 86(4).
[20] *c.f.* **Gough v. Gough** [1891] 2 Q.B. 665.
[21] See para. 17.4 above.
[22] *c.f.* **Bennett v. Stone** [1902] 1 Ch. 226, where the vendor was in the position of a trustee

17.7 General provisions in regard to charges

The charge will include costs properly incurred as well as the sum payable.[23] The order will be made in favour of the person obtaining the charge and his executors, administrators and assigns, and will make such provision for the payment of interest and the payment of the sum charged by instalments, and certain such directions for giving effect to the charge, as the Minister things fit.[24] In the case of a landlord's charge under section 86 the sum charged is to be a charge on the holding (or the part thereof charged as the case may be) for the landlord's interest therein and all interests therein subsequent to that of the landlord, but so that where the landlord has a leasehold interest only the charge shall not extend beyond the interest of the landlord, his executors, administrators and assigns.[25] Further, in the case of a landlord's charge under section 86, where the landlord is not the absolute beneficial owner of the holding no instalment of capital or payment of interest is to be made payable after the time when the improvement in respect of which compensation is paid will, in the Minister's opinion have become exhausted.[26] The usual type of clause in settlements and wills which provides for the determination or forfeiture of interests which are charged does not apply to a tenant's charge under section 85(2) or a landlord's charge under section 86.[27] Any charge under section 85, and an occupier's charge under section 74 of the 1948 Act,[28] have absolute priority over all other charges, however and whenever created or arising.[29] This would give priority even over a Crown charge.[30] As between themselves charges under the above sections rank in the order of their creation (not registration).[31]

Any company incorporated by Parliament and having power to advance money for land improvement may take an assignment of any charge created under section 85(2) or 86(1), upon such terms and conditions as may be agreed upon between the company and the person entitled to the charge, and may assign any charge of which they have taken an assignment.[32]

Charges created under section 85 or 86 are land charges within the meaning of

---

for the purchaser; in such a case the vendor who paid compensation to the tenant would presumably be able to obtain such a charge.

[23] s. 87(1).
[24] s. 87(2).
[25] s. 87(3). Thus a life tenant can obtain a charge which is binding on the remaindermen (subject to any direction of the Minister limiting the operation of the charge) but a lessee cannot obtain a charge that will bind the reversioner.
[26] s. 87(4).
[27] s. 87(5).
[28] This relates to the special provision in s. 66 of the 1948 Act (repealed together with s. 74 of that Act by the 1984 Act), which provided for compensation in the case of a tenancy not binding on a mortgagee. For a discussion, see pp.134–137 of the 12th edition of this book. The scope for s. 66 was virtually non-existent before its repeal and the present saving for s. 74 charges must relate to a small and diminishing, if not now vanished, category.
[29] s. 87(6).
[30] s. 87(8).
[31] s. 87(6). It may be noted that s. 93 of the 1948 Act (revocation and variation of orders) is not consolidated in the 1986 Act.
[32] The Agricultural Mortgage Corporation and the Lands Improvement Company are within this category.

the Land Charges Act 1972 and may be registered accordingly. If not so registered they will be void against a purchaser for value of the land charged.[33] A potential purchaser should search the register. It is understood that the Ministry in practice requires an applicant for a charge who is not absolutely entitled for his own benefit to give notice of the application to other persons likely to be affected. Such notice has to be served personally or by registered letter. There is no official form of charge or form of application for a charge.

LIMITED OWNERS

The Trusts of Land and Appointment of Trustees Act 1996 — 17.8
The Trusts of Land and Appointment of Trustees Act 1996[34] prevents any new Settled Land Act settlements being created after the commencement of that Act. Existing settlements remain in existence and it is for those settlements that the provisions discussed in the following paragraphs are important. The 1996 Act also operated to amend the terms of section 89 of the Agricultural Holdings Act 1986 so as to remove any reference to powers conferred by the Law of Property Act 1925. In the original version of the 1986 Act those words had operated to permit trustees of a trust for sale to exercise the same powers and be treated in the same way as a tenant for life of settled land. The provisions are no longer necessary in relation to trusts of land[35] because trustees of land in relation to land which is subject to their trust have all the powers of an absolute owner.[36] Accordingly the scope of sections 89 and 90 has been significantly reduced as from January 1, 1997. The 1996 Act does not apply to land within the University and College Estates Act 1925.

Limited owners: power of limited owners to consent — 17.9
A landlord of an agricultural holding may, for the purposes of the 1986 Act, notwithstanding the fact that his estate or interest is limited, give any consent, make any agreement or enter into any transaction which would have been within his competence if he had been the owner in fee simple or, if his interest is an interest in a leasehold, he had been absolutely entitled to that leasehold.[37]

Limited owners: application of capital money — 17.10
Where, under powers conferred by the Settled Land Act 1925 or the Law of Property Act 1925, capital money is applied in or about the execution of any

---

[33] Land Charges Act 1972, Sched. 2, para. 1, as amended and extended by 1986 Act, Sched. 17, para. 51.
[34] 1996 c.47 coming into force on January 1, 1997 (S.I. 1996 No.2974).
[35] Into which all pre-existing trusts for sale were converted and into which all future trusts whether express bare or implied will fall where they constitute trusts of land.
[36] s. 6(1) of the Trusts of Land and Appointment of Trustees Act 1996.
[37] 1986 Act, s. 88. This power is expressed in general terms, so that it covers not only the matters originally covered by s. 80 of the 1948 Act, but also those which arose under ss. 9–15 of the 1968 Act and under Part II of the 1976 Act and Sched. 2 to the 1984 Act (now ss. 60–63 and Part IV of the 1986 Act). See on this Law Com: No. 153 and the Minutes and Report of the Joint Committee on Consolidation Bills (H.L. 56-II and H.C. 178-II).

improvement specified in Schedule 7 to the 1986 Act, no provision is to be made for requiring the money or any part of it to be replaced out of income, and, accordingly, any such improvement is to be deemed to be an improvement authorised by Part I of Schedule 3 to the Settled Land Act 1925.[38] There is a similar provision relating to powers conferred by the University and College Estates Act 1925 and 1964, with the proviso that the Minister or (where applicable) the university or college itself may decide that the money should be so replaced.[39] Neither provision itself confers any power to apply capital money: this must be sought in the parent statute.[40] In the case of settled land the relevant statutory power is to apply capital money "in payment as for an improvement authorised by this Act[41] of any money expended and costs incurred by a landlord under or in pursuance of the Agricultural Holdings Act 1986, or any similar previous enactment, or under custom or agreement or otherwise, in or about the execution of any improvement comprised in Schedule 7 to the said Agricultural Holdings Act".[42]

Section 89 of the 1986 Act is a short and apparently simple and straightforward section on the face of it, but the background of law is somewhat complex, as the interaction of the 1925 legislation and successive Agricultural Holdings Acts has produced, in the words of one Chancery judge, a "welter of confused and confusing enactments".[43] The position appears to be as follows.

17.11 **Limited owners: capital money not to be applied directly in compensation**

It was decided by Plowman J. in *Re Duke of Wellington's Parliamentary Estates*,[44] rejecting a dictum of Joyce J. in an earlier case,[45] that the words quoted above from section 73(1)(iv) of the Settled Land Act 1925, as amended, did not enable money to be applied directly by a tenant for life in the payment of compensation to agricultural tenants on the termination of their tenancies. The words quoted are directed to the payment of the landlord's costs in carrying out the improvements, not the payment of compensation to an outgoing tenant, which is based, not on the cost of the improvement but on the increase attributable to the improvement in the value of the holding as a holding.[46] The same principle applies *a fortiori* to compensation for tenant-right matters and disturbance.

---

[38] s. 89(1).
[39] s. 89(2). See s. 26(5) of the University and College Estates Act 1925 as modified by Sched. 1 to the 1964 Act.
[40] See s. 73(1) of the Settled Land Act 1925 as amended by Sched. 14, para. 11, to the 1986 Act; s. 28(1) of the Law of Property Act 1925; s. 26(1) of the Universities and College Estates Act 1925 as amended by Sched. 14, para. 13, to the 1986 Act.
[41] *i.e.*, the Settled Land Act 1925.
[42] See s. 73(1)(iv) of the Settled Land Act 1925 as amended by Sched. 14, para. 11, to the 1986 Act.
[43] *per* Vaisey J. in *Re Duke of Northumberland* [1951] Ch. 202 at 208.
[44] [1972] Ch. 374.
[45] *Re Earl De La Warr's Cooden Beach Settled Estate* [1913] 1 Ch. 142 at 144.
[46] An interpretation given in 1951 by E.H. Scamell in 15 Conv. (N.S.) 415, and supported by s. 13 of the Landlord and Tenant Act 1927, which, after a provision similar to s. 73(1)(iv) of the Settled Land Act, goes on to provide expressly that capital money may be applied in payment of a sum due to a tenant for compensation under the 1927 Act.

Limited owners: tenant for life may obtain a charge 17.12

In *Re Duke of Wellington's Parliamentary Estates* (above) Plowman J. made the following statement by way of dictum about the possibility of the tenant for life obtaining reimbursement out of capital money by means of a charge on the holding:

> "The fact that compensation to an outgoing tenant for improvements is outside the provisions of section 73 of the Settled Land Act does not mean that it is necessarily irrecoverable by the landlord, since section 82 of the Agricultural Holdings Act 1948 [section 86 of the 1986 Act] contains a provision enabling a landlord to obtain from the Minister an order charging the holding with repayment of the compensation, and the trustees can redeem that charge out of capital moneys, pursuant to section 73(1)(ii) of the Settled Land Act."

This entitlement to a charge must be understood as subject to certain conditions and qualifications. It must be appreciated that the ability to obtain a charge and the right to have that charge redeemed or discharged out of capital money are not necessarily co-extensive. Further, as will be seen later, the redemption of a charge out of capital money does not necessarily decide the final reckoning between tenant for life and remainderman.

If a tenant for life has actually paid compensation to the tenant of a holding in respect of improvements or tenant-right or for disturbance, he is entitled to obtain an order charging the holding with the amount paid.[47] If the landlord is entitled to receive the rents and profits of the holding "otherwise than for his own benefit" he is entitled to obtain a charge even before he has paid compensation agreed or awarded to the tenant.[48] However, a tenant for life of settled land does not appear to come within this category. Although he is a trustee he is also, by virtue of his equitable life interest, interested in the rents and profits.

It may be noted that where the landlord is a limited owner no instalment or interest in respect of the charge shall become payable after the time when the improvement for which compensation is paid will, in the opinion of the Minister, become exhausted.[49]

Limited owners: redemption of charges out of capital money 17.13

As already mentioned, the fact that a charge can be obtained does not necessarily mean that it can be redeemed or discharged out of capital money. Whether it can or not depends on whether the case comes within the wording of section 73(1)(ii) of the Settled Land Act 1925. This paragraph as amended now refers to "an improvement created on a holding under the Agricultural Holdings Act 1986 or any similar previous enactment".[50] The word "improvement" would cover anything in Schedule 7, Part I of Schedule 8 and Schedule 10 to the 1986 Act, but

---

[47] s. 86(1)(a). But market garden improvements in Sched. 10 are not included (though improvement No. 5 would be suitable).
[48] s. 86(3).
[49] s. 87(4).
[50] As amended by 1986 Act, Sched. 14, para. 11.

not Part II of Schedule 8 (tenant-right matters) or, of course, disturbance. Thus, although landlords can obtain charges in respect of compensation paid to tenants for tenant-right matters and disturbance under section 86(1) of the 1986 Act, a tenant for life cannot require the trustees of the settlement to redeem such charges out of capital money by virtue of section 73(1)(ii) of the Settled Land Act.

17.14 Limited owners: ultimate liability between tenant for life and remainderman

It would be contrary to the principles of equity which underly the Settled Land Act if the redemption of a charge out of capital money were automatically to close the account as between tenant for life and remainderman. It would be inequitable if compensation for improvements which are likely to be exhausted within a short time should become a permanent burden on capital. The decision of Eve J. in *Re Duke of Manchester's Settlement*[51] demonstrates that the redemption of a charge out of capital money under section 73(1)(ii) does not preclude a subsequent accounting as between tenant for life and remainderman. Section 89(1) of the 1986 Act, which provides that capital money "applied in or about the execution of any improvement specified in Schedule 7 to this Act" is not required to be replaced out of income, has no application to the redemption of a charge out of capital money under section 73(1)(ii) of the Settled Land Act. As Harman J. pointed out in *Re Wynn*,[52] all that what is now section 89(1) says is that "if capital is spent on such improvements, it cannot be recouped out of income". That is very different from saying that all such improvements must be defrayed out of capital and also very different from saying that a charge in respect of compensation for such improvements must ultimately be borne by capital.

17.15 Limited owners: direct expenditure by tenant for life "in or about the execution" of improvements: position in regard to repairs

The decision in *Re Duke of Wellington's Parliamentary Estates*;[53] mentioned above, made it clear that section 73(1)(iv) of the Settled Land Act relates to the application of capital money in payment of costs incurred directly by the tenant for life, not in the reimbursement of compensation paid by the tenant for life to the farm tenant. Even as so qualified, however, the effect of this provision is sufficiently striking to have been described by Harman J. in *Re Wynn* as "revolutionary".[54] One of the improvements now listed in Schedule 7 to the 1986 Act (formerly in Schedule 3 to the 1948 Act) is "Repairs to fixed equipment, being equipment reasonably required for the proper farming of the holding, other than repairs which the tenant is under an obligation to carry out".[55] The somewhat startling result is that in some circumstances repairs can be paid for out of capital money without any need to replace out of income the amount spent. In a series of cases in the 1950s even more remarkable conclusions were reached. Vaisey J. in

---

[51] [1910] 1 Ch. 106.
[52] [1955] 1 W.L.R 940 at 947.
[53] [1972] Ch. 374.
[54] [1955] 1 W.L.R 940 at 948.
[55] Sched. 7, para. 26.

Re Duke of Northumberland[56] decided that capital money could be applied in payment for repairs in pursuance of section 73(1)(iv) whether the land was let or not. In the subsequent case of ***Re Lord Brougham and Vaux's Settled Estates***[57] Vaisey J. carried further his venturesome interpretation by jettisoning the words "other than repairs which the tenant is under an obligation to carry out".[58] The result in that case was that the tenant for life was entitled to be paid out of capital money for repairs which he had carried out to fixed equipment for the repair of which the tenant was contractually liable.[59] In two later cases this doctrine was not applied to trusts for sale[60] on the ground that trustees for sale were in a different position from that of a tenant for life. The authorities have not been reviewed by the Court of Appeal.[61]

Although there is no statutory power to apply capital money in payment of compensation for disturbance, such a power can, of course, be given to a tenant for life by the trust instrument.

A tenant for life has no statutory power to apply capital money for the provision of fixed equipment as such, but many kinds of fixed equipment are in fact covered by Part I of Schedule 3 to the Settled Land act 1925 and by Schedule 7 to the 1986 Act. The same was true, prior to the Trusts of Land and Appointment of Trustees Act 1996 in relation to trustees of a trust for sale.[62]

Limited owners: lease at best rent 17.16

Limited owners, such as tenants for life, are sometimes given, either by an instrument or statute, powers of letting land subject to their obtaining the best rent that can reasonably be obtained. Section 90 provides that, in estimating the best rent, or reservation in the nature of rent, it shall not be necessary to take into account against the tenant any increase in the value of the holding arising from any improvements made or paid for by him.

SERVICE OF NOTICES

Service of notices: section 93: General 17.17

Section 93 affords special, and in some instances quite extensive, service provisions for instruments served "under" the Agricultural Holdings Act 1986.

---

[56] [1951] Ch. 202.
[57] [1954] Ch. 24.
[58] In what is now Sched. 7, para. 26 to the 1986 Act.
[59] Although Vaisey J. had been in error in ***Re Duke of Northumberland*** in holding that expenditure on repairs incurred before March 1, 1948 could be paid for out of capital money (and he acknowledged this minor error in ***Re Lord Brougham & Vaux's Settled Estates***), his decision so far as it relates to repairs after that date has not been overruled. The minor error as to the date was regarded by Harman J. in ***Re Sutherland Settlement Trusts*** [1953] Ch. 792 at 809, as "a case of *bonus dormitat Homerus*". But Harman J. did not suggest that Homer had nodded on the substantive issue.
[60] ***Re Wynn*** [1955] 1 W.L.R 940 and ***Re Boston's Will Trusts*** [1956] Ch. 395.
[61] In ***Re Pelly's Will Trusts*** (1957) Ch.1, a CA decision, the issue did not arise; Lord Evershed M.R. said at 12 in relation to the ***Northumberland*** and ***Sutherland*** cases, "I do not propose to express any view on that matter".
[62] See para. 17.8 above.

The terms of section 93 are permissive and do not preclude successful reliance on some alternative method of service authorised by the contract of tenancy or expressly agreed for that purpose between the parties. But it must be recollected that the service of legal proceedings and the service of notices required by statutes other than the 1986 Act do not fall within the terms of section 93.[63] In the case of legal proceedings Rules of Court make separate provision.[64] The terms of section 93 are not the same as the terms of section 36 of the Agricultural Tenancies Act 1995[65] and care must be taken to check that the correct 1986 Act procedures are followed. The section covers "any notice, request, demand or other instrument" which is a comprehensive coverage.[66]

17.18 Due service: delivery to the recipient: section 93(1)

Any notice, request, demand or other instrument to be given under the 1986 Act is duly given or served on the person to or on whom it is to be given or served if it is delivered to him.[67] This means delivery to the tenant personally.[68] In short, if the intended recipient refuses to take the copy it is not necessary to leave it in his actual physical possession but it is enough to inform him of the nature of the document and to throw it down in his presence. However there are complex variants of this procedure, which readers may wish to consult. Where an instrument is to be given to or served on an incorporated company or body it should be given to or served on the secretary or clerk of that company or body.[69] It would seem that delivery to the wife of the intended recipient, being a person authorised to receive and deal with the document, is likely to count as good service on the intended recipient even if he never in fact got it.[70] The fact that the tenant may have appointed an agent for the purpose of receiving notices and the fact that the Act provides service on one class of agents is sufficient[71] does not mean that a landlord is precluded thereby from serving the tenant personally.[72]

---

[63] *e.g.* a notice under ss. 47 and 48 of the Landlord and Tenant Act 1987.

[64] See the *County Court Practice* for the County Court and the *Supreme Court Practice* for the High Court. The latter in particular contains useful notes under Ord. 65 summarising case law relating to service and also identifying means of serving particular types of body corporate.

[65] See paras 7.8–7.14 above.

[66] Notices to quit are clearly included within the above. "Any notice" covers notices served under all the provisions consolidated in the Act: see Law Com. No. 153, pp. 7–8 and Minutes and Report of the Joint Committee on Consolidation Bills (H.L. 56-II; H.C. 178-II).

[67] s. 93(1).

[68] There are collected in the *Supreme Court Practice*, 1997, under the notes to Ord. 65 at 65/2/1 a variety of cases, mostly quite amusing, identifying what amounts to personal service.

[69] s. 93(2).

[70] *Hosier v. Goodall* [1962] 2 Q.B. 401.

[71] s. 93(3).

[72] *Hallinan (Lady) v. Jones* [1984] 2 E.G.L.R. 20, CC, at 23E.

Due service: leaving the document at the recipient's proper address: section 93(1) 17.19

Any notice, request, demand or other instrument under the 1986 Act is duly given to or served on the intended recipient if it is left at his proper address.[73] The proper address in the case of the secretary or clerk or an incorporated company or body is that of the registered or principal office of the company or body.[74] In all other cases the proper address is the last known address of the person in question.[75] The words "last known address" are perfectly general and are not limited to either a business or a residential address. Either would suffice.[76] The words "last known" relate directly to actual knowledge of the person giving the notice.[77] This particular provision of section 93(1) is satisfactorily relied on even though the intended recipient does not actually receive the document in question provided the document has been left in a manner which a reasonable person would adopt to bring it to the notice of the addressee[78].

Due service: sending by registered or recorded delivery service: section 93(1) 17.20

Any notice, request, demand or other instrument under the 1986 Act is duly given to or served on the person to or on whom it is to be given or served if it is sent to him by post in a registered letter or by the recorded delivery service.[79] There may be evidential advantages in using this means of service and problems are unlikely to arise in circumstances where the document in question is signed for. However this particular provision gives rise to a difficult and unresolved issue of law namely whether the act of sending the document by post by registered or recorded delivery service is in itself good service whether or not the recipient ever got the document. In the normal way clear statutory wording will be required to rebut a construction that service will not be effected unless the document has been received.[80] Whether or not actual receipt is necessary really turns on the wording of section 93(1) itself and in particular the meaning, in that context, of "sent". It is clear that section 93(1) contemplates, in the two methods previously described, satisfactory service in the one case where delivery is effected to the recipient or his agent and, in the other case, where it is left at the correct address whether or not the recipient got it. Accordingly there appears to be no policy in section 93(1) in either direction and, if

---

[73] s. 93(1).
[74] s. 93(4).
[75] *ibid.*
[76] Even a limited phrase such as "place of abode" has been generously construed to include a business address—see *Price v. West London Investment Building Society Ltd* [1964] 1 W.L.R. 616 and *Italica Holdings SA v. Bayadea* [1985] 1 E.G.L.R. 70.
[77] *Price v. West London Investment Building Society Ltd* (above).
[78] *Newborough (Lord) v. Jones* [1975] 1 Ch. 90 (notice pushed under the side door normally used but it went under the linoleum and was not found for months); *Datnow v. Jones* [1985] 2 E.G.L.R. 1 (notice put through the letter box in a door in the back porch of the farmhouse).
[79] s. 93(1).
[80] *R. v. County of London Quarter Sessions Appeals Committee, ex p. Rossi* [1956] 1 Q.B. 682, not an agricultural case.

anything, the case law[81] relating to section 93(3) suggests that the section as a whole is not particularly concerned with actual receipt by the intended recipient. There is genuine disagreement in the authorities on this issue.[82] Cases decided on earlier agricultural legislation, differently worded, are unlikely to assist.[83] Perhaps some guidance is to be found by comparing similarly worded legislation being legislation in general terms of a similar type. The closest example appears to be *Moody v. Godstone Rural District Council*.[84] Accordingly it is suggested, but very cautiously, that simply sending a document by registered letter or recorded delivery service is in itself sufficient service for the purposes of section 93(1) whether or not it was received.[85]

17.21 Due service: use of the ordinary post

There is no specific sub-section in section 93 that deals with the ordinary post. There is only an oblique reference in section 93(4) but from that oblique reference

---

[81] Discussed in para. 17.23 below.

[82] In *Hallinan (Lady) v. Jones* [1984] 2 E.G.L.R. 20 at 23 Mr. Peter Langdon-Davies sitting as an Assistant Recorder in the County Court at 23A-B stated: "Mr. Jones urged upon me the dictum of Megaw J., as he then was, in *Re Poyser & Mills' Arbitration* [1964] 2 Q.B. 467 at 479 where he accepted the proposition that if notice is sent by registered post it is good service whether it is received or not. That remark was an *obiter dictum* within an *obiter dictum*, but in my view it was not intended to go any further than saying that if the notice was proved to have been duly sent by registered post that in itself established a prima facie case of service, though rebuttable, while if the notice was sent by ordinary post it was necessary to prove receipt before a prima facie case was made out."

[83] e.g. *Van Grutten v. Trevenen* [1902] 2 K.B. 82 under the Agricultural Holdings Act 1883 to which the Interpretation Act did not apply (a case where the tenant refused to accept a registered letter).

[84] [1966] 1 W.L.R 1085 CA. The notice in question was given under s. 45 of the Town & Country Planning Act 1962 requiring the Defendant to remove from his land caravans placed there without permission. The Defendant failed to comply with the notice within 28 days of its taking effect and an information was preferred against him. The notice in question had been sent by pre-paid registered post but on the unchallenged evidence it was never in fact received. The enforcement notice was distinguished in its nature by the Court from notices of a forthcoming event such as the hearing of an appeal or an intended prosecution. The service provisions of s. 214 of the 1962 Act were: "(1) Subject to the provisions of this section, any notice or other document required or authorised to be served or given under this Act may be served or given either- (c) by sending it in a pre-paid registered letter, or by the recorded delivery service, addressed to that person at his usual or last known place of abode, or, in a case where an address for service has been given by that person, at that address." It was held that service had been duly made in the circumstances. Although in a different context, service was deemed to have been properly effected by compliance with Ord. 8, r. 8(2) of the CCR 1936 where, again, a document had been sent but not received: *Cooper v. Scott-Farnell* [1969] 1 W.L.R. 120, CA. The relevant wording of Ord. 8, r. 8(2) was: "Where the plaintiff or his solicitor gives a certificate for postal service in Form 6 ... the summons shall, unless the Registrar otherwise directs, be served by an officer of the Court sending it by ordinary post to the defendant named in the certificate at the address stated in the *praecipe*". In *Beer v. Davies* [1958] 2 Q.B. 187 sending a document by registered post was held not to be in itself sufficient compliance with s. 21 of the Road Traffic Act 1930 but part of the proviso to that section probably makes this result inevitable: "(2) The requirement of this section shall in every case be deemed to have been complied with unless and until the contrary is proved".

[85] There is also a point to be made, although perhaps not a very strong one, that section 93(5)

it may be deduced that ordinary service by the post is a method contemplated of achieving the situation where a document is left at the proper address of the intended recipient.[86] From this it may further be deduced that where it can be proved that, using the ordinary post, the document was left at the proper address service will be completed.[87] There may therefore be circumstances in which the statutory context of section 93 may require the wording of section 7 of the Interpretation Act 1978 to be modified or overridden so as to allow service to be complete as and when the document is appropriately left at the proper address using the postal service.[88] In so far as section 7 of the Interpretation Act is being used to establish the time of service it is important to note that section 7, for the purposes of the RSC, is, subject to proof to the contrary, to be construed as indicating ordinary delivery in the case of first class mail on the second working day after posting and in the case of second class mail on the fourth working day after posting.[89]

Due service: transmission by fax or other electronic means 17.22

There is no specific provision which contemplates service by fax or other electronic means (*e.g.* e-mail or direct computer link).[90] Of the various electronic means of transmission, fax is the longest established. Section 93, it is submitted, does not contemplate electronic transmission as a means of service.[91] It is submitted that it is quite impossible to describe materials electronically transmitted

---

is sensitive to the distinction between sending and receipt since that sub-section refers to a notice being "received".

[86] Section 93(4) is designed to ascertain "the proper address", a term exclusively referable to the second method of service contemplated by s. 93(1) namely leaving the document at the proper address.

[87] See para. 17.19 above from which it is clear that actual receipt by the tenant is not necessary.

[88] In all other circumstances use of the ordinary post will only result in successful service provided there is actual delivery (*i.e.* delivery by means of the post falling within the first method contemplated by s. 93(1): see para. 17.18 above). Section 7 of the Interpretation Act 1978 provides: "Where an Act authorises or requires any document to be served by post (whether the expression "serve" or the expression "give" or "send" or any other expression is used) then, *unless the contrary intention appears*, the service is deemed to be effected by properly addressing, pre-paying and posting a letter containing the document and, unless the contrary is proved, to have been effected at the time at which the letter would be delivered in the ordinary course of post".

[89] Practice Direction (1985) 1 All E.R. 889. The explanatory note with the Practice Direction indicates that it is no longer safe to assume that letters posted by first class mail will always be delivered on the following day. Paragraphs 1 and 2 of the Practice Direction are perhaps of more general interest: "1. Under section 7 of the Interpretation Act 1978 service by post is deemed to have been effected, unless the contrary has been proved, at the time when the letter would be delivered in the ordinary course of post. 2. To avoid uncertainty as to the date of service it will be taken (subject to proof to the contrary) that delivery in the ordinary course of post was effected (a) in the case of first class mail, on the second working day after posting, (b) in the case of second class mail, on the fourth working day after posting. 'Working days' are Monday to Friday, excluding any bank holiday".

[90] Contrast s. 36(3) of the Agricultural Tenancies Act, and see para. 7.11 above.

[91] None of the wording is appropriate to it and the wording itself derives materially unchanged from s. 92 of the Agricultural Holdings Act 1948.

as "left" at the proper address of the intended recipient and accordingly that part of section 93(1) is not an appropriate place to categorise this method of communication. In so far as the first method of service contemplated by section 93(1) is concerned namely "delivery" to the recipient it is submitted that simply sending a fax or other electronic transmission does not constitute service for the purposes of section 93(1) at all. It is submitted that section 93(1) should not be construed so as to place the risk of electronic failure or corruption on the recipient of the notice and accordingly transmitting by this means does not constitute delivery. Conversely there appears to be no reason of principle why a document transmitted successfully without corruption and correctly received should not be regarded as "delivered".[92] Consequently it is submitted that, for example, whilst the landlord may try to serve his tenant by fax, e-mail, or computer link, it is only likely he will be able to demonstrate a successful delivery if the tenant is willing to co-operate by acknowledging a complete and legible document being received.

17.23 Due service: agent or servant responsible for the control of the management or farming: section 93(3)

Any notice, request, demand or other instrument under the 1986 Act to be given to or served on a landlord or tenant is, where an agent or servant is responsible for the control of the management or farming duly given or served if given to or served on that agent or servant.[93] It is in general terms difficult to see how far this sub-section in fact goes. It appears that on its true (wide) construction the sub-section effects service on the landlord or the tenant where the notice in question is not just served on but also addressed to the agent or servant who has responsibilities of the kind described by the sub-section. However there are large grey areas in particular as to whether the agency or employment is to be presumed conclusively from the exercise of the relevant responsibilities and further as to whether it always matters whether the notice is addressed to the correct person if it is served on someone exercising these particular responsibilities. The case law is confused.[94] What is

---

[92] Although, for the purposes of comparison, one may see that service by fax is permitted by Ord. 65 of the RSC it is striking how many safeguards are written into the Order limiting reliance on that means and further deeming the document never to have been served by fax unless a copy of the document is also sent by the more orthodox means permitted by the Order. *Hastie & Jenkerson v. McMahon* [1990] 1 W.L.R. 1575, under the earlier version of Ord. 65, resulted in the decision that transmission by fax was an available means of service provided that receipt by the recipient could be demonstrated of a copy in a clearly legible form. In other words, there was no risk of corruption placed on the recipient.

[93] s. 93(3).

[94] In *Egerton v. Rutter* [1951] 1 K.B. 472, a reserved judgment of Lord Goddard C.J. a notice to quit was upheld when it was served on relatives of the deceased tenant who continued in possession. The notice was in fact wrongly addressed to the executors, when the tenant had died intestate. The persons occupying were regarded as the agents of the President of the Probate, Divorce and Admiralty Division purely on the basis that it was necessary that the farm should be carried on and the occupiers for that reason were regarded as falling within s. 92(3) of the Agricultural Holdings Act 1948 (the direct predecessor of the current section). It was further held that, apart from s. 92, on the death of a yearly tenant the landlord was not bound to raise a personal representative as a condition precedent to determining the tenancy by notice to quit but might treat any party

clear is that where the tenant has died the Courts are keen to save notices to quit served on the persons farming, almost regardless of who is addressed as the tenant in the notice. It may be questioned whether this line of authority will be developed so far as to allow a tenant to serve the landlord's agent responsible for the management of the holding with a notice intended for the landlord but in fact addressed to somebody else. From a practical point of view the problem may be avoided by, in all cases of doubt, addressing the relevant document to "the tenant" or "the landlord", as the case may be, and serving that document under section 93(3).[95] This sub-section is to be contrasted with the requirements of section 146 of the Law of Property Act 1925.[96] It is even possible that the liberal use of this sub-section in the three cases noted and discussed here will be confined to circumstances where the actual tenant has died.[97] On balance it is concluded that section 93(3) of the 1986 Act is indeed concerned only with service and not with contents and accordingly the *obiter dicta* of Lord Denning to that effect in ***Jones v. Lewis*** are correct. It would appear likely that the three first instance decisions, if correct, should not be extended beyond the circumstance of serving notice to quit when the tenant has died.

---

in possession as the tenant. This last conclusion may be insecurely founded on prior authority (see 477–478). However it has considerable practical merit and the same conclusion was reached, on different reasoning, by Cassels J. in ***Harrowby (Earl) v. Snelson*** [1951] 1 All E.R. 140 at 145A-C: "The President is not in possession. He has no responsibility for the rent. The estate of the deceased is merely vested in him. The landlord is not deprived of all rights over the property merely because his tenant has died intestate." In that case, a decision at first instance, it was held that although the legal estate had vested in the President the notice to quit could be validly served on the occupiers (again, the surviving relatives of the deceased). It was held that occupation of the farm and management of it was sufficient to validate the notice to quit notwithstanding that the notice was addressed to the executors. It was further assumed that the occupiers must be regarded as agents for the President because they were not trespassers. The notice to quit was addressed to "the executors of the late FS and to all others whom it may concern" and may in fact have been wider than simply a notice addressed to the executors. In ***Wilbraham v. Colclough*** [1952] 1 All E.R. 979 Jones J. applied ***Egerton v. Rutter*** (above) so as to give effect to a notice to quit which was given to the real tenant although it was addressed to him and his brother in a different capacity. He held "The notice seems to me to be clear though not addressed to the real tenant".

[95] But service on the President of the Family Division, in circumstances where he was not farming, and was further not vested with the tenancy was of no effect: ***Thorlby v. Olivant*** [1960] E.G.D. 257, which is hardly surprising.

[96] See ***Blewett v. Blewett*** [1936] 2 All E.R. 188, CA, where a notice under that section was held to be bad because it was not served on all the lessees (one of the lessees, who managed the affairs of all the lessees, was in fact served).

[97] The CA in ***Jones v. Lewis*** (1973) 25 P.&C.R. 375 held to be invalid a notice to do work under the equivalent of Sched. 3 Case D addressed to only one of two joint tenants in circumstances where the person in whose name the notice was addressed (and on whom it was in fact served) was farming to the exclusion of the other tenant. Lord Denning M.R. at 377 rejected an attempt to rely on s. 92(3) of the 1948 Act because "It is only dealing with the service of the form. It does not deal with the contents of it". The three first instance

17.24 Due service: change of landlord: section 93(5)
This section is in terms materially identical to section 36(7) of the Agricultural Tenancies Act.[98] In short, until the tenant has received notice[99] of the name and address of any new landlord, any notice or other document served on the original landlord is deemed to have been served on the actual landlord. It is not clear from the drafting of section 93(5) whether the notice to be received by the tenant is in fact necessarily a notice in writing. It remains an open question as to whether or not such a notice may be served on the tenant before the actual transfer of the entitlement to receive the rents and profits has taken place.[1]

OTHER

17.25 Crown land within the 1986 Act: section 95
All Crown land, whether or not held for the purposes of a Government Department, is within the scope of the 1986 Act. In particular this includes the Duchies of Lancaster and Cornwall. Section 95 provides extensively for this. The only exception to the general application of the 1986 Act is the general exclusion relating to section 11 of the 1986 Act, which does not apply to Crown land.[2] No modifications in the application of the Act to Crown land have been prescribed for the purposes of section 95(1).

---

decisions discussed in this paragraph appear not to have been cited.
[98] See para. 7.14 above.
[99] For a precedent see Form 21 in Part V of this work.
[1] See *Railtrack Plc v. Gojra* (1998) 8 E.G. 158 noted at para. 7.14 above.
[2] See s. 95(3).

SECTION THREE

MILK QUOTAS AND THE AGRICULTURE ACT 1986

CHAPTER 18

MILK QUOTAS GENERALLY

18.1 General

18.3 Legal framework of the Common Agricultural Policy and the relationship between Community and domestic legislation.

18.9 The system at Community level.

18.10 General implementation at domestic level in the United Kingdom.

18.11 Meanings of "producer", "purchaser" and "holding".

18.16 Scheme of the domestic regulations, arbitrations and apportionment.

18.19 Temporary transfers of quota.

18.20 Transfers of quota without land.

18.21 Permanent transfers and the marketing quota.

18.23 Milk quota protection clauses and disposals of quota.

18.28 Milk quotas and partnerships.

18.31 Milk quotas and mortgages.

PROCEDURAL TABLES RELATING TO MILK QUOTAS GENERALLY

Part VI of this work contains Procedural Table 13: Apportionment of Milk Quota by Arbitration. The content of Chapter 19 is directed, amongst other things, to compensation claims in respect of milk quota on termination of the tenancy. For arbitrations caused by such claims readers are referred to Procedural Table 11: Compensation on Quitting.

General Introduction 18.1

This chapter is not intended to do more than give a basic understanding of those parts of the law relating to milk quotas which are essential to a correct appreciation of its impact upon agricultural holdings. The provisions of the Agriculture Act 1986[1] cannot be digested without some knowledge of the broader legal picture. That statute relies critically upon the definitions in the relevant Dairy Produce Quotas Regulations and contains ambiguities of expression which can only be assessed in terms of valuation by reference to the workings of the milk quota

---

[1] See Chapter 19.

market and consideration of its legal structure. Beyond that it may confidently be said that milk is one of the principal temperate agricultural products and the ownership and destination of quota, which enables it to be sold without crippling levy, is of great interest to both landlords and tenants: in the last decade agricultural tenancies have usually dealt expressly with quota. For lawyers, the question remains as to how far and in what way the best clauses may be enforceable and what form such clauses might take. Were quota not "tied" to land no doubt it would occupy considerably less space in this work than it does. It is the peculiar nature of the tie to the land, a tie conceived outside the confines of the English law of property, which gives to the study of milk quota its slightly, in places, uncertain character. This work focuses on the current law at Community and domestic levels and as far as possible avoids investigation of earlier versions of either.

It is not considered fruitful to pursue the question as to whether, in some abstract sense, quota should be considered as an asset.[2]

18.2 Economic purpose of milk quotas

The milk regime forms an important part of the Common Agricultural Policy[3] and there is within the confines of Regulation 804/68[4] a single marketing system and pricing system for milk and milk products. Economic studies have demonstrated that by 1980 milk and its by-products constituted an extremely important factor in contributing to farm incomes within the Community[5] although only 75 per cent of total production was regularly consumed within the Community. Various techniques to deal with over-supply had over the years failed.[6] Since it was not politically acceptable to poison the surplus, it had to be stored[7] or disposed of by other means[8]: eventually the cost of storage including in particular the cost of electricity brought the entire Community to the edge of financial failure. It was therefore as a result of crisis that in the end milk quotas were introduced, and had to be introduced quickly. It is doubtful whether there was any way of fairly limiting production other than by reference to a percentage of historic production.

---

[2] The debate is sterile and there appears to be now considerable guidance in the case law as to how any specific problem is to be dealt with. In *Harries v. Barclays Bank* [1997] 2 E.G.L.R. 14 the CA indicated a marked reluctance to become involved in that "metaphysical question". Having reviewed both property and tax case law Morritt L.J. at 18M stated: "Milk quota is the creation of the legislation both European and domestic to which I have referred. In determining where the benefit of it lies and how it got there it is necessary to apply that legislation to the facts of the case. I do not find it helpful in that context to seek to label or categorise milk quota as an asset or as an asset of a particular description, not least when the description is one of English law which may not be recognised by the domestic laws of other member states."

[3] See para. 18.3 below.

[4] O.J. L148/13. The original system did not cater for long-term structural surplus in production although it did allow for levies and export refunds at the borders of the Community and within the Community common quality standards and free movement of milk products (recitals to Regulation 804/68 and implementation within it).

[5] See Brian E. Hill, *The Common Agricultural Policy: Past, Present and Future*, (Methuen, 1984), Table 5.03, p. 78.

[6] For example co-responsibility levy on milk delivered to dairies and on certain dairy items sold direct by the producer: Regulation 1079/77, [1977] O.J. L131/6.

[7] As butter and skimmed milk.

[8] Trading it out at below cost abroad, for example.

The legal means chosen took the form of a new Article 5(c) introduced into 804/68 by 856/84.[9] The system was essentially simple: the reference quantity (known in the United Kingdom as quota) was fixed for the entire Community[10] which was then allocated as between individual countries. This amount at national level was available either for producers or purchasers[11], the latter being entitled to pass the levy burden to producers responsible for any excess of production over quota.[12] The initial regime ran for five years commencing on April 1, 1984[13], Member States being entitled to choose implementation either according to Formula A or Formula B or a mixture of the two by regions.[14] Under Formula A levy was paid on deliveries to a purchaser in excess of quota; under Formula B the purchaser paid the levy but passed the burden on in price to producers on proportionate contribution where the purchaser's quota was exceeded.[15] In so far as producers sold directly from farms to consumption they also had to pay levy (known as direct sales levy) on excess over quota. What this meant in real terms was that those people who produced in excess of their quota were at risk of severe financial punishment. If, by contrast, milk was produced and not sold this obviously did not attract levy. Whilst some people initially gambled that the United Kingdom as a whole would not go over its threshold (this being the trigger for the imposition of levy across the board), quota itself became valuable since there would always be some people who wished to expand their production in any event and others who simply miscalculated estimated productivity. The current regime, similar in many respects but restructured in others, is described below.[16]

Whether or not the introduction of milk quotas has been an overall financial success for the Community is still not settled. It appears to have limited the amount of milk produced but, of course, farmers consequently went into other forms of production for which subsidy has been available. Consequently, the Court of Auditors concluded that the quota regime had achieved its specific objective but the wider financial implications were not as optimistic as one might otherwise have supposed.[17]

Legal framework of the Common Agricultural Policy 18.3

Part Three Title II of the E.C. Treaty, Arts 38–47[18] enshrine the essential legal framework for far-reaching changes and policies in the control of the production and marketing of agricultural produce within the Member States. The general milk

---

[9] [1984] O.J. L90/10.
[10] 97.2m tonnes of milk or milk equivalent corresponding to the 1983 guarantee threshold.
[11] *i.e.* dairies buying product from producers.
[12] See 857/84, O.J. L90/13, Art. 1.1.
[13] 804/68 Art. 5c.1.
[14] The U.K. chose Formula B for England and Wales; contrast Scotland which was originally within Formula A.
[15] Levy has always been at a deterrent rate: in 1986 for example it stood under Formula B at 100% of the target price for milk (857/84 Art. 1.1).
[16] See paras 18.9–18.10 below.
[17] See the Court of Auditors's Special Report No. 4/93 on the Implementation of the Quota System intended to control Milk Production (94/C 12/01).
[18] This text does not use the numbering of the as yet unratified Treaty of Amsterdam signed on October 2, 1997, as to which see Part IV of this work.

regime referred to above,[19] 804/68, was made under Article 43 establishing, amongst other things, a milk year from April 1 to March 31. Although the introduction of a quota system had been proposed by the Commission in discussion documents,[20] the perspective of the Community institutions is sometimes not fully appreciated from a United Kingdom standpoint. In one sense one might wonder why, instead of introducing quotas, there was not simply a substantial drop in the target price for milk. The explanation is the fear that the effect on the income of farmers would be too serious. That this should be a worry to the Commission is really a reflection of the diverse objectives of the Common Agricultural Policy which, even in total financial crisis at Community level, operated to some extent to protect farmers from the full force of a corrective scheme. Article 39 declares those objectives to be:

(a) to increase agricultural productivity by promoting technical progress and by ensuring the rational development of agricultural production and the optimum utilisation of the factors of production, in particular labour;

(b) thus to ensure a fair standard of living for the agricultural community, in particular by increasing the individual earnings of persons engaged in agriculture;

(c) to stabilise markets;

(d) to assure the availability of supplies;

(e) to ensure that supplies reach consumers at reasonable prices.

It is unclear how far the long term ramifications of the chosen policy were foreseen at the outset. Doubtless to some extent it was appreciated that whilst in legal terms milk quotas represented a constraint on production, in economic terms they represented a disguised subsidy making the market more difficult for new entrants and offering to farmers with quota, even in legal systems which did not permit transfer, the opportunity to surrender the quota for cash in the form of outgoers' schemes. These aspects of the chosen scheme were consistent with some of the objectives of the CAP of a not exclusively financial nature.[21]

18.4 Governing E.C. legislation: Council Regulation 3950/92, Commission Regulation 536/93

The current governing E.C. legislation is, in combination, Council Regulation 3950/92[22] and Commission Regulation 536/93[23] laying down detailed rules in

---

[19] para. 18.2 above.
[20] COM (83) 500; see the commentary in M. Cardwell, *Milk Quotas* (Clarendon Press, 1996) pp.8–11.
[21] See further Art. 39.2 of the E.C. Treaty. For more general discussion of the objectives of the CAP see F.G. Snyder, *Law of the Common Agricultural Policy* (Sweet & Maxwell, 1985) and J.A. Usher, *Legal Aspects of Agriculture in the European Community*, (Clarendon Press, 1988), both works in other respects now rather out of date. For a more recent survey see M. Cardwell, *Milk Quotas*, (Clarendon Press, 1996).
[22] Of [1992] O.J. L405/1.
[23] Of [1993] O.J. L57/12.

relation to the additional levy on milk and milk products established by 3950/92. The main amendment to 3950/92 is contained in Council Regulation 1560/93[24] which alters the definitions of "producer" and "holding" so as to limit the same to the geographical territory of a Member State as distinct from the territory of the Community.[25] Although there are numerous amendments to the main Council and Commission Regulations, these have little impact on discussion for the purposes of this work.[26] Council Regulation 3950/92 is in part a consolidation of earlier versions of legislation governing the sector but it also represents in parts significant reformulation of policy, as indicated by the recitals.[27] Consequently when reading case law which discusses versions of the Community legislation predating the current version, care should be taken to check what if any changes have occurred since that time. The earlier versions are contained in two main cycles each of which was frequently amended before being replaced.[28]

Governing domestic legislation: the Dairy Produce Quotas Regulations 1997 18.5
The current domestic regulations are the Dairy Produce Quotas Regulations 1997 (S.I. 1997 No.733)[29] coming into force on the April 1, 1997. These Regulations operate in tandem with the Community legislation[30] partly by providing adaptation for the United Kingdom and its land tenure but partly by applying the Community scheme directly[31]. The current domestic Regulations replace and revoke all previous domestic legislation, the effect of which is preserved only for the purpose of apportionment as at historic dates.[32] The domestic legislation has gone through a number of earlier versions and there have been changes over time, sometimes, but not always, corresponding with changes at European level.[33] It is occasionally

---

[24] Of [1993] O.J. L154/30.
[25] See para. 18.11 below.
[26] Commission Regulation 647/94, O.J. L80/16; Council Regulation 1883/94 O.J. L197/25; Commission Regulation 630/95 O.J. L66/11; Council Regulation 1552/95 O.J. L148/43; Commission Regulation 635/96 O.J. L90/17; Commission Regulation 1109/96 O.J. L148/13; Commission Regulation 2186/96 O.J. L292/6.
[27] See para. 18.9 below.
[28] Council Regulation 857/84 of [1984] O.J. L90/13 made pursuant to the amendment of 804/68 by 856/84; Commission Regulation 1371/84 of [1984] O.J. L132/11 containing the detailed rules necessary to 857/84; Commission Regulation 1546/88 [1988] O.J. L139/12 repealing 1371/84. The numerous amendments to these main Regulations are beyond the scope of this work.
[29] Made under s.2(2) of the European Communities Act 1972.
[30] See para. 18.4 above.
[31] For example in reg. 2 where a number of key definitions are imported at domestic level from the relevant EEC legislation.
[32] See Sched. 2, para. 3(3) in respect of arbitrations in England and Wales and corresponding provisions for Northern Ireland in Sched. 4, para. 5(3).
[33] The first domestic regulations were the Dairy Produce Quotas Regulations 1984 (S.I. 1984 No.1047) which proceeded on the basis, in relation to transfers, of minor and major changes of occupation. They were amended by S.I. 1985 No.509 and replaced by the 1986 Regulations (S.I. 1986 No.470) which by an amendment in 1988 (S.I. 1988 No.534) abandoned the classification of minor/major change of occupation and instead introduced a series of exemptions from quota transfer consequences. In addition those amending regulations introduced the ability to lease out on a temporary basis part of a producer's wholesale quota. New regulations appeared in 1989 (S.I. 1989 No.380) which were

necessary to consult the earlier versions of the Regulations not only for historic apportionment or litigation on a historic basis but also in order to understand some of the case law and the extent to which it is helpful in relation to the current Regulations.

18.6 Construction of Community legislation

It is neither possible nor permissible to try to construe the domestic legislation without the corresponding EEC provisions upon which it is based. This is not only because the domestic legislation imports a variety of definitions but also because the domestic provisions must be construed to produce the result intended by the Community legislation. This work is not the place for detailed commentary on this issue but it is to be noted that all the general principles of construction and of substantive law applicable to Community law apply to domestic legislation introduced pursuant to Community legislation.[34] The various general approaches to construction at Community level differ markedly from the domestic canons of interpretation.[35] For the purposes of the milk scheme perhaps the most important aspect or approach to interpretation is the contextual interpretive technique.[36] Specifically it is to be noted that an unhappy result may be taken as an indicator that a particular construction is wrong even if it is the construction which is literally correct.[37]

18.7 Construction of domestic Regulations implementing the Community Regulations

Attention is drawn to the sometimes extreme efforts made to interpret United Kingdom legislation consistently with matching E.C. provisions. Even where the Community legislation is no more than a directive (and therefore not directly applicable as are Regulations, which are the usual vehicles for the Common Agricultural Policy), a considerable amount of omitted material will be "read into" subordinate United Kingdom legislation in order to produce the result intended at Community level.[38] Furthermore what appears to be clear on the English text must not necessarily be taken to be clear as a matter of interpretation where other language versions may pose a problem.[39]

---

themselves replaced in 1991 (S.I. 1991 No.2232). By the replacing 1993 Regulations (S.I. 1993 No.923) temporary transfers of all of a producer's quota were permitted (reg. 14). Regulation 32 introduced a confiscation procedure where quota was neither used for production nor let out on a temporary basis. The replacing 1994 Regulations (S.I. 1994 No.672) by reg. 13 permitted transfer of quota without transfer of land but subject to such strict conditions that the provision was not initially significantly in use.

[34] See the HL in *R. v. Home Secretary, ex p. Brind* [1991] A.C. 696.
[35] See in particular Neville Brown and Kennedy, *the Court of Justice of the European Communities*, (4th ed., Sweet & Maxwell, 1994), Chapter 14.
[36] Discussed at page 311 and following *ibid*.
[37] See Case 174/88 *R. v. Dairy Produce Quota Tribunal for England & Wales, ex p. Hall & Sons (Dairy Farmers) Ltd* [1990] E.C.R. I-2237 at paras 13–17.
[38] For an example of this, where it was expressly pointed out that the same result could not have been reached by using the ordinary domestic canons of construction see the HL in *Lister v. Forth Dry Dock & Engineering Company Ltd* [1990] 1 A.C. 546.
[39] See *R v. Henn & Darby* [1981] A.C. 850, HL.

Relevance of general principles in Community law 18.8

Apart from the issue of construction it is to be noted that the United Kingdom authorities are constrained by general principles of Community law, in the same way that Community institutions are so constrained. The Community institutions must, for example, respect the general principles of law in framing Community legislation and where those principles are not observed the relevant law will be void (with the consequence that United Kingdom implementing legislation will also be void). The most dramatic example of this is in the *Mulder* litigation[40] where there was a failure at Community level to respect the principle of legitimate expectation of producers who entered into Community non-marketing undertakings for five years, only to find that within that five years they became permanently barred from re-entering production because the allocation of quota was based on historic achievement of milk production at a time when they themselves were not producing. This type of problem may affect United Kingdom legislation even though it may not be visible on the face of the relevant legislation.[41]

The system at Community level 18.9

Reference is made to paragraph 18.4 above identifying the current governing E.C. legislation. The main provisions of the current scheme are set out in Council Regulation 3950/92[42] which introduces for the seven years commencing on April 1, 1993 super levy for milk production over quota at 115 per cent of the target price for milk.[43] The levy is payable on milk or milk equivalent marketed in excess of quota[44]. Essentially the Regulation relates to milk, cream, butter, cheese and ice cream.[45] The previously available choice between Formulas A and B was abolished in the interests of simplification[46] but Member States remained limited to an overall guaranteed total quantity beyond which production would be punished by the imposition of levy. Within each Member State individual overruns were to be equalled out over all the individual reference quantities but Member States continued to be allowed to decide which of two methods of dealing with equalling out overruns they wished to choose.[47] Conversion of wholesale to direct sales quota and vice versa was expressly permitted[48] and the temporary transfer system was for the first time extended to all producers whether or not they continued to produce.[49] In the case of sales leases or transfers by inheritance of land the principle

---

[40] Case 120/86 *J. Mulder v. Minister van Landbouw en Visserij* [1988] E.C.R. 2321.
[41] For discussion of the general principles see Weatherill & Beaumont, *E.C. Law* (2nd ed. 1995, Penguin); Craig & de Burca, *E.C. Law, text cases and materials*, (Clarendon Press 1995), and Hartley & Others, *The Foundations of European Community Law* (3rd ed., 1994, Clarendon Press).
[42] [1992] O.J. L405/1.
[43] Art. 1.
[44] Milk or milk equivalent which is destroyed does not attract levy: see Art. 2.
[45] See the definitions in Art. 9(a) and (b), the words "in particular" having been added in order to cover ice cream (which appeared to have been omitted from some earlier versions of the Regulations and became in consequence a means of evading quota restrictions).
[46] See second recital.
[47] See the 7th recital.
[48] See the 12th recital.
[49] See the 14th recital and Art. 6.

was reimposed that a corresponding element of quota should go with the land transferred away.[50] In order to allow or facilitate restructuring of milk production and improving the environment, transfers of quota without corresponding transfers of land were authorised.[51] Article 9 contains a number of specific definitions, some of which are discussed below.[52] In so far as producers do not either themselves use or lease out quota for a 12-month period, their quota will on a mandatory basis be absorbed into the national reserve of the Member State and may subsequently be re-allocated.[53]

For the purposes of this work, and the concerns of landlords and tenants of agricultural land, it is the workings of Articles 5–9, which are of most interest. In combination Articles 5 and 6 have created the phenomenon known as "non-active quota holders".[54] It will be a matter of great importance to any person who comes into possession of land used or previously used for dairy production to ensure that the relevant quota does not fall into the national reserve: this difficulty is frequently experienced by persons, taking by operation of law, such as executors, receivers or trustees in bankruptcy.[55] Article 7 requires quota to be apportioned between blocks of land where there is a transfer in the case of sale, lease or inheritance and where transactions occur which have "comparable legal effects for producers". Those circumstances are covered by general wording in the corresponding domestic Regulations.[56] Article 7.1(b) and 7.2 appear to require, in the English version, that in some circumstances the departing occupier or tenant be permitted to take the quota with him.[57] Although Article 8 was designed to permit Member States to choose to allow, by way of detailed rules, the transfer of quota without corresponding transfer of land, or vice versa, this opportunity is available only where the relevant transaction is done "with the aim of improving the structure of milk production at the level of the holding or to allow for extensification of production".[58] In other words, this is not a general opportunity to abolish the link between land and quota on a transfer of land but simply a special exemption for those circumstances chosen by the Community.

The levy, in order to be fair, is based on the fat content of milk and this is dealt

---

[50] See the 15th recital and Art. 7.
[51] See 16th recital and Art. 8.
[52] For "producer" see paras 18.11–8.12; for "purchaser" see para. 18.13 and for "holding" see para. 18.14 below.
[53] See Art. 5.
[54] See para. 18.12 below.
[55] See generally para. 18.10 below.
[56] See paras 18.16 and 18.18 below.
[57] However these provisions in previous versions of the Community legislation were expressed as options for the Member States and there is no indication in the recitals of 3950/92 that these options were to become mandatory. In fact the U.K. never adopted either option and it would appear unlikely that so dramatic a change was intended. For the time being it is therefore assumed by this work that the optional status of the original provisions remains, applying the construction to the English version that the mandatory language relates to the ancillary arrangements if and in so far as the Member State has chosen the relevant option.
[58] "Extensification" means reducing the intensiveness or productivity per hectare of land. This may be desirable either to reduce production overall or, frequently, to reduce negative environmental impact.

with in some detail by Commission Regulation 536/93.[59] That Regulation also contains detailed instructions for the calculation and payment of levy together with the maintenance of detailed records and checking procedures by Member States. It additionally provides for penalties in circumstances where there is a failure to comply with the Regulation.[60]

General implementation at domestic level in the United Kingdom 18.10

The Dairy Produce Quotas Regulations 1997[61] establish direct sales quota and wholesale quota for any person and purchaser quota for any purchaser in respect of specific quota years as provided by the domestic Regulations and the relevant Community legislation.[62] The overall Regulations apply to England, Wales, Scotland and Northern Ireland and cover both ordinary quota and special quota allocated following the *Mulder* litigation[63]. Levy is established at the level of the purchaser (*i.e.* the dairy)[64] although producers are required to contribute towards over-production as against the purchaser's levy.[65] Calculations are based on the fat content of milk.[66] Of particular interest for the purposes of this work are the provisions relating to transfer of quota with transfer of land,[67] apportionment of quota,[68] prospective apportionment of quota[69] and the provisions for implementing apportionment by arbitration.[70] In limited circumstances quota may be transferred without land[71]; temporary transfer of quota may be made pursuant to Regulation 13; and there is now a national reserve within the United Kingdom[72] from which temporary re-allocations of quota may be made.[73] The payment of levy and the functions of the Intervention Board are the subject of detailed provisions[74] and criminal penalties attend failure to comply with the Regulations.[75] The all important confiscation and restoration provisions are to be found in Regulation 32 whereby quota which is neither the subject of a temporary lease nor used to offset production will be swallowed into the national reserve. The provisions relating to transfers and registration of quota are discussed further below.[76]

---

[59] [1993] O.J. L57/12.
[60] For example Art. 7.1(a) provides for withdrawal of approval of purchasers (*i.e.* dairies) for repeated failure to comply with either the Commission or Council Regulations.
[61] S.I. 1997 No.733 coming into force April 1, 1997.
[62] Reg. 3.
[63] See para. 18.15 below.
[64] Now covering both the largest purchaser, Milk Marque, and a number of independent dairies.
[65] Reg. 4.
[66] Reg. 5.
[67] Reg. 7.
[68] Reg. 8.
[69] Reg. 9 (although rarely used).
[70] See for England and Wales, Sched. 2 and the special powers of the Intervention Board under Reg. 10.
[71] Reg. 11 implementing Art. 8 of the Council Regulation, 3950/92.
[72] Reg. 12.
[73] Reg. 14.
[74] Reg. 20–30.
[75] Reg. 31, although the form of these Regulations is not entirely satisfactory.
[76] See paras 18.16–18.22 below.

18.11 The meaning of "producer"
The definition of "producer" is one of the key definitions in the overall structure of the relevant Regulations. Regulation 2(1) of the domestic scheme[77] defines the word as having the meaning assigned to it by Article 9(c) of Council Regulation 3950/92.[78] This definition provides[79]:

> "'Producer' means a natural or legal person or a group of natural or legal persons farming a holding[80] within the geographical territory of a Member State:
> — selling milk or other milk products directly to the consumer,
> — and/or supplying the purchaser."[81]

In most cases the definition is satisfactory to cover the circumstances in hand, that is to say the calculation of and payment of levy where there is production beyond the level of quota held by the individual producing and marketing the milk. It is at the margins, that is to say where there is a change of circumstances, that doubt or occasionally litigation may arise. For example, it does not appear to be appropriate to construe the definition literally in all circumstances although the literal construction gives a clear idea as to what, in general terms, is intended to be comprised within the word "producer". However, in context, the word may require a wider, non-literal, definition in order to ensure that the purpose of Regulation 3950/92 and implementing domestic legislation is achieved. Even within Regulation 3950/92 there are examples of the word "producer" being used to designate persons not currently in production.[82] In addition there are clear indications in the case law that certain people are classified as "producers" when their entire complaint is that they are not at any material time actually in production.[83] It is probably not possible to imagine every set of circumstances which might arise but it is submitted that, at a practical level, the question can always be answered by taking a functional, contextual interpretation of the European Regulations where the literal construction produces an unsatisfactory result or one which lessens the effectiveness of the Regulations in terms of their apparent intention.[84] It has, perhaps not surprisingly, been held that where the holding is let the lessor (as opposed to the lessee) is no longer the producer.[85] The producer is a person who will operate on his own account.[86] It is submitted that the producer is, in effect, the person who has control of the holding and is able to exercise such control if he wishes to farm.[87] In terms of quota transfer, it is further

---

[77] Dairy Produce Quotas Regulations 1997 (S.I. 1997 No.733).
[78] Of [1992] O.J. L405/1.
[79] As amended by Council Regulation 1560/93 of [1993] at O.J. L154/30.
[80] See para. 18.14 below.
[81] See para. 18.13 below.
[82] For example Art. 5 and Art. 6.
[83] See Case C-120/86 *Mulder v. Minister van Landbouw en Visserij* [1988] E.C.R. 2321.
[84] See for example *Wachauf v. The State* [1991] 1 C.M.L.R. 328, judgment paras 7–11; *Holdcroft v. Staffordshire County Council* [1994] 2 E.G.L.R. 1 at 3–4.
[85] Case C-236/90 *Maier v. Freistaat Bayern* [1992] E.C.R. I-4483.
[86] Case C-463/93 *Katholische Kirchengemeinde St Martinus Elten v. Landwirtschaftskammer Rheinland* judgment of the Court, January 23, 1997, para. 17.
[87] Although it should be noted that the literal definition, perhaps unsurprisingly, was used so as to deprive a claimant of compensation for definitively ceasing milk production when at

submitted that persons without such control should not have corresponding control over the relevant quota apportionable to the farm.[88] Consequently land may be transferred from one "producer" to another "producer" even though the business of the original producer is not transferred as a going concern.[89] It is not easy to separate a consideration of the word "producer" from consideration of the word "holding".[90]

Non-active quota holders 18.12

Non-active quota holders are persons not currently farming by way of milk production but who are registered as quota holders in the records kept by the Intervention Board pursuant to regulation 24 of the domestic Regulations.[91] These may be persons who have entered into temporary transfers of quota in favour of a third party who is himself producing milk.[92] Alternatively the non-active quota holder may be a person shown as the quota holder on the records who has not as yet made deliveries of milk during that quota year.[93] It has always been assumed that only a "producer" could be a non-active quota holder and that accordingly the definition of "producer" should be regarded as sufficiently wide to embrace such persons, since without that wider view there would be serious gaps in the system of supervision of quota. However in *Harries v. Barclays Bank*[94] the Court of Appeal expressly refused to define "producer" in the context of non-active quota holders and, instead, held that the determining issue on a transfer of milk quota was whether or not there had been a transfer where a bank took possession as mortgagee such that pursuant to the domestic Regulations the bank was entitled to be registered in respect of the quota and consequently itself to make temporary

---

the time he had already voluntarily gone out of production: Case C152/95 *Michel Macon v. Prefet de l'Aisne*, judgment of the E.C.J. dated October 9, 1997.

[88] Although the landlord, whilst the tenant is in possession, will not be regarded as the producer it is tolerably clear that for the purposes of apportionment or re-registration of quota at the end of a lease (unless the Member State has made special provisions) the landlord will be regarded as the producer on retaking possession: See *Katholische Kirchengemeinde St Martinus Elten v. Landwirtschaftskammer Rheinland* (above) at paras 29–31 of the judgment.

[89] This is the effect of the European Regulations, a state of affairs made clearer in the domestic Regulations by the definitions in Reg. 2(1) of "transferor", "transferee" and "occupier".

[90] See for an excellent assessment of the two concepts together M. Cardwell, Milk Quotas, (Clarendon Press, 1996) pp. 28–31 where, however, the assessment is too generous to the case of *Carson v. Cornwall County Council* [1993] 1 E.G.L.R. 21 the underlying reasoning of which must by now be regarded as incorrect and which in any case cannot stand in the light of *R. v. Ministry of Agriculture, Fisheries & Food, ex p. Bostock* [1994] E.C.R. I-955. As for *Carson v. Cornwall County Council* generally see para. 19.17 below.

[91] S.I. 1997 No.733.

[92] See Reg. 13 of the domestic Regulations and Art. 6 of Council Regulation 3950/92 of [1992] O.J. L405/1.

[93] If ultimately no temporary lease of the quota is made and for one year no quota is used against production there will be a confiscation of the quota pursuant to Reg. 32 of the domestic Regulations into the national reserve.

[94] [1997] 2 E.G.L.R. 14.

transfers as an incident of possession.[95] Non-active quota holders are a well known and important feature of the United Kingdom quota market. They were thoroughly investigated by the Agriculture Committee of the House of Commons in its Third Report "Trading of Milk Quota"[96] in which the economic importance of these persons was stressed.[97] The Committee considered fluctuation in prices of milk quota and found that there was no evidence that speculators or quota agents had manipulated the market in milk quota to any significant degree. Non-active quota holders were discussed not in relation to high prices but on the moral question as to whether they should hold quota at all[98]; without the non-active quota holders there would be great pressure on smaller farmers and considerably less flexibility in the quota market generally. Such persons might be retired farmers, those farmers who have moved away from milk production into some other kind of enterprise, persons taking land by operation of law for example executors or trustees in bankruptcy and, pending any re-letting, a landlord or, as in the reported case, a mortgagee in possession.

18.13 **The meaning of "purchaser"**
"Purchaser" by the domestic Regulations[99] is defined to mean a purchaser satisfying the definition in Article 9(e) of Council Regulation 3950/92 who is approved by the Intervention Board pursuant to Article 7(1)(a) of Commission Regulation 536/93. The Council Regulation defines a "purchaser" to mean:

> "An undertaking or grouping which purchases milk or other milk products from a producer:
> — to treat or process them,
> — to sell them to one or more undertakings treating or processing milk or other milk products."

> " However, any group of purchasers in the same geographical area which carries out administrative and accounting obligations necessary for the payment of the levy on behalf of its members shall be regarded as a purchaser. For the purposes of applying this provision, Greece shall be deemed a single geographical area and it may deem an official body to be a group of purchasers as referred to above."

By Article 7.1(a) a purchaser may be approved by its Member State only where it is able to demonstrate its status as a milk dealer and where it has premises in the relevant Member State where stock accounts, registers and other documents may be checked. Further it must give an undertaking to keep up to date stock accounts, registers and other documents for checking and also must undertake to forward to the Member State every year prior to the May 15, a summary of statements drawn

---

[95] The Court held that the bank did have those powers and that there had been, when possession was taken, a "transfer" within the meaning of the relevant domestic Regulations.
[96] Printed on July 12, 1995.
[97] Para. 15 of the conclusions.
[98] Paras 14–15 of the conclusions.
[99] Reg. 2(1).

up for each producer showing milk delivered and the fat content of that milk. Where these conditions are not observed approval may be withdrawn. Producers are required to ensure that purchasers to whom they deliver are approved.[1]

The meaning of "holding" 18.14
By Regulation 2(1) of the domestic Regulations[2] holding is stated to have the meaning assigned to it by Article 9(d) of Council Regulation 3950/92.[3] Article 9(d) provides:

> "'holding' means all production units operated by the single producer and located within the geographical territory of a Member State".[4]

The use of the present tense in this definition is not, it is submitted, a necessary ingredient in all applications of the definition,[5] and the Court of Appeal has expressly rejected the submission that quota cannot attach to land on which no milk production is currently carried out.[6] A "holding" for these purposes may comprise one or more different types of tenure and the word is not used to indicate the tenanted status of land, in contrast to its usual meaning in the context of the Agricultural Holdings Act 1986.

S.L.O.M. quota 18.15
This is the quota referred to as "special quota" by regulation 1 of the domestic Regulations,[7] and it may be withdrawn as to the whole or any part where the Minister considers that a false or misleading statement in the application for special quota has been made or if there is a failure to comply with any special requirements relating to it.[8] Essentially this type of quota was introduced consequent on the *Mulder*[9] litigation whereby parts of the original EEC legislation were found to be void.[10] Subsequent litigation has resulted in additional allocations

---

[1] Art. 7.1(b): an obligation apparently missing from the corresponding domestic Regulations.
[2] The Dairy Produce Quotas Regulations 1997 (S.I. 1997 No.733).
[3] The relevant definition is amended by Council Regulation 1560/93 of [1993] O.J. L154/30.
[4] The previous wording referred to location "within the geographical territory of the Community" which has been held to mean that there was no territorial principle in the allocation originally of milk quotas: see Case C-463/93 *Katholische Kirchengemeinde St Martinus Elten v. Landwirtschaftskammer Rheinland*, January 23, 1997, judgment paras 19–20.
[5] A feature which it probably shares with the definition of "producer"—see paras 18.11–18.12 above.
[6] "It is plain, in my judgment, from the answers to those questions that a farm is perfectly capable of being a holding even if the cows have all gone": McCowan L.J. at page 4A in *Holdcroft v. Staffordshire County Council* [1992] 2 E.G.L.R. 1.
[7] Defined to mean the quota referred to in Art. 4(3) of Council Regulation 3950/92 and Art. 1(1) of Council Regulation 2055/93.
[8] Reg. 33.
[9] This case is summarised and referenced at para. 18.8 above.
[10] Ultimately resulting in the amendment of previous Council Regulation 857/84 by the insertion of a new Article 3(a), carried through into the then domestic Regulations of 1989 by an amendment in 1990 (S.I. 1990 No.132). The sorry story leading to the first allocation in favour of the S.L.O.M. producers is set out in the recitals to Council Regulation 764/89 of [1989] O.J. L84/2.

to S.L.O.M.[11] producers[12] and in due course there was a successful damages claim against the Community for its handling of the S.L.O.M. producers.[13] For present purposes the full story of the S.L.O.M. producers is not directly relevant. What is to be noted is that persons dealing with special quota (which should be shown as such on the register) should take indemnities or otherwise satisfy themselves that conditions imposed whether by domestic or Community legislation have been satisfied and that the relevant quota is not liable to be withdrawn pursuant to Regulation 33.

18.16 The scheme of the domestic regulations

The general programme of implementation at domestic level has been outlined elsewhere.[14] The overall scheme of the domestic Regulations[15] is, in regard to transfer, relatively clearly drafted. The complexity arises more in terms of the application of the provisions than in, essentially, understanding what is intended. It must be recalled that a large number of definitions in regulation 2 have either special meanings or meanings which are to be found only in the corresponding European legislation. The three most useful of such imported definitions have been discussed above.[16] Permanent transfers of quota must be made in circumstances where land is the subject of an appropriate "transfer". This word clearly derives in essence from the corresponding European provisions.[17] However this concept is not itself defined by the domestic Regulations although some help may be gained from the definitions of "transferee" and "transferor" in regulation 2(1). The Court of Appeal in *Holdcroft v. Staffordshire County Council*[18] stated that in the domestic scheme the expression "transfer means a change of occupation not a change of legal title".[19] Council Regulation 3950/92, Art. 7, specifically identifies the cases of sale, lease or transfer by inheritance as transfers bearing quota consequences; they also require that the same provisions are to apply to "other cases of transfers involving comparable legal effects for producers". The reasoning of the Court of Appeal in *Holdcroft v. Staffordshire County Council* assists in the classification of various changes of occupation which might otherwise give rise to difficulty. It is now settled that a mortgagee entering into

---

[11] This is a Dutch acronym, since Mr Mulder was Dutch.
[12] The complaint that 60% on the original allocation was not enough resulted in an 80% allocation ultimately.
[13] This in turn in most instances was compromised by producers taking advantage of a block offer of settlement.
[14] para. 18.10 above.
[15] The Dairy Produce Quotas Regulations 1997 (S.I. 1997 No.733).
[16] "Producer" at paras 18.11–18.12; "purchaser" at 18.13 above and "holding" at 18.14 above.
[17] Council Regulation 3950/92 of [1992] at O.J. L405/1, Art. 7.
[18] (1994) 2 E.G.L.R. 1.
[19] "If A and B and C occupy a production unit for milk quota purposes and A and B drop out bringing that partnership to an end, there is, in my judgment, clearly a change of occupation when C and D form a new and distinct partnership and take occupation. That C figures in both partnerships is neither here nor there ... It is plain from this, in my judgment, that when the regulations talk about 'transfer' they are talking in terms of occupation and not of legal title." (McCowan L.J.) at 4D.

possession gives rise to a transfer requiring re-registration of the quota pursuant to Regulation 7.[20]

Equally clear is the situation of a landlord retaking possession, for example following a surrender.[21] Perhaps more problematic is the entering into control of a business by a receiver appointed under a charge, usually under the Agricultural Credits Act 1928. In such a case, it is submitted, that although the receiver is the agent of the chargor and acts in his name, the reality is that the business is being run and/or the assets controlled for the benefit of the charge holder whose interests become paramount. In these circumstances, in substance, there is a real change in the control of the holding and therefore a change in occupation for milk quota registration purposes. The form of a transaction does not determine its classification: it is the effect which should be considered as determinative.[22] Perhaps the most troublesome case is that of a squatter: if transfer related to a matter of change in the legal title[23] such a person would not be capable of being registered with the quota; however following *Holdcroft v. Staffordshire County Council* it would appear that a squatter may, following a change of occupation, be entitled to quota pending his being ejected from the land.

Where an entire holding[24] is transferred to another person then regulation 7 (transfer of quota with transfer of land) applies so as to require registration of the entire quota in the incomer's name. Where only part of the holding is the subject of a change of occupation it is provided that the quota in the unitary registration must be apportioned and effectively split as between holdings.[25] It is the process of apportionment of quota which will give rise to determination if necessary by arbitration under the domestic Regulations.[26] Transfers of quota without land are available in the case of restructuring of holdings and are dealt with separately.[27] Temporary transfers of quota are the subject of regulation 13[28] and are colloquially known as "leasing" but they have nothing to do with any lease in the sense known to the Law of Property Act 1925. Such transactions have no permanent effect on the registration of the quota save that the existence of a lease of quota in any particular year will stop the confiscation provisions in Regulation 32 coming into play.

---

[20] See *Harries v. Barclays Bank*, [1997] 2 E.G.L.R. 14.
[21] See the reasoning in Case 5/88 *Harries v. Barclays Bank* (above) and also *Wachauf v. The State* (1991) 1 C.M.L.R. 328.
[22] See Case C-44/89 *Von Deetzen v. Hauptzollamt Oldenburg* [1991] E.C.R. I-5119 and the discussion regarding the concept of a sale, Advocate General Jacobs, paras 23–36 at pp. I-5143–5147 and the judgment of the Court paras 37 and 38, I-5159.
[23] A hitherto tenable view of the European legislation.
[24] See para. 18.14 above.
[25] See para. 18.18 below.
[26] See para. 18.17 below.
[27] Reg. 11 and see para. 18.20 below.
[28] See para. 18.19 below.

18.17 Arbitrations under the Dairy Produce Quotas Regulations 1997

The 1997 Regulations[29] provide at various points for apportionment of quota to different blocks of land to be effected by arbitration[30]; however, the two most important and frequently encountered types of arbitration relate to apportionment of quota under the general provisions of regulations 8 (on the transfer of part of a holding in relation to quota or special quota) and 10 (where the Intervention Board has reason to believe that the areas used for milk production were not as specified in documents submitted or were not as agreed by the parties at the time of the apportionment where no notice or application under regulations 7 or 9(1) has been submitted). The latter is, in reality, a means of depriving fraudulent or grossly negligent parties of the benefit of an incorrect registration. The process of the apportionment itself is discussed later.[31] Schedule 2, in relation to England and Wales, governs any arbitration for these purposes. It should be noted at the outset that the Arbitration Act 1996 is disapplied to such an arbitration[32] and that this has particular impact not only on the appeals procedure[33] but also upon the conduct of the arbitration itself.[34] Schedule 2, paragraph 1 governs the appointment and remuneration of the arbitrator. In the normal way in the case of an arbitration under regulation 8 the transferor and the transferee have the opportunity within 28 days after the change of occupation on the holding to appoint an arbitrator, which must be done in writing,[35] subject to a requirement to give notice of the appointment to the Intervention Board within 14 days.[36] There is a concurrent unilateral power in the hands of the transferor or of the transferee at any time to apply to the President of the RICS for the appointment of an arbitrator[37] but if after the 28 days following the change of occupation no arbitrator has been applied for or appointed, the Intervention Board is required to apply to the President of the RICS for the arbitrator to be appointed.[38] The Intervention Board has the duty in the case of apportionment under regulation 10 to apply to the President of the RICS for the appointment of an arbitrator. In the case of an apportionment under regulation 32(5) the producer can only appoint by agreement with all persons having an interest in the holding; alternatively he may apply to the President of the RICS for an appointment to be made. Prospective apportionment arbitrations are subject to the appointment procedures in Schedule 2, paragraph 2. Applications made to the President of the RICS for the appointment of an arbitrator will not be valid unless accompanied by the prescribed fee.[39] The Intervention Board can recover any fee it

---

[29] S.I. 1997 No.733
[30] For example in relation to prospective apportionment of quota, Regulation 9(1)(b); in relation to the retention of the right to request restoration of quota which has been confiscated, Reg. 32(5)(b)(iii).
[31] See para. 18.18.
[32] Sched. 2, para. 35.
[33] See Sched. 2, paras 29–31.
[34] In so far as there may be special powers or procedures available under the 1996 Act they are not applicable to a milk quota apportionment arbitration.
[35] Sched. 2, para. 11.
[36] Sched. 2, para. 1(1).
[37] Sched. 2, para. 1(2).
[38] Sched. 2, para. 1(3).
[39] Sched. 2, para. 4.

pays as a debt due from the other parties to the arbitration.[40] The President is required to deal with the request for appointment as soon as possible,[41] and where the holding is in Wales and a party requires it, the President must appoint a person with a knowledge of Welsh. Once appointed the arbitrator remains seized of the reference notwithstanding the death of any party and his appointment can only be revoked where all parties consent.[42] There are provisions for a new arbitrator to be appointed where the previous one dies, becomes incapable of acting or fails to act for seven days after notice requiring him to do so.[43] The arbitrator's fees are dealt with by Schedule 2, paragraph 12.

The conduct of proceedings and matters arising in relation to witnesses are the subject of Schedule 12, paragraphs 13–21. The general framework is similar to that under arbitrations under the Agricultural Holdings Act, Sched. 11[44] but there are some peculiarities in the Schedule. Perhaps the most notable is the arbitrator's power to join as a party to the arbitration any person having an interest in the holding, provided that the person consents to be joined, whether or not that person has applied to become a party. In this matter the arbitrator has an absolute discretion but subject to the mandatory provisions of Schedule 2, paragraph 13(2) requiring joinder as a party of any person with an interest in the holding who in the case of an apportionment arbitration under regulation 32(5) has refused to sign the statement referred to in regulation 32(5)(b)(ii). In most arbitrations, therefore, the arbitrator has the opportunity to join as a party anyone who comes along to the arbitration because he has an interest in the holding, if it would be desirable to do so. It may frequently be desirable for the arbitrator not simply to hear evidence from a person having an interest in the holding but also to give that person the opportunity to cross-examine other witnesses and, if their contentions are not accepted, to punish that person in costs. Otherwise the unsatisfactory position is reached whereby some but not all of the parties bound by an award have the ability to participate fully in the proceedings or may cause matters to be investigated but without allowing the arbitrator control over who should pay the costs of the investigation. Clearly, if a person invited to be joined as a party declines to do so the arbitrator will not allow that person to act as though he were a party or to conduct litigation or put forward questions if he is unwilling to carry the risk in costs. It is further submitted that since Schedule 2, paragraph 13 gives the arbitrator an absolute discretion, circumscribed only as expressly stated in sub-paragraph (2), it is not appropriate for the parties appointing the arbitrator to seek to disable him from the full powers in paragraph 13. Persons having an interest in the holding have an absolute right to "make representations" to the arbitrator[45] but this does not entitle such a person to be fully active in the arbitration as though he were a party[46]

---

[40] Sched. 2, para. 5.
[41] Sched. 2, para. 6.
[42] Sched. 2, para. 10. A person who is purely an interested person does not have any rights under this paragraph unless made a party.
[43] Sched. 2, para. 9.
[44] As to which see Chapter 16.
[45] Sched. 2, para. 16.
[46] Contrast Sched. 2, para. 13(1).

nor does it require such a person to be a witness on oath.[47]

There is a 35-day time-limit for the submission of a Statement of Case, familiar from the 1986 Act, Sched. 11,[48] but with a power for the arbitrator to extend the time.[49]

There is a 56-day time-limit from the arbitrator's appointment for his award to be made[50] but this time may be enlarged even after the period has expired.[51] His powers in relation to the award are set out in Schedule 2, paragraphs 22–24 and he is required to notify the Intervention Board within eight days of delivery of the terms of the award[52] and by Schedule 2, paragraph 22(4) the award must fix a date not later than one month after delivery of the award for payment of any costs awarded pursuant to paragraph 26. Some guidance on the question of costs is to be found in paragraphs 26–28. However there is no express power to issue an interim award final on all matters save as to costs. Perhaps the cautious arbitrator, in a difficult case, will choose to take submissions on the question of costs having first made a provisional finding as to the merits which would then enable him to issue a single final award and thereby enable him to comply more easily with Schedule 2, paragraph 22(3).

The provisions for a special case for the opinion of the County Court on any question of law or as to the jurisdiction of the arbitrator[53] will be familiar from parallel provisions in Schedule 11 under the 1986 Act.[54] The County Court may remove the arbitrator for misconduct, alternatively set the award aside where there is misconduct, an improperly procured award or an error of law on the face of the award.[55] Remission of the award to the arbitrator in an appropriate case is also possible and in a proper case the County Court may extend time for making the remitted award.[56]

In so far as the question arises as to the time of the arbitrator's appointment[57] the time of appointment will depend on the method of its being made. Contractual appointments will be dealt with in accordance with principles discussed

---

[47] Para. 16 entitles parties outside of the jurisdiction to state their opinion or make a request to the arbitrator without being joined or appearing personally at the hearing. The arbitrator may be alerted to possibilities by such representations, if amounting to suspicions, but should not treat such representations as evidence. In so far as representations amount to submissions of law, it is submitted that the arbitrator ought correctly to allow all parties sight of the submissions and the opportunity to comment on them.
[48] See para. 16.27 above.
[49] Sched. 2, para. 14.
[50] Sched. 2, para. 22(1).
[51] Enlargement by the President of the RICS under Sched. 2, para. 22(2).
[52] Sched. 2, para. 22(3).
[53] Sched. 2, para. 29.
[54] As to which see paras 16.61–16.65 above.
[55] Sched. 2, para. 30.
[56] Sched. 2, para. 31(4).
[57] For example in connection with the time limited for service of Statement of Case under para. 14 or the making of an award under para. 22.

elsewhere[58]; appointments by the President of the RICS are made when he executes the instrument of appointment.[59]

Apportionment of quota 18.18

For the general circumstances in which the need for apportionment will arise see above.[60] Nowadays, pursuant to Council Regulation 3950/92,[61] Article 7 an apportionment must be made "in accordance with detailed rules to be determined by the Member States taking account of the areas used for dairy production or other objective criteria and, where applicable, of any agreement between the parties. In so far as any part of the reference quantity is not transferred with the holding it must be added to the national reserve".[62] The language of this part of the Regulation differs a little from the language of the previous versions of the governing EEC Regulations.[63] Although there is a slight change it is submitted that the effect of it is to allow agreement between the parties as to the areas used for dairy production, subject to Member State rules, where the parties have made *an honest attempt to assess the areas used for dairy production* even though that assessment may not be fully accurate.[64] Furthermore the change in wording would be appropriate to cover an agreement on a current use basis (assuming that dairy farming continues) as opposed to undergoing a full investigation of the history of the holding over a number of years.[65]

In terms of the domestic legislation, apportionment is effected pursuant to regulation 7 of the Dairy Produce Quotas Regulations 1997. In the case of a

---

[58] See para. 16.22 above.
[59] Sched. 2, para. 33 and see para. 16.23 above.
[60] Para. 18.16.
[61] Of [1992] O.J. L405/1.
[62] Art. 7.1.
[63] Council Regulation 590/85 of [1985] O.J. L68/1 provided a replacement to Art. 7 for Council Regulation 857/84 whereby, continuing previous wording, "where a holding is sold leased or transferred by inheritance, all or part of the corresponding reference quantity shall be transferred to the purchaser tenant or heir according to procedures to be determined". Corresponding Commission Regulation 1546/88 of [1988] O.J. L139/12, Art. 7.2 required that "where one or several parts of a holding is sold, leased or transferred by inheritance, the corresponding reference quantity shall be distributed among the producers operating the holding in proportion to the areas used for milk production or according to other objective criteria laid down by Member States ...". The phrase "in proportion to the areas used for milk production" has been held to be a purely mathematical relationship, not allowing for any more intensified use on specific parts of the holding: *Posthumus v. Oosterwoud* [1992] 2 C.M.L.R. 336, whereby (in default of specific legislation providing objective criteria) the quota was to be apportioned to only the areas used for milk production, disregarding other parts of the farm including other buildings.
[64] It is further submitted that the change in language is not great enough to allow agreement as to areas used for milk production on a differential basis with a greater intensity of use on one part being reflected in a higher level of quota. Such a departure would markedly differ from the objective nature of the criteria required for the purposes of Art. 7.1.
[65] It is of interest to note that in the context of S.L.O.M. quota apportionment according to areas used for milk production has been adopted from the main transfer provisions discussed here: see Case C165/95, *R v. M.A.F.F. ex p. Lay*, judgment of the E.C.J., October 16, 1997.

transfer of part of a holding it is necessary to submit to the Intervention Board,[66] if available, a statement signed by the transferor and transferee accompanied by a consent or sole interest notice[67] agreeing apportionment "taking account of the areas used for milk production as specified in the statement". This document establishes the apportionment for registration purposes[68] and in its absence there must be an arbitration determining the apportionment.[69] The Intervention Board has powers to request arbitration if it has grounds for believing, amongst other things, that the areas used for milk production are not as specified in a notice submitted.[70]

If there is an arbitration under the Regulations,[71] the arbitrator must base his award on findings made by him in accordance with the law in force at the time the event giving rise to an application for arbitration took place.[72] The arbitrator is required[73] to:

"base his award on findings made by him as to areas used for milk production in the last five year period during which production took place before the change of occupation, or in the case of a prospective apportionment in the last five year period during which production took place before the appointment of the arbitrator."

There is a special provision in relation to arbitrations apportioning under Regulation 32(5).[74] It must be recalled that, because of the temporary leasing provisions there may well be holdings where there has not been dairy production for some time, possibly for some years. The temporary transfers do not affect the registration on a permanent basis of the quota. One may wonder why there is a reference to a period of five years when there is no reference to any apportionment over time, in stark contrast to the requirement to apportion by areas. It is submitted that the best reconciliation of the drafting is to regard the stipulation as to period as indicating to the arbitrator simply that he must investigate what has been going on for a substantial period of time with a view to checking that he has a sufficiently long perspective to make a confident apportionment as at the date material to his purposes. This is not perhaps so odd as it may at first sound.[75] As to what may amount to an area used for milk production, this appears to be taken on a wide basis so as to include areas used to support the entire dairy herd and in particular this will

---

[66] reg. 7(2).
[67] Defined by reg. 2(1).
[68] reg. 8(a).
[69] reg. 8(b).
[70] reg. 10.
[71] Sched. 2.
[72] Sched. 2, para. 3(3).
[73] Sched. 2, para. 3(1).
[74] Sched. 2, para. 3(3).
[75] It must be recalled that the CA has confirmed that a holding on which no production is taking place at the material time may nevertheless carry quota: *Holdcroft v. Staffordshire County Council* [1994] 2 E.G.L.R. 1.

include areas supporting it by growing fodder.[76] Although applying an objective test, the finding of material facts is a highly skilled business whereby stocking densities have to be considered to see whether or not use for dairy purposes has been substantial or minimal and whether, in consequence, areas should be included or excluded in the description "area used for milk production".[77]

Temporary transfers of quota 18.19

Pursuant to authorisation in Article 6 of Council Regulation 3950/92[78] a "producer"[79] may agree with any other producer to make a transfer of quota permanently held by him.[80] The domestic Regulations provide that the transfer may relate to all or any part of the producer's unused quota[81] but there is a restriction in relation to special quota[82] applicable until December 31, 1997.[83] For these purposes the Intervention Board under Regulation 24 must keep full up to date accurate records as to direct sales and wholesale quota in relation to each purchaser and producer and for these purposes "producer" and "direct seller" expressly include a person who occupies land with quota whether or not that person is engaged in the sale or delivery of dairy produce.[84] Records may be inspected pursuant to regulation 25 and there are extensive obligations on direct sellers and producers, including persons who have temporarily ceased or who intend temporarily to cease making wholesale deliveries.[85] A temporary transfer[86] is in force for a period of one quota year and enables a person other than the permanent owner of the quota to take advantage of it. Such a transferee is required to notify the Intervention Board under regulation 13(3) in such form as the Intervention Board may require.[87] The Scottish Islands area[88] is ring fenced.[89] Entering into a temporary lease of quota which is not being used by the registered holder avoids the problem of confiscation of quota pursuant to regulation 32. In so

---

[76] See for a general consideration of this problem *Puncknowle Farms Ltd v. Kane* [1985] 3 All E.R. 790.
[77] The arbitrator's task is not usually helped by the kind of records which parties without guidance make available. It is suggested that the arbitrator will be assisted by considering June Census returns, livestock movement books and any relevant computer records kept either by the farmer or any third party, such as the dairy, which may be available either directly in the producer's possession or kept to his order elsewhere. Accountants and bank managers frequently have copies of useful documents and annual valuations produced for accounting or loan purposes can sometimes be used to check assertions as to what has been going on. IACS returns will afford very precise descriptions of land areas and may prove useful, especially as regards forage.
[78] Of [1992] O.J. L405/1.
[79] As to which see paras 18.11–18.12 above.
[80] reg. 13 of the Dairy Produce Quotas Regulations 1997 (S.I. 1997 No.733).
[81] See the definition in reg. 2(1).
[82] See para. 18.15 above.
[83] See reg. 13(5).
[84] r. 24(6).
[85] r. 26.
[86] Colloquially known as a "lease".
[87] And must pay the Intervention Board's administrative charge.
[88] Defined by reg. 2(1).
[89] r. 13(4).

far as leasing transactions are entered into by a mortgagee in possession, the mortgagee is entitled to retain the benefit of the proceeds since they represent a realisation of his security.[90]

18.20 Transfers of quota without land
Pursuant to authorisation in Council Regulation 3950/92,[91] the United Kingdom in regulation 11 of the domestic Regulations[92] has provided the opportunity for quota to be transferred from one holding to another direct without any underlying transaction in land. There is no restriction on the dealings as between themselves to be entered into by producers save that the Scottish Islands area[93] is ring fenced.[94] The Intervention Board's approval must be obtained and the relevant application made in the form prescribed for that purpose by the Board.[95] Although to some extent used, these provisions have not provided a general easily available means of transferring quota without land transfers because the application must demonstrate, before approval is granted, "how the transfer is necessary to improve the structure of the business of the transferor and transferee".[96] As usual, a consent or sole interest notice is required from the transferor in relation to the entire holding.[97] In addition undertakings are required from both the transferor[98] and the transferee[99] which severely restrict further dealings in quota and stop anti-avoidance action in relation to the undertakings. The only general exemptions apply where milk quota is transferred by way of inheritance[1] or where the Intervention Board releases the transferee from his undertakings on being satisfied that stipulated exceptional circumstances apply which have resulted in a significant fall in milk production, the circumstances being unavoidable or unforeseeable when the original application under regulation 11 was made.[2] The exceptional circumstances are set out in regulation 11(8) and, significantly, include in the quota year commencing April 1, 1997 the slaughter of animals as a result of being exposed to BSE. What "the structure of the business" may mean in any given set of circumstances[3] is unclear. Potential applicants will no doubt discuss evolving policy with the Intervention Board before becoming too far committed to an individual transaction. There is a significant restraint on utilisation of these provisions for so long as they are construed to require improvement in the structure of the business of both the transferor and, separately, the transferee. This double

---

[90] See *Harries v. Barclays Bank*, [1997] 2 E.G.L.R. 14.
[91] [1992] O.J. L405/1, 5th indent.
[92] The Dairy Produce Quotas Regulations 1997 (S.I. 1997 No.733).
[93] Defined by reg. 2(1).
[94] reg. 11(9).
[95] reg. 11(1).
[96] reg. 11(2)(a).
[97] reg. 11(2)(a); "consent or sole interest notice" is defined by reg. 2(1).
[98] Pursuant to reg. 11(2)(c).
[99] Pursuant to reg. 11(2)(d).
[1] reg. 11(3).
[2] reg. 11(7);
[3] reg. 11(2)(a) offers no guidance.

requirement appears in the domestic Regulations when it does not appear at E.C. level.[4]

Permanent transfers of quota 18.21

Any permanent transfer of quota results in a corresponding entry in the records kept by the Intervention Board. Such permanent transfers may be the result either of transfers of quota without land or of transfers of quota where there has been a land transaction. In relation to the latter reference is made to the text above and specifically the commentary under regulation 7 and Schedule 2.[5] Clearly where control over and occupation of an entire holding takes place there is no complication generated by the need to apportion quota. However, owing to the complexity usually associated with farmers' holdings, apportionment is virtually inevitable on the majority of changes of occupation. The type of transaction normally giving rise to a change of occupation is discussed above[6] but it should be noted that there are certain transactions which are exempt from quota consequences[7]: the creation of a licence to occupy land, the creation of any tenancy by which land is occupied for a period of less than 10 months (in England and Wales), and the termination of any such licence or tenancy. Just as the creation of exempt transfers is balanced by an exemption for the termination of any interest so created, it should be noted that any transaction which carries quota consequences at the outset also carries them at the conclusion.[8] Where parties intend to avoid the permanent transfer of quota as a result of their land transactions, care must be taken to ensure that one of the exemptions in regulation 7(5) does apply. For these purposes it is important to realise that there is no true "licence" if that licence contains terms which specify a payment, a period and exclusive possession in favour of the occupier. In these circumstances, as a matter of law, a tenancy will result.[9] Unless it is non-exclusive, a "licence" conferring grazing rights may well be a grazing tenancy. Such a tenancy will not affect the quota of either the land owner or the occupier provided that the relevant occupation is for less than 10 months.[10] These exemptions do not correspond to the exemptions from long term security of tenure available under the Agricultural Holdings Act.[11]

---

[4] The wording of Art. 8 of 3950/92 simply states that the application is to be made by the producer where the objective is the "aim of improving the structure of milk production at the level of the holding or to allow for extensification of production". Whilst these may be the objectives of the transaction it does not follow that the demonstrated benefit must be in relation to the holding of the person selling the quota: indeed there is an apparent contrast between the two objectives and it would appear more logical to suppose that the first would naturally benefit the acquiring transferee and the second would naturally benefit the person selling the quota, thereby raising money for supporting a less intensive operation.
[5] See paras 18.16–18.18 above.
[6] para. 18.16.
[7] See reg. 7(5).
[8] Thus the creation of a tenancy which does carry quota consequences will in due course be followed by the determination of that tenancy which determination also carries quota consequences: see para. 18.16.
[9] See *Street v. Mountford* [1985] A.C. 809, HL.
[10] Therefore the traditional 364 day grazing tenancy will affect quota.
[11] Hence the popularity of 11 month grazing tenancies or *Gladstone v. Bower* agreements

Where a "change of occupation" triggers a transfer under regulation 7, this will mean an investigation into the actual farming going on. It is not enough for matters to be dealt with purely on paper[12] and certain arrangements quite commonly encountered must be viewed in this context with suspicion.[13] Although usefully stressing the importance of actual occupation, the *Cox* decision ought to be treated with caution.[14]

18.22 The market in permanent transfers of quota

Ever since 1986 there has been a market in the United Kingdom in the permanent transfer of milk quota by means of creating short term leases in land which, on termination, leave quota on the purchaser's property. This market has been trading openly from the outset[15] and the market itself has developed in response to the needs of farmers and, to a significant extent, the willingness of lenders to treat the quota as an acceptable security.[16] The United Kingdom is one of a number of countries where in response to market demand trading in the quota has evolved by implementing, not avoiding, the apportionment requirements in the Community legislation.[17] For practitioners the following points are important:

(i) the Community and domestic legislation override contract;

(ii) permanent sales of quota depend on apportionment which in turn is dependent on the actual farming conducted;

---

for more than one and less than two years where parties deliberately intend to sell quota but ultimately intend that the land will revert to the original owners (see para. 18.22).

[12] See ***R. v. Ministry of Agriculture Fisheries & Food, ex p. Cox*** [1993] 1 E.G.L.R. 17.

[13] *e.g.* the so-called contracting scheme whereby the original owner "becomes" a contractor for the purchaser of the quota, on whose behalf he purports to occupy. Even if such an arrangement were fully implemented (and many are not) the arrangement as a whole remains open to the accusation of invalidity because it is designed as a scheme to take a benefit from the milk quota regime which was not intended to be conferred. It is easy to see the dividing line between open market arms length transactions which are fully followed through in farming consequences on the one hand and, on the other, arrangements where the control of the farming never changes at all, with the milk quota simply being absorbed into the purchaser's enterprise. Some of these "contracting" agreements even go so far as to provide that the original owner's animals should be "hired" to the purchaser of the quota: not all lawyers would consider these arrangements, cumulatively, to be safe.

[14] In particular the conclusion of Popplewell J. at 20A-B that 1371/84, Art. 5(2) "is to be read as requiring the transferee to be operating the holding before he or she is entitled to the transfer of the milk quota". This clearly cannot stand in the light of two subsequent decisions of the CA in ***Holdcroft v. Staffordshire County Council*** [1994] 2 E.G.L.R. 1 and ***Harries v. Barclays Bank***, [1997] 2 E.G.L.R. 14.

[15] Contrast the position in France where transactions are illegal and have been driven underground: see the article "Les droits a produire: Rapport de synthese", Professor Lorvellec (*Review de Droit Rural* 227/November 1994).

[16] See further paras 18.31–18.32 below.

[17] See the Special Report No. 4/93 of the Court of Auditors (94/C 12/01) and the Commissions Reply at 94/C 12/59. The Commission has not pursued action against the U.K. under Art. 169 of the Treaty of Rome; it must now be assumed that the U.K. system of trading will not be challenged by the Commission.

(iii) when the cycle of transactions is over there is always a risk that quota will finish in the wrong hands. It is normal and highly desirable to provide for appropriate indemnities or cross-payments so that the person who takes an unintended benefit in the form of quota pays for it to the person who ought to have had the quota; and

(iv) any arrangement whereby the Intervention Board or MAFF may have indicated that no questions will be raised provided a transfer does not involve a density of quota higher than 20,000 litres per hectare is not binding and should not be relied on.

The clearest description of the structure of the market in permanent transfers of quota is to be found in the judgment of Rattee J. in *Harries v. Barclays Bank* at first instance quoted in the judgment of Morritt L.J. in the same case on appeal.[18]

Occasionally readers may come across the so-called "reverse grazing agreement"[19] but these arrangements are rare.[20]

Milk quota protection clauses: types 18.23

To a large extent paragraphs 18.23–18.30 of this work are based on practitioner experience with only very limited guidance from the Courts. There are two main areas where clauses may be considered for inclusion in order to try to control the destination or ownership of milk quota. The first is in connection with an intended sale of the quota itself and the second is in the course of normal conveyancing

---

[18] [1997] 2 E.G.L.R. 14 at 18B: the quoted words are: "However, it is clear that a market has developed in quota as a valuable commodity apart from the holding to which it relates, in the following way. It has become common practice that, where farmer A has quota in respect of his holding but no longer wishes to carry on a dairy farming business and, therefore, wishes to dispose of his quota without the land, he will grant a short lease for, say, 11 months, of his holding to farmer B, who wishes to acquire farmer A's quota. It will be a term of the arrangement that the land let by farmer A to farmer B shall not be used for dairy production. On taking the lease farmer B will be registered as the holder of what was farmer A's quota in respect of the holding comprised in the lease. Farmer A's land and farmer B's land will thereafter during the continuance of the lease form one holding for the purposes of the quota regulations. As a result, when the lease in respect of farmer A's land terminates, an apportionment will have to be made of the quota enjoyed during the term of the lease in respect of the composite holding, and that apportionment will fall to be made according to the use made of the two parts of that composite holding. Since farmer A's land will not have been used during the lease for dairy farming, the whole of the quota will be apportioned to farmer B's land, which will have been used for dairy farming. Thus farmer A recovers his land, leaving farmer B with the quota previously enjoyed by farmer A in respect of that land. By such artificial means permanent transfers of quota are apparently frequently made. It follows that by this means a permanent transfer can be effected of quota without the land comprised in the holding to which that quota was originally attached, whereas no permanent transfer can be made of the land, leaving the quota in the original owner's enjoyment."

[19] An arrangement whereby it is the vendor of the quota who uses land belonging to the purchaser of quota, under cover of a grazing agreement, in order to effect the milk quota transfer.

[20] Understandably since the purchaser of quota is nearly always using his own land to the full and does not have grazing land within his own holding available for the vendor of quota to use for some other operation.

including the drawing up of leases. The provision of suitable indemnities has been mentioned elsewhere.[21] Where part of a farmer's holding is sold in freehold it will be quite usual to identify and preferably agree the amount of quota which is to be transferred with it. The mechanisms for and basis of such agreement are set out in regulation 7 of the domestic Regulations.[22] It is also appropriate in this type of transaction to provide for the circumstance that too much or too little quota is transferred in the event of there being an apportionment of quota by arbitration.[23] Sometimes a person intending to take the identified level of quota will not wish to take a sum of money on a valuation[24] but will instead prefer to buy quota on an arms length basis in the market and may instead ask the original vendor of quota to refund to him the capital cost of the purchase.[25] In the case of leases the objective of the landlord is nearly always to keep a minimum stipulated level of quota on the holding and only very rarely will he intend to prevent quota from "appearing" on the holding.[26] The most commonly encountered types of clauses, other than the indemnity provisions mentioned above, are: prohibition on certain types of activity; requirements as to the provision of specified documentation during the tenancy; and the requirement for co-operation in the completion of forms for the Intervention Board. The disclosure of documentation during the course of the tenancy nearly always relates to milk records and any correspondence with the Intervention Board.

18.24 Milk quota protection clauses: efficacy

Clauses which are designed to result in payments of money appear to have a greater chance of success than other types of clause, although they do suffer from problems of enforceability where parties other than the original contracting parties are involved. It remains to be decided whether or not some of these clauses will run with land where the original parties fail to require each other to procure a novation of the original terms with any further party who in other respects takes over the subject matter of the main transaction. Quota "massaging" is a phenomenon whereby quota will be moved around by the farmer within his holding by means straightforwardly of changing his farming pattern. Where part of the holding is tenanted land there is but limited control that can be obtained over this type of activity.[27] Where the change in farming pattern occurs, the quota will, on an

---

[21] See para. 18.22(iii) above.
[22] See paras 18.16–18.18 and 18.21 above.
[23] The value of the quota can conveniently be ascertained by contractual arbitration and valuation by reference to the open market value on an arms length basis of unused quota per litre, if possible stipulating an appropriate assumption as to the butter fat base. Another way of ascertaining such value is to nominate a person regularly involved in the market to make the valuation as an expert which will avoid any need for submissions or a hearing or a reasoned award.
[24] Which inevitably involves an expression of opinion rather than market fact.
[25] *i.e.* excluding any grazing rent or other money paid to the vendor on the second transaction.
[26] This is because for reasons connected with the decision in ***Carson v. Cornwall County Council***, discussed at para. 19.17 below, payment out on the Agriculture Act 1986 compensation claim may be at a level lower than the market value at which the quota could be sold.
[27] This is quite apart from the various freedoms available to the tenant of an Agricultural

apportionment, be dealt with according to the reality. This leaves, for example, a landlord who has a prohibition on certain types of farming with only a remedy in damages as opposed to the actual quota. If that same landlord during the tenancy becomes aware of what is going on it would appear that his best remedy is to claim an injunction to stop an unauthorised activity.[28] The most restrictive clauses in a tenancy agreement are those which prohibit the tenant from farming any other land and require him to use the farm for a dairy enterprise only.[29] The following must be borne in mind:

(i) it is not possible to contract out of the Agriculture Act or the European or domestic Regulations dealing with milk quota;

(ii) where the market in permanent transfers of quota depends on land transactions, for certain types of contract it will be necessary either to provide the relevant land or to identify it with particularity. Problems of certainty must be confronted at the beginning and if they cannot be resolved the transaction is likely to be ineffective.

Milk quota protection clauses: reservations on sale 18.25
Because it is not possible to contract out of the European or domestic milk quota Regulations it is not possible on a sale of freehold land to reserve the milk quota to the vendor. This is the case whether or not the vendor retains other land: the destination of the milk quota is governed exclusively by the operation of the apportionment provisions where the sale relates to part of a holding and where the sale relates to the entire holding the quota must be transferred to the purchaser of the land.[30]

Disposal of quota on break up or sale of holding 18.26
Where the vendor of an entire holding wishes to dispose of the quota on that holding to someone other than the purchaser of the land he will require a long run-up period to the sale of the freehold. This is because the disposal of the quota on the holding, whether to one or more purchasers, must allow time for the creation and expiry of those short term leases necessary to effect a separate sale of the quota.[31] Where the vendor intends to sell only part of his holding but to do so

---

Holdings Act tenancy as discussed in paras 10.55–10.66 above.

[28] The Court would not grant a positive order for specific performance in relation to running a farming business or a particular type of enterprise within such a business: compare enforcement of the covenant to keep open and trade in *Co-operative Insurance Society Ltd v. Argyll Stores (Holdings) Ltd* [1997] 2 W.L.R. 893, HL.

[29] This type of documentation is common with County Councils but clearly the landlord will suffer on a rent review and in any case many tenants would simply not be prepared to make an agreement along these lines precisely because they need additional areas of land or the flexibility of allowing their enterprise to grow over a period of years.

[30] Attempts to "re-identify" the holding as some other parcel prior to sale of freehold land intending to transfer no quota will fail: see *Walker v. Titterton*, County Court decision of His Honour Judge Granville Styler, Stoke on Trent County Court (December 23, 1993, unreported, Case No. 9304964).

[31] See para. 18.22 above.

without relinquishing quota to the purchaser of that part he has various options. One possibility is simply to ensure that for a very substantial period prior to the freehold sale the land to be sold off is not used for milk production.[32] Another possibility is to sell off part of his quota in advance of selling the freehold part of the holding and, once again, sufficient time must be allowed for the creation and expiry of any lease created in order to effect this result.[33] A third possibility, but less satisfactory, is for a freehold sale of part of the holding to take place but coupled with the creation by the purchaser in favour of the vendor of a grazing agreement over the land sold off.[34] On the expiry of the grazing agreement this time the quota will be re-deposited on the rump of the original holding provided that during the course of the lease the land sold off has not been used for milk production. It will be recalled that conveyancing delay can bring problems of its own if the farming meanwhile comes to an end. Attention is drawn to the possibility of entering into temporary transfers of quota[35] if there is any danger of the quota being taken into the national reserve under regulation 32 of the domestic Regulations.[36]

18.27 Absence of milk quota protection clauses: landlord's position
Because the agricultural holdings code was developed decades before the introduction of milk quota there is little help to be found in it to cope with the management problems which milk quota may generate. Sometimes the landlord may secure an injunction to enforce a contractual clause as to user; sometimes the notice to remedy procedures under Case D[37] may halt or reverse an undesirable trend in farming. Very occasionally the tenant will sell off quota in breach of a prohibition on sub-letting which, because of the loss of milk quota, will result in material prejudice to the landlord's interest for the purposes of Case E.[38] Where the tenant has land other than the tenanted holding available to him and the loss of quota results from a change in the pattern of farming over a period of years it would be unusual indeed to find a contractual clause of a general character which protects the landlord's position at all. The loss of quota from a tenanted holding is not waste in any traditional sense.[39] Similarly claims under section 71 of the Agricultural Holdings Act 1986 appear designed to cover physical damage or physical disrepair as opposed to economic loss or enforced change in the type of farming viable on

---

[32] Therefore on an apportionment under reg. 7 and Sched. 2 he reduces the likelihood of milk quota attaching to that particular land.
[33] See para. 18.22 above.
[34] This is the rare use of the "reverse grazing agreement" referred to at the end of para. 18.22 above.
[35] See para. 18.19 above.
[36] Dairy Produce Quotas Regulations 1997 (S.I. 1997 No.733).
[37] See para. 12.75 above.
[38] See paras 12.76–12.77 above. Although it may be argued in some cases where Agriculture Act compensation would otherwise be available that the landlord has been relieved of an obligation and has therefore not suffered material prejudice.
[39] This concept is confined to physical changes on the land and is not therefore usually appropriate: *West Ham Central Charity Board v. East London Waterworks Co.* [1900] 1 Ch. 624.

the holding.[40] Although it might theoretically be possible to maintain a claim under section 72 of the Agricultural Holdings Act 1986 where there is a total loss of quota or a reduction so serious that dairy farming cannot be continued at all in circumstances where there is no other viable type of farming, the authors are not aware of a single case of such damages being awarded or upheld.[41] A landlord who has no clauses designed to protect quota may consider a variation of the tenancy agreement in order to improve his position.

Milk quotas and partnerships: equitable cross-accounting 18.28

In circumstances where land used by a partnership is owned in freehold by some but not all of the partners, the question is asked as to whether the landowners should be compelled to make some allowance in the accounts to the partnership to reflect the acquisition or allocation of milk quota which on dissolution of the partnership remains on the land. It is clear that, in principle, such a claim may be sometimes sustainable.[42] However, the application of the general principle to particular facts is not straightforward. It seems reasonably clear that the acquisition by the partnership of quota on a basis of it being transferred from another property has a good chance of giving rise to cross-accounting in the dissolution accounts. Ordinary expenditure and ordinary investment in the course of running a business which during its lifetime benefited from quota by allocation in 1984 is unlikely to give rise to cross accounting.[43] There is some suggestion that "exceptional expenditure ... incurred by the partnership over and above what was inherent in running a dairy enterprise on the farm" may give rise to cross accounting,[44] but the element of expenditure which might be regarded as exceptional and the amount which it would be fair to reflect in the dissolution accounts may be predictably contentious. Furthermore, a decision would have to be taken as to how such exceptional expenditure related to levels of quota found on the land.[45]

---

[40] The language of s. 71 is limited to "dilapidation or deterioration of, or damage to, any part of the holding or anything in or on the holding caused by non-fulfilment by the tenant of his responsibilities to farm in accordance with the rules of good husbandry".

[41] The problem is that s. 11 of the Agriculture Act 1947 is drafted with an eye to a reasonable standard of efficient production and long pre-dates the type of restriction represented by milk quota.

[42] *Pawsey v. Armstrong* [1881] 18 Ch.D. 698 and *Miles v. Clarke* [1953] 1 W.L.R. 537 discussed by Chadwick J. in *Faulks v. Faulks* [1992] 1 E.G.L.R. 9 at 17: "The principle in those cases appears to me to be this: that where partnership money has been expended in maintaining or enhancing the value of land which is the exclusive property of one partner, then in taking the partnership accounts on a dissolution it may be fair and right to make some allowance to the partnership against that partner for the money which has been so expended or, perhaps, for a portion of the enhanced value. In making such an allowance the Court does not, I think, treat the land or anything on it as an asset of the partnership which is to be valued as such; rather, it adjusts the accounts between the partners by debiting the account of the partner who benefited from the expenditure in order to do what is just and equitable."

[43] See *Davies v. H&R Ecroyd Ltd* [1996] 2 E.G.L.R. 5.

[44] *Davies v. Ecroyd Ltd* (above) at 9C.

[45] This is not a case where the land would otherwise have had no quota since it is only the exceptional element which will be reflected in the accounting procedures. This is a difficult exercise, experienced as acute difficulty where there is no tenancy in the hands of the partnership: see further para. 18.30 below.

18.29 Milk quotas and partnerships: cross-accounting where there is a tenancy

Where quota is purchased by the partnership in the circumstances contemplated above[46] by the quota being transferred onto the landowning partner's property it would seem reasonable to take as the basis of an accounting adjustment the value to the landowner[47] of that transferred quota. It is considered that this is in any case the measure in relation to transferred quota in calculations under the Agriculture Act 1986[48] and where there is no compensation claim under that Act this basis of assessment appears appropriate. Insofar as a claim under the Agriculture Act 1986 is made and relates to transferred quota no further or additional adjustment in the accounts is appropriate in respect of the same quota.[49] Where quota is allocated in 1984 to the partnership there is every likelihood that a claim in respect of it under the Agriculture Act 1986 should be treated as the appropriate adjustment in the accounts. Presumably Parliament chose a basis that was fair and reasonable on average.[50] If, although there is a tenancy, no claim in respect of allocated quota is made (or perhaps possible), the question of any adjustment should be dealt with, it is submitted, on the same basis as where there is no tenancy.[51]

18.30 Milk quotas and partnerships: cross-accounting where there is no tenancy

As stated in paragraph 18.29 above it is suggested that market value provides an appropriate starting point for accounting adjustments in relation to quota transferred onto the relevant holding. In relation to quota allocated in 1984 and ultimately deposited on the landowning partner's land at the dissolution of the partnership a suitable starting point is not so easy to identify. It is impossible to ignore the existence of the Agriculture Act 1986 even though that Act is obviously not applicable where there is no tenancy. The importance of the statute is that it provides guidance as to what elements may be considered suitable for compensation as between parties who are at arms length. However it is probably not desirable and in many instances may not be possible to apply directly (even with a few necessary adjustments)[52] the statutory measure. But the construction of the Agriculture Act 1986 has generated problems and the primary concern of the court on a cross-accounting exercise is to focus on what it is fair to make allowance for and it would appear unlikely that in this connection too technical a view of the 1986 Act would be considered appropriate. It is suggested that a broadly parallel measure of adjustment between statutory and equitable claims should be adopted.

---

[46] para. 18.28.
[47] Particularly having regard to his ability to sell on the open market.
[48] See para. 19.17 below.
[49] In effect the statutory claim is the adjustment.
[50] It is suggested that the limited grounds of adjustment contemplated in *Davies v. Ecroyd* (above) mirrors the statutory basis in so far as the tenant is not regarded as obtaining an entitlement in respect of quota generated by ordinary farming, (the parallel being with "standard quota" under the Agriculture Act: see para. 19.14 below).
[51] See para. 18.30 below.
[52] For example the partnership may have been paying a rent equivalent as distinct from an actual rent at the time material to the calculation.

Milk quotas and mortgages created after March 1, 1948 but before September 1, 1995 18.31

Where the mortgagee is in possession and from that moment he is entitled to treat milk quota apportionable to the property as within his security both for the purposes of a sale and for the purposes of entering into temporary leases of quota[53] pending sale.[54] Before the mortgagee takes possession a mortgagor in possession and occupation will normally have the quota registered in his name and will be able to control it by means of his leasing powers pursuant to section 99 of the Law of Property Act 1925.[55] For so long as the mortgagor is in possession and in occupation he will normally also enjoy the powers of creating temporary transfers of the quota,[56] which may indeed be beneficial to his business. If the mortgage purports to exclude the powers of leasing under section 99, the validity of this exclusion should be carefully considered. In relation to agricultural land within the meaning of the Agriculture Act 1947 any ability to exclude the leasing powers[57] is unavailable in relation to a mortgage made after the March 1, 1948 but before the September 1, 1995. During the period March 1, 1948 to September 1, 1995 a mortgage of agricultural land could not exclude the mortgagor's leasing powers by virtue, in succession, of the Agricultural Holdings Act 1948, Sched. 7, para. 2 and the corresponding 1986 Act, Sched. 14, para. 12. Ultimately section 31 of the Agricultural Tenancies Act 1995 amended section 99 of the 1925 Act.[58] The net result is to disallow the exclusion of the leasing powers for mortgages created between March 1, 1948 and September 1, 1995, thereby empowering the mortgagor to create sub-leases and thereby sell the quota permanently away. Charges under the Agricultural Credits Act 1928 cannot create a security over milk quota and are irrelevant for these purposes. Finally, it should be pointed out that the leasing powers under section 99 of the 1925 Act are no longer exercisable once a receiver of the income of the mortgaged property or any part of it has been appointed by the mortgagee under his statutory power.[59]

Milk quotas and mortgages created on or after September 1, 1995 18.32

Reference is made to paragraph 18.31 above. For mortgages created on or after the September 1, 1995[60] the relevant amendment to section 99 of the Law of Property

---

[53] See para, 18.19 above.
[54] See *Harries v. Barclays Bank* [1997] 2 E.G.L.R. 14, CA.
[55] It is the leasing powers which enable permanent transfers of quota to be made (see para. 18.22 above).
[56] See para. 18.19 above.
[57] Pursuant to s. 99(13).
[58] By the addition of a new subs. (13A): "Sub-section (13) of this section—(a) shall not enable the application of any provision of this section to be excluded or restricted in relation to any mortgage of agricultural land made after 1st March 1948 but before 1st September 1995, and (b) shall not enable the power to grant a lease of an agricultural holding to which, by virtue of section 4 of the Agricultural Tenancies Act 1995, the Agricultural Holdings Act 1986 will apply, to be excluded or restricted in relation to any mortgage or agricultural land made on or after 1st September 1995." By a new subs. (13B) 'agricultural holding' is defined to mean a holding within the 1986 Act and "agricultural land" to be land with that meaning in the Agriculture Act 1947.
[59] See s. 99(19): the power passes to the mortgagee who may delegate it to the receiver.
[60] The commencement date of the Agricultural Tenancies Act 1995: see s. 41(2).

Act 1925[61] has the effect of validating a contractual bar on the exercise of the leasing powers save only where the mortgagor creates a tenancy falling within section 4 of the Agricultural Tenancies Act 1995. These tenancies are protected by the Agricultural Holdings Act 1986.[62] To some extent this will give a mortgagee a better degree of control over the quota where the holding falls within the mortgage and there is no other land.[63]

---

[61] See the new s. 99(13A)(b) cited in the preceding paragraph.
[62] See paras 1.7–1.14 above.
[63] It still leaves the problem of a "reverse grazing agreement" as mentioned in para. 18.22 above.

CHAPTER 19

THE AGRICULTURE ACT 1986

19.1 General Introduction and definitions

19.4 Treatment of milk quotas on rent arbitration under the Agricultural Holdings Act 1986

19.7 Compensation to outgoing tenants for milk quota

19.9 Entitlement in the tenant

19.13 Framework of calculations

19.14 Standard quota

19.15 Tenant's fraction

19.16 Relevant period

19.17 Valuation of milk quota

19.18 Procedures for claims

19.20 Miscellaneous: termination of tenancy of part of tenanted land, severance of reversion, service of notices

19.24 Farm business tenancies

General Introduction 19.1
The Agriculture Act 1986, ss. 13, 15 and Sched. 1 make adaptations in the law relating to agricultural holdings to provide specifically for milk quotas. The Agriculture Act 1986 represents a response to political conditions in the United Kingdom and its provisions were not introduced pursuant to any obligation of European Community law.[1] It is not clear whether general principles of Community law apply to the Agriculture Act, but it is submitted that they probably do not.[2] In consequence the construction of the Agriculture Act 1986 is a matter for domestic law entirely. However since milk quota is a creature of Community law,

---

[1] See Case C-2/92 *R. v. Ministry of Agriculture, Fisheries and Food*, ex p. Dennis Clifford **Bostock** [1994] E.C.R. I-955.
[2] Logically if the scheme were a domestic scheme outside the requirements imposed by Community legislation it is difficult to see why Community law should apply. This line was taken expressly by A.G. Gulmann in ***Bostock*** (above) in his opinion at para. 33. It may be inferred from the judgment of the court: in so far as Member States implement Community Rules they must observe fundamental rights (judgment para. 16) but relations between lessees and lessors on expiry of a lease are governed by Member State law and not by Community law (judgment para. 26) and the law of unjust enrichment is not part of Community law (para. 27) and further the Agriculture Act scheme was not introduced pursuant to any requirement of Community law (judgment para. 27).

the way in which milk quota is held and the rules relating to it are all governed by Community law.[3]

19.2 Structure of the statute

The adaptations provided by the Agriculture Act 1986 relate to two areas only. The first is statutory rent review under section 12 of the Agricultural Holdings Act 1986; the second relates to the availability of compensation on termination of the tenancy for milk quota left when the tenant quits. The provisions which relate to rent are voluntary[4]: those relating to compensation are mandatory.[5] For convenience all matters relating to milk quota on rent review are treated in this Chapter[6] and, for the same reason, compensation in relation to milk quota is dealt with here[7] rather than in Chapter 13.[8]

19.3 Definitions in relation to rent and compensation provisions: section 15(3) and Schedule 1, paragraph 18

In relation to milk quotas and rent arbitrations section 15(3) provides definitions of "quota", "holding", "tenant" and "tenancy". The first two of these definitions are stated to have the same meanings as in the Dairy Produce Quotas Regulations 1986. This is very curious since those Regulations have long since been revoked and their current equivalent is the Dairy Produce Quotas Regulations 1997.[9] In both the 1986 and the 1997 Regulations relevant definitions are set out in regulation 2(1). The individual definitions, in each case, are preceded by the words "unless the context otherwise requires". The definition of "quota" is the same in the 1986 and 1997 versions.[10] However when the component parts of the identical definition are chased through each respective version of regulation 2(1) there are differences to be observed mainly attributable to the fact that the underlying Community legislation to which the 1986 version refers has itself been revoked and replaced.[11] In these circumstances it is submitted that the words "unless the context otherwise requires" allows where necessary the current Community and domestic legislation to be effective for the purposes of section 15 of the Agriculture Act 1986.

The definitions of "holding" in the 1986 and 1997 Regulations differ.[12] It is

---

[3] See generally Chapter 18.
[4] See para. 19.5 below.
[5] See para. 19.8 below.
[6] paras 19.4 and 19.6 below.
[7] paras 19.7 and following.
[8] That Chapter deals with all other types of compensation and in particular those generated under the Agricultural Holdings Act 1986.
[9] S.I. 1997 No.733.
[10] "'quota' means direct sales quota or wholesale quota, as the case may be".
[11] See para. 18.4 above.
[12] The 1986 version is: "'holding' has the meaning assigned to it by Article 12 of Council Regulation 857/84, but—(a) in relation to any region, it means the division of the holding in that region, and (b) in relation to any register entry identifying a holding and used under these regulations, it means (for the purpose of making calculations in respect of changes of occupation) the land identified in that register entry". The 1997 version simply provides: "'holding' has the meaning assigned to it by Article 9(d) of the Council Regulation". As to the latter see further the discussion in para. 18.14 above.

submitted that the words "unless the context otherwise requires" would allow the construction of "holding" in whatever form was appropriate to achieve the evident purposes of section 15: in relation to any given problem the likelihood is that the content of a definition is that applicable from time to time.[13]

"Tenant" and "tenancy" are stated to have the same meanings as in the Agricultural Holdings Act 1986.[14]

In relation to compensation claims for milk quota a glossary of definitions is provided by Schedule 1, paragraph 18.[15] For the most part these definitions involve cross-references to other parts of Schedule 1 and are accordingly discussed elsewhere.[16] It is noteworthy that the definition of "tenancy" includes not only yearly or fixed term tenancies enjoying full security of tenure but also fixed term tenancies within section 5 of the 1986 Act, that is to say leases which by reason of a Ministerial approval do not enjoy full security. *Gladstone v. Bower* tenancies are excluded.[17] Where there is reference to the "termination" of a tenancy this includes any form of termination[18]: in this respect the availability of a compensation claim corresponds to the occasions available for a tenant right claim generally.

Finally, there exists in relation to the definitions in Schedule 1, paragraph 18 the same problem visible in relation to the definitions contained within section 15(3) of the Agriculture Act namely continued references to the now revoked Dairy Produce Quotas Regulations 1986. In a number of instances, where definitions are stated to be derived from the 1986 Regulations, it may be possible to include by construction the current version of those Regulations.[19] However a literal construction simply cannot be satisfied where there is the use of the present tense coupled with a reference to activity under the 1986 Regulations.[20] In such cases it is submitted that Schedule 1, paragraph 18 should as far as possible be construed to include a reference to current Regulations on the footing that otherwise a mischief, namely lack of compensation to outgoing tenants, would occur which Parliament had intended to prevent.[21]

---

[13] This may occasionally necessitate checking definitions in a now revoked cycle of domestic Regulations: see para. 18.5 above.

[14] See for the general definition of "tenant" s. 96(1). In respect of particular parts of the 1986 Act there are further sub-definitions which have been collected under the list of statutory definitions contained in Chapter 8.

[15] The following are defined: "allocated quota", "holding", "landlord", "sub-landlord", "milk quota", "the Minister", "registered", "relevant quota", "standard quota", "the 1986 Regulations", "tenancy", "tenant's fraction", "termination", "transferred quota", "land used for the feeding of dairy cows kept on the land" and "dairy cows". It is further provided that the designations of landlord and tenant shall continue to apply to the parties until the conclusion of any proceedings under the Schedule.

[16] In this work under the paragraph where the main definition is to be found.

[17] *i.e.* interests for more than one but less than two years: see para. 9.20 above. These are neither tenancies from year to year nor interests to which s. 3 of the Agricultural Holdings Act 1986 applies.

[18] By notice to quit, by effluxion of time, forfeiture, surrender or any other reason.

[19] See the argument above in relation to "quota" and "holding" in s. 15(3) of the Agriculture Act 1986.

[20] For example in relation to "registered".

[21] Regrettably the wider interpretative techniques available in relation to Community legislation appear not to be available for the construction of the Agriculture Act 1986

19.4 Treatment of milk quotas on rent arbitration—general: section 15

It is important to make it clear that, subject to the statutory exception in section 15, the possession of milk quota by the sitting tenant is a benefit to which regard should be had in assessing the rent properly payable. The fact that it is necessary to legislate to disregard it in the particular circumstances defined in section 15 implies that in general it is a factor to be regarded. This is in accordance with common sense. The registered quota is clearly relevant to the "related earning capacity" mentioned in Schedule 2 to the Agricultural Holdings Act 1986.[22] Whatever milk quota means in terms of strict legal definition, it is clear that the hypothetical competent tenant, practising a suitable system of husbandry, must be assumed to be entitled to the benefit of the quota in fact registered in respect of the land which constitutes the agricultural holding at the date of the reference. Any other view would be unrealistic.

19.5 Treatment of milk quotas on rent arbitration: non-mandatory nature of provisions

Essentially section 15 of the Agriculture Act 1986 offers a limited disregard for what is defined to be "transferred" quota.[23] The direction to the arbitrator to disregard increases in rental value due to transferred quota for which the tenant has paid is "subject to any agreement between the landlord and the tenant to the contrary".[24] It remains to be seen in any individual case in what circumstances parties will agree that this disregard, which on the face of it is entirely in the tenant's interest, should be excluded. There may be occasions when it would be worthwhile for the tenant to accept some benefit for agreeing to pay an undiminished rent.

19.6 Treatment of milk quota on rent arbitration: method of application

On a rent review under section 12 of the Agricultural Holdings Act 1986 quota "transferred to the tenant by virtue of a transaction the cost of which was borne wholly or partly by him"[25] is to be disregarded where by reason of it there is an increase in the rental value of the tenanted holding. This apparently simple concept raises certain problems. The first, which the Courts may choose to ignore, is the fact that section 15(1) refers to quota which is "registered under the Dairy Produce Quotas Regulations 1986" whereas in fact those Regulations have long since been revoked. The second problem relates to any perceived difference between quota regarded as "transferred" for the purposes of section 15 and quota regarded as "transferred quota" for the purposes of Schedule 1, paragraph 1(2). Since the introduction of the possibility of acquiring quota by transfers not involving the transfer of land[26], it would appear that quota regarded as transferred for the

---

since it is not part of a Community scheme: see para. 19.1 above.
[22] Agricultural Holdings Act 1986, Sched. 2, para. 1(1) and (2). *cf. McGill v. Bury Management Ltd* (1986) S.L.Ct., Strath, R.N. 293.
[23] See para. 19.6 below.
[24] Agriculture Act 1986, s. 15(1).
[25] Agriculture Act 1986, s. 15(1).
[26] A possibility available only since authorising legislation in 1992: see generally para. 18.20 above.

purposes of section 15(1) includes quota transferred without an underlying land transaction.[27] This difference of meaning may be inadvertent but it is probably too clear to be avoidable.[28]

Cost of transfer 19.6.1

"Transaction" suggests something which is intended to result in legal consequences, to create a change in legal relations, such as a contract or conveyance. The cost must be borne by the tenant.[29] Thus a gratuitous transfer of quota in conjunction with the transfer of an interest in land would not bring the disregard provision into play for the benefit of the tenant. An important provision in section 15(2)(a) is that "any payment made by the tenant in consideration for the grant or assignment to him of the tenancy or any previous tenancy of any land comprised in the holding shall be disregarded".[30] This is a disregard of a disregard, *i.e.* such a payment shall be regarded. It would appear from this that an agreement by an incoming tenant to pay to the landlord the amount of compensation paid by the latter to the outgoing tenant would not qualify as a payment of the cost of the transferred quota within section 15(1). It seems to be essential to show that the payment has been made specifically and identifiably for the cost of the transfer of the quota itself.

The benefit of section 15 in the disregard of rental value extends beyond the tenant who has paid the cost to any person who would be treated under paragraph 2, 3 or 4 of Schedule 1 to the Agriculture Act 1986 as having had quota transferred to him or having paid the whole or part of the cost of any transaction for the purpose of a claim to compensation under that Schedule. This covers close relatives obtaining a new tenancy on the death or retirement of the previous tenant, certain assignees, and tenants who have sub-let where the sub-letting has terminated.[31]

Calculation of the increase in rental value to be disregarded 19.6.2

The calculation of the increase of rental value which has to be disregarded is likely to be an exercise not free from difficulties. Apart from the proportion sums to be done where the agricultural holding is part only of the holding or where the cost was only partly borne by the tenant, the "increase in the rental value" to be disregarded may present problems. Calculations may involve considerations of "productive capacity", "related earnings capacity", registered quota and transferred quota. There may be cases where the transferred quota would make no difference to the rental value, so that there is nothing to be disregarded. The question is: to what extent has the transferred quota increased the rental value? It may not have done so, for example, in a case where the registered quota, after

---

[27] The definition of "transferred quota" in Sched. 1, para. 1(2) is narrower by being limited to quota transferred to the tenant "by virtue of the transfer to him of the whole or part of a holding".

[28] It results from a change in the law since the last edition of this work which at p. 228 considered that it would be odd if there should be a material difference between quota regarded as transferred for the purposes of s. 15 and Sched. 1, para. 1(2).

[29] It is by no means clear whether it would fulfil this condition if the cost was borne by a partnership or a company in which the tenant was interested.

[30] Agriculture Act 1986, s. 15(2)(a).

[31] Agriculture Act 1986, s. 15(2)(b), (c); see below paras 19.10–19.12.

deducting the transferred quota, exceeds the productive capacity of the agricultural holding. There may, on the other hand, be cases where the registered quota is much less than the tenant, being an extremely efficient producer, could achieve in view of the productive capacity and related earning capacity of the holding. In such a situation it does not appear possible to attribute to the hypothetical tenant in the rental formula a notional quota in excess of the actual quota registered in relation to the holding. Does the disregard of transferred quota paid for by the tenant involve simply an arithmetical deduction of an amount equal to the quota to be disregarded? Or is there a value judgment involved? The disregard is to be of "any increase in the rental value of the land which is due to that quota",[32] which suggests a "valuing out" principle. On the other hand, a quota, as distinct from an improvement, may not afford much scope for valuing out.[33]

19.7 Compensation to outgoing tenants for milk quota: section 13 and Schedule 1

Although it has long been possible for Member States to allow an outgoing tenant to take the milk quota with him if he intends to continue milk production,[34] the United Kingdom did not avail itself of this opportunity. Instead a voluntary domestic scheme was enacted by virtue of section 13 and Schedule 1 of the Agriculture Act 1986 which permitted certain tenants to apply for compensation where, broadly, as a result of their own investment additional quota was available in respect of dairy land. Any tenancy coming to an end prior to July 25, 1986 fell outside the scope of this possible compensation claim and it is now settled that the United Kingdom was not in breach of any duty in Community law by failing to make provision for tenancies ending prior to that time.[35] The terms of Schedule 1 have given rise to a limited base of case law but it may be observed that the calculations under the Schedule are complex, technical and not in every respect clear.

19.8 Mandatory nature of compensation to outgoing tenants for milk quota: section 13

In stark contrast to the provisions of section 15 of the Agriculture Act, section 13 states that the compensation provisions "shall" have effect. From this it may be deduced that it is not possible to contract out in advance of the compensation claim and, secondly, that there is every likelihood that tenancy terms which incidentally have the effect of depriving the tenant of such a claim in full will be treated as

---

[32] Agriculture Act 1986, s. 15(1).
[33] See generally comments on valuation by Forbes J. in *GREA Real Property Investments Ltd v. Williams* (1979) 250 E.G. 651 and *Estates Projects Ltd v. Greenwich London Borough* (1979) 251 E.G. 851.
[34] Originally Council Regulation 857/84 of [1984] O.J. L90/13, Art. 7.4; now Council Regulation 3950/92 of [1992] O.J. L405/1, Art. 7.2, see further para. 18.9 above.
[35] See Case C-2/92 *R. v. Ministry of Agriculture, Fisheries and Food, ex p. Dennis Clifford Bostock* [1994] E.C.R. I-955. It seems tolerably clear that neither the court nor the Advocate General felt able to see any duty on the U.K. to provide for persons with tenancies terminating prior to July 25, 1986 in a political context where the U.K. was the only country making any provision whatsoever for this type of compensation to tenants.

void.[36] However it would seem likely that a crystallised claim may be settled once the tenancy has ended.

Tenant's rights to compensation: Schedule 1, paragraph 1   19.9
Schedule 1, paragraph 1 establishes a right for certain tenants to claim compensation on quitting tenanted land. The entitlement relates to quota "registered as" the tenant's and further relates to two specific categories of quota apportionable at quitting to the tenanted land. These categories are the subject of special definition and are identified in general terms as "allocated quota" and "transferred quota". It should be noted that there is no compensation claim available during the currency of the tenancy and it is only on termination that the claim arises.

"Registered as his": Schedule 1, paragraph 1(1)   19.9.1
The statutory entitlement relates only to quota "registered as his" (*i.e.* the tenant's). This would appear to include cases where the quota was registered in the name of a farming partnership of which the tenant was one of the partners: it is probable that the registration should be regarded as joint and several in the name of each partner since, as a matter of law, there is no independent personality of the partnership itself.[37] It would seem that registration in favour of one partner where the tenancy is held by two partners would not prevent a claim being made.[38] Since in many cases the quota registration may be an accident of history, some tenants may perhaps[39] be able to bring themselves within the wording of Schedule 1, paragraph 1(1) simply by requiring the register to be corrected to show the tenant as the current registered quota holder. Further problems are generated where quota is registered in the name of a company. Where the problem cannot be corrected by re-registration in the name of the tenant careful examination of the registration in the company's favour will be required. The relationship of the tenant to the company whether as a director or even a majority shareholder would appear to be irrelevant. Even where there is quota held on trust for the tenant this will not necessarily secure the availability of a compensation claim.[40] Where the company has a real and independent existence there is a distinct possibility that the statutory wording simply cannot be satisfied: it would seem that the only avenue of argument will be where the very limited possibility exists of arguing that the veil of incorporation

---

[36] See by way or comparison para. 13.2 above. Although not protected by the equivalent of s. 78(1) of the Agricultural Holdings Act 1986, mandatory language is likely to be given the same treatment as is displayed in the early case law relating to tenant-right and other compensation claims.

[37] Since this statute is not part of a Community scheme (see para. 19.1 above) the reader is not troubled in this context with the possibility that for some purposes European legislation may ascribe personality to a partnership.

[38] The analogy is with ***Howson v. Buxton*** [1928] 97 L.J.K.B. 749 which suggests that courts are reluctant to defeat claims without substantial reason.

[39] This possibility presupposes a difference between "registered" and "allocated", *i.e.* on the assumption that the latter may include beneficial entitlement: see para. 19.9.3 below.

[40] Compare under the Landlord and Tenant Act 1954 the case of ***Cristina v. Seear*** [1985] 2 E.G.L.R. 128.

should be pierced but the Courts display an extreme reluctance to do this.[41] The definition of "registered" provided by Schedule 1, paragraph 18 is considered above.[42] The milk quota capable of generating a compensation payment may be either direct sales quota or wholesale quota as the case may be.[43] Throughout Schedule 1 the words "tenant" and "tenancy" must be construed in accordance with paragraph 18.[44]

19.9.2 Meaning of "the relevant quota": Schedule 1, paragraph 1(2)
The definition in Schedule 1, paragraph 1(2) limits the compensation claim to quota which on termination of the tenancy is registered exclusively in respect of or apportionable to the tenanted land.[45]

19.9.3 Claim in respect of allocated quota: Schedule 1, paragraph 1(1)(a)
The tenant's claim for milk quota compensation will be partly in respect of "allocated quota" which is loosely defined to mean "milk quota allocated to him (the tenant) in relation to land comprised in the holding".[46] The claim itself is further limited to that part of the allocated quota as is "relevant quota".[47] It is assumed that "allocated" means registered in the tenant's name in 1984 when milk quota first came in. The language "allocated to him" may be slightly less exact than "registered as his"[48]: therefore in so far as there is a contrast it may be that the reference to "registered as his" is limited to the person whose name appears on the register whereas "allocated to him" may allow a person beneficially entitled, but who did not have the registration in his own name, to assert successfully that quota was "allocated to him". The requirement in Schedule 1, paragraph 1(1)(a) that the allocation be in relation "to land comprised in the holding" is not normally investigated further than ascertaining that the agricultural tenanted holding was originally part of the milk quota holding. In other words, it is almost unknown for a cross-check to be made as to the amount of quota which as at the date of allocation would have attached to the tenanted part of a larger original holding. It is suggested that all steps in the calculation ought to be done and that it is necessary to trace the element carrying compensation not only as properly relating on a current basis to the tenanted property but also as being originally allocated in respect of that precise property. The historical details of the original allocation need only now be stated in brief. The allocation was based in the main on dairy produce (by wholesale producers) in 1983. In the case of direct sales the allocations were made in respect of transactions in 1981. This was done in accordance with provisions in the Dairy

---

[41] See *DHN Food Distributors Ltd v. Tower Hamlets LBC* [1976] 1 W.L.R. 852 and *Woolfson v. Strathclyde Regional Council* (1978) 38 P.&C.R. 521, both HL decisions.
[42] See para. 19.3 above.
[43] See the definition of "milk quota" in Schedule 1, paragraph 18, which is also further considered at para. 19.3 above.
[44] See para. 19.3 above.
[45] See the definition of "holding" for milk quota legislation purposes in para. 18.14 above and as to apportionment paras 18.16–18.18 above.
[46] See para. 18.14.
[47] See para. 19.9.2 above.
[48] Contrast para. 19.9.1 above.

CLAIM IN RESPECT OF ALLOCATED QUOTA: SCHEDULE 1, PARAGRAPH 1(1)(A)

Produce Quotas Regulations 1984.[49] A special allocation could be made by an award of the Dairy Produce Quota Tribunal for reasons such as "a serious natural disaster affecting the various producer's farm to a substantial extent" or "exceptional hardship". A further special situation was a development claim based on capital investment.

Entitlement in respect of transferred quota: Schedule 1, paragraph 1(1)(b)   19.9.4

"Transferred quota" is defined by Schedule 1, paragraph 1(2) to mean "milk quota transferred to the tenant by virtue of the transfer to him of the whole or part of a holding". The claim itself is restricted to transferred quota which can further be described as transferred to the tenant "by virtue of a transaction the cost of which was borne wholly or partly by him".[50] Accordingly there is a double condition first as to the nature of the transaction which resulted in the quota being transferred,[51] and, secondly, as to the identity of the person bearing all or part of the cost. A gratuitous transaction therefore does not result in a compensation claim in the tenant's favour.[52] Schedule 1, paragraph 1(1)(b) further contains a condition as to dates which effectively limits claims (subject to express statutory exceptions in Schedule 1, paras 2, 3 and 4) to persons occupying the tenanted land on April 2, 1984. It follows that persons becoming tenants (unless falling within the specific statutory exemptions) after April 2, 1984 are not eligible to make a claim for milk quota compensation under the Agriculture Act 1986. The condition as to time is expressed in the alternative and is satisfied:

(i) if the tenant had milk quota allocated to him in respect of land comprised in the holding[53]; or

(ii) if the tenant was in occupation of the tenanted land as a tenant on April 2, 1984. It is expressly stated that the relevant tenancy need not be the tenancy which on termination gives rise to the milk quota compensation claim.

One compensation payment only in respect of the same land   19.9.5

Schedule 1, paragraph 1(3) restricts a tenant's entitlement to one payment in respect of the same land.

Right to compensation: succession on death or retirement of tenant: 19.10
Schedule 1, paragraph 2

Where statutory succession takes place on the death or retirement of the tenant under Part IV of the Agricultural Holdings Act 1986 the right to compensation in respect of quota passes to the statutory successor, not to the deceased tenant's estate or to the retiring tenant. This is a form of compulsory "roll over" whereby the

---

[49] S.I. 1984 No.1047.
[50] Sched. 1, para. 1(1)(b).
[51] *i.e.* a transfer consequent on the transfer of the whole or part of a holding: contrast corresponding provisions in relation to rent review, as to which see para. 19.6 above.
[52] But see below for "roll over" of claims to successor tenants, assignees, and sub-landlords: paras 19.10–19.12 respectively.
[53] As identified by Sched. 1, para. 1(1)(a) (see para. 19.9.3) above.

technical requirements of Schedule 1, paragraph 1 are modified such that the successor tenant is eligible to make a claim. The relevant modifications are that milk quota allocated or transferred to the former tenant is treated as if instead it had been allocated or transferred to the new tenant[54]; in the case of transferred quota transaction costs carried by the former tenant are treated as carried by the new tenant[55]; and where the former tenant was in occupation of land on April 2, 1984 the new tenant is treated as being in occupation on that date.[56] The modifications are mandatory and they strip the former tenant or his estate of any possible claim. Schedule 2, paragraph 2 applies only in those circumstances identified by sub-paragraph (1).[57] Where the new tenancy is granted prior to the commencement of the Agricultural Holdings Act 1986 the "roll over" is still available where the succession took place under equivalent provisions of earlier legislation.[58]

19.11 Right to compensation: assignments: Schedule 1 paragraph 3

Where a tenancy is assigned after April 2, 1984, whether by deed or by operation of law, there is a "roll over" of any milk quota compensation claim away from the assignor into the hands of the assignee.[59] Again the mechanism chosen is to treat an allocation or transfer of quota as being to the assignee,[60] to treat the assignee as having carried the cost of a transaction actually carried by the assignor[61]; and to treat the assignee as being in occupation in place of the assignor in relation to historical periods.[62] Paragraph 3 applies only in the case of assignment and not, for example, where there is a surrender and re-grant.

19.12 Right to compensation: sub-tenancies: Schedule 1, paragraph 4

Special provisions are required to deal with the situation of a sub-landlord. Such a person, without special provisions in the statute, might be faced with a claim from his own tenant which could not be passed up to the head landlord. The mechanism of rendering the sub-landlord eligible to make a claim is similar to that chosen in respect of the successions and assignments under the two preceding paragraphs. Thus, quota allocated or transferred to the sub-tenant is treated as so allocated or transferred to the sub-landlord[63]; transaction costs carried by the sub-tenant are treated as carried by the sub-landlord[64]; and occupation of the land by the sub-tenant on April 2, 1984 is treated as that of the sub-landlord.[65] These provisions do not disentitle the sub-tenant from making his own claim against his

---

[54] Sched. 1, para. 2(2)(a).
[55] Sched. 1, para. 2(2)(b)(i).
[56] Sched. 1, para. 2(2)(b)(ii).
[57] Tenancy obtained by virtue of a direction under s. 39 (succession on death) or s. 53 (succession on retirement); tenancy granted following a direction under s. 39 in the circumstances within s. 45(6) (see para. 14.96 above); tenancy granted within s. 37(1)(b) or (2) by agreement to a close relative (see respectively paras 14.16 and 14.17 above).
[58] See Sched. 1, para. 2(3).
[59] Sched. 1, para. 3.
[60] Sched. 1, para. 3(a).
[61] Sched. 1, para. 3(b)(i).
[62] Sched. 1, para. 3(b)(ii).
[63] Sched. 1, para. 4(a).
[64] Sched. 1, para. 4(b)(i).
[65] Sched. 1, para. 4(b)(ii).

RIGHT TO COMPENSATION—SUB-TENANCIES: SCHEDULE 1, PARAGRAPH 4

own landlord but simply operate for the purpose of determining the sub-landlord's entitlement as against his own (*i.e.* the head) landlord. If the sub-landlord does not occupy the land after the sub-tenancy has ended, the sub-tenant having quitted, the sub-landlord is deemed to have quitted when the sub-tenant left.[66] Without this special provision the sub-landlord would be unable to demonstrate a "quitting" so as to qualify him under Schedule 1, paragraph 1(1). But this provision does not accelerate the sub-landlord's claim which arises only on termination of his own tenancy.

Steps in the calculation of a claim 19.13

In outline, the steps which are necessary to ascertain the quota for which the tenant is to be compensated at the end of the tenancy are as follows:

(i) identify the relevant quota (which may require an apportionment);

(ii) separate, within the relevant quota, the transferred quota from the allocated quota;

(iii) ascertain the "standard quota"[67];

(iv) calculate the "tenant's fraction".[68]

The composition of the tenant's compensation is then broadly as follows:

(a) the value of the excess, if any, of the allocated quota over the standard quota;

(b) the value of the tenant's fraction of the standard quota;

(c) the value of the transferred quota, to the extent to which the tenant has paid for it[69];

(d) in cases where the allocated quota is equal to or less than the standard quota—(i) where it is equal, the tenant is entitled to the tenant's fraction of the allocated quota, (ii) where it is less, the tenant is entitled to the value of such proportion of the tenant's fraction of the allocated quota as the allocated quota bears to the standard quota.[70]

Amount of compensation payable: calculation of payment: Schedule 1, 19.13.1
paragraph 5

The calculation of the payment due must be made in accordance with Schedule 1, paragraph 5. As stated in the previous paragraph the treatment of allocated quota and transferred quota differs. The former is dealt with under paragraph 5(2) according to its relationship to "standard quota",[71] whereas the latter under

---

[66] Sched. 1, para. 4(c).
[67] See para. 19.14 below.
[68] See para. 19.15 below.
[69] Sched. 1, para. 5(3).
[70] Sched. 1, para. 5(2).
[71] See para. 19.14 below.

paragraph 5(3) forms part of a claim according to the extent to which the tenant himself met the cost of a relevant transaction. Much of the remainder of Schedule 1 is concerned with providing the detailed assessment of concepts required to calculate the payment due in respect of allocated quota. It would appear that the payment itself should reflect the extent of the tenant's own investment in the holding and therefore to a significant extent the statute contemplates that the landlord of dairy land will certainly receive some quota by way of allocated quota for which no payment is due. This can be seen in the use of the "tenant's fraction".[72]

19.14 Amount of compensation payable: "standard quota": Schedule 1 paragraph 6

Schedule 1, paragraph 6 provides a complicated definition of "standard quota" for the purposes of computing compensatable milk quota.[73] There are different possible bases for the calculation of standard quota set out respectively in Schedule 1, paragraph 6(1) and (2). In each instance the standard quota relates to "any land" which, in context, clearly includes buildings.[74] The calculation under sub-paragraph (1) is made by multiplying the "relevant number of hectares"[75] by the "prescribed quota per hectare".[76] Where, for specific identifiable reasons, "the reasonable amount"[77] differs from the prescribed average yield per hectare, a calculation under paragraph 6(2) will apply.

19.14.1 "The relevant number of hectares"

"The relevant number of hectares" is defined by paragraph 6(1)(a) to mean either:

"the average number of hectares of the land in question used[78] during the relevant period[79] for the feeding of dairy cows[80] kept on the land", or"

"if different, the average number of hectares of the land which could reasonably be expected to have been so used (having regard to the number of grazing animals other than dairy cows kept on the land during that period)."

Each of these alternative calculations is designed to ascertain an average number

---

[72] See para. 19.15 below.
[73] The steps in the calculation of claim are set out at para. 19.13 above.
[74] The compensation right arises where the tenancy "of any land" comes to an end (Sched. 1, para. 1(1)) which, where any were included within the tenancy, necessarily includes buildings.
[75] Defined by sub-para. (1)(a).
[76] Defined by sub-para. (1)(b).
[77] para. 6(2).
[78] There is an express statutory exclusion of land "used for growing cereal crops for feeding to dairy cows in the form of loose grain" (para. 6(5)(a)). This is a curious provision because, as noted in *Grounds v. Att.-Gen. of the Duchy of Lancaster* [1989] 1 E.G.L.R. 6, CA there is no farming practice which literally involves the feeding of loose grain to cows. This can only mean, as recorded in the judgment of Glidewell L.J. at 9E that land is excluded where grain grown on it is then processed and fed to the cattle.
[79] See Sched. 6 para. 8 and para. 19.16 below.
[80] This means "cows kept for milk production (other than uncalved heifers)": para. 6(5)(b).

of hectares which either was actually used or ought reasonably to have been used for a particular purpose. The figure is therefore a theoretical figure, even in terms of actual use, since it will have to be calculated over a period of time. The theoretical tool used to attempt ascertainment of the average number of hectares used during the relevant period for the purpose of feeding dairy cows kept on particular land is the "livestock unit". Although widely used, this concept is one which derives entirely from land agency expertise and it has no statutory expression. For this reason it is impossible for a solicitor, without expert land agency advice, to calculate a statutory compensation payment. It must be obvious that the dairy herd will include animals which fall outside the definition of "dairy cows".[81] Furthermore there will sometimes be changes within the pattern of land use during the relevant period and/or shared use of some land by other animals which are in no way connected with the dairy herd. These problems can only be resolved by the use of the livestock unit and in every case the calculation will be made on a retrospective basis for a purpose for which no records were kept at the time in question. In terms of the land use during the relevant period it is often possible to obtain some information from surviving cropping books, valuations and/or June census returns to the Ministry. Since accuracy in the calculation is important where the overall use of a piece of land can be ascertained, the precise extent of the land is often most clearly identifiable, if available, from subsequent IACS. returns filed for subsidy purposes. It is clearly necessary to identify, in addition, the number of dairy cows kept during the relevant period. Although not expressly stated to be an average number, quite obviously this must be the case since there will be changes in numbers caused by deaths, sales, births and purchases. The most accurate information will be, if available, in the livestock movement books although the annual valuation may, at a specific date, provide a "snapshot" of animal numbers. Sometimes correspondence with the Ministry in connection with other matters[82] will also yield further information.

It remains an open question as to whether the average number of hectares used during the relevant period for the feeding of dairy cows kept on the land should or should not include buildings. Although buildings are involved in the wider concept "land" it is quite likely that they are excluded since in a general way the wording seems apt to describe only grazing land as distinct from land used for "accommodation or milking".[83]

The second alternative basis on which "the relevant number of hectares" may be calculated is what is sometimes referred to as the "if different" calculation. It must be almost impossible that there would be a precise coincidence between the first and second alternatives in any given case and whether or not the "if different" calculation comes into play will depend on the evidence and on the case which is run by the parties to any arbitration. Sometimes parties simply choose to consider the actual calculation (*i.e.* the first alternative) without involving themselves in the complexities and uncertainties of the "if different" alternative calculation.

It is very difficult to see what the second alternative formulation of "relevant

---

[81] *e.g.* uncalved heifers of various ages and steers.
[82] *e.g.* in relation to development claims for milk quota.
[83] Contrast Sched. 1, para. 7(1)(b).

number of hectares" is really designed to do. The problem relates to the words in brackets and the extent to which, if at all, they qualify or throw light on the introductory words about reasonable expectation for hectares used for keeping dairy cows. In short, if the provision had been directed exclusively to, in general terms, ascertaining the reasonable use of land as distinct from the actual use of land, the bracketed words would not have been necessary at all. Since those bracketed words are there the only way of preserving that interpretation (*i.e.* a general consideration of what would reasonably be expected to have been used) is to regard the bracketed words as evidential in content. Thus the bracketed words, on that hypothesis, might indicate the quality of the grassland which, if it was actually used for a certain number of sheep, would assist in determining how many dairy cows could be kept on that same land. A diametrically opposed construction of the alternative formulation of "the relevant number of hectares" begins with the assumption that the bracketed words require, in all calculations on this, the assumption to be made of the actual animals really grazing and the remaining assessment of what would be reasonable in terms of use by dairy cows to be predicated on that basis. This would seem to be a somewhat pointless construction since it will frequently return to the actuality which forms the basis of the first alternative. The explanation for the curious "if different" calculation may be that the statutory draftsman did not anticipate the development of the "livestock unit" technique. If that were the case then the first part of the calculation for "the relevant number of hectares" would fit easily with actual exclusive use by dairy cows whereas the "if different" provision would allow a calculation to take place where there was mixed use with other grazing animals together with the dairy cows.

19.14.2 **"The prescribed quota per hectare"**
This is defined[84] to mean such number of litres as the Minister[85] may from time to time by order prescribe for this purpose.[86]

19.14.3 **Calculations under Schedule 1, paragraph 6(2)**
The provisions of Schedule 1, paragraph 6(2) only come into play where specific circumstances apply. Essentially if the reasonable expectation as to milk yield differs from the prescribed quota per hectare[87] a substituted calculation is made. The trigger is limited to only some of the many circumstances which might affect the reasonable expectation as to milk production. These are first the quality of the land in question and, alternatively, climatic conditions in the area. It is not necessary in every case for an arbitrator to make the paragraph 6(2) calculation, although he may do so, since he may be satisfied on the evidence before him that

---

[84] Sched. 1, para. 6(1)(b).
[85] Defined by Sched. 1, para. 18(1).
[86] Currently the Milk Quota (Calculation of Standard Quota) (Amendment) Order 1992 (S.I. 1992 No.1225) inserted by amendment into the Milk Quota (Calculation of Standard Quota) Order 1986 (S.I. 1986 No.1530). The Order offers different figures depending on whether the land is severely disadvantaged or disadvantaged or neither of those and also depending on the breed of animal. There is no overt assumption as to buildings.
[87] See the preceding paragraph.

"the quality of the land and the climatic conditions are not so unorthodox that they would affect the milk yield either way".[88] It is not immediately obvious whether the phrase "quality of the land in question" allows a tenant to rely on the paragraph 6(2) calculation in circumstances where his complaint is the absence or type of buildings provided on the holding by his landlord. There are clearly arguments in support of land, for these purposes, including or excluding buildings. In the normal way "land" will include buildings[89] and furthermore it appears that "land" for the purposes of Schedule 6, paragraph 1 does in the general way include land with buildings on it. However the paragraph 6(2) calculation is intended to replace in part figures deriving from paragraph 6(1) and it is questionable whether land used during the relevant period for the feeding of dairy cows kept on the land includes land with buildings or relates to grazing land only. Finally, and perhaps most telling, is the choice of language in paragraph 6(2) itself since one would normally take the phrase "quality of the land" to refer to soil type and fertility rather than the absence of quality of buildings. Whereas it is possible to have a reasonable expectation about land quality which is visible it is, for example, almost impossible to have a reasonable expectation as to productivity from land over which buildings are absent. The presence of buildings transforms expectation. On balance, therefore, it is suggested that probably "quality of the land" is used in context to refer only to land and not to the presence or quality of buildings. It is observed that this reading may be more consistent with paragraph 6(2) allowing an alternative calculation in circumstances where nature, not the failings of the parties, is responsible for a departure in terms of expectation from the Minister's prescribed figures. "Climatic conditions in the area" is not further defined, although it is suggested that as a matter of common sense this must refer to a reasonably close locality. The word "area" appears considerably more localised than, for example, "region". Information as to relevant climatic conditions can normally be obtained from the Meteorological Office and it will be important to ascertain the distance from the holding to the point at which any relevant readings were taken.

Paragraph 6(2) requires that where "the reasonable amount"[90] is greater or less than the prescribed average yield per hectare standard quota must be calculated in accordance with sub-paragraph (2). In forming a view as to "the reasonable amount" the arbitrator is entitled to include the effect of concentrates fed to the cows in accordance with normal practice in addition to grass grown on the relevant hectares.[91] Standard quota will then be calculated by multiplying the relevant number of hectares[92] by "such proportion of the prescribed quota per hectare[93] as the reasonable amount[94] bears to the prescribed average yield per hectare". The

---

[88] His Honour Judge Slot in *Surrey County Council v. Main* [1992] 1 E.G.L.R. 26 at 27L.
[89] Compare *Mann v. Gardner* [1991] 1 E.G.L.R. 9, CA.
[90] Defined by reference to a reasonable expectation in relation to one hectare of the land during the relevant period.
[91] *Grounds v. Att.-Gen. of the Duchy of Lancaster* [1989] 1 E.G.L.R. 6, CA.
[92] See para. 6(1)(a).
[93] See para. 6(1)(b).
[94] See above.

amount of milk to be taken as the average yield per hectare has been prescribed by order by the Minister.[95]

19.14.4 Milk quota allocated by the Dairy Produce Quota Tribunal

Where the relevant quota[96] includes an amount allocated by an award of the Dairy Produce Quota Tribunal which has not been allocated in full, adjustments must be made in the calculation of the standard quota in accordance with Schedule 1, paragraph 6(3) and (4).

19.15 Amount of compensation payable: "tenant's fraction": Schedule 1, paragraph 7

The tenant's fraction is defined as a fraction of which:

(a) The numerator[97] is the annual rental value at the end of the relevant period[98] of the tenant's dairy improvements and fixed equipment[99]; and

(b) The denominator[1] is the sum of that value and such part of the rent payable[2] by the tenant in respect of the relevant period as is attributable to the land used in that period for the feeding, accommodation or milking of dairy cows kept on the land."

---

[95] See the Milk Quota (Calculation of Standard Quota) Order 1986 (S.I. 1986 No.1530) as amended by S.I. 1992 No.1225.

[96] See para. 19.9.2.

[97] The top part of the fraction.

[98] See Sched. 1, para. 8 and para. 19.16 below. If the relevant period is less or greater than 12 months, or the rent was only payable by the tenant in respect of part of the relevant period, the average rent payable in respect of one month is determined and the rent payable is taken to be the corresponding annual amount: this is expressly provided by Sched. 1, para. 7(3).

[99] By Sched. 1, para. 7(2) this amount is to be arrived at by the method of asking what amount would fall to be disregarded in a rental arbitration under s. 12 of the Agricultural Holdings Act 1986 in so far as attributable to improvements or fixed equipment on land used for the feeding, accommodation or milking of dairy cows kept on the land in question: as to this see para. 11.21 above. Some adjustments or modifications are necessary in the application of the rental arbitration provisions for this purpose, as the calculation relates to the position in the past, not to a current rental valuation. Accordingly Sched. 1, para. 7(4) makes these adjustments.

[1] The bottom part of the fraction.

[2] This means the actual rent payable under the tenancy agreement. This may sometimes produce a curious result where the rent is out of line with what at the time would have been the market rent. Thus: "Where, as in the present case, the rent is concessionary or unusually low, the effect of reducing the denominator by taking the actual rent instead of the rental value, is artificially to increase the tenant's fraction and therefore the compensation payable to the tenant in respect of his milk quota on quitting the holding. Conversely, if the rent payable under the tenancy agreement was above the market rent, the effect of the definition in paragraph (b) is artificially to reduce the tenant's fraction and the amount of the compensation he will receive. The advantage that the tenant obtained by a low rent, or the disadvantage which he suffered by a high rent, is thus reflected in the amount of compensation, so that the tenant receives a double benefit or detriment." (Millett L.J. in *Creear v. Fearon* [1994] 2 E.G.L.R. 12 at 14E). That case confirms the obvious and natural reading of para. 7(1).

Ascertainment of the tenant's fraction is often a peculiarly troublesome part of the necessary calculation. The difficulty is sometimes generated by a simple absence of information as to what was provided when and it is occasionally impossible to demonstrate that particular installations or works were provided prior to the expiry of the relevant period. Usually the calculation as to the value of individual items will be done many years after acquisition and at a time or in circumstances when the condition or usefulness of them may be unclear. Depreciation is often extremely difficult to allow for, for that reason. Care must also be taken to ensure that chattels, properly so viewed, do not form part of this calculation.[3] The establishment of the rental value of the relevant dairy improvements and fixed equipment will be an exercise familiar to valuers under the rent review provisions of section 12 of the Agricultural Holdings Act.[4] As with all mathematically applied assessment criteria, the apparent justice of any individual case may be undermined by the strict and correct application of the statutory wording.[5]

Amount of compensation payable: "relevant period": Schedule 1, paragraph 8   19.16

"The relevant period" is a necessary ingredient in the calculation of both standard quota and tenant's fraction. It is defined for both purposes by Schedule 1, paragraph 8 as being referable to the period in which the allocated quota was determined.[6] Normally the relevant period will mean the calendar year 1983 but this is a matter which should be checked in each case. It is information which the producer and/or Intervention Board records will normally be able to identify.

Amount of compensation payable: valuation of milk quota: Schedule 1, paragraph 9   19.17

The valuation of milk quota for the purposes of Schedule 1 is in accordance with paragraph 9 of that Schedule. The requirement is to ascertain "the value of the milk quota at the time of the termination of the tenancy in question". This is the aim and purpose of the valuation exercise and the remainder of the paragraph is directed to evidential matters, requiring that the arbitrator must take into account "such evidence as is available". This is phrased in an extremely wide way, and the

---

[3] As to what may be regarded as a chattel, readers are referred to extensive commentary in *Woodfall, Landlord and Tenant*, Vol. 1 (Sweet & Maxwell, looseleaf) and more specifically to ***Elitestone Ltd v. Morris*** [1997] 27 E.G. 116 in which the HL definitively reviewed the law relating to the classification of items as fixtures or chattels. These authors consider on balance that in the normal way (and subject of course to examination of the facts of each case) the bulk milk tank will be a chattel not a fixture if fixed only for the purpose of better operation of the equipment and/or the prevention of fraud in the readings given. But if the bulk milk tank physically forms part of a larger configuration of equipment which comprises fixtures, then it also is probably a fixture.

[4] See para. 11.21 above. It should be noted in passing that improvements effected off the tenanted holding cannot be material to the calculation of tenant's fraction—*e.g.* the improvement of access roads or clearing of woodland.

[5] See ***Creear v. Fearon*** (above).

[6] Sub-para. (a); or where quota was determined in relation to more than one period, the period in relation to which the majority was determined; or, if equal amounts were determined in relation to different periods, the later of those periods (sub-para. (b)).

inclusiveness of the search for evidence is underlined by the statute expressly encouraging parties to look at evidence related to land sales.[7] As has been stated above[8] there is no Community law of unjust enrichment which impacts on the Agriculture Act scheme and, further, the scheme itself is not a creature of Community law but derives exclusively from U.K. legislation. It is suggested that Parliament in Schedule 1, paragraph 9 took the view that if and in so far as milk quota had a value at the time of termination of the tenancy this value was to be ascertained on the basis of all available evidence. Whether or not there may be legal uncertainty as to the status of the market in milk quotas must, it is submitted, be irrelevant since that is a factor which features in the amounts which purchasers wish to pay.[9] In relation to any accrued date the risk of illegality lies where it falls: thus if Parliament requires the valuation of milk quota to be made as at the date of termination of a tenancy and it is subsequently discovered that open market transactions current at that date were legally unsound this would not undermine a valuation based on those open market transactions. A change of circumstances after the valuation date still less a subsequent change in or clarification of the law is beside the point where the statutory wording is as clear as it is in Schedule 1, paragraph 9. The net result, it is submitted, is that open market transactions whereby milk quota changes hands in consideration of money can and ought properly to form part of the valuation exercise which the arbitrator must undertake. It is further suggested that in most cases this must be the best evidence of the true value of the quota as opposed to requiring the arbitrator to value quota by reference to land sales as contemplated by the extended wording at the end of paragraph 9. That type of valuation, it is suggested, is a fall back situation since it attempts to establish indirectly what may be established directly by reference to the market in quota. Accordingly this work is critical of and would ignore both the decision and the reasoning in *Carson v. Cornwall County Council*[10] a decision of Mr Recorder

---

[7] The arbitrator must take into account "such evidence as is available, including evidence as to the sums being paid for interests in land—(a) in cases where milk quota is registered in relation to the land; and (b) in cases where no milk quota is so registered".

[8] para. 19.1.

[9] This subject is covered in Chapter 18 of this work and in particular para. 18.22.

[10] [1993] 1 E.G.L.R. 21. The arbitration award was made with the benefit of the advice of the legal adviser, Professor Usher. It was attacked for rejecting an open market valuation based on transactions in the open market by way of sale of milk quota. The arbitrator preferred to use a method of valuation involving the capitalisation of the value of annual quota leasing. On grounds of evidential reliability he also rejected a method of valuation based on land transactions. The appeal against the arbitrator's award was dismissed by the Judge. The arbitrator had declined to use open market evidence of quota sales which had been effected by means of grazing agreements or short term tenancies in the fashion described in para. 18.22 of this work because his legal adviser "doubted (a) whether grazing licences or tenancies had the effect of transferring quota by virtue of Art. 7, para. 1 of Regulation 857/84 or (b) whether a licence or tenancy for less than one marketing year could have the effect of transferring quota and (c) reminded the arbitrator that land which the producer could not use for milk production, in the way many of the short term licences or tenancies prohibit, does not constitute part of the holding under Regulation 857/84".

These authors are relatively unperturbed by doubts (a) and (b) in terms of legal risk. The judge rejected these doubts in any case on the footing that they could have been resolved by evidence of entries in the register. These authors do not necessarily share

Burgess in the Bodmin County Court on an arbitration reference, which is the only reported case under this paragraph of Schedule 1.

Determination of standard quota and tenant's fraction before end of tenancy: Schedule 1, paragraph 10

19.18

It may be convenient for the landlord or tenant to obtain advance information, before the end of the tenancy, of what the standard quota and the tenant's fraction would be. Either party may seek to establish the position by means of an informal approach to the other or by demanding a reference to arbitration under the 1986 Act. The latter course may be taken by serving a notice demanding the reference.[11] It will be seen below that such an agreement or determination by the arbitrator before the end of the tenancy can have a binding effect on an arbitration after the termination of the tenancy.[12] The arbitrator will determine only the standard quota and/or the tenant's fraction and would do so in circumstances where on termination of the tenancy the tenant "may" be entitled to a payment under Schedule 1, paragraph 1. In other words, any dispute as to whether or not there is an entitlement

> doubt (c). The judge appears to consider that the case of *Wachauf v. Bundesamt fuer Ernaehrung und Forstwirtschaft* [1989] E.C.R. 2609 establishes the scheme of the Agriculture Act as introduced according to a Community law duty or as governed by general principles of Community law. We now know this is not correct, following the *Bostock* case discussed at para. 19.1 of this work. However, even on its face the judge's reasoning is extremely difficult to follow. He refers to *Wachauf* as not precluding the opportunity for a departing lessee to obtain compensation and concludes: "from this it is quite clear that the compensation one is considering is not concerned with sums paid by farmers or graziers, possibly in urgent need of additional grazing or pasture, who may be prepared to pay very much 'above the odds' for short term licences or grazing agreements or *Gladstone v. Bower's* type tenancies. The compensation is to go to those tenants who have been concerned with the building up of milk production on the holding. In the light of the plain guidance there given by the court, it is clear that the arbitrator is not to be concerned with valuations which have been found by the method A [open market sales] type of valuation." (at 22K).
>
> It is submitted that the identity of the persons who participate in the open market as purchasers or the possibility of the market being "high" at any particular time simply establishes the value of the quota and is not in any way connected with the availability of the compensation scheme to individual tenants under the 1986 Act. It is difficult to see why the departing tenant's compensation should be valued at a lower level simply because, if the landlord chose to sell the quota on the open market, the people giving him the money would be willing to pay it because of their own risk of over-production. Whether or not to sell the quota once the tenant has left is an investment decision in the landlord's hands. In so far as the scheme of the Agriculture Act is designed to benefit the tenant to the extent that the Act provides it is curious that in the particular market conditions the effect of the *Carson* case was to give the landlord an element of "unjust enrichment" and the U.K. statutory scheme is not expressly or by implication related to "the building up of the holding": compensation is to be calculated as the statute overtly describes and statutory policy is to be ascertained from the wording of the statute alone, as required by Millett L.J. at 15B in *Creear v. Fearon* (above). Finally, persons wishing to use the arbitrator's method as described in the *Carson* case should note that in some market conditions it will produce a figure which is actually higher than that obtainable from quota sales on the open market. This is a somewhat ironic twist.

[11] Sched. 1, para. 10.
[12] Sched. 1, para. 11(6), (7).

19.19 Settlement of tenant's claim on termination of tenancy: Schedule 1, paragraph 11

The tenant's claim on the termination of the tenancy may be settled either by agreement or by arbitration. The provisions are modelled on section 83 of the 1986 Act and the arbitration provisions of section 84 and Schedule 11 apply.[13] See **Procedural Table 11 "Compensation on Quitting" in Part VI**. No such claim is enforceable unless before the expiry of two months from the determination of the tenancy the tenant serves notice in writing on his landlord of his intention to make the claim.[14] The parties have a period of eight months from the termination of the tenancy to settle the claim by agreement in writing; but if not so settled it must be determined by arbitration.[15] In cases where, on the termination of the tenancy, a new tenancy may be granted to a successor by virtue of a direction under section 39 of the 1986 Act, different times are substituted for the normal termination of the tenancy, according to the circumstances; for example, when the Tribunal gives a direction the time is the "relevant time" for the purpose of section 46 of the 1986 Act. No notice of intention to claim may be served before the substituted time.[16] Where a tenant lawfully remains in occupation of part of the land after the termination of the tenancy (or after the substituted time) the period of two months for notifying a claim, and the period of eight months for settling a claim before arbitration, begin to run from the termination of the occupation.[17] The arbitration provisions of the 1986 Act, s. 84 and Sched. 11, apply, but in the application of paragraph 18 of Schedule 11 the date fixed for the payment of money awarded is to be not later than three months (instead of one month) after the delivery of the award.[18]

Where before the termination of the tenancy there has been an agreement in writing or an award as to the amount of the standard quota or the tenant's fraction or the value of milk quota, the arbitrator in determining the claim after the termination of the tenancy is required to award payment in accordance with these figures.[19] But he must disregard so much of the earlier agreement or award as appears to him materially affected by a relevant change of circumstances.[20]

---

[13] The reader is referred generally to commentary under s. 83 at para. 13.115–13.124.

[14] Sched. 1, para. 11(1). What is required in a notice of intention to make a claim is that the notice should be in terms which are sufficiently clear to bring home to the ordinary landlord that the tenant is purporting to exercise his rights: this is the test set out in *Amalgamated Estates Ltd v. Joystretch Manufacturing Ltd* (1980) 257 E.G. 489, applied in this area by *Walker v. Crocker* [1992] 1 E.G.L.R. 29 and applicable elsewhere under the Agricultural Holdings Act 1986 in relation to the giving of notice (see in relation to notice by executors under Case G para. 12.81.1 above and, in relation to compensation claims commentary at para. 13.119 above).

[15] Sched. 1, para. 11(2).
[16] Sched. 1, para. 11(3).
[17] Sched. 1, para. 11(4).
[18] Sched. 1, para. 11(5).
[19] Sched. 1, para. 11(6).
[20] Sched. 1, para. 11(7).

Termination of tenancy of part of tenanted land: Schedule 1, paragraph 13   19.20

A compensation claim in respect of milk quota is available where the tenant quits part only of the tenanted land, provided that the occasion of the quitting falls within Schedule 1, paragraph 13. Not all quittings of part of a tenancy (*e.g.* by surrender) will therefore qualify. The qualifying occasions are following notices to quit part by the landlord either under section 31 of the Agricultural Holdings Act, a contractual provision, or exercise of rights under section 140 of the Law of Property Act 1925.[21] In addition the claim is available where the landlord serves notice to quit part pursuant to section 43(2) of the Agricultural Holdings Act 1986 (consent by the Tribunal to the operation of the notice to quit under section 44 following the tenant's death).[22]

Severance of reversion: Schedule 1, paragraph 14   19.21

Where the reversion is severed the tenant is entitled to require that his milk quota compensation claim under Schedule 1 should be determined as if the reversionary estate were not severed.[23] This means that the tenant is entitled to require a single arbitration as to determination of his claim, thereby saving duplication in cost and administration. The arbitrator is expressly empowered, where necessary, to apportion the amount of any award between the landlords and costs of dispute on that issue must be paid by those landlords as the arbitrator determines.[24]

Service of notices: Schedule 1, paragraph 16   19.22

Schedule 1, paragraph 16 makes provision for service of notices in terms similar to those of section 93 of the Agricultural Holdings Act 1986. Where there has been a change of landlord the tenant is entitled to serve the original landlord unless he has received notice of the name and address of the person subsequently entitled to receive the rents and profits.[25] Attention is accordingly drawn to observations made in relation to section 93 of the Agricultural Holdings Act 1986.[26]

Miscellaneous: Schedule 1, paragraphs 12, 15 and 17   19.23

The general enforcement provisions in section 85 of the 1986 Act and the charges provisions in section 86(1), (3), and (4) apply to sums due to a tenant under the above rules.[27] There are provisions in regard to limited owners authorising anything to be done as it could be by an absolute owner[28] and as to administration in regard to Crown.[29]

Farm business tenancies   19.24

Compensation on termination in relation to milk quota may be available pursuant to section 15 of the Agricultural Tenancies Act 1995 by way of an intangible

---

[21] See generally paras 12.17–12.22 above.
[22] See para. 14.82 above.
[23] Sched. 1, para. 14(1).
[24] Sched. 1, para. 14(2).
[25] Sched. 1, para. 16(5).
[26] See para. 17.17–17.24 above.
[27] Sched. 1, para. 12.
[28] Sched. 1, para. 15. Compare s. 88 of the Agricultural Holdings Act 1986.
[29] Sched. 1, para. 17. No regulations have as yet been made under this paragraph.

advantage falling within sub-section (b). In relation to a farm business tenancy, however, the provisions of the Agriculture Act 1986 are expressly disapplied.[30] The process of making a claim in relation to an intangible advantage is described above.[31] In relation to milk quota, in so far as the statutory rent review applies in relation to a farm business tenancy, the milk quota, it is submitted, will be something which can be taken account of. In so far as an increase in rental value is due to a tenant's improvement, it is disregarded.[32] Because of the definition of "tenant's improvement" which expressly covers an intangible advantage, it is submitted that the status of milk quota under section 13 of the 1995 Act is by way of tenant's improvement.[33] Accordingly where, under the 1995 Act, a tenant's improvement would be capable of generating an increase in the rental value on a statutory rent review,[34] these circumstances will also apply to the treatment of milk quota. Of course, where the statutory rent review does not apply[35] the terms of section 13 of the 1995 Act will not have any impact on the rent review.

---

[30] s. 16(3) of the Agricultural Tenancies Act 1995.
[31] See para. 5.4 above.
[32] s. 13(3) of the Agricultural Tenancies Act 1995.
[33] This contrasts with the need to categorise it only as a "relevant factor" under s. 12 of the Agricultural Holdings Act 1986.
[34] An improvement provided pursuant to obligation (s. 13(3)(a)), an improvement to the extent allowance or benefit was made by the landlord in consideration of its provision (subs. (b)) and to the extent the tenant has received compensation from the landlord in respect of it (subs. (c)).
[35] See para. 2.11 above.

PART II

STATUTES

	PAGE
Law of Property Act 1925 (part)	649
Agriculture Act 1947 (part)	650
Agriculture (Miscellaneous Provisions) Act 1954 (part)	659
Agriculture Act 1986 (part)	661
Agriculture Holdings Act 1986	672
Agriculture Tenancies Act 1995	798

LAW OF PROPERTY ACT
(1925 c. 20)

* * * * *

Apportionment of conditions on severance   A.2

140.—(1) Notwithstanding the severance by conveyance, surrender, or otherwise of the reversionary estate in any land comprised in a lease, and notwithstanding the avoidance or cesser in any other manner of the term granted by a lease as to part only of the land comprised therein, every condition or right of re-entry, and every other condition contained in the lease, shall be apportioned, and shall remain annexed to the severed parts of the reversionary estate as severed, and shall be in force with respect to the term whereon each severed part is reversionary, or the term in the part of the land as to which the term has not been surrendered, or has not been avoided or has not otherwise ceased, in like manner as if the land comprised in each severed part, or the land as to which the term remains subsisting, as the case may be, had alone originally been comprised in the lease.

(2) In this section "right of re-entry" includes a right to determine the lease by notice to quit or otherwise; but where the notice is served by a person entitled to a severed part of the reversion so that it extends to part only of the land demised, the lessee may within one month determine the lease in regard to the rest of the land by giving to the owner of the reversionary estate therein a counter notice expiring at the same time as the original notice.[...][1]

(3) This section applies to leases made before or after the commencement of this Act and whether the severance of the reversionary estate or the partial avoidance or cesser of the term was effected before or after such commencement: Provided that, where the lease was made before the first day of January eighteen hundred and eighty-two nothing in this section shall affect the operation of a severance of the reversionary estate or partial avoidance or cesser of the term which was effected before the commencement of this Act.

* * * * *

---

[1] Proviso repealed with savings by Agricultural Holdings Act 1948 (c. 63), Sched. 8, paras 98–100.

AGRICULTURE ACT 1947
(1947 c. 48)

* * * * *

PART II
GOOD ESTATE MANAGEMENT AND HUSBANDRY

RULES OF GOOD ESTATE MANAGEMENT AND GOOD HUSBANDRY

A.3 *Good estate management*

10.—(1) For the purposes of this Act, an owner of agricultural land shall be deemed to fulfil his responsibilities to manage it in accordance with the rules of good estate management in so far as his management of the land and (so far as it affects the management of that land) of other land managed by him is such as to be reasonably adequate, having regard to the character and situation of the land and other relevant circumstances, to enable an occupier of the land reasonably skilled in husbandry to maintain efficient production as respects both the kind of produce and the quality and quantity thereof.

(2) In determining whether the management of land is such as aforesaid, regard shall be had, but without prejudice to the generality of the provisions of the last foregoing subsection, to the extent to which the owner is providing, improving, maintaining and repairing fixed equipment on the land in so far as is necessary to enable an occupier of the land reasonably skilled in husbandry to maintain efficient production as aforesaid.

(3) The responsibilities under the rules of good estate management of an owner of land in the occupation of another person shall not in relation to the maintenance and repair of fixed equipment include an obligation to do anything which that other person is under an obligation to do by virtue of any agreement.

Good husbandry

11.—(1) For the purposes of this Act, the occupier of an agricultural unit shall be deemed to fulfil his responsibilities to farm it in accordance with the rules of good husbandry in so far as the extent to which and the manner in which the unit is being farmed (as respects both the kind of operations carried out and the way in which they are carried out) is such that, having regard to the character and situation of the unit, the standard of management thereof by the owner and other relevant circumstances, the occupier is maintaining a reasonable standard of efficient production, as respects both the kind of produce and the quality and quantity thereof, while keeping the unit in a condition to enable such a standard to be maintained in the future.

(2) In determining whether the manner in which a unit is being farmed is such as aforesaid, regard shall be had, but without prejudice to the generality of the provisions of the last foregoing subsection, to the extent to which—

   (*a*) permanent pasture is being properly mown or grazed and maintained in a good state of cultivation and fertility and in good condition;

(b) the manner in which arable land is being cropped is such as to maintain that land clean and in a good state of cultivation and fertility and in good condition;

(c) the unit is properly stocked where the system of farming practised requires the keeping of livestock, and an efficient standard of management of livestock is maintained where livestock are kept and of breeding where the breeding of livestock is carried out;

(d) the necessary steps are being taken to secure and maintain crops and livestock free from disease and from infestation by insects and other pests;

(e) the necessary steps are being taken for the protection and preservation of crops harvested or lifted, or in course of being harvested or lifted;

(f) the necessary work of maintenance and repair is being carried out.

(3) The responsibilities under the rules of good husbandry of an occupier of an agricultural unit which is not owned by him shall not include an obligation to carry out any work of maintenance or repair which the owner of the unit or any part thereof is under an obligation to carry out in order to fulfil his responsibilities to manage in accordance with the rules of good estate management.

PART V
ADMINISTRATIVE AND GENERAL

AGRICULTURAL LAND TRIBUNALS

Establishment, constitution and procedure of Agricultural Land Tribunals **A.4**

73.—(1) For the purposes of this section [the Lord Chancellor][2] shall by order constitute such number of areas, together comprising the whole of England and Wales as he may consider expedient, and for each area so constituted there shall be established an Agricultural Land Tribunal which shall be charged with the duty of [hearing and determining references and applications made to them under any enactment].[3]

(2) The provisions in that behalf of the Ninth Schedule to this Act shall have effect as to the constitution of Agricultural Land Tribunals and otherwise in relation thereto.

(3) [The Lord Chancellor][4] may by order make provision for the procedure of Agricultural Land Tribunals, and in particular—

---

[2] Words substituted by Agriculture Act 1958 (c. 71), Sched. 1, Pt. I, para. 3(a).
[3] Words substituted by Agriculture Act 1958 (c. 71), Sched. 1, Pt. I, para. 3(b).
[4] Words substituted by Agriculture Act 1958 (c. 71), Sched. 1, Pt. I, para. 3(a).

[(*aa*) as to the manner in which applications are to be made to the Tribunals and the time within which they are made;[5]
   (*a*) for the taking of evidence on oath, affirmation or otherwise, the cross-examination of witnesses, and for the summoning of witnesses in like manner as for the purposes of an arbitration under [the Agricultural Holdings Act 1986][6];
   (*b*) for the recording and proof of the decisions of the Tribunals, and for enabling the Tribunals to decide by a majority;
   (*c*) [...][7]

(4) An order under the last foregoing subsection may make different provision for the procedure on different classes of reference [or application][8] to the Tribunals.

[(5) An Agricultural Land Tribunal may, for the purpose of hearing and determining applications and references made to them under any enactment, sit in two or more divisions, and, in relation to the hearing and determination of any such application or reference by such a division, that division shall be deemed to be the Tribunal[9]].

Amendment

S. 73 (3) extended by Agriculture (Miscellaneous Provisions) Act 1954 (c. 39), s. 6(4)(6) and Agriculture (Miscellaneous Provisions) Act 1976 (c. 55), s. 20(14)

Proceedings before Agricultural Land Tribunal on reference of Minister's proposals.

74.—(1) In any case where by any of the provisions of this Act a person is empowered to require that a proposal of the Minister to take any action shall be referred to the Agricultural Land Tribunal, then if within the prescribed time and in the prescribed manner the said person so requires, the proposal shall be referred accordingly.

(2) On any such reference the Tribunal shall determine—
   (*a*) whether the conditions as to which the Minister must be satisfied before taking the action are fulfilled, and
   (*b*) whether, having regard to their determination under the foregoing paragraph and to all the circumstances of the case, the Minister should or should not take the action proposed, and shall report to the Minister accordingly and the Minister shall forward a copy of the report to any person who availed himself of an opportunity to make representations to the Minister afforded to him under the provisions in question of this Act.

---

[5] S. 73(3)(aa) inserted by Agriculture Act 1958 (c. 71), Sched. 1, Pt. I, para. 3(c).
[6] Words substituted by Agricultural Holdings Act 1986 (c. 5), ss. 99, 100, Sched. 13, para. 3, Sched. 14, para. 18.
[7] S. 73(3)(c) repealed by Agriculture Act 1958 (c. 71), Sched. 2, Pt. I.
[8] Words inserted by Agriculture Act 1958 (c. 71), Sched. 1, Pt. I, para. 3(d).
[9] S. 73(5) added by Agriculture Act 1958 (c. 71), Sched. 1, Pt. I, para. 3(e).

(3) In any such case as is mentioned in subsection (1) of this section the Minister shall not give effect to the proposal until the expiration of the period within which a reference to the Tribunal may be required.

(4) Where such a reference is duly required the Minister shall act in accordance with the report of the Tribunal and not otherwise.

(5) Forthwith after taking action in any such case as is mentioned in subsection (1) of this section the Minister shall serve notice thereof in writing on any person who under the provisions in question of this Act was entitled to be afforded an opportunity to make representations to the Minister.

* * * * *

Interpretation

109.—(1) In this Act the expression "agricultural land" means land used for agriculture which is so used for the purposes of a trade or business, or which is designated by the Minister for the purposes of this subsection, and includes any land so designated as land which in the opinion of the Minister ought to be brought into use for agriculture. Provided that no designation under this subsection shall extend—

(*a*) to land used as pleasure grounds, private gardens or allotment gardens, or

(*b*) to land kept or preserved mainly or exclusively for the purposes of sport or recreation, except

where the Minister is satisfied that its use or agriculture would not be inconsistent with its use for the said purposes and it is so stated in the designation.

(2) In this Act the expression "agricultural unit" means land which is occupied as a unit for agricultural purposes, including—

(*a*) any dwelling-house or other building occupied by the same person for the purpose of farming the land, and

(*b*) any other land falling within the definition in this Act of the expression "agricultural land" which is in the occupation of the same person, being land as to which the Minister is satisfied that having regard to the character and situation thereof and other relevant circumstances it ought in the interests of full and efficient production to be farmed in conjunction with the agricultural unit, and directs accordingly: Provided that the Minister shall not give a direction under this subsection as respects any land unless it is for the time being not in use for any purpose which appears to him to be substantial having regard to the use to which it might be put for agriculture.

(3) In this Act the following expressions have the meanings hereby respectively assigned to them, that is to say:-

"agriculture" includes horticulture, fruit growing, seed growing, dairy farming and livestock breeding and keeping, the use of land as grazing land, meadow land, osier land, market gardens and nursery grounds, and the use of land for woodlands where that use is ancillary to the farming of land for other agricultural purposes, and "agricultural" shall be construed accordingly;

"allotment garden" means an allotment not exceeding [0.10 hectare][10] in extent which is wholly or mainly cultivated by the occupier for the production of vegetables or fruit for consumption by himself or his family;

"fixed equipment" includes any building or structure affixed to land and any works on, in, over or under land, and also includes anything grown on land for a purpose other than use after severance from the land, consumption of the thing grown or of produce thereof, or amenity, and references to fixed equipment on land shall be construed accordingly;

"functions" includes powers and duties;

"livestock" includes any creature kept for the production of food, wool, skins or fur, or for the purpose of its use in the farming of land;

"pasture" includes meadow;

"prescribed" has the meaning assigned to it by the last foregoing section;

"produce" includes anything (whether live or dead) produced in the course of agriculture;

"relevant circumstances," in relation to an owner or occupier, includes all circumstances affecting management or farming other than the personal circumstances of the owner or occupier.

(4) References in this Act to any enactment shall be construed, except where the context otherwise requires, as references to that enactment as amended by or under any other enactment, including this Act.

(5) References in this Act to the farming of land include references to the carrying on in relation to the land of any agricultural activity; and in relation to any agricultural activity the person having the right to carry it on shall be deemed to be the occupier of the land.

(6) References in this Act to the use of land for agriculture include in relation to land forming part of an agricultural unit, references to any use of the land in connection with the farming of the unit.

* * * * *

SCHEDULE 9

CONSTITUTION ETC. OF COMMISSION, SUB-COMMISSION, COMMITTEES AND TRIBUNALS

* * * * *

---

[10] Words substituted by S.I. 1978/446, reg. 2(1).

SECTION 13

AGRICULTURAL LAND TRIBUNALS

13.—(1) The Lord Chancellor shall appoint a chairman for each Agricultural Land Tribunal, who shall be a [person who has a 7 years' general qualification, within the meaning of section 71 of the Courts and Legal Services Act 1990].[11]

(2) Subject to sub-paragraph (2A) of this paragraph,][12] the chairman shall hold office for [such period as may be specified in the terms of his appointment],[13] and a chairman whose term of office expires shall be eligible to be re-appointed as chairman.

[(2A) No appointment of a person to be the chairman shall be such as to extend beyond the day on which he attains the age of seventy years; but this sub-paragraph is subject to section 26 (4) to (6) of the Judicial Pensions and Retirement Act 1993 (power to authorise continuance in office up to the age of seventy-five years).][14]

(3) The chairman may resign his office by notice in writing to the Lord Chancellor.

(4) If the Lord Chancellor is satisfied that the chairman is incapacitated by infirmity of mind or body from discharging the duties of his office, or if the chairman is adjudged bankrupt or makes a composition or arrangement with his creditors, the Lord Chancellor may revoke the appointment of the chairman.[15]

14.—(1) The Lord Chancellor shall draw up for each Agricultural Land Tribunal and from time to time revise a panel of deputy-chairmen, who shall be [persons eligible for appointment under paragraph 13 (1)][16+17]

[(2) A member of the panel of deputy-chairmen shall vacate his office on the day on which he attains the age of seventy years; but this sub-paragraph is subject to section 26(4) to (6) of the Judicial Pensions and Retirement Act 1993 (power to authorise continuance in office up to the age of seventy-five years).][18]

15.—(1) The Lord Chancellor shall draw up for each Agricultural Land Tribunal and from time to time revise a panel of persons appearing to him to represent the interests of farmers and a panel of persons appearing to him to represent the interests of owners of agricultural land.

[(1A) A member of either of the panels drawn up under sub-paragraph (1) of this

---

[11] Words substituted by Courts and Legal Services Act 1990 (c. 41), s. 71(2), Sched. 10, para. 6 (1).

[12] Words added by Judicial Pensions and Retirement Act 1993 (c. 8), s. 26, Sched. 6.

[13] Words substituted by Judicial Pensions and Retirement Act 1993 (c. 8), s. 26, Sched. 6.

[14] Subsection (2A) added by Judicial Pensions and Retirement Act 1993 (c. 8), s. 26, Sched. 6.

[15] Paras 13–16, 16A substituted for paras. 13–16 by Agriculture Act 1958 (c. 71), Sched. 1, Pt. I, para. 5(1)(2).

[16] Words substituted by Courts and Legal Services Act 1990 (c. 41), s. 71(2), Sched. 10, para. 6(2). Paras. 13–16, 16A substituted for paras. 13–16 by Agriculture Act 1958 (c. 71), Sched. 1.

[17] Paragraph 14 renumbered as paragraph 14(1) by Judicial Pensions and Retirement Act 1993 (c. 8), s. 26, Sched. 6.

[18] Sub-paragraph (2) added by Judicial Pensions and Retirement Act 1993 (c. 8), s. 26, Sched. 6.

paragraph shall vacate his office on the day on which he attains the age of seventy years; but this sub-paragraph is subject to section 26(4) to (6) of the Judicial Pensions and Retirement Act 1993 (power to authorise continuance in office up to the age of seventy-five years).][19]

(2) Subject to the following sub-paragraph, the persons to be placed on either panel shall be selected by the Lord Chancellor from nominations made at his request by persons appearing to him to represent the interests of farmers or of owners of agricultural land, as the case may be.

(3) The last foregoing sub-paragraph shall not prevent the Lord Chancellor from placing on either of the panels a person not nominated in accordance with that sub-paragraph, if the persons requested to make the nominations for that purpose do not make the required number of nominations, or the nominations they make do not include enough persons who appear to the Lord Chancellor to be suitable.[20]]

16.—(1) For each hearing by an Agricultural Land Tribunal of an application or reference thereto the members of the Tribunal shall be—
  (a) the chairman, or a person nominated by the chairman either from the panel of deputy-chairmen (whether for that Tribunal or for any other Agricultural Land Tribunal) or from among the chairmen of other Agricultural Land Tribunals, and
  (b) one person nominated by the chairmen from each of the panels for that Tribunal drawn up under the last foregoing paragraph or from a corresponding panel for any other Agricultural Land Tribunal.

(2) The chairman may, if it appears to him expedient so to do, nominate two assessors to be added to the Tribunal for the hearing of an application or reference thereto in order to assist the Tribunal in the hearing.

(3) The assessors shall be selected by the chairman from a panel of persons nominated by the President of the Royal Institution of Chartered Surveyors.[21]

Amendment

Para. 16 (1) modified by Land Drainage Act 1976 (c. 70), s. 42 (1).

16A. If the chairman of an Agricultural Land Tribunal is prevented by sickness or any other reason from making nominations under sub-paragraphs (1) and (2) of the last foregoing paragraph or from otherwise discharging the duties of his office, those duties may be discharged by a person appointed from the panel of deputy-chairmen for that Tribunal by the chairman or, if the chairman is unable to make the appointment, by the Lord Chancellor.[22]

---

[19] Sub-paragraph (1A) added by Judicial Pensions and Retirement Act 1993 (c. 8), s. 26, Sched. 6.
[20] Paras. 13–16, 16A substituted for paras 13–16 by Agriculture Act 1958 (c. 71), Sched. 1, Pt. I, para. 5(1)(2).
[21] Paras. 13–16, 16A substituted for paras, 13–16 by Agriculture Act 1958 (c. 71), Sched. 1, Pt. I, para. 5(1)(2).
[22] Words substituted by Agriculture Act 1958 (c. 71), Sched. 1, Pt. I, para. 5(1)(3).

SCHEDULE 9

Amendment

Para. 16(1) extended by Land Drainage Act 1976 (c. 70), s. 42(2)

17.—(1) [The Lord Chancellor][23] may by order direct that the foregoing provisions of this Schedule as to the nominated members of Agricultural Land Tribunals shall have effect subject to such modification of the number of such members, and such additions to the classes of persons referred to in paragraph 15 of this Schedule, as may be specified in the order.

(2) Any order under this paragraph shall be of no effect unless approved by resolution of each House of Parliament.

18.—[...][24]

DISQUALIFICATIONS FOR APPOINTMENT

19.—(1) [...][25]

(2) A person shall be disqualified for being appointed or being a member of, or assessor to, an Agricultural Land Tribunal so long as he is a member of any other body mentioned in the last foregoing sub-paragraph.

VALIDITY OF ACTS

20.—(1) Any body mentioned in the last foregoing paragraph shall have power to act notwithstanding any vacancy among its members.

(2) All acts done at any meeting of any such body shall, notwithstanding that it is afterwards discovered that there was a defect in the appointment or disqualification of a person purporting to be a member thereof, be as valid as if that defect had not existed.

(3) Nothing in sub-paragraph (1) of this paragraph shall affect any requirement as to the number of members necessary to constitute a meeting of any such body as aforesaid.

21.—[...][26]

OFFICERS AND SERVANTS

22.—(1) [...][27]

(2) The Minister shall attach to [...].[28] Agricultural Land Tribunals such officers and servants of the Ministry as he may with the approval of [the Minister for the

---

[23] Paras. 13–16, 16A substituted for paras. 13–16 by Agriculture Act 1958 (c. 71), Sched. 1, Pt. I, para. 5(1)(2).
[24] Repealed by Agriculture Act 1958 (c. 71), Sched. 2, Pt. I.
[25] Repealed by House of Commons Disqualification Act 1957 (c. 20), Sched. 4, Pt. 1.
[26] Repealed by Agriculture (Miscellaneous Provisions) Act 1972 (c. 62), Sched. 6.
[27] Repealed by Agriculture (Miscellaneous Provisions) Act 1963 (c. 11), Sched., Pt. 1.
[28] Words repealed by Agriculture (Miscellaneous Provisions) Act 1972 (c. 62), Sched. 6.

Civil Service][29] determine to be required for providing the [...] [30] Tribunals with the necessary officers and servants.

(3) —[...][31]

REMUNERATION AND EXPENSES

23.—(1) The Minister may pay to members of [...][32] Agricultural Land Tribunals such remuneration (whether by way of salaries or of fees) as he may with the approval of [the Minister, for the Civil Service][33] determine)

(2) The Minister may pay to the members of any body mentioned in paragraph 19 of this Schedule and to the assessors to Agricultural Land Tribunals such allowances as he may with the approval of [the Minister for the Civil Service][34] determine.

(3) The expenses of any body mentioned in paragraph 19 of this Schedule shall be defrayed by the Minister.

PROOF OF INSTRUMENTS

24.—(1) Any document purporting to be a document duly executed or issued [...][35] on behalf of any such body as aforesaid shall, until the contrary is proved, be deemed to be a document so executed or issued, as the case may be.

* * * * *

AGRICULTURE (MISCELLANEOUS PROVISIONS) ACT 1954

* * * * *

A.6 *Power of Agricultural Land Tribunal to award costs*

5.—(1) An Agricultural Land Tribunal, where it appears to them that any person concerned in a reference [or application] to them (including any Minister of the Crown or Government department so concerned) has acted frivolously, vexatiously or oppressively in applying for or in connection with the reference [or application][36], may order that person to pay any other person either a specified sum in respect of the costs incurred by him at or with a view to the hearing or the taxed

---

[29] Words substituted by virtue of S.I. 1971/No.2099, arts. 2, 3, 6(5).
[30] Words repealed by Agriculture (Miscellaneous Provisions) Act 1972 (c. 62), Sched. 6.
[31] Repealed by Agriculture (Miscellaneous Provisions) Act 1963 (c. 11), Sched., Pt. I.
[32] Words repealed by Agriculture (Miscellaneous Provisions) Act 1963 (c. 11), Sched., Pt. I.
[33] Words substituted by virtue of S.I. 1971/No.2099, arts 2, 3, 6(5).
[34] Words substituted by virtue of S.I. 1971/No.2099, arts 2, 3, 6(5).
[35] Words repealed by Agriculture (Miscellaneous Provisions) Act 1963 (c. 11), Sched., Pt. I.
[36] Words inserted by Agriculture Act 1958 (c. 71, SIF 2:3), Sched., 1 Pt. I, para. 26.

SCHEDULE 9

amount of those costs; and an order may be made under this subsection whether or not the reference [or application][37] proceeds to a hearing.

(2) Any costs required by an order under this section to be taxed may be taxed in the county court according to such of the scales prescribed by county court rules for proceedings in the county court as may be directed by the order or, if the order gives no direction, by the county court.

(3) Any sum payable by virtue of an order of an Agricultural Land Tribunal under this section shall, if the county court so orders, be recoverable by execution issued from the county court or otherwise as if payable under an order of that court; and, subject to county court rules, an application for an order of the county court under this subsection may be made *ex parte*.

(4) The powers of the county court under this section may be exercised by the registrar.

Power of Agricultural Land Tribunal to refer questions of law to High Court.

6.—(1) Any question of law arising in the course of proceedings before an Agricultural Land Tribunal may, at the request of any party to the proceedings, be referred by the Tribunal to the High Court for decision, whether before or after the Tribunal have given their decision in the proceedings.

(2) Subject to the following provisions of this section, if an Agricultural Land Tribunal, after giving their decision in any proceedings, refuse any such request to refer a question to the High Court under this section, any person aggrieved by the refusal may apply to the High Court for an order directing them to do so.

(3) —[...][38]

(4) Provision shall be made by order under subsection (3) of section 73 of the Agriculture Act, 1947 (which relates to the procedure of Agricultural Land Tribunals), for limiting the time for requesting a Tribunal to refer a question to the High Court under this section, and for requiring notice to be given to a Tribunal within a time limited by the order of any intended application to the High Court under this section; and provision shall be made by rules of court for limiting the time for instituting proceedings in the High Court under subsection (2) of this section.

(5) Where, after an Agricultural Land Tribunal have given their decision in any proceedings, they refer a question to the High Court under this section, or receive notice of an intended application to the High Court for an order directing them to do so, effect shall not be given to the Tribunal's decision unless and until the Tribunal otherwise order after the proceedings in the High Court and any proceedings arising therefrom have been concluded (or the right to take or continue any such proceedings has lapsed); and any such order of the Tribunal shall, where necessary, modify their decisions so as to give effect to the decision on any reference to the High Court and, in a case relating to a notice to quit, may postpone (or further postpone) the date at which the tenancy is to be terminated by the notice, if it has effect.

---

[37] Words inserted by Agriculture Act 1958 (c. 71, SIF 2:3), Sched., 1, Pt. I, para. 26.
[38] Repealed by Agriculture Act 1958 (c. 71, SIF 2:3), Sched. 2, Pt. I.

(6) [The Minister of Agriculture, Fisheries and Food][39] may, by order under subsection (3) of section 73 of the Agriculture Act, 1947, make such provision as he thinks necessary or expedient for enabling the chairman of an Agricultural Land Tribunal to exercise all or any of the Tribunal's powers under the last foregoing subsection, and for regulating any proceedings before an Agricultural Land Tribunal which are consequent on the reference of any question to the High Court under this section or on the decision on such a reference, and enabling any such proceedings to be dealt with by an Agricultural Land Tribunal constituted for the purpose, where they cannot conveniently be dealt with by the Tribunal originally constituted for the purpose of the proceedings in the course of which the question arose.

(7) This section shall come into force on such date as [the Minister of Agriculture, Fisheries and Food][40]

may appoint by order made by statutory instrument.

Amendments

S 6 (5) modified by S.I. 1978/259, art. 34.

S. 6 (6) amended by Agriculture Act 1958 (c. 71, SIF 2:1), Sched., 1 Pt. I, para. 27.

*　*　*　*　*

---

[39] Words substituted by virtue of S.I. 1955/No.554 (1955 I, p. 1200), art. 3.
[40] Words substituted by virtue of S.I. 1955/No. 554 (1955 I, p. 1200), art. 3.

SECTION 13

AGRICULTURE ACT 1986
[(1986 c. 49)]

An Act to make further provision relating to agriculture and agricultural and other food products, horticulture and the countryside; and for connected matters.

A.7

[25th July 1986]

* * * * *

COMPENSATION TO TENANTS FOR MILK QUOTAS

Compensation to outgoing tenants for milk quota

13.—Schedule 1 to this Act shall have effect in connection with the payment to certain agricultural tenants on the termination of their tenancies of compensation in respect of milk quota (within the meaning of that Schedule).

* * * * *

Rent arbitrations milk quotas

15.—(1) Where there is a reference under section 12 of the Agricultural Holdings Act 1986 (arbitration of rent) in respect of land which comprises or is part of a holding in relation to which quota is registered under the Dairy Produce Quotas Regulations 1986 which was transferred to the tenant by virtue of a transaction the cost of which was borne wholly or partly by him, the arbitrator shall (subject to any agreement between the landlord and tenant to the contrary) disregard—
  (*a*) in a case where the land comprises the holding, any increase in the rental value of the land which is due to that quota (or, as the case may be, the corresponding part of that quota); or
  (*b*) in a case where the land is part of the holding, any increase in that value which is due to so much of that quota (or part) as would fall to be apportioned to the land under those Regulations on a change of occupation of the land.

(2) In determining for the purposes of this section whether quota was transferred to a tenant by virtue of a transaction the cost of which was borne wholly or partly by him—
  (*a*) any payment made by the tenant in consideration for the grant or assignment to him of the tenancy or any previous tenancy of any land comprised in the holding, shall be disregarded;
  (*b*) any person who would be treated under paragraph 2, 3 or 4 of Schedule 1 to this Act as having had quota transferred to him or having paid the whole or part of the cost of any transaction for the purposes of a claim under that Schedule shall be so treated for the purposes of this section; and
  (*c*) any person who would be so treated under paragraph 4 of that Schedule if a sub-tenancy to which his tenancy is subject had terminated, shall be so treated for the purposes of this section.

(3) In this section—
"quota" and "holding" have the same meanings as in the Dairy Produce Quotas Regulations 1986;
"tenant" and "tenancy" have the same meanings as in the Agricultural Holdings Act 1986.

(4) Section 95 of that Act (Crown land) applies to this section as it applies to the provisions of that Act.

Rent arbitrations milk quotas Scotland

* * * * *

SCHEDULE 1

Section 13

TENANTS COMPENSATION FOR MILK QUOTA

Part I
RIGHT TO COMPENSATION

Tenants' Rights to Compensation

A.8 1.—(1) Subject to the following provisions of this Schedule, where on the termination of the tenancy of any land the tenant has milk quota registered as his in relation to a holding consisting of or including the land, the tenant shall be entitled, on quitting the land, to obtain from his landlord a payment—
  (a) if the tenant had milk quota allocated to him in relation to land comprised in the holding ("allocated quota"), in respect of so much of the relevant quota as consists of allocated quota; and
  (b) if the tenant had milk quota allocated to him as aforesaid or was in occupation of the land as a tenant on 2nd April 1984 (whether or not under the tenancy which is terminating), in respect of so much of the relevant quota as consists of transferred quota transferred to him by virtue of a transaction the cost of which was borne wholly or partly by him.

(2) In sub-paragraph (1) above—
"the relevant quota" means—
  (a) in a case where the holding mentioned in sub-paragraph (1) above consists only of the land subject to the tenancy, the milk quota registered in relation to the holding; and
  (b) otherwise, such part of that milk quota as falls to be apportioned to that land on the termination of the tenancy;
"transferred quota" means milk quota transferred to the tenant by virtue of the transfer to him of the whole or part of a holding.

SCHEDULE 1

(3) A tenant shall not be entitled to more than one payment under this paragraph in respect of the same land.

Succession on death or retirement of tenant

2.—(1) This paragraph applies where on the termination of the tenancy of any land after 2nd April 1984 a new tenancy of the land or part of the land has been granted to a different tenant ("the new tenant") and that tenancy—
   (*a*) was obtained by virtue of a direction under section 39 or 53 of the Agricultural Holdings Act 1986 (direction for grant of tenancy to successor on death or retirement of previous tenant);
   (*b*) was granted (following a direction under section 39 of that Act) in circumstances within section 45(6) of that Act (new tenancy granted by agreement to persons entitled to tenancy under direction); or
   (*c*) is such a tenancy as is mentioned in section 37(1)(*b*) or (2) of that Act (tenancy granted by agreement to close relative).

(2) Where this paragraph applies—
   (*a*) any milk quota allocated or transferred to the former tenant (or treated as having been allocated or transferred to him) in respect of the land which is subject to the new tenancy shall be treated as if it had instead been allocated or transferred to the new tenant; and
   (*b*) in a case where milk quota is treated under paragraph (*a*) above as having been transferred to the new tenant, he shall be treated for the purposes of any claim in respect of that quota—
      (i) as if he had paid so much of the cost of the transaction by virtue of which the milk quota was transferred as the former tenant bore (or is treated as having borne); and
      (ii) in a case where the former tenant was in occupation of the land on 2nd April 1984 (or is treated as having been in occupation of the land on that date), as if he had been in occupation of it on that date.

(3) Sub-paragraph (1) above applies in relation to the grant of a new tenancy before the date on which the Agricultural Holdings Act 1986 comes into force as if the references in that sub-paragraph to sections 39, 53 and 45(6) of that Act were references to section 20 of the Agriculture (Miscellaneous Provisions) Act 1976, paragraph 5 of Schedule 2 to the Agricultural Holdings Act 1984 and section 23(6) of the said Act of 1976 respectively.

Assignments

3. Where the tenancy of any land has been assigned after 2nd April 1984 (whether by deed or by operation of law)—
   (*a*) any milk quota allocated or transferred to the assignor (or treated as having been allocated or transferred to him) in respect of the land shall be treated as if it had instead been allocated or transferred to the assignee; and

(b) in a case where milk quota is treated under paragraph (a) above as having been transferred to the assignee, he shall be treated for the purposes of any claim in respect of that quota—
  (i) as if he had paid so much of the cost of the transaction by virtue of which the milk quota was transferred as the assignor bore (or is treated as having borne); and
  (ii) in a case where the assignor was in occupation of the land on 2nd April 1984 (or is treated as having been in occupation of the land on that date), as if he had been in occupation of it on that date;
and accordingly the assignor shall not be entitled to a payment under paragraph 1 above in respect of that land.

Sub-tenancies

4. Where the sub-tenancy of any land terminates after 2nd April 1984 then, for the purposes of determining the sub-landlord's entitlement under paragraph 1 above—
  (a) any milk quota allocated or transferred to the sub-tenant (or treated as having been allocated or transferred to him) in respect of the land shall be treated as if it had instead been allocated or transferred to the sub-landlord;
  (b) in a case where milk quota is treated under paragraph (a) above as having been transferred to the sub-landlord, he shall be treated for the purposes of any claim in respect of that quota—
    (i) as if he had paid so much of the cost of the transaction by virtue of which the milk quota was transferred as the sub-tenant bore (or is treated as having borne); and
    (ii) in a case where the sub-tenant was in occupation of the land on 2nd April 1984 (or is treated as having been in occupation of the land on that date), as if he had been in occupation of it on that date;
  (c) if the sub-landlord does not occupy the land after the sub-tenancy has ended and the sub-tenant has quitted the land, the sub-landlord shall be taken to have quitted the land when the sub-tenant quitted it.

Part II

AMOUNT OF COMPENSATION PAYABLE

Calculation of payment

5.—(1) The amount of the payment to which the tenant of any land is entitled under paragraph 1 above on the termination of his tenancy shall be determined in accordance with the following provisions of this paragraph.

(2) The amount of the payment to which the tenant is entitled under paragraph 1 above in respect of allocated quota shall be an amount equal—
  (a) in a case where the allocated quota exceeds the standard quota for the land, to the value of the sum of—

SCHEDULE 1

    (i) the tenant's fraction of the standard quota, and

    (ii) the amount of the excess;

  (b) in a case where the allocated quota is equal to the standard quota, to the value of the tenant's fraction of the allocated quota; and

  (c) in a case where the allocated quota is less than the standard quota, to the value of such proportion of the tenant's fraction of the allocated quota as the allocated quota bears to the standard quota.

(3) The amount of the payment the tenant is entitled to under paragraph 1 above in respect of transferred quota shall be an amount equal—

  (a) in a case where the tenant bore the whole of the cost of the transaction by virtue of which the transferred quota was transferred to him, to the value of the transferred quota; and

  (b) in a case where the tenant bore only part of that cost, to the value of the corresponding part of the transferred quota.

"Standard quota"

6.—(1) Subject to the following provisions of this paragraph the standard quota for any land for the purposes of this Schedule shall be calculated by multiplying the relevant number of hectares by the prescribed quota[41] per hectare; and for the purposes of this paragraph—

  (a) "the relevant number of hectares" means the average number of hectares of the land in question used during the relevant period for the feeding of dairy cows kept on the land or, if different, the average number of hectares of the land which could reasonably be expected to have been so used (having regard to the number of grazing animals other than dairy cows kept on the land during that period); and

  (b) "the prescribed quota per hectare" means such number of litres as the Minister may from time to time by order prescribe for the purposes of this sub-paragraph.

(2) Where by virtue of the quality of the land in question or climatic conditions in the area the amount of milk which could reasonably be expected to have been produced from one hectare of the land during the relevant period ("the reasonable amount") is greater or less than the prescribed average yield per hectare, then sub-paragraph (1) above shall not apply and the standard quota shall be calculated by multiplying the relevant number of hectares by such proportion of the prescribed quota per hectare as the reasonable amount bears to the prescribed average yield per hectare; and the Minister shall by order prescribe the amount of milk to be taken as the average yield per hectare for the purposes of this sub-paragraph.

(3) Where the relevant quota of the land includes milk quota allocated in pursuance of an award of quota made by the Dairy Produce Quota Tribunal for England and Wales which has not been allocated in full, the standard quota for the land shall be reduced by the amount by which the milk quota allocated in

---

[41] See for prescribed matters the Milk Quota (Calculation of Standard Quota) Order (No.1986/s.1530) amended by S.I. 1992 No. 1225.

pursuance of the award falls short of the amount awarded (or, in a case where only part of the milk quota allocated in pursuance of the award is included in the relevant quota, by the corresponding proportion of that shortfall).

(4) In sub-paragraph (3) above the references to milk quota allocated in pursuance of an award of quota include references to quota allocated by virtue of the amount awarded not originally having been allocated in full.

(5) In this paragraph—
   (a) references to land used for the feeding of dairy cows kept on the land do not include land used for growing cereal crops for feeding to dairy cows in the form of loose grain; and
   (b) references to dairy cows are to cows kept for milk production (other than uncalved heifers).

(6) An order under this paragraph may make different provision for different cases.

(7) The power to make an order under this paragraph shall be exercisable by statutory instrument and any instrument containing such an order shall be subject to annulment in pursuance of a resolution of either House of Parliament.

"Tenant's fraction"

7.—(1) For the purposes of this Schedule "the tenant's fraction" means the fraction of which—
   (a) the numerator is the annual rental value at the end of the relevant period of the tenant's dairy improvements and fixed equipment; and
   (b) the denominator is the sum of that value and such part of the rent payable by the tenant in respect of the relevant period as is attributable to the land used in that period for the feeding, accommodation or milking of dairy cows kept on the land.

(2) For the purposes of sub-paragraph (1)(a) above the rental value of the tenant's dairy improvements and fixed equipment shall be taken to be the amount which would fall to be disregarded under paragraph 2(1) of Schedule 2 to the Agricultural Holdings Act 1986 on a reference made in respect of the land in question under section 12 of that Act (arbitration of rent), so far as that amount is attributable to tenant's improvements to, or tenant's fixed equipment on, land used for the feeding, accommodation or milking of dairy cows kept on the land in question.

(3) Where—
   (a) the relevant period is less than or greater than 12 months; or
   (b) rent was only payable by the tenant in respect of part of the relevant period,
the average rent payable in respect of one month in the relevant period or, as the case may be, in that part shall be determined and the rent referred to in sub-paragraph (1)(b) above shall be taken to be the corresponding annual amount.

(4) For the purposes of sub-paragraph (2) above "tenant's improvements" and "tenant's fixed equipment" have the same meanings as in paragraph 2 of Schedule 2 to the 1986 Act, except that—

SCHEDULE 1

(a) any allowance made or benefit given by the landlord after the end of the relevant period in consideration of the execution of improvements wholly or partly at the expense of the tenant shall be disregarded for the purposes of sub-paragraph (2)(a) of that paragraph;

(b) any compensation received by the tenant after the end of the relevant period in respect of any improvement or fixed equipment shall be disregarded for the purposes of sub-paragraph (3) of that paragraph; and

(c) where paragraph 2 above applies in respect of any land, improvements or equipment which would be regarded as tenant's improvements or equipment on the termination of the former tenant's tenancy (if he were entitled to a payment under this Schedule in respect of that land) shall be regarded as the new tenant's improvements or equipment.

"Relevant period"

8. In this Schedule "the relevant period" means—
   (a) the period in relation to which the allocated quota was determined; or
   (b) where it was determined in relation to more than one period, the period in relation to which the majority was determined or, if equal amounts were determined in relation to different periods, the later of those periods.

Valuation of milk quota

9. The value of milk quota to be taken into account for the purposes of paragraph 5 above is the value of the milk quota at the time of the termination of the tenancy in question and in determining that value at that time there shall be taken into account such evidence as is available, including evidence as to the sums being paid for interests in land—
   (a) in cases where milk quota is registered in relation to the land; and
   (b) in cases where no milk quota is so registered.

Part III

SUPPLEMENTAL PROVISIONS

Determination of standard quota and tenant's fraction before end of tenancy

10.—(1) Where, on the termination of a tenancy of any land, the tenant may be entitled to a payment under paragraph 1 above, the landlord or tenant may at any time before the termination of the tenancy by notice in writing served on the other demand that the determination of the standard quota for the land or the tenant's fraction shall be referred to arbitration.

(2) On a reference under this paragraph the arbitrator shall determine the standard quota for the land or, as the case may be, the tenant's fraction (so far as determinable at the date of the reference).

(3) Section 84 of the Agricultural Holdings Act 1986 (arbitrations) shall apply as

if the matters mentioned in this paragraph were required by that Act to be determined by arbitration under that Act.

Settlement of tenant's claim on termination of tenancy

11.—(1) Subject to the provisions of this paragraph, any claim arising under paragraph 1 above shall be determined by arbitration under the Agricultural Holdings Act 1986 and no such claim shall be enforceable unless before the expiry of the period of two months from the termination of the tenancy the tenant serves notice in writing on his landlord of his intention to make the claim.

(2) The landlord and tenant may within the period of eight months from the termination of the tenancy by agreement in writing settle the claim but where the claim has not been settled during that period it shall be determined by arbitration under the Agricultural Holdings Act 1986.

(3) In any case where on the termination of the tenancy in question a new tenancy of the land or part of the land may be granted to a different tenant by virtue of a direction under section 39 of the Agricultural Holdings Act 1986 then, as respects any claim in respect of that land or part, references in sub-paragraphs (1) and (2) above to the termination of the tenancy shall be construed as references to the following time, namely—

  (*a*) in a case where no application is made under that section within the period within which such an application may be made, the expiry of that period;
  (*b*) in a case where every such application made within that period is withdrawn, the expiry of that period or the time when the last outstanding application is withdrawn (whichever is the later);
  (*c*) in a case where the Agricultural Land Tribunal refuse every such application for a direction under that section, the time when the last outstanding application is refused; and
  (*d*) in a case where the Tribunal give such a direction, the relevant time for the purposes of section 46 of that Act;
and no notice may be served under sub-paragraph (1) above before that time.

(4) Where a tenant lawfully remains in occupation of part of the land subject to the tenancy after the termination of the tenancy or, in a case where sub-paragraph (3) above applies, after the time substituted for the termination of the tenancy by virtue of that sub-paragraph, the references in sub-paragraphs (1) and (2) above to the termination of the tenancy shall be construed as references to the termination of the occupation.

(5) Section 84 of the Agricultural Holdings Act 1986 (arbitrations) shall apply as if the requirements of this paragraph were requirements of that Act, but paragraph 18 of Schedule 11 to that Act (arbitration award to fix day for payment not later than one month after award) shall have effect for the purposes of this paragraph as if for the words "one month" there were substituted the words "three months".

(6) Where—

  (*a*) before the termination of the tenancy of any land the landlord and tenant have agreed in writing the amount of the standard quota for the land or the tenant's fraction or the value of milk quota which is to be used for the

SCHEDULE 1

purpose of calculating the payment to which the tenant will be entitled under this Schedule on the termination of the tenancy; or

(b) the standard quota or the tenant's fraction has been determined by arbitration in pursuance of paragraph 10 above, the arbitrator determining the claim under this paragraph shall, subject to sub-paragraph (7) below, award payment in accordance with that agreement or determination.

(7) Where it appears to the arbitrator that any circumstances relevant to the agreement or determination mentioned in sub-paragraph (6) above were materially different at the time of the termination of the tenancy from those at the time the agreement or determination was made, he shall disregard so much of the agreement or determination as appears to him to be affected by the change in circumstances.

Enforcement

12.—Section 85 of the Agricultural Holdings Act 1986 (enforcement) and section 86(1), (3) and (4) of that Act (power of landlord to obtain charge on holding) shall apply to any sum which becomes due to a tenant by virtue of this Schedule as they apply to the sums mentioned in those sections.

Termination of tenancy of part of tenanted land

13.—References in this Schedule to the termination of a tenancy of land include references to the resumption of possession of part of the land subject to the tenancy—
(a) by the landlord by virtue of section 31 or 43(2) of the Agricultural Holdings Act 1986 (notice to quit part);
(b) by the landlord in pursuance of a provision in the contract of tenancy; or
(c) by a person entitled to a severed part of the reversionary estate in the land by virtue of a notice to quit that part given to the tenant by virtue of section 140 of the Law of Property Act 1925;

and in the case mentioned in paragraph (c) above this Schedule shall apply as if the person resuming possession were the landlord of the land of which he resumes possession.

Severing of reversionary estate

14.—(1) Where the reversionary estate in the land is for the time being vested in more than one person in several parts, the tenant shall be entitled, on quitting all the land, to require that any amount payable to him under this Schedule shall be determined as if the reversionary estate were not so severed.

(2) Where sub-paragraph (1) above applies, the arbitrator shall, where necessary, apportion the amount awarded between the persons who for the purposes of this Schedule together constitute the landlord of the land, and any additional costs of the award caused by the apportionment shall be paid by those persons in such proportions as the arbitrator may determine.

Powers of limited owners

15.—Notwithstanding that a landlord of any land is not the owner in fee simple of the land or, in a case where his interest is an interest in a leasehold, that he is not absolutely entitled to the leasehold, he may for the purposes of this Schedule do anything which he might do if he were such an owner or, as the case may be, were so entitled.

Notices

16.—(1) Any notice under this Schedule shall be duly served on the person on whom it is to be served if it is delivered to him, or left at his proper address, or sent to him by post in a registered letter or by the recorded delivery service.

(2) Any such notice shall be duly served on an incorporated company or body if it is served on the secretary or clerk of the company or body.

(3) Any such notice to be served on a landlord or tenant of any land shall, where an agent or servant is responsible for the control of the management or farming, as the case may be, of the land, be duly served if served on that agent or servant.

(4) For the purposes of this paragraph and of section 7 of the Interpretation Act 1978 (service by post), the proper address of any person on whom any such notice is to be served shall, in the case of the secretary or clerk of an incorporated company or body, be that of the registered or principal office of the company or body, and in any other case be the last known address of the person in question.

(5) Unless or until the tenant of any land has received—
  (*a*) notice that the person who before that time was entitled to receive the rents and profits of the land ("the original landlord") has ceased to be so entitled; and
  (*b*) notice of the name and address of the person who has become entitled to receive the rents and profits,
any notice served on the original landlord by the tenant shall be deemed for the purposes of this Schedule to have been served on the landlord of the land.

Crown land

17.—(1) The provisions of this Schedule shall apply to land which belongs to Her Majesty in right of the Crown or to the Duchy of Lancaster, the Duchy of Cornwall or a Government department or which is held in trust for Her Majesty for the purposes of a Government department, subject in each case to such modifications as the Minister may by regulations prescribe.

(2) For the purposes of this Schedule—
  (*a*) as respects land belonging to Her Majesty in right of the Crown, the Crown Estate Commissioners or the proper officer or body having charge of the land for the time being, or, if there is no such officer or body, such person as Her Majesty may appoint in writing under the Royal Sign Manual, shall represent Her Majesty and shall be deemed to be the landlord,

SCHEDULE 1

(b) as respects land belonging to Her Majesty in right of the Duchy of Lancaster, the Chancellor of the Duchy shall represent Her Majesty and shall be deemed to be the landlord;

(c) as respects land belonging to the Duchy of Cornwall, such person as the Duke of Cornwall or the possessor for the time being of the Duchy of Cornwall appoints shall represent the Duchy and shall be deemed to be the landlord and may do any act or thing which a landlord is authorised or required to do under this Act.

(3) Any sum payable under this Schedule by the Duke of Cornwall (or any other possessor for the time being of the Duchy of Cornwall) may be raised and paid as if it were an expense incurred in permanently improving the possessions of the Duchy as mentioned in section 8 of the Duchy of Cornwall Management Act 1863.

(4) Any sum payable under this Schedule by the Chancellor of the Duchy of Lancaster may—

(a) be raised and paid as if it were an expense incurred in the improvement of land belonging to Her Majesty in right of the Duchy within section 25 of the Duchy of Lancaster Act 1817; or

(b) be paid out of the annual revenues of the Duchy.

(5) The power to make regulations under this paragraph shall be exercisable by statutory instrument and any statutory instrument containing such regulations shall be subject to annulment in pursuance of a resolution of either House of Parliament.

Interpretation

18.—(1) In this Schedule—

"allocated quota" has the meaning given in paragraph 1(1) above;

"holding" has the same meaning as in the 1986 Regulations;

"landlord" means any person for the time being entitled to receive the rents and profits of any land and "sub-landlord" shall be construed accordingly;

"milk quota" means—

(a) in the case of a tenant registered in the direct sales register maintained under the 1986 Regulations, a direct sales quota (within the meaning of the 1986 Regulations); and

(b) in the case of a tenant registered in the wholesale register maintained under those Regulations, a wholesale quota (within the meaning of those Regulations);

"the Minister" means—

(a) in the case of land in England, the Minister of Agriculture, Fisheries and Food; and

(b) in the case of land in Wales, the Secretary of State;

"registered", in relation to milk quota, means—

(a) in the case of direct sales quota (within the meaning of the 1986 Regulations) registered in the direct sales register maintained under those Regulations; and

(b) in the case of a wholesale quota (within the meaning of those Regulations) registered in a wholesale register maintained under those Regulations;

"relevant quota" has the meaning given in paragraph 1(2) above;
"standard quota" has the meaning given in paragraph 6 above;
"the 1986 Regulations" means the Dairy Produce Quotas Regulations 1986;
"tenancy" means a tenancy from year to year (including any arrangement which would have effect as if it were such a tenancy by virtue of section 2 of the Agricultural Holdings Act 1986 if it had not been approved by the Minister) or a tenancy to which section 3 of that Act applies (or would apply apart from section 5 of that Act); and "tenant" and "sub-tenant" shall be construed accordingly;

"tenant's fraction" has the meaning given in paragraph 7 above;

"termination", in relation to a tenancy, means the cesser of the letting of the land in question or the agreement for letting the land, by reason of effluxion of time or from any other cause;

"transferred quota" has the meaning given in paragraph 1(2) above.

(2) In this Schedule references to land used for the feeding of dairy cows kept on the land and to dairy cows have the same meaning as in paragraph 6 above.

(3) The designations of landlord and tenant shall continue to apply to the parties until the conclusion of any proceedings taken under or in pursuance of this Schedule.

Note

See for prescribed matters the Milk Quota (Calculation of Standard Quota) Order (S.I. 1986 No.1530) amended by S.I. 1992 No. 1225.

* * * * *

AGRICULTURAL HOLDINGS ACT 1986

(1986 c. 5)

Arrangement of Sections

Part I

Introductory

SECTION
1. Principal definitions.
2. Restriction on letting agricultural land for less than from year to year.
3. Tenancies for two years or more to continue from year to year unless terminated by notice.
4. Death of tenant before term date.
5. Restriction on agreements excluding effect of section 3.

Part II

Provisions Affecting Tenancy During its Continuance

Written tenancy agreements

6. Right to written tenancy agreement.

ARRANGEMENT OF SECTIONS

Fixed equipment

7. The model clauses.
8. Arbitration where terms of written agreement are inconsistent with the model clauses.
9. Transitional arrangements where liability in respect of fixed equipment transferred.
10. Tenant's right to remove fixtures and buildings.
11. Provision of fixed equipment necessary to comply with statutory requirements.

Variation of rent

12. Arbitration of rent.
13. Increases of rent for landlord's improvements.

Cultivation of land and disposal of produce

14. Variation of terms of tenancies as to permanent pasture.
15. Disposal of produce and cropping.

Distress

16. No distress for rent due more than a year previously.
17. Compensation to be set off against rent for purposes of distress.
18. Restrictions on distraining on property of third party.
19. Settlement of disputes as to distress.

Miscellaneous

20. Compensation for damage by game.
21. Extension of tenancies in lieu of claims to emblements.
22. Rights to require certain records to be made.
23. Landlord's power of entry.
24. Restriction of landlord's remedies for breach of contract of tenancy.

Part III

Notices to Quit

Notices to quit whole or part of agricultural holding

25. Length of notice to quit.
26. Restriction on operation of notices to quit.
27. Tribunal's consent to operation of notice to quit.
28. Additional restrictions on operation of notice to quit given under Case D.
29. Power to make supplementary provision.
30. Notice to quit where tenant is a service man.

Notices to quit part of agricultural holding

31. Notice to quit part of holding valid in certain cases.

AGRICULTURAL HOLDINGS ACT 1986

32. Right to treat notice to quit part of holding as notice to quit entire holding.
33. Reduction of rent where notice is given to quit part of holding.

Part IV

Succession on Death or Retirement Tenant

Tenancies to which Part IV applies
34. Tenancies to which Part IV applies.

Succession on death of tenant
35. Application of sections 36 to 48.
36. Right of any eligible person to apply for new tenancy on death of tenant.
37. Exclusion of statutory succession where two successions have already occurred.
38. Other excluded cases.
39. Applications for tenancy of holding.
40. Provisions supplementary to section 39.
41. Application by not fully eligible person to be treated as eligible.
42. Procedure where deceased held more than one holding.
43. Restriction on operation of notice to quit given by reason of death of tenant.
44. Opportunity for landlord to obtain Tribunal's consent to operation of noticeto quit.
45. Effect of direction under section 39.
46. Interpretation of section 45.
47. Terms of new tenancy unless varied by arbitration.
48. Arbitration on terms of new tenancy.

Succession on retirement of tenant
49. Application of sections 50 to 58.
50. Right to apply for new tenancy on retirement of tenant.
51. Excluded cases.
52. Notices to quit restricting operation of section 53.
53. Application for tenancy of holding by nominated successor.
54. Restriction on operation of certain notices to quit.
55. Effect of direction under section 53.
56. Terms of new tenancy.
57. Effect of death of retiring tenant on succession to the holding.
58. Effect of direction under section 53 on succession to other holdings.

Interpretation
59. Interpretation of Part IV.

Part V

Compensation on Termination of Tenancy

Compensation to tenant for disturbance

ARRANGEMENT OF SECTIONS

60. Right to, and measure of, compensation for disturbance.
61. Cases where compensation under section 60 is not payable.
62. Compensation on termination in pursuance of early resumption clause.
63. Compensation for disturbance: supplementary provisions.

Compensation to tenant for improvements and tenant-right matters
64. Tenant's right to compensation for improvements.
65. Tenant's right to compensation for tenant-right matters.
66. Measure of compensation.
67. Compensation for long-term improvements: consent required.
68. Improvements: special cases.
69. Improvements: successive tenancies.

Compensation to tenant for adoption of special system of farming
70. Compensation for special system of farming.

Compensation to landlord for deterioration of holding
71. Compensation for deterioration of particular parts of holding.
72. Compensation for general deterioration of holding.
73. Deterioration of holding: successive tenancies.

Supplementary provisions with respect to compensation
74. Termination of tenancy of part of holding.
75. Compensation where reversionary estate in holding is severed.
76. Restrictions on compensation for things done in compliance with this Act.
77. No compensation under custom for improvement or tenant-right matter.
78. Extent to which compensation recoverable under agreements.

Part VI

Market Gardens and Smallholdings
79. Additional rights with respect to improvements for tenants of market gardens.
80. Power of Tribunal to direct holding to be treated as market garden.
81. Agreements as to compensation relating to market gardens.
82. Application of section 15 to smallholdings.

Part VII

Miscellaneous and Supplemental
83. Settlement of claims on termination of tenancy.
84. Arbitrations.
85. Enforcement.
86. Power of landlord to obtain charge on holding.
87. General provisions as to charges under this Act on holdings.
88. Power of limited owners to give consents etc.
89. Power of limited owners to apply capital for improvements.
90. Estimation of best rent for purposes of Acts and other instruments.

91. Power of Minister to vary Schedules 7, 8 and 10.
92. Advisory committee on valuation of improvements and tenant-right matters.
93. Service of notices.
94. Orders and regulations.
95. Crown land.
96. Interpretation.
97. Saving for other rights etc.
98. Application of Act to old tenancies etc.
99. Transitional provisions and savings.
100. Consequential amendments.
101. Repeals and revocations.
102. Citation, commencement and extent.

Schedules:
Schedule 1 - Matters for which provision is to be made in written tenancy agreements.
Schedule 2 - Arbitration of rent: provisions supplementary to section 12.
Schedule 3 - Cases where consent of Tribunal to operation of notice to quit is not required.
Schedule 4 - Matters for which provision may be made by order under section 29.
Schedule 5 - Notice to quit where tenant is a service man.
Schedule 6 - Eligibility to apply for new tenancy under Part IV of this Act.
Schedule 7 - Long-term improvements begun on or after 1st March 1948 for which compensation is payable.
Schedule 8 - Short-term improvements begun on or after 1st March 1948, and othermatters, for which compensation is payable.
Schedule 9 - Compensation to tenant for improvements begun before 1st March 1948.
Schedule 10 - Market garden improvements.
Schedule 11 - Arbitrations.
Schedule 12 - Modifications applicable to old tenancies and other similar cases.
Schedule 13 - Transitional provisions and savings.
Schedule 14 - Consequential amendments.
Schedule 15 - Repeals and revocations.

An Act to consolidate certain enactments relating to agricultural holdings, with amendments to give effect to recommendations of the Law Commission.
[18th March 1986]

Part 1: Introductory

Principal definitions

1.—(1) In this Act "agricultural holding" means the aggregate of the land (whether agricultural land or not) comprised in a contract of tenancy which is a contract for an agricultural tenancy, not being a contract under which the land is let to the tenant during his continuance in any office, appointment or employment held under the landlord.

(2) For the purposes of this section, a contract of tenancy relating to any land is a contract for an agricultural tenancy if, having regard to -
   (a) the terms of the tenancy,
   (b) the actual or contemplated use of the land at the time of the conclusion of the contract and subsequently, and
   (c) any other relevant circumstances, the whole of the land comprised in the contract, subject to such exceptions only as do not substantially affect the character of the tenancy, is let for use as agricultural land.

(3) A change in user of the land concerned subsequent to the conclusion of a contract of tenancy which involves any breach of the terms of the tenancy shall be disregarded for the purpose of determining whether a contract which was not originally a contract for an agricultural tenancy has subsequently become one unless it is effected with the landlord's permission, consent or acquiescence.

(4) In this Act "agricultural land" means -
   (a) land used for agriculture which is so used for the purposes of a trade or business, and
   (b) any other land which, by virtue of a designation under section 109 (1) of the Agriculture Act 1947, is agricultural land within the meaning of that Act.

(5) In this Act "contract of tenancy" means a letting of land, or agreement for letting land, for a term of years or fromyear to year; and for the purposes of this definition a letting of land, or an agreement for letting land, which, by virtue of subsection (6) of section149 of the Law of Property Act 1925, takes effect as such a letting of land or agreement for letting land as is mentioned in that subsection shall be deemed to be a letting of land or, as the case may be, an agreement for letting land, for a term of years.

Restriction on letting agricultural land for less than from year to year

2.—(1) An agreement to which this section applies shall take effect, with the necessary modifications, as if it were an agreement for the letting of land for a tenancy from year to year unless the agreement was approved by the Minister before it was entered into.

(2) Subject to subsection (3) below, this section applies to an agreement under which -
   (a) any land is let to a person for use as agricultural land for an interest less than a tenancy from year to year, or
   (b) a person is granted a licence to occupy land for use as agricultural land, if the circumstances are such that if his interest were a tenancy from year to year he would in respect of that land be the tenant of an agricultural holding.

(3) This section does not apply to an agreement for the letting of land, or the granting of a licence to occupy land -
   (a) made (whether or not it expressly so provides) in contemplation of the use of the land only for grazing or mowing (or both) during some specified period of the year, or

(b) by a person whose interest in the land is less than a tenancy from year to year and has not taken effect as such a tenancy by virtue of this section.

(4) Any dispute arising as to the operation of this section in relation to any agreement shall be determined by arbitration under this Act.

Tenancies for two years or more to continue from year to year unless terminated by notice

3.—(1) Subject to section 5 below, a tenancy of an agricultural holding for a term of two years or more shall, instead of terminating on the term date, continue (as from that date) as a tenancy from year to year, but otherwise on the terms of the original tenancy so far as applicable, unless -
- (a) not less than one year nor more than two years before the term date a written notice has been given by either party to the other of his intention to terminate the tenancy, or
- (b) section 4 below applies.

(2) A notice given under subsection (1) above shall be deemed, for the purposes of this Act, to be a notice to quit.

(3) This section does not apply to a tenancy which, by virtue of subsection (6) of section 149 of the Law of Property Act 1925, takes effect as such a term of years as is mentioned in that subsection.

(4) In this section "term date", in relation to a tenancy granted for a term of years, means the date fixed for the expiry of that term.

Death of tenant before term date

4.—(1) This section applies where -
- (a) a tenancy such as is mentioned in subsection (1) of section3 above is granted on or after 12th September 1984 to any person or persons,
- (b) the person, or the survivor of the persons, dies before the term date, and
- (c) no notice effective to terminate the tenancy on the term date has been given under that subsection.

(2) Where this section applies, the tenancy, instead of continuing as mentioned in section 3 (1) above -
- (a) shall, if the death is one year or more before the term date, terminate on that date, or
- (b) shall, if the death is at any other time, continue (as from the term date) for a further period of twelve months, but otherwise on the terms of the tenancy so far as applicable, and shall accordingly terminate on the first anniversary of the term date.

(3) For the purposes of the provisions of this Act with respect to compensation any tenancy terminating in accordance with this section shall be deemed to terminate by reason of a notice to quit given by the landlord of the holding.

(4) In this section "term date" has the same meaning as in section 3 above.

Restriction on agreements excluding effect of section 3

5.—(1) Except as provided in this section, section 3 above shall have effect notwithstanding any agreement to the contrary.

(2) Where before the grant of a tenancy of an agricultural holding for a term of not less than two, and not more than five, years -
  (a) the persons who will be the landlord and the tenant in relation to the tenancy agree that section 3 above shall not apply to the tenancy, and
  (b) those persons make a joint application in writing to the Minister for his approval of that agreement, and
  (c) the Minister notifies them of his approval, section 3 shall not apply to the tenancy if it satisfies the requirements of subsection (3) below.

(3) A tenancy satisfies the requirements of this subsection if the contract of tenancy is in writing and it, or a statement endorsed upon it, indicates (in whatever terms) that section 3 does not apply to the tenancy.

Part II
Provisions Affecting Tenancy During its Continuance

WRITTEN TENANCY AGREEMENTS

Right to written tenancy agreement

6.—(1) Where in respect of a tenancy of an agricultural holding -
  (a) there is not in force an agreement in writing embodying all the terms of the tenancy (including any model clauses incorporated in the contract of tenancy by virtue of section 7 below), or
  (b) such an agreement in writing is in force but the terms of the tenancy do not make provision for one or more of the matters specified in Schedule 1 to this Act, the landlord or tenant of the holding may, if he has requested the other to enter into an agreement in writing embodying all the terms of the tenancy and containing provision for all of the said matters but no such agreement has been concluded, refer the terms of the tenancy to arbitration under this Act.

(2) On any such reference the arbitrator in his award -
  (a) shall specify the existing terms of the tenancy, subject to any variations agreed between the landlord and the tenant,
  (b) in so far as those terms as so varied neither make provision for, nor make provision inconsistent with, the matters specified in Schedule 1 to this Act, shall make provision for all of the said matters having such effect as may be agreed between the landlord and the tenant or, in default of agreement, as appears to the arbitrator to be reasonable and just between them, and
  (c) may include any further provisions relating to the tenancy which may be agreed between the landlord and the tenant.

(3) Where it appears to the arbitrator on a reference under this section that, by reason of any provision which he is required to include in his award, it is equitable that the rent of the holding should be varied, he may vary the rent accordingly.

(4) The award of an arbitrator under this section shall have effect as if the terms and provisions specified and made in the award were contained in an agreement in writing entered into by the landlord and the tenant and having effect (by way of variation of the agreement previously in force in respect of the tenancy) as from the

making of the award or, if the award so provides, from such later date as may be specified in it.

(5) Where in respect of a tenancy of an agricultural holding -
  (a) the terms of the tenancy neither make provision for, nor make provision inconsistent with, the matter specified in paragraph 9 of Schedule 1 to this Act, and
  (b) the landlord requests the tenant in writing to enter into such an agreement as is mentioned in subsection (1) above containing provision for all of the matters specified in that Schedule, the tenant may not without the landlord's consent in writing assign, sub-let or part with possession of the holding or any part of it during the period while the determination of the terms of the tenancy is pending; and any transaction entered into in contravention of this subsection shall be void.

(6) The period mentioned in subsection (5) above is the period beginning with the date of service of the landlord's request on the tenant and ending with the date on which an agreement is concluded in accordance with that request or (as the case may be) with the date on which the award of an arbitrator on a reference under this section relating to the tenancy takes effect.

FIXED EQUIPMENT

The model clauses

7.—(1) The Minister may, after consultation with such bodies of persons as appear to him to represent the interests of landlords and tenants of agricultural holdings, make regulations prescribing terms as to the maintenance, repair and insurance of fixed equipment (in this Act referred to as "the model clauses").

(2) Regulations[42] under this section may make provision for any matter arising under them to be determined by arbitration under this Act.

(3) The model clauses shall be deemed to be incorporated in every contract of tenancy of an agricultural holding except in so far as they would impose on one of the parties to an agreement in writing a liability which under the agreement is imposed on the other.

Arbitration where terms of written agreement are inconsistent with the model clauses

8.—(1) This section applies where an agreement in writing relating to a tenancy of an agricultural holding effects substantial modifications in the operation of regulations under section 7 above.

(2) Where this section applies, then, subject to subsection (6) below, the landlord or tenant of the holding may, if he has requested the other to vary the terms of the tenancy as to the maintenance, repair and insurance of fixed equipment so as

---

[42] The Agriculture (Maintenance, Repair and insurance of Fixed Equipment) Regulations 1973 (S.I.1973/No.1473) as amended by the Agriculture (Maintenance, Repair and Insurance of Fixed Equipment) (Amendment) Regulations 1988 (S.I.1988/No.281). The amended Regulations apply with effect from March 24, 1988: see the Agriculture (Time Limit) Regulations 1988 (S.I.1988/No.282).

to bring them into conformity with the model clauses but no agreement has been reached on the request, refer those terms of the tenancy to arbitration under this Act.

(3) On any reference under this section the arbitrator shall consider whether (disregarding the rent payable for the holding) the terms referred to arbitration are justifiable having regard to the circumstances of the holding and of the landlord and the tenant, and, if he determines that they are not so justifiable, he may by his award vary them in such manner as appears to him reasonable and just between the landlord and tenant.

(4) Where it appears to the arbitrator on any reference under this section that by reason of any provision included in his award it is equitable that the rent of the holding should be varied, he may vary the rent accordingly.

(5) The award of an arbitrator under this section shall have effect as if the terms and provisions specified and made in the award were contained in an agreement in writing entered into by the landlord and the tenant and having effect (by way of variation of the agreement previously in force in respect of the tenancy) as from the making of the award or, if the award so provides, from such later date as may be specified in it.

(6) Where there has been a reference under this section relating to a tenancy, no further such reference relating to that tenancy shall be made before the expiry of three years from the coming into effect of the award of the arbitrator on the previous reference.

Transitional arrangements where liability in respect of fixed equipment transferred

9.—(1)Where by virtue of section 6, 7 or 8 above the liability for the maintenance or repair of any item of fixed equipmentis transferred from the tenant to the landlord, the landlord may within the prescribed period beginning with the date on which the transfer takes effect require that there shall be determined by arbitration under this Act and paid by the tenant the amount of any relevant compensation.

(2) In subsection (1) above "relevant compensation" means compensation which would have been payable either under subsection (1) of section 71 below or in accordance with subsection (3) of that section, in respect of any previous failure by the tenant to discharge the liability mentioned in subsection (1) above, if the tenant had quitted the holding on the termination of his tenancy at the date on which the transfer takes effect.

(3) Where by virtue of section 6, 7 or 8 above the liability for the maintenance or repair of any item of fixed equipment is transferred from the landlord to the tenant, any claim by the tenant in respect of any previous failure by the landlord to discharge the said liability shall, if the tenant within the prescribed period beginning with the date on which the transfer takes effect so requires, be determined by arbitration under this Act.

(4) Where the terms of a tenancy of an agricultural holding as to the maintenance, repair or insurance of fixed equipment (whether established by the operation of regulations under section 7 above or by agreement) are varied by new

regulations made under that section, then, if a reference is made under section 6 above within the prescribed period after the coming into operation of the new regulations, the arbitrator shall, for the purposes of subsection (2) of the said section 6, disregard the variation.

Tenant's right to remove fixtures and buildings

10.—(1) Subject to the provisions of this section -
- (a) any engine, machinery, fencing or other fixture (of whatever description) affixed, whether for the purposes of agriculture or not, to an agricultural holding by the tenant, and
- (b) any building erected by him on the holding, shall be removable by the tenant at any time during the continuance of the tenancy or before the expiry of two months from its termination, and shall remain his property so long as he may remove it by virtue of this subsection.

(2) Subsection (1) above shall not apply -
- (a) to a fixture affixed or a building erected in pursuance of some obligation,
- (b) to a fixture affixed or a building erected instead of some fixture or building belonging to the landlord,
- (c) to a building in respect of which the tenant is entitled to compensation under this Act or otherwise, or
- (d) to a fixture affixed or a building erected before 1st January 1884.

(3) The right conferred by subsection (1) above shall not be exercisable in relation to a fixture or building unless the tenant -
- (a) has paid all rent owing by him and has performed or satisfied all his other obligations to the landlord in respect of the holding, and
- (b) has, at least one month before both the exercise of the right and the termination of the tenancy, given to the landlord notice in writing of his intention to remove the fixture or building.

(4) If, before the expiry of the notice mentioned in subsection (3) above, the landlord gives to the tenant a counter-notice in writing electing to purchase a fixture or building comprised in the notice, subsection (1) above shall cease to apply to that fixture or building, but the landlord shall be liable to pay to the tenant the fair value of that fixture or building to an incoming tenant of the holding.

(5) In the removal of a fixture or building by virtue of subsection (1) above, the tenant shall not do any avoidable damage to any other building or other part of the holding, and immediately after the removal shall make good all damage so done that is occasioned by the removal.

(6) Any dispute between the landlord and the tenant with respect to the amount payable by the landlord under subsection (4) above in respect of any fixture or building shall be determined by arbitration under this Act.

(7) This section shall apply to a fixture or building acquired by a tenant as it applies to a fixture or building affixed or erected by him.

(8) This section shall not be taken as prejudicing any right to remove a fixture that subsists otherwise than by virtue of this section.

SECTION 11

Provision of fixed equipment necessary to comply with statutory requirements

11.—(1) Where, on an application by the tenant of an agricultural holding, the Tribunal are satisfied that it is reasonable, having regard to the tenant's responsibilities to farm the holding in accordance with the rules of good husbandry, that he should carry on on the holding an agricultural activity specified in the application to the extent and in the manner so specified and -
- (a) that, unless fixed equipment is provided on the holding, the tenant, in carrying on that activity to that extent and in that manner, will contravene requirements imposed by or under any enactment, or
- (b) that it is reasonable that the tenant should use, for purposes connected with that activity, fixed equipment already provided on the holding, but that, unless that equipment is altered or repaired, the tenant, in using the equipment for those purposes, will contravene such requirements, the Tribunal may direct the landlord to carry out, within a period specified in the direction, such work for the provision or, as the case may be, the alteration or repair of that fixed equipment as will enable the tenant to comply with the said requirements.

(2) Where it appears to the Tribunal that an agricultural activity specified in the tenant's application has not been carried on on the holding continuously for a period of at least three years immediately preceding the making of the application the Tribunal shall not direct the landlord to carryout work in connection with that activity unless they are satisfied that the starting of the activity did not or, where the activity has not yet been started, will not constitute or form part of a substantial alteration of the type of farming carried on on the holding.

(3) The Tribunal shall not direct the landlord to carry out work under this section unless they are satisfied -
- (a) that it is reasonable to do so having regard to the landlord's responsibilities to manage the land comprised in the holding in accordance with the rules of good estate management and also to the period for which the holding may be expected to remain a separate holding and to any other material consideration, and
- (b) that the landlord has refused to carry out that work on being requested in writing to do so by the tenant or has not agreed to carry it out within a reasonable time after being so requested.

(4) The Tribunal shall not direct the landlord to carry out work under this section if he is under a duty to carry out the work in order to comply with a requirement imposed on him by or under any enactment or if provision is made by the contract of tenancy, or by any other agreement between the landlord and the tenant, for the carrying out of work by one of them.

(5) If the landlord fails to comply with a direction under this section the tenant shall have the same remedies as if the contract of tenancy had contained an undertaking by the landlord to carry out the work required by the direction within the period allowed by the Tribunal.

(6) Notwithstanding any term in the contract of tenancy restricting the carrying out by the tenant of alterations to the holding, the remedies referred to in subsection

(5) above shall include the right of the tenant to carry out the work himself and recover the reasonable cost of the work from the landlord.

(7) The Tribunal, on an application by the landlord, may extend or further extend the period specified in a direction under this section if it is shown to their satisfaction that the period so specified, or that period as previously extended under this subsection, as the case may be, will not allow sufficient time both for the completion of preliminary arrangements necessary or desirable in connection with the work required by the direction (including, in appropriate cases, the determination of an application by the landlord for a grant out of money provided by Parliament in respect of that work) and for the carrying out of the said work.

(8) The reference in subsection (6) above to the reasonable cost of work carried out by a tenant shall, where the tenant has received a grant in respect of the work out of money provided by Parliament, be construed as a reference to the reasonable cost reduced by the amount of the grant.

VARIATION OF RENT

Arbitration of rent

12.—(1) Subject to the provisions of Schedule 2 to this Act, the landlord or tenant of an agricultural holding may by notice in writing served on the other demand that the rent to be payable in respect of the holding as from the next termination date shall be referred to arbitration under this Act.

(2) On a reference under this section the arbitrator shall determine what rent should be properly payable in respect of the holding at the date of the reference and accordingly shall, with effect from the next termination date following the date of the demand for arbitration, increase or reduce the rent previously payable or direct that it shall continue unchanged.

(3) A demand for arbitration under this section shall cease to be effective for the purposes of this section on the next termination date following the date of the demand unless before the said termination date -
  (a) an arbitrator has been appointed by agreement between the parties, or
  (b) an application has been made to the President of the Royal Institution of Chartered Surveyors for the appointment of an arbitrator by him.

(4) References in this section (and in Schedule 2 to this Act) in relation to a demand for arbitration with respect to the rent of any holding, to the next termination date following the date of the demand are references to the next day following the date of the demand on which the tenancy of the holding could have been determined by notice to quit given at the date of the demand.

(5) Schedule 2 to this Act shall have effect for supplementing this section.

INCREASES OF RENT FOR LANDLORD'S IMPROVEMENTS

13.—(1) Where the landlord of an agricultural holding has carried out on the holding any improvement to which this section applies he may by notice in writing served on the tenant within six months from the completion of the improvement increase the rent of the holding as from the completion of the improvement by an amount equal to the increase in the rental value of the holding attributable to the carrying out of the improvement.

(2) This section applies to -
- (a) an improvement carried out at the request of, or in agreement with, the tenant,
- (b) an improvement carried out in compliance with a direction given by the Tribunal under section 11 above,
- (c) an improvement carried out in pursuance of a notice served by the landlord under section 67 (5) below,
- (d) an improvement carried out in compliance with a direction given by the Minister under powers conferred on him by or under any enactment,
- (e) works executed on the holding for the purpose of complying with the requirements of a notice under section 3 of the Agriculture (Safety, Health and Welfare Provisions) Act 1956 (provision of sanitary conveniences and washing facilities),
- (f) an improvement carried out in compliance with an improvement notice served, or an undertaking accepted, under Part VII of the Housing Act 1985 or Part VIII of the Housing Act 1974.

(3) No increase of rent shall be made under subsection (1) above in respect of an improvement within paragraph (*a*), (*b*) or (*f*) of subsection (2) above if within six months from its completion the landlord and tenant agree on any increase of rent or other benefit to the landlord in respect of the improvement.

(4) The increase in rent provided for by subsection (1) above shall be reduced proportionately -
- (a) in the case of an improvement within paragraph (*b*) of subsection (2) above, where a grant has been made to the landlord in respect of the improvement out of money provided by Parliament,
- (b) in the case of an improvement within any other paragraph of that subsection, where a grant has been made to the landlord in respect of the improvement out of money provided by Parliament or local government funds, and
- (c) in the case of an improvement within paragraph (f) of that subsection, where the tenant has contributed to the cost incurred by his landlord in carrying out the improvement.

(5) Where, on the failure of a landlord to carry out an improvement specified in such a direction as is referred to in subsection (2)(b) above, the tenant has himself carried out the improvement, the provisions of this section shall apply as if the improvement had been carried out by the landlord and as if any grant made to the tenant in respect of the improvement out of money provided by Parliament had been made to the landlord.

(6) No increase in rent shall take effect by virtue of subsection (5) above until the tenant has recovered from the landlord the reasonable cost of the improvement reduced by the amount of any grant made to the tenant inrespect of the improvement out of money provided by Parliament.

(7) Any dispute arising between the landlord and the tenant of the holding under this section shall be determined by arbitration under this Act.

(8) This section applies to an improvement whether or not it is one for the carrying out of which compensation is provided under Part V or VI of this Act.

Amendment

Section 13 modified by Opencast Coal Act 1958 (c.69), s. 14(7) as substituted by Housing and Planning Act 1986 (c.63), s. 39 (3), Sched. 8, para. 5.

CULTIVATION OF LAND AND DISPOSAL OF PRODUCE

Variation of terms of tenancies as to permanent pasture

14.—(1) This section applies where a contract for a tenancy of an agricultural holding provides for the maintenance of specified land, or a specified proportion of the holding, as permanent pasture.

(2) Where this section applies, the landlord or tenant may, by notice in writing served on the other, demand a reference to arbitration under this Act of the question whether it is expedient in order to secure the full and efficient farming of the holding that the area of land required to be maintained as permanent pasture should be reduced.

(3) On a reference under subsection (2) above the arbitrator may by his award direct that the provisions of the contract of tenancy as to land which is to be maintained as permanent pasture or is to be treated as arable land and as to cropping shall have effect subject to such modifications as may be specified in the direction.

(4) If, on a reference under subsection (2) above, the arbitrator gives a direction reducing the area of land which under the contract of tenancy is to be maintained as permanent pasture, he may order that the contract of tenancy shall have effect as if it provided that on quitting the holding on the termination of the tenancy the tenant should leave -
- (a) as permanent pasture, or
- (b) as temporary pasture sown with seeds mixture of such kind as maybe specified in the order, such area of land (in addition to the area of land required by the contract of tenancy, as modified by the direction, to be maintained as permanent pasture) as may be so specified.

(5) The area of land specified in an order made under subsection (4) above shall not exceed the area by which the land required by the contract of tenancy to be maintained as permanent pasture has been reduced by virtue of the direction.

Disposal of produce and cropping

15.—(1) Subject to the provisions of this section and to section 82 below, the tenant of an agricultural holding shall (notwithstanding any custom of the country or the provisions of the contract of tenancy or of any agreement respecting the disposal of crops or the method of cropping of arable land) have, without incurring any penalty, forfeiture or liability, the following rights, namely -
- (a) to dispose of the produce of the holding, other than manure produced on the holding, and
- (b) to practise any system of cropping of the arable land on the holding.

(2) Subsection (1) above shall not apply -

SECTION 15

    (a) in the case of a tenancy from year to year, as respects the year before the tenant quits the holding or any period after he has given or received notice to quit which results in his quitting the holding, or

    (b) in the case of any other tenancy, as respects the year before its termination.

(3) Subject to any agreement in writing to the contrary, the tenant of an agricultural holding shall not at any time after he has given or received notice to quit the holding sell or remove from the holding any manure or compostor any hay or straw or roots grown in the last year of the tenancy unless the landlord's written consent has been obtained before the sale or removal.

(4) Before, or as soon as possible after, exercising his rights under subsection (1) above, a tenant shall make suitable and adequate provision -

    (a) in the case of an exercise of the right to dispose of produce, to return to the holding the full equivalent manurial value of all crops sold off or removed from the holding in contravention of the custom, contract or agreement, and

    (b) in the case of an exercise of the right to practise any system of cropping, to protect the holding from injury or deterioration.

(5) If the tenant of an agricultural holding exercises his rights under subsection (1) above in such manner as to, or to be likely to, injure or deteriorate the holding, the landlord shall have the following remedies, but no other, namely -

    (a) the right to obtain, if the case so requires, an injunction to restrain the exercise of those rights in that manner, and

    (b) the right in any case, on the tenant's quitting the holding on the termination of the tenancy, to recover damages for any injury to or deterioration of the holding attributable to the exercise by the tenant of those rights.

(6) For the purposes of any proceedings for an injunction brought under paragraph (*a*) of subsection (5) above, the question whether the tenant is exercising, or has exercised, his rights under subsection (1) above in such a manner as to, or to be likely to, injure or deteriorate his holding shall be determined by arbitration under this Act; and the award of the arbitrator shall, for the purposes of any proceedings brought under subsection (5) (including an arbitration under paragraph (*b*))be conclusive proof of the facts stated in the award.

(7) In this section -

"arable land" does not include land in grass which, by the terms of a contract of tenancy,is to be retained in the same condition throughout the tenancy; and

"roots" means the produce of any root crop of a kind normally grown for consumption on the holding.

DISTRESS

No distress for rent due more than a year previously

16.—(1) Subject to subsection (2) below, the landlord of an agricultural holding shall not be entitled to distrain for rent which became due in respect of that holding more than one year before the making of the distress.

(2) Where it appears that, according to the ordinary course of dealing between

the landlord and the tenant of the holding, the payment of rent has been deferred until the expiry of a quarter or half-year after the date at which the rent legally became due, the rent shall, for the purposes of subsection (1) above, be deemed to have become due at the expiry of that quarter or half-year and not at the date at which it became legally due.

Compensation to be set off against rent for purposes of distress

17.—Where the amount of any compensation due to the tenant of an agricultural holding, whether under this Act or under custom or agreement, has been ascertained before the landlord distrains for rent, that amount may be set off against the rent and the landlord shall not be entitled to distrain for more than the balance.

Restrictions on distraining on property of third party

18.—(1) Property belonging to a person other than the tenant of an agricultural holding shall not be distrained for rent if -
  (a) the property is agricultural or other machinery and is on the holding under an agreement with the tenant for its hire or use in the conduct of his business, or
  (b) the property is livestock and is on the holding solely for breeding purposes.

(2) Agisted livestock shall not be distrained by the landlord of an agricultural holding for rent where there is other sufficient distress to be found; and if such livestock is distrained by him by reason of other sufficient distress not being found, there shall not be recovered by that distress a sum exceeding the amount of the price agreed to be paid for the feeding, or any part of the price which remains unpaid.

(3) The owner of the agisted livestock may, at any time before it is sold, redeem it by paying to the distrainer a sum equal to the amount mentioned in subsection (2) above, and payment of that sum to the distrainer shall be in full discharge as against the tenant of any sum of that amount which would otherwise be due from the owner of the livestock to the tenant in respect of the price of feeding.

(4) Any portion of the agisted livestock shall, so long as it remains on the holding, continue liable to be distrained for the amount for which the whole of the livestock is distrainable.

(5) In this section "livestock" includes any animal capable of being distrained; and "agisted livestock" means livestock belonging to another person which has been taken in by the tenant of an agricultural holding to be fed at a fair price.

Settlement of disputes as to distress

19.—(1)Where a dispute arises -
  (a) in respect of any distress having been levied on an agricultural holding contrary to the provisions of this Act,

(b) as to the ownership of any livestock distrained or as to the price to be paid for the feeding of that stock, or

(c) as to any other matter or thing relating to a distress on an agricultural holding, the dispute may be determined by the county court or on complaint by a magistrates' court, and the court may make an order for restoration of any livestock or things unlawfully distrained, may declare the price agreed to be paid for feeding or may make any other order that justice requires.

(2) Any person aggrieved by a decision of a magistrates' court under this section may appeal to the Crown Court.

(3) In this section "livestock" includes any animal capable of being distrained.

MISCELLANEOUS

Compensation for damage by game

20.—(1) Where the tenant of an agricultural holding has sustained damage to his crops from any wild animals or birds the right to kill and take which is vested in the landlord or anyone (other than the tenant himself) claiming under the landlord, being animals or birds which the tenant has not permission in writing to kill, he shall, if he complies with the requirements of subsection (2) below, be entitled to compensation from his landlord for the damage.

(2) The requirements of this subsection are that the tenant shall give his landlord -

(a) notice in writing within one month after the tenant first became, or ought reasonably to have become, aware of the occurrence of the damage,

(b) a reasonable opportunity to inspect the damage -
   (i) in the case of damage to a growing crop, before the crop is begun to be reaped, raised or consumed, and
   (ii) in the case of damage to a crop which has been reaped or raised, before the crop is begun to be removed from the land, and

(c) notice in writing of the claim, together with particulars of it, within one month after the expiry of the year in respect of which the claim is made.

(3) For the purposes of subsection (2) above -

(a) seed once sown shall be treated as a growing crop whether or not it has germinated, and

(b) "year" means any period of twelve months ending, in any year, with 29th September or with such other date as may by agreement between the landlord and tenant be substituted for that date.

(4) The amount of compensation under this section shall, in default of agreement made after the damage has been suffered, be determined by arbitration under this Act.

(5) Where the right to kill and take the wild animals or birds that did the damage is vested in some person other than the landlord, the landlord shall be entitled to be indemnified by that other person against all claims for compensation under this section; and any question arising under this subsection shall be determined by arbitration under this Act.

Extension of tenancies in lieu of claims to emblements

21.—(1) Where the tenancy of an agricultural holding held by a tenant at a rack rent determines by the death or cesser of the estate of any landlord entitled for his life, or for any other uncertain interest, instead of claims to emblements the tenant shall continue to hold and occupy the holding until the occupation is determined by a twelve months' notice to quit expiring at the end of a year of the tenancy, and shall then quit upon the terms of his tenancy in the same manner as if the tenancy were then determined by effluxion of time or other lawful means during the continuance of his landlord's estate.

(2) The succeeding landlord shall be entitled to recover from the tenant, in the same manner as his predecessor could have done, a fair proportion of the rent for the period which may have elapsed from the date of the death or cesser of the estate of his predecessor to the time of the tenant so quitting.

(3) The succeeding landlord and the tenant respectively shall as between themselves and as against each other be entitled to all the benefits and advantages and be subject to the terms, conditions and restrictions to which the preceding landlord and the tenant respectively would have been entitled and subject if the tenancy had determined in manner aforesaid at the expiry of the said twelve months' notice.

Rights to require certain records to be made

22.—(1) At any time during the tenancy of an agricultural holding -
  (a) the landlord or the tenant may require the making of a record of the condition of the fixed equipment on the holding and of the general condition of the holding itself (including any parts not under cultivation), and
  (b) the tenant may require the making of a record of any fixtures or buildings which, under section 10 above, he is entitled to remove and of existing improvements executed by him or in respect of the execution of which he, with the written consent of the landlord, paid compensation to an outgoing tenant.

(2) Any such record shall be made by a person appointed, in default of agreement between the landlord and tenant, by the President of the Royal Institution of Chartered Surveyors (referred to in this section as "the President"); and any person so appointed may, on production of evidence of his appointment, enter the holding at all reasonable times for the purpose of making any such record.

(3) The cost of making any such record shall, in default of agreement between the landlord and tenant, be borne by them in equal shares.

(4) No application may be made to the President for a person to be appointed by him under subsection (2) above unless the application is accompanied by such fee as may be prescribed as the fee for such an application.

(5) Any instrument of appointment purporting to be made by the President by virtue of subsection (2) above and to besigned by or on behalf of the President shall be taken to be such an instrument unless the contrary is shown.

Landlord's power of entry

23.—The landlord of an agricultural holding or any person authorised by him may at all reasonable times enter on the holding for any of the following purposes, namely -
  (a) viewing the state of the holding,
  (b) fulfilling the landlord's responsibilities to manage the holding in accordance with the rules of good estate management,
  (c) providing or improving fixed equipment on the holding otherwise than in fulfilment of those responsibilities.

Restriction of landlord's remedies for breach of contract of tenancy

24.—Notwithstanding any provision in a contract of tenancy of an agricultural holding making the tenant liable to pay a higher rent or other liquidated damages in the event of a breach or non-fulfilment of a term or condition of the contract, the landlord shall not be entitled to recover in consequence of any such breach or non-fulfilment, by distress or otherwise, any sum in excess of the damage actually suffered by him in consequence of the breach or non- fulfilment.

PART III
NOTICES TO QUIT

NOTICES TO QUIT WHOLE OR PART OF AGRICULTURAL HOLDING

Length of notice to quit

25.—(1) A notice to quit an agricultural holding or part of an agricultural holding shall (notwithstanding any provision to the contrary in the contract of tenancy of the holding) be invalid if it purports to terminate the tenancy before the expiry of twelve months from the end of the then current year of tenancy.
  (2) Subsection (1) above shall not apply -
  (a) where the tenant is insolvent,
  (b) to a notice given in pursuance of a provision in the contract of tenancy authorising the resumption of possession of the holding or some part of it for some specified purpose other than the use of the land for agriculture,
  (c) to a notice given by a tenant to a sub-tenant,
  (d) where the tenancy is one which, by virtue of subsection (6) of section 149 of the Law of Property Act 1925, has taken effect as such a term of years as is mentioned in that subsection.
  (3) Where on a reference under section 12 above with respect to an agricultural holding the arbitrator determines that the rent payable in respect of the holding shall be increased, a notice to quit the holding given by the tenant at least six months before it purports to take effect shall not be invalid by virtue of subsection (1) above if it purports to terminate the tenancy at the end of the year of the tenancy beginning with the date as from which the increase of rent is effective.
  (4) On an application made to the Tribunal with respect to an agricultural

holding under paragraph 9 of Part II of Schedule 3 to this Act, the Tribunal may, if they grant a certificate in accordance with the application -
  (a) specify in the certificate a minimum period of notice for termination of the tenancy (not being a period of less than two months), and
  (b) direct that that period shall apply instead of the period of notice required in accordance with subsection (1) above; and in any such case a notice to quit the holding which states that the Tribunal have given a direction under this subsection shall not be invalid by virtue of subsection (1) above if the notice given is not less than the minimum notice specified in the certificate.

(5) A notice to quit within subsection (3) or (4) above shall not be invalid by virtue of any term of the contract of tenancy requiring a longer period of notice to terminate the tenancy, and a notice to quit within subsection (4) above shall not be invalid by reason of its terminating at a date other than the end of a year of the tenancy.

Restriction on operation of notices to quit

26.—(1) Where -
  (a) notice to quit an agricultural holding or part of an agricultural holding is given to the tenant, and
  (b) not later than one month from the giving of the notice to quit the tenant serves on the landlord a counter-notice in writing requiring that this subsection shall apply to the notice to quit, then, subject to subsection (2) below, the notice to quit shall not have effect unless, on an application by the landlord, the Tribunal consent to its operation.

Amendment

Section 26 (1) modified by S.I. 1987 No. 710, arts 11, 17 (4); excluded by S.I. 1987 No. 710, art. 16

(2) Subsection (1) above shall not apply in any of the Cases set out in Part I of Schedule 3 to this Act; and in this Act "Case A", "Case B" (and so on) refer severally to the cases set out and so named in that Part of that Schedule.

(3) Part II of that Schedule shall have effect in relation to the cases there specified.

Tribunal's consent to operation of notice to quit

27.—(1) Subject to subsection (2) below, the Tribunal shall consent under section 26 above to the operation of a notice to quit an agricultural holding or part of an agricultural holding if, but only if, they are satisfied as to one or more of the matters mentioned in subsection (3) below, being a matter or matters specified by the landlord in his application for their consent.

(2) Even if they are satisfied as mentioned in subsection (1) above, the Tribunal shall withhold consent under section 26 above to the operation of the notice to quit if in all the circumstances it appears to them that a fair and reasonable landlord would not insist on possession.

(3) The matters referred to in subsection (1) above are -
  (a) that the carrying out of the purpose for which the landlord proposes to terminate the tenancy is desirable in the interests of good husbandry as respects the land to which the notice relates, treated as a separate unit;
  (b) that the carrying out of the purpose is desirable in the interests of sound management of the estate of which the land to which the notice relates forms part or which that land constitutes;
  (c) that the carrying out of the purpose is desirable for the purposes of agricultural research, education, experiment or demonstration, or for the purposes of the enactments relating to small holdings;
  (d) that the carrying out of the purpose is desirable for the purposes of the enactments relating to allotments;
  (e) that greater hardship would be caused by withholding than by giving consent to the operation of the notice;
  (f) that the landlord proposes to terminate the tenancy for the purpose of the land's being used for a use, other than for agriculture, not falling within Case B.

(4) Where the Tribunal consent under section 26 above to the operation of a notice to quit, they may impose such conditions as appear to them requisite for securing that the land to which the notice relates will be used for the purpose for which the landlord proposes to terminate the tenancy.

(5) Where, on an application by the landlord, the Tribunal are satisfied that, by reason of any change of circumstances or otherwise, any condition imposed under subsection (4) above ought to be varied or revoked, they shall vary or revoke the condition accordingly.

(6) Where -
  (a) on giving consent under section 26 above to the operation of a notice to quit the Tribunal imposed a condition under subsection (4) above, and
  (b) it is proved on an application to the Tribunal on behalf of the Crown that the landlord has acted in contravention of the condition or has failed within the time allowed by the condition to comply with it, the Tribunal may by order impose on the landlord a penalty of an amount not exceeding two years' rent of the holding at the rate at which rent was payable immediately before the termination of the tenancy, or, where the notice to quit related to a part only of the holding, of an amount not exceeding the proportion of the said two years' rent which it appears to the Tribunal is attributable to that part.

(7) The Tribunal may, in proceedings under this section, by order provide for the payment by any party of such sum as the Tribunal consider a reasonable contribution towards costs.

(8) A penalty imposed under subsection (6) above shall be a debt due to the Crown and shall, when recovered, be paid into the Consolidated Fund.

(9) An order under subsection (6) or (7) above shall be enforceable in the same manner as a judgment or order of the county court to the like effect.

Amendments

Section 27 (1) modified by Opencast Coal Act 1958 (c.69), s. 14(5) as substituted by Housing and Planning Act 1986 (c.63), s. 39 (3), Sched. 8, para. 5

Section 27 (3) modified by Opencast Coal Act 1958 (c.69), s. 14(5) as substituted by Housing and Planning Act 1986 (c.63), s. 39 (3), Sched. 8, para. 5

Additional restrictions on operation of notice to quit given under Case D.

28.—(1) This section applies where -
  (a) notice to quit an agricultural holding or part of an agricultural holding is given to the tenant, and
  (b) the notice includes a statement in accordance with Case D to the effect that it is given by reason of the tenant's failure to comply with a notice to do work.

(2) If the tenant serves on the landlord a counter-notice in writing in accordance with subsection (3) or (4) below requiring that this subsection shall apply to the notice to quit, the notice to quit shall not have effect (whether as a notice to which section 26 (1) above does or does not apply) unless, on an application by the landlord, the Tribunal consent to its operation.

(3) Subject to subsection (4) below, a counter-notice under subsection (2) above shall be served not later than one month from the giving of the notice to quit.

(4) Where the tenant not later than one month from the giving of the notice to quit serves on the landlord an effective notice requiring the validity of the reason stated in the notice to quit to be determined by arbitration under this Act -
  (a) any counter-notice already served under subsection (2) above shall be of no effect, but
  (b) if the notice to quit would, apart from this subsection, have effect in consequence of the arbitration, the tenant may serve a counter-notice under subsection (2) not later than one month from the date on which the arbitrator's award is delivered to him.

(5) The Tribunal shall consent under subsection (2) above to the operation of the notice to quit unless it appears to them, having regard -
  (a) to the extent to which the tenant has failed to comply with the notice to do work,
  (b) to the consequences of his failure to comply with it in any respect, and
  (c) to the circumstances surrounding any such failure, that a fair and reasonable landlord would not insist on possession.

(6) In this section "notice to do work" means a notice served on a tenant of an agricultural holding for the purposes of paragraph (*b*) of Case D, being a notice requiring the doing of any work of repair, maintenance or replacement.

Power to make supplementary provision

29.—The Lord Chancellor may by order provide for any of the matters specified in Schedule 4 to this Act.[43]

---

[43] See the Agricultural Holdings (Arbiration on Notices) Order 1987 (S.I. 1987 No. 710).

SECTION 30

Notice to quit where tenant is a service man

30.—Schedule 5 to this Act[44], which makes provision as to notices to quit in cases where the tenant of an agricultural holding is a service man[45], shall have effect.

NOTICES TO QUIT PART OF AGRICULTURAL HOLDING

Notice to quit part of holding valid in certain cases

31.—(1) A notice to quit part of an agricultural holding held on a tenancy from year to year given by the landlord of the holding shall not be invalid on the ground that it relates to part only of the holding if it is given -
   (a) for the purpose of adjusting the boundaries between agricultural units or amalgamating agricultural units or parts of such units, or
   (b) with a view to the use of the land to which the notice relates for any of the objects mentioned in subsection (2) below, and the notice states that it is given for that purpose or with a view to any such use, as the case may be.

(2) The objects referred to in subsection (1) above are -
   (a) the erection of cottages or other houses for farm labourers, whether with or without gardens;
   (b) the provision of gardens for cottages or other houses for farm labourers;
   (c) the provision of allotments;
   (d) the letting of land (with or without other land) as a small holding under Part III of the Agriculture Act 1970;
   (e) the planting of trees;
   (f) the opening or working of a deposit of coal, ironstone, limestone, brick-earth or other mineral, or a stone quarry or a clay, sand or gravel pit, or the construction of any works or buildings to be used in connection therewith;
   (g) the making of a watercourse or reservoir;
   (h) the making of a road, railway, tramroad, siding, canal or basin, or a wharf, pier, or other work connected therewith.

Right to treat notice to quit part of holding as notice to quit entire holding

32.—(1) Where there is given to the tenant of an agricultural holding a notice to quit part of the holding, being either -
   (a) such a notice as is rendered valid by section 31 above, or
   (b) a notice given by a person entitled to a severed part of the reversionary estate in the holding, subsection (2) below shall apply.

(2) If -
   (a) within twenty-eight days after the giving of the notice, or
   (b) where the operation of the notice depends on any proceedings under this Part of this Act, within twenty-eight days after the time at which it is

---

[44] Section 29 powers applied to Sched. 5 by Schedule 5, para 5.
[45] See the Reserve and Auxiliary Forces (Agricultural Tenants) Regulations 1959 (S.I. 1959 No. 84) and the Agricultural Holdings (Arbitration on Notices) Order 1987 (S.I. 1987 No. 710) Article 17.

determined that the notice has effect, the tenant gives to the landlord or (as the case may be) to the persons severally entitled to the severed parts of the reversion a counter-notice in writing to the effect that he accepts the notice to quit as a notice to quit the entire holding given by the landlord or (as the case may be) those persons, to take effect at the same time as the original notice, the notice to quit shall have effect accordingly.

Reduction of rent where notice is given to quit part of holding

33.—(1)Where the landlord of an agricultural holding resumes possession of part of the holding either -
   (a) by virtue of section 31 (1) above, or
   (b) in pursuance of a provision in that behalf contained in the contract of tenancy, the tenant shall be entitled to a reduction of rent proportionate to that part of the holding and in respect of any depreciation of the value to him of the residue of the holding caused by the severance or by the use to be made of the part severed.

(2) The amount of any reduction of rent under this section shall, in default of agreement made after the landlord resumes possession of the part of the holding concerned, be determined by arbitration under this Act.

(3) In a case falling within subsection (1)(*b*) above that falls to be determined by arbitration under this Act the arbitrator, in assessing the amount of the reduction, shall take into consideration any benefit or relief allowed to the tenant under the contract of tenancy in respect of the land possession of which is resumed by the landlord.

Amendment

Pt. III excluded by Housing Act 1988 (c.50), s. 101

Part IV
Succession on Death or Retirement of Tenant

TENANCIES TO WHICH PART IV APPLIES

Tenancies to which Part IV applies

34.—(1) The provisions of this Part of this Act shall have effect with respect to -
   (a) any tenancy of an agricultural holding granted before 12th July 1984, and
   (b) a tenancy granted on or after that date if (but only if) -
       (i) the tenancy was obtained by virtue of a direction of the Tribunal under section 39 or 53 below,
       (ii) the tenancy was granted (following a direction under section 39 below) in circumstances within section 45 (6) below,
       (iii) the tenancy was granted by a written contract of tenancy indicating (in whatever terms) that this Part of this Act is to apply in relation to the tenancy, or

(iv) the tenancy was granted otherwise than as mentioned in the preceding provisions of this subsection to a person who, immediately before that date, was a tenant of the holding or of any agricultural holding which comprised the whole or a substantial part of the land comprised in the holding.

(2) In this section "tenant" does not include an executor, administrator, trustee in bankruptcy or other person deriving title from a tenant by operation of law.

SUCCESSION ON DEATH OF TENANT

Application of sections 36 to 48

35.—(1) Sections 36 to 48 below (except sections 40 (5), 42 and 45 (8) which are of general application) shall apply where -
- (a) an agricultural holding is held under a tenancy which falls within paragraph (*a*) or (*b*) of section 34 (1) above, and
- (b) the sole (or sole surviving) tenant (within the meaning of that section) dies and is survived by a close relative of his.

(2) In sections 36 to 48 below (and in Part I of Schedule 6 to this Act) -
"close relative" of a deceased tenant means -
- (a) the wife or husband of the deceased;
- (b) a brother or sister of the deceased;
- (c) a child of the deceased;
- (d) any person (not within (*b*) or (*c*) above) who, in the case of any marriage to which the deceased was at any time a party, was treated by the deceased as a child of the family in relation to that marriage;

"the date of death" means the date of the death of the deceased;
"the deceased" means the deceased tenant of the holding;
"the holding" (except where the context otherwise requires) means the agricultural holding mentioned in subsection (1) above;
"related holding" means, in relation to the holding, any agricultural holding comprising the whole or a substantial part of the land comprised in the holding;
"the tenancy" means the tenancy of the holding.

Right of any eligible person to apply for new tenancy on death of tenant

36.—(1) Any eligible person may apply under section 39 below to the Tribunal for a direction entitling him to a tenancy of the holding unless excluded by subsection (2) or section 37 or 38 below.

(2) Subsection (1) above (and section 41 below) shall not apply if on the date of death the holding was held by the deceased under -
- (a) a tenancy for a fixed term of years of which more than twenty-seven months remained unexpired, or
- (b) a tenancy for a fixed term of more than one but less than two years.

(3) For the purposes of this section and sections 37 to 48 below, "eligible person" means (subject to the provisions of Part I of Schedule 6 to this Act and without prejudice to section 41 below) any surviving close relative of the deceased in whose case the following conditions are satisfied -

(a) in the seven years ending with the date of death his only or principal source of livelihood throughout a continuous period of not less than five years, or two or more discontinuous periods together amounting to not less than five years, derived from his agricultural work on the holding or on an agricultural unit of which the holding forms part, and

(b) he is not the occupier of a commercial unit of agricultural land.

(4) In the case of the deceased's wife the reference in subsection (3)(*a*) above to the relative's agricultural work shall be read as a reference to agricultural work carried out by either the wife or the deceased (or both of them).

(5) Part I of Schedule 6 to this Act, which supplements subsection (3) above and makes provision with respect to the assessment of the productive capacity of agricultural land for the purposes of paragraph (b) of that subsection, shall have effect.

Exclusion of statutory succession where two successions have already occurred

37.—(1) Section 36 (1) above (and section 41 below) shall not apply if on each of the last two occasions when there died a sole (or sole surviving) tenant of the holding or of a related holding there occurred one or other of the following things, namely -

(a) a tenancy of the holding or of a related holding was obtained by virtue of a direction of the Tribunal under section 39 below, or such a tenancy was granted (following such a direction) in circumstances within section 45 (6) below, or

(b) a tenancy of the holding or of a related holding was granted by the landlord to a person who, being a close relative of the tenant who died on that occasion, was or had become the sole or sole remaining applicant for such a direction.

(2) If on any occasion prior to the date of death, as a result of an agreement between the landlord and the tenant for the time being of the holding or of a related holding, the holding or a related holding became let -

(a) under a tenancy granted by the landlord, or

(b) by virtue of an assignment of the current tenancy, to a person who, if the said tenant had died immediately before the grant or assignment would have been his close relative, that occasion shall for the purposes of subsection (1) above be deemed to be an occasion such as is mentioned in that subsectionon which a tenancy of the holding or a related holding was obtained by virtue of a direction of the Tribunal under section 39 below.

(3) If any such tenancy was granted as mentioned in subsection (2) above for a term commencing later than the date of the grant, the holding under that tenancy shall for the purposes of that subsection not be taken to have become let under that tenancy until the commencement of the term.

(4) Subsections (1) and (2) above -

(a) shall apply whether or not any tenancy granted or obtained (otherwise than by virtue of an assignment) as mentioned in those provisions related to the whole of the land held by the tenant on the occasion of whose death, or with whose agreement, the tenancy was so granted or obtained, as the case may be, and

(b) shall apply where a joint tenancy is granted by the landlord to persons one of whom is a person such as is mentioned in either of those subsections as they apply where a tenancy is granted by the landlord to any such personal one.

(5) Subsection (2) above shall apply where a tenancy is assigned to joint tenants one of whom is a person such as is mentioned in that subsection as it applies where a tenancy is assigned to any such person alone.

(6) Where a tenancy of the holding or of a related holding was obtained by virtue of a direction of the Tribunal under section 53 (7) below, that occasion shall for the purposes of subsection (1) above be deemed to be an occasion such as is mentioned in that subsection on which a tenancy of the holding or a related holding was obtained by virtue of a direction of the Tribunal under section 39 below.

(7) Subsection (2) above shall, in relation to any time before 12th September 1984, have effect with the substitution for the words from "as a result" to "grant or assignment" of the words "the holding or a related holding became let under a new tenancy granted by the landlord, with the agreement of the outgoing tenant, to a person who, if the outgoing tenant had died immediately before the grant".

(8) Subsections (4) and (5) above shall not apply in relation to any tenancy if -
(a) it was granted before 12th September 1984,
(b) it was obtained by virtue of any direction given in any proceedings arising out of an application made under Part II of the Agriculture (Miscellaneous Provisions) Act 1976 before 12th September 1984, or
(c) it was granted (following such a direction) in circumstances within section 23(6) of the said Act of 1976.

(9) In this section "tenant" has the same meaning as in section 34 above.

Other excluded cases

38.—(1) Section 36 (1) above (and section 41 below) shall not apply if on the date of death the tenancy is the subject of a valid notice to quit to which subsection (1) of section 26 above applies, being a notice given before that date in the case of which -
(a) the month allowed by that subsection for serving a counter-notice under that subsection expired before that date without such a counter-notice having been served, or
(b) the Tribunal consented before that date to its operation.

(2) Section 36 (1) (and section 41) shall not apply if on the date of death the tenancy is the subject of a valid notice to quit given before that date and falling within Case C or F.

(3) Those sections shall not apply if on the date of death the tenancy is the subject of a valid notice to quit given before that date and falling within Case B, D or E, and
(a) the time within which the tenant could have required any question arising in connection with the notice to be determined by arbitration under this Act expired before that date without such a requirement

having been made by the tenant, and the month allowed for serving any counter-notice in respect of the notice expired before that date without any such counter-notice having been served, or

(b) questions arising in connection with the notice were referred to arbitration under this Act before that date and were determined before that date in such a way as to uphold the operation of the notice and (where applicable) the month allowed for serving any counter-notice in respect of the notice expired before that date without a counter-notice having been served, or

(c) the Tribunal consented before that date to the operation of the notice.

(4) Those sections shall not apply if the holding consists of land held by a small holdings authority or the Minister for the purposes of small holdings within the meaning of Part III of the Agriculture Act 1970 (whether the tenancy was granted before or after the commencement of the said Part III).

(5) Those sections shall not apply if the tenancy was granted by trustees in whom the land is vested on charitable trusts the sole or principal object of which is the settlement or employment in agriculture of persons who have served in any of Her Majesty's naval, military or air forces.

Applications for tenancy of holding

39.—(1) An application under this section by an eligible person to the Tribunal for a direction entitling him to a tenancy of the holding shall be made within the period of three months beginning with the day after the date of death.

(2) Where only one application is made under this section the Tribunal, if satisfied -
   (a) that the applicant was an eligible person at the date of death, and
   (b) that he has not subsequently ceased to be such a person, shall determine whether he is in their opinion a suitable person to become the tenant of the holding.

(3) Where two or more applications are made under this section, then, subject to subsection (4) below, subsection (2) above shall apply to each of the applicants as if he were the only applicant.

(4) If the applicants under this section include a person validly designated by the deceased in his will as the person he wished to succeed him as tenant of the holding, the Tribunal shall first make a determination under subsection (2) above as regards that person, and shall do so as regards the other applicant or each of the other applicants only if the Tribunal determine that the person so designated is not in their opinion a suitable person to become the tenant of the holding.

(5) If under the preceding provisions of this section only one applicant is determined by the Tribunal to be in their opinion a suitable person to become the tenant of the holding, the Tribunal shall, subject to subsection (10) and section 44 below, give a direction entitling him to a tenancy of the holding.

(6) If under the preceding provisions of this section each of two or more applicants is determined by the Tribunal to be in their opinion a suitable person to become the tenant of the holding, the Tribunal -

(a) shall, subject to subsection (9) below, determine which of those applicants is in their opinion the more or most suitable person to become the tenant of the holding, and

(b) shall, subject to subsection (10) and section 44 below, give a direction entitling that applicant to a tenancy of the holding.

(7) Before making a determination under subsection (2) above in the case of any applicant the Tribunal shall afford the landlord an opportunity of stating his views on the suitability of that applicant.

(8) In making a determination under subsection (2) above in the case of a particular applicant, or a determination under subsection (6) above as between two or more applicants, the Tribunal shall have regard to all relevant matters including -

(a) the extent to which the applicant or each of those applicants has been trained in, or has had practical experience of, agriculture,

(b) the age, physical health and financial standing of the applicant or each of those applicants, and

(c) the views (if any) stated by the landlord on the suitability of the applicant or any of those applicants.

(9) Where subsection (6) above would apply apart from this subsection, the Tribunal may, with the consent of the landlord, give instead a direction specifying any two, any three or any four of the applicants within that subsection, and entitling the specified applicants to a joint tenancy of the holding.

(10) Where the person or persons who would, subject to section 44 below, be entitled to a direction under this section entitling him or them to a tenancy or (as the case may be) to a joint tenancy of the holding agree to accept instead a tenancy or joint tenancy of a part of the holding, any direction given by the Tribunal under subsection (5), (6) or (9) above shall relate to that part of the holding only.

Provisions supplementary to section 39

40.—(1) In section 39 above "will" includes codicil, and for the purposes of that section a person shall be taken to be validly designated by the deceased in his will as the person he wishes to succeed him as tenant of the holding if, but only if, a will of the deceased which is the subject of a grant of probate or administration -

(a) contains an effective specific bequest to that person of the deceased's tenancy of the holding, or

(b) does not contain an effective specific bequest of that tenancy, but does contain a statement specifically mentioning the holding or the deceased's tenancy of the holing and exclusively designating that person (in whatever words, and whether by name or description) as the person whom the deceased wishes to succeed him as tenant of the holding.

(2) For the purposes of subsection (1) above a statement which is framed so as to designate as mentioned in paragraph (b) of that subsection different persons in different circumstances shall be taken to satisfy that paragraph if, in the events which have happened, the statement exclusively designates a particular person.

(3) A direction under section 39 above given in favour of a person by reason of his being a person validly designated by the deceased as mentioned in subsection

(4) of that section shall be valid even if the probate or administration by virtue of which he was such a person at the giving of the direction is subsequently revoked or varied.

(4) For the purposes of this Part of this Act an application under section 39 above which is withdrawn or abandoned shall be treated as if it had never been made.

(5) Provision shall be made by order under section 73 (3) of the Agriculture Act 1947 (procedure of Agricultural Land Tribunals) for requiring any person making an application to the Tribunal under section 39 above or section 41 below to give notice of the application to the landlord of the agricultural holding to which the application relates and to take such steps as the order may require for bringing the application to the notice of other persons interested in the outcome of the application.[46]

Application by not fully eligible person to be treated as eligible

41.—(1) This section applies to any surviving close relative of the deceased who for some part of the seven years ending with the date of death engaged (whether full-time or part-time) in agricultural work on the holding, being a person in whose case -
   (a) the condition specified in paragraph (*b*) of the definition of "eligible person" in section 36(3) above is satisfied, and
   (b) the condition specified in paragraph (*a*) of that definition, though not fully satisfied, is satisfied to a material extent.

(2) A person to whom this section applies may within the period of three months beginning with the day after the date of death apply to the Tribunal for a determination that he is to be treated as an eligible person for the purposes of sections 36 to 48 of this Act.

(3) If on an application under this section -
   (a) the Tribunal are satisfied that the applicant is a person to whom this section applies, and
   (b) it appears to the Tribunal that in all the circumstances it would be fair and reasonable for the applicant to be able to apply under section 39 above for a direction entitling him to a tenancy of the holding, the Tribunal shall determine that he is to be treated as an eligible person for the purposes of sections 36 to 48 of this Act, but shall otherwise dismiss the application.

(4) In relation to a person in respect of whom the Tribunal have determined as mentioned in subsection (3) above sections 36 to 48 of this Act shall apply as if he were an eligible person.

(5) A person to whom this section applies may make an application under section 39 above as well as an application under this section; and if the Tribunal determine as mentioned in subsection (3) above in respect of a person who has made an application under that section, the application under that section shall (without prejudice to subsection (4) above) be treated as made by an eligible person.

---

[46] See the Agricultural Land Tribunals (Succession to Agricultural Tenancies) Order 1984 (S.I. 1984 No. 1301).

(6) Without prejudice to the generality of paragraph (b) of subsection (1) above, cases where the condition mentioned in that paragraph might be less than fully satisfied include cases where the close relative's agricultural work on the holding fell short of prodding him with his principal source of livelihood because the holding was too small.

Procedure where deceased held more than one holding

42.—(1) Subsections (2) and (3) below shall have effect where at the expiry of the period of three months beginning with the day after the date of death of a tenant there are pending before the Tribunal separate applications made under section 39 above by any person, or (as the case may be) by each one of a number of persons, in respect of more than one agricultural holding held by the tenant at that date.

(2) The applications referred to in subsection (1) above (together with, in each case, any associated application made under section 41 above) shall, subject to and in accordance with the provisions of any such order as is referred to in section 40 (5) above, be heard and determined by the Tribunal in such order as may be decided -
   (a) where the applications were made by one person, by that person,
   (b) where the applications were made by two or more persons, by agreement between those persons or, in default of agreement, by the chairman of the Tribunal.[47]

(3) Any decision made by the chairman under subsection (2)(*b*) above shall be made according to the respective sizes of the holdings concerned so that any application in respect of any holding which is larger than any other of those holdings shall be heard and determined by the Tribunal before any application in respect of that other holding.

Restriction on operation of notice to quit given by reason of death of tenant

43.—(1) A notice to quit the holding given to the tenant of the holding by reason of the death of the deceased and falling within Case G shall not have effect unless -
   (a) no application to become the tenant of the holding is made (or has already at the time of the notice to quit been made) under section 39 above within the period mentioned in subsection (1) of that section, or
   (b) one or more such applications having been made within that period -
       (i) none of the applicants is determined by the Tribunal to be in their opinion a suitable person to become the tenant of the holding, or
       (ii) the Tribunal consent under section 44 below to the operation of the notice to quit in relation to the whole or part of the holding.

(2) Where the Tribunal consent under section 44 below to the operation of a notice to quit to which subsection (1) above applies in relation to part only of the holding, the notice shall have effect accordingly as a notice to quit that part and shall not be invalid by reason that it relates only to part of the holding.

---

[47] The Agricultural Land Tribunals (Succession to Agricultural Tenancies) Order 1984 (S.I. 1984 No. 1301). There are no provisions in this Order affecting the rules laid down in section 42.

Opportunity for landlord to obtain Tribunal's consent to operation of notice to quit

44.—(1) Before giving a direction under section 39(5) or (6) above in a case where a notice to quit to which section 43(1) above applies has been given the Tribunal shall afford the landlord an opportunity of applying for their consent under this section to the operation of the notice.

(2) Subject to subsection (5) below, section 27 above shall apply in relation to an application for, or the giving of, the Tribunal's consent under this section as it applies in relation to an application for, or the giving of, their consent under section 26 above.

(3) The Tribunal shall not entertain an application for their consent to the operation of a notice to quit to which section 43(1) above applies unless it is made in pursuance of subsection (1) above.

(4) Subject to subsection (5) below, if the Tribunal give their consent on an application made in pursuance of subsection (1) above, they shall dismiss the application or each of the applications made under section 39 above.

(5) Where in any case -
   (a) a notice to quit to which section 43(1) above applies has been given, and
   (b) section 39(10) above applies, the Tribunal shall give their consent to the operation of the notice to quit in relation to the part of the holding which would, in accordance with section 39(10), be excluded from any direction given by the Tribunal with respect to the holding under section 39; and subsections (2)and (4) above shall not apply.

(6) If on an application made in pursuance of subsection (1) above the Tribunal give their consent to the operation of a notice to quit -
   (a) within the period of three months ending with the date on which the notice purports to terminate the tenancy ("the original operative date"), or
   (b) at any time after that date, the Tribunal may, on the application of the tenant, direct that the notice shall have effect from a later date ("the new operative date").

(7) The new operative date, in the case of a notice to quit, must be a date not later than the end of the period of three months beginning with -
   (a) the original operative date, or
   (b) the date on which the Tribunal give their consent to the operation of the notice, whichever last occurs.

Effect of direction under section 39

45.—(1) A direction by the Tribunal -
   (a) under section 39(5) or (6) above entitling an applicant to a tenancy of the holding, or
   (b) under section 39(9) above entitling two or more applicants to a joint tenancy of the holding, shall entitle him or them to a tenancy or joint tenancy of the holding as from the relevant time on the terms provided by sections 47 and 48 below; and accordingly such a tenancy or joint tenancy shall be deemed to be at that time granted by the landlord to, and accepted by, the person or persons so entitled.

(2) Where the deceased's tenancy was not derived from the interest held by the landlord at the relevant time, the tenancy or joint tenancy deemed by virtue of subsection (1) above to be granted to, and accepted by, the person or persons so entitled shall be deemed to be granted by the person for the time being entitled to the interest from which the deceased's tenancy was derived, instead of by the landlord, with like effect as if the landlord's interest and any other supervening interest were not subsisting at the relevant time.

(3) The reference in subsection (2) above to a supervening interest is a reference to any interest in the land comprised in the deceased's tenancy, being an interest created subsequently to that tenancy and derived (whether immediately or otherwise) from the interest from which that tenancy was derived and still subsisting at the relevant time.

(4) Subsection (2) above shall not be read as affecting the rights and liabilities of the landlord under this Part of this Act.

(5) Any tenancy of the holding inconsistent with the tenancy to which a direction such as is mentioned in subsection (1) above entitles the person or persons concerned shall, if it would not cease at the relevant time apart from this subsection, cease at that time as if terminated at that time by a valid notice to quit given by the tenant.

(6) If the person or persons whom such a direction entitles to a tenancy or joint tenancy of the holding as from the relevant time becomes or become the tenant or joint tenants of the holding before that time under a tenancy granted by the landlord to, and accepted by, the person or persons concerned, the direction shall cease to have effect and section 48 below shall not apply.

(7) The rights conferred on any person by such a direction (as distinct from his rights under his tenancy of the holding after he has become the tenant or joint tenant of the holding) shall not be capable of assignment.

(8) The Lord Chancellor may by regulations provide for all or any of the provisions of sections 36 to 48 of this Act (except this subsection) to apply, with such exceptions, additions or other modifications as may be specified in the regulations, in cases where the person or any of the persons whom such a direction entitles to a tenancy or joint tenancy of the holding dies before the relevant time.[48]

Interpretation of section 45

46.—(1) Subject to subsection (2) below, in sections 45 above and 48 below "the relevant time" -
- (a) except where the following paragraph applies, means the end of the twelve months immediately following the end of the year of tenancy in which the deceased died,
- (b) if a notice to quit the holding was given to the tenant by reason of the death of the deceased, being a notice falling within Case G which, apart from section 43 above, would have terminated the tenancy at a time after the end of those twelve months, means that time.

(2) Where the Tribunal give a direction under section 39(5), (6) or (9) above in

---

[48] See the Agriculture (Miscellaneous Provisions) Act 1976 (Application of Provisions) Regulations 1977 (S.I. 1977 No. 1215).

relation to the holding at any time after the beginning of the period of three months ending with the relevant time apart from this subsection ("the original relevant time"), then -
> (a) if the direction is given within that period, the Tribunal may, on the application of the tenant, specify in the direction, as the relevant time for the purposes of this section and section 48 below, such a time falling within the period of three months immediately following the original relevant time as they think fit,
> (b) if the direction is given at any time after the original relevant time the Tribunal shall specify in the direction, as the relevant time for those purposes, such a time falling within the period of three months immediately following the date of the giving of the direction as they think fit, and any time so specified shall be the relevant time for those purposes accordingly.

(3) Where in accordance with section 39(10) above, the tenancy to which a direction under that section entitles the person or persons concerned is a tenancy of part of the deceased's holding, references in sections 45 above and 48 below to the holding shall be read as references to the whole of the deceased's holding or to the part of that holding to which the direction relates, as the context requires.

Terms of new tenancy unless varied by arbitration

47.—(1) Subject to the provisions of this section and section 48 below, the terms of the tenancy or joint tenancy to which a direction under section 39(5), (6) or (9) above entitles the person or persons concerned shall be the same as the terms on which the holding was let immediately before it ceased to be let under the contract of tenancy under which it was let at the date of death.

(2) If on the date of death the holding was held by the deceased under a tenancy for a fixed term of years, subsection (1) above shall have effect as if the tenancy under which the holding was let at the date of death had before that date become a tenancy from year to year on (with that exception) the terms of the actual tenancy as far as applicable.

(3) If the terms of the tenancy to which such a direction entitles the person or persons concerned would not, apart from this subsection, include a covenant by the tenant or each of the tenants not to assign, sub-let or part with possession of the holding or any part of it without the landlord's consent in writing, subsection (1) above shall have effect as if those terms included such a covenant.

Arbitration on terms of new tenancy

48.—(1) Where the Tribunal give a direction such as is mentioned in subsection (1) of section 45 above, the provisions of this section shall apply unless excluded by subsection (6) of that section.

(2) In the following provisions of this section -

"the landlord" means the landlord of the holding;

"prescribed period" means the period between the giving of the direction and -
> (a) the end of the three months immediately following the relevant time, or

SECTION 48

    (b) the end of the three months immediately following the date of the giving of the direction, whichever last occurs;

"the relevant time" has the meaning given by subsection (1) or (as the case may require) subsection (2) of section 46 above;

"the tenant" means the person or persons entitled to a tenancy or joint tenancy of the holding by virtue of the direction;

and references to the holding shall be read in accordance with section 46(3) above.

(3) At any time within the prescribed period the landlord or the tenant may by notice in writing served on the other demand a reference to arbitration under this Act of one or both of the questions specified in subsection (4) below.

(4) Those questions (referred to in the following provisions of this section as "question (*a*)" and "question (*b*)" respectively) are -

    (a) what variations in the terms of the tenancy which the tenant is entitled to or has obtained by virtue of the direction are justifiable having regard to the circumstances of the holding and the length of time since the holding was first let on those terms;

    (b) what rent should be or should have been properly payable in respect of the holding at the relevant time.

(5) Where question (*a*) is referred to arbitration under subsection (3) above (with or without question (*b*)), the arbitrator -

    (a) shall determine what variations, if any, in the terms mentioned in that question are justifiable as there mentioned, and

    (b) without prejudice to the preceding paragraph, shall include in his award such provision, if any, as are necessary -

        (i) for entitling the landlord to recover from the tenant under those terms a sum equal to so much as is in all the circumstances fair and reasonable of the aggregate amount of the compensation mentioned in subsection (8)(*a*) below, and

        (ii) for entitling the tenant to recover from the landlord under those terms a sum equal to so much as is in all the circumstances fair and reasonable of the aggregate amount of the compensation mentioned in subsection (8)(*b*) below, and shall accordingly, with effect from the relevant time, vary those terms in accordance with his determination or direct that they are to remain unchanged.

(6) Where question (*a*) but not question (*b*) is referred to arbitration under subsection (3) above and it appears to the arbitrator that by reason of any provision included in his award under subsection (5) above (not being a provision of a kind mentioned in paragraph (*b*) of that subsection) it is equitable that the rent of the holding should be varied, he may vary the rent accordingly with effect from the relevant time.

(7) Where question (*b*) is referred to arbitration under subsection (3) above (with or without question (*a*)), the arbitrator shall determine what rent should be or should have been properly payable in respect of the holding at the relevant time and accordingly shall, with effect from that time, increase or reduce the rent which would otherwise be or have been payable or direct that it shall remain unchanged.

(8) The compensation referred to in subsection (5)(b) above is -

(a) the compensation paid or payable by the landlord, whether under this Act or under agreement or custom, on the termination of the deceased's tenancy of the holding,

(b) the compensation paid or payable to the landlord, whether under this Act or under agreement, on that termination in respect of any such dilapidation or deterioration of, or damage to, any part of the holding or anything in or on the holding as the tenant is or will be liable to make good under the terms of his tenancy.

(9) For the purposes of this section the rent properly payable in respect of the holding shall be the rent at which the holding might reasonably be expected to be let by a prudent and willing landlord to a prudent and willing tenant, taking into account all relevant factors, including (in every case) the terms of the tenancy or prospective tenancy (including those relating to rent) and any such other matters as are specifically mentioned in sub-paragraph (1) of paragraph 1 of Schedule 2 to this Act (read with sub-paragraphs (2) and (3) of that paragraph).

(10) On any reference under subsection (3) above the arbitrator may include in his award such further provisions, if any, relating to the tenancy which the tenant is entitled to or has obtained by virtue of the direction as may be agreed between the landlord and the tenant.

(11) If the award of an arbitrator under this section is made before the relevant time, section 47(1) above shall have effect subject to, and in accordance with, the award.

(12) If the award of an arbitrator under this section is made after the relevant time, it shall have effect as if the terms of the award were contained in an agreement in writing entered into by the landlord and the tenant and having effect as from the relevant time.

SUCCESSION ON RETIREMENT OF TENANT

Application of sections 50 to 58

49.—(1) Sections 50 to 58 below (except sections 53(11) and 55(7) which are of general application) shall apply where -
  (a) an agricultural holding is held under a tenancy from year to year, being a tenancy which falls within paragraph (*a*) or (*b*) of section 34(1) above, and
  (b) a notice is given to the landlord by the tenant, or (in the case of a joint tenancy) by all the tenants, of the holding indicating (in whatever terms) that he or they wish a single eligible person named in the notice to succeed him or them as tenant of the holding as from a date specified in the notice, being a date on which the tenancy of the holding could have been determined by notice to quit given at the date of the notice and which falls not less than one year, but not more than two years, after the date of the notice.

(2) In subsection (1) above "tenant" has the same meaning as in section 34 above.

(3) In this section and sections 50 to 58 below (and in Part I of Schedule 6 to this Act as applied by section 50 (4)) -

SECTION 49

"close relative" of the retiring tenant means -
  (a) the wife or husband of the retiring tenant;
  (b) a brother or sister of the retiring tenant;
  (c) a child of the retiring tenant;
  (d) any person (not within (b) or (c) above) who, in the case of any marriage to which the retiring tenant has been at any time a party, has been treated by the latter as a child of the family in relation to that marriage;

"eligible person" has the meaning given by section 50 below;

"the holding" means the holding in respect of which the retirement notice is given;

"the nominated successor" means the eligible person named in the retirement notice;

"related holding" means, in relation to the holding, any agricultural holding comprising the whole or a substantial part of the land comprised in the holding;

"the retirement date" means the date specified in the retirement notice as the date as from which the proposed succession is to take place;

"the retirement notice" means the notice mentioned in subsection (1) above;

"the retiring tenant" means the tenant by whom the retirement notice was given, or, where it was given by joint tenants (and the context so permits), any one of those tenants, and "the retiring tenants" accordingly means those tenants;

"the tenancy" means the tenancy of the holding.

Right to apply for new tenancy on retirement of tenant

50.—(1) The eligible person named in the retirement notice may (subject to section 57(2) below) apply under section 53 below to the Tribunal for a direction entitling him to a tenancy of the holding unless excluded by section 51 below.

(2) For the purposes of sections 49 to 58 of this Act, "eligible person" means (subject to the provisions of Part I of Schedule 6 to this Act as applied by subsection (4) below) a close relative of the retiring tenant in whose case the following conditions are satisfied -
  (a) in the last seven years his only or principal source of livelihood throughout a continuous period of not less than five years, or two or more discontinuous periods together amounting to not less than five years, derived from his agricultural work on the holding or on an agricultural unit of which the holding forms part, and
  (b) he is not the occupier of a commercial unit of agricultural land.

(3) In the case of the wife of the retiring tenant the reference in subsection (2)(a) above to the relative's agricultural work shall be read as a reference to agricultural work carried out by either the wife or the retiring tenant (or both of them).

(4) Part I of Schedule 6 to this Act shall apply for the purposes of supplementing subsection (2) above and making provision with respect to the assessment of the productive capacity of agricultural land for the purposes of paragraph (b) of that subsection, but subject to the modifications set out in Part II of that Schedule.

AGRICULTURAL HOLDINGS ACT 1986

Excluded cases

51.—(1) Sections 37 and 38 above shall apply for the purpose of excluding the application of section 50(1) above, but subject to the following modifications -
  (a) references to sections 36(1) and 41 above shall be read as references to section 50(1),
  (b) references to the holding, a related holding and the tenancy shall be read in accordance with section 49(3) above, and
  (c) references to the date of death shall be read as references to the date of the giving of the retirement notice.

(2) Section 50(1) shall not apply if the retiring tenant has at any time given any other notice under section 49(1) above in respect of the holding or a related holding and an application to become the tenant of the holding or a related holding has been duly made by any person under section 53 below in respect of that notice.

(3) Section 50(1) shall not apply if at the retirement date the retiring tenant will be under sixty-five, unless the retirement notice is given on the grounds that -
  (a) the retiring tenant or (where the notice is given by joint tenants) each of the retiring tenants is or will at the retirement date be incapable, by reason of bodily or mental infirmity, of conducting the farming of the holding in such a way as to secure the fulfilment of the responsibilities of the tenant to farm in accordance with the rules of good husbandry, and
  (b) any such incapacity is likely to be permanent, and that fact is stated in the notice.

(4) If on the date of the giving of the retirement notice the tenancy is the subject of a valid notice to quit given before that date and including a statement that it is given for any such reason as is referred to in Case B, D or E (not being a notice to quit falling within section 38(3) above as applied by subsection (1) above), section 50(1) shall not apply unless one of the events mentioned in subsection (5) below occurs.

(5) Those events are as follows -
  (a) it is determined by arbitration under this Act that the notice to quit is ineffective for the purposes of section 26(2) above on account of the invalidity of any such reason as aforesaid, or
  (b) where a counter-notice is duly served under section 28(2) above -
    (i) the Tribunal withhold consent to the operation of the notice to quit, or
    (ii) the period for making an application to the Tribunal for such consent expires without such an application having been made.

(6) Where one of the events mentioned in subsection (5) above occurs the relevant period shall for the purposes of sections 53(1) and 54(2) below be the period of one month beginning with the date on which the arbitrator's award is delivered to the tenant, with the date of the Tribunal's decision to withhold consent, or with the expiry of the said period for making an application (as the case may be).

SECTION 52

Notices to quit restricting operation of section 53

52.—(1) If the tenancy becomes the subject of a valid notice to quit given on or after the date of the giving of the retirement notice (but before the Tribunal have begun to hear any application by the nominated successor under section 53 below in respect of the retirement notice) and the notice to quit -
- (a) falls within Case C and is founded on a certificate granted under paragraph 9 of Part II of Schedule 3 to this Act in accordance with an application made before that date, or
- (b) falls within Case F, the retirement notice shall be of no effect and no proceedings, or (as the case may be) no further proceedings, shall be taken under this Part of this Act in respect of it.

(2) If the tenancy becomes the subject of a valid notice to quit given on or after the date of the giving of the retirement notice (but before the Tribunal have begun to hear any application by the nominated successor under section 53 below in respect of the retirement notice) and the notice to quit -
- (a) includes a statement that it is given for any such reason as is referred to in Case B, or
- (b) includes a statement that it is given for any such reason as is referred to in Case D and is founded on a notice given for the purposes of that Case before that date, the retirement notice shall be of no effect and no proceedings, or (as the case may be) no further proceedings, shall be taken under this Part of this Act in respect of it unless one of the events mentioned in subsection (3) below occurs.

(3) Those events are as follows -
- (a) it is determined by arbitration under this Act that the notice to quit is ineffective for the purposes of section 26(2) above on account of the invalidity of any such reason as aforesaid, or
- (b) where a counter-notice is duly served under section 28(2) above -
    - (i) the Tribunal withhold consent to the operation of the notice to quit, or
    - (ii) the period for making an application to the Tribunal for such consent expires without such an application having been made.

(4) Where -
- (a) one of the events mentioned in subsection (3) above occurs, and
- (b) the notice to quit was given before the time when the relevant period for the purposes of sections 53(1) and 54(2) would expire apart from this subsection, that period shall for those purposes expire at the end of the period of one month beginning with the date on which the arbitrator's award is delivered to the tenant, with the date of the Tribunal's decision to withhold consent, or with the expiry of the said period for making an application (as the case may be).

(5) For the purposes of this Part of this Act an application by the nominated successor under section 53 below which is invalidated by subsection (1) or (2) above shall be treated as if it had never been made.

AGRICULTURAL HOLDINGS ACT 1986

Application for tenancy of holding by nominated successor

53.—(1) An application under this section by the nominated successor to the Tribunal for a direction entitling him to a tenancy of the holding shall be made within the relevant period.

(2) In subsection (1) above "the relevant period" means (subject to sections 51(6) and 52(4) above) the period of one month beginning with the day after the date of the giving of the retirement notice.

(3) Any such application -
 (a) must be accompanied by a copy of the retirement notice, and
 (b) must be signed by both the nominated successor and the retiring tenant or, where the notice was given by joint tenants, by each of the retiring tenants.

(4) If the retirement notice includes a statement in accordance with section 51(3) above that it is given on the grounds mentioned in that provision, then, before the nominated successor's application is further proceeded with under this section, the Tribunal must be satisfied -
 (a) that the retiring tenant or (as the case may be) each of the retiring tenants either is or will at the retirement date be incapable, by reason of bodily or mental infirmity, of conducting the farming of the holding in such a way as to secure the fulfilment of the responsibilities of the tenant to farm in accordance with the rules of good husbandry, and
 (b) that any such incapacity is likely to be permanent.

(5) If the Tribunal are satisfied -
 (a) that the nominated successor was an eligible person at the date of the giving of the retirement notice, and
 (b) that he has not subsequently ceased to be such a person, the Tribunal shall determine whether he is in their opinion a suitable person to become the tenant of the holding.

(6) Before making a determination under subsection (5) above the Tribunal shall afford the landlord an opportunity of stating his views on the suitability of the nominated successor; and in making any such determination the Tribunal shall have regard to all relevant matters, including -
 (a) the extent to which the nominated successor has been trained in, or has had practical experience of, agriculture,
 (b) his age, physical health and financial standing,
 (c) the views (if any) stated by the landlord on his suitability.

(7) If the nominated successor is determined under that sub-section to be in their opinion a suitable person to become the tenant of the holding, the Tribunal shall, subject to subsection (8) below, give a direction entitling him to a tenancy of the holding.

(8) The Tribunal shall not give such a direction if, on an application made by the landlord, it appears to the Tribunal that greater hardship would be caused by giving the direction than by refusing the nominated successor's application under this section.

(9) If the Tribunal dispose of the nominated successor's application otherwise

than by the giving of a direction under subsection (7) above the retirement notice shall be of no effect (but without prejudice to section 51(2) above).

(10) For the purposes of this Part of this Act, an application by the nominated successor under this section which is withdrawn or abandoned shall be treated as if it had never been made.

(11) Provision shall be made by order under section 73(3) of the Agriculture Act 1947 (procedure of Agricultural Land Tribunals) for requiring any person making an application to the Tribunal for a direction under this section to give notice of the application to the landlord of the agricultural holding to which the application relates.[49]

Restriction on operation of certain notices to quit

54.—(1) This section applies to any notice to quit the holding or part of it given to the tenant of the holding (whether before or on or after the date of the giving of the retirement notice), not being a notice to quit falling within any provision of section 38 above (as applied by section 51(1) above) or section 51 or 52 above.

(2) A notice to quit to which this section applies shall not, if it would otherwise be capable of so having effect, have effect -
    (a) at any time during the relevant period, or
    (b) where an application to become the tenant of the holding is made by the nominated successor under section 53 above within that period, at any time before the application has been finally disposed of by the Tribunal or withdrawn or abandoned, and shall in any event not have effect if any such application is disposed of by the Tribunal by the giving of a direction under section 53(7) above.

(3) In subsection (2) above "the relevant period" means (subject to sections 51(6) and 52(4) above) the period of one month beginning with the day after the date of the giving of the retirement notice.

Effect of direction under section 53

55.—(1) A direction by the Tribunal under section 53(7) above entitling the nominated successor to a tenancy of the holding shall entitle him to a tenancy of the holding as from the relevant time on the terms provided by section 56 below; and accordingly such a tenancy shall be deemed to be at that time granted by the landlord to, and accepted by, the nominated successor.

(2) Where the tenancy of the retiring tenant or (as the case may be) of the retiring tenants was not derived from the interest held by the landlord at the relevant time, the tenancy deemed by virtue of subsection (1) above to be granted to, and accepted by, the nominated successor shall be deemed to be granted by the person for the time being entitled to the interest from which the tenancy of the retiring tenant or tenants was derived, instead of by the landlord, with like effect as if the landlord's interest and any other supervening interest were not subsisting at the relevant time.

---

[49] See the Agricultural Land Tribunals (Succession to Agriculturing Tenancies) Order 1984 (S.I. 1984 No. 1301) Rule 24.

(3) The reference in subsection (2) above to a supervening interest is a reference to any interest in the land comprised in the tenancy of the retiring tenant or tenants, being an interest created subsequently to that tenancy and derived (whether immediately or otherwise) from the interest from which that tenancy was derived and still subsisting at the relevant time.

(4) Subsection (2) above shall not be read as affecting the rights and liabilities of the landlord under this Part of this Act.

(5) Any tenancy of the holding inconsistent with the tenancy to which the nominated successor is entitled by virtue of a direction under section 53(7) above shall, if it would not cease at the relevant time apart from this subsection, cease at that time as if terminated at that time by a valid notice to quit given by the tenant.

(6) The rights conferred on any person by such a direction (as distinct from his rights under his tenancy of the holding after he has become the tenant) shall not be capable of assignment.

(7) The Lord Chancellor may by regulations provide for all or any of the provisions of sections 37(6) and 50 to 58 of this Act (except this subsection) to apply, with such exceptions, additions or other modifications as may be specified in the regulations, in cases where the nominated successor, being entitled to a tenancy of the holding by virtue of such a direction, dies before the relevant time.[50]

(8) In this section "the relevant time" means the retirement date, except that -
   (a) where such a direction is given within the period of three months ending with the retirement date, the Tribunal may, on the application of the tenant, specify in the direction, as the relevant time for the purposes of this section, such a time falling within the period of three months immediately following the retirement date as they think fit,
   (b) where such a direction is given at any time after the retirement date, the Tribunal shall specify in the direction, as the relevant time for those purposes, such a time falling within the period of three months immediately following the date of the giving of the direction as they think fit, and any time so specified shall be the relevant time for those purposes accordingly.

Terms of new tenancy

56.—(1) Subject to subsections (2) and (3) below, the terms of the tenancy to which a direction under section 53(7) above entitles the nominated successor shall be the same as the terms on which the holding was let immediately before it ceased to be let under the contract of tenancy under which it was let at the date of the giving of the retirement notice.

(2) If the terms of the tenancy to which the nominated successor is entitled as

---

[50] No such regulations have yet been made. The Agriculture (Miscellaneous Provisions) Act 1976 (Application of Provisions) Regulations 1977 (S.I. 1977 No. 1215) makes the necessary provisions for a similar contingency in the case of a person entitled to a tenancy under a direction following the deceased tenants's death himself dying before the relevant time; but the regulations have not been added to our ammended to cover nominated successors dying before the relevant time set out in sub-section (8).

mentioned in subsection (1) above would not, apart from this subsection, include a covenant by the tenant not to assign, sub-let or part with possession of the holding or any part of it without the landlord's consent in writing, subsection (1) above shall have effect as if those terms included that covenant.

(3) Where the Tribunal give a direction under section 53(7) above, subsections (3) to (12) of section 48 above shall have effect in relation to the tenancy which the nominated successor is entitled to or has obtained by virtue of the direction, but with the substitution -
- (a) in subsection (8)(*a*) of a reference to the tenancy of the retiring tenant or (as the case may be) tenants for the reference to the deceased's tenancy,
- (b) in subsection (11) of a reference to subsection (1) above for the reference to section 47(1).

(4) In those provisions, as extended by subsection (3) above -

"the landlord" means the landlordof the holding;

"the prescribed period" means the period between the giving of the direction and-
- (a) the end of the three months immediately following the relevant time, or
- (b) the end of the three months immediately following the date of the giving of the direction, whichever last occurs;

"the relevant time" has the meaning given by section 55(8) above;

"the tenant" means the nominated successor.

Effect of death of retiring tenant on succession to the holding

57.—(1) Subsections (2) to (4) below apply where the retiring tenant, being the sole (or sole surviving) tenant of the holding, dies after giving the retirement notice.

(2) If the tenant's death occurs at a time when no application by the nominated successor has been made under section 53 above or such an application has not been finally disposed of by the Tribunal, the retirement notice shall be of no effect and no proceedings, or (as the case may be) no further proceedings, shall be taken under section 53 above in respect of it; and accordingly sections 36 to 48 above shall apply on the tenant's death in relation to the holding.

(3) If the tenant's death occurs at a time when any such application has been so disposed of by the giving of a direction such as is mentioned in subsection (1) of section 55 above,but before the relevant time (within the meaning of that section), that section and section 56 above shall continue to have effect in relation to the holding; and accordingly sections 36 to 48 above shall not apply on the tenant's death in relation to the holding.

(4) If the tenant's death occurs at a time when any such application has been so disposed of otherwise than by the giving of any such direction, sections 36 to 48 above shall apply on the tenant's death in relation to the holding, but no application under section 39 (or 41)above may be made on that occasion by the nominated successor in relation to the holding.

(5) Where the retirement notice was given by joint tenants and one of those tenants, not being the sole surviving tenant of the holding, dies, his death shall not affect any rights of the nominated successor under sections 50 to 56 above.

AGRICULTURAL HOLDINGS ACT 1986

Effect of direction under section 53 on succession to other holdings

58.—Where -
- (a) the retiring tenant, being the sole (or sole surviving) tenant of the holding, dies, and
- (b) the nominated successor is for the time being entitled to a tenancy of the holding by virtue of a direction under section 53(7) above, then for the purpose of determining whether, in relation to any other agricultural holding held by the retiring tenant at the date of his death, the nominated successor is a person in whose case the condition specified in paragraph (*b*) of section 36(3) above is satisfied, the nominated successor shall be deemed to be in occupation of the holding.

INTERPRETATION

Interpretation of Part IV

59.—(1) In sections 36 to 48 above (and in Part I of Schedule 6 to this Act) -
"close relative" of a deceased tenant,
"the date of death",
"the deceased",
"the holding",
"related holding", and
"the tenancy",
have the meanings given by section 35(2) above; and in those sections "eligible person" has the meaning given by section 36(3) above.

(2) In sections 49 to 58 above (and in Part I of Schedule 6 to this Act as applied by section 50 (4) above) -
"close relative" of the retiring tenant,
"the holding",
"the nominated successor",
"related holding",
"the retirement date",
"the retirement notice",
"the retiring tenant",
"the retiring tenants", and
"the tenancy",
have the meanings given by section 49(3) above; and in those sections "eligible person" has the meaning given by section 50(2) above.

Amendment
Pt. IV excluded by Housing Act 1988 (c. 50), s. 101.
Part V
Compensation on Termination of Tenancy

SECTION 60

COMPENSATION TO TENANT FOR DISTURBANCE

Right to, and measure of, compensation for disturbance

60.—(1) This section applies where the tenancy of an agricultural holding terminates by reason -
  (a) of a notice to quit the holding given by the landlord, or
  (b) of a counter-notice given by the tenant under section 32 above after the giving to him of such a notice to quit part of the holding as is mentioned in that section, and the tenant quits the holding in consequence of the notice or counter-notice.

(2) Subject to section 61 below, where this section applies there shall be payable by the landlord to the tenant by way of compensation for disturbance -
  (a) a sum computed under subsection (3) below (in this section referred to as "basic compensation"), and
  (b) a sum computed under subsection (4) below (in this section referred to as "additional compensation").

(3) The amount of basic compensation shall be -
  (a) an amount equal to one year's rent of the holding at the rate at which rent was payable immediately before the termination of the tenancy, or
  (b) where the tenant has complied with the requirements of subsection (6) below, a greater amount equal to either the amount of the tenant's actual loss or two years' rent of the holding whichever is the smaller.

(4) The amount of additional compensation shall be an amount equal to four years' rent of the holding at the rate at which rent was payable immediately before the termination of the tenancy of the holding.

(5) In subsection (3) above "the amount of the tenant's actual loss" means the amount of the loss or expense directly attributable to the quitting of the holding which is unavoidably incurred by the tenant upon or in connection with the sale or removal of his household goods, implements of husbandry, fixtures, farmproduce or farm stock on or used in connection with the holding, and includes any expenses reasonably incurred by him in the preparation of his claim for basic compensation (not being costs of an arbitration to determine any question arising under this section or section 61 below).

(6) The requirements of this subsection are -
  (a) that the tenant has not less than one month before the termination of the tenancy given to the landlord notice in writing of his intention to make a claim for an amount under subsection (3)(*b*) above, and
  (b) that the tenant has, before their sale, given to the landlord a reasonable opportunity of making a valuation of any such goods, implements, fixtures, produce or stock as are mentioned in subsection (5) above.

(7) Compensation payable under this section shall be in addition to any compensation to which the tenant may be entitled apart from this section.

Cases where compensation under section 60 is not payable

61.—(1) Neither basic compensation nor additional compensation shall be payable under section 60 above where the operation of section 26(1) above in relation to the relevant notice is excluded by virtue of Case C, D, E, F or G.

(2) Additional compensation shall not be so payable where the operation of section 26(1) above in relation to the relevant notice is excluded by virtue of Case A or H.

(3) Except as provided by subsection (4) below, additional compensation shall not be payable under section 60 above where -
- (a) the relevant notice contains a statement either that the carrying out of the purpose for which the landlord proposes to terminate the tenancy is desirable on any of the grounds mentioned in paragraphs (*a*) to (*c*) of section 27(3) above or that the landlord will suffer hardship unless the notice has effect, and
- (b) if an application for consent in respect of the notice is made to the Tribunal in pursuance of section 26(1) above, the Tribunal consent to its operation and state in the reasons for their decision that they are satisfied as to any of the matters mentioned in paragraphs (*a*), (*b*), (*c*) and (*e*) of section 27(3).

(4) Additional compensation shall be payable in a case falling within subsection (3) above where such an application as is mentioned in paragraph (*b*) of that subsection is made and -
- (a) the reasons given by the Tribunal also include the reason that they are satisfied as to the matter mentioned in paragraph (*f*) of section 27(3) above, or
- (b) the Tribunal include in their decision a statement under subsection (5) below.

(5) Where such an application as is mentioned in subsection (3)(*b*) above is made in respect of the relevant notice and the application specifies the matter mentioned in paragraph (*b*) of section 27(3) above (but not that mentioned in paragraph (*f*) of that subsection), the Tribunal shall if they are satisfied as to the matter mentioned in paragraph (b) but would, if it had been specified in the application, have been satisfied also as to the matter mentioned in paragraph (*f*) include a statement to that effect in their decision.

(6) In this section -

"basic compensation" and "additional compensation" have the same meanings as in section 60 above;

"the relevant notice" means the notice to quit the holding or part of the holding, as the case may be, mentioned in section 60(1) above.

Compensation on termination in pursuance of early resumption clause

62.—(1) Where -
- (a) the tenancy of an agricultural holding terminates by reason of a notice to quit the holding given in pursuance of a provision in the contract of tenancy authorising the resumption of possession of the holding for some specified purpose other than the use of the land for agriculture, and

(b) the tenant quits the holding in consequence of the notice, compensation shall be payable by the landlord to the tenant, in addition to any other compensation so payable apart from this section in respect of the holding.

(2) The amount of compensation payable under this section shall be equal to the value of the additional benefit (if any) which would have accrued to the tenant if the tenancy had, instead of being terminated as provided by the notice, been terminated by it on the expiration of twelve months from the end of the year of tenancy current when the notice was given.

(3) For the purposes of subsection (2) above, the current year of a tenancy for a term of two years or more is the year beginning with such day in the period of twelve months ending with the date on which the notice is served as corresponds to the day on which the term would expire by the effluxion of time.

Compensation for disturbance: supplementary provisions

63.—(1) Where -
  (a) the tenant of an agricultural holding has sub-let the holding, and
  (b) the sub-tenancy terminates by operation of law in consequence of the termination of the tenancy by reason of any such notice or counter-notice as is referred to in section 60(1)(*a*) or (*b*) above, section 60 shall apply if the sub-tenant quits the holding in consequence of the termination of the sub-tenancy as mentioned in paragraph (*b*) above as it applies where a tenant quits a holding in consequence of any such notice or counter-notice.

(2) Where the tenant of an agricultural holding has sub-let the holding and in consequence of a notice to quit given by his landlord becomes liable to pay compensation under section 60 or 62 above to the sub-tenant, the tenant shall not be debarred from recovering compensation under that section by reason only that, owing to not being in occupation of the holding, on the termination of his tenancy he does not quit the holding.

(3) Where the tenancy of an agricultural holding terminates by virtue of such a counter-notice as is mentioned in section 60(1)(*b*) above, and -
  (a) the part of the holding affected by the notice to quit together with any part of the holding affected by any relevant previous notice rendered valid by section 31 above is less than one-fourth of the original holding, and
  (b) the holding as proposed to be diminished is reasonably capable of being farmed as a separate holding, compensation shall not be payable under section 60 above except in respect of the part of the holding to which the notice to quit relates.

(4) In subsection (3) above "relevant previous notice" means any notice to quit given by the same person who gave the current notice to quit or, where that person is a person entitled to a severed part of the reversionary estate in the holding, by that person or by any other person so entitled.

AGRICULTURAL HOLDINGS ACT 1986

COMPENSATION TO TENANT FOR IMPROVEMENTS AND TENANT-RIGHT MATTERS

Tenant's right to compensation for improvements

64.—(1) The tenant of an agricultural holding shall, subject to the provisions of this Act, be entitled on the termination of the tenancy, on quitting the holding, to obtain from his landlord compensation for an improvement specified in Schedule 7 or Part I of Schedule 8 to this Act carried out on the holding by the tenant, being an improvement begun on or after 1st March 1948.

(2) In this Act "relevant improvement" means an improvement falling within subsection (1) above.

(3) Subsection (1) above shall have effect as well where the tenant entered into occupation of the holding before 1st March 1948 as where he entered into occupation on or after that date.

(4) The provisions of Part I of Schedule 9 to this Act shall have effect with respect to the rights of the tenant of an agricultural holding with respect to compensation for improvements specified in Part II of that Schedule carried out on the holding, being improvements begun before 1st March 1948.

Tenant's right to compensation for tenant-right matters

65.—(1) The tenant of an agricultural holding shall, subject to the provisions of this Act, be entitled on the termination of the tenancy, on quitting the holding, to obtain from his landlord compensation for any such matter as is specified in Part II of Schedule 8 to this Act.

(2) The tenant shall not be entitled to compensation under subsection (1) above for crops or produce grown, seeds sown, cultivations, fallows or acts of husbandry performed, or pasture laid down, in contravention of the terms of a written contract of tenancy unless -
  (a) the growing of the crops or produce, the sowing of the seeds, the performance of the cultivations, fallows or acts of husbandry, or the laying down of the pasture was reasonably necessary in consequence of the giving of a direction under the Agriculture Act 1947, or
  (b) the tenant shows that the term of the contract contravened was inconsistent with the fulfilment of his responsibilities to farm the holding in accordance with the rules of good husbandry.

(3) Subject to paragraphs 6 and 7 of Schedule 12 to this Act, subsection (1) above shall apply to a tenant on whatever date he entered into occupation of the holding.

Measure of compensation

66.—(1) The amount of any compensation under this Act for a relevant improvement specified in Schedule 7 to this Act shall be an amount equal to the increase attributable to the improvement in the value of the agricultural holding as a holding, having regard to the character and situation of the holding and the average requirements of tenants reasonably skilled in husbandry.

(2) The amount of any compensation under this Act for a relevant improvement specified in Part I of Schedule 8 to this Act, or for any matter falling within Part II

of that Schedule, shall be the value of the improvement or matter to an incoming tenant calculated in accordance with such method, if any, as may be prescribed.[51]

(3) Where the landlord and the tenant of an agricultural holding have entered into an agreement in writing whereby any benefit is given or allowed to the tenant in consideration of his carrying out an improvement specified in Part I of Schedule 8 to this Act, the benefit shall be taken into account in assessing compensation under this Act for the improvement.

(4) Nothing in this Act shall prevent the substitution, in the case of matters falling within Part II of Schedule 8 to this Act, for the measure of compensation specified in subsection (2) above, of such measure of compensation, to be calculated according to such method, if any, as may be specified in a written contract of tenancy.

(5) Where a grant out of money provided by Parliament or local government funds has been or will be made to the tenant of an agricultural holding in respect of a relevant improvement, the grant shall be taken into account in assessing compensation under this Act for the improvement.

Compensation for long-term improvements: consent required

67.—(1) The tenant of an agricultural holding shall not be entitled to compensation for a relevant improvement specified in Schedule 7 to this Act unless the landlord has given his consent in writing to the carrying out of the improvement.

(2) Any such consent may be given by the landlord unconditionally or upon such terms as to compensation or otherwise as may be agreed upon in writing between the landlord and the tenant; and the provisions of section 66(1) above shall have effect subject to the provisions of any such agreement as is made.

(3) Where, in the case of an improvement specified in Part II of Schedule 7 to this Act, a tenant is aggrieved by the refusal of his landlord to give his consent under subsection (1) above, or is unwilling to agree to any terms subject to which the landlord is prepared to give his consent, the tenant may apply to the Tribunal for approval of the carrying out of the improvement, and the following provisions of this section shall have effect with respect to the application.

(4) The Tribunal may approve the carrying out of the improvement, either unconditionally or upon such terms, whether as to reduction of the compensation which would be payable if the Tribunal approved unconditionally or as to other matters, as appear to them to be just, or may withhold their approval.

(5) If the Tribunal grant their approval, the landlord may, within the prescribed period from receiving notification of the Tribunal's decision, serve notice in writing on the Tribunal and the tenant that the landlord proposes himself to carry out the improvement.

(6) Where the Tribunal grant their approval, then if -
   (a) no notice is duly served by the landlord under subsection (5) above, or
   (b) such a notice is duly served, but on an application made by the tenant the Tribunal determines that the landlord has failed to carry out the

---

[51] See the Agriculture (Calculation of Valuation for Compensation) Regulations 1978 (S.I. 1978 No. 809).

improvement within a reasonable time, the approval of the Tribunal shall have effect for the purposes of subsection (1) above as if it were the consent of the landlord, and any terms subject to which the approval was given shall have effect as if they were contained in an agreement in writing between the landlord and the tenant.

(7) In subsection (5) above, "the prescribed period" means the period prescribed by the Lord Chancellor by order.[52]

Improvements: special cases

68.—(1) The tenant of an agricultural holding shall not be entitled to compensation for a relevant improvement specified in paragraph 1 of Schedule 8 to this Act unless, not later than one month before the improvement was begun, he gave notice in writing to the landlord of his intention to carry out the improvement.

(2) Where, on an application of the sub-tenant of an agricultural holding, the Tribunal have directed the immediate landlord of the sub-tenant to carry out work under section 11 above being work which constitutes an improvement specified in Schedule 7 to this Act -

(a) section 67 above shall not apply as respects a claim by the immediate landlord against his superior landlord for compensation in respect of that work, and

(b) if, on the failure of the immediate landlord to comply with the direction of the Tribunal, the sub-tenant has himself carried out the work, sections 64 and 66 above shall have effect for the purposes of a claim for compensation by the immediate landlord against his superior landlord as if the work had been carried out by the immediate landlord and as if any grant made to the sub-tenant in respect of the workout of money provided by Parliament had been made to the immediate landlord.

(3) Where the tenant of an agricultural holding has carried out on the holding an improvement specified in Schedule 7 to this Act in accordance with provision for the making of the improvement and for the tenant's being responsible for doing the work in a hill farming land improvement scheme approved under section 1 of the Hill Farming Act 1946, being provision included in the scheme at the instance or with the consent of the landlord -

(a) the landlord shall be deemed to have consented as mentioned in subsection (1) of section 67 above,

(b) any agreement as to compensation or otherwise made between the landlord and the tenant in relation to the improvement shall have effect as if it had been such an agreement on terms as is mentioned in subsection (2) of that section, and

(c) the provisions of subsections (5) and (6) of that section as to the carrying out of improvements by the landlord shall not apply.

(4) In assessing the amount of any compensation payable under custom or agreement to the tenant of an agricultural holding, if it is shown to the satisfaction of the person assessing the compensation that the cultivations in respect of which the compensation is claimed were wholly or in part the result of or incidental to

---

[52] See the Agricultural Land Tribunals (Rules) Order 1978 (S.I. 1978 No. 259), rule 7.

work in respect of the cost of which an improvement grant has been paid under section 1 of the Hill Farming Act 1946, the amount of the grant shall be taken into account as if it had been a benefit allowed to the tenant in consideration of his executing the cultivations and the compensation shall be reduced to such extent as that person considers appropriate.

(5) Where the tenant of an agricultural holding claims compensation in respect of works carried out in compliance with an improvement notice served, or an undertaking accepted, under Part VII of the Housing Act 1985 or Part VIII of the Housing Act 1974 -
- (a) section 67 above shall not apply as respects the works, and
- (b) if a person other than the tenant has contributed to the cost of carrying out the works, compensation in respect of the works as assessed under section 66 above shall be reduced proportionately.

Improvements: successive tenancies

69.—(1) Where the tenant of an agricultural holding has remained in the holding during two or more tenancies, he shall not be deprived of his right to compensation under this Act in respect of relevant improvements by reason only that the improvements were made during a tenancy other than the one at the termination of which he quits the holding.

(2) Where, on entering into occupation of an agricultural holding, the tenant -
- (a) with the consent in writing of his landlord paid to an outgoing tenant any compensation payable by the landlord under or in pursuance of this Act (or the Agricultural Holdings Act 1948 or Part III of the Agriculture Act 1947) in respect of the whole or part of a relevant improvement, or
- (b) has paid to the landlord the amount of any such compensation payable to an outgoing tenant, the tenant shall be entitled, on quitting the holding, to claim compensation in respect of the improvement or part in the same manner, if at all, as the outgoing tenant would have been entitled if the outgoing tenant had remained tenant of the holding and quitted it at the time at which the tenant quits it.

(3) Where, in a case not falling within subsection (2) above, the tenant, on entering into occupation of an agricultural holding, paid to his landlord any amount in respect of the whole or part of a relevant improvement, he shall, subject to any agreement in writing between the landlord and the tenant, be entitled on quitting the holding to claim compensation in respect of the improvement or part in the same manner, if at all, as he would have been entitled if he had been tenant of the holding at the time when the improvement was carried out and the improvement or part had been carried out by him.

COMPENSATION TO TENANT FOR ADOPTION OF SPECIAL SYSTEM OF FARMING

Compensation for special system of farming

70.—(1) Where the tenant of an agricultural holding shows that, by the continuous adoption of a system of farming which has been more beneficial to the holding -

(a) than the system of farming required by the contract of tenancy, or

(b) in so far as no system of farming is so required, than the system of farming normally practised on comparable agricultural holdings, the value of the holding as a holding has been increased during the tenancy, having regard to the character and situation of the holding and the average requirements of tenants reasonably skilled in husbandry, the tenant shall be entitled, on quitting the holding on the termination of the tenancy, to obtain from the landlord compensation of an amount equal to the increase.

(2) Compensation shall not be recoverable under this section unless -

(a) the tenant has, not later than one month before the termination of the tenancy, given to the landlord notice in writing of his intention to claim compensation under this section, and

(b) a record has been made under section 22 above of the condition of the fixed equipment on the holding and of the general condition of the holding.

(3) Compensation shall not be recoverable under this section in respect of any matter arising before the date of the making of the record referred to in subsection (2) above or, if more than one such record has been made, the first of them.

(4) In assessing the value of an agricultural holding for the purposes of this section due allowance shall be made for any compensation agreed or awarded to be paid to the tenant for an improvement falling within section 64(1) or (4) above or (subject to paragraph 8 of Schedule 12 to this Act) for any such matter as is specified in Part II of Schedule 8 to this Act, being an improvement or matter which has caused, or contributed to, the benefit.

(5) Nothing in this section shall entitle a tenant to recover for an improvement falling within section 64(1) or (4) above or an improvement to which the provisions of this Act relating to market gardens apply or (subject to the said paragraph 8) for any such matter as is specified in Part II of Schedule 8 to this Act, any compensation which he is not entitled to recover apart from this section.

COMPENSATION TO LANDLORD FOR DETERIORATION OF HOLDING

Compensation for deterioration of particular parts of holding

71.—(1) The landlord of an agricultural holding shall be entitled to recover from a tenant of the holding, on the tenant's quitting the holding on the termination of the tenancy, compensation in respect of the dilapidation or deterioration of, or damage to, any part of the holding or anything in or on the holding caused by non-fulfilment by the tenant of his responsibilities to farm in accordance with the rules of good husbandry.

(2) Subject to subsection (5) below, the amount of the compensation payable under subsection (1) above shall be the cost, as at the date of the tenant's quitting the holding, of making good the dilapidation, deterioration or damage.

(3) Notwithstanding anything in this Act, the landlord may, in lieu of claiming compensation under subsection (1) above, claim compensation in respect of matters specified in that subsection under and in accordance with a written contract of tenancy.

(4) Where the landlord claims compensation in accordance with subsection (3) above -
   (a) compensation shall be so claimed only on the tenant's quitting the holding on the termination of the tenancy, and
   (b) compensation shall not be claimed in respect of any one holding both under such a contract as is mentioned in that subsection and under subsection (1) above; and for the purposes of paragraph (b) above any claim under section 9(1) above shall be disregarded.

(5) The amount of the compensation payable under subsection (1) above, or in accordance with subsection (3) above, shall in no case exceed the amount (if any) by which the value of the landlord's reversion in the holding is diminished owing to the dilapidation, deterioration or damage in question.

Compensation for general deterioration of holding

72.—(1) This section applies where, on the quitting of an agricultural holding by the tenant on the termination of the tenancy, the landlord shows that the value of the holding generally has been reduced by reason of any such dilapidation, deterioration or damage as is mentioned in section 71(1) above or otherwise by non-fulfilment by the tenant of his responsibilities to farm in accordance with the rules of good husbandry.

(2) Where this section applies, the landlord shall be entitled to recover from the tenant compensation for the matter in question, in so far as the landlord is not compensated for it under subsection (1), or in accordance with subsection (3), of section 71 above.

(3) The amount of the compensation payable under this section shall be equal to the decrease attributable to the matter in question in the value of the holding as a holding, having regard to the character and situation of the holding and the average requirements of tenants reasonably skilled in husbandry.

(4) Compensation shall not be recoverable under this section unless the landlord has, not later than one month before the termination of the tenancy, given notice in writing to the tenant of his intention to claim such compensation.

Deterioration of holding: successive tenancies

73.—(1) Where the tenant of an agricultural holding has remained on the holding during two or more tenancies his landlord shall not be deprived of his right to compensation under section 71 or 72 above in respect of any dilapidation, deterioration or damage by reason only that the tenancy during which an act or omission occurred which in whole or in part caused the dilapidation, deterioration or damage was a tenancy other than the tenancy at the termination of which the tenant quits the holding.

SUPPLEMENTARY PROVISIONS WITH RESPECT TO COMPENSATION

Termination of tenancy of part of holding

74.—(1) Where the landlord of an agricultural holding resumes possession of part of the holding by virtue of section 31 or 43(2) above, the provisions of this Act with respect to compensation shall apply to that part of the holding as if it were a separate holding which the tenant had quitted in consequence of a notice to quit.

(2) Where the landlord of an agricultural holding resumes possession of part of the holding in pursuance of a provision in that behalf contained in the contract of tenancy -
   (a) the provisions of this Act with respect to compensation shall apply to that part of the holding as if it were a separate holding which the tenant had quitted in consequence of a notice to quit, but
   (b) the arbitrator in assessing the amount of compensation payable to the tenant, except the amount of compensation under section 60(2)(*b*) above, shall take into consideration any benefit or relief allowed to the tenant under the contract of tenancy in respect of the land possession of which is resumed by the landlord.

(3) Where a person entitled to a severed part of the reversionary estate in an agricultural holding resumes possession of part of the holding by virtue of a notice to quit that part given to the tenant by virtue of section 140 of the Law of Property Act 1925 the provisions of this Act with respect to compensation shall apply to that part of the holding as if -
   (a) it were a separate holding which the tenant had quitted in consequence of the notice to quit, and
   (b) the person resuming possession were the landlord of that separate holding.

(4) References in this Act to the termination of the tenancy of, or (as the case may be) of part of, an agricultural holding include references to the resumption of possession of part of an agricultural holding in circumstances within subsection (1), (2) or (3) above.

Compensation where reversionary estate in holding is severed

75.—(1) Where the reversionary estate in an agricultural holding is for the time being vested in more than one person in several parts, the tenant shall be entitled, on quitting the entire holding, to require that any compensation payable to him under this Act shall be determined as if the reversionary estate were not so severed.

(2) Where subsection (1) above applies, the arbitrator shall where necessary, apportion the amount awarded between the persons who for the purposes of this Act together constitute the landlord of the holding, and any additional costs of the award caused by the apportionment shall be directed by the arbitrator to be paid by those persons in such proportions as he shall determine.

Restrictions on compensation for things done in compliance with this Act

76.—(1) Notwithstanding anything in this Act or any custom or agreement -
   (a) no compensation shall be payable to the tenant of an agricultural holding in respect of anything done in pursuance of an order under section 14(4) above,
   (b) in assessing compensation to an outgoing tenant of an agricultural holding where land has been ploughed up in pursuance of a direction under that section, the value per hectare of any tenant's pasture

comprised in the holding shall be taken not to exceed the average value per hectare of the whole of the tenant's pasture comprised in the holding on the termination of the tenancy.

(2) In subsection (1) above "tenant's pasture" means pasture laid down at the expense of the tenant or paid for by the tenant on entering on the holding.

(3) The tenant of an agricultural holding shall not be entitled to any compensation for a relevant improvement specified in Part I of Schedule 8 to this Act or (subject to paragraph 8 of Schedule 12 to this Act) for any such matter as is specified in Part II of Schedule 8 if it is an improvement or matter made or effected for the purposes of section 15(4) above.

No compensation under custom for improvement or tenant-right matter

77.—(1) A landlord or tenant of an agricultural holding shall not be entitled under custom to any compensation from the other for any improvement, whether or not one in respect of the carrying out of which compensation is provided under this Act, or (subject to paragraph 8 of Schedule 12 to this Act) for any matter specified in Part II of Schedule 8 to this Act or otherwise.

(2) Subsection (1) above shall not apply to compensation for an improvement of a kind specified in Schedule 7 or Part I of Schedule 8 to this Act begun before 1st March 1948.

Extent to which compensation recoverable under agreements

78.—(1) Save as expressly provided in this Act, in any case for which apart from this section the provisions of this Act provide for compensation, a tenant or landlord shall be entitled to compensation in accordance with those provisions and not otherwise, and shall be so entitled notwithstanding any agreement to the contrary.

(2) Where the landlord and tenant of an agricultural holding enter into an agreement in writing for any such variation of the terms of the contract of tenancy as could be made by direction or order under section 14 above, the agreement may provide for the exclusion of compensation in the same manner as under section 76(1) above.

(3) Nothing in the provisions of this Act, apart from this section, shall be construed as disentitling a tenant or landlord to compensation in any case for which the said provisions do not provide for compensation, but (subject to paragraph 8 of Schedule 12 to this Act) a claim for compensation in any such case shall not be enforceable except under an agreement in writing.

Amendment
Pt. V excluded by Housing Act 1988 (c.50), s. 101.
Part VI
Market Gardens and Smallholdings

Additional rights with respect to improvements for tenants of market gardens

79.—(1) Subsections (2) to (5) below apply in the case of an agricultural holding in respect of which it is agreed by an agreement in writing that the holding shall be let or treated as a market garden; and where the land to which such agreement relates consists of part of an agricultural holding only, those subsections shall apply as if that part were a separate holding.

(2) The provisions of this Act shall apply as if improvements of a kind specified in Schedule 10 to this Act begun on or after 1st March 1948 were included amongst the improvements specified in Part I of Schedule 8 to this Act and as if improvements begun before that day consisting of the erection or enlargement of buildings for the purpose of the trade or business of a market gardener were included amongst the improvements specified in Part II of Schedule 9 to this Act.

(3) In section 10 above -
   (a) subsection (2)(c) shall not exclude that section from applying to any building erected by the tenant on the holding or acquired by him for the purposes of his trade or business as a market gardener, and
   (b) subsection (2)(d) shall not exclude that section from applying to any building acquired by him for those purposes (whenever erected).

(4) It shall be lawful for the tenant to remove all fruit trees and fruit bushes planted by him on the holding and not permanently set out, but if the tenant does not remove them before the termination of his tenancy they shall remain the property of the landlord and the tenant shall not be entitled to any compensation in respect of them.

(5) The right of an incoming tenant to claim compensation in respect of the whole or part of an improvement which he has purchased may be exercised although his landlord has not consented in writing to the purchase.

Power of Tribunal to direct holding to be treated as market garden

80.—(1) Where the tenant of an agricultural holding desires to make on the holding or any part of it an improvement specified in Schedule 10 to this Act and the landlord refuses, or fails within a reasonable time, to agree in writing that the holding or that part of it, as the case may be, shall be treated as a market garden, the tenant may apply to the Tribunal for a direction under subsection (2) below.

(2) On such an application, the Tribunal may, after being satisfied that the holding or part is suitable for the purposes of market gardening, direct that subsections (2) to (5) of section 79 above shall, either in respect of all the improvements specified in the said Schedule 10 or in respect of some only of those improvements, apply to the holding or to that part of it; and the said subsections shall apply accordingly as respects any improvements executed after the date on which the direction is given.

(3) Where a direction is given under subsection (2) above, then, if the tenancy is terminated by notice to quit given by the tenant or by reason of the tenant becoming insolvent, the tenant shall not be entitled to compensation in respect of improvements specified in the direction unless the conditions mentioned in subsection (4) below are satisfied.

(4) Those conditions are that -
   (a) the tenant not later than one month after the date on which the notice to quit is given or the date of the insolvency, as the case may be, or such later date as may be agreed, produces to the landlord an offer in writing by a substantial and otherwise suitable person (being an offer which is to

hold good for a period of three months from the date on which it is produced) -
   (i) to accept a tenancy of the holding from the termination of the existing tenancy, and on the terms and conditions of that tenancy so far as applicable, and,
   (ii) subject as hereinafter provided, to pay to the outgoing tenant all compensation payable under this Act or under the contract of tenancy, and
(b) the landlord fails to accept the offer within three months after it has been produced.

(5) If the landlord accepts any such offer as is mentioned in subsection (4) above, the incoming tenant shall pay to the landlord on demand all sums payable to him by the outgoing tenant on the termination of the tenancy in respect of rent or breach of contractor otherwise in respect of the holding, and any amount so paid may, subject to any agreement between the outgoing tenant and incoming tenant, be deducted by the incoming tenant from any compensation payable by him to the outgoing tenant.

(6) A direction under subsection (2) above may be given subject to such conditions (if any) for the protection of the landlord as the Tribunal think fit.

(7) Without prejudice to the generality of subsection (6) above, where a direction relates to part only of an agricultural holding, it may, on the application of the landlord, be given subject to the condition that it shall become operative only in the event of the tenant's consenting to the division of the holding into two parts, of which one shall be that to which the direction relates, to be held at rents settled, in default of agreement, by arbitration under this Act, but otherwise on the same terms and conditions (so far as applicable) as those on which the holding is held.

(8) A new tenancy created by the acceptance of a tenant in accordance with the provisions of this section on the terms and conditions of the existing tenancy shall be deemed for the purposes of Schedule 2 to this Act not to be a new tenancy.

(9) For the purposes of subsection (3) above a person has become insolvent if any of the events mentioned in section 96(2)(*a*) or (*b*) below has occurred; and the reference in subsection (4) above to the date of the insolvency is a reference to the date of the occurrence of the event in question.

Agreements as to compensation relating to market gardens

81.—(1) Where an agreement in writing secures to the tenant, of an agricultural holding, for an improvement for which compensation is payable by virtue of section 79 or section 80 above, fair and reasonable compensation having regard to the circumstances existing when the agreement was made, the compensation so secured shall, as respects that improvement, be substituted for compensation under this Act.

(2) The landlord and tenant of an agricultural holding who have agreed that the holding shall be let or treated as a market garden may by agreement in writing substitute, for the provisions as to compensation which would otherwise be applicable to the holding, the provisions as to compensation known as the "Evesham custom", and set out in subsections (3) to (5) of section 80 above.

Application of section 15 to small-holdings

82.—(1) Section 15(1) above shall not apply to a tenancy of land let as a small holding by a small holdings authority or by the Minister in pursuance of a scheme, approved by the Minister for the purposes of this section, which -
- (a) provides for the farming of such holdings on a cooperative basis,
- (b) provides for the disposal of the produce of such holdings, or
- (c) provides other centralised services for the use of the tenants of such holdings.

(2) Where it appears to the Minister that the provisions of any scheme approved by him for the purposes of this section are not being satisfactorily carried out, he may, in accordance with subsection (3) below, withdraw his approval to the scheme.

(3) Before withdrawing his approval to a scheme the Minister shall -
- (a) serve a notice on the persons responsible for the management of the scheme specifying a date (not being earlier than one month after the service of the notice) and stating that on that date his approval to the scheme will cease to have effect and that, accordingly, section 15(1) will then apply to the tenancies granted in pursuance of the scheme,
- (b) give to those persons an opportunity of making representations to him; and, if the said notice is not withdrawn by the Minister before the said date, section 15(1) shall as from that date apply to the said tenancies.

Amendment

Pt. VII excluded by Housing Act 1988 (c.50), s. 101.

Part VII
Miscellaneous and Supplemental

Settlement of claims on termination of tenancy

83.—(1) Without prejudice to any other provision of this Act, any claim of whatever nature by the tenant or landlord of an agricultural holding against the other, being a claim which arises -
- (a) under this Act or any custom or agreement, and
- (b) on or out of the termination of the tenancy of the holding or part of it, shall, subject to the provisions of this section, be determined by arbitration under this Act.

(2) No such claim as is mentioned in subsection (1) above shall be enforceable unless before the expiry of two months from the termination of the tenancy the claimant has served notice in writing on his landlord or tenant, as the case may be, of his intention to make the claim.

(3) A notice under subsection (2) above shall specify the nature of the claim; but it shall be sufficient if the notice refers to the statutory provision, custom or term of an agreement under which the claim is made.

(4) The landlord and tenant may, within the period of eight months from the termination of the tenancy, by agreement in writing settle any such claim as is mentioned in subsection (1) above.

(5) Where by the expiry of the said period any such claim as is mentioned in subsection (1) above has not been settled, it shall be determined by arbitration under this Act.

(6) Where a tenant lawfully remains in occupation of part of an agricultural holding after the termination of a tenancy, references in subsections (2) and (4) above to the termination of the tenancy shall, in the case of a claim relating to that part of the holding, be construed as references to the termination of the occupation.

Arbitrations

84.—(1) Any matter which by or by virtue of this Act or regulations made under this Act is required to be determined by arbitration under this Act shall, notwithstanding any agreement (under a contract of tenancy or otherwise) providing for a different method of arbitration, be determined by the arbitration of a single arbitrator in accordance with the provisions of any order under this section, together with the provisions of Schedule 11 to this Act (as for the time being in force); and [Part I of the Arbitration Act 1996] (*Words substituted by Arbitration Act 1996 (c.23), s. 107(1), Sched. 3, para. 45*) shall not apply to any such arbitration.

(2) The Lord Chancellor may by order make provision as to the procedure to be followed in, or in connection with, proceedings on arbitrations under this Act.[53]

(3) An order under this section may in particular -
  (a) provide for the provisions of Schedule 11 to this Act, exclusive of those mentioned in subsection (4) below, to have effect subject to such modifications as may be specified in the order;
  (b) prescribe forms for proceedings on arbitrations under this Act which, if used, shall be sufficient;
  (c) prescribe the form in which awards in such proceedings are to be made.

(4) An order under this section shall not make provision inconsistent with the following provisions of Schedule 11 to this Act, namely paragraphs 1 to 6, 11 to 13, 14(2), 17, 19, 21, 22, 26 to 29 and 32.

(5) In this section "modifications" includes additions, omissions and amendments.

Minor amendments, which relate mainly to the substitution of the president of the RICS for the Minister as the authority for the appointment of arbitrators, were made by the Agricultural Holdings (England and Wales) Rules (Variation) Order 1985 (S.I. 1985 No. 1829) under section 77 of the 1948 act as amended by the 1984 Act (Sched. 3, para, 19 and Sched. 5, para, 14).

Enforcement

85.—(1) Subject to subsection (3) below, where a sum agreed or awarded under this Act to be paid for compensation, costs or otherwise by a landlord or tenant of an agricultural holding is not paid within fourteen days after the time when the

---

[53] See the Agricultural Holdings (Form of Award in Arbitration Proceedings) Order 1990 (S.I. 1990 No. 1472).

payment becomes due, it shall be recoverable, if the county court so orders, as if it were payable under an order of that court.

(2) Where a sum becomes due to a tenant of an agricultural holding in respect of compensation from the landlord, and the landlord fails to discharge his liability within the period of one month from the date on which the sum becomes due, the tenant shall be entitled to obtain from the Minister an order charging the holding with payment of the amount due.

(3) Where the landlord of an agricultural holding is entitled to receive the rents and profits of the holding otherwise than for his own benefit (whether as trustee or in any other character) -
- (a) he shall not be under any liability to pay any sum agreed or awarded under this Act to be paid to the tenant or awarded under this Act to be paid by the landlord, and it shall not be recoverable against him personally, but
- (b) if he fails to pay any such sum to the tenant for one month after it becomes due, the tenant shall be entitled to obtain from the Minister an order charging the holding with payment of the sum.

Power of landlord to obtain charge on holding

86.—(1) Where the landlord of an agricultural holding -
- (a) has paid to the tenant of the holding an amount due to him under this Act, or under custom or agreement, or otherwise, in respect of compensation for an improvement falling within section 64(1) or (4) above, for any such matter as is specified in Part II of Schedule 8 to this Act or for disturbance, or
- (b) has defrayed the cost of the execution by him, in pursuance of a notice served under section 67(5) above, of an improvement specified in Part II of Schedule 7 to this Act, he shall be entitled to obtain from the Minister an order charging the holding or any part of it with repayment of the amount of the compensation or the amount of the cost, as the case may be.

(2) Where there falls to be determined by arbitration under this Act the amount of compensation for an improvement falling within 64(1) or (4) above or for any such matter as is specified in Part II of Schedule 8 to this Act payment of which entitles the landlord to obtain a charge under subsection (1) above, the arbitrator shall, at the request and cost of the landlord, certify -
- (a) the amount of the compensation, and
- (b) the term for which the charge may properly be made having regard to the time at which each improvement or matter in respect of which compensation is awarded is to be deemed to be exhausted.

(3) Where the landlord of an agricultural holding is entitled to receive the rents and profits of the holding otherwise than for his own benefit (whether as trustee or in any other character) he shall, either before or after paying to the tenant of the holding any sum agreed or awarded under this Act to be paid to the tenant for compensation or awarded under this Act to be paid by the landlord, be entitled to obtain from the Minister an order charging the holding with repayment of that sum.

(4) The rights conferred by this section on a landlord of an agricultural holding to obtain an order charging land shall not be exercised by trustees for ecclesiastical or charitable purposes except with the approval in writing of the Charity Commissioners.

General provisions as to charges under this Act on holdings

87.—(1) An order of the Minister under this Act charging an agricultural holding or any part of an agricultural holding with payment or repayment of a sum shall charge it, in addition, with payment of all costs properly incurred in obtaining the charge.

(2) Any such order shall be made in favour of the person obtaining the charge and of his executors, administrators and assigns, and the order shall make such provision as to the payment of interest and the payment of the sum charged by instalments, and shall contain such directions for giving effect to the charge, as the Minister thinks fit.

(3) In the case of a charge under section 86 above the sum charged shall be a charge on the holding or the part of the holding charged, as the case may be, for the landlord's interest in the holding and for all interests in the holding subsequent to that of the landlord, but so that in any case where the landlord's interest is an interest in a leasehold, the charge shall not extend beyond the interest of the landlord, his executors, administrators and assigns.

(4) In the case of a charge under section 86 above where the landlord is not absolute owner of the holding for his own benefit, no instalment or interest shall be made payable after the time when the improvement in respect of which compensation is paid will, in the opinion of the Minister, have become exhausted.

(5) Notwithstanding anything in any deed, will or other instrument to the contrary, where the estate or interest in an agricultural holding of the landlord is determinable or liable to forfeiture by reason of his creating or suffering any charge on it, that estate or interest shall not be determined or forfeited by reason that the tenant obtains a charge on the holding under section 85(2) above or that the landlord obtains a charge on the holding under section 86 above.

(6) A charge created under section 85 above or section 74 of the Agricultural Holdings Act 1948 shall rank in priority to any other charge, however and whenever created or arising; and charges created under those sections shall, as between themselves, rank in the order of their creation.

(7) Any company now or hereafter incorporated by Parliament, and having power to advance money for the improvement of land, may take an assignment of any charge created under section 85(2) or 86(1) above upon such terms and conditions as may be agreed upon between the company and the person entitled to the charge, and may assign any charge of which they have taken an assignment under this subsection.

(8) Subsection (6) above shall bind the Crown.

Power of limited owners to give consents etc

88.—The landlord of an agricultural holding, whatever his estate or interest in it, may, for the purposes of this Act, give any consent, make any agreement or do or have done to him any other act which he might give, make, do or have done to him if he were owner in fee simple or, if his interest is an interest in a leasehold, were absolutely entitled to that leasehold.

Power of limited owners to apply capital for improvements

89.—(1) Where under powers conferred by the Settled Land Act 1925 [...][54] capital money is applied in or about the execution of any improvement specified in Schedule 7 to this Act no provision shall be made for requiring the money or any part of it to be replaced out of income, and accordingly any such improvement shall be deemed to be an improvement authorised by Part I of Schedule 3 to the Settled Land Act 1925.

(2) Where under powers conferred by the Universities and College Estates Act 1925 capital money is applied in payment for any improvement specified in Schedule 7 to this Act no provision shall be made for replacing the money out of income unless the Minister requires such provision to be made under section 26(5) of that Act or, in the case of a university or college to which section 2 of the Universities and College Estates Act 1964 applies, it appears to the university or college to be necessary to make such provision under the said section 26(5) as modified by Schedule I to the said Act of 1964.

Estimation of best rent for purposes of Acts and other instruments

90.—In estimating the best rent or reservation in the nature of rent of an agricultural holding for the purposes of any Act of Parliament, deed or other instrument, authorising a lease to be made provided that the best rent, or reservation in the nature of rent, is reserved, it shall not be necessary to take into account against the tenant any increase in the value of the holding arising from any improvements made or paid for by him.

Power of Minister to vary Schedules 7, 8 and 10

91.—(1) The Minister may, after consultation with such bodies of persons as appear to him to represent the interests of landlords and tenants of agricultural holdings, by order vary the provisions of Schedules 7, 8 and 10 to this Act.[55]

(2) An order under this section may make such provision as to the operation of this Act in relation to tenancies current when the order takes effect as appears to the Minister to be just having regard to the variation of the said Schedules effected by the order.

Advisory committee on valuation of improvements and tenant-right matters

92.—(1) The Minister shall appoint a committee to advise him as to the provisions to be included in regulations under section 66(2) above, consisting of

---

[54] Words repealed by Trusts of Land and Appointment of Trustees Act 1996 (c.47), s. 25(2), Sched. 4.

[55] No variations have been made under this power. Under a similar power in the 1948 Act, in relation to Schedules 3, 4 and 5 of that Act, the Minister varied Schedule 4 three times, by S.I. 1951 No. 2168, S.I. 1978 No. 742 and S.I. 1985 No. 1947. These instruments were revoked by Schedule 15, Part II to the present Act.

such number of persons, having such qualifications, as the Minister thinks expedient, including persons appointed by the Minister as having experience in land agency, farming, estate management and the valuation of tenant-right.[56]

(2) The Minister may pay to the members of the committee such travelling and other allowances as he may with the consent of the Treasury determine.

Service of notices

93.—(1) Any notice, request, demand or other instrument under this Act shall be duly given to or served on the person to or on whom it is to be given or served if it is delivered to him, or left at his proper address, or sent to him by post in a registered letter or by the recorded delivery service.

(2) Any such instrument shall be duly given to or served on an incorporated company or body if it is given or served on the secretary or clerk of the company or body.

(3) Any such instrument to be given to or served on a landlord or tenant shall, where an agent or servant is responsible for the control of the management or farming, as the case may be, of the agricultural holding, be duly given or served if given to or served on that agent or servant.

(4) For the purposes of this section and of section 7 of the Interpretation Act 1978 (service by post), the proper address of any person to or on whom any such instrument is to be given or served shall, in the case of the secretary or clerk of an incorporated company or body, be that of the registered or principal office of the company or body, and in any other case be the last known address of the person in question.

(5) Unless or until the tenant of an agricultural holding has received -
  (a) notice that the person who before that time was entitled to receive the rents and profits of the holding ("the original landlord") has ceased to be so entitled, and
  (b) notice of the name and address of the person who has become entitled to receive the rents and profits, any notice or other document served upon or delivered to the original landlord by the tenant shall be deemed for the purposes of this Act to have been served upon or delivered to the landlord of the holding.

Orders and regulations

94.—(1) Any power to make an order or regulations conferred on the Minister or the Lord Chancellor by any provision of this Act (except section 85 or 86) shall be exercisable by statutory instrument.[57]

(2) Any statutory instrument containing an order or regulations made under any provision of this Act (except section 22(4) or 91 or paragraph 1(2) of Schedule 11)

---

[56] This is the Committee on Agricultural Valuation. The Committee have published four reports, in 1948, 1950, 1969 and 1977 respectively. The reports have been followed by changes based on their recommendation in regard to improvements and tenant right matters and have resulted in the making of regulations under section 66(2).

[57] Readers with queries related to the procedure whereby statutory instruments are made are referred to the current edition of Erskine May's *Parliamentary Practice* (Butterworths).

shall be subject to annulment in pursuance of a resolution of either House of Parliament.

(3) No regulations shall be made under section 22(4) above or paragraph 1(2) of Schedule 11 to this Act unless a draft of the regulations has been laid before and approved by a resolution of each House of Parliament.

(4) An order made under section 91 above shall be of no effect unless approved by a resolution of each House of Parliament.

Crown land

95.—(1) The provisions of this Act, except section 11 above, shall apply to land belonging to Her Majesty in right of the Crown or the Duchy of Lancaster and to land belonging to the Duchy of Cornwall, subject in either case to such modifications as may be prescribed.[58]

(2) For the purposes of this Act -
  (a) as respects land belonging to Her Majesty in right of the Crown, the Crown Estate Commissioners or other the proper officer or body having charge of the land for the time being, or, if there is no such officer or body, such person as Her Majesty may appoint in writing under the Royal Sign Manual, shall represent Her Majesty and shall be deemed to be the landlord,
  (b) as respects land belonging to Her Majesty in right of the Duchy of Lancaster, the Chancellor of the Duchy shall represent Her Majesty and shall be deemed to be the landlord,
  (c) as respects land belonging to the Duchy of Cornwall, such person as the Duke of Cornwall or other the possessor for the time being of the Duchy of Cornwall appoints shall represent the Duke of Cornwall or other the possessor aforesaid, and shall be deemed to be the landlord and may do any act or thing which a landlord is authorised or required to do under this Act.

(3) Without prejudice to subsection (1) above it is hereby declared that the provisions of this Act, except section 11 above, apply to land notwithstanding that the interest of the landlord or tenant is held on behalf of Her Majesty for the purposes of any government department; but those provisions shall, in their application to any land in which an interest is so held, have effect subject to such modifications as may be prescribed.[59]

(4) Any compensation payable under this Act by the Chancellor of the Duchy of Lancaster for long-term improvements shall, and any compensation so payable under section 60(2)(*b*) or 62 above may, be raised and paid as an expense incurred in improvement of land belonging to Her Majesty in right of the Duchy within section 25 of the Duchy of Lancaster Act 1817; and any compensation so payable under this Act for short-term improvements and tenant-right matters shall be paid out of the annual revenues of the Duchy.

(5) Any compensation payable under this Act by the Duke of Cornwall or other the possessor for the time being of the Duchy of Cornwall for long-term

---

[58] No regulations have been made.
[59] No regulations have been made.

improvements shall, and any compensation so payable under section 60(2)(b) or 62 above may, be paid and advances therefor made in the manner and subject to the provisions of section 8 of the Duchy of Cornwall Management Act 1863 with respect to improvements of land mentioned in that section.

(6) Nothing in subsection (5) above shall be taken as prejudicing the operation of the Duchy of Cornwall Management Act 1982.

(7) In this section -

"long-term improvements" means relevant improvements specified in Schedule 7 to this Act, improvements falling within section 64(4) above and improvements specified in Schedule 10 to this Act;

"short-term improvements and tenant-right matters" means relevant improvements specified in Part I of Schedule 8 to this Act and such matters as are specified in Part II of that Schedule.

Amendment

Section 95 extended by Agriculture Act 1986 (c.49), s. 15(4)

Interpretation

96.—(1) In this Act, unless the context otherwise requires—

"agreement" includes an agreement arrived at by means of valuation or otherwise, and "agreed" has a corresponding meaning;

"agricultural holding" has the meaning given by section 1 above;

"agricultural land" has the meaning given by section 1 above;

"agricultural unit" means land which is an agricultural unit for the purposes of the Agriculture Act 1947;

"agriculture" includes horticulture, fruit growing, seed growing, dairy farming and livestock breeding and keeping, the use of land as grazing land, meadow land, osier land, market gardens and nursery grounds, and the use of land for woodlands where that use is ancillary to the farming of land for other agricultural purposes, and "agricultural" shall be construed accordingly;

"building" includes any part of a building;

"Case A", "Case B" (and so on) refer severally to the Cases set out and so named in Part I of Schedule 3 to this Act;

"contract of tenancy" has the meaning given by section 1 above;

"county court", in relation to an agricultural holding, means the county court within the district in which the holding or the larger part of the holding is situated;

"fixed equipment" includes any building or structure affixed to land and any works on, in, over or under land, and also includes anything grown on land for a purpose other than use after severance from the land, consumption of the thing grown or of its produce, or amenity, and any reference to fixed equipment on land shall be construed accordingly;

"landlord" means any person for the time being entitled to receive the rents and profits of any land;

"livestock" includes any creature kept for the production of food, wool, skins, or fur or for the purpose of its use in the farming of land or the carrying on in relation to land of any agricultural activity;

"local government funds" means, in relation to any grant in respect of an improvement executed by the landlord or tenant of an agricultural holding, the funds of any body which, under or by virtue of any enactment, has power to make grants in respect of improvements of the description in question within any particular area (whether or not it is a local authority for that areas);

"the Minister" means—
  (a) in relation to England, the Minister of Agriculture, Fisheries and Food, and
  (b) in relation to Wales, the Secretary of State;

"the model clauses" has the meaning given by section 7 above;

"pasture" includes meadow;

"prescribed" means prescribed by the Minister by regulations;

"relevant improvement"has the meaning given by section 64(2) above;

"tenant" means the holder of land under a contract of tenancy, and includes the executors, administrators, assigns, or trustee in bankruptcy of a tenant, or other person deriving title from a tenant;

"termination", in relation to a tenancy, means the cesser of the contract of tenancy by reason of effluxion of time or from any other cause;

"the Tribunal" means an Agricultural Land Tribunal established under Part V of the Agriculture Act 1947.

(2) For the purposes of this Act, a tenant is insolvent if—
  (a) he has been adjudged bankrupt or has made a composition or arrangement with his creditors, or
  (b) where the tenant is a body corporate, a winding-up order has been made with respect to it or a resolution for voluntary winding-up has been passed with respect to it (other than a resolution passed solely for the purposes of its reconstruction or of its amalgamation with another body corporate).

(3) Sections 10 and 11 of the Agriculture Act 1947 (which specify the circumstances in which an owner of agricultural land is deemed for the purposes of that Act to fulfil his responsibilities to manage the land in accordance with the rules of good estate management and an occupier of such land is deemed for those purposes to fulfil his responsibilities to farm it in accordance with the rules of good husbandry) shall apply for the purposes of this Act.

(4) References in this Act to the farming of land include references to the carrying on in relation to the land of any agricultural activity.

(5) References in this Act to the use of land for agriculture include, in relation to land forming part of an agricultural unit, references to any use of the land in connection with the farming of the unit.

(6) The designations of landlord and tenant shall continue to apply to the parties until the conclusion of any proceedings taken under or in pursuance of this Act in respect of compensation.

SAVING FOR OTHER RIGHTS ETC.

97.—Subject to sections 15(5) and 83(1) above in particular, and to any other provision of this Act which otherwise expressly provides, nothing in this Act shall prejudicially affect any power, right or remedy of a landlord, tenant or other person vested in or exercisable by him by virtue of any other Act or law or under any custom of the country or otherwise, in respect of a contract of tenancy or other contract, or of any improvements, deteriorations, waste, emblements, tillages, away-going crops, fixtures, tax, rate, tithe rentcharge, rent or other thing.

APPLICATION OF ACT TO OLD TENANCIES ETC.

98.—(1) Subject to sections 4 and 34 above, to the provisions of Schedule 12 to this Act and to any other provision to the contrary, this Act applies in relation to tenancies of agricultural holdings whenever created, agreements whenever made and other things whenever done.

(2) The provisions of this Act shall apply in relation to tenancies of agricultural holdings granted or agreed to be granted, agreements made and things done before the dates specified in paragraphs 1 to 5 and 10 of Schedule 12 to this Act (being dates no later than 1st March 1948) subject to the modifications there specified.

(3) Paragraphs 6 to 9 of Schedule 12 to this Act, which make provision with respect to compensation for tenant-right matters in relation to tenants of agricultural holdings who entered into occupation before the dates specified in those paragraphs (being dates no later than 31st December 1951), shall have effect.

TRANSITIONAL PROVISIONS AND SAVINGS

99.—(1) Schedule 13 to this Act, which excepts from the operation of this Act certain cases current at the commencement of this Act and contains other transitional provisions and savings, shall have effect.

(2) The re-enactment in paragraphs 6 to 8 of Schedule 12 to this Act of provisions contained in the Agricultural Holdings Act (Variation of Fourth Schedule) Order 1951[60] shall be without prejudice to the validity of those provisions; and any question as to the validity of any of those provisions shall be determined as if the re-enacting provisions of this Act were contained in a statutory instrument made under the powers under which the original provision was made.

(3) Nothing in this Act (except paragraph 8 of Schedule 13) shall be taken as prejudicing the operation of sections 16 and 17 of the Interpretation Act 1978 (which relate to the effect of repeals).

CONSEQUENTIAL AMENDMENTS

100.—Schedule 14 to this Act shall have effect.

REPEALS AND REVOCATIONS

101.—(1) The enactments specified in Part I of Schedule 15 to this Act are hereby repealed to the extent specified in the third column of that Schedule.

(2) The instruments specified in Part II of Schedule 15 to this Act are hereby revoked to the extent specified in the third column of that Schedule.

CITATION, COMMENCEMENT AND EXTENT

102.—(1) This Act may be cited as the Agricultural Holdings Act 1986.

---

[60] The Agricultural Holdings Act (Variation of Fourth Schedule) Order 1951 (S.I. 1951 No. 2168) is revoked by Schedule 15, Part II. See now Sched. 8, para. 10 and Sched. 12, paras. 6-8.

(2) This Act shall come into force at the end of the period of three months beginning with the day on which it is passed.[61]

(3) Subject to subsection (4) below, this Act extends to England and Wales only.

(4) Subject to subsection (5) below and to paragraph 26(6) of Schedule 14 to this Act, the amendment or repeal by this Act of an enactment which extends to Scotland or Northern Ireland shall also extend there.

(5) Subsection (4) above does not apply to the amendment or repeal by this Act of section 9 of the Hill Farming Act 1946, section 48(4) of the Agriculture Act 1967 or an enactment contained in the Agriculture (Miscellaneous Provisions) Act 1968.

SCHEDULES

SCHEDULE 1

MATTERS FOR WHICH PROVISION IS TO BE MADE IN WRITTEN TENANCY AGREEMENTS

Section 6

1. The names of the parties.

2. Particulars of the holding with sufficient description, by reference to a map or plan, of the fields and other parcels of land comprised in the holding to identify its extent.

3. The term or terms for which the holding or different parts of it is or are agreed to be let.

4. The rent reserved and the dates on which it is payable.

5. The incidence of the liability for rates (including drainage rates).

6. A covenant by the tenant in the event of the destruction by fire of harvested crops grown on the holding for consumption on it to return to the holding the full equivalent manurial value of the crops destroyed, in so far as the return of that value is required for the fulfilment of his responsibilities to farm in accordance with the rules of good husbandry.

7. A covenant by the tenant (except where the interest of the tenant is held for the purposes of a government department or where the tenant has made provision approved by the Minister in lieu of such insurance) to insure against damage by fire all dead stock on the holding and all harvested crops grown on the holding for consumption on it.

8. A power for the landlord to re-enter on the holding in the event of the tenant not performing his obligations under the agreement.

---

[61] The Act was passed on March 18, 1986 and came into force on June 18, 1986.

SCHEDULE 1

9. A covenant by the tenant not to assign, sub-let or part with possession of the holding or any part of it without the landlord's consent in writing.

SCHEDULE 2

Arbitration of Rent: Provisions Supplementary to Section 12

Section 12

Amount of rent

1.—(1) For the purposes of section 12 of this Act, the rent properly payable in respect of a holding shall be the rent at which the holding might reasonably be expected to be let by a prudent and willing landlord to a prudent and willing tenant, taking into account (subject to sub-paragraph (3) and paragraphs 2 and 3 below) all relevant factors, including (in every case) the terms of the tenancy (including those relating to rent), the character and situation of the holding (including the locality in which it is situated), the productive capacity of the holding and its related earning capacity, and the current level of rents for comparable lettings, as determined in accordance with sub-paragraph (3) below.

(2) In sub-paragraph (1) above, in relation to the holding—
  (a) "productive capacity" means the productive capacity of the holding (taking into account fixed equipment and any other available facilities on the holding) on the assumption that it is in the occupation of a competent tenant practising a system of farming suitable to the holding, and
  (b) "related earning capacity" means the extent to which, in the light of that productive capacity, a competent tenant practising such a system of farming could reasonably be expected to profit from farming the holding.

(3) In determining for the purposes of that sub-paragraph the current level of rents for comparable lettings, the arbitrator shall take into account any available evidence with respect to the rents (whether fixed by agreement between the parties or by arbitration under this Act) which are, or (in view of rents currently being tendered) are likely to become, payable in respect of tenancies of comparable agricultural holdings on terms (other than terms fixing the rent payable) similar to those of the tenancy under consideration, but shall disregard—
  (a) any element of the rents in question which is due to an appreciable scarcity of comparable holdings available for letting on such terms compared with the number of persons seeking to become tenants of such holdings on such terms,
  (b) any element of those rents which is due to the fact that the tenant of, or a person tendering for, any comparable holding is in occupation of other land in the vicinity of that holding that may conveniently be occupied together with that holding, and

(c) any effect on those rents which is due to any allowances or reductions made in consideration of the charging of premiums.

2.—(1) On a reference under section 12 of this Act, the arbitrator shall disregard any increase in the rental value of the holding which is due to—
   (a) tenant's improvements or fixed equipment other than improvements executed or equipment provided under an obligation imposed on the tenant by the terms of his contract of tenancy, and
   (b) landlord's improvements, in so far as the landlord has received or will receive grants out of money provided by Parliament or local government funds in respect of the execution of those improvements.

(2) In this paragraph—
   (a) "tenant's improvements" means any improvements which have been executed on the holding, in so far as they were executed wholly or partly at the expense of the tenant (whether or not that expense has been or will be reimbursed by a grant out of money provided by Parliament or local government funds) without any equivalent allowance or benefit made or given by the landlord in consideration of their execution,
   (b) "tenant's fixed equipment" means fixed equipment provided by the tenant, and
   (c) "landlord's improvements" means improvements executed on the holding by the landlord.

(3) Where the tenant has held a previous tenancy of the holding, then—
   (a) in the definition of "tenant's improvements" in sub-paragraph (2)(a) above, the reference to any such improvements as are there mentioned shall extend to improvements executed during that tenancy, and
   (b) in the definition of "tenant's fixed equipment" in sub-paragraph (2)(b), the reference to such equipment as is there mentioned shall extend to equipment provided during that tenancy, excluding, however, any improvement or fixed equipment so executed or provided in respect of which the tenant received any compensation on the termination of that (or any other) tenancy.

(4) For the purpose of sub-paragraph (2)(a) above, the continuous adoption by the tenant of a system of farming more beneficial to the holding—
   (a) than the system of farming required by the contract of tenancy, or
   (b) in so far as no system is so required, than the system of farming normally practised on comparable agricultural holdings, shall be treated as an improvement executed at his expense.

3.—On a reference under section 12 of this Act the arbitrator
   (a) shall disregard any effect on the rent of the fact that the tenant who is a party to the arbitration is in occupation of the holding, and
   (b) shall not fix the rent at a lower amount by reason of any dilapidation or deterioration of, or damage to, buildings or land caused or permitted by the tenant.

SCHEDULE 2

Frequency of arbitrations under section 12

4.—(1) Subject to the following provisions of this Schedule, a demand for arbitration shall not be effective for the purposes of section 12 of this Act if the next termination date following the date of the demand falls earlier than the end of three years from any of the following dates, that is to say—
  (a) the commencement of the tenancy, or
  (b) the date as from which there took effect a previous increase or reduction of rent (whether made under that section or otherwise), or
  (c) the date as from which there took effect a previous direction of an arbitrator under that section that the rent should continue unchanged.

(2) The following shall be disregarded for the purposes of sub-paragraph (1)(*b*) above—
  (a) an increase or reduction of rent under section 6(3) or 8(4) of this Act;
  (b) an increase of rent under subsection (1) of section 13 of this Act or such an increase as is referred to in subsection (3) of that section, or any reduction of rent agreed between the landlord and the tenant of the holding in consequence of any change in the fixed equipment provided on the holding by the landlord;
  (c) a reduction of rent under section 33 of this Act.

5.—(1) This paragraph applies in any case where a tenancy of an agricultural holding ("the new holding") commences under a contract of tenancy between—
  (a) a person who immediately before the date of the commencement of the tenancy was entitled to a severed part of the reversionary estate in an agricultural holding ("the original holding") in which the new holding was then comprised, and
  (b) the person who immediately before that date was the tenant of the original holding, and where the rent payable in respect of the new holding at the commencement of the tenancy of that holding represents merely the appropriate portion of the rent payable in respect of the original holding immediately before the commencement of that tenancy.

(2) In any case to which this paragraph applies—
  (a) paragraph (*a*) of sub-paragraph (1) of paragraph 4 above shall be read as referring to the commencement of the tenancy of the original holding, and
  (b) references to rent in paragraphs (*b*) and (*c*) of that sub-paragraph shall be read as references to the rent payable in respect of the original holding, until the first occasion following the commencement of the tenancy of the new holding on which any such increase or reduction of, or direction with respect to, the rent of the new holding as is mentioned in paragraph (*b*) or (*c*) takes effect.

6.—Where under an agreement between the landlord and the tenant of the holding (not being an agreement expressed to take effect as a new contract of tenancy between the parties) provision is made for adjustment of the boundaries of

the holding or for any other variation of the terms of the tenancy, exclusive of those relating to rent, then, unless the agreement otherwise provides—
  (a) that provision shall for the purposes of sub-paragraph (1) of paragraph 4 above be treated as not operating to terminate the tenancy, and accordingly as not resulting in the commencement of a new contract of tenancy between the parties, and
  (b) any increase or reduction of rent solely attributable to any such adjustment or variation as aforesaid shall be disregarded for the purposes of paragraph (*b*) of that sub-paragraph.

SCHEDULE 3

CASES WHERE CONSENT OF TRIBUNAL TO OPERATION OF NOTICE TO QUIT IS NOT REQUIRED

Section 26

PART I

THE CASES

Case A

The holding is let as a smallholding by a smallholdings authority or the Minister in pursuance of Part III of the Agriculture Act 1970 and was so let on or after 12th September 1984, and
  (a) the tenant has attained the age of sixty-five, and
  (b) if the result of the notice to quit taking effect would be to deprive the tenant of living accommodation occupied by him under the tenancy, suitable alternative accommodation is available for him, or will be available for him when the notice takes effect, and
  (c) the instrument under which the tenancy was granted contains an acknowledgment signed by the tenant that the tenancy is subject to the provisions of this Case (or to those of Case I in section 2(3) of the Agricultural Holdings (Notices to Quit) Act 1977),
and it is stated in the notice to quit that it is given by reason of the said matter.

Case B

The notice to quit is given on the ground that the land is required for a use, other than for agriculture—
  (a) for which permission has been granted on an application made under the enactments relating to town and country planning,
  (b) for which permission under those enactments is granted by a general development order by reason only of the fact that the use is authorised by—
    (i) a private or local Act,

SCHEDULE 3

      (ii) an order approved by both Houses of Parliament,
      (iii) an order made under section 14 or 16 of the Harbours Act 1964,
(c) for which any provision that—
      (i) is contained in an Act, but
      (ii) does not form part of the enactments relating to town and country planning,

deems permission under those enactments to have been granted,

(d) which any provision deems not to constitute development for the purposes of those enactments, or

(e) for which permission is not required under the enactments relating to town and country planning by reason only of Crown immunity,

and that fact is stated in the notice.[62]

Case C

Not more than six months before the giving of the notice to quit, the Tribunal granted a certificate under paragraph 9 of Part II of this Schedule that the tenant of the holding was not fulfilling his responsibilities to farm in accordance with the rules of good husbandry, and that fact is stated in the notice.

Case D

At the date of the giving of the notice to quit the tenant had failed to comply with a notice in writing served on him by the landlord, being either—

(a) a notice requiring him within two months from the service of the notice to pay any rent due in respect of the agricultural holding to which the notice to quit relates, or

(b) a notice requiring him within a reasonable period specified in the notice to remedy any breach by the tenant that was capable of being remedied of any term or condition of his tenancy which was not inconsistent with his responsibilities to farm in accordance with the rules of good husbandry,

and it is stated in the notice to quit that it is given by reason of the said matter.

Case E

At the date of the giving of the notice to quit the interest of the landlord in the agricultural holding had been materially prejudiced by the commission by the tenant of a breach, which was not capable of being remedied, of any term or condition of the tenancy that was not inconsistent with the tenant's responsibilities to farm in accordance with the rules of good husbandry, and it is stated in the notice that it is given by reason of the said matter.

---

[62] Sched. 3, Pt. I, Case B substituted by Agricultural Holdings (Amendment) Act 1990 (c.15), ss. 1(1)(2), 2.

Case F

At the date of the giving of the notice to quit the tenant was a person who had become insolvent, and it is stated in the notice that it is given by reason of the said matter.

Case G

The notice to quit is given—
  (a) following the death of a person who immediately before his death was the sole (or sole surviving) tenant under the contract of tenancy, and
  (b) not later than the end of the period of three months beginning with the date of any relevant notice,

and it is stated in the notice to quit that it is given by reason of that person's death.

Case H

The notice to quit is given by the Minister and—
  (a) the Minister certifies in writing that the notice to quit is given in order to enable him to use or dispose of the land for the purpose of effecting any amalgamation (within the meaning of section 26(1) of the Agriculture Act 1967) or the reshaping of any agricultural unit, and
  (b) the instrument under which the tenancy was granted contains an acknowledgement signed by the tenant that the tenancy is subject to the provisions of this Case (or to those of Case H in section 2(3) of the Agricultural Holdings (Notices to Quit) Act 1977 or of section 29 of the Agriculture Act 1967).

PART II

SUPPLEMENTARY PROVISIONS APPLICABLE TO CASES A, B, C, D, E AND G

Provisions applicable to Case A

1.—Paragraphs 2 to 7 below have effect for determining whether, for the purposes of paragraph (*b*) of Case A, suitable alternative accommodation is or will be available for the tenant.

2.—For the purposes of paragraph (*b*) of Case A, a certificate of the housing authority for the district in which the living accommodation in question is situated, certifying that the authority will provide suitable alternative accommodation for the tenant by a date specified in the certificate, shall be conclusive evidence that suitable alternative accommodation will be available for him by that date.

3.—Where no such certificate as is mentioned in paragraph 2 above has been

SCHEDULE 3

issued, accommodation shall be deemed to be suitable for the purposes of paragraph (*b*) of Case A if it consists of either—
- (a) premises which are to be let as a separate dwelling such that they will then be let on a protected tenancy (within the meaning of the Rent Act 1977), or
- (b) premises to be let as a separate dwelling on terms which will afford to the tenant security of tenure reasonably equivalent to the security afforded by Part VII of that Act in the case of a protected tenancy, [or] (Word inserted by Housing Act 1988 (c.50), s. 140, Sch. 17 para. 69(1))
- [(c) premises which are to be let as a separate dwelling such that they will then be let on an assured tenancy which is not an assured shorthold tenancy (construing those terms in accordance with Part I of the Housing Act 1988), or
- (d) premises to be let as a separate dwelling on terms which will afford to the tenant security of tenure reasonably equivalent to the security afforded by Chapter I of Part I of that Act in the case of an assured tenancy which is not an assured shorthold tenancy.][63] and the accommodation fulfils the conditions in paragraph 4 below.

[(2) Any reference in sub-paragraph (1) above to an assured tenancy does not include a reference to any tenancy in respect of which possession might be recovered on any of Grounds 1 to 5 in Schedule 2 to the Housing Act 1988.] [64]

4.—(1) The accommodation must be reasonably suitable to the needs of the tenant's family as regards proximity to place of work and either—
- (a) similar as regards rental and extent to the accommodation afforded by dwelling-houses provided in the neighbourhood by any housing authority for persons whose needs as regards extent are similar to those of the tenant and his family, or
- (b) reasonably suitable to the means of the tenant and to the needs of the tenant and his family as regards extent and character.

(2) For the purposes of sub-paragraph (1)(*a*) above, a certificate of a housing authority stating—
- (a) the extent of the accommodation afforded by dwelling-houses provided by the authority to meet the needs of tenants with families of such number as may be specified in the certificate, and
- (b) the amount of the rent charged by the authority for dwelling-houses affording accommodation of that extent, shall be conclusive evidence of the facts so stated.

(3) If any furniture was provided by the landlord for use under the tenancy in question, furniture must be provided for use in the alternative accommodation which is either—
- (a) similar to that so provided, or
- (b) reasonably suitable to the needs of the tenant and his family.

---

[63] Sched. 3, Pt. II, para. 3(c)(d) inserted by Housing Act 1988 (c.50), s. 140, Sched. 17, para. 69(1).

[64] Sched. 3, Pt. II, para. 3(2) inserted by Housing Act 1988 (c.50), s. 140, Sched. 17, para. 69(2).

AGRICULTURAL HOLDINGS ACT 1986

5.—Accommodation shall not be deemed to be suitable to the needs of the tenant and his family if the result of their occupation of the accommodation would be that it would be an overcrowded dwelling-house for the purposes of Part X of the Housing Act 1985.

6.—Any document purporting—
   (a) to be a certificate of a housing authority named in it issued for the purposes of this Schedule, and
   (b) to be signed by the proper officer of the authority, shall be received in evidence and, unless the contrary is shown, shall be deemed to be such a certificate without further proof.

7.—(1) In paragraphs 2, 4 and 6 above "housing authority", and "district" in relation to such an authority, mean a local housing authority and their district within the meaning of the Housing Act 1985.

(2) For the purposes of paragraphs 4 and 5 a dwelling-house may be a house or part of a house.

Provisions applicable to Case B

8.—(1) For the purposes of Case B no account shall be taken of any permission granted as mentioned in paragraph (a) of that Case if the permission—
   (a) [...][65]
   (b) relates to the working of coal by opencast operations, and
   (c) was granted subject to a restoration condition and to an aftercare condition in which the use specified is use for agriculture or use for forestry.

(2) In this paragraph "restoration condition" and "aftercare condition" have the meaning given by [section 336(1) of the Town and Country Planning Act 1990][66].

[8A.—(1) For the purposes of Case B—
   (a) "general development order" means an order under section 59 of the Town and Country Planning Act 1990 which is made as a general order, and
   (b) "the enactments relating to town and country planning" means the planning Acts (as defined in section 336(1) of the Town and Country Planning Act 1990 and any enactment amending or replacing any of those Acts.

(2) In relation to any time before the commencement of Part III of the Town and Country Planning Act 1990, sub-paragraph (1) above shall have effect as if—
   (a) in paragraph (*a*), for '59' there were substituted '24' and for '1990' there were substituted '1971', and

---

[65] Repealed by Coal Industry Act 1994 (c.21), s. 67, Sched. 9, para. 35, Sched. 11, Pt. II.
[66] Words substituted by Planning (Consequential provisions) Act 1990 (c.11), s. 4, Sched. 2, para. 72.

SCHEDULE 3

(b) in paragraph (*b*), for the words from 'planning Acts' onwards there were substituted 'repealed enactments (as defined in section 1(1) of the Planning (Consequential Provisions) Act)'[67].]

Provisions applicable to Case C

9.—(1) For the purposes of Case C the landlord of an agricultural holding may apply to the Tribunal for a certificate that the tenant is not fulfilling his responsibilities to farm in accordance with the rules of good husbandry; and the Tribunal, if satisfied that the tenant is not fulfilling his said responsibilities, shall grant such a certificate.

(2) In determining whether to grant a certificate under this paragraph the Tribunal shall disregard any practice adopted by the tenant in pursuance of any provision of the contract of tenancy, or of any other agreement with the landlord, which indicates (in whatever terms) that its object is the furtherance of one or more of the following purposes, namely—
  (a) the conservation of flora or fauna or of geological or physiographical features of special interest;
  (b) the protection of buildings or other objects of archaeological, architectural or historic interest;
  (c) the conservation or enhancement of the natural beauty or amenity of the countryside or the promotion of its enjoyment by the public.

[(3) In determining whether to grant a certificate under this paragraph, the Tribunal shall disregard any practice adopted by the tenant in compliance with any obligation accepted or imposed on the tenant under [section 94 or 95 of the Water Resources Act 1991][68] and [69]

Provisions applicable to Case D

10.—(1) For the purposes of Case D—
  (a) a notice such as that mentioned in paragraph (*a*) or (*b*) of that Case must be in the prescribed form,[70]
  (b) where such a notice in the prescribed form requires the doing of any work of repair, maintenance or replacement, any further notice requiring the doing of any such work which is served on the tenant less than twelve months after the earlier notice shall be disregarded unless the earlier notice was withdrawn with his agreement in writing,
  (c) a period of less than six months shall not be treated as a reasonable period within which to do any such work, and

---

[67] Sched. 3, Pt. II, para. 8A inserted by Agricultural Holdings (Amendment) Act 1990 (c.15), ss. 1(3)(2), 2.
[68] Words substituted by Water Consolidation (Consequential Provisions) Act 1991 (c.60), s. 2, Sched. 1, para. 43.
[69] Sched. 3, Pt. II, para. 9(3) inserted by Water Act 1989 (c.15), ss. 58(7), 101(1), 141(6), 160(1)(2)(4), 189(4)-(10), 190, 193(1), Sched. 25, para. 75(a), Sched. 26, paras. 3(1)(2), 17, 40(4), 57(6), 58.
[70] Forms are prescribed by the Agricultural Holdings (Forms of Notice to Pay Rent or to Remedy) Regulations 1987 (S.I. 1987 No. 711).

(d) any provision such as is mentioned in paragraph 9(2) above shall (if it would not otherwise be so regarded) be regarded as a term or condition of the tenancy which is not inconsistent with the tenant's responsibilities to farm in accordance with the rules of good husbandry.

(2) Different forms may be prescribed for the purpose of paragraph (*b*) of Case D in relation to different circumstances.

[(3) For the purposes of that Case compliance with any obligation accepted or imposed on the tenant under [section 94 or 95 of the Water Resources Act 1991] [71] Words substituted by Water Consolidation (Consequential Provisions) Act 1991 (c.60), s. 2, Sched. 1, para. 43. shall not be capable of constituting a breach by the tenant of the terms or conditions of his tenancy.[72]]

Provisions applicable to Case E

11.—(1) Where—
(a) the landlord is a small holdings authority, or
(b) the landlord is the Minister and the holding is on land held by him for the purposes of small holdings, then, in considering whether the interest of the landlord has been materially prejudiced as mentioned in Case E, regard shall be had to the effect of the breach in question not only on the holding itself but also on the carrying out of the arrangements made by the small holdings authority or the Minister (as the case may be) for the letting and conduct of small holdings.

(2) For the purposes of Case E any provision such as is mentioned in paragraph 9(2) above shall (if it would not otherwise be so regarded) be regarded as a term or condition of the tenancy which is not inconsistent with the tenant's responsibilities to farm in accordance with the rules of good husbandry.

[(3) For the purposes of that Case compliance with any obligation accepted or imposed on the tenant under [section 94 or 95 of the Water Resources Act 1991][73] shall not be capable of constituting a breach by the tenant of the terms or conditions of his tenancy.[74]]

Provisions applicable to Case G

12.—For the purposes of Case G—
(a) "tenant" does not include an executor, administrator, trustee in bankruptcy or other person deriving title from a tenant by operation of law, and

---

[71] Words substituted by Water Consolidation (Consequential Provisions) Act 1991 (c.60), s. 2, Sched. 1, para. 43.

[72] Sched. 3, Pt. II, para. 10(3) inserted by Water Act 1989 (c.15), ss. 58(7), 101(1), 141(6), 160(1)(2)(4), 189(4)-(10), 190, 193(1), Sched. 25, para. 75(b), Sched. 26, 57(6), 58.

[73] Words substituted by Water Consolidation (Consequential Provisions) Act 1991 (c.60), s. 2, Sched. 1, para. 43.

[74] Note 2 Sched. 3, Pt. II, para. 11(3) inserted by Water Act 1989 (c.15), ss. 58(7), 101(1), 141(6), 160(1)(2)(4), 189(4)-(10), 190, 193(1), Sched. 25, para. 75(b), Sched. 26, paras 57(6), 58.

(b) the reference to the date of any relevant notice shall be construed as a reference—
   (i) to the date on which a notice in writing was served on the landlord by or on behalf of an executor or administrator of the tenant's estate informing the landlord of the tenant's death or the date on which the landlord was given notice by virtue of section 40(5) of this Act of any application with respect to the holding under section 39 or 41, or
   (ii) where both of those events occur, to the date of whichever of them occurs first.

SCHEDULE 4

MATTERS FOR WHICH PROVISION MAY BE MADE BY ORDER UNDER SECTION 29[75]

Section 29

1. Requiring any question arising under the provisions of section 26(2) of, and Schedule 3 to, this Act to be determined by arbitration under this Act.

2. Limiting the time within which any such arbitration may be required or within which an arbitrator may be appointed by agreement between the parties, or (in default of such agreement) an application may be made under paragraph 1 of Schedule 11 to this Act for the appointment of an arbitrator, for the purposes of any such arbitration.

3. Extending the period within which a counter-notice may be given by the tenant under section 26(1) of this Act where any such arbitration is required.

4. Suspending the operation of notices to quit until the expiry of any time fixed in pursuance of paragraph 2 above for the making of any such appointment by agreement or application as is there mentioned or, where any such appointment or application has been duly made, until the termination of any such arbitration.

5. Postponing the date at which a tenancy is to be terminated by a notice to quit which has effect in consequence of any such arbitration or of an application under section 26(1) or 28(2) of this act or under provisions made by virtue of paragraph 12 below.

6. Excluding the application of section 26(1) of this Act in relation to sub-tenancies in such cases as may be specified in the order.

7. Making such provision as appears to the Lord Chancellor expedient for the purpose of safeguarding the interests of sub-tenants including provision enabling

---

[75] See the Agricultural Holdings (Arbitration on notices) Order 1987 (SI.1987 No.710).

the Tribunal, where the interest of a tenant is terminated by notice to quit, to secure that a sub-tenant will hold from the landlord on the like terms as he held from the tenant.

8. The determination by arbitration under this Act of any question arising under such a notice as is mentioned in paragraph (b) of Case D, being a notice requiring the doing of any work of repair, maintenance or replacement (including the question whether the notice is capable of having effect for the purposes of that Case).

9. Enabling the arbitrator, on an arbitration under this Act relating to such a notice as is mentioned in paragraph 8 above, to modify the notice—
   (a) by deleting any item or part of an item of work specified in the notice as to which, having due regard to the interests of good husbandry as respects the agricultural holding to which the notice relates and of sound management of the estate of which that holding forms part or which that holding constitutes, the arbitrator is satisfied that it is unnecessary or unjustified, or
   (b) by substituting, in the case of any item or part of an item of work so specified, a different method or material for the method or material which the notice would otherwise require to be followed or used where, having regard to the purpose which that item or part is intended to achieve, the arbitrator is satisfied that—
      (i) the last-mentioned method or material would involve undue difficulty or expense,
      (ii) the first-mentioned method or material would be substantially as effective for the purpose, and
      (iii) in all the circumstances the substitution is justified.

10. Enabling the time within which anything is to be done in pursuance of such a notice as is mentioned in paragraph (b) of Case D to be extended or to be treated as having been extended.

11. Enabling a tenancy, in a case where that time is extended, to be terminated either by a notice to quit served less than twelve months before the date on which it is to be terminated, or at a date other than the end of a year of the tenancy, or both by such a notice and at such a date.

12. Securing that, where a subsequent notice to quit is given in accordance with provisions made by virtue of paragraph 11 above in a case where the original notice to quit fell within section 28(1) of this Act, then, if the tenant serves on the landlord a counter-notice in writing within one month after the giving of the subsequent notice to quit (or, if the date specified in that notice for the termination of the tenancy is earlier, before that date), the subsequent notice to quit shall not have effect unless the Tribunal consent to its operation, and applying section 28(5) of this Act as regards the giving of that consent.

13. The recovery by a tenant of the cost of any work which is done by him in

compliance with a notice requiring him to do it, but which is found by arbitration under this Act to be work which he was not under an obligation to do.

SCHEDULE 5

NOTICE TO QUIT WHERE TENANT IS A SERVICEMAN

Section 30

1. In this Schedule—

"the 1951 Act" means the Reserve and Auxiliary Forces (Protection of Civil Interests) Act 1951;

"period of residence protection" in the case of a service man who performs a period of relevant service, other than a short period of training, means the period comprising that period of service and the four months immediately following the date on which it ends;

"relevant service" means service (as defined in section 64(1) of the 1951 Act) of a description specified in Schedule 1 to that Act;

"serviceman" means a man or woman who performs a period of relevant service;

"short period of training" has the meaning given by section 64(1) of the 1951 Act.

2.—(1) Paragraph 3 below shall have effect where—
   (a) the tenant of an agricultural holding to which this Schedule applies performs a period of relevant service, other than a short period of training, and
   (b) during his period of residence protection there is given to him—
      (i) notice to quit the holding, or
      (ii) notice to quit a part of it to which this Schedule applies.

(2) This Schedule applies to—
   (a) any agricultural holding which comprises such a dwelling-house as is mentioned in section 10 of the Rent Act 1977, that is to say a dwelling-house occupied by the person responsible for the control (whether as tenant or as servant or agent of the tenant) of the farming of the holding, and
   (b) any part of an agricultural holding, being a part which consists of or comprises such a dwelling-house.

3.—(1) Section 26(1) of this Act shall apply notwithstanding the existence of any such circumstances as are mentioned in Cases B to G; but where the Tribunal are satisfied that such circumstances exist, then, subject to sub-paragraph (2) below, the Tribunal shall not be required to withhold their consent to the operation of the notice to quit by reason only that they are not satisfied that circumstances exist such as are mentioned in paragraphs (*a*) to (*f*) of section 27(3) of this Act.

(2) In determining whether to give or withhold their consent under section 26 of this Act the Tribunal—

(a) if satisfied that circumstances exist such as are mentioned in Cases B to G or in section 27(3) of this Act, shall consider to what extent (if at all) the existence of those circumstances is directly or indirectly attributable to the service man's performing or having performed the period of service in question, and

(b) in any case, shall consider to what extent (if at all) the giving of such consent at a time during the period of protection would cause special hardship in view of circumstances directly or indirectly attributable to the service man's performing or having performed that period of service,and the Tribunal shall withhold their consent to the operation of the notice to quit unless in all the circumstances they consider it reasonable to give their consent.

4.—Where the tenant of an agricultural holding to which this Schedule applies performs a period of relevant service, other than a short period of training, and—
  (a) a notice to quit the holding, or a part of it to which this Schedule applies, is given to him before the beginning of his period of residence protection,and
  (b) the tenant duly serves a counter-notice under section 26(1) of this Act, and
  (c) the Tribunal have not before the beginning of his period of residence protection decided whether to give or withhold consent to the operation of the notice to quit, paragraph 3(2) above shall (with the necessary modifications) apply in relation to the giving or withholding of consent to the operation of the notice to quit given in the circumstances mentioned in paragraph 2(1) above.

5. The Lord Chancellor's power under section 29 of this Act to provide for the matters specified in paragraphs 1 to 7 of Schedule 4 to this Act shall apply in relation to the provisions of sections 26 and 27 of this Act as modified by the preceding provisions of this Schedule as they apply in relation to the provisions of those sections apart from this Schedule.[76]

6.—(1) The Lord Chancellor may make regulations—
  (a) for enabling a counter-notice under section 26(1) of this Act to be served on behalf of a service man at a time when he is serving abroad, in a case where a notice to quit is given to him as mentioned in paragraph 2(1) above, and
  (b) for enabling an act or proceedings consequential upon the service of a counter-notice under section 26(1) to be performed or conducted on behalf of a service man at a time when he is serving abroad, either in such a case as is mentioned in paragraph (a) above or in a case where paragraph 4 above applies in relation to him.[77]

---

[76] See the Agricultural Holdings (Arbitration on Notices) Order 1987 (S.I. 1987 No. 710) art.17.
[77] See the Reserve and Auxillary Forces (Agricultural Tenants) Regulations 1959 (S.I. 1959 No. 84).

SCHEDULE 5

(2) References in sub-paragraph (1) above to a time when a serviceman is serving abroad are references to a time when he is performing a period of relevant service and is outside the United Kingdom.

(3) Regulations under this paragraph may contain such incidental and consequential provisions as appear to the Lord Chancellor to be necessary or expedient for the purposes of the regulations.

SCHEDULE 6

ELIGIBILITY TO APPLY FOR NEW TENANCY UNDER PART IV OF THIS ACT

Sections 36 and 50

PART I

"ELIGIBLE PERSON": SUPPLEMENTARY PROVISIONS

Preliminary

1.—(1) In this Schedule—
"the livelihood condition" means paragraph (*a*) of the definition of "eligible person" in section 36(3) of this Act;
"the occupancy condition" means paragraph (*b*) of that definition.

(2) For the purposes of this Schedule a body corporate is controlled by a close relative of the deceased if he or his spouse, or he and his spouse together, have the power to secure—

  (a) by means of the holding of shares or the possession of voting power in or in relation to that or any other body corporate, or

  (b) by virtue of any powers conferred by the articles of association or other document regulating that or any other body corporate, that the affairs of that body corporate are conducted in accordance with his, her or their wishes, respectively.

(3) Any reference in this Schedule to the spouse of a close relative of the deceased does not apply in relation to any time when the relative's marriage is the subject of a decree of judicial separation or a decree of divorce or of nullity of marriage.

The livelihood condition

2.—For the purposes of the livelihood condition, any period during which a close relative of the deceased was, in the period of seven years mentioned in that condition, attending a full-time course at a university, college or other [establishment of higher or further education][78] shall be treated as a period throughout which

---

[78] Words substituted by Education Reform Act 1988 (c.40), ss. 231(7), 235(6), 237, Sched. 12, para. 96.

his only or principal source of livelihood derived from his agricultural work on the holding; but not more than three years in all shall be so treated by virtue of this paragraph.

Commercial unit of agricultural land

3.—(1) In the occupancy condition "commercial unit of agricultural land" means a unit of agricultural land which is capable, when farmed under competent management, of producing a net annual income of an amount not less than the aggregate of the average annual earnings of two full-time, male agricultural workers aged twenty or over.

(2) In so far as any units of production for the time being prescribed by an order under paragraph 4 below are relevant to the assessment of the productive capacity of a unit of agricultural land when farmed as aforesaid, the net annual income which that unit is capable of producing for the purposes of this paragraph shall be ascertained by reference to the provisions of that order.

4.—The Minister shall by order[79]—
   (a) prescribe such units of production relating to agricultural land as he considers appropriate, being units framed by reference to any circumstances whatever and designed for the assessment of the productive capacity of such land, and
   (b) for any period of twelve months specified in the order, determine in relation to any unit of production so prescribed the amount which is to be regarded for the purposes of paragraph 3 above as the net annual income from that unit in that period.

Ministerial statements as to net annual income of land

5.—(1) For the purposes of any proceedings under sections 36 to 48 of this Act in relation to the holding, the Minister shall—
   (a) at the request of any of the following persons, namely any close relative of the deceased, the landlord or the secretary of the Tribunal, and
   (b) in relation to any relevant land, determine by reference to the provisions of any order for the time being in force under paragraph 4 above the net annual income which, in his view, the land is capable of producing for the purposes of paragraph 3 above, and shall issue a written statement of his view and the grounds for it to the person making the request.

(2) In sub-paragraph (1) above "relevant land" means agricultural land which is—
   (a) occupied (or, by virtue of section 58 of this Act or this Part of this Schedule, deemed to be occupied) by any close relative of the deceased (whether he is, where the request is made by such a relative, the person making the request or not), or

---

[79] At the time of writing the current Order is the Agricultural Holdings (Units of Production) Order (S.I. 1996 No. 2163). The Notes to Schedule are those of MAFF and form part of the Order.

SCHEDULE 6

    (b) the subject of an application made under section 39 of this Act by any such relative.

(3) Where—
    (a) for the purposes of any proceedings under sections 36 to 48 of this Act the Minister has issued a statement to any person containing a determination under sub-paragraph (1) above made by reference to the provisions of an order under paragraph 4 above, and
    (b) before any hearing by the Tribunal in those proceedings is due to begin it appears to him that any subsequent order under that paragraph has affected any matter on which that determination was based, he shall make a revised determination under sub-paragraph (1) above and shall issue a written statement of his view and the grounds for it to the person in question.

(4) Any statement issued by the Minister in pursuance of this paragraph shall be evidence of any facts stated in it as facts on which his view is based.

(5) Any document purporting to be a statement issued by the Minister in pursuance of this paragraph and to be signed for or on behalf of the Minister shall be taken to be such a statement unless the contrary is shown.

Occupation to be disregarded for purposes of occupancy condition

6.—(1) Occupation by a close relative of the deceased of any agricultural land shall be disregarded for the purposes of the occupancy condition if he occupies it only—
    (a) under a tenancy approved by the Minister under subsection (1) of section 2 of this Act or under a tenancy falling within subsection (3)(a) of that section,
    (b) under a tenancy for more than one year but less than two years,
    (c) under a tenancy not falling within paragraph (*a*) or (*b*) above and not having effect as a contract of tenancy,
    (d) under a tenancy to which section 3 of this Act does not apply by virtue of section 5 of this Act,

[(dd) under a farm business tenancy, within the meaning of the Agricultural Tenancies Act 1995, for less than five years (including a farm business tenancy which is a periodic tenancy).][80]
    (e) as a licensee, or
    (f) as an executor, administrator, trustee in bankruptcy or person otherwise deriving title from another person by operation of law.

(2) Paragraphs (*a*) to (*e*) of sub-paragraph (1) above do not apply in the case of a tenancy or licence granted to a close relative of the deceased by his spouse or by a body corporate controlled by him.

(3) References in the following provisions of this Schedule to the occupation of land by any person do not include occupation under a tenancy, or in a capacity, falling within paragraphs (*a*) to (*f*) of that sub-paragraph.

---

[80] Sched. 6, para. 6(1)(dd) inserted by Agricultural Tenancies Act 1995 (c.8), s. 40, Sched., para. 32.

Joint occupation

7.—(1) Where any agricultural land is jointly occupied by a close relative of the deceased and one or more other persons as—
- (a) beneficial joint tenants,
- (b) tenants in common,
- (c) joint tenants under a tenancy, or
- (d) joint licensees,the relative shall be treated for the purposes of the occupancy condition as occupying the whole of the land.

(2) If, however, the Tribunal in proceedings under section 39 of this Act determine on the application of the close relative that his appropriate share of the net annual income which the land is, or was at any time, capable of producing for the purposes of paragraph 3 above is or was then less than the aggregate of the earnings referred to in that paragraph, then, for the purpose of determining whether the occupancy condition is or was then satisfied in his case, the net annual income which the land is, or (as the case may be) was, capable of so producing shall be treated as limited to his appropriate share.

(3) For the purposes of sub-paragraph (2) above the appropriate share of the close relative shall be ascertained—
- (a) where he is a beneficial or other joint tenant or a joint licensee, by dividing the net annual income which the land is or was at the time in question capable of producing for the purposes of paragraph 3 above by the total number of joint tenants or joint licensees for the time being,
- (b) where he is a tenant in common, by dividing the said net annual income in such a way as to attribute to him and to the other tenant or tenants in common shares of the income proportionate to the extent for the time being of their respective undivided shares in the land.

Deemed occupation in case of Tribunal direction

8.—(1) Where a close relative of the deceased is, by virtue of a direction of the Tribunal under section 39 of this Act, for the time being entitled (whether or not with any other person) to a tenancy of the whole or part of any agricultural holding held by the deceased at the date of death other than the holding, he shall, for the purposes of the occupancy condition, be deemed to be in occupation of the land comprised in that holding or (as the case may be) in that part of that holding.

(2) Where by virtue of sub-paragraph (1) above any land is deemed to be occupied by each of two or more close relatives of the deceased as a result of a direction entitling them to a joint tenancy of the land, the provisions of paragraph 7 above shall apply to each of the relatives as if the land were jointly occupied by him and the other relative or relatives as joint tenants under that tenancy.

Occupation by spouse or controlled company

9.—(1) For the purposes of the occupancy condition and of paragraph 7 above, occupation—
- (a) by the spouse of a close relative of the deceased, or

SCHEDULE 6

(b) by a body corporate controlled by a close relative of the deceased, shall be treated as occupation by the relative.

(2) Where, in accordance with sub-paragraph (1) above, paragraph 7 above applies to a close relative of the deceased in relation to any time by virtue of the joint occupation of land by his spouse or a body corporate and any other person or persons, sub-paragraphs (2) and (3) of that paragraph shall apply to the relative as if he were the holder of the interest in the land for the time being held by his spouse or the body corporate, as the case may be.

Deemed occupation in case of tenancy or licence granted by close relative, spouse or controlled company

10.—(1) Where—
  (a) any agricultural land is occupied by any person under such a tenancy as is mentioned in paragraphs (*a*) to (*d*) of paragraph 6(1) above or as a licensee, and
  (b) that tenancy or licence was granted by a close relative of the deceased or a connected person (or both), being at the time it was granted a person or persons entitled to occupy the land otherwise than under a tenancy, or in a capacity, falling within paragraphs (*a*) to (*f*) of paragraph 6(1), then, unless sub-paragraph (2) below applies, the close relative shall, for the purposes of the occupancy condition, be deemed to be in occupation of the whole of the land.

(2) Where the tenancy or licence referred to in sub-paragraph (1) above was granted by the person or persons there referred to and one or more other persons who were at the time it was granted entitled to occupy the land as mentioned in paragraph (*b*) of that sub-paragraph, sub-paragraphs (2) and (3) of paragraph 7 above shall apply to the close relative as if the land were jointly occupied by him and the said other person or persons as holders of their respective interests for the time being in the land.

(3) In this paragraph "connected person", in relation to a close relative of the deceased, means—
  (a) the relative's spouse, or
  (b) a body corporate controlled by the relative;

and for the purposes of sub-paragraph (2) above and the provisions of paragraph 7 there mentioned any interest in the land for the time being held by a connected person by whom the tenancy or licence was granted shall be attributed to the relative.

PART II

MODIFICATIONS OF PART I OF THIS SCHEDULE IN ITS APPLICATION TO SUCCESSION ON RETIREMENT

11.—The modifications of Part I of this Schedule referred to in section 50(4) of this Act are as follows.

12.—The reference in paragraph 1(1) to section 36(3) of this Act shall be read as a reference to section 50(2) of this Act.

13.—References to a close relative of the deceased shall be read as references to the nominated successor.

14.—In paragraph 5—
  (a) references to sections 36 to 48 of this Act shall be read as references to sections 50 to 58 of this Act,
  (b) the reference in sub-paragraph (1) to any close relative of the deceased shall be read as a reference to the nominated successor, and
  (c) for sub-paragraph (2) there shall be substituted—

"(2) In sub-paragraph (1) above 'relevant land' means agricultural land which is occupied (or, by virtue of this Part of this Schedule, is deemed to be occupied) by the nominated successor."

15.—The reference in paragraph 7(2) to section 39 of this Act shall be read as a reference to section 53 of this Act.

16.—For paragraph 8 there shall be substituted—"8.—Where the nominated successor is, by virtue of a direction of the Tribunal under section 53(7) of this Act, for the time being entitled to a tenancy of any agricultural holding held by the retiring tenant other than the holding he shall, for the purposes of the occupancy condition, be deemed to be in occupation of that holding."

SCHEDULE 7

LONG-TERM IMPROVEMENTS BEGUN ON OR AFTER 1ST MARCH 1948 FOR WHICH COMPENSATION IS PAYABLE

Sections 64, 66, etc.

PART I

IMPROVEMENTS TO WHICH CONSENT OF LANDLORD REQUIRED

1. Making or planting of osier beds.

2. Making of water meadows.

3. Making of watercress beds.

4. Planting of hops.

5. Planting of orchards or fruit bushes.

6. Warping or weiring of land.

SCHEDULE 7

7. Making of gardens.

8. Provision of underground tanks.

Part II

Improvements to which Consent of Landlord or Approval of Tribunal Required

9. Erection, alteration or enlargement of buildings, and making or improvement of permanent yards.

10. Carrying out works in compliance with an improvement notice served, or an undertaking accepted, under Part VII of the Housing Act 1985 or Part VIII of the Housing Act 1974.

11. Erection or construction of loading platforms, ramps, hard standings for vehicles or other similar facilities.

12. Construction of silos.

13. Claying of land.

14. Marling of land.

15. Making or improvement of roads or bridges.

16. Making or improvement of water courses, culverts, ponds, wells or reservoirs, or of works for the application of water power for agricultural or domestic purposes or of works for the supply, distribution or use of water for such purposes (including the erection or installation of any structures or equipment which form part of or are to be used for or in connection with operating any such works).

17. Making or removal of permanent fences.

18. Reclaiming of waste land.

19. Making or improvement of embankments or sluices.

20. Erection of wirework for hop gardens.

21. Provision of permanent sheep-dipping accommodation.

22. Removal of bracken, gorse, tree roots, boulders or other like obstructions to cultivation.

23. Land drainage (other than improvements falling within paragraph 1 of Schedule 8 to this Act).

24. Provision or laying-on of electric light or power.

25. Provision of facilities for the storage or disposal of sewage or farm waste.

26. Repairs to fixed equipment, being equipment reasonably required for the proper farming of the holding, other than repairs which the tenant is under an obligation to carry out.

27. The grubbing up of orchards or fruit bushes.

28. Planting trees otherwise than as an orchard and bushes other than fruit bushes.

SCHEDULE 8

Short-term improvements begun on or after 1st March 1948, and other matters, for which compensation payable

Sections 64, 65, etc.

Part I

Improvements (to which no Consent Required)

1. Mole drainage and works carried out to secure its efficient functioning.

2. Protection of fruit trees against animals.

3. Clay burning.

4. Liming (including chalking) of land.

5. Application to land of purchased manure and fertilizer, whether organic or inorganic.

6. Consumption on the holding of corn (whether produced on the holding or not), or of cake or other feeding stuff not produced on the holding, by horses, cattle, sheep, pigs or poultry.

Part II

Tenant-Right Matters

7. Growing crops and severed or harvested crops and produce, being in either case crops or produce grown on the holding in the last year of tenancy, but not including crops or produce which the tenant has a right to sell or remove from the holding.

8. Seeds sown and cultivations, fallows and acts of husbandry performed on the holding at the expense of the tenant (including the growing of herbage crops for commercial seed production).

9. Pasture laid down with clover, grass, lucerne, sainfoin or other seeds, being either—
   (a) pasture laid down at the expense of the tenant otherwise than in compliance with an obligation imposed on him by an agreement in writing to lay it down to replace temporary pasture comprised in the holding when the tenant entered on the holding which was not paid for by him, or
   (b) pasture paid for by the tenant on entering on the holding.

10.—(1) Acclimatisation, hefting or settlement of hill sheep on hill land.
(2) In this paragraph—
"hill sheep" means sheep which—
   (a) have been reared and managed on a particular hill or mountain,
   (b) have developed an instinct not to stray from the hill or mountain,
   (c) are able to withstand the climatic conditions typical of the hill or mountain, and
   (d) have developed resistance to diseases which are likely to occur in the area in which the hill or mountain is situated;
"hill land" means any hill or mountain where only hill sheep are likely to thrive throughout the year.

11.—(1) In areas of the country where arable crops can be grown in an unbroken series of not less than six years and it is reasonable that they should be grown on the holding or part of it, the residual fertility value of the sod of the excess qualifying leys on the holding, if any.
(2) For the purposes of this paragraph—
   (a) the growing of an arable crop includes the growing of clover, grass, lucerne, sainfoin or other seeds grown for a period of less than one year but does not include the laying down of a ley continuously maintained as such for more than one year,
   (b) the qualifying leys comprising the excess qualifying leys shall be those indicated to be such by the tenant, and
   (c) qualifying leys laid down at the expense of the landlord without reimbursement by the tenant or any previous tenant of the holding or laid

down by and at the expense of the tenant pursuant to agreement by him with the landlord for the establishment of a specified area of leys on the holding as a condition of the landlord giving consent to the ploughing or other destruction of permanent pasture or pursuant to a direction given by an arbitrator on a reference under section 14(2) of this Act, shall not be included in the excess qualifying leys.

(3) In this paragraph—

"leys" means land laid down with clover, grass, lucerne, sainfoin or other seeds, but does not include permanent pasture;

"qualifying leys" means—
   (a) leys continuously maintained as such for a period of three or more growing seasons since being laid down excluding, if the leys were undersown or autumn-sown, the calendar year in which the sowing took place, and
   (b) arable land which within the three growing seasons immediately preceding the termination of the tenancy was ley continuously maintained as aforesaid before being destroyed by ploughing or some other means for the production of a tillage crop or crops; and for the purpose of paragraph (*a*) above the destruction of a ley (by ploughing or some other means) followed as soon as practicable by re-seeding to a ley without sowing a crop in the interval between such destruction and such re-seeding shall be treated as not constituting a break in the continuity of the maintenance of the ley;

"the excess qualifying leys" means the area of qualifying leys on the holding at the termination of the tenancy which is equal to the area (if any) by which one-third of the aggregate of the areas of leys on the holding on the following dates, namely,
   (a) at the termination of the tenancy,
   (b) on the date one year prior to such termination, and
   (c) on the date two years prior to such termination, exceeds the accepted proportion at the termination of the tenancy;

"the accepted proportion" means the area which represents the proportion which the total area of the leys on the holding would, taking into account the capability of the holding, be expected to bear to the area of the holding, excluding the permanent pasture on the holding, or, if a greater proportion is provided for by or under the terms of the tenancy, that proportion.

SCHEDULE 9

COMPENSATION TO TENANT FOR IMPROVEMENTS BEGUN BEFORE 1ST MARCH 1948

Sections 64 and 79

SCHEDULE 9

PART I

TENANT'S RIGHT TO COMPENSATION FOR OLD IMPROVEMENTS

1.—

(1) The tenant of an agricultural holding shall, subject to the provisions of this Act, be entitled on the termination of the tenancy, on quitting the holding, to obtain from his landlord compensation for an improvement specified in Part II of this Schedule carried out on the holding by the tenant, being an improvement begun before 1st March 1948.

(2) Improvements falling within sub-paragraph (1) above are in this Schedule referred to as "old improvements".

(3) The tenant of an agricultural holding shall not be entitled to compensation under this Schedule for an improvement which he was required to carry out by the terms of his tenancy where the contract of tenancy was made before 1st January 1921.

(4) Nothing in this Schedule shall prejudice the right of a tenant to claim any compensation to which he may be entitled under custom or agreement, or otherwise, in lieu of any compensation provided by this Schedule.

(5) The tenant of an agricultural holding shall not be entitled to compensation under this Schedule for an old improvement made on land which, at the time when the improvement was begun, was not a holding within the meaning of the Agricultural Holdings Act 1923, as originally enacted, and would not have fallen to be treated as such a holding by virtue of section 33 of that Act.

2.—(1) The amount of any compensation under this Schedule for an old improvement shall be an amount equal to the increase attributable to the improvement in the value of the agricultural holding as a holding, having regard to the character and situation of the holding and the average requirements of tenants reasonably skilled in husbandry.

(2) In the ascertainment of the amount of the compensation payable under this Schedule to the tenant of an agricultural holding in respect of an old improvement, there shall be taken into account any benefit which the landlord has given or allowed to the tenant in consideration of the tenant's executing the improvement, whether expressly stated in the contract of tenancy to be so given or allowed or not.

3.—(1) Compensation under this Schedule shall not be payable for an old improvement specified in any of paragraphs 1 to 15 of Part II of this Schedule unless, before the execution of the improvement, the landlord consented in writing (whether unconditionally or upon terms as to compensation or otherwise agreed between him and the tenant) to the execution of the improvement.

(2) Where the consent was given upon agreed terms as to compensation, compensation payable under the agreement shall be substituted for compensation under this Schedule.

4.—(1) Compensation under this Schedule shall not be payable for an old improvement consisting of that specified in paragraph 16 of Part II of this Schedule

unless the tenant gave to the landlord, not more than three nor less than two months before beginning to execute the improvement, notice in writing under section 3 of the Agricultural Holdings Act 1923 of his intention to execute the improvement and of the manner in which he proposed to execute it, and—
- (a) the landlord and tenant agreed on the terms on which the improvement was to be executed, or
- (b) in a case where no agreement was reached and the tenant did not withdraw the notice, the landlord failed to exercise the right conferred on him by that section to execute the improvement himself within a reasonable time.

(2) Subsection (1) above shall not have effect if the landlord and tenant agreed, by the contract of tenancy or otherwise, to dispense with notice under the said section 3.

(3) If the landlord and tenant agreed (whether after notice was given under the said section 3 or by an agreement to dispense with notice under that section) upon terms as to compensation upon which the improvement was to be executed, compensation payable under the agreement shall be substituted for compensation under this Schedule.

5.—(1) Where the tenant of an agricultural holding has remained in the holding during two or more tenancies, he shall not be deprived of his right to compensation under this Schedule in respect of old improvements by reason only that the improvements were made during a tenancy other than the one at the termination of which he quits the holding.

(2) Where, on entering into occupation of an agricultural holding, the tenant, with the consent in writing of his landlord, paid to an outgoing tenant any compensation payable under or in pursuance of this Schedule (or the Agricultural Holdings Act 1948 or the Agricultural Holdings Act 1923) in respect of the whole or part of an old improvement, he shall be entitled, on quitting the holding, to claim compensation for the improvement or part in the same manner, if at all, as the outgoing tenant would have been entitled if the outgoing tenant had remained tenant of the holding and quitted it at the time at which the tenant quits it.

Part II

Old Improvements for which Compensation is Payable

1. Erection, alteration or enlargement of buildings.

2. Formation of silos.

3. Making and planting of osier beds.

4. Making of water meadows or works of irrigation.

5. Making of gardens.

SCHEDULE 9

6. Making or improvement of roads or bridges.

7. Making or improvement of water courses, ponds, wells or reservoirs or of works for the application of water power or for supply of water for agricultural or domestic purposes.

8. Making or removal of permanent fences.

9. Planting of hops.

10. Planting of orchards or fruit bushes.

11. Reclaiming of waste land.

12. Warping or weiring of land.

13. Embankments and sluices against floods.

14. Erection of wirework in hop gardens.

15. Provision of permanent sheep-dipping accommodation.

16. Drainage.

SCHEDULE 10

MARKET GARDEN IMPROVEMENTS

Sections 79 and 80

1. Planting of standard or other fruit trees permanently set out.

2. Planting of fruit bushes permanently set out.

3. Planting of strawberry plants.

4. Planting of asparagus, rhubarb and other vegetable crops which continue productive for two or more years.

5. Erection, alteration or enlargement of buildings for the purpose of the trade or business of a market gardener.

SCHEDULE 11

ARBITRATIONS

Sections 84 and 94

AGRICULTURAL HOLDINGS ACT 1986

Appointment and remuneration of arbitrator

1.—(1) The arbitrator shall be a person appointed by agreement between the parties or, in default of agreement, a person appointed on the application of either of the parties by the President of the Royal Institution of Chartered surveyors (referred to in this Schedule as "the President") from among the members of the panel constituted for the purposes of this paragraph.

(2) No application may be made to the President for an arbitrator to be appointed by him under this paragraph unless the application is accompanied by such fee as may be prescribed as the fee for such an application,[81] but once the fee has been paid in connection with any such application no further fee shall be payable in connection with any subsequent application for the President to exercise any function exercisable by him in relation to the arbitration by virtue of this Schedule (including an application for the appointment by him in an appropriate case of a new arbitrator).

(3) Any such appointment by the President shall be made by him as soon as possible after receiving the application; but where the application is referable to a demand for arbitration made under section 12 of this Act any such appointment shall in any event not be made by him earlier than four months before the next termination date following the date of the demand (as defined by subsection (4) of that section).

(4) A person appointed by the President as arbitrator shall, where the arbitration relates to an agricultural holding in Wales, be a person who possesses a knowledge of Welsh agricultural conditions, and, if either party to the arbitration so requires, a knowledge also of the Welsh language.

(5) For the purposes of this Schedule there shall be constituted a panel consisting of such number of persons as the Lord Chancellor may determine, to be appointed by him.

[(6) A member of the panel constituted for the purpose of this Schedule shall vacate his office on the day on which he attains the age of seventy years; but this sub-paragraph is subject to section 26(4) to (6) of the Judicial Pensions and Retirement Act 1993 (power to authorise continuance in office up to the age of seventy-five years).][82]

2.—If the arbitrator dies, or is incapable of acting, or for seven days after notice from either party requiring him to act fails to act, a new arbitrator may be appointed as if no arbitrator had been appointed.

3.—In relation to an arbitrator who is appointed in place of another arbitrator (whether under paragraph 2 above or otherwise) the reference in section 12(2) of this Act to the date of the reference shall be construed as a reference to the date when the original arbitrator was appointed.

---

[81] See the Agricultural Holdings (Fee) Regulations 1985 (S.I. 1985 No. 1967): £70. The applications forms are avaliable in Part V: the RICS can be contacted at 12 Great George Street, Parliament Square, London SWIP 3AD (telephone 0171-222-7000).

[82] Sched. 11, para. 1(6) inserted by Judicial Pensions and Retirement Act 1993 (c.8), s. 26, Sched. 6, para. 45.

SCHEDULE 11

4.—Neither party shall have power to revoke the appointment of the arbitrator without the consent of the other party; and his appointment shall not be revoked by the death of either party.

5.—Every appointment, application, notice, revocation and consent under the foregoing paragraphs must be in writing.

6.—The remuneration of the arbitrator shall be—
   (a) where he is appointed by agreement between the parties, such amount as may be agreed upon by him and the parties or, in default of agreement, fixed by the registrar of the county court (subject to an appeal to the judge of the court) on an application made by the arbitrator or either of the parties,
   (b) where he is appointed by the President, such amount as may be agreed upon by the arbitrator and the parties or, in default of agreement, fixed by the President, and shall be recoverable by the arbitrator as a debt due from either of the parties to the arbitration.

Conduct of proceedings and witnesses

7.—The parties to the arbitration shall, within thirty-five days from the appointment of the arbitrator, deliver to him a statement of their respective cases with all necessary particulars and—
   (a) no amendment or addition to the statement or particulars delivered shall be allowed after the expiry of the said thirty-five days except with the consent of the arbitrator,
   (b) a party to the arbitration shall be confined at the hearing to the matters alleged in the statement and particulars delivered by him and any amendment or addition duly made.

Amendment

Sched. 11, para. 7 applied (with modifications) by S.I. 1986 No. 1611, reg. 16(2) and S.I. 1987 No. 908, art. 16(2).

8.—The parties to the arbitration and all persons claiming through them respectively shall, subject to any legal objection, submit to be examined by the arbitrator, on oath or affirmation, in relation to the matters in dispute and shall, subject to any such objection, produce before the arbitrator all samples and documents within their possession or power respectively which may be required or called for, and do all other things which during the proceedings the arbitrator may require.

9.—Witnesses appearing at the arbitration shall, if the arbitrator thinks fit, be examined on oath or affirmation, and the arbitrator shall have power to administer oaths to, or to take the affirmation of, the parties and witnesses appearing.

10.—The provisions of county court rules as to the issuing of witness summonses shall, subject to such modifications as may be prescribed by such rules, apply for the purposes of the arbitration as if it were an action or matter in the county court.

11.—(1) Subject to sub-paragraphs (2) and (3) below, any person who—
  (a) having been summoned in pursuance of county court rules as a witness in the arbitration refuses or neglects, without sufficient cause, to appear or to produce any documents required by the summons to be produced, or
  (b) having been so summoned or being present at the arbitration and being required to give evidence, refuses to be sworn or give evidence, shall forfeit such fine as the judge of the county court may direct.

(2) A judge shall not have power under sub-paragraph (1) above to direct that a person shall forfeit a fine of an amount exceeding £10.

(3) No person summoned in pursuance of county court rules as a witness in the arbitration shall forfeit a fine under this paragraph unless there has been paid or tendered to him at the time of the service of the summons such sum in respect of his expenses (including, in such cases as may be prescribed by county court rules, compensation for loss of time) as may be so prescribed for the purposes of section 55 of the County Courts Act 1984.

(4) The judge of the county court may at his discretion direct that the whole or any part of any such fine, after deducting costs, shall be applicable towards indemnifying the party injured by the refusal or neglect.

12.—(1) Subject to sub-paragraph (2) below, the judge of the county court may, if he thinks fit, upon application on affidavit by either party to the arbitration, issue an order under his hand for bringing up before the arbitrator any person (in this paragraph referred to as a "prisoner") confined in any place under any sentence or [following the transfer of proceedings against him][83] for trial or otherwise, to be examined as a witness in the arbitration.

(2) No such order shall be made with respect to a person confined under process in any civil action or matter.

(3) Subject to sub-paragraph (4) below, the prisoner mentioned in any such order shall be brought before the arbitrator under the same custody, and shall be dealt with in the same manner in all respects, as a prisoner required by a writ of habeas corpus to be brought before the High Court and examined there as a witness.

(4) The person having the custody of the prisoner shall not be bound to obey the order unless there is tendered to him a reasonable sum for the conveyance and maintenance of a proper officer or officers and of the prisoner in going to, remaining at, and returning from, the place where the arbitration is held.

13.—The High Court may order that a writ of habeas corpus ad testificandum shall issue to bring up a prisoner for examination before the arbitrator, if the prisoner is confined in any prison under process in any civil action or matter.

---

[83] Words substituted by Criminal Justice and Public Order Act 1994 (c.33), s. 44, Sched. 4, para. 63.

SCHEDULE 11

Award

14.—(1) Subject to sub-paragraph (2) below, the arbitrator shall make and sign his award within fifty-six days of his appointment.

(2) The President may from time to time enlarge the time limited for making the award, whether that time has expired or not.

Amendment

Sched. 11, para. 14 applied (with modifications) by S.I. 1986 No. 1611, reg. 16(3) and S.I. 1987 No. 908, art. 16(3).

15.—The arbitrator may if he thinks fit make an interim award for the payment of any sum on account of the sum to be finally awarded.

16.—The arbitrator shall—
   (a) state separately in the award the amounts awarded in respect of the several claims referred to him, and
   (b) on the application of either party, specify the amount awarded in respect of any particular improvement or any particular matter the subject of the award.

17.—Where by virtue of this Act compensation under an agreement is to be substituted for compensation under this Act for improvements or for any such matters as are specified in Part II of Schedule 8 to this Act, the arbitrator shall award compensation in accordance with the agreement instead of in accordance with this Act.

18.—The award shall fix a day not later than one month after the delivery of the award for the payment of the money awarded as compensation, costs or otherwise.

Amendment

Sched. 11, para. 14 applied (with modifications) by Agriculture Act 1986 (c.49), s. 13, Sched. 1, Pt. III, para. 11(5), S.I. 1986 No. 1611, reg. 16(4) and S.I. 1987 No. 908, art. 16(4).

19.—The award shall be final and binding on the parties and the persons claiming under them respectively.

20.—The arbitrator shall have power to correct in the award any clerical mistake or error arising from any accidental slip or omission.

Reasons for award

21.—[Section 10 of the Tribunals and Inquiries Act 1992][84] (reasons to be given for decisions of tribunals etc.) shall apply in relation to the award of an arbitrator

---

[84] Words substituted by Tribunals and Inquiries Act 1992 (c.53), s. 18(1), Sched. 3, para. 18.

appointed under this Schedule by agreement between the parties as it applies in relation to the award of an arbitrator appointed under this Schedule otherwise than by such agreement.

Interest on awards

22.—Any sum directed to be paid by the award shall, unless the award otherwise directs, carry interest as from the date of the award and at the [same rate as that specified in section 17 of the Judgments Act 1838 at the date of the award].[85]

Costs

23.—The costs of, and incidental to, the arbitration and award shall be in the discretion of the arbitrator who may direct to and by whom and in what manner the costs, or any part of the costs, are to be paid.

24.—On the application of either party, any such costs shall be taxable in the county court according to such of the scales prescribed by county courtrules for proceedings in the county court as may be directed by the arbitrator under paragraph 23 above, or, in the absence of any such direction, by the county court.

25.—(1) The arbitrator shall, in awarding costs, take into consideration—
   (a) the reasonableness or unreasonableness of the claim of either party, whether in respect of amount or otherwise,
   (b) any unreasonable demand for particulars or refusal to supply particulars, and
   (c) generally all the circumstances of the case.

(2) The arbitrator may disallow the costs of any witness whom he considers to have been called unnecessarily and any other costs which he considers to have been unnecessarily incurred.

Special case, setting aside award and remission

26.—The arbitrator may, at any stage of the proceedings, and shall, upon a direction in that behalf given by the judge of the county court upon an application made by either party, state in the form of a special case for the opinion of the county court any question of law arising in the course of the arbitration and any question as to the jurisdiction of the arbitrator.

27.—(1) Where the arbitrator has misconducted himself, the county court may remove him.

(2) Where the arbitrator has misconducted himself, or an arbitration or award has been improperly procured, or there is an error of law on the face of the award, the county court may set the award aside.

---

[85] Words substituted by Private International Law (Miscellaneous Provisions) Act 1995 (c.42), s. 4.

SCHEDULE 11

28.—(1) The county court may from time to time remit the award, or any part of the award, to the reconsideration of the arbitrator.

(2) In any case where it appears to the county court that there is an error of law on the face of the award, the court may, instead of exercising its power of remission under sub-paragraph (1) above, vary the award by substituting for so much of it as is affected by the error such award as the court considers that it would have been proper for the arbitrator to make in the circumstances; and the award shall there upon have effect as so varied.

(3) Where remission is ordered under that sub-paragraph, the arbitrator shall, unless the order otherwise directs, make and sign his award within thirty days after the date of the order.

(4) If the county court is satisfied that the time limited for making the said award is for any good reason insufficient, the court may extend or further extend that time for such period as it thinks proper.

Miscellaneous

29.—Any amount paid, in respect of the remuneration of the arbitrator by either party to the arbitration, in excess of the amount, if any, directed by the award to be paid by him in respect of the costs of the award shall be recoverable from the other party.

30.—The provisions of this Schedule relating to the fixing and recovery of the remuneration of an arbitrator and the making and enforcement of an award as to costs, together with any other provision in this Schedule applicable for the purposes of or in connection with those provisions, shall apply where the arbitrator has no jurisdiction to decide the question referred to him as they apply where the arbitrator has jurisdiction to decide that question.

31.—For the purposes of this Schedule, an arbitrator appointed by the president shall be taken to have been so appointed at the time when the President executed the instrument of appointment; and in the case of any such arbitrator the periods mentioned in paragraphs 7 and 14 above shall accordingly run from that time.

32.—Any instrument of appointment or other document purporting to be made in the exercise of any function exercisable by the President under paragraph 1, 6 or 14 above and to be signed by or on behalf of the President shall be taken to be such an instrument or document unless the contrary is shown.

SCHEDULE 12

MODIFICATIONS APPLICABLE TO OLD TENANCIES AND OTHER SIMILAR CASES

Sections 65, 70, 76, 77, 78, 98

AGRICULTURAL HOLDINGS ACT 1986

General

1.—Section 2 of this Act shall not apply to an agreement made before 1st March 1948.

2.—Section 3 of this Act shall not apply to a tenancy granted or agreed to be granted before 1st January 1921.

Right to remove fixtures

3.—A tenant shall not be entitled by virtue of section 10(1) or 79 of this Act (or the said section 79 as applied by paragraph 10 below) to remove a fixture or building acquired by him before 1st January 1901.

Notices to quit

4.—(1) Where a tenancy of an agricultural holding subsists under an agreement entered into before 25th March 1947, section 25(1) of this Act does not apply—
   (a) to a notice given by or on behalf of the Secretary of State under the provisions of any agreement of tenancy, where possession of the land is required for naval, military or air force purposes, or
   (b) to a notice given by a corporation carrying on a railway, dock, canal, water or other undertaking in respect of land acquired by the corporation for the purposes of their undertaking or by a government department or local authority, where possession of the land is required by the corporation, government department or authority for the purpose (not being the use of the land for agriculture) for which it was acquired by the corporation, department or authority or appropriated under any statutory provision.

(2) In the application of sub-paragraph (1)(*b*) above to a Board, the reference to land acquired by the corporation for the purposes of their undertaking shall be construed as including a reference to land transferred to that Board by section 31 of the Transport Act 1962 or, in the case of London Regional Transport, by section 16 of the Transport (London) Act 1969, being land—
   (a) acquired, for the purpose of an undertaking vested in the British Transport Commission by Part II of the Transport Act 1947, by the body carrying on that undertaking, or
   (b) acquired by a body carrying on an undertaking vested in any such undertaking as is mentioned in paragraph (*a*) above by virtue of an amalgamation or absorption scheme under the Railways Act 1921, being a scheme that came into operation on or after 7th July 1923,and the reference to the purpose for which the land was acquired or appropriated by the corporation shall be construed accordingly.

(3) In sub-paragraph (2) above "a Board" means any of the following, namely—
   (i) Associated British Ports,
   (ii) the British Railways Board,
   (iii) the British Waterways Board, and

SCHEDULE 12

(iv) London Regional Transport.

(4) Sub-paragraph (2) above shall have effect in relation to a subsidiary of London Regional Transport (within the meaning of the London Regional Transport Act 1984) as it has effect in relation to London Regional Transport, so far as relates to land transferred to London Regional Transport as there mentioned and subsequently transferred to that subsidiary by a scheme made under section 4 or 5 of that Act.

(5) Where by a scheme under section 7 of the Transport Act 1968 relevant land has been transferred by the British Railways Board to another body, sub-paragraph (2) above shall (so far as relates to relevant land so transferred) have effect in relation to that body as it has effect in relation to the British Railways Board; and in this sub-paragraph "relevant land" means land falling within paragraph (*a*) or (*b*) of sub-paragraph (2) above and transferred to the British Railways Board as there mentioned.

(6) Where, by virtue of an Act (whether public, general or local) passed, or an instrument having effect under an Act made, after 7th July 1923 and before 30th July 1948, any right of a corporation carrying on a water undertaking or of a local authority to avail itself of the benefit conferred by section 25(2)(*b*) of the Agricultural Holdings Act 1923 was transferred to some other person, that other person shall have the same right to avail himself of the benefit conferred by sub-paragraph (1)(*b*) above as the corporation or authority would have had if the Act or instrument by virtue of which the transfer was effected had not been passed or made.

Compensation for improvements

5.—The tenant of an agricultural holding shall not be entitled to compensation under section 64(1) of this Act for an improvement which he was required to carry out by the terms of his tenancy where the contract of tenancy was made before 1st January 1921.

Compensation for tenant-right matters

6.—(1) Where the tenant of an agricultural holding entered into occupation of the holding before 1st March 1948, section 65(1) of this Act shall not apply to him as regards the matters specified in paragraphs 7 to 10 of Part II of Schedule 8 to this Act, unless, before the termination of the tenancy, he gives notice in writing to the landlord stating that he elects that it is to apply to him as regards those matters.

(2) Where the tenancy terminates by reason of a notice to quit and at any time while the notice to quit is current the landlord gives notice in writing to the tenant requiring him to elect whether section 65(1) of this Act is to apply to him as regards the matters specified in paragraphs 7 to 10 of Part II of Schedule 8 to this Act, the tenant shall not be entitled to give a notice under sub-paragraph (1) above after the expiry of—

(a) one month from the giving of the notice under this sub-paragraph, or

(b) if the operation of the notice to quit depends upon any proceedings under section 26 or 27 of this Act (including any proceedings under Schedule 3 to this Act), one month from the termination of those proceedings.

7.—(1) This paragraph applies where the tenant of an agricultural holding entered into occupation of the holding before 31st December 1951 and immediately before that date subsection (1) of section 47 of the Agricultural Holdings Act 1948 applied to him as regards the matters now specified in paragraphs 7 to 9 of Part II of Schedule 8 to this Act (whether by virtue of his having entered into occupation of the holding on or after 1st March 1948 or by virtue of a notice having been given under paragraph (c) of the proviso to subsection (1) of the said section 47).

(2) Where this paragraph applies, section 65(1) of this Act shall not apply to the tenant as regards the matters specified in paragraph 10 of Part II of Schedule 8 to this Act unless, before the termination of the tenancy, he gives notice in writing to the landlord that it is to apply to him as regards those matters.

(3) Paragraph 6(2) above shall have effect in relation to a notice under this paragraph as if in that provision there were substituted—
   (a) for the reference to the matters specified in paragraphs 7 to 10 of Part II of Schedule 8 to this Act a reference to the matters specified in paragraph 10 of Part II of that Schedule, and
   (b) for the reference to a notice under paragraph 6(1) above, a reference to a notice under this paragraph.

8.—(1) In a case where, by virtue of paragraph 6 or 7 above, section 65(1) above does not apply to a tenant as regards all or any of the matters specified in paragraphs 7 to 10 of Part II of Schedule 8 to this Act—
   (a) sections 70(4) and (5) and 76(3) of this Act shall have effect with the omission of references to the excluded matters,
   (b) section 77(1) of this Act shall not apply to compensation to the tenant for the excluded matters, and
   (c) section 78(3) of this Act, in so far as it provides that a claim for compensation in a case for which the provisions of this Act do not provide for compensation shall not be enforceable except under an agreement in writing, shall not apply to a claim by a tenant for compensation for the excluded matters.

(2) In this paragraph "the excluded matters" means, in relation to a case to which this paragraph applies, the matters as regards which section 65(1) does not apply to the tenant.

9.—The Minister may revoke or vary the provisions of paragraphs 6 to 8 above so far as they relate to the matters specified in paragraph 10 of Part II of Schedule 8 to this Act as if those provisions were contained in an order made under section 91 of this Act.

SCHEDULE 12

Market gardens

10.—(1) Except as provided by this paragraph, subsections (2) to (5) of section 79 of this Act shall not apply unless the agreement in writing mentioned in subsection (1) of that section was made on or after 1st January 1896.

(2) Where—
(a) under a contract of tenancy current on 1st January 1896 an agricultural holding was at that date in use or cultivation as a market garden with the knowledge of the landlord, and
(b) the tenant had then executed on the holding, without having received before the execution a written notice of dissent by the landlord, an improvement of a kind specified in Schedule 10 to this Act (other than one consisting of such an alteration of a building as did not constitute an enlargement of it), subsections (2) to (5) of section 79 (and section 81) of this Act shall apply in respect of the holding as if it had been agreed in writing after that date that the holding should be let or treated as a market garden.

(3) The improvements in respect of which compensation is payable under subsections (2) to (5) of section 79 of this Act as applied by this paragraph shall include improvements executed before, as well as improvements executed after, 1st January 1896.

(4) Where the land used and cultivated as mentioned in sub-paragraph (2) above consists of part of an agricultural holding only, this paragraph shall apply as if that part were a separate holding.

SCHEDULE 13

TRANSITIONAL PROVISIONS AND SAVINGS

Section 99

Construction of references to old and new law[86]

1.—(1) Any reference, whether express or implied, in any enactment, instrument or document (including this Act and any enactment amended by Schedule 14 to this Act) to, or to things done or falling to be done under or for the purposes of, any provision of this Act shall, if and so far as the nature of the reference permits, be construed as including, in relation to the times, circumstances or purposes in relation to which the corresponding provision repealed by this Act has or had effect, a reference to, or as the case may be, to things done or falling to be done under or for the purposes of, that corresponding provision.

(2) Any reference, whether express or implied, in any enactment, instrument or

---

[86] It is under the provisions of paragraph 1 that statutory instruments made under earlier Acts such as the 1948 Act continue to be operative until new orders or regulations are made under section 94.

document (including the enactments repealed by this Act and enactments, instruments and documents passed or made after the passing of this Act) to, or to things done or falling to be done under or for the purposes of, any provision repealed by this Act shall, if and so far as the nature of the reference permits, be construed as including, in relation to the times, circumstances or purposes in relation to which the corresponding provision of this Act has effect, a reference to, or as the case may be, to things done or falling to be done under or for the purposes of, that corresponding provision.

(3) In this paragraph references to any provision repealed by this Act include references to any earlier provision, corresponding to a provision so repealed, which was repealed by the Agricultural Holdings (Notices to Quit) Act 1977, the Agricultural Holdings Act 1948, the Agricultural Holdings Act 1923 or the Agricultural Holdings Act 1908.

2.—References, in whatever terms, in any enactment a holding within the meaning of the Agricultural Holdings Act 1923 shall be construed as references to an agricultural holding within the meaning of this Act.

Continuation of old law for certain pending cases[87]

3.—(1) Nothing in this Act shall apply in relation to—
  (a) a notice to quit an agricultural holding or part of an agricultural holding—
    (i) given before the commencement of this Act, or
    (ii) in the case of a notice to quit given after that time which includes a statement that it is given by reason of the death of a former tenant, where the date of death was before that time,
  (b) an agricultural holding—
    (i) the tenancy of which terminated before the commencement of this Act, or
    (ii) the tenant of which quitted the holding before the commencement of this Act or quitted after that time in consequence of a notice to quit falling within paragraph (*a*) above,
  (c) an arbitration where the arbitrator was appointed under the Agricultural Holdings Act 1948 before the commencement of this Act,
  (d) an application made before the commencement of this Act to the Tribunal under any of the enactments repealed by this Act, or

---

[87] Attention is drawn to paragraph 3 for the position where a notice to quit has been given, or a death has taken place, before the commencement of the present Act (*i.e.* before June 18, 1986). It will also be noted that the Act does not apply, *i.e.* that the old law will still apply to an arbitration where the arbitrator was appointed under the 1948 Act before that date, and where an application to the Agricultural Land Tribunal was made before that date. Again, the previous enactments will apply even before that date. Again, the previous enactments will apply even where an application was made after that date for a direction entitling the applicant to a tenancy on the death or retirement of the tenant, where the date of death or the date of the giving of he retirement notice took place after that date. But the provisions of paragraph 3 are subject in certain respects to paragraph 11 below.

(e) an application made after the commencement of this Act to the Tribunal for a direction entitling the applicant to a tenancy of an agricultural holding on the death or retirement of the tenant where the date of death or the date of the giving of the retirement notice was before that time; and accordingly the enactments repealed or amended by this Act shall in relation to any such notice to quit, agricultural holding, arbitration (including an award made in such an arbitration) or application (including any proceedings arising out of any such application or any direction given in any such proceedings) continue to have effect as if this Act had not been passed.

(2) This paragraph shall have effect subject to paragraph 1 above and paragraph 11 below.

Periods of time

4.—Where a period of time specified in any enactment repealed by this Act is current at the commencement of this Act, this Act shall have effect as if the corresponding provision of this Act had been in force when the period began to run.

Transfer of functions

5.—Any reference, whether express or implied, in this Act (or any enactment amended by Schedule 14 to this Act) to, or to anything done by, the Minister, the Tribunal, an arbitrator or the President of the Royal Institution of Chartered Surveyors shall where the relevant function has been transferred to that person be construed, in relation to any time before the transfer, as including a reference to, or to the corresponding thing done by, the person by whom the function was then exercisable.

6.—Section 22 of this Act shall have effect in relation to the appointment of a person in pursuance of an application made before 1st January 1986 under section 16(2) of the Agricultural Holdings Act 1948 as if for references to the President of the Royal Institution of Chartered Surveyors there were substituted references to the Minister and as if subsections (4) and (5) were omitted.

7.—(1) Schedule 11 to this Act shall have effect in relation to the appointment of an arbitrator in pursuance of an application made before 1st January 1986 under Schedule 6 to the Agricultural Holdings Act 1948 and in relation to an arbitrator appointed in pursuance of such an application as if—
 (a) for references to the President of the Royal Institution of Chartered Surveyors there were substituted references to the Minister,
 (b) paragraphs 1(2) and 32 were omitted, and
 (c) at the end there were inserted—"33. Where the Minister or any other person acting on behalf of Her Majesty is a party to the arbitration, anything which under this Schedule is to be done by the Minister in relation to the appointment or remuneration of the arbitrator or the

extension of time for making and signing his award shall be done instead by the President of the Royal Institution of Chartered Surveyors."

(2) An order under section 84 of this Act shall not make provision inconsistent with the modifications of Schedule 11 effected by sub-paragraph (1) above.

Compensation

8.—Notwithstanding section 16 of the Interpretation Act 1978, rights to compensation conferred by this Act shall be in lieu of rights to compensation conferred by any enactment repealed by this Act.

Right to remove fixtures

9.—Sections 13 and 67 of the Agricultural Holdings Act 1948 shall continue to have effect (to the exclusion of sections 10 and 79 of this Act) in relation to an agricultural holding in a case where the tenant gave notice under subsection (2)(*b*) of the said section 13 before 12th September 1984 as the said sections 13 and 67 had effect before that date.

Compensation for damage by game

10.—Section 14 of the Agricultural Holdings Act 1948 shall continue to have effect (to the exclusion of section 20 of this Act) in relation to an agricultural holding in a case where a notice was given to the landlord under paragraph (*a*) of the proviso to subsection (1) of the said section 14 before 12th September 1984 as the said section 14 had effect before that date.

Succession on death or retirement

11.—(1) Where Part IV of this Act has effect in relation to an application under that Part, references in that Part to notices to quit[88] shall include references to notices to quit given before the commencement of this Act and, in particular, section 54 of this Act shall apply (to the exclusion of paragraph 4 of Schedule 2 to the Agricultural Holdings Act 1984) in relation to a notice to quit given before the commencement of this Act as it applies in relation to a notice to quit given after that time.

(2) Where, by virtue of paragraph 3(1) above, Part II of the Agriculture (Miscellaneous Provisions) Act 1976 or Schedule 2 to the Agricultural Holdings

---

[88] Paragraph 11 clarifies the position where owing to the date of the application, the succession provisions as enacted in the consolidation Act apply, but notices to quit are given before its commencement, and (the converse case) where, owing to the date of application, the succession provisions, as amended by the 1984 Act apply, but notices to quit are given after the commencement of the consolidation Act. The solution is that in the former case the consolidation Act will apply to notices to quit given before the commencement as well as to those given after; and in the latter case Schedule 2 to the 1984 Act will apply to those given after the commencement as well as to those given before. These provisions apply in particular to section 54 of the present Act and Schedule 2 paragraph 4 to the 1984 Act.

SCHEDULE 13

Act 1984 has effect in relation to an application under the said Part II or, as the case may be, under the said Schedule 2, references in the said Part II or the said Schedule 2 to notices to quit shall include references to notices to quit given after the commencement of this Act and, in particular, paragraph 4 of the said Schedule 2 shall apply (to the exclusion of section 54 of this Act) in relation to a notice to quit given after the commencement of this Act as it applies in relation to a notice to quit given before that time.

(3) This paragraph is without prejudice to the generality of paragraph 1 above.

12.—[...][89]

Record of condition of holding

13.—(1) In section 70(2)(b) of this Act the reference to a record made under section 22 of this Act shall include a reference to a record made before 12th September 1984 under section 16 of the Agricultural Holdings Act 1948 as it had effect before that date.

(2) Sub-paragraph (1) above is without prejudice to the generality of paragraph 1 above.

Insolvency

14.—Sections 80(9) and 96(2) of this Act shall have effect—
  (a) until the date on which Part III of the Insolvency Act 1985 comes into force, and
  (b) on or after that date, in any case in which a petition of bankruptcy was presented, or a receiving order or adjudication in bankruptcy was made, before that date as if for paragraph (*a*) of section 96(2) there were substituted—
  "(*a*) he has become bankrupt or has made a composition or arrangement with his creditors or a receiving order is made against him"."

Forms for arbitration

15.—Any form specified in pursuance of paragraph 15 or 27 of Schedule 6 to the Agricultural Holdings Act 1948 and in force immediately before 12th September 1984 shall have effect as if prescribed by an order under section 84 of this Act, and may be varied or revoked accordingly.

Notices to quit

16.—Paragraphs 10(1)(d) and 11(2) of Part II of Schedule 3 to this Act shall not apply in relation to any act or omission by a tenant which occurred before 12th September 1984.

---

[89] Repealed by Agricultural Tenancies Act 1995 (c.8), s. 31(4).

AGRICULTURAL HOLDINGS ACT 1986

SCHEDULE 14

CONSEQUENTIAL AMENDMENTS

Section 100

The Small Holdings and Allotments Act 1908

1.—(1) Section 47 of the Small Holdings and Allotments Act 1908 shall be amended as follows.

(2) In subsection (1) for the words "section forty-two of the Agricultural Holdings Act 1908" there shall be substituted the words "subsections (2) to (5) of section 79 of the Agricultural Holdings Act 1986".

(3) In subsection (2)—
  (a) for the words "Agricultural Holdings Act 1908", in the first place where they occur, there shall be substituted the words "Agricultural Holdings Act 1986",
  (b) for the words "section forty-two of the Agricultural Holdings Act 1908" there shall be substituted the words "subsections (2) to (5) of section 79 of the Agricultural Holdings Act 1986", and
  (c) for the words "Part III of the First Schedule to the Agricultural Holdings Act 1908" there shall be substituted the words "Schedule 8 to the Agricultural Holdings Act 1986".

(4) In subsection (3) for the words "Agricultural Holdings Act 1908" there shall be substituted the words "Agricultural Holdings Act 1986".

2.—In section 58 of that Act for the words "Agricultural Holdings Act 1908" there shall be substituted the words "Agricultural Holdings Act 1986".

3.—In paragraph (3) of Part II of Schedule 1 to that Act for the words "Agricultural Holdings Act 1908" there shall be substituted the words "Agricultural Holdings Act 1986".

The Law of Distress Amendment Act 1908

4.—In section 4(1) of the Law of Distress Amendment Act 1908 for the words from "live stock" to "Act 1908" there shall be substituted the words "agisted livestock within the meaning of section 18 of the Agricultural Holdings Act 1986 to which that section".

The Chequers Estate Act 1917

5.—In clauses 6B(*b*) and 8D of the Deed set out in the Schedule to the Chequers Estate act 1917 for the words "Agricultural Holdings Act 1948"there shall be substituted the words "Agricultural Holdings Act 1986, except section 60(2)(*b*) or 62 of that Act".

SCHEDULE 14

The Land Settlement (Facilities) Act 1919

6.—In section 2(3) of the Land Settlement (Facilities Act) 1919 for the words "Second Schedule of the Agricultural Holdings Act 1908" there shall be substituted the words "Agricultural Holdings Act 1986".

7.—In section 11(4) of that Act for the words "Second Schedule to the Agricultural Holdings Act 1908" there shall be substituted the words "Agricultural Holdings Act 1986".

8.—[Repealed by Statute Law (Repeals) Act 1993 (c.50), Sched. 1, Pt. II]

The Allotments Act 1922

9.—In section 3(5) of the Allotments Act 1922—
  (a) for the words "Agricultural Holdings Acts 1908 to 1921" there shall be substituted the words "Agricultural Holdings Act 1986",
  (b) for the words "to which those Acts apply" there shall be substituted the words "which is an agricultural holding within the meaning of that Act", and
  (c) for the words "those Acts", in the second and third places where they occur, there shall be substituted the words "that Act".

10.—In section 11(2) of that Act for the words "Second Schedule to the Agricultural Holdings Act 1908" there shall be substituted the words "Agricultural Holdings Act 1986".

The Settled Land Act 1925

11.—In section 73(1) of the Settled Land Act 1925—
  (a) for the words "Agricultural Holdings Act 1923", in both places where they occur, there shall be substituted the words "Agricultural Holdings Act 1986", and
  (b) for the words "Part I or Part II of the First Schedule" there shall be substituted the words "Schedule 7".

The Law of Property Act 1925

12.—(1) In section 99 of the Law of Property Act 1925 (which provides for the making by a mortgagee or mortgagor of such leases as are authorised by that section, which shall be binding on the mortgagor or mortgagee), subsection (13), which provides that the section applies only if and so far as the contrary intention is not expressed in the mortgage deed or otherwise in writing and that the section has effect subject to the terms of the mortgage deed or of any such writing, shall continue not to have effect in relation to a mortgage made after 1st March 1948 of agricultural land within the meaning of the Agriculture Act 1947.

(2) This paragraph shall be construed as one with the said section 99.

The Universities and College Estates Act 1925

13.—In section 26(1) of the Universities and College Estates Act 1925—
  (a) for the words "Agricultural Holdings Act 1923", in both places where they occur, there shall be substituted the words "Agricultural Holdings Act 1986", and
  (b) for the words "Part I and Part II of the First Schedule" there shall be substituted the words "Schedule 7".

The Landlord and Tenant Act 1927

14.—In section 17(1) of the Landlord and Tenant Act 1927 for the words "Agricultural Holdings Act 1923" there shall be substituted the words "Agricultural Holdings Act 1986".

15.—In section 19(4) of that Act for the words "Agricultural Holdings Act 1923" there shall be substituted the words "Agricultural Holdings Act 1986".

The Agricultural Credits Act 1928

16.—In section 5(7) of the Agricultural Credits Act 1928 for the words "Agricultural Holdings Act 1923" there shall be substituted the words "Agricultural Holdings Act 1986, except under section 60(2)(*b*) or 62,".

The Leasehold Property (Repairs) Act 1938

17.—In section 7(1) of the Leasehold Property (Repairs) Act 1938 for the words "Agricultural Holdings Act 1948" there shall be substituted the words "Agricultural Holdings Act 1986".

The Agriculture Act 1947

18.—In section 73(3)(*a*) of the Agriculture Act 1947 for the words "Agricultural Holdings Act 1923" there shall be substituted the words "Agricultural Holdings Act 1986".

19.—In Schedule 2 to that Act—
  (a) in paragraph 1 for the words "any provision of Part III of this Act" there shall be substituted the words "section 14 of the Agricultural Holdings Act 1986", and
  (b) in paragraph 3 for the words "Part III of this Act" there shall be substituted the words "the Agricultural Holdings Act 1986" and for the words "a holding (as defined in the Agricultural Holdings Act 1923)" there shall be substituted the words "an agricultural holding within the meaning of the Agricultural Holdings Act 1986".

SCHEDULE 14

The Reserve and Auxiliary Forces (Protection of Civil Interests) Act 1951

20.—In section 27(1) of the Reserve and Auxiliary Forces (Protection of Civil Interests) Act 1951 for the words "Agricultural Holdings Act 1948" there shall be substituted the words "Agricultural Holdings Act 1986".

The Landlord and Tenant Act 1954

21.—In section 43(1)(*a*) of the Landlord and Tenant Act 1954 for the words from "the proviso" to "the said subsection (1)" there shall be substituted the words "subsection (3) of section 2 of the Agricultural Holdings Act 1986 did not have effect or, in a case where approval was given under subsection (1) of that section".

22.—In section 69(1) of that Act for the words "Agricultural Holdings Act 1948" there shall be substituted the words "Agricultural Holdings Act 1986".

The Agriculture (Safety, Health and Welfare Provisions) Act 1956

23.—In section 24(1) of the Agriculture (Safety, Health and Welfare Provisions) Act 1956 for the words "Agricultural Holdings Act 1948" there shall be substituted the words "Agricultural Holdings Act 1986".

The Coal-Mining (Subsidence) Act 1957

24.—[...][90]

The Opencast Coal Act 1958

[25.—(1) Section 14 of the Opencast Coal Act 1958 shall be amended as follows.
(2) In subsection (2)—
  (a) for the words "Agricultural Holdings Act 1948" there shall be substituted the words "Agricultural Holdings Act 1986", and
  (b) for the words "Act of 1948" there shall be substituted the words "Act of 1986".
(3) In subsections (3) and (4) for the words "Act of 1948" there shall be substituted the words "Act of 1986".
(4) In subsection (5) for the words "Case B in section 2(3) of the Agricultural Holdings (Notices to Quit) Act 1977" there shall be substituted the words "Case B in Part I of Schedule 3 to the Agricultural Holdings Act 1986"; and that subsection shall continue to have effect with the substitution of the words "that Case" for the words "that paragraph" made by paragraph 3(3) of Schedule 1 to the Agricultural Holdings (Notices to Quit) Act 1977.
(5) In subsection (6)—
  (a) for the words from "section 3" to "section 2" there shall be substituted the words "section 27 of the Agricultural Holdings Act 1986 (in which

---

[90] Repealed by Coal Mining Subsidence Act 1991 (c.45), s. 53(2), Sched. 8.

subsections (1) to (3) specify conditions for the giving of consent under section 26", and (*b*) for the words "paragraph (*e*) of the said subsection (3)" there shall be substituted the words "paragraph (*f*) of the said subsection (3)".

(6) In subsection (7) for the words "section 8 of the Act of 1948" there shall be substituted the words "section 12 of the Act of 1986".

(7) In subsection (8) for the words "section 9 of the Act of 1948" there shall be substituted the words "section 13 of the Act of 1986".

[(8) In subsection (9) for paragraph (*a*) there shall be substituted—

"(a) for the references—
  (i) to the Act of 1986 and sections 12, 13 and 26 of that Act there shall be substituted respectively references to the Agricultural Holdings (Scotland) Act 1949 (in this Act referred to as "the Scottish Act of 1949") and sections 7, 8 and 25 of that Act,
  (ii) to section 27 of the Act of 1986, subsections (1) to (3) of that section and paragraph (*f*) of the said subsection (3) there shall be substituted respectively references to section 26 of the Scottish Act of 1949, subsection (1) of that section and paragraph (*e*) of the said sub-section (1), and
  (iii) to Case B in Part I of Schedule 3 to the Act of 1986 there shall be substituted references to paragraph (*c*) of subsection (2) of section 25 of that Act."][91] and [92]

26.—(1) Section 24 of that Act shall be amended as follows.

(2) In subsection (1) for the words "Act of 1948" there shall be substituted the words "Act of 1986".

(3) In subsection (2) for the words "Act of 1948" there shall be substituted the words "Act of 1986".

(4) In subsection (3) for the words "Act of 1948", in each place where they occur, there shall be substituted the words "Act of 1986".

(5) In subsection (5)—
  (a) for the words "section forty-four or section fifty-four of the Act of 1948" there shall be substituted the words "section 69(1) of the Act of 1986 or paragraph 5(1) of Part I of Schedule 9 to that Act", and
  (b) for the words "section forty-five or section fifty-five of the Act of 1948" there shall be substituted the words "section 69(2) or (3) of the Act of 1986 or paragraph 5(2) of Part I of Schedule 9 to that Act".

(6) In subsection (6)—
  (a) for the words "Act of 1948", in both places where they occur, there shall be substituted the words "Act of 1986", and
  (b) for the words "subsection (3) of section seventy" there shall be substituted the words "section 83(4)"; and that subsection in its application to England and Wales shall continue to have effect with the

---

[91] Repealed (S.) by Agricultural Holdings (Scotland) Act 1991 (c.55), s. 88, Sched. 13, Pt. II.
[92] Sched. 14, para. 25 repealed (E.W.) by Housing and Planning Act 1986 (c.63), s. 39(4), Sched. 12, Pt. II.

SCHEDULE 14

substitution for each of the words "four" and "five" of the word "eight" made by paragraph 29 of Schedule 3 to the Agricultural Holdings Act 1984.

(7) In subsection (7)—
   (a) for the words "Act of 1948", in both places where they occur, there shall be substituted the words "Act of 1986" and
   (b) for the words "section fifty-six" there shall be substituted the words "section 70".

(8) In subsection (8) for the words "Act of 1948" there shall be substituted the words "Act of 1986".

(9) In subsection (9) for the words "the Third Schedule to the Act of 1948" there shall be substituted the words "Schedule 7 to the Act of 1986".

(10) After subsection (9) there shall be inserted—

"(9A) In this section the references to the Act of 1986 in subsections (1)(*b*), (7) and (8) and the second and fourth references to that Act in subsection (3) include references to the Agricultural Holdings Act 1948 (in this Act called the Act of 1948) and the reference to section 70 of the Act of 1986 in subsection (7)(*b*) includes a reference to section 56 of the Act of 1948."

[(11) For subsection (10) there shall be substituted—

"(10) In the application of this section to Scotland, for references—
   (a) to the Act of 1986 and to sections 70 and 83(4) of that Act there shall be substituted respectively references to the Scottish Act of 1949 and to sections 56 and 68(3) of that Act,
   (b) to subsections (1), (2) and (3) of section 69 of the Act of 1986 there shall be substituted respectively references to sections 54, and subsections (1) and (2) of section 55 of the Scottish Act of 1949,
   (c) to Parts I and II of Schedule 7 to the Act of 1986 and to the first day of March 1948 there shall be substituted references to Parts I and II of Schedule 1 to the Scottish Act of 1949 and to the first day of November 1948, and
   (d) to sub-paragraphs (1) and (2) of paragraph 5 of Part I of Schedule 9 to the 1986 Act there shall be substituted respectively references to sections 45 and 46 of the Scottish Act of 1949.]"[93]

27.—(1) Section 25 of that Act shall be amended as follows.

(2) In subsection (1)—
   (a) for the words "section fifty-seven of the Act of 1948" there shall be substituted the words "section 71 of the Act of 1986", and
   (b) for the words "section fifty-eight" there shall be substituted the words "section 72".

(3) In subsection (2) for the words "Act of 1948" there shall be substituted the words "Act of 1986".

---

[93] Repealed (S.) by Agricultural Holdings (Scotland) Act 1991 (c.55), s. 88, Sched. 13, Pt. II.

(4) After subsection (2) there shall be inserted—

"(2A) In this section references to the Act of 1986 and to sections 71 and 72 of that Act include respectively references to the Act of 1948 and to sections 57 and 58 of that Act"."

(5) In subsection (3) for the words from "Act of 1948" to "fifty-eight" there shall be substituted the words "Act of 1986 and to sections 71 and 72 ".

28.—(1) Section 26 of that Act shall be amended as follows.

(2) In subsection (3) for the words "Act of 1948" there shall be substituted the words "Act of 1986".

(3) In subsection (5) for the words "section seventy-eight of the Act of 1948, the provisions of the Fourth Schedule" there shall be substituted the words "section 91 of the Act of 1986, the provisions of Schedule 8".

(4) After subsection (5) there shall be inserted—

"(5A) the reference in subsection (3) of this section to the 1986 Act includes a reference to the 1948 Act"."

(5) In subsection (6)—
  (a) for the words "Act of 1948", in the first place where they occur, there shall be substituted the words "Act of 1986", and
  (b) for the words "section seventy-eight of the Act of 1948 and to the Fourth Schedule" there shall be substituted the words "section 91 of the Act of 1986 and to Schedule 8".

29.—(1) Section 27 of that Act shall be amended as follows.

(2) In subsection (1)(*b*) for the words "section thirteen of the Act of 1948" there shall be substituted the words "section 10 of the Act of 1986 ".

(3) In subsection (4) for the words "section thirteen of the Act of 1948" there shall be substituted the words "section 10 of the Act of 1986".

30.—(1) Section 28 of that Act shall be amended as follows.

(2) In subsection (3)—
  (a) for the words "section sixty-seven of the Act of 1948" there shall be substituted the words "subsections (2) to (5) of section 79 of the Act of 1986", and
  (b) for the words "subsection (1) of section sixty-eight" there shall be substituted the words "subsection (2) of section 80".

(3) In subsection (4)—
  (a) for the words "section thirteen of the Act of 1948" there shall be substituted the words "section 10 of the Act of 1986", and
  (b) for the words "paragraph (*b*) of subsection (1) of section sixty-seven of the Act of 1948" there shall be substituted the words "subsection (3) of section 79 of the Act of 1986 ".

(4) In subsection (5) for the words from "section seventy-eight" to "Fifth Schedule" there shall be substituted the words "section 91 of the Act of 1986 the provisions of Schedule 10".

(5) In subsection (6)—

SCHEDULE 14

(a) for the words "section sixty-seven of the Act of 1948 and to paragraph (*b*) of subsection (1)" there shall be substituted the words "subsections (2) to (5) of section 79 of the Act of 1986 and subsection (3) of that section",

(b) for the words "subsection (1) of section sixty-eight of the Act of 1948 and to section thirteen" there shall be substituted the words "subsection (2) of section 80 of the Act of 1986 and to section 10 ", and

(c) for the words "section seventy-eight of the Act of 1948 and to the Fifth Schedule" there shall be substituted the words "section 91 of the Act of 1986 and to Schedule 10".

31.—In section 51(1) of that Act—
(a) after the definition of "the Acquisition of Land Act" there shall be inserted—"'the Act of 1986' means the Agricultural Holdings Act 1986;" and
(b) in the definition of "agricultural holding" for the words "Act of 1948" there shall be substituted the words "Act of 1986".

32.—(1) Schedule 6 to that Act shall be amended as follows.

(2) In paragraph 20(*a*) for the words from "made" to "year" there shall be substituted the words "falling within section 2(3)(*a*) of the 1986 Act".

(3) In paragraph 24—
(a) for the words from "by the Minister" to "1948 ("" there shall be substituted the words "under section 2 of the Act of 1986 or of the Act of 1948 (each of", and
(b) for the words from "by the said Minister" to "of the section)" there shall be substituted the words "under that section from the operation of that section)".

(4) In paragraph 25 for the words from "by the Minister" to "section two" there shall be substituted the words "under section 2 of the Act of 1986 or".

(5) In paragraph 31 for the words from "for the letting" to "Secretary of State" there shall be substituted the words "failing within section 2(3)(*a*) of the 1986 Act, to an agreement for the letting of land and to section 2 of the Act of 1986 there shall be substituted respectively references to a lease of land entered into in contemplation of the use of the land only for grazing or mowing falling within the proviso to section 2(1) of the Scottish Act of 1949, to a lease".

33.—(1) Schedule 7 to that Act shall be amended as follows.

(2) In paragraph 1(2) for the words "Act of 1948" there shall be substituted the words "Act of 1986".

(3) In paragraph 2—
(a) for the words "Act of 1948", in each place where they occur, there shall be substituted the words "Act of 1986", and
(b) after sub-paragraph (3) there shall be inserted—
"(3A) The references in sub-paragraph (1)(*a*) of this paragraph to the Act of 1986 include references to the Act of 1948"."

(4) In paragraph 3—

(a) in sub-paragraph (1) for the words "Act of 1948" there shall be substituted the words "Act of 1986", and
(b) in sub-paragraph (2) for the words "section nine of the Act of 1948 in so far as the said section nine" there shall be substituted the words "section 13 of the Act of 1986 in so far as the said section 13".

(5) In paragraph 4—
(a) in sub-paragraph (2) for the words "Act of 1948" there shall be substituted the words "Act of 1986",
(b) in sub-paragraph (4) for the words "section seventy-seven of the Act of 1948" there shall be substituted the words "section 84 of the Act of 1986" and for the words "Act of 1948", in the second place where they occur, there shall be substituted the words "Act of 1986",
(c) in sub-paragraph (5) for the words "section eight or section nine of the Act of 1948" there shall be substituted the words "section 12 or section 13 of the Act of 1986", and
(d) in sub-paragraph (6) for the words "section nine of the Act of 1948" there shall be substituted the words "section 13 of the Act of 1986".

(6) In paragraph 5—
(a) in sub-paragraph (1) for the words "section thirteen of the Act of 1948" there shall be substituted the words "section 10 of the Act of 1986".
(b) in sub-paragraph (2) for the words "subsection (2)"there shall be substituted the words "subsection (3)",
(c) in sub-paragraph (3) for the words "subsection (2)"there shall be substituted the words "subsection (3)" and for the words "subsection (3)" there shall be substituted the words "subsection (4)", and
(d) in sub-paragraph (5) for the words "section thirteen of the Act of 1948" there shall be substituted the words "section 10 of the Act of 1986" and for the words "paragraph (*b*) of subsection(1) of section sixty-seven" there shall be substituted the words "subsection (3) of section 79".

(7) In paragraph 6(2) for the words "section seventeen of the Act of 1948" there shall be substituted the words "section 23 of the Act of 1986".

[(8) In paragraph 25, for sub-paragraph (*a*) there shall be substituted—
"(a) for references—
(i) to the Act of 1986 and to sections 12, 13, 23 and 84 of that Act there shall be substituted respectively references to the Scottish Act of 1949 and to sections 7, 8, 18 and 75 of that Act.
(ii) to section 10 of the Act of 1986 and to subsections (3) and (4) of that section there shall be substituted respectively references to section 14 of the Scottish Act of 1949 and to subsections (2) and (3) of that section, and
(iii) to subsection (3) of section 79 of the Act of 1986 there shall be substituted references to paragraph (*b*) of subsection (1) of section 65 of the Scottish Act of 1949.][94]

---

[94] Repealed (S.) by Agricultural Holdings (Scotland) Act 1991 (c.55), s. 88, Sched. 13, Pt. II.

SCHEDULE 14

The Chevening Estate Act 1959

34.—In clauses 15(i) and 23(*b*) of the Trust Instrument set out in the Schedule to the Chevening Estate Act 1959 for the words "Agricultural Holdings Act 1948" there shall be substituted the words "Agricultural Holdings Act 1986, except section 60(2)(*b*) or 62 of that Act,".

The Horticulture Act 1960

35.—[...][95]

The Agriculture (Miscellaneous Provisions) Act 1963

36.—In subsections (1)(*a*) and (6)(*c*) of section 22 of the Agriculture (Miscellaneous Provisions) Act 1963 for the words "Agricultural Holdings Act 1948" there shall be substituted the words "Agricultural Holdings Act 1986".

The Agriculture Act 1967

37.—In section 26(1) of the Agriculture Act 1967 for the words "Agricultural Holdings Act 1948", in both places where they occur, there shall be substituted the words "Agricultural Holdings Act 1986".

38.—In section 27(5B)(*a*) of that Act for the words "Agricultural Holdings Act 1948" there shall be substituted the words "Agricultural Holdings Act 1986".

39.—In section 28(1)(*a*) of that Act for the words "section 34 of the Agricultural Holdings Act 1948" there shall be substituted the words "section 60(2)(*a*) of the Agricultural Holdings Act 1986".

40.—In section 29(3)(*a*) of that Act for the words "section 34 of the Agricultural Holdings Act 1948" there shall be substituted the words "section 60(2)(*a*) of the Agricultural Holdings Act 1986".

41.—(1) Section 48 of that Act shall be amended as follows.
(2) In subsection (2)(*a*) for the words "section 34 of the Agricultural Holdings Act 1948" there shall be substituted the words "section 60(2)(*a*) of the Agricultural Holdings Act 1986".
(3) For subsection (4) there shall be substituted—
"(4) Case H in Part I of Schedule 3 to the Agricultural Holdings Act 1986 shall apply in relation to a Rural Development Board as it applies in relation to the Minister within the meaning of that Act."

42.—In paragraph 7(4) of Schedule 3 to that Act for the words "section 77 of the Agricultural Holdings Act 1948" there shall be substituted the words "section 84 of the Agricultural Holdings Act 1986".

---

[95] Repealed by Statute Law (Repeals) Act 1993 (c.50), Sched. 1, Pt. II.

The Leasehold Reform Act 1967

43.—In section 1(3)(*b*) of the Leasehold Reform Act 1967 for the words "Agricultural Holdings Act 1948" there shall be substituted the words "Agricultural Holdings Act 1986".

The Agriculture (Miscellaneous Provisions) Act 1968

44.—In section 12(1) of the Agriculture (Miscellaneous Provisions) Act 1968 for the words from "section 9" to the end there shall be substituted the words "subsection (2)(*b*) of section 60 of the Agricultural Holdings Act 1986(additional compensation to tenant for disturbance) shall apply as if the acquiring authority were the landlord of the holding and on the date of the acquisition or taking of possession the tenancy of the holding or part of it had terminated, and the tenant had quitted the holding or part of it, inconsequence of such a notice or counter-notice as is mentioned in subsection (1) of that section; and section 61 of that Act (exceptions to section 60) shall not apply in such a case."

45.—In section 15(1) of that Act for the words "section 2(1) of the principal Act" there shall be substituted the words "section 2(2) of the Agricultural Holdings Act 1986".

46.—(1) Section 17 of that Act shall be amended as follows.

(2) In subsection (1) for the words "principal Act", in the second place where they occur, there shall be substituted the words "Agricultural Holdings Act 1986".

(3) In subsection (3) for the words "section 87(1) and (2) of the principal Act" there shall be substituted the words "section 95(1), (2) and (3) of the Agricultural Holdings Act 1986".

47.—In section 42(2) of that Act, as it has effect for the purposes of section 48(6) of the Land Compensation Act 1973, for the words "section 24 of the principal Act" there shall be substituted the words "section 26 of the Agricultural Holdings Act 1986" and for the words "principal Act", in the second place where they occur, there shall be substituted the words "Agricultural Holdings Act 1986".

48.—(1) Schedule 3 to that Act shall be amended as follows.
(2) In paragraph 2—
  (a) for the words "section 9(2) of this Act" there shall be substituted the words "section 60(4) of the Agricultural Holdings Act 1986", and
  (b) for the words "section 8 or section 9 of the principal Act" there shall be substituted the words "section 12 or section 13 of the Agricultural Holdings Act 1986".
(3) In paragraph 3—
  (a) for the words "section 8 of the principal Act" there shall be substituted the words "section 12 of the Agricultural Holdings Act 1986", and
  (b) for the words "section 9(2)" there shall be substituted the words "section 60(4)".

SCHEDULE 14

The Tribunals and Inquiries Act 1971

49.—[...]⁹⁶

The Town and Country Planning Act 1971

50.—In section 27(7) of the Town and Country Planning Act 1971 for the words "Agricultural Holdings Act 1948" there shall be substituted the words "Agricultural Holdings Act 1986".

The Land Charges Act 1972

51.—(1) Schedule 2 to the Land Charges Act 1972 shall be amended as follows.

(2) In paragraph (*g*) for the words from "sections" to "tenant or" there shall be substituted the words "section 74 (charge in respect of sums due to" and the words from "section 82" to "improvements)" shall be omitted.

(3) After paragraph 1(*h*) there shall be inserted—
"(i) The Agricultural Holdings Act 1986
Section 85 (charges in respect of sums due to tenant of agricultural holding).
Section 86 (charges in favour of landlord of agricultural holding in respect of compensation for or cost of certain improvements)."

(4) In paragraph 3 for the words from the beginning to "Act 1948" there shall be substituted the words "The reference in paragraph 1(*g*) above to section 74 of the Agricultural Holdings Act 1948 and the references in paragraph 1(i) above to section 85 and 86 of the Agricultural Holdings Act 1986".

The Land Compensation Act 1973

52.—In section 34(3)(*c*) of the Land Compensation Act 1973 for the words "Agricultural Holdings Act 1948" there shall be substituted the words "Agricultural Holdings Act 1986".

53.—(1) Section 48 of that Act shall be amended as follows.
(2) In subsection (2)—
  (a) for the words "Case B in section 2(3) of the Agricultural Holdings (Notices to Quit) Act 1977" there shall be substituted the words "Case B in Part I of Schedule 3 to the Agricultural Holdings Act 1986",
  (b) for the words "section 3(3)(*e*)" there shall be substituted the words "section 27(3)(*f*)"; and that subsection shall continue to have effect with the substitution of the words "the said Case B" for the words "section 24(2)(*b*)" made by paragraph 6 of Schedule 1 to the Agricultural Holdings (Notices to Quit) Act 1977.
(3) In subsection (3) for the words "Case B and section 3(3)(*e*)" there shall be substituted the words "Case B and section 27(3)(*f*)".

---

⁹⁶ Repealed by Tribunals and Inquiries Act 1992 (c.53), s. 18(2), Sched. 4, pt. land consolidated by Tribunals and Inquiries Act 1992 (c.53), Sched. 1, para. 1(*b*).

(4) After subsection (6) there shall be inserted—

"(6A) In assessing the tenant's compensation no account shall be taken of any benefit which might accrue to the tenant by virtue of section 60(2)(*b*) of the Agricultural Holdings Act 1986 (additional payments by landlord for disturbance); and in this subsection the reference to the said section 60(2)(*b*) does not include a reference to it as applied by section 12 of the Agriculture (Miscellaneous Provisions) Act 1968."

54.—(1) Section 56 of that Act shall be amended as follows.

(2) In subsection (3)(*d*) for the words "Agricultural Holdings Act 1948" there shall be substituted the words "Agricultural Holdings Act 1986".

(3) In subsection (4) for the words "section 58 of the Agricultural Holdings Act 1948" there shall be substituted the words "section 72 of the Agricultural Holdings Act 1986 " and for the words "the proviso" there shall be substituted the words "subsection (4) of that section".

55.—(1) Section 59 of that Act shall be amended as follows.

(2) In subsection (1)(*b*)—
  (a) in paragraph (i) for the words "subsection (1) of section 2 of the Agricultural Holdings (Notices to Quit) Act 1977" there shall be substituted the words "section 26(1) of the Agricultural Holdings Act 1986" and for the words "Case B in subsection (3) of that section" there shall be substituted the words "Case B in Part I of Schedule 3 to that Act", and
  (b) in paragraph (ii) for the words "section 3(3)(*e*) "there shall be substituted the words "section 27(3)(*f*)"; and that subsection shall continue to have effect with the substitution of the words "the said Case B" for the words "section 24(2)(*b*)" made by paragraph 6 of Schedule 1 to the Agricultural Holdings (Notices to Quit) Act 1977.

(3) In subsection (2)(*b*) for the words from "Agricultural Holdings Act 1948" to "notice to quit)" there shall be substituted the words "Agricultural Holdings Act 1986 relating to compensation to a tenant on the termination of his tenancy".

(4) In subsection (6) for the words "section 9 of the Agricultural Holdings (Notices to Quit) Act 1977" there shall be substituted the words "section 32 of the Agricultural Holdings Act 1986".

56.—In section 87(1) for the words "Agricultural Holdings Act 1948" there shall be substituted the words "Agricultural Holdings Act 1986".

The Rent (Agriculture) Act 1976

57.—In section 9(3) and (4)(*c*) of the Rent (Agriculture) Act 1976 for the words "Agricultural Holdings Act 1948" there shall be substituted the words "Agricultural Holdings Act 1986".

58.—In paragraph 2 of Schedule 2 to that Act for the words "Agricultural Holdings Act 1948" there shall be substituted the words "Agricultural Holdings Act 1986".

SCHEDULE 14

The Rent Act 1977

59.—In section 10 of the Rent Act 1977 for the words "Agricultural Holdings Act 1948" there shall be substituted the words "Agricultural Holdings Act 1986".

60.—In section 137(3) and (4)(*c*) of that Act for the words "Agricultural Holdings Act 1948" there shall be substituted the words "Agricultural Holdings Act 1986".

The Protection from Eviction Act 1977

61.—In section 8(1)(*d*) of the Protection from Eviction Act 1977 for the words "Agricultural Holdings Act 1948" there shall be substituted the words "Agricultural Holdings Act 1986".

The Cycle Tracks Act 1984

62.—In section 3(2) of the Cycle Tracks Act 1984 for the words "section 1(2) of the Agricultural Holdings Act 1948" there shall be substituted the words "section 1(4) of the Agricultural Holdings Act 1986".

The Housing Act 1985

63.—In paragraph 8 of Schedule 1 to the Housing Act 1985 for the words "Agricultural Holdings Act 1948" there shall be substituted the words "Agricultural Holdings Act 1986".

The Landlord and Tenant Act 1985

64.—In section 14(3) of the Landlord and Tenant Act 1985 for the words "Agricultural Holdings Act 1948" there shall be substituted the words "Agricultural Holdings Act 1986".

SCHEDULE 15

REPEALS AND REVOCATIONS

Section 101

PART I

REPEALS

Chapter	Short title	Extent of repeal
9 & 10 Geo. 6. c. 73.	The Hill Farming Act 1946.	Section 9.

11 & 12 Geo. 6. c. 63.	The Agricultural Holdings Act 1948.	The whole Act. In the Schedule, Part III.
12 & 13 Geo. 6. c. 37.	The Agriculture (Miscellaneous Provisions) Act 1949.	
6 & 7 Eliz. 2. c. 71.	The Agriculture Act 1958.	Section 4. In section 9(1), in the definition of "agricultural holding" the words from "as respects England" to "1948 and", the definitions of "contract of tenancy" and "fixed equipment" and in the definition of "landlord and tenant" the words from "as respects England" to "1948 and". In Schedule 1, in Part I, paragraphs 6, 7, 14 to 18, 20 and 21. In Schedule 4, paragraphs 5, 9 and 11.
1963 c. 11.	The Agriculture (Miscellaneous Provisions) Act 1963.	In section 20, paragraph (*b*), the words "and the period within which the arbitrator is to make his award", the words "the said paragraph 6 or" and paragraph (ii).
1964 c. 51.	The Universities and College Estates Act 1964.	In Schedule 3, in Part I, the entry relating to the Agricultural Holdings Act 1948.
1968 c. 34.	The Agriculture (Miscellaneous Provisions) Act 1968.	Sections 9 and 10. In section 15, subsection (2), in subsection (4) the words from the beginning to "section and", the words "subsection (2) or" and the words "as the case may be" and in subsection (5)(*a*) the words "or subsection (2)". In section 17, in subsection (1) the definition of "the principal Act" and in subsection (2) the words from "references to the termination" to "holding and".
1970 c. 40.	The Agriculture Act 1970.	In Schedule 4, the entry relating to the Agricultural Holdings Act 1948.
1971 c. 23.	The Courts Act 1971.	In Schedule 9, in Part I, the entry relating to the Agricultural Holdings Act 1948.

SCHEDULE 15

1972 c. 61.	The Land Charges Act 1972.	In Schedule 2, in paragraph 1(*g*), the words from "Section 82" to "improvements)".
1972 c. 62.	The Agriculture (Miscellaneous Provisions) Act 1972.	Section 15.
1976 c. 55.	The Agriculture (Miscellaneous Provisions) Act 1976.	Sections 17 to 24. In section 27(5), the words "and Part II". In Schedule 3, the entries relating to the Agricultural Holdings Act 1948. Schedule 3A.
1977 c. 12.	The Agricultural Holdings (Notices to Quit) Act 1977.	The whole Act.
1984 c. 32.	The London Regional Transport Act 1984.	In Schedule 6, paragraph 13.
1984 c. 41.	The Agricultural Holdings Act 1984.	The whole Act.
1985 c. 65.	The Insolvency Act 1985.	In Schedule 8, paragraphs 9 and 30.
1985 c. 63.	The Housing Act 1985.	Section 231.
1985 c. 71.	The Housing (Consequential Provisions) Act 1985.	In Schedule 2, paragraph 34.

PART II

REVOCATIONS

Number	Title	Extent of Revocation
S.I. 1951/2168.	The Agricultural Holdings Act (Variation of Fourth Schedule) Order 1951.	The whole order.
S.I. 1978/447.	The Agricultural Holdings Act 1948 (Amendment) Regulations 1978.	The whole instrument.
S.I. 1978/742.	The Agricultural Holdings Act 1948 (Variation of Fourth Schedule) Order 1978.	The whole order.
S.I. 1985/1947.	The Agricultural Holdings Act 1948 (Variation of Fourth Schedule) Order 1985.	The whole order.

AGRICULTURAL TENANCIES ACT 1995

1995 c. 8

Arrangement of sections

Part I

General provisions

SECTION

Farm business tenancy
1. Meaning of "farm business tenancy".
2. Tenancies which cannot be farm business tenancies.
3. Compliance with notice conditions in cases of surrender and regrant.

Exclusion of Agricultural Holdings Act 1986
4. Agricultural Holdings Act 1986 not to apply in relation to new tenancies except in special cases.

Termination of the tenancy
5. Tenancies for more than two years to continue from year to year unless terminated by notice.
6. Length of notice to quit.
7. Notice required for exercise of option to terminate tenancy or resume possession of part.

Tenant's right to remove fixtures and buildings
8. Tenant's right to remove fixtures and buildings.

Part II

Rent review under farm business tenancy

9. Application of Part II.
10. Notice requiring statutory rent review.
11. Review date where new tenancy of severed part of reversion.
12. Appointment of arbitrator.
13. Amount of rent.
14. Interpretation of Part II.

Part III

Compensation on termination of farm business tenancy

Tenant's entitlement to compensation
15. Meaning of "tenant's improvement".
16. Tenant's right to compensation for tenant's improvement.

ARRANGEMENT OF SECTIONS

Conditions of eligibility

17. Consent of landlord as condition of compensation for tenant's improvement.
18. Conditions in relation to compensation for planning permission.
19. Reference to arbitration of refusal or failure to give consent or of condition attached to consent.

Amount of compensation

20. Amount of compensation for tenant's improvement not consisting of planning permission.
21. Amount of compensation for planning permission.
22. Settlement of claims for compensation.
23. Successive tenancies.

Supplementary provisions with respect to compensation

24. Resumption of possession of part of holding.
25. Compensation where reversionary estate in holding is severed.
26. Extent to which compensation recoverable under agreements.
27. Interpretation of Part III.

Part IV

Miscellaneous and supplemental

Resolution of disputes

28. Resolution of disputes.
29. Cases where right to refer claim to arbitration under section 28 does not apply.
30. General provisions applying to arbitrations under Act.

Miscellaneous

31. Mortgages of agricultural land.
32. Power of limited owners to give consents etc.
33. Power to apply and raise capital money.
34. Estimation of best rent for purposes of Acts and other instruments.
35. Preparation of documents etc. by valuers and surveyors.

Supplemental

36. Services of notices.
37. Crown land.
38. Interpretation.
39. Index of defined expressions.
40. Consequential amendments.
41. Short title, commencement and extent.

Schedule

Consequential Amendments

AGRICULTURAL TENANCIES ACT 1995

1995 c. 8

An Act to make further provision with respect to tenancies which include agricultural land.

[9th May 1995]

PART I

GENERAL PROVISIONS

FARM BUSINESS TENANCIES

Meaning of "farm business tenancy"

1.—(1) A tenancy is a "farm business tenancy" for the purposes of this Act if-
   (a) it meets the business conditions together with either the agriculture condition or the notice conditions, and
   (b) it is not a tenancy which, by virtue of section 2 of this Act, cannot be a farm business tenancy.

(2) The business conditions are-
   (a) that all or part of the land comprised in the tenancy is farmed for the purposes of a trade or business, and
   (b) that, since the beginning of the tenancy, all or part of the land so comprised has been so farmed.

(3) The agriculture condition is that, having regard to-
   (a) the terms of the tenancy,
   (b) the use of the land comprised in the tenancy,
   (c) the nature of any commercial activities carried on on that land, and
   (d) any other relevant circumstances,
the character of the tenancy is primarily or wholly agricultural.

(4) The notice conditions are-
   (a) that, on or before the relevant day, the landlord and the tenant each gave the other a written notice-
      (i) identifying (by name or otherwise) the land to be comprised in the tenancy or proposed tenancy, and
      (ii) containing a statement to the effect that the person giving the notice intends that the tenancy or proposed tenancy is to be, and remain, a farm business tenancy, and
   (b) that, at the beginning of the tenancy, having regard to the terms of the tenancy and any other relevant circumstances, the character of the tenancy was primarily or wholly agricultural.

(5) In subsection (4) above "the relevant day" means whichever is the earlier of the following—

(a) the day on which the parties enter into any instrument creating the tenancy, other than an agreement to enter into a tenancy on a future date, or

(b) the beginning of the tenancy.

(6) The written notice referred to in subsection (4) above must not be included in any instrument creating the tenancy.

(7) If in any proceedings—
  (a) any question arises as to whether a tenancy was a farm business tenancy at any time, and
  (b) it is proved that all or part of the land comprised in the tenancy was farmed for the purposes of a trade or business at that time,

it shall be presumed, unless the contrary is proved, that all or part of the land so comprised has been so farmed since the beginning of the tenancy.

(8) Any use of land in breach of the terms of the tenancy, any commercial activities carried on in breach of those terms, and any cessation of such activities in breach of those terms, shall be disregarded in determining whether at any time the tenancy meets the business conditions or the agriculture condition, unless the landlord or his predecessor in title has consented to the breach or the landlord has acquiesced in the breach.

Tenancies which cannot be farm business tenancies

2.—(1) A tenancy cannot be a farm business tenancy for the purposes of this Act if—
  (a) the tenancy begins before 1st September 1995, or
  (b) it is a tenancy of an agricultural holding beginning on or after that date with respect to which, by virtue of section 4 of this Act, the Agricultural Holdings Act 1986 applies.

(2) In this section "agricultural holding" has the same meaning as in the Agricultural Holdings Act 1986.

Compliance with notice conditions in cases of surrender and regrant

3.—(1) This section applies where—
  (a) a tenancy ("the new tenancy") is granted to a person who, immediately before the grant, was the tenant under a farm business tenancy ("the old tenancy") which met the notice conditions specified in section 1(4) of this Act,
  (b) the condition in subsection (2) below or the condition in subsection (3) below is met, and
  (c) except as respects the matters mentioned in subsections (2) and (3) below and matters consequential on them, the terms of the new tenancy are substantially the same as the terms of the old tenancy.

(2) The first condition referred to in subsection (1)(b) above is that the land comprised in the new tenancy is the same as the land comprised in the old tenancy, apart from any changes in area which are small in relation to the size of the holding and do not affect the character of the holding.

(3) The second condition referred to in subsection (1)(b) above is that the old

tenancy and the new tenancy are both fixed term tenancies, but the term date under the new tenancy is earlier than the term date under the old tenancy.

(4) Where this section applies, the new tenancy shall be taken for the purposes of this Act to meet the notice conditions specified in section 1(4) of this Act.

(5) In subsection (3) above, "the term date", in relation to a fixed term tenancy, means the date fixed for the expiry of the term.

EXCLUSION OF AGRICULTURAL HOLDINGS ACT 1986

Agricultural Holdings Act 1986 not to apply in relation to new tenancies except in special cases

4.—(1) The Agricultural Holdings Act 1986 (in this section referred to as "the 1986 Act") shall not apply in relation to any tenancy beginning on or after 1st September 1995 (including any agreement to which section 2 of that Act would otherwise apply beginning on or after that date), except any tenancy of an agricultural holding which—

   (*a*) is granted by a written contract of tenancy entered into before 1st September 1995 and indicating (in whatever terms) that the 1986 Act is to apply in relation to the tenancy,
   (*b*) is obtained by virtue of a direction of an Agricultural Land Tribunal under section 39 or 53 of the 1986 Act,
   (*c*) is granted (following a direction under section 39 of that Act) in circumstances falling within section 45(6) of that Act,
   (*d*) is granted on an agreed succession by a written contract of tenancy indicating (in whatever terms) that Part IV of the 1986 Act is to apply in relation to the tenancy,
   (*e*) is created by the acceptance of a tenant, in accordance with the provisions as to compensation known as the "Evesham custom" and set out in subsections (3) to (5) of section 80 of the 1986 Act, on the terms and conditions of the previous tenancy, or
   (*f*) is granted to a person who, immediately before the grant of the tenancy, was the tenant of the holding, or of any agricultural holding which comprised the whole or a substantial part of the land comprised in the holding, under a tenancy in relation to which the 1986 Act applied ("the previous tenancy") and is so granted merely because a purported variation of the previous tenancy (not being an agreement expressed to take effect as a new tenancy between the parties) has effect as an implied surrender followed by the grant of the tenancy.

(2) For the purposes of subsection (1)(*d*) above, a tenancy ("the current tenancy") is granted on an agreed succession if, and only if,—

   (*a*) the previous tenancy of the holding or a related holding was a tenancy in relation to which Part IV of the 1986 Act applied, and
   (*b*) the current tenancy is granted otherwise than as mentioned in paragraph (*b*) or (*c*) of subsection (1) above but in such circumstances that if—
      (i) Part IV of the 1986 Act applied in relation to the current tenancy, and

(ii) a sole (or sole surviving) tenant under the current tenancy were to die and be survived by a close relative of his, the occasion on which the current tenancy is granted would for the purposes of subsection (1) of section 37 of the 1986 Act be taken to be an occasion falling within paragraph (*a*) or (*b*) of that subsection.

(3) In this section—
  (*a*) "agricultural holding" and "contract of tenancy" have the same meaning as in the 1986 Act, and
  (*b*) "close relative" and "related holding" have the meaning given by section 35(2) of that Act.

TERMINATION OF THE TENANCY

Tenancies for more than two years to continue from year to year unless terminated by notice

5.—(1) A farm business tenancy for a term of more than two years shall, instead of terminating on the term date, continue (as from that date) as a tenancy from year to year, but otherwise on the terms of the original tenancy so far as applicable, unless at least twelve months but less than twenty-four months before the term date a written notice has been given by either party to the other of his intention to terminate the tenancy.

(2) In subsection (1) above "the term date", in relation to a fixed term tenancy, means the date fixed for the expiry of the term.

(3) For the purposes of section 140 of the Law of Property Act 1925 (apportionment of conditions on severance of reversion), a notice under subsection (1) above shall be taken to be a notice to quit.

(4) This section has effect notwithstanding any agreement to the contrary.

Length of notice to quit

6.—(1) Where a farm business tenancy is a tenancy from year to year, a notice to quit the holding or part of the holding shall (notwithstanding any provision to the contrary in the tenancy) be invalid unless—
  (*a*) it is in writing,
  (*b*) it is to take effect at the end of a year of the tenancy, and
  (*c*) it is given at least twelve months but less than twenty-four months before the date on which it is to take effect.

(2) Where, by virtue of section 5(1) of this Act, a farm business tenancy for a term of more than two years is to continue (as from the term date) as a tenancy from year to year, a notice to quit which complies with subsection (1) above and which is to take effect on the first anniversary of the term date shall not be invalid merely because it is given before the term date; and in this subsection "the term date" has the meaning given by section 5(2) of this Act.

(3) Subsection (1) above does not apply in relation to a counter-notice given by the tenant by virtue of subsection (2) of section 140 of the Law of Property Act 1925 (apportionment of conditions on severance of reversion).

Notice required for exercise of option to terminate tenancy or resume possession of part

7.—(1) Where a farm business tenancy is a tenancy for a term of more than two years, any notice to quit the holding or part of the holding given in pursuance of any provision of the tenancy shall (notwithstanding any provision to the contrary in the tenancy) be invalid unless it is in writing and is given at least twelve months but less than twenty-four months before the date on which it is to take effect.

(2) Subsection (1) above does not apply in relation to a counter-notice given by the tenant by virtue of subsection (2) of section 140 of the Law of Property Act 1925 (apportionment of conditions on severance of reversion).

(3) Subsection (1) above does not apply to a tenancy which, by virtue of subsection (6) of section 149 of the Law of Property Act 1925 (lease for life or lives or for a term determinable with life or lives or on the marriage of the lessee), takes effect as such a term of years as is mentioned in that subsection.

TENANT'S RIGHT TO REMOVE FIXTURES AND BUILDINGS

Tenant's right to remove fixtures and buildings

8.—(1) Subject to the provisions of this section—
 (a) any fixture (of whatever description) affixed, whether for the purposes of agriculture or not, to the holding by the tenant under a farm business tenancy, and
 (b) any building erected by him on the holding,
may be removed by the tenant at any time during the continuance of the tenancy or at any time after the termination of the tenancy when he remains in possession as tenant (whether or not under a new tenancy), and shall remain his property so long as he may remove it by virtue of this subsection.

(2) Subsection (1) above shall not apply—
 (a) to a fixture affixed or a building erected in pursuance of some obligation,
 (b) to a fixture affixed or a building erected instead of some fixture or building belonging to the landlord,
 (c) to a fixture or building in respect of which the tenant has obtained compensation under section 16 of this Act or otherwise, or
 (d) to a fixture or building in respect of which the landlord has given his consent under section 17 of this Act on condition that the tenant agrees not to remove it and which the tenant has agreed not to remove.

(3) In the removal of a fixture or building by virtue of subsection (1) above, the tenant shall not do any avoidable damage to the holding.

(4) Immediately after removing a fixture or building by virtue of subsection (1) above, the tenant shall make good all damage to the holding that is occasioned by the removal.

(5) This section applies to a fixture or building acquired by a tenant as it applies to a fixture or building affixed or erected by him.

(6) Except as provided by subsection (2)(d) above, this section has effect notwithstanding any agreement or custom to the contrary.

(7) No right to remove fixtures that subsists otherwise than by virtue of this section shall be exercisable by the tenant under a farm business tenancy.

Part II

Rent Review Under Farm Business Tenancy

Application of Part II

9.—This Part of this Act applies in relation to a farm business tenancy (notwithstanding any agreement to the contrary) unless the tenancy is created by an instrument which—
- (*a*) expressly states that the rent is not to be reviewed during the tenancy, or
- (*b*) provides that the rent is to be varied, at a specified time or times during the tenancy—
  - (i) by or to a specified amount, or
  - (ii) in accordance with a specified formula which does not preclude a reduction and which does not require or permit the exercise by any person of any judgment or discretion in relation to the determination of the rent of the holding,

but otherwise is to remain fixed.

Notice requiring statutory rent review

10.—(1) The landlord or tenant under a farm business tenancy in relation to which this Part of this Act applies may by notice in writing given to the other (in this Part of this Act referred to as a "statutory review notice") require that the rent to be payable in respect of the holding as from the review date shall be referred to arbitration in accordance with this Act.

(2) In this Part of this Act "the review date", in relation to a statutory review notice, means a date which—
- (*a*) is specified in the notice, and
- (*b*) complies with subsections (3) to (6) below.

(3) The review date must be at least twelve months but less than twenty-four months after the day on which the statutory review notice is given.

(4) If the parties have agreed in writing that the rent is to be, or may be, varied as from a specified date or dates, or at specified intervals, the review date must be a date as from which the rent could be varied under the agreement.

(5) If the parties have agreed in writing that the review date for the purposes of this Part of this Act is to be a specified date or dates, the review date must be that date or one of those dates.

(6) If the parties have not agreed as mentioned in subsection (4) or (5) above, the review date-
- (*a*) must be an anniversary of the beginning of the tenancy or, where the landlord and the tenant have agreed in writing that the review date for the purposes of this Act is to be some other day of the year, that day of the year, and

(b) must not fall before the end of the period of three years beginning with the latest of any of the following dates—
   (i) the beginning of the tenancy,
   (ii) any date as from which there took effect a previous direction of an arbitrator as to the amount of the rent,
   (iii) any date as from which there took effect a previous determination as to the amount of the rent made, otherwise than as arbitrator, by a person appointed under an agreement between the landlord and the tenant, and
   (iv) any date as from which there took effect a previous agreement in writing between the landlord and the tenant, entered into since the grant of the tenancy, as to the amount of the rent.

Review date where new tenancy of severed part of reversion

11.—(1) This section applies in any case where a farm business tenancy ("the new tenancy") arises between—
   (a) a person who immediately before the date of the beginning of the tenancy was entitled to a severed part of the reversionary estate in the land comprised in a farm business tenancy ("the original tenancy") in which the land to which the new tenancy relates was then comprised, and
   (b) the person who immediately before that date was the tenant under the original tenancy,
and the rent payable under the new tenancy at its beginning represents merely the appropriate portion of the rent payable under the original tenancy immediately before the beginning of the new tenancy.
   (2) In any case where this section applies—
   (a) references to the beginning of the tenancy in subsection (6) of section 10 of this Act shall be taken to be references to the beginning of the original tenancy, and
   (b) references to rent in that subsection shall be taken to be references to the rent payable under the original tenancy,
until the first occasion following the beginning of the new tenancy on which any such direction, determination or agreement with respect to the rent of the new holding as is mentioned in that subsection takes effect.

Appointment of arbitrator

12.—Where a statutory review notice has been given in relation to a farm business tenancy, but—
   (a) no arbitrator has been appointed under an agreement made since the notice was given, and
   (b) no person has been appointed under such an agreement to determine the question of the rent (otherwise than as arbitrator) on a basis agreed by the parties,
either party may, at any time during the period of six months ending with the review date, apply to the President of the Royal Institution of Chartered Surveyors (in this Act referred to as "the RICS") for the appointment of an arbitrator by him.

Amount of rent

13.—(1) On any reference made in pursuance of a statutory review notice the arbitrator shall determine the rent properly payable in respect of the holding at the review date and accordingly shall, with effect from that date, increase or reduce the rent previously payable or direct that it shall continue unchanged.

(2) For the purposes of subsection (1) above, the rent properly payable in respect of a holding is the rent at which the holding might reasonably be expected to be let on the open market by a willing landlord to a willing tenant, taking into account (subject to subsections (3) and (4) below) all relevant factors, including (in every case) the terms of the tenancy (including those which are relevant for the purposes of section 10(4) to (6) of this Act, but not those relating to the criteria by reference to which any new rent is to be determined).

(3) The arbitrator shall disregard any increase in the rental value of the holding which is due to tenant's improvements other than—

(a) any tenant's improvement provided under an obligation which was imposed on the tenant by the terms of his tenancy or any previous tenancy and which arose on or before the beginning of the tenancy in question,

(b) any tenant's improvement to the extent that any allowance or benefit has been made or given by the landlord in consideration of its provision, and

(c) any tenant's improvement to the extent that the tenant has received any compensation from the landlord in respect of it.

(4) The arbitrator—

(a) shall disregard any effect on the rent of the fact that the tenant who is a party to the arbitration is in occupation of the holding, and

(b) shall not fix the rent at a lower amount by reason of any dilapidation or deterioration of, or damage to, buildings or land caused or permitted by the tenant.

(5) In this section "tenant's improvement", and references to the provision of such an improvement, have the meaning given by section 15 of this Act.

Interpretation of Part II

14.—In this Part of this Act, unless the context otherwise requires—

"the review date", in relation to a statutory review notice, has the meaning given by section 10(2) of this Act;

"statutory review notice" has the meaning given by section 10(1) of this Act.

PART III

COMPENSATION ON TERMINATION OF FARM BUSINESS TENANCY

TENANT'S ENTITLEMENT TO COMPENSATION

Meaning of "tenant's improvement"

15.—For the purposes of this Part of this Act a "tenant's improvement", in relation to any farm business tenancy, means—

(a) any physical improvement which is made on the holding by the tenant by his own effort or wholly or partly at his own expense, or
(b) any intangible advantage which—
  (i) is obtained for the holding by the tenant by his own effort or wholly or partly at his own expense, and
  (ii) becomes attached to the holding,

and references to the provision of a tenant's improvement are references to the making by the tenant of any physical improvement falling within paragraph (a) above or the obtaining by the tenant of any intangible advantage falling within paragraph (b) above.

Tenant's right to compensation for tenant's improvement

16.—(1) The tenant under a farm business tenancy shall, subject to the provisions of this Part of this Act, be entitled on the termination of the tenancy, on quitting the holding, to obtain from his landlord compensation in respect of any tenant's improvement.

(2) A tenant shall not be entitled to compensation under this section in respect of—
  (a) any physical improvement which is removed from the holding, or
  (b) any intangible advantage which does not remain attached to the holding.

(3) Section 13 of, and Schedule 1 to, the Agriculture Act 1986 (compensation to outgoing tenants for milk quota) shall not apply in relation to a farm business tenancy.

CONDITIONS OF ELIGIBILITY

Consent of landlord as condition of compensation for tenant's improvement

17.—(1) A tenant shall not be entitled to compensation under section 16 of this Act in respect of any tenant's improvement unless the landlord has given his consent in writing to the provision of the tenant's improvement.

(2) Any such consent may be given in the instrument creating the tenancy or elsewhere.

(3) Any such consent may be given either unconditionally or on condition that the tenant agrees to a specified variation in the terms of the tenancy.

(4) The variation referred to in subsection (3) above must be related to the tenant's improvement in question.

(5) This section does not apply in any case where the tenant's improvement consists of planning permission.

Conditions in relation to compensation for planning permission

18.—(1) A tenant shall not be entitled to compensation under section 16 of this Act in respect of a tenant's improvement which consists of planning permission unless-
  (a) the landlord has given his consent in writing to the making of the application for planning permission,
  (b) that consent is expressed to be given for the purpose—

SECTION 18

      (i) of enabling a specified physical improvement falling within paragraph (*a*) of section 15 of this Act lawfully to be provided by the tenant, or

      (ii) of enabling the tenant lawfully to effect a specified change of use, and

  (*c*) on the termination of the tenancy, the specified physical improvement has not been completed or the specified change of use has not been effected.

(2) Any such consent may be given either unconditionally or on condition that the tenant agrees to a specified variation in the terms of the tenancy.

(3) The variation referred to in subsection (2) above must be related to the physical improvement or change of use in question.

Reference to arbitration of refusal or failure to give consent or of condition attached to consent

19.—(1) Where, in relation to any tenant's improvement, the tenant under a farm business tenancy is aggrieved by—

  (*a*) the refusal of his landlord to give his consent under section 17(1) of this Act,

  (*b*) the failure of his landlord to give such consent within two months of a written request by the tenant for such consent, or

  (*c*) any variation in the terms of the tenancy required by the landlord as a condition of giving such consent,

the tenant may by notice in writing given to the landlord demand that the question shall be referred to arbitration under this section; but this subsection has effect subject to subsections (2) and (3) below.

(2) No notice under subsection (1) above may be given in relation to any tenant's improvement which the tenant has already provided or begun to provide, unless that improvement is a routine improvement.

(3) No notice under subsection (1) above may be given—

  (*a*) in a case falling within paragraph (*a*) or (*c*) of that subsection, after the end of the period of two months beginning with the day on which notice of the refusal or variation referred to in that paragraph was given to the tenant, or

  (*b*) in a case falling within paragraph (*b*) of that subsection, after the end of the period of four months beginning with the day on which the written request referred to in that paragraph was given to the landlord.

(4) Where the tenant has given notice under subsection (1) above but no arbitrator has been appointed under an agreement made since the notice was given, the tenant or the landlord may apply to the President of the RICS, subject to subsection (9) below, for the appointment of an arbitrator by him.

(5) The arbitrator shall consider whether, having regard to the terms of the tenancy and any other relevant circumstances (including the circumstances of the tenant and the landlord), it is reasonable for the tenant to provide the tenant's improvement.

(6) Subject to subsection (9) below, the arbitrator may unconditionally approve the provision of the tenant's improvement or may withhold his approval, but may

not give his approval subject to any condition or vary any condition required by the landlord under section 17(3) of this Act.

(7) If the arbitrator gives his approval, that approval shall have effect for the purposes of this Part of this Act and for the purposes of the terms of the farm business tenancy as if it were the consent of the landlord.

(8) In a case falling within subsection (1)(c) above, the withholding by the arbitrator of his approval shall not affect the validity of the landlord's consent or of the condition subject to which it was given.

(9) Where, at any time after giving a notice under subsection (1) above in relation to any tenant's improvement which is not a routine improvement, the tenant begins to provide the improvement—
- (a) no application may be made under subsection (4) above after that time,
- (b) where such an application has been made but no arbitrator has been appointed before that time, the application shall be ineffective, and
- (c) no award may be made by virtue of subsection (6) above after that time except as to the costs of the reference and award in a case where the arbitrator was appointed before that time.

(10) For the purposes of this section-"fixed equipment" includes any building or structure affixed to land and any works constructed on, in, over or under land, and also includes anything grown on land for a purpose other than use after severance from the land, consumption of the thing grown or its produce, or amenity;"routine improvement", in relation to a farm business tenancy, means any tenant's improvement which—
- (a) is a physical improvement made in the normal course of farming the holding or any part of the holding, and
- (b) does not consist of fixed equipment or an improvement to fixed equipment,

but does not include any improvement whose provision is prohibited by the terms of the tenancy.

AMOUNT OF COMPENSATION

Amount of compensation for tenant's improvement not consisting of planning permission

20.—(1) The amount of compensation payable to the tenant under section 16 of this Act in respect of any tenant's improvement shall be an amount equal to the increase attributable to the improvement in the value of the holding at the termination of the tenancy as land comprised in a tenancy.

(2) Where the landlord and the tenant have entered into an agreement in writing whereby any benefit is given or allowed to the tenant in consideration of the provision of a tenant's improvement, the amount of compensation otherwise payable in respect of that improvement shall be reduced by the proportion which the value of the benefit bears to the amount of the total cost of providing the improvement.

(3) Where a grant has been or will be made to the tenant out of public money in respect of a tenant's improvement, the amount of compensation otherwise payable in respect of that improvement shall be reduced by the proportion which the

amount of the grant bears to the amount of the total cost of providing the improvement.

(4) Where a physical improvement which has been completed or a change of use which has been effected is authorised by any planning permission granted on an application made by the tenant, section 18 of this Act does not prevent any value attributable to the fact that the physical improvement or change of use is so authorised from being taken into account under this section in determining the amount of compensation payable in respect of the physical improvement or in respect of any intangible advantage obtained as a result of the change of use.

(5) This section does not apply where the tenant's improvement consists of planning permission.

Amount of compensation for planning permission

21.—(1) The amount of compensation payable to the tenant under section 16 of this Act in respect of a tenant's improvement which consists of planning permission shall be an amount equal to the increase attributable to the fact that the relevant development is authorised by the planning permission in the value of the holding at the termination of the tenancy as land comprised in a tenancy.

(2) In subsection (1) above, "the relevant development" means the physical improvement or change of use specified in the landlord's consent under section 18 of this Act in accordance with subsection (1)(*b*) of that section.

(3) Where the landlord and the tenant have entered into an agreement in writing whereby any benefit is given or allowed to the tenant in consideration of the obtaining of planning permission by the tenant, the amount of compensation otherwise payable in respect of that permission shall be reduced by the proportion which the value of the benefit bears to the amount of the total cost of obtaining the permission.

Settlement of claims for compensation

22.—(1) Any claim by the tenant under a farm business tenancy for compensation under section 16 of this Act shall, subject to the provisions of this section, be determined by arbitration under this section.

(2) No such claim for compensation shall be enforceable unless before the end of the period of two months beginning with the date of the termination of the tenancy the tenant has given notice in writing to his landlord of his intention to make the claim and of the nature of the claim.

(3) Where—
   (*a*) the landlord and the tenant have not settled the claim by agreement in writing, and
   (*b*) no arbitrator has been appointed under an agreement made since the notice under subsection (2) above was given,

either party may, after the end of the period of four months beginning with the date of the termination of the tenancy, apply to the President of the RICS for the appointment of an arbitrator by him.

(4) Where—

(*a*) an application under subsection (3) above relates wholly or partly to compensation in respect of a routine improvement (within the meaning of section 19 of this Act) which the tenant has provided or has begun to provide, and

(*b*) that application is made at the same time as an application under section 19(4) of this Act relating to the provision of that improvement,

the President of the RICS shall appoint the same arbitrator on both applications and, if both applications are made by the same person, only one fee shall be payable by virtue of section 30(2) of this Act in respect of them.

(5) Where a tenant lawfully remains in occupation of part of the holding after the termination of a farm business tenancy, references in subsections (2) and (3) above to the termination of the tenancy shall, in the case of a claim relating to that part of the holding, be construed as references to the termination of the occupation.

SUPPLEMENTARY PROVISIONS WITH RESPECT TO COMPENSATION

Successive tenancies

23.—(1) Where the tenant under a farm business tenancy has remained in the holding during two or more such tenancies, he shall not be deprived of his right to compensation under section 16 of this Act by reason only that any tenant's improvement was provided during a tenancy other than the one at the termination of which he quits the holding.

(2) The landlord and tenant under a farm business tenancy may agree that the tenant is to be entitled to compensation under section 16 of this Act on the termination of the tenancy even though at that termination the tenant remains in the holding under a new tenancy.

(3) Where the landlord and the tenant have agreed as mentioned in subsection (2) above in relation to any tenancy ("the earlier tenancy"), the tenant shall not be entitled to compensation at the end of any subsequent tenancy in respect of any tenant's improvement provided during the earlier tenancy in relation to the land comprised in the earlier tenancy.

Resumption of possession of part of holding

24.—(1) Where—
(*a*) the landlord under a farm business tenancy resumes possession of part of the holding in pursuance of any provision of the tenancy, or

(*b*) a person entitled to a severed part of the reversionary estate in a holding held under a farm business tenancy resumes possession of part of the holding by virtue of a notice to quit that part given to the tenant by virtue of section 140 of the Law of Property Act 1925,

the provisions of this Part of this Act shall, subject to subsections (2) and (3) below, apply to that part of the holding (in this section referred to as "the relevant part") as if it were a separate holding which the tenant had quitted in consequence of a notice to quit and, in a case falling within paragraph (*b*) above, as if the person resuming possession were the landlord of that separate holding.

(2) The amount of compensation payable to the tenant under section 16 of this

Act in respect of any tenant's improvement provided for the relevant part by the tenant and not consisting of planning permission shall, subject to section 20(2) to (4) of this Act, be an amount equal to the increase attributable to the tenant's improvement in the value of the original holding on the termination date as land comprised in a tenancy.

(3) The amount of compensation payable to the tenant under section 16 of this Act in respect of any tenant's improvement which consists of planning permission relating to the relevant part shall, subject to section 21(3) of this Act, be an amount equal to the increase attributable to the fact that the relevant development is authorised by the planning permission in the value of the original holding on the termination date as land comprised in a tenancy.

(4) In a case falling within paragraph (*a*) or (*b*) of subsection (1) above, sections 20 and 21 of this Act shall apply on the termination of the tenancy, in relation to the land then comprised in the tenancy, as if the reference in subsection (1) of each of those sections to the holding were a reference to the original holding.

(5) In subsections (2) to (4) above-"the original holding" means the land comprised in the farm business tenancy—

    (*a*) on the date when the landlord gave his consent under section 17 or 18 of this Act in relation to the tenant's improvement, or

    (*b*) where approval in relation to the tenant's improvement was given by an arbitrator, on the date on which that approval was given,

"the relevant development", in relation to any tenant's improvement which consists of planning permission, has the meaning given by section 21(2) of this Act, and "the termination date" means the date on which possession of the relevant part was resumed.

Compensation where reversionary estate in holding is severed

25.—(1) Where the reversionary estate in the holding comprised in a farm business tenancy is for the time being vested in more than one person in several parts, the tenant shall be entitled, on quitting the entire holding, to require that any compensation payable to him under section 16 of this Act shall be determined as if the reversionary estate were not so severed.

(2) Where subsection (1) applies, the arbitrator shall, where necessary, apportion the amount awarded between the persons who for the purposes of this Part of this Act together constitute the landlord of the holding, and any additional costs of the award caused by the apportionment shall be directed by the arbitrator to be paid by those persons in such proportions as he shall determine.

Extent to which compensation recoverable under agreements

26.—(1) In any case for which apart from this section the provisions of this Part of this Act provide for compensation, a tenant shall be entitled to compensation in accordance with those provisions and not otherwise, and shall be so entitled notwithstanding any agreement to the contrary.

(2) Nothing in the provisions of this Part of this Act, apart from this section, shall be construed as disentitling a tenant to compensation in any case for which those provisions do not provide for compensation.

Interpretation of Part III

27.—In this Part of this Act, unless the context otherwise requires-"planning permission" has the meaning given by section 336(1) of the Town and Country Planning Act 1990; "tenant's improvement", and references to the provision of such an improvement, have the meaning given by section 15 of this Act.

PART IV

MISCELLANEOUS AND SUPPLEMENTAL

RESOLUTION OF DISPUTES

Resolution of disputes

28.—(1) Subject to subsections (4) and (5) below and to section 29 of this Act, any dispute between the landlord and the tenant under a farm business tenancy, being a dispute concerning their rights and obligations under this Act, under the terms of the tenancy or under any custom, shall be determined by arbitration.

(2) Where such a dispute has arisen, the landlord or the tenant may give notice in writing to the other specifying the dispute and stating that, unless before the end of the period of two months beginning with the day on which the notice is given the parties have appointed an arbitrator by agreement, he proposes to apply to the President of the RICS for the appointment of an arbitrator by him.

(3) Where a notice has been given under subsection (2) above, but no arbitrator has been appointed by agreement, either party may, after the end of the period of two months referred to in that subsection, apply to the President of the RICS for the appointment of an arbitrator by him.

(4) [...][97] and [98].

(5) Subsections (1) to (3) above do not apply in relation to—
   (a) the determination of rent in pursuance of a statutory review notice (as defined in section 10(1) of this Act),
   (b) any case falling within section 19(1) of this Act, or
   (c) any claim for compensation under Part III of this Act.

Cases where right to refer claim to arbitration under section 28 does not apply

29.—(1) Section 28 of this Act does not apply in relation to any dispute if—
   (a) the tenancy is created by an instrument which includes provision for disputes to be resolved by any person other than—
      (i) the landlord or the tenant, or
      (ii) a third party appointed by either of them without the consent or concurrence of the other, and
   (b) either of the following has occurred—
      (i) the landlord and the tenant have jointly referred the dispute to the third party under the provision, or

---

[97] Repealed by Arbitration Act 1996 (c.23), s.107(2), Sched. 4.
[98] Words repealed by Trusts of Land and Appointment of Trustees Act 1996 (c.47), s. 25(2), Sched. 4, section 26 of the Universities and College Estates Act 1925.

(ii) the landlord or the tenant has referred the dispute to the third party under the provision and notified the other in writing of the making of the reference, the period of four weeks beginning with the date on which the other was so notified has expired and the other has not given a notice under section 28(2) of this Act in relation to the dispute before the end of that period.

(2) For the purposes of subsection (1) above a term of the tenancy does not provide for disputes to be "resolved" by any person unless that person (whether or not acting as arbitrator) is enabled under the terms of the tenancy to give a decision which is binding in law on both parties.

General provisions applying to arbitrations under Act

30.—(1) Any matter which is required to be determined by arbitration under this Act shall be determined by the arbitration of a sole arbitrator.

(2) Any application under this Act to the President of the RICS for the appointment of an arbitrator by him must be made in writing and must be accompanied by such reasonable fee as the President may determine in respect of the costs of making the appointment.

(3) Where an arbitrator appointed for the purposes of this Act dies or is incapable of acting and no new arbitrator has been appointed by agreement, either party may apply to the President of the RICS for the appointment of a new arbitrator by him.

MISCELLANEOUS

Mortgages of agricultural land

31.—(1) Section 99 of the Law of Property Act 1925 (leasing powers of mortgagor and mortgagee in possession) shall be amended in accordance with subsections (2) and (3) below.

(2) At the beginning of subsection (13), there shall be inserted "Subject to subsection (13A) below,".

(3) After that subsection, there shall be inserted—

"(13A) Subsection (13) of this section—
   (a) shall not enable the application of any provision of this section to be excluded or restricted in relation to any mortgage of agricultural land made after 1st March 1948 but before 1st September 1995, and
   (b) shall not enable the power to grant a lease of an agricultural holding to which, by virtue of section 4 of the Agricultural Tenancies Act 1995, the Agricultural Holdings Act 1986 will apply, to be excluded or restricted in relation to any mortgage of agricultural land made on or after 1st September 1995."

(13B) In subsection (13A) of this section-'agricultural holding' has the same meaning as in the Agricultural Holdings Act 1986; and'agricultural land' has the same meaning as in the Agriculture Act 1947."

(4) Paragraph 12 of Schedule 14 to the Agricultural Holdings Act 1986 (which excludes the application of subsection (13) of section 99 of the Law of Property

Act 1925 in relation to a mortgage of agricultural land and is superseded by the amendments made by subsections (1) to (3) above) shall cease to have effect.

Power of limited owners to give consents etc

32.—The landlord under a farm business tenancy, whatever his estate or interest in the holding, may, for the purposes of this Act, give any consent, make any agreement or do or have done to him any other act which he might give, make, do or have done to him if he were owner in fee simple or, if his interest is an interest in a leasehold, were absolutely entitled to that leasehold.

Power to apply and raise capital money

33.—(1) The purposes authorised by section 73 of the Settled Land Act 1925[...][99]
  (a) the payment of expenses incurred by a landlord under a farm business tenancy in, or in connection with, the making of any physical improvement on the holding,
  (b) the payment of compensation under section 16 of this Act, and
  (c) the payment of the costs, charges and expenses incurred by him on a reference to arbitration under section 19 or 22 of this Act.
(2) The purposes authorised by section 71 of the Settled Land Act 1925[...][101]
(3) Where the landlord under a farm business tenancy—
  (a) is a tenant for life or in a fiduciary position, and
  (b) is liable to pay compensation under section 16 of this Act,
he may require the sum payable as compensation and any costs, charges and expenses incurred by him in connection with the tenant's claim under that section to be paid out of any capital money held on the same trusts as the settled land.

(4) In subsection (3) above-"capital money" includes any personal estate held on the same trusts as the land[...][102]

Estimation of best rent for purposes of Acts and other instruments

34.—(1) In estimating the best rent or reservation in the nature of rent of land comprised in a farm business tenancy for the purposes of a relevant instrument, it shall not be necessary to take into account against the tenant any increase in the value of that land arising from any tenant's improvements.

(2) In subsection (1) above-"a relevant instrument" means any Act of Parliament, deed or other instrument which authorises a lease to be made on the condition that the best rent or reservation in the nature of rent is reserved; "tenant's improvement" has the meaning given by section 15 of this Act.

---

[99] Words repealed by Trusts of Land and Appointment of Trustees Act 1996 (c.47), s.25(2), Sched. 4; s.16 of this Act.
[1] Words repealed by Trusts of Land and Appointment of Trustees Act 1996 (c.47), s.25(2), Sched. 4; s.16 of this Act.
[2] Definition of "settled land" repealed by Trusts of Land and Appointment of Trustees Act

Preparation of documents etc. by valuers and surveyors

35.—(1) Section 22 of the Solicitors Act 1974 (unqualified person not to prepare certain instruments) shall be amended as follows.

(2) In subsection (2), after paragraph (*ab*) there shall be inserted—

"(*ac*) any accredited person drawing or preparing any instrument—

(i) which creates, or which he believes on reasonable grounds will create, a farm business tenancy (within the meaning of the Agricultural Tenancies Act 1995), or

(ii) which relates to an existing tenancy which is, or which he believes on reasonable grounds to be, such a tenancy;".

(3) In subsection (3A), immediately before the definition of "registered trade mark agent" there shall be inserted-'accredited person' means any person who is—

(*a*) a Full Member of the Central Association of Agricultural Valuers,

(*b*) an Associate or Fellow of the Incorporated Society of Valuers and Auctioneers, or

(*c*) an Associate or Fellow of the Royal Institution of Chartered Surveyors;".

SUPPLEMENTAL

Service of notices

36.—(1) This section applies to any notice or other document required or authorised to be given under this Act.

(2) A notice or other document to which this section applies is duly given to a person if—

(*a*) it is delivered to him,

(*b*) it is left at his proper address, or

(*c*) it is given to him in a manner authorised by a written agreement made, at any time before the giving of the notice, between him and the person giving the notice.

(3) A notice or other document to which this section applies is not duly given to a person if its text is transmitted to him by facsimile or other electronic means otherwise than by virtue of subsection (2)(*c*) above.

(4) Where a notice or other document to which this section applies is to be given to a body corporate, the notice or document is duly given if it is given to the secretary or clerk of that body.

(5) Where—

(*a*) a notice or other document to which this section applies is to be given to a landlord under a farm business tenancy and an agent or servant of his is responsible for the control of the management of the holding, or

(*b*) such a document is to be given to a tenant under a farm business tenancy and an agent or servant of his is responsible for the carrying on of a business on the holding,

the notice or document is duly given if it is given to that agent or servant.

1996 (c. 47), s.25(2), Sched. 4.

(6) For the purposes of this section, the proper address of any person to whom a notice or other document to which this section applies is to be given is—
   (a) in the case of the secretary or clerk of a body corporate, the registered or principal office of that body, and
   (b) in any other case, the last known address of the person in question.

(7) Unless or until the tenant under a farm business tenancy has received—
   (a) notice that the person who before that time was entitled to receive the rents and profits of the holding ("the original landlord") has ceased to be so entitled, and
   (b) notice of the name and address of the person who has become entitled to receive the rents and profits,
any notice or other document given to the original landlord by the tenant shall be deemed for the purposes of this Act to have been given to the landlord under the tenancy.

Crown land

37.—(1) This Act shall apply in relation to land in which there subsists, or has at any material time subsisted, a Crown interest as it applies in relation to land in which no such interest subsists or has ever subsisted.

(2) For the purposes of this Act—
   (a) where an interest belongs to Her Majesty in right of the Crown and forms part of the Crown Estate, the Crown Estate Commissioners shall be treated as the owner of the interest,
   (b) where an interest belongs to Her Majesty in right of the Crown and does not form part of the Crown Estate, the government department having the management of the land or, if there is no such department, such person as Her Majesty may appoint in writing under the Royal Sign Manual shall be treated as the owner of the interest,
   (c) where an interest belongs to Her Majesty in right of the Duchy of Lancaster, the Chancellor of the Duchy shall be treated as the owner of the interest,
   (d) where an interest belongs to a government department or is held in trust for Her Majesty for the purposes of a government department, that department shall be treated as the owner of the interest, and
   (e) where an interest belongs to the Duchy of Cornwall, such person as the Duke of Cornwall or the possessor for the time being of the Duchy of Cornwall appoints shall be treated as the owner of the interest and, in the case where the interest is that of landlord, may do any act or thing which a landlord is authorised or required to do under this Act.

(3) If any question arises as to who is to be treated as the owner of a Crown interest, that question shall be referred to the Treasury, whose decision shall be final.

(4) In subsections (1) and (3) above "Crown interest" means an interest which belongs to Her Majesty in right of the Crown or of the Duchy of Lancaster or to the Duchy of Cornwall, or to a government department, or which is held in trust for Her Majesty for the purposes of a government department.

(5) Any compensation payable under section 16 of this Act by the Chancellor of the Duchy of Lancaster may be raised and paid under section 25 of the Duchy of Lancaster Act 1817 (application of monies) as an expense incurred in improvement of land belonging to Her Majesty in right of the Duchy.

(6) In the case of land belonging to the Duchy of Cornwall, the purposes authorised by section 8 of the Duchy of Cornwall Management Act 1863 (application of monies) for the advancement of parts of such gross sums as are there mentioned shall include the payment of compensation under section 16 of this Act.

(7) Nothing in subsection (6) above shall be taken as prejudicing the operation of the Duchy of Cornwall Management Act 1982.

Interpretation

38.—(1) In this Act, unless the context otherwise requires—

"agriculture" includes horticulture, fruit growing, seed growing, dairy farming and livestock breeding and keeping, the use of land as grazing land, meadow land, osier land, market gardens and nursery grounds, and the use of land for woodlands where that use is ancillary to the farming of land for other agricultural purposes, and "agricultural" shall be construed accordingly;

"building" includes any part of a building;

"fixed term tenancy" means any tenancy other than a periodic tenancy;

"holding", in relation to a farm business tenancy, means the aggregate of the land comprised in the tenancy;

"landlord" includes any person from time to time deriving title from the original landlord;

"livestock" includes any creature kept for the production of food, wool, skins or fur or for the purpose of its use in the farming of land;

"the RICS" means the Royal Institution of Chartered Surveyors;

"tenancy" means any tenancy other than a tenancy at will, and includes a sub-tenancy and an agreement for a tenancy or sub-tenancy;

"tenant" includes a sub-tenant and any person deriving title from the original tenant or sub-tenant;

"termination", in relation to a tenancy, means the cesser of the tenancy by reason of effluxion of time or from any other cause.

(2) References in this Act to the farming of land include references to the carrying on in relation to land of any agricultural activity.

(3) A tenancy granted pursuant to a contract shall be taken for the purposes of this Act to have been granted when the contract was entered into.

(4) For the purposes of this Act a tenancy begins on the day on which, under the terms of the tenancy, the tenant is entitled to possession under that tenancy; and references in this Act to the beginning of the tenancy are references to that day.

(5) The designations of landlord and tenant shall continue to apply until the conclusion of any proceedings taken under this Act in respect of compensation.

AGRICULTURAL TENANCIES ACT 1995

Index of defined expressions

39.—In this Act the expressions listed below are defined by or otherwise fall to be construed in accordance with the provisions indicated—

Consequential amendments

40.—The Schedule to this Act (which contains consequential amendments) shall have effect.

Short title, commencement and extent

41.—(1) This Act may be cited as the Agricultural Tenancies Act 1995.

(2) This Act shall come into force on 1st September 1995.

(3) Subject to subsection (4) below, this Act extends to England and Wales only.

(4) The amendment by a provision of the Schedule to this Act of an enactment which extends to Scotland or Northern Ireland also extends there, except that paragraph 9 of the Schedule does not extend to Northern Ireland.

SCHEDULE

CONSEQUENTIAL AMENDMENTS

Section 40

The Small Holdings and Allotments Act 1908 (c. 36)

1.—(1) Section 47 of the Small Holdings and Allotments Act 1908 (compensation for improvements) shall be amended as follows.

(2) In subsection (1), after "to any tenant" there shall be inserted "otherwise than under a farm business tenancy".

(3) In subsection (2), after "small holdings or allotments" there shall be inserted "otherwise than under a farm business tenancy".

(4) In subsection (3), after "if" there shall be inserted "he is not a tenant under a farm business tenancy and".

(5) In subsection (4), after "allotment" there shall be inserted "who is not a tenant under a farm business tenancy".

(6) After that subsection, there shall be inserted—

"(5)—In this section, 'farm business tenancy' has the same meaning as in the Agricultural Tenancies Act 1995."

The Law of Distress Amendment Act 1908 (c. 53)

2.—In section 4(1) of the Law of Distress Amendment Act 1908 (exclusion of certain goods), for "to which that section applies" there shall be substituted "on land comprised in a tenancy to which that Act applies".

SCHEDULE

The Allotments Act 1922 (c. 51)

3.—In section 3(7) of the Allotments Act 1922 (provision as to cottage holdings and certain allotments), after "landlord" there shall be inserted "otherwise than under a farm business tenancy (within the meaning of the Agricultural Tenancies Act 1995)".

4.—In section 6(1) of that Act (assessment and recovery of compensation), after "contract of tenancy" there shall be inserted "(not being a farm business tenancy within the meaning of the Agricultural Tenancies Act 1995)".

The Landlord and Tenant Act 1927 (c. 36)

5.—In section 17(1) of the Landlord and Tenant Act 1927 (holdings to which Part I applies), for the words from "not being" to the end there is substituted "not being—
 (a) agricultural holdings within the meaning of the Agricultural Holdings Act 1986 held under leases in relation to which that Act applies, or
 (b) holdings held under farm business tenancies within the meaning of the Agricultural Tenancies Act 1995."

6.—In section 19(4) of that Act (provisions as to covenants not to assign etc. without licence or consent), after "the Agricultural Holdings Act 1986" there shall be inserted "which are leases in relation to which that Act applies, or to farm business tenancies within the meaning of the Agricultural Tenancies Act 1995".

The Agricultural Credits Act 1928 (c. 43)

7.—In section 5(7) of the Agricultural Credits Act 1928 (agricultural charges on farming stock and assets) in the definition of "other agricultural assets", after "otherwise" there shall be inserted "a tenant's right to compensation under section 16 of the Agricultural Tenancies Act 1995,".

The Leasehold Property (Repairs) Act 1938 (c. 34)

8.—In section 7(1) of the Leasehold Property (Repairs) Act 1938 (interpretation), at the end there shall be added "which is a lease in relation to which that Act applies and not being a farm business tenancy within the meaning of the Agricultural Tenancies Act 1995".

The Reserve and Auxiliary Forces (Protection of Civil Interests) Act 1951 (c. 65)

9.—(1) Section 27 of the Reserve and Auxiliary Forces (Protection of Civil Interests) Act 1951 (renewal of tenancy expiring during period of service or within two months thereafter) shall be amended as follows.
(2) In subsection (1), for the words from "are an agricultural holding" onwards there shall be substituted—

"(*a*) are an agricultural holding (within the meaning of the Agricultural Holdings Act 1986) held under a tenancy in relation to which that Act applies,

(*b*) are a holding (other than a holding excepted from this provision) held under a farm business tenancy, or

(*c*) consist of or comprise premises (other than premises excepted from this provision) licensed for the sale of intoxicating liquor for consumption on the premises."

(3) In subsection (5), after paragraph (*b*) there shall be inserted—

"(*bb*) the expressions 'farm business tenancy' and 'holding', in relation to such a tenancy, have the same meaning as in the Agricultural Tenancies Act 1995;"

(4) After that subsection, there shall be inserted—

"(5A)— In paragraph (*b*) of the proviso to subsection (1) of this section the reference to a holding excepted from the provision is a reference to a holding held under a farm business tenancy in which there is comprised a dwelling-house occupied by the person responsible for the control (whether as tenant or servant or agent of the tenant) of the management of the holding."

(5) In subsection (6), for the words from the beginning to "liquor" there shall be substituted "In paragraph (*c*) of the proviso to subsection (1) of this section, the reference to premises excepted from the provision".

The Landlord and Tenant Act 1954 (c. 56)

10.—In section 43(1) of the Landlord and Tenant Act 1954 (tenancies excluded from Part II)—

(*a*) in paragraph (*a*), for the words from "or a tenancy" to "1986" there shall be substituted "which is a tenancy in relation to which the Agricultural Holdings Act 1986 applies or a tenancy which would be a tenancy of an agricultural holding in relation to which that Act applied if subsection (3) of section 2 of that Act", and

(*b*) after that paragraph there shall be inserted—

"(*aa*) to a farm business tenancy;"

11.—In section 51(1) of that Act (extension of Leasehold Property (Repairs) Act 1938), for paragraph (*c*) there shall be substituted—

"(*c*) that the tenancy is neither a tenancy of an agricultural holding in relation to which the Agricultural Holdings Act 1986 applies nor a farm business tenancy"

12.—In section 69(1) of that Act (interpretation), after the definition of "development corporation"there shall be inserted-"'farm business tenancy' has the same meaning as in the Agricultural Tenancies Act 1995;".

SCHEDULE

The Opencast Coal Act 1958 (c. 69)

13.—(1) Section 14 of the Opencast Coal Act 1958 (provisions as to agricultural tenancies in England and Wales) shall be amended as follows.

(2) In subsection (1)(b), for "or part of an agricultural holding" there shall be substituted "held under a tenancy in relation to which the Agricultural Holdings Act 1986 (in this Act referred to as 'the Act of 1986') applies or part of such an agricultural holding".

(3) In subsection (2), for the words from "Agricultural" to "of 1986")" there shall be substituted "Act of 1986".

14.—After section 14A of that Act, there shall be inserted-"Provisions as to farm business tenancies (14B)—(1). Without prejudice to the provisions of Part III of this Act as to matters arising between landlords and tenants in consequence of compulsory rights orders, the provisions of this section shall have effect where—
 (*a*) opencast planning permission has been granted subject to a restoration condition, and
 (*b*) immediately before that permission is granted, any of the land comprised therein consists of the holding or part of the holding held under a farm business tenancy,
whether any of that land is comprised in a compulsory rights order or not.

(2) For the purposes of section 1 of the Agricultural Tenancies Act 1995 (in this Act referred to as 'the Act of 1995'), the land shall be taken, while it is occupied or used for the permitted activities, to be used for the purposes for which it was used immediately before it was occupied or used for the permitted activities.

(3) For the purposes of the Act of 1995, nothing done or omitted by the tenant or by the landlord under the tenancy by way of permitting any of the land in respect of which opencast planning permission has been granted to be occupied for the purpose of carrying on any of the permitted activities, or by way of facilitating the use of any of that land for that purpose, shall be taken to be a breach of any term or condition of the tenancy, either on the part of the tenant or on the part of the landlord.

(4) In determining under subsections (1) and (2) of section 13 of the Act of 1995 the rent which should be properly payable for the holding, in respect of any period for which the person with the benefit of the opencast planning permission is in occupation of the holding, or of any part thereof, for the purpose of carrying on any of the permitted activities, the arbitrator shall disregard any increase or diminution in the rental value of the holding in so far as that increase or diminution is attributable to the occupation of the holding, or of that part of the holding, by that person for the purpose of carrying on any of the permitted activities.

(5) In this section 'holding', in relation to a farm business tenancy, has the same meaning as in the Act of 1995.

(6) This section does not extend to Scotland."

15.—(1) Section 24 of that Act (tenant's right to compensation for improvements and other matters) shall be amended as follows.

(2) In subsection (1)(*a*), after "holding" there shall be inserted "held under a tenancy in relation to which the Act of 1986 applies".

(3) In subsection (10), after "Scotland" there shall be inserted "the words 'held under a tenancy in relation to which the Act of 1986 applies' in subsection (1)(*a*) of this section shall be omitted and".

16.—After section 25 of that Act, there shall be inserted- "Tenant's right to compensation for improvements etc.: farm business tenancies.(25A)—(1) The provisions of this section shall have effect where—
   (*a*) any part of the land comprised in a compulsory rights order is held, immediately before the date of entry, under a farm business tenancy;
   (*b*) there have been provided in relation to the land which is both so comprised and so held ('the tenant's land') tenant's improvements in respect of which, immediately before that date, the tenant had a prospective right to compensation under section 16 of the Act of 1995 on quitting the holding on the termination of the tenancy;
   (*c*) at the end of the period of occupation, the tenant's land has lost the benefit of any such improvement; and
   (*d*) immediately after the end of that period, the tenant's land is comprised in the same tenancy as immediately before the date of entry, or is comprised in a subsequent farm business tenancy at the end of which the tenant is not deprived, by virtue of section 23(3) of that Act, of his right to compensation under section 16 of that Act in respect of any tenant's improvement provided during the earlier tenancy in relation to the tenant's land.

(2) For the purposes of subsection (1) of this section, subsection (2) of section 22 of the Act of 1995 (which requires notice to be given of the intention to make a claim) shall be disregarded.

(3) Subject to subsection (4) of this section, Part III of the Act of 1995 shall apply as if—
   (*a*) the tenant's land were in the state in which it was immediately before the date of entry, and
   (*b*) the tenancy under which that land is held at the end of the period of occupation had terminated immediately after the end of that period and the tenant had then quitted the holding.

(4) Where the tenant's land has lost the benefit of some tenant's improvements but has not lost the benefit of all of them, Part III of the Act of 1995 shall apply as mentioned in subsection (3) above, but as if the improvements of which the tenant's land has not lost the benefit had not been tenant's improvements.

(5) For the purposes of subsections (1) and (4) of this section, the tenant's land shall be taken to have lost the benefit of a tenant's improvement if the benefit of that improvement has been lost (wholly or in part) without being replaced by another improvement of comparable benefit to the land.

(6) In this section 'holding', in relation to a farm business tenancy, 'tenant's improvement', 'termination', in relation to a tenancy, and references to the provision of a tenant's improvement have the same meaning as in the Act of 1995.

(7) This section does not extend to Scotland."

SCHEDULE

17.—(1) Section 26 of that Act (compensation for short-term improvements and related matters) shall be amended as follows.

(2) In subsection (1), after "agricultural land" there shall be inserted "and was not comprised in a farm business tenancy".

(3) In subsection (6), after "Scotland" there shall be inserted—
"(za) in subsection (1) of this section, the words 'and was not comprised in a farm business tenancy' shall be omitted;"."

18.—(1) Section 28 of that Act (special provision as to market gardens) shall be amended as follows.

(2) In subsection (1), after "market garden" there shall be inserted "and was not comprised in a farm business tenancy."

(3) In subsection (6), after "Scotland" there shall be inserted "in subsection (1) of this section, the words 'and was not comprised in a farm business tenancy' shall be omitted; and".

19.—In section 51 of that Act (interpretation) in subsection (1)—
   (a) after the definition of "the Act of 1986" there shall be inserted-"'the Act of 1995' means the Agricultural Tenancies Act 1995;"and
   (b) after the definition of "emergency powers" there shall be inserted-"'farm business tenancy' has the same meaning as in the Act of 1995;".

20.—(1) Schedule 7 to that Act (adjustments between landlords and tenants and in respect of mortgages and mining leases and orders) shall be amended as follows.

(2) After paragraph 1, there shall be inserted-"(1A.)—
(1) The provisions of this paragraph shall have effect where—
   (a) paragraphs (a) and (b) of subsection (1) of section 25A of this Act apply, and
   (b) the farm business tenancy at the end of which the tenant could have claimed compensation for tenant's improvements terminates on or after the date of entry, but before the end of the period of occupation, without being succeeded by another such subsequent tenancy.

(2) In the circumstances specified in sub-paragraph (1) of this paragraph, the provisions of Part III of the Act of 1995—
   (a) shall apply, in relation to the tenancy mentioned in that sub-paragraph, as if, at the termination of that tenancy, the land in question were in the state in which it was immediately before the date of entry, and
   (b) if the tenant under that tenancy quitted the holding before the termination of his tenancy, shall so apply as if he had quitted the holding on the termination of his tenancy.

(3) In sub-paragraph (2) of this paragraph, 'holding', in relation to a farm business tenancy, and 'termination', in relation to a tenancy, have the same meaning as in the Act of 1995."

(3) In paragraph 2, in sub-paragraph (1), after "agricultural holding" there shall be inserted "held under a tenancy in relation to which the Act of 1986 applies".

(4) After that paragraph there shall be inserted-"(2A.)—
(1) The provisions of this paragraph shall have effect where land comprised in a

farm business tenancy is comprised in a compulsory rights order (whether any other land is comprised in the holding, or comprised in the order, or not), and—
  (a) before the date of entry there had been provided in relation to the land in question tenant's improvements (in this paragraph referred to as 'the former tenant's improvements') in respect of which, immediately before that date, the tenant had a prospective right to compensation under section 16 of the Act of 1995 on quitting the holding on the termination of the tenancy, and
  (b) at the end of the period of occupation the circumstances are such that Part III of that Act would have applied as mentioned in subsections (3) and (4) of section 25A of this Act, but for the fact that the benefit of the former tenant's improvements has been replaced, on the restoration of the land, by other improvements (in this paragraph referred to as 'the new improvements') of comparable benefit to the land.

(2) In the circumstances specified in sub-paragraph (1) of this paragraph, Part III of the Act of 1995 shall have effect in relation to the new improvements as if those improvements were tenant's improvements.

(3) Subsections (2) and (6) of section 25A of this Act shall apply for the purposes of this paragraph as they apply for the purposes of that section."

(5) After paragraph 3 there shall be inserted-"(3A.)—Where by virtue of section 25A of this Act a tenant is entitled to compensation for tenant's improvements as mentioned in that section and—
  (a) after the end of the period of occupation expenses are incurred in replacing the benefit of the tenant's improvements by other improvements of comparable benefit to the land, and
  (b) the person incurring those expenses (whether he is the landlord or not) is entitled to compensation in respect of those expenses under section 22 of this Act,
section 13 of the Act of 1995 shall apply as if the works in respect of which those expenses are incurred were not tenant's improvements, if apart from this paragraph they would constitute such improvements."

(6) At the end of paragraph 4, there shall be added—
  "(7)—In this paragraph 'agricultural holding' does not include an agricultural holding held under a farm business tenancy."

(7) After that paragraph there shall be inserted-"4A.—

(1) The provisions of this paragraph shall apply where—
  (a) immediately before the operative date of a compulsory rights order, any of the land comprised in the order is subject to a farm business tenancy, and
  (b) that tenancy continues until after the end of the period of occupation.

(2) The landlord or tenant under the tenancy may, by notice in writing served on his tenant or landlord, demand a reference to arbitration of the question whether any of the terms and conditions of the tenancy (including any term or condition relating to rent) should be varied in consequence of any change in the state of the land resulting from the occupation or use of the land in the exercise of rights conferred by the order; and subsection (3) of section 28 of the Act of 1995 shall

SCHEDULE

apply in relation to a notice under this sub-paragraph as it applies in relation to a notice under subsection (2) of that section.

(3) On a reference by virtue of this paragraph, the arbitrator shall determine what variations (if any) should be made in the terms and conditions of the tenancy, and the date (not being earlier than the end of the period of occupation) from which any such variations are to take effect or to be treated as having taken effect; and as from that date the tenancy shall have effect, or, as the case may be, shall be treated as having had effect, subject to any variations determined by the arbitrator under this paragraph.

(4) The provisions of this paragraph shall not affect any right of the landlord or the tenant, or the jurisdiction of the arbitrator, under Part II of the Act of 1995; but where—

(a) there is a reference by virtue of this paragraph and a reference under Part II of that Act in respect of the same tenancy, and

(b) it appears to the arbitrator that the reference under Part II of that Act relates wholly or mainly to the consequences of the occupation or use of the land in the exercise of rights conferred by the order,

he may direct that proceedings on the two references shall be taken concurrently."

(8) In paragraph 5(1), after "agricultural holding" there shall be inserted "held under a tenancy in relation to which the Act of 1986 applies".

(9) In paragraph 6—

(a) in sub-paragraph (1), for "an agricultural holding" there shall be substituted"—

(a) an agricultural holding held under a tenancy in relation to which the Act of 1986 applies, or

(b) a holding under a farm business tenancy,"; and

(b) after sub-paragraph (2) there shall be added-

"(2A) In sub-paragraph (1) of this paragraph, 'holding', in relation to a farm business tenancy, has the same meaning as in the Act of 1995."

(10) In paragraph 7—

(a) after "The provisions of" there shall be inserted "sub-paragraphs (1) to (6) of";

(b) for "that paragraph" there shall be substituted "those sub-paragraphs"; and

(c) after "subject to a mortgage" there shall be inserted "but not comprised in a farm business tenancy".

(11) After that paragraph there shall be inserted-"(7A.)—The provisions of paragraph 4A of this Schedule shall apply in relation to mortgages of land comprised in farm business tenancies as they apply in relation to such tenancies, as if any reference in that paragraph to such a tenancy were a reference to such a mortgage, and any reference to a landlord or to a tenant were a reference to a mortgagee or to a mortgagor, as the case may be."

(12) In paragraph 12(1)(a), for the words from "did" to "holding" there shall be substituted "was not comprised in a tenancy in relation to which the Act of 1986 applies or in a farm business tenancy".

(13) In paragraph 13, after "or to a tenancy" there shall be inserted "(other than a reference to a tenancy in relation to which the Act of 1986 applies or a farm business tenancy)".

(14) In paragraph 25—
   (*a*) in sub-paragraph (*a*), at the beginning there shall be inserted "subject to sub-paragraphs (*ba*), (*bc*), (*bd*)(*i*) and (*be*) of this paragraph,";
   (*b*) after sub-paragraph (*b*), there shall be inserted—

"(*ba*) in sub-paragraph (1) of paragraph 2, the words 'held under a tenancy in relation to which the Act of 1986 applies' shall be omitted;

(*bb*) sub-paragraph (7) of paragraph 4 shall be omitted;

(*bc*) in sub-paragraph (1) of paragraph 5, the words 'held under a tenancy in relation to which the Act of 1986 applies' shall be omitted;

(*bd*) in paragraph (6)—

(i) for paragraphs (*a*) and (*b*) of sub-paragraph (1) there shall be substituted the words 'an agricultural holding'; and

(ii) sub-paragraph (2A) shall be omitted;

(*be*) in sub-paragraph (1)(*a*) of paragraph 12, for the words 'was not comprised in a tenancy in relation to which the Act of 1986 applies or in a farm business tenancy' there shall be substituted the words 'did not constitute or form part of an agricultural holding';" and"
   (*c*) in sub-paragraph (*c*), for "7" there shall be substituted "1A, 2A, 3A, 4A, 7, 7A".

The Agriculture (Miscellaneous Provisions) Act 1963 (c. 11)

21.—(1) Section 22 of the Agriculture (Miscellaneous Provisions) Act 1963 (allowances to persons displaced from agricultural land) shall be amended as follows.

(2) In subsection (1), for paragraph (*a*) there shall be substituted—

"(*a*) the land—

(i) is used for the purposes of agriculture (within the meaning of the Agricultural Tenancies Act 1995) and is so used by way of a trade or business, or

(ii) is not so used but is comprised in a farm business tenancy (within the meaning of the Agricultural Tenancies Act 1995) and used for the purposes of a trade or business,"

(3) In subsection (6)(*c*), for "the Agricultural Holdings Act 1986" there shall be substituted ", the Agricultural Tenancies Act 1995".

The Leasehold Reform Act 1967 (c. 88)

22.—In section 1(3) of the Leasehold Reform Act 1967 (tenants entitled to enfranchisement or extension), for paragraph (*b*) there shall be substituted—

"(*b*) it is comprised in—

(i) an agricultural holding within the meaning of the Agricultural Holdings Act 1986 held under a tenancy in relation to which that Act applies, or

SCHEDULE

(ii) the holding held under a farm business tenancy within the meaning of the Agricultural Tenancies Act 1995."

The Agriculture (Miscellaneous Provisions) Act 1968 (c. 34)

23.—In section 12 of the Agriculture (Miscellaneous Provisions) Act 1968 (additional payments in consequence of compulsory acquisition etc of agricultural holdings), after subsection (1) there shall be inserted-"(1A) No sum shall be payable by virtue of subsection (1) of this section in respect of any land comprised in a farm business tenancy within the meaning of the Agricultural Tenancies Act 1995."

The Land Compensation Act 1973 (c. 26)

24.—In section 48 of the Land Compensation Act 1973 (compensation in respect of agricultural holdings) at the beginning of subsection (1) there shall be inserted "Subject to subsection (1A) below" and after subsection (1) there shall be inserted-"(1A)—This section does not have effect where the tenancy of the agricultural holding is a tenancy to which, by virtue of section 4 of the Agricultural Tenancies Act 1995, the Agricultural Holdings Act 1986 does not apply."

The Rent (Agriculture) Act 1976 (c. 80)

25.—(1) Section 9 of the Rent (Agriculture) Act 1976 (effect of determination of superior tenancy, etc) shall be amended as follows.

(2) In subsection (3), after "the Agricultural Holdings Act 1986" there shall be inserted "held under a tenancy in relation to which that Act applies and land comprised in a farm business tenancy within the meaning of the Agricultural Tenancies Act 1995."

(3) In subsection (4), for the words from "or" at the end of paragraph (*b*) onwards there shall be substituted—

"(*c*) a tenancy of an agricultural holding within the meaning of the Agricultural Holdings Act 1986 which is a tenancy in relation to which that Act applies; or

(*d*) a farm business tenancy within the meaning of the Agricultural Tenancies Act 1995."

26.—In Schedule 2 to that Act (meaning of "relevant licence" and "relevant tenancy"), in paragraph 2 for the words from "and a tenancy" to the end there shall be substituted ", a tenancy of an agricultural holding within the meaning of the Agricultural Holdings Act 1986 which is a tenancy in relation to which that Act applies, and a farm business tenancy within the meaning of the Agricultural Tenancies Act 1995."

The Rent Act 1977 (c. 42)

27.—For section 10 of the Rent Act 1977 there shall be substituted-(10.)- "Agricultural holdings etc. (1) A tenancy is not a protected tenancy if—

(a) the dwelling-house is comprised in an agricultural holding and is occupied by the person responsible for the control (whether as tenant or as servant or agent of the tenant) of the farming of the holding, or

(b) the dwelling-house is comprised in the holding held under a farm business tenancy and is occupied by the person responsible for the control (whether as tenant or as servant or agent of the tenant) of the management of the holding.

(2) In subsection (1) above-'agricultural holding' means any agricultural holding within the meaning of the Agricultural Holdings Act 1986 held under a tenancy in relation to which that Act applies, and 'farm business tenancy', and 'holding' in relation to such a tenancy, have the same meaning as in the Agricultural Tenancies Act 1995."

28.—(1) Section 137 of that Act (effect on sub-tenancy of determination of superior tenancy) shall be amended as follows.

(2) In subsection (3), after "the Agricultural Holdings Act 1986" there shall be inserted "held under a tenancy to which that Act applies and land comprised in a farm business tenancy within the meaning of the Agricultural Tenancies Act 1995."

(3) In subsection (4), in paragraph (c), for the words from "applies" onwards there shall be substituted "applies—

(i) a tenancy of an agricultural holding within the meaning of the Agricultural Holdings Act 1986 which is a tenancy in relation to which that Act applies, or

(ii) a farm business tenancy within the meaning of the Agricultural Tenancies Act 1995."

The Protection from Eviction Act 1977 (c. 43)

29.—In section 8(1) of the Protection from Eviction Act 1977 (interpretation)—

(a) in paragraph (d), after "Agricultural Holdings Act 1986" there shall be inserted "which is a tenancy in relation to which that Act applies", and

(b) at the end there shall be added—

"(g) a farm business tenancy within the meaning of the Agricultural Tenancies Act 1995."

The Housing Act 1985 (c. 68)

30.—In Schedule 1 to the Housing Act 1985 (tenancies which are not secure tenancies), for paragraph 8 there shall be substituted—

"Agricultural holdings etc.

8.— (1) A tenancy is not a secure tenancy if—

(a) the dwelling-house is comprised in an agricultural holding and is occupied by the person responsible for the control (whether as tenant or as servant or agent of the tenant) of the farming of the holding, or

SCHEDULE

(b) the dwelling-house is comprised in the holding held under a farm business tenancy and is occupied by the person responsible for the control (whether as tenant or as servant or agent of the tenant) of the management of the holding."

(2) In sub-paragraph (1) above-'agricultural holding' means any agricultural holding within the meaning of the Agricultural Holdings Act 1986 held under a tenancy in relation to which that Act applies, and 'farm business tenancy', and 'holding' in relation to such a tenancy, have the same meaning as in the Agricultural Tenancies Act 1995."

The Landlord and Tenant Act 1985 (c. 70)

31.—In section 14(3) of the Landlord and Tenant Act 1985 (leases to which section 11 does not apply), at the end there shall be added "and in relation to which that Act applies or to a farm business tenancy within the meaning of the Agricultural Tenancies Act 1995."

The Agricultural Holdings Act 1986 (c. 5)

32.—In Schedule 6 to the Agricultural Holdings Act 1986 (eligibility to apply for a new tenancy under Part IV of that Act), in paragraph 6 (occupation to be disregarded for purposes of occupancy condition), in sub-paragraph (1) after paragraph (d) there shall be inserted—

"(dd) under a farm business tenancy, within the meaning of the Agricultural Tenancies Act 1995, for less than five years (including a farm business tenancy which is a periodic tenancy),"

The Housing Act 1988 (c. 50)

33.—[...][103]

34.—In Schedule I to that Act (tenancies which cannot be assured tenancies), for paragraph 7 there shall be substituted—

"Tenancies of agricultural holdings etc.

7.— (1) A tenancy under which the dwelling-house—
(a) is comprised in an agricultural holding, and
(b) is occupied by the person responsible for the control (whether as tenant or as servant or agent of the tenant) of the farming of the holding.

(2) A tenancy under which the dwelling-house—
(a) is comprised in the holding held under a farm business tenancy, and
(b) is occupied by the person responsible for the control (whether as tenant or as servant or agent of the tenant) of the management of the holding.

(3) In this paragraph-'agricultural holding' means any agricultural holding within the meaning of the Agricultural Holdings Act 1986 held under a tenancy in relation to which that Act applies, and 'farm business tenancy' and 'holding', in

---

[3] Repealed by Housing Act 1996 (c.52), s.227, Sched. 19, Pt. IX.

relation to such a tenancy, have the same meaning as in the Agricultural Tenancies Act 1995."

The Town and Country Planning Act 1990 (c. 8)

35.—(1) Section 65 of the Town and Country Planning Act 1990 (notice etc. of applications for planning permissions) shall be amended as follows.

(2) In subsection (2), for "a tenant of any agricultural holding any part of which is comprised in that land" there shall be substituted "an agricultural tenant of that land".

(3) In subsection (8), for the definition of "agricultural holding" there shall be substituted-"'agricultural tenant', in relation to any land, means any person who
  (*a*) is the tenant, under a tenancy in relation to which the Agricultural Holdings Act 1986 applies, of an agricultural holding within the meaning of that Act any part of which is comprised in that land; or
  (*b*) is the tenant, under a farm business tenancy (within the meaning of the Agricultural Tenancies Act 1995), of land any part of which is comprised in that land;".

The Coal Mining Subsidence Act 1991 (c. 45)

36.—In section 21 of the Coal Mining Subsidence Act 1991 (property belonging to protected tenants) in subsection (3), after paragraph (*a*) there shall be inserted—
  "(*aa*) a tenant under a farm business tenancy within the meaning of the Agricultural Tenancies Act 1995;"

37.—In Schedule 3 to that Act (property belonging to protected tenants) in paragraph 1(2), after paragraph (*b*) there shall be inserted—
  "(*bb*) section 20 of the Agricultural Tenancies Act 1995;"

PART III

STATUTORY INSTRUMENTS

	PAGE
The Reserve and Auxiliary Forces (Agricultural Tenants) Regulations 1959 (S.I. 1959 No. 84)	835
The Agriculture (Miscellaneous Time-Limits) Regulations 1959 (S.I. 1959 No. 171)	836
The Agriculture (Maintenance, Repair and Insurance of Fixed Equipment) Regulations 1973 (S.I. 1973 No. 1473)	837
The Agriculture (Time-Limit) Regulations 1973 (S.I. 1973 No. 1482)	846
The Agriculture (Miscellaneous Provisions) Act 1976 (Application of Provisions) Regulations 1977 (S.I. 1977 No. 1215)	846
The Agricultural Land Tribunals (Rules) Order 1978 (S.I. 1978 No. 259)	849
The Agricultural Land Tribunals (Areas) Order 1982 (S.I. 1982 No. 97)	877
The Agricultural Land Tribunals (Succession to Agricultural Tenancies) Order 1984 (S.I. 1984 No. 1301)	879
The Milk Quota (Calculation of Standard Quota) Order 1986 (S.I. 1986 No. 1530)	890
The Agricultural Holdings (Arbitration on Notices) Order 1987 (S.I. 1987 No. 710)	893
The Agricultural Holdings (Forms of Notice to Pay Rent or to Remedy) Regulations 1987 (S.I. 1987 No. 711)	900
The Agricultural Holdings (Form of Award in Arbitration Proceedings) Order 1990 (S.I. 1990 No. 1472)	902
The Agricultural Holdings (Fee) Regulations 1996 (S.I. 1996 No. 337)	903
The Agricultural Holdings (Units of Production) Order 1996 (S.I. 1996 No. 2163)	904
The Diary Produce Quotas Regulations 1997 (S.I. 1997 No. 733)	909
The Agricultural Holdings (Units of Production) Order 1997 (S.I. 1997 No. 1962)	952
The Agricultural Holdings (Units of Production) Order 1998 (S.I. 1998 No. 2025)	958

REGULATION 1

THE RESERVE AND AUXILIARY FORCES (AGRICULTURAL TENANTS) REGULATIONS 1959

A.12

(S.I. 1959 No. 84)

I, David Viscount Kilmuir, Lord High Chancellor of Great Britain, in exercise of the powers conferred on me by section 22 of the Reserve and Auxiliary Forces (Protection of Civil Interests) Act, 1951, as amended by section 8 of and the First Schedule to the Agriculture Act, 1958, do hereby make the following Regulations:-

1. These Regulations, which may be cited as the Reserve and Auxiliary Forces (Agricultural Tenants) Regulations, 1959, shall come into operation on the 26th day of January, 1959.

2. The Reserve and Auxiliary Forces (Protection of Civil Interests) (Agricultural Tenants' Representation) Regulations, 1951, are hereby revoked, so however that any direction given under those Regulations shall have effect as if it has been given under these Regulations.

3. In these Regulations, unless the context otherwise requires-
"1948 Act" means the Agricultural Holdings Act, 1948, as amended;
"1951 Act" means the Reserve and Auxiliary Forces (Protection of Civil Interests) Act, 1951, as amended;
"chairman" means the chairman of an Agricultural Land Tribunal established under section 73 of the Agriculture Act, 1947, for the area in which the holding which is the subject of a notice to quit or of proceedings to which these Regulations apply is wholly or in the greater part situate, or a person nominated under paragraph 16(1)(a) or appointed under paragraph 16A of the Ninth Schedule to that Act to act as chairman in that area, and "secretary" means the secretary of that tribunal.

4. The Interpretation Act, 1889, shall apply to the interpretation of these Regulations as it applies to the interpretation of an Act of Parliament.

5. Where the chairman is satisfied on an application by any person that-
   (a) a notice to quit has been given to a service man as mentioned in sub-section (1) of section 21 of the 1951 Act,
   (b) the service man is serving abroad,
   (c) the applicant is a fit person to serve a counter-notice under subsection (1) of section 24 of the 1948 Act on the service man's behalf but is not duly authorised to do so, and
   (d) the application is made in good faith in the interests of the service man, the chairman may direct that the applicant be deemed to be duly authorised to serve the counter-notice on the service man's behalf.

6. Where a counter-notice under subsection (1) of section 24 of the 1948 Act has been served-

(a) in a case where a notice to quit has been given to a service man as mentioned in subsection (1) of section 21 of the 1951 Act, or
(b) in a case where subsection (5) of the said section 21 applies in relation to a service man,

and it appears to the chairman that-
   (i) it is necessary for any act or proceedings consequential upon the service of the counter-notice to be performed or conducted by the service man;
   (ii) the service man is serving abroad, and
   (iii) no person has been duly authorised to perform the act or conduct the proceedings on the service man's behalf,

the chairman may, whether on an application by any person or otherwise, direct that some fit person who is willing to perform the act or conduct the proceedings shall be deemed to be authorised for that purpose and to take all such steps as may be necessary or incidental thereto.

7.—(1) An application to the chairman for a direction under these Regulations shall be made in writing and delivered or sent to the secretary.

(2) The chairman may, for the purpose of deciding whether to give the direction, require the applicant to furnish such testimonial or other evidence in support of his application as the chairman may think fit.

Dated the 15th day of January, 1959

GENERAL NOTE

The Reserve and Auxiliary Forces (Protection of Civil Interests) Act, 1951, provides that in certain circumstances a tenant of an agricultural holding, who is performing a period of service, shall have special protection in addition to that given by the Agricultural Holdings Act, 1948. These Regulations provide that, where a service man is entitled to this special protection, but is serving abroad and therefore unable to serve a counter-notice under section 24(1) of the 1948 Act, or to take some necessary step in subsequent proceedings, and has not authorised anyone to do so on his behalf, the chairman of an Agricultural Land Tribunal may authorise a suitable person to do so.

A.13   **THE AGRICULTURE (MISCELLANEOUS TIME-LIMITS) REGULATIONS 1959**

(S.I. 1959 No. 171)

The Minister of Agriculture, Fisheries and Food, in exercise of the powers conferred upon him by sub-section (2) of section 30, sub-sections (1) and (2) of section 7, and sub-section (1) of section 94 of the Agricultural Holdings Act, 1948, and of all other powers enabling him in that behalf, hereby makes the following regulations:—

1.—(1) These regulations may be cited as the Agriculture (Miscellaneous

Time-Limits) Regulations, 1959, and shall come into operation on the 4th day of February, 1959.

(2) The Agriculture (Miscellaneous Time-Limits) Regulations, 1948, to the extent that those regulations are in force immediately before the coming into operation of these regulations, are hereby revoked.

(3) In these regulations the expression "the Act" means the Agricultural Holdings Act, 1948.

(4) The Interpretation Act, 1889, shall apply to the interpretation of these Regulations as it applies to the interpretation of an Act of Parliament.

2.—(1) The time within which a landlord shall give notice in writing to the tenant, pursuant to paragraph (*a*) of subsection (2) of section 30 of the Act, that a contract has been made for the sale of the landlord's interest in land of which the tenant has been given notice to quit, shall be whichever is the shorter of the two following periods, namely, one month from the making of the said contract, or the period remaining before the expiration of the said notice to quit.

(2) The time within which a landlord may, pursuant to sub-section (1) of section 7 of the Act, require that there shall be determined by arbitration and paid by the tenant the amount of any compensation referred to in the said sub-section, shall be one month from the date on which there takes effect by virtue of section 5 or section 6 of the Act any transfer from the tenant to the landlord of liability for the maintenance or repair of any item of fixed equipment.

(3) The time within which a tenant may, pursuant to sub-section (2) of section 7 of the Act, require that any claim in respect of a previous failure by the landlord to discharge a liability for the maintenance or repair of any item of fixed equipment shall be determined by arbitration, shall be one month from the date on which there takes effect by virtue of section 5 or section 6 of the Act any transfer from the landlord to the tenant of the said liability for the maintenance or repair of any item of fixed equipment.

Minister of Agriculture, Fisheries and Food.

GENERAL NOTE

These regulations are made in the exercise of various powers under the Agricultural Holdings Act, 1948, to prescribe the time within which certain actions are to be carried out. Previous similar regulations made under similar powers conferred by the Agriculture Act, 1947, were S.I. 1948/No. 188. They were continued in force for the purposes of the 1948 Act by section 100 thereof, and their effect is reproduced in the present regulations, except to the extent that the 1948 regulations have been superseded by later provisions, or have become spent.

THE AGRICULTURE (MAINTENANCE, REPAIR AND INSURANCE OF FIXED EQUIPMENT) REGULATIONS 1973   A.14

(S.I. 1973 No. 1473)

The Minister of Agriculture, Fisheries and Food (hereinafter referred to as "the Minister"), in exercise of the powers conferred on him by section 6(1) of the

AGRICULTURE (MAINTENANCE, REPAIR, ETC.) REGULATIONS 1973

Agricultural Holdings Act 1948 as read with section 15(2) of the Agriculture (Miscellaneous Provisions) Act 1972, and of all other powers enabling him in that behalf, and after consultation with such bodies of persons as appear to him to represent the interests of landlords and tenants of agricultural holdings, hereby makes the following regulations:—

Citation and commencement

1. These regulations may be cited as the Agriculture (Maintenance, Repair and Insurance of Fixed Equipment) Regulations 1973, and shall come into operation on 29th September 1974.

Interpretation

2. The Interpretation Act 1889 shall apply for the interpretation of these regulations as it applies for the interpretation of an Act of Parliament and as if these regulations and the regulations hereby revoked were Acts of Parliament.

Incorporation of provisions in tenancy agreements

3. The provisions set forth in the Schedule hereto relating to the maintenance, repair and insurance of fixed equipment shall be deemed to be incorporated in every contract of tenancy of an agricultural holding, whether made before or after the commencement of the Agricultural Holdings Act 1948, except in so far as they would impose on one of the parties to an agreement in writing a liability which under the agreement is imposed on the other: Provided that where the interest of the landlord is held for the purposes of a Government department, or where a person representing Her Majesty or the Duke of Cornwall under section 87 of the Agricultural Holdings Act 1948 is deemed to be the landlord, or where the landlord has made provision approved by the Minister for defraying the cost of any such works of repair or replacement as are referred to in sub-paragraph (1)(*b*) of paragraph 2 of the Schedule hereto, the provision of sub-paragraph (1)(*a*) of the said paragraph 2 requiring the landlord to insure against loss or damage by fire shall not apply.

Revocation

4. The Agriculture (Maintenance, Repair and Insurance of Fixed Equipment) Regulations 1948 are hereby revoked. Minister of Agriculture, Fisheries and Food.

SCHEDULE

MAINTENANCE, REPAIR AND INSURANCE OF THE FIXED EQUIPMENT OF A HOLDING

PART I

RIGHTS AND LIABILITIES OF THE LANDLORD

1.—(1) To execute all repairs and replacements to the under-mentioned parts of the farmhouse, cottages and farm buildings, namely: roofs, including chimney stacks, chimney pots, eaves-guttering and downpipes, main walls and exterior walls, howsoever constructed, including walls and fences of open and covered yards and garden walls, together with any interior repair or decoration made necessary as a result of structural defect to such roofs or walls, floors, floor joists, ceiling joists and timbers, exterior and interior staircases and fixed ladders (including banisters or handrails) of the farmhouse and cottages, and doors, windows and skylights, including the frames of such doors, windows and skylights (but excepting glass or glass substitute, sashcords, locks and fastenings): provided that in the case of repairs and replacements to floorboards, interior staircases and fixed ladders (including banisters of handrails), doors and windows and opening skylights (including frames), eaves-guttering and downpipes, the landlord may recover one-half of the reasonable cost thereof from the tenant.

(2) To execute all repairs and replacements to underground water supply pipes, wells, bore-holes and reservoirs and all underground installations connected therewith, and to sewage disposal systems, including septic tanks, filtering media and cesspools (but excluding covers and tops).

(3) Except as provided by paragraph 8, to replace anything mentioned in paragraph 5(1) which has worn out or otherwise become incapable of further repair unless the tenant is himself liable to replace it under paragraph 6.

2.—(1)
  (a) To keep the farmhouse, cottages and farm buildings insured to their full value against loss or damage by fire; and
  (b) as often as the farmhouse, cottages and farm buildings or any, or any part, of them shall be destroyed or damaged by fire, to execute all works of repair or replacement thereto necessary to make good damage by fire and to cause all money received in respect of such destruction or damage by virtue of such insurance to be laid out in the execution of such works.

(2) The proviso to paragraph 1(1) shall not apply to works falling within sub-paragraph (1)(b) of this paragraph.

3.—(1) As often as may be necessary in order to prevent deterioration, and in any case at intervals of not more than five years, properly to paint with at least two coats of a suitable quality or properly and adequately to gas-tar, creosote or otherwise effectively treat with a preservative material all outside wood and ironwork of the farmhouse, cottages and farm buildings, the inside wood and ironwork of all external outward opening doors and windows of farm buildings (but not of the farmhouse or cottages), and the interior structural steelwork of open-sided farm buildings which have been previously painted, gas-tarred, creosoted or otherwise treated with preservative material or which it is necessary in order to prevent deterioration of the same so to paint, gas-tar, creosote or treat with preservative material provided that in respect of doors, windows, eaves-guttering and downpipes the landlord may recover one-half of the reasonable cost of such work from the tenant, but if any such work to any of those items is completed before the commencement of the fifth year of the tenancy the sum which the landlord may so recover from the tenant shall be restricted to an amount equal to the aggregate of one-tenth part of such reasonable cost in respect of each year that has elapsed between the commencement of the tenancy and the completion of such work.

(2) In the last foregoing sub-paragraph "open-sided" means having the whole or the greater part of at least one side or end permanently open, apart from roof supports, if any.

4.—(1) The landlord shall be under no liability—
   (a) to execute repairs or replacements or to insure buildings or fixtures which are the property of the tenant, or
   (b) subject to paragraph 2(1)(b), to execute repairs or replacements rendered necessary by the wilful act or the negligence of the tenant or any members of his household or his employees.

(2) If the tenant does not start work on the repairs or replacements for which he is liable under paragraphs 5, 6, 7 and 8 within two months, or if he fails to complete them within three months of receiving from the landlord a written notice (not being a notice to remedy breach of tenancy agreement by doing work of repair, maintenance or replacement in a form prescribed under section 19(1) and (3) of the Agriculture (Miscellaneous Provisions) Act 1963 specifying the necessary repairs or replacements and calling on him to execute them the landlord may enter and execute such repairs or replacements and recover the reasonable cost from the tenant forthwith.

(3)
   (a) If the tenant wishes to contest his liability to execute any repairs or replacements specified in a notice served upon him by the landlord under the last foregoing sub-paragraph he shall within one month serve a counter-notice in writing upon the landlord specifying the grounds on which and the items of repair or replacement in respect of which he denies liability and requiring the question of liability in respect thereof to be determined by arbitration under the Act.
   (b) Upon service of the counter-notice on the landlord, the operation of the notice (including the running of time thereunder) shall be suspended, in so far as it relates to the items specified in the counter-notice, until the termination of an arbitration determining the question of liability in respect of those items.
   (c) In this sub-paragraph, "termination", in relation to an arbitration, means the date on which the arbitrator's award is delivered to the tenant.

Part II
Rights and Liabilities of the Tenant

Except in so far as such liabilities fall to be undertaken by the landlord under Part 1 hereof:

5.—(1) To repair and to keep and leave clean and in good tenantable repair, order and condition the farmhouse, cottages and farm buildings together with all fixtures and fittings, boilers, ranges and grates, drains, sewers, gulleys, grease-traps, manholes and inspection chambers, electrical supply systems and fittings, water supply systems and fittings in so far as they are situated above ground, including pipes, tanks, cisterns, sanitary fittings, drinking troughs and pumping equipment, hydraulic rams (whether situated above or below ground), fences, hedges, field walls, stiles, gates and posts, cattle grids, bridges, culverts, ponds, watercourses, sluices, ditches, roads and yards in and upon the holding, or which during the tenancy may be erected or provided thereon.

(2) To repair or replace all removable covers to manholes, to inspection chambers and to sewage disposal systems.

(3) To keep clean and in good working order all roof valleys, eaves-guttering and downpipes, wells, septic tanks, cesspools and sewage disposal systems.

(4) To use carefully so as to protect from wilful, reckless or negligent damage all items for the repair or replacement of which the landlord is responsible under paragraph 1; and also to report in writing immediately to the landlord any damage, however caused, to items for the repair or replacement of which the landlord is responsible.

6. Subject to paragraph 2(1)(*b*)—

(1) to replace or repair and, upon replacement or repair, adequately to paint, gas-tar, creosote or otherwise treat with effective preservative material as may be proper, all items of fixed equipment, and to do any work, where such replacement, repair or work is rendered necessary by the wilful act or negligence of the tenant or any members of his household or his employees; and

(2) to replace anything mentioned in paragraph 5(1) which has worn out or otherwise become incapable of repair if its condition has been brought about by or is substantially due to the tenant's failure to repair it.

7. As often as may be necessary, and in any case at intervals of not more than seven years, properly to clean, colour, whiten, paper, paint, limewash or otherwise treat with materials of suitable quality the inside of the farmhouse, cottages and farm buildings, including the interior of outward opening doors and windows of the farmhouse and cottages, which have been previously so treated and in the last year of the tenancy to limewash the inside of all buildings which previously have been limewashed.

8. [(1) Notwithstanding the general liability of the landlord for repairs and replacements, to renew all broken or cracked tiles or slates and to replace all slipped tiles or slates from time to time as the damage occurs, but so that the cost shall not exceed £100 in any one year of the tenancy.]

[(2) This paragraph shall not have effect so as to render a tenant liable for the cost of any renewals or replacement of tiles in excess of £25 which have been carried out by the landlord prior to 24th March 1988.]

Note

The words in square brackets were amended or added by The Agricultural (Maintenance, Repair and Insurance of Fixed Equipment) (Amendment) Regulations 1988, S.I. 1988 No. 281.

9. To cut, trim or lay a proper proportion of the hedges in each year of the tenancy so as to maintain them in good and sound condition.

10. To dig out, scour and cleanse all ponds, watercourses, ditches and grips, as may be necessary to maintain them at sufficient width and depth, and to keep clear from obstruction all field drains and their outlets.

11.—(1) If the last year of the tenancy is not a year in which such cleaning, colouring, whitening, papering, painting, limewashing or other treatment as is mentioned in paragraph 7 is due to be carried out, the tenant shall pay to the landlord at the end of such last year either the estimated reasonable cost thereof or a sum equal to the aggregate of one-seventh part of that cost in respect of each year that has elapsed since such last cleaning, colouring, whitening, papering, painting, limewashing or other treatment as aforesaid, was completed, whichever is the less.

(2) If the last year of the tenancy is not a year in which the landlord is liable, under paragraph 3, to paint, gas-tar, creosote or otherwise treat the doors, windows, eaves-guttering and downpipes of buildings, the tenant shall pay to the landlord at the end of such last year either one-half of the estimated reasonable cost thereof or a sum equal to the aggregate of one-tenth part of that cost in respect of each year that has elapsed since such last painting, gas-tarring, creosoting or other treatment as aforesaid, was completed, whichever is the less.

(3) In the assessment of any compensation payable by the tenant on the termination of the tenancy in respect of dilapidation, any accrued liability under the two preceding sub-paragraphs shall be taken into account.

[12.—(1) If the landlord fails to execute repairs other than repairs to an underground waterpipe which are his liability within three months of receiving from the tenant a written notice specifying the necessary repairs and calling on him to execute them, the tenant may execute such repairs and, except to the extent to which under the terms of Part I hereof the tenant is liable to bear the cost, recover (subject to the landlord's right to require arbitration under sub-paragraph (5) below) the reasonable cost from the landlord forthwith.

(2) If the landlord fails to execute any repairs which are his liability to an underground waterpipe within one week of receiving from the tenant a written notice specifying the necessary repairs and calling on him to execute them, the tenant may execute such repairs and, except to the extent to which under the terms of Part I hereof the tenant is liable to bear the cost, recover (subject to the landlord's right to require arbitration under sub-paragraph (5) below) the reasonable cost from the landlord upon the expiry of a period of one month from the execution of the repairs.

(3) Subject to sub-paragraph (4) below, if the landlord fails to execute any replacements which are his liability within three months of receiving from the tenant a written notice specifying the necessary replacements and calling on him to execute them, the tenant may execute such replacements and, except to the extent to which under the terms of Part I hereof the tenant is liable to bear the cost, recover (subject to the landlord's right to require arbitration under sub-paragraph (5) below) the reasonable cost from the landlord forthwith.

(4) The tenant shall not be entitled to recover, in respect of the aggregate of the replacements executed by him after being specified in a notice given in pursuance of sub-paragraph (3) above, in any year of the tenancy any sum in excess of

SCHEDULE

whichever of the following sums is hereinafter specified in relation to the replacements so executed, that is to say—

(a) in relation to replacements executed in any year of the tenancy terminating on or before 24th March 1988, a sum equal to the rent of the holding for that year or £500, whichever is the smaller, or

(b) in relation to replacements executed in any year of the tenancy terminating after 24th March 1988, a sum equal to the rent of the holding for that year or £2,000, whichever is the smaller.

(5) (a) If the landlord wishes to contest his liability to execute any repairs or replacements specified in a notice served upon him by the tenant under sub-paragraph (1), (2) or (3) above he shall within one month of the service of that notice serve a counter-notice in writing upon the tenant specifying the grounds on which and the items of repair or replacement in respect of which he denies liability and requiring the question of liability in respect thereof to be determined by arbitration under the Act.

(b) Upon service of a counter-notice on the tenant which relates to a notice served on the landlord under sub-paragraph (1) or (3) above, the operation of the notice so served under sub-paragraph (1) or (3) (including the running of time thereunder) shall be suspended, in so far as it relates to the items specified in the counter-notice, until the termination of an arbitration determining the question of liability in respect of those items.

(c) Upon service of a counter-notice on the tenant which relates to a notice served on the landlord under sub-paragraph (2) above, the tenant's right under that sub-paragraph to recover the reasonable cost of the repairs specified in the counter-notice shall not arise unless the question of liability to execute those repairs is first determined by arbitration in favour of the tenant, and shall thereupon arise from the termination of the arbitration.

(d) In this sub-paragraph "termination" in relation to an arbitration means the date on which the arbitrator's award is deliver to the landlord.]

Note

Paragraph 12 was amended by The Agricultural (Maintenance, Repair and Insurance of Fixed Equipment) (Amendment) Regulations 1988, S.I. 1988 No. 281.

PART III
GENERAL PROVISIONS

13.—(1) If at any time and from time to time the landlord or the tenant shall be of opinion that any item of fixed equipment is, or before the same was damaged or destroyed by fire was, redundant to the farming of the holding, the landlord or the tenant may by giving two months' notice in writing to the other of them require that the question whether such item of fixed equipment is, or before such damage or destruction was, so redundant shall be determined, in default of agreement, by arbitration under the Act, and if the arbitrator shall award that the said item of fixed equipment is, or before such damage or destruction by fire was, redundant to the farming of the holding then, as from the date of such award, paragraph 14(1) shall apply to that item and both the landlord and the tenant shall be relieved from all liability in respect of any antecedent breach of any obligation to maintain, repair or replace the item of fixed equipment so awarded to be redundant and the landlord shall be entitled to demolish and remove such item of fixed equipment and to enter upon the holding for those purposes.

(2) In any arbitration to which sub-paragraph (1) of this paragraph applies, no item of fixed equipment shall be determined to be, or to have been before damage or destruction by fire, as the case may be, redundant to the farming of the holding, unless the arbitrator shall be satisfied that the repair or replacement of such item is or, as the case may be, was, not reasonably required having regard to-

(a)
    (i) the landlord's responsibilities to manage the holding in accordance with the rules of good estate management; and
    (ii) the period for which the holding may reasonably be expected to remain a separate holding; and

(b) the character and situation of the holding and the average requirements of a tenant reasonably skilled in husbandry.

14. Nothing contained in Part I or Part II hereof shall create any liability on the part of either landlord or tenant:

(1) to maintain, repair, replace or insure any item of fixed equipment which the landlord and the tenant agree in writing to be obsolete or redundant to the farming of the holding or which in the event of any dispute between them as to whether it is, or before the same was damaged or destroyed by fire was, redundant to the farming of the holding, shall be awarded to be so redundant by an arbitrator in an arbitration as mentioned in paragraph 13; or

(2) to execute any work if and so far as the execution of such work is rendered impossible (except at prohibitive or unreasonable expense) by reason of subsidence of any land or the blocking of outfalls which are not under the control of either the landlord or the tenant.

15. If any claim, question or difference shall arise between the landlord and the tenant under the foregoing provisions hereof, not being a matter which, otherwise than under the provisions of this paragraph, is required by or by virtue of the Act or section 19 of the Agriculture (Miscellaneous Provisions) Act 1963 (notice to remedy breach of tenancy agreement) or regulations or orders made thereunder or the foregoing provisions hereof to be determined by arbitration under the Act, such claim, question or difference shall be determined, in default of agreement, by arbitration under the Act.

Interpretation

16.—(1) In this Schedule, unless the context otherwise requires, "the Act" means the Agricultural Holdings Act 1948 as amended by any other enactment.

SCHEDULE

(2) Any reference in this Schedule to a numbered paragraph is a reference to the paragraph bearing that number in this Schedule.

GENERAL NOTE

These Regulations revoke and replace the Agriculture (Maintenance, Repair and Insurance of Fixed Equipment) Regulations 1948. They come into operation on September 29, 1974. These Regulations prescribe terms, set out in the Schedule, as to the maintenance, repair and insurance of fixed equipment which are to be deemed to be incorporated in every contract of tenancy of an agricultural holding. The Schedule to the Regulations divides between the landlord and the tenant of a holding the responsibility for maintaining, repairing and insuring fixed equipment, and imposes upon each party certain specific liabilities in regard to those matters. The prescribed terms do not apply where an agreement in writing is in existence, or is entered into, which imposes on one of the parties to the agreement a liability which the prescribed terms would impose on the other. The prescribed term requiring the landlord to insure against loss or damage by fire does not apply in the circumstances specified in the proviso to Regulation 3. Under section 6(2) of the Agricultural Holdings Act 1948, where a written agreement substantially modifies the rights and liabilities of the parties under the prescribed terms, it is open to either party to refer the terms of the tenancy relating to the maintenance, repair and insurance of fixed equipment to arbitration under the Act and the arbitrator may by his award vary the terms referred to arbitration in such manner as appears to him to be just and reasonable between the landlord and the tenant. The substance of the revoked Regulations is reproduced in these Regulations with certain differences, the main ones being the following:—

(a) Certain items have been added to the general repair and maintenance obligations of the landlord and the tenant respectively;

(b) The list of items in respect of the cost of repair of which the landlord is entitled to recover one-half from the tenant has been extended;

(c) The landlord is made liable to replace any items for the repair of which the tenant is liable (with certain exceptions) and which have become incapable of further repair, unless the tenant is expressly made liable for their replacement;

(d) Limits are placed on the amounts which the landlord and the tenant may recover from the other of them at the commencement or end of the tenancy as part of the cost of certain specified items of work carried out by them;

(e) The limit on the tenant's liability for replacement of roof tiles or slates in any one year is increased from £5 to £25;

(f) The tenant may recover from the landlord in any one year the cost of replacements carried out by him, but which are the landlord's liability, up to a limit of £500 or the year's rent whichever is the less; and

(g) Provisions are made enabling the landlord or the tenant on whom a notice has been served by the other of them requiring him to execute specified repairs or replacements, to contest his liability, and for determination of such disputes by arbitration under the Agricultural

Holdings Act 1948. Provision is also made for settling disputes concerning the redundancy of any building, and for settling other disputes arising under the Schedule, by arbitration under the Act.

A.15 THE AGRICULTURE (TIME-LIMIT) REGULATIONS 1973

(S.I. 1973 No. 1482)

The Minister of Agriculture, Fisheries and Food, in exercise of the powers conferred upon him by section 7(4) of the Agricultural Holdings Act 1948, and of all other powers enabling him in that behalf, hereby makes the following regulations:—

1. These regulations may be cited as the Agriculture (Time-Limit) Regulations 1973, and shall come into operation on 29th September 1974.

2.—(1) In these regulations "the Act" means the Agricultural Holdings Act 1948.

(2) The Interpretation Act 1889 shall apply for the interpretation of these regulations as it applies for the interpretation of an Act of Parliament.

3. The time within which the landlord or the tenant of a holding may refer the terms of the tenancy of a holding to arbitration under subsection (1) of section 5 of the Act so that, pursuant to section 7(4) of the Act, the arbitrator shall, for the purposes of subsection (2) of the said section 5, disregard any variation effected by the Agriculture (Maintenance, Repair and Insurance of Fixed Equipment) Regulations 1973 of the terms of the tenancy as to maintenance, repair or insurance of fixed equipment, shall be one year after the coming into operation of the said Regulations.

Minister of Agriculture, Fisheries and Food.

A.16 THE AGRICULTURE (MISCELLANEOUS PROVISIONS) ACT 1976 (APPLICATION OF PROVISIONS) REGULATIONS 1977

(S.I. 1977 No. 1215)

The Lord Chancellor, in exercise of the powers conferred on him by section 23(8) of the Agriculture (Miscellaneous Provisions) Act 1976, hereby makes the following Regulations:—

Citation, commencement and interpretation

1.—(1) These Regulations may be cited as the Agriculture (Miscellaneous Provisions) Act 1976 (Application of Provisions) Regulations 1977 and shall come into operation on 23rd August 1977.

(2) In these Regulations "the Act" means the Agriculture (Miscellaneous Provisions) Act 1976.

(3) The Interpretation Act 1889 shall apply to the interpretation of these Regulations as it applies to the interpretation of an Act of Parliament.

SCHEDULE

Application of the Act in cases of death before succession

2.—(1) Where a person entitled to a joint tenancy of an agricultural holding by virtue of a direction under section 20(9) of the Act dies before the relevant time (as defined in section 23(2) of the Act) without having become the tenant or a joint tenant of that holding, that direction shall from the date of his death cease to have effect in relation to that person if he is survived by any other person jointly entitled under the direction; but the direction shall continue to have effect (subject to the provisions of the Act) in relation to the other person or persons as if the dead person had not been named therein; and the provisions of Part II of the Act, so far as relevant, shall apply accordingly.

(2) Where—
  (a) a person entitled to a tenancy of an agricultural holding by virtue of a direction under section 20(5) or (6) of the Act; or
  (b) the sole survivor of two or more persons entitled to a joint tenancy of an agricultural holding by virtue of a direction under section 20(9) of the Act

dies before the relevant time (as defined in section 23(2) of the Act) without having become the tenant or joint tenant of that holding, the provisions of Part II of the Act, except section 23(8), shall apply in accordance with the provisions of the Schedule to these Regulations subject to the exceptions, additions and modifications set out therein.

(3) Where two or more persons who are jointly entitled to a tenancy of the holding by virtue of a direction under section 20(9) of the Act have died in circumstances rendering it uncertain which of them survived the other, such deaths shall for the purposes of these Regulations be presumed to have occurred in order of seniority, and accordingly the younger shall be deemed to have survived the elder.

Dated 21st July 1977.

SCHEDULE

APPLICATION OF PART II OF THE ACT

1. Sections 16 and 17 shall not apply.

2. Section 18 shall apply—
  (a) with the addition of the following subsection after subsection (1):—
   "(1A) In subsection (1) and in the definition of "the deceased" in subsection (2), the expression "tenant"includes a person who is—
     (i) entitled to a tenancy of an agricultural holding by virtue of a direction by the Tribunal under section 20(5) or (6) of this Act; or
     (ii) the sole survivor of two or more persons entitled to a joint tenancy of an agricultural holding by virtue of such a direction under section 20(9) of this Act,
  and who dies before the time at which, had he survived, he would have been deemed to have been granted and to have accepted that tenancy or joint tenancy";

(b) with the addition in subsection (4) of the words "(except section 19A)" after the words "this Part of this Act";
(c) as if the reference in subsection (4)(e) to subsection (1) included a reference to subsection (1A);
(d) with the exception of subsection (5).

3. Section 19 shall not apply, but instead the following section shall be added:—"19A—(1) Where at the date of death of the deceased the holding is the subject of a relevant notice to quit, the operation of that notice shall, subject to subsection (2) below and notwithstanding any provision of this Act having effect prior to the death of the deceased, take effect at the date specified in the notice for the termination of the tenancy to which it relates:Provided that where, in the case of a relevant notice to quit, there remains at the date of death of the deceased a period of less than twelve months before the date specified in the notice for the termination of the tenancy of the holding, the operation of the notice shall be postponed for a period of twelve months.

(2) A relevant notice to quit shall not have effect unless either—
(a) no application to become the tenant of the holding is made under section 20 of this Act within the relevant period; or
(b) one or more such applications having been made within that period, either—
 (i) none of the applications is determined by the Tribunal to be in their opinion a suitable person to become the tenant of the holding; or
 (ii) the Tribunal consent under section 22 of this Act to the operation of the notice to quit.

(3) In this section "relevant notice to quit" means a notice to quit the holding falling within section 24(2)(g) of the 1948 Act."

4. Sections 20 and 21 shall apply.

5. Section 22 shall apply as if the references to section 19 of the Act were references to section 19A.

6. Section 23 shall apply:—
(a) as if, in subsection (1), for the words "the date of death", there were substituted the words "the date when the original tenant died";
(b) as if for subsection (2) there were substituted the following sub-section:—
"(2A) In this and the following section "the relevant time" means the end of the twelve months immediately following the end of the year of tenancy in which the deceased died.";
(c) as if, in subsection (3), for the words "on the date of death the holding was held by the deceased" there were substituted the words "immediately before the death of the original tenant he held the holding";
(d) as if the following subsection were added:—
"(9) In this and the next following section "the original tenant" means the tenant of the holding to whose tenancy the deceased would have

SCHEDULE

succeeded, had he survived, by virtue of the provisions of this Part of this Act.".

7. Section 24 shall apply as if in subsection (5)(*a*) for the word "deceased's" there were substituted the words "the original tenant's".

GENERAL NOTE

These Regulations apply, with certain exceptions, additions and modifications, the provisions of Part II of the Agriculture (Miscellaneous Provisions) Act 1976 (which make provision for succession on the death of a tenant of an agricultural holding) in cases where the person or any of the persons whom a direction by an Agricultural Land Tribunal entitles to a tenancy or joint tenancy of the holding dies before he becomes the tenant thereof.

THE AGRICULTURAL LAND TRIBUNALS (RULES) ORDER 1978   A.17

(S.I. 1978 No. 259)

The Lord Chancellor, in exercise of the powers conferred on him by section 73(3) and (4) of the Agriculture Act 1947, as amended[1], section 50(3) of the Agricultural Holdings Act 1948 as amended[2] and section 6(4) and (6) of the Agriculture (Miscellaneous Provisions) Act 1954, as amended[3], and after consultation with the Council on Tribunals in accordance with section 10 of the Tribunals and Inquiries Act 1971, hereby makes the following Order:—

Citation, commencement and interpretation

1.—(1) This Order may be cited as the Agricultural Land Tribunals (Rules) Order 1978 and shall come into operation on 7th April 1978.

(2) The Interpretation Act 1889 shall apply to the interpretation of this Order as it applies to the interpretation of an Act of Parliament.

Rules of procedure

2. The Rules set out in Schedule 1 to this Order shall apply for the purposes of proceedings before Agricultural Land Tribunals other than proceedings arising from any application made under Part II of the Agriculture (Miscellaneous Provisions) Act 1976 [or under Schedule 2 to the Agricultural Holdings Act 1984].

Note

The words in square brackets were added by The Agricultural Land Tribunals (Succession to Agricultural Tenancies) Order 1984 (1984 No. 1301), as from 12 September 1984.

---

[1] Proviso repealed with savings by Agricultural Holdings Act 1948 (c. 63), Sched. 8, paras 98–100.
[2] Words substituted by Agriculture Act 1958 (c. 71), Sched. 1, pt I para. 3(a).
[3] Words substituted by Agriculture Act 1958 (c. 71), Sched. 1, pt. I para. 3(b).

Amendment of other rules

3. The Agricultural Land Tribunals (Succession to Agricultural Tenancies) Order 1976 shall be amended to the extent shown in Schedule 2 to this Order.

Revocation of orders

4.—(1) The Agricultural Land Tribunals and Notices to Quit Order 1959,the Agricultural Land Tribunals (Amendment) Order 1959,the Agricultural Land Tribunals (Amendment) Order 1961, and the Agricultural Land Tribunals (Amendment) Order 1974,are hereby revoked except to such extent as may be necessary for the disposal of an application pending at the commencement of this Order.

(2) The Agriculture (Procedure of Agricultural Land Tribunals) Order 1954 (which was revoked with a saving in 1959) shall continue to have effect for the purpose of references to an Agricultural Land Tribunal under section 86 of the Agriculture Act 1947.

Dated 27th February 1978.

Schedule 1

RULES OF PROCEDURE FOR AGRICULTURAL LAND TRIBUNALS

Arrangement of Rules

Rule

Preliminary

1. Citation and interpretation.

Form of Application

2. Consent to operation of notice to quit.
3. Postponement of operation of notice to quit.
4. Certificate of bad husbandry (Case C).
5. Variation or revocation of conditions.
6. Directions relating to fixed equipment.
7. Approval of long-term improvements.
8. Treating agricultural holding as market garden.
9. Restrictions on burning of heather or grass.
10. Section 20(5) of the Mineral Workings Act 1951.
11. Applications under Land Drainage Act 1976.

Parties etc.

12. Persons affected to be parties.
13. Sub-tenancies.

SCHEDULE 1

14. Joinder of parties.

FORM OF REPLY

15. Reply.

GENERAL PROVISIONS AS TO APPLICATIONS AND REPLIES

16. Application, reply and supporting documents.
17. Services of documents by secretary.
18. Withdrawal of application or reply.

PREPARATION FOR HEARING

19. Interlocutory applications.
20. Disclosure of documents.
21. Minister's report in drainage cases.
22. Summary determination in drainage cases.
23. Notice of hearing.

THE HEARING

24. Tribunal to sit in public.
25. Right of audience.
26. Procedure at hearing.
27. Default of appearance.

EVIDENCE

28. Evidence.
29. Witnesses.
30. Inspection of land.

THE DECISION

31. Decision of tribunal.
32. Variation of order in drainage cases.

REFERENCE TO HIGH COURT

33. Request under section 6 of Agriculture (Miscellaneous Provisions) Act 1954.
34. Modification of tribunal's decision following High Court proceedings.

SUPPLEMENTAL

35. Mode of service.
36. Substituted service.
37. Extension of time.
38. Failure to comply with rules.

APPENDIX
Forms

Preliminary

Citation and interpretation

1.—(1) These Rules may be cited as the Agricultural Land Tribunals Rules 1978.

(2) In these Rules, unless the context otherwise requires—

"the 1948 Act" means the Agricultural Holdings Act 1948;

"the 1977 Act" means the Agricultural Holdings (Notices to Quit) Act 1977;[4]

"chairman" means the chairman of the tribunal or a person nominated under paragraph 16(1)(*a*) or appointed under paragraph 16A of the Ninth Schedule to the Agriculture Act 1947 to act as chairman;

"drainage case" means proceedings on an application under section 40 or 41 of the Land Drainage Act 1976;[5]

"secretary" means the secretary of the tribunal;

"tribunal" means the Agricultural Land Tribunal for the area in which the agricultural holding which is the subject of an application, or the greater part of that holding, is situate.

(3) A form referred to by number means the form so numbered in the Appendix to these Rules, or a form substantially to the like effect, with such variations as the circumstances may require.

(4) Any reference in these Rules to any rule or enactment shall, unless the context otherwise requires, be construed as a reference to that rule or enactment as amended, extended or applied by any other rule or enactment.

(5) Expressions defined in or used for the purposes of the 1977 Act have the same meaning in the Rules.

Form of Application

Consent to operation of notice to quit

2.—(1) An application for the tribunal's consent to the operation of a notice to quit under section 2(1) of the 1977 Act which is made by the landlord before the giving of the said notice shall be made not more than twelve months and not less than three months before the commencement of the period at the expiration of which the notice to quit is intended to have effect.

(2) An application for the tribunal's consent to the operation of a notice to quit under section 2(1) or 4(2) or (3) of the 1977 Act which is made by the landlord after service upon him by the tenant of a counter-notice shall be made within one month of the service of the counter-notice.

---

[4] 1977 c.12.
[5] 1976 c.70.

SCHEDULE 1

(3) An application under this rule shall be made in form 1.

Postponement of operation of notice to quit

3. An application under Article 12(1) of the Agriculture Holdings (Arbitration on Notices) Order 1978[6] to postpone the termination of a tenancy shall, unless made at the hearing of the proceedings before the tribunal on an application under the 1977 Act, be made in form 2.

Certificate of bad husbandry (Case C)

4. An application under section 2(4) of the 1977 Act shall be made in form 3.

Variation or revocation of conditions

5. An application under section 3(5) of the 1977 Act shall be made in form 4.

Directions relating to fixed equipment

6.—(1) An application under section 4(1) of the Agriculture Act 1958[7] for a direction for the provision, alteration or repair of fixed equipment shall be made in form 5.

(2) An application under section 4(4) of the Agriculture Act 1958 for the extension of the period specified in a direction under section 4(1) shall be made in writing and shall state the grounds of the application.

Approval of long-term improvements

7.—(1) An application under section 50(1) of the 1948 Act for the tribunal's approval of the carrying out of a long-term improvement shall be made in form 6.

(2) The time within which a landlord may serve a notice under section 50(3) of the 1948 Act that he proposes himself to carry out an improvement shall be one month from the date on which he receives notice in writing of the tribunal's approval of the carrying out of the improvement.

(3) An application under section 50(4)(*b*) of the 1948 Act for a determination that the landlord has failed to carry out an improvement within a reasonable time shall be made in form 7.

Treating agricultural holdings as market garden

8. An application under section 68 of the 1948 Act for a direction that an agricultural holding shall be treated as a market garden shall be made in form 8.

Restrictions on burning of heather or grass

9. An application under section 21 of the Hill Farming Act 1946[8] for a direction shall be made in form 9.

---

[6] S.I. 1978/257.
[7] 1958 c.71.
[8] 1946 c.73.

Section 20(5) of the Mineral Workings Act 1951

10.—(1) An application under section 21(2)(*b*) of the Agriculture Act 1947 as it applies for the purposes of section 20(5) of the Mineral Workings Act 1951[9] for a determination that some person should be treated as owner of the land other than the person who would be so treated apart from the determination shall be made in form 10.

(2) Any person who is specified in an application under paragraph (1) as being affected by the determination shall be party to the proceedings on the application for the purposes of the Rules.

Applications under Land Drainage Act 1976

11.—(1) An application under section 40 or 41 of the Land Drainage Act 1976 for an order requiring the carrying out of work for putting a ditch in proper order or authorising the applicant to carry out drainage work on land shall be made in form 11.

(2) Without prejudice to rule 12(1), on any application under section 40 of the Land Drainage Act 1976, the occupier of any land which may be entered in pursuance of the order shall be a party to the application.

(3) Without prejudice to rule 12(1), on any application under section 41 of the Land Drainage Act 1976, the owner of any land on which it is proposed that any work should be carried out and the occupier of any land which may be entered in pursuance of the order shall be parties to the application.

(4) Where, on hearing of an application under section 40, the applicant states that he desires also to apply under section 41 for an order authorising him to carry out the same or substantially the same work as that referred to in his application, the tribunal may, if they think fit, deal with the application as if it had been made under section 41 as well as under section 40.

PARTIES ETC.

Persons affected to be parties

12.—(1) Without prejudice to rule 10(2), any person against whom any relief is sought on an application under rules 2 to 11 (or on an application by the Crown under section 6 of the 1977 Act) shall be a party to the proceedings on that application.

(2) Any authority having power to enforce the statutory requirement specified in an application under rule 6(1) shall be entitled to be heard on the proceedings on an application under that paragraph, and shall be treated as a party thereto except for the purposes of rule 15.

---

[9] 1951 c.60.

SCHEDULE 1

Sub-tenancies

13.—(1) Where an application is made to the tribunal in respect of an agricultural holding the whole or any part of which has been sublet, every landlord, tenant and sub-tenant of that holding shall be a party to the proceedings on that application.

(2) Paragraph (1) shall not apply in a drainage case.

Joinder of parties

14. If it appears to the chairman or to the tribunal, whether on the application of a party or otherwise, that it is desirable to join any person as a party to the proceedings, the chairman or the tribunal, as the case may be, may order such person to be joined and may give such consequential directions as may be just, including directions as to the service of documents on any person so joined and as to the time within which he may reply to the application.

FORM OF REPLY

Reply

15.—(1) Any party who intends to oppose the whole or any part of an application to the tribunal shall, within one month of a copy of the application being served on him under rule 17 (or, in a drainage case, within the time allowed by rule 21 (5)), reply thereto in the form appended to the copy of the application served on him.

(2) Where no reply is received by the secretary within the time allowed by paragraph (1), the tribunal may decide to make an order in the terms of the application without a formal hearing.

(3) Paragraph (1) does not apply to an application under rule 5 or to an application by the Crown under section 6 of the 1977 Act, and paragraph (2) does not apply in a drainage case.

GENERAL PROVISIONS AS TO APPLICATIONS AND REPLIES

Application, reply and supporting documents

16.—(1) Every application and reply shall be signed by the party making it or by some person authorised to do so on his behalf, and shall be delivered or sent in duplicate to the secretary.

(2) Every application shall be accompanied by two copies of a map of the land which is the subject of the application on a scale of 6" to one mile or 1/10,000 or larger.

(3) Where a party intends to give evidence about any land which is not shown on the map referred to in paragraph (2), his application or reply shall be accompanied by two copies of a map of that land on a scale of 6" to one mile or 1/10,000 or larger.

(4) Every application and reply shall be accompanied by two copies of any plan or other document which the party making the application or reply intends to adduce in support of his case.

(5) Where there are more than two parties to proceedings, the party making an application or reply, as the case may be, shall deliver or send to the secretary one additional copy thereof, and of any map, plan or other document accompanying the application or reply, for service on each additional party.

(6) The chairman may, on such terms as he thinks fit, dispense with any map, plan or other document required to be furnished by any party under this rule where it appears to him that the map, plan or other document, or a copy thereof, is already in the possession of the tribunal or of some other party to the proceedings, or that to require it to be furnished would be unreasonable on the ground of expense or otherwise.

(7) A request for the chairman's direction under this rule shall be made in writing and shall be delivered or sent to the secretary on or before the delivery of the application or reply of the party making the request.

Service of documents by secretary

17.—On receiving from any party an application, reply or other document referred to in rule 16, the secretary shall forthwith serve one copy thereof on every other party to the proceedings.

Withdrawal of applications or reply

18.—(1) A party may withdraw his application or reply by giving notice in writing to the secretary at any time before the hearing and on receipt of such a notice the secretary shall forthwith notify all other parties.

(2) Where a reply is withdrawn the tribunal may, except in a drainage case, decide to make an order in the terms of the application without a formal hearing.

(3) If, on the withdrawal of an application or reply, it appears to the chairman that the case is a proper one for the award of costs under the power conferred by section 5 of the Agriculture (Miscellaneous Provisions) Act 1954, he shall cause the tribunal to be convened for the purpose of determining whether costs should be awarded, and the secretary shall give to all parties not less than seven days' notice of the date, time and place appointed for that purpose.

PREPARATION FOR HEARING

Interlocutory applications

19.—Unless the chairman otherwise orders, an application for directions on any matter which the chairman has power to determine under these Rules shall be made in writing stating the grounds of the application and shall be delivered or sent to the secretary together with a sufficient number of copies for service on the other party or parties.

Disclosure of documents

20.—(1) A party shall furnish to the secretary on his request any document or other information which the tribunal may require and which it is in the power of

SCHEDULE 1

that party to furnish, and shall afford to all other parties an opportunity to inspect such document or a copy of such document, and to take copies thereof.

(2) Nothing in paragraph (1) shall require the furnishing of any information which it would be contrary to the public interest to disclose.

Minister's report in drainage cases

21.—(1) On receipt of an application in a drainage case, the tribunal shall call on the Minister of Agriculture, Fisheries and Food to provide a report on the matters to which the application relates, and for that purpose the tribunal may authorise any officer of the Minister to enter and inspect any land specified by the tribunal.

(2) A report made under paragraph (1) may recommend that no order or that an order in the terms set out in the report be made by the tribunal.

(3) On receipt of the report the secretary shall serve a copy thereof on every party.

(4) Within one month of a copy of the report being served on him the applicant shall serve a notice on the tribunal in form 12 stating whether or not he agrees with the facts stated and the recommendations made in the report; and rules 16(1) and (5) and 17 shall apply to the notice as if it were an application.

(5) The time within which a party is required by rule 15 to reply to the application shall, in a drainage case, run from the date of the service on him of the notice under paragraph (4).

(6) A report under this rule shall be *prima facie* evidence of the facts set out therein, but the maker of the report shall, unless the tribunal otherwise direct, attend any formal hearing of the application for the purpose of being examined and cross-examined on the contents of the report.

Summary determination in drainage cases

22. Where, in a drainage case,—
    (*a*) the report received under rule 21—
        (i) recommends that an order be made and
        (ii) in the case of an application under section 40 of the Land Drainage Act 1976 names a party to the application as the person whom it recommends should be required to carry out any work; and
    (*b*) the applicant has notified the tribunal of his acceptance of the recommendation, and
    (*c*) every other party has either—
        (i) notified the tribunal of his acceptance of the recommendation, or
        (ii) failed to reply to the application within the time allowed by rule 21(5), or
        (iii) withdrawn his reply,
the tribunal may decide to make an order on the application substantially in the terms of the recommendation without a formal hearing.

Notice of hearing

23.—(1) As soon as practicable after receipt of the reply or, as the case may be, after the time for replying has expired, the chairman shall fix a date, time and place for the hearing of the application.

(2) Where rule 15(1) does not apply, the chairman shall fix a date, time and place for the hearing as soon as practicable after receipt of the application.

(3) The chairman may alter the date, time or place fixed for any hearing if it appears to him necessary or desirable to do so to avoid hardship to the parties or for other good cause.

(4) The secretary shall send to every party notice in form 13 of the date, time and place of any hearing which, except with the consent of the parties, shall not be earlier than fourteen days after the date on which the notice is sent.

THE HEARING

Tribunal to sit in public

24. The tribunal shall sit in public unless it appears to them that there are exceptional reasons which make it desirable that the hearing or some part of it should take place in private:

Provided that where a hearing or part of a hearing takes place in private, a member of the Council on Tribunals in his capacity as such shall be entitled to attend.

Right of audience

25. Any party may appear and be heard in person or by counsel or solictor or by a representative appointed in writing.

Procedure at hearing

26.—(1) At the hearing the party making the application shall begin and other parties shall be heard in such order as the tribunal may determine.

(2) Subject to the provisions of these Rules and to any direction given by the chairman, the procedure at the hearing shall be such as the tribunal may direct.

(3) The tribunal may adjourn the hearing from time to time if for any reason it appears to them necessary or desirable to do so.

Default of appearance

27. If a party fails to appear at the time fixed for the hearing, the tribunal, if they are satisfied that the party has been afforded an adequate opportunity of attending, may—

   (a) where the party failing to appear is the applicant, dismiss the application, or
   (b) in any other case, proceed to determine the application in the absence of that party.

SCHEDULE 1

EVIDENCE

Evidence

28.—(1) The tribunal may admit evidence notwithstanding that it would not be admissible in a court of law.

(2) Evidence before the tribunal may be given —
   (a) orally, on oath or on affirmation or otherwise,
   (b) by affidavit, if the parties consent, or
   (c) by means of written statements produced by the maker when giving evidence or, if the tribunal consent, by another witness.

(3) At any stage of the proceedings the tribunal may, of their own motion or on the application of any party, order the personal attendance of a deponent or of the maker of any written statement for examination and cross-examination, or admit any map, plan or other document in evidence.

Witnesses

29.—(1) The tribunal shall give each party an opportunity to call witnesses and to cross-examine any witness called by or on behalf of any other party and to re-examine his own witnesses after cross-examination, and a party may, if he so desires, give evidence as a witness on his own behalf.

(2) The tribunal may call a witness who may, after giving evidence, be cross-examined by any party.

(3) The tribunal may require any witness to give evidence on oath or affirmation.

(4) The provisions of the County Court Rules 1936 as to the issuing of witness summonses shall apply for the purposes of any proceedings before the tribunal as they apply for the purposes of an arbitration under 1948 Act.

Inspection of land

30.—(1) The tribunal may enter on and inspect an agricultural holding owned or occupied by any party (whether the holding is the subject of the proceedings or not) and inspect any fixed or other equipment, produce or livestock thereon.

(2) Notice of the tribunal's intention to inspect a holding shall be given by the secretary to all parties and to any other occupier of the holding and, unless given orally at the hearing, shall be given in writing at least twenty-four hours before the intended entry.

(3) The parties, their representatives and expert witnesses and any other occupier of the holding may attend the inspection.

THE DECISION

Decision of the tribunal

31.—(1) The decision of the tribunal, which in the event of disagreement between the members shall be the decision of the majority, shall be given in writing, together with a statement of the tribunal's reasons for their decision.

(2) The chairman may correct any clerical mistake in the written record of the tribunal's decision.

(3) The secretary shall send to each party a copy of the tribunal's decision and reasons.

(4) The secretary may supply a further copy of the tribunal's decision and reasons or any part thereof to any party who appears reasonably to require it.

(5) A copy issued under paragraph (3) or (4) shall be certified by the secretary as a true copy and shall be *prima facie* evidence of the matters contained therein.

Variation of order in drainage cases

32. Any order made following a decision of the tribunal in a drainage case may be varied whether as to the time within which any work is to be carried out or otherwise and on an application to vary the order which shall be made in form 14 the chairman may give all such directions as may be just.

REFERENCE TO HIGH COURT

Request under section 6 of Agriculture (Miscellaneous Provisions) Act 1954

33.—(1) A request to the High Court of a question of law arising in the course of proceedings before the tribunal shall, unless made at the hearing, be made in writing to the secretary not later than fourteen days from the date on which a copy of the tribunal's decion was sent to the party making the request and shall be accompanied by as many copies of the request as there are other parties; and the secretary shall thereupon serve a copy of the request on every such party.

(2) If the tribunal refuse the request, the secretary shall, not later than fourteen days from the date of his receipt of the request, notify all parties of the refusal; and if the party making the request, being aggrieved by the refusal, intends to apply for an order directing the tribunal to refer the question of law to the High Court, he shall, within seven days after receiving notice of the refusal, serve on the secretary notice in writing of the intended application accompanied by as many copies of the notice as there are other parties; and the secretary shall thereupon serve a copy of the notice on every such party.

(3) A case stated on a question of law for the decision of the High Court shall set out the question of law and the facts found by the tribunal and shall be signed by the chairman and sent to the party who requested the reference within two months after the date of the request or, as the case may be, within two months after the making of an order by the High Court directing the reference.

Modification of tribunal's decision following High Court proceedings

34.—(1) The powers of the tribunal under section 6(5) of the Agriculture (Miscellaneous Provisions) Act 1954 may be exercised by the chairman in any case where he does not consider it necessary to convene the tribunal for that purpose; but if it appears to the chairman that there should be a further hearing before the tribunal, he shall fix a date, time and place for the hearing.

(2) Where a further hearing consequent on the reference to the High Court cannot conveniently take place before the tribunal as originally constituted, the chairman shall cause a fresh tribunal to be constituted for that purpose.

SCHEDULE 1

SUPPLEMENTAL

Mode of service

35.—(1) Every application, reply or other document required or authorised by these Rules to be served on any person shall be deemed to have been duly served if it is delivered to him or left at his proper address, or sent to him by post in a registered letter or by recorded delivery.

(2) Any such document required or authorised to be given to, or served on, an incorporated company or body shall be duly given or served if given to or served on the secretary or clerk of the company or body.

(3) The proper address of any person to or on whom any such document is to be given or served shall, in the case of a secretary or clerk of any incorporated company or body, be that of the registered or principal office of the company or body and, in any other case, be the last known address of the person in question.

(4) Where any such document is to be given to, or served on, any person as being the owner of land and the land belongs to an ecclesiastical benefice, a copy thereof shall be served on the Church Commissioners.

Substituted service

36. If any person on whom any document is required to be served for the purpose of these Rules cannot be found, or has died and has no known personal representative, or is out of the United Kingdom, or if for any other reason service on him cannot be readily effected, the chairman may dispense with service on such person or may make an order for substituted service on such other person or in such other form (whether by advertisement in a newspaper or otherwise) as the chairman may think fit.

Extension of time

37. The time appointed by or under these Rules for doing any act or taking any step in connection with any proceedings may be extended by the chairman on such terms and conditions, if any, as appear to him just.

Failure to comply with rules

38. Any failure on the part of any person to comply with the provisions of these Rules shall not render the proceedings, or anything done in pursuance thereof, invalid unless the chaiman or the tribunal so direct.

APPENDIX

Form 1 and Form 1R
Application by landlord for Agricultural Land Tribunal's consent to notice to quit and tenant's reply (section 26(1) and section 28(2), (2) and (4) (prescribed forms)).
[printed as Forms 40 and 40A in Part V, paras A.78 and A.79 of this work]

Form 2 and Form 2R
Application by tenant to the Agricultural Land Tribunal to postpone operation of notice to quit and landlord's reply (prescribed forms).
[printed as Forms 42 and 42A in Part V, paras A.81 and A.82 of this work]

Form 3 and Form 3R
Application by landlord to Agricultural Land Tribunal for a Certificate of bad husbandry and tenant's reply (Schedule 3, Part I, Case C, and Part II, Paragraph 9) (prescribed forms).
[printed as Forms 26 and 26A in Part V, paras A.63 and A.64 of this work]

Form 4
Application by landlord under section 27(5) for variation or revocation of condition imposed by Tribunal under section 27 (4) in consenting to operation of notice to quit (prescribed forms).
[printed as Form 41 in Part V, para. A.80 of this work]

Forms 5 and 5R
Application by tenant to Agricultural Land Tribunal for a direction under section 11 in regard to fixed equipment and landlord's reply (prescribed forms).
[printed as Forms 13 and 13A in Part V, paras A.49 and A.50 of this work]

Forms 6 and 6A
Application by tenant to Agricultural Land Tribunal for approval to improvements in Part II of Schedule 7, and landlord's reply (section 67(3)) (prescribed forms).
[printed as Forms 57 and 57A in Part V, paras A.100 and A.101 of this work]

Forms 7 and 7R
Application by tenant to Agricultural Land Tribunal for a determination that the landlord has failed to carry out improvements within a reasonable time, and the landlord's reply (section 67(4)) (prescribed forms).
[printed as Forms 59 and 59A in Part V, paras A.103 and A.104 of this work]

Forms 8 and 8R
Application by tenant to Agricultural Land Tribunal for holding to be treated as a market garden and landlord's reply (section 80) (prescribed forms).
[printed as Forms 64 and 64A in Part V, paras A.109 and A.110 of this work]

Form 9

rule 9

Ref. No.
To be
inserted
by the
Secretary.

AGRICULTURE LAND TRIBUNAL

Application for Direction to Avoid or Relax Covenant against the Burning of Heather or Grass

To the Secretary of the Agricultural Land Tribunal

  for the .... Area.

  1. I, ... [*block capitals*]

SCHEDULE 1

of .... [*address*],

tenant of .... [*name or description of holding*],

hereby apply under section 21 of the Hill Farming Act 1946 (as amended by the Agriculture Act 1958) for the Tribunal's direction that the covenants, conditions or agreements contained in my lease and specified in paragraph 3 below be avoided or relaxed.

    2. My landlord is .... [*block capitals*] of .... [*address*].

    3. The *covenant(s)/condition(s)/agreement(s) to which I refer is (are) numbered .... in my lease and I ask the Tribunal to direct that it (they) be—
*(*a*) avoided completely;
*(*b*) relaxed in the following way:—
    *(i) permanently;
    *(ii) for the following period:—

    4. The holding consists of:—
(*a*) .... hectares of arable land (including temporary grass)
                                (Ordnance Survey Field Nos. ....);
(*b*) .... hectares of permanent pasture
                                (Ordnance Survey Field Nos. ....);
(*c*) .... hectares of rough grazing
                                (Ordnance Survey Field Nos. ....);
(*d*) .... hectares of other land (including orchards)
                                (Ordnance Survey Field Nos. ....);
Total .... hectares.

    5. The *covenant(s)/condition(s)/agreement(s) mentioned in paragraph 3 above is (are)   *impeding the proper use of the land for agricultural purposes in
               preventing
the following way:—

and I wish it (them) to be   *avoided so as to allow me to burn .... hectares
                               relaxed
of   *heather.
     grass.

    6. I attach:—
    (*a*) two[10] copies of my lease[11];

---

[10] Two copies of the application and of any map and document must be sent to the Secretary, and if there are more than two parties (*e.g.*, if the land is held under a sub-tenancy), an additional copy of the application, etc., must be supplied for, and the Secretary must be informed of the name and address of, each additional party.

[11] The Chairman of the Tribunal has power in all cases to dispense with maps or other documents (*e.g.*, where the landlord already has a copy of the lease). A request for a direction on this subject should be made in writing before or at the time of sending the

(b) two[10] copies of a 6" to one mile or 1/10,000[12] map of the land described in paragraph 4 above;

(c) two[10] copies each of the following other documents[13]:—

Date .... Signed[14] ....

*Strike out whichever is inapplicable

Form 9R

Ref. No.
To be
inserted
by the
Secretary.

AGRICULTURE LAND TRIBUNAL

Reply to Application for Direction to Avoid or Relax Covenant against Burning of Heather or Grass

To the Secretary of the Agricultural Land Tribunal

for the .... Area.

I, ... [block capitals]

of .... [address],

landlord of .... [name or description of holding],

having received a copy of the application (bearing the above reference number) for the Tribunal's direction that certain covenants, conditions or agreements in the applicant's lease should be avoided or relaxed, reply as follows:—

1. The facts contained in the first four paragraphs of the application are correct except that:—

    2. *(a) I do not wish any covenant, condition or agreement to be avoided or relaxed in any way.

       *(b) I would agree to the following *covenant(s)/condition(s)/agreement(s) being *avoided / relaxed as follows:—

3. For the following main reasons I do not agree that the *covenant(s)/condition(s)/agreement(s) is (are) impeding or preventing the proper use of the land for agricultural purposes or that (except as agreed in paragraph (2) (b) above) it would be expedient to relax or avoid it (them):—

---

application.

[12] A larger scale map may be used if preferred. Ordnance Survey Field Numbers must be marked on the map.

[13] Mention any other document which is attached to this application.

[14] If signed by any person other than the applicant himself, he should state in what capacity or by what authority he signs.

SCHEDULE 1

4. I attach copies of the following relevant documents[15]:—

Date .... Signed[16] ....
*Strike out whichever is inapplicable

Form 10

rule 10(1) Ref. No.
 To be
 inserted
 by the
 Secretary.

AGRICULTURAL LAND TRIBUNAL

Application for Determination that a Person be Treated as Owner of Land

To the Secretary of the Agricultural Land Tribunal

for the .... Area.

1. I, ... [*block capitals*]

of .... [*address*],

hereby apply to the Tribunal to determine under section 21 of the Agriculture Act 1947 that—

*(a) .... [*block capitals*]

of .... [*address*]

*(b) I

be treated for the purposes of section 20 of the Mineral Workings Act 1951 as the owner of the land known as:— ....

.... [*name or description*].

2. My own interest in the land is:—

3. The following person(s) would be affected by the granting of this application[17]:—

4. The land consists of:—

---

[15] (*a*) Two copies of the reply and of any document which you wish to submit to the Tribunal must be sent to the Secretary, and, if there are more than two parties (*e.g.*, if the holding is sub-let), an additional copy of each must be supplied for each additional party.
(*b*) If you disagree with any map or plan attached to the application, your reply should be accompanied by two copies of a 6" to one mile or 1/10,000 (or larger) map showing what you consider to be the true position and marking the Ordnance Survey Field Numbers.
[16] If signed by any person other than the landlord himself, he should state in what capacity or by what authority he signs.
[17] State name and address of any person mentioned and whether he is owner or occupier or what other interest he has in the land.

RULES OF PROCEDURE FOR AGRICULTURAL LAND TRIBUNALS

(a) .... hectares of arable land (including temporary grass)
(Ordnance Survey Field Nos. ....);
(b) .... hectares of permanent pasture
(Ordnance Survey Field Nos. ....);
(c) .... hectares of rough grazing
(Ordnance Survey Field Nos. ....);
(d) .... hectares of other land (including orchards)
(Ordnance Survey Field Nos. ....);
Total .... hectares.

5. The land includes the following buildings:—[*give a general description*]

6. The Minister of Agriculture, Fisheries and Food proposes to make the following arrangements for the purpose of taking the following special steps (as referred to in the said section 20):—[*describe briefly*]

7. My main reasons for this application are:—

8. I attach the following documents which I intend to produce in support of my case:—
   (a) two[18] copies of a 6" to one mile or 1/10,000[19] map of the land described in paragraph 4 above;
   (b) two[18] copies of[20]:—

Date ....   Signed[21]

Form 10R

Ref. No.
To be
inserted
by the
Secretary.

AGRICULTURAL LAND TRIBUNAL

Reply to Application for Determination that a Person be Treated as Owner of Land

To the Secretary of the Agricultural Land Tribunal
   for the ....Area.
   I, ... [*block capitals*]

---

[18] Two copies of the application and of any map and document must be sent to the Secretary, and if there is more than one party named in paragraph 3, an additional copy of the application, etc., must be supplied for each additional party.

[19] A larger scale map may be used if preferred. Ordnance Survey Field Numbers must be marked on the map.

[20] Mention any other document which is attached to the application.

[21] If signed by any person other than the applicant himself, he should state in what capacity or by what authority he signs.

SCHEDULE 1

of .... [*address*],
having received a copy of the application (bearing the above reference number), reply as follows:—

1. The facts stated in the first five paragraphs of the application are correct except that:—

2. My main reasons for resisting the application are:

3. I attach copies of the following relevant documents[22]—

   Date ....   Signed[23] ....

Form 11

rule 11(1)   Ref. No.
                                                                To be
                                                                inserted
                                                                by the
                                                                Secretary.

AGRICULTURAL LAND TRIBUNAL
Application under Land Drainage Act 1976

To the Secretary of the Agricultural Land Tribunal

для the ....Area.

*1. I, ... [*block capitals*]
of .... [*address*],
hereby apply to the Tribunal for an order under section 40 of the Land Drainage Act 1976 requiring ....

[*state name(s) of persons(s) against whom order is sought*][24] to carry out the work mentioned in paragraph 6 on the ground that [the land mentioned in paragraph 3, of which I am the † owner/occupier, is being injured] [*or* the improvement of the drainage of the land mentioned in paragraph 3, of which I am the † owner/occupier, is being prevented] by the condition of the ditch mentioned in paragraph 4.

*To be used for application under s. 40.
†Strike out whichever is inapplicable.

---

[22] (a) Two copies of the reply and of any document which you wish to submit to the Tribunal must be sent to the Secretary, and, if there are more than two parties, an additional copy of each must be supplied for each additional party.
(b) If you disagree with any map or plan attached to the application, your reply should be accompanied by two copies of a 6″ to one mile or 1/10,000 (or larger) map showing what you consider to be the true position and marking the Ordnance Survey Field Numbers.
[23] If signed by any person other than the party himself, he should state in what capacity or by what authority he signs.
[24] Section 40 enables an order to be made against the owner or occupier of land through which the ditch passes or which abuts on the ditch or against any person who, although not such an owner or occupier, has a right to carry out the work specified in the order.

RULES OF PROCEDURE FOR AGRICULTURAL LAND TRIBUNALS

‡[In the event of the Tribunal deciding not to make such an order I hereby apply in the alternative under section 41 of the said Act for an order authorising me to carry out the said work.]

‡Strike out if inapplicable.

OR

*[1. I, ... [block capitals] of .... [address], hereby apply to the Tribunal under section 41 of the Land Drainage Act 1976 for an order authorising me to carry out the work mentioned in paragraph 6 on the ground that the drainage of the land mentioned in paragraph 3, of which I am the † owner/occupier, requires the carrying out of such work.]

*To be used for application under s. 41.

†Strike out whichever is inapplicable.

*[2. I ask that the said order should authorise me [*or* the person required to carry out the said work] to enter on the land mentioned in paragraph 4 [and paragraph 7] so far as may be necessary for the carrying out of the said work.]

*To be used for application under s. 40 or s. 41: strike out if no such authority is asked for.

3. I am the *owner/occupier of [*describe the land affected by application and give Ordnance Survey Field Numbers*].

*Strike out whichever is inapplicable.

*4. Injury to my said land is being caused [and/or the improvement of the drainage of my said land is being prevented] by the condition of the under-mentioned ditch [*specify ditch, stating land through which it passes and if possible the Ordnance Survey Field Numbers of that land*].

*To be used for application under s. 40.

OR

*[4. The drainage of my said land requires:—

    †(*a*) the carrying out of work in connection with the under-mentioned ditch:

    †(*b*) and/or the replacement or construction of the under-mentioned ditch:

    †(*c*) and/or the alteration or removal of drainage work in connection with the under-mentioned ditch:

[*specify ditch, stating land through which it passes and if possible the Ordnance Survey Field Numbers of that land*].

*To be used for application under s. 41.

†Strike out whichever is inapplicable.

5. The condition of the said ditch and its effect on my land is as follows [and/or the construction of the said ditch is required for the following reason]:

SCHEDULE 1

6. The work which is required to be carried out is as follows:—

*[7. For the purpose of carrying out the said work it will be necessary to enter the under-mentioned land in addition to that mentioned in paragraph 4 [*describe land, stating Ordnance Survey Field Numbers if possible*].
   *Strike out if inapplicable.

8. This application affects the interests of the following persons:[25]

   (a) .... [*block capitals*]

   of .... [*address*]
   who is the *owner/occupier of [the following part of] the land mentioned in paragraph 4 [*or* 7] of this application [*or as the case may be*][26]

   (b) .... [*block capitals*]

   of .... [*address*]
   who is the *owner/occupier of [the following part of] the land mentioned in paragraph 4 [*or* 7] of this application [*or as the case may be*].[26]
   *Strike out whichever is inapplicable.

*[9. To the best of my information and belief the following persons in addition to those named in paragraph 8 have rights in or over the said ditch and the land through which it passes:

   (a) .... [*block capitals*]

      of .... [*address*]

      who is ....

   (b) .... [*block capitals*]

      of .... [*address*]

      who is ....]
   *Strike out if inapplicable.

10. I attach the following documents which I intend to produce in support of my case:—

---

[25] State the names of all persons who are to be parties to the proceedings. These must include any person against whom an order is applied for under section 40 as well as the name of the occupier of any land on which entry may be necessary for carrying out work under section 40 or 41 and, in the case of an application under section 41, the name of the owner of any land on which it is proposed that any work should be carried out. If more than two persons are named, continue on separate sheet.
[26] State whether owner or occupier of the land or persons having a right to carry out the

(a) two[27] copies of a 6″ to one mile or 1/10,000[28] map of the land described in paragraphs 3 and 4 [and 7] above;

(b) two[27] copies of [29]:—

Date .... Signed[30] ....

Form 11R

Ref. No.
To be
inserted
by the
Secretary.

AGRICULTURAL LAND TRIBUNAL
Reply to Application under Land Drainage Act 1976

To the Secretary of the Agricultural Land Tribunal

for the ....Area.

I, ... [block capitals]
of .... [address],
having received a copy of the application (bearing the above reference number) and of the report provided by the Minister of Agriculture, Fisheries and Food for the purpose thereof and of the applicant's notice in Form 12 reply as follows:—

1. The facts stated in the said application and in the said report are correct except that:—

2. *(a) I agree to an order being made
    * (i) in the terms of the recommendation in the report; or
    * (ii) in the terms asked for in the application [*if different from those recommended in the report*]; or
    *(iii) in the terms stated in the applicant's notice.

  *(b) I resist the application

*Strike out whichever is inapplicable.

---

proposed work on the ditch mentioned in paragraph 4.
[27] Two copies of the application and of any map and document must be sent to the Secretary, and if there are more than two parties, an additional copy of the application, etc., must be supplied for each additional party.
[28] A larger scale map may be used if preferred. Ordnance Survey Field Numbers must be marked on the map where required.
[29] Mention any other document which is attached to this application.
[30] If signed by any person other than the applicant himself, he should state in what capacity or by what authority he signs.

SCHEDULE 1

3. *My main reasons for resisting the application are:—
*Strike out if inapplicable.

4. I attach copies of the following relevant documents[31]:—

Date .... Signed[32] ....

Form 12

rule 21 (4)

Ref No.
To be
inserted
by the
Secretary

AGRICULTURAL LAND TRIBUNAL
Land Drainage Act 1976
Notice by Applicant under Rule 21 (4) of
the Agricultural Land Tribunals Rules 1978

To the Secretary of the Agricultural Land Tribunal

for the ....Area.

I, ... [*block capitals*]

of .... [*address*]

having applied to the Tribunal on the   day of   19   (under reference number ....) for an order under section 40 [and/or section 41]* of the Land Drainage Act 1976, and having received a copy of the report provided by the Minister of Agriculture, Fisheries and Food for the purpose of my application, state as follows:

*Strike out whichever is inapplicable.

1. I accept the facts stated in the report with the exception of:

2. *(a) I accept the recommendation made in the report and hereby request the Tribunal to make an order on my application in the terms of the recommendation.

---

[31] (a) Two copies of the reply and of any document which you wish to submit to the Tribunal must be sent to the Secretary, and, if there are more than two parties, an additional copy of each must be supplied for each additional party.
(b) If you disagree with any map or plan attached to the application or if, in your reply, you mention any land not shown thereon, your reply should be accompanied by two copies of a 6″ to one mile or 1/10,000 (or larger) map showing what you consider to be the true position or showing the other land mentioned in your reply, as the case may be, and marking the Ordnance Survey Field Numbers.
[32] If signed by any person other than the party himself, he should state in what capacity or by what authority he signs.

*(b) I do not accept the recommendation made in the report and I request the Tribunal to make an order on my application in the terms asked for therein [*or* in the following modified terms].

*Strike out whichever is inapplicable.

3. I attach the following documents which I intend to produce in support of my case:—[33]

Date .... Signed[34] ....

rule 23(4)

Form 13

AGRICULTURAL LAND TRIBUNAL

Notice of Hearing

Land at:

Applicant/s:

Respondent/s:

TAKE NOTICE that the HEARING of the APPLICATION in respect of the above named Holding will be held on   at
commencing at

Dated .... 197....... Signed ....

(Secretary of the Tribunal)

NOTE TO PARTIES

You may find of assistance the following note of rules of evidence and procedure, which apply to this hearing and which are contained in the Agricultural Land Tribunals Rules 1878.

1. *Rules of Evidence*

(*a*) Any evidence may be admitted by the tribunal, including evidence that would not be admissible in a court of law.

(*b*) Evidence before the tribunal may be given—

(i) orally, on oath or on affirmation or otherwise,

(ii) by affidavit, if the parties consent, or

(iii) by means of written statements produced by the maker when giving evidence or, if the tribunal consent, by another witness.

---

[33] Two copies of this notice must be sent to the Secretary together with two copies of any map or document which you wish to submit to the Tribunal and which has not already been submitted with the application. If there are more than two parties, an additional copy of the notice, etc., must be supplied for each additional party.

[34] If signed by any person other than the applicant himself, he should state in what capacity or by what authority he signs.

If evidence is tendered in the form of a written statement, four copies of the statement should be available at the hearing for the tribunal and two copies for the other parties.

(c) At any stage of the proceedings the tribunal may, of their own motion or on the application of any party, order the personal attendance of the maker of any written statement for examination and cross-examination.

(d) The secretary may require a party to give to the tribunal documents or other information, and to afford to all other parties an opportunity to inspect such documents, or copies of them, and to take copies of them.

If the parties intend to produce documents at the hearing, they should if possible agree them beforehand, list them in order and put them into one agreed bundle. Four copies of this bundle should be available if possible for the use of the tribunal.

(e) The tribunal may, after giving notice to all parties and to any other occupier of the land, enter and inspect any agricultural holding owned or occupied by any party, whether the holding is the subject of the proceedings or not, and may inspect any fixed or other equipment, produce or livestock thereon.

2. *Procedure at the Hearing*

(a) The tribunal sit in public unless exceptional circumstances make it desirable that the hearing, or some part of it, should take place in private.

(b) A party may appear and be heard in person or by counsel or solicitor or by a representative appointed in writing.

(c) The party making the application will begin and the other parties will be heard in such order as the tribunal may determine.

3. *Witnesses*

(a) Each party will be given an opportunity to call and cross-examine witnesses, and a party may if he wishes give evidence as a witness on his own behalf.

(b) The tribunal may call witnesses, who may after giving evidence be cross-examined by any party.

(c) The provisions of the County Court Rules 1936, as amended, as to the issue of witness summonses (Order 20, rule 8) apply for the purposes of any proceedings before the tribunal. Under these Rules, a party desiring a person to be summoned as a witness must apply to the county court registrar by filling in the prescribed form in the county court office.

4. *Default of Appearance*

If a party fails to appear at the time fixed for the hearing, the tribunal may—

    (i) dismiss the application where the party failing to appear is the applicant, or

    (ii) proceed in any other case to determine the application in the party's absence, if satisfied that the party failing to appear has been afforded an adequate opportunity of attending.

Form 14

rule 32

Ref No.
To be
inserted
by the
Secretary

AGRICULTURAL LAND TRIBUNAL
Application for Variation of Order made under Land Drainage Act 1976

To the Secretary of the Agricultural Land Tribunal
for the ....Area.

1. I, ... [*block capitals*]
of .... [*address*],
hereby apply to the Tribunal to vary its order dated the   day of
19

2. The order was made on *[my application] [the application of ....
.... [*block capitals*]
of .... [*address*]]
bearing the reference number ....
*Strike out whichever is inapplicable.

3. The variation for which I apply is:—

4. My main reasons for making this application are:—

5. I attach copies of the following documents which I intend to produce in support of my case[35]:—

Date ....   Signed[36] ....

---

[35] Two copies of this application and of any document which you wish to submit to the Tribunal must be sent to the Secretary, and, if there are more than two parties, an additional copy of each must be supplied for each additional party.

[36] If signed by any person other than the applicant himself, he should state in what capacity or by what authority he signs.

SCHEDULE 2

SCHEDULE 2

Article 3

AMENDMENTS TO OTHER RULES OF PROCEDURE

1. In Article 2 of the Agricultural Land Tribunals (Succession to Agricultural Tenancies) Order 1976, the words from "and, accordingly," to the end shall be omitted.

2. The Agricultural Land Tribunals (Succession) Rules 1976 (which are set out in the Schedule to that Order) shall be amended as follows:—

1. (*a*) in rule 1(2), in the definition of "the principal rules", for the expression "1959" there shall be substituted the expression "1978";

(*b*) for rule 10 there shall be substituted the following rule:—

"Application of principal rules relating to applications and replies

10.—(1) Rules 16 (except for paragraph (5)) and 18 (except for paragraph (2)) of the principal rules shall apply with the necessary modifications to applications and replies under these Rules.

(2) Rule 15(2) of the principal rules shall apply in the case of an application by the landlord.

(3) Rule 18(2) of the principal rules shall apply to a reply under rule 6 of these Rules if the relevant period has expired and, following the withdrawal of the reply, there is no other outstanding reply to the application by the landlord.";

(*c*) for rule 13 there shall be substituted the following rule:—

"Application of principal rules relating to prepration for hearing and to hearing

13. Rules 19, 20, 23(3) and (4), 24, 25, 26(2) and (3) and 27 of the principal rules shall apply with the necessary modifications to applications under these Rules.";

(*d*) for rule 14(2) there shall be substituted the following paragraph:—

"(2) Where pursuant to rule 15(2) or 18(2) of the principal rules (as applied by rule 10(2) and (3) of these Rules), the tribunal decide to make an order in the

875

terms of the application by the landlord without a formal hearing, any application under rule 2(1) in respect of the holding shall be dismissed.";

(*e*) for rule 19 there shall be substituted the following rule:—

"*Application of principal rules relating to evidence, decisions, etc.*

19.—(1) Rules 28 to 31 and 33 to 38 of the principal rules shall apply with the necessary modifications to proceedings under these Rules as they apply to other proceedings before the tribunal.

(2) For the purposes of rules 31, 33 and 34 of the principal rules, any dismissal of an application under these Rules shall be a decision, and all such decisions, and the reasons for them, may be given in a single document at the conclusion of the proceedings unless the chairman otherwise decides.";

(*f*) Form 2 in the Appendix shall be amended as follows:—

(*i*) for paragraph 5 there shall be substituted the following paragraph:—

"5. The grounds upon which I make this application are those provided in paragraph(s)   of section 3(3) of the Agricultural Holdings (Notices to Quit) Act 1977 as read with section 22(2) of the Agriculture (Miscellaneous Provisions) Act 1976. (*It is important to refer to note* (1)].", and

(*ii*) in footnote (1), for paragraph (*e*) there shall be substituted the following paragraph:—

"(*e*) that the landlord proposes to terminate the tenancy for the purpose of the land's being used for a use, other than for agriculture, not falling within Case B (i.e. in section 2(3) of the Agricultural Holdings (Notices to Quit) Act 1977).".

GENERAL NOTE

This Order consolidates the instruments relating to rules of procedure for Agricultural Land Tribunals (other than rules for application under Part II of the Agriculture (Miscellaneous Provisions) Act 1976). Some amendments are also introduced, including amendments necessitated by the Agricultural Holdings (Notices to Quit) Act 1977 and the Agricultural Holdings (Arbitration on Notices) Order 1978. The most important of these amendments are:—

(1) Applications under section 4(2) or (3) of the Agricultural Holdings (Notices to Quit) Act 1977 for the Tribunal's consent to the operation of a notice to quit are to be made in Form 1 in Schedule 1 to the Order, and Form 1 is enlarged accordingly (Rule 2(2) and Form 1).

SCHEDULE 2

(2) If a Tribunal hearing takes place (exceptionally) in private, a member of the Council on Tribunals may now attend (Rule 24).

THE AGRICULTURAL LAND TRIBUNALS (AREAS) ORDER 1982   A.19

(S.I. 1982 No. 97)

The Lord Chancellor, in exercise of the powers conferred on him by section 73(1) of the Agriculture Act 1947, hereby makes the following Order:—

1. This Order may be cited as the Agricultural Land Tribunals (Areas) Order 1982 and shall come into operation on 2nd March 1982.

2.—(1) For the purposes of section 73 of the Agriculture Act 1947 there shall be eight areas as specified in column 1 of the Schedule to this Order.

(2) Each area shall comprise the counties and the London Boroughs which are set out in respect of it in column 2 of the said Schedule.

(3) For the purposes of the preceding paragraph and of the said Schedule the Isles of Scilly shall be treated as if they were a county.

3. Any proceedings which on the coming into operation of this Order are pending before an Agricultural Land Tribunal may thereafter be continued before the Agricultural Land Tribunal for the area in which the whole or the greater part of the agricultural holding to which the proceedings relate is situate, and that tribunal shall have power to hear and determine them.

4. The Agricultural Land Tribunals (Areas) Order 1974 and the Agricultural Land Tribunals (Areas) (Amendment) Order 1976 are hereby revoked.

Dated 29th January 1982.

SCHEDULE

Column 1	Column 2
Areas	Counties and London Boroughs
Northern	Cleveland Cumbria Durham Northumberland Tyne and Wear
Yorkshire and Humberside	Humberside North Yorkshire South Yorkshire West Yorkshire
Eastern	Bedfordshire Cambridgeshire Essex Hertfordshire Lincolnshire Norfolk Northamptonshire Suffolk London Boroughs north of the river Thames except Richmond upon Thames
Midlands	Derbyshire Herefordshire and Worcestershire Leicestershire Nottinghamshire Warwickshire West Midlands
Western	Cheshire Greater Manchester Lancashire Merseyside Shropshire Staffordshire
South Western	Avon Cornwall Devon Dorset Gloucestershire Somerset

SCHEDULE

South Eastern	Berkshire Buckinghamshire East Sussex Hampshire Isle of Wight Kent Oxfordshire Surrey West Sussex London Boroughs south of the river Thames including Richmond upon Thames
Welsh	Clwyd Dyfed Gwent Gwynedd Mid Glamorgan Powys South Glamorgan West Glamorgan

GENERAL NOTE

This Order constitutes new areas for Agricultural Land Tribunals. The Yorkshire and Lancashire, East Midland and West Midland Areas cease to exist and the counties formerly included in those areas become part of the areas to be known as Yorkshire and Humberside, Midlands, Western and Eastern.

THE AGRICULTURAL LAND TRIBUNALS (SUCCESSION TO AGRICULTURAL TENANCIES) ORDER 1984

A.20

(S.I. 1984 No. 1301)

The Lord Chancellor, in exercise of the powers conferred on him by sections 73(3) and (4) and 108(3) of the Agriculture Act 1947[37], after consultation with the Council on Tribunals as required by section 10 of the Tribunals and Inquiries Act 1971, hereby makes the following Order:—

Citation and commencement

1. This Order may be cited as the Agricultural Land Tribunals (Succession to Agricultural Tenancies) Order 1984 and shall come into operation on 12th September 1984.

---

[37] Section 73(3) and (4) was amended by the Agriculture Act 1958 (c.71), Sched. 1, para. 3.

Rules of procedure

2. The rules set out in the Schedule to this Order shall apply to any proceedings before Agricultural Land Tribunals arising from any application made after the commencement of this Order under Part II of the Agriculture (Miscellaneous Provisions) Act 1976[38] or under Schedule 2 to the Agricultural Holdings Act 1984.

Variation of the Agricultural Land Tribunals (Rules) Order 1978

3. The Agricultural Land Tribunals (Rules) Order 1978 shall be varied by inserting at the end of article 2 thereof (rules of procedure) the words "or under Schedule 2 to the Agricultural Holdings Act 1984".

Revocations

4. The Agricultural Land Tribunals (Succession to Agricultural Tenancies) Order 1976[39] is hereby revoked except to such extent as may be necessary for the disposal of an application pending at the commencement of this Order.

Dated 26th July 1984.

Part I
Preliminary

Citation and interpretation

1.—(1) These rules may be cited as the Agricultural Land Tribunals (Succession) Rules 1984.

(2) In these rules "the principal rules" means the Agricultural Land Tribunals Rules 1978 and expressions defined in the principal rules have the same meaning in these rules.

(3) Unless the context otherwise requires, any reference in these rules—
   (*a*) to a numbered rule shall be construed as a reference to the rule bearing that number in these rules; or
   (*b*) to a numbered form shall be construed as a reference to the form bearing that number in the Appendix to these rules, or a form substantially to the like effect with such variations as the circumstances may require.

Part II
Application for Succession on Death of Tenant Under Part II of the Agriculture (Miscellaneous Provisions) Act 1976

Interpretation of Part II

2.—(1) In this Part of these rules, unless the context otherwise requires—"the 1976 Act" means the Agriculture (Miscellaneous Provisions) Act 1976;"applicant" means a person who has made an application under rule 3(1); "designated

---

[38] Part II of the Act was amended by the Agricultural Holdings Act 1984 (c.41), s. 3 and Sched. 1.
[39] amended by S.I. 1978/No. 259.

applicant" means an applicant who has been validly designated by the deceased in his will in accordance with section 20(10) of the 1976 Act; "holding" means a holding in respect of which an application under rule 3(1) is made; "landlord" means the landlord of the holding; "the relevant period" means the period of three months beginning with the day after the date of death.

(2) Other expressions defined for the purposes of, or of any provision in, sections 18 to 23 of the 1976 Act (notably in sections 18(1), (2) and (7), 20(10), 22(6) and 23(2)) have the same meaning in this Part of these rules.

Forms of Application and Reply

Application by eligible person or by person wishing to be treated as eligible person

3.—(1) An application to the tribunal under section 20 of the 1976 Act for a direction entitling the applicant to a tenancy of an agricultural holding shall be made in Form 1.

(2) An application to the tribunal under section 21 of the 1976 Act for a determination that the applicant is to be treated as an eligible person shall be made in Form 1 and if the applicant also makes an application under section 20 of that Act, both applications shall be made at the same time and in the same Form.

(3) An application made under this rule shall not be entertained by the tribunal if it is not made within the relevant period.

Landlord's application for consent to operation of notice to quit

4.—(1) An application by the landlord under section 22 of the 1976 Act for the tribunal's consent to the operation of a notice to quit shall be in Form 2 and, subject to paragraphs (3) and (4), may be made at any time after the landlord receives notice of an application under rule 3(1).

(2) Where the landlord bases his application under section 22 of the 1976 Act on the ground of hardship to a person or persons other than himself, he shall give particulars in his application of that person or those persons and of the hardship on which he relies.

(3) Where, at the expiry of the relevant period, only one application under rule 3(1) in respect of the holding is pending, any application by the landlord shall be made within four months after a copy of the application under rule 3(1) is served on him.

(4) Where, at the expiry of the relevant period, more than one application under rule 3(1) in respect of the holding is pending, any application by the landlord shall be made—
   (a) within four months after a copy of the first application under rule 3(1) is served on him, or
   (b) within one month after the date on which the number of applications under rule 3(1) which are pending is reduced to one or within one month after such earlier date as the tribunal may direct,
whichever of those periods expires last.

(5) The secretary shall forthwith inform the landlord of the start of any period of

four months under paragraph (3) or paragraph (4) and any period of one month under paragraph (4).

Notice of application

5.—(1) An applicant shall at the time of making his application serve notice of the application in Form 3 on the landlord and on any person who, to the knowledge of the applicant, has made or may be able to make an application under rule 3(1), and shall inform the tribunal in his application of the name and address of every person to be notified by him.

(2) The applicant shall also inform the tribunal in his application of the name and address of—
- (a) the personal representatives of the deceased, or, if a grant of probate or of letters of administration has not been made, any person who appears to be responsible for the management of the holding on behalf of the deceased's estate;
- (b) any other person who to the knowledge of the applicant may be interested in the outcome of the application,

and in each case shall give the tribunal an indication of the nature of that person's interest in the outcome of the application.

Landlord's reply

6. A landlord who intends to oppose the whole or any part of an application under rule 3(1) shall, within one month after a copy of the application has been served on him, reply thereto in Form 1R (which is the form appended to the copy of the application served on him).

Applicant's reply to landlord's application

7. An applicant who intends to oppose an application to the tribunal under rule 4 shall, within one month after a copy of the application has been served on him, reply thereto in Form 2R (which is the form appended to the copy of the application served on him).

Applicant's reply to other applications under rule 3(1)

8.—(1) An applicant who intends to oppose any application under rule 3(1) by any other person shall, within one month after the expiry of the relevant period, reply to that application in Form 4.

(2) Any request by two, three or four applicants for the consent of the landlord to a direction entitling them to a joint tenancy of the holding under section 20(9) of the 1976 Act may be made in the reply of each of them under this rule.

PARTIES, ETC.

Applications to be heard together, and parties

9. Subject to the following provision of these rules, all applications under rule 3(1) or (2) in respect of any particular holding which are made within the relevant

period, and any applications in respect thereof by the landlord, shall be heard and determined together as if each of them other than the first had been made by a party in the course of the proceedings on the first of them to be made, and, accordingly, there shall be parties to the proceedings on each application by an applicant—
- (*a*) that applicant,
- (*b*) the landlord, and
- (*c*) any other applicant whose application was made within the relevant period and is still pending.

General Provisions as to Applications and Replies

Service of documents by secretary

10.—(1) As soon as possible after receiving from any person any document under rule 3, 4, 6, 7 or 8 the secretary shall serve one copy thereof on every other person who, in accordance with rule 9, is a party to the proceedings on that application.

(2) As soon as possible after any fresh application under rule 3(1) is made in respect of a holding, the secretary shall serve on the fresh applicant one copy of every document which has not already been served on him but which would have been served on him had he been a party from the outset to the proceedings.

(3) As soon as possible after the expiry of the relevant period, the secretary shall serve on all those persons whose names and addresses were supplied under rule 5(2) by any applicant notice of the existence of the proceedings in respect of the holding and of the names and addresses of the parties thereto, and shall inform each of those persons that, if he so requests in writing, a copy of the eventual decision of the tribunal will be sent to him by the secretary.

Application of principal rules relating to applications and replies

11.—(1) Rules 16 (except for paragraph (5)) and 18 (except for paragraph (2)) of the principal rules shall apply to applications and replies under this Part of these rules.

(2) Rule 15(2) of the principal rules shall apply in the case of an application by the landlord under this Part of these rules.

(3) Rule 18(2) of the principal rules shall apply to a reply under rule 7 of these rules if the relevant period has expired and, following the withdrawal of the reply, there is no other outstanding reply to the application by the landlord.

Hearings

Date and place of hearing

12. As soon as practicable the chairman shall fix a date, time and place for the hearing of all applications made in the proceedings under this Part of these rules.

Duty to adjourn part of hearing

13.—(1) Where on the date of the hearing the landlord has not made an application under rule 4(3) but the time allowed for him to do so has not expired, the tribunal shall not proceed to give a direction under section 20 of the 1976 Act except with the consent of the landlord.

(2) Where on the date of the hearing the time allowed for a reply under rule 7 has not expired, or has not started to run, the tribunal shall not proceed to hear the application of the landlord except with the consent of every applicant who has not yet replied thereto.

(3) Where under this rule consent is required but is not given the tribunal shall adjourn the proceedings and the chairman shall give such directions as he thinks fit for the further hearing of the proceedings.

Application of principal rules relating to preparation for hearing and to hearing

14. Rules 19, 20, 23(3) and (4), 24, 25, 26(2) and (3) and 27 of the principal rules shall apply with the necessary modifications to applications under this Part of these rules.

FURTHER PROVISIONS RELATING TO HEARINGS

Sanctions for failure to reply

15.—(1) If no reply to an application under rule 3(1) is received from the landlord by the secretary within the time allowed by rule 6, then, subject to section 20(7) of the 1976 Act, the landlord shall not be entitled to dispute any matter alleged in that application, but this paragraph does not affect any right of the landlord to rely upon his own application under rule 4.

(2) Where pursuant to rule 15(2) or 18(2) of the principal rules (as applied by rule 11(2) and (3) of these rules), the tribunal decide to make an order in the terms of the application by the landlord without a formal hearing, any application under rule 3(1) in respect of the holding shall be dismissed.

(3) If no reply to an application under rule 3(1) is received from an applicant by the secretary within the time allowed by rule 8(1), the applicant who has not replied shall not be entitled to dispute any matter alleged in the application, but this paragraph does not affect the right of that applicant to claim before the tribunal that he is more suitable than the other applicant.

Procedure at hearing in case of sole applicant

16. Where on the date of the hearing only one application under rule 3(1) is pending before the tribunal, the applicant shall begin, and the order of proceedings shall be the same as in civil proceedings in the High Court as if the application were an action begun by writ and as if any application by the landlord were a counterclaim.

Procedure at hearing in case of multiple applicants where designation is claimed

17.—(1) Where any applicant under rule 3(1) claims to be a designated applicant the tribunal shall first hear him as to the validity of his claim to be a designated applicant (and if more than one applicant so claims, the tribunal shall hear them on those respective claims in the order determined by the tribunal), and shall then afford any other applicant (including any applicant who himself so claims) an opportunity to reply to that claim.

(2) The tribunal shall thereupon determine the validity of each claim to be a designated applicant.

(3) If the tribunal determine that an applicant under rule 3(1) is a designated applicant, they shall then hear that person's application as if he were the only applicant.

(4) If under paragraph (3) the tribunal determine that the designated applicant is a suitable person to become the tenant of the holding, they—
- (a) shall dismiss all other applications under rule 3(1), and
- (b) shall, subject to rule 13, hear any application by the landlord.

(5) If under paragraph (3) the tribunal determine that the designated applicant is not a suitable person to become the tenant of the holding, they—
- (a) shall dismiss his application, and
- (b) shall, unless there is any remaining issue to be determined under paragraph (2) above, hear the remaining applications under rule 3(1) in accordance with rules 13 and 16 (or, in the case of two or more such applications, under rule 18) as if no applicant had claimed to be a designated applicant.

(6) If under paragraphs (1) and (2) the tribunal determine that there is no designated applicant, rule 18 shall apply.

Procedure at hearing in case of multiple applicants where designation is not claimed

18.—(1) Where the tribunal have to hear more than one application under rule 3(1) and no applicant claims or has been determined to be a designated applicant, then, subject to any direction by the chairman, the tribunal shall—
- (a) dispose of the various matters before them in the following order, that is to say—
  - (i) any determination as to eligibility under section 21(3) of the 1976 Act;
  - (ii) any remaining issue as to eligibility under section 20(3) of the 1976 Act;
  - (iii) any determination as to suitability under section 20(3) of the 1976 Act;
  - (iv) any question of exercising the discretion conferred by section 20(9) of the 1976 Act;
  - (v) any determination as to relative suitability under section 20(6) of the 1976 Act;
  - (vi) any question arising under section 20(9A) of the 1976 Act;
  - (vii) subject to rule 13, any question arising on an application by the landlord under section 22 of the 1976 Act, and
- (b) hear the person who is in the position of applicant in respect of any of the matters referred to in subparagraph (a) above and then the other parties in such order as the tribunal may determine, and, for the purpose of this

subparagraph, any request for the landlord's consent made under rule 8(2) or at the hearing shall be treated as if it were an application.

(2) Where, under paragraph (1)(*a*)(iii), two or more applicants are determined to be suitable persons to become the tenant of the holding, then—
- (*a*) the tribunal shall ask the landlord if he will consent to the giving of a direction in accordance with section 20(9) of the 1976 Act specifying any two, any three, or any four of the suitable applicants and entitling them to a joint tenancy of the holding, and if the landlord then consents the tribunal may (after hearing such of the suitable applicants as wish to be heard) give a direction specifying the applicants in respect of whom the landlord's consent is given, and entitling them to a joint tenancy of the holding;
- (*b*) the tribunal may give the landlord an opportunity to consent within such time as they may allow, and may regard his consent as refused if not given within that time.

(3) Where the tribunal dispose of any matter under paragraph (1)(*a*)(i), (ii), (iii), (v) or (vii) in such a way that any particular application can no longer succeed, that application shall be dismissed.

Further provisions relating to notice to quit

19. Where the proceedings are adjourned under rule 13(1) and the landlord then fails to make an application under rule 4 within the time allowed by that rule, the tribunal may, without a formal hearing, give a direction under section 20(5) or 20(6) of the 1976 Act (as the case may be) entitling the suitable applicant to a tenancy of the holding.

Application of principal rules relating to evidence, decisions, etc

20.—(1) Rules 28 to 31 and 33 to 38 of the principal rules shall apply with the necessary modifications to proceedings under this Part of these rules as they apply to other proceedings before the tribunal.

(2) For the purposes of rules 31, 33 and 34 of the principal rules, any dismissal of an application under these rules shall be a decision, and all such decisions, and the reasons for them, may be given in a single document at the conclusion of the proceedings unless the chairman otherwise decides.

Postponement of operation of notice to quit or direction

21.—(1) Where the tribunal give their consent to the operation of a notice to quit under section 22 of the 1976 Act within the period of three months ending with the original operative date or at any time after that date, any application by the tenant under subsection (6) of that section for the notice to have effect from a later date shall be made in writing to the secretary before the hearing or verbally at the hearing.

(2) Where the tribunal give a direction under section 20(5), (6) or (9) of the 1976 Act within the period of three months ending with the relevant time apart from section 23(2A) of that Act, any application by the tenant under that subsection for

the direction to have effect from a later time shall be made in writing to the secretary before the hearing or verbally at the hearing.

Part III
Application for Succession by Person Nominated by Retiring Tenant under Schedule 2 to the Agricultural Holdings Act 1984

Interpretation of Part III

22.—(1) In this Part of these rules "the 1984 Act" means the Agricultural Holdings Act 1984.

(2) Expressions defined for the purposes of, or of any provision in, paragraphs 1 to 6 of Schedule 2 to the 1984 Act (notably in paragraphs 1(1) and (2) and 6(7)) have the same meaning in this Part of these rules.

Form of Application and Reply

Application by nominated successor

23.—(1) An application by the nominated successor to the tribunal under paragraph 5(1) of Schedule 2 to the 1984 Act for a direction entitling him to a tenancy of an agricultural holding shall be made in Form 5.

(2) An application made under this rule shall not be entertained by the tribunal if it is not made within the relevant period.

Notice of application

24. The nominated successor shall at the time of making his application serve notice of the application in Form 6 on the landlord.

Landlord's reply

25. A landlord who intends to oppose the whole or any part of an application under rule 23(1) shall, within one month after a copy of the application has been served on him, reply thereto in Form 5R (which is the form appended to the copy of the application served on him).

Parties

Parties

26. There shall be parties to the proceedings on an application by the nominated successor—
- (*a*) the nominated successor,
- (*b*) the landlord, and
- (*c*) the retiring tenant or (in the case of a joint tenancy) all the retiring tenants.

General Provisions as to Applications and Replies

Service of documents by secretary

27. As soon as possible after receiving from any person any document under rule 23 or 25 the secretary shall serve one copy thereof on every other person who, in accordance with rule 26, is a party to the proceedings on that application.

Application of principal rules relating to applications and replies

28. Rules 16 (except for paragraph (5)) and 18 (except for paragraph (2)) of the principal rules shall apply to applications and replies under this Part of these rules.

Hearings

Date and place of hearing

29. As soon as practicable the chairman shall fix a date, time and place for the hearing of an application made under this Part of these rules.

Application of principal rules relating to preparation for hearing and to hearing

30. Rules 19, 20, 23(3) and (4), 24, 25, 26(2) and (3) and 27 of the principal rules shall apply with the necessary modifications to applications under this Part of these rules.

Further Provisions Relating to Hearings

Sanctions for failure to reply

31. If no reply to an application under rule 23(1) is received from the landlord by the secretary within the time allowed by rule 25, then, subject to paragraph 5(5) of Schedule 2 to the 1984 Act, the landlord shall not be entitled to dispute any matter alleged in that application.

Procedure at hearing

32.—(1) Subject to paragraph (2), at the hearing the nominated successor shall begin and the other parties shall be heard in such order as the tribunal may determine.

(2) Where the retirement notice to which the nominated successor's application relates includes a statement in accordance with paragraph 2(3) of Schedule 2 to the 1984 Act that the notice is given on the grounds mentioned in that provision, the tribunal shall first consider whether the conditions specified in paragraph 5(3)(*a*) and (*b*) of that Schedule are satisfied and, if the tribunal determine that those conditions are not satisfied, they shall dismiss the nominated successor's application.

Application of principal rules relating to evidence, decisions, etc

33.—(1) Rules 28 to 31 and 33 to 38 of the principal rules shall apply with the necessary modifications to proceedings under this Part of these rules as they apply to other proceedings before the tribunal.

(2) For the purposes of rules 31, 33 and 34 of the principal rules, any dismissal of an application under these rules shall be a decision, and all such decisions, and the reasons for them, may be given in a single document at the conclusion of the proceedings unless the chairman otherwise decides.

Postponement of operation of direction

34. Where the tribunal give a direction under paragraph 5(6) of Schedule 2 to the 1984 Act within the period of three months ending with the retirement date, any application by the tenant under paragraph 6(7) of that Schedule for the direction to have effect from a later time shall be made in writing to the secretary before the hearing or verbally at the hearing.

APPENDIX
FORMS

Rule 1(3)(*b*)

Form 1 (Succession on Death) Agricultural Land Tribunal, rule 3(1) and (2)

Form 1R (Succession on Death) Agricultural Land Tribunal, rule 6
Application for direction giving entitlement to tenancy of agricultural holding and application that applicant be treated as an eligible person (combined prescribed form) and landlord's reply (prescribed forms).
[printed as Forms 43 and 43A in Part V, paras A.83 and A84 of this work]

Form 2 (Succession on Death) Agricultural Land Tribunal, rule 4(1)

Form 2R (Succession on Death) Agricultural Land Tribunal, rule 7
Application by the landlord following the tenant's death for consent to operation of notice to quit and tenant's reply (prescribed forms).
[printed as Forms 44 and 44A in Part V, paras A.85 and A.86 of this work]

Form 3 (Succession on Death), rule 5(1)
Notice by applicant of application for entitlement to tenancy on the death of the tenant (prescribed form).
[printed as Form 45 in Part V, para. A.87 of this work]

Form 4 (Succession on Death) Agricultural Land Tribunal, rule 8
Applicant's reply to other applications for direction giving entitlement to tenancy (prescribed form).
[printed as Form 46 in Part V, para. A.88]

Form 5 (Succession on Retirement) Agricultural Land Tribunal, rule 23(1)

Form 5R (Succession on Retirement) Agricultural Land Tribunal, rule 25
Application (following a retirement notice) for a direction giving entitlement to tenancy of holding and landlord's reply (prescribed forms).

[printed as Forms 48 and 48A in Part V, paras A.90 and A91 of this work]

Form 6 (Succession on Retirement) Agricultural Land Tribunal, rule 24
Notice given to landlord by nominated successor of application for entitlement to tenancy on tenant's retirement (prescribed form).
[printed as Form 49 in Part V, para. A.92 of this work]

GENERAL NOTE

This Order consolidates with amendments the Agricultural Land Tribunals (Succession to Agricultural Tenancies) Order 1976, as amended. The Order—
(a) amends the rules of procedure for Agricultural Land Tribunals in relation to applications for succession to an agricultural holding on the death of a tenant under Part II of the Agriculture (Miscellaneous Provisions) Act 1976, as amended by the Agricultural Holdings Act 1984;
(b) introduces rules of procedure for Agricultural Land Tribunals in relation to applications for succession to an agricultural holding by a person nominated by a retiring tenant under Schedule 2 to the 1984 Act.

The most important changes to the procedural rules relating to succession on death are—
(a) the substitution of new time limits for the landlord's application for consent to the operation of a notice to quit (rule 4(3) and (4));
(b) a provision specifying the stage at which the tribunal is to consider any question arising under section 20 (9A) of the 1976 Act, as amended (rule 18(1)(a));
(c) the requirement that any application by the tenant to postpone the operation of a notice to quit or a direction under section 20 of the 1976 Act must be made in writing to the secretary before the hearing or verbally at the hearing (rule 21);
(d) the introduction of further questions in Form 1 which are necessary as a result of amendments to the 1976 Act effected by the 1984 Act.

The new procedural rules relating to succession on retirement regulate the form of application by the nominated successor (rule 23 and Form 5) and any reply by the landlord (rule 25 and Form 5R). Provision is also made for the service of notice of the application (rule 24 and Form 6) and for general matters relating to applications, replies and the hearing. So far as material, the Agricultural Land Tribunals Rules 1978 are applied to the proceedings (rules 28, 30 and 33).

A.21 **THE MILK QUOTA (CALCULATION OF STANDARD QUOTA) ORDER 1986**

(S.I 1986 No. 1530)

The Minister of Agriculture, Fisheries and Food, in the case of land in England, and the Secretary of State, in the case of land in Wales, in exercise of the powers conferred on them by paragraph 6 of Schedule 1 to the Agriculture Act 1986, and

APPLICATION OF PART II OF THE ACT

of all other powers enabling them in that behalf, hereby make the following order:—

Application, title and commencement

1. This order, which applies to land in England and Wales, may be cited as the Milk Quota (Calculation of Standard Quota) Order 1986 and shall come into operation on 25th September 1986.

Interpretation

[2. In this Order, the expressions "disadvantaged land" and "severely disadvantaged land" have the same meaning as in the Hill Livestock (Compensatory Allowances) Regulations 1992 S.I. 1992/269.]
Note:
Art. 2 was substituted, as from June 19, 1992, by Art. 2(2) of the Milk Quota (Calculation of Standard Quota) (Amendment) Order 1992 (S.I. 1992 No. 1225).

Prescribed quota

3. The number of litres prescribed for the purposes of sub-paragraph 6(1)(*b*) of Schedule 1 to the Agriculture Act 1986 (calculation of standard quota) in respect of each of the breeds shown in Column 1 of the Schedule to this order is the number shown opposite that breed in—
   (*a*) column 2(*a*) in relation to severely disadvantaged land;
   (*b*) column 3(*a*) in relation to disadvantaged land; and
   (*c*) column 4(*a*) in relation to any other land.

Average yield per hectare

4. The amount of milk to be taken as the average yield per hectare for the purposes of sub-paragraph 6(2) of Schedule 1 to the Agriculture Act 1986 (calculation of standard quota in exceptional cases) in respect of each of the breeds shown in Column 1 of the Schedule to this order is the amount shown opposite that breed in—
   (*a*) column 2(*b*) in relation to severely disadvantaged land;
   (*b*) column 3(*b*) in relation to disadvantaged land; and
   (*c*) column 4(*b*) in relation to any other land.

Minister of State,
Ministry of Agriculture, Fisheries and Food.
Secretary of State for Wales.

27th August 1986.

THE MILK QUOTA (CALCULATION OF STANDARD QUOTA) ORDER 1986

SCHEDULE

Article 3 and 4

(1)	(2)		(3)		(4)	
Breed	Severely disadvantaged Land		Disadvantaged land		Other land	
	(a) Quota/ Hectare	(b) Average Yield/ Hectare	(a) Quota/ Hectare	(b) Average Yield/ Hectare	(a) Quota/ Hectare	(b) Average Yield/ Hectare
	litres	litres	litres	litres	litres	litres
Channel Island and South Devon, and breeds with similar characteristics	4,550	5,737	5,310	6,694	6,070	7,650
Ayrshire and Dairy Shorthorn and breeds with similar characteristics	5,205	6,562	6,075	7,656	6,940	8,750
Other	5,355	6,750	6,250	7,875	7,140	9,000

Note:

This Schedule was substituted, as from June 19, 1992, by Art. 2(3) of the Milk Quota (Calculation of Standard Quota) (Amendment) Order 1992 (S.I. 1992 No. 1225).

GENERAL NOTE

Where, on the termination of a tenancy of land in England or Wales the tenant has milk quota registered as his in relation to a holding consisting of or including the land, Schedule 1 to the Agriculture Act 1986 gives him a right in certain circumstances, on quitting the land, to obtain from his landlord a payment in respect of all or part of the milk quota which was allocated to him in relation to land comprised in the holding. The amount of payment to which the tenant is entitled in respect of that milk quota is calculated by reference to the "standard quota" for the land, and the "standard quota" is in turn calculated by reference to the "prescribed quota per hectare" and the "prescribed average yield per hectare". This order prescribes the quota per hectare and the average yield per hectare to be taken into account in determining the "standard quota" for the purposes of calculating the payment to which the tenant is entitled under the Act.

ARTICLE 1

THE AGRICULTURAL HOLDINGS (ARBITRATION ON NOTICES) ORDER 1987

(S.I. 1987 No. 710)

The Lord Chancellor, in exercise of the powers conferred on him by section 29 of, and paragraphs 1 to 6 (inclusive) and 8 to 13 (inclusive) of Schedule 4 and paragraph 5 of Schedule 5 to, the Agricultural Holdings Act 1986, and of all other powers enabling him in that behalf, after consultation with the Council on Tribunals as required by section 10 of the Tribunals and Inquiries Act 1971, hereby makes the following Order:

[PART I: PRELIMINARY]

Citation and commencement

1. This Order may be cited as the Agricultural Holdings (Arbitration on Notices) Order 1987 and shall come into force on 12th May 1987.

Interpretation

2.—(1) In this Order, unless the context otherwise requires-
"the 1986 Act" means the Agricultural Holdings Act 1986;
"notice to remedy" means a notice served on the tenant of an agricultural holding for the purposes of Case D requiring him to remedy a breach of a term or condition of his tenancy;
"notice to do work" means a notice to remedy which requires the doing of any work of repair, maintenance or replacement;
"termination", in relation to an arbitration, means the date on which the arbitrator's award is delivered to the tenant.

(2) Any reference in this Order to a numbered article shall be construed as a reference to the article bearing that number in this Order.

[PART II: NOTICES TO DO WORK]

[NOTICES REQUIRING ARBITRATION]

Notice where arbitration is available at the notice to remedy stage only

3.—(1) Where a tenant on whom a notice to do work has been served wishes to have determined by arbitration under the 1986 Act any of the following questions, namely-
  (a) his liability under the terms or conditions of his tenancy to do any of the work specified in the notice,
  (b) the deletion from the notice of any item or part of an item of work on the ground that it is unnecessary or unjustified, or
  (c) the substitution, in the case of any item or part of an item of work, of a different method or material for the method or material which the notice would otherwise require to be followed or used,

he shall do so by service of a notice requiring the question or questions to be determined by arbitration under the 1986 Act.

(2) A notice under paragraph (1) above shall be in writing, and shall be served on the landlord within one month after the service on the tenant of the notice to do work.

(3) A notice under paragraph (1) above shall specify, as the case may be-
   (a) any items in respect of which the tenant denies liability,
   (b) any items or parts of items which the tenant claims to be unnecessary or unjustified, and
   (c) any method or material in respect of which the tenant desires a substitution to be made.

Notice on other questions or in other cases

4.—(1) Where the tenant on whom a notice to do work has been served wishes to have determined by arbitration under the 1986 Act in addition to a question specified in article 3(1) any other question arising under that notice which is not a question so specified, he shall do so by serving on the landlord within one month after the service of the notice to do work a notice in writing requiring the question to be so determined.

(2) Where the tenant on whom a notice to do work has been served does not wish any question specified in article 3(1) to be determined by arbitration under the 1986 Act but wishes to have determined by such arbitration any other question arising under that notice, he shall do so-
   (a) by serving on the landlord within one month after the service of the notice to do work a notice in writing requiring the question to be so determined, or
   (b) by serving a notice in accordance with article 9.

(3) Nothing in this article shall preclude a tenant who has required arbitration under this article and who has been found liable to comply with a notice to do work or with any part of it from subsequently requiring arbitration under article 9 on the ground that, in consequence of anything happening before the expiration of the time for doing the work as extended by the arbitrator in pursuance of article 6(2), it would have been unreasonable to require the tenant to do the work within that time.

[POWERS OF ARBITRATOR]

Power to modify notice

5. In addition to any powers otherwise available to him, an arbitrator may-
   (a) in relation to any question specified in article 3(1)(b), modify a notice to do work by deleting any item or part of an item of work specified in the notice as to which, having due regard to the interests of good husbandry as respects the agricultural holding to which the notice relates and of sound management of the estate of which that holding forms part or which that holding constitutes, the arbitrator is satisfied that it is unnecessary or unjustified, and

(b) in relation to a question specified in article 3(1)(c), modify a notice to do work by substituting, in the case of any item or part of an item of work specified in the notice, a different method or material for the method or material which the notice would otherwise require to be followed or used where, having regard to the purpose which that item or part is intended to achieve, the arbitrator is satisfied that-
   (i) the last-mentioned method or material would involve undue difficulty or expense,
   (ii) the first-mentioned method or material would be substantially as effective for that purpose, and
   (iii) in all the circumstances the substitution is justified.

[SUPPLEMENTARY]

Extension of time for doing work

6.—(1) Where a tenant requires any question to be determined by arbitration under article 3 or 4, the time specified for doing the work which is the subject of the arbitration shall be extended until the termination of the arbitration.

(2) Where the arbitrator finds that the tenant is liable to comply with a notice to do work or with any part of it, he shall extend the time for doing that work by such further period as he thinks fit.

Date of termination of tenancy on failure to do work

7.—(1) Where the time specified for doing any work is extended under article 6(2), the arbitrator may, either of his own motion or on the application of the landlord made not later than fourteen days after the termination of the arbitration, specify a date for the termination of the tenancy by notice to quit in the event of the tenant's failure to do the work within the extended time.

(2) A date specified under paragraph (1) above shall not be earlier than-
   (a) the date on which the tenancy could have been terminated by notice to quit served on the expiration of the time originally specified in the notice to do work, or
   (b) six months after the expiration of the extended time,
whichever is the later.

(3) Where the landlord applies to the arbitrator under paragraph (1) above, he shall at the same time give written notice of the application to the tenant (except where the application is made at the arbitration) and the tenant shall be entitled to be heard on the application.

(4) A notice to quit on a date specified under paragraph (1) above shall be served on the tenant within one month after the expiration of the extended time, and shall (subject to any right to contest its effectiveness available to the tenant) be valid notwithstanding that it is served less than twelve months before the date on which the tenancy is to be terminated or that that date is not the end of a year of the tenancy.

THE AGRICULTURAL HOLDINGS (ARBITRATION ON NOTICES) ORDER 1987

Recovery of cost of work

8. Where, on an arbitration relating in whole or in part to the question specified in article 3(1)(*a*), it appears to the arbitrator that the tenant has done work required by a notice to do work which he was under no obligation to do, the arbitrator shall determine the reasonable cost of such work, which shall be recoverable from the landlord by the tenant in accordance with section 85(1) of the 1986 Act.

[PART III: NOTICES TO QUIT]
[ARBITRATION CONCERNING NOTICES TO QUIT]

Notice requiring arbitration

9. Where it is stated in a notice to quit an agricultural holding or part thereof that the notice is given for one or more of the reasons specified in Case A, B, D or E and the tenant wishes to contest any question arising under the provisions of section 26(2) of, and Schedule 3 to, the 1986 Act relating to any of the reasons so stated, he shall within one month after the service of the notice serve on the landlord notice in writing requiring the question to be determined by arbitration under the 1986 Act.

Appointment of arbitrator

10. A notice under article 9 requiring arbitration under the 1986 Act shall cease to be effective three months after the date of the service of that notice unless before the expiry of those three months-
    (*a*) an arbitrator has been appointed by agreement between the parties, or
    (*b*) (in default of such agreement) an application has been made by the tenant or the landlord under paragraph 1 of Schedule 11 to that Act for the appointment of an arbitrator,
for the purposes of that arbitration.

Service of counter-notice

11. Where-
(1) an arbitration is required under article 9 in respect of a notice to quit which is capable of taking effect either as a notice to quit to which section 26(2) of the 1986 Act applies or in the alternative as a notice to quit to which section 26(1) of that Act applies, and
(2) in consequence of the arbitration that notice takes effect as a notice to quit to which section 26(1) applies,
the time within which a counter-notice may be served by the tenant on the landlord under section 26(1) of the 1986 Act shall be one month from the termination of the arbitration.

[POSTPONEMENT OF OPERATION OF NOTICE TO QUIT]

During arbitration

12. Where a tenant requires a question arising out of a notice to quit to be determined by arbitration under article 9, the operation of the notice shall be suspended until-

(a) the expiry of the time fixed in article 10 for appointing an arbitrator by agreement or for making an application under paragraph 1 of Schedule 11 to the 1986 Act, or

(b) where any such appointment or application has been duly made, the termination of the arbitration.

After arbitration or proceedings

13.—(1) Where-
 (a) a notice to quit has effect in consequence of an arbitration under article 9, or the Tribunal have consented to the operation of the notice under section 26(1) or 28(2) of the 1986 Act or article 15(5), and
 (b)
  the notice would, but for the provisions of this article, come into operation on or within six months after the termination of the arbitration, or the giving of the consent,

the arbitrator or the Tribunal may, either of his or their own motion or on the application of the tenant made not later than fourteen days after the termination of the arbitration or the giving of the consent, postpone the termination of the tenancy for a period not exceeding twelve months.

(2) Where the tenant applies to the arbitrator or the Tribunal under paragraph (1) above, he shall at the same time give written notice of the application to the landlord (except where the application is made at the arbitration or at the hearing before the Tribunal) and the landlord shall be entitled to be heard on the application.

[EXTENSION OF TIME UNDER NOTICE TO REMEDY AFTER NOTICE TO QUIT]

Extension by arbitrator

14. Where-
 (a) notice to quit is stated to be given by reason of the tenant's failure to remedy a breach of any term or condition of his tenancy-
  (i) within the time specified in a notice to remedy, or
  (ii) within that time as extended by the landlord, or in pursuance of article 6 or of this article, and
(b) it appears to the arbitrator on an arbitration under article 9 that, notwithstanding that the time originally specified or extended was reasonable, it would, in consequence of anything happening before the expiration of that time, have been unreasonable to require the tenant to remedy the breach within that time,

the arbitrator may treat the time as having been extended, or further extended, and may make his award as if the time had not expired; and where the breach has not been remedied at the date of the award, the arbitrator may extend the time by such period as he considers reasonable, having regard to the length of time which has elapsed since the service of the notice to remedy.

THE AGRICULTURAL HOLDINGS (ARBITRATION ON NOTICES) ORDER 1987

Termination of tenancy following extension

15.—(1) Where the time specified for doing any work is extended under article 14, the arbitrator may, either of his own motion or on the application of the landlord made not later than fourteen days after the termination of the arbitration, specify a date for the termination of the tenancy by a subsequent notice to quit in the event of the tenant's failure to do the work within the extended time.

(2) A date specified under paragraph (1) above shall not be earlier than-
- (*a*) the date on which the tenancy could have been terminated by the original notice to quit (that is, the notice which was the subject of the arbitration), or
- (*b*) six months after the expiration of the extended time,

whichever is the later.

(3) Where the landlord applies to the arbitrator under paragraph (1) above, he shall at the same time give written notice of the application to the tenant (except where the application is made at the arbitration) and the tenant shall be entitled to be heard on the application.

(4) A notice to quit on a date specified under paragraph (1) above shall be served on the tenant within one month after the expiration of the extended time, and, subject to paragraph (5) below, shall be valid notwithstanding it is served less than twelve months before the date on which the tenancy is to be terminated or that that date is not the end of a year of the tenancy.

(5) Where a subsequent notice to quit is given in accordance with paragraph (1) above in a case where the original notice to quit included a statement in accordance with Case D to the effect that it was given by reason of the tenant's failure to comply with a notice to do work, then, if the tenant serves on the landlord a counter-notice in writing within one month after the giving of the subsequent notice to quit (or, if the date specified in that notice for the termination of the tenancy is earlier, before that date), the subsequent notice to quit shall not have effect unless the Tribunal consent to its operation.

(6) On an application made for the consent of the Tribunal under paragraph (5) above on the part of the landlord, the Tribunal shall consent to the operation of the notice to quit unless it appears to them, having regard-
- (*a*) to the extent to which the tenant has failed to comply with the notice to do work,
- (*b*) to the consequences of his failure to comply with it in any respect, and
- (*c*) to the circumstances surrounding any such failure,

that a fair and reasonable landlord would not insist on possession.

[SUPPLEMENTARY]

Notice to sub-tenants

16.—(1) Section 26(1) of the 1986 Act shall not apply where notice to quit an agricultural holding or part thereof is given to a sub-tenant by a tenant who has himself been given notice to quit that holding or part thereof and the fact that the tenant has been given such notice is stated in the notice given to the sub-tenant.

(2) Such a notice given to a sub-tenant shall have effect only if the notice to quit given to the tenant by the landlord itself has effect.

(3) Where a tenant accepts notice to quit part of a holding as notice to quit the whole under section 32 of the 1986 Act, then, for the purpose of this article, the notice given by him shall be deemed to be a notice to quit the entire holding.

Service men

17.—(1) In any case to which, notwithstanding the existence of any such circumstances as are mentioned in Cases B to G, section 26(1) of the 1986 Act applies by virtue of the modification of that section by paragraph 3 of Schedule 5 to that Act, paragraphs (2) to (4) below shall have effect.

(2) Where, on an application by the landlord for the consent of the Tribunal to the operation of a notice to quit, it appears to the Tribunal that the notice to quit was given for one or more of the reasons specified in Case B, D or E, and that it is expedient that any question arising under the provisions of section 26(2) of, and Schedule 3 to, the 1986 Act relating to any of the reasons so stated should be determined by arbitration between the landlord and tenant under that Act before the Tribunal consider whether to grant or withhold consent to the operation of the notice to quit, they may require that the question be determined accordingly.

(3) Article 9 shall apply with the addition of the following words-
"so, however, that the tenant's failure to serve such a notice shall not affect his right to contest the question in proceedings before the Tribunal consequent upon the service of a counter-notice under section 26(1) of the 1986 Act or in any arbitration by which the Tribunal may require any such question to be determined."

(4) Article 11 shall not apply, but where a tenant requires a question to be determined by arbitration in pursuance of article 9, the time within which a counter-notice under section 26(1) of the 1986 Act may be served by the tenant on the landlord under that subsection shall be one month from the termination of the arbitration.

[PART IV: REVOCATION]

Revocation

18. The Agricultural Holdings (Arbitration on Notices) Order 1978 and the Agricultural Holdings (Arbitration on Notices) (Variation) Order 1984 are hereby revoked, but without prejudice to their application in relation to notices to do work and notices to quit which have been served before the commencement of this Order, and to any proceedings relating to or consequent upon any such notices.

Dated 8th April 1987

GENERAL NOTE

This Order consolidates with an amendment the Agricultural Holdings (Arbitration on Notices) Order 1978, as varied ("the 1978 Order"). In particular, the Order brings up to date references in the 1978 Order to statutory provisions which have been consolidated by the Agricultural Holdings Act 1986 ("The 1986

Act"). The Order makes detailed provision in relation to the reference to arbitration under the 1986 Act of questions arising under-
  (*a*) a notice served on the tenant of an agricultural holding for the purposes of Case D in Part I of Schedule 3 to the 1986 Act requiring him to remedy a breach of a term or condition of his tenancy by doing any work of repair, maintenance or replacement (articles 3 to 8);
  (*b*) a notice to quit given for one or more of the reasons specified in Case A, B, D or E in the said Part I (articles 9 to 17).

The Order contains an amendment in relation to the three months' time-limit after service of a notice requiring arbitration on a notice to quit within which an arbitrator must be appointed or application must be made under the 1986 Act for such an appointment if the notice requiring arbitration is not to cease to be effective. The Order now specifically provides that an application by either the landlord or the tenant within the three months' time-limit will preserve the effectiveness of such a notice (article 10).

A.23   THE AGRICULTURAL HOLDINGS (FORMS OF NOTICE TO PAY RENT OR TO REMEDY) REGULATIONS 1987

(S.I. 1987 No. 711)

The Minister of Agriculture, Fisheries and Food in relation to England and the Secretary of State in relation to Wales, in exercise of the powers conferred on them by paragraph 10(1)(*a*) and (2) of Part II of Schedule 3 to the Agricultural Holdings Act 1986, and of all other powers enabling them in that behalf, hereby make the following Regulations:

Citation and commencement

1. These Regulations may be cited as the Agricultural Holdings (Forms of Notice to Pay Rent or to Remedy) Regulations 1987 and shall come into force on 12th May 1987.

Interpretation

2.—(1) In these Regulations-
"the 1986 Act" means the Agricultural Holdings Act 1986;
"notice to pay rent" means a notice served on the tenant of an agricultural holding for the purposes of Case D requiring him to pay rent due;
"notice to remedy" means a notice served on the tenant of an agricultural holding for the purposes of Case D requiring him to remedy a breach of a term or condition of his tenancy.

(2) A form referred to by number in these Regulations means the form so numbered in the Schedule to these Regulations or a form substantially to the same effect.

Form of notice to pay rent

3. A notice to pay rent shall be in Form 1.

Forms of notice to remedy

4. A notice to remedy which requires the doing of any work of repair, maintenance or replacement shall be in Form 2 and any other notice to remedy shall be in Form 3.

Revocation

5. The Agricultural Holdings (Forms of Notice to Pay Rent or to Remedy) Regulations 1984 are hereby revoked, but without prejudice to their application in relation to any notice served before the coming into operation of these Regulations.

Minister of Agriculture, Fisheries and Food
Secretary of State for Wales
30th March 1987

SCHEDULE

Regulations 2(2), 3 and 4

Form 1
Agricultural Holdings Act 1986
[printed as Form 22 in Part V, para. A.59 of this work]

Form 2
Agricultural Holdings Act 1986
[printed as Form 23 in Part V, para. A.60 of this work]

Form 3
Agricultural Holdings Act 1986
[printed as Form 25 in Part V, paras A.62 of this work]

GENERAL NOTE

These Regulations revoke and replace the Agricultural Holdings (Forms of Notice to Pay Rent or to Remedy) Regulations 1984 ("the 1984 Regulations"). The Regulations bring up to date references in the 1984 Regulations to provisions which have been consolidated by the Agricultural Holdings Act 1986 and the Agricultural Holdings (Arbitration on Notices) Order 1987 ("the 1987 Order"). The Regulations continue to prescribe-

(a) a form to be used by the landlord of an agricultural holding when serving on his tenant a notice to pay rent due for the purposes of Case D in Part I of Schedule 3 to that Act (regulation 3 and Form 1 in Schedule);

(b) two different forms for the notice to remedy breaches of the terms and conditions of the tenancy for the purposes of the said Case D according to whether or not any work of repair, maintenance or replacement is required to remedy the breach (regulation 4 and Forms 2 and 3 in Schedule).

The reference in the Notes to the Forms to the time-limit in article 10 of the 1987 Order (appointment of arbitrator) reflects an amendment made by that article.

Note 4 to Form 2 has been expanded to give an example of a further question which may be referred to arbitration.

A.24 THE AGRICULTURAL HOLDINGS (FORM OF AWARD IN ARBITRATION PROCEEDINGS) ORDER 1990

(S.I. 1990 No. 1472)

The Lord Chancellor, in exercise of the powers conferred on him by section 84(2) and (3)(c) of, and paragraph 15 of Schedule 13 to, the Agricultural Holdings Act 1986, after consultation with the Council on Tribunals as required by section 10 of the Tribunals and Inquiries Act 1971, hereby makes the following Order:-

Citation and commencement

1. This Order may be cited as the Agricultural Holdings (Form of Award in Arbitration Proceedings) Order 1990 and shall come into force on 19th July 1990.

Saving

2. Articles 3 and 4 below shall not apply in relation to an arbitration where the arbitrator was appointed under the Agricultural Holdings Act 1948 before 18th June 1986.

Form of award

3. An award in proceedings on an arbitration under the Agricultural Holdings Act 1986 shall be made in the form set out in the Schedule to this Order, or in a form to the like effect, with such omissions or modifications as the circumstances may require.

Revocation

4. The Agricultural Holdings (England and Wales) Rules 1948, the Agricultural Holdings (England and Wales) (Amendment) Rules 1978 and the Agricultural Holdings (England and Wales) Rules (Variation) Order 1985 are hereby revoked.

Lord Chancellor
Dated 4th July 1990

SCHEDULE

AGRICULTURAL HOLDINGS ACT 1986 (NOTE 1)

Article 3

FORM OF AWARD [printed as Form 75 in Part V, para. A.122 of this work].

GENERAL NOTE

This Order, which applies to England and Wales only, prescribes the form in which awards are to be made in proceedings on arbitrations under the Agricultural Holdings Act 1986 (article 3 and Schedule) and revokes the Agricultural Holdings (England and Wales) Rules 1948, as varied ("the 1948 Rules") (article 4). The new form of award makes specific reference for the first time to rent cases, questions arising out of a notice to quit and the giving of reasons for the award, where appropriate. Arbitrators are required to omit or otherwise modify the items prescribed in the form only as far as circumstances require.

This Order does not prescribe forms of application for the appointment of arbitrators and for an extension of the time for making an award, which were prescribed in the 1948 Rules.

The prescribed forms in the 1948 Rules continue to apply where the arbitrator was appointed before 18th June 1986 (article 2).

THE AGRICULTURAL HOLDINGS (FEE) REGULATIONS 1996   A.25

(S.I. 1996 No. 337)

The Minister of Agriculture, Fisheries and Food in relation to England and the Secretary of State in relation to Wales, in exercise of the powers conferred on them by sections 22(4) and 96(1) of and paragraph 1(2) of Schedule 11 to the Agricultural Holdings Act 1986[40], and of all others powers enabling them in that behalf, and both Houses of Parliament having approved a draft of the Regulations, hereby make the following Regulations:-

Title and commencement

1.—These Regulations may be cited as the Agricultural Holdings (Fee) Regulations 1996 and shall come into force on 1st March 1996.

Prescribed fee

2.—The fee for an application to the President of the Royal Institution of Chartered Surveyors—
 (*a*) for a person to be appointed by him under section 22(2) of the Agricultural Holdings Act 1986, or
 (*b*) for an arbitrator to be appointed by him under paragraph 1(1) of Schedule 11 to that Act
is hereby increased from £70 to £115.

Revocation

3.—The Agriculture Holdings (Fee) Regulations 1985[41] are hereby revoked.

Tim Boswell
Parliamentary Secretary,
19th February 1996   Ministry of Agriculture, Fisheries and Food

Signed by the authority of the Secretary of State for Wales

Gwilym Jones
15th February 1996   Parliamentary Under Secretary of State for Wales

---

[40] 1986 c.5; Section 96(1) of the Act defines the "Minister" and "prescribed".
[41] S.I. 1985/1967.

THE AGRICULTURAL HOLDINGS (FEE) REGULATIONS 1996

GENERAL NOTE

These Regulations revoke the Agricultural Holdings (Fee) Regulations 1985 (S.I. 1985 No. 1967) which prescribed a fee of £70 for an application to the President of the Royal Institution of Chartered Surveyors for a person to be appointed by him to make a record of the condition of an agricultural holding or for an arbitrator to be appointed by him under the Agricultural Holdings Act 1986.

These Regulations increase the prescribed fee to £115.

A compliance cost assessment relating to these Regulations has been placed in the libraries of both Houses of Parliament.

A.26
THE AGRICULTURAL HOLDINGS (UNITS OF PRODUCTION) ORDER 1996

(S.I. 1996 No. 2163)

The Minister of Agriculture, Fisheries and Food in relation to England and the Secretary of State in relation to Wales, in exercise of the powers conferred on them by paragraph 4 of Schedule 6 to the Agricultural Holdings Act 1986[42], and of all other powers enabling them in that behalf, hereby make the following Order:—

Title, commencement and interpretation

1.—(1) This Order may be cited as the Agricultural Holdings (Units of Production) Order 1996 and shall come into force on 12th September 1996.

(2) Any reference in this Order to "the Schedule" shall be construed as a reference to the Schedule to this Order.

(3) Any reference in this Order to a Community instrument is a reference to that instrument as amended on the date this Order is made.

(4) In this Order, unless the context requires otherwise:

"Council Regulation 805/68" means Council Regulation (EEC) No. 805/68 on the common organisation of the market in beef and veal[43];

"Council Regulation 3013/89" means Council Regulation (EEC) No. 3013/89 on the common organization of the market in sheepmeat and goatmeat[44];

"Council Regulation 1765/92" means Council Regulation (EEC) No. 1765/92 establishing a support system for producers of certain arable crops[45];

"Council Regulation 1357/96" means Council Regulation (EC) No. 1357/96 providing for additional payments to be made in 1996 with the premiums referred to in Regulation (EEC) No. 805/68 on the common organization of the market in beef and veal and amending that Regulation.

Assessment of productive capacity of land

2.—(1) Paragraph (2) of this article has effect for the purpose of the assessment of the productive capacity of a unit of agricultural land, in order to determine

---

[42] Section 96(1) of the Act defines "the Minister".
[43] (O.J./S.E. 1968 (I) p.187), as amended in particular by Council Regulation (EEC) No. 2066/92, and as last amended by Council Regulation (EC) No. 894/96.
[44] As last amended by Council Regulation (EC) No. 1265/95.
[45] As last amended by Council Regulation (EC) No. 2989/95.

ARTICLE 2

whether that unit is a commercial unit of agricultural land within the meaning of subparagraph (1) of paragraph 3 of Schedule 6 to the Agricultural Holdings Act 1986.

(2) Where the land in question is capable, when farmed under competent management, of carrying or producing any such livestock, crop, etc. as is mentioned in any entry in column 1 of the Schedule—

  (*a*) the unit of production prescribed in relation to that use of the land shall be the unit specified in column 2 of the Schedule opposite to that entry, and

  (*b*) the amount determined, for the period of 12 months beginning with 12th September 1996, as the net annual income from the unit of production in that period shall be the amount specified in column 3 of the Schedule opposite that unit of production.

(3) The Schedule has effect subject to the Notes to the Schedule.

Revocation

3. The Agricultural Holdings (Units of Production) Order 1995 is hereby revoked.

Minister of State, Minister of Agriculture, Fisheries and Food
7th August 1996

12th August 1996

Parliamentary Under Secretary of State,
Welsh Office

SCHEDULE

Article 1(2) and 2

PRESCRIBED UNITS OF PRODUCTION AND DETERMINATION OF NET ANNUAL INCOME

Column 1[1] Farming use	Column 2 Unit of production	Column 3[2] Net annual income from unit of production
		£
1. *Livestock*		
Dairy cows:		
Channel Islands breeds	cow	294
Other breeds	cow	350
Beef breeding cows:		
On eligible land under the Hill Livestock (Compensatory Allowances) Regulations 1996	cow	75[1]
On other land	cow	60[1]
Beef fattening cattle (semi-		

THE AGRICULTURAL HOLDINGS (UNITS OF PRODUCTION) ORDER 1996

intensive)	head	102[2]
Dairy replacements	head	85[3]
Ewes:		
On eligible land under the Hill Livestock (Compensatory Allowances) Regulations 1996	ewe	28[4]
On other land	ewe	24[5]
Store lambs (including ewe lambs sold as shearlings)	head	
Pigs:		
Sows and gilts in pig	sow or gilt	103
Porker	head	2.83
Cutter	head	5.01
Bacon	head	6.22
Poultry:		
Laying hens	bird	1.16
Broilers	bird	0.16
Point-of-lay pullets	bird	0.32
Turkeys	bird	1.44
2. *Farm arable crops*		
Barley	hectare	429[6]
Beans	hectare	185[7]
Herbage seed	hectare	208
Linseed	hectare	282[8]
Oats	hectare	349[9]
Oilseed rape	hectare	380[10]
Peas:		
Dried	hectare	204[11]
Vining	hectare	311
Potatoes:		
First early	hectare	1207
Maincrop (including seed)	hectare	1226
Sugar Beet	hectare	513
Wheat	hectare	453[12]
3. *Set-aside(1)*	hectare	97
4. *Outdoor horticultural crops*		
Broad beans	hectare	512
Brussels sprouts	hectare	1313
Cabbage, savoys and sprouting broccoli	hectare	1559
Carrots	hectare	1994
Cauliflower and winter broccoli	hectare	1140
Celery	hectare	4060
Leeks	hectare	3074

SCHEDULE

Lettuce	hectare	3414
Onions:		
Dry bulb	hectare	2008
Salad	hectare	4403
Outdoor bulbs	hectare	1687
Parsnips	hectare	2026
Rhubarb (natural)	hectare	2581
Turnips and swedes	hectare	1210
5. *Protected crops*		
Forced narcissi	1000 square metres	6338
Forced tulips	1000 square metres	6167
Mushrooms	1000 square metres	11452
6. *Orchard fruit*		
Apples:		
Cider	hectare	505
Cooking	hectare	1265
Dessert	hectare	1462
Cherries	hectare	1090
Pears	hectare	1110
Plums	hectare	933
7. **Soft fruit**		
Blackcurrants	hectare	961
Gooseberries	hectare	1490
Raspberries	hectare	2860
Strawberries	hectare	3117
8. *Miscellaneous*		
Hops	hectare	2103

Notes

Note to column 1: [1] This refers to land which is set-aside under Article 2(5) of Council Regulation 1765/92, except where such land is used (in accordance with Article 7(4) of Council Regulation 1765/92) for the provision of materials for the manufacture within the Community of products not primarily intended for human or animal consumption.

Notes

Notes to column 3: [1] Deduct £147 from this figure in the case of animals for which the net annual income does not include: (i) a sum in respect of the premium for maintaining suckler cows (suckler cow premium) provided for in Article 4d of Council Regulation 805/68, and (ii) a sum provided for by Council Regulation 1357/96.

Add £31 to the figure in column 3 in the case of animals for which the net annual income is to include a sum in respect of the additional amount (extensification premium) provided for in Article 4h of Council Regulation 805/68.

(2) This is the figure for animals which are kept for 12 months. Deduct £113 in the case of animals which are kept for 12 months and for which the net annual income does not include: (i) a sum in respect of the special premium for holding male bovine animals (beef special premium) provided for in Article 4b of Council Regulation 805/68, and (ii) a sum provided for by Council Regulation 1357/96.

Add £31 to the figure in column 3 in the case of animals which are kept for 12 months and for which the net annual income is to include a sum in respect of extensification premium.

In the case of animals which are kept for less than 12 months and for which the net annual income does not include a sum in respect of beef special premium, the net annual income is to be calculated by deducting £113 from the figure in column 3 and then making a pro rata adjustment of the resulting figure.In the case of animals which are kept for less than 12 months and for which the net annual income includes a sum in respect of beef special premium, the net annual income is to be calculated by first deducting £113 from the figure in column 3, then making a pro rata adjustment of the resulting figure, then adding to that figure the sum of £113 and (where the net annual income includes a sum in respect of extensification premium) the sum of £31.

(3) This indicates the figure for animals (irrespective of age) which are kept for 12 months. In the case of animals which are kept for less than 12 months a pro rata adjustment of this figure is to be made.

(4) Deduct £24 from this figure in the case of animals for which the net annual income does not include a sum in respect of the premium for offsetting income loss sustained by sheep meat producers (sheep annual premium) provided for in Article 5 of Council Regulation 3013/89.

(5) Deduct £18 from this figure in the case of animals for which the net annual income does not include a sum in respect of sheep annual premium.

(6) Deduct £266 from this figure in the case of land for which the net annual income does not include a sum in respect of the compensatory payment for which producers of arable crops may apply (area payment) provided for in Article 2 of Council Regulation 1765/92.

(7) Deduct £385 from this figure in the case of land for which the net annual income does not include a sum in respect of area payment.

(8) Deduct £515 from this figure in the case of land for which the net annual income does not include a sum in respect of area payment.

(9) Deduct £265 from this figure in the case of land for which the net annual income does not include a sum in respect of area payment.

(10) Deduct £423 from this figure in the case of land for which the net annual income does not include a sum in respect of area payment.

(11) Deduct £385 from this figure in the case of land for which the net annual income does not include a sum in respect of area payment.

(12) Deduct £267 from this figure in the case of land for which the net annual income does not include a sum in respect of area payment.

GENERAL NOTE

This Order prescribes units of production for the assessment of the productive capacity of agricultural land and sets out the amount which is to be regarded as the net annual income from each such unit for the year September 12, 1996 to September 11, 1997 inclusive. This Order supersedes the Agricultural Holdings (Units of Production) Order 1995 (S.I. 1995 No. 2125).

An assessment of the productive capacity of agricultural land is required in determining whether or not the land in question is a "commercial unit of agricultural land" for the purposes of the succession provisions in the Agricultural Holdings Act 1986 ("the 1986 Act"): see in particular sections 36(3) and 50(2).

A "commercial unit of agricultural land" is land which, when farmed under competent management, is capable of producing a net annual income which is not less than the aggregate of the average annual earnings of two full-time male agricultural workers aged 20 years or over paragraph 3 of Schedule 6 to the 1986 Act). In determining this annual income figure, neither the system of farming carried out on a particular holding nor historical data from that holding will necessarily be used. Instead, whenever a particular farming use mentioned in column 1 of the Schedule to this Order is relevant to this determination, the units of production and the net annual income specified in columns 2 and 3 respectively will form the basis of the assessment of the productive capacity of the land in question.

The net annual income figures in column 3 of the Schedule specify the net annual income from one unit of production. In some cases the net annual income is derived from a unit which will be on the land for the full twelve-month period. In other cases the net annual income is derived from a unit which will be on the land for only part of the year, and there may be more than one production cycle in the twelve-month period. The assessment of the productive capacity of the land will take account of the total production in the course of a year.

THE DAIRY PRODUCE QUOTAS REGULATIONS 1997   A.27

(S.I. 1997 No. 733)

The Minister of Agriculture, Fisheries and Food and the Secretary of State, being Ministers designated[46] for the purposes of section 2(2) of the European Communities Act 1972 in relation to the common agricultural policy of the European Community, acting jointly, in exercise of the powers conferred on them by that section and of all other powers enabling them in that behalf, hereby make the following Regulations:

Title and commencement

1.—These Regulations may be cited as the Dairy Produce Quotas Regulations 1997 and shall come into force on 1st April 1997.

---

[46] S.I. 1972 No. 1811.

Interpretation

2.—(1) In these Regulations, unless the context otherwise requires-

"agricultural area" includes areas used for horticulture, fruit growing, seed growing, dairy farming and livestock breeding and keeping, areas of land used as grazing land, meadow land, osier land, market gardens and nursery grounds and areas of land used for woodlands where that use is ancillary to the farming of land for other agricultural purposes;

"authorised officer" means any person who is authorised by the Intervention Board, in writing, either generally or specifically, to act in matters arising under these Regulations or the Community legislation;

"the Commission Regulation" means Commission Regulation (EEC) No.536/93, laying down detailed rules on the application of the levy on milk and milk products, as last amended by Commission Regulation (EEC) No.470/94 and as corrected by the first corrigendum at OJ No. L273, 16.11.95, p. 54;

"the Community compensation scheme" means the scheme instituted by Council Regulation (EEC) No. 2187/93 providing for an offer of compensation to certain producers of milk and milk products temporarily prevented from carrying on their trade and Commission Regulation (EEC) No. 2648/93 laying down detailed rules for the application of Council Regulation (EEC) No. 2187/93;

"the Community legislation" means the Commission Regulation, the Council Regulation, Council Regulation 2055/93 and the legislation listed in Schedule 1;

"consent or sole interest notice" means a notice, in relation to a holding or part of a holding, provided by the person required under these Regulations to provide the notice, and certifying—

(a) either that he is the occupier of that holding or part of a holding and that no other person has an interest in that holding or part of the holding, or

(b) that all persons having an interest in the holding or part of the holding the value of which interest might be reduced by the apportionment or prospective apportionment to which the notice relates agree to that apportionment or proposed prospective apportionment;

"the Council Regulation" means Council Regulation (EEC) No. 3950/92 establishing an additional levy in the milk and milk products sector, as last amended by Commission Regulations (EC) No. 1109/96;

"Council Regulation 2055/93" means Council Regulation (EEC) No. 2055/93 allocating a special reference quantity to certain producers of milk and milk products;

"cow" includes a heifer that has calved;

"dairy enterprise" means an area stated by the occupier of that area to be run as a self-contained dairy produce business;

"dairy produce" means the produce, expressed in kilograms or litres of milk (one kilogram being 0.971 litres), in respect of which levy is payable under the Community legislation;

"Dairy Produce Quota Tribunal" has the meaning assigned to it by regulation 34;

"delivery" has the meaning assigned to it by Article 9(g) of the Council

Regulation (which sets out definitions) and "deliver" shall be construed accordingly;

"direct sale" means a sale which comes within Article 9(*h*) of the Council Regulation;

"direct sales quota" means the quantity of dairy produce which may be sold by direct sale from a holding in a quota year without the direct seller in occupation of that holding being liable to pay levy;

"direct seller" means a person who produces milk and treats or processes that milk into milk or milk products on his holding and subsequently sells or transfers free of charge that milk or those milk products without their having been treated or processed by an undertaking which treats or processes milk or milk products;

"eligible heifer" means any heifer, which, at the date of service of a notice referred to in regulation 14(2)(*b*)(i), was on land subject to the notice and calves for the first time on a day when the notice has effect, or which at the date of the coming into force of an order referred to in regulation 14(2)(*b*)(ii), was on land designated by the order and calves for the first time on a day when the order is in force;

"holding" has the meaning assigned to it by Article 9(*d*) of the Council Regulation;

"interest" includes the interest of a mortgage or heritable creditor and a trustee, but does not include the interest of a beneficiary under a trust or settlement or, in Scotland, the estate of a superior;

"Intervention Board" means the Intervention Board for Agricultural Produce established under section 6(1) of the European Communities Act 1972;

"levy" means the levy, payable under the Community legislation and these Regulations to the Intervention Board and described in Article 1 of the Council Regulation (which deals with the fixing of the levy);

"Minister", as regards anything in these Regulations relating to—

    (*a*) England and Wales, means the Minister of Agriculture, Fisheries and Food and the Secretary of State for Wales acting jointly;

    (*b*) Scotland, means the Secretary of State for Scotland;

    (*c*) Northern Ireland, shall be construed in accordance with paragraph (3); and

    (*d*) the United Kingdom, means the Ministers;

"Ministers" means all those to whom the definition of "the Minister" relates, acting jointly;

"national reserve" means the reserve described in regulation 12, constituted so as to comply with Article 5 of the Council Regulation (which deals with confiscation and distribution of quota);

"occupier" includes, in relation to land in respect of which there is no occupier, the person entitled to grant occupation of that land to another person, and during the currency of an interest referred to in regulation 7(5)(*a*), the person entitled to grant occupation when that interest terminates, and "occupation" shall be construed accordingly;

"producer" has the meaning assigned to it by Article 9(*c*) of the Council Regulation;

"prospective apportionment" in relation to quota on a holding means apportionment of quota under regulation 9 which will take place if there is a change of occupation of a part of the holding to which the prospective apportionment relates (other than a change to which regulation 7(5) applies) within six months of that prospective apportionment;

"purchaser" means a purchaser as defined in Article 9(e) of the Council Regulation and approved by the Intervention Board pursuant to Article 7(1)(a) of the Commission Regulation;

"purchaser quota" means the quantity of dairy produce which may be delivered by wholesale delivery to a purchaser during a quotas year without that purchaser being liable to pay levy;

"purchaser special quota" means the quantity of dairy produce which may be delivered by wholesale deliveries against producers' special quotas to a purchaser during a quota year without that purchaser being liable to pay levy;

"qualifying cow" means, any eligible heifer which calves at a time when the number of eligible heifers exceeds the replacement number;

"qualifying day" means, in respect of any qualifying cow, the day it calves and each day or part of a day thereafter during which the notice referred to in regulation 14(2)(b)(i) has effect or during which the order referred to in regulation 14(2)(b)(ii) is in force;

"quota" means direct sales quota or wholesale quota, as the case may be;

"quota year" means any of the periods of 12 months described in Article 1 of the Council Regulation (which deals with the fixing of the levy);

"registered wholesale quota" means quota registered in accordance with regulation 24(2)(a);

"the 1984 Regulations" means the Dairy Produce Quotas Regulations 1984[47];

"replacement number" means the nearest integer to 20 per cent of the total number of dairy cows on the land subject to the notice referred to in regulation 14(2)(b)(i), or designated by the order referred to in regulation 14(2)(b)(ii), as at the date of service of the notice or (as the case may be) the coming into force of the order, and where 20 per cent of the total number is half way between two integers the nearest even integer shall be deemed to be the nearest integer;

"Scottish Islands area" means any one of—
- (a) the islands of Shetland;
- (b) the islands of Orkney; or
- (c) the islands of Islay, Jura, Gigha, Arran, Bute, Great Cumbrae and Little Cumbrae and the Kintyre peninsula south of Tarbert;

"special quota" means the quota referred to in Article 4(3) of the Council Regulation and in Article 1(1) of Council Regulation 2055/93;

"submit" means, in relation to a document submitted to the Intervention Board, the act of sending that document as evidenced by proof of posting or delivery to a courier service;

"total direct sales quota" means the total quantity of dairy produce which may be sold by direct sale from a holding in a quota year without the direct seller in occupation of that holding being liable to pay levy;

"total wholesale quota" means the total quantity of dairy produce which may be

---

[47] Amended by S.I. 1984 Nos. 1538, 1787 and S.I. 1985 No. 509, and revoked by S.I. 1986 No. 470.

delivered by wholesale delivery from a holding in a quota year without the producer in occupation of that holding being liable to pay levy;

"transferee", means—
- (a) where quota is transferred with land, a person who replaces another person as occupier of that holding or part of a holding; and
- (b) in any other case, the transferee of quota;

"transferor", means—
- (a) where quota is transferred with land, a person who is replaced by another person as occupier of a holding or part of a holding; and
- (b) in any other case, the transferor of quota;

"unused quota" means quota remaining unused after any direct sales or wholesale deliveries have been taken into account, adjusted in accordance with Article 2(2) of the Commission Regulation (which deals with the fat content of milk), and "used quota" shall be construed accordingly;

"wholesale delivery" means delivery from a producer to a purchaser;

"wholesale quota" means the quantity of dairy produce which may be delivered by wholesale delivery to a purchaser (to the extent specified in relation to that purchaser under these Regulations), from a holding in a quota year without the producer in occupation of that holding being liable to pay levy.

(2) In these Regulations, unless the context otherwise requires—
- (a) any reference to a numbered regulation or Schedule shall be construed as a reference to the regulation or Schedule so numbered in these Regulations;
- (b) any reference in a regulation or Schedule to a numbered paragraph shall be construed as a reference to the paragraph so numbered in that regulation or Schedule; and
- (c) any reference in a paragraph to a numbered or lettered sub-paragraph shall be construed as a reference to the sub-paragraph so numbered or lettered in that paragraph.

(3) In their application to Northern Ireland these Regulations shall have effect with the substitution, for references to the Minister, of references to the Department of Agriculture for Northern Ireland.[48]

Establishment of quota

3.—Total direct sales quota and total wholesale quota for any person and purchaser quota for any purchaser in respect of any quota year shall be established in accordance with these Regulations and the Community legislation.

Determination of levy

4.—For the purposes of Article 2(1) of the Council Regulation (which deals with the calculation of the levy), the contribution of producers who make wholesale deliveries towards the levy shall be established, in accordance with the provisions of that Article, at the level of the purchaser.

---

[48] Words substituted by S.I. 1997/No. 1093, reg. 2(2).

THE DAIRY PRODUCE QUOTAS REGULATIONS 1997

Milk equivalence of dairy produce

5.—(1) For the purposes of Article 1(2) of the Commission Regulation (which deals with milk equivalence of dairy produce) the milk equivalence of dairy produce shall be calculated on the basis that each kilogram of dairy produce shall equal such quantity of milk referred to in paragraph (2) as is required to make that kilogram of dairy produce.

(2) The milk to which paragraph (1) relates is milk the fat content of which has not been altered since milking.

Adjustment of purchaser quota

6.—(1) Where any wholesale quota is increased or reduced in accordance with the Community legislation or these Regulations, the purchaser quota of any purchaser to whom that quota is applicable shall be correspondingly increased or reduced.

(2) On any transaction to which the second sub-paragraph of Article 2(2) of the Council Regulation (which deals with replacements of purchasers and changes of purchasers by producers) applies, or on any permanent conversion of quota under regulation 16, any purchaser whose purchaser quota has been increased by virtue of such a transaction (other than as a result of a temporary transfer of quota under regulation 13) or such a conversion of quota shall submit to the Intervention Board—

(a) no later than 21st May 1997 or 28 days after the date on which the transaction or conversion of quota takes place (whichever is the later)[49], a statement setting out particulars of the transaction or conversion; and

(b) where appropriate, a declaration made and signed by the producer that the purchaser whose purchaser quota is to decrease has been notified of the particulars set out in the statement referred to in sub-paragraph (a).

(3) The statement referred to in paragraph (2)(a) and the declaration referred to in paragraph (2)(b) shall be made in such form as may reasonably be required by the Intervention Board.

(4) Where during a quota year a producer changes from being registered with a purchaser to being registered with any other purchaser—

(a) for the purposes of calculation of levy liability under regulation 18 in that quota year, any purchaser with whom he is newly registered shall have his purchaser quota increased by an amount equivalent to such part of that producer's registered wholesale quota as that producer shall determine;

(b) the amount of the increase of purchaser quota determined in accordance with sub-paragraph (a) shall not include the amount of quota necessary to cover the deliveries made by the producer before the date of the change of purchaser, adjusted if necessary in accordance with the second sub-paragraph of Article 2(2) of the Commission Regulation, and such amount of quota shall remain available to the original purchaser; and

---

[49] Words substituted by S.I. 1997 No. 1093, reg. 2(2).

(c) at the beginning of the quota year following the quota year referred to in sub-paragraph (a), the purchaser with whom the producer is newly registered shall have his purchaser quota increased by such part of the producer's remaining registered wholesale quota as that producer shall determine;

and corresponding reductions of the purchaser quota of the original purchaser shall be made and where there are adjustments of quota of a producer registered with more than one purchaser, similar adjustments of purchaser quota shall be made.

(5) Where the amount of wholesale quota available to a producer changes as a result of a transfer of quota under regulation 7, 11 or 13; or as a result of a conversion of quota under regulation 16, that producer shall notify each purchaser with whom his wholesale quota is registered within seven working days of the change.

Transfer of quota with transfer of land

7.—(1) For the purposes of Article 7 of the Council Regulation (which deals with transfer of quota with a holding when the holding is sold, leased, transferred by inheritance or subjected to other cases of transfer involving comparable legal effects for producers), on a transfer of any holding or part of a holding, other than a transfer of a kind to which paragraph (5) or (7) refers, the transferee shall submit to the Intervention Board—
- (a) no later than 28 days after the change of occupation of the holding or part of the holding, and in any event no later than 7 working days after the end of the quota year in which the transfer takes place, a notice of transfer in such a form as may reasonably be required by the Intervention Board; and
- (b) such other information relating to the transfer, and within such time, as the Intervention Board may reasonably require.

(2) The notice referred to in paragraph (1)(a) shall, in the case of a transfer of part of a holding, include—
- (a) a statement, signed by the transferor and transferee, that they have agreed that the quota shall be apportioned taking account of the areas used for milk production as specified in the statement or to the effect that no such apportionment has been agreed; and
- (b) where such an apportionment has been agreed, a consent or sole interest notice, provided by the transferor in respect of the entirety of the holding.

(3) Where there is a transfer of part of a holding—
- (a) an apportionment of the quota relating to the holding shall be carried out in accordance with regulation 8; and
- (b) any dairy produce which has been sold by direct sale or delivered by wholesale delivery from the holding during the quota year in which the change of occupation takes place and prior to that transfer shall be deemed, for the purposes of any levy calculation, to have been sold or

delivered from each part of the holding in proportion to that apportionment, unless the parties agree otherwise and notify the Intervention Board of the agreement in such a form as the Intervention Board may reasonably require, no later than 28 days after the change of occupation, and in any event no later than 7 working days after the end of the quota year in which the transfer takes place.

(4) A prospective apportionment of quota in respect of a part of a holding may be made in accordance with regulation 9.

(5) No person shall transfer quota on a transfer of any holding or part of a holding in the following cases—
  (a) the grant of:
    (i) a licence to occupy land;
    (ii) the tenancy of any land under which a holding, or part of a holding, in England and Wales is occupied for a period of less than ten months;
    (iii) the lease of any land under which a holding, or part of a holding, in Scotland is occupied for a period of less than eight months;
    (iv) the tenancy of any land under which a holding, or part of a holding, in Northern Ireland is occupied for a period of less than twelve months;
  (b) the termination of a licence, tenancy or lease to which sub-paragraph (a) applies.

(6) Where a transferee fails to submit the notice referred to in paragraph (1)(a) no later than seven working days after the end of the quota year in which the transfer takes place, then for the purposes of any levy calculation—
  (a) the unused quota transferred with such transfer shall not be treated as a part of the transferee's quota entitlement for the quota year in which the transfer takes effect but shall be treated as if it remained unused quota available where appropriate for reallocation by the Intervention Board in that quota year in accordance with paragraph 7 of Schedule 5;
  (b) the notice shall be disregarded by the Intervention Board for the quota year to which it applies and shall not be noted on any register maintained under regulation 24 until the following quota year; and
  (c) a transferee shall not be entitled to demand that, by reason of such a transfer, an amendment be made to the amount of quota, if any, which has been reallocated to him under Schedule 5 for the quota year in which the transfer takes effect.

(7) No person shall transfer quota on a transfer of a holding or part of a holding where the transfer would result in an increase or reduction in the total direct sales quota or total wholesale quota available for use by dairy enterprises located within a Scottish Islands area.

Apportionment of quota

8.—Subject to regulations 7(5) and (7), 9(4) and (5) and 10, where there is a transfer of part of a holding, the apportionment of the quota or special quota, relating to that holding, shall be carried out—

(a) in accordance with the agreed apportionment set out in the notice referred to in regulation 7(1)(*a*); or
(b) where there is no such agreement—
   (i) in England and Wales and Northern Ireland, by arbitration in accordance with Schedules 2 and 4 respectively;
   (ii) in Scotland, in accordance with Schedule 3.

Prospective apportionment of quota

9.—(1) The occupier of a holding who intends that a prospective apportionment of quota will be applied to it shall submit to the Intervention Board an application in such a form as may reasonably be required for this purpose by the Intervention Board, requesting either—
  (*a*) that a prospective apportionment of quota relating to the holding be made taking account of areas used for milk production as set out in the application; or
  (*b*) that a prospective apportionment of quota be ascertained by arbitration in accordance with Schedule 2 in England and Wales and with Schedule 4 in Northern Ireland, or in Scotland in accordance with Schedule 3.

(2) A request for a prospective apportionment of quota may be revoked by a notice in writing to the Intervention Board, signed by the occupier of the holding to which the prospective apportionment relates.

(3) Where the occupier of a holding requests that a prospective apportionment be made in accordance with paragraph (1)(*a*), or gives notice in writing of the revocation of such a request, that request or notice shall be accompanied by a consent or sole interest notice in respect of the entirety of the holding.

(4) Where there is a change of occupation of part of a holding (other than a change to which regulation 7(5) applies) and within the six months preceding that change of occupation—
  (*a*) the occupier of that holding has requested a prospective apportionment of quota in respect of that part of the holding and has submitted a notice in accordance with regulation 7(1), indicating that an apportionment of quota has been agreed; or
  (*b*) a prospective apportionment of quota relating to that part of that holding has been or is in the process of being made by virtue of Schedule 2, 3 or 4,
the apportionment of quota shall be carried out in accordance with paragraph (5).

(5) Where quota is apportioned in accordance with this paragraph, the apportionment shall be carried out in accordance with—
  (*a*) any prospective apportionment of quota relating to that part of that holding made under paragraph (1) unless the request for that prospective apportionment was revoked before the change of occupation to which it relates takes place;
  (*b*) if no such prospective apportionment has been made, any prospective apportionment which is in the process of being made under paragraph (1); and

(c) in any other case, regulation 8.

Notification by the Intervention Board of apportionment of quota by arbitration

10.—(1) Where the Intervention Board has reasonable grounds for believing—
   (a) that the areas used for milk production on a holding are not as specified in a notice or application submitted for the purposes of regulation 7 or 9(1) respectively; or
   (b) that the areas used for milk production on a holding were not as agreed between the parties at the time of apportionment in a case where no notice or application has yet been submitted for the purposes of the aforementioned regulations,
it may give notice of this fact to the person who submitted the form, or in a case where no such notice or application was made, to the transferee.

(2) In any case to which paragraph (1) applies the apportionment or prospective apportionment of that quota shall be made—
   (a) in England and Wales and Northern Ireland by arbitration in accordance with Schedules 2 and 4 respectively;
   (b) in Scotland in accordance with Schedule 3.

Transfer of quota without transfer of land

11.—(1) For the purposes of the fifth indent of the first paragraph of Article 8 of the Council Regulation (which permits the authorisation of a transfer of quota without transfer of the corresponding land, with the aim of improving the structure of milk production at the level of the holding), an application for transfer of quota without transfer of land, other than an application for transfer of a kind to which paragraph (9) below refers, shall be submitted by the transferee to the Intervention Board for approval no later than 8th May 1997 or ten working days before the intended date of the transfer (whichever is the later)[50] and that application shall be in such form as may be reasonably required for that purpose by the Intervention Board.

(2) The application referred to in paragraph (1) shall include—
   (a) a statement, signed by the transferor and transferee, that they have agreed to the transfer of quota and explaining how the transfer is necessary to improve the structure of the business of the transferor and transferee;
   (b) a consent or sole interest notice signed by the transferor in respect of the entirety of the holding from which the quota is to be transferred;
   (c) an undertaking by the transferor that he—
      (i) has not transferred quota onto his holding in accordance with the provisions of this regulation other than by a transfer in respect of which, pursuant to paragraph (7), he has been released from the undertaking referred to in sub-paragraph (d)(i) in the course of the quota year in which the application is made, or in the preceding quota year;

---

[50] Words substituted by S.I. 1997 No. 1093, reg. 2(3).

(ii) will not transfer quota onto his holding under regulations 7, 11 or 13 in the period between the date of submission of the application and the end of the quota year following the quota year in which the transfer without land takes place; and

(iii) will not, through his connection with or involvement in another business, seek to circumvent the restrictions at paragraphs (i) and (ii) above; and

(d) an undertaking by the transferee that he—

(i) will not transfer quota from his holding under regulation 7, 11 or 13 in the period between the date of submission of the application and the end of the quota year following the quota year in which the transfer without land takes place;

(ii) will not, through his connection with or involvement in another business, seek to circumvent the restriction at paragraph (i) above.

(3) The reference to the transfer of quota in sub-paragraphs (c)(ii) and (d)(i) of paragraph (2) shall include temporary transfer under regulation 13 but exclude transfer on inheritance.

(4) Where it has received an application under paragraph (1), the Intervention Board may require that the transferor or transferee shall produce such other information relating to the application, and within such time, as the Intervention Board reasonably may determine.

(5) Where the Intervention Board approves an application under paragraph (1), the transferee shall, no later than 28 days after the transfer takes place, and in any event no later than seven working days after the end of the quota year in which the transfer takes place, submit to the Intervention Board, in such form as the Intervention Board may reasonably require, a statement of the amounts of used and unused quota available to the transferor and transferee on the date of the transfer.

(6) Where a transferee fails to submit a statement in accordance with the requirements of paragraph (5), the Intervention Board shall revoke its approval.

(7) Where an application to transfer quota without transfer of land has been approved by the Intervention Board, and the statement required by paragraph (5) has been submitted in accordance with that paragraph, the Intervention Board may release a transferee from the undertaking referred to in paragraph (2)(d)(i), where the Intervention Board is satisfied that exceptional circumstances, resulting in a significant fall in milk production which could not have been avoided or foreseen by the transferee at the time of the submission of the application under paragraph (1), justify that release.

(8) The exceptional circumstances referred to in paragraph (7) are—

(a) the inability of the transferee to conduct his business over a prolonged period as a result of the onset of ill-health, injury or disability;

(b) a natural disaster seriously affecting the holding;

(c) the accidental destruction of buildings used for the purposes of milk production;

(d) without prejudice to sub-paragraph (e), an outbreak of illness or disease seriously affecting the dairy herd;

(e) the serving of a notice or the making of a declaration under an order made under section 17 of the Animal Health Act 1981 (in respect of places or areas in Great Britain) or the making of a declaration under an order made under article 12(1) of the Diseases of Animals (Northern Ireland) Order 1981 (in respect of places or areas in Northern Ireland) or the adoption of an emergency order under section 1 of the Food and Environment Protection Act 1985;

(f) the loss of a significant proportion of the forage area as a result of the compulsory purchase of the holding or part of the holding;

(g) where the transferee is a tenant, the serving of an incontestable notice to quit under the provisions of section 26 of and Schedule 3 to the Agricultural Holdings Act 1986 dealing with the serving of incontestable notices to quit where the tenant is not at fault; and

(h) in the quota year commencing 1st April 1997, the slaughter of animals forming part of the dairy herd pursuant to the powers conferred upon the Minister under section 32(1)(b) of the Animal Health Act 1981, as animals having been exposed to the infection of bovine spongiform encephalopathy.

(9) As provided for in the fourth indent of the first paragraph of Article 8 of the Council Regulation (which provides for the determination of regions within which such transfers may be authorised), no applications for a transfer of quota may be submitted pursuant to paragraph (1) where the transfer would result in an increase or reduction in the total direct sales quota or total wholesale quota available for use by dairy enterprises located within a Scottish Islands area.

National reserve

12.—(1) The national reserve shall comprise such wholesale and direct sales quota as is not for the time being allocated to any person, including any quota withdrawn under these Regulations.

(2) The Minister may make allocations from the national reserve in accordance with the Community legislation and these Regulations.

Temporary transfer of quota

13.—(1) For the purposes of Article 6 of the Council Regulation (which deals with the temporary transfer of quota), and subject to paragraph (5) below, a producer may agree with any other producer to make a temporary transfer, other than a temporary transfer of a kind to which paragraph (4) below refers, of all or part of any unused quota which is registered under regulation 24 as permanently held by him for a period of one quota year to that other producer.

(2) The Intervention Board may require a reasonable charge to be paid for the registration of any temporary transfer of a quota, but only if the transfer takes place within a quota year in respect of which it has announced before the beginning of that quota year that it intends to make such a charge, in such a manner as it considered likely to come to the attention of producers.

(3) Where there is an agreement to make a temporary transfer of quota under paragraph (1), the transferee shall notify the Intervention Board of the agreement in such form as may reasonably be required by the Intervention Board, and shall submit the notice, accompanied by any charge payable under paragraph (2), to the

Intervention Board no later than 31st December in the quota year in which the agreement is made.

(4) No producer shall agree with any other producer to make a temporary transfer of quota which would result in a reduction in the total direct sales quota or total wholesale quota available for use by dairy enterprises located within a Scottish Islands area.

(5) Until 31st December 1997, where a producer who holds special quota received under Council Regulation 2055/93, temporarily transfers of any quota held by him, the special quota shall be taken into the national reserve for the duration of the quota year in which such temporary transfer takes place.

Temporary reallocation of quota

14.—(1) For the purposes of Article 2(4) of the Council Regulation and Article 5 of the Commission Regulation (which together deal with the reallocation of excess levy), the Intervention Board may, for any quota year, award to a producer referred to in paragraph (2) a temporary reallocation of an amount of any surplus quota corresponding to a proportion of any levy collected in excess of the levy actually due in that year, in accordance with the provisions of this regulation.

(2) This regulation shall apply to—
 (*a*) a producer who is affected by a formal acknowledgment of an error in the levy calculation, made pursuant to Article 5(1)(*a*) of the Commission Regulation; and
 (*b*) a producer who has quota registered as his in relation to a holding which—
  (i) is in whole or in part subject to a notice prohibiting or regulating the movement of dairy cows pursuant to an order made under the Animal Health Act 1981 or the Diseases of Animals (Northern Ireland) Order 1981, or
  (ii) is situated wholly or partly within an area which at any time during that quota year has been designated by an emergency order under section 1 of the Food and Environment Protection Act 1985.

(3) Subject to paragraphs (4) and (5), a producer referred to in paragraph (2)(*b*) may be awarded a temporary reallocation of surplus quota for any quota year in which the notice referred to in paragraph (2)(*b*)(i) or (as the case may be) the order referred to in paragraph (2)(*b*)(ii) has effect, and the amount of any such award shall be calculated either—
 (*a*) as the amount equal to 16 litres per qualifying cow per qualifying day in any quota year; or
 (*b*) as the amount by which in the quota year in question the producer's production exceeds his quota entitlement,
whichever amount is less.

(4) Where the notice referred to in paragraph (2)(*b*)(i) continues in effect or the order referred to in paragraph (2)(*b*)(ii) remains in force for a period beyond the quota year in respect of which a producer has received an award under paragraph (3), any award under that paragraph for the following quota year shall be calculated as if the number of the producer's qualifying cows were equal to that of his eligible

heifers which calved during that period or (if the period extends beyond that following quota year) during that following quota year, notwithstanding the fact that when any such heifers calved the number of eligible heifers did not exceed the replacement number.

(5) An award under paragraph (3) above shall not be available in the same quota year to a producer who transfers unused quota under regulation 7 or 11, makes a temporary transfer of quota under regulation 13, or purchases cows or in-calf heifers for dairy purposes, unless the Intervention Board is satisfied that the agreement to transfer, temporarily transfer or purchase, was entered into before service of the notice to which paragraph (2)(*b*)(i) refers, or (as the case may be) before the coming into force of the order to which paragraph (2)(*b*)(ii) refers.

(6) A producer referred to in paragraph (2)(*a*) above may be awarded a temporary reallocation of surplus quota, for any quota year in respect of which the formal acknowledgement referred to in the Commission Regulation applies, which wholly or partially offsets the error in levy calculation to which the acknowledgement relates.

(7) In awarding a temporary reallocation of surplus quota for the purpose of this regulation the Intervention Board shall give priority to the producers referred to in paragraph (2)(*a*).

Special allocation of quota

15. Where, by reason of a mistake made by the Minister or any person acting on his behalf, a person has not been allocated any quota or has been allocated a smaller quantity of any such quota than he would have been allocated if the mistake had not been made, the Minister may allocate to that person such quota as will compensate, in whole or in part, for that mistake from the national reserve.

Conversion of quota

16.—(1) For the purposes of the provisions of Article 4(2) of the Council Regulation (which deals with changes from direct sales to wholesale delivery and vice versa), the second sub-paragraph of Article 2(2) of the Council Regulation (which deals with replacements of purchasers) and this regulation, a producer may apply to convert, temporarily or permanently, direct sales quota for wholesale quota or wholesale quota for direct sales quota.

(2) Where a producer wishes to convert quota permanently or temporarily in any quota year, he shall submit to the Intervention Board an application in such a form as the Intervention Board may reasonably require for that purpose and such application shall—

    (*a*) state the amount (if any) of the producer's direct sales quota, wholesale quota, direct sales and wholesale deliveries for the quota year in which the application is made, and the amount of unused quota which he holds at the time of the application and which he wishes the Intervention Board to convert; and

    (*b*) include such other information as the Intervention Board may reasonably require in order to assess whether the requirements of Article 4(2) of the Council Regulation and Article 2 of the Commission Regulation are fulfilled.

(3) The application referred to in paragraph (2) above shall be submitted by the producer to the Intervention Board by—

(a) 31st December in any year in the case of permanent conversion of quota; or

(b) 14th May in any year following the end of the quota year in which the temporary conversion of quota takes place, in the case of temporary conversion of quota.

(4) Subject to paragraph (5), where a producer has permanently converted quota in any quota year, he shall not subsequently in that quota year transfer out quota, of the type to which he has converted, whether temporarily or otherwise.

(5) In the quota year commencing 1st April 1997, where the Minister in accordance with section 32(1)(b) of the Animal health Act 1981 has caused animals forming part of a producer's dairy herd, to be slaughtered as having been exposed to the infection of bovine spongiform encephalopathy, paragraph (4) above shall not apply to that producer.

Representative fat content of milk

17.—A producer who in any quota year comes within the first indent of Article 2(1)(e) of the Commission Regulation (which deals with the representative fat content of milk from certain new producers) may benefit from the negative correction provided for in the second indent of Article 2(2) thereof only if, before 1st March in that quota year, he confirms to the Intervention Board that in that quota year as he has maintained in his dairy herd breeds of cow with characteristics similar to those in the herd in the first twelve months of production and undertakes to maintain such breeds in his dairy herd for the remainder of that quota year.

Reallocation of quota and calculation of levy liability

18. Schedule 5 shall apply in respect of the reallocation of quota and the calculation of levy liability for the purposes of Article 2(1) of the Council Regulation (which deals with the calculation of the levy).

Prevention of avoidance of levy

19.—(1) Subject to paragraph (2), where in any quota year a producer makes sales or deliveries of milk or milk products from milk produced by any cows and subsequently in the same quota year another producer makes sales or deliveries of milk or milk products from milk produced by any or all of the same cows, the second producer shall be deemed for the purposes of these Regulations to have made those sales or deliveries in the capacity of agent for the first producer.

(2) Paragraph (1) shall not apply where—

(a) an agreement has been entered into by the first producer for the sale or lease of the cows in question or the second producer has inherited them from the first producer; and

(b) the cows are kept on the second producer's holding.

Payment of levy

20.—(1) For the purposes of Article 2(3) of the Council Regulation and Article 4 of the Commission Regulation (both of which deal with payment of levy by direct sellers), or Article 2(2) of the Council Regulation and Article 3 of the Commission Regulation (both of which deal with payment of levy by purchasers in respect of wholesale deliveries), levy shall be paid to the Intervention Board.

(2) Where any part of the levy remains unpaid after 1st September in any year, the Intervention Board may recover from the direct seller or (as the case may be) the purchaser, the amount of the levy outstanding at that date together with interest in respect of each day thereafter until the said amount is recovered at the rate of one percentage point above the sterling three month London interbank offered rate.

(3) For the purposes of the third sub-paragraph of Article 2(2) of the Council Regulation (which deals with deduction of levy liability), where a producer making wholesale deliveries to a purchaser exceeds his wholesale quota, following adjustment of that quota where appropriate and in accordance with Article 2(2) of the Commission Regulation, that purchaser may immediately deduct an amount corresponding to the amount of levy potentially payable by him in respect of the excess from the sums owed to the producer in respect of the deliveries.

Functions of the Intervention Board

21.—The Intervention Board shall be the competent body for the purposes of Article 2(3) of the Council Regulation (which deals with payment of levy by direct sellers), and the competent authority for the purposes of Articles 1, 3, 4 and 7 of the Commission Regulation (which together deal with matters relating to the assessment of levy and the payment of levy by direct sellers and purchasers).

Annual statements

22.—(1) The Intervention Board may, in respect of—
   (a) any person in whose name any direct sales quota is registered and who fails to submit to the Intervention Board by 14th May in any year any declaration which he is required to forward by Article 4(2) of the Commission Regulation, or
   (b) any purchaser approved by the Intervention Board in accordance with Article 7 of the Commission Regulation and who fails to submit to the Intervention Board by 14th May in any year any summary which he is required to forward by Article 3(2) of the Commission Regulation,

recover a reasonable charge in respect of any visit to any premises which the Intervention Board has reasonably considered that it should make in order to obtain the declaration or summary in question.

Disapplication of enactments

23.—Nothing in section 47(2) of the Agricultural Marketing Act 1958[51] or Article 29 of the Agricultural Marketing (Northern Ireland) Order 1982[52] (which

---

[51] To which there are amendments not relevant to these Regulations.
[52] Article 29 was amended by S.I. 1984 No. 1822 (N.I. 12), Article 7(b) and Sched. 2, Part

restrict the disclosure of certain information obtained under those enactments) shall restrict or apply to the disclosure of any information if, and in so far as, the disclosure is required or authorised by these Regulations or the Community legislation.

Registers to be prepared and maintained by the Intervention Board

24.—(1) The Intervention Board shall—
   (a) prepare a direct sales register entry in respect of each direct seller setting out in particular-
      (i) his name;
      (ii) his trading address;
      (iii) a reference number which serves to identify the direct seller;
      (iv) the direct sales quota available to him for the quota year excluding the quota referred to in paragraph (v) below; and
      (v) quota issued to him as special quota,
   and shall send each direct seller a copy of the entry relating to him; and
   (b) maintain—
      (i) a direct sales register (being a register of entries referred to in sub-paragraph (1)(a)), and
      (ii) a register of particulars of direct sales by each direct seller.

(2) The Intervention Board shall—
   (a) prepare a wholesale register entry in respect of each producer setting out in particular-
      (i) his name;
      (ii) his trading address;
      (iii) a reference number which serves to identify the producer;
      (iv) the wholesale quota available to him for the quota year excluding the quota referred to in sub-paragraph (v);
      (v) quota issued to him as special quota; and
      (vi) a list of the names and addresses of each purchaser whose purchaser quota will be calculated to take into account all or part of that producer's total wholesale quota, and of the wholesale quota registered with each purchaser, showing the representative fat content base of that quota calculated in accordance with Article 2 of the Commission Regulation,
   and shall send to each producer a copy of the entry relating to him and to each purchaser named on the list referred to in paragraph (vi) above a copy of that part of the entry relating to his purchaser quota; and
   (b) maintain a wholesale register (being a register of entries referred to in sub-paragraph (a)).

(3) The Intervention Board shall—
   (a) prepare a purchaser notice in respect of each purchaser setting out—
      (i) his name,
      (ii) his purchaser quota,
      (iii) his purchaser special quota,

III.

and shall send each purchaser a copy of the notice relating to him; and

  (*b*) maintain a register of purchaser notices.

(4) For the purposes of paragraphs (1) and (2) above, where a holding comprises more than one dairy enterprise, a direct seller or a producer may, on presenting to the Intervention Board a consent or sole interest notice in respect of that holding, agree with the Intervention Board the partition of that holding between separate direct sales register entries or wholesale register entries as specified in the agreement.

(5) The Intervention Board may make such enquiries as it reasonably considers to be necessary for the purposes of ensuring the accuracy of the registers which it is required to maintain pursuant to this regulation and shall amend such registers—

  (*a*) to record any allocations or adjustments made under or by virtue of these Regulations, or

  (*b*) to make any correction or amendment which it reasonably considers to be necessary,

and where it makes a correction or amendment, it shall notify any person affected by that correction or amendment.

(6) In this regulation "direct seller" and "producer" include a person who occupies land with quota whether or not that person is engaged in the sale or delivery of dairy produce.

Inspection of entries in the Intervention Board's registers

25. The Intervention Board may, in response to a request in writing regarding a quota register entry referred to in regulation 24(1) or (2)—

  (*a*) by any person who is the direct seller or producer identified in that entry, or who gives the Intervention Board a statement in writing that he has an interest in the holding of the producer or direct seller identified in that entry; or

  (*b*) by a purchaser in relation to a specific purchaser in the register referred to in regulation 24(3)(*b*),

on payment of a reasonable charge, supply to such a person a copy of that quota register entry.

Obligations of direct sellers and purchasers with respect to registration and deliveries

26.—(1) Each direct seller shall register his quota with the Intervention Board.

(2) Each producer (as defined in regulation 24(6)) who holds registered wholesale quota (including any producer who has temporarily ceased or who intends temporarily to cease making wholesale deliveries) shall register his quota with a purchaser and, if making deliveries, shall deliver to a purchaser.

(3) Each purchaser shall maintain, in respect of all producers whose register entries include that purchaser's name on the list referred to in regulation 24(2)(*a*)(vi)—

  (*a*) a register as indicated in regulation 24(2)(*b*) in respect of that part of his purchaser quota attributable to each of those producers;

(b) a register of particulars of wholesale deliveries from each of those producers to that purchaser;

(c) the information required by Article 7 of the Commission Regulation (which deals with the records required in connection with levy assessment); and

(d) a system approved by the Intervention Board for sampling the milk of each producer and determining its fat content.

(4) Each purchaser shall amend the register referred to in paragraph (3)(a) on each occasion when, under these Regulations, the equivalent register maintained by the Intervention Board is required to be amended in relation to producers registered in that purchaser's register.

(5) Each purchaser shall register with the Intervention Board and shall—

(a) give an undertaking to the Intervention Board to abide by the provisions of these Regulations and the Community legislation and comply with that undertaking;

(b) inform the Intervention Board of any factor or change in circumstance which affect that purchaser's registration or its ability to comply with the undertaking referred to in sub-paragraph (a);

(c) confirm to each producer supplying that purchaser that the purchaser is registered and supply on request details of that registration; and

(d) notify each producer supplying that purchaser if that registration is rescinded.

Registers as evidence

27.—Any entry in a register or notice required by these Regulations to be maintained by the Intervention Board shall in any proceedings be evidence of the matters stated therein.

Information

28.—(1) Each purchaser or producer shall provide such information to the Intervention Board as the Intervention Board may reasonably require in order to perform its functions under these Regulations and the Community legislation.

(2) Each purchaser shall submit to the Intervention Board on request, in a form from time to time to be determined by the Intervention Board, such statistics and forecasts relating to deliveries made or to be made to him, as reasonably may be required by the Intervention Board for the purpose of monitoring deliveries in relation to the total quantity for the United Kingdom referred to in Article 3(2) of the Council Regulation, and any such statistics shall be submitted within three working days of the end of the period to which the statistics relate, and any such forecast shall be submitted within 28 days of receipt by the purchaser of the request to provide such forecast.

(3) The Intervention Board shall copy such records to each purchaser as that purchaser reasonably may require for the purposes of his registration obligations under these Regulations and Article 3 of the Commission Regulation (which deals with the assessment and payment of levy).

THE DAIRY PRODUCE QUOTAS REGULATIONS 1997

Withholding or recovery of compensation

29. Where a producer has submitted an application for compensation in accordance with the Community compensation scheme and it appears to the Minister that the producer has made a false or misleading statement in his application or has failed to comply with any of the requirements of that scheme, the Minister may withhold or recover on demand from that producer the whole or any part of the compensation payable or paid to him.

Powers of authorised officers

30.—(1) An authorised officer may, at all reasonable hours and on producing some duly authenticated document showing his authority, exercise the powers specified in this regulation for the purposes of ascertaining whether an offence under regulation 31(1)(*a*)(*b*), or (*c*) has been or is being committed.

(2) For the purposes of this Regulation, an authorised officer may enter upon a holding.

(3) An authorised officer who has entered upon a holding by virtue of this regulation may—
   (*a*) inspect any land (other than land used only as a dwelling) and any record or document, including any document kept by means of a computer, which relates to the allocation or transfer of quota or the trade in, or production of milk or milk products;
   (*b*) seize and retain any such record or document which he has reason to believe may be required as evidence in proceedings under regulation 31(1)(*a*), (*b*) or (*c*).

(4) A producer shall render all reasonable assistance to the authorised officer in relation to the matters mentioned in paragraph (1) above and in particular shall produce any such record or document and supply such additional information relating to the allocation to him of quota, the transfer to or from him of quota and the trade in or production of milk or milk products, as the authorised officer may reasonably require.

(5) In the case of a record or document kept by means of a computer a producer shall, if so required, provide any such record or document in a form in which it may be taken away.

Penalties

31.—(1) Any person who—
   (*a*) fails without reasonable excuse to comply with a requirement imposed on him by or under these Regulations or the Community legislation, or
   (*b*) in connection with these Regulations or the Community legislation, makes a statement or uses a document which he knows to be false in a material particular or recklessly makes a statement or uses a document which is false in a material particular; or
   (*c*) disposes of quota which he knows or might reasonably be expected to know is incorrectly registered in his name,

shall be guilty of an offence and liable, on summary conviction, to a fine not exceeding level 5 on the standard scale or, on conviction on indictment, to a fine.

(2) The Minister may, following any conviction under paragraph (1)(*b*) against which there is no successful appeal, by notice served (within the period of 12 months following the date specified in paragraph (3) on the person to whose quota that conviction relates withdraw his quota to such extent as may reasonably be regarded by the Minister as being attributable to the falsehood on which the conviction was founded.

(3) The date referred to in paragraph (2) above is—
- (*a*) in the case of a conviction against which there is no appeal, the date on which the right to appeal against that conviction expires; and
- (*b*) in the case of a conviction against which there is an unsuccessful appeal—
  - (i) if there is no right of appeal against the result of that unsuccessful appeal, the date of that result; and
  - (ii) if there is a right of appeal against that result but no appeal is made, the date on which that right of appeal expires.

(4) If any person—
- (*a*) intentionally obstructs an authorised officer acting in the exercise of the powers conferred to him by regulation 30(4) or (5); or
- (*b*) fails without reasonable excuse to comply with a requirement of an authorised officer pursuant to regulation 30(4) or (5),

he shall be guilty of an offence and be liable on summary conviction to a fine not exceeding level 3 on the standard scale.

(5) In this regulation "requirement" does not include a requirement imposed on an authority or a person acting as arbitrator or arbiter, nor does it include any restriction or obligation in or under regulation 7(5) or (7), 9(1), 11(9), 13(2) or (4) or 16(2).

Confiscation and restoration of quota

32.—(1) Within forty-five days after the end of each quota year, each purchaser shall supply to the Intervention Board a list of those producers registered with that purchaser (whether for the whole or part of the quota year) who have not made deliveries to him during that year.

(2) Pursuant to Article 5 of the Council Regulation (which deals with the confiscation and restoration of quota), the Intervention Board shall notify—
- (*a*) any producer who from information available to the Intervention Board appears not to have made deliveries or direct sales or a temporary transfer of quota under regulation 13 during the previous quota year, that his quota has been taken into the national reserve;
- (*b*) any producer who is a direct seller and to whom the third sub-paragraph of Article 4(2) of the Commission Regulation (which deals with the late submission of declarations) applies that, unless that producer submits to the Intervention Board a declaration under the first sub-paragraph thereof within 30 days of the notification, his quota will be confiscated to the national reserve.

(3) Any quota withdrawn pursuant to Article 5 of the Council Regulation shall be placed in the national reserve with effect from the beginning of the quota year following the quota year for which the list referred to paragraph (1) was supplied, the quota year for which the declaration indicating no direct sales was made, or the quota year for which no declaration was submitted, as the case may be.

(4) Any quota withdrawn pursuant to Article 5 of the Council Regulation may be restored to the producer in respect of the holding from which it was withdrawn within a period of six years from the beginning of the quota year in which it was withdrawn, in accordance with the provisions of this regulation.

(5) A producer who receives a notification of confiscation under paragraph (2) above shall—

    (*a*) within 28 days of receipt of that notification notify any person with an interest in the holding of the content of that notification; and

    (*b*) within six months of receipt of that notification, submit a notification to the Intervention Board, in such form as may reasonably be required by the Intervention Board for that purpose, whether he wishes to retain the right to request restoration of the quota and such a notification shall include—

        (i) a statement that he is the occupier of the entirety of the holding and that no other person has an interest in all or any of it;

        (ii) a statement of the agreed apportionment of quota taking account of the areas used for milk production, signed by every person with an interest in the holding; or

        (iii) a statement requesting apportionment of the quota in accordance with an arbitration under paragraphs 1(5), 3, 4 and 6 to 35 of Schedule 2 in respect of England and Wales, paragraphs 1, 2, 3(4) and 5 to 28 of Schedule 3 in respect of Scotland, and paragraphs 1, 2, 3(5), 5, 6, and 8 to 19 of Schedule 4 in respect of Northern Ireland.

(6) Where a producer has notified the Intervention Board under paragraph (5)(*b*) that he wishes to retain the right to restoration of quota, he may request the Intervention Board to restore to him the quota relating to that holding or part holding provided that the request is submitted to the Intervention Board by 15th July in the quota year following the quota year to which the request relates.

(7) Where a producer has notified the Intervention Board that he wishes to retain the right to restoration of quota and there is a change of occupation of all or part of the holding to which the quota relates, the new occupier may request the Intervention Board to restore to him the quota relating to that holding or part holding, provided that the request is received by the Intervention Board at least six months before the end of the six-year period referred to in paragraph (4) or within six months of the change of occupation, whichever is the earlier.

(8) Where quota is restored to part of a holding in respect of which an apportionment of quota has been made in accordance with or under paragraph 5(*b*)(ii) or (iii); in accordance with a request made under paragraph (6), or following a change of occupation of part of a holding under paragraph (7), the amount of quota to be restored to that part shall be determined in accordance with—

(a) the apportionment referred to in paragraph (5)(*b*)(ii) or (iii) and within that apportionment in proportion to the agricultural areas concerned; or

(b) where no such apportionment has been carried out, in the same proportion which the agricultural area concerned bears to the total agricultural area of the holding from which quota was withdrawn.

(9) Where a producer—

(*a*). fails to submit a notification in accordance with paragraph (5)(*b*);

(*b*) indicates on the notification submitted under paragraph (5)(*b*) that he does not wish to retain the right to restoration of quota;

(*c*) fails to request the restoration of quota in accordance with paragraph (6) or (7);

(*d*) having had quota restored to him in accordance with paragraph (6), fails to make deliveries or direct sales of dairy produce from the holding to which the quota relates within six months after his application for the restoration of quota or the end of the six year period, whichever is the earlier; or

(*e*) having had quota restored to him following a change of occupation referred to in paragraph (7), fails to make deliveries or direct sales of dairy produce from the holding within eighteen months of the change of occupation or the end of the six year period, whichever is the earlier,

the relevant quota shall be taken into the national reserve.

Withdrawal of Special Quota

33.—Where a producer has special quota registered in his name and it appears to the Minister that the producer has made a false or misleading statement in his application for special quota or has failed to comply with the requirements in relation to special quota, the Minister may withdraw the whole or any part of the special quota.

Dairy produce Quota Tribunals

34.—(1) For the purpose of completing the discharge of any functions exercisable by it under the Regulations revoked by these Regulations, the Dairy Produce Quota Tribunal for England and Wales, the Dairy Produce Quota Tribunal for Scotland and the Dairy Produce Quota Tribunal for Northern Ireland constituted under regulation 6 of the 1984 Regulations shall continue in existence and, in respect of a holding situated in more than one area of a Dairy Produce Quota Tribunal, the Dairy Produce Quota Tribunal the functions of which shall relate to that holding shall continue to be the Dairy Produce Quota Tribunal chosen for the purpose by the Ministers.

(2) Schedule 6 shall apply in respect of the constitution, appointment of members, remuneration of members, staffing and procedure of Dairy Produce Quota Tribunals.

Revocation

35.—The Dairy Produce Quotas Regulations 1994, the Dairy Produce Quotas (Amendment) Regulations 1994, the Dairy Produce Quotas (Amendment) (No. 2)

THE DAIRY PRODUCE QUOTAS REGULATIONS 1997

Regulations 1994, the Dairy Produce Quotas (Amendment) Regulations 1995, the Dairy Produce Quotas (Amendment) Regulations 1996 and the Dairy Produce Quotas (Amendment) Regulations 1997 shall be revoked.

10th March 1997

Minister of State
Ministry of Agriculture, Fisheries and Food
Parliamentary Under Secretary of State,
11th March 1997
Scottish Office

SCHEDULE 1

MEANING OF COMMUNITY LEGISLATION

Regulation 2(1)

1. Council Regulation (EEC) No. 857/84, adopting general rules for the application of the levy referred to in Article 5c of Regulation (EEC) No. 804/68 in the milk and milk products sector, OJ No. L90, 1.4.84, p.13.

2. Council Regulation (EEC) No. 764/89, amending Regulation (EEC) No. 857/84, OJ No. L84, 29.3.89, p.2.

3. Council Regulation (EEC) No. 1639/91, amending Regulation (EEC) No. 857/84, OJ No. L150, 15.6.91, p.35.

4. Commission Regulation (EEC) No. 1756/93, fixing the operative events for the agricultural conversion rate applicable to milk and milk products, OJ No. L161, 2.7.93, p.48.

5. Council Regulation (EEC) No. 2187/93, providing for an offer of compensation to certain producers of milk and milk products temporarily prevented from carrying on their trade, OJ No. L196, 5.8.93, p.6.

6. Commission Regulation (EEC) No. 2562/93, laying down detailed rules for the application of Council Regulation 2055/93, OJ No. L253, 18.9.93, p.18.

7. Commission Regulation (EEC) No. 2648/93, laying down detailed rules for the application of Council Regulation (EEC) No. 2187/93, OJ No. L243, 29.9.93, p.1.

SCHEDULE 2

APPORTIONMENTS AND PROSPECTIVE APPORTIONMENTS BY
ARBITRATION—ENGLAND AND WALES

Regulations 8, 9, 10 and 32

SCHEDULE 2

Appointment and remuneration of arbitrator

1.—(1) In any case where an apportionment is to be carried out by arbitration an arbitrator shall be appointed by agreement between the transferor and transferee within the period of 28 days referred to in regulation 7(1)(*a*) (referred to in this paragraph as "the relevant period") and the transferee shall give notice of the appointment of the arbitrator to the Intervention Board within fourteen days of the date of the appointment.

(2) Notwithstanding sub-paragraph (1), the transferor or the transferee may at any time within the relevant period make an application to the President of the Royal Institution of Chartered Surveyors (referred to in this Schedule as "the President") for the appointment of an arbitrator from amongst the members of the panel referred to in paragraph 8 and the person who makes such an application to the President shall give notice of that fact to the Intervention Board within fourteen days of the date of the application.

(3) If at the expiry of the relevant period an arbitrator has not been appointed by agreement between the transferor and the transferee and no application has been made to the President under sub-paragraph (2), the Intervention Board shall make an application to the President for the appointment of an arbitrator.

(4) Where the Intervention Board gives a notice in accordance with regulation 10 it shall make an application to the President for the appointment of an arbitrator and the Intervention Board shall be a party to the arbitration.

(5) Where an apportionment under regulation 32(5) is to be carried out by arbitration, the producer shall either appoint by agreement with all persons with an interest in the holding or make an application to the President for the appointment of an arbitrator from amongst the members of the panel referred to in paragraph 8.

2.—(1) In any case where a prospective apportionment is to be made by arbitration an arbitrator shall be appointed—
  (*a*) where regulation 10 applies, by the President,
  (*b*) in any other case, by agreement between the occupier of the relevant holding and any other interested party, or, in default, by the President on an application by the occupier.

(2) Where sub-paragraph (1)(*b*) applies, the occupier shall give notice to the Intervention Board of the appointment of the arbitrator pursuant to the agreement, or of the application to the President for the appointment of an arbitrator, with fourteen days of the date of the appointment of the arbitrator or the date of the application to the President, as the case may be.

3.—(1) An arbitrator appointed in accordance with paragraphs 1(1) to (4) and 2 shall conduct the arbitration in accordance with this Schedule and shall base his award on findings made by him as to areas used for milk production in the last five year period during which production took place before the change of occupation, or in the case of a prospective apportionment in the last five year period during which production took place before the appointment of the arbitrator.

(2) An arbitrator appointed in accordance with paragraph 1(5) shall conduct the arbitration in accordance with this Schedule and shall base his award on findings

made by him as to the areas used for milk production in the last five-year period during which production took place.

(3) An arbitrator appointed under any paragraph of this Schedule shall base his award on findings made by him in accordance with the law in force at the time the event giving rise to an application for arbitration took place.

4.—(1) No application may be made to the President for an arbitrator to be appointed by him under this Schedule unless the application is accompanied by the prescribed fee for such an application; but once the fee has been paid in connection with any such application no further fee shall be payable in connection with any subsequent application for the President to exercise any function exercisable by him in relation to the arbitration by virtue of this Schedule (including an application for the appointment by him in an appropriate case of a new arbitrator).

(2) The prescribed fee for the purposes of this paragraph shall be that which from time to time is prescribed as the fee payable to the President under paragraph 1(2) of Schedule 11 to the Agricultural Holdings Act 1986.

5.—Where the Intervention Board makes an application to the President under paragraphs 1(3) or (4), the fee payable to the President in respect of that application referred to in paragraph 4 shall be recoverable by the Intervention Board as a debt due from the other parties to the arbitration jointly or severally.

6.—Any appointment of an arbitrator by the President shall be made by him as soon as possible after receiving the application.

7.—A person appointed by the President as arbitrator shall, where the arbitration relates to a holding in Wales, and any party to the arbitration so requires, be a person who possesses a knowledge of the Welsh language.

8.—For the purposes of paragraph 1(2) the panel of arbitrators shall be the panel appointed by the Lord Chancellor under paragraph 1(5) of Schedule 11 to the Agricultural Holdings Act 1986.

9.—If the arbitrator dies, or is incapable of acting, or for seven days after notice from any party requiring him to act fails to act, a new arbitrator may be appointed as if no arbitrator had been appointed.

10.—No party to the arbitration shall have power to revoke the appointment of the arbitrator without the consent of any other party, and his appointment shall not be revoked by the death of any party.

11.—Every appointment, application, notice, revocation and consent under paragraphs 1 to 10 must be in writing.

12.—The remuneration of the arbitrator shall be—
    (*a*) where he is appointed by agreement between the parties, such amount as may be agreed upon by him and the parties or, in default of agreement,

SCHEDULE 2

fixed by the registrar of the county court (subject to an appeal to the judge of the court) on an application made by the arbitrator or any party;

(b) where he is appointed by the President, such amount as may be agreed upon by the arbitrator and the parties or, in default of agreement, fixed by the President,

and shall be recoverable by the arbitrator as a debt due from the parties to the arbitration, jointly or severally.

Conduct of proceedings and witnesses

13.—(1) In any arbitration to which this Schedule applies, the arbitrator may, in his absolute discretion, subject to sub-paragraph (2), join as a party to the arbitration any person having an interest in the holding, whether or not such person has applied to become a party to the arbitration, provided that such person consents to be so joined.

(2) Where an apportionment under regulation 32(5) is to be carried out by arbitration, any person with an interest in the holding who has refused to sign the statement referred to in regulation 32(5)(b)(ii) shall be a party to the arbitration.

14.—The parties to the arbitration shall, within thirty-five days of the appointment of the arbitrator, or within such further period as the arbitrator may determine, deliver to him a statement of their respective cases with all necessary particulars and—

(a) no amendment or addition to the statement or particulars delivered shall be allowed after the expiry of the said thirty-five days except with the consent of the arbitrator; and

(b) a party to the arbitration shall be confined at the hearing to the matters alleged in the statement and particulars delivered by him and any amendment or addition duly made.

15.—The parties to the arbitration and all persons claiming through them shall, subject to any legal objection, submit to be examined by the arbitrator, on oath or affirmation, in relation to the matters in dispute and shall, subject to any such objection, produce before the arbitrator all samples and documents within their possession or power which may be required or called for, and do such other things as the arbitrator reasonably may require for the purposes of the arbitration.

16.—Any person having an interest in the holding to which the arbitration relates shall be entitled to make representations to the arbitrator.

17.—Witnesses appearing at the arbitration shall, if the arbitrator thinks fit, be examined on oath or affirmation, and the arbitrator shall have power to administer oaths to, or to take the affirmation of, the parties and witnesses appearing.

18.—The provisions of county court rules as to the issuing of witness summonses shall, subject to such modifications as may be prescribed by such rules, apply for the purposes of the arbitration as if it were an action or matter in the county court.

19.—(1) Subject to sub-paragraphs (2) and (3), any person who—
   (a) having been summoned in pursuance of county court rules as a witness in the arbitration refuses or neglects, without sufficient cause, to appear or to produce any documents required by the summons to be produced, or
   (b) having been so summoned or being present at the arbitration and being required to give evidence, refuses to be sworn or give evidence,

shall forfeit such fine as the judge of the county court may direct.

(2) A judge shall not have power under sub-paragraph (1) above to direct that a person shall forfeit a fine of an amount exceeding £400.

(3) No person summoned in pursuance of county court rules as a witness in the arbitration shall forfeit a fine under this paragraph unless there has been paid or tendered to him at the time of the service of the summons such sum in respect of his expenses (including, in such cases as may be prescribed by county court rules, compensation for loss of time) as may be so prescribed for the purposes of section 55 of the County Courts Act 1984

(4) The judge of the county court may at his discretion direct that the whole or any part of any such fine, after deducting costs, shall be applicable towards indemnifying the party injured by the refusal or neglect.

20.—(1) Subject to sub-paragraph (2), the judge of the county court may, if he thinks fit, upon application on affidavit by any party to the arbitration, issue an order under his hand for bringing up before the arbitrator any person (in this paragraph referred to as a "prisoner") confined in any place under any sentence or under committal for trial or otherwise, to be examined as a witness in the arbitration.

(2) No such order shall be made with respect to a person confined under process in any civil action or matter.

(3) Subject to sub-paragraph (4), the prisoner mentioned in any such order shall be brought before the arbitrator under the same custody, and shall be dealt with in the same manner in all respects, as a prisoner required by a writ of habeas corpus to be brought before the High Court and examined there as a witness.

(4) The person having the custody of the prisoner shall not be bound to obey the order unless there is tendered to him a reasonable sum for the conveyance and maintenance of a proper officer or officers and of the prisoner in going to, remaining at, and returning from, the place where the arbitration is held.

21.—The High Court may order that a writ of habeas corpus ad testificandum shall issue to bring up a prisoner for examination before the arbitrator, if the prisoner is confined in any prison under process in any civil action or matter.

Award

22.—(1) Subject to sub-paragraph (2), the arbitrator shall make and sign his award within fifty-six days of his appointment.

(2) The President may from time to time enlarge the time limited for making the award, whether that time has expired or not.

(3) The arbitrator shall notify the terms of his award to the Intervention Board within eight days of delivery of that award.

(4) The award shall fix a date not later than one month after the delivery of the award for the payment of any costs awarded under paragraph 26.

23.—The award shall be final and binding on the parties and any persons claiming under them.

24.—The arbitrator shall have power to correct in the award any clerical mistake or error arising from any accidental slip or omission.

Reasons for award

25.—Where the arbitrator is requested by any party to the arbitration, on or before the making of the award, to make a statement, either written or oral, of the reasons for the award, the arbitrator shall furnish such a statement.

Costs

26.—The costs of and incidental to the arbitration and award shall be in the discretion of the arbitrator who may direct to and by whom and in what manner the costs, or any part of the costs, are to be paid. The costs for the purposes of this paragraph shall include any fee paid to the President in respect of the appointment of an arbitrator and any sum paid to the Intervention Board pursuant to paragraph 5.

27.—On the application of any party, any such costs shall be taxable in the county court according to such of the scales prescribed by county court rules for proceedings in the county court as may be directed by the arbitrator under paragraph 26, or, in the absence of any such direction, by the county court.

28.—(1) The arbitrator shall, in awarding costs, take into consideration—
- (*a*) the reasonableness or unreasonableness of the claim of any party, whether in respect of the amount or otherwise,
- (*b*) any unreasonable demand for particulars or refusal to supply particulars, and
- (*c*) generally all the circumstances of the case.

(2) The arbitrator may disallow any costs which he considers to have been unnecessarily incurred, including the costs of any witness whom he considers to have been called unnecessarily.

Special case, setting aside award and remission

29.—The arbitrator may at any stage of the proceedings and shall, upon a direction in that behalf given by the judge of the county court upon an application made by any party, state in the form of a special case for the opinion of the county court any question of law arising in the course of the arbitration and any question as to the jurisdiction of the arbitrator.

30.—(1) Where the arbitrator has misconducted himself, the county court may remove him.

(2) Where the arbitrator has misconducted himself, or an arbitration or award has been improperly procured, or there is an error of law on the face of the award, the county court may set the award aside.

31.—(1) The county court may from time to time remit the award, or any part of the award, to the reconsideration of the arbitrator.

(2) In any case where it appears to the county court that there is an error of law on the face of the award, the court may, instead of exercising its power of remission under sub-paragraph (1), vary the award by substituting for so much of it as is affected by the error such award as the court considers that it would have been proper for the arbitrator to make in the circumstances; and the award shall thereupon have effect as so varied.

(3) Where remission is ordered under that sub-paragraph, the arbitrator shall, unless the order otherwise directs, make and sign his award within thirty days of the date of the order.

(4) If the county court is satisfied that the time limited for making the said award is for any good reason insufficient, the court may extend or further extend that time for such period as it thinks proper.

Miscellaneous

32.—Any amount paid, in respect of the remuneration of the arbitrator by any party to the arbitration in excess of the amount, if any, directed by the award to be paid by him in respect of the costs of the award, shall be recoverable from the other party or jointly from the other parties.

33.—For the purposes of this Schedule, an arbitrator appointed by the President shall be taken to have been so appointed at the time when the President executed the instrument of appointment, in accordance with the law in force at the time of such execution and in the case of any such arbitrator the periods mentioned in paragraphs 14 and 22 shall accordingly run from that time.

34.—Any instrument of appointment or other document purporting to be made in the exercise of any function exercisable by the President under paragraph 1, 2, 6, 7, 12 or 22 and to be signed by or on behalf of the President shall be taken to be such an instrument or document unless the contrary is shown.

35.—The Arbitration Act 1996 shall not apply to an arbitration determined in accordance with this Schedule.

SCHEDULE 3

APPORTIONMENTS AND PROSPECTIVE APPORTIONMENTS BY ARBITRATION OR SCOTTISH LAND COURT SCOTLAND

Regulations 8, 9, 10 and 32

SCHEDULE 3

PART I
GENERAL

1.—(1) Subject to sub-paragraphs (2) and (3) below, all apportionments and prospective apportionments in respect of holdings in Scotland shall be carried out by arbitration and the provisions of Part II of this Schedule shall apply.

(2) The Scottish Land Court shall carry out the apportionment or prospective apportionment where the holding or any part of the holding constitutes or, immediately prior to the transfer giving rise to the apportionment, constituted—
   (a) a croft within the meaning of section 3 of the Crofters (Scotland) Act 1993,
   (b) a holding within the meaning of section 2 of the Small Landholders (Scotland) Act 1911,
   (c) the holding of a statutory small tenant under section 32 of the Small Landholders (Scotland) Act 1911.

(3) Where sub-paragraph (2) above does not apply and the holding or any part of the holding constitutes or, immediately prior to the transfer giving rise to the apportionment, constituted an agricultural holding within the meaning of section 1 of the Agricultural Holdings (Scotland) Act 1991, the Scottish Land Court shall carry out the apportionment or prospective apportionment if requested to do so by a joint application of all parties interested in the apportionment, made within the period of 28 days referred to in regulation 7(1)(a).

(4) Where the Scottish Land Court carries out any apportionment or prospective apportionment, Part III of this Schedule shall apply.

2.—(1) An arbiter or the Scottish Land Court, as the case may be, shall decide the apportionment on the basis of findings made as to areas used for milk production in the last five-year period during which production took place before the change of occupation or, in the case of a prospective apportionment, in the last five-year period during which production took place before the appointment of the arbiter or the application to the Scottish Land Court.

(2) Notwithstanding sub-paragraph (1), an arbiter appointed in accordance with paragraph 3(4) shall conduct the arbitration in accordance with this Schedule and shall base his award on findings made by him as to the areas used for milk production in the last five year period during which production took place.

PART II
APPORTIONMENTS CARRIED OUT BY ARBITRATION

Appointment and remuneration of arbiter

3.—(1) In any case where the apportionment is to be carried out by arbitration, an arbiter shall be appointed by agreement between the transferor and transferee within the period of 28 days referred to in regulation 7(1)(a) (referred to in this paragraph as "the relevant period") and the transferee shall give notice of the appointment of the arbiter to the Minister within fourteen days from the date of the appointment.

(2) Notwithstanding sub-paragraph (1), the transferor or the transferee may at

any time within the relevant period make an application to the Minister for the appointment of an arbiter.

(3) If at the expiry of the relevant period an arbiter has not been appointed by agreement between the transferor and the transferee not an application made to the Minister under sub-paragraph (2), the Minister shall at his own instance proceed to appoint an arbiter.

(4) Where an apportionment under regulation 32(5) is to be carried out by arbitration, the producer shall either appoint an arbiter with the agreement of all persons with an interest in the holding or make an application to the Minister for the appointment of an arbiter.

4.—(1) In any case where a prospective apportionment is to be made by arbitration, an arbiter shall be appointed by agreement between the occupier and any other interested party or, in default of agreement, by the Minister on an application by the occupier.

(2) Where an arbiter is appointed by agreement in terms of sub-paragraph (1), the occupier shall give notice of the appointment of the arbiter to the Minister within fourteen days from the date of the appointment.

5.—(1) Where, in terms of a notice given by the Intervention Board under regulation 10, an apportionment or prospective apportionment is to be carried out by arbitration, the Intervention Board shall apply to the Scottish Land Court for the appointment of an arbiter.

(2) Any fee payable by the Intervention Board on an application to the Scottish Land Court under sub-paragraph (1) shall be recoverable by it as a debt due from the other parties to the arbitration jointly or severally.

(3) Where the Minister is to be a party to an arbitration (otherwise than in terms of a notice given under regulation 10, the arbiter shall, in lieu of being appointed by the Minister, be appointed by the Scottish Land Court.

6.—If the person appointed arbiter dies, or is incapable of acting, or for seven days after notice from any party requiring him to act fails to act, a new arbiter may be appointed as if no arbiter had been appointed.

7.—No party to the arbitration shall have power to revoke the appointment of the arbiter without the consent of any other party.

8.—Every appointment, application, notice, revocation and consent under paragraphs 1 to 7 must be in writing.

9.—The remuneration of the arbiter shall be—
   (a) where he is appointed by agreement between the parties, such amount as may be agreed upon by him and the parties or, in default of agreement, fixed by the auditor of the sheriff court (subject to an appeal to the sheriff) on an application made by the arbiter or one of the parties;
   (b) where he is appointed by the Minister, such amount as may be fixed by the Minister;

SCHEDULE 3

(c) where he is appointed by the Scottish Land Court, such amount as may be fixed by that Court;

and shall be recoverable by the arbiter as a debt due from any one of the parties to the arbitration.

Conduct of proceedings and witnesses

10.—The parties to the arbitration shall within twenty-eight days of the appointment of the arbiter deliver to him a statement of their respective cases with all necessary particulars; and—
  (a) no amendment or addition to the statement or particulars delivered shall be allowed after the expiry of the said twenty-eight days except with the consent of the arbiter;
  (b) a party to the arbitration shall be confined at the hearing to the matters alleged in the statement and particulars delivered by him and any amendment or addition duly made.

11.—The parties to the arbitration, and all persons claiming through them, shall, subject to any legal objection, submit to be examined by the arbiter on oath or affirmation in relation to the matters in dispute and shall, subject to any such objection, produce before the arbiter all samples, books, deeds, papers, accounts, writings and documents, within their possession or power which may be required or called for, and do all other things as the arbiter reasonably may require for the purposes of the arbitration.

12.—Any person having an interest in the holding to which the arbitration relates shall be entitled to make representations to the arbiter. The Intervention Board may make such representations where the arbitration follows on a notice given by it under regulation 10.

13.—The arbiter shall have power to administer oaths, and to take the affirmation of parties and witnesses appearing, and witnesses shall, if the arbiter thinks fit, be examined on oath or affirmation.

Award

14.—(1) The arbiter shall make and sign his award within three months of his appointment or within such longer period as may, either before or after the expiry of the aforesaid period, be agreed to in writing by the parties or fixed by the Minister.

(2) The arbiter shall notify the terms of his award to the Minister within eight days of the delivery of that award.

(3) The award shall fix a date not later than one month after the delivery of the award for the payment of any expenses awarded under paragraph 17.

15.—The award to be made by the arbiter shall be final and binding on the parties and the persons claiming under them respectively.

16.—The arbiter may correct in an award any clerical mistake or error arising from any accidental slip or omission.

Expenses

17.—The expenses of and incidental to the arbitration and award shall be in the discretion of the arbiter, who may direct to and by whom and in what manner those expenses or any part thereof are to be paid, and the expenses shall be subject to taxation by the auditor of the sheriff court on the application of any party, but that taxation shall be subject to review by the sheriff.

18.—(1) The arbiter shall, in awarding expenses, take into consideration—
   (*a*) the reasonableness or unreasonableness of the claim of any party, whether in respect of amount or otherwise;
   (*b*) any unreasonable demand for particulars or refusal to supply particulars; and
   (*c*) generally all the circumstances of the case.

(2) The arbiter may disallow any expenses which he considers to have been incurred unnecessarily, including the expenses of any witness whom he considers to have been called unnecessarily.

19.—It shall not be lawful to include in the expenses of and incidental to the arbitration and award, or to charge against any of the parties, any sum payable in respect of remuneration or expenses to any person appointed by the arbiter to act as clerk or otherwise to assist him in the arbitration unless such appointment was made after submission of the claim and answers to the arbiter and with either the consent of the parties to the arbitration or the sanction of the sheriff.

Statement of case

20.—The arbiter may at any stage of the proceedings, and shall, if so directed by the sheriff (which direction may be given on the application of any party), state a case for the opinion of the sheriff on any questions of law arising in the course of the arbitration. The opinion of the sheriff on any case shall be final.

Removal of arbiter and setting aside of award

21.—Where an arbiter has misconducted himself the sheriff may remove him.

22.—When an arbiter has misconducted himself, or an arbitration or award has been improperly procured, the sheriff may set the award aside.

Miscellaneous

23.—Any amount paid in respect of the remuneration of the arbiter by any party to the arbitration in excess of the amount, if any, directed by the award to be paid by him in respect of the expenses of the award shall be recoverable from the other party or jointly from the other parties.

SCHEDULE 3

24.—The Arbitration (Scotland) Act 1894 shall not apply to any arbitration carried out under this Schedule.

PART III
APPORTIONMENTS CARRIED OUT BY THE SCOTTISH LAND COURT

25.—The provisions of the Small Landholders (Scotland) Acts 1886 to 1931 with regard to the Scottish Land Court shall, with any necessary modifications, apply for the purpose of the determination of any matter which they are required, in terms of paragraph 1, to determine, in like manner as those provisions apply for the purpose of the determination by the Land Court of matters referred to them under those Acts.

26.—Where an apportionment or prospective apportionment is to be dealt with by the Scottish Land Court, the party making application to that Court shall notify the Minister in writing of the application within fourteen days of its being lodged with the Court.

27.—Where, in terms of a notice given by the Intervention Board under regulation 10, an apportionment or prospective apportionment is to be carried out by the Scottish Land Court, any fee payable by the Intervention Board to the Court shall be recoverable by it as a debt due from the other parties to the case jointly or severally.

28.—Any person having an interest in the holding to which the apportionment or prospective apportionment relates shall be entitled to be a party to the proceedings before the Scottish Land Court. The Intervention Board shall be entitled to be a party where the apportionment follows on a notice given by it under regulation 10.

SCHEDULE 4

APPORTIONMENTS AND PROSPECTIVE APPORTIONMENTS BY
ARBITRATION—NORTHERN IRELAND

Regulations 8, 9, 10 and 32

1.—Paragraphs 3 to 19 shall apply to every arbitration in Northern Ireland.

2.—(1) Parts I, II and IV of the Arbitration Act 1996 shall, except insofar as they are inconsistent with paragraphs 3 to 19, apply to every arbitration in Northern Ireland as if that arbitration were pursuant to an arbitration agreement and as if paragraphs 3 to 11 and 13 to 18 were contained in an arbitration agreement.

(2) For the purposes of this paragraph "arbitration agreement" shall be construed in accordance with sections 5(1) and 6 of the Arbitration Act 1996.

Appointment of arbitrator

3.—(1) In any case where an apportionment is to be carried out by arbitration an arbitrator shall be appointed by agreement between the transferor and transferee within the period of 28 days referred to in regulation 7(1)(*a*)(referred to in this paragraph as "the relevant period") and the transferee shall give notice of the appointment of the arbitrator to the Intervention Board within fourteen days of the date of the appointment.

(2) Notwithstanding sub-paragraph (1) above, the transferor or the transferee may at any time within the relevant period make an application to the president of the Law Society of Northern Ireland (referred to in this Schedule as "the President") for the appointment of an arbitrator and the person who makes such an application to the President shall give notice of that fact to the Intervention Board within fourteen days of the date of the application.

(3) If at the expiry of the relevant period an arbitrator has not been appointed by agreement between the transferor and the transferee nor an application made to the President under sub-paragraph (2), the Intervention Board shall make an application to the President for the appointment of an arbitrator.

(4) Where the Intervention Board gives a notice in accordance with regulation 10 he shall make an application to the President for the appointment of an arbitrator and the Intervention Board shall be a party to the arbitration.

(5) Where an apportionment under regulation 32(5) is to be carried out by arbitration, the producer shall either appoint an arbitrator by agreement with all persons with an interest in the holding or make an application to the President for the appointment of an arbitrator.

4.—(1) In any case where a prospective apportionment is to be made by arbitration an arbitrator shall be appointed—
  (*a*) where regulation 10 applies, by the President;
  (*b*) in any other case, by agreement between the occupier of the holding to which the prospective apportionment relates and any other interested party, or, in default, by the President on an application by that occupier.

(2) Where sub-paragraph (1)(*b*) applies, the occupier shall give notice to the Intervention Board of the appointment of the arbitrator pursuant to the agreement, or of the application to the President for the appointment of an arbitrator, within fourteen days of the date of the appointment of the arbitrator or the date of the application to the President, as the case may be.

5.—(1) An arbitrator appointed in accordance with paragraphs 3(1) to (4) and 4 shall conduct the arbitration in accordance with this Schedule and shall base his award on findings made by him as to areas used for milk production in the last five year period during which production took place before the change of occupation, or in the case of a prospective apportionment in the last five year period during which production took place before the appointment of the arbitrator.

(2) An arbitrator appointed in accordance with paragraph 3(5) shall conduct the arbitration in accordance with this Schedule and shall base his award on findings

made by him as to areas used for milk production in the last five year period during which production took place.

(3) An arbitrator appointed under any paragraph of this Schedule shall base his award on findings made by him in accordance with the law in force at the time the event giving rise to an application for arbitration took place.

6.—No application may be made to the President for an arbitrator to be appointed by him under this Schedule unless the application is accompanied by the fee which shall be £50 for such an application; but once the fee has been paid in connection with any such application no further fee shall be payable in connection with any subsequent application for the President to exercise any function exercisable by him in relation to the arbitration by virtue of this Schedule (including an application for the appointment by him in an appropriate case of a new arbitrator).

7.—Where the Intervention Board makes an application to the President under paragraph 3(3) or (4), the fee payable to the President in respect of that application referred to in paragraph 6 above shall be recoverable by the Intervention Board as a debt due from the parties to the arbitration jointly or severally.

8.—Any appointment of an arbitrator by the President shall be made by him within fourteen days after receiving the application.

9.—If the arbitrator dies, or is incapable of acting, or for seven days after notice from any party requiring him to act fails to act, a new arbitrator may be appointed as if no arbitrator had been appointed.

10.—A party to the arbitration shall have power to revoke the appointment of the arbitrator with the consent of all other parties.

11.—Every appointment, application, notice, revocation and consent under paragraphs 1 to 10 shall be in writing.

Persons with an interest in the holding

12.—(1) In an arbitration to which this Schedule applies, the arbitrator may, in his absolute discretion, subject to sub-paragraph (2), join as a party to the arbitration any person having an interest in the holding, whether or not such person has applied to become a party to the arbitration, provided that such person consents to be so joined.

(2) Where an apportionment under regulation 32(5) is to be carried out by arbitration, any person with an interest in the holding who has refused to sign the statement referred to in regulation 32(5)(*b*)(ii) shall be a party to the arbitration.

Statement of case

13.—The parties to the arbitration shall, within thirty-five days of the appointment of the arbitrator, deliver to him a statement of their respective cases with all necessary particulars and—

(*a*) no amendment or addition to the statement or particulars delivered shall be allowed after the expiry of the said thirty-five days except with the consent of the arbitrator;

(*b*) a party to the arbitration shall be confined at the hearing to the matters alleged in the statement and particulars delivered by him and any amendment or addition duly made.

Award

14.—The arbitrator shall make and sign his award within fifty-six days of his appointment.

15.—The arbitrator shall notify the terms of his award to the Intervention Board within eight days of the delivery of that award.

16.—The arbitrator shall have power to correct in the award any clerical mistake or error arising from any accidental slip or omission.

Reasons for award

17.—If requested by any party to the arbitration, on or before the making of the award, to make a statement, either written or oral, of the reasons for the award the arbitrator shall furnish such a statement.

18.—For the purposes of this Schedule, an arbitrator appointed by the President shall be taken to have been so appointed at the time when the President executed the instrument of appointment; and in the case of any such arbitrator the periods mentioned in paragraphs 13 and 14 shall run from that time.

19. Any person having an interest in the holding to which the arbitration relates shall be entitled to make representations to the arbitrator.

SCHEDULE 5

Reallocation of Quota and Calculation of Levy Liability

Regulation 18

Wholesale quota

1. The Intervention Board shall determine the amount, if any, by which the wholesale deliveries of dairy produce to each purchaser exceeds his purchaser quota.

2. In making that determination the Intervention Board shall complete in sequence the steps required by paragraphs 3 to 7.

3. The Intervention Board shall where necessary authorise an adjustment of the amount, if any, by which the quantity of wholesale deliveries of dairy produce to

SCHEDULE 5

each purchaser must be adjusted to take account of its fat content, calculated in accordance with Article 2(2) of the Commission Regulation.

4. The Intervention Board shall authorise the adjustment by purchasers (to the extent possible from within the quota available to the purchaser (to the extent possible from within the quota available to the purchaser to whom the producer makes deliveries) of the quota of any producer making wholesale deliveries to whom a temporary reallocation of quota has been made, to take account of that reallocation, in accordance with the order of priority set out in regulation 14(7) and any purchaser who has insufficient quota unused by producers registered with him to meet that temporary reallocation shall notify the Intervention Board of the amount of the shortfall in such form as may reasonably be required by the Intervention Board.

5. The Intervention Board shall determine for each purchaser the amount, if any, by which the purchaser quota of each purchaser exceeds or falls short of the quantity of wholesale deliveries of dairy produce made to him taking into account the amount of quota converted in accordance with regulation 16, and any temporary reallocation made in accordance with paragraph 4.

6. The Intervention Board shall determine the total amount, if any, of excess quota remaining for any purchaser whose purchaser quota exceeds the quantity of wholesale deliveries of dairy produce made to him, as determined in accordance with paragraph 5, and shall add that amount to the national reserve.

7. The Intervention Board shall reallocate the amount, if any, referred to in paragraph 6—
   (*a*) in the first instance, to meet any award of a temporary reallocation of quota which has not been met by the adjustment referred to in paragraph 4 above in accordance with the order of priority set out in regulation 14(7);
   (*b*) thereafter, to offset the amount by which the deliveries made to any purchaser exceed his purchaser quota, such allocation being made proportionately to the amount of quota; and
   (*c*) where the allocations referred to in sub-paragraph (*b*) exceed the amount required by the purchaser, the surplus shall be allocated to all purchasers where the deliveries exceed purchaser quota, until all unallocated quota has been exhausted.

8. Where a purchaser fails to notify the Intervention Board within 45 days of the end of the quota year of the actual quantity of milk or milk products delivered to him in that year, the Intervention Board may decide that that purchaser shall not benefit from the reallocation of quota referred to in paragraph 7(*b*).

9. The Intervention Board shall determine the total amount of the levy payable by a purchaser by multiplying the amount, if any, by which deliveries to him exceed his purchaser quota following the steps specified in paragraphs 3 to 7 by the rate of levy calculated in accordance with Article 1 of the Council Regulation.

THE DAIRY PRODUCE QUOTAS REGULATIONS 1997

10. Where, for any quota year, a purchaser is unable to supply such proof of the quantities of dairy produce delivered to him that year as the Intervention Board may reasonably require, the Intervention Board shall make its own determination of those quantities, based on all the information available to it, for the purposes of calculating any levy payable by that purchaser, and shall inform the purchaser of such determination.

Direct sales quota

11. The Intervention Board shall determine for each direct seller the amount, if any, after taking into account the amount of quota converted in accordance with regulation 16, by which his direct sales quota exceeds the quantity of dairy produce sold by direct sale by him, and shall add this to any quantities available in the national reserve.

12. The Intervention Board shall make an award of a temporary reallocation of direct sales quota, under the terms of regulation 14, and in accordance with the order of priority set out in regulation 14(7) from the aggregate of amounts, if any, referred to in paragraph 11.

13. The Intervention Board shall determine the aggregate amount, if any, by which the direct sales quota of all direct sellers falls short of the total quantity of dairy produce sold by direct sales by them, after taking into account the amount of quota converted in accordance with regulation 16, and any temporary reallocation made in accordance with paragraph 12.

14. The Intervention Board shall determine for each direct seller the amount, if any, by which his direct sales quota falls short of the quantity of dairy produce sold by direct sale by him, taking into account the amount of quota converted in accordance with regulation 16, and any temporary reallocation of quota made in accordance with paragraph 12.

15. The Intervention Board shall determine the aggregate of the amounts, if any, referred to in paragraph 14.

16. The Intervention Board shall determine the total amount of the levy payable by multiplying the amount, if any, referred to in paragraph 13 by the rate of levy calculated in accordance with Article 1 of the Council Regulation.

17. The Intervention Board shall calculate the rate of levy per litre, if any, to be paid by each direct seller on the amount, if any, at paragraph 14 by dividing the amount calculated in accordance with paragraph 16 by the aggregate referred to in paragraph 15.

18. Where a direct seller fails to notify the Intervention Board within 45 days of the end of the quota year of the total quantity of milk products sold by him by direct sales in that year, the Intervention Board may require that the rate of levy per litre to be paid by that direct seller on the quantity not notified shall be the rate calculated in accordance with Article 1 of the Council Regulation.

SCHEDULE 5

19. Where for any quota year a direct seller is unable to supply such proof as the Intervention Board may reasonably require of the quantities of dairy produce sold by him in that year, the Intervention Board shall make its own determination of those quantities, based on all the information available to it, for the purposes of calculating any levy payable by that direct seller, and shall inform the direct seller of its determination.

SCHEDULE 6

Dairy Produce Quota Tribunals

Regulation 34

PART I
Dairy Produce Quota Tribunals (Other than for Scotland)

1. Each Dairy Produce Quota Tribunal shall consist of up to ninety members appointed by the Minister. The Minister shall designate one of the members of each Tribunal as the Chairman of that Tribunal and may, if he thinks fit, designate another member as the Deputy Chairman.

2. The quorum for any determination by a Dairy Produce Quota Tribunal shall be three.

3. Any determination to be made by a Dairy Produce Quota Tribunal shall be made by a majority.

4. Each Dairy Produce Quota Tribunal may be serviced by a Secretary and such other staff as the Minister may appoint.

5. Any document purporting to be signed by the Chairman or Deputy Chairman of, or the Secretary to, a Dairy Produce Quota Tribunal and purporting to state a determination (or guidance) of the Dairy Produce Quota Tribunal shall in any proceedings be evidence of such a determination (or such guidance).

6. The terms of appointment and the remuneration of the members, Secretary and other staff of a Dairy Produce Quota Tribunal shall be determined by the Minister.

7. Except as otherwise provided in these Regulations, the procedure of a Dairy Produce Quota Tribunal shall be such as the Chairman or, in the absence of the Chairman, the Deputy Chairman shall determine.

Part II
The Dairy Produce Quota Tribunal for Scotland

8. The Dairy Produce Quota Tribunal shall consist of up to twenty members appointed by the Minister.

9. The Dairy Produce Quota Tribunal shall sit in separate panels, and a determination of any such panel shall be treated as the determination of the Tribunal for the purpose of these Regulations.

10. Each panel constituted under paragraph 9 shall choose their own Chairman.

11. The quorum for any determination by the Dairy Produce Quota Tribunal shall be three.

12. Any determination to be made by the Dairy Produce Quota Tribunal shall be made by a majority.

13. Each panel constituted under paragraph 9 shall be serviced by a Secretary and such other staff as the Minister may appoint.

14. Any document purporting to be signed by the Chairman of or the Secretary to a panel constituted under paragraph 9 and purporting to state a determination of the Dairy Produce Quota Tribunal shall in any proceedings be evidence of such a determination.

15. The terms of appointment and the remuneration of—
   (a) the members of the Dairy Produce Quota Tribunal, and
   (b) the Secretary and other staff of a panel constituted under paragraph 9
   shall be determined by the Minister.

16. Except as otherwise provided in these Regulations, the procedure of a panel constituted under paragraph 9 shall be such as their Chairman shall in his discretion determine.

17. A panel constituted under paragraph 9 may consult with any person whom the panel consider to be capable of assisting them in reaching their determination and, in the event of such consultation, the applicant whose special case claim under the Regulations revoked by these Regulations is being examined by the panel shall be afforded the opportunity to comment, before the panel reach their determination, on any advice given by that person.

PART III
GENERAL

18. The Dairy Produce Quota Tribunals for England and Wales, Scotland and Northern Ireland shall, if so required by the Minister, issue a joint written statement of general guidance in respect of the criteria to be used in reaching any determination and each Dairy Produce Quota Tribunal shall make its determinations in accordance with those criteria.

GENERAL NOTE

These Regulations revoke and replace the Dairy Produce Quotas Regulations 1994, as amended. They implement in the United Kingdom Council Regulation

SCHEDULE 6

(EEC) No. 3950/92 establishing an additional levy in the milk and milk products sector and Commission Regulation (EEC) No. 536/93 establishing detailed rules for the levy, both as amended, which consolidate earlier legislation relating to the levy.

Under the Community legislation (including the legislation listed in Schedule 1), a levy continues to be payable on dairy produce sold by direct sale by a producer or delivered by him wholesale to a dairy business, unless the sales or deliveries are within a reference quantity described in that legislation. The Community legislation establishes the system of what are commonly called "milk quotas" and in these Regulations the term "quota" is used to refer to the reference quantity described in the Community legislation.

Apart from drafting changes and the revocation of spent provisions, the new provisions included in these Regulations are as follows:

1. A variation in the ring fencing of Scottish Islands areas (as defined in regulation 2(1)) is made by permitting temporary transfers of quota which increase quantities available to dairy enterprises within them (regulation 13(4)).

2. Any special quota within the meaning of Council Regulation (EEC) No. 2055/93, held by a producer who, before December 31, 1997, makes a temporary transfer of any quota held by him, is to be taken into the national reserve for the duration of the quota year in which that temporary transfer takes place regulation 13(5)).

3. A producer who is awarded a temporary reallocation of quota under regulation 14(2)(*b*)(i) or (2)(*b*)(ii) of these Regulations is to have his award calculated on the basis of a maximum of 16 litres per qualifying cow per qualifying day in any quota year (regulation 14(3)(*a*)).

4. The date by which a producer who wishes to convert quota temporarily in any quota year from wholesale to direct sales quota or the other way must submit his application to do so to the Intervention Board has changed from April 28 to May 14 in any quota year following the end of the quota year in which the temporary conversion of quota takes place (regulation 16(3)(b)).

5. A producer who permanently converts quota in any quota year is not permitted in that same quota year to transfer out quota of the same type as that which he has converted whether temporarily or otherwise (regulation 16(4)), but this restriction does not apply, in the quota year commencing April 1, 1997, to producers who have had animals forming part of their dairy herd slaughtered as animals having been exposed to bovine spongiform encephalopathy, in accordance with section 32(1)(*b*) of the Animal Health Act 1981 (1981 c.22) (regulation 16(5)).

6. A provision is introduced defining and extending the powers of authorised officers of the Intervention Board to include a power to enter upon a holding in order to ascertain whether an offence under regulation 31(1)(*a*), (*b*) or (*c*) of these

Regulations has been or is being committed, to inspect any record or document relating to milk production (including a document kept by means of a computer), and to seize and retain such document or record if he has reason to believe that it may be required in evidence in criminal proceedings under these Regulations (regulation 30).

7. Provisions are introduced making it a criminal offence to dispose of quota which a producer has reason to believe is incorrectly registered in his name, to intentionally obstruct an authorised officer in the exercise of his powers under regulation 30(4) and (5) of these Regulations or to fail without reasonable excuse to comply with a requirement of an authorised officer pursuant to regulation 30(4) or (5) of these Regulations (regulation 31).

A compliance cost assessment has been prepared and a copy has been placed in the library of each House of Parliament.

A.29   THE AGRICULTURAL HOLDINGS (UNITS OF PRODUCTION) ORDER 1997

(S.I.1997 No. 1962)

The Minister of Agriculture, Fisheries and Food in relation to England and the Secretary of State in relation to Wales, in exercise of the powers conferred on them by paragraph 4 of Schedule 6 to the Agricultural Holdings Act 1986[53], and of all other powers enabling them in that behalf, hereby make the following Order:—

Title, commencement and interpretation

1.—(1) This Order may be cited as the Agricultural Holdings (Units of Production) Order 1997 and shall come into force on 12th September 1997.

(2) Any reference in this Order to "the Schedule" is a reference to the Schedule to this Order.

(3) Any reference in this Order to a Community instrument is a reference to that instrument and any amendment of such instrument as may exist on the date this Order is made.

(4) In this Order:

"Council Regulation 805/68" means Council Regulation (EEC) No. 805/68 on the common organisation of the market in beef and veal[54];

"Council Regulation 3013/89" means Council Regulation (EEC) No. 3013/89 on the common organization of the market in sheepmeat and goatmeat[55];

"Council Regulation 1765/92" means Council Regulation (EEC) No. 1765/92 establishing a support system for producers of certain arable crops[56].

---

[53] Section 96(1) of the Act defines "the Minister".
[54] (OJ/SE 1968 (I) p. 187) as last amended by Council Regulation (EC) No. 2222/96
[55] As last amended by Council Regulation (EC) No. 1589/96.
[56] As last amended by Council Regulation (EC) No. 1598/96.

ARTICLE 2

Assessment of productive capacity of land

2.—(1) Paragraph (2) of this article has effect for the purpose of the assessment of the productive capacity of a unit of agricultural land, in order to determine whether that unit is a commercial unit of agricultural land within the meaning of subparagraph (1) of paragraph 3 of Schedule 6 to the Agricultural Holdings Act 1986.

(2) Where the land in question is capable, when farmed under competent management, of being used to produce any livestock, crop, fruit, etc. or as set-aside land, as is mentioned in any of the entries 1 to 8 in column 1 of the Schedule, then—
- (*a*) the unit of production prescribed in relation to that use of the land shall be the unit specified in column 2 of the Schedule opposite to that entry, and
- (*b*) the amount determined, for the period of 12 months beginning with 12th September 1997, as the net annual income from that unit of production in that period shall be the amount specified in column 3 of the Schedule opposite that unit of production.

(3) The Schedule has effect subject to the Notes to the Schedule.

Revocation

3. The Agricultural Holdings (Units of Production) Order 1996 is revoked.

28th July 1997

Parliamentary Secretary,
Ministry of Agriculture, Fisheries and Food

4th August 1997

Parliamentary Under Secretary of State,
Welsh Office

THE AGRICULTURAL HOLDINGS (UNITS OF PRODUCTION) ORDER 1997

SCHEDULE

Articles 1(2) and 2

PRESCRIBED UNITS OF PRODUCTION AND DETERMINATION OF NET ANNUAL INCOME

Column 1[(1)] Farming use	Column 2 Unit of production	Column 3[(2)] Net annual income from unit of production
		£
1. *Livestock*		
Dairy cows:		
Channel Islands breeds	cow	289
Other breeds	cow	345
Beef breeding cows:		
On eligible land under the Hill Livestock (Compensatory Allowances) Regulations 1996 [(1)]	cow	60[(1)]
On other land	cow	45[(1)]
Beef fattening cattle (semi-intensive)	head	83[(2)]
Dairy replacements	head	77[(3)]
Ewes:		
On eligible land under the Hill Livestock (Compensatory Allowances) Regulations 1996	ewe	25[(4)]
On other land	ewe	23[(5)]
Store lambs (including ewe lambs sold as shearlings)	head	2.05
Pigs:		
Sows and gilts in pig	sow or gilt	153
Porker	head	3.78
Cutter	head	6.73
Bacon	head	9.10
Poultry:		
Laying hens	bird	1.80
Broilers	bird	0.22
Point-of-lay pullets	bird	0.43
Turkeys	bird	1.93
2. *Farm arable crops*		

SCHEDULE

Barley	hectare	396[6]
Beans	hectare	153[7]
Herbage seed	hectare	270
Linseed	hectare	241[8]
Oats	hectare	330[9]
Oilseed rape	hectare	382[10]
Peas:		
Dried	hectare	197[11]
Vining	hectare	290
Potatoes:		
First early	hectare	1204
Maincrop (including seed)	hectare	1124
Sugar Beet	hectare	533
Wheat	hectare	438[12]
3. *Set-aside*[1]	hectare	83
4. *Outdoor horticultural crops*		
Broad beans	hectare	478
Brussels sprouts	hectare	1287
Cabbage, savoys and sprouting broccoli	hectare	1531
Carrots	hectare	2146
Cauliflower and winter broccoli	hectare	1050
Celery	hectare	4390
Leeks	hectare	3112
Lettuce	hectare	3444
Onions:		
Dry bulb	hectare	1851
Salad	hectare	4000
Outdoor bulbs	hectare	1919
Parsnips	hectare	2124
Rhubarb (natural)	hectare	2807
Turnips and swedes	hectare	1183
5. *Protected crops*		
Forced narcissi	1000 square metres	8400
Forced tulips	1000 square metres	6471
Mushrooms	1000 square metres	11861
6. *Orchard fruit*		
Cider	hectare	531
Cooking	hectare	1265
Dessert	hectare	1350
Cherries	hectare	1403
Pears	hectare	1058
Plums	hectare	981

7. *Soft fruit*		
Blackcurrants	hectare	1025
Gooseberries	hectare	1586
Raspberries	hectare	2892
Strawberries	hectare	2833
8. *Miscellaneous*		
Hops	hectare	2100

Notes

Note to column 1: [1] This refers to land which is set-aside under Article 2(5) of Council Regulation 1765/92, except where such land is used (in accordance with Article 7(4) of Council Regulation 1765/92) for the provision of materials for the manufacture within the Community of products not primarily intended for human or animal consumption.

Notes to column 3: [1] Deduct £117 from this figure in the case of animals for which the net annual income does not include a sum in respect of the premium for maintaining suckler cows (suckler cow premium) provided for in Article 4d of Council Regulation 805/68.

Add £29 to the figure in column 3 in the case of animals for which the net annual income includes a sum in respect of the lower rate of extensification premium provided for in Article 4h of Council Regulation 805/68.

Add £42 to the figure in column 3 in the case of animals for which the net annual income includes a sum in respect of the higher rate of extensification premium provided for in Article 4h of Council Regulation 805/68.

[2] This is the figure for animals which are kept for 12 months. Deduct £107 in the case of animals which are kept for 12 months and for which the net annual income does not include a sum in respect of the special premium for holding male bovine animals (beef special premium) provided for in Article 4b of Council Regulation 805/68.

Add £29 to the figure in column 3 in the case of animals which are kept for 12 months and for which the net annual income includes a sum in respect of the lower rate of extensification premium.

Add £42 to the figure in column 3 in the case of animals which would be kept for that period and for which the net annual income includes a sum in respect of the higher rate of extensification premium.

In the case of animals which are kept for less than 12 months and for which the net annual income does not include a sum in respect of beef special premium, the net annual income is to be calculated by deducting £107 from the figure in column 3 and then making a pro rata adjustment of the resulting figure.

In the case of animals which are kept for less than 12 months and for which the net annual income includes a sum in respect of beef special premium, the net annual income is to be calculated by first deducting £107 from the figure in column 3, then making a pro rata adjustment of the resulting figure, then adding to that figure the sum of £107 and (where the net annual income includes a sum in respect of extensification premium) the sum of £29 (where the extensification premium is paid at the lower rate) or £42 (where the extensification premium is paid at the higher rate).

SCHEDULE

(3) This indicates the figure for animals (irrespective of age) which are kept for 12 months. In the case of animals which are kept for less than 12 months a pro rata adjustment of this figure is to be made.

(4) Deduct £19 from this figure in the case of animals for which the net annual income does not include a sum in respect of the premium for offsetting income loss sustained by sheep meat producers (sheep annual premium) provided for in Article 5 of Council Regulation 3013/89.

(5) Deduct £13 from this figure in the case of animals for which the net annual income does not include a sum in respect of sheep annual premium.

(6) Deduct £256 from this figure in the case of land for which the net annual income does not include a sum in respect of the compensatory payment for which producers of arable crops may apply (area payment) provided for in Article 2 of Council Regulation 1765/92.

(7) Deduct £371 from this figure in the case of land for which the net annual income does not include a sum in respect of area payment.

(8) Deduct £497 from this figure in the case of land for which the net annual income does not include a sum in respect of area payment.

(9) Deduct £256 from this figure in the case of land for which the net annual income does not include a sum in respect of area payment.

(10) Deduct £432 from this figure in the case of land for which the net annual income does not include a sum in respect of area payment.

(11) Deduct £371 from this figure in the case of land for which the net annual income does not include a sum in respect of area payment.

(12) Deduct £257 from this figure in the case of land for which the net annual income does not include a sum in respect of area payment.

GENERAL NOTE

This Order prescribes units of production for the assessment of the productive capacity of agricultural land and sets out the amount which is to be regarded as the net annual income from each such unit for the year September 12, 1997 to September 11, 1998 inclusive. This Order supersedes the Agricultural Holdings (Units of Production) Order 1996 (S.I. 1996/No. 2163).

An assessment of the productive capacity of agricultural land is required in determining whether or not the land in question is a "commercial unit of agricultural land" for the purposes of the succession provisions in the Agricultural Holdings Act 1986 ("the 1986 Act"): see in particular sections 36(3) and 50(2).

A "commercial unit of agricultural land" is land which, when farmed under competent management, is capable of producing a net annual income which is not less than the aggregate of the average annual earnings of two full-time male agricultural workers aged 20 years or over (paragraph 3 of Schedule 6 to the 1986 Act). In determining this annual income figure, neither the system of farming carried out on a particular holding not historical data from that holding will necessarily be used. Instead, whenever a particular farming use mentioned in column 1 of the Schedule to this Order is relevant to this determination, the units of production and the net annual income specified in columns 2 and 3 respectively will form the basis of the assessment of the productive capacity of the land in question.

The net annual income figures in column 3 of the Schedule specify the net annual income from one unit of production. In some cases the net annual income is derived from a unit which will be on the land for the full twelve-month period. In other cases the net annual income is derived from a unit which will be on the land for only part of the year, and there may be more than one production cycle in the twelve-month period. The assessment of the productive capacity of the land will take account of the total production in the course of a year.

A.30   **THE AGRICULTURAL HOLDINGS (UNITS OF PRODUCTION ORDER) 1998**

(S.I. 1998 No. 2025)

The Minister of Agriculture, Fisheries and Food in relation to England and the Secretary of State in relation to Wales, in exercise of the powers conferred on them by paragraph 4 of Schedule 6 to the Agricultural Holdings Act 1986[57], and of all other powers enabling them in that behalf, hereby make the following Order:

Title, commencement and interpretation

1.—(1) This Order may be cited as the Agricultural Holdings (Units of Production) Order 1998 and shall come into force on 12th September 1998.

(2) Any reference in this Order to "the Schedule" is a reference to the Schedule to this Order.

(3) Any reference in this Order to a Community instrument is a reference to that instrument and any amendment of such instrument in force on the date this Order is made.

(4) In this Order:
"Council Regulation 805/68" means Council Regulation (EEC) No. 805/68 on the common organisation of the market in beef and veal.[58];
"Council Regulation 3013/89" means Council Regulation (EEC) No. 3013/89 on the common organisation of the market in sheepmeat and goatmeat[59];
"Council Regulation 1765/92" means Council Regulation (EEC) No. 1765/92 establishing a support system for producers of certain arable crops[60].

---

[57] 1986 c.5; section 96(1) of the Act defines the "Minister".
[58] OJ No. L148, 28.6.68, p.24 (OJ/SE 1968 (I) p.187) as last amended by Council Regulation (EC) No. 1633/98 (OJ No. L210, 28.7.98, p.17).
[59] OJ No. L289, 7.10.89, p.1 as last amended by Council Regulation (EC) No. 1589/96 (OJ No. L206, 16.8.96, p.25).
[60] OJ No. L181, 1.7.92, p.12 as last amended by Council Regulation (EC) No. 1625/98 (OJ No. L210, 28.7.98, p.3).

RULE 1

Assessment of productive capacity of land

2.—(1) Paragraphs (2) and (3) of this article have effect for the purpose of the assessment of the productive capacity of a unit of agricultural land, in order to determine whether that unit is a commercial unit of agricultural land within the meaning of subparagraph (1) of paragraph 3 of Schedule 6 to the Agricultural Holdings Act 1986.

(2) Where the land in question is capable, when farmed under competent management, of being used to produce any livestock, crop, fruit, etc., as is mentioned in any of the entries 1 to 7 in column 1 of the Schedule, then
    (a) the unit of production prescribed in relation to that use of the land shall be the unit specified in column 2 of the Schedule opposite to that entry, and
    (b) the amount determined, for the period of 12 months beginning with 12th September 1998, as the net annual income from that unit of production in that period shall be the amount specified in column 3 of the Schedule opposite that unit of production.

(3) Where land capable, when farmed under competent management, of producing a net annual income is designated as set aside land, as is mentioned in entry 8 in column 1 of the Schedule, then—
    (a) the unit of production prescribed in relation to that use of the land shall be the unit specified in column 2 of the Schedule opposite to that entry, and
    (b) the amount determined, for the period of 12 months beginning with 12th September 1998, as the net annual income from that unit of production in that period shall be the amount specified in column 3 of the Schedule opposite that unit of production.

(4) The Schedule has effect subject to the Notes to the Schedule.

Revocation

3. The Agricultural Holdings (Units of Production) Order 1997[61] is revoked.

Elliot Morley
Parliamentary Secretary,
8th August 1998   Ministry of Agriculture, Fisheries and Food

Signed by authority of the Secretary of State for Wales

Jon Owen Jones
Parliamentary Under Secretary of State.
6th August 1998   Welsh Office

---

[61] S.I. 1997/1962.

THE AGRICULTURAL HOLDINGS (UNITS OF PRODUCTION) ORDER 1998

SCHEDULE Articles 1(2) and 2

PRESCRIBED UNITS OF PRODUCTION AND DETERMINATION OF NET ANNUAL INCOME

Column 1 Farming use	Column 2 Unit of production	Column 3 Net annual income from unit of production
		£
1. *Livestock*		
Dairy cows:		
Channel Islands breeds	cow	269
Other breeds	cow	314
Beef breeding cows:		
On eligible land under the Hill Livestock (Compensatory Allowances) Regulations 1996[62]	cow	49(1)
On other land	cow	40(1)
Beef fattening cattle (semi-intensive)	head	66(2)
Dairy replacements	head	54(3)
Ewes:		
On eligible land under the Hill Livestock (Compensatory Allowances) Regulations 1996	ewe	25(4)
On other land	ewe	26(5)
Store lambs (including ewe lambs sold as shearlings	head	0.87
Pigs:		
Sows and gilts in pig	sow or gilt	135
Porker	head	3.17
Cutter	head	5.74
Bacon	head	7.98
Poultry:		
Laying hens	bird	1.47
Broilers	bird	0.18
Point-of-lay-pullets	bird	0.39
Turkeys	bird	1.75
2. *Farm arable crops*		
Barley	hectare	246(6)

[62] S.I. 1996/1500, as amended by S.I. 1997/33 and S.I. 1998/206.

SCHEDULE

Column 1 Farming use	Column 2 Unit of production	Column 3 Net annual income from unit of production
Beans	hectare	115(7)
Herbage seed	hectare	238
Linseed	hectare	172(8)
Oats	hectare	197(9)
Oilseed rape	hectare	294(10)
Peas:		
Dried	hectare	103(11)
Vining	hectare	257
Potatoes:		
First early	hectare	675
Maincrop (including seed)	hectare	833
Sugar Beet	hectare	398
Wheat	hectare	353(12)
3. *Outdoor horticultural crops*		
Broad beans	hectare	386
Brussels sprouts	hectare	1406
Cabbage, savoys and sprouting broccoli	hectare	1631
Carrots	hectare	2136
Cauliflower and winter broccoli	hectare	976
Celery	hectare	5891
Leeks	hectare	3004
Lettuce	hectare	3800
Onions:		
Dry bulb	hectare	989
Salad	hectare	4174
Outdoor bulbs	hectare	1735
Parsnips	hectare	2480
Rhubarb (natural)	hectare	2815
Turnips and swedes	hectare	1172
4. *Protected crops*		
Forced narcissi	1000 square metres	9425
Forced tulips	1000 square metres	7075
Mushrooms	1000 square metres	11868
5. *Orchard fruit*		
Apples:		
Cider	hectare	603
Cooking	hectare	1412
Dessert	hectare	1378

Column 1 Farming use	Column 2 Unit of production	Column 3 Net annual income from unit of production
Cherries	hectare	1297
Pears	hectare	1100
Plums	hectare	1030
6. *Soft fruit*		
Blackcurrants	hectare	1093
Gooseberries	hectare	1579
Raspberries	hectare	2974
Strawberries	hectare	3093
7. *Miscellaneous*		
Hops	hectare	1800
8. *Set-aside*	hectare	66

NOTES TO THE SCHEDULE Article 2(4)

Note to column 1

(1) This refers to land which is set-aside under Article 2(5) of Council Regulation 1765/92, except where such land is used (in accordance with Article 7(4) of Council Regulation 1765/92) for the provision of materials for the manufacture within the Community of products not primarily intended for human or animal consumption.

Notes to column 3

(1) Deduct £112 from this figure in the case of animals for which the net annual income does not include a sum in respect of the premium for maintaining suckler cows (suckler cow premium) provided for in Article 4d of Council Regulation 805/68.

Add £28 to the figure in column 3 in the case of animals for which the net annual income includes a sum in respect of the lower rate of extensification premium provided for in Article 4h of Council Regulation 805/68.

Add £40 to the figure in column 3 in the case of animals for which the net annual income includes a sum in respect of the higher rate of extensification premium provided for in Article 4h of Council Regulation 805/68.

(2) This is the figure for animals which are kept for 12 months.

Deduct £90 in the case of animals which are kept for 12 months and for which the net annual income does not include a sum in respect of the special premium for holding male bovine animals (beef special premium) provided for in Article 4b of Council Regulation 805/68.

Add £28 to the figure in column 3 in the case of animals which are kept for 12 months and for which the net annual income includes a sum in respect of the lower rate of extensification premium.

SCHEDULE

Add £40 to the figure in column 3 in the case of animals which would be kept for that period and for which the net annual income includes a sum in respect of the higher rate of extensification premium.

In the case of animals which are kept for less than 12 months and for which the net annual income does not include a sum in respect of beef special premium, the net annual income is to be calculated by deducting £90 from the figure in column 3 and then making a pro rata adjustment of the resulting figure.

In the case of animals which are kept for less than 12 months and for which the net annual income includes a sum in respect of beef special premium, the net annual income is to be calculated by first deducting £90 from the figure in column 3, then making a pro rata adjustment of the resulting figure, then adding to that figure the sum of £90 and (where the net annual income includes a sum in respect of extensification premium) the sum of £28 (where the extensification premium is paid at the lower rate) or £40 (where the extensification premium is paid at the higher rate).

(3) This indicates the figure for animals (irrespective of age) which are kept for 12 months. In the case of animals which are kept for less than 12 months a pro rata adjustment of this figure is to be made.

(4) Deduct £24 from this figure in the case of animals for which the net annual income does not include a sum in respect of the premium for offsetting income loss sustained by sheep meat producers (sheep annual premium) provided for in Article 5 of Council Regulation 3013/89.

(5) Deduct £19 from this figure in the case of animals for which the net annual income does not include a sum in respect of sheep annual premium.

(6) Deduct £241 from this figure in the case of land for which the net annual income does not include a sum in respect of the compensatory payment for which producers of arable crops may apply (area payment) provided for in Article 2 of Council Regulation 1765/92.

(7) Deduct £349 from this figure in the case of land for which the net annual income does not include a sum in respect of area payment.

(8) Deduct £467 from this figure in the case of land for which the net annual income does not include a sum in respect of area payment.

(9) Deduct £240 from this figure in the case of land for which the net annual income does not include a sum in respect of area payment.

(10) Deduct £331 from this figure in the case of land for which the net annual income does not include a sum in respect of area payment.

(11) Deduct £349 from this figure in the case of land for which the net annual income does not include a sum in respect of area payment.

(12) Deduct £241 from this figure in the case of land for which the net annual income does not include a sum in respect of area payment.

GENERAL NOTE

This Order prescribes units of production for the assessment of the productive capacity of agricultural land and sets out the amount which is to be regarded as the net annual income from each such unit for the year 12th September 1998 to 11th September 1999 inclusive. This Order supersedes the Agricultural Holdings (Units of Production) Order 1997 (S.I. 1997/1962).

THE AGRICULTURAL HOLDINGS (UNITS OF PRODUCTION) ORDER 1998

An assessment of the productive capacity of agricultural land is required in determining whether or not the land in question is a "commercial unit of agricultural land" for the purposes of the succession provisions in the Agricultural Holdings Act 1986 ("the 1986 Act"): see in particular sections 36(3) and 50(2). A "commercial unit of agricultural land" is land which, when farmed under competent management, is capable of producing a net annual income which is not less than the aggregate of the average annual earnings of two full-time male agricultural workers aged 20 years or over (paragraph 3 of Schedule 6 to the 1986 Act). In determining this annual income figure, neither the system of farming carried out on a particular holding nor historical data from that holding will necessarily be used. Instead, whenever a particular farming use mentioned in column 1 of the Schedule to this Order is relevant to this determination, the units of production and the net annual income specified in columns 2 and 3 respectively will form the basis of the assessment of the productive capacity of the land in question.

The net annual income figures in column 3 of the Schedule specify the net annual income from one unit of production. In some cases the net annual income is derived from a unit which will be on the land for the full twelve-month period. In other cases the net annual income is derived from a unit which will be on the land for only part of the year, and there may be more than one production cycle in the twelve-month period. The assessment of the productive capacity of the land will take account of the total production in the course of a year.

PART IV

EEC REGULATIONS

A.31

PAGE

Council Regulation (EEC) No. 3950/92, of 28 December 1992, establishing an additional levy in the milk and milk products sector   967

Commission Regulation (EEC) No. 536/93, of 9 March 1993 laying down detailed rules on the application of the additional levy on milk and milk products   978

The Treaty of Rome as amended by the Treaty of Amsterdam, excerpt from "The Treaty of Amsterdam in Perspective - Consolidated Treaty on European Union", Title II, pages 31-33   988

THE COUNCIL OF THE EUROPEAN COMMUNITIES

COUNCIL REGULATION (EEC) NO 3950/92 OF 28 DECEMBER 1992 ESTABLISHING AN ADDITIONAL LEVY IN THE MILK AND MILK PRODUCTS SECTOR

A.32

THE COUNCIL OF THE EUROPEAN COMMUNITIES,

Having regard to the Treaty establishing the European Economic Community, and in particular Article 43 thereof,

Having regard to the proposal from the Commission (1),

Having regard to the opinion of the European Parliament (2),

Whereas, pursuant to Council Regulation (EEC) No 856/84 of 31 March 1984 amending Regulation (EEC) No 804/68 on the common organization of the market in milk and milk products (3), an additional levy scheme was introduced from 2 April 1984 in the said sector; whereas the purpose of this scheme, introduced for nine years and due to expire of 31 March 1993, was to reduce the imbalance between supply and demand on the milk and milk-products market and the resulting structural surpluses; whereas the scheme remains necessary in the future in order to achieve a better market balance; whereas it should therefore continue to be applied for seven further consecutive 12-month periods starting on 1 April 1993;

Whereas, in order to make full use of the experience gained in this area and in the interests of simplification and clarification with a view to ensuring the legal certainty of producers and other parties concerned, the basic rules of the extended scheme should be laid down in a separate regulation, their scope and diversity should be reduced and Council Regulation (EEC) No 2074/92 of 30 June 1992 establishing an additional levy on the milk and milk-products sector (4), adopted as an interim measure by the Council, and Regulation (EEC) No 857/84 of 31 March 1984 laying down general rules for the application of the levy referred to in Article 5c of Regulation (EEC) No 804/68 in the milk and milk-products sector (5), should both be repealed, without prejudice to the obligations and undertakings entered into under the said Regulation;

Whereas the method adopted in 1984, consisting of the application of a levy to quantities of milk collected or sold for direct consumption above a certain guarantee threshold, must be maintained; whereas the said threshold is expressed for each Member State by a guaranteed total quantity which may not be exceeded by the sum of the individually allocated quantities for both deliveries and sales for direct consumption; whereas the quantities are established for the seven periods as from 1 April 1993 and take account of the various factors relating to the scheme in the past;

Whereas in particular, a Community reserve was created at the start of the scheme to take account of the difficulties created for certain Member States by the implementation of a scheme for controlling milk production; whereas the said reserve had been increased several times to meet the special needs of certain Member States and certain producers; whereas in the light of this experience the various parts of the Community reserve should be incorporated into the guaranteed total quantities and the reserve be abolished;

Whereas the Council has decided, in the context of the reform of the common agricultural policy, to take a definitive decision on the level of the total quantities to apply during the first of the two periods of twelve months, in the light, in particular, of a report on the market situation which the Commission will present before each of these periods;

Whereas if any of the total guaranteed quantities is overrun, the consequence for the Member State is that the producers who contributed to the overrun must pay the levy; whereas the levy on deliveries and sales for direct consumption should be fixed at 115% of the target price for milk; whereas a difference in rates is no longer justified if producers are placed in a comparable position as regards the calculation of the levy;

Whereas, in order to keep the management of the scheme sufficiently flexible, provision should be made for individual overruns to be equalled out over all the individual reference quantities of the same type within the territory of a Member State; whereas in the case of deliveries, which constitute nearly all the quantities marketed, the need to ensure that the levy is fully effective throughout the Community justifies, in principle, continuing to allow Member States the choice between two methods of equalling out overruns of individual reference quantities, bearing in mind the variety of milk production and collection structures; whereas, in this connection, Member States should be authorized not to reallocate unused reference quantities at the end of a period, whether nationally or between purchasers, and to use the amount collected in excess of the levy due for funding national restructuring programmes and/or to refund it to producers of certain categories or producers who find themselves in an exceptional situation;

Whereas, in order to avoid, as in the past, long delays between collection and payment of the levy, which are incompatible with the scheme's objective, provision should be made for the purchaser, who seems in the best position to carry out the necessary operations, to be liable for the levy, and for him to be given the means to collect the levy from the producers who owe it;

Whereas the individual reference quantity should be defined as the quantity available, irrespective of any quantities which may have been transferred temporarily, on 31 March 1993, the expiry date of the nine initial periods of application of the levy scheme; whereas the principles or provisions pursuant to which the said quantity must or may be reduced or increased under the extended scheme should be specified;

Whereas, therefore, under the rules for determining the individual reference quantities, account should be taken of producers who have provisionally received a specific quantity under the scheme in the past;

Whereas it has been agreed that application of the arrangements to control milk production must not jeopardize the restructuring of agricultural holdings in the territory of the former German Democratic Republic; whereas the difficulties encountered make it necessary to extend for a further period the flexibility introduced into those arrangements for that territory, while ensuring that it remains the sole beneficiary;

Whereas reference quantities for deliveries and direct sales should be adapted to reflect economic realities and whereas a producer should therefore be entitled to have a reference quantity increased or established where another is reduced or abolished commensurately, on condition that the request is duly justified by the need to take account of changes in his marketing requirements;

THE COUNCIL OF THE EUROPEAN COMMUNITIES,

Whereas experience has shown that that implementation of this scheme presupposes the existence of a national reserve to accommodate all those quantities which, for whatever reasons, are not, or are no longer, allocated individually; whereas a Member State may need to have reference quantities available to cater for special situations, determined by objective criteria; whereas it should be authorized, to this end, to top up its national reserve, especially following a linear reduction in all reference quantities;

Whereas the temporary transfer of parts of individual reference quantities in Member States which have authorized this has proven to be an improvement to the scheme; whereas this facility should therefore be extended to all producers; whereas, however, implementation of this principle should not stand in the way of further structural change and adjustment, nor fail to take account of the resulting administrative difficulties;

Whereas when the additional levy system was brought in in 1984, the principle was established that when an undertaking was sold, leased or transferred by inheritance, the corresponding reference quantity was transferred to the purchaser, tenant or heir; whereas this original decision should not be changed; whereas, however, national provisions to safeguard the legitimate interests of the parties should be implemented in all cases of transfer, where the parties are not in agreement;

Whereas, in order to continue restructuring milk production and improving the environment, certain derogations to the principle linking reference quantities to holdings should be extended, and Member States should be authorized to continue implementing national restructuring programmes and to organize some degree of mobility for reference quantities within a given geographical area, on the basis of objective criteria;

Whereas the purpose of the levy provided for in this Regulation is to stabilize the market in milk products; whereas the revenue accruing from this Regulation should therefore be used for financing expenditure in the milk sector,

HAS ADOPTED THIS REGULATION:[*]

ARTICLE 1

For seven new consecutive periods of twelve months commencing on 1 April 1993, an additional levy shall be payable by producers of cow's milk on quantities of milk or milk equivalent delivered to a purchaser or sold directly for consumption during the 12-month period in question in excess of a quantity to be determined.

The levy shall be 115% of the target price for milk.

ARTICLE 2

1. The levy shall be payable on all quantities of milk or milk equivalent marketed during the 12-month period in question in excess of the relevant quantity referred to in Article 3. It shall be shared between the producers who contributed to the overrun.

Note
[*] Printed as current as at April 1998. Last incorporated amendment by Regulation No. 614/97.

COUNCIL REGULATION (EEC) NO. 3950/92 OF 28 DECEMBER 1992

In accordance with a decision of the Member State, the contribution of producers towards the levy payable shall be established, after the unused reference quantities have been reallocated or not, either at the level of the purchaser, in the light of the overrun remaining after unused reference quantities have been allocated in proportion to the reference quantities of each producer, or at national level, in the light of the overrun in the reference quantity of each individual producer.

2. As regards deliveries, before a date and in accordance with detailed rules to be laid down, the purchaser liable for the levy shall pay to the competent body of the Member State the amount payable, which he shall deduct from the price of milk paid to producers who owe the levy or, failing this, collect by any appropriate means.

Whereas a purchaser replaces in whole or in part one or more purchasers, the individual reference quantities available to producers shall be taken into account for the remainder of the twelve-month period in progress, less quantities already delivered and account being taken of their fat content. The same provisions shall apply where a producer transfers from one purchaser to another.

Where quantities delivered by a producer exceed his reference quantity, the purchaser shall be authorized, by way of an advance on the levy payable, in accordance with detailed rules laid down by the Member State, to deduct an amount from the price of the milk in respect of any delivery by that producer in excess of his reference quantity.

3. As regards direct sales, the producer shall pay the levy payable to the competent body of the Member State before a date and in accordance with rules to be laid down.

4. Where the levy is payable and the amount collected is greater than that levy, the Member State may use the excess to finance the measures referred to in the first indent of Article 8 and/or redistribute it to producers who fall within priority categories established by the Member State on the basis of objective criteria to be determined or who are affected by an exceptional situation resulting from a national provision unconnected with this scheme.

ARTICLE 3

[1. The sum of the individual reference quantities of the same type may not exceed the corresponding total quantities for each Member State.

2. The following total quantities shall be fixed without prejudice to possible review in the light of the general market situation and particular conditions existing in certain member states:

ARTICLE 3

Member State	Deliveries	Direct sales
Belgium	3 109 639	200 792
Denmark	4 454 639	709
Germany (1)	27 764 778	100 038
Greece	629 817	696
Spain	5 438 118	128 832
France	23 749 650	486 148
Ireland	5 235 723	10 041
Italy	9 698 399	231 661
Luxembourg	268 098	951
Netherlands	10 988 039	86 653
Austria	2 382 377	367 000
Portugal	1 835 461	37 000
Finland	2 384 327	10 000
Sweden	3 300 000	3 000
United Kingdom	14 338 375	251 672

(1) Of which 6, 244 566 tonnes for deliveries by producers in the new Länder and 8,801 tonnes for direct sales in the new Länder.

The increase in the total quantities for Belgium, Denmark, Germany, France, Ireland, Luxembourg, The Netherlands and the United Kingdom shall be granted in order to permit the allocation of additional reference quantities to: - producers who, by virtue of the second indent of Article 3a (1) of Regulation (EEC) No. 857/84 (*), had been excluded from allocation of a special reference quantity; producers situated in the mountain areas as defined in Article 3 (3) of Directive 75/268/EEC (**) or to the producers referred to in Article 5 of this regulation or to all producers. The increase in the total quantity for Portugal shall be granted as a matter of priority to contribute towards satisfying the requests for additional reference quantities from producers whose production during the 1990 reference year was substantially affected by exceptional events which took place during the period 1988 to 1990 or to the producers referred to in article 5. The increase in total quantities of deliveries granted for the period 1993/94 for Greece, Spain and Italy shall be established for Spain and shall be extended for the period 1994/95 for Greece and Italy. The total quantity of deliveries for Italy includes a reserve of 347,701 tonnes for allocation, in so far as necessary and in agreement with the Commission, of reference quantities to producers who have brought legal proceedings against a national administration following withdrawal of their reference quantities and obtain judgment in their favour. The increase in the total quantities of deliveries granted for the period 1994/95 for Greece and Italy shall be established with effect from 1995/96. The overall quantity for the Austrian deliveries quota may be increased to compensate Austrian 'slom' producers, up to a maximum of 180, 000 tonnes, to be allocated in accordance with community legislation. This reserve must be non-transferable and used exclusively on behalf of producers whose right to take up production again will be affected as a result of accession. The overall quantity for the Finnish deliveries quota may be increased to compensate Finnish 'slom' producers, up to a maximum of 200, 000 tonnes, to be allocated in accordance with community legislation. This reserve must be non-transferable and used exclusively on behalf of producers whose right to take up production again will be affected as a result of accession. The increase in overall quantities, and the conditions under which the individual reference quantities provided for in the two preceding subparagraphs shall be granted, shall be decided upon in accordance with the procedure referred to in article 11.

3. When the Council decides to adjust the abovementioned total quantities to the market situation, the adjustments shall be expressed as a percentage of the total quantities to be complied with for the preceding period.]

Note

The words in square brackets were added, amended or deleted by council Regulations No. 748/93, No. 1560/93, No. 697/94, No. 1883/94, 194NN01/05/B1, No. 630/95, No. 1552/95, No. 1552/96, No. 204/96, No. 635/96, No. 1109/96, No. 614/96.

ARTICLE 4

1. The individual reference quantity available on the holding shall be equal to the quantity available on 31 March 1993 and shall be adjusted, where appropriate, for each of the periods concerned, so that the sum of the individual reference quantities of the same type does not exceed the corresponding global quantities referred to in Article 3, taking account of any reductions made for allocation to the national reserve provided for in Article 5.

[However, for Austria, Finland and Norway, the date of 31 March 1993 shall be replaced by that of 31 March 1995 and for Sweden by that of 31 March 1996.]

2. Individual reference quantities shall be increased or established at the duly justified request of producers to take account of changes affecting their deliveries and/or direct sales. The increase or establishment of such a reference quantity shall be subject to a corresponding reduction or cancellation of the other reference quantity the producer owns. Such adjustments may not lead to an increase in the sum of the deliveries and direct sales referred to in Article 3 for the Member State concerned.

Where the individual reference quantities undergo a definitive change, the quantities referred to in Article 3 shall be adjusted in accordance with the procedure laid down in Article 11.

3. If a producer who has provisionally received a specific individual reference quantity pursuant to the last subparagraph of Article 3a(1) of Regulation (EEC) No 857/84 can prove before 1 July 1993 to the satisfaction

of the competent authority that he has actually resumed sales and/or deliveries and that his direct sales and/or his deliveries have in the course of the preceding twelve months reached a level equal to or higher than 80% of the provisional reference quantity, the specific reference quantity shall be allocated definitively to him. Otherwise, the reference quantity definitively allocated shall be equal to the quantity actually delivered or sold direct.

Actual deliveries and/or direct sales shall be determined in the light of the trend in production on the producer's holding, seasonal conditions and any exceptional circumstances.

4. In the case of agricultural holdings situated in the territory of the former German Democratic Republic, the reference quantity may be allocated provisionally for the period from 1 April 1993 to 31 March 1994, provided that the quantity thus allocated is not modified during that period.

[However, in order to complete the restructuring of the said holdings, the first subparagraph shall continue to apply until the end of the period 1997/98.]

Note
The words in square brackets have been added; amended or deleted by Regulations 194NN01/05/B1 and No. 1883/94.

ARTICLE 5

[1. Within the quantities referred to in Article 3, the Member State may replenish the national reserve following an across-the-board reduction in all the individual reference quantities in order to grant additional or specific quantities to producers determined in accordance with objective criteria agreed with the Commission, without prejudice to the provisions of the second and third subparagraphs of Article 3 (2).;]

Without prejudice to Article 6 (1), reference quantities available to producers who have not marketed milk or other milk products for one of the twelve-month periods shall be allocated to the national reserve and may be reallocated in accordance with the first subparagraph. Where the producer resumes production of milk or other milk products within a period to be determined by the Member State, he shall be granted a reference quantity in accordance with Article 4 (1) no later than 1 April following the date of his application.

Note
The words in square brackets were added, amended or deleted by Regulation No. 1560/93.

ARTICLE 6

1. Before a date that they shall determine and by 31 December at the latest, Member States shall authorize, for the 12-month period concerned,

temporary transfers of individual reference quantities which producers who are entitled thereto do not intend to use. However, the reference quantities referred to in Article 4 (3) may not be the subject of such temporary transfers until 31 March 1995.

Member States may vary transfer operations depending on the category of producers or dairy production structures, may limit them at the level of the purchaser within regions and may determine to what extent transfer operations may be renewed.

2. Any Member State may decide not to implement paragraph 1 on the basis of one or both of the following criteria:

- the need to facilitate structural developments and adjustments,
- overriding administrative needs.

ARTICLE 7

1. Reference quantities available on a holding shall be transferred with the holding in the case of sale, lease or transfer by inheritance to the producers taking it over in accordance with detailed rules to be determined by the Member States taking account of the areas used for dairy production or other objective criteria and, where applicable, of any agreement between the parties. Any part of the reference quantity which is not transferred with the holding shall be added to the national reserve.

The same provisions shall apply to other cases of transfers involving comparable legal effects for producers.
However:

(a) until 30 June 1994, the reference quantity referred to in Article 4 (3) shall be added to the national reserve in the case of sale or leasing of the holding;

(b) where land is transferred to public authorities and/or for use in the public interest, or where the transfer is carried out for non-agricultural purposes, Member States shall provide that the measures necessary to protect the legitimate interests of the parties are implemented, and in particular that the departing producer is in a position to continue milk production, if such is his intention.

2. Where there is no agreement between the parties, in the case of rural leases due to expire without any possibility of renewal on similar terms, or in situations involving comparable legal effects, the reference quantities

Article 7

available on the holdings in question shall be transferred in whole or in part to the producers taking them over, in accordance with provisions adopted or to be adopted by the Member States, taking account of the legitimate interests of the parties.

Article 8

With a view to completing restructuring of milk production at national, regional or collection area level, or to environmental improvement, Member States may take one or more of the following actions in accordance with detailed rules which they shall lay down taking account of the legitimate interests of the parties:

- grant compensation in one or more annual instalments to producers who undertake to abandon definitively all or part of their milk production and place the reference quantities thus released in the national reserve,

- determine on the basis of objective criteria the conditions under which producers may obtain, in return for payment, at the beginning of a 12-month period, the reallocation by the competent authority or by the body designated by that authority, of reference quantities released definitively at the end of the preceding twelve-month period by other producers in return for compensation in one or more annual instalments equal to the abovementioned payment,

- provide, in the case of land transferred with a view to improving the environment, for the allocation of the reference quantity available on the holding concerned to the departing producer if he intends continuing milk production,

- determine, on the basis of objective criteria, the regions or collection areas within which the transfer of reference quantities between certain producer categories without transfer of the corresponding land is authorized, with the aim of improving the structure of milk production,

- authorize, upon application by the producer to the competent authority or the body designated by that authority, the transfer of reference quantities without transfer of the corresponding land, or vice versa, with the aim of improving the structure of milk production at the level of the holding or to allow for extensification of production.

However, until 30 June 1994, producers with a reference quantity as referred to in Article 4 (3) may not benefit from the provisions of this Article, with the exception of the third indent.

[For the implementation, during the 1993/94 period in each Member State, of a programme for the restructuring of milk production, and, if necessary, to replenish the national reserve with a view to allocating the additional quantities referred to in the first indent of the second subparagraph of Article 3 (2), Community financing shall be granted, limited to the amounts in ecus indicated below; the method of

COUNCIL REGULATION (EEC) NO. 3950/92 OF 28 DECEMBER 1992

applying such financing and in particular the maximum amount of the indemnity shall be adopted in accordance with the procedure referred to in Article 11:

Belgium 1 106 613 Denmark 1 678 207 Germany 10 460 461 Greece 235 842 Spain 1 959 115 France 8 854 814 Ireland 1 970 627 Italy 3 470 719 Luxembourg 101 007 Netherlands 4 133 772 Portugal 679 994 United Kingdom 5 348 829

These amounts shall be converted into national currencies with the aid of the conversion rate applicable for the entry in the accounts of the expenditure of the general budget of the European Communities valid on 20 July 1993.

The financing of payments made under this programme shall be deemed intervention within the meaning of Article 3 of Regulation (EEC) No 729/70 (*).

The expenditure commitment must be made by virtue of the appropriations of the 1993 financial year, at the request of the Member States and by 30 September 1993 at the latest. The payments made by the disbursing agencies must be effected before 15 October 1994.]

Note
The words in square brackets have been added, amended or deleted by Council Regulation No. 1560/93.

ARTICLE 9

For the purposes of this Regulation:
(a) 'milk' means the produce of the milking of one or more cows;
(b) 'other milk products' means cream, butter and cheese in particular;
(c) 'producer' means a natural or legal person or a group of natural or legal persons farming a holding within the geographical territory of [a Member State]:

- selling milk or other milk products directly to the consumer,
- and/or supplying the purchaser;

(d) 'holding' means all production units operated by the single producer and located within the geographical territory of [a Member State];
(e) 'purchaser' means an undertaking or grouping which purchases milk or other milk products from a producer:

- to treat or process them,
- to sell them to one or more undertakings treating or processing milk or other milk products.

However, any group of purchasers in the same geographical area which carries out administrative and accounting operations necessary for the payment of the levy on behalf of its members shall be regarded as a purchaser. For the purposes of applying this provision, Greece shall be deemed a single geographical area and it may deem an official body to be a group of purchasers as referred to above;

(f) 'undertaking treating or processing milk or other milk products' means an undertaking or grouping which is involved in collection, packaging, storage,

ARTICLE 9

chilling and processing operations or whose dairying activities are restricted to one of those operations;

(g) 'delivery' means any delivery of milk or other milk products, whether the transport is carried out by the producer, a purchaser, an undertaking processing or treating such products or a third party;

(h) 'milk or milk equivalent sold directly for consumption' means milk or milk products converted into milk equivalent, sold or transferred free without going through an undertaking treating or processing milk or other milk products.

Note
The words in square brackets have been added or amended by Council Regulation No. 1560/93.

ARTICLE 10

The levy shall be considered as intervention to stabilize agricultural markets and shall be used to finance expenditure in the milk sector.

ARTICLE 11

The detailed rules for the application of this Regulation and in particular the characteristics of milk, including fat content, which are considered representative for the purposes of establishing the quantities of milk delivered or purchased shall be adopted in accordance with the procedure provided for in Article 30 of Regulation (EEC) No 804/68 (1).

[However, for Norway, Austria, Finland and Sweden, the characteristics of the milk considered as representative shall be those of the 1992 calendar year, and the national average representative fat content of the milk delivered shall be set at 3,87% for Norway, at 4,03% for Austria, at 4,34% for Finland and at 4,33% for Sweden.]

Note
The words in square brackets have been added, amended or deleted by Regulation No. 194NN01/05/B1.

ARTICLE 12

Regulations (EEC) Nos 857/84 and 2074/92 are hereby repealed.

ARTICLE 13

This Regulation shall enter into force on the third day following that of its publication in the Official Journal of the European Communities.

It shall apply from 1 April 1993.

This Regulation shall be binding in its entirety and directly applicable in all Member States.

Done at Brussels, 28 December 1992.
For the Council
The President
J. GUMMER

A.33 COMMISSION REGULATION (EEC) NO 536/93 OF 9 MARCH 1993 LAYING DOWN DETAILED RULES ON THE APPLICATION OF THE ADDITIONAL LEVY ON MILK AND MILK PRODUCTS

THE COMMISSION OF THE EUROPEAN COMMUNITIES,

Having regard to the Treaty establishing the European Economic Community,

Having regard to Council Regulation (EEC) No 3950/92 of 28 December 1992 establishing an additional levy in the milk and milk products sector (1), and in particular Article 11 thereof,

Having regard to Council Regulation (EEC) No 3813/92 of 28 December 1992 on the unit of account and the conversion rates to be applied for the purposes of the common agricultural policy (2), and in particular Article 1 thereof,

Whereas the application of the arrangements regarding the additional levy on milk and milk products were extended in accordance with Regulation (EEC) No 3950/92 for a further seven consecutive 12 month periods from 1 April 1993; whereas that Regulation repeals the previous provisions concerned and replaces them; whereas new detailed rules for the application of Regulation (EEC) No 3950/92 should accordingly be laid down and the detailed rules which the Commission adopted under the previous arrangements should be repealed;

Whereas this Regulation concerns firstly the additional factors necessary for the final calculation of the levy payable by producers, secondly the measures to ensure payment of the levy in good time and lastly the rules on checks permitting verification of proper collection of the levy;

Whereas the characteristics of milk which are considered to be representative and in particular the way its fat content is to be taken into account when the final quantities is based on a reference fat content, which must, like the individual reference quantity to which it is related, be that available on 31 March 1993; whereas special provisions must cover cases where the reference quantity for deliveries is increased or established by converting a reference quantity for direct sales; whereas the experience gained demonstrates the need for very specific rules applicable to milk producers beginning production;

Whereas it is necessary to make it quite clear that under no circumstances can individual downward corrections relating to the fat content of delivered milk result in a deduction from the levy payment of any quantity in excess of the guaranteed total quantity in a Member State;

Whereas experience gained has shown that major delays in both the transmission of figures on collections or direct sales and payment of the levy, have prevented the arrangements from being fully effective; whereas, therefore, lessons should be learned from the past and the necessary conclusions drawn by laying down strict requirements as regards notification and payment deadlines and providing for penalties where deadlines are not met;

Whereas pursuant to Article 2 (4) of Regulation (EEC) No 3950/92 the Commission is responsible for laying down criteria for determining which priority categories of producer are to benefit from reimbursement of the levy where the Member State has decided not to fully reallocate unused quantities in its territory; whereas a Member State may only be authorized to use other criteria, in agreement

THE COMMISSION OF THE EUROPEAN COMMUNITIES

with the Commission, in the event that the criteria laid down by the Commission cannot be fully applied in that Member State;

Whereas under Regulation (EEC) No 3950/92 purchasers bear chief responsibility for the correct implementation of the arrangements; whereas it is therefore essential that Member States approve the purchasers operating in their territory;

Whereas, lastly, the Member States must have suitable means of conducting ex-post checks to verify whether and to what extent the levy has been collected in accordance with the provisions in force; whereas such checks must involve at least a certain number of measures which should be specified;

Whereas the Management Committee for Milk and Milk Products has not delivered an opinion within the time limit set by its chairman,

HAS ADOPTED THIS REGULATION:[*]

ARTICLE 1

For the purposes of calculating the additional levy introduced by Regulation (EEC) No 3950/92:

1. Within the meaning of Article 2 (1) of that Regulation 'quantities of milk or milk equivalent marketed' in a Member State means all quantities of milk or milk equivalent which leave any holding in the territory of that Member State.

Quantities presented by producers for treatment or processing under contract shall be deemed deliveries;

2. The equivalence formulae to be used shall be:

   - 1 kg cream = 26,3 kg milk × % fat content of cream 100
   - 1 kg butter = 22,5 kg milk.

In the case of cheese and all other milk products, Member States may determine equivalences using the dry-extract content and the fat content of the types of cheese or products concerned or fix the quantities of milk equivalent on a flat-rate basis by reference to the number of dairy cows held by the producer and an average milk yield per cow representative of the herd.

If the producer can provide proof to the satisfaction of the competent authority of the quantities actually used for the manufacture of the products in question, the Member State shall use such proof in place of the abovementioned equivalences;

3. Where wholly or partly skimmed milk is delivered, the producer must prove to the satisfaction of the competent authority that the fat content of the milk has been used to calculate the levy. In the absence of such proof, deliveries of such milk shall be treated as whole milk when the levy is calculated;

---

[*] Printed as current as at April 1998. Last incorporated amendment by Regulation No. 2186/96.

COMMISSION REGULATION (EEC) NO. 536/93 OF 9 MARCH 1993

[4. The target price shall be that applying on the last day of the 12 month period concerned.]

Note
The words in square brackets have been amended by Regulation No. 1456/93.

ARTICLE 2

1. The characteristics of milk, including fat content, considered representative within the meaning of Article 11 of Regulation (EEC) No 3950/92 shall be those associated with the individual reference quantity available on 31 March 1993.
[Where the individual reference quantity is changed, the following provisions shall apply:

   (a) the representative fat content of milk shall remain unchanged where additional reference quantities are allocated from the national reserve;

   (b) where, pursuant to Article 4 (2) of Regulation (EEC) No 3950/92, the reference quantity for deliveries is increased or established, the representative fat content associated with the reference quantity converted into deliveries shall be 3, 8%.

   However; the representative fat content of the reference quantity for deliveries shall remain unchanged if the producer provides justification therefore to the satisfaction of the competent authority;

   (c) where Articles 6 and 7 and the third, fourth and fifth indents of Article 8 of Regulation (EEC) No 3950/92 are applied, the representative fat content shall be transferred with the reference quantity with which it is associated;

   (d) in the cases referred to in the first subparagraph of (b) and (c), the resulting representative fat content shall be equal to the average of the initial and transferred or converted representative contents, weighted by the initial and transferred or converted reference quantities;

   (e) in the case of producers whose entire reference quantities come from the national reserve and who have commenced production after 1 April 1992, the representative fat content of their milk shall be the average fat content of milk delivered during the first 12 months of production. However, if the representative content exceeds the average national fat content of milk collected in the Member State during the twelve-month reference period during which they commenced production:

Article 2

- the producers concerned may not benefit from the negative correction provided for in the second indent of paragraph 2 unless they provide supporting evidence to the contrary,
- where Articles 6 and 7 and the fourth and fifth indents of Article 8 of Regulation (EEC) No 3950/92 are applied, the representative fat content of milk associated with the transferred reference quantity shall be reduced to the abovementioned national average content.]

Note
The words in square brackets have been added, amended or deleted by Regulation No. 470/94.

2. In order to draw up the definitive statement for purposes of the levy as referred to in Article 3 for each producer, the average fat content of the milk and/or milk equivalent he has delivered shall be compared with the representative fat content of his production:

- if the difference is positive, the quantity of milk or milk equivalent delivered shall be increased by 0, 18, % per 0, 1 gram of additional fat per kilogram of milk,
- if the difference is negative, the quantity of milk or milk equivalent delivered shall be reduced by 0, 18 % per 0, 1 gram of fat lacking per kilogram of milk.

where the quantity of milk delivered is expressed in litres, the 0, 18 % adjustment per 0,1 gram of fat content shall be multiplied by the coefficient 0,971.

3. If the quantity of milk collected in a Member State is greater than the quantity as corrected in accordance with paragraph 2, the levy shall be payable on the difference between the quantity collected and the guaranteed total quantity of deliveries available in the Member State.

Article 3

1. At the end of each of the periods referred to in Article 1 of Regulation (EEC) No 3950/92, the purchaser shall establish a statement for each producer showing, opposite the producer's reference quantity and the representative fat content of his production, the quantity and fat content of the milk and/or milk equivalent which he has delivered during the period.

In the case of leap years, the quantity of milk or milk equivalent shall be reduced by one sixtieth of the quantities delivered in February and March.

2. Before 15 May each year, the purchasers shall forward to the competent authority of the Member State a summary of the statements drawn up for each producer or, where appropriate, by decision of the Member State, the total quantity, the quantity corrected in accordance with Article 2 (2) and average fat content of the milk and/or milk equivalent delivered to it by producers and the sum of the individual reference quantities and the average representative fat content of such producers' production.

Where that time limit is not observed, the purchaser shall be liable to a penalty equal to the amount of the levy due for a 0,1% overrun on the quantities of milk and milk equivalent delivered to them by producers. Such penalty may not exceed ECU 20 000.

3. Member States may provide that the competent authority shall notify the purchaser of the levies payable by him after reallocating, or not, by decision of the Member State, all or part of the unused reference quantities either directly to the producers concerned or to purchasers with a view to their subsequent allocation among the producers concerned.

4. Before 1 September each year, the purchaser liable for levies shall pay the competent body the amount due in accordance with rules laid down by the Member State.

Where the time limit for payment is not met, the sums due shall bear interest at a rate per annum fixed by the Member State and which shall not be lower than the rate of interest which the latter applies for the recovery of wrongly paid amounts.

Article 4

1. In the case of direct sales, at the end of each of the periods referred to in Article 1 of Regulation (EEC) No 3950/92, the producer shall make a declaration summarizing by product the quantities of milk and/or other milk products sold directly for consumption and/or to wholesalers, cheese maturers and the retail trade.

In the case of leap years, the quantity of milk or milk equivalent shall be reduced by 1 / 60 of the quantities sold directly in February and March or by 1 / 336 of the quantities sold directly in the 12-month period in question.

2. Before 15 May each year, the producer shall forward declarations to the competent authority of the Member State.

[Where that time limit is not observed, the producer shall be liable to the levy on all the quantities of milk and milk equivalent sold directly in excess of his reference quantity or, where there is no overrun, to a penalty equal to the levy due for a 0,1% overrun of his reference quantity. That penalty may not, however, be less than ECU 20 or exceed ECU 1 000.]

Article 4

Where a declaration is not submitted before 1 July, the second paragraph of Article 5 of Regulation (EEC) No 3950/92 shall apply 30 days after the Member State has served notice.

3. The Member State may provide that the competent authority shall notify the producer of the levies payable by him after reallocating, or not, by decision of the Member State, all or part of the unused reference quantities to the producers concerned.

4. Before 1 September each year, the producer shall pay the amount due to the competent body in accordance with rules laid down by the Member State.

Where the time limit for payment is not met, the sums due shall bear interest at a rate por annum fixed by the Member State and which shall not be lower than the rate of interest which the latter applies for the recovery of amounts wrongly paid.

Note
The words in square brackets were added, amended or deleted by Regulation No. 2186/96.

Article 5

1. Where appropriate, Member States shall determine the priority categories of producers as referred to in Article 2 (4) of Regulation (EEC) No 3950/92 on the basis of one or more of the following objective criteria, in order of priority:

    (a) formal acknowledgement by the competent authority of the Member State that all or part of the levy has been wrongly charged;

    (b) the geographical location of the holding, and primarily mountain areas as defined in Article 3 (3) of Council Directive 75/268/EEC (3);

    (c) the maximum stocking density on the holding for the purposes of extensive livestock production;

    (d) the amount by which the individual reference quantity is exceeded;

    (e) the volume of the producer's reference quantity.

Where the financial resources available for a given period are not used up after the abovementioned criteria have been applied, the Member State may adopt other objective criteria with the agreement of the Commission.

2. Member States shall take any additional measures necessary to ensure payment of levies due to the Community within the time limit laid down.

Where the set of documents referred to in Article 3 (5) of Commission Regulation (EEC) No 2776/88 (4), which the Member States must transmit to the

COMMISSION REGULATION (EEC) NO. 536/93 OF 9 MARCH 1993

Commission each month, shows that this time limit has not been met, the Commission shall reduce advances on entry in the accounts of agricultural expenditure in proportion to the amount due or an estimate thereof.

Interest paid pursuant to Article 3 (4) and Article 4 (4) shall be deducted by the Member States from expenditure on milk and milk products.

ARTICLE 6

Reference quantities not or no longer allocated to individuals shall be included in the national reserve referred to in Article 5 of Regulation (EEC) No 3950/92. Reference quantities for deliveries and those for direct sales shall be recorded separately.

ARTICLE 7

1. Member States shall take all the verification measures necessary to ensure payment of the levy on quantities of milk and milk equivalent marketed in excess of any of the quantities referred to in Article 3 of Regulation (EEC) No 3950/92. To that end:

   (a) all purchasers operating in the territory of a Member State must be approved by that Member State.

   Purchasers shall be approved only where they:

   - provide proof of their status as dealers from the viewpoint of national laws,

   - have premises in the Member State concerned where the stock accounts, registers and other documents referred to in (c) may be consulted by the competent authority,

   - undertake to keep up to date the stock accounts, registers and other documents referred to in (c),

   - undertake to forward the declarations provided for in Article 3 (2) to the competent authority of the Member State concerned.

   Approval shall be withdrawn where the above-mentioned provisions are not observed; it may be withdrawn where it is ascertained that the purchaser has repetedly failed to comply with any other obligation under Regulation (EEC) No 3950/92 or this Regulation;

   (b) producers shall be required to ensure that purchasers to whom they deliver are approved;

   (c) purchasers shall keep available to the competent authority of the Member State for at least three years stock accounts per 12-month period

ARTICLE 7

with details of the name and address of each producer, the reference quantity available at the beginning and at the end of each period, the quantities of milk or milk equivalent which he has delivered per month or four-week period, the representative and average fat contents of his deliveries, together with the commercial documents, correspondance and other information referred to in Council Regulation (EEC) No 4045/89 (5) permitting such stock accounts to be verified;

(d) purchasers shall be responsible for recording under the additional levy arrangements all quantities of milk and/or other milk products delivered to them; to that end they shall keep available to the competent authority for at least three years the list of purchasers and undertakings treating or processing milk and/or other milk products supplying them with milk or other milk products and, per month, the quantities delivered by each supplier;

(e) on collection at holdings, milk and/or other milk products shall be accompanied by a document identifying the delivery. In addition, purchasers shall keep recors of each individual delivery for at least three years;

(f) producers with reference quantities for direct sales shall keep available to the competent authority of the Member State for at least three years stock accounts by 12-month period with details of the quantities, per month and per product, of milk and/or milk products sold directly for consumption and/or to wholesalers, cheese maturers and the retail trade, together with registers of livestock held on holdings and used for milk production, in accordance with Article 4 (1) of Council Directive 92/102/EEC (6), and supporting documents enabling such stock accounts to be verified.

2. The Member States shall take any further measures necessary to:

- verify cases of total or partial abandonment of milk production and/or reference quantities in accordance with Article 8 of Regulation (EEC) No 3950/92 where relevant provisions thereof are applied,

- ensure that the parties concerned are aware of the penal or administrative sanctions to which they are liable where they fail to comply with the provisions of Regulation (EEC) No 3950/92 and this Regulation.

3. Member States shall physically verify the accuracy of the accounting with regard to the quantities of milk and milk equivalent marketed and, to that end, shall check milk transport during collection at farms and shall, in particular, check:

COMMISSION REGULATION (EEC) NO. 536/93 OF 9 MARCH 1993

(a) at the permises of the purchasers, the statements referred to in Article 3 (1), the credibility of stock accounts and supplies as referred to in paragraph 1 (c) and (d) with regard to the commercial documents and other documents proving now the collected milk and milk equivalent have been used;

(b) at the permises of the producers with a reference quantity for direct sales, the credibility of the declaration referred to in Article 4 (1) and the stock accounts referred to in paragraph 1 (f).

The checks shall be determined by the Member States on the basis of a risk analysis. The number of checks per year may not be less than:

- 40% of the number of purchasers, in the case of (a),
- 5% of the number of producers concerned, in the case of (b).

ARTICLE 8

Member States shall notify the Commission of:

- the measures adopted for the application of Regulation (EEC) No 3950/92 and this Regulation, and any amendments thereto, within one month following their adoption,

- their duly reasoned decisions where recourse 13 had to Article 6 (2) of Regulation (EEC) No 3950/92,

- before 1 March each year, the quantities transferred in accordance with the second subparagraph of Article 4 (2) of Regulation (EEC) No 3950/92,

- before 1 September each year, the duly completed questionnaire as set out in the Annex. Where that time limit is not observed, the Commission shall make a flat-rate reduction to advances on the entry of agricultural expenditure in the accounts. [Where the information changes, in particular as a result of the checks provided for in Article 7, an update shall be communicated to the Commission before 1 December, 1 March and 1 July of each year,]

- the results and information necessary to evaluate measures implemented pursuant to the first and second indents of Article 8 of Regulation (EEC) No 3950/92.

Note
The words in square brackets were added by Regulation No. 82/96.

ARTICLE 9

Commission Regulation (EEC) No 1546/88 (7) is hereby repealed.

However, it shall continue to apply to ensure the fulfilment of obligations regarding the implementation of the additional levy scheme for the ninth period and, if necessary, previous periods.

To ensure the continuity of the national measures enforcing compliance with the additional levy scheme, references to Article 5c of Council Regulation (EEC) No 804/68 (8), to Regulation (EEC) No 857/84 (9) or to Regulation (EEC) No 1546/88 may, during a transitional period, be treated as reference to Regulation (EEC) No 3950/92 and this Regulation.

ARTICLE 10

This Regulation shall enter into force on the seventh day following its publication in the Official Journal of the European Communities.

It shall apply from the 12-month period commencing on 1 April 1993.

However, in the event of administrative difficulties, the Member States concerned may postpone application of Article 7 (1) (a), (b) and (e) until 31 December 1993.

This Regulation shall be binding in its entirety and directly applicable in all Member States.

Done at Brussels, 9 March 1993.
For the Commission
René STEICHEN
Member of the Commission

ANNEX

Annual questionnaire on the application of the arrangements on additional levies on milk and milk products introduced by Regulation (EEC) No 3950/92

PERIOD OF APPLICATION: MEMBER STATE:

1. Deliveries 1.1. Number of purchasers of which groups of purchasers

1.2. Sum of individual reference quantities allocated for deliveries before the quantities under 1.4. are taken into account (tonnes)

1.3. Number of procedure of which producers with reference quantities for direct sales also

1.4. Number of temporary conversions of the reference quantities requested pursuant to Article 4 (2) of Regulation (EEC) No 3950/92 - deliveries into direct sales and quantities concerned (tonnes) - direct sales into deliveries and quantities concerned (tonnes)

1.5. Average representative fat content (g/kg)

1.6. Quantity of deliveries of milk and milk equivalent (tonnes) of which milk products in milk equivalent (tonnes)

1.7. Average real fat content of deliveries (g/kg)

1.8. Adjustment of deliveries to representative fat content (tonnes)

COMMISSION REGULATION (EEC) NO. 536/93 OF 9 MARCH 1993

1.9. Number of temporary transfers of reference quantities recorded at 31 December and quantities concerned (tonnes)

1.10. Unused reference quantities before possible reallocation (tonnes)

1.11. Number of producers by category benefiting under Article 2 (4) of Regulation (EEC) No 3950/92 amounts redistributed by category of producers (national currency) amounts allocated to finance measures under the first indent of Article 8 of Regulation (EEC) No 3950/92 (national currency)

2. Direct sales

2.1. Sum of individual reference quantities allocated for direct sales before the quantities under 1.4. are taken into account (tonnes)

2.2. Number of producers

2.3. Quantities covered by direct sales of milk and milk equivalent (tonnes) of which milk products in milk equivalent (tonnes)

of which
- cream and butter
- cheese
- yoghurt
- other

2.4. Unused reference quantities before possible reallocation (tonnes)

2.5. Amount of levies collected allocated for measures under the first indent of Article 8 of Regulation (EEC) No 3950/92 (national currency)

Note
The Annex was replaced by Regulation No. 82/96.

THE TREATY OF ROME

The text of all the changes and additions incorporated into the Title on Agriculture in the **Treaty of Rome** by the **Treaty of Amsterdam.**[*]

TITLE II
AGRICULTURE

A.34   ARTICLE 32 (ex Article 38)

1. The common market shall extend to agriculture and trade in agricultural products. 'Agricultural products' means the products of the soil, of stock farming and of fisheries and products of first-stage processing directly related to these products.

2. Save as otherwise provided in Articles **33** to **38,** the rules laid down for the establishment of the common market shall apply to agricultural products.

3. The products subject to the provisions of Articles **33** to **38** are listed in **Annex I** to this Treaty. *Second Sentence shall be deleted.*

4. The operation and development of the common market for agricultural products must be accompanied by the establishment of a common agricultural policy. *Remainder of sentence shall be deleted.*

Note
[*] Excerpt printed from *The Treaty of Amsterdam in Perspective - Consolidated Treaty on European Union*, by Anthony Cowgill and Andrew Cowgill, British Management Data Foundation, 1998, with the kind permission of the authors and publishers.

ARTICLE 33 (ex Article 39)

1. The objectives of the common agricultural policy shall be:
(a) to increase agricultural productivity by promoting technical progress and by ensuring the rational development of agricultural production and the optimum utilisation of the factors of production, in particular labour;
(b) thus to ensure a fair standard of living for the agricultural community, in particular by increasing the individual earnings of persons engaged in agriculture;
(c) to stabilise markets;
(d) to assure the availability of supplies;
(e) to ensure that supplies reach consumers at reasonable prices.

2. In working out the common agricultural policy and the special methods for its application, account shall be taken of:
(a) the particular nature of agricultural activity, which results from the social structure of agriculture and from structural and natural disparities between the various agricultural regions;
(b) the need to effect the appropriate adjustments by degrees;
(c) the fact that in the Member States agriculture constitutes a sector closely linked with the economy as a whole.

ARTICLE 34 (ex Article 40)

Paragraph 1 shall be repealed.

1. In order to attain the objectives set out in Article 33, a common organisation of agricultural markets shall be established.

This organisation shall take one of the following forms, depending on the product concerned:
(a) common rules on competition;
(b) compulsory co-ordination of the various national market organisations;
(c) a European market organisation.

2. The common organisation established in accordance with **paragraph 1** may include all measures required to attain the objectives set out in Article 33, in particular regulation of prices, aids for the production and marketing of the various products, storage and carryover arrangements and common machinery for stabilising imports or exports.

The common organisation shall be limited to pursuit of the objectives set out in Article 33 and shall exclude any discrimination between producers or consumers within the Community.

Any common price policy shall be based on common criteria and uniform methods of calculation.

3. In order to enable the common organisation referred to in **paragraph 1** to attain its objectives, one or more agricultural guidance and guarantee funds may be set up.

ARTICLE 35 (ex Article 41)

To enable the objectives set out in Article 33 to be attained, provision may be made within the framework of the common agricultural policy for measures such as:
(a) an effective co-ordination of efforts in the spheres of vocational training, of research and of the dissemination of agricultural knowledge; this may include joint financing of projects or institutions;
(b) joint measures to promote consumption of certain products.

ARTICLE 36 (ex Article 42)

The provisions of the Chapter relating to rules on competition shall apply to production of and trade in agricultural products only to the extent determined by the Council within the framework of Article 37(2) and (3) and in accordance with the procedure laid down therein, account being taken of the objectives set out in Article 33.

The Council may, in particular, authorise the granting of aid:
(a) for the protection of enterprises handicapped by structural or natural conditions;
(b) within the framework of economic development programmes.

ARTICLE 37 (ex Article 43)

1. In order to evolve the broad lines of a common agricultural policy, the Commission shall, immediately this Treaty enters into force, convene a conference of the Member States with a view to making a comparison of their agricultural policies, in particular by producing a statement of their resources and needs.

2. Having taken into account the work of the conference provided for in paragraph 1, after consulting the Economic and Social Committee and within two years of the entry into force of this Treaty, the Commission shall submit proposals for working out and implementing the common agricultural policy, including the replacement of the national organisations by one of the forms of common organisation provided for in **Article 34(1),** and for implementing the measures specified in this Title.

These proposals shall take account of the interdependence of the agricultural matters mentioned in this Title. The Council shall, on a proposal from the Commission and after consulting the European Parliament, **acting by a qualified majority,** make regulations, issue directives, or take decisions, without prejudice to any recommendations it may also make.

3. The Council may, acting by a qualified majority and in accordance with paragraph 2, replace the national market organisations by the common organisation provided for in **Article 34(1)** if:
(a) the common organisation offers Member States which are opposed to this measure and which have an organisation of their own for the production in question equivalent safeguards for the employment and standard of living of the producers concerned, account being taken of the adjustments that will be possible and the specialisation that will be needed with the passage of time;

(b) such an organisation ensures conditions for trade within the Community similar to those existing in a national market.

4. If a common organisation for certain raw materials is established before a common organisation exists for the corresponding processed products, such raw materials as are used for processed products intended for export to third countries may be imported from outside the Community.

ARTICLES 44 and 45 shall be repealed.

ARTICLE **38** (ex Article 46)
Where in a Member State a product is subject to a national market organisation or to internal rules having equivalent effect which affect the competitive position of similar production in another Member State, a countervailing charge shall be applied by Member States to imports of this product coming from the Member State where such organisation or rules exist, unless that State applies a countervailing charge on export.
The Commission shall fix the amount of these charges at the level required to redress the balance; it may also authorise other measures, the conditions and details of which it shall determine.

ARTICLE 47 shall be repealed.

PART V

FORMS

PART V

LIST OF FORMS

A.35

SECTION 1: TENANCIES PROTECTED BY THE AGRICULTURAL HOLDINGS ACT 1986

Matters arising during the tenancy

Form No.		Page
1.	Reference to arbitration as to operation of section 2(1) of the 1986 Act (not a prescribed form).	1003
2.	Request by landlord or tenant to other party to enter into or supplement a written tenancy agreement (section 6) (not a prescribed form).	1003
3.	Reference to arbitration of the terms of a tenancy where no agreement has been reached as to the terms to be embodied in writing (section 6) (not a prescribed form).	1004
4.	Request by tenant or landlord for variation of agreement to conform with the "model clauses", i.e. the Agriculture (Maintenance, Repair and Insurance of Fixed Equipment) Regulations 1973 (S.I. 1973 No. 1473) (section 8) (not a prescribed form).	1005
5.	Reference to arbitration on failure to reach agreement in regard to the variation of tenancy agreement to conform with the "model clauses", i.e. the Agriculture (Maintenance, Repair and Insurance of Fixed Equipment) Regulations 1973 (S.I. 1973 No. 1473) (section 8) (not a prescribed form).	1005
6.	Counter-notice by tenant or landlord to other party requiring contested question of liability under the Agriculture (Maintenance, Repair and Insurance of Fixed Equipment) Regulations 1973 S.I. 1973 No. 1473) to be referred to arbitration (not a prescribed form).	1006
7.	Notice by landlord or tenant requiring arbitration to determine amount due on transfer of liability as to fixed equipment (section 9) (not a prescribed form).	1007

SECTION 1: TENANCIES PROTECTED BY THE AGRICULTURAL HOLDINGS ACT 1986

Form No. **Page**

8. Notice by landlord or tenant under the Agriculture (Maintenance, Repair and Insurance of Fixed Equipment) Regulations 1973 (S.I. 1973 No. 1473) requiring arbitration as to redundant fixed equipment. 1007

9. Notice by tenant of intention to remove fixtures or buildings (section 10(3)) (not a prescribed form). 1008

10. Counter-notice by landlord electing to purchase fixtures and buildings (section 10(4)) (not a prescribed form). 1008

11. Tenant's request to landlord to carry out work for the provision, alteration or repair of fixed equipment (section 11) (short form : not a prescribed form). 1009

12. Tenant's request to landlord to carry out work for the provision, alteration or repair of fixed equipment (section 11) (fuller form : not a prescribed form). 1009

13 and 13A. Application by tenant to Agricultural Land Tribunal for a direction under section 11 in regard to fixed equipment and landlord's reply (prescribed forms). 1010

14. Demand by landlord or tenant for arbitration as to rent (section 12) (not a prescribed form). 1014

15. Notice by landlord to tenant requiring an increase of rent on completion of improvements (section 13) (not a prescribed form). 1014

16. Demand for arbitration in regard to variation of a contract of tenancy as to permanent pasture (section 14) (not a prescribed form). 1015

17. Demand for arbitration (for the purpose of injunction proceedings) on exercise of tenant's rights of disposal of produce or freedom of cropping (section 15) (not a prescribed form). 1016

18. Notice by tenant of occurrence of damage by "game" (section 20(2)(a)) (not a prescribed form). 1016

19. Notice by tenant of claim for damage by "game", with particulars (section 20(2)(c)) (not a prescribed form). 1017

20. Request by landlord or tenant for a record to be made (section 22) (not a prescribed form). 1018

21. Notice to tenant of change of landlord (section 93(5)) (not a prescribed form). 1018

22. Notice to pay rent due (prescribed form). 1019

23. Notice to do work (notice to tenant to remedy breach of tenancy agreement by doing work of repair, maintenance or replacement) (prescribed form). 1020

LIST OF FORMS

Form No. **Page**

24. Notice by tenant requiring arbitration on notice to do work under Part II of the Agricultural Holdings (Arbitration on Notice) Order 1987 (S.I. 1987 No. 710) (not a prescribed form).   1024

25. Notice to tenant to remedy breach of tenancy agreement, not being a notice to do any work of repair, maintenance or replacement (prescribed form).   1026

26 and 26A. Application by landlord to Agricultural Land Tribunal for a certificate of bad husbandry and tenant's reply (Schedule 3, Part I, Case C, and Part II, paragraph 9) (prescribed forms).   1028

Termination of tenancy: notices to quit and counter-notices

27. Notice of landlord's intention to terminate a tenancy for a fixed term of two years or upwards at the date fixed for the expiry of the term (section 3) (not a prescribed form).   1030

28. Notice to quit by landlord (ordinary notice without reasons stated) (not a prescribed form).   1031

29. Notice to quit by landlord to tenant stating reasons, in accordance with section 61(3) of the 1986 Act, for the purpose of excluding "additional compensation" for disturbance (not a prescribed form).   1031

30. Notice to quit by landlord relying on one or more of the Cases in Schedule 3 and specifying the relevant reason as appropriate (not a prescribed form).   1032

31. Notice to quit to personal representatives of deceased tenant, given not later than three months beginning with the date of a "relevant notice" of death of tenant or of an application for succession (not a prescribed form).   1034

32. Notice to quit by landlord relying on one or more of the Cases in Schedule 3, specifying the relevant reasons, and in the alternative expressing the notice as a simple notice to which section 26(1) applies (not a prescribed form).   1035

33. Tenant's notice to landlord requiring arbitration in regard to reasons stated in a notice to quit given in pursuance of Cases A, B, D or E in Schedule 3 to the 1986 Act (not a prescribed form).   1036

34. Notice to quit part of a holding for one of the purposes mentioned in section 31 of the 1986 Act (as an example, erection of farm labourers' cottages) (not a prescribed form).   1036

35. Notice to quit part of a holding given by landlord for a non-agricultural use, planning permission having been obtained. Less than 12 months' notice given under clause in contract of tenancy (section 25(2)(b) and Case B) (not a prescribed form).   1037

SECTION 1: TENANCIES PROTECTED BY THE AGRICULTURAL HOLDINGS ACT 1986

Form No. **Page**

36. Counter-notice by tenant (section 26(1)) (not a prescribed form), with variant for section 28(2) when appropriate. **1038**

37. Counter-notice by tenant accepting notice to quit as a notice to quit the entire holding; variation where the reversion is severed (section 32) (not a prescribed form). **1038**

38. Notice to quit by tenant to landlord (not a prescribed form). **1039**

39. Notice to quit by tenant to sub-tenant (not a prescribed form). **1039**

40 and 40A. Application by landlord for Agricultural Land Tribunal's consent to notice to quit and tenant's reply (section 26(1) and section 28(2), (3) and (4) (prescribed forms)). **1040**

41. Application by landlord under section 27(5) for variation or revocation of condition imposed by Tribunal under section 27(4) in consenting to operation of notice to quit (prescribed forms). **1044**

42 and 42A. Application by tenant to the Agricultural Land Tribunal to postpone operation of notice to quit and landlord's reply (prescribed forms). **1045**

Succession on death or retirement

43 and 43A. Application for direction giving entitlement to tenancy of agricultural holding and application that applicant be treated as an eligible person (combined prescribed form) and landlord's reply (prescribed forms). **1047**

44 and 44A. Application by the landlord following the tenant's death for consent to operation of notice to quit and tenant's reply (prescribed forms). **1055**

45. Notice by applicant of application for entitlement to tenancy on the death of the tenant (prescribed form). **1058**

46. Applicant's reply to other applications for direction giving entitlement to tenancy (prescribed form). **1059**

47. Retirement notice given by tenant to landlord indicating his wish that a single named person should succeed him as tenant of the holding (section 49) (not a prescribed form). **1060**

48 and 48A. Application (following a retirement notice) for a direction giving entitlement to tenancy of holding and landlord's reply (prescribed forms). **1061**

49. Notice given to landlord by nominated successor of application for entitlement to tenancy on tenant's retirement (prescribed form). **1067**

LIST OF FORMS

Form No.		Page
50.	Demand for arbitration by successful applicant following direction in his favour on death or retirement of previous tenant (not a prescribed form).	**1067**

Compensation on termination of tenancy

51.	Notice of tenant's intention to claim the higher level of basic compensation for disturbance (section 60(3)(b)) (not a prescribed form).	**1068**
52.	Tenant's notice of election in favour of statutory basis of compensation for tenant-right matters (Schedule 12, paragraphs 6 to 9) (not a prescribed form).	**1069**
53.	Notice by landlord requiring tenant to elect in regard to the basis of compensation for Part II of Schedule 8 matters (Schedule 12, paragraph 6(2)) (not a prescribed form).	**1069**
54.	Consent by landlord to payment of compensation by incoming to outgoing tenant (section 69(2)) (not a prescribed form).	**1070**
55.	Application by tenant to landlord for written consent to Schedule 7 improvements (section 67) (not a prescribed form).	**1070**
56.	Consent by landlord to improvements (section 67) (not a prescribed form).	**1071**
57 and 57A.	Application by tenant to Agricultural Land Tribunal for approval to improvements in Part II of Schedule 7, and landlord's reply (section 67(3)) (prescribed forms).	**1071**
58.	Notice by landlord to the Agricultural Land Tribunal and the tenant that the landlord proposes himself to carry out approved improvements (section 67(5)) (not a prescribed form).	**1074**
59 and 59A.	Application by tenant to the Agricultural Land Tribunal for a determination that the landlord has failed to carry out improvements within a reasonable time, and the landlord's reply (section 67(4)) (prescribed forms).	**1075**
60.	Notice of tenant's intention to carry out mole drainage (section 68(1) and Schedule 8, paragraph 1) (not a prescribed form).	**1077**
61.	Notice by tenant of intention to claim compensation for the continuous adoption of a special system of farming "high farming" (section 70) (not a prescribed form).	**1078**
62.	Notice by landlord of intention to claim compensation for general deterioration of the holding (section 72) (not a prescribed form).	**1078**
63.	Request by tenant to landlord to agree that holding or part of it shall be treated as a market garden (section 79) (not a prescribed form).	**1079**
64 and 64A.	Application by tenant to Agricultural Land Tribunal for	**1079**

SECTION 1: TENANCIES PROTECTED BY THE AGRICULTURAL HOLDINGS ACT 1986

Form No. **Page**

holding to be treated as a market garden and landlord's reply (section 80) (prescribed forms).

65. Landlord's or tenant's notice of intention to claim compensation on the termination of the tenancy (section 83(2)), including for milk quota (not a prescribed form).   1082

Arbitration

66. Appointment of valuer with full powers, including power to secure the appointment of an arbitrator.   1084

67A. Form for application to the President of the Royal Institution of Chartered Surveyors for the appointment of an arbitrator in a section 12 rent review (prescribed by the RICS).   1085

67B. Form for application to the President of the Royal Institution of Chartered Surveyors for appointment of arbitrator, all cases other than section 12 rent review (prescribed by the RICS).   1087

68. Notice requiring arbitrator to act (Schedule 11, paragraph 2) (not a prescribed form).   1095

69. Revocation of appointment of arbitrator (form for signature by valuers duly authorised to do so) (Schedule 11, paragraph 4) (not a prescribed form).   1096

70. Statement of Case: example is of a landlord's Statement of Case in a rent arbitration (Schedule 11, paragraph 7) (not a prescribed form).   1096

71. Statement of Case with particulars for arbitrator in respect of claims on termination of tenancy: tenant's Statement of Case with claim for milk quota included (Schedule 11, paragraph 7) (not a prescribed form).   1098

72. Forms of oath or affirmation for witness in arbitrations.   1101

73. Notice by arbitrator to produce documents (Schedule 11, paragraph 8) (not a prescribed form).   1101

74. Outline of statement by arbitrator of special case for opinion of the County Court (not a prescribed form).   1102

75. Form of award in arbitration (prescribed form).   1103

LIST OF FORMS

Forms relating to matters subsequent to Agricultural Land Tribunal proceedings

Form No.		Page
76.	Request to Agricultural Land Tribunal for reference of question of law to the High Court (not a prescribed form).	1105
77.	Notice to Agricultural Land Tribunal (after refusal by Tribunal to refer a question of law to the High Court) of intention to apply for a direction (not a prescribed form).	1106

SECTION 2: TENANCIES PROTECTED BY THE AGRICULTURAL TENANCIES ACT 1995

A.36

All forms are non-statutory.

Character of tenancy
Form

101.	Notice of farm business tenancy (section 1(4)).	1106
102.	Recital for lease or tenancy agreement.	1107

Termination

103.	Fixed term: Termination notice at expiry (section 5).	1107
104.	Fixed term: Tenant's break notice (section 7).	1108
105.	Fixed term: Landlord's break notice (section 7).	1108
106.	Fixed term: Tenant's notice to quit part (section 7).	1109
107.	Fixed term: Landlord's notice to quit part (section 7).	1109
108.	Periodic tenancies: Annual tenancy, tenant's notice to quit (section 6).	1109
109.	Periodic tenancies: Annual tenancy, landlord's notice to quit (section 6).	1110
110.	Periodic tenancies: Annual tenancy, tenant's notice to quit part (section 6).	1110
111.	Periodic tenancies: Annual tenancy, landlord's notice to quit part (section 6).	1111
112.	Lease for life: Notice of termination on tenant's death (section 149(6) of the Law of Property Act 1925 and section 7(3) of the Agricultural Tenancies Act 1995).	1111

SECTION 2: TENANCIES PROTECTED BY THE AGRICULTURAL TENANCIES ACT 1995

General notices

Form No.		**Page**
113.	Landlord's notice of severance of the reversion.	1111
114.	Landlord's notice of change of landlord and giving landlord's address in England and Wales (sections 47 and 48 of the Landlord and Tenant Act 1987 and section 36(7) of the Agricultural Tenancies Act 1995).	1112
115.	Notice giving landlord's address in England and Wales (sections 47 and 48 of the Landlord and Tenant Act 1987).	1112

Rent review

116.	Statutory rent review notice (section 10).	1113
117.	Rent agreement (section 10).	1113

Notices related to compensation/improvements

118.	Tenant's request for consent to improvement (section 17).	1114
119.	Tenant's application for consent to the making of an application for planning permission (section 18).	1114
120.	Tenant's application for consent to implement planning permission (section 17).	1115
121.	Tenant's reference to arbitration on improvements after landlord's refusal (section 19).	1115
122.	Tenant's reference to arbitration on improvements after landlord's failing to respond (section 19).	1115
123.	Tenant's reference to arbitration on improvements after landlord's required conditions (section 19).	1116
124.	Landlord's consent to improvements (section 17).	1116
125.	Landlord's consent to tenant applying for planning permission for physical improvement and making that physical improvement (sections 17 and 18).	1117
126.	Landlord's consent to tenant applying for planning permission for change of use (section 18).	1118
127.	Landlord's consent to tenant applying for planning permission but not to tenant making physical improvement (section 18).	1119
128.	Tenant's notice of intention to claim compensation (section 22).	1119
129.	Agreement regarding compensation (section 23(2)).	1120

Disputes

Form No.		Page
130.	Tenancy clause for third party dispute resolution (an example).	**1120**
131.	Joint reference of dispute by landlord and tenant to third party.	**1120**
132.	Reference of dispute by landlord or tenant to third party.	**1121**
133.	Notice by landlord or tenant to other party of his unilateral reference of dispute to third party.	**1121**
134.	Notice of dispute (section 28(2)).	**1122**

SECTION 1: TENANCIES PROTECTED BY THE AGRICULTURAL HOLDINGS ACT 1986

Matters arising during the tenancy

Form 1. Reference to arbitration as to operation of section 2(1) of the 1986 Act (not a prescribed form) — A.37

Agricultural Holdings Act 1986, section 2

The holding known as [name/OS numbers]

To: A.B. landlord of [address]

I require to be determined by arbitration under the above section of the Act the question of what modifications are necessary in the agreement dated [*] under which the holding was let to me [*or* under which I was granted a licence to occupy the holding] by reason of such agreement taking effect under the above section as if it were an agreement for the letting of the holding for a tenancy from year to year.

Dated:

Signed:

Form 2. Request by landlord or tenant to other party to enter into or supplement a written tenancy agreement (section 6) (not a prescribed form) — A.38

Agricultural Holdings Act 1986, section 2

To: A.B. landlord of [address]

Or

SECTION 1: TENANCIES PROTECTED BY THE AGRICULTURAL HOLDINGS ACT 1986

To: C.D. tenant of [address]

Re: The holding known as [name/OS numbers]

In accordance with section 6(1) of the Act I request you to enter into an agreement in writing embodying the terms of the tenancy under which I hold [or you hold] the holding and containing provision for all the matters included in Schedule 1 to the Act.

[*If there is in existence a written tenancy agreement, but it contains no provision for one or more of the matters included in Schedule 1, use the following variation.*]

In accordance with section 6(1) of the Act, I request you to enter into an agreement in writing making provision for the matter [matters] set out in the Schedule hereto which is [are] not provided for in the tenancy agreement under which I hold [or you hold] the holding.

Dated:

Signed:

SCHEDULE

[*Specify matter or matters in Schedule 1 to the Act for which provision is required.*]

A.39 Form 3. Reference to arbitration of the terms of a tenancy where no agreement has been reached as to the terms to be embodied in writing (section 6) (not a prescribed form)

Agricultural Holdings Act 1986, section 6

To: A.B. landlord of [address]

Or

To: C.D. tenant of [address]

Re: The holding known as [name/OS numbers]

As no agreement has been reached following my request to you dated [*] to enter into an agreement in writing embodying the terms of the tenancy under which I hold [or you hold] the holding and making provision for all the matters included in Schedule 1 to the Act, I require, in accordance with section 6 of the Act that the terms of the said tenancy be referred to arbitration under the Act.

FORM 3

Dated:

Signed:

Form 4. Request by tenant or landlord for variation of agreement to conform with "model clauses", i.e. the Agriculture (Maintenance, Repair and Insurance of Fixed Equipment) Regulations 1973 (S.I. 1973 No. 1473), (section 8) (not a prescribed form) A.40

Agricultural Holdings Act 1986, section 8

To: A.B. landlord of [address]

Or

To: C.D. tenant of [address]

Re: The holding known as [name/OS numbers]

I request you, in accordance with section 8(2) of the Act, to vary the agreement dated [*] under which I hold [*or* you hold] the holding in order to bring the terms of the said agreement into conformity with the "model clauses" mentioned in the said subsection, namely, the provisions set out in the Schedule to the Agriculture (Maintenance, Repair and Insurance of Fixed Equipment) Regulations 1987 (S.I. 1987 No.1473).

Dated:

Signed:

Form 5. Reference to arbitration on failure to reach agreement in regard to the variation of tenancy agreement to conform with the "model clauses", i.e. the Agriculture (Maintenance, Repair and Insurance of Fixed Equipment) Regulations 1973 (S.I. 1973 No. 1473) (section 8) (not a prescribed form) A.41

Agricultural Holdings Act 1986, section 8

To: C.D. tenant of [address]

Re: The holding known as [name/OS numbers]

As no agreement has been reached between us on my request dated [*] to vary the

SECTION 1: TENANCIES PROTECTED BY THE AGRICULTURAL HOLDINGS ACT 1986

tenancy agreement dated [*] under which you hold the holding, in order to bring the said tenancy agreement into conformity with the model clauses set out in the Agriculture (Maintenance, Repair and Insurance of Fixed Equipment) Regulations 1973, I require the terms of the said tenancy in regard to the maintenance, repair and insurance of fixed equipment to be referred to arbitration in accordance with section 8(2) of the Act.

Dated:

Signed:

A.42 Form 6. **Counter-notice by tenant or landlord to other party requiring contested question of liability under the Agriculture (Maintenance, Repair and Insurance of Fixed Equipment) Regulations 1973 (S.I. 1973 No. 1473) to be referred to arbitration (not a prescribed form)**

Agricultural Holdings Act 1986 and the Agriculture (Maintenance, Repair and Insurance of Fixed Equipment) Regulations 1973

To: A.B. landlord of [address]

Or

To: C.D. tenant of [address]

Re: The holding known as [name/OS numbers]

I have received from you a notice dated [*] calling upon me to execute works of repair or replacement specified in the said notice on the ground that they are my liability under the Agriculture (Maintenance, Repair and Insurance of Fixed Equipment) Regulations 1973 in respect of the holding of which I am your tenant [*or* of which you are my tenant].

I wish in accordance with the said regulations to contest my liability to execute such of the said works of repair or replacement as are specified in the Schedule hereto on the grounds therein set out and I require the question of my liability to execute such works to be determined by arbitration under the Act.

SCHEDULE

Items of repair or replacement in respect of which liability is contested	Grounds on which liability is contested

Dated:

Signed:

Form 7. Notice by landlord or tenant requiring arbitration to determine amount due on transfer of liability as to fixed equipment (section 9) (not a prescribed form) A.43

Agricultural Holdings Act 1986, section 9

To: A.B. landlord of [address]

Or

To: C.D. tenant of [address]

Re: The holding known as [name/OS numbers]

I give you notice, in accordance with section 9 of the Acct, that I require to be determined by arbitration under the Act the amount due from you to me in respect of your failure to discharge the liability for the maintenance or repair of the items of fixed equipment mentioned in the Schedule hereto prior to the transfer of the said liability to me with effect from [date] under the agreement dated [*] made between us [or under the award dated [*] issued by Mr [*]] pursuant to the provisions of section 6 [or section 7 or section 8] of the said Act.

SCHEDULE

[*Set out items of fixed equipment, liability for which was transferred by sections 6, 7 or 8 (or a combination of these sections) where there has been a previous failure by the other party to maintain or repair.*]

Dated:

Signed:

Form 8. Notice by landlord or tenant under the Agriculture (Maintenance, Repair and Insurance of Fixed Equipment) Regulations 1973 (S.I. 1973 No. 1473) requiring arbitration as to redundant fixed equipment A.44

Agricultural Holdings Act 1986 and the Agriculture (Maintenance, Repair and Insurance of Fixed Equipment) Regulations 1973

To: A.B. landlord of [address]

Or

To: C.D. tenant of [address]

Re: The holding known as [name/OS numbers]

SECTION 1: TENANCIES PROTECTED BY THE AGRICULTURAL HOLDINGS ACT 1986

As it has not proved possible for us to reach agreement I require to be determined by arbitration under the Act in accordance with the above regulations the question whether the item of fixed equipment described in the Schedule hereto is [or was before it was damaged [or destroyed] [on or about the day of [*] 19[*]]] redundant to the farming of the holding of which you are my tenant [or of which I am your tenant].

SCHEDULE

[Here give description of item claimed to be redundant.]

Dated:

Signed:

A.45   Form 9.   **Notice by tenant of intention to remove fixtures or buildings (section 10(3)) (not a prescribed form)**

Agricultural Holdings Act 1986, section 10(3)

To: A.B. landlord of [address]

Re: The holding known as [name/OS numbers]

It is my intention, in accordance with the above section, after expiration of one month from the date of service of this notice, to remove from the holding of which I am your tenant, the fixtures [and buildings] of which particulars are given below.

PARTICULARS OF FIXTURES [AND BUILDINGS] TO BE REMOVED

[Set out here, with sufficient particulars to identify them clearly, the fixtures and/or buildings which it is proposed to remove.]

Dated:

Signed:

A.46   Form 10.   **Counter-notice by landlord electing to purchase fixtures and buildings (section 10(4)) (not a prescribed form)**

Agricultural Holdings Act 1986, section 10(4)

To: C.D. tenant of [address]

FORM 10

Re: The holding known as [name/OS numbers]

With reference to your notice dated [*] of your intention to remove from the holding certain fixtures [and buildings], specified in the said notice, in accordance with the above section, I elect to purchase at the fair value thereof to an incoming tenant the following fixtures [and buildings] which are referred to in the said notice:

[*Set out particulars of fixtures and/or buildings which the landlord wishes to take over.*]

Dated:

Signed:

Form 11. Tenant's request to landlord to carry out work for the provision, alteration or repair of fixed equipment (section 11) (short form: not a prescribed form) A.47

Agricultural Holdings Act 1986, section 11

To: A.B. landlord of [address]

Re: The holding known as [name/OS numbers]

I request you, in accordance with section 11(3) of the Act, to carry out on the holding, of which I am your tenant, the work for the [provision] [alteration] [repair] of fixed equipment specified in the Schedule below.

SCHEDULE

[*Here set out precise particulars of the proposed work necessary to comply with prescribed requirements as mentioned in section 11.*]

Dated:

Signed:

Form 12. Tenant's request to landlord to carry out work for the provision, alteration or repair of fixed equipment (section 11) (fuller form: not a prescribed form) A.48

Agricultural Holdings Act 1986, section 11

To: A.B. landlord of [address]

SECTION 1: TENANCIES PROTECTED BY THE AGRICULTURAL HOLDINGS ACT 1986

Re: The holding known as [name/OS numbers]

1. I desire to carry on the agricultural activity specified in Part I of the Schedule hereto, to the extent and in the manner therein specified, on the holding of which I am your tenant.

2. Unless the work specified in Part II of the said Schedule is carried out, being work of a kind mentioned in section 11 of the Act, I shall, in carrying on the said activity on the holding, contravene the requirements of [*state relevant provision of Act or prescribed instrument*].

3. Accordingly I request you, pursuant to the said section 11, to carry out the work specified in Part II of the said Schedule.

4. If you refuse to carry out the said work, or if you do not within [*] of the receipt of this request agree to carry it out, I propose to apply to the Agricultural Land Tribunal for [*] for a direction under the said section 11 that you should carry out the said work.

SCHEDULE

[*Specify the agricultural activity which the tenant desires to carry out. The extent to which and the manner in which it is proposed to carry on the activity should be specified.*]

[*Specify, as the case may be, either the new fixed equipment which requires to be provided or the existing fixed equipment which requires to be altered or repaired, stating in the latter case what alterations or repairs are needed.*]

Dated:

Signed:

A.49 Form 13. **Application by tenant to Agricultural Land Tribunal for a direction under section 11 of the Agricultural Holdings Act 1986 in regard to fixed equipment (prescribed form)**

Form 5

rule 6(1)

Ref. No.
To be inserted
by the Secretary.

FORM 13

AGRICULTURAL LAND TRIBUNAL

Application for Direction to Provide Fixed Equipment

To the Secretary of the Agricultural Land Tribunal
for the .... Area.

1. I .... [block capitals]
of .... [address]
tenant of .... [name or description of holding],
hereby apply under section 4 of the Agriculture Act 1958 for the Tribunal to direct
my landlord .... [block capitals]
of .... [address]
to carry out the following work on the said holding:—

2.(a) On the .... day of ...., 19 , I
requested my landlord in writing to carry out the said work and he
* refused on the .... day of ....,19.......

_____

has had reasonable time to agree but has not done so.

(b) No term in my contract of tenancy or in any other agreement binds me or my landlord to carry out the said work.

(c) My landlord is not bound by any enactment to carry out the said work.

3. The holding consists of:—

(a) .... hectares of arable land (including temporary grass)
(Ordnance Survey Field Nos. ....);
(b) .... hectares of permanent pasture
(Ordnance Survey Field Nos. ....);
(c) .... hectares of rough grazing
(Ordnance Survey Field Nos. ....);
(d) .... hectares of other land (including orchards)
(Ordnance Survey Field Nos. ....);

Total .... hectares.

4. The holding includes the following buildings:

5. The type of farming carried on on the holding is ([1]):—

_____

[1] Under section 4(1) of the Agriculture Act 1958 the Tribunal cannot direct a landlord to carry out work in connection with an agricultural activity specified in the tenant's application where the activity has not been carried on on the holding for a period of at least three years immediately preceding the making of the application unless they are satisfied that the starting of the activity did not or, where it has not yet been started, will not constitute or form part of a substantial alteration of the type of farming carried on on the holding.

SECTION 1: TENANCIES PROTECTED BY THE AGRICULTURAL HOLDINGS ACT 1986

6. I wish to carry on the following agricultural activity on the said holding to the extent and in the manner specified, *viz.*:—

7. If I were to do so without the said work being carried out, I should contravene the following prescribed requirements in the following respects:—

8. I attach the following documents which I intend to produce in support of my case:

(a) two ([2]) copies of a 6" to one mile or 1/10,000([3]) map of the holding described in paragraph 3 above;

(b) two([2]) copies of the following plan:—

(c) two ([2]) copies of my contract of tenancy and any other document([4]):—

Date ....   Signed([5]) ....

* Strike out whichever is inapplicable.

A.50   Form 13A. **Landlord's reply to application by tenant to Agricultural Land Tribunal for a direction under section 11 of the Agricultural Holdings Act 1986 in regard to fixed equipment (prescribed form)**

Form 5R

Ref. No.
To be inserted
by the Secretary.

---

[2] Two copies of the application and of any map and document must be sent to the Secretary, and if there are more than two parties (*e.g.*, if the land is held under a sub-tenancy) an additional copy of the contract of tenancy and of the application, etc., must be supplied for, and the Secretary must be informed of the name and address of, each additional party.

[3] A larger scale map may be used if preferred. Ordnance Survey Field Numbers must be marked on the map.

[4] Mention any other document which is attached to this application. The Chairman of the Tribunal has power in all cases to dispense with maps or other documents (*e.g.*, where the landlord already has a copy of the contract of tenancy). A request for a direction on this subject should be made in writing before or at the time of sending the application.

[5] If signed by any person other than the applicant himself, he should state in what capacity or by what authority he signs.

FORM 13A

AGRICULTURAL LAND TRIBUNAL

Reply to Application for Direction to Provide Fixed Equipment

To the Secretary of the Agricultural Land Tribunal for the .... Area.

I .... [*block capitals*]
of .... [*address*]
landlord (¹) of .... [*name or description of holding*],
having received a copy of the application (bearing the above reference number) for the Tribunal's direction to me to carry out certain work on the said holding, reply as follows:—

1. With regard to paragraph 2(a) of the application, I—
   * (a) agree that the request was made and refused;
   * (b) agree that the request was made, but
      * (i) deny that it was refused,
      * (ii) say that I have not yet had a reasonable time to agree to it;
   * (c) deny that the request was made.

2. The other facts stated in the first four paragraphs of the application are correct, except that:—

3. My main reasons for resisting the application are:—
   * (a) that the carrying on of the activity specified in paragraph 6 of the application to the extent and in the manner specified therein—
      * (i) will not involve the contravention of any prescribed requirement even if the said work is not carried out;
      * (ii) would be unreasonable having regard to the tenant's responsibilities to farm the holding in accordance with the rules of good husbandry;
   * (b) that the activity specified in paragraph 6 of the application has not been carried on on the holding for a period of at least three years immediately preceding the making of the application and that the starting of the activity * constitutes/forms part of a substantial alteration of the type of farming carried on on the holding;
   * (c) that the direction asked for would be unreasonable having regard to-
      * (i) my responsibilities to manage the land comprised in the holding in accordance with the rules of good estate management;
      * (ii) the period for which the holding may be expected to remain a separate holding;
      * (iii) [*any other reasons*].

4. I attach copies of the following relevant documents(²):—

---

¹ If this form is completed by a superior landlord he should omit paragraph 1.
² (a) Two copies of the reply and of any document which you wish to submit to the Tribunal

SECTION 1: TENANCIES PROTECTED BY THE AGRICULTURAL HOLDINGS ACT 1986

Date .... Signed([3]) ....

* Strike out whichever is inapplicable.

A.51 **Form 14. Demand by a landlord or tenant for arbitration as to rent (section 12) (not a prescribed form)**

Agricultural Holdings Act 1986, section 12

To: A.B. landlord of [address]

Or

To: C.D. tenant of [address]

Re: The holding known as [name/OS numbers]

I demand, in accordance with section 12 of the Act, that the question of the rent to be paid for the holding of which I am your tenant [*or* of which you are my tenant] as from the [*], being the next termination date within the meaning of subsection (4) of the said section, be referred to arbitration under the Act.

Dated:

Signed:

A.52 **Form 15. Notice by landlord to tenant requiring an increase of rent on completion of improvements (section 13) (not a prescribed form)**

Agricultural Holdings Act 1986, section 13

To: C.D. tenant of [address]

Re: The holding known as [name/OS numbers]

---

must be sent to the Secretary, and, if there are more than two parties (*e.g.*, if the holding is sub-let), an additional copy of each must be supplied for each additional party.
(b) If you disagree with any map or plan attached to the application, your reply should be accompanied by two copies of a 6" to one mile or 1/10,000 (or larger) map showing what you consider to be the true position and marking the Ordnance Survey Field Numbers.
[3] If signed by any person other than the landlord himself, he should state in what capacity or by what authority he signs.

FORM 15

You are notified under section 13 of the Act that I require the rent of the holding of which you are my tenant to be increased as from [*], the date of completion of the improvement whereof particulars are given below, being an improvement to which the said section 13 applies, by an amount equal to the increase in the rental value of the holding attributable to the carrying out of the said improvement.

I propose that the said rent be increased by £[*] per annum on account of the said improvement and I shall be obliged if you will let me know in writing whether you agree. In the event of a failure to agree the said Act provides for the matter to be determined by arbitration.

Particulars of the improvement above referred to

[*Set out a brief specification of the improvement*].

Dated:

Signed:

Form 16. Demand for arbitration in regard to variation of a contract of tenancy as to permanent pasture (section 14) (not a prescribed form) A.53

Agricultural Holdings Act 1986, section 14

To: A.B. landlord of [address]

Or

To: C.D. tenant of [address]

Re: The holding known as [name/OS numbers]

I demand, in accordance with section 14 of the Act, a reference to arbitration of the question whether it is expedient in order to secure the full and efficient farming of the holding that the area of land required to be maintained as permanent pasture by the contract of tenancy should be reduced.

Particulars of the existing provisions of the said contract of tenancy in regard to permanent pasture, and of the modifications which I suggest should be made in the said contract, are given in the Schedule hereto.

SCHEDULE ABOVE REFERRED TO

Part I

Existing contractual provisions in regard to permanent pasture

SECTION 1: TENANCIES PROTECTED BY THE AGRICULTURAL HOLDINGS ACT 1986

It is provided by clause [*] of the contract of tenancy, dated [*], and made between [*] that [*state relevant provisions in regard to permanent pasture*].

Part II

Proposed modifications of the contract of tenancy

[*State modifications sought*].

Dated:

Signed:

A.54   **Form 17.   Demand for arbitration (for the purpose of injunction proceedings) on exercise of tenant's rights of disposal of produce or freedom of cropping (section 15) (not a prescribed form)**

Agricultural Holdings Act 1986, section 15

To: C.D. tenant of [address]

Re: The holding known as [name/OS numbers]

I demand, in accordance with section 15 of the Act, a reference to arbitration of the question whether you are exercising [*or* have exercised] your rights [to dispose of produce] [and] [to practice any system of cropping of arable land] under the said section in such manner as to injure or deteriorate or to be likely to injure or deteriorate the holding of which you are my tenant. This reference is demanded for the purpose of proceedings for an injunction which I intend to bring against you [*or* which I have commenced against you in the [*] court] to restrain you from exercising your said rights in the said manner.

Dated:

Signed:

A.55   **Form 18.   Notice by tenant of occurrence of damage by "game" (section 20(2)(a)) (not a prescribed form)**

Agricultural Holdings Act 1986, section 20

To: A.B. landlord of [address]

Re: The holding known as [name/OS numbers]

FORM 18

I give you notice under section 20 of the Act that I have suffered the damage set out below from wild animals or birds within the meaning of subsection (1) of that section on the holding of which I am your tenant:

Damage to my growing crop of [*] in [identify field or fields]

Damage to my harvested crop of [*] in [identify field or fields]

I intend to claim compensation from you in respect of the said damage.

You may inspect the said damage within [*] days of the receipt by you of this notice.

Dated:

Signed:

Form 19. Notice by tenant of claim for damage by "game" with particulars (section 20(2)(c)) (not a prescribed form) A.56

Agricultural Holdings Act 1986, section 20

To: A.B. landlord of [address]

Re: The holding known as [name/OS numbers]

I give you notice in accordance with section 20 of the Act of the particulars of my claim for compensation for damage done by wild animals or birds within the meaning of subsection (1) of that section to my crops on the holding of which I am your tenant. The occurrence of the damage was notified to you in a notice from me dated the [*] 19[*]. The particulars of the damage are set out below.

Particulars of damage

Damage [by pheasants] in the month of [*] to [*] hectares of growing [wheat] in the field [known as Blackacre O.S. Nos.....] at £[*] per hectare   £ _____

Damage [by grouse] in the month of [*] to [*] hectares of [barley] in the field [known as Whiteacre O.S. Nos.....] at £[*] per hectare   £ _____

Total £ _____

Dated:

Signed:

SECTION 1: TENANCIES PROTECTED BY THE AGRICULTURAL HOLDINGS ACT 1986

A.57   Form 20.   **Request by landlord or tenant for a record to be made (section 22) (not a prescribed form)**

Agricultural Holdings Act 1986, section 22

To: A.B. landlord of [address]

Or

To: C.D. tenant of [address]

Re: The holding known as [name/OS numbers]

I require, in accordance with section 22 of the Act that a record be made of the holding of which I am your tenant [*or* of which you are my tenant].

[*Insert appropriate alternative, below*]

Dated:

Signed:

Request by landlord or tenant	[the fixed equipment on and the general condition (including the condition of any parts not under cultivation) of]
Request by tenant only	[the fixtures or buildings which, under section 10 of the said Act, I am entitled to remove from]
	[the existing improvements executed by me on]
	[the existing improvements in respect of the execution of which I paid compensation, with your written consent, to the outgoing tenant of]

A.58   Form 21.   **Notice to tenant of change of landlord (section 93(5)) (not a prescribed form)**

Agricultural Holdings Act 1986, section 93(5)

To: C.D. tenant of [address]

Re: The holding known as [name/OS numbers]

I give you notice, in accordance with section 93(5) of the Act that as from the date hereof I have ceased to be entitled to receive the rents and profits of the holding and that E.F. of [*] has been entitled to receive the same.

All notices or other documents which require to be served upon or delivered to the landlord of the said holding should henceforth be served upon or delivered to the said E.F. [You are hereby notified that the address of E.F. within England and Wales at which notices including notices in proceedings may be served is [*]].

Dated:

Signed:

Form 22. Notice to pay rent due (prescribed form) A.59

FORM 1

AGRICULTURAL HOLDINGS ACT 1986

SCHEDULE 3, PART I, CASE D

Notice to tenant to pay rent due

Re: the holding known as ....
To ....
....

(Name and address of tenant)

> IMPORTANT—FAILURE TO COMPLY WITH THIS NOTICE MAY BE RELIED ON AS A REASON FOR A NOTICE TO QUIT UNDER CASE D. IF YOU WANT YOUR TENANCY TO CONTINUE YOU MUST ACT QUICKLY. READ THE NOTICE AND ALL THE NOTES CAREFULLY. IF YOU ARE IN ANY DOUBT ABOUT THE ACTION YOU SHOULD TAKE, GET ADVICE IMMEDIATELY, e.g. FROM A SOLICITOR, SURVEYOR OR CITIZENS ADVICE BUREAU.

1. I hereby give you notice that I require you to pay within two months from the date of service of this Notice* the rent due in respect of the above holding as set out below:

* Note: This Notice may not be served before the rent is due.

Particulars of rent not paid

Date when due   Amount due

SECTION 1: TENANCIES PROTECTED BY THE AGRICULTURAL HOLDINGS ACT 1986

....

2. This Notice is given in accordance with Case D in Part I of Schedule 3 to the Agricultural Holdings Act 1986, and failure to comply with it within the period specified above may be relied on as a reason for a notice to quit under Case D.

3. Your attention is drawn to the Notes following the signature to this Notice.

Signed .... Date ....

(If signed by any person other than the landlord of the holding, state in what capacity or by what authority the signature is affixed.)

Address ....
....
....
....

Notes

1. You cannot at this stage refer to arbitration either your liability to comply with this Notice to pay rent or any other question as to the validity of the Notice. You will, however, be entitled to do so later if a notice to quit is served on you on the ground that you have failed to comply with this Notice to pay rent. That is the only opportunity you will have to challenge this Notice.

2. At that stage under article 9 of the Agricultural Holdings (Arbitration on Notice) Order 1987 (S.I. 1987/710) you have one month after the service of the notice to quit within which you can serve on your landlord a notice in writing requiring the question to be determined by arbitration under the Agricultural Holdings Act 1986 (clause 5).

3. You will then have three months from the date of service of that notice in which to appoint an arbitrator by agreement or (in default of such an agreement) to make an application under paragraph 1 of Schedule 11 to that Act for the appointment of an arbitrator. If this is not done by you or your landlord your notice requiring arbitration ceases to be effective (see article 10 of that Order).

A.60 Form 23. **Notice to do work (notice to tenant to remedy breach of tenancy agreement by doing work of repair, maintenance or replacement) (prescribed form)**

FORM 2

AGRICULTURAL HOLDINGS ACT 1986

FORM 23

SCHEDULE 3, PART I, CASE D

Notice to tenant to remedy breach of tenancy by doing work of repair, maintenance or replacement

Re: the holding known as ....
To ....
....

(Name and address of tenant)

> IMPORTANT—FAILURE TO COMPLY WITH THIS NOTICE MAY BE RELIED ON AS A REASON FOR A NOTICE TO QUIT UNDER CASE D. IF YOU WANT YOUR TENANCY TO CONTINUE YOU MUST ACT QUICKLY. READ THE NOTICE AND ALL THE NOTES CAREFULLY. IF YOU ARE IN ANY DOUBT ABOUT THE ACTION YOU SHOULD TAKE, GET ADVICE IMMEDIATELY, e.g. FROM A SOLICITOR, SURVEYOR OR CITIZENS ADVICE BUREAU.

1. I hereby give you notice that I require you to remedy within [*] months* from the date of service of this Notice the breaches, set out below, of the terms or conditions of your tenancy, being breaches which are capable of being remedied of terms or conditions which are not inconsistent with your responsibilities to farm the holding in accordance with the rules of good husbandry.

* Note: This period must be a reasonable period for the tenant to remedy the breaches and must in any event be not less than six months.

2. This Notice requires the doing of the work of repair, maintenance or replacement specified below.

Particulars of breaches of terms or conditions of tenancy

Term or condition of tenancy	Particulars of breach and work required to remedy it
....	....
....	....

3. This Notice is given in accordance with Case D in Part I of Schedule 3 to the Agricultural Holdings Act 1986, and failure to comply with it within the period specified above may be relied on as a reason for a notice to quit under Case D.

4. Your attention is drawn to the Notes following the signature to this Notice.

SECTION 1: TENANCIES PROTECTED BY THE AGRICULTURAL HOLDINGS ACT 1986

Signed .... Date ....

(If signed by any person other than the landlord of the holding, state in what capacity or by what authority the signature is affixed.)

Address ....
....
....
....

Notes

In these Notes "the Order" means the Agricultural Holdings (Arbitration on Notices) Order 1987 (S.I. 1987/710).

What to do if you wish—

(a) to contest you liability to do the work, or any part of the work, required by this Notice to remedy (Question (a)); or

(b) to request the deletion from this Notice to remedy of any item or part of an item of work on the ground that it is unnecessary or unjustified (Question (b)); or

(c) to request the substitution in the case of any item or part of an item of work of a different method or material for the method or material which this Notice to remedy would otherwise require to be followed or used (Question (c)).

1. Questions (a), (b) and (c) mentioned in the heading to these Notes can be referred to arbitration under article 3(1) of the Order. To do so you *must* serve a notice in writing upon your landlord *within one month* of the service upon you of this Notice to remedy. The notice you serve upon your landlord should specify—

    (a) if you are referring Question (a), the items for which you deny liability,
    (b) if you are referring Question (b), the items you wish to be deleted,
    (c) if you are referring Question (c), the different methods or materials you wish to be substituted,

    and in each case should require the matter to be determined by arbitration under the Agricultural Holdings Act 1986 (clause 5). You will not be able to refer Question (a), (b) or (c) to arbitration later, on receipt of a notice to quit. This action does not prevent you settling the matter in writing by agreement with your landlord.

Carrying out the work

Form 23

2. If you refer any of these Questions (a), (b) and (c) to arbitration, you are not obliged to carry out the work which is the subject of the reference to arbitration unless and until the arbitrator decides that you are liable to do it; but you *must* carry out any work which you are not referring to arbitration.

3. If you are referring Question (a) to arbitration you may if you wish carry out any of the work which is the subject of that reference to arbitration without waiting for the arbitrator's award. If you do this and the arbitrator finds that you have carried out any such work which you were under no obligation to do, he will determine at the time he makes his award the reasonable cost of any such work which you have done and you will be entitled to recover this from your landlord (see article 8 of the Order). This provision does not apply in the case of work referred to arbitration under Question (b) or Question (c).

What to do if you wish to contest any other question arising under this Notice to remedy.

4. If you wish to contest any other question arising under this Notice other than Question (a), (b) or (c), such as whether the time specified in the Notice to do work is a reasonable period in which to carry out the work, you should refer the question to arbitration in either of the following ways, according to whether or not you are also at the same time referring Question (a), (b) or (c) to arbitration—

   (a) If you are referring Question (a), (b) or (c) to arbitration, then you must also refer to arbitration at the same time any other questions relevant to this Notice which you may wish to dispute.

   To do this, you should include in the Notice to your landlord referred to in Note 1 above a statement of the other questions which you require to be determined by arbitration under the Agricultural Holdings Act 1986 (see article 4(1) of the Order).

   (b) If you are not referring Question (a), (b) or (c) to arbitration, but wish to contest some other question arising under this Notice to remedy, you may refer that question to arbitration either now, on receipt of this Notice, or later, if you get a notice to quit.

   To refer the question to arbitration now, you should serve on your landlord *within one month* after the service of this Notice to remedy a notice in writing setting out what it is you require to be determined by arbitration under the Agricultural Holdings Act 1986 (see article 4(2)(a) of the Order).

   Alternatively, you have one month after the service of the notice to quit within which you can serve on your landlord a notice in writing requiring the question to be determined by arbitration under the 1986 Act (see

SECTION 1: TENANCIES PROTECTED BY THE AGRICULTURAL HOLDINGS ACT 1986

article 9 of the Order). You will then have three months from the date of service of that notice in which to appoint an arbitrator by agreement or (in default of such an agreement) to make an application under paragraph 1 of Schedule 11 to that Act for the appointment of an arbitrator. If this is not done by you or your landlord your notice requiring arbitration ceases to be effective (see article 10 of that Order).

Warning

5. Notes 1 to 4 above outline the *only* opportunities you have to challenge this Notice to remedy.

Extensions of time allowed for complying with this Notice to remedy

6. If you refer to arbitration now any question arising from this Notice to remedy, the time allowed for complying with the Notice will be extended until the termination of the arbitration. If the arbitrator decides that you are liable to do any of the work specified in this Notice to remedy, he will extend the time in which the work is to be done by such period as he thinks fit (see article 6(2) of the Order).

Warning as to the effect which any extension of the time allowed for complying with this Notice may have upon a subsequent notice to quit

7. If your time for doing the work is extended as mentioned in note 6 above, the arbitrator can specify a date for the termination of your tenancy should you fail to complete the work you are liable to do within the extended time. Then, if you did fail to complete that work within the extended time, your landlord could serve a notice to quit upon you expiring on the date on which the arbitrator had specified, and the notice would be valid even though that date might be less than 12 months after the next term date, and might not expire on a term date. The arbitrator cannot, however, specify a termination date which is less than six months after the expiry of the extended time to do the work. Nor can he specify a date which is earlier than would have been possible if you had not required arbitration on this Notice to remedy and had failed to do the work (see article 7 of the Order).

A.61 Form 24. **Notice by tenant requiring arbitration on notice to do work under Part II of the Agricultural Holdings (Arbitration on Notices) Order 1987 (S.I. 1987 No. 710) (not a prescribed form)**

AGRICULTURAL HOLDINGS ACT 1986, AGRICULTURAL HOLDINGS (ARBITRATION ON NOTICES) ORDER 1987

To: A.B. landlord of [address]

FORM 24

Re: The holding known as [name/OS numbers]

[1] I give you notice that I wish to have determined by arbitration under the Act the following question[s], namely—

- (a) my liability under the terms or conditions of the tenancy under which I hold the holding as your tenant to do certain items of the work specified in the notice to do work dated [*] which you have served on me. The items in respect of which I deny liability are specified in [Part I of] the Schedule hereto;

- [(b) the deletion from the said notice to do work of the items [or the parts of items] specified in Part II of the Schedule hereto on the ground that the said items [parts of items] are unnecessary or unjustified;]

- [(c) the substitution in the case of the items [or parts of items] specified in Part III of the Schedule hereto of the method [or material or method and material] specified in the said Part III for that required to be followed [or used or followed and used] in the said notice to do work.]

SCHEDULE

[Part I]

[Specify items in respect of which tenant denies liability.]

[Part II]

[Specify items or parts of items which tenant claims to be unnecessary or unjustified.]

[Part III]

[Specify items or parts of items in respect of which tenant wishes to substitute a different method or material or method and material, as follows:

Description of item or part of item;

Method or material or method and material required by notice to do work;

Method or material or method and material which it is desired to substitute.]

([1])[2] I also give you notice that I require to have determined by arbitration the

---

[1] If the tenant wishes to raise questions as to his liability to do work, deletion of items or substitution of methods or materials, it must be done at this stage and any additional questions must be raised at the same time.

SECTION 1: TENANCIES PROTECTED BY THE AGRICULTURAL HOLDINGS ACT 1986

following additional question[s] arising under the said notice to do work, namely: [*Here set out the additional question or questions which the tenant wishes to raise under the notice to do work, e.g. whether the time specified was a reasonable time in which to carry out the required work or whether the notice to do work was invalid because it was not in the prescribed form or not properly served.*]

(^{2})[I hereby give you notice that I wish to have determined by arbitration the questions set out in the Schedule hereto arising under the notice to do work dated [*] which you have served on me in respect of the holding.]

SCHEDULE

[*Here set out the question or questions to be determined (other than questions mentioned in article 3(1) of the Agricultural Holdings (Arbitration on Notices) Order 1986), e.g. whether the time specified in the notice to do work was a reasonable time in which to carry out the required work or whether the notice was invalid because not in the prescribed form or not properly served.*]

Dated:

Signed:

A.62 Form 25. **Notice to tenant to remedy breach of tenancy agreement, not being a notice to do any work of repair, maintenance or replacement (prescribed form)**

FORM 3

AGRICULTURAL HOLDINGS ACT 1986

SCHEDULE 3, PART I, CASE D

Notice to tenant to remedy breach of tenancy (not being a notice requiring the doing of any work of repair, maintenance or replacement)

Re: the holding known as ....
To ....
....

(Name and address of tenant)

---

[2] If the tenant wishes to raise other questions only (not as to liability, deletion of items or substitution of methods or materials), he has an option to raise them at this stage or after the notice to quit: see article 4 of the Order above mentioned.

FORM 25

> IMPORTANT—FAILURE TO COMPLY WITH THIS NOTICE MAY BE RELIED ON AS A REASON FOR A NOTICE TO QUIT UNDER CASE D. IF YOU WANT YOUR TENANCY TO CONTINUE YOU MUST ACT QUICKLY. READ THE NOTICE AND ALL THE NOTES CAREFULLY. IF YOU ARE IN ANY DOUBT ABOUT THE ACTION YOU SHOULD TAKE, GET ADVICE IMMEDIATELY, e.g. FROM A SOLICITOR, SURVEYOR OR CITIZENS ADVICE BUREAU.

1. I hereby give you notice that I require you to remedy within [*] months* from the date of service of this Notice the breaches, set out below, of the terms or conditions of your tenancy, being breaches which are capable of being remedied of terms or conditions which are not inconsistent with your responsibilities to farm the holding in accordance with the rules of good husbandry.

Particulars of breaches of terms or conditions of tenancy

Term or condition of tenancy   Particulars of breach

....

....

2. This Notice is given in accordance with Case D in Part I of Schedule 3 to the Agricultural Holdings Act 1986, and failure to comply with it within the period specified may be relied on as a reason for a notice to quit under Case D.

3. Your attention is drawn to the Notes following the signature to this Notice.

   Signed .... Date ....

(If signed by any person other than the landlord of the holding, state in what capacity or by what authority the signature is affixed.)

                                    Address ....
                                    ....
                                    ....
                                    ....

Notes

1. You cannot at this stage refer to arbitration either your liability to comply with this Notice to remedy or any other question as to the validity of the Notice. You will, however, be entitled to do so later if a notice to quit is served on you on the ground that you have failed to comply with this Notice to remedy. That is the only opportunity you will have to challenge this Notice.

2. At that stage under article 9 of the Agricultural Holdings (Arbitration on

SECTION 1: TENANCIES PROTECTED BY THE AGRICULTURAL HOLDINGS ACT 1986

Notices) Order 1987 (S.I. 1987/710), you have one month after the service of the notice to quit within which you can serve on your landlord a notice in writing requiring the question to be determined by arbitration under the Agricultural Holdings Act 1986 (clause 5).

3. You will then have three months from the date of service of that notice in which to appoint an arbitrator by agreement or (in default of such an agreement) to make an application under paragraph 1 of Schedule 11 to that Act for the appointment of an arbitrator. If this is not done by you or your landlord your notice requiring arbitration ceases to be effective (see article 10 of that Order).

A.63 **Form 26. Application by landlord to Agricultural Land Tribunal for a certificate of bad husbandry (prescribed form)**

Form 3

rule 4

Ref. No.
To be inserted
by the Secretary.

AGRICULTURAL LAND TRIBUNAL

Application for Certificate of Bad Husbandry

To the Secretary of the Agricultural Land Tribunal for the .... Area.

1. I .... [*block capitals*]
of .... [*address*]
hereby apply under section 2(4) of the Agricultural Holdings (Notices to Quit) Act 1977 for a certificate that my tenant, ...
.... [*block capitals*]
of .... [*address*]
is not fulfilling his responsibility to farm ....
.... [*name or description of holding*]
in accordance with the rules of good husbandry.

2. The land consists of:—

(a) .... hectares of arable land (including temporary grass)
(Ordnance Survey Field Nos. ....);
(b) .... hectares of permanent pasture
(Ordnance Survey Field Nos. ....);

FORM 26

(c) .... hectares of rough grazing
(Ordnance Survey Field Nos. ....);
(d) .... hectares of other land (including orchards)
(Ordnance Survey Field Nos. ....);

Total .... hectares.

3. The holding includes the following buildings [*give a general description*]:—

4. If a certificate of bad husbandry is granted I propose to serve a notice to quit.

5. The main grounds on which I allege bad husbandry are:—

6. I attach the following documents which I intend to produce in support of my case:

(a) two (^{1}) copies of a 6" to one mile or 1/10,000(^{2}) map of the holding described in paragraph 3 above;

(b) two(^{1}) copies of(^{3}):—

Date .... Signed(^{4}) ....

Form 26A. Tenant's reply to application by landlord to Agricultural Land Tribunal for a certificate of bad husbandry (prescribed form) A.64

Form 3R

Ref. No.
To be inserted
by the Secretary.

---

^{1} Two copies of the application and of any map and document must be sent to the Secretary, and if there are more than two parties (e.g., if the holding or part of it is sub-let) an additional copy of the application, etc., must be supplied for, and the Secretary must be informed of the name and address of, each additional party.

^{2} A larger scale map may be used if preferred. Ordnance Survey Field Numbers must be marked on the map.

^{3} Mention any other document which is attached to this application.

^{4} If signed by any person other than the applicant himself, he should state in what capacity or by what authority he signs.

SECTION 1: TENANCIES PROTECTED BY THE AGRICULTURAL HOLDINGS ACT 1986

AGRICULTURAL LAND TRIBUNAL

Reply to Application for Certificate of Bad Husbandry

To the Secretary of the Agricultural Land Tribunal for the .... Area.

I .... [*block capitals*]
of .... [*address*]
tenant (^{1}) of .... [*name or description of holding*],
having received a copy of the application (bearing the above reference number) for the Tribunal's certificate of bad husbandry, reply as follows:

1. The facts stated in the first three paragraphs of the application are correct except that:—

2. My main reasons for resisting the application are:—

3. I attach copies of the following relevant documents (^{2})

    Date .... Signed(^{3}) ....

Termination of tenancy: notices to quit and counter-notices

A.65   Form 27.   **Notice of landlord's intention to terminate a tenancy for a fixed term of two years or upwards at the date fixed for the expiry of the term (section 3) (not a prescribed form)**

Agricultural Holdings Act 1986, section 3(1)

To: C.D. tenant of [address]

Re: The holding known as [name/OS numbers]

I give you notice that I hereby terminate your tenancy of the holding under a lease dated [*], and made between (1) [*] and (2) [*] on the [*], being the date fixed by the lease for the expiry of the term granted by the lease.

---

^{1} If this form is completed by a sub-tenant, he should state whether he is sub-tenant of the whole or part of the holding; if of part, he should describe the part with reference to paragraphs 2 and 3 of the application and should state Ordnance Survey Field Numbers.
^{2} (a) Two copies of the reply and of any document which you wish to submit to the Tribunal must be sent to the Secretary, and, if there are more than two parties (e.g., if the holding or part of it sub-let), an additional copy of each must be supplied for each additional party.
(b) If you disagree with any map or plan attached to the application, your reply should be accompanied by two copies of a 6" to one mile or 1/10,000 (or larger) map showing what you consider to be the true position and marking the Ordnance Survey Field Numbers.
^{3} If signed by any person other than the tenant himself, he should state in what capacity or by what authority he signs.

Dated:

Signed:

Form 28. Notice to quit by landlord (ordinary notice without reasons stated) (not a prescribed form)   **A.66**

Agricultural Holdings Act 1986

To: C.D. tenant of [address]

Re: The holding known as [name/OS numbers]

I give you notice to quit the holding of which you are tenant on [*] [or at the expiration of the year of your tenancy which shall expire next after the end of 12 months from the service of this notice].

Dated:

Signed:

Form 29. Notice to quit by landlord to tenant stating reasons, in accordance with section 61(3) of the 1986 Act, for the purpose of excluding "additional compensation" for disturbance (not a prescribed form)   **A.67**

Agricultural Holdings Act 1986, section 61(3)

To: C.D. tenant of [address]

Re: The holding known as [name/OS numbers]

I give you notice to quit the holding on [*] or at the expiration of the year of your tenancy which shall expire next after the end of twelve months from the service of this notice. I give you notice that in accordance with section 61(3) of the above Act:

*   the carrying out of the purpose for which I propose to terminate the tenancy is desirable in the interests of good husbandry as respects the land to which this notice relates treated as a separate unit; and/or

*   the carrying out of the purpose for which I propose to terminate the tenancy is desirable in the interests of sound management of the estate of which the land to which this notice relates forms part [or is desirable in the interests of sound management of the estate which the land to which this notice relates constitutes]; and/or

SECTION 1: TENANCIES PROTECTED BY THE AGRICULTURAL HOLDINGS ACT 1986

* the carrying out of the purpose for which I propose to terminate the tenancy is desirable for the purposes of agricultural research, experiment or demonstration, or for the purposes of enactments relating to smallholdings; and/or

* I shall suffer hardship unless this notice has effect.

Dated:

Signed:

* Delete whatever is inapplicable.

A.68 Form 30. **Notice to quit by landlord relying on one or more of the Cases in Schedule 3 and specifying the relevant reason as appropriate (not a prescribed form)**

Agricultural Holdings Act 1986

To: C.D. tenant of [address]

Re: The holding known as [name/OS numbers]

I give you notice to quit the holding which you hold as tenant, on [*] [or at the expiration of the year of your tenancy which shall expire next after the end of 12 months from the service of this notice].

Statement for the purposes of Schedule 3 to the Act:

* Case A. This notice to quit is given by reason that the land which is the subject of this notice is let as a smallholding by a smallholdings authority [or by the Minister of Agriculture, Fisheries and Food or by the Secretary of State for Wales] and was so let on or after September 12, 1984 and

    (a) you have obtained the age of sixty-five, and

    (b) suitable alternative accommodation is available to you, or will be available to you when this notice takes effect, and

    (c) the instrument under which this tenancy was granted contains an acknowledgement signed by you that the tenancy was subject to the provisions of this Case.

* Case B. This notice to quit is given by reason that the land which is the subject of this notice is required for a use other than for agriculture—

FORM 30

* (a) for which permission has been granted on [* date] by [* local authority *or* the Secretary of State] on an application made under the enactments relating to town and country planning *or*

* (b) for which permission under the enactments relating to town and country planning is granted by a general development order by reason only of the fact that the use is authorised by (i) a private or local Act/(ii) an order approved by both Houses of Parliament or (iii) an order made under sections 14 or 16 of the Harbours Act 1964 *or*

* (c) for which a provision that (i) is contained in an Act but (ii) does not form part of the enactments relating to town and country planning deems permission under those enactments to have been granted *or*

* (d) which the provisions referred to in Case B(c) deem not to constitute development for the purposes of the enactments relating to town and country planning *or*

* (e) for which permission is not required under the enactments relating to town and country planning by reason only of Crown immunity.

* Case C. This notice to quit is given by reason that not more than six months before the giving of this notice the Agricultural Land Tribunal for the [*] Area granted a certificate under paragraph 9 of Part II of Schedule 3 to the Agricultural Holdings Act 1986 that you were not fulfilling your responsibilities to farm in accordance with the rules of good husbandry.

* Case D(a). This notice to quit is given by reason that at the date of the giving of this notice you have failed to comply with a notice in writing dated the [*] day of [*] served on you by me requiring you within two months from the service of the notice to pay rent in respect of the above-mentioned holding.

* Case D(b). This notice to quit is given by reason that at the date of the giving of this notice you have failed to comply with a notice in writing dated the [*] day of [*] requiring you within such reasonable period as was specified in the said notice [and as subsequently extended] to remedy the breaches set out in the said notice of the terms or conditions of your tenancy being breaches capable of being remedied by you of terms or conditions not inconsistent with your responsibilities to farm in accordance with the rules of good husbandry.

* Case E. This notice to quit is given by reason that at the date of the giving of this notice the interest of the landlord in the above-mentioned holding has been materially prejudiced by the commission by you of the

SECTION 1: TENANCIES PROTECTED BY THE AGRICULTURAL HOLDINGS ACT 1986

under-mentioned breaches, which are not capable of being remedied, of terms or conditions of your tenancy, being terms or conditions which are not inconsistent with the fulfilment of your responsibilities to farm in accordance with the rules of good husbandry.

PARTICULARS OF BREACHES OF TERMS OR CONDITIONS OF TENANCY

(Set out breaches, not capable of being remedied, which are relied on.)

* Case F. This notice to quit is given by reason that at the date of the giving of this notice the tenant has become insolvent.

(Case G. For precedent of a notice to quit served pursuant to Case G, see Form 31 below.)

(Case H. This relates to a notice to quit given by the Minister of Agriculture, Fisheries and Food or the Secretary of State for Wales: see section 96(1). It is not thought appropriate to include a precedent here. The departments no doubt have their own forms).

Dated:

Signed:

* Delete whatever is inapplicable. Under Case B it is unlikely that more than one variant will be required.

A.69 Form 31. **Notice to quit to personal representatives of deceased tenant, given not later than three months beginning with the date of a "relevant notice" of death of tenant or of an application for succession (not a prescribed form)**

Agricultural Holdings Act 1986

To: The personal representatives of the late C.D. tenant of [address]

(And/or)

To: The Public Trustee

Re: The holding known as [name/OS numbers]

I give you notice to quit the holding which was held by the late C.D. as tenant until his death on or about the [*] day of [*], (and which you now hold as his personal representatives), on the [*] [or at the expiration of the year of your tenancy which shall expire next after the end of 12 months from the service of this notice].

In accordance with Case G in Schedule 3 to the Agricultural Holdings Act 1986 this notice to quit—

> is given by reason of the death of C.D., who immediately before his death was the sole (or sole surviving) tenant under the contract of tenancy of the holding.

Dated:

Signed:

Form 32. Notice to quit by landlord relying on one or more of the Cases in Schedule 3, specifying the relevant reasons, and in the alternative expressing the notice as a simple notice to which section 26(1) applies (not a prescribed form) A.70

Agricultural Holdings Act 1986

To: C.D. tenant of [address]

Re: The holding known as [name/OS numbers]

I give you notice to quit and deliver up possession of the holding of which you are my tenant on the [*] [or at the expiration of the year of your tenancy which shall expire next after the end of twelve months from the service of this notice].

This notice is given in accordance with section 26(2) of and the under-mentioned Case(s) in Schedule 3 to the Agricultural Holdings Act 1986 and for the following reason(s):

[Here set out the reference to the relevant Case(s) with a statement of the reason(s) as in the body of Form 30/31.]

In the alternative, if this notice does not have effect as a notice to which section 26(2) of and Schedule 3 to the Act apply, I will rely on it as a notice to quit which section 26(1) of the Act applies. In that event I give you notice, in accordance with section 61(3) of the Act, that the purpose for which I proposed to terminate the tenancy is desirable in the interests of good husbandry as respects the land to which the notice relates treated as a separate unit [*or* is desirable in the interests of sound management of the estate of which the land to which this notice relates forms part].

Dated:

Signed:

SECTION 1: TENANCIES PROTECTED BY THE AGRICULTURAL HOLDINGS ACT 1986

A.71 **Form 33. Tenant's notice to landlord requiring arbitration in regard to reasons stated in a notice to quit given in pursuance of Cases A, B, D or E in Schedule 3 to the Agricultural Holdings Act 1986 (not a prescribed form)**

Agricultural Holdings Act 1986 and the Agriculture Holdings (Notices to Quit) Order 1987, Article 9

To: A.B. landlord of [address]

Re: The holding known as [name/OS numbers]

With reference to the notice to quit dated [*], which you have served on me in respect of the holding, I wish to contest questions arising under the provisions of section 26(2) of, and Schedule 3 to, the Act relating to the reason(s) stated in the said notice to quit, and I require the question(s) to be determined by arbitration under the Act.

[This notice is given without prejudice to any rights which I may have to contend that the said notice is invalid, which rights are hereby expressly reserved.]

Dated:

Signed:

A.72 **Form 34. Notice to quit part of a holding for one of the purposes mentioned in section 31 of the 1986 Act (as an example, erection of farm labourers' cottages) (not a prescribed form)**

Agricultural Holdings Act 1986, section 31

To: C.D. tenant of [address]

Re: The holding known as [name/OS numbers]

I hereby give you notice to quit on [*] or at the expiration of the year of your tenancy which shall expire next after the end of twelve months from service of this notice the land shown edged red on the attached plan and identified by the Schedule attached hereto being part of the holding of which you are tenant from year to year.

In accordance with section 31 of the Act, you are notified that this notice is given with a view to the use of the said part of the holding for the erection of cottages for farm labourers.

This notice is also given in accordance with Case B in Schedule 3 to the Act on the ground that the said part of the holding is required for a use other than for

FORM 34

agriculture, namely, for the erection of the said cottages, for which planning permission has been granted by [*] by a planning decision dated [*] on an application made in that behalf under the enactments relating to town and country planning.

SCHEDULE

[*Describe exactly in sufficient detail for identification the part of the holding concerned.*]

Dated:

Signed:

Form 35. Notice to quit part of a holding given by landlord for a non-agricultural use, planning permission having been obtained. Less than twelve months' notice given under clause in contract of tenancy (section 25(2)(b) and Case B) (not a prescribed form) A.73

Agricultural Holdings Act 1986, Schedule 3 Case B

To: C.D. tenant of [address]

Re: The holding known as [name/OS numbers]

I hereby give you notice to quit all that part of the above named holding which is identified edged red on the plan annexed hereto and specified by the Schedule forming part hereof of which you are tenant on [*]. I require possession of the said part for the following non-agricultural purpose namely [*] and this notice is given in accordance with clause [*] of the tenancy agreement dated [*] which provides that I may resume possession of the same for the said purpose on giving [*] months' notice.

You are also hereby notified in accordance with Case B in Part I of Schedule 3 to the Act that the said part is required for a use other than for agriculture, namely, the use specified above, for which planning permission has been granted on an application made under the enactments relating to town and country planning by the [*] Council by a planning decision dated [*].

SCHEDULE

[*Describe exactly in sufficient detail for identification the part of the holding concerned.*]

Dated:

Signed:

SECTION 1: TENANCIES PROTECTED BY THE AGRICULTURAL HOLDINGS ACT 1986

A.74 **Form 36. Counter-notice by tenant (section 26(1)) (not a prescribed form) with variant for section 28(2) when appropriate**

Agricultural Holdings Act 1986, section 26(1) [*or* section 28(2)]

To: A.B. landlord of [address]

Re: The holding known as [name/OS numbers]

I require subsection (1) of section 26 of the Act to apply to the notice to quit served on me in respect of the holding, of which I am the tenant, and which notice is dated [*].

[*or:*

I require subsection (2) of section 28 of the Act to apply to the notice to quit served on me in respect of the holding, of which I am the tenant, and which notice is dated[*]].

[This counter-notice is given without prejudice to the exercise of my right to contest reasons stated in the said notice to quit insofar as it relies on a Case or Cases set out in Schedule 3 to the said Act and to require the question or questions so raised to be determined by arbitration under the said Act.]

[This counter-notice is also given without prejudice to the exercise of any rights which I may have to contend that the said notice to quit is invalid, which rights are hereby expressly reserved.]

Dated:

Signed:

A.75 **Form 37. Counter-notice by tenant accepting notice to quit the entire holding (section 32), variation where reversion is severed: (section 32) (not a prescribed form)**

Agricultural Holdings Act 1986, section 32

To: A.B. landlord of [address]

Re: The holding known as [name/OS numbers]

I have received your notice to quit dated [*] referring to part of the above named holding and I hereby give you a counter-notice in accordance with section 32 of the Act that I accept the said notice to quit as a notice to quit the entirety of the holding to take effect at the same time as the said notice to quit.

† *[I have received from [*] (being a person entitled to a severed part of the reversionary estate in the above named holding) a notice to quit dated [*] referring to part of the holding and I give you and all the other persons severally entitled to the severed parts of the reversion in the holding a counter-notice, in accordance with section 32 of the Act that I accept the said notice to quit as a notice to quit the entirety of the holding to take effect at the same time as the said notice to quit.]*

Dated:

Signed:

† This variation applies where the notice to quit part is given by the owner of the severed part of the reversion not by the owner of the entirety.

Form 38. Notice to quit by tenant to landlord (not a prescribed form)   A.76

Agricultural Holdings Act 1986

To: A.B. landlord of [address]

Re: The holding known as [name/OS numbers]

I intend to quit and deliver up possession of the holding, of which I am the tenant, on the [*] [or at the expiration of the year of my tenancy which shall expire next after the end of twelve months from the service of this notice].

Dated:

Signed:

Form 39. Notice to quit by tenant to sub-tenant (not a prescribed form)   A.77

Agricultural Holdings Act 1986

To: E.F. [name and address of sub-tenant]

I hereby give you notice to quit and deliver up possession of the holding, of which you are my tenant, on [*].

I have myself been given notice to quit the holding on [*] by [name of superior landlord] from whom I hold as tenant.

Dated:

Signed:

SECTION 1: TENANCIES PROTECTED BY THE AGRICULTURAL HOLDINGS ACT 1986

A.78 **Form 40. Application by landlord for Agricultural Land Tribunal's consent to notice to quit (section 26(1)) (prescribed form); (section 28(2) (prescribed form)**

Form 1

rule 2(3)

Ref. No.
To be inserted
by the Secretary.

AGRICULTURAL LAND TRIBUNAL

Application for Consent to Operation of Notice to Quit

To the Secretary of the Agricultural Land Tribunal for the .... Area.

1. I .... [*block capitals*]
of .... [*address*]
hereby apply under—

    *   (a) Section 2(1)
    *   (b) Section 4(2)
    *   (c) Section 4(3)

of the Agricultural Holdings (Notices to Quit) Act 1977 for the consent of the Tribunal to the operation of a notice to quit which I * propose to give/have given to my tenant, ... [*block capitals*]
of .... [*address*]

2.
  *(a) I propose to serve the notice before the .... day of .... 19........
  *(b) The notice was served on the ..... day of ..... 19 ....., and a counter-notice was served by the tenant on the .... day of .... 19 ....

3. The holding in respect of which the notice * will be/has been given is known as
....
and consists of:—

(a)	....	hectares of arable land (including temporary grass) (Ordnance Survey Field Nos. ....);
(b)	....	hectares of permanent pasture (Ordnance Survey Field Nos. ....);
(c)	....	hectares of rough grazing (Ordnance Survey Field Nos. ....);

FORM 40

(d) .... hectares of other land (including orchards)
(Ordnance Survey Field Nos. ....);

Total .... hectares.   ANNUAL RENT £

4. The holding includes the following buildings [*give a general description*]:—

†5. I apply for the Tribunal's consent to the operation of the notice to quit on the following ground(s) provided in paragraph(s) .... of section 3(3) of the Agricultural Holdings (Notices to Quit) Act 1977 (^{1}). [*This paragraph is relevant to an application under section 2(1) of the Act, in which case it is important to refer to footnote (^{1}). In other cases the paragraph should be struck out.*]

6. The main facts on which I base my case are [*give a brief outline*]:—(^{2})

7. If I obtain possession of the land I intend:—

    (a) to farm it myself;
    (b) to let it to another tenant [*state name and address if known*].

8. I/The future tenant*(^{3}) at present farm(s) other and consisting of:—

(a) .... hectares of arable land (including temporary grass)
(Ordnance Survey Field Nos. ....);
(b) .... hectares of permanent pasture
(Ordnance Survey Field Nos. ....);
(c) .... hectares of rough grazing

---

^{1} The applicant must state on which paragraph or paragraphs of the subsection he intends to rely. The five paragraphs, as amended, are as follows:
(a) that the carrying out of the purpose for which the landlord proposes to terminate the tenancy is desirable in the interests of good husbandry as respects the land to which the notice relates, treated as a separate unit; or
(b) that the carrying out thereof is desirable in the interests of sound management of the estate of which the land to which the notices relates forms part or which that land constitutes (*see footnote (^{31}) below*); or
(c) that the carrying out thereof is desirable for the purposes of agricultural research, education, experiment or demonstration, or for the purposes of the enactments relating to small-holdings or allotments; or
(d) that greater hardship would be caused by withholding than by giving consent to the operation of the notice; or
(e) that the landlord proposes to terminate the tenancy for the purpose of the land's being us ed for a use, other than for agricultural, not falling within Case B (i.e. section 2(3) of the Agricultural Holdings (Notices to Quit) Act 1977).

^{2} Where the tenant is a serviceman within the meaning of section 11 of the Agricultural Holdings (Notices to Quit) Act 1977, and the notice to quit is given for one or more of the reasons specified in Case B, D or E, the reasons for the giving of the notice must be stated and, if any question arising out of them has been determined by arbitration, the determination should also be stated.

^{3} (3) Paragraph 8 need not be completed if the name of the future tenant is unknown. Where land is described, a map should be provided (*footnote (^{6}) below*).

SECTION 1: TENANCIES PROTECTED BY THE AGRICULTURAL HOLDINGS ACT 1986

(d) .... hectares of other land (including orchards)
(Ordnance Survey Field Nos. ....);
(Ordnance Survey Field Nos. ....);

Total .... hectares.

9. I attach the following documents which I intend to produce in support of my case:—

   (a) two ([4]) copies of a 6" to one mile or 1/10,000([5]) map of the holding described in paragraph 3 above (and of any other land referred to in paragraph 8†([6]);

   (b) two([4]) copies of ([7]):—

   Date .... Signed([8]) ....

* Strike out whichever is inapplicable.

†Strike out if inapplicable

A.79   **Form 40A. Tenant's reply to landlord's application for consent to notice to quit (prescribed form)**

Form 1R

Ref. No.
To be inserted
by the Secretary.

AGRICULTURAL LAND TRIBUNAL

Reply to Application for Consent to Operation of Notice to Quit

To the Secretary of the Agricultural Land Tribunal for the .... Area.

I .... [*block capitals*]

---

[4] Two copies of the application and of any map and document must be sent to the Secretary, and if there are more than two parties (e.g. if the holding or part of it is sub-let), an additional copy of the application, etc, must be supplied for, and the Secretary of State must be informed of the name and address of, each additional party.

[5] A larger scale map may be used if preferred. Ordnance Survey Field Numbers must be marked on the map.

[6] Where it is intended to give evidence about any land other than that which is the subject of the notice to quit, it must be shown either on the map produced or on a separate map of a scale of 6" to one mile or 1/10,000 or larger.

[7] Mention any other document which is attached to this application.

[8] If signed by any person other than the applicant himself, he should state in what capacity or by what authority he signs.

FORM 40A

of .... [address]
tenant (^{1}) of .... [name or description of holding],
having received a copy of the application (bearing the above reference number) for the Tribunal's consent to the operation of a notice to quit, reply as follows:

1. The facts stated in the first four paragraphs of the application are correct except that:—

2. In addition to the land which is the subject of the application, I farm the following land(^{2}):—
   which includes the following buildings [give a general description]:—

3. My main reasons for restricting the application are:—

4. My landlord is not acting fairly and reasonably because(^{3}):—

5. I attach copies of the following relevant documents(^{4}):—

   Date .... Signed(^{5}) ....

---

^{1} (a) If this form is completed by a sub-tenant, he should state whether he is sub-tenant of the whole or part of the holding; if of part, he should describe the part with reference to paragraphs 3 and 4 of the application and should state Ordnance Survey Field Numbers.
(b) If this form is completed by a superior landlord, he should omit paragraph 2.
^{2} (a) If you farm other land as part of the same unit with that which is the subject of the application, give a description, stating the area (in hectares) which is arable (including temporary grass), pasture (including rough grazing) and other land (including orchards) and giving the Ordnance Survey Field Numbers. If the land is farmed separately, give a general description, stating area, kind of farming and approximate distance from the holding in question.
(b) If the other land is not shown on the map produced by the landlord, you should produce a map of it of a scale of 6" to one mile or 1/10,000 (or larger) and giving the Ordnance Survey Field Numbers. If the land is not farmed as part of the same unit, or for any other good reason, you may, before or at the time of sending your reply, apply to the Secretary of the Tribunal in writing for the Chairman to dispense with the map.
^{3} The Tribunal will not give consent if, in all the circumstances, it appears to them that a fair and reasonable landlord would not insist on possession. If you have any special reasons for saying your landlord is acting unfairly or unreasonably which do not appear under paragraph 3, you should state them under paragraph 4.
^{4} (a) Two copies of the reply and of any document which you wish to submit to the Tribunal must be sent to the Secretary, and, if there are more than two parties (e.g., if the holding or part of it is sub-let), an additional copy of each must be supplied for each additional party.
(b) If you disagree with any map or plan attached to the application, your reply should be accompanied by two copies of a 6" to one mile or 1/10,000 (or larger) map showing what you consider to be the true position and marking the Ordnance Survey Field Numbers.
^{5} If signed by any person other than the landlord himself, he should state in what capacity or by what authority he signs.

SECTION 1: TENANCIES PROTECTED BY THE AGRICULTURAL HOLDINGS ACT 1986

A.80 Form 41. Application by landlord under section 27(5) for variation or revocation of condition imposed by Tribunal under section 27(4) in consenting to operation of a notice to quit (prescribed form)

Form 4

rule 5

Ref. No.
To be inserted
by the Secretary.

AGRICULTURAL LAND TRIBUNAL

Application for Variation of Revocation of Condition Imposed by the Tribunal

To the Secretary of the Agricultural Land Tribunal for the .... Area.

1. I .... [*block capitals*]
of .... [*address*]
hereby apply under section 3(5) of the Agricultural Holdings (Notices to Quit) Act 1977 for the Tribunal to vary or revoke the condition imposed by them under section 3(4) thereof granting my application bearing the reference number ....

2. *(a) I wish the Tribunal to revoke the condition.
   *(b) I wish the Tribunal to revoke the condition; but if they are unwilling to do so, I request them to make the following variation:—
   *(c) I do not wish the Tribunal to revoke the condition, but only to make the following variation:—

3. The main reasons for my application are:—

4. I attach two(^{1}) copies of a 6" to one mile or 1/10,000(^{2}) map of the holding which was the subject of the notice to quit(^{3}) and the following documents which I intend to produce in support of my case(^{4}):—

Date .... Signed(^{5}) ....

---

[1] Two copies of the application and of any map and document must be sent to the Secretary.
[2] A larger scale map may be used if preferred. Ordnance Survey Field Numbers must be marked on the map.
[3] The Chairman of the Tribunal has power in all cases to dispense with maps, etc (e.g. if they are already in the possession of the Tribunal). A request for a direction on this subject should be made in writing before or at the time of sending the application.
[4] Mention any other document which is attached to the application.
[5] If signed by any person other than the applicant himself, he should state in what capacity or by what authority he signs.

FORM 41

* Strike out whichever is inapplicable.

Form 42. Application by tenant to the Agricultural Land Tribunal to postpone operation of notice to quit (prescribed form) A.81

Form 2

rule 3

Ref. No.
To be inserted
by the Secretary.

AGRICULTURAL LAND TRIBUNAL

Application for Consent to Operation of Notice to Quit

To the Secretary of the Agricultural Land Tribunal for the .... Area.

1. I .... [*block capitals*]
of .... [*address*]
hereby apply under Article 12(1) of the Agricultural Holdings (Arbitration on Notices) Order 1978 for the Tribunal to postpone the operation of the Notice to Quit served on me by my landlord:—
.... [*block capitals*]
of .... [*address*]
in respect of ....
.... [*name or description of holding*].

2. The Tribunal consented on the .... day of .... 19 ...., to the operation of the said notice on the application of my landlord bearing reference number ....

3. If its operation is not postponed the Notice will expire on the .... day of .... 19.........

4. My main reasons for this application are:—

5. I attach two (^{1}) copies of a 6" to one mile or 1/10,000(^{2}) map of the land which was the subject of the notice to quit(^{3}) and of the following documents

---

[1] Two copies of the application and any map or document must be sent to the Secretary, and if there are more than two parties (e.g. if the land is held under a sub-tenancy), an additional copy of the application etc. must be supplied for, and the Secretary of State must be informed of the name and address of, each additional party. A written notice is required (by Article 12(2) of the 1978 Order referred to above) to be given at the same time to the landlord.

[2] A larger scale map may be used if preferred. Ordnance Survey Field Numbers must be marked on the map.

[3] The Chairman of the Tribunal has power in all cases to dispense with maps, etc. A request for a direction on this subject should be made in writing before or at the time of sending the application.

SECTION 1: TENANCIES PROTECTED BY THE AGRICULTURAL HOLDINGS ACT 1986

which I intend to produce in support of my case:—

Date ……………………… Signed(⁴) ………………………

A.82 **Form 42A. Landlord's reply to application by tenant to the Agricultural Land Tribunal to postpone operation of notice to quit (prescribed form)**

Form 2R

Ref. No.
To be inserted
by the Secretary.

AGRICULTURAL LAND TRIBUNAL

Reply to Application to Postpone Operation of Notice to Quit

To the Secretary of the Agricultural Land Tribunal for the ……………… Area.

I ……………………………………………………………… [*block capitals*]
of ……………………………………………………………… [*address*]
landlord of ………………………………… [*name or description of holding*], having received a copy of the application (bearing the above reference number) for the Tribunal to postpone the operation of the notice to quit the above named holding, reply as follows:

1. The facts stated in the first three paragraphs of the application are correct except that:—

2. *(a) I request that there should be no postponement.
   *(b) I would agree to postponement up to the …….. day of …….. 19 ……..

3. My main reasons for restricting the application are:—

4. I attach copies of the following relevant documents(¹):—

   Date ……………………… Signed(²) ………………………

---

⁴ If signed by any person other than the applicant himself, he should state in what capacity or by what authority he signs.

¹ (a) Two copies of the reply and of any document which you wish to submit to the Tribunal must be sent to the Secretary, and, if there are more than two parties (e.g., if the land is sub-let), an additional copy of each must be supplied for each additional party.
(b) If you disagree with any map or plan attached to the application, your reply should be accompanied by two copies of a 6" to one mile or 1/10,000 (or larger) map showing what you consider to be the true position and marking the Ordnance Survey Field Numbers.

² If signed by any person other than the landlord himself, he should state in what capacity or by what authority he signs.

FORM 42A

* Strike out whichever is inapplicable.

Succession on death or retirement
Succession on death

Form 43. Application for direction giving entitlement to tenancy of agricul-   **A.83**
tural holding and application that applicant be treated as an
eligible person (prescribed form)

                Form 1 (Succession on Death)   Rule 3(1) and (2)

                                                        Ref. No.
                                                         To be inserted
                                                          by the secretary.

AGRICULTURAL LAND TRIBUNAL

**Application for Direction giving Entitlement
to Tenancy of Agricultural Holding**

Application for Determination that Applicant be Treated as an Eligible Person

[*In completing this form it is important to refer to the notes*]

PART A—To be completed by all applicants

To the Secretary of the Agricultural Land Tribunal for the .... Area.

1. I .... [*block capitals*]
of .... [*address*]
hereby apply under section 20(1) of the Agriculture (Miscellaneous Provisions) Act 1976 for a direction entitling me to a tenancy of the holding specified in paragraph 2 below.

2. The holding in respect of which the application is made is known as

and consists of:—

(a)   ....   hectares of arable land (including temporary grass)
                              (Ordnance Survey Field Nos. ....);
(b)   ....   hectares of permanent pasture
                              (Ordnance Survey Field Nos. ....);
(c)   ....   hectares of rough grazing
                              (Ordnance Survey Field Nos. ....);
(d)   ....   hectares of other land (including orchards)

SECTION 1: TENANCIES PROTECTED BY THE AGRICULTURAL HOLDINGS ACT 1986

(Ordnance Survey Field Nos. ....);

Total .... hectares   ANNUAL RENT £

3. The current year of the tenancy of the holding expires on ....

4. The holding includes the following buildings [*give a general description*]:—

†5. The holding forms part of a larger agricultural unit known as and consisting of [*give a general description*]:—

6. The application arises on the death of formerly the tenant of the holding referred to in paragraph 2, who died on;(¹);

His/her tenancy was—

* (a) granted before 12th July 1984.
* (b) obtained on or after 12th July 1984 by virtue of a direction of the Agricultural Land Tribunal under section 20 of the 1976 Act.
* (c) granted on or after 12th July 1984 following a direction of the Agricultural Land Tribunal under section 20 of the 1976 Act but commenced before the relevant time for the purposes of section 23 of that Act.
* (d) granted on or after the 12th July 1984 by a written contract of tenancy indicating that the succession provisions in Part II off the 1976 Act should apply.
* (e) granted on or after 12th July 1984 to a person who, immediately before that date, was a tenant of the holding or of any agricultural holding which comprised the whole or a substantial part of the land comprised in the holding.

7. The landlord of the holding is ....
of .... [*address*].

†8. I am the sole person validly designated by the deceased tenant of the holding in his will as the person he wished to succeed him as tenant of the holding. A copy of the relevant part of the will in which I am designated is attached [*attach a copy of or extract from the will marking the relevant passage*](²).

---

[1] Formal proof of the date of death will be required at the hearing.

[2] This paragraph should be completed only if the applicant received a specified bequest of the deceased's tenancy under his will or is specifically named in the will as the person whom the deceased tenant wished to succeed him as tenant of the holding. It will be necessary for a grant of probate or administration to be obtained from the Family Division of the High Court in respect of the will before the tribunal can hear any claim to be a designated applicant. Where an applicant establishes that he is so designated under the deceased tenant's will, no other application will be considered unless the tribunal determine that the designated applicant is not an eligible person or is not a suitable person to become the tenant of the holding.

FORM 43

9. †(a) I am the *wife/*husband/*brother/*sister/*child of the deceased tenant(^{3}).

   †(b) I was treated by the deceased tenant as a child of the family in relation to his marriage to .... (^{4})
   on .... [*give date of marriage*]

10. †(a) During the seven years ending with the date of death of the deceased tenant my only or my principal source of livelihood was derived from—
    * (i) my agricultural work on the holding, or on an agricultural unit of which the holding forms a part;
    * (ii) his/her and my agricultural work on the holding, or on an agricultural unit of which the holding forms a part;
    during the following period(s) and in the following manner [*give details of the way livelihood derived from agricultural work on the holding*];(^{5}):—
    (b) During the period(s) specified in paragraph 10(a) I had the following source(s) of livelihood other than those derived from the holding or from an agricultural unit of which the holding forms a part [*give details of other sources of livelihood*]:—
    * (c) During the period(s) specified in paragraph 10(a) I had no other source of livelihood.

†11. During the seven years ending with the date of death of the deceased tenant attended a full time course at [*name of university, college or other establishment of further education*] during the following period(s) [*give details of time spent at university, etc*]; (^{5}), (^{6}):—

---

^{3} Formal proof of the relationship to the deceased, e.g. by production of marriage or birth certificate, may be required at the hearing. Adopted children should complete this sub-paragraph, and not paragraph 9(b) following.

^{4} Paragraph 9(b) may apply where the applicant was the step-child or foster child of the deceased or was otherwise treated by him as his child. An outline should be given of the circumstances relied on as establishing that the applicant was treated by the deceased as his child in relation to the marriage. Production of the relevant marriage certificate and any relevant birth certificate may be required at the hearing.

^{5} To qualify under paragraph 10(a)(i) the applicant should have derived his only or principal source of livelihood from his agricultural work on the holding (or on a larger unit of which the holding forms part) during a total of five years of the seven years ending with the death of the deceased tenant. Paragraph 10(a)(ii) is available only to a widow of the deceased tenant. The total of five years may be made up of one continuous period or one or more separate periods. A period of full-time education at university etc, may, in the circumstances set out in note (^{6}) count towards the five-year period of earning a livelihood from the holding, and reference should be made to paragraph 11 and note (^{6}) in deciding whether the requirements of this paragraph can be satisfied. An applicant who cannot satisfy the requirements of paragraph 10(a) fully but who believes he can satisfy them to a material extent should not complete paragraphs 10 and 11 but should complete instead paragraph 15, together with paragraphs 16, 17 (if relevant) and 18 in Part B of the Form. The notes to those paragraphs should also be consulted. Where an applicant is in any doubt as to whether or not he can satisfy the requirements of paragraph 10 fully, he is advised to complete paragraphs 10 and 11 (if relevant) and Part B of the Form.

^{6} Any period or periods (up to an aggregate total of three years) during the seven years ending with the date of death of the deceased tenant during which the applicant was

SECTION 1: TENANCIES PROTECTED BY THE AGRICULTURAL HOLDINGS ACT 1986

During this period/these period(s), I studied the following subjects and obtained the following qualifications [*give details of subjects studied and any qualifications obtained*]:—

†12. (a) The following agricultural land is occupied by me, my spouse or a company under my control, the control of my spouse or our joint control as owner-occupier/tenant/licensee, whether alone or jointly with others [*give particulars of any land occupied, including area and any land occupied jointly with others*]: (^{7}):—

†(b) The following agricultural land is occupied by a person under a licence or such a tenancy as is mentioned in paragraph 2(1)(a) to (d) of Schedule 3A to the 1976 Act(^{8}) granted by *me and/or *my spouse and/or *a company controlled by me and/or my spouse (together with one or more other persons, being at the time it was granted a person or persons entitled to occupy the land otherwise than under a tenancy, or in a capacity, falling within paragraph 2(1)(a) to (f) of that Schedule (^{8}) [*give particulars of any land occupied, including area*]:—

†(c) I apply under paragraph 4(2) of Schedule 3A to the 1976 Act for the net annual income from the following agricultural land which is—
  * (i) jointly occupied;
  * (ii) deemed by virtue of paragraph 6(2) of that Schedule to be jointly occupied;
by me and one or more other persons (not being only my spouse or a company

---

attending a full-time course at a university, college or other establishment of further education will be treated as a period throughout which his only or principal source of livelihood was derived from his agricultural work on the holding. Any subject may have been studied.

^{7} Land occupied by the applicant's spouse or by a company controlled by that person or jointly by that person and the applicant should not be included in paragraph 12 where either of the parties had obtained a decree of judicial separation or a decree nisi of divorce or of a nullity of marriage and in each case that decree remains unrescinded. In addition, land should not be included in paragraph 12 if it is occupied by the applicant, his spouse or a controlled company—
(a) under a tenancy approved under section 2(1) of the Agricultural Holdings Act 1948 or under such a tenancy relating to the use of land for grazing or mowing as is referred to in the proviso to that provision;
(b) under a tenancy for more than one year but less than two years;
(c) under a tenancy not falling within (a) or (b) above and not having effect as a contract of tenancy;
(d) under a tenancy to which section 3 of the 1948 Act does not apply by virtue of section 3B of that Act;
(e) as a licensee; or
(f) as an executor, administrator, trustee in bankruptcy or person otherwise deriving title from another person by operation of law.
However, where the applicant occupies land in accordance with (a) to (e) above under a licence or tenancy granted to him by his spouse or by a body corporate controlled by him, that land should be included in paragraph 12.

^{8} Paragraph 2(1)(a) to (f) of Schedule 3A to the Agriculture (Miscellaneous Provisions) Act 1976 is set out in note (^{7}).

under my control, the control of my spouse or our joint control) to be treated as limited to my appropriate share of that net annual income [*give particulars of any land in joint occupation or deemed joint occupation*](^{9}):—

13. I was born on ....

14. I claim to be a suitable person to receive the tenancy of this holding because (^{10}):—

Part B—To be completed if you think that you may not fully satisfy the requirements of paragraph 10(a)

15. Further to the application set out in the preceding paragraphs of this Form, I, ... [*block capitals*] of the above address also apply under section 21(2) of the 1976 Act for a determination that I am to be treated as an eligible person for the purposes of Part II of that Act(^{11}).

16.(a) During the seven years ending with the date of death of the deceased tenant my livelihood was derived from—
* (i) my agricultural work on the holding referred to in paragraph 2, or on an agricultural unit of which the holding forms a part;
* (ii) his/her and my agricultural work on the holding referred to in paragraph 2, or on an agricultural unit of which the holding forms a part;

to a material extent during the following period(s) and in the following manner [*give details of the extent to which livelihood was derived from agricultural work on the holding*](^{12}):—

---

^{9} If the applicant occupies land jointly with one or more other persons (not being only his spouse or a company under the control of the applicant or his spouse or under their joint control), or if the applicant is deemed to occupy land jointly with one or more such persons, he may in either case complete the application set out in paragraph 12(c) of the Form for the net annual income which the land is or was capable of producing to be treated as limited to his appropriate share.

^{10} All matters relied on as supporting the claim to be a suitable person to become the tenant of the holding should be summarised. These should include details of the applicant's training and practical experience of agriculture, physical health, financial standing and any educational qualifications not already listed in paragraph 11 or 17.

^{11} This paragraph should be completed (together with paragraphs 16, 17 (if relevant) and 18) in any case where the applicant, while otherwise meeting the conditions contained in paragraphs (a) and (c) of the definition of "eligible person" in section 18(2) of the 1976 Act cannot fully satisfy the conditions as to deriving his principal or main source of livelihood from the holding contained in paragraph (b) of that subsection. (It is also necessary for the application set out in paragraph 1 of the Form to be completed in addition to completing this paragraph.) An applicant who fully satisfies the requirements of paragraph 10(a) need not complete this paragraph or paragraphs 16, 17 and 18.

^{12} The applicant should state to what extent he has derived his livelihood from his agricultural work on the holding (or on a larger unit of which the holding forms part) during a total of five years of the seven years ending with the death of the deceased tenant. Paragraph 16(a)(ii) applies only to a widow of the deceased tenant. The total of five years may be made up of one continuous period, or one or more separate periods. A period of

SECTION 1: TENANCIES PROTECTED BY THE AGRICULTURAL HOLDINGS ACT 1986

†(b) During the period(s) specified in paragraph 16(a) I had the following source(s) of livelihood other than those derived from the holding or from an agricultural unit of which the holding forms a part [*give details of other sources of livelihood*]:—

†(c) During the period(s) specified in paragraph 16(a) I had no other source of livelihood.

†17. During the seven years ending with the date of death of the deceased tenant I attended a full-time course at [*name of university, college or other establishment of further education*] during the following period(s) [*give details of time spent at university, etc*]([16]):—

During this period/these periods I studied the following subjects and obtained the following qualifications [*give details of subjects studied and any qualifications obtained*]:—

†18. I claim that, because of the following circumstances, it is fair and reasonable for me to be able to apply under section 20 of the 1976 Act for a direction entitling me to a tenancy of the holding referred to in paragraph 2([13]):—

PART C—To be completed by all applicants

19. I attach the following documents which I intend to produce in support of my case:—
    (a) two([14]) copies of a 6" to one mile or 1/10,000([15]) map of the holding described in paragraph 2 above (and of other land referred to in paragraph 5);
    (b) two([14]) copies of([16]):—

20. The persons whom I shall notify of this application/these applications are([17]):—

---

full-time education at a university, etc., may in certain circumstances count in relation to the five year period as a period in which a livelihood was derived from agricultural work on the holding, and paragraph 17 should also be completed where relevant.

[13] A summary should be given of matters relied on as establishing that it is fair and reasonable that the applicant should be entitled to apply under section 20 of the 1976 Act for a tenancy of the holding, though not fully satisfying the conditions specified in paragraph (b) of the definition of "eligible person" in section 18(2) of that Act. The length of time the applicant has lived on the holding, details of work done by him on the holding (apart from those already given in paragraph 16) and any special circumstances which have prevented him from qualifying in full as an eligible person under paragraph (b) of the definition of "eligible person" should be given. (Note ([5]) describes the requirements needed to qualify fully under paragraph (b) of the definition.)

[14] By virtue of rule 11(1) of the Agricultural Land Tribunals (Succession) Rules 1984 two copies of the application and of any map and document must be sent to the secretary.

[15] A larger scale map may be used if preferred. Ordnance Survey Field Numbers must be marked on the map.

[16] Mention any other document which is attached to this application.

[17] The applicant is required to send to the landlord of the holding, and to every other person who to his knowledge has made or may be able to make an application for a tenancy of the holding, notice of this application in Form 3 (Succession on Death) which is set out in the

(a) the landlord of the holding whose name and address are:—
(b)
(c)
(d)

21. (a) The following is/are the personal representative(s) of the deceased tenant or [*if there are no personal representatives*] the person or persons responsible for the management of the holding on behalf of the deceased's estate([18]):—

Name(s) ....
Address(es) ....
 ....
 ....

(b) The following person(s) is/are or may be interested in the outcome of this application([18]):—

Name(s) ....
Address(es) ....

Nature of ....
interest ....

Date .... Signed([19]) ....

* Strike out whichever is inapplicable.

†Strike out if inapplicable.

Form 43A. Landlord's reply to application for direction giving entitlement to tenancy of agricultural holding and application that applicant be treated as an eligible person (prescribed form)   **A.84**

Form 1R (Succession on Death)   Rule 6
Ref. No.
To be inserted
by the secretary.

Appendix to the Agricultural Land Tribunals (Succession) Rules 1984. The applicant should enter the name and address of the landlord at (a) and the names and addresses of appropriate other persons (if any) respectively at (b), (c) and (d), etc.

[18] This information is required by rule 5(2) of those Rules.
[19] If signed by any person other than the applicant himself, he should state in what capacity or by what authority he signs.

SECTION 1: TENANCIES PROTECTED BY THE AGRICULTURAL HOLDINGS ACT 1986

AGRICULTURAL LAND TRIBUNAL

Reply to Application for Direction giving Entitlement to Tenancy of Agricultural Holding

Reply to Application for Determination that Applicant be Treated as an Eligible Person

To the secretary of the Agricultural Land Tribunal for the .... Area.

1. I, ... [block capitals]
    of .... [address]
    landlord of .... [name or description of holding]
    having received a copy of the application bearing the above reference number reply as follows:—

1. The facts stated in paragraphs 1, 2, 4 and 7 of the application are, to the best of my knowledge, information and belief, correct †except that:—

†2. I dispute the claim of the applicant to be an eligible person([1]) on the following grounds:—

†3. I dispute the claim of the applicant to be treated as an eligible person([2]) on the following grounds:—

4. I have the following comments on the suitability of the applicant to become the tenant of the above holding:—

5. I attach two copies of the following relevant documents([3]):—

6. I consider the application to be invalid by reason of([4]):—

   Date ....   Signed([5]) ....

†Strike out if inapplicable.

---

[1] The paragraphs of the application which (where completed) will be relevant to the applicant's claim to be an eligible person are paragraphs 9, 10, 11 and 12.

[2] The paragraphs of the application which (where completed) will be relevant to the applicant's claim to be treated as an eligible person are paragraphs 15, 16, 17 and 18.

[3] By virtue of rule 11(1) of the Agricultural Land Tribunals (Succession) Rules 1984 two copies of this reply and of any document which you wish to submit to the tribunal must be sent to the secretary. If you disagree with any map or plan attached to the application, your reply should be accompanied by two copies of a 6" to one mile or 1/10,000 (or larger) map showing what you consider to be the true position and marking the Ordnance Survey Field Numbers.

[4] If you consider that, for any reason, the applicant is not legally entitled to make his application, you should state succinctly the grounds on which you rely.

[5] If signed by any person other than the landlord himself, he should state in what capacity or by what authority he signs.

FORM 43A

TAKE NOTICE THAT IF YOU DO NOT REPLY IN THIS FORM WITHIN ONE MONTH OF THE DATE OF SERVICE ON YOU OF THE ATTACHED APPLICATION, THEN, SUBJECT TO SECTION 20(7) OF THE AGRICULTURE (MISCELLANEOUS PROVISIONS) ACT 1976, YOU WILL NOT BE ENTITLED AT THE HEARING OF THE APPLICATION TO DISPUTE ANY MATTER ALLEGED IN IT.

Form 44. Application by landlord following tenant's death for consent to operation of notice to quit (prescribed form)   A.85

Form 2 (Succession on Death)   Rule 4(1)
                                     Ref. No.
                                     To be inserted
                                     by the secretary.

AGRICULTURAL LAND TRIBUNAL

Application for Consent to Operation of Notice to Quit

To the secretary of the Agricultural Land Tribunal for the .... Area.

1. I, ... [block capitals] of .... [address] hereby apply under section 22(1) of the Agriculture (Miscellaneous Provisions) Act 1976 for the consent of the tribunal to the operation of a notice to quit which I gave to .... and .... being the personal representative(s) of ....[block capitals] deceased, formerly of .... [address]

   I was officially notified of his/her death by .... on ....

2. The notice to quit was served on [insert date] in respect of the holding known as ....

3. An application (bearing reference number ....) to the tribunal under Part II of the 1976 Act for a tenancy of this holding was made on ....

Full particulars of the holding are set out in that application †(as amended in my reply to that application dated ....).

4. I apply for the tribunal's consent to the operation of the notice to quit in the event of an applicant under the application referred to in paragraph 3, or any other such applicant, being determined by the tribunal to be a suitable person to become the tenant of the holding.

1055

SECTION 1: TENANCIES PROTECTED BY THE AGRICULTURAL HOLDINGS ACT 1986

5. The grounds upon which I make this application are those provided in paragraph(s)   of section 3(3) of the Agricultural Holdings (Notices to Quit) Act 1977 as read with section 22(2) of the 1976 Act, as amended. [*It is important to refer to note*(¹).]

6. The main facts on which I will base my case are:—

7. If I obtain possession of the land I intend:—
   * (a) to farm it myself.
   * (b) to let it to another tenant [*state name and address if known*].
   * (c) [*state any other intention*].

†8. The future tenant referred to in paragraph 7(b)(²) at present farms other land consisting of:—

(a) .... hectares of arable land (including temporary grass)
     (Ordnance Survey Field Nos. ....);
(b) .... hectares of permanent pasture
     (Ordnance Survey Field Nos. ....);
(c) .... hectares of rough grazing
     (Ordnance Survey Field Nos. ....);
(d) .... hectares of other land (including orchards)
     (Ordnance Survey Field Nos. ....);

Total .... hectares.

---

¹ The applicant must state on which paragraph or paragraphs of the subsection he intends to rely. The five paragraphs state as follows:—
  (a) that the carrying out of the purpose for which the landlord proposes to terminate the tenancy is desirable in the interests of good husbandry as respects the land to which the notice relates, treated as a separate unit;
  (b) that the carrying out thereof is desirable in the interests of sound management of the estate of which the land to which the notice relates forms part or which that land constitutes (see note (⁵) below);
  (c) that the carrying out thereof is desirable for the purposes of agricultural research, education, experiment or demonstration, or for the purposes of the enactments relating to smallholdings or allotments;
  (d) that greater hardship would be caused by withholding than by giving consent to the operation of the notice;
  (e) that the landlord proposes to terminate the tenancy for the purposes of the land's being used for a use, other than for agriculture, not falling within Case B in section 2(3) of the Agricultural Holdings (Notices to Quit) Act 1977.
If, under paragraph (d) above, the applicant intends to rely on hardship to a person or persons other than himself, he should set out in paragraph 6 the name of every person who will be so affected, and the relationship of that person to himself, and should state the nature of the hardship on which he relies.
² Paragraph 8 need not be completed if the name of the future tenant is unknown. Where land is described, a map should be provided (see note (⁵) below).

FORM 44

9. I attach the following documents which I intend to produce in support of my case:—

   (a) two copies (^{3}) of a 6" to one mile or 1/10,000(^{4}) map of the land described in paragraph 8(^{5}) above;

   (b) two copies(^{3}) of(^{6}):—

   Date .... Signed(^{7}) ....

   * Strike out whichever is inapplicable.

   †Strike out if inapplicable.

Form 44A. Tenant's reply to application by landlord following tenant's death for consent to operation of notice to quit (prescribed form)   A.86

Form 2R (Succession on Death)

Rule 7

Ref. No.
To be inserted
by the secretary.

AGRICULTURAL LAND TRIBUNAL

Reply to Application for Consent to Operation of Notice to Quit

To the secretary of the Agricultural Land Tribunal for the .... Area.

I, ... [*block capitals*]
of .... [*address*]
having applied to the tribunal on .... for a direction entitling me
to a tenancy of ....

---

^{3} By virtue of rule 11(1) of the Agricultural Land Tribunals (Succession) Rules 1984 two copies of the application and of any map and document must be sent to the secretary.
^{4} A larger scale map may be used if preferred. Ordnance Survey Field Numbers must be marked on the map.
^{5} Where it is intended to give evidence about any land other than that which is the subject of the notice to quit, it must be shown either on the map produced or on a separate map of a scale of 6" to one mile or 1/10,000 (or larger).
^{6} Mention any other document which is attached to this application.
^{7} If signed by any person other than the landlord himself, he should state in what capacity or by what authority he signs.

SECTION 1: TENANCIES PROTECTED BY THE AGRICULTURAL HOLDINGS ACT 1986

and having received a copy of the application (bearing the above reference number) for the tribunal's consent to the operation of a notice to quit, reply as follows:—

1. The facts stated in the first three paragraphs of the application are correct †except that:—

2. My main reasons for resisting the application are:—

†3. The landlord is not acting fairly and reasonably because(^{1}):—

4. I attach two copies of the following relevant documents(^{2}):—

Date .... Signed(^{3}) ....

TAKE NOTICE THAT IF YOU DO NOT REPLY IN THIS FORM WITHIN ONE MONTH OF THE DATE OF SERVICE ON YOU OF THE ATTACHED APPLICATION BY THE LANDLORD OF THE HOLDING FOR THE TRIBUNAL'S CONSENT TO THE OPERATION OF THE LANDLORD'S NOTICE TO QUIT, THE TRIBUNAL MAY GIVE THAT CONSENT SUMMARILY AND SUMMARILY DISMISS YOUR OWN APPLICATION TO BE GRANTED A TENANCY OF THE HOLDING, WITHOUT HEARING YOUR CASE.

†Strike out if inapplicable.

A.87 Form 45. **Notice by applicant of application for entitlement to tenancy on the death of the tenant (prescribed form)**

Form 3 (Succession on Death)   Rule 5(1)
Ref. No.
To be inserted
by the secretary.

---

[1] The tribunal must withhold consent if, in all the circumstances, it appears that a fair and reasonable landlord would not insist on possession. If you have any special reasons for saying the landlord is acting unfairly or unreasonably which do not appear under paragraph 2, you should state them under paragraph 3.

[2] By virtue of rule 11(1) of the Agricultural Land Tribunals (Succession) Rules 1984 two copies of the reply and of any document which you wish to submit to the tribunal must be sent to the secretary.

If you disagree with any map or plan attached to the application, your reply should be accompanied by two copies of a 6" to one mile or 1/10,000 (or larger) map showing what you consider to be the true position and marking the Ordnance Survey Field Numbers.

[3] If signed by any person other than the applicant himself, he should state in what capacity or by what authority he signs.

FORM 45

AGRICULTURAL LAND TRIBUNAL

Notice of Application for Entitlement to Tenancy under Part II of the Agriculture (Miscellaneous Provisions) Act 1976

To: .... [*name*]
of .... [*address*]
[*block capitals*]

I, ...
of .... [*address*]
hereby give you notice that I applied on .... [*date of application*] under Part II of the above-named Act for a direction entitling me to a tenancy of the agricultural holding known as

[*address or brief description of holding*] in succession to [*name of deceased tenant of the holding*] who died on

Date ....   Signed ....

A copy of the full application will in due course be sent to the landlord and any other applicants by the secretary to the tribunal.

Form 46. Applicant's reply to other applications for direction giving entitlement to tenancy (prescribed form)   A.88

Form 4 (Succession on Death)   Rule 8

Ref. No.
To be inserted
by the secretary.

AGRICULTURAL LAND TRIBUNAL

Reply to Application for Direction giving Entitlement to Tenancy of Agricultural Holding

To the secretary of the Agricultural Land Tribunal for the .... Area.
I, ... [*block capitals*]
of .... [*address*]
having received a copy of the application of .... (hereinafter called "the applicant") bearing the above reference number, reply as follows:—

1. The facts stated in the first seven paragraphs of the application are correct †except that:—

SECTION 1: TENANCIES PROTECTED BY THE AGRICULTURAL HOLDINGS ACT 1986

2. *I accept the applicant's claim to be a designated applicant, as stated in paragraph 8 of the application.

OR

*I dispute the applicant's claim to be a designated applicant, as stated in paragraph 8 of the application, on the following grounds:—

3. I do not dispute any of the matters stated in paragraphs 9–13, 16, and 17 of the application †except that:—

4. I claim to be a more suitable person than the applicant to be granted a tenancy of the holding; and I base this claim on the following grounds:—

5. The applicant and I †(and) have agreed to request the landlord's consent to a direction entitling us to a joint tenancy of the holding.

Date .... Signed ....

†Strike out if inapplicable.

* Strike out whichever is inapplicable.

A.89 Form 47. Retirement notice given by tenant to landlord indicating his wish that a single named person should succeed him as tenant of the holding (not a prescribed form)

Agricultural Holdings Act 1986, Part IV

To: A.B. landlord of [address]

Re: The holding known as [name/OS numbers]

I, as the tenant of the holding give you notice, in accordance with section 49(1) of the Act, that I wish to nominate [*name and address of nominated successor*], being an eligible person, to succeed me as tenant of the holding.

I declare that the retirement date as from which I nominate the said .... to succeed me as tenant is the [*] day of [*], being a date at which the tenancy of the holding could have been determined by a notice to quit given at the date of this notice and being not less than one year, but not more than two years, after the date of this notice. *[I declare that I shall have attained the age of 65 years by the said retirement date.]

*[I declare that in accordance with section 51(3) of the Act that this notice is given on the ground that I am [*or* will at the said retirement date be] incapable, by reason of bodily or mental infirmity, of conducting the farming of the said holding in such a way as to secure the fulfilment of my responsibility as a tenant to farm in

accordance with the rules of good husbandry and I declare that the said incapacity is likely to be permanent.]

* Delete if not applicable

Dated:

Signed:

Form 48. **Application (following a retirement notice) for a direction giving entitlement to tenancy of agricultural holding (prescribed form)** A.90

Form 5 (Succession on retirement)

Rule 23(1)

Ref. No.
To be inserted
by the secretary.

AGRICULTURAL LAND TRIBUNAL

Application for Direction giving Entitlement of Agricultural Holding

[*In completing this form it is important to refer to the notes*]

To the Secretary of the Agricultural Land Tribunal for the .... Area.

1. I, ... [*block capitals*] of .... [*address*] hereby apply under paragraph 5(1) of Schedule 2 to the Agricultural Holdings Act 1984 for a direction entitling me to a tenancy of the holding specified in paragraph 2 below.

2. The holding in respect of which the application is made is known as and consists of:—

(a) .... hectares of arable land (including temporary grass)
     (Ordnance Survey Field Nos. ....);
(b) .... hectares of permanent pasture
     (Ordnance Survey Field Nos. ....);
(c) .... hectares of rough grazing
     (Ordnance Survey Field Nos. ....);
(d) .... hectares of other land (including orchards)
     (Ordnance Survey Field Nos. ....);

SECTION 1: TENANCIES PROTECTED BY THE AGRICULTURAL HOLDINGS ACT 1986

Total ....hectares   ANNUAL RENT £

3. The current year of the tenancy of the holding expires on

4. The holding includes the following buildings [*give a general description*]:—

†5. The holding forms part of a larger agricultural unit known as and consisting of [*give a general description*]:—

6. The landlord of the holding is
of .... [*address*].

The tenant(s) of the holding is/are
of .... [*address(es)*].

7. This application arises as a result of a retirement notice given by the tenant(s) to the landlord on

8. I am the nominated successor.

9. †(a) I am the *wife/*husband/*brother/*sister/*child of the tenant [*where there is more than one tenant, specify which*](¹).
†(b) I am treated by the tenant [*where there is more than one tenant, specify which*] as a child of the family in relation to his marriage to (²) on .... [*give date of marriage*].

10. (a) During the seven years ending with the date on which the tenant(s) gave the retirement notice to the landlord my only or principal source of livelihood was derived from—
    * (i) my agricultural work on the holding, or on an agricultural unit of which the holding forms a part;
    * (ii) the tenant's/the tenant's and my [*where there is more than one tenant, specify which*] agricultural work on the holding, or on an agricultural unit of which the holding forms a part;
during the following period(s) and in the following manner [*give details of the way livelihood derived from agricultural work on the holding*](³):—

---

¹ Formal proof of the relationship of the tenant, e.g. by production of marriage or birth certificates, may be required at the hearing. Adopted children should complete this sub-paragraph, and not paragraph 9(b) following.

² Paragraph 9(b) may apply where the applicant is the step-child or foster child of the tenant or is otherwise treated by him as his child. An outline should be given of the circumstances relied on as establishing that the applicant is treated by the tenant as his child in relation to the marriage. Production of the relevant marriage certificate and any relevant birth certificate may be required at the hearing.

³ To qualify under paragraph 10(a)(i) the applicant should have derived his only or principal source of livelihood from his agricultural work on the holding (or on a larger unit of which the holding forms part) during a total of five years of the seven years ending with the date on which the tenant(s) gave the landlord the retirement notice. Paragraph 10(a)(ii) is available only to a tenant(s) wife. The total of five years may be made up of one continuous period or one or more separate periods. A period of full-time education at university etc., may, in the circumstances set out in note (⁴), count towards the five-year period of earning a livelihood from the holding, and reference should be made to paragraph 11 and

FORM 48

* (b) During the period(s) specified in paragraph 10(a) I had the following source(s) of livelihood other than those derived from the holding or from an agricultural unit of which the holding forms a part [*give details of other sources of livelihood*]:—

* (c) During the period(s) specified in paragraph 10(a) I had no other source of livelihood.

†11. During the seven years ending with the date on which the tenant(s) gave the retirement notice to the landlord I attended a full time course at [*name of university, college or other establishment of further education*] during the following period(s) [*give details of time spent at university, etc.*](^{4}):—

During this period/these period(s), I studied the following subjects and obtained the following qualifications [*give details of subjects studied and any qualifications obtained*]:—

†12. (a) The following agricultural land is occupied by me, my spouse or a company under my control, the control of my spouse or our joint control as owner-occupier/tenant/licensee, whether alone or jointly with others [*give particulars of any land occupied, including area and any land occupied jointly with others*](^{5}):—

†(b) The following agricultural land is occupied by a person under a licence or

---

note (^{4}) in deciding whether the requirements of this paragraph can be satisfied.

^{4} Any period or periods (up to an aggregate total of three years) during the seven years ending with the date on which the tenant(s) gave the retirement notice to the landlord during which the applicant was attending a full-time course at a university, college or other establishment of further education will be treated as a period throughout which his only or principal source of livelihood was derived from his agricultural work on the holding. Any subject may have been studied.

^{5} Land occupied by the applicant's spouse or by a company controlled by that person or jointly by that person and the applicant should not be included in paragraph 12 where either of the parties has obtained a decree of judicial separation or a decree nisi of divorce or of nullity of marriage and in each case that decree remains unrescinded. In addition, land should not be included in paragraph 12 if it is occupied by the applicant, his spouse or a controlled company—

(a) under a tenancy approved under section 2(1) of the Agricultural Holdings Act 1948 or under such a tenancy relating to the use of land for grazing or mowing as is referred to in the proviso to that provision;
(b) under a tenancy for more than one year but less than two years;
(c) under a tenancy not falling within (a) or (b) above and not having effect as a contract of tenancy;
(d) under a tenancy to which section 3 of the 1948 Act does not apply by virtue of section 3B of that Act;
(e) as a licensee; or
(f) as an executor, administrator, trustee in bankruptcy or person otherwise deriving title from another person by operation of law.

However, where the applicant occupies land in accordance with (a) to (e) above under a licence or tenancy granted to him by his spouse or by a body corporate controlled by him, that land should be included in paragraph 12.

SECTION 1: TENANCIES PROTECTED BY THE AGRICULTURAL HOLDINGS ACT 1986

such a tenancy as is mentioned in paragraph 2(1)(a) to (d) of Schedule 3A to the Agriculture (Miscellaneous Provisions) Act 1976([6]) granted by *me and/or *my spouse and/or *a company controlled by me and/or my spouse (together with one or more other persons, being at the time it was granted a person or persons entitled to occupy the land otherwise than under a tenancy, or in a capacity, falling within paragraph 2(1)(a) to (f) of that Schedule([6]) [*give particulars of any land occupied, including area*]:—

[†](c) I apply under paragraph 4(2) of Schedule 3A to the 1976 Act, as applied by paragraph 1(4)(b) of Schedule 2 to the 1984 Act, for the net annual income from the following agricultural land which is—
    * (i)   jointly occupied;
    * (ii) deemed by virtue of paragraph 6(2) of the said Schedule 3A, as applied by the said paragraph 1(4)(b), to be jointly occupied;
by me and one or more other persons (not being only my spouse or a company under my control, the control of my spouse or our joint control) to be treated as limited to my appropriate share of that net annual income [*give particulars of any land in joint occupation or deemed joint occupation*]([7]):—

13. I was born on

14. I claim to be a suitable person to receive the tenancy of this holding because ([8]):—

15. I attach the following documents which I intend to produce in support of my case:—
    (a) two([9]) copies of a 6" to one mile or 1/10,000([10]) map of the holding described in paragraph 2 above (and of other land referred to in paragraph 5);
    (b) two([9]) copies of the retirement notice;
    (c) two([9]) copies of([11]):—

---

[6] Paragraph 2(1)(a) to (f) of Schedule 3A to the Agriculture (Miscellaneous Provisions) Act 1976 is set out in note ([5]).

[7] If the applicant occupies land jointly with one or more other persons (not being only his spouse or a company under the control of the applicant or his spouse or under their joint control), or if the applicant is deemed to occupy land jointly with one or more such persons, he may in either case complete the application set out in paragraph 12(c) of the Form for the net annual income which the land is or was capable of producing to be treated as limited to his appropriate share.

[8] All matters relied on as supporting the claim to be a suitable person to become the tenant of the holding should be summarised. These should include details of the applicant's training and practical experience of agriculture, physical health, financial standing and any educational qualifications not already listed in paragraph 11.

[9] By virtue of rule 28 of the Agricultural Land Tribunals (Succession) Rules 1984 two copies of the application and of any map and document must be sent to the secretary.

[10] A larger scale map may be used if preferred. Ordnance Survey Field Numbers must be marked on the map.

[11] Mention any other document which is attached to this application.

FORM 48

16. I shall notify the landlord of this application(^{12}).

Date .... Signed(^{13}) ....

Signature of retiring tenant(s) ....
....
....
....

* Strike out whichever is inapplicable.

†Strike out if inapplicable.

Form 48A. Landlord's reply to application (following a retirement notice) for a direction giving entitlement to tenancy of agricultural holding (prescribed form) A.91

Form 5R (Succession on Retirement)   Rule 25

Ref. No.
To be inserted
by the secretary.

AGRICULTURAL LAND TRIBUNAL

Reply to Application for Direction giving Entitlement to Tenancy of Agricultural Holding

To the secretary of the Agricultural Land Tribunal for the .... Area.

I, ... [*block capitals*]
of .... [*address*]
landlord of .... [*name or description of holding*]
having received a copy of the application bearing the above reference number reply as follows:—

1. The facts stated in paragraphs 1, 2, 4, 6 and 7 of the application are, to the best of my knowledge, information and belief, correct †except that:—

†2. I dispute the claim of the applicant to be an eligible person(^{1}) on the following grounds:—

---

^{12} The applicant is required to send to the landlord of the holding notice of this application in Form 6 (Succession on Retirement) which is set out in the Appendix to the Agricultural Land Tribunals (Succession) Rules 1984.
^{13} If signed by any person other than the applicant himself, he should state in what capacity or by what authority he signs.
^{1} The paragraphs of the application which (where completed) will be relevant to the

SECTION 1: TENANCIES PROTECTED BY THE AGRICULTURAL HOLDINGS ACT 1986

3. I have the following comments on the suitability of the applicant to become the tenant of the above holding:—

†4. I claim that greater hardship would be caused by the tribunal giving the direction sought by the applicant than by refusing his application and my reasons for this claim are:—

†5. The tenancy is the subject of a notice to quit Case *B/*C/*D/*E/*F served on [*date*].

†[*For Case C only*] The notice to quit is founded on a certificate granted in accordance with an application made on [*date*].

([*For Case D only*] The notice to quit is founded on a notice given for the purposes of that Case on [*date*].

6. I attach two copies of the following relevant documents(^{2}):—

7. I consider the application to be invalid by reason of(^{3}):—

Date .... Signed(^{4}) ....

* Strike out whichever is inapplicable.

†Strike out if inapplicable.

TAKE NOTICE THAT IF YOU DO NOT REPLY IN THIS FORM WITHIN ONE MONTH OF THE DATE OF SERVICE ON YOU OF THE ATTACHED APPLICATION, THEN, SUBJECT TO PARAGRAPH 5(5) OF SCHEDULE 2 TO THE AGRICULTURAL HOLDINGS ACT 1984, YOU WILL NOT BE ENTITLED AT THE HEARING OF THE APPLICATION TO DISPUTE ANY MATTER ALLEGED IN IT.

---

applicant's claim to be an eligible person are paragraphs 9, 10, 11 and 12.
[2] By virtue of rule 28 of the Agricultural Land Tribunals (Succession) Rules 1984 two copies of this reply and of any document which you wish to submit to the tribunal must be sent to the secretary. If you disagree with any map or plan attached to the application, your reply should be accompanied by two copies of a 6" to one mile or 1/10,000 (or larger) map showing what you consider to be the true position and marking the Ordnance Survey Field Numbers.
[3] If you consider that, for any reason, the applicant is not legally entitled to make his application, you should state succinctly the grounds on which you rely.
[4] If signed by any person other than the landlord himself, he should state in what capacity or by what authority he signs.

Form 49. Notice given to landlord by nominated successor of application A.92
for entitlement to tenancy on tenant's retirement (prescribed
form)

Form 6 (Succession on Retirement)　　　　Rule 24

Ref. No.
To be inserted
by the secretary.

AGRICULTURAL LAND TRIBUNAL

Notice of Application for Entitlement to Tenancy under Schedule 2 to the Agricultural Holdings Act 1984

To:　　　　　　　　　　　　　　　　　　　　　　　　　　[name]
of　　　　　　　　　　　　　　　　　　　　　　　　　　[address]
I,　　　　　　　　　　　　　　　　　　　　　　　　[block capitals]
of　　　　　　　　　　　　　　　　　　　　　　　　　　[address]
hereby give you notice that I applied on　　　　[date of application]
under Schedule 2 to the above-named Act for a direction entitling me to a tenancy of the agricultural holding known as
[address or brief description of holding] in succession to
　　　　　　　　　　　　　　　[name of present tenant(s) of the holding]
who served on you his/their retirement notice on

Date ....　　Signed ....

A copy of the full application will in due course be sent to you by the secretary to the tribunal.

Form 50. Demand for arbitration by successful applicant following direc- A.93
tion in his favour on death of previous tenant (not a prescribed
form)([1])

Agricultural Holdings Act 1986, Part IV

To: A.B. landlord of [address]

Re: The holding known as [name/OS numbers]

1. I, C.D. am entitled by virtue of a direction dated [*] by the Agricultural Land Tribunal for [*] Area to a tenancy of the holding.

2. I hereby, within the prescribed period mentioned in section 48(2) of the Act, demand a reference to arbitration under the Act of the following questions:

---

[1] A form on similar lines may be used in the case of succession on retirement.

SECTION 1: TENANCIES PROTECTED BY THE AGRICULTURAL HOLDINGS ACT 1986

    (a) What variations in the terms of the tenancy to which I am entitled under the said direction are justifiable having regard to the circumstances of the holding and the length of time since the holding was first let on those terms;

    (b) What rent should be or should have been properly payable in respect of the holding at the relevant time.

3. I also desire that the award shall include such provisions as are necessary to entitle me to recover from you a sum equal to so much as is in all the circumstances fair and reasonable of the aggregate amount of the compensation mentioned in section 48(8)(b) of the Act.

Dated:

Signed:

Compensation on termination of tenancy

A.94 Form 51. Notice of tenant's intention to claim the higher level of basic compensation for disturbance (section 60(3)(b)) (not a prescribed form)

Agricultural Holdings Act 1986, section 60(3)(b)

To: A.B. landlord of [address]

Re: The holding known as [name/OS numbers]

I give you notice that on quitting the holding of which I am your tenant, in consequence of the notice to quit served by you on me dated [*], [and of the counter-notice dated [*] served on you by me under section 32 of the Act] I intend to claim under section 60(3)(b) of the Act as basic compensation for disturbance a greater amount than one year's rent of the holding.

You, at any reasonable time before the sale thereof, may inspect and make a valuation of my household goods, implements of husbandry, fixtures, farm produce or farm stock on or used in connection with the holding.

Dated:

Signed:

Form 52. Tenant's notice of election in favour of statutory basis of compensation for tenant-right matters (Schedule 2, paragraphs 6 to 9) (not a prescribed form)   A.95

Agricultural Holdings Act 1986, Schedule 12, paragraph 6

To: A.B. landlord of [address]

Re: The holding known as [name/OS numbers]

In accordance with paragraph 6 of Schedule 12 to the Act I elect that section 65(1) of the Act shall apply to me as regards compensation for the matters specified in paragraphs 7 to 10 of Part II of Schedule 8 to the Act on the termination of my tenancy of the holding of which I am your tenant and of which I entered into occupation before March 1, 1948.

Dated:

Signed:

Form 53. Notice by landlord requiring tenant to elect in regard to the basis of compensation for Part II of Schedule 8 matters (Schedule 12, paragraph 6(2)) (not a prescribed form)   A.96

Agricultural Holdings Act 1986, Schedule 12, paragraph 6(2)

To: C.D. tenant of [address]

Re: The holding known as [name/OS numbers]

In accordance with paragraph 6(2) of Schedule 12 to the Act, I require you within one month from the giving of this notice to elect whether section 65(1) of the Act is to apply to you in regard to the matters specified in paragraphs 7 to 10 of Part II of Schedule 8 thereto on the termination of the tenancy of the holding of which you are the tenant and of which you entered into occupation before March 1, 1948.

This notice is given, as required by the said paragraph 6(2), during the currency of a notice to quit which I have served on you dated [*] and expiring on [*].

Dated:

Signed:

SECTION 1: TENANCIES PROTECTED BY THE AGRICULTURAL HOLDINGS ACT 1986

A.97 Form 54. Consent by landlord to payment of compensation by incoming to outgoing tenant (section 69(2)) (not a prescribed form)

Agricultural Holdings Act 1986, section 69(2)(a)

To: C.D. [name and address of incoming tenant]

Re: The holding known as [name/OS numbers]

I consent under section 69(2)(a) of the Act, on your entering into occupation of the holding, to your paying E.F. [*name and address of outgoing tenant*], the outgoing tenant thereof, the sum of £[*], being the amount of compensation payable by me under or in pursuance of the Act [or the Agricultural Holdings Act 1948] in respect of the relevant improvements, as defined in section 64(1) of the Act, of which particulars are set out below.

Particulars of the improvements mentioned above

Dated:

Signed:

Note: If there has been an arbitration award reference should be made to it.

A.98 Form 55. Application by tenant to landlord for written consent to Schedule 7 improvements (section 67) (not a prescribed form)

Agricultural Holdings Act 1986, section 67

To: A.B. landlord of [address]

Re: The holding known as [name/OS numbers]

I give you notice that I wish to carry out on the holding of which I am your tenant, the improvements specified in the Schedule hereto, and I request you to give your consent in writing to the carrying out of the said improvements [*or* I request you to give your consent in writing to the carrying out of the said improvements upon such terms as to compensation or otherwise as may be agreed upon in writing between us. I suggest that the terms which I have set out in the said Schedule would be appropriate].

The Schedule above referred to

(*Here set out the specifications of the proposed improvements and any terms which it is desired to suggest.*)

Dated:

Signed:

Form 56. Consent by landlord to improvements (section 67) (not a prescribed form)   A.99

Agricultural Holdings Act 1986, section 67

To: C.D. tenant of [address]

Re: The holding known as [name/OS numbers]

[In reply to your application dated [*]] I give my consent to the carrying out by you on the holding of the improvements specified in the Schedule hereto [upon the terms and conditions set out].

The SCHEDULE above referred to

PARTICULARS OF IMPROVEMENTS

(*Describe improvements with sufficient particularity to avoid any doubt or ambiguity as to their nature or location.*)

[TERMS AND CONDITIONS OF CONSENT

(*Set out terms and conditions on which landlord is willing to give consent.*)]

Dated:

Signed:

Form 57. Application by tenant to Agricultural Land Tribunal for approval to improvements in Part II of Schedule 7 (section 67) (prescribed form)   A.100

                       Form 6   rule 7(1)

                                                 Ref. No.
                                                 To be inserted
                                                 by the Secretary.

AGRICULTURAL LAND TRIBUNAL

Application for Approval of Long-Term Improvement

To the Secretary of the Agricultural Land Tribunal for the .... Area.

SECTION 1: TENANCIES PROTECTED BY THE AGRICULTURAL HOLDINGS ACT 1986

1.   I .... [block capitals]
of .... [address]
tenant of .... [name or description of holding],
hereby apply for the Tribunal's approval under section 50 of the Agricultural Holdings Act 1948 (as amended by the Agriculture Act 1958) of the carrying out of the following improvement(s) on the said holding:—

2.   My landlord is .... [block capitals]
of .... [address]

3.   The holding consists of:—

(a)   ....   hectares of arable land (including temporary grass)
                          (Ordnance Survey Field Nos. ....);
(b)   ....   hectares of permanent pasture
                          (Ordnance Survey Field Nos. ....);
(c)   ....   hectares of rough grazing
                          (Ordnance Survey Field Nos. ....);
(d)   ....   hectares of other land (including orchards)
                          (Ordnance Survey Field Nos. ....);

Total .... hectares.

4.   The holding includes the following buildings:—[give a general description]

5.   I requested my landlord on the .... day of .... 19........, to consent in writing to the carrying out of the said improvement(s), but he—
   * (a) refuses to give his consent.
   * (b) will only consent subject to the following terms to which I am unwilling to agree:—[state the terms and your reasons for not agreeing].

6.   My main reasons for wishing for the improvements to be carried out are:—

7.   I attach the following documents which I intend to produce in support of my case:

   (a) two(^{1}) copies of a 6" to one mile or 1/10,000(^{2}) map of the holding described in paragraph 4 above;

   (b) two(^{1}) copies of the following plan:—

---

^{1} Two copies of the application and of any map and document must be sent to the Secretary, and if there are more than two parties (e.g., if the holding is held under a sub-tenancy) an additional copy of the application, etc., must be supplied for, and the Secretary must be informed of the name and address of, each additional party.
^{2} A larger scale map may be used if preferred. Ordnance Survey Field Numbers must be marked on the map.

FORM 57

(c) two(¹) copies (³):—

Date .... Signed(⁴) ....

Form 57A. Landlord's reply to application by tenant to Agricultural Land Tribunal for approval to improvements in Part II of Schedule 7 (section 67(3)) (prescribed form)   A.101

Form 6R

Ref. No.
To be inserted
by the Secretary.

AGRICULTURAL LAND TRIBUNAL

Reply to Application for Approval of Long-Term Improvement

To the Secretary of the Agricultural Land Tribunal for the .... Area.

I .... [block capitals]
of .... [address]
landlord of .... [name or description of holding], having received a copy of the application (bearing the above reference number) for the Tribunal's approval under section 50 of the Agricultural Holdings Act 1948 (as amended) of the carrying out on the said holding of the improvement(s) specified therein, reply as follows:

1. The facts stated in the first four paragraphs of the application are correct except that:—

2.* (a) I deny that the request referred to in paragraph 5 of the application was made.
   * (b) I do not wish the improvements to be carried out because—
   * (c) I agree the improvements being carried out subject to the following terms:—[state terms and any special reasons]

3. My main reasons for resisting the application are:—

---
³ Mention any other document which is attached to this application.
⁴ If signed by any person other than the applicant himself, he should state in what capacity or

SECTION 1: TENANCIES PROTECTED BY THE AGRICULTURAL HOLDINGS ACT 1986

4. I attach copies of the following relevant documents(^{1}):—

Date .... Signed(^{2}) ....

* Strike out whichever is inapplicable.

A.102 **Form 58. Notice by landlord to Agricultural Land Tribunal and to the tenant that the landlord proposes himself to carry out approved improvements (section 67(5)) (not a prescribed form)**

Agricultural Holdings Act 1986, section 67

To: The Secretary to the Agricultural Land Tribunal for the [*] Area

and

To: C.D. tenant of [address]

Re: The holding known as [name/OS numbers]

1. On an application made by the tenant of the holding the Agricultural Land Tribunal for the [*] Area decided on the [*] to give their approval under section 67(4) of the Act to the carrying out by the said tenant of the improvements described in the Schedule hereto, and I, the landlord of the said holding, received notification of the Tribunal's approval on the [*].

2. By virtue of section 67(5) of the Act and rule 7(2) of the Agricultural Land Tribunals Rules 1978 in the Schedule to the Agricultural Land Tribunals (Rules) Order 1978 (S.I. 1978/259), I, as the said landlord, am entitled within one month from the date of receipt of the said notification to give notice to the Tribunal and the tenant that I propose myself to carry out the said improvements.

3. Accordingly in pursuance of the said provisions I give notice that I, as landlord of the said holding, propose myself to carry out the said improvements.

---

by what authority he signs.
^{1} (a) Two copies of the reply and of any document which you wish to submit to the Tribunal should be sent to the Secretary, and, if there are more than two parties (e.g., if the holding is sub-let), an additional copy of each must be supplied for each additional party.
(b) If you disagree with any map or plan attached to the application, your reply should be accompanied by two copies of a 6" to one mile or 1/10,000 (or larger) map showing what you consider to be the true position and marking the Ordnance Survey Field Numbers.
^{2} If signed by any person other than the landlord himself, he should state in what capacity or by what authority he signs.

FORM 58

THE SCHEDULE ABOVE REFERRED TO

(Set out description of improvements)

Dated:

Signed:

Form 59. Application by tenant to the Agricultural Land Tribunal for a determination that the landlord has failed to carry out improvements within a reasonable time (section 67(4)) (prescribed form)   A.103

Form 7   rule 7(3)

Ref. No.
To be inserted
by the Secretary.

AGRICULTURAL LAND TRIBUNAL

Application for Determination that Landlord has Failed to carry out Improvement within a Reasonable Time

To the Secretary of the Agricultural Land Tribunal for the .... Area.

1. I .... [*block capitals*]
   of .... [*address*]
   tenant of .... [*name or description of holding*], hereby apply to the Tribunal in pursuance of section 50(4)(b) of the Agricultural Holdings Act 1948 (as amended by the Agriculture Act 1958) to determine that my landlord: .... [*block capitals*]
   of .... [*address*]
   has failed within a reasonable time to carry out the following improvements to the said holding:—

2. The said improvement was approved by the Tribunal on my application bearing reference number ....

3. The Tribunal's decision was dated .... day of .... 19............, and my landlord notified me of his proposal to carry out the said improvement himself on the .... day of .... 19.........

4. My landlord has failed to carry out the said improvements:—[*if he has done any part of them, give particulars*]

5. My main reasons for saying that the delay is unreasonable are:—

SECTION 1: TENANCIES PROTECTED BY THE AGRICULTURAL HOLDINGS ACT 1986

6. I attach two(^{1}) copies each of—
   (a) a 6" to one mile or 1/10,000(^{2}) map of the holding(^{3});
   (b) the following plan showing the intended improvement(s):—
   (c) the following other document(s)(^{4}):—

   Date .... Signed(^{5}) ....

A.104 **Form 59A. Landlord's reply to application by tenant to the Agricultural Land Tribunal for a determination that the landlord has failed to carry out improvements within a reasonable time (section 67(4)) (prescribed form)**

Form 7R

Ref. No.
To be inserted
by the Secretary.

AGRICULTURAL LAND TRIBUNAL

Reply to Application for Determination that Landlord has Failed to carry out the Improvement within a Reasonable Time

To the Secretary of the Agricultural Land Tribunal for the .... Area.

I .... [*block capitals*]
of .... [*address*]
landlord of .... [*name or description of holding*], having received a copy of the application (bearing the above reference number) for the Tribunal's determination that I have failed within a reasonable time to carry out on the said holding the improvement(s) specified therein, reply as follows:—

1. The facts stated in the first three paragraphs of the application are correct except that:—

---

^{1} Two copies of the application and of any map and document must be sent to the Secretary, and if there are more than two parties (*e.g.*, if the holding is held under a sub-tenancy) an additional copy of the application, etc., must be supplied for, and the Secretary must be informed of the name and address of, each additional party.
^{2} A larger scale map may be used if preferred. Ordnance Survey Field Numbers must be marked on the map.
^{3} The Chairman of the Tribunal has power in all cases to dispense with maps, etc., (*e.g.* if they are already in possession of the Tribunal or the other parties). A request for a direction on this subject should be made in writing before or at the time of sending the application.
^{4} Mention any other documents which are attached to the application.
^{5} If signed by any person other than the applicant himself, he should state in what capacity or by what authority he signs.

FORM 59A

2. My main reasons for resisting the application are:—
   * (a) I have adequately carried out the said improvement(s);
   * (b) I intend to carry out the said improvement(s) but have not yet had reasonable time to do so for the following reasons:—
     [*give particulars*]
   * (c) [*any other reasons*]

3. I attach copies of the following relevant documents([1]):—

   Date ………………………… Signed([2]) …………………………

* Strike out whichever is inapplicable.

Form 60. Notice of tenant's intention to carry out mole drainage (section 68(1) and Schedule 8, paragraph 1) (not a prescribed form)   A.105

Agricultural Holdings Act 1986, section 68(1) and Schedule 8, paragraph 1

To: A.B. landlord of [address]

Re: The holding known as [name/OS numbers]

It is my intention after the expiration of one month from the service of this notice, which is given in accordance with section 68(1) of the Act, to proceed to drain the fields known as Whiteacre and Blackacre (O.S. Nos.*), part of the holding of which I am your tenant, by means of mole drainage. I shall also carry out any works required to secure the efficient functioning of the said mole drainage system.

Dated:

Signed:

---

[1] Two copies of the reply and of any document which you wish to submit to the Tribunal must be sent to the Secretary, and, if there are more than two parties (*e.g.*, if the holding is sub-let) an additional copy of each must be supplied for each additional party.
(b) If you disagree with any map or plan attached to the application your reply should be accompanied by two copies of a 6" to one mile or 1/10,000 (or larger) map or plan showing what you consider to be the true position and marking the Ordnance Survey Field Numbers.
[2] If signed by any person other than the landlord himself, he should state in what capacity or by what authority he signs.

SECTION 1: TENANCIES PROTECTED BY THE AGRICULTURAL HOLDINGS ACT 1986

A.106   Form 61.   **Notice by tenant of intention to claim compensation for the continuous adoption of a special system of farming ("high farming") (section 70) (not a prescribed form)**

Agricultural Holdings Act 1986, section 70

To: A.B. landlord of [address]

Re: The holding known as [name/OS numbers]

It is my intention on quitting the holding on the termination of my tenancy to claim compensation under section 70 of the Act on the ground that the value of the holding has been increased during my tenancy by the continuous adoption of a system of farming which has been more beneficial to the holding than the system of farming required by the contract of tenancy [*or* the system of farming normally practised on comparable holdings], namely (*state briefly the system adopted*).

Dated:

Signed:

A.107   Form 62.   **Notice by landlord of intention to claim compensation for general deterioration of the holding (section 72) (not a prescribed form)**

Agricultural Holdings Act 1986, section 72

To: C.D. tenant of [address]

Re: The holding known as [name/OS numbers]

In accordance with section 72 of the Agricultural Holdings Act 1986 it is my intention to claim compensation on your quitting on the termination of your tenancy of the holding of which you are my tenant, on the ground that the value of the holding generally has been reduced by reason of such dilapidation, deterioration or damage as is mentioned in section 71(1) of the said Act or otherwise by your failure to fulfil your responsibilities to farm in accordance with the rules of good husbandry.

Dated:

Signed:

Form 63. Request by tenant to landlord to agree that holding or part of it shall be treated as a market garden (section 79) (not a prescribed form)

A.108

Agricultural Holdings Act 1986, section 79

To: A.B. landlord of [address]

Re: The holding known as [name/OS numbers]

I request you to agree in writing within one month from the date of receipt by you of this notice that the arable fields (O.S. Nos.....) forming part of the holding, of which I am your tenant under an agreement of tenancy dated [*] may be treated as a market garden in accordance with section 79 of the Act.

[And I give you notice that in the event of your refusing or failing within the said month to agree to this request I shall make an application to the Agricultural Land Tribunal for the [*] Area under section 80 of the Act for a direction that section 79(2) to (5) shall apply to the above-mentioned fields.]

Dated:

Signed:

Form 64. Application by tenant to Agricultural Land Tribunal for holding to be treated as a market garden (section 80) (prescribed form)

A.109

Form 8   rule 8

Ref. No.
To be inserted
by the Secretary.

AGRICULTURAL LAND TRIBUNAL

Application for Direction to Treat an Agricultural Holding as a Market Garden

To the Secretary of the Agricultural Land Tribunal for the .... Area.

1. I .... [block capitals]
   of .... [address]
   tenant of .... [name or description of holding],
   hereby apply for the Tribunal to direct under section 68 of the Agricultural Holdings Act 1948 (as amended by the Agriculture Act 1958) that the said

SECTION 1: TENANCIES PROTECTED BY THE AGRICULTURAL HOLDINGS ACT 1986

holding/the part of the said holding specified in paragraph 6 below shall be treated as a market garden so that section 67 of the said Act shall apply.

2. My landlord is .... [*block capitals*]
   of .... [*address*].

3. I requested him on the .... day of .... 19............, to agree in writing to the (part of the) holding being so treated, but he * refused on the day .... 19............... /has had reasonable time but has failed to do so.

4. The holding consists of:—

(a) .... hectares of arable land (including temporary grass)
    (Ordnance Survey Field Nos. ....);
(b) .... hectares of permanent pasture
    (Ordnance Survey Field Nos. ....);
(c) .... hectares of rough grazing
    (Ordnance Survey Field Nos. ....);
(d) .... hectares of other land (including orchards)
    (Ordnance Survey Field Nos. ....);

Total .... hectares.

5. The holding includes the following buildings:—[*give a general description*]

6. I wish to make the following improvements:—

   Ordnance Survey Field Nos. Improvements

7. For the following main reasons I request the Tribunal to direct that the *holding/part of the holding described in paragraph 6 above be treated as a market garden:—

8. I attach the following documents which I intend to produce in support of my case:

   (a) two (^{1}) copies of a 6" to one mile or 1/10,000(^{2}) map of the holding described in paragraph 4 above;

   (b) two(^{1}) copies of the following plan:—

---

^{1} Two copies of the application and of any map and document must be sent to the Secretary, and if there are more than two parties (*e.g.*, if the holding is held under a sub-tenancy), an additional copy of the application, etc., must be supplied for, and the Secretary must be informed of the name and address of, each additional party.

^{2} A larger scale map may be used if preferred. Ordnance Survey Field Numbers must be marked on the map.

FORM 64

(c) two (^{1}) copies of (^{3}):—

Date .... Signed(^{4}) ....

* Strike out whichever is inapplicable.

Form 64A. Landlord's reply to application by tenant to Agricultural Land Tribunal for the holding to be treated as a market garden (prescribed form) A.110

Form 8R

Ref. No.
To be inserted
by the Secretary.

AGRICULTURAL LAND TRIBUNAL

Reply to Application for Direction to Treat an Agricultural Holding as a Market Garden

To the Secretary of the Agricultural Land Tribunal for the .... Area.

I .... [*block capitals*]
of .... [*address*]
landlord(^{1}) of .... [*name or description of holding*], having received a copy of the application (bearing the above reference number) for the Tribunal's direction under section 68 of the Agricultural Holdings Act 1948 (as amended) that the said holding or part thereof should be treated as a market garden in respect of the improvement(s) specified therein, reply as follows:—

1. With regard to paragraph 3 of the application, I—
    * (a) agree that the request was made and refused;
    * (b) agree that the request was made, but say that
        * (i) I did agree to it in writing on the .... day of .... 19........
        * (ii) I have not yet had reasonable time to agree to it;
    (c) deny that the request was made.

2. The other facts stated in the application are correct except that:—

3. My main reasons for resisting the application are:—

---

^{3} Mention any other document which is attached to this application.
^{4} If signed by any person other than the applicant himself, he should state in what capacity or by what authority he signs.
^{1} If this form is completed by a superior landlord, he should omit paragraph 1.

SECTION 1: TENANCIES PROTECTED BY THE AGRICULTURAL HOLDINGS ACT 1986

      (a) the land is unsuitable for market gardening for the following reasons:—
      (b) [*any other reasons*]

4. (1) If the Tribunal decide to give the direction applied for, I request them to limit its effect to the following improvement(s):—

(2) My main reasons for this would be:—

5. I attach copies of the following relevant documents(^{2}):—

    Date .... Signed(^{3}) ....

* Strike out whichever is inapplicable.

A.111   **Form 65. Landlord's or tenant's notice of intention to claim compensation on termination of the tenancy (section 83(2) (not a prescribed form) [Notice of tenant's intention to claim milk quota compensation under the Agriculture Act 1986]**

Agricultural Holdings Act 1986
[Agriculture Act 1986]

To: A.B. landlord of [address]

Or

To: C.D. tenant of [address]

Re: The holding known as [name/OS numbers]

I give you notice in accordance with section 83(2) of the Agricultural Holdings Act 1986, that it is my intention to make against you the claims specified in the Schedule hereto, being claims which arise on or out of the termination of my [*or* your] tenancy of the holding of which I was your [*or* you were my] tenant.

[I also give you notice, under Schedule 1, paragraph 11 of the Agriculture Act 1986, that it is my intention to make against you the claim specified in the Schedule hereto, being a claim for compensation in respect of milk quota arising under paragraph 1 of Schedule 1 to the said Act.]

---

[2] (a) Two copies of the reply and of any document which you wish to submit to the Tribunal must be sent to the Secretary, and, if there are more than two parties (*e.g.*, if the holding is sub-let) an additional copy of each must be supplied for each additional party.
(b) If you disagree with any map or plan attached to the application your reply should be accompanied by two copies of a 6" to one mile or 1/10,000 (or larger) map or plan showing what you consider to be the true position and marking the Ordnance Survey Field Numbers.
[3] If signed by any person other than the landlord himself, he should state in what capacity or by what authority he signs.

FORM 65

The Schedule of Claims above referred to

Nature of Claim	Reference to statutory provision or term of agreement under which claim is made	Amount £

Examples of tenant's claims

Nature of Claim	Reference to statutory provision or term of agreement under which claim is made
Compensation for disturbance	Agricultural Holdings Act 1986
Basic (one year's rent)	section 60(3)(a)
Basic (loss amounting to more than one year's rent)	section 60(3)(b)
Additional	section 60(4)
Compensation for relevant improvements—	Agricultural Holdings Act 1986
Construction of silos	section 64 and Schedule 7, paragraph 12
Land drainage (other than mole drainage)	section 64 and Schedule 7, paragraph 23
Application of fertilisers	section 64 and Schedule 8, paragraph 5
Consumption in the holding of cake or other feeding stuff not produced on the holding	section 64 and Schedule 8, paragraph 6
Compensation for tenant-right matters—	
Growing crops and severed or harvested crops and produce	section 65 and Schedule 8, paragraph 7
Pasture land down at the expense of the tenant	section 65 and Schedule 8, paragraph 9
Acclimatisation, hefting or settlement of hill sheep on hill land	section 65 and Schedule 8, paragraph 10
Residual fertility value of sod of excess qualifying leys	section 65 and Schedule 8, paragraph 11
Compensation for tenant-right matters under terms of a written agreement	Clause of contract of tenancy dated and made between and
Compensation in respect of milk quota	Agriculture Act 1986, section 13 and Schedule 1

SECTION 1: TENANCIES PROTECTED BY THE AGRICULTURAL HOLDINGS ACT 1986

The total claim made by me is ....
This is based on allocated quota of ....
The tenant's fraction of standard quota is ....
Transferred quota is ....
of which the tenant has carried the entire cost

Examples of landlord's claims

Dilapidations—
    Foul condition of land: Injury to or deterioration of the holding due to cross-cropping;
    Failure to scour and cleanse ditches and water courses;   section 71(1) of the Agricultural Holdings Act 1986
    Failure to return to the holding the manurial equivalent of produce sold off

(Alternative claim for dilapidations)
Dilapidations—
    Failure to repair farm buildings; selling off and removal of hay, straw and roots after receipt of notice to quit; failure to repair fences and gates   section 71(3) of 1986 Act and the following clauses of the Contract of tenancy, dated .... and made between .... and ....
(Describe each clause briefly, not merely by number unless there is no room for doubt or confusion)

General deterioration of the holding   section 72 of the 1986 Act

Dated:

Signed:

Arbitration

A.112   **Form 66.   Appointment of a valuer with full powers, including power to secure the appointment of an arbitrator**

I hereby appoint [*] of [*] to be my valuer and agent to ascertain, determine, agree and settle on my behalf all matters, questions, differences, claims and valuations arising as between landlord and tenant in respect of the holding known as [*] and situate at [*] in the County of [*], whether arising under the Agricultural Holdings

Act 1986, the Agriculture Act 1986, other statutory provisions, the contract of tenancy, custom or otherwise, and I authorise the said [*] to prepare, sign and serve on my behalf all forms, applications, notices, claims or other documents required for or incidental to the carrying out of the purposes for which he is appointed and to receive claims and other documents as relate to such purposes. I further authorise the said [*] in case of disagreement or dispute to refer all such matters, questions, differences, claims or valuations to arbitration under the Agricultural Holdings Act 1986, or, if necessary, the Arbitration Acts 1950 and 1979, or any amendment, statutory modification or re-enactment of the said Acts or any of them for the time being in force, and for this purpose to nominate and appoint, or to concur in the nomination and appointment of, as a single arbitrator, any person he may think fit, and, in default of agreement upon a person to act as arbitrator, to apply to the President of the Royal Institution of Chartered Surveyors to appoint a single arbitrator or to take such steps as are prescribed by law to secure such appointment and to concur in the revocation of the appointment of any arbitrator. And I hereby undertake to confirm, adopt, and allow any act, agreement, settlement, compromise or thing done, made, suffered or allowed by the said [*] in or in connection with such matters, questions, differences, claims and valuations.

Dated:

Signed:

Form 67A. Form for application to the President of the Royal Institution of Chartered Surveyors (RICS) for the appointment of an arbitrator in a section 12 rent review (prescribed by the RICS)   **A.113**

AGRICULTURAL HOLDINGS ACT 1986

APPLICATION FOR THE APPOINTMENT OF AN ARBITRATOR (FOR USE IN S.12 RENT CASES)

To the President,
The Royal Institution of Chartered Surveyors
(Arbitrations Section)
Surveyor Court
Westwood Way
Coventry CV4 8JE

SECTION 1: TENANCIES PROTECTED BY THE AGRICULTURAL HOLDINGS ACT 1986

A. The landlord and tenant having failed to agree as to the person to act as arbitrator and there being no provision in any agreement between them relating to the appointment of such arbitrator, I/We* hereby apply to the President of the Royal Institution of Chartered Surveyors for the appointment of an arbitrator((from among the Lord Chancellor's panel of arbitrators) to determine the rent to be paid for the holding referred to below as from the next termination date following the date of the demand for arbitration served by the landlord/tenant* on his tenant/landlord.*

B. I/We enclose a cheque for £115 made out to "The Royal Institution of Chartered Surveyors".**

C. I/We* understand that unless the application, accompanied by the fee, is received at the address given above **before the next termination date following the date of the demand for arbitration**, it will be invalid and the appointment of the arbitrator will not be made.

Signature .... Date ....

PARTICULARS REQUIRED	REPLIES
1. Name and address of the agricultural holding (as defined in Section 1 of the Agricultural Holdings Act 1986).	Holding(s): Parish: County:
2. Name and address of landlord	
3. Name and address of landlord's agent (please quote reference)	
4. Name and address of tenant	
5. Name and address of tenant's agent (please quote reference)	
6. Approximate area of holding	Hectares/acres*
7. Description of holding (for example, mixed, arable, dairying, market garden)	
8. Has a demand in writing for an arbitration as to the rent to be	

	paid for the holding been made by one party to the other? If so, state the date of such demand and whether it was made by the landlord or the tenant.	
9.	State the next termination date following the date of the demand.	
10.	(a) On what date did the tenancy commence? (b) On what date did any previous increase or reduction of the rent take place? (c) On what date took effect any previous direction of an arbitrator that the rent should continue unchanged?	
11.	(Holdings in Wales) Do you require the appointment of an arbitrator with a knowledge of the Welsh language?	

NOTES

* Delete as appropriate

** VAT is not payable and **the fee is non-returnable**.
If more than one holding is to be referred to arbitration, a fee is payable (and a separate form must be submitted) in respect of each holding.

†Under paragraph 7 of the Eleventh Schedule to the Agricultural Holdings Act 1986, the parties to the arbitration must, within 35 days from the appointment of the arbitrator, deliver to him a statement of their respective cases, with all necessary particulars. Such a statement cannot afterwards be amended, except with the arbitrator's consent; and the parties will be bound by it when the hearing takes place.

Form 67B. Form for application to the President of the Royal Institution of Chartered Surveyors for appointment of arbitrator, in all cases other than section 12 rent review (prescribed by the RICS) A.114

AGRICULTURAL HOLDINGS ACT 1986

APPLICATION FOR THE APPOINTMENT OF AN ARBITRATOR TO

SECTION 1: TENANCIES PROTECTED BY THE AGRICULTURAL HOLDINGS ACT 1986

DETERMINE CLAIMS, QUESTIONS, OR DIFFERENCES BETWEEN THE LANDLORD AND TENANT OF A HOLDING EXCEPT FOR S.12 RENT CASES

PART I

To the President, The Royal Institution of Chartered Surveyors, (Arbitration Section), Surveyor Court, Westwood Way, Coventry CV4 8JE

A. The landlord and tenant having failed to agree as to the person to act as arbitrator and there being no provision in any agreement between them relating to the appointment of such arbitrator, I/We* hereby apply to the President of the Royal Institution of Chartered Surveyors for the appointment of an arbitrator** (from among the Lord Chancellor's panel of arbitrators) for the purpose of settling the claims, questions or differences set out below.

B. I/We enclose a cheque for £115 made out to "The Royal Institution of Chartered Surveyors".***

C. I/We* understand that, where the request for an arbitrator is in respect of cases A, B, D or E notices to quit, the application, accompanied by the fee, must be received at the address given above **before the expiry of 3 months after the date of the service of the notice under Article 9 of the Agricultural Holdings (Arbitration on Notices) Order 1987**, *requiring arbitration under the 1986 Act*, and that if it is not so received within that period, the application will be invalid and the appointment of the arbitrator will not be made.

Signature .... Date ....

State whether landlord or tenant or duly authorised agent of either.

....

NOTES

* Delete as appropriate

** Under paragraph 7 of the Eleventh Schedule to the Agricultural Holdings Act 1986, the parties to the arbitration must, within 35 days from the appointment of the arbitrator, deliver to him a statement of their respective cases, with all necessary particulars. Such a statement cannot afterwards be amended, except with the arbitrator's consent; and the parties will be bound by it when the hearing takes place.

*** VAT is not payable and **the fee is non-returnable**. If more than one holding is

FORM 67B

to be referred to arbitration, a fee is payable (and a separate form must be submitted) in respect of each holding.

N.B. This form is also appropriate for use under S.22 of the Agricultural Holdings Act 1986 and Schedule 1 of the Agriculture Act 1986.

PARTICULARS REQUIRED	**REPLIES**
1. Name and address of the agricultural holding (as defined in Section 1 of the Agricultural Holdings Act 1986).	Holding(s): Parish: County:
2. Name and address of landlord.	
3. Name and address of landlord's agent (please quote reference).	
4. Name and address of tenant.	
5. Name and address of tenant's agent (please quote reference).	
6. Approximate area of holding.	Hectares/acres* (Delete as appropriate)
7. Description of holding (for example, mixed, arable, dairying, market garden).	
8. State the provision of the agricultural holdings legislation (naming the provision in the relevant Act or Statutory Instrument) in respect of which arbitration is required and, where appropriate, give the particulars listed in Column 2 of the Table contained in Part II of this Form in relation to the provision (no additional information is needed for applications under S.2(4) of the Agricultural Holdings Act 1986).	
9. (Holdings in Wales) Do you require the appointment of an arbitrator with a knowledge of the Welsh language?	

SECTION 1: TENANCIES PROTECTED BY THE AGRICULTURAL HOLDINGS ACT 1986

PART II

NOTE It may be necessary to set out some of the following particulars in your answer to question 8 or Part I of this form, but only Part I should be submitted to the President.

AGRICULTURAL HOLDINGS ACT 1986

Column 1

Section 6—(securing written tenancy agreements)

Section 8(1) & (2) (terms of tenancy relating to maintenance, repair and insurance of fixed equipment)

Section 9(1)—(compensation on transfer of liability for maintenance or repair of fixed equipment from tenant to landlord)

Section 9(3)—(compensation to the tenant for the landlord's failure to comply with existing terms on transfer of liability for maintenance or

Column 2

(a) The date of service of the request to the landlord or tenant from the tenant or landlord seeking to enter into a written tenancy agreement, or to provide in the existing agreement for any matter specified in the First Schedule to the 1986 Act that is not included in the existing agreement.

(a) The date of service of the landlord's or tenant's request to bring the existing tenancy agreement into conformity with regulations made under Section 7(1) of the 1986 Act prescribing terms as to maintenance, repair and insurance of fixed equipment. (The current regulations are The Agriculture (Maintenance, Repair and Insurance of Fixed Equipment) Regulations 1973 SI No 1473).

(a) The date on which the liability for the maintenance or repair of any item of fixed equipment was transferred (by virtue of Section 6, Section 7 or Section 8 of the 1986 Act).
(b) The date of service of the landlord's demand for the matter to be determined by arbitration (this must be within one month from the date when the transfer takes effect as laid down in the Agriculture (Miscellaneous Time-Limits) Regulations 1959: SI No 171 Regulation 2(2)).

(a) The date on which the liability for the maintenance or repair of any item of fixed equipment was transferred (by virtue of Section 6, Section 7 or Section 8 of the 1986 Act).

FORM 67B

repair of fixed equipment from landlord to tenant)	(b) The date of service of the tenant's demand for the matter to be determined by arbitration (this must be within one month from the date when the transfer takes effect as laid down in the Agriculture (Miscellaneous Time-Limits) Regulations 1959: SI No 171 Regulation 2(3)).
Section 10—(tenant's right to remove fixtures and buildings)	(a) The date the tenancy terminated (if applicable). (b) The date of service of the notice by the tenant on the landlord of his intention to remove fixtures or buildings (Notice must have been served at least one month before the right is exercised and the tenancy is terminated). (c) The date of service of the landlord's counter-notice electing to purchase the fixtures or buildings. (Counter-notice must have been served before the expiry of the tenant's notice above).
Section 13—(increase of rent for landlord's improvement)	(a) The date of completion of the improvement. (b) The date of service of the landlord's notice requiring the rent to be increased (notice must have been served within six months from the completion of the improvement).
Section 14—(terms of tenancy as to area of permanent pasture)	The date of service of the notice by the landlord or tenant on his tenant or landlord demanding arbitration on the question whether the area of land required to be maintained as permanent pasture should be reduced.
Section 15—(claims under S.15(6) for injury or deterioration of holding as a result of the tenant's exercising rights under S.15(1))	State whether or not the arbitration is required for the purposes of any proceedings for an injunction to restrain the exercise of the tenant's rights under Section 15(5) of the 1986 Act.
Section 20—(tenant's right to compensation for damage by wild animals or birds)	(a) The date of service of the tenant's notice to the landlord before the expiration of one month after the tenant first became or ought reasonably to have become aware of the damage. (b) The date of service of the claim given to the landlord within one month after

SECTION 1: TENANCIES PROTECTED BY THE AGRICULTURAL HOLDINGS ACT 1986

	the expiration of the year in respect of which the claim is made. (c) The date which is the end of the year for the purposes of question (b) above. (Unless the landlord or tenant agree on a different date, 29 September will be taken as the year-ending date).
Section 33—(reduction of rent following resumption of possession of part of holding by landlord)	The date the landlord resumed possession of part of the holding.
Section 48(3) & (4) (succession on death—rent and/or terms of new tenancy, please specify)	(a) The annual term date of the tenancy. (b) The date the tenant died. (c) The ALT which gave the direction under Section 39 of the 1986 Act. (d) The date of the direction. (e) The date of service of the notice to quit (if applicable). (f) The date of service of the demand for arbitration by the landlord or the tenant. (g) If the ALT extended the relevant time under Section 46(2) of the 1986 Act, give the extended date.
Section 56(1) & (3) (succession on retirement—rent and/or terms of new tenancy, please specify)	(a) The annual term date of the tenancy. (b) The date of service of the retirement notice under Section 49(1)(b). (c) The ALT which gave the direction under Section 53(7). (d) The date of the direction. (e) The retirement date. (f) If the ALT extended the relevant time under Section 55(8) give the extended date. (g) The date of service of the demand for arbitration by the landlord or tenant.
Section 83—(settlement of claims on termination of the tenancy)	(a) The date of the termination of the tenancy. (b) The date of service of the notice(s) by the landlord/tenant on the tenant/landlord of his/their intention to make a claim. (For the claim to be enforceable, the landlord/tenant must, before the expiry of 2 months from the termination of the tenancy, have served notice in writing on his tenant/landlord of his intention to make the claim).

FORM 67B

    (c) In the case of a claim for disturbance under Section 60 of the 1986 Act:
    (i) the date of service of the notice to quit;
    (ii) the date of service of the tenant's counter-notice under section 32 of the 1986 Act (if applicable);
    (iii) the date of service of the tenant's notice, on the landlord, before the termination of the tenancy stating his intention to make a claim greater than that stated in Section 60(3)(a) of the 1986 Act (if applicable).

The Agriculture (Maintenance, Repair and Insurance of Fixed Equipment) Regulations 1973 SI 1973/1473

Schedule Paragraph 4(3)(a)— (right and liabilities of the landlord with respect to repairs and replacements)	(a) The date of service of the landlord's notice under paragraph 4(2) of the Schedule to the 1973 Regulations calling on the tenant to execute necessary repairs or replacements.
	(b) The date of service of the tenant's counter-notice denying liability and requiring arbitration. (This must be served within one month of service of the landlord's notice).
Schedule Paragraph 12(3)(a)— rights and liabilities of the tenant with respect to repairs and replacements)	(a) The date of service of the tenant's notice under paragraph 12(1) and/or (2) calling on the landlord to execute the necessary repairs and/or replacements.
	(b) The date of service of the landlord's counter-notice denying liability and requiring arbitration.
Schedule paragraph 13— (redundant fixed equipment)	(a) The date of service of the notice by the landlord or tenant requiring arbitration on the question whether any item of fixed equipment is redundant to the farming of the holding.

SECTION 1: TENANCIES PROTECTED BY THE AGRICULTURAL HOLDINGS ACT 1986

Schedule paragraph 15— (other matters)

If any claim, question or difference shall arise between the landlord and the tenant under the foregoing provisions hereof, not being a matter which, otherwise than under the provisions of this paragraph, is required by or by virtue of the Act or regulations or orders made thereunder or the foregoing provisions hereof to be determined by arbitration under the Act, such claim, question or difference shall be determined, in default or agreement, by arbitration under the Act.

The Agricultural Holdings (Arbitration on Notices) Order 1987 SI 1987/710, as varied

Articles 3 and 4— (notices served on the tenant to remedy breach of tenancy agreement by doing work of repair maintenance or replacement)

(a) The date Form 2 of the Agricultural Holdings (Forms of Notices to Pay Rent or to Remedy) Regulations 1984 was served on the tenant.

(b) The date of service of the tenant's notice requiring arbitration (must be within one month of (a) above).

(c) State whether the demand for arbitration requires matters to be determined in respect of Article 3 only, Article 4 only, or both Articles 3 and 4 of the Agricultural Holdings (Arbitration on Notices) Order 1987.

Article 9— (notices to quit served on the tenant under S.26 & Schedule 3: Part I of the Agricultural Holdings Act 1986, cases A, B, D or E)

(a) The date of service of the notice to quit.

(b) State the Case under which the notice to quit was given (A, B, D or E).

(c) The date of the tenant's notice requiring arbitration (must be

FORM 67B

within one month of the service of the notice to quit).

Agriculture Act 1986 (Milk Quotas)

Schedule 1 paragraph 10 (Determination of standard quota and tenant's fraction before end of tenancy)	(a) The termination date of the tenancy. (b) The date of service of the notice by the landlord or tenant demanding the determination by arbitration of the standard quota for the land or the tenant's fraction (the notice must be served before the termination of the tenancy).
Schedule 1 paragraph 11 (Settlement of tenant's claim on termination of tenancy)	(a) The termination of the tenancy as defined in paragraph 11. (b) The date of service of the tenant's notice to the landlord of his intention to make a claim. (This must be before the expiry of two months from the termination of the tenancy as defined in paragraph 11).

A.115
Form 68. Notice requiring arbitrator to act (Schedule 11, paragraph 2) (not a prescribed form)

Agricultural Holdings Act 1986, Schedule 11, paragraph 2

[Agriculture Act 1986]([1])

To: E.F. [name and address of arbitrator]

Re: The holding known as [name/OS numbers]

I require you to act within seven days from the receipt of this notice in the matter of the arbitration between [name and address of other party] and myself under the Act in respect of the holding.

Dated:

Signed:

---

[1] Arbitrations under the Agriculture Act are governed by Schedule 11 of the 1986 Act. Insert if necessary.

SECTION 1: TENANCIES PROTECTED BY THE AGRICULTURAL HOLDINGS ACT 1986

A.116 Form 69. Revocation of the appointment of arbitrator (revocation by valuers duly authorised to do so) (Schedule 11, paragraph 4) (not a prescribed form)

Agricultural Holdings Act 1986, Schedule 11, paragraph 4

To: E.F. [name and address of arbitrator]

Re: The holding known as [name/OS numbers]

We [*] and [*] Valuers and Agents for [*] ("the landlord") and [*] ("the tenant") give you notice that in accordance with the authority given to us by the landlord and the tenant respectively we revoke your appointment dated [*] to act as arbitrator under the Act to determine questions arising between the landlord and the tenant in respect of the holding. [*or state more specifically the question or questions referred to arbitration in the words of the appointment, care being taken that the revocation is co-extensive with the appointment.*]

Dated .... 19...............
(Signed)
Landlord's Valuers and Agents.
Tenant's Valuers and Agents.
(Address)

A.117 Form 70. Statement of Case, Schedule 11, paragraph 7 (not a prescribed form). The example given is of the landlord's Statement of Case in a rent arbitration

AGRICULTURAL HOLDINGS ACT 1986, SECTION 12

RE: THE HOLDING KNOWN AS BLACKACRE FARM NEAR BLACKTOWN, BLACKSHIRE

IN THE MATTER OF AN ARBITRATION

BETWEEN:

A.B.   Landlord

and

C.D.   Tenant

<u>LANDLORD'S STATEMENT OF CASE</u>

1. A.B. of [*address*] is the freehold owner of Blackacre Farm, Blacktown, Blackshire shown edged red on the attached plan drawn to a scale of [*].

2. C.D. of [*address*] is the tenant of the farm pursuant to an agreement in writing made on [*] between the parties hereto. A copy is attached to this Statement of Case.

3. The current rent is £[*] annually. The landlord on [*] served notice under section 12 of the Agricultural Holdings Act 1986 to review the rent of the holding with effect from [*].

4. On [*] Mr [*] of [*address*] was duly appointed by the parties to determine the rent as arbitrator under section 12.

5. The landlord in this arbitration contends that the new rent should be fixed at £[*] annually. He relies on the following matters.

6. Attention is drawn in particular to the following terms of the tenancy namely [*insert numbers/details*].

7. Attached hereto is a Schedule containing full details of all fixed equipment and improvements on the holding stating whether the same are provided by the landlord or whether the same are tenant's improvements or fixed equipment and indicating which are grant-aided and to what extent. Also attached is a plan showing all buildings including redundant buildings and cross-referring by letters/numbers to the said list.

8. The character and situation of the holding is [*full description*].

9. The productive capacity of the holding and its related earning capacity are as shown in the attached budget assuming here that the competent tenant would practice the following system of husbandry [*give details*].

10. The current level of rent for comparable lettings of other holdings on similar terms is established by two holdings namely Whiteacre Farm, Blacktown, Blackshire and Blueacre Farm, Blacktown, Blackshire. Full details of the relevant transactions and the landlord's analysis of those transactions is set out in two appendices attached hereto. Included within those appendices is a copy of the tenancy agreement and a letter from agents involved in the relevant transactions confirming the accuracy of the details given.

11. The landlord wishes to make the following allowance/comment in relation to tenant's improvements and/or fixed equipment [*give full details*].

12. The landlord will wish to comment on any information put forward by the tenant. It may be necessary to amend or supplement this Statement of Case, with the arbitrator's leave.

Dated:

Signed:

SECTION 1: TENANCIES PROTECTED BY THE AGRICULTURAL HOLDINGS ACT 1986

As duly authorised agent for the above-named landlord

A.118 Form 71. **Statement of Case with all necessary particulars for the arbitrator, claims on termination of tenancy (Schedule 11, paragraph 7). Claim in respect of milk quota included (not a prescribed form)**

AGRICULTURE ACT 1986

IN THE MATTER OF AN ARBITRATION

BETWEEN:

A.B.   Landlord

and

C.D.   Tenant

TENANT'S STATEMENT OF CASE

1. By a written tenancy agreement dated [*] the farm known as Greenacre at [*] in the County of [*] ("the holding") was let by A.B. ("the landlord") to C.D. ("the tenant") on a yearly tenancy commencing on the [*]. A copy of the said tenancy agreement is attached hereto as Annex No.1. A plan of the holding, which is [*] hectares in size, is attached hereto as Annex No.2.

2. By a notice to quit dated [*], the landlord terminated the tenancy on the [*]. The tenant duly delivered up possession of the holding in consequence of the notice.

3. The tenant, having delivered up possession of the holding on the termination of the tenancy, and having on the [*] served on the landlord a notice of intention to claim in accordance with section 83(2) of the Agricultural Holdings Act 1986, now claims from the landlord compensation for disturbance (both basic and additional), improvements, tenant-right matters and fixtures in accordance with the said Act or otherwise. Particulars of the tenant's claims under these heads are set out below.

[4. The tenant, having on [*] served notice under Schedule 1 paragraph 11 of the Agriculture Act 1986 of intention to claim compensation in respect of milk quota, now claims payment from the landlord in accordance with the particulars of entitlement to quota included in the Schedule below.]

[5. With reference to the landlord's claim for dilapidations in respect of the

FORM 71

farmhouse and farm buildings, mentioned in the landlord's notice of intention to claim dated the [*], the tenant will object that the said sum is excessive and should be reduced. And the tenant will contend that there is no foundation for the claims in respect of foul land and general deterioration of the holding mentioned in the landlord's said notice. The land in question is not foul land and the holding has not suffered any deterioration.]

Particulars

Claim	Authority	Amount £ p
Basic compensation for disturbance, equal to one year's rent of the holding	Agricultural Holdings Act 1986, section 60(3)(a).	
Additional compensation for disturbance, equal to four year's rent of holding	AHA 1986, section 60(4).	
Compensation for relevant improvements.		
(a) Erection of building for with consent of landlord in writing dated	AHA 1986, section 64 and Schedule 7, paragraph 9.	
(b) Laying on of electric light and power to outbuildings completed on	Agreement between landlord and tenant, dated	
(c) Construction of silo in stockyard, completed on with approval of Agricultural Land Tribunal for .... Area.	AHA 1986, section 64 and Schedule 7, paragraph 12.	
(d) Mole drainage in field OS No .... completed on ...., one month's notice of intention having been given to the landlord on	AHA 1986, section 64 and Schedule 8, paragraph 1.	
Compensation for other matters		

SECTION 1: TENANCIES PROTECTED BY THE AGRICULTURAL HOLDINGS ACT 1986

(calculated in accordance with the Agriculture (Calculation of Value for Compensation) Regulations 19..		
(a) Baled hay filling two bays of dutch barns in stockyard	AHA 1986, section 65 and Schedule 8, paragraph 7.	
(b) Tenant's pasture in field OS No.............................	AHA 1986, section 65 and Schedule 8, paragraph 9.	
Fixture Implements shed erected by tenant which landlord has elected to purchase by notice date	AHA 1986, section 10.	
Milk Quota	Agriculture Act 1986, section 13 and Schedule 1.	
Excess of allocated quota (1,000,000 litres) over standard quota (800,000 litres) = 200,000 litres		
Tenant's fraction of standard quota, 40 per cent of 800,000 litres = 320,000 litres		
Transferred quota of 50,000 litres, to cost of which tenant contributed 1/2 = 25,000 litres		
Total = 545,000 litres		
Quota valued at xp per litre		

Dated:

Signed:

As duly authorised agent for the above-named tenant

Form 72. Forms of oath or affirmation for witnesses in arbitrations A.119

Oath

I swear by Almighty God that the evidence I shall give in this arbitration shall be the truth, the whole truth, and nothing but the truth.

Affirmation (for witnesses who have conscience objections to an oath)

I solemnly, sincerely and truly affirm and declare that the evidence I shall give in this arbitration shall be the truth, the whole truth, and nothing but the truth.

Form 73. Notice by arbitrator to produce documents (Schedule 11, paragraph 8) (not a prescribed form) A.120

AGRICULTURAL HOLDINGS ACT 1986

IN THE MATTER OF AN ARBITRATION

BETWEEN:

A.B.   Landlord

and

C.D.   Tenant

Re: The holding known as [name/OS numbers]

To: A.B. landlord of [address]

Or

To: C.D. tenant of [address]

I, [*] the arbitrator appointed to act in the above-mentioned arbitration, hereby require you, in accordance with paragraph 8 of Schedule 11 to the Agricultural Holdings Act 1986, to attend at [*] on [*], at [*] o'clock on the hearing of the said arbitration and there produce before me the several samples and documents specified in the Schedule hereto being samples of documents within your possession or power which relate to the matters to be determined by me in the said arbitration.

SCHEDULE ABOVE REFERRED TO

Consent of A.B., dated [*], to the erection of a building on the holding.

SECTION 1: TENANCIES PROTECTED BY THE AGRICULTURAL HOLDINGS ACT 1986

Plans and specifications relating to the drainage of fields O.S. [*] and O.S. [*] on the holding.

Sample of [*] and receipts showing the payment for the total amount included in the tenant's claim in respect of such compensation, namely £[*].

      Dated   19[*]
      (Signed) X.Y.
      Arbitrator in the
      above-mentioned arbitration.
      (Address)

A.121   **Form 74. Outline of statement by arbitrator of special case for the opinion of the County Court (not a prescribed form)**

IN THE [*] COUNTY COURT

AGRICULTURAL HOLDINGS ACT 1986

IN THE MATTER OF AN ARBITRATION

BETWEEN

A.B.   Landlord

and

C.D.   Tenant

Special case stated for the opinion of the Court by [*] Arbitrator, of [address], appointed in the above-mentioned arbitration.

1. [*Material facts in regard to the tenancy of the holding, with reference to lease or tenancy agreement.*]

2. [*Material facts as proved in the arbitration and references to any material documents. A logical sequence should be observed and the statement should be as succinct as possible, omitting irrelevant matter and including precis of, or reference to, evidence which has resulted in the strict proof of facts being avoided.*]

3. The landlord contended:

4. The tenant contended:

5. The questions of law which are submitted for the opinion of the Court are:

[The questions should be set out in numbered subparagraphs, and should, if possible, be in such a form that the Court can answer them by a simple affirmative or negative.]

Dated:

Signed:

Arbitrator of
(Address)

A.122

Form 75. Form of award in arbitration (prescribed form)

AGRICULTURAL HOLDINGS ACT 1986 (Note 1)

FORM OF AWARD

Arbitrator: [name and address]

Date of appointment:

Time for making award extended to:

Present landlord [name and address]

Present tenant [name and address]

Rent payable prior to arbitration:

Award of the Arbitrator

The claims or questions set out in the Schedule to this award have been referred to arbitration and, having considered the evidence and the submissions of the parties, I, the arbitrator, award as follows: (Note 2)

1. The landlord is to pay to the tenant in respect of the claims set out in Column 1 of Part I of the Schedule the sum(s) set out in Column 2 thereof.

2. The tenant is to pay to the landlord in respect of the claims set out in Column 1 of Part II of the Schedule the sum(s) set out in Column 2 thereof.

3. As from   (the next day on which the tenancy could have been brought to an end by notice to quit given at the date of the notice demanding arbitration under section 12 of the Act) the rent previously payable [is [increased] [reduced] to £......] [continues unchanged at £......] being the rent properly payable in respect of the holding at the date of the reference to arbitration.

SECTION 1: TENANCIES PROTECTED BY THE AGRICULTURAL HOLDINGS ACT 1986

4. The notice to quit referred to in Part IV of the Schedule shall [not] have effect. [I postpone the termination of the tenancy until   ].

5. My award in respect of the claims set out in Column 1 of Part V of the Schedule is set out in Column 2 thereof.

6. The landlord must pay to the tenant the sum(s) awarded by me to the tenant on the day .... (Note 3) after delivery of this award, and the tenant must pay to the landlord the sum(s) awarded by me to the landlord on the same day.

7. The costs of and incidental to the arbitration and the award shall be dealt with as follows:
   (a) My costs of the award amounting to £................ must be paid by the [landlord] [tenant] [landlord and the tenant in the following proportions]:
   (b) As respects the costs of and incidental to this arbitration [each party must bear his own costs] [the landlord must pay [........ % of] the costs of the tenant] [the tenant must pay [............. % of] the costs of the landlord] [to be taxed in the County Court] [according to Scale [................] as prescribed by the County Court Rules] [[the landlord] [the tenant] must pay £............. to the [tenant] [landlord] on account of his costs]:
   (c) All costs ordered by me to be paid shall be paid on the .... day (Note 3) after delivery of this award.

Signed by the arbitrator in the presence of: (Note 4)

Date:

This award was delivered to the [landlord] [tenant] on [date].

THE SCHEDULE

Part I

| Column 1 | Column 2 |
| Claims made by the landlord | Sum(s) awarded |

Part II

| Column 1 | Column 2 |
| Claims made by the tenant | Sum(s) awarded |

Part III

Rent

Part IV

Question(s) arising out of a notice to quit

FORM 75

Part V

| Column 1 | Column 2 |
| Other claims | Award |

APPENDIX

Statement of reasons for award (Note 5)

Notes for the arbitrator

1. This form must be followed as closely as possible, with only such omissions or modifications as circumstances may require. Paragraphs 1 to 6 inclusive will not all be relevant in every case, and any which are not relevant should be omitted.

2. The arbitrator must state separately in the award the amounts awarded in respect of the several claims referred to him. If either party applies to him to specify the amount awarded in respect of any particular improvement or any particular matter, he must do so.

3. The day on which payment is to be made must not be later than one month after the delivery of the award. Paragraph 22 of Schedule 11 to the Act provides for interest to be payable on sums directed by the award to be paid.

4. The award must be endorsed with the date of delivery so that there is no doubt as to the date upon which payments are to be made under paragraphs 6 and 8, and upon the date from which interest runs.

5. The arbitrator must furnish a statement of his reasons for the award if the landlord of the tenant so requests "on or before the giving or notification of the decision"—see section 12 of the Tribunals and Inquiries Act 1971. The statement may deal with different matters under different headings as appropriate; for example—
the facts he found to be admitted or proved;
the submissions of the parties and his rulings on them;
the method of valuation he applied to the facts so as to arrive at his determination;
the costs of, and incidental to, the arbitration and award.

Forms relating to matters subsequent to Agricultural Land Tribunal proceedings.

Form 76. Request to Agricultural Land Tribunal for reference of a question of law to the High Court (not a prescribed form) A.123

Ref. No.

To the Secretary of the Agricultural Land Tribunal for the [*] Area.

SECTION 1: TENANCIES PROTECTED BY THE AGRICULTURAL HOLDINGS ACT 1986

I, [*] of [*], the landlord [tenant] of the holding known as [*] and situate at [*] in the County of [*], having received a copy of the Tribunal's decision, dated [*] and bearing the above reference number, on the application [*here state briefly the nature of the application and by whom it was made*] request, in accordance with section 6 of the Agriculture (Miscellaneous Provisions) Act 1954, that the following question(s) of law arising in the course of the proceedings before the Tribunal shall be referred to the High Court for decision, namely: [*here set out the question or questions of law*].

Dated:

Signed:

A.124   77. **Notice to Agricultural Land Tribunal (after refusal by Tribunal to refer a question of law to the High Court) of intention to apply for a direction (not a prescribed form)**

                                                                                                  Ref. No.

To the Secretary of the Agricultural Land Tribunal for the [*] Area.

I, [*] of [*], the landlord [tenant] of the holding known as [*] and situate at [*] in the County of [*], having received notice dated [*] and bearing the above reference number, of the refusal of my request dated [*] to refer a question [*or* certain questions] of law to the High Court for decision, give notice, in accordance with section 6 of the Agriculture (Miscellaneous Provisions) Act 1954, that I intend to apply to the High Court for an order directing the Tribunal to refer the said question [questions] to the Court.

Dated:

Signed:

SECTION 2: TENANCIES PROTECTED BY THE AGRICULTURAL TENANCIES ACT 1995

All forms are non-statutory.

Character of tenancy

A.125   **Form 101. Notice of farm business tenancy (section 1(4)).**

Agricultural Tenancies Act 1995, section 1(4)

To: AB (name and address of landlord)

Or

To: CD [name and address of tenant]

Re: the holding known as [insert name of tenancy/OS numbers]

I hereby give you notice that the above land which is to be comprised in a tenancy between ourselves is intended by me to be held under a tenancy which will be and will remain a farm business tenancy within the meaning of the said Act.

Dated:

Signed:

Form 102. Recital for Lease or Tenancy Agreement A.126

Whereas:

(1) before the creation of the tenancy/term hereby granted the landlord has served upon the tenant and the tenant has served upon the landlord a notice identifying the land to be let and containing a statement to the effect that each party intends the tenancy to be and remain a farm business tenancy and

(2) the parties hereby confirm that at the date hereof the character of the tenancy to be granted is primarily or wholly agricultural and

(3) any use of the land hereby agreed to be let after the date hereof in breach of the terms of this tenancy, any commercial activities carried on in breach of those terms and any cessation of such activities in breach of those terms are to be disregarded as set out in section 1(8) of the Agricultural Tenancies Act 1995:

Now it is agreed (this Deed witnesseth) as follows:

Termination

Form 103. Fixed term: Termination notice at expiry (section 5) A.127

Agricultural Tenancies Act 1995: section 5

To: AB [landlord] of [address] or

To: CD [tenant] of [address]

Re: The holding known as [name/OS numbers]

SECTION 2: TENANCIES PROTECTED BY THE AGRICULTURAL TENANCIES ACT 1995

The lease dated [*] made between [*] and [*] expires on [*]. I hereby give you notice to terminate the tenancy of the above holding created by the said lease on [*] being a date not less than 12 and not more than 24 months after service of this notice.

Dated:

Signed:

A.128   **Form 104. Fixed term: Tenant's break notice, section 7**

Agricultural Tenancies Act 1995, section 7

To: CD, landlord, of [address]

Re: The Holding known as [name/OS numbers]

Pursuant to clause [*] of a tenancy agreement/lease dated [*] made between [*] and [*] I hereby give you notice that I will quit and deliver up possession of the above holding on [*] being a date not less than 12 and not more than 24 months after service of this notice whereupon the term granted by the said agreement/lease shall determine.

Dated:

Signed:

A.129   **Form 105. Fixed term: Landlord's break notice, section 7**

Agricultural Tenancies Act 1995, section 7

To: CD, tenant, of [address]

Re: The Holding known as [name/OS numbers]

Pursuant to clause [*] of the agreement/lease dated [*] made between [*] and [*] I hereby give you notice to quit and deliver up possession of the above holding on [*] being a date not less than 12 and not more than 24 months after service of this notice whereupon the term created by the said agreement/lease shall determine.

Dated:

Signed:

Form 106. Fixed term: Tenant's notice to quit part (section 7) A.130

Agricultural Tenancies Act 1995, section 7

To: AB, landlord, of [address]

Re: The Holding known as [name/OS numbers]

Pursuant to clause [*] of a lease/agreement dated [*] made between [*] and [*] I hereby give notice that I shall quit and deliver up possession of certain land comprised within the said agreement being land identified edged red on the attached plan on [*] being a date not less than 12 and not more than 24 months after service of this notice. I shall continue as tenant of the remainder of the land comprised within the said agreement/lease.

Dated:

Signed:

Form 107. Fixed term: Landlord's notice to quit part (section 7) A.131

Agricultural Tenancies Act 1995, section 7

To: CD, tenant, of [address]

Re: The Holding known as [name/OS numbers]

Pursuant to clause [*] of the agreement/lease dated [*] made between [*] and [*] I hereby give you notice to quit and deliver up possession of the land identified edged red on the attached plan being part of the land comprised within the said agreement/lease on [*] being a date not less than 12 and not more than 24 months after service of this notice upon you.

Dated:

Signed:

Form 108. Periodic tenancies: Annual tenancy, tenant's notice to quit (section 6) A.132

Agricultural Tenancies Act 1995, section 6

To: AB Landlord, of [address]

Re: The holding known as [name/OS numbers]

SECTION 2: TENANCIES PROTECTED BY THE AGRICULTURAL TENANCIES ACT 1995

I hereby give notice that I shall quit and deliver up possession of the above named holding on [*] or at the expiration of 12 months from the end of the now current year of my tenancy.

Dated:

Signed:

A.133 **Form 109. Periodic tenancies: Annual tenancy, landlord's notice to quit (section 6)**

Agricultural Tenancies Act 1995, section 6

To: CD, tenant of [address]

Re: The holding known as [name/OS numbers]

I hereby give you notice to quit and deliver up possession of the above named holding on [*] or at the expiration of 12 months from the end of the now current year of your tenancy.

Dated:

Signed:

A.134 **Form 110. Periodic tenancies: Annual tenancy, tenant's notice to quit part (section 6)**

Agricultural Tenancies Act 1995

To: AB, landlord of [address]

Re: The holding known as [name/OS numbers]

Pursuant to clause [*] of an agreement dated [*] made between [*] and [*] I hereby give you notice that I shall quit and deliver up possession of certain land comprised within the said agreement being land identified edged red on the attached plan on [*] or at the expiration of 12 months from the end of the now current year of my tenancy.

Dated:

Signed:

Form 111. Periodic tenancies: Annual tenancy, landlord's notice to quit part (section 6)

A.135

Agricultural Tenancies Act 1995, section 6

To: CD, tenant of [address]

Re: The holding known as [name/OS numbers]

Pursuant to clause [*] of the agreement dated [*] made between [*] and [*] I hereby give you notice to quit deliver up possession of the land identified edged red on the attached plan being part of the land comprised within the said agreement on [*] or at the expiration of 12 months from the end of the now current year of your tenancy.

Dated:

Signed:

Form 112. Lease for life: notice of termination on tenant's death (section 149(6) of the Law of Property Act 1925 and section 7(3) of the Agricultural Tenancies Act 1995)

A.136

Section 149(6) Law of Property Act 1925

To: The Personal Representatives of CD (the deceased tenant) of [address]

[And To: The Public Trustee]

Re: The holding known as [name/OS numbers]

This notice is given under the above named section following the death of CD who died on or about [*] being at that time the tenant holding under a lease dated [*] made between [*] and [*]. I hereby give you notice to quit and deliver up possession of the above named holding on [*] or on the quarter day falling next after the expiration of one month following service on you of this notice.

Dated:

Signed:

General notices

Form 113. Landlord's notice of severance of the reversion

A.137

Agricultural Tenancies Act 1995

SECTION 2: TENANCIES PROTECTED BY THE AGRICULTURAL TENANCIES ACT 1995

To: CD, tenant, of [address]

Re: The holding known as [name/OS numbers]

You are hereby notified that the reversion expectant on your tenancy has been severed on [*]. The land within your tenancy identified edged red by the plan attached hereto has £[*] rent apportioned to it and you are requested and authorised to pay such apportioned rent in respect of the said land as from the next rent day to [*] or as that person may direct.

Dated:

Signed:

A.138   **Form 114. Landlord's notice of change of landlord and giving landlord's address in England and Wales (sections 47 and 48 of the Landlord and Tenant Act 1987 and section 36(7) of the Agricultural Tenancies Act 1995)**

Agricultural Tenancies Act 1995, section 36(7)

Landlord and Tenant Act 1987, sections 47 and 48

To: CD, tenant, of [address]

Re: The holding known as [name/OS numbers]

You are hereby notified that AB [* previous landlord] who was previously entitled to receive the rents and profits of the above holding has ceased to be so entitled and I am now entitled to receive the said rents and profits as of [*]. My full name and address are [* name and address] and my address within England and Wales at which notices (including notices in proceedings) may be served on me is [* address].

Dated:

Signed:

A.139   **Form 115. Notice giving landlord address in England and Wales (sections 47 and 48 of the Landlord and Tenant Act 1987)**

Landlord and Tenant Act 1987, sections 47 and 48

To: CD, tenant, of [address]

Re: The holding known as [name/OS numbers]

You are hereby notified that my address within England and Wales at which notices including notices in proceedings may be served on me is [*].

Dated:

Signed:

Rent review

Form 116. Statutory rent review notice (section 10) A.140

Agricultural Tenancies Act 1995, section 10

To: AB, landlord, of [address]

Or: CD, tenant, of [address]

Re: The holding known as [name/OS numbers]

I hereby require that the rent payable in respect of the above holding as from [*] be referred to arbitration in accordance with the above-named Act.

Dated:

Signed:

Form 117. Rent agreement A.141

Agricultural Tenancies Act 1995, section 10

This Agreement is made between

    (1) AB, landlord, of [address] and

    (2) CD, tenant, of [address]

Re: The holding known as [name/OS numbers]

It is hereby agreed that with effect from [*] the rent properly payable in respect of the above named holding shall be £[*] per annum.

Dated:

Signed:

SECTION 2: TENANCIES PROTECTED BY THE AGRICULTURAL TENANCIES ACT 1995

(AB, landlord)

Signed:

(CD, tenant)

Notices related to compensation/improvements

A.142 **Form 118. Tenant's request for consent to improvement (section 17)**

Agricultural Tenancies Act 1995, section 17

To: AB, landlord of [address]

Re: The holding known as [name/OS numbers]

As tenant of the above named holding I hereby request you to give your consent to the provision of the tenant's improvements identified below.

Schedule

[*Description of improvement*]

Dated:

Signed:

A.143 **Form 119. Tenant's application for consent to the making of an application for planning permission (section 18)**

Agricultural Tenancies Act 1995, section 18

To: AB, landlord, of [address]

Re: The holding known as [name/OS numbers]

As tenant of the above named holding I hereby request you to give your consent in writing to the making of an application for planning permission as set out below.

Schedule

[*Details of planning permission*]

Dated:

Signed:

Form 120. Tenant's application for consent to implement planning permission (section 17)   A.144

Agricultural Tenancies Act 1995, section 17

To: AB, landlord, of [address]

Re: The holding known as [name/OS numbers]

As tenant of the above named holding I hereby request your written consent for the implementation by me of the planning permission referred to below.

Schedule

[*Details of planning permission*]

Dated:

Signed:

Form 121. Tenant's reference to arbitration on improvements after landlord's refusal (section 19)   A.145

Agricultural Tenancies Act 1995, section 19

To: AB, landlord, of [address]

Re: The holding known as [name/OS numbers]

You have refused to give your consent under section 17(1) of the above named Act in response to my application for consent dated [*] and accordingly I hereby demand that the question shall be referred to arbitration under section 19 of the Agricultural Tenancies Act 1995.

Dated:

Signed:

Form 122. Tenant's reference to arbitration on improvements after landlord's failing to respond (section 19)   A.146

Agricultural Tenancies Act 1995, section 19

To: AB, landlord, of [address]

SECTION 2: TENANCIES PROTECTED BY THE AGRICULTURAL TENANCIES ACT 1995

Re: The holding known as [name/OS numbers]

By notice dated [*] I requested consent under section 17(1) of the above named Act and you have failed within two months of that request being made to give any such consent. Accordingly I hereby demand that the question shall be referred to arbitration under section 19 of the Agricultural Tenancies Act 1995.

Dated:

Signed:

A.147 **Form 123. Tenant's reference to arbitration on improvements after landlord's required conditions (section 19)**

Agricultural Tenancies Act 1995, section 19

To: AB, landlord, of [address]

Re: The holding known as [name/OS numbers]

By notice dated [*] I requested consent from you as landlord of the above named holding pursuant to section 17 of the above named Act. By letter dated [*] you have required a variation or variations in the terms of the tenancy as a condition of giving such consent. I hereby demand that the question shall be referred to arbitration under section 19 of the Agricultural Tenancies Act 1995.

Dated:

Signed:

A.148 **Form 124. Landlord's consent to improvements (section 17)**

Agricultural Tenancies Act 1995, section 17

To: CD, tenant, of [address]

Re: The holding known as [name/OS numbers]

By a written request dated [*] you have requested my consent pursuant to section 17 of the above named Act.

Either

I hereby consent unconditionally to the making of the improvement[s] specified by the said request.

Or

I hereby give consent to the making of the improvement specified by the said request but such consent is conditional to the variations in the terms of tenancy which are identified by the Schedule hereto.

Schedule

[*Specify tenancy variations*]

Dated:

Signed:

Form 125. Landlord's consent to tenant applying for planning permission for physical improvement and making that physical improvement (sections 17 and 18)   **A.149**

Agricultural Tenancies Act 1995, sections 17 and 18

To: CD, tenant, of [address]

Re: The holding known as [name/OS numbers]

You have made to me a written request dated [*] for consent under section 17 of the above named Act.

Either

I hereby consent unconditionally to you making the physical improvement referred to in the said request for my consent.

Or

I hereby consent to you making the physical improvements specified by the said request for my consent but my consent is conditional upon you agreeing to a specified variation in the terms of tenancy as set out in the Schedule hereto.

Schedule

[*Specify variation in tenancy terms*]

This consent is given

Either

to enable the physical improvement specified by your request for my consent (being an improvement falling within paragraph (a) of section 15 of the said Act) lawfully to be provided by the tenant.

SECTION 2: TENANCIES PROTECTED BY THE AGRICULTURAL TENANCIES ACT 1995

Or

to enable you as tenant lawfully to effect a change of use specified by your said request for my consent.

Dated:

Signed:

A.150 **Form 126. Landlord's consent to tenant applying for planning permission for change of use (section 18)**

Agricultural Tenancies Act 1995, section 18

To: CD, tenant, of [address]

Re: The holding known as [name/OS numbers]

You have served on me a request dated [*] for the giving of my consent under section 17 of the above Act. This consent relates only to the application for planning permission and not to any implementation of that planning permission.

Either

I hereby give my consent unconditionally to the making of the application for planning permission as specified by your said written request and my consent is given in order to enable you as tenant lawfully to effect the change of use specified by your said request to me.

Or

I hereby consent to the making of the application for planning permission specified by your said written request but my consent is conditional upon you agreeing to a specified variation in the terms of tenancy as set out in the Schedule hereto. Further my consent is given in order to enable you as tenant lawfully to effect the change of use specified by your said request to me.

Schedule

[*Specify variation in tenancy terms.*]

Dated:

Signed:

Form 127. Landlord's consent to tenant applying for planning permission but not to tenant making physical improvement (section 18)   A.151

Agricultural Tenancies Act 1995, section 18

To: CD, tenant, of [address]

Re: The holding known as [name/OS numbers]

You have made a written request to me dated [*] requesting my consent in writing to the making of an application for planning permission as set out in your said request. This consent relates only to the application for planning permission and not to any implementation of it.

Either

I hereby consent unconditionally to the making of an application for planning permission as set out in your said request and my consent is given in order to enable a physical improvement falling within paragraph (a) of section 15 of this Act as specified by your said request to me lawfully to be provided by you as tenant.

Or

I hereby consent to the making of an application for planning permission as set out in your said request but my consent is conditional upon you agreeing to a specified variation in the terms of tenancy as set out in the Schedule hereto. Further my consent is given in order to enable a physical improvement falling within paragraph (a) of section 15 of this Act as specified by your request to me lawfully to be provided by you as tenant.

Schedule

[*Specify variation in tenancy terms*]

Dated:

Signed:

Form 128. Tenant's notice of intention to claim compensation (section 22)   A.152

Agricultural Tenancies Act 1995, section 18

To: AB, landlord, of [address]

Re: The holding known as [name/OS numbers]

SECTION 2: TENANCIES PROTECTED BY THE AGRICULTURAL TENANCIES ACT 1995

I hereby notify you of my intention to claim compensation under section 16 of the Agricultural Tenancies Act 1995 in respect of an improvement namely [*] for which you consented in writing on [*] [alternatively, in respect of an improvement for which approval was given by an arbitration award dated [*]].

Dated:

Signed:

A.153   **Form 129. Agreement regarding compensation (section 23(2))**

Agricultural Tenancies Act 1995

Re: The holding known as [name/OS numbers]

This agreement is made between

    (1)   AB, landlord, of [address] and

    (2)   CD, tenant, of [address]

It is agreed between the above named landlord and tenant that the tenant is entitled to compensation under section 16 of the Agricultural Tenancies Act 1995 on termination of the tenancy even though at such termination the tenant may remain in the holding under a new tenancy.

Dated:

Signed:

Disputes

A.154   **Form 130. Tenancy clause for third party dispute resolution an example (section 29(1)(a))**

Clause [*] Any dispute as to whether or not the tenant is currently in residence in the farmhouse shall be determined by Mr. Smith, senior partner in Smith & Smith, solicitors of [address]. Mr. Smith may be appointed by either the landlord or the tenant without the agreement of the other party to the tenancy agreement.

A.155   **Form 131. Joint reference of dispute by landlord and tenant to third party**

Agricultural Tenancies Act 1995, section 29(1)

Landlord: AB of [address]

FORM 131

Tenant: CD of [address]

Re: The holding known as [name/OS numbers]

The landlord and the tenant hereby jointly refer a dispute to Mr. Smith of Smith & Co., solicitors, of [address] as set out in the Schedule below, being a dispute which clause [*] of the tenancy agreement provides may be resolved by him.

Schedule

[*Insert details of dispute*]

Dated:

Signed:

Form 132. Reference of dispute by landlord or tenant to third party. A.156

Agricultural Tenancies Act 1995, section 29

Re: The holding known as [name/OS numbers]

Either

I, AB, landlord of the above named holding whose address is [*]

Or

I, CD, as tenant of the above named holding whose address is [*]

hereby refer to Mr. Smith of Smith & Smith, solicitors, of [address] a dispute which has arisen with my landlord/tenant as set out in the Schedule below and this reference is made pursuant to clause [*] of the tenancy agreement.

Schedule

[*Details of dispute*]

Dated:

Signed:

Form 133. Notice by landlord or tenant to other party of his unilateral reference of dispute to third party A.157

Agricultural Tenancies Act 1995, section 29(1)

SECTION 2: TENANCIES PROTECTED BY THE AGRICULTURAL TENANCIES ACT 1995

To: AB, landlord, of [address]

Or

To: CD, tenant, of [address]

Re: The holding known as [name/OS numbers]

I hereby notify you that by a reference dated [*] a copy of which is attached I have referred to Mr. Smith of Messrs. Smith & Smith of [address] a dispute which has arisen between ourselves as specified in that reference. The reference to Mr. Smith was made pursuant to clause [*] of the tenancy agreement.

Dated:

Signed:

A.158   Form 134.   Notice of dispute (section 28(2))

Agricultural Tenancies Act 1995, section 28(2)

To: AB, landlord, of [address]

Or

To: CD, tenant, of [address]

Re: The holding known as [name/OS numbers]

I hereby give you notice that a dispute has arisen between us as set out in the Schedule hereto. Unless before the end of the period of two months beginning with the day on which this notice is given we as parties have appointed an arbitrator by agreement, I propose to apply to the President of the RICS for the appointment of an arbitrator by him. This notice is given under section 28(2) of the above named Act.

Schedule

[*Details of dispute*]

Dated:

Signed:

PART VI

PROCEDURAL TABLES

A.159 INDEX OF PROCEDURAL TABLES

		PAGE
Table 1	Notices to quit capable of reference to the A.L.T. [Chapter 12]	1125
Table 2	Notices to quit: Cases A, B and E [Chapter 12]	1126
Table 3	Notice to quit: Case C [Chapter 12]	1127
Table 4	Notices to quit under Case D following notice to pay rent [Chapter 12]	1128
Table 5	Notice to quit: Case D and notice to do work of repair, maintenance or replacement [Chapter 12]	1129
Table 6	Notice to quit under Case D following notice to remedy not including work of repair, maintenance or replacement [Chapter 12]	1134
Table 7	Succession on death where Case G notice to quit has been served [Chapter 14]	1136
Table 8	Succession on death where no Case G notice to quit is served [Chapter 14]	1141
Table 9	Succession on retirement [Chapter 14]	1143
Table 10	Arbitration following succession direction [Chapter 14]	1145
Table 11	Compensation on quitting [fixtures, Chapter 10; compensation, Chapter 13; compensation for milk quota, Chapter 19]	1146
Table 12	Variation of rent by arbitration [Chapter 11]	1149
Table 13	Apportionment of milk quota by arbitration [Chapter 18]	1150

TABLE 1: NOTICES TO QUIT CAPABLE OF REFERENCE TO THE A.L.T.   A.160

	Step	Time Limit	Authority	Form	Consequence if step taken	Consequence if step not taken
1.	Service by landlord of notice to quit		Agricultural Holdings Act 1986, s. 25	Form 28 (not prescribed)		
2.	Tenant's counter-notice requiring that section 26(1)(b) shall apply to notice to quit	One month from giving of notice to quit	Agricultural Holdings Act 1986, s. 26(1)(b)	Form 36 (not prescribed)	Notice to quit rendered ineffective unless and until Agricultural Land Tribunal gives consent to operation of notice to quit	Notice to quit takes effect
3.	Landlord's application to the Agricultural Land Tribunal for consent to operation of notice to quit	Within one month of receipt of counter-notice	Agricultural Land Tribunals (Rules) Order 1978, r. 2(2)	Form 40 (prescribed)	Application proceeds	Application may be made for extension of time for filing application to Tribunal (1978 Order, rule 37)
4.	Tenant's reply	One month after service of landlord's application on tenant	Agricultural Land Tribunals (Rules) Order 1978, r. 15(1)	Form 40A (prescribed)	Agricultural Land Tribunal proceedings continue	Agricultural Land Tribunal may make an order in the terms of the application without formal hearing (1978 Order r. 15(2))
5.	Agricultural Land Tribunal's decision					
6.	Application by tenant for postponement of tenancy termination [and notice of its making to be given to landlord]	Within 14 days after giving of consent [as above]	Agricultural Land Tribunals (Rules) Order 1978, Sched. 1, r. 3, Form 2, and Agricultural Holdings (Arbitration on Notices) Order 1987, art. 13 [as above]	Form 42 (prescribed) [None prescribed]	Tribunal have power to postpone termination of tenancy for period not exceeding 12 months	Notice to quit takes effect

A.161 TABLE 2: NOTICES TO QUIT: CASES A, B AND E

	Step	Time Limit	Authority	Form	Consequence if step taken	Consequence if step not taken
1.	Service of Notice to Quit	None	Agricultural Holdings Act 1986, Sched. 3	Form 30 (not prescribed)		
2.	Tenant's demand for arbitration	One month after service of notice to quit	Agricultural Holdings (Arbitration and Notices) Order 1987, art. 9	Form 33 (not prescribed)	Suspension of notice to quit pending arbitration (1987 Order, art. 12)	Notice to quit takes effect
3.	Appointment of arbitrator by parties *or* application to President of RICS by either party	Before expiry of three months after service of notice to quit	Agricultural Holdings (Arbitration and Notices) Order 1987, art. 10	Appointment: none given. Application: Form 67 (excluding section 12 rent review) (prescribed)	Arbitration continues	Arbitration demand lapses. Notice to quit takes effect
4.	Service of Statement of Case	Within 35 days from appointment of arbitrator	Agricultural Holdings Act 1986 Sched. 11, para. 7	None prescribed: See Forms 70 & 71 for comparison	Party confined to matters alleged	Party not able to adduce evidence at hearing
5.	Arbitrator's Award	Within 56 days of his appointment	Agricultural Holdings Act 1986, Sched. 11, para. 14(1)	Form 75 (prescribed)	Award determines issues raised	
6.	Extension of time for making award	Before or after expiry of time limited for making award	Agricultural Holdings Act 1986, Sched. 11, para. 14(2)			
7.	Application by tenant for postponement of tenancy termination [and notice of its making to be given to landlord]	Within 14 days after termination of arbitration [as above]	Agricultural Holdings (Arbitration on Notices) Order 1987, art. 13 [as above]	None prescribed [None prescribed]	Arbitrator has power to postpone termination of tenancy for period not exceeding 12 months	Notice to quit takes effect

TABLE 3: NOTICE TO QUIT: CASE C

A.162

	Step	Time Limit	Authority	Form	Consequence if step taken	Consequence if step not taken
1.	Application by Landlord to Agricultural Land Tribunal for Certificate of bad husbandry	None	Agricultural Land Tribunals (Rules) Order 1978, r. 4	Form 26 (prescribed)		Agricultural Land Tribunal proceedings commence
2.	Filing of tenant's reply in proceedings	Within one month of service of application on tenant	Agricultural Land Tribunals (Rules) Order 1978, r. 15	Form 26A (prescribed)	Tenant's challenges made at hearing	Extension of time may be requested for filing reply (1978 Order, r. 37)
3.	Service of Notice to Quit	Within six months of grant of certificate by Agricultural Land Tribunal	Agricultural Holdings Act 1986, Sched. 3, Case C	Form 30 (not prescribed)	Notice to Quit takes effect	After six months certificate cannot be relied on by landlord for purposes of Case C
4.	[No demand for arbitration or counter-notice by the tenant is possible]					

A.163 TABLE 4: NOTICES TO QUIT UNDER CASE D FOLLOWING NOTICE TO PAY RENT

Step	Time Limit	Authority	Form	Consequence if step taken	Consequence if step not taken
1. Service by landlord of a notice to pay rent		Agricultural Holdings Act 1986, Sched. 3, Pt II, para. 10(1)(a) and Agricultural Holdings (Forms of Notice to Pay Rent or to Remedy) Regulations 1987, reg. 3, Form 1	Form 22 (prescribed)		
2. Service by landlord of notice to quit under Case D if tenant fails to pay during specified two months			Form 30 (not prescribed)		
3. Tenant's demand for arbitration	One month after service of notice to quit	Agricultural Holdings (Arbitration on Notices) Order 1987, art. 9	Form 33 (not prescribed)	Suspension of notice to quit pending arbitration or pending lapse of demand (1987 Order, art. 12)	Notice to quit takes effect
4. Appointment of arbitrator by parties *or* application to President of RICS by either party	Before expiry of three months after service of notice to quit	Agricultural Holdings (Arbitration on Notices) Order 1987, art. 10	Appointment: none given. Application: Form 67 (excluding section 12 rent review) (prescribed)	Arbitration continues	Arbitration demand lapses. Notice to quit takes effect

PROCEDURAL TABLE 4

	Step	Time Limit	Authority	Form	Consequence if step taken	Consequence if step not taken
5.	Service of Statement of Case	Within 35 days from appointment of arbitrator	Agricultural Holdings Act 1986, Sched. 11, para. 7	None prescribed: see Forms 70 & 71 for comparison	Party confined to matters alleged	Party not able to adduce evidence at hearing
6.	Arbitrator's Award	Within 56 days of his appointment	Agricultural Holdings Act 1986, Sched. 11, para. 14(1)	Form 75 (prescribed)	Award determines issues raised	
7.	Extension of time for making award	Before or after expiry of time limited for making award	Agricultural Holdings Act 1986 Sched. 11, para. 14(2)			
8.	Application by tenant for postponement of tenancy termination [and notice of its making to be given to landlord]	Within 14 days after termination of arbitration [as above]	Agricultural Holdings (Arbitration on Notices) Order 1987, art. 13 [as above]	Form 42 (prescribed) [None prescribed]	Arbitrator has power to postpone termination of tenancy for period not exceeding 12 months	Notice to quit takes effect

TABLE 5: NOTICE TO QUIT: CASE D AND NOTICE TO DO WORK OF REPAIR, MAINTENANCE OR REPLACEMENT A.164

	Step	Time Limit	Authority	Form	Consequence if step taken	Consequence if step not taken
1.	Service by landlord of notice to do work of repair and maintenance or replacement giving not less than six months for doing work	Service cannot be less than 12 months from service of a previous notice to do work unless withdrawn with the tenant's agreement	Agricultural Holdings Act 1986 Sched. 3, para. 10 and Agricultural Holdings (Forms of Notice to Pay Rent or to Remedy) Regulations 1987, reg. 4, Form 2	Form 23 (prescribed)		

2.	Tenant's demand for arbitration on (i) liability to do the work and/or (ii) deletion of work as unnecessary or unjustified and/or (iii) substitution of a different method or material for compliance	Within one month after service of notice to do work	Agricultural Holdings (Arbitration on Notices) Order 1987, art. 3	Form 24 (not prescribed but requirements set out in Agricultural Holdings (Arbitration on Notices) Order 1987, art. 3)	Arbitration proceedings available and time for doing work extended until termination of arbitration (Agricultural Holdings (Arbitration on Notices) Order 1987, art. 6(1))	Tenant may not contest these items on receipt of notice to quit
3.	Further or alternatively a tenant's demand for arbitration on an issue not listed in Step 2	Within one month after service of notice to do work	Agricultural Holdings (Arbitration on Notices) Order 1987, art. 4	Form 24 (not prescribed: a notice under Step 2 can be drawn to incorporate additional items for Step 4)	Arbitration proceedings available and time for doing work is extended until termination of arbitration (Agricultural Holdings (Arbitration on Notices) Order 1987, art. 6(1)).	Tenant is free to contest all unresolved issues on receipt of notice to quit
4.	Appointment of arbitrator by parties *or* by the President of the RICS on application by either party	None		Appointment: none given. Application: Form 67 (excluding section 12 rent review) (prescribed)	Arbitration continues	On subsequent art. 9 (Notice to Quit) arbitration proceedings arbitrator may under article 14 extend time for doing work if completion of work within the specified period would not be reasonable

PROCEDURAL TABLE 5

5.	Service of Statement of Case	Within 35 days from appointment of arbitrator	Agricultural Holdings Act 1986, Sched. 11, para. 7	None prescribed: see Forms 70 & 71 for comparison	Party confined to matters alleged	Party not able to adduce evidence at hearing
6.	Arbitrator's Award including (a) power to modify the notice: article 5 of the 1987 Order and (b) extension of time for doing work: art. 6(2) of the 1987 Order	Within 56 days of his appointment	Agricultural Holdings Act 1986, Sched. 11, para. 14(1)	Form 75 (prescribed)	Award determines issues raised	
7.	Extension of time for making award	Before or after expiry of time limited for making award	Agricultural Holdings Act 1986, Sched. 11, para. 14(2)			
8.	[Only where the arbitrator extends time under art. 6(2)]: arbitrator specifies a date for termination of tenancy if the tenant fails to do the work	On arbitrator's own motion *or* on landlord's application not later than 14 days after termination of arbitration	Agricultural Holdings (Arbitration on Notices) Order 1987, art. 7	None prescribed: a suitable letter would suffice	Arbitrator must hear tenant's views. Notice to quit must be served within one month after expiry of extended time and may validly expire in under 12 months or not at the end of the year of tenancy (1987 Order, art. 7(4))	Any notice to quit must expire at the end of the year of tenancy not less than 12 months from service
9.	Landlord serves notice to quit under Case D	(See Step 8 consequences)	Agricultural Holdings Act 1986, Sched. 3	Form 30 (not prescribed)		
10.	Tenant's demand for arbitration [and/or see Step 16]	Within one month after service of notice to quit	Agricultural Holdings (Arbitration on Notices) Order 1987, art. 9	Form 33 (not prescribed)	Suspension of notice to quit pending arbitration or pending lapse of demand (1987 Order, art. 12)	Notice to quit takes effect (unless Step 16 is followed)

1131

11.	Appointment of arbitrator by parties *or* application to President of RICS by either party	Before expiry of three months after service of notice to quit	Agricultural Holdings (Arbitration on Notices) Order 1987, art. 10	Appointment: none given. Application: Form 67 (excluding section 12 rent review) (prescribed)	Arbitration continues	Arbitration demand lapses. Notice to quit takes effect
12.	Service of Statement of Case	Within 35 days from appointment of arbitrator	Agricultural Holdings Act 1986 Sched. 11, para. 7	None prescribed: see Forms 70 & 71 for comparison	Party confined to matters alleged	Party not able to adduce evidence at hearing
13.	Extension of time by arbitrator for compliance with notice to do work		Agricultural Holdings (Arbitration on Notices) Order 1987, art. 14		Possible application by landlord under article 15 not later than 14 days after termination of arbitration for specification of termination date of tenancy if tenant fails to comply in time. If landlord subsequently serves notice to quit for such failure he must do so within one month of expiry of the extension period (1987 Order Art. 15)	No extension of time
14.	Arbitrator's Award	Within 56 days of his appointment	Agricultural Holdings Act 1986 Sched. 11, para. 14(1)	Form 75 (prescribed)	Award determines issues raised. If the tenant loses he can apply to the Agricultural Land Tribunal	
15.	Extension of time for making award	Before or after expiry of time limited for making award	Agricultural Holdings Act 1986, Sched. 11 para. 14(2)			

16.	Tenant's counter-notice under section 28	*Either* (i) within one month of service of notice to quit *or* (ii) within one month of delivery of the arbitrator's award	In relation to (i) section 28(3); and in relation to (ii) section 28(4) of the Agricultural Holdings Act 1986	Form 36A	In relation to (i) notice to quit is ineffective unless the Agricultural Land Tribunal consent. If the counter-notice is served it is invalidated by timely service of a demand for arbitration: section 28(4)(a). In relation to (ii) notice to quit is ineffective unless the Agricultural Land Tribunal consent	In relation to (i) the step is unnecessary if a demand for arbitration is served. If no demand is served the notice to quit takes effect. In relation to (ii) the notice to quit takes effect
17.	Landlord's application to the Agricultural Land Tribunal	Within one month of service of the counter-notice	Agricultural Land Tribunals (Rules) Order 1978, r. 2(2)	Form 40 (prescribed) (See the 1978 Order, r. 2(2))	Application proceeds	Application may be made for extension of time for filing application to Tribunal (1978 Order, r. 37)
18.	Tenant's reply	One month after service of landlord's application on the tenant	Agricultural Land Tribunals (Rules) Order 1978, r. 15(1)	Form 40A (prescribed)	Agricultural Land Tribunal proceedings continue	Agricultural Land Tribunal may make an order in terms of the application without formal hearing (1978 Order r. 15(2))
19.	Agricultural Land Tribunal's decision					
20.	Application by tenant for postponement of tenancy termination [and notice of its making to be given to landlord]	Within 14 days after termination of arbitration or giving of consent [as above]	Agricultural Holdings (Arbitration on Notices) Order 1987, art. 13 [as above]	Form 42 (prescribed) [None prescribed]	Arbitrator/Tribunal have power to postpone termination of tenancy for period not exceeding 12 months	Notice to quit takes effect

1133

A.165 TABLE 6: NOTICE TO QUIT UNDER CASE D FOLLOWING NOTICE TO REMEDY NOT INCLUDING WORK OF REPAIR, MAINTENANCE OR REPLACEMENT

Step	Time Limit	Authority	Form	Consequence if step taken	Consequence if step not taken
1. Service by landlord of notice to remedy breach of tenancy (not being a notice requiring the doing of any work of repair, maintenance or replacement) giving time to remedy breach	None	Agricultural Holdings Act 1986, Sched. 3, Pt II, para. 10(1)(a) and Agricultural Holdings (Forms of Notice to Pay Rent or to Remedy) Regulations 1987, reg. 4, Form 3	Form 25 (prescribed)	Tenant has no option of reference to arbitration at this stage	
2. Landlord serves notice to quit under Case D if tenant fails to comply with notice to remedy	None	Agricultural Holdings Act 1986, Sched. 3, Pt I	Form 30 (not prescribed)		
3. Tenant's demand for arbitration	Within one month after service of notice to quit	Agricultural Holdings (Arbitration on Notices) Order 1987, art. 9	Form 33 (not prescribed)	Suspension of notice to quit pending arbitration or pending lapse of demand (1987 Order, art. 12)	Notice to quit takes effect
4. Appointment of arbitrator by parties *or* application to President of RICS by either party	Before expiry of three months after service of notice to quit	Agricultural Holdings (Arbitration on Notices) Order 1987, art. 10	Appointment: none given. Application: Form 67 (excluding section 12 rent review) (prescribed)	Arbitration continues	Arbitration demand lapses. Notice to quit takes effect

PROCEDURAL TABLE 6

5.	Service of statement of case	Within 35 days from appointment of arbitrator	Agricultural Holdings Act 1986, Sched. 11, para. 7	None prescribed: see Forms 70 & 71 for comparison	Party confined to matters alleged, subject to amendment with consent of arbitrator	Party not able to adduce evidence at hearing
6.	Extension of time by arbitrator for compliance with notice to remedy		Agricultural Holdings (Arbitration on Notices) Order 1987, art. 14		Possible application by landlord under article 15 not later than 14 days after termination of arbitration for specification of termination date of tenancy if tenant fails to comply in time. If landlord subsequently serves notice to quit for such failure he must do so within one month of expiry of the extension period (1987 Order, art. 15)	
7.	Arbitrator's Award	Within 56 days of his appointment	Agricultural Holdings Act 1986 Sched. 11, para. 14(1)	Form 75 (prescribed)	Award determines issues raised	
8.	Extension of time for making award	Before or after expiry of time limited for making award	Agricultural Holdings Act 1986, Sched. 11, para. 14(2)			
9.	Application by tenant for postponement of tenancy termination [and notice of its making to be given to landlord]	Within 14 days after termination of arbitration [as above]	Agricultural Holdings (Arbitration on Notices) Order 1987, art. 13 [as above]	Form 42 (prescribed) [None prescribed]	Arbitrator has power to postpone termination of tenancy for period not exceeding 12 months	Notice to quit takes effect

1135

A.166   TABLE 7: SUCCESSION ON DEATH WHERE CASE G NOTICE TO QUIT HAS BEEN SERVED[1]

Step		Time Limit	Authority	Form	Consequence if step taken	Consequence if step not taken
1.	Tenant's personal representatives give landlord written notice of the tenant's death		Agricultural Holdings Act 1986, Sched. 3, Pt II, para. 12(b)		Period within which landlord can serve Case G notice to quit begins to run	
2.	Application by eligible person to Agricultural Land Tribunal for a direction entitling him to a tenancy of the holding	Within three months beginning with the day after the date of death	Agricultural Holdings Act 1986, s. 39(1) and Agricultural Land Tribunal (Succession to Agricultural Tenancies) Order 1984, r. 3, Form 1	Form 43 (prescribed)	Tenant required to give notice of application, Step 4 below	Application out of time is invalid. No power to extend time limit
3.	If necessary, application by not fully eligible person to Agricultural Land Tribunal to be treated as eligible	At the same time as Step 2 above	Agricultural Holdings Act 1986, s. 41(2) and Agricultural Land Tribunal (Succession to Agricultural Tenancies) Order 1984, r. 3(2), Form 1	Form 43 (prescribed)	Agricultural Land Tribunal determine whether applicant is to be treated as an eligible person for purposes of sections 36 to 48 of the 1986 Act	If person is not fully eligible, application for direction fails

---

[1] Assuming a single applicant: for provisions relating to multiple applicants, see sections 39 to 46 of the 1986 Act, and regulations thereunder.

PROCEDURAL TABLE 7

4.	Notice of application under Step 2 above given to the landlord of holding	At the time of making the application	Agricultural Holdings Act 1986, s. 40(5) and Agricultural Land Tribunal (Succession to Agricultural Tenancies) Order 1984, r. 5, Form 3	Form 45 (prescribed)	Time for service of Case G notice by landlord, if not running, begins to run	Agricultural Land Tribunal can, by discretion, extend time for giving notice: Agricultural Land Tribunal (Rules) Order 1978, rr. 36 to 38
5.	Service by landlord of notice to quit under Case G	Not later than the end of three months from the date that the landlord receives notice under Step 1 or Step 4 above, or, if both served, the earlier of the two	Agricultural Holdings Act 1986, Sched. 3, Pt II, para. 12(b)	Form 31 (not prescribed)	If no application is made by the eligible person for a succession tenancy under Step 2, notice to quit takes effect: 1986 Act, s. 43(1)(a)	The right to give a notice to quit is lost
6.	Landlord's reply to application for a direction entitling the applicant to a tenancy	Within one month after copy of application served on him	Agricultural Holdings Act 1986, s. 39(7) and Agricultural Land Tribunal (Succession to Agricultural Tenancies) Order 1984, r. 6, Form 1R	Form 43A (prescribed)		Agricultural Land Tribunal may extend time for reply: 1978 Order, rr. 36 to 38. If no reply is received, landlord not entitled to dispute any matter alleged in application: 1984 Order, r. 15(1)

1137

PROCEDURAL TABLES

7.	Landlord applies to Agricultural Land Tribunal for consent to operation of notice to quit. Section 27 of the 1986 Act applies to such an application	Within four months of service of notice under Step 4	Agricultural Holdings Act 1986, s. 44, and Agricultural Land Tribunal (Succession to Agricultural Tenancies) Order 1984, r. 4(1), (3), Form 2	Form 44 (prescribed)		Hearing of application of eligible person postponed until time limit above has expired, save with the consent of the landlord: 1984 Order, r. 13(1)
8.	Applicant opposes landlord's application for consent	Within one month after copy of application served on him	Agricultural Land Tribunal (Succession to Agricultural Tenancies) Order 1984, r. 7, Form 2R	Form 44A (prescribed)		Agricultural Land Tribunal shall not proceed to hear application of landlord until time under r. 7 has expired, save with the consent of every applicant who has not replied: 1984 Order, r. 13(2)
9.	Agricultural Land Tribunal decision on consent					
10 A.	Agricultural Land Tribunal consent to operation of notice to quit				Agricultural Land Tribunal dismiss application for direction (Step 2): 1986 Act, s. 44(4). Notice to quit takes effect	

PROCEDURAL TABLE 7

	Step	Time	Reference		Tribunal action	Effect
11A.	Application by tenant for postponement of tenancy termination	Within three months before the notice to quit takes effect or any time after that date	Agricultural Holdings Act 1986, s. 44(6), and Agricultural Land Tribunal (Succession to Agricultural Tenancies) Order 1984, r. 21(1)		Agricultural Land Tribunal has power to direct that notice shall have effect from the latest of three months from the original date of termination or three months from the date of consent: 1986 Act, s. 44(7)	Notice to quit takes effect
10.	Agricultural Land Tribunal do not consent to operation of notice to quit					
11.	Agricultural Land Tribunal considers any application under Step 3 above, and if satisfied in that regard considers application for direction (Step 2)					
12.	Agricultural Land Tribunal gives direction for a new tenancy		Agricultural Holdings Act 1986, s. 39(5)(8)		Title to new tenancy vests in applicant at end of 12 month period following the end of year of tenancy when deceased tenant died: 1986 Act, s. 46(1)(a), or when Case G notice expires, if later: 1986 Act, s. 46(1)(b)	

13.	Application by tenant to postpone vesting of new tenancy		Agricultural Holdings Act 1986, s. 46(2), and Agricultural Land Tribunal (Succession to Agricultural Tenancies) Order 1984, r. 21(2)		Agricultural Land Tribunal may specify later date	Tenancy vests as Step 12 above
14.	[Applicant and landlord enter tenancy by agreement]	[Before vesting of new tenancy]			[Tribunal's direction ceases to have effect: 1986 Act, s. 45(6)]	[Tenancy vests as Step 12 above]

TABLE 8: SUCCESSION ON DEATH WHERE NO CASE G NOTICE TO QUIT IS SERVED[2]

A.167

	Step	Time Limit	Authority	Form	Consequence if step taken	Consequence if step not taken
1.	Tenant's personal representatives give landlord written notice of the tenant's death		Agricultural Holdings Act 1986, Sched. 3, Pt II, para. 12(b)		Period within which landlord can serve Case G notice to quit begins to run	
2.	Application by eligible person to Agricultural Land Tribunal for a direction entitling him to a tenancy of the holding	Within three months beginning with the day after the date of death	Agricultural Holdings Act 1986, s. 39(1), and Agricultural Land Tribunal (Succession to Agricultural Tenancies) Order 1984, r. 3, Form 1	Form 43 (prescribed)	Tenant required to give notice of application, Step 4 below	Application out of time is invalid. No power to extend time limit
3.	If necessary, application by not fully eligible person to Agricultural Land Tribunal to be treated as eligible	At the same time as Step 2 above	Agricultural Holdings Act 1986, s. 41(2), and Agricultural Land Tribunal (Succession to Agricultural Tenancies) Order 1984, r. 3(2), Form 1	Form 43 (prescribed)	Agricultural Land Tribunal determine whether applicant is to be treated as an eligible person for purposes of sections 36 to 48 of the 1986 Act	If person is not fully eligible, application for directions fails
4.	Notice of application under Step 2 above given to the landlord of holding	At the time of making the application	Agricultural Holdings Act 1986, s. 40(5), and Agricultural Land Tribunal (Succession to Agricultural Tenancies) Order 1984, r. 5, Form 3	Form 45 (prescribed)	Time for service of Case G notice by landlord, if not running, begins to run	Agricultural Land Tribunal can, by discretion, extend time for giving notice: Agricultural Land Tribunal (Rules) Order 1978, rr. 36 to 38

[2] Assuming a single applicant: for provisions relating to multiple applicants, see sections 39 to 46 of the 1986 Act, and regulations thereunder.

5.	Landlord's reply to application for a direction entitling the applicant to a tenancy	Within one month after copy of application served on him	Agricultural Holdings Act 1986, s. 39(7), and Agricultural Land Tribunal (Succession to Agricultural Tenancies) Order 1984, r. 6, Form 1R	Form 43A (prescribed)		Agricultural Land Tribunal may extend time for reply: 1978 Order, rr. 36 to 38. If no reply is received, landlord not entitled to dispute any matter alleged in application: 1984 Order, r. 15(1)
6.	Agricultural Land Tribunal considers any application under Step 3 above, and if satisfied in that regard considers application for direction (Step 2)					
7.	Agricultural Land Tribunal gives direction for a new tenancy		Agricultural Holdings Act 1986, s. 39(5) (8)		Title to new tenancy vests in applicant at end of 12 month period following the end of year of tenancy when deceased tenant died: 1986 Act, s. 46(1)(a)	

	Step	Time Limit	Authority	Form	Consequence if step taken	Consequence if step not taken
8.	Application by tenant to postpone vesting of new tenancy		Agricultural Holdings Act 1986, s. 46(2), and Agricultural Land Tribunal (Succession to Agricultural Tenancies) Order 1984, r. 21(2)		Agricultural Land Tribunal may specify later date	Tenancy vests as Step 7 above
9.	[Applicant and landlord enter tenancy by agreement]	[Before vesting of new tenancy]			[Tribunal's direction ceases to have effect: 1986 Act, s. 45(6)]	[Tenancy vests as Step 7 above]

TABLE 9: SUCCESSION ON RETIREMENT   A.168

	Step	Time Limit	Authority	Form	Consequence if step taken	Consequence if step not taken
1.	Retiring tenant serves a retirement notice on the landlord nominating an eligible person to succeed him as tenant of the holding from a date specified in the notice		Agricultural Holdings Act 1986, s. 49(1)(b)	Form 47 (not prescribed)	Any previous notice to quit other than that within Case B,C,D,E or F (see sections 38, 51 and 52 of the 1986 Act) is suspended pending the outcome of any application to Tribunal pursuant to the retirement notice	
2.	Nominated successor applies to Agricultural Land Tribunal for a direction entitling him to a tenancy of the holding	Within one month beginning with the day after the date of giving of the retirement notice	Agricultural Holdings Act 1986, s. 53(1) and (2)	Form 48 (prescribed)		If no application made within the relevant period, application will not be entertained

1143

3.	Nominated successor serves notice of application to Tribunal at Step 2 on landlord	At time of application to Tribunal within one month beginning with the day after the date of giving of the retirement notice	Agricultural Land Tribunal (Succession to Agricultural Tenancies) Order 1984, Pt III, r. 24, Form 6	Form 49 (prescribed)		Not a statutory requirement; failure does not invalidate application
4.	Landlord who intends to oppose whole or any part of tenant's application serves reply on applicant	Within one month after copy of application is served on him	Agricultural Land Tribunal (Succession to Agricultural Tenancies) Order 1984, Pt III, r. 25, Form 5R	Form 48A (prescribed)		Landlord not entitled to dispute any matter alleged in application, 1984 Order, r. 31. Landlord may apply for extension of time for filing under 1978 Order, r. 37; 1984 Order, r. 33
5.	Landlord applies to Tribunal to refuse application on ground of greater hardship	No time limit expressly stated	Agricultural Holdings Act 1986, s. 53(7), (8), Form 5R	Form 48A (prescribed)	If it appears to Tribunal that direction for tenancy would cause greater hardship to landlord than refusal Tribunal shall not give direction	Tribunal gives direction entitling eligible and suitable applicant to new tenancy
6.	Agricultural Land Tribunal considers application					
7.	Tribunal gives direction in favour of applicant		Agricultural Holdings Act 1986, s. 53(7)		Title to new tenancy vests in applicant on date specified in retirement notice: 1986 Act, s. 55(1)	Retirement notice of no effect: 1986 Act, s. 53(9)

PROCEDURAL TABLE 9

8.	Application by tenant to postpone vesting of new tenancy		Agricultural Holdings Act 1986, s. 55(8) and Agricultural Land Tribunal (Succession to Agricultural Tenancies) Order 1984, r. 34		Tribunal may specify later date	Tenancy vests as in Step 7 above

TABLE 10: ARBITRATION FOLLOWING SUCCESSION DIRECTION   A.169

	Step	Time Limit	Authority	Form	Consequence if step taken	Consequence if step not taken
1.	Landlord or tenant under new tenancy demands reference to arbitration on (i) justifiable variations in terms of tenancy; and/or (ii) review of rent properly payable	Before the expiry of three months from the date on which the new tenancy takes effect or from the date of the giving of the direction, whichever last occurs	Agricultural Holdings Act 1986, s. 56(3), (4); s. 46(1), (2), s. 48(2), (3)	Form 50 (not prescribed)		Arbitration precluded if mandatory time limit missed
2.	Appointment of arbitrator by parties *or* by application to President of RICS by either party					
3.	Service of Statement of Case	Within 35 days from appointment of arbitrator	Agricultural Holdings Act 1986, Sched. 11, para. 7	None prescribed	Party confined to matters alleged subject to amendment by consent of the arbitrator	Party not able to adduce evidence at hearing

1145

PROCEDURAL TABLES

4.	Arbitrator's award, including (i) directions required by determination of matters referred to him: 1986 Act, s. 48(5) to (7) and (ii) further provisions relating to tenancy that landlord and tenant agree are to be included: 1986 Act, s. 48(10)	Within 56 days of his appointment	Agricultural Holdings Act 1986, Sched. 11, para. 14(1)	Form 75 (prescribed)	Award determines issues raised
5.	Extension of time for making award	Before or after expiry of time limited for making award	Agricultural Holdings Act 1986, Sched. 11, para. 14(2)		

A.170   **TABLE 11: COMPENSATION ON QUITTING**

	Time Limit	Step	Authority	Form
1.	Not less than one month before termination of the tenancy	Tenant gives to landlord written notice of his intention to claim: (i) Additional compensation for disturbance: under section 60(3)(b); (ii) Compensation for special system of farming: under section 70(1). Landlord gives to tenant written notice of his intention to claim compensation for	(i) Agricultural Holdings Act 1986, s. 60(6)(a) (ii) Agricultural Holdings Act 1986, s. 70(2)(a)	Form 51 (not prescribed) Form 61 (not prescribed)

1146

PROCEDURAL TABLE 11

		general deterioration of holding: section 72(1)	Agricultural Holdings Act 1986, s. 72(4)	Form 62 (not prescribed)
2.	At least one month before both termination of tenancy and the exercise of tenant's right to remove fixtures and buildings	Tenant gives landlord at least one month's written notice of intention to remove fixture or building: section 10(1)	Agricultural Holdings Act 1986, s. 10(3)(b)	Form 9 (not prescribed)
3.	Before termination of tenancy	(If applicable) tenant gives landlord written notice of his election in favour of statutory basis of compensation for tenant-right matters: section 65	Agricultural Holdings Act 1986, Sched. 12, para. 6-9	Form 52 (not prescribed)
4.	Termination of tenancy			
5.	Before expiry of notice in Step 2 above	Landlord gives to tenant written counter-notice electing to purchase the fixture or building comprised in the tenant's notice: landlord thereby becomes liable to pay to tenant the fair value of that fixture or building to an incoming tenant	Agricultural Holdings Act 1986, s. 10(4)	Form 10 (not prescribed)
6.	Before the expiry of two months from termination of the tenancy	Landlord or tenant gives the other written notice of his intention to claim: (i) compensation under the Agricultural Holdings Act 1986 (see above) or any custom or agreement (ii) compensation for milk quota	(i) Agricultural Holdings Act 1986, s. 83(2) (ii) Agriculture Act 1986, Sched. 1, para. 11(1)	Form 65 (not prescribed) Form 65 (not prescribed)
7.	Within eight months from termination of tenancy	Landlord and tenant may settle claim under (i) or (ii) of Step 6 above by agreement in writing. Any claim not		

		so settled shall be determined by arbitration under the Agricultural Holdings Act 1986	(i) Agricultural Holdings Act 1986 s. 83(4) and (5) (ii) Agriculture Act 1986, Sched. 1, para. 11(2)	
8.	Thereafter (no time limit expressed)	Appointment of arbitrator by agreement between the parties *or* an application of either party to the President of RICS	Agricultural Holdings Act 1986, Sched. 11, para. 1(1)	Form 67 (prescribed)
9.	Within 35 days from appointment of arbitrator	Service by each party of Statement of Case	Agricultural Holdings Act 1986, Sched. 11, para. 7.	None prescribed: see Forms 70 and 71 for comparison
10.	Within 56 days of appointment of arbitrator	Arbitrator to make his award	Agricultural Holdings Act 1986, Sched. 11, para. 14(1)	Form 75 (prescribed)
11.	Before or after expiry of time limited for making award	President of RICS may enlarge the time for making award	Agricultural Holdings Act 1986, Sched. 11, para. 14(2)	
12.	Not later than one month (or in relation to milk quota compensation, three months) after delivery of award	Day fixed by arbitrator for payment of money awarded as compensation	Agricultural Holdings Act 1986, Sched. 11, para. 18 (in relation to milk quota, Agriculture Act 1986, Sched. 1, para. 11(5))	

TABLE 12: VARIATION OF RENT BY ARBITRATION A.171

	Time Limit	Step	Authority	Form
1.	As long before the term day on which it is proposed the variation of rent should take effect as a notice to quit would have to be given to terminate the tenancy on that day, and such that that day ("next termination date") does not fall earlier than the end of three years from the commencement of the tenancy, or the date as from which there took effect a previous increase or reduction of rent or a previous direction of the arbitrator under section 12: Agricultural Holdings Act 1986, Sched. 2, para. 4(1)	Landlord or tenant gives written notice to the other to demand that the rent payable in respect of the holding as from "next termination date" shall be referred to arbitration under the 1986 Act	Agricultural Holdings Act 1986, s. 12(1)	Form 14 (not prescribed)
2.	Before the "next termination date" following demand	Appointment of arbitrator by agreement between the parties *or* an application of either party to the President of RICS. If no arbitrator is appointed the demand at Step 1 above will cease to be effective on the next termination date following demand	Agricultural Holdings Act 1986, s. 12(3)	
3.	Not earlier than four months before the next termination date following date of demand	If so requested, President shall appoint arbitrator	Agricultural Holdings Act 1986, Sched. 11, para. 1(3)	
4.	Within 35 days from appointment of arbitrator	Service by each party of Statement of Case	Agricultural Holdings Act 1986, Sched. 11, para. 7	None prescribed: see Forms 70 and 71 for comparison
5.	Within 56 days of appointment of arbitrator	Arbitrator to make his award	Agricultural Holdings Act 1986, Sched. 11, para. 14(1)	Form 75 (prescribed)

PROCEDURAL TABLES

6.	Before or after expiry of time limited for making award	President of RICS may enlarge the time for making award	Agricultural Holdings Act 1986, Sched. 11, para. 14(2)	
7.	Next termination date following demand	Arbitrator's determination takes effect	Agricultural Holdings Act 1986, s. 12(2)	

A.172
TABLE 13: APPORTIONMENT OF MILK QUOTA BY ARBITRATION

	Time Limit	Step	Authority	Form
1A.(1)	**Arbitration commenced under regulation 8**: within 28 days after change of occupation of the holding after transfer of part	Arbitrator appointed: (i) by agreement between transferor and transferee; or, in default of agreement, (ii) by application of either party to the President of the RICS	The Dairy Produce Quotas Regulations 1997, reg. 8 and Sched. 2, para. 1(1) and (2)	
1A.(2)	Within 14 days of the date of: (i) appointment or (ii) application under 1A(1) above	(i) Transferee or (ii) applicant to give notice of (i) appointment or (ii) application to the Intervention Board	The Dairy Produce Quotas Regulations 1997, Sched. 2, para. 1(1) and (2)	
1A.(3)	At the expiry of 28 days referred to in 1A(1) above, in the absence of appointment by agreement within 1A(1)(i) or any application within 1A(1)(ii)	Intervention Board to make application to President of RICS for appointment of arbitrator	The Dairy Produce Quotas Regulations 1997, Sched. 2, para. 1(3)	
1B.(1)	**Arbitration commenced under regulation 9**: following application to Intervention Board by occupier of holding requesting prospective apportionment of quota by arbitration (reg. 9(1)(b))	Arbitrator appointed by (i) agreement between occupier of holding and any other interested party; or, in default, (ii) the President of the RICS on application by occupier. No express time limit applies	The Dairy Produce Quotas Regulations 1997, Sched. 2, para. 2(1)(b)	

PROCEDURAL TABLE 13

1B.(2)	Within 14 days of: (i) date of appointment of arbitrator pursuant to agreement; or (ii) application to the President of RICS for appointment of arbitrator	Occupier to give notice to Intervention Board of (i) appointment of arbitrator; or (ii) application	The Dairy Produce Quotas Regulations 1997, Sched. 2, para. 2(2)	
1C.(1)	**Arbitration commenced under regulation 10:** following notification by Intervention Board of apportionment of quota by arbitration (regulation 10(1))	Arbitrator to be appointed by the President of RICS on application by the Intervention Board	The Dairy Produce Quotas Regulations 1997, Sched. 2, para. 2(1) and 1(4)	
1D.(1)	**Arbitration commenced under regulation 32:** following notification by producer to Intervention Board requesting apportionment of quota by arbitration (regulation 32(5)(b)(iii))	Producer shall appoint arbitrator: (i) by agreement with all persons with an interest in the holding; or (ii) by application to the President of RICS. No express time limit applies	The Dairy Produce Quotas Regulations 1997, Sched. 2, para. 1(5)	
2.	Within 35 days of appointment of arbitrator or within such further period as arbitrator shall determine	Service by each party of Statement of Case	The Dairy Produce Quotas Regulations 1997, Sched. 2, para. 14	None prescribed: see Forms 70 and 71 for comparison
3.	Within 56 days of appointment of arbitrator	Arbitrator to make his award	The Dairy Produce Quotas Regulations 1997, Sched. 2, para. 22(1)	
4.	Before or after expiry of time limited for making award	President of RICS may enlarge the time for making award	The Dairy Produce Quotas Regulations 1997, Sched. 2, para. 22(2)	
5.	Within eight days of delivery of award	Arbitrator shall notify terms of award to Intervention Board	The Dairy Produce Quotas Regulations 1997, Sched. 2, para. 22(3)	
6.	Not later than one month after delivery of award	Date fixed by award for payment of any costs awarded by award	The Dairy Produce Quotas Regulations 1997, Sched. 2, para. 22(4)	

PART VII

ARBITRATION ACT 1996

ARBITRATION ACT 1996

(1996 c. 23)

Arrangement of sections

PART I
ARBITRATION PURSUANT TO AN ARBITRATION AGREEMENT

INTRODUCTORY

SECTION

1. General principles.
2. Scope of application of provision.
3. The seat of the arbitration.
4. Mandatory and non-mandatory provisions.
5. Agreements to be in writing.

The arbitration agreement

6. Definition of arbitration agreement.
7. Separability of arbitration agreement.
8. Whether agreement discharged by death of a party.

Stay of legal proceedings

9. Stay of legal proceedings.
10. Reference of interpleader issue to arbitration.
11. Retention of security where Admiralty proceedings stayed.

Commencement of arbitral proceedings

12. Power of court to extend time for beginning arbitral proceedings etc.
13. Application of Limitation Acts.
14. Commencement of arbitral proceedings.

The arbitral tribunal

15. The arbitral tribunal.
16. Procedure for appointment of arbitrators.
17. Power in case of default to appoint sole arbitrator.
18. Failure of appointment procedure.
19. Court to have regard to agreed qualifications.
20. Chairman.
21. Umpire.
22. Decision-making where no chairman or umpire.

23. Revocation of arbitrator's authority.
24. Power of court to remove arbitrator.
25. Resignation of arbitrator.
26. Death of arbitrator or person appointing him.
27. Filling of vacancy, etc.
28. Joint and several liability of parties to arbitrators for fees and expenses.
29. Immunity of arbitrator.

Jurisdiction of the arbitral tribunal

30. Competence of tribunal to rule on its own jurisdiction.
31. Objection to substantive jurisdiction of tribunal.
32. Determination of preliminary point of jurisdiction.

The arbitral proceedings

33. General duty of the tribunal.
34. Procedural and evidential matters.
35. Consolidation of proceedings and concurrent hearings.
36. Legal or other representation.
37. Power to appoint experts, legal advisers or assessors.
38. General powers exercisable by the tribunal.
39. Power to make provisional awards.
40. General duty of parties.
41. Powers of tribunal in case of party's default.

Powers of court in relation to arbitral proceedings

42. Enforcement of peremptory orders of tribunal.
43. Securing the attendance of witnesses.
44. Court powers exercisable in support of arbitral proceedings.
45. Determination of preliminary point of law.

The award

46. Rules applicable to substance of dispute.
47. Awards on different issues, etc.
48. Remedies.
49. Interest.
50. Extension of time for making award.
51. Settlement.
52. Form of award.
53. Place where award treated as made.
54. Date of award.
55. Notification of award.
56. Power to withhold award in case of non-payment.
57. Correction of award or additional award.
58. Effect of award.

Costs of the arbitration

59. Costs of the arbitration.
60. Agreement to pay costs in any event.
61. Award of costs.
62. Effect of agreement or award about costs.
63. The recoverable costs of the arbitration.
64. Recoverable fees and expenses of arbitrators.
65. Power to limit recoverable costs.

Powers of the court in relation to award

66. Enforcement of the award.
67. Challenging the award: substantive jurisdiction.
68. Challenging the award: serious irregularity.
69. Appeal on point of law.
70. Challenge or appeal: supplementary provisions.
71. Challenge or appeal: effect of order of court.

Miscellaneous

72. Saving for rights of person who takes no part in proceedings.
73. Loss of right to object.
74. Immunity of arbitral institutions, etc.
75. Charge to secure payment of solicitors' costs.

Supplementary

76. Service of notices, etc.
77. Powers of court in relation to service of documents.
78. Reckoning periods of time.
79. Power of court to extend time limits relating to arbitral proceedings.
80. Notice and other requirements in connection with legal proceedings.
81. Saving for certain matters governed by common law.
82. Minor definitions.
83. Index of defined expressions: Part I.
84. Transitional provisions.

PART II
OTHER PROVISIONS RELATING TO ARBITRATION

Domestic arbitration agreements

85. Modification of Part I in relation to domestic arbitration agreement.
86. Staying of legal proceedings.
87. Effectiveness of agreement to exclude court's jurisdicition.
88. Power to repeal or amend sections 85 to 87.

Consumer arbitration agreements

    89. Application of unfair terms regulations to consumer arbitration agreements.
    90. Regulations apply where consumer is a legal person.
    91. Arbitration agreement unfair where modest amount sought.

Small claims arbitration in the county court

    92. Exclusion of Part I in relation to small claims arbitration in the county court.

Appointment of judges as arbitrators

    93. Appointment of judges as arbitrators.

Statutory arbitrations

    94. Application of Part I to statutory arbitrations.
    95. General adaptation of provisions in relation to statutory arbitrations.
    96. Specific adaptations of provisions in relation to statutory arbitrations.
    97. Provisions excluded from applying to statutory arbitrations.
    98. Powers to make further provisions by regulations.

PART III
RECOGNITION AND ENFORCEMENT OF CERTAIN FOREIGN AWARDS

Enforcement of Geneva Convention awards

    99. Continuation of Part II of the Arbitration Act 1950.

Recognition and enforcement of New York Convention awards

    100. New York Convention awards.
    101. Recognition and enforcement of awards.
    102. Evidence to be produced by party seeking recognition or enforcement.
    103. Refusal of recogniton or enforcement.
    104. Saving for other bases of recognition or enforcement.

PART IV
GENERAL PROVISIONS

    105. Meaning of ''the court'': jurisdiction of High Court and county court.
    106. Crown application.
    107. Consequential amendements and repeals.
    108. Extent.
    109. Commencement.
    110. Short title.

ARRANGEMENT OF SECTIONS

SCHEDULES

Schedule 1—Mandatory provisions of Part I.
Schedule 2—Modifications of Part I in relation to judge-arbitrators.
Schedule 3—Consequential amendments.
Schedule 4—Repeals.

ARBITRATION ACT 1996

(1996 c. 23) A.174

An Act to restate and improve the law relating to arbitration pursuant to an arbitration agreement; to make other provision relating to arbitration and arbitration awards; and for connected purposes.

[17th June 1996]

PART I
ARBITRATION PURSUANT TO AN ARBITRATION AGREEMENT

INTRODUCTORY

General principles

1.—The provisions of this Part are founded on the following principles, and shall be construed accordingly—
   (*a*) the object of arbitration is to obtain the fair resolution of disputes by an impartial tribunal without unnecessary delay or expense;
   (*b*) the parties should be free to agree how their disputes are resolved, subject only to such safeguards as are necessary in the public interest;
   (*c*) in matters governed by this Part the court should not intervene except as provided by this Part.

Scope of application of provisions

2.—(1) The provisions of this Part apply where the seat of the arbitration is in England and Wales or Northern Ireland.

(2) The following sections apply even if the seat of the arbitration is outside England and Wales or Northern Ireland or no seat has been designated or determined—
   (*a*) sections 9 to 11 (stay of legal proceedings, etc.), and
   (*b*) section 66 (enforcement of arbitral awards).

(3) The powers conferred by the following sections apply even if the seat of the arbitration is outside England and Wales or Northern Ireland or no seat has been designated or determined—
   (*a*) section 43 (securing the attendance of witnesses), and
   (*b*) section 44 (court powers exercisable in support of arbitral proceedings);
but the court may refuse to exercise any such power if, in the opinion of the court, the fact that the seat of the arbitration is outside England and Wales or

Northern Ireland, or that when designated or determined the seat is likely to be outside England and Wales or Northern Ireland, makes it inappropriate to do so.

(4) The court may exercise a power conferred by any provision of this Part not mentioned in subsection (2) or (3) for the purpose of supporting the arbitral process where—
- (*a*) no seat of the arbitration has been designated or determined, and
- (*b*) by reason of a connection with England and Wales or Northern Ireland the court is satisfied that it is appropriate to do so.

(5) Section 7 (separability of arbitration agreement) and section 8 (death of a party) apply where the law applicable to the arbitration agreement is the law of England and Wales or Northern Ireland even if the seat of the arbitration is outside England and Wales or Northern Ireland or has not been designated or determined.

The seat of the arbitration

3.—In this Part "the seat of the arbitration" means the juridical seat of the arbitration designated—
- (*a*) by the parties to the arbitration agreement, or
- (*b*) by any arbitral or other institution or person vested by the parties with powers in that regard, or
- (*c*) by the arbitral tribunal if so authorised by the parties,

or determined, in the absence of any such designation, having regard to the parties agreement and all the relevant circumstances.

Mandatory and non-mandatory provisions

4.—(1) The mandatory provisions of this Part are listed in Schedule 1 and have effect notwithstanding any agreement to the contrary.

(2) The other provisions of this Part (the "non-mandatory provisions") allow the parties to make their own arrangements by agreement but provide rules which apply in the absence of such agreement.

(3) The parties may make such arrangements by agreeing to the application of institutional rules or providing any other means by which a matter may be decided.

(4) It is immaterial whether or not the law applicable to the parties' agreement is the law of England and Wales or, as the case may be, Northern Ireland.

(5) The choice of a law other than the law of England and Wales or Northern Ireland as the applicable law in respect of a matter provided for by a non-mandatory provision of this Part is equivalent to an agreement making provision about that matter. For this purpose an applicable law determined in accordance with the parties' agreement, or which is objectively determined in the absence of any express or implied choice, shall be treated as chosen by the parties.

Agreements to be in writing

5.—(1) The provisions of this Part apply only where the arbitration agreement is in writing, and any other agreement between the parties as to any matter is effective for the purposes of this Part only if in writing. The expressions "agreement", "agree" and "agreed" shall be construed accordingly.

(2) There is an agreement in writing—

(a) if the agreement is made in writing (whether or not it is signed by the parties),
(b) if the agreement is made by exchange of communications in writing, or
(c) if the agreement is evidenced in writing.

(3) Where parties agree otherwise than in writing by reference to terms which are in writing, they make an agreement in writing.

(4) An agreement is evidenced in writing if an agreement made otherwise than in writing is recorded by one of the parties, or by a third party, with the authority of the parties to the agreement.

(5) An exchange of written submissions in arbitral or legal proceedings in which the existence of an agreement otherwise than in writing is alleged by one party against another party and not denied by the other party in his response constitutes as between those parties an agreement in writing to the effect alleged.

(6) References in this Part to anything being written or in writing include its being recorded by any means.

THE ARBITRATION AGREEMENT

Definition of arbitration agreement

6.—(1) In this Part an "arbitration agreement" means an agreement to submit to arbitration present or future disputes (whether they are contractual or not).

(2) The reference in an agreement to a written form of arbitration clause or to a document containing an arbitration clause constitutes an arbitration agreement if the reference is such as to make that clause part of the agreement.

Separability of arbitration agreement

7.—Unless otherwise agreed by the parties, an arbitration agreement which forms or was intended to form part of another agreement (whether or not in writing) shall not be regarded as invalid, non-existent or ineffective because that other agreement is invalid, or did not come into existence or has become ineffective, and it shall for that purpose be treated as a distinct agreement.

Whether agreement discharged by death of a party

8.—(1) Unless otherwise agreed by the parties, an arbitration agreement is not discharged by the death of a party and may be enforced by or against the personal representatives of that party.

(2) Subsection (1) does not affect the operation of any enactment or rule of law by virtue of which a substantive right or obligation is extinguished by death.

STAY OF LEGAL PROCEEDINGS

Stay of legal proceedings

9.—(1) A party to an arbitration agreement against whom legal proceedings are brought (whether by way of claim or counterclaim) in respect of a matter which under the agreement is to be referred to arbitration may (upon notice to the other parties to the proceedings) apply to the court in which the proceedings have been brought to stay the proceedings so far as they concern that matter.

(2) An application may be made notwithstanding that the matter is to be referred to arbitration only after the exhaustion of other dispute resolution procedures.

(3) An application may not be made by a person before taking the appropriate procedural step (if any) to acknowledge the legal proceedings against him or after he has taken any step in those proceedings to answer the substantive claim.

(4) On an application under this section the court shall grant a stay unless satisfied that the arbitration agreement is null and void, inoperative, or incapable of being performed.

(5) If the court refuses to stay the legal proceedings, any provision that an award is a condition precedent to the bringing of legal proceedings in respect of any matter is of no effect in relation to those proceedings.

Reference of interpleader issue to arbitration

10.—(1) Where in legal proceedings relief by way of interpleader is granted and any issue between the claimants is one in respect of which there is an arbitration agreement between them, the court granting the relief shall direct that the issue be determined in accordance with the agreement unless the circumstances are such that proceedings brought by a claimant in respect of the matter would not be stayed.

(2) Where subsection (1) applies but the court does not direct that the issue be determined in accordance with the arbitration agreement, any provision that an award is a condition precedent to the bringing of legal proceedings in respect of any matter shall not affect the determination of that issue by the court.

Retention of security where Admiralty proceedings stayed

11.—(1) Where Admiralty proceedings are stayed on the ground that the dispute in question should be submitted to arbitration, the court granting the stay may, if in those proceedings property has been arrested or bail or other security has been given to prevent or obtain release from arrest—
  (*a*) order that the property arrested be retained as security for the satisfaction of any award given in the arbitration in respect of that dispute, or
  (*b*) order that the stay of those proceedings be conditional on the provision of equivalent security for the satisfaction of any such award.

(2) Subject to any provision made by rules of court and to any necessary modifications, the same law and practice shall apply in relation to property retained in pursuance of an order as would apply if it were held for the purposes of proceedings in the court making the order.

COMMENCEMENT OF ARBITRAL PROCEEDINGS

Power of court to extend time for beginning arbitral proceedings etc.

12.—(1) Where an arbitration agreement to refer future disputes to arbitration provides that a claim shall be barred, or the claimant's right extinguished, unless the claimant takes within a time fixed by the agreement some step—

(a) to begin arbitral proceedings, or

(b) to begin other dispute resolution procedures which must be exhausted before arbitral proceedings can be begun,

the court may by order extend the time for taking that step.

(2) Any party to the arbitration agreement may apply for such an order (upon notice to the other parties), but only after a claim has arisen and after exhausting any available arbitral process for obtaining an extension of time.

(3) The court shall make an order only if satisfied

(a) that the circumstances are such as were outside the reasonable contemplation of the parties when they agreed the provision in question, and that it would be just to extend the time, or

(b) that the conduct of one party makes it unjust to hold the other party to the strict terms of the provision in question.

(4) The court may extend the time for such period and on such terms as it thinks fit, and may do so whether or not the time previously fixed (by agreement or by a previous order) has expired.

(5) An order under this section does not affect the operation of the Limitation Acts (see section 13).

(6) The leave of the court is required for any appeal from a decision of the court under this section.

Application of Limitation Acts

13.—(1) The Limitation Acts apply to arbitral proceedings as they apply to legal proceedings.

(2) The court may order that in computing the time prescribed by the Limitation Acts for the commencement of proceedings (including arbitral proceedings) in respect of a dispute which was the subject matter—

(a) of an award which the court orders to be set aside or declares to be of no effect, or

(b) of the affected part of an award which the court orders to be set aside in part, or declares to be in part of no effect,

the period between the commencement of the arbitration and the date of the order referred to in paragraph (a) or (b) shall be excluded.

(3) In determining for the purposes of the Limitation Acts when a cause of action accrued, any provision that an award is a condition precedent to the bringing of legal proceedings in respect of a matter to which an arbitration agreement applies shall be disregarded.

(4) In this Part "the Limitation Acts" means—

(a) in England and Wales, the Limitation Act 1980, the Foreign Limitation Periods Act 1984 and any other enactment (whenever passed) relating to the limitation of actions;

(b) in Northern Ireland, the Limitation (Northern Ireland) Order 1989, the Foreign Limitation Periods (Northern Ireland) Order 1985 and any other enactment (whenever passed) relating to the limitation of actions.

Commencement of arbitral proceedings

14.—(1) The parties are free to agree when arbitral proceedings are to be regarded as commenced for the purposes of this Part and for the purposes of the Limitation Acts.

(2) If there is no such agreement the following provisions apply.

(3) Where the arbitrator is named or designated in the arbitration agreement, arbitral proceedings are commenced in respect of a matter when one party serves on the other party or parties a notice in writing requiring him or them to submit that matter to the person so named or designated.

(4) Where the arbitrator or arbitrators are to be appointed by the parties, arbitral proceedings are commenced in respect of a matter when one party serves on the other party or parties notice in writing him or them to appoint an arbitrator or to agree to the appointment of an arbitrator in respect of that matter.

(5) Where the arbitrator or arbitrators are to be appointed by a person other than a party to the proceedings, arbitral proceedings are commenced in respect of a matter when one party gives notice in writing to that person requesting him to make the appointment in respect of that matter.

THE ARBITRAL TRIBUNAL

The arbitral tribunal

15.—(1) The parties are free to agree on the number of arbitrators to form the tribunal and whether there is to be a chairman or umpire.

(2) Unless otherwise agreed by the parties, an agreement that the number of arbitrators shall be two or any other even number shall be understood as requiring the appointment of an additional arbitrator as chairman of the tribunal.

(3) If there is no agreement as to the number of arbitrators, the tribunal shall consist of a sole arbitrator.

Procedure for appointment of arbitrators

16.—(1) The parties are free to agree on the procedure for appointing the arbitrator or arbitrators, including the procedure for appointing any chairman or umpire.

(2) If or to the extent that there is no such agreement, the following provisions apply

(3) If the tribunal is to consist of a sole arbitrator, the parties shall jointly appoint the arbitrator not later than 28 days after service of a request in writing by either party to do so.

(4) If the tribunal is to consist of two arbitrators, each party shall appoint one arbitrator not later than 14 days after service of a request in writing by either party to do so.

(5) If the tribunal is to consist of three arbitrators—
- (a) each party shall appoint one arbitrator not later than 14 days after service of a request in writing by either party to do so, and
- (b) the two so appointed shall forthwith appoint a third arbitrator as the chairman of the tribunal.

(6) If the tribunal is to consist of two arbitrators and an umpire—
- (*a*)　each party shall appoint one arbitrator not later than 14 days after service of a request in writing by either party to do so, and
- (*b*)　the two so appointed may appoint an umpire at any time after they themselves are appointed and shall do so before any substantive hearing or forthwith if they cannot agree on a matter relating to the arbitration.

(7) In any other case (in particular, if there are more than two parties) section 18 applies as in the case of a failure of the agreed appointment procedure.

Power in case of default to appoint sole arbitrator

17.—(1) Unless the parties otherwise agree, where each of two parties to an arbitration agreement is to appoint an arbitrator and one party ("the party in default") refuses to do so, or fails to do so within the time specified, the other party, having duly appointed his arbitrator, may give notice in writing to the party in default that he proposes to appoint his arbitrator to act as sole arbitrator.

(2) If the party in default does not within 7 clear days of that notice being given—
- (*a*)　make the required appointment, and
- (*b*)　notify the other party that he has done so,

the other party may appoint his arbitrator as sole arbitrator whose award shall be binding on both parties as if he had been so appointed by agreement.

(3) Where a sole arbitrator has been appointed under subsection (2), the party in default may (upon notice to the appointing party) apply to the court which may set aside the appointment.

(4) The leave of the court is required for any appeal from a decision of the court under this section.

Failure of appointment procedure

18.—(1) The parties are free to agree what is to happen in the event of a failure of the procedure for the appointment of the arbitral tribunal. There is no failure if an appointment is duly made under section 17 (power in case of default to appoint sole arbitrator), unless that appointment is set aside.

(2) If or to the extent that there is no such agreement any party to the arbitration agreement may (upon notice to the other parties) apply to the court to exercise its powers under this section.

(3) Those powers are—
- (*a*)　to give directions as to the making of any necessary appointments;
- (*b*)　to direct that the tribunal shall be constituted by such appointments (or any one or more of them) as have been made;
- (*c*)　to revoke any appointments already made;
- (*d*)　to make any necessary appointments itself.

(4) An appointment made by the court under this section has effect as if made with the agreement of the parties.

(5) The leave of the court is required for any appeal from a decision of the court under this section.

ARBITRATION ACT 1996

Court to have regard to agreed qualifications

19.—In deciding whether to exercise, and in considering how to exercise, any of its powers under section 16 (procedure for appointment of arbitrators) or section 18 (failure of appointment procedure), the court shall have due regard to any agreement of the parties as to the qualifications required of the arbitrators.

Chairman

20.—(1) Where the parties have agreed that there is to be a chairman, they are free to agree what the functions of the chairman are to be in relation to the making of decisions, orders and awards.

(2) If or to the extent that there is no such agreement, the following provisions apply.

(3) Decisions, orders and awards shall be made by all or a majority of the arbitrators (including the chairman).

(4) The view of the chairman shall prevail in relation to a decision, order or award in respect of which there is neither unanimity nor a majority under subsection (3).

Umpire

21.—(1) Where the parties have agreed that there is to be an umpire, they are free to agree what the functions of the umpire are to be, and in particular—
   (*a*) whether he is to attend the proceedings, and
   (*b*) when he is to replace the other arbitrators as the tribunal with power to make decisions, orders and awards.

(2) If or to the extent that there is no such agreement, the following provisions apply.

(3) The umpire shall attend the proceedings and be supplied with the same documents and other materials as are supplied to the other arbitrators.

(4) Decisions, orders and awards shall be made by the other arbitrators unless and until they cannot agree on a matter relating to the arbitration. In that event they shall forthwith give notice in writing to the parties and the umpire, whereupon the umpire shall replace them as the tribunal with power to make decisions, orders and awards as if he were sole arbitrator.

(5) If the arbitrators cannot agree but fail to give notice of that fact, or if any of them fails to join in the giving of notice, any party to the arbitral proceedings may (upon notice to the other parties and to the tribunal) apply to the court which may order that the umpire shall replace the other arbitrators as the tribunal with power to make decisions, orders and awards as if he were sole arbitrator.

(6) The leave of the court is required for any appeal from a decision of the court under this section.

Decision-making where no chairman or umpire

22.—(1) Where the parties agree that there shall be two or more arbitrators with no chairman or umpire, the parties are free to agree how the tribunal is to make decisions, orders and awards.

(2) If there is no such agreement, decisions, orders and awards shall be made by all or a majority of the arbitrators.

Revocation of arbitrator's authority

23.—(1) The parties are free to agree in what circumstances the authority of an arbitrator may be revoked.

(2) If or to the extent that there is no such agreement the following provisions apply.

(3) The authority of an arbitrator may not be revoked except—
- (*a*) by the parties acting jointly, or
- (*b*) by an arbitral or other institution or person vested by the parties with powers in that regard.

(4) Revocation of the authority of an arbitrator by the parties acting jointly must be agreed in writing unless the parties also agree (whether or not in writing) to terminate the arbitration agreement.

(5) Nothing in this section affects the power of the court—
- (*a*) to revoke an appointment under section 18 (powers exercisable in case of failure of appointment procedure), or
- (*b*) to remove an arbitrator on the grounds specified in section 24.

Power of court to remove arbitrator

24.—(1) A party to arbitral proceedings may (upon notice to the other parties, to the arbitrator concerned and to any other arbitrator) apply to the court to remove an arbitrator on any of the following grounds—
- (*a*) that circumstances exist that give rise to justifiable doubts as to his impartiality,
- (*b*) that he does not possess the qualifications required by the arbitration agreement;
- (*c*) that he is physically or mentally incapable of conducting the proceedings or there are justifiable doubts as to his capacity to do so;
- (*d*) that he has refused or failed—
  - (i) properly to conduct the proceedings, or
  - (ii) to use all reasonable despatch in conducting the proceedings or making an award,

and that substantial injustice has been or will be caused to the applicant.

(2) If there is an arbitral or other institution or person vested by the parties with power to remove an arbitrator, the court shall not exercise its power of removal unless satisfied that the applicant has first exhausted any available recourse to that institution or person.

(3) The arbitral tribunal may continue the arbitral proceedings and make an award while an application to the court under this section is pending.

(4) Where the court removes an arbitrator, it may make such order as it thinks fit with respect to his entitlement (if any) to fees or expenses, or the repayment of any fees or expenses already paid.

(5) The arbitrator concerned is entitled to appear and be heard by the court before it makes any order under this section.

(6) The leave of the court is required for any appeal from a decision of the court under this section.

Resignation of arbitrator

25.—(1) The parties are free to agree with an arbitrator as to the consequences of his resignation as regards—
  (*a*) his entitlement (if any) to fees or expenses, and
  (*b*) any liability thereby incurred by him.
(2) If or to the extent that there is no such agreement the following provisions apply.
(3) An arbitrator who resigns his appointment may (upon notice to the parties) apply to the court—
  (*a*) to grant him relief from any liability thereby incurred by him, and
  (*b*) to make such order as it thinks fit with respect to his entitlement (if any) to fees or expenses or the repayment of any fees or expenses already paid.
(4) If the court is satisfied that in all the circumstances it was reasonable for the arbitrator to resign, it may grant such relief as is mentioned in subsection (3)(*a*) on such terms as it thinks fit.
(5) The leave of the court is required for any appeal from a decision of the court under this section.

Death of arbitrator or person appointing him

26.—(1) The authority of an arbitrator is personal and ceases on his death.
(2) Unless otherwise agreed by the parties, the death of the person by whom an arbitrator was appointed does not revoke the arbitrator's authority.

Filling of vacancy etc.

27.—(1) Where an arbitrator ceases to hold office, the parties are free to agree—
  (*a*) whether and if so how the vacancy is to be filled,
  (*b*) whether and if so to what extent the previous proceedings should stand, and
  (*c*) what effect (if any) his ceasing to hold office has on any appointment made by him (alone or jointly).
(2) If or to the extent that there is no such agreement, the following provisions apply.
(3) The provisions of section 16 (procedure for appointment of arbitrators) and 18 (failure of appointment procedure) apply in relation to the filling of the vacancy as in relation to an original appointment.
(4) The tribunal (when reconstituted) shall determine whether and if so to what extent the previous proceedings should stand. This does not affect any right of a party to challenge those proceedings on any ground which had arisen before the arbitrator ceased to hold office.
(5) His ceasing to hold office does not affect any appointment by him (alone or jointly) of another arbitrator, in particular any appointment of a chairman or umpire.

Joint and several liability of parties to arbitrators for fees and expenses

28.—(1) The parties are jointly and severally liable to pay to the arbitrators such reasonable fees and expenses (if any) as are appropriate in the circumstances.

(2) Any party may apply to the court (upon notice to the other parties and to the arbitrators) which may order that the amount of the arbitrators' fees and expenses shall be considered and adjusted by such means and upon such terms as it may direct.

(3) If the application is made after any amount has been paid to the arbitrators by way of fees or expenses, the court may order the repayment of such amount (if any) as is shown to be excessive, but shall not do so unless it is shown that it is reasonable in the circumstances to order repayment.

(4) The above provisions have effect subject to any order of the court under section 24(4) or 25(3)(*b*) (order as to entitlement to fees or expenses in case of removal or resignation of arbitrator).

(5) Nothing in this section affects any liability of a party to any other party to pay all or any of the costs of the arbitration (see sections 59 to 65) or any contractual right of an arbitrator to payment of his fees and expenses.

(6) In this section references to arbitrators include an arbitrator who has ceased to act and an umpire who has not replaced the other arbitrators.

Immunity of arbitrator

29.—(1) An arbitrator is not liable for anything done or omitted in the discharge or purported discharge of his functions as arbitrator unless the act or omission is shown to have been in bad faith.

(2) Subsection (1) applies to an employee or agent of an arbitrator as it applies to the arbitrator himself.

(3) This section does not affect any liability incurred by an arbitrator by reason of his resigning (but see section 25).

JURISDICTION OF THE ARBITRAL TRIBUNAL

Competence of tribunal to rule on its own jurisdiction

30.—(1) Unless otherwise agreed by the parties, the arbitral tribunal may rule on its own substantive jurisdiction, that is, as to—
   (*a*) whether there is a valid arbitration agreement,
   (*b*) whether the tribunal is properly constituted, and
   (*c*) what matters have been submitted to arbitration in accordance with the arbitration agreement.

(2) Any such ruling may be challenged by any available arbitral process of appeal or review or in accordance with the provisions of this Part.

Objection to substantive jurisdiction of tribunal

31.—(1) An objection that the arbitral tribunal lacks substantive jurisdiction at the outset of the proceedings must be raised by a party not later than the time he takes the first step in the proceedings to contest the merits of any matter in relation to which he challenges the tribunal's jurisdiction. A party is not precluded from raising such an objection by the fact that he has appointed or participated in the appointment of an arbitrator.

(2) Any objection during the course of the arbitral proceedings that the arbitral tribunal is exceeding its substantive jurisdiction must be made as soon as possible after the matter alleged to be beyond its jurisdiction is raised.

(3) The arbitral tribunal may admit an objection later than the time specified in subsection (1) or (2) if it considers the delay justified.

(4) Where an objection is duly taken to the tribunal's substantive jurisdiction and the tribunal has power to rule on its own jurisdiction, it may—

(a) rule on the matter in an award as to jurisdiction, or

(b) deal with the objection in its award on the merits.

If the parties agree which of these courses the tribunal should take, the tribunal shall proceed accordingly.

(5) The tribunal may in any case, and shall if the parties so agree, stay proceedings whilst an application is made to the court under section 32 (determination of preliminary point of jurisdiction).

Determination of preliminary point of jurisdiction

32.—(1) The court may, on the application of a party to arbitral proceedings (upon notice to the other parties), determine any question as to the substantive jurisdiction of the tribunal. A party may lose the right to object (see section 73).

(2) An application under this section shall not be considered unless—

(a) it is made with the agreement in writing of all the other parties to the proceedings, or

(b) it is made with the permission of the tribunal and the court is satisfied—

(i) that the determination of the question is likely to produce substantial savings in costs,

(ii) that the application was made without delay, and

(iii) that there is good reason why the matter should be decided by the court.

(3) An application under this section, unless made with the agreement of all the other parties to the proceedings, shall state the grounds on which it is said that the matter should be decided by the court.

(4) Unless otherwise agreed by the parties, the arbitral tribunal may continue the arbitral proceedings and make an award while an application to the court under this section is pending.

(5) Unless the court gives leave, no appeal lies from a decision of the court whether the conditions specified in subsection (2) are met.

(6) The decision of the court on the question of jurisdiction shall be treated as a judgment of the court for the purposes of an appeal. But no appeal lies without the leave of the court which shall not be given unless the court considers that the question involves a point of law which is one of general importance or is one which for some other special reason should be considered by the Court of Appeal.

The Arbitral Proceedings

General duty of the tribunal

33.—(1) The tribunal shall—
  (*a*) act fairly and impartially as between the parties, giving each party a reasonable opportunity of putting his case and dealing with that of his opponent, and
  (*b*) adopt procedures suitable to the circumstances of the particular case, avoiding unnecessary delay or expense, so as to provide a fair means for the resolution of the matters falling to be determined.

(2) The tribunal shall comply with that general duty in conducting the arbitral proceedings, in its decisions on matters of procedure and evidence and in the exercise of all other powers conferred on it.

Procedural and evidential matters

34.—(1) It shall be for the tribunal to decide all procedural and evidential matters, subject to the right of the parties to agree any matter.

(2) Procedural and evidential matters include—
  (*a*) when and where any part of the proceedings is to be held;
  (*b*) the language or languages to be used in the proceedings and whether translations of any relevant documents are to be supplied;
  (*c*) whether any and if so what form of written statements of claim and defence are to be used, when these should be supplied and the extent to which such statements can be later amended;
  (*d*) whether any and if so which documents or classes of documents should be disclosed between and produced by the parties and at what stage;
  (*e*) whether any and if so what questions should be put to and answered by the respective parties and when and in what form this should be done;
  (*f*) whether to apply strict rules of evidence (or any other rules) as to the admissibility, relevance or weight of any material (oral, written or other) sought to be tendered on any matters of fact or opinion, and the time, manner and form in which such material should be exchanged and presented;
  (*g*) whether and to what extent the tribunal should itself take the initiative in ascertaining the facts and the law;
  (*h*) whether and to what extent there should be oral or written evidence or submissions.

(3) The tribunal may fix the time within which any directions given by it are to be complied with, and may if it thinks fit extend the time so fixed (whether or not it has expired).

Consolidation of proceeding and concurrent hearings

35.—(1) The parties are free to agree—
  (*a*) that the arbitral proceedings shall be consolidated with other arbitral proceedings, or
  (*b*) that concurrent hearings shall be held,

on such terms as may be agreed.

(2) Unless the parties agree to confer such power on the tribunal, the tribunal has no power to order consolidation of proceedings or concurrent hearings.

Legal or other representation

36.—Unless otherwise agreed by the parties, a party to arbitral proceedings may be represented in the proceedings by a lawyer or other person chosen by him.

Power to appoint experts, legal advisers or assessors

37.—(1) Unless otherwise agreed by the parties—
  (*a*) the tribunal may—
    (i) appoint experts or legal advisers to report to it and the parties, or
    (ii) appoint assessors to assist it on technical matters,
and may allow any such expert, legal adviser or assessor to attend the proceedings; and
  (*b*) the parties shall be given a reasonable opportunity to comment on any information, opinion or advice offered by any such person.

(2) The fees and expenses of an expert, legal adviser or assessor appointed by the tribunal for which the arbitrators are liable are expenses of the arbitrators for the purposes of this Part.

General powers exercisable by the tribunal

38.—(1) The parties are free to agree on the powers exercisable by the arbitral tribunal for the purposes of and in relation to the proceedings.

(2) Unless otherwise agreed by the parties the tribunal has the following powers.

(3) The tribunal may order a claimant to provide security for the costs of the arbitration. This power shall not be exercised on the ground that the claimant is—
  (*a*) an individual ordinarily resident outside the United Kingdom, or
  (*b*) a corporation or association incorporated or formed under the law of a country outside the United Kingdom, or whose central management and control is exercised outside the United Kingdom.

(4) The tribunal may give directions in relation to any property which is the subject of the proceedings or as to which any question arises in the proceedings, and which is owned by or is in the possession of a party to the proceedings—
  (*a*) for the inspection, photographing, preservation, custody or detention of the property by the tribunal, an expert or a party, or
  (*b*) ordering that samples be taken from, or any observation be made of or experiment conducted upon, the property.

(5) The tribunal may direct that a party or witness shall be examined on oath or affirmation, and may for that purpose administer any necessary oath or take any necessary affirmation.

(6) The tribunal may give directions to a party for the preservation for the purposes of the proceedings of any evidence in his custody or control.

SECTION 39

Power to make provisional awards

39.—(1) The parties are free to agree that the tribunal shall have power to order on a provisional basis any relief which it would have power to grant in a final award.

(2) This includes, for instance, making—
- (*a*) a provisional order for the payment of money or the disposition of property as between the parties, or
- (*b*) an order to make an interim payment on account of the costs of the arbitration.

(3) Any such order shall be subject to the tribunal's final adjudication; and the tribunal's final award, on the merits or as to costs, shall take account of any such order.

(4) Unless the parties agree to confer such power on the tribunal, the tribunal has no such power. This does not affect its powers under section 47 (awards on different issues, etc.).

General duty of parties

40.—(1) The parties shall do all things necessary for the proper and expeditious conduct of the arbitral proceedings.

(2) This includes—
- (*a*) complying without delay with any determination of the tribunal as to procedural or evidential matters, or with any order or directions of the tribunal, and
- (*b*) where appropriate, taking without delay any necessary steps to obtain a decision of the court on a preliminary question of jurisdiction or law (see sections 32 and 45).

Powers of tribunal in case of party's default

41.—(1) The parties are free to agree on the powers of the tribunal in case of a party's failure to do something necessary for the proper and expeditious conduct of the arbitration.

(2) Unless otherwise agreed by the parties, the following provisions apply.

(3) If the tribunal is satisfied that there has been inordinate and inexcusable delay on the part of the claimant in pursuing his claim and that the delay—
- (*a*) gives rise, or is likely to give rise, to a substantial risk that it is not possible to have a fair resolution of the issues in that claim, or
- (*b*) has caused, or is likely to cause, serious prejudice to the respondent,

the tribunal may make an award dismissing the claim.

(4) If without showing sufficient cause a party—
- (*a*) fails to attend or be represented at an oral hearing of which due notice was given, or
- (*b*) where matters are to be dealt with in writing, fails after due notice to submit written evidence or make written submissions,

the tribunal may continue the proceedings in the absence of that party or, as the case may be, without any written evidence or submissions on his behalf, and may make an award on the basis of the evidence before it.

(5) If without showing sufficient cause a party fails to comply with any order or directions of the tribunal, the tribunal may make a peremptory order to the same effect, prescribing such time for compliance with it as the tribunal considers appropriate.

(6) If a claimant fails to comply with a peremptory order of the tribunal to provide security for costs, the tribunal may make an award dismissing his claim.

(7) If a party fails to comply with any other kind of peremptory order, then, without prejudice to section 42 (enforcement by court of tribunal's peremptory orders), the tribunal may do any of the following—

    (*a*) direct that the party in default shall not be entitled to rely upon any allegation or material which was the subject matter of the order;

    (*b*) draw such adverse inferences from the act of non-compliance as the circumstances justify;

    (*c*) proceed to an award on the basis of such materials as have been properly provided to it;

    (*d*) make such order as it thinks fit as to the payment of costs of the arbitration incurred in consequence of the non-compliance.

POWERS OF COURT IN RELATION TO ARBITRAL PROCEEDINGS

Enforcement of peremptory orders of tribunal

42.—(1) Unless otherwise agreed by the parties, the court may make an order requiring a party to comply with a peremptory order made by the tribunal.

(2) An application for an order under this section may be made—

    (*a*) by the tribunal (upon notice to the parties),

    (*b*) by a party to the arbitral proceedings with the permission of the tribunal (and upon notice to the other parties), or

    (*c*) where the parties have agreed that the powers of the court under this section shall be available.

(3) The court shall not act unless it is satisfied that the applicant has exhausted any available arbitral process in respect of failure to comply with the tribunal's order.

(4) No order shall be made under this section unless the court is satisfied that the person to whom the tribunal's order was directed has failed to comply with it within the time prescribed in the order or, if no time was prescribed, within a reasonable time.

(5) The leave of the court is required for any appeal from a decision of the court under this section.

Securing the attendance of witnesses

43.—(1) A party to arbitral proceedings may use the same court procedures as are available in relation to legal proceedings to secure the attendance before the tribunal of a witness in order to give oral testimony or to produce documents or other material evidence.

(2) This may only be done with the permission of the tribunal or the agreement of the other parties.

(3) The court procedures may only be used if—
   (a) the witness is in the United Kingdom, and
   (b) the arbitral proceedings are being conducted in England and Wales or, as the case may be, Northern Ireland.

(4) A person shall not be compelled by virtue of this section to produce any document or other material evidence which he could not be compelled to produce in legal proceedings.

Court powers exercisable in support of arbitral proceedings

44.—(1) Unless otherwise agreed by the parties, the court has for the purposes of and in relation to arbitral proceedings the same power of making orders about the matters listed below as it has for the purposes of and in relation to legal proceedings.

(2) Those matters are—
   (a) the taking of the evidence of witnesses;
   (b) the preservation of evidence;
   (c) making orders relating to property which is the subject of the proceedings or as to which any question arises in the proceedings—
      (i) for the inspection, photographing, preservation, custody or detention of the property, or
      (ii) ordering that samples be taken from, or any observation be made of or experiment conducted upon, the property;
   and for that purpose authorising any person to enter any premises in the possession or control of a party to the arbitration;
   (d) the sale of any goods the subject of the proceedings;
   (e) the granting of an interim injunction or the appointment of a receiver.

(3) If the case is one of urgency, the court may, on the application of a party or proposed party to the arbitral proceedings, make such orders as it thinks necessary for the purpose of preserving evidence or assets.

(4) If the case is not one of urgency, the court shall act only on the application of a party to the arbitral proceedings (upon notice to the other parties and to the tribunal) made with the permission of the tribunal or the agreement in writing of the other parties.

(5) In any case the court shall act only if or to the extent that the arbitral tribunal, and any arbitral or other institution or person vested by the parties with power in that regard, has no power or is unable for the time being to act effectively.

(6) If the court so orders, an order made by it under this section shall cease to have effect in whole or in part on the order of the tribunal or of any such arbitral or other institution or person having power to act in relation to the subject-matter of the order.

(7) The leave of the court is required for any appeal from a decision of the court under this section.

Determination of preliminary point of law

45.—(1) Unless otherwise agreed by the parties, the court may on the application of a party to arbitral proceedings (upon notice to the other parties) determine any question of law arising in the course of the proceedings which the court is satisfied substantially affects the rights of one or more of the parties. An agreement to dispense with reasons for the tribunal's award shall be considered an agreement to exclude the court's jurisdiction under this section.

(2) An application under this section shall not be considered unless—
- (*a*) it is made with the agreement of all the other parties to the proceedings, or
- (*b*) it is made with the permission of the tribunal and the court is satisfied—
  - (i) that the determination of the question is likely to produce substantial savings in costs, and
  - (ii) that the application was made without delay.

(3) The application shall identify the question of law to be determined and, unless made with the agreement of all the other parties to the proceedings, shall state the grounds on which it is said that the question should be decided by the court.

(4) Unless otherwise agreed by the parties, the arbitral tribunal may continue the arbitral proceedings and make an award while an application to the court under this section is pending.

(5) Unless the court gives leave, no appeal lies from a decision of the court whether the conditions specified in subsection (2) are met.

(6) The decision of the court on the question of law shall be treated as a judgment of the court for the purposes of an appeal. But no appeal lies without the leave of the court which shall not be given unless the court considers that the question is one of general importance, or is one which for some other special reason should be considered by the Court of Appeal.

THE AWARD

Rules applicable to substance of dispute

46.—(1) The arbitral tribunal shall decide the dispute—
- (*a*) in accordance with the law chosen by the parties as applicable to the substance of the dispute, or
- (*b*) if the parties so agree, in accordance with such other considerations as are agreed by them or determined by the tribunal.

(2) For this purpose the choice of the laws of a country shall be understood to refer to the substantive laws of that country and not its conflict of laws rules.

(3) If or to the extent that there is no such choice or agreement, the tribunal shall apply the law determined by the conflict of laws rules which it considers applicable.

SECTION 47

Awards on different issues etc.

47.—(1) Unless otherwise agreed by the parties, the tribunal may make more than one award at different times on different aspects of the matters to be determined.

(2) The tribunal may, in particular, make an award relating—
  (*a*) to an issue affecting the whole claim, or
  (*b*) to a part only of the claims or cross-claims submitted to it for decision.

(3) If the tribunal does so, it shall specify in its award the issue, or the claim or part of a claim, which is the subject matter of the award.

Remedies

48.—(1) The parties are free to agree on the powers exercisable by the arbitral tribunal as regards remedies.

(2) Unless otherwise agreed by the parties, the tribunal has the following powers.

(3) The tribunal may make a declaration as to any matter to be determined in the proceedings.

(4) The tribunal may order the payment of a sum of money, in any currency.

(5) The tribunal has the same powers as the court—
  (*a*) to order a party to do or refrain from doing anything;
  (*b*) to order specific performance of a contract (other than a contract relating to land);
  (*c*) to order the rectification, setting aside or cancellation of a deed or other document.

Interest

49.—(1) The parties are free to agree on the powers of the tribunal as regards the award of interest.

(2) Unless otherwise agreed by the parties the following provisions apply.

(3) The tribunal may award simple or compound interest from such dates, at such rates and with such rests as it considers meets the justice of the case—
  (*a*) on the whole or part of any amount awarded by the tribunal, in respect of any period up to the date of the award;
  (*b*) on the whole or part of any amount claimed in the arbitration and outstanding at the commencement of the arbitral proceedings but paid before the award was made, in respect of any period up to the date of payment.

(4) The tribunal may award simple or compound interest from the date of the award (or any later date) until payment, at such rates and with such rests as it considers meets the justice of the case, on the outstanding amount of any award (including any award of interest under subsection (3) and any award as to costs).

(5) References in this section to an amount awarded by the tribunal include an amount payable in consequence of a declaratory award by the tribunal.

(6) The above provisions do not affect any other power of the tribunal to award interest.

Extension of time for making award

50.—(1) Where the time for making an award is limited by or in pursuance of the arbitration agreement, then, unless otherwise agreed by the parties, the court may in accordance with the following provisions by order extend that time.

(2) An application for an order under this section may be made—
   (*a*) by the tribunal (upon notice to the parties), or
   (*b*) by any party to the proceedings (upon notice to the tribunal and the other parties),

but only after exhausting any available arbitral process for obtaining an extension of time.

(3) The court shall only make an order if satisfied that a substantial injustice would otherwise be done.

(4) The court may extend the time for such period and on such terms as it thinks fit, and may do so whether or not the time previously fixed (by or under the agreement or by a previous order) has expired.

(5) The leave of the court is required for any appeal from a decision of the court under this section.

Settlement

51.—(1) If during arbitral proceedings the parties settle the dispute, the following provisions apply unless otherwise agreed by the parties.

(2) The tribunal shall terminate the substantive proceedings and, if so requested by the parties and not objected to by the tribunal, shall record the settlement in the form of an agreed award.

(3) An agreed award shall state that it is an award of the tribunal and shall have the same status and effect as any other award on the merits of the case.

(4) The following provisions of this Part relating to awards (sections 52 to 58) apply to an agreed award.

(5) Unless the parties have also settled the matter of the payment of the costs of the arbitration, the provisions of this Part relating to costs (sections 59 to 65) continue to apply.

Form of award

52.—(1) The parties are free to agree on the form of an award.

(2) If or to the extent that there is no such agreement, the following provisions apply.

(3) The award shall be in writing signed by all the arbitrators or all those assenting to the award.

(4) The award shall contain the reasons for the award unless it is an agreed award or the parties have agreed to dispense with reasons.

(5) The award shall state the seat of the arbitration and the date when the award is made.

Place where award treated as made

53.—Unless otherwise agreed by the parties, where the seat of the arbitration is in England and Wales or Northern Ireland, any award in the proceedings shall be treated as made there, regardless of where it was signed, despatched or delivered to any of the parties.

Date of award

54.—(1) Unless otherwise agreed by the parties, the tribunal may decide what is to be taken to be the date on which the award was made.

(2) In the absence of any such decision, the date of the award shall be taken to be the date on which it is signed by the arbitrator or, where more than one arbitrator signs the award, by the last of them.

Notification of award

55.—(1) The parties are free to agree on the requirements as to notification of the award to the parties.

(2) If there is no such agreement, the award shall be notified to the parties by service on them of copies of the award, which shall be done without delay after the award is made.

(3) Nothing in this section affects section 56 (power to withhold award in case of non-payment).

Power to withhold award in case of non-payment

56.—(1) The tribunal may refuse to deliver an award to the parties except upon full payment of the fees and expenses of the arbitrators.

(2) If the tribunal refuses on that ground to deliver an award, a party to the arbitral proceedings may (upon notice to the other parties and the tribunal) apply to the court, which may order that—

   (a) the tribunal shall deliver the award on the payment into court by the applicant of the fees and expenses demanded, or such lesser amount as the court may specify,
   (b) the amount of the fees and expenses properly payable shall be determined by such means and upon such terms as the court may direct, and
   (c) out of the money paid into court there shall be paid out such fees and expenses as may be found to be properly payable and the balance of the money (if any) shall be paid out to the applicant.

(3) For this purpose the amount of fees and expenses properly payable is the amount the applicant is liable to pay under section 28 or any agreement relating to the payment of the arbitrators.

(4) No application to the court may be made where there is any available arbitral process for appeal or review of the amount of the fees or expenses demanded.

(5) References in this section to arbitrators include an arbitrator who has ceased to act and an umpire who has not replaced the other arbitrators.

(6) The above provisions of this section also apply in relation to any arbitral or

other institution or person vested by the parties with powers in relation to the delivery of the tribunal's award. As they so apply, the references to the fees and expenses of the arbitrators shall be construed as including the fees and expenses of that institution or person.

(7) The leave of the court is required for any appeal from a decision of the court under this section.

(8) Nothing in this section shall be construed as excluding an application under section 28 where payment has been made to the arbitrators in order to obtain the award.

Correction of award or additional award

57.—(1) The parties are free to agree on the powers of the tribunal to correct an award or make an additional award.

(2) If or to the extent there is no such agreement, the following provisions apply.

(3) The tribunal may on its own initiative or on the application of a party—
   (*a*) correct an award so as to remove any clerical mistake or error arising from an accidental slip or omission or clarify or remove any ambiguity in the award, or
   (*b*) make an additional award in respect of any claim (including a claim for interest or costs) which was presented to the tribunal but was not dealt with in the award.

These powers shall not be exercised without first affording the other parties a reasonable opportunity to make representations to the tribunal.

(4) Any application for the exercise of those powers must be made within 28 days of the date of the award or such longer period as the parties may agree.

(5) Any correction of an award shall be made within 28 days of the date the application was received by the tribunal or, where the correction is made by the tribunal on its own initiative, within 28 days of the date of the award or, in either case, such longer period as the parties may agree.

(6) Any additional award shall be made within 56 days of the date of the original award or such longer period as the parties may agree.

(7) Any correction of an award shall form part of the award.

Effect of award

58.—(1) Unless otherwise agreed by the parties, an award made by the tribunal pursuant to an arbitration agreement is final and binding both on the parties and on any persons claiming through or under them.

(2) This does not affect the right of a person to challenge the award by any available arbitral process of appeal or review or in accordance with the provisions of this Part.

COSTS OF THE ARBITRATION

Costs of the arbitration

59.—(1) References in this Part to the costs of the arbitration are to—
   (*a*) the arbitrators' fees and expenses,

(b) the fees and expenses of any arbitral institution concerned, and
  (c) the legal or other costs of the parties.
(2) Any such reference includes the costs of or incidental to any proceedings to determine the amount of the recoverable costs of the arbitration (see section 63).

Agreement to pay costs in any event

60.—An agreement which has the effect that a party is to pay the whole or part of the costs of the arbitration in any event is only valid if made after the dispute in question has arisen.

Award of costs

61.—(1) The tribunal may make an award allocating the costs of the arbitration as between the parties, subject to any agreement of the parties.

(2) Unless the parties otherwise agree, the tribunal shall award costs on the general principle that costs should follow the event except where it appears to the tribunal that in the circumstances this is not appropriate in relation to the whole or part of the costs.

Effect of agreement or award about costs

62.—Unless the parties otherwise agree, any obligation under an agreement between them as to how the costs of the arbitration are to be borne, or under an award allocating the costs of the arbitration, extends only to such costs as are recoverable.

The recoverable costs of the arbitration

63.—(1) The parties are free to agree what costs of the arbitration are recoverable.

(2) If or to the extent there is no such agreement, the following provisions apply.

(3) The tribunal may determine by award the recoverable costs of the arbitration on such basis as it thinks fit. If it does so, it shall specify—
  (a) the basis on which it has acted, and
  (b) the items of recoverable costs and the amount referable to each.

(4) If the tribunal does not determine the recoverable costs of the arbitration, any party to the arbitral proceedings may apply to the court (upon notice to the other parties) which may—
  (a) determine the recoverable costs of the arbitration on such basis as it thinks fit, or
  (b) order that they shall be determined by such means and upon such terms as it may specify.

(5) Unless the tribunal or the court determines otherwise—
  (a) the recoverable costs of the arbitration shall be determined on the basis that there shall be allowed a reasonable amount in respect of all costs reasonably incurred, and
  (b) any doubt as to whether costs were reasonably incurred or were reasonable in amount shall be resolved in favour of the paying party.

(6) The above provisions have effect subject to section 64 (recoverable fees and expenses of arbitrators).

(7) Nothing in this section affects any right of the arbitrators, any expert, legal adviser or assessor appointed by the tribunal, or any arbitral institution, to payment of their fees and expenses.

Recoverable fees and expenses of arbitrators

64.—(1) Unless otherwise agreed by the parties, the recoverable costs of the arbitration shall include in respect of the fees and expenses of the arbitrators only such reasonable fees and expenses as are appropriate in the circumstances.

(2) If there is any question as to what reasonable fees and expenses are appropriate in the circumstances, and the matter is not already before the court on an application under section 63(4), the court may on the application of any party (upon notice to the other parties)—
  (*a*) determine the matter, or
  (*b*) order that it be determined by such means and upon such terms as the court may specify.

(3) Subsection (1) has effect subject to any order of the court under section 24(4) or 25(3)(*b*) (order as to entitlement to fees or expenses in case of removal or resignation of arbitrator).

(4) Nothing in this section affects any right of the arbitrator to payment of his fees and expenses.

Power to limit recoverable costs

65.—(1) Unless otherwise agreed by the parties, the tribunal may direct that the recoverable costs of the arbitration, or of any part of the arbitral proceedings, shall be limited to a specified amount.

(2) Any direction may be made or varied at any stage, but this must be done sufficiently in advance of the incurring of costs to which it relates, or the taking of any steps in the proceedings which may be affected by it, for the limit to be taken into account.

POWERS OF THE COURT IN RELATION TO AWARD

Enforcement of the award

66.—(1) An award made by the tribunal pursuant to an arbitration agreement may, by leave of the court, be enforced in the same manner as a judgment or order of the court to the same effect.

(2) Where leave is so given, judgment may be entered in terms of the award.

(3) Leave to enforce an award shall not be given where, or to the extent that, the person against whom it is sought to be enforced shows that the tribunal lacked substantive jurisdiction to make the award. The right to raise such an objection may have been lost (see section 73).

(4) Nothing in this section affects the recognition or enforcement of an award under any other enactment or rule of law, in particular under Part II of the Arbitration Act 1950 (enforcement of awards under Geneva Convention) or the

provisions of Part III of this Act relating to the recognition and enforcement of awards under the New York Convention or by an action on the award.

Challenging the award: substantive jurisdiction

67.—(1) A party to arbitral proceedings may (upon notice to the other parties and to the tribunal) apply to the court—
- (*a*) challenging any award of the arbitral tribunal as to its substantive jurisdiction; or
- (*b*) for an order declaring an award made by the tribunal on the merits to be of no effect, in whole or in part, because the tribunal did not have substantive jurisdiction.

A party may lose the right to object (see section 73) and the right to apply is subject to the restrictions in section 70(2) and (3).

(2) The arbitral tribunal may continue the arbitral proceedings and make a further award while an application to the court under this section is pending in relation to an award as to jurisdiction.

(3) On an application under this section challenging an award of the arbitral tribunal as to its substantive jurisdiction, the court may by order—
- (*a*) confirm the award,
- (*b*) vary the award, or
- (*c*) set aside the award in whole or in part.

(4) The leave of the court is required for any appeal from a decision of the court under this section.

Challenging the award: serious irregularity

68.—(1) A party to arbitral proceedings may (upon notice to the other parties and to the tribunal) apply to the court challenging an award in the proceedings on the ground of serious irregularity affecting the tribunal, the proceedings or the award. A party may lose the right to object (see section 73) and the right to apply is subject to the restrictions in section 70(2) and (3).

(2) Serious irregularity means an irregularity of one or more of the following kinds which the court considers has caused or will cause substantial injustice to the applicant—
- (*a*) failure by the tribunal to comply with section 33 (general duty of tribunal);
- (*b*) the tribunal exceeding its powers (otherwise than by exceeding its substantive jurisdiction: see section 67);
- (*c*) failure by the tribunal to conduct the proceedings in accordance with the procedure agreed by the parties;
- (*d*) failure by the tribunal to deal with all the issues that were put to it;
- (*e*) any arbitral or other institution or person vested by the parties with powers in relation to the proceedings or the award exceeding its powers;
- (*f*) uncertainty or ambiguity as to the effect of the award;
- (*g*) the award being obtained by fraud or the award or the way in which it was procured being contrary to public policy;
- (*h*) failure to comply with the requirements as to the form of the award; or

(i) any irregularity in the conduct of the proceedings or in the award which is admitted by the tribunal or by any arbitral or other institution or person vested by the parties with powers in relation to the proceedings or the award.

(3) If there is shown to be serious irregularity affecting the tribunal, the proceedings or the award, the court may—
   (a) remit the award to the tribunal, in whole or in part, for reconsideration,
   (b) set the award aside in whole or in part, or
   (c) declare the award to be of no effect, in whole or in part.

The court shall not exercise its power to set aside or to declare an award to be of no effect, in whole or in part, unless it is satisfied that it would be inappropriate to remit the matters in question to the tribunal for reconsideration.

(4) The leave of the court is required for any appeal from a decision of the court under this section.

Appeal on point of law

69.—(1) Unless otherwise agreed by the parties, a party to arbitral proceedings may (upon notice to the other parties and to the tribunal) appeal to the court on a question of law arising out of an award made in the proceedings. An agreement to dispense with reasons for the tribunal's award shall be considered an agreement to exclude the court's jurisdiction under this section.

(2) An appeal shall not be brought under this section except—
   (a) with the agreement of all the other parties to the proceedings, or
   (b) with the leave of the court.

The right to appeal is also subject to the restrictions in section 70(2) and (3).

(3) Leave to appeal shall be given only if the court is satisfied—
   (a) that the determination of the question will substantially affect the rights of one or more of the parties,
   (b) that the question is one which the tribunal was asked to determine,
   (c) that, on the basis of the findings of fact in the award—
      (i) the decision of the tribunal on the question is obviously wrong, or
      (ii) the question is one of general public importance and the decision of the tribunal is at least open to serious doubt, and
   (d) that, despite the agreement of the parties to resolve the matter by arbitration, it is just and proper in all the circumstances for the court to determine the question.

(4) An application for leave to appeal under this section shall identify the question of law to be determined and state the grounds on which it is alleged that leave to appeal should be granted.

(5) The court shall determine an application for leave to appeal under this section without a hearing unless it appears to the court that a hearing is required.

(6) The leave of the court is required for any appeal from a decision of the court under this section to grant or refuse leave to appeal.

(7) On an appeal under this section the court may by order—
   (a) confirm the award,
   (b) vary the award,

(c) remit the award to the tribunal, in whole or in part, for reconsideration in the light of the court's determination, or

(d) set aside the award in whole or in part.

The court shall not exercise its power to set aside an award, in whole or in part, unless it is satisfied that it would be inappropriate to remit the matters in question to the tribunal for reconsideration.

(8) The decision of the court on an appeal under this section shall be treated as a judgment of the court for the purposes of a further appeal. But no such appeal lies without the leave of the court which shall not be given unless the court considers that the question is one of general importance or is one which for some other special reason should be considered by the Court of Appeal.

Challenge or appeal: supplementary provisions

70.—(1) The following provisions apply to an application or appeal under section 67, 68 or 69.

(2) An application or appeal may not be brought if the applicant or appellant has not first exhausted—

(a) any available arbitral process of appeal or review, and

(b) any available recourse under section 57 (correction of award or additional award).

(3) Any application or appeal must be brought within 28 days of the date of the award or, if there has been any arbitral process of appeal or review, of the date when the applicant or appellant was notified of the result of that process.

(4) If on an application or appeal it appears to the court that the award—

(a) does not contain the tribunal's reasons, or

(b) does not set out the tribunal's reasons in sufficient detail to enable the court properly to consider the application or appeal,

the court may order the tribunal to state the reasons for its award in sufficient detail for that purpose.

(5) Where the court makes an order under subsection (4), it may make such further order as it thinks fit with respect to any additional costs of the arbitration resulting from its order.

(6) The court may order the applicant or appellant to provide security for the costs of the application or appeal, and may direct that the application or appeal be dismissed if the order is not complied with. The power to order security for costs shall not be exercised on the ground that the applicant or appellant is—

(a) an individual ordinarily resident outside the United Kingdom, or

(b) a corporation or association incorporated or formed under the law of a country outside the United Kingdom, or whose central management and control is exercised outside the United Kingdom.

(7) The court may order that any money payable under the award shall be brought into court or otherwise secured pending the determination of the application or appeal, and may direct that the application or appeal be dismissed if the order is not complied with.

(8) The court may grant leave to appeal subject to conditions to the same or

Challenge or appeal: effect of order of court

71.—(1) The following provisions have effect where the court makes an order under section 67, 68 or 69 with respect to an award.

(2) Where the award is varied, the variation has effect as part of the tribunal's award.

(3) Where the award is remitted to the tribunal, in whole or in part, for reconsideration, the tribunal shall make a fresh award in respect of the matters remitted within three months of the date of the order for remission or such longer or shorter period as the court may direct.

(4) Where the award is set aside or declared to be of no effect, in whole or in part, the court may also order that any provision that an award is a condition precedent to the bringing of legal proceedings in respect of a matter to which the arbitration agreement applies, is of no effect as regards the subject matter of the award or, as the case may be, the relevant part of the award.

MISCELLANEOUS

Saving for rights of person who takes no part in proceedings

72.—(1) A person alleged to be a party to arbitral proceedings but who takes no part in the proceedings may question—
 (a) whether there is a valid arbitration agreement,
 (b) whether the tribunal is properly constituted, or
 (c) what matters have been submitted to arbitration in accordance with the arbitration agreement,

by proceedings in the court for a declaration or injunction or other appropriate relief.

(2) He also has the same right as a party to the arbitral proceedings to challenge an award—
 (a) by an application under section 67 on the ground of lack of substantive jurisdiction in relation to him, or
 (b) by an application under section 68 on the ground of serious irregularity (within the meaning of that section affecting him;

and section 70(2) (duty to exhaust arbitral procedures) does not apply in his case.

Loss of right to object

73.—(1) If a party to arbitral proceedings takes part, or continues to take part, in the proceedings without making, either forthwith or within such time as is allowed by the arbitration agreement or the tribunal or by any provision of this Part, any objection—
 (a) that the tribunal lacks substantive jurisdiction,
 (b) that the proceedings have been improperly conducted,

(c) that there has been a failure to comply with the arbitration agreement or with any provision of this Part, or

(d) that there has been any other irregularity affecting the tribunal or the proceedings,

he may not raise that objection later, before the tribunal or the court, unless he shows that, at the time he took part or continued to take part in the proceedings, he did not know and could not with reasonable diligence have discovered the grounds for the objection.

(2) Where the arbitral tribunal rules that it has substantive jurisdiction and a party to arbitral proceedings who could have questioned that ruling—

(a) by any available arbitral process of appeal or review, or

(b) by challenging the award,

does not do so, or does not do so within the time allowed by the arbitration agreement or any provision of this Part, he may not object later to the tribunal's substantive jurisdiction on any ground which was the subject of that ruling.

Immunity of arbitral institutions

74.—(1) An arbitral or other institution or person designated or requested by the parties to appoint or nominate an arbitrator is not liable for anything done or omitted in the discharge or purported discharge of that function unless the act or omission is shown to have been in bad faith.

(2) An arbitral or other institution or person by whom an arbitrator is appointed or nominated is not liable, by reason of having appointed or nominated him, for anything done or omitted by the arbitrator (or his employees or agents) in the discharge or purported discharge of his functions as arbitrator.

(3) The above provisions apply to an employee or agent of an arbitral or other institution or person as they apply to the institution or person himself.

Charge to secure payment of solicitors costs

75.—The powers of the court to make declarations and orders under section 73 of the Solicitors Act 1974 or Article 71H of the Solicitors (Northern Ireland) Order 1976 (power to charge property recovered in the proceedings with the payment of solicitors' costs) may be exercised in relation to arbitral proceedings as if those proceedings were proceedings in the court.

SUPPLEMENTARY

Service of notices etc.

76.—(1) The parties are free to agree on the manner of service of any notice or other document required or authorised to be given or served in pursuance of the arbitration agreement or for the purposes of the arbitral proceedings.

(2) If or to the extent that there is no such agreement the following provisions apply.

(3) A notice or other document may be served on a person by any effective means.

(4) If a notice or other document is addressed, pre-paid and delivered by post—

(*a*) to the addressee's last known principal residence or, if he is or has been carrying on a trade, profession or business, his last known principal business address, or

(*b*) where the addressee is a body corporate, to the body's registered or principal office,

it shall be treated as effectively served.

(5) This section does not apply to the service of documents for the purposes of legal proceedings, for which provision is made by rules of court.

(6) References in this Part to a notice or other document include any form of communication in writing and references to giving or serving a notice or other document shall be construed accordingly.

Powers of court in relation to service of documents

77.—(1) This section applies where service of a document on a person in the manner agreed by the parties, or in accordance with provisions of section 76 having effect in default of agreement, is not reasonably practicable.

(2) Unless otherwise agreed by the parties, the court may make such order as it thinks fit—

(*a*) for service in such manner as the court may direct, or

(*b*) dispensing with service of the document.

(3) Any party to the arbitration agreement may apply for an order, but only after exhausting any available arbitral process for resolving the matter.

(4) The leave of the court is required for any appeal from a decision of the court under this section.

Reckoning periods of time

78.—(1) The parties are free to agree on the method of reckoning periods of time for the purposes of any provision agreed by them or any provision of this Part having effect in default of such agreement.

(2) If or to the extent there is no such agreement, periods of time shall be reckoned in accordance with the following provisions.

(3) Where the act is required to be done within a specified period after or from a specified date, the period begins immediately after that date.

(4) Where the act is required to be done a specified number of clear days after a specified date, at least that number of days must intervene between the day on which the act is done and that date.

(5) Where the period is a period of seven days or less which would include a Saturday, Sunday or a public holiday in the place where anything which has to be done within the period falls to be done, that day shall be excluded.

In relation to England and Wales or Northern Ireland, a "public holiday" means Christmas Day, Good Friday or a day which under the Banking and Financial Dealings Act 1971 is a bank holiday.

Power of court to extend time limits relating to arbitral proceedings

79.—(1) Unless the parties otherwise agree, the court may by order extend any time limit agreed by them in relation to any matter relating to the arbitral proceedings or specified in any provision of this Part having effect in default of such agreement. This section does not apply to a time limit to which section 12 applies (power of court to extend time for beginning arbitral proceedings, etc.).

(2) An application for an order may be made—
- (*a*) by any party to the arbitral proceedings (upon notice to the other parties and to the tribunal), or
- (*b*) by the arbitral tribunal (upon notice to the parties).

(3) The court shall not exercise its power to extend a time limit unless it is satisfied—
- (*a*) that any available recourse to the tribunal, or to any arbitral or other institution or person vested by the parties with power in that regard, has first been exhausted, and
- (*b*) that a substantial injustice would otherwise be done.

(4) The court's power under this section may be exercised whether or not the time has already expired.

(5) An order under this section may be made on such terms as the court thinks fit.

(6) The leave of the court is required for any appeal from a decision of the court under this section.

Notice and other requirements in connection with legal proceedings

80.—(1) References in this Part to an application, appeal or other step in relation to legal proceedings being taken "upon notice" to the other parties to the arbitral proceedings, or to the tribunal, are to such notice of the originating process as is required by rules of court and do not impose any separate requirement.

(2) Rules of court shall be made—
- (*a*) requiring such notice to be given as indicated by any provision of this Part, and
- (*b*) as to the manner, form and content of any such notice.

(3) Subject to any provision made by rules of court, a requirement to give notice to the tribunal of legal proceedings shall be construed—
- (*a*) if there is more than one arbitrator, as a requirement to give notice to each of them; and
- (*b*) if the tribunal is not fully constituted, as a requirement to give notice to any arbitrator who has been appointed.

(4) References in this Part to making an application or appeal to the court within a specified period are to the issue within that period of the appropriate originating process in accordance with rules of court.

(5) Where any provision of this Part requires an application or appeal to be made to the court within a specified time, the rules of court relating to the reckoning of periods, the extending or abridging of periods, and the consequences of not taking a step within the period prescribed by the rules, apply in relation to that requirement.

(6) Provision may be made by rules of court amending the provisions of this Part—
- (*a*) with respect to the time within which any application or appeal to the court must be made,

(b) so as to keep any provision made by this Part in relation to arbitral proceedings in step with the corresponding provision of rules of court applying in relation to proceedings in the court, or

(c) so as to keep any provision made by this Part in relation to legal proceedings in step with the corresponding provision of rules of court applying generally in relation to proceedings in the court.

(7) Nothing in this section affects the generality of the power to make rules of court.

Saving for certain matters governed by common law

81.—(1) Nothing in this Part shall be construed as excluding the operation of any rule of law consistent with the provisions of this Part, in particular, any rule of law as to—

(a) matters which are not capable of settlement by arbitration;

(b) the effect of an oral arbitration agreement; or

(c) the refusal of recognition or enforcement of an arbitral award on grounds of public policy.

(2) Nothing in this Act shall be construed as reviving any jurisdiction of the court to set aside or remit an award on the ground of errors of fact or law on the face of the award.

Minor definitions

82.—(1) In this Part—

"arbitrator" unless the context otherwise requires, includes an umpire;

"available arbitral process", in relation to any matter, includes any process of appeal to or review by an arbitral or other institution or person vested by the parties with powers in relation to that matter;

"claimant", unless the context otherwise requires, includes a counterclaimant, and related expressions shall be construed accordingly;

"dispute" includes any difference;

"enactment" includes an enactment contained in Northern Ireland legislation;

"legal proceedings" means civil proceedings in the High Court or a county court;

"peremptory order" means an order made under section 41(5) or made in exercise of any corresponding power conferred by the parties;

"premises" includes land, buildings, moveable structures, vehicles, vessels, aircraft and hovercraft;

"question of law" means—

(a) for a court in England and Wales, a question of the law of England and Wales, and

(b) for a court in Northern Ireland, a question of the law of Northern Ireland;

"substantive jurisdiction", in relation to an arbitral tribunal, refers to the matters specified in section 30(1)(a) to (c), and references to the tribunal exceeding its substantive jurisdiction shall be construed accordingly.

(2) References in this Part to a party to an arbitration agreement include any person claiming under or through a party to the agreement.

SECTION 83

Index of defined expressions: Part I

83.—In this Part the expressions listed below are defined or otherwise explained by the provisions indicated—

agreement, agree and agreed	section 5(1)
agreement in writing	section 5(2) to (5)
arbitration agreement	sections 6 and 5(1)
arbitrator	section 82(1)
available arbitral process	section 82(1)
claimant	section 82(1)
commencement (in relation to arbitral proceedings)	section 14
costs of the arbitration	section 59
the court	section 105
dispute	section 82(1)
enactment	section 82(1)
legal proceedings	section 82(1)
Limitation Acts	section 13(4)
notice (or other document)	section 76(6)
party—in relation to an arbitration agreement	section 82(2)
—where section 106(2) or (3) applies	section 106(4)
peremptory order	section 82(1) (and see section 41(5))
premises	section 82(1)
question of law	section 82(1)
recoverable costs	section 63 and 64
seat of the arbitration	section 3
serve and service (of notice or other document)	section 76(6)
substantive jurisdiction (in relation to an arbitral tribunal)	section 82(1) (and see section 30(1)(*a*) to (*c*))
upon notice (to the parties or the tribunal)	section 80
written and in writing	section 5(6)

Transitional provisions

84.—(1) The provisions of this Part do not apply to arbitral proceedings commenced before the date on which this Part comes into force.

(2) They apply to arbitral proceedings commenced on or after that date under an arbitration agreement whenever made.

(3) The above provisions have effect subject to any transitional provision made by an order under section 109(2) (power to include transitional provisions in commencement order).

PART II
OTHER PROVISIONS RELATING TO ARBITRATION

DOMESTIC ARBITRATION AGREEMENTS

Modification of Part I in relation to domestic arbitration agreement

85.—(1) In the case of a domestic arbitration agreement the provisions of Part I are modified in accordance with the following sections.

(2) For this purpose a "domestic arbitration agreement" means an arbitration agreement to which none of the parties is—
   (a) an individual who is a national of, or habitually resident in, a state other than the United Kingdom, or
   (b) a body corporate which is incorporated in, or whose central control and management is exercised in, a state other than the United Kingdom,

and under which the seat of the arbitration (if the seat has been designated or determined) is in the United Kingdom.

(3) In subsection (2) "arbitration agreement" and "seat of the arbitration" have the same meaning as in Part I (see sections 3, 5(1) and 6).

Staying of legal proceedings

86.—(1) In section 9 (stay of legal proceedings), subsection (4) (stay unless the arbitration agreement is null and void, inoperative, or incapable of being performed) does not apply to a domestic arbitration agreement.

(2) On an application under that section in relation to a domestic arbitration agreement the court shall grant a stay unless satisfied—
   (a) that the arbitration agreement is null and void, inoperative, or incapable of being performed, or
   (b) that there are other sufficient grounds for not requiring the parties to abide by the arbitration agreement.

(3) The court may treat as a sufficient ground under subsection (2)(b) the fact that the applicant is or was at any material time not ready and willing to do all things necessary for the proper conduct of the arbitration or of any other dispute resolution procedures required to be exhausted before resorting to arbitration.

(4) For the purposes of this section the question whether an arbitration agreement is a domestic arbitration agreement shall be determined by reference to the facts at the time the legal proceedings are commenced.

Effectiveness of agreement to exclude court's jurisdiction

87.—(1) In the case of a domestic arbitration agreement any agreement to exclude the jurisdiction of the court under—
   (a) section 45 (determination of preliminary point of law), or
   (b) section 69 (challenging the award: appeal on point of law),

is not effective unless entered into after the commencement of the arbitral proceedings in which the question arises or the award is made.

(2) For this purpose the commencement of the arbitral proceedings has the same meaning as in Part I (see section 14).

(3) For the purposes of this section the question whether an arbitration agreement is a domestic arbitration agreement shall be determined by reference to the facts at the time the agreement is entered into.

Power to repeal or amend sections 85 to 87

88.—(1)The Secretary of State may by order repeal or amend the provisions of section 85 to 87

(2) An order under this section may contain such supplementary, incidental and transitional provisions as appear to the Secretary of State to be appropriate.

(3) An order under this section shall be made by statutory instrument and no such order shall be made unless a draft of it has been laid before and approved by a resolution of each House of Parliament.

CONSUMER ARBITRATION AGREEMENTS

Application of unfair terms regulations to consumer arbitration agreements

89.—(1) The following section extend the application of the Unfair Terms in Consumer Contracts Regulations 1994 in relation to a term which constitutes an arbitration agreement. For this purpose "arbitration agreement" means an agreement to submit to arbitration present or future disputes or differences (whether or not contractual).

(2) In those sections "the Regulations" means those regulations and includes any regulations amending or replacing those regulations.

(3) Those sections apply whatever the law applicable to the arbitration agreement.

Regulations apply where consumer is a legal person

90.—The Regulations apply where the consumer is a legal person as they apply where the consumer is a natural person.

Arbitration agreement unfair where modest amount sought

91.—(1) A term which constitutes an arbitration agreement is unfair for the purposes of the Regulations so far as it relates to a claim for a pecuniary remedy which does not exceed the amount specified by order for the purposes of this section.

(2) Orders under this section may make different provision for different cases and for different purposes.

(3) The power to make orders under this section is exercisable—
  (*a*) for England and Wales, by the Secretary of State with the concurrent of the Lord Chancellor,
  (*b*) for Scotland, by the Secretary of State with the concurrence of the Lord Advocate, and
  (*c*) for Northern Ireland, by the Department of Economic Development for Northern Ireland with the concurrence of the Lord Chancellor.

(4) Any such order for England and Wales or Scotland shall be made by

statutory instrument which shall be subject to annulment in pursuance of a resolution of either House of Parliament.

(5) Any such order for Northern Ireland shall be a statutory rule for the purposes of the Statutory Rules (Northern Ireland) Order 1979 and shall be subject to negative resolution, within the meaning of section 41(6) of the Interpretation Act (Northern Ireland) 1954.

SMALL CLAIMS ARBITRATION IN THE COUNTY COURT

Exclusion of Part I in relation to small claims arbitration in the county court

92.—Nothing in Part I of this Act applies to arbitration under section 64 of the County Courts Act 1984.

APPOINTMENT OF JUDGES AS ARBITRATORS

Appointment of judges as arbitrators

93.—(1) A judge of the Commercial Court or an official referee may, if in all the circumstances he thinks fit, accept appointment as a sole arbitrator or as umpire by or by virtue of an arbitration agreement.

(2) A judge of the Commercial Court shall not do so unless the Lord Chief Justice has informed him that, having regard to the state of business in the High Court and the Crown Court, he can be made available.

(3) An official referee shall not do so unless the Lord Chief Justice has informed him that, having regard to the state of official referees' business, he can be made available.

(4) The fees payable for the services of a judge of the Commercial Court or official referee as arbitrator or umpire shall be taken in the High Court.

(5) In this section—"arbitration agreement" has the same meaning as in Part I; and "official referee" means a person nominated under section 68(1)(a) of the Supreme Court Act 1981 to deal with official referees' business.

(6) The provisions of Part I of this Act apply to arbitration before a person appointed under this section with the modifications specified in Schedule 2.

STATUTORY ARBITRATIONS

Application of Part I to statutory arbitrations

94.—(1) The provisions of Part I apply to every arbitration under an enactment (a "statutory arbitration"), whether the enactment was passed or made before or after the commencement of this Act, subject to the adaptations and exclusions specified in sections 95 to 98.

(2) The provisions of Part I do not apply to a statutory arbitration if or to the extent that their application—
    (*a*) is inconsistent with the provisions of the enactment concerned, with any rules or procedure authorised or recognised by it, or
    (*b*) is excluded by any other enactment.

(3) In this section and the following provisions of this Part "enactment"—

(a) in England and Wales, includes an enactment contained in subordinate legislation within the meaning of the Interpretation Act 1978;

(b) in Northern Ireland, means a statutory provision within the meaning of section 1(f) of the Interpretation Act (Northern Ireland) 1954.

General adaptation of provisions in relation to statutory arbitrations

95.—(1) The provisions of Part I apply to a statutory arbitration—
  (a) as if the arbitration were pursuant to an arbitration agreement and as if the enactment were that agreement, and
  (b) as if the persons by and against whom a claim subject to arbitration in pursuance of the enactment may be or has been made were parties to that agreement.
(2) Every statutory arbitration shall be taken to have its seat in England and Wales or, as the case may be, in Northern Ireland.

Specific adaptations of provisions in relation to statutory arbitrations

96.—(1) The following provisions of Part I apply to a statutory arbitration with the following adaptations.
(2) In section 30(1) (competence of tribunal to rule on its own jurisdiction), the reference in paragraph (a) to whether there is a valid arbitration agreement shall be construed as a reference to whether the enactment applies to the dispute or difference in question.
(3) Section 35 (consolidation of proceedings and concurrent hearings) applies only so as to authorise the consolidation of proceedings, or concurrent hearings in proceedings, under the same enactment.
(4) Section 46 (rules applicable to substance of dispute) applies with the omission of subsection (1)(b) (determination in accordance with considerations agreed by parties).

Provisions excluded from applying to statutory arbitrations

97.—The following provisions of Part I do not apply in relation to a statutory arbitration—
  (a) section 8 (whether agreement discharged by death of a party);
  (b) section 12 (power of court to extend agreed time limits);
  (c) section 9(5), 10(2) and 71(4) (restrictions on effect of provision that award condition precedent to right to bring legal proceedings).

Power to make further provision by regulations

98.—(1) The Secretary of State may make provision by regulations for adapting or excluding any provision of Part I in relation to statutory arbitrations in general or statutory arbitratins of any particular description.
(2) The power is exercisable whether the enactment concerned is passed or made before or after the commencement of this Act.
(3) Regulations under this section shall be made by statutory instrument which

shall be subject to annulment in pursuance of a resolution of either House of Parliament.

PART III
RECOGNITION AND ENFORCEMENT OF CERTAIN FOREIGN AWARDS

ENFORCEMENT OF GENEVA CONVENTION AWARDS

Continuation of Part II of the Arbitration Act 1950

99.—Part II of the Arbitration Act 1950 (enforcement of certain foreign awards) continues to apply in relation to foreign awards within the meaning of that Part which are not also New York Convention awards.

RECOGNITION AND ENFORCEMENT OF NEW YORK CONVENTION AWARDS

New York Convention awards

100.—(1) In this Part a "New York Convention award" means an award made, in pursuance of an arbitration agreement, in the territory of a state (other than the United Kingdom) which is a party to the New York Convention.

(2) For the purposes of subsection (1) and of the provisions of this Part relating to such awards—
 (*a*) "arbitration agreement" means an arbitration agreement in writing, and
 (*b*) an award shall be treated as made at the seat of the arbitration, regardless of where it was signed, despatched or delivered to any of the parties.
In this subsection "agreement in writing" and "seat of the arbitration" have the same meaning as in Part I.

(3) If Her Majesty by Order in Council declares that a state specified in the Order is a party to the New York Convention, or is a party in respect of any territory so specified, the Order shall, while in force, be conclusive evidence of that fact.

(4) In this section "the New York Convention" means the Convention on the Recognition and Enforcement of Foreign Arbitral Awards adopted by the United Nations Conference on International Commercial Arbitration on 10th June 1958.

Recognition and enforcement of awards

101.—(1) A New York Convention award shall be recognised as binding on the persons as between whom it was made, and may accordingly be relied on by those persons by way of defence, set-off or otherwise in any legal proceedings in England and Wales or Northern Ireland.

(2) A New York Convention award may, by leave of the court, be enforced in the same manner as a judgment or order of the court to the same effect.

As to the meaning of "the court" see section 105.

(3) Where leave is so given, judgment may be entered in terms of the award.

Section 102

Evidence to be produced by party seeking recognition or enforcement

102.—(1) A party seeking the recognition or enforcement of a New York Convention award must produce—

    (*a*) the duly authenticated original award or a duly certified copy of it, and

    (*b*) the original arbitration agreement or a duly certified copy of it.

(2) If the award or agreement is in a foreign language, the party must also produce a translation of it certified by an official or sworn translator or by a diplomatic or consular agent.

Refusal of recognition or enforcement

103.—(1) Recognition or enforcement of a New York Convention award shall not be refused except in the following cases.

(2) Recognition or enforcement of the award may be refused if the person against whom it is invoked proves—

    (*a*) that a party to the arbitration agreement was (under the law applicable to him) under some incapacity;

    (*b*) that the arbitration agreement was not valid under the law to which the parties subjected it or, failing any indication thereon, under the law of the country where the award was made;

    (*c*) that he was not given proper notice of the appointment of the arbitrator or of the arbitration proceedings or was otherwise unable to present his case;

    (*d*) that the award deals with a difference not contemplated by or not falling within the terms of the submission to arbitration or contains decisions on matters beyond the scope of the submission to arbitration (but see subsection (4));

    (*e*) that the composition of the arbitral tribunal or the arbitral procedure was not in accordance with the agreement of the parties or, failing such agreement, with the law of the country in which the arbitration took place;

    (*f*) that the award has not yet become binding on the parties, or has been set aside or suspended by a competent authority of the country in which, or under the law of which, it was made.

(3) Recognition or enforcement of the award may also be refused if the award is in respect of a matter which is not capable of settlement by arbitration, or if it would be contrary to public policy to recognise or enforce the award.

(4) An award which contains decisions on matters not submitted to arbitration may be recognised or enforced to the extent that it contains decisions on matters submitted to arbitration which can be separated from those on matters not so submitted.

(5) Where an application for the setting aside or suspension of the award has been made to such a competent authority as is mentioned in subsection (2)(*f*), the court before which the award is sought to be relied upon may, if it considers it proper, adjourn the decision on the recognition or enforcement of the award.

It may also on the application of the party claiming recognition or enforcement of the award order the other party to give suitable security.

Saving for other bases of recognition or enforcement

104.—Nothing in the preceding provisions of this Part affects any right to rely upon or enforce a New York Convention award at common law or under section 66.

PART IV
GENERAL PROVISIONS

Meaning of "the court": jurisdiction of High Court and county court

105.—(1) In this Act "the court" means the High Court or a county court, subject to the following provisions.

(2) The Lord Chancellor may by order make provision—
   (a) allocating proceedings under this Act to the High Court or to county courts; or
   (b) specifying proceedings under this Act which may be commenced or taken only in the High Court or in a county court.

(3) The Lord Chancellor may by order make provision requiring proceedings of any specified description under this Act in relation to which a county court has jurisdiction to be commenced or taken in one or more specified county courts. Any jurisdiction so exercisable by a specified county court is exercisable throughout England and Wales or, as the case may be, Northern Ireland.

(4) An order under this section—
   (a) may differentiate between categories of proceedings by reference to such criteria as the Lord Chancellor sees fit to specify, and
   (b) may make such incidental or transitional provision as the Lord Chancellor considers necessary or expedient.

(5) An order under this section for England and Wales shall be made by statutory instrument which shall be subject to annulment in pursuance of a resolution of either House of Parliament.

(6) An order under this section for Northern Ireland shall be a statutory rule for the purposes of the Statutory Rules (Northern Ireland) Order 1979 which shall be subject to annulment in pursuance of a resolution of either House of Parliament in like manner as a statutory instrument and section 5 of the Statutory Instruments Act 1946 shall apply accordingly.

Crown application

106.—(1) Part I of this Act applies to any arbitration agreement to which Her Majesty, either in right of the Crown or of the Duchy of Lancaster or otherwise, or the Duke of Cornwall, is a party.

(2) Where Her Majesty is party to an arbitration agreement otherwise than in right of the Crown, Her Majesty shall be represented for the purposes of any arbitral proceedings—

(a) where the agreement was entered into by Her Majesty in right of the Duchy of Lancaster, by the Chancellor of the Duchy or such person as he may appoint, and

(b) in any other case, by such person as Her Majesty may appoint in writing under the Royal Sign Manual.

(3) Where the Duke of Cornwall is party to an arbitration agreement, he shall be represented for the purposes of any arbitral proceedings by such person as he may appoint.

(4) References in Part I to a party or the parties to the arbitration agreement or to arbitral proceedings shall be construed, where subsection (2) or (3) applies, as references to the person representing Her Majesty or the Duke of Cornwall.

Consequential amendments and repeals

107.—(1) The enactments specified in Schedule 3 are amended in accordance with that Schedule, the amendments being consequential on the provisions of this Act.

(2) The enactments specified in Schedule 4 are repealed to the extent specified.

Extent

108.—(1) The provisions of this Act extend to England and Wales and, except as mentioned below, to Northern Ireland.

(2) The following provisions of Part II do not extend to Northern Ireland—section 92 (exclusion of Part I in relation to small claims arbitration in the county court), and section 93 and Schedule 2 (appointment of judges as arbitrators).

(3) Sections 89, 90 and 91 (consumer arbitration agreements) extend to Scotland and the provisions of Schedules 3 and 4 (consequential amendments and repeals) extend to Scotland so far as they relate to enactments which so extend, subject as follows.

(4) The repeal of the Arbitration Act 1975 extends only to England and Wales and Northern Ireland.

Commencement

109.—(1) The provisions of this Act come into force on such day as the Secretary of State may appoint by order made by statutory instrument, and different days may be appointed for different purposes.

(2) An order under subsection (1) may contain such transitional provisions as appear to the Secretary of State to be appropriate.

Short title

110.—this Act may be cited as the Arbitration Act 1996.
SCHEDULES

ARBITRATION ACT 1996

SCHEDULE 1

Section 4(1)

MANDATORY PROVISIONS OF PART I

Sections 9 to 11 (stay of legal proceedings);
Section 12 (power of court to extend agreed time limits);
Section 13 (application of Limitation Acts);
Section 24 (power of court to remove arbitrator);
Section 26(1) (effect of death of arbitrator);
Section 28 (liability of parties for fees and expenses of arbitrators);
Section 29 (immunity of arbitrator);
Section 31 (objection to substantive jurisdiction of tribunal);
Section 32 (determination of preliminary point of jurisdiction);
Section 33 (general duty of tribunal);
Section 37(2) (items to be treated as expenses of arbitrators);
Section 40 (general duty of parties);
Section 43 (securing the attendance of witnesses);
Section 56 (power to withhold award in case of non-payment);
Section 60 (effectiveness of agreement for payment of costs in any event);
Section 66 (enforcement of award);
Sections 67 and 68 (challenging the award; substantive jurisdiction and serious irregularity), and sections 70 and 71 (supplementary provisions; effect of order of court) so far as relating to those sections;
Section 72 (saving for rights of person who takes no part in proceedings);
Section 73 (loss of right to object);
Section 74 (immunity of arbitral institutions etc.);
Section 75 (charge to secure payment of solicitors' costs).

SCHEDULE 2

Section 93(6)

MODIFICATIONS OF PART I IN RELATION TO JUDGE-ARBITRATORS

Introductory

1.—In this Schedule "judge-arbitrator" means a judge of the Commercial Court or official referee appointed as arbitrator or umpire under section 93.

General

2.—(1) Subject to the following provisions of this Schedule, references in Part I to the court shall be construed in relation to a judge-arbitrator, or in relation to the appointment of a judge-arbitrator, as references to the Court of Appeal.

SCHEDULE 2

(2) The references in sections 32(6), 45(6) and 69(8) to the Court of Appeal shall in such a case be construed as references to the House of Lords.

Arbitrator's fees

3.—(1) The power of the court in section 28(2) to order consideration and adjustment of the liability of a party for the fees of an arbitrator may be exercised by a judge-arbitrator.

(2) Any such exercise of the power is subject to the powers of the Court of Appeal under sections 24(4) and 25(3)(*b*) (directions as to entitlement to fees or expenses in case of removal or resignation).

Exercise of court powers in support of arbitration

4.—(1) Where the arbitral tribunal consists of or includes a judge-arbitrator the powers of the court under sections 42 to 44 (enforcement of peremptory orders, summoning witnesses, and other court powers) are exercisable by the High Court also by the judge-arbitrator himself.

(2) Anything done by a judge-arbitrator in the exercise of those powers shall be regarded as done by him in his capacity as judge of the High Court and have effect as if done by that court.

Nothing in this sub-paragraph prejudices any power vested in him as arbitrator or umpire.

Extension of time for making award

5.—(1) The power conferred by section 50 (extension of time for making award) is exercisable by the judge-arbitrator himself.

(2) Any appeal from a decision of a judge-arbitrator under that section lies to the Court of Appeal with the leave of that court.

Withholding award in case of non-payment

6.—(1) The provisions of paragraph 7 apply in place of the provisions of section 56 (power to withhold award in the case of non-payment) in relation to the withholding of an award for non-payment of the fees and expenses of a judge-arbitrator.

(2) This does not affect the application of section 56 in relation to the delivery of such an award by an arbitral or other institution or person vested by the parties with powers in relation to the delivery of the award.

7.—(1) A judge-arbitrator may refuse to deliver an award except upon payment of the fees and expenses mentioned in section 56(1).

(2) The judge-arbitrator may, on an application by a party to the arbitral proceedings, order that if he pays into the High Court the fees and expenses demanded, or such lesser amount as the judge-arbitrator may specify—
  (*a*) the award shall be delivered,
  (*b*) the amount of the fees and expenses properly payable shall be determined by such means and upon such terms as he may direct, and

(c) out of the money paid into court there shall be paid out such fees and expenses as may be found to be properly payable and the balance of the money (if any) shall be paid out to the applicant.

(3) For this purpose the amount of fees and expenses properly payable is the amount the applicant is liable to pay under section 28 or any agreement relating to the payment of the arbitrator.

(4) No application to the judge-arbitrator under this paragraph may be made where there is any available arbitral process for appeal or review of the amount of the fees or expenses demanded.

(5) Any appeal from a decision of a judge-arbitrator under this paragraph lies to the Court of Appeal with the leave of that court.

(6) Where a party to arbitral proceedings appeals under sub-paragraph (5), an arbitrator is entitled to appear and be heard.

Correction of award or additional award

8.—Subsections (4) to (6) of section 57 (correction of award or additional award: time limit for application or exercise of power) do not apply to a judge-arbitrator.

Costs

9.—Where the arbitral tribunal consists of or includes a judge-arbitrator the powers of the court under section 63(4) (determination of recoverable costs) shall be exercised by the High Court.

10.—(1) The power of the court under section 64 to determine an arbitrator's reasonable fees and expenses may be exercised by a judge-arbitrator.

(2) Any such exercise of the power is subject to the powers of the Court of Appeal under sections 24(4) and 25(3)(*b*) (directions as to entitlement to fees or expenses in case of removal or resignation).

Enforcement of award

11.—The leave of the court required by section 66 (enforcement of award) may in the case of an award of a judge-arbitrator be given by the judge-arbitrator himself.

Solicitors' costs

12.—The powers of the court to make declarations and orders under the provisions applied by section 75 (power to charge property recovered in arbitral proceedings with the payment of solicitors' costs) may be exercised by the judge-arbitrator.

Powers of court in relation to service of documents

13.—(1) The power of the court under section 77(2) (powers of court in relation to service of documents) is exercisable by the judge-arbitrator.

(2) Any appeal from a decision of a judge-arbitrator under that section lies to the Court of Appeal with the leave of that court.

Powers of court to extend time limits relating to arbitral proceedings

14.—(1) The power conferred by section 79 (power of court to extend time limits relating to arbitral proceedings) is exercisable by the judge-arbitrator himself.

(2) Any appeal from a decision of a judge-arbitrator under that section lies to the Court of Appeal with the leave of that court.

SCHEDULE 3

Section 107(1)

CONSEQUENTIAL AMENDMENTS

Merchant Shipping Act 1894 (c.60)

1.—In section 496 of the Merchant Shipping Act 1894 (provisions as to deposits by owners of goods), after subsection (4) insert—
> "(5) In subsection (3) the expression "legal proceedings" includes arbitral proceedings and as respects England and Wales and Northern Ireland the provisions of section 14 of the Arbitration Act 1996 apply to determine when such proceedings are commenced."

Stannaries Court (Abolition) Act 1896 (c. 45)

2.—In section 4(1) of the Stannaries Court (Abolition) Act 1896 (references of certain disputes to arbitration), for the words from "tried before" to "any such reference" substitute "referred to arbitration before himself or before an arbitrator agreed on by the parties or an officer of the court".

Tithe Act 1936 (c. 43)

3.—In section 39(1) of the Tithe Act 1936 (proceedings of Tithe Redemption Commission)—
  (a) for "the Arbitration Acts 1889 to 1934" substitute "Part I of the Arbitration Act 1996";
  (b) for paragraph (e) substitute—
   "(e) the making of an application to the court to determine a preliminary point of law and the bringing of an appeal to the court on a point of law.;"
  (c) for "the said Acts" substitute "Part I of the Arbitration Act 1996".

Education Act 1944 (c. 31)

[…][1]

---

[1] Repealed by the Education Act 1996, c. 56, Sched. 38, Pt I.

Commonwealth Telegraphs Act 1949 (c. 39)

5.—In section 8(2) of the Commonwealth Telegraphs Act 1949 (proceedings of referees under the Act) for "the Arbitration Acts 1889 to 1934; or the Arbitration Act (Northern Ireland) 1937," substitute "Part I of the Arbitration Act 1996".

Lands Tribunal Act 1949 (c. 42)

6.—In section 3 of the Lands Tribunal Act 1949 (proceedings before the Lands Tribunal)—
  (a) in subsection (6)(c) (procedural rules: power to apply Arbitration Acts), and
  (b) in subsection (8) (exclusion of Arbitration Acts except as applied by rules),
for "the Arbitration Acts 1889 to 1934" substitute "Part I of the Arbitration Act 1996".

Wireless Telegraphy Act 1949 (c. 54)

7.—In the Wireless Telegraphy Act 1949, Schedule 2 (procedure of appeals tribunal), in paragraph 3(1)—
  (a) for the words "the Arbitration Acts 1889 to 1934" substitute "Part I of the Arbitration Act 1996";
  (b) after the word "Wales" insert "or Northern Ireland"; and
  (c) for "the said Acts" substitute "Part I of that Act".

Patents Act 1949 (c. 87)

8.—In section 67 of the Patents Act 1949 (proceedings as to infringement of pre-1978 patents referred to comptroller), for "The Arbitration Acts 1889 to 1934" substitute "Part I of the Arbitration Act 1996".

National Health Service (Amendment) Act 1949 (c. 93)

9.—In section 7(8) of the National Health Service (Amendment) Act 1949 (arbitration in relation to hardship arising from the National Health Service Act 1946 or the Act), for "the Arbitration Acts 1889 to 1934" substitute "Part I of the Arbitration Act 1996" and for "the said Acts" substitute "Part I of that Act".

Arbitration Act 1950 (c. 27)

10.—In section 36(1) of the Arbitration Act 1950 (effect of foreign awards enforceable under Part II of that Act) for "section 26 of this Act" substitute "section 66 of the Arbitration Act 1996".

Interpretation Act (Northern Ireland) 1954 (c. 33)

11.—In section 46(2) of the Interpretation Act (Northern Ireland) 1954 (miscellaneous definitions), for the definition of "arbitrator" substitute—"arbitrator" has the same meaning as in Part I of the Arbitration Act 1996;".

SCHEDULE 3

Agricultural Marketing Act 1958 (c. 47)

12.—In section 12(1) of the Agricultural Marketing Act 1958 (application of provisions of Arbitration Act 1950)—
- (*a*) for the words from the beginning to "shall apply" substitute "Sections 45 and 69 of the Arbitration Act 1996 (which relate to the determination by the court of questions of law) and section 66 of that Act (enforcement of awards) apply"; and
- (*b*) for "an arbitration" substitute "arbitral proceedings".

Carriage by Air Act 1961 (c. 27)

13.—(1) The Carriage by Air Act 1961 is amended as follows.
(2) In section 5(3) (time for bringing proceedings)—
- (*a*) for "an arbitration" in the first place where it occurs substitute "arbitral proceedings"; and
- (*b*) for the words from "and subsections (3) and (4)" to the end substitute "and the provisions of section 14 of the Arbitration Act 1996 apply to determine when such proceedings are commenced."

(3) In section 11(c) (application of section 5 to Scotland)—
- (*a*) for "subsections (3) and (4)" substitute "the provisions of section 14 of the Arbitration Act 1996"; and
- (*b*) for "an arbitration" substitute "arbitral proceedings".

Factories Act 1961 (c. 34)

14.—In the Factories Act 1961, for section 171 (application of Arbitration Act 1950), substitute—
Application of the Arbitration Act 1996
"71.—Part I of the Arbitration Act 1996 does not apply to proceedings under this Act except in so far as it may be applied by regulations made under this Act."

Clergy Pensions Measure 1961 (No. 3)

15.—In the Clergy Pensions Measure 1961, section 38(4) (determination of questions), for the words "The Arbitration Act 1950" substitute "Part I of the Arbitration Act 1996".

Transport Act 1962 (c. 46)

16.—(1) The Transport Act 1962 is amended as follows.
(2) In section 74(6)(*f*) (proceedings before referees in pension disputes), for the words "the Arbitration Act 1950" substitute "Part I of the Arbitration Act 1996".
(3) In section 81(7) (proceedings before referees in compensation disputes), for the words "the Arbitration Act 1950" substitute "Part I of the Arbitration Act 1996".
(4) In Schedule 7, Part IV (pensions), in paragraph 17(5) for the words "the Arbitration Act 1950" substitute "Part I of the Arbitration Act 1996".

Corn Rents Act 1963 (c. 14)

17.—In the Corn Rents Act 1963, section 1(5) (schemes for apportioning corn rents, etc.), for the words "the Arbitration Act 1950" substitute "Part I of the Arbitration Act 1996".

Plant Varieties and Seeds Act 1964 (c. 14)

18.—In section 10(6) of the Plant Varieties and Seeds Act 1964 (meaning of "arbitration agreement"), for "the meaning given by section 32 of the Arbitration Act 1950" substitute "the same meaning as in Part I of the Arbitration Act 1996".

Lands Tribunal and Compensation Act (Northern Ireland) 1964 (c. 29)

19.—In section 9 of the Lands Tribunal and Compensation Act (Northern Ireland) 1964 (proceedings of Lands Tribunal), in subsection (3) (where Tribunal acts as arbitrator) for "the Arbitration Act (Northern Ireland) 1937" subsitute "Part I of the Arbitration Act 1996".

Industrial and Provident Societies Act 1965 (c. 12)

20.—(1) Section 60 of the Industrial and Provident Societies Act 1965 is amended as follows.

(2) In subsection (8) (procedure for hearing disputes between society and member, etc.)—
- (*a*) in paragraph (*a*) for "the Arbitration Act 1950" substitute "Part I of the Arbitration Act 1996"; and
- (*b*) in paragraph (*b*) omit "by virtue of section 12 of the said Act of 1950".

(3) For subsection (9) substitute—

"(9) The court or registrar to whom any dispute is referred under subsections (2) to (7) may at the request of either party state a case on any question of law arising in the dispute for the opinion of the High Court or, as the case may be the Court of Session."

Carriage of Goods by Road Act 1965 (c. 37)

21.—In section 7(2) of the Carriage of Goods by Road Act 1965 (arbitrations: time at which deemed to commence), for paragraphs (a) and (b) substitute—

"(*a*) as respects England and Wales and Northern Ireland, the provisions of section 14(3) to (5) of the Arbitration Act 1996 (which determine the time at which an arbitration is commenced) apply."

Factories Act (Northern Ireland) 1965 (c. 20 (N.I.))

22.—In section 171 of the Factories Act (Northern Ireland) 1965 (application of Arbitration Act), for "The Arbitration Act (Northern Ireland) 1937" substitute "Part I of the Arbitration Act 1996".

SCHEDULE 3

Commonwealth Secretariat Act 1966 (c. 10)

23.—In section 1(3) of the Commonwealth Secretariat Act 1966 (contracts with Commonwealth Secretariat to be deemed to contain provision for arbitration), for "the Arbitration Act 1950 and the Arbitration Act (Northern Ireland) 1937" substitute "Part I of the Arbitration Act 1996".

Arbitration (International Investment Disputes) Act 1966 (c. 41)

24.—In the Arbitration (International Investment Disputes) Act 1966, for section 3 (application of Arbitration Act 1950 and other enactments) substitute—
Application of provisions of Arbitration Act 1996

"3.—(1) The Lord Chancellor may by order direct that any of the provisions contained in section 36 and 38 to 44 of the Arbitration Act 1996 provisions concerning the conduct of arbitral proceedings, etc.) shall apply to such proceedings pursuant to the Convention as are specified in the order with or without any modifications or exceptions specified in the order.

(2) Subject to subsection (1), the Arbitration Act 1996 shall not apply to proceedings pursuant to the Convention, but this subsection shall not be taken as affecting section 9 of that Act (stay of legal proceedings in respect of matter subject to arbitration).

(3) An order made under this section—
(a) may be varied or revoked by a subsequent order so made, and
(b) shall be contained in a statutory instrument."

Poultry Improvement Act (Northern Ireland) 1968 (c. 12 (N.I.))

25.—In paragraph 10(4) of the Schedule to the Poultry Improvement Act (Northern Ireland) 1968 (reference of disputes), for "The Arbitration Act (Northern Ireland) 1937" substitute "Part I of the Arbitration Act 1996".

Industrial and Provident Societies Act (Northern Ireland) 1969 (c. 24 (N.I.))

26.—(1) Section 69 of the Industrial and Provident Societies Act (Northern Ireland) 1969 (decision of disputes) is amended as follows.

(2) In subsection (7) (decision of disputes)—
(a) in the opening words, omit the words from "and without prejudice" to "1937";
(b) at the beginning of paragraph (a) insert "without prejudice to any powers exercisable by virtue of Part I of the Arbitration Act 1996,"; and
(c) in paragraph (b) omit "the registrar or" and "registrar or" and for the words from "as might have been granted by the High Court" to the end substitute "as might be granted by the registrar".

(3) For subsection (8) substitute—
"(8) The court or registrar to whom any dispute is referred under subsections (2) to (6) may at the request of either party state a case on any question of law arising in the dispute for the opinion of the High Court."

Health and Personal Social Services (Northern Ireland) Order 1972 (N.I. 14)

27.—In Article 105(6) of the Health and Personal Social Services (Northern Ireland) Order 1972 (arbitrations under the Order), for "the Arbitration Act (Northern Ireland) 1937" substitute "Part I of the Arbitration Act 1996".

Consumer Credit Act 1974 (c. 39)

28.—(1) Section 146 of the Consumer Credit Act 1974 is amended as follows.

(2) In subsection (2) (solicitor engaged in contentious business), for "section 86(1) of the Solicitors Act 1957" substitute "section 87(1) of the Solicitors Act 1974".

(3) In subsection (4) (solicitor in Northern Ireland engaged in contentious business), for the words from "business done" to "Administration of Estates (Northern Ireland) Order 1979" substitute "contentious business (as defined in Article 3(2) of the Solicitors (Northern Ireland) Order 1976".

Friendly Societies Act 1974 (c. 46)

29.—(1) The Friendly Societies Act 1974 is amended as follows.

(2) For section 78(1) (statement of case) substitute—

"(1) Any arbitrator, arbiter or umpire to whom a dispute falling within section 76 above is referred under the rules of a registered society or branch may at the request of either party state a case on any question of law arising in the dispute for the opinion of the High Court or, as the case may be, the Court of Session."

(3) In section 83(3) (procedure on objections to amalgamations etc. of friendly societies), for "the Arbitration Act 1950 or, in Northern Ireland, the Arbitration Act (Northern Ireland) 1937" substitute "Part I of the Arbitration Act 1996".

Industry Act 1975 (c. 68)

30. In Schedule 3 to the Industry Act (arbitration of disputes relating to vesting and compensation orders), in paragraph 14 (application of certain provisions of Arbitration Acts—
  (*a*) for "the Arbitration Act 1950 or, in Northern Ireland, the Arbitration Act (Northern Ireland) 1937" substitute "Part I of the Arbitration Act 1996", and
  (*b*) for "that Act" substitute "that Part".

Industrial Relations (Northern Ireland) Order 1976 (N.I. 16)

[…][2]

Aircraft and Shipbuilding Industries Act 1977 (c. 3)

32.—In Schedule 7 to the Aircraft and Shipbuilding Industries Act 1977 (procedure of Arbitration Tribunal), in paragraph 2—

---

[2] Repealed by The Industrial Tribunals (Northern Ireland) Order 1996, No. 1921, Sched. 3.

(a) for "the Arbitration Act 1950 or, in Northern Ireland, the Arbitration Act (Northern Ireland) 1937" substitute "Part I of the Arbitration Act 1996", and

(b) for "that Act" substitute "that Part".

Patents Act 1977 (c. 37)

33.—In section 130 of the Patents Act 1977 (interpretation), in subsection (8) (exclusion of Arbitration Act) for "The Arbitration Act 1950" substitute "Part I of the Arbitration Act 1996".

Judicature (Northern Ireland) Act 1978 (c. 23)

34.—(1) The Judicature (Northern Ireland) Act 1978 is amended as follows.

(2) In section 35(2) (restrictions on appeals to the Court of Appeal) paragraph (f), after insert—

"(fa) except as provided by Part I of the Arbitration Act 1996, from any decision of the High Court under that Part."

(3) In section 55(2) (rules of court) after paragraph (c) insert—

"(cc) providing for any prescribed part of the jurisdiction of the High Court in relation to the trial of any action involving matters of account to be exercised in the prescribed manner by a person agreed by the parties and for the remuneration of any such person;".

Health and Safety at Work (Northern Ireland) Order 1978 (N.I. 9)

35.—In Schedule 4 to the Health and Safety at Work (Northern Ireland) Order 1978 (licensing provisions), in paragraph 3, for "The Arbitration Act (Northern Ireland) 1937" substitute "Part I of the Arbitration Act 1996".

County Courts (Northern Ireland) Order 1980 (N.I. 3)

36.—(1) The County Courts (Northern Ireland) Order 1980 is amended as follows.

(2) In Article 30 (civil jurisdiction exercisable by district judge)—

(a) for paragraph (2) substitute—

"(2) Any order, decision or determination made by a district judge under this Article (other than one made in dealing with a claim by way of arbitration under paragraph (3)) shall be embodied in a decree which for all purposes (including the right of appeal under Part VI) shall have the like effect as a decree pronounced by a county court judge.";

(b) for paragraphs (4) and (5) substitute—

"(4) Where in any action to which paragraph (1) applies the claim is dealt with by way of arbitration under paragraph (3)—

(a) any award made by the district judge in dealing with the claim shall be embodied in a decree which for all purposes (except the right of appeal under Part VI) shall have the like effect as a decree pronounced by a county court judge;

(b) the district judge may, and shall if so required by the High Court, state for the determination of the High Court any question of law arising out of an award so made;

(c) except as provided by sub-paragraph (b) any award so made shall be final; and

(d) except as otherwise provided by county court rules, no costs shall be awarded in connection with the action."

(5) Subject to paragraph (4) county court rules may—

(a) apply any of the provisions of Part I of the Arbitration Act 1996 to arbitrations under paragraph (3) with such modifications as may be prescribed;

(b) prescribe the rules of evidence to be followed on any arbitration under paragraph (3) and, in particular, make provision with respect to the manner of taking and questioning evidence."

(5A) Except as provided by virtue of paragraph (5)(a), Part I of the Arbitration Act 1996 shall not apply to an arbitration under paragraph (3)."

(3) After Article 61 insert—

Appeals from decisions under Part I of Arbitration Act 1996

"61A.—(1) Article 61 does not apply to a decision of a county court judge made in the exercise of the jurisdiction conferred by Part I of the Arbitration Act 1996.

(2) Any party dissatisfied with a decision of the county court made in the exercise of the jurisdiction conferred by any of the following provisions of Part I of the Arbitration Act 1996, namely—

(a) section 32 (question as to substantive jurisdiction of arbitral tribunal);

(b) section 45 (question of law arising in course of arbitral proceedings);

(c) section 67 (challenging award of arbitral tribunal: substantive jurisdiction);

(d) section 68 (challenging award of arbitral tribunal: serious irregularity);

(e) section 69 (appeal on point of law),"

may, subject to the provisions of that Part, appeal from that decision to the Court of Appeal.

(3) Any party dissatisfied with any decision of a county court made in the exercise of the jurisdiction conferred by any other provision of Part I of the Arbitration Act 1996 may, subject to the provisions of that Part, appeal from that decision to the High Court.

(4) The decision of the Court of Appeal on an appeal under paragraph (2) shall be final."

SCHEDULE 3

Supreme Court Act 1981 (c. 54)

37.—(1) The Supreme Court Act 1981 is amended as follows.

(2) In section 18(1) (restrictions on appeals to the Court of Appeal), for paragraph (g) substitute—

"(g) except as provided by Part I of the Arbitration Act 1996, from any decision of the High Court under that Part;".

(3) In section 151 (interpretation, etc.), in the definition of "arbitration agreement", for "the Arbitration Act 1950 by virtue of section 32 of that Act;" substitute "Part I of the Arbitration Act 1996;".

Merchant Shipping (Liner Conferences) Act 1982 (c. 37)

38.—In section 7(5) of the Merchant Shipping (Liner Conferences) Act 1982 (stay of legal proceedings), for the words from "section 4(1)" to the end substitute "section 9 of the Arbitration Act 1996 (which also provides for the staying of legal proceedings).".

Agricultural Marketing (Northern Ireland) Order 1982 (N.I. 12)

39.—In Article 14 of the Agricultural Marketing (Northern Ireland) Order 1982 (application of provisions of Arbitration Act (Northern Ireland) 1937—
   (a) for the words from the beginning to "shall apply" substitute "Section 45 and 69 of the Arbitration Act 1996 (which relate to the determination by the court of questions of law) and section 66 of that Act (enforcement of awards)" apply; and
   (b) for "an arbitration" substitute "arbitral proceedings".

Mental Health Act 1983 (c. 20)

40.—In section 78 of the Mental Health Act 1983 (procedure of Mental Health Review Tribunals), in subsection (9) for "The Arbitration Act 1950" substitute "Part I of the Arbitration Act 1996".

Registered Homes Act 1984 (c. 23)

41.—In section 43 of the Registered Homes Act 1984 (procedure of Registered Homes Tribunals), in subsection (3) for "The Arbitration Act 1950" substitute "Part I of the Arbitration Act 1996".

Housing Act 1985 (c. 68)

42.—In section 47(3) of the Housing Act 1985 (agreement as to determination of matters relating to service charges) for "section 32 of the Arbitration Act 1950" substitute "Part I of the Arbitration Act 1996".

Landlord and Tenant Act 1985 (c. 70)

[...]³

---

³ Repealed by the Housing Act 1996, c. 52, Sched. 19, Pt III.

Credit Unions (Northern Ireland) Order 1985 (N.I. 12)

44.—(1) Article 72 of the Credit Unions (Northern Ireland) Order 1985 (decision of disputes) is amended as follows.

(2) In paragraph (7)—
  (a) in the opening words, omit the words from "and without prejudice" to "1937";
  (b) at the beginning of sub-paragraph (a) insert "without prejudice to any powers exercisable by virtue of Part I of the Arbitration Act 1996,"; and
  (c) in sub-paragraph (b) omit "the registrar or" and "registrar or" and for the words from "as might have been granted by the High Court" to the end substitute "as might be granted by the registrar".

(3) For paragraph (8) substitute—

"(8) The court or registrar to whom any dispute is referred under paragraphs (2) to (6) may at the request of either party state a case on any question of law arising in the dispute for the opinion of the High Court."

Agricultural Holdings Act 1986 (c. 5)

45.—In section 84(1) of the Agricultural Holdings Act 1986 (provisions relating to arbitration), for "the Arbitration Act 1950" substitute "Part I of the Arbitration Act 1996".

Insolvency Act 1986 (c. 45)

46.—In the Insolvency Act 1986, after section 349 insert—

Arbitration agreements to which bankrupt is party

"349A.—(1) This section applies where a bankrupt had become party to a contract containing an arbitration agreement before the commencement of his bankruptcy.

(2) If the trustee in bankruptcy adopts the contract, the arbitration agreement is enforceable by or against the trustee in relation to matters arising from or connected with the contract.

(3) If the trustee in bankruptcy does not adopt the contract and a matter to which the arbitration agreement applies requires to be determined in connection with or for the purposes of the bankruptcy proceedings—
  (a) the trustee with the consent of the creditors' committee, or
  (b) any other party to the agreement,

may apply to the court which may, if it thinks fit in all the circumstances of the case, order that the matter be referred to arbitration in accordance with the arbitration agreement.

(4) In this section—"arbitration agreement" has the same meaning as in Part I of the Arbitration Act 1996; and "the court" means the court which has jurisdiction in the bankruptcy proceedings."

Building Societies Act 1986 (c. 53)

47.—In Part II of Schedule 14 to the Building Societies Act 1986 (settlement of disputes: arbitration), in paragraph 5(6) for "the Arbitration Act 1950 and the

SCHEDULE 3

Arbitration Act 1979 or, in Northern Ireland, the Arbitration Act (Northern Ireland) 1937" substitute "Part I of the Arbitration Act 1996".

Mental Health (Northern Ireland) Order 1986 (N.I. 4)

48.—In Article 83 of the Mental Health (Northern Ireland) Order 1986 (procedure of Mental Health Review Tribunal), in paragraph (8) for "The Arbitration Act (Northern Ireland) 1937" substitute "Part I of the Arbitration Act 1996".

Multilateral Investment Guarantee Agency Act 1988 (c. 8)

49.—For section 6 of the Multilateral Investment Guarantee Agency Act 1988 (application of Arbitration Act substitute—
Application of Arbitration Act
  "6.—(1) The Lord Chancellor may by order made by statutory instrument direct that any of the provisions of sections 36 and 38 to 44 of the Arbitration Act 1996 (provisions in relation to the conduct of the arbitral proceedings, etc.) apply, with such modifications or exceptions as are specified in the order, to such arbitration proceedings pursuant to Annex II to the Convention as are specified in the order.
  (2) Except as provided by an order under subsection (1) above, no provision of Part I of the Arbitration Act 1996 other than section 9 (stay of legal proceedings) applies to any such proceedings."

Copyright, Designs and Patents Act 1988 (c. 48)

50.—In section 150 of the Copyright, Designs and Patents Act 1988 (Lord Chancellor's power to make rules for Copyright Tribunal), for subsection (2) substitute—
  "(2) The rules may apply in relation to the Tribunal, as respects proceedings in England and Wales or Northern Ireland, any of the provisions of Part I of the Arbitration Act 1996."

Fair Employment (Northern Ireland) Act 1989 (c. 32)

51.—In the Fair Employment (Northern Ireland) Act 1989, section 5(7) (procedure of Fair Employment Tribunal), for "The Arbitration Act (Northern Ireland) 1937" substitute "Part I of the Arbitration Act 1996".

Limitation (Northern Ireland) Order 1989 (N.I. 11)

52.—In Article 2(2) of the Limitation (Northern Ireland) Order 1989 (interpretation), in the definition of "arbitration agreement", for "the Arbitration Act (Northern Ireland) 1937" substitute "Part I of the Arbitration Act 1996".

Insolvency (Northern Ireland) Order 1989 (N.I. 19)

53.—In the Insolvency (Northern Ireland) Order 1989, after Article 320 insert—
  "*Arbitration agreements to which bankrupt is party*

320A.—(1) This Article applies where a bankrupt had become party to a contract containing an arbitration agreement before the commencement of his bankruptcy.

(2) If the trustee in bankruptcy adopts the contract, the arbitration agreement is enforceable by or against the trustee in relation to matters arising from or connected with the contract.

(3) If the trustee in bankruptcy does not adopt the contract and a matter to which the arbitration agreement applies requires to be determined in connection with or for the purposes of the bankruptcy proceedings—

(*a*) the trustee with the consent of the creditors' committee, or

(*b*) any other party to the agreement."

may apply to the court which may, if it thinks fit in all the circumstances of the case, order that the matter be referred to arbitration in accordance with the arbitration agreement.

(4) In this Article—"arbitration agreement" has the same meaning as in Part I of the Arbitration Act 1996; and "the court" means the court which has jurisdiction in the bankruptcy proceedings."

Social Security Administration Act 1992 (c. 5)

54.—In section 59 of the Social Security Administration Act 1992 (procedure for inquiries, etc.), in subsection (7), for "The Arbitration Act 1950" substitute "Part I of the Arbitration Act 1996".

Social Security Administration (Northern Ireland) Act 1992 (c. 8)

55.—In section 57 of the Social Security Administration (Northern Ireland) Act 1992 (procedure for inquiries, etc.), in subsection (6) for "the Arbitration Act (Northern Ireland) 1937" substitute "Part I of the Arbitration Act 1996".

Trade Union and Labour Relations (Consolidation) Act 1992 (c. 52)

56.—In sections 212(5) and 263(6) of the Trade Union and Labour Relations (Consolidation) Act 1992 (application of Arbitration Act) for "the Arbitration Act 1950" substitute "Part I of the Arbitration Act 1996".

Industrial Relations (Northern Ireland) Order 1992 (N.I. 5)

57.—In Articles 84(9) and 92(5) of the Industrial Relations (Northern Ireland) Order 1992 (application of Arbitration Act) for "The Arbitration Act (Northern Ireland) 1937" substitute "Part I of the Arbitration Act 1996".

Registered Homes (Northern Ireland) Order 1992 (N.I. 20)

58.—In Article 33(3) of the Registered Homes (Northern Ireland) Order 1992 (procedure of Registered Homes Tribunal) for "The Arbitration Act (Northern Ireland) 1937" substitute "Part I of the Arbitration Act 1996".

SCHEDULE 3

Education Act 1993 (c. 35)

[…]⁴

Roads (Northern Ireland) Order 1993 (N.I. 15)

60.—(1) The Roads (Northern Ireland) Order 1993 is amended as follows.

(2) In Article 131 (application of Arbitration Act) for "the Arbitration Act (Northern Ireland) 1937" substitute "Part I of the Arbitration Act 1996".

(3) In Schedule 4 (disputes), in paragraph 3(2) for "the Arbitration Act (Northern Ireland) 1937" substitute "Part I of the Arbitration Act 1996".

Merchant Shipping Act 1995 (c. 21)

61.—In Part II of Schedule 6 to the Merchant Shipping Act 1995 (provisions having effect in connection with Convention Relating to the Carriage of Passengers and Their Luggage by Sea), for paragraph 7 substitute—

> "7. Article 16 shall apply to arbitral proceedings as it applies to an action; and, as respects England and Wales and Northern Ireland, the provisions of section 14 of the Arbitration Act 1996 apply to determine for the purposes of that Article when an arbitration is commenced."

Industrial Tribunals Act 1996 (c. 17)

62.—In section 6(2) of the Industrial Tribunals Act 1996 (procedure of industrial tribunals), for "The Arbitration Act 1950" substitute "Part I of the Arbitration Act 1996".

SCHEDULE 4

Section 107(2)

REPEALS

Chapter	Short title	Extent of repeal
1892 c. 43.	Military Lands Act 1892.	In section 21(b), the words "under the Arbitration Act 1889".
1922 c. 51.	Allotments Act 1922.	In section 21(3), the words "under the Arbitration Act 1889".
1937 c. 8 (N.I.).	Arbitration Act (Northern Ireland) 1937.	The whole Act.
1949 c. 54.	Wireless Telegraphy Act 1949.	In Schedule 2, paragraph 3(3).
1949 c. 97.	National Parks and Access to the Countryside Act 1949.	In section 18(4), the words from "Without prejudice" to "England or Wales".

---

⁴ Repealed by the Education Act 1996, c. 56, Sched. 38, Pt I.

1950 c. 27.	Arbitration Act 1950.	Part I. Section 42(3).
1958 c. 47.	Agricultural Marketing Act 1958.	Section 53(8).
1962 c. 46.	Transport Act 1962.	In Schedule 11, Part II, paragraph 7.
1964 c. 14.	Plant Varieties and Seeds Act 1964.	In section 10(4) the words from "or in section 9" to "three arbitrators)". Section 39(3)(*b*)(i).
1964 c. 29 (N.I.).	Lands Tribunal and Compensation Act (Northern Ireland) 1964.	In section 9(3) the words from "so, however, that" to the end.
1965 c. 12.	Industrial and Provident Societies Act 1965.	In section 60(8)(*b*), the words "by virtue of section 12 of the said Act of 1950".
1965 c. 37.	Carriage of Goods by Road Act 1965.	Section 7(2)(*b*).
1965 c. 13 (N.I.).	New Towns Act (Northern Ireland) 1965.	In section 27(2), the words from "under and in accordance with" to the end.
1969 c. 24 (N.I.).	Industrial and Provident Societies Act (Northern Ireland) 1969.	In section 69(7)—(*a*) in the opening words, the words from "and without prejudice" to "1937"; (*b*) in paragraph (b), the words "the registrar or" and "registrar or".
1970 c. 31.	Administration of Justice Act 1970.	Section 4. Schedule 3.
1973 c. 41.	Fair Trading Act 1973.	Section 33(2)(*d*).
1973 N.I. 1.	Drainage (Northern Ireland) Order 1973.	In Article 15(4), the words from "under and in accordance" to the end. Article 40(4). In Schedule 7, in paragraph 9(2), the words from "under and in accordance" to the end.
1974 c. 47.	Solicitors Act 1974.	In section 87(1), in the definition of "contentious business", the words "appointed under the Arbitration Act 1950".
1975 c. 3.	Arbitration Act 1975.	The whole Act.

SCHEDULE 4

1975 c. 74.	Petroleum and Submarine Pipe-Lines Act 1975.	In Part II of Schedule 2—(*a*) in model clause 40(2), the words "in accordance with the Arbitration Act 1950"; (*b*) in model clause 40(2B), the words "in accordance with the Arbitration Act (Northern Ireland) 1937". In Part II of Schedule 3, in model clause 38(2), the words "in accordance with the Arbitration Act 1950".
1976 N.I. 12.	Solicitors (Northern Ireland) Order 1976.	In Article 3(2), in the entry "contentious business", the words "appointed under the Arbitration Act (Northern Ireland) 1937". Article 71H(3).
1977 c. 37.	Patents Act 1977.	In section 52(4) the words "section 21 of the Arbitration Act 1950 or, as the case may be, section 22 of the Arbitration Act (Northern Ireland) 1937 (statement of cases by arbitrators); but". Section 131(*e*).
1977 c. 38.	Administration of Justice Act 1977.	Section 17(2).
1978 c. 23.	Judicature (Northern Ireland) Act 1978.	In section 35(2), paragraph (*g*) (y). In Schedule 5, the amendment to the Arbitration Act 1950.
1979 c. 42.	Arbitration Act 1979.	The whole Act.
1980 c. 58.	Limitation Act 1980.	Section 34.
1980 N.I. 3.	County Courts (Northern Ireland) Order 1980.	Article 31(3).
1981 c. 54.	Supreme Court Act 1981.	Section 148.
1982 c. 27.	Civil Jurisdiction and Judgments Act 1982.	Section 25(3)(*c*) and (5). In section 26—(*a*) in subsection (1), the words "to arbitration or"; (*b*) in subsection (1)(*a*)(i), the words "arbitration or"; (*c*) in subsection (2), the words "arbitration or".
1982 c. 53.	Administration of Justice Act 1982.	Section 15(6). In Schedule 1, Part IV.
1984 c. 5.	Merchant Shipping Act 1984.	Section 4(8).
1984 c. 12.	Telecommunications Act 1984.	Schedule 2, paragraph 13(8).

1984 c. 16.	Foreign Limitation Periods Act 1984.	Section 5.
1984 c. 28.	County Courts Act 1984.	In Schedule 2, paragraph 70.
1985 c. 61.	Administration of Justice Act 1985.	Section 58. In Schedule 9, paragraph 15.
1985 c. 68.	Housing Act 1985.	In Schedule 18, in paragraph 6(2) the words from "and the Arbitration Act 1950" to the end.
1985 N.I. 12.	Credit Unions (Northern Ireland) Order 1985.	In Article 72(7)—(*a*) in the opening words, the words from "and without prejudice" to "1937"; (*b*) in sub-paragraph (*b*), the words "the registrar or" and "registrar or".
1986 c. 45.	Insolvency Act 1986.	In Schedule 14, the entry relating to the Arbitration Act 1950.
1988 c. 8.	Multilateral Investment Guarantee Agency Act 1988.	Section 8(3).
1988 c. 21.	Consumer Arbitration Agreements Act 1988.	The whole Act.
1989 N.I. 11.	Limitation (Northern Ireland) Order 1989.	Article 72. In Schedule 3, paragraph 1.
1989 N.I. 19.	Insolvency (Northern Ireland) Order 1989	In Part II of Schedule 9, paragraph 66.
1990 c. 41.	Courts and Legal Services Act 1990.	Sections 99 and 101 to 103.
1991 N.I. 7.	Food Safety (Northern Ireland) Order 1991.	In Articles 8(8) and 11(10) the words from "and the provisions" to the end.
1992 c. 40.	Friendly Societies Act 1992	In Schedule 16, paragraph 30(1).
1995 c. 8.	Agricultural Tenancies Act 1995.	Section 28(4).
1995 c. 21.	Merchant Shipping Act 1995.	Section 96(10) Section 264(9).
1995 c. 42.	Private International Law (Miscellaneous Provisions) Act 1995.	Section 3.

TABLE OF DERIVATIONS

This table was passed as part of Schedule 15, Part II of the Agriculture Holdings Act 1986.

TABLE OF DERIVATIONS A.175

Note: The following abbreviations are used in this Table:—

1948	=	The Agricultural Holdings Act 1948 (11 & 12 Geo. 6. c. 63)
1949	=	The Agriculture (Miscellaneous Provisions) Act 1949 (12 & 13 Geo. 6. c. 37)
1958	=	The Agriculture Act 1958 (6 & 7 Eliz. 2. c. 71)
1963	=	The Agriculture (Miscellaneous Provisions) Act 1963 (c. 11)
1968	=	The Agriculture (Miscellaneous Provisions) Act 1968 (c. 34)
1970	=	The Agriculture Act 1970 (c. 40)
1972	=	The Agriculture (Miscellaneous Provisions) Act 1972 (c. 62)
1976	=	The Agriculture (Miscellaneous Provisions) Act 1976 (c. 55)
1977	=	The Agricultural Holdings (Notices to Quit) Act 1977 (c. 12)
1984	=	The Agricultural Holdings Act 1984 (c. 41)
S.I. 1951/2168	=	The Agricultural Holdings Act (Variation of Fourth Schedule) Order 1951 (S.I. 1951/2168)
S.I. 1955/554	=	The Transfer of Functions (Ministry of Food) Order 1955 (S.I. 1955/554)
S.I. 1978/272	=	The Transfer of Functions (Wales) (No. 1) Order 1978 (S.I. 1978/272)
S.I. 1978/447	=	The Agricultural Holdings Act 1948 (Amendment) Regulations 1978 (S.I. 1978/447)
S.I. 1978/742	=	The Agricultural Holdings Act 1948 (Variation of Fourth Schedule) Order 1978 (S.I. 1978/742)
S.I. 1985/1947	=	The Agricultural Holdings Act 1948 (Variation of Fourth Schedule) Order 1985 (S.I. 1985/1947)
R (followed by a number)	=	The recommendation set out in the paragraph of that number in the Appendix to the Report of the Law Commission on this Act (Cmnd. 9665).

Provision	Derivation
1(1)	1948 s. 1(1); 1984 Sch. 3 para. 1(2).
(2)(3)	1948 s. 1(1A)(1B); 1984 Sch. 3 para. 1(3).
(4)	1948 s. 1(2); 1976 s. 18(2); 1984 Sch. 1 para. 1, Sch. 2 para. 1(2).
(5)	1948 s. 94(1).
2	1948 s.2; R.1.
3(1)	1948 s. 3(1); 1984 Sch. 3 para. 2(1)(*a*).
(2)	1948 s. 3(2).

TABLE OF DERIVATIONS

(3)	1948 s. 3(3).
(4)	1948 s. 3(1).
4(1)	1948 s. 3A(1)(2)(3); 1984 Sch. 3 para. 2(2).
(2)	1948 s. 3A(2)(3); 1984 Sch. 3 para. 2(2).
(3)	1948 s. 3A(4); 1984 Sch. 3 para. 2(2).
(4)	1948 s. 3A(2)(3); 1984 Sch. 3 para. 2(2).
5(1)	1948 s. 3(4); 1984 Sch. 3 para. 2(1)(*b*).
(2)(3)	1948 s. 3B; 1984 Sch. 3 para. 2(2).
6(1)	1948 s. 5(1); 1984 Sch. 3 para. 3(2).
(2)	1948 s. 5(2)(3).
(3)	1948 s. 7(3).
(4)	1948 s. 7(5); 1984 Sch. 3 para. 4.
(5)	1948 s. 5(4)(6); 1984 Sch. 3 para. 3(3).
(6)	1948 s. 5(5); 1984 Sch. 3 para. 3(3).
7(1)	1948 s. 6(1).
(2)	1972 s. 15(2).
(3)	1948 s. 6(1).
8(1)(2)	1948 s. 6(2).
(3)	1948 s. 6(3).
(4)	1948 s. 7(3).
(5)	1948 s. 7(5); 1984 Sch. 3 para. 4.
(6)	1948 s. 6(2).
9(1)(2)	1948 s. 7(1).
(3)	1948 s. 7(2).
(4)	1948 s. 7(4).
10(1)	1948 s. 13(1)(4A); 1984 Sch. 3 para. 6(2)(3).
(2)	1948 s. 13(1)(5)(*b*).
(3) to (5)	1948 s. 13(2) to (4).
(6)	1948 s. 13(4B); 1984 Sch. 3 para. 6(3).
(7)	1948 s. 13(5)(*a*).
(8)	1948 s. 13(4A); 1984 Sch. 3 para. 6(3).
11(1)	1958 s. 4(1).
(2)	1958 s. 4(1); 1984 Sch. 3 para. 30.
(3) to (7)	1958 s. 4(2) to (4).
(8)	1958 s. 4(7).
12(1)(2)	1948 s. 8(1)(2); 1984 s. 1.
(3)	1948 s. 8(13); 1984 ss. 1, 8(2).
(4)	1948 s. 8A(2); 1984 s. 1.
(5)	Introduces Schedule 2.
13(1)	1948 s. 9(1).
(2)	1948 s. 9(1); 1958 s. 4(5); 1984 Sch. 3 para. 5(2)(*b*); Housing Act 1985 (c. 68) s. 231(1).
(3)	1948 s. 9(2); 1958 s. 4(5); 1984 Sch. 3 para. 5(3); Housing Act 1985 (c. 68) s. 231(1).
(4)	1948 s. 9(1); 1958 s. 4(5); 1984 Sch. 3 para. 5(2)(*c*); Housing Act 1985 (c. 68) s. 231(1)(2).
(5)(6)	1958 s. 4(5)(7).

TABLE OF DERIVATIONS

(7)	1948 s. 9(4).
(8)	1948 s. 9(1).
14(1)(2)	1948 s. 10(1); 1958 Sch. 1 Pt. I para. 6.
(3)	1948 s. 10(2)(*a*); 1958 Sch. 1 Pt. I para. 6.
(4)(5)	1948 s. 10(2)(*b*); 1958 Sch. 1 Pt. I para. 6.
15(1)	1948 s. 11(1).
(2)	1948 s. 11(4)(*a*)(*b*).
(3)	1948 s. 12(1).
(4)(5)	1948 s. 11(1)(2).
(6)	1948 s. 11(3); 1958 Sch. 1 Pt. I para. 7.
(7)	1948 ss. 11(5), 12(2).
16	1948 s. 18.
17	1948 s. 22.
18(1)	1948 s. 20(1).
(2)(3)(4)	1948 s. 19(1)(2)(3).
(5)	1948 ss. 19(1)(4), 20(2).
19(1)	1948 s. 21(1)(2).
(2)	1948 s. 21(3); Courts Act 1971 (c. 23) Sch. 9 Pt. I.
(3)	1948 s. 21(4).
20(1)(2)(3)	1948 s. 14(1); 1984 Sch. 3 para. 7(2).
(4)	1948 s. 14(2).
(5)	1948 s. 14(3); 1984 Sch. 3 para. 7(3).
21(1)(2)(3)	1948 s. 4(1)(2)(3).
22(1)	1948 s. 16(1); 1984 Sch. 3 para. 8(*a*).
(2)	1948 s. 16(2); 1984 s. 8(1)(2), Sch. 3 para. 8(*b*).
(3)	1948 s. 16(3).
(4)	1948 s. 8(3)(4).
(5)	1984 s. 8(5).
23	1948 s. 17.
24	1948 s. 15.
25(1)	1977 s. 1(1).
(2)	1977 s. 1(2); 1984 Sch. 3 para. 36.
(3) to (5)	1977 s. 1(5) to (7); 1984 s. 5.
26(1)	1977 s. 2(1).
(2)	1977 ss. 2(2), 12(1).
(3)	Introduces Schedule 3.
27(1) to (5)	1977 s. 3.
(6)	1977 s. 6(1).
(7)	1977 s. 6(3).
(8)	1977 s. 6(2).
(9)	1977 s. 6(4).
28(1)	1977 s. 4(1).
(2)	1977 s. 4(2)(3).
(3)	1977 s. 4(2).
(4)	1977 s. 4(2)(3).
(5)	1977 s. 4(4), 1984 s. 7.
(6)	1977 s. 4(5).

TABLE OF DERIVATIONS

29	Introduces Schedule 4.
30	Introduces Schedule 5.
31(1)	1977 s. 8(1).
(2)	1977 s. 8(2); 1984 Sch. 3 para. 39.
32	1977 s. 9.
33(1)	1977 s. 10(1); 1984 Sch. 3 para. 40(*a*).
(2)	1977 s. 10(1A); 1984 Sch. 3 para. 40(*b*).
(3)	1977 s. 10(2); 1984 Sch. 3 para. 40(*c*).
34(1)	1984 s. 2(1)(2), Sch. 2 paras. 1(1)(*a*), 10(1)(*a*).
(2)	1984 s. 2(3).
35(1)	1976 s. 18(1); 1984 s. 2(1)(2), Sch. 1 para. 5(1).
(2)	1976 s. 18(1)(2); 1984 Sch. 1 para. 1.
36(1)	1976 ss. 18(1), 20(1).
(2)	1976 s. 18(4)(*d*).
(3)	1976 s. 18(2).
(4)	1976 s. 18(2); 1984 s. 3(2)(*b*).
(5)	Introduces Schedule 6.
37(1)	1976 s. 18(4)(*e*); 1984 Sch. 1 para. 2(5).
(2)(3)	1976 s. 18(5); 1984 Sch. 1 para. 2(7).
(4)(5)	1976 s. 18(5A); 1984 Sch. 1 para. 2(7).
(6)	1984 Sch. 2 para. 10(1)(*b*), (2).
(7)	1984 Sch. 5 para. 2(2)(*a*).
(8)	1984 Sch. 5 para. 2(2)(*b*).
(9)	1976 s. 18(4)(*e*), (5); 1984 Sch. 1 para. 2(5), (7).
38(1)	1976 s.18(4)(*a*); 1977 Sch. 1 para. 7(2)(*b*); 1984 Sch. 1 para. 2(2).
(2)	1976 s. 18(4)(*b*); 1977 Sch. 1 para. 7(2)(*c*); 1984 Sch. 3 para. 34.
(3)	1976 s. 18(4)(*c*); 1977 Sch. 1 para. 7(2)(*d*); 1984 Sch. 1 para. 2(3).
(4)	1976 s. 18(4)(*f*); 1984 Sch. 1 para. 2(6).
(5)	1976 s. 18(4)(*g*).
39(1)	1976 ss. 18(2), 20(1).
(2)	1976 s. 20(2); 1984 Sch. 1 para. 4.
(3)	1976 s. 20(3).
(4)	1976 s. 20(4).
(5)	1976 s. 20(5); 1984 Sch. 1 para. 3(3)(*a*).
(6)	1976 s. 20(6); 1984 Sch. 1 para. 3(3)(*a*).
(7) to (9)	1976 s. 20(7) to (9).
(10)	1976 s. 20(9A); 1984 Sch. 1 para. 3(3)(*b*).
40(1) to (5)	1976 s. 20(10) to (14).
41	1976 ss. 18(2), 21.
42	1976 s. 20(15), 1984 Sch. 1 para. 5(2).
43	1976 s. 19; 1977 Sch. 1 para. 7(3); 1984 s. 6(9), Sch. 1 para. 3(2).
44(1)	1976 s. 22(1).

TABLE OF DERIVATIONS

(2)	1976 s. 22(2); 1977 Sch. 1 para. 7(4); 1984 Sch. 1 para. 3(4)(*a*).
(3)	1976 s. 22(3).
(4)	1976 s. 22(4); 1984 Sch. 1 para. 3(4)(*a*).
(5)	1976 s. 22(5); 1984 Sch. 1 para. 3(4)(*b*).
(6)	1976 s. 22(6); 1984 Sch. 1 para. 6.
(7)	1976 s. 22(7); 1984 Sch. 1 para. 6.
45(1)	1976 s. 23(1).
(2) to (4)	1976 s. 23(1A); 1984 s. 3(1).
(5) to (8)	1976 s. 23(5) to (8).
46(1)	1976 s. 23(2); 1977 Sch. 1 para. 7(5); 1984 Sch. 1 para. 7(1).
(2)	1976 s. 23(2A); 1984 Sch. 1 para. 7(2).
(3)	1976 s. 23(9); 1984 Sch. 1 para. 3(5).
47(1)	1976 s. 23(1).
(2)	1976 s. 23(3).
(3)	1976 s. 23(4).
48(1)	1976 s. 24(1).
(2)	1976 s. 24(2); 1984 Sch. 1 paras. 3(6), 7(3).
(3)(4)	1976 s. 24(3).
(5)	1976 s. 24(4)(*a*).
(6)	1976 s. 24(4)(*b*).
(7)	1976 s. 24(4)(*c*).
(8)	1976 s. 24(5).
(9)	1976 s. 24(6); 1984 Sch. 3 para. 35.
(10)	1976 s. 24(7).
(11)	1976 s. 24(4).
(12)	1976 s. 24(8).
49(1)(2)	1984 Sch. 2 para. 1(1)(2).
(3)	1984 Sch. 2 para. 1(2), 2(2).
50(1)	1984 Sch. 2 paras. 1(1), 5(1).
(2)(3)	1984 Sch. 2 para. 1(2).
(4)	Introduces Schedule 6.
51(1)	1984 Sch. 2 para. 2(1)(*a*)(*b*)(*c*)(*f*)(*g*), (4).
(2)	1984 Sch. 2 para. 2(1)(*d*).
(3)	1984 Sch. 2 para. 2(1)(*e*), (3).
(4)	1984 Sch. 2 para. 2(5).
(5)(6)	1984 Sch. 2 para. 2(6).
52(1)(2)	1984 Sch. 2 para. 3(1)(2).
(3)(4)	1984 Sch. 2 para. 3(3).
(5)	1984 Sch. 2 para. 3(4).
53(1)	1984 Sch. 2 para. 5(1).
(2)	1984 Sch. 2 para. 1(2).
(3) to (11)	1984 Sch. 2 para. 5(2) to (10).
54(1)(2)	1984 Sch. 2 para. 4.
(3)	1984 Sch. 2 para. 1(2).
55(1)	1984 Sch. 2 paras. 6(1).
(2) to (4)	1984 Sch. 2 para. 6(2).

TABLE OF DERIVATIONS

(5) to (8)	1984 Sch. 2 para. 6(4) to (7).
56(1)	1984 Sch. 2 para. 6(1).
(2)	1984 Sch. 2 para. 6(3).
(3)(4)	1984 Sch. 2 para. 7(1)(2).
57	1984 Sch. 2 para. 8.
58	1984 Sch. 2 para. 9.
59	Index of definitions.
60(1)(2)	1948 s. 34(1); 1968 s. 9(1); 1977 Sch. 1 para. 1(3)(*a*).
(3)	1948 s. 34(2)(*a*)(*d*).
(4)	1968 s. 9(2).
(5)	1948 s. 34(2).
(6)	1948 s. 34(2)(*b*)(*c*).
(7)	1948 s. 34(5); 1968 s. 9(1).
61(1)	1948 s. 34(1); 1968 s. 9(1); 1977 Sch. 1 para. 1(3)(*b*).
(2)	1968 s. 10(1)(*d*)(*e*); 1977 Sch. 1 para. 5; 1984 Sch. 3 para. 32(*b*).
(3)(4)	1968 s. 10(1)(*b*)(*c*), (2), (8); 1977 Sch. 1 para. 5; 1984 Sch. 3 para. 32(1)(*a*).
(5)	1968 s. 10(2); 1977 Sch. 1 para. 5.
(6)	1948 s. 34(1); 1968 s. 10(8).
62(1)(2)	1968 s. 15(2).
(3)	1968 S. 15(5).
63(1)	1948 s. 34(2A); 1968 s. 9(1); 1984 Sch. 3 para. 9(2).
(2)	1948 s. 34(3); 1968 ss. 10(5), 15(4).
(3)	1948 s. 34(4); 1968 s. 9(1); 1977 Sch. 1 para. 1(3)(*c*); 1984 Sch. 3 para. 9(3)(*a*)(*b*).
(4)	1948 s. 34(4); 1984 Sch. 3 para. 9(3)(*c*).
64(1)	1948 ss. 46(1), 47(1).
(2)	1948 s. 46(2).
(3)	1948 s. 46(1).
(4)	1948 s. 35(1).
65(1)	1948 ss. 46(1), 47(1).
(2)	1948 s. 47(1)(*b*).
(3)	1948 s. 46(1).
66(1)	1948 s. 48.
(2)	1948 s. 51(1).
(3)	1948 s. 51(3).
(4)	1948 s. 51(2).
(5)	1948 s. 53; 1984 Sch. 3 para. 11.
67(1)	1948 s. 49(1).
(2)	1948 s. 49(1)(2).
(3) to (6)	1948 s. 50(1) to (4); 1958 Sch. 1 Pt. I para. 14.
(7)	1948 s. 50(3); 1958 Sch. 1 Pt. I para. 15.
68(1)	1948 s. 52.
(2)	1958 s. 4(6); R.2.
(3)(4)	Hill Farming Act 1946 (c. 73) s. 9(2)(4); 1948 Sch. 7 para. 4.

TABLE OF DERIVATIONS

(5)	Housing Act 1985 (c. 68) s. 231(3)(4).
69(1)	1948 s. 54.
(2)(3)	1948 s. 55(1)(2).
70(1)	1948 s. 56(1).
(2)(3)	1948 s. 56(1); 1984 Sch. 3 para. 12.
(4)(5)	1948 s. 56(2)(3).
71(1)	1948 s. 57(1).
(2)	1948 s. 57(2); 1984 Sch. 3 para. 13(*a*).
(3)(4)	1948 s. 57(3).
(5)	1948 s. 57(4); 1984 Sch. 3 para. 13(*b*).
72	1948 s. 58.
73	1958 s. 59.
74(1)	1948 s. 60(1); 1968 s. 9(1)(2); 1977 Sch. 1 para. 1(5); 1984 Sch. 3 para. 14(*a*).
(2)	1948 s. 60(1); 1968 ss. 9(1)(2), 15(2).
(3)	1948 s. 60(2); 1968 s. 9(1A); 1984 Sch. 3 paras. 14(*b*), 31.
(4)	1948 s. 60(3); 1968 s. 17(2); 1984 Sch. 3 paras. 14(*b*), 33.
75	1948 s. 61; 1968 ss. 10(5), 15(4); 1984 Sch. 3 para. 15.
76(1)	1948 s. 63(1); 1958 Sch. 1 Pt. I para. 16; S.I. 1978/447 reg. 2(2).
(2)	1948 s. 63(1).
(3)	1948 s. 63(2).
77	1948 s. 64.
78(1)(2)	1948 s. 65(1); 1968 ss. 10(4), 15(4).
(3)	1948 s. 65(2).
79	1948 s. 67(1)(3)(4); 1984 Sch. 3 paras. 16 and 27(*b*).
80(1)(2)	1948 s. 68(1); 1958 Sch. 1 Pt. I para. 17.
(3)(4)	1948 s. 68(2); 1984 Sch. 3 para. 17(*a*).
(5)	1948 s. 68(3).
(6)	1948 s. 68(4); 1958 Sch. 1 Pt. I para. 17.
(7)	1948 s. 68(4).
(8)	1948 s. 68(5).
(9)	1948 s. 68(6); 1984 Sch. 3 para. 17(*b*).
81	1948 s. 69.
82(1)	1948 s. 11(4)(*c*); 1949 s. 10(1); 1970 Sch. 4.
(2)(3)	1949 s. 10(2); S.I. 1955/554 art. 3; S.I. 1978/272 art. 2(1), Sch. 1.
83(1) to (3)	1948 s. 70(1)(2); 1968 ss. 10(5), 15(4).
(4)	1948 s. 70(3); 1984 Sch. 3 para. 18(*a*).
(5)	1948 s. 70(4); 1984 Sch. 3 para. 18(*b*).
(6)	1948 s. 70(5).
84(1)	1948 s. 77(1); Arbitration Act 1950 (c. 27) s. 44(3); 1968 ss. 10(5), 15(4); 1976 s. 24(9); 1984 Sch. 2 para. 7(3), Sch. 3 para. 19(2).
(2) to (5)	1948 s. 77(2) to (4), (6); 1984 Sch. 3 para. 19(3).
85(1)	1948 s. 71; 1968 ss. 10(5), 15(4); R. 3.
(2)	1948 s. 72; 1968 ss. 10(5), 15(4).

TABLE OF DERIVATIONS

(3)	1948 s. 73; 1968 ss. 10(5), 15(4); R.3.
86(1) to (3)	1948 s. 82(1)(2); 1968 ss. 10(5), 15(4).
(4)	1948 s. 89; 1968 ss. 10(5), 15(4).
87	1948 s. 83; 1968 ss. 10(5), 15(4).
88	1948 s. 80; 1968 ss. 10(5), 15(4); R.4.
89(1)	1948 s. 81(1).
(2)	1948 s. 81(2); Universities and College Estates Act 1964 (c. 51) Sch. 3 Pt. I.
90	1948 s. 86.
91	1948 s. 78; Housing Act 1985 (c. 68) s. 231(2).
92	1948 s. 79.
93(1)	1948 s. 92(1); 1968 ss. 10(5), 15(4); 1977 s. 12(2)(*a*); 1984 Sch. 2 para. 1(7), Sch. 3 para. 21; R.5.
(2)(3)	1948 s. 92(2)(3).
(4)	1948 s. 92(4); Interpretation Act 1978 (c. 30) s. 25(2).
(5)	1948 s. 92(5); 1968 ss. 10(5), 15(4); 1977 s. 12(2)(*a*); 1984 Sch. 2 para. 1(7); R.5.
94(1)(2)	1948 ss. 6(4), 50(3), 77(5), 78(1), 94(1); 1958 Sch. 1 Pt. I para. 15; 1976 ss. 18(3B), 23(8); 1977 ss. 5(2), 11(9); 1984 ss. 3(3), 8(4), Sch. 2 para. 6(6), Sch. 3 para. 19(3).
(3)	1984 s. 8(4).
(4)	1978 s. 78(3).
95	1948 s. 87; Crown Estate Act 1956 (c. 73); Crown Estate Act 1961 (c. 55); 1968 ss. 10(5), 15(4), 17(3); 1976 s. 18(8); 1977 s. 12(2)(*a*); 1984 s. 9(3).
96(1)	1948 s. 94(1); 1958 s. 9(1); 1968 s. 17(1); 1976 s. 18(2)(7); 1977 ss. 2(3) Case H, 12(1)(2)(*a*); 1984 ss. 8(4), 9(2), Sch. 1 para. 1(*a*), Sch. 2 para. 1(2), Sch. 3 para. 23.
(2)	1948 s. 68(6); 1977 s. 12(1A); 1984 Sch. 3 paras. 17(*b*), 42(*b*); Insolvency Act 1985 (c. 65) Sch. 8 paras. 9 and 30.
(3)	1948 s. 94(2); 1958 s. 4(8); 1977 s. 12(2)(*a*); 1984 s. 9(2).
(4)(5)	1948 s. 94(3)(4).
(6)	1948 s. 94(5), 1968 ss. 10(5), 15(4).
97	1948 s. 101; 1968 ss. 10(5), 15(4).
98	1948 ss. 5(1), 6(1)(2), 8A(1), 9(1), 10(1); 1984 s. 1.
99-102 -	
Sch. 1	
paras. 1 to 5	1948 Sch. 1 paras. 1 to 5.
6 and 7	1948 Sch. 1 para. 8.
8	1948 Sch. 1 para. 9.
9	1948 Sch. 1 para. 10; 1976 s. 17.
Sch. 2	
para. 1(1) to (3)	1948 s. 8(3) to (5); 1984 s. 1.
2(1)	1948 s. 8(6); 1984 s. 1.
(2) to (4)	1948 s. 8A(3) to (5); 1984 s. 1.
3	1948 s. 8(7); 1984 s. 1.
4(1)	1948 s. 8(8); 1984 s. 1.

TABLE OF DERIVATIONS

(2)	1948 s. 8(12); 1984 s. 1.
5(1)	1948 s. 8(9); 1984 s. 1.
(2)	1948 s. 8(10); 1984 s. 1.
6	1948 s. 8(11); 1984 s. 1.
Sch. 3	
Pt. I	
Case A	1977 s. 2(3) Case I; 1984 ss. 6(6), 11(2).
Case B	1977 s. 2(3) Case B.
Case C	1977 s. 2(3) Case C; 1984 s. 6(3).
Case D	1977 s. 2(3) Case D.
Case E	1977 s. 2(3) Case E.
Case F	1977 s. 2(3) Case F; 1984 Sch. 3 para. 37.
Case G	1977 s. 2(3) Case G; 1984 s. 6(5)(*a*).
Case H	1977 s. 2(3) Case H.
Pt. II	
para. 1	1977 s. 2(3) Case I; 1984 s. 6(6).
2 to 7	1977 Sch. 1A paras. 1 to 6; 1984 Sch. 3 para. 43; Housing (Consequential Provisions) Act 1985 (c. 71) Sch. 2 para. 34.
8	1977 s. 2(3A); 1984 s. 6(7).
9(1)	1977 s. 2(4).
(2)	1977 s. 2(4A); 1984 s. 6(8).
10(1)	1977 s. 2(3) Case D, (4B); 1984 s. 6(4)(8).
(2)	1977 s. 2(6).
11(1)	1977 s. 2(5).
(2)	1977 s. 2(4B); 1984 s. 6(8).
12	1977 s. 2(3) Case G; 1984 s. 6(5)(*b*).
Sch. 4	1977 s. 5(1); 1984 Sch. 3 para. 38.
Sch. 5	
para. 1	1977 s. 11(10).
2	1977 s. 11(1), (2).
3	1977 s. 11(3), (4); 1984 Sch. 3 para. 41.
4	1977 s. 11(5).
5	1977 s. 11(6).
6	1977 s. 11(7), (8).
Sch. 6	
Pt. I.	
1	1976 Sch. 3A para. 1; 1984 Sch. 1 para. 3, Sch. 2 para. 1(4).
2	1976 s. 18(3); 1984 Sch. 2 para. 1(3).
3	1976 s. 18(3A); 1984 s. 3(3), Sch. 2 para. 1(4).
4	1976 s. 18(3B); 1984 s. 3(3); Sch. 2 para. 1(4).
5(1)	1976 s. 18(6); 1984 s. 3(4); Sch. 2 para. 1(5).
(2)	1976 s. 18(6); Sch. 3A para. 7; 1984 s. 3(4); Sch. 1 para. 8, Sch. 2 paras. 1(5), 9.
(3)	1976 s. 18(6A); 1984 s. 3(4), Sch. 2 para. 1(5).
(4)(5)	1976 s. 18(6B); 1984 s. 3(4), Sch. 2 para. 1(5).
6	1976 Sch. 3A para. 2; 1984 Sch. 1 para. 8; Sch. 2 para. 1(4).

TABLE OF DERIVATIONS

7	1976 Sch. 3A para. 4(1) to (3); 1984 Sch. 1 para. 8; Sch. 2 para. 1(4).
8(1)	1976 Sch. 3A para. 3; 1984 Sch. 1 para. 8.
(2)	1976 Sch. 3A para. 4(4); 1984 Sch. 1 para. 8.
9	1976 Sch. 3A para. 5; 1984 Sch. 1 para. 8; Sch. 2 para. 1(4).
10	1976 Sch. 3A para. 6; 1984 Sch. 1 para. 8; Sch. 2 para. 1(4).
Pt. II	1984 Sch. 2 para. 1(3) to (6).
Sch. 7	
Pt. I	
para. 1	1948 Sch. 3 Pt. I para. 1.
2	1948 Sch. 3 Pt. I para. 2.
3 to 7	1948 Sch. 3 Pt. I paras. 3 to 7.
8	1948 Sch. 3 Pt. I para. 7A; 1984 Sch. 3 para. 25(1)(*b*).
Pt. II	
para. 9	1948 Sch. 3 Pt. II para. 8.
10	Housing Act 1985 (c. 68) s. 231(2).
11	1948 Sch. 3 Pt. II para. 8A; 1984 Sch. 3 para. 25(2)(*a*).
12 to 15	1948 Sch. 3 Pt. II paras. 9 to 12.
16	1948 Sch. 3 Pt. II para. 13; 1984 Sch. 3 para. 25(2)(*b*).
17 to 24	1948 Sch. 3 Pt. II paras. 14 to 21.
25	1948 Sch. 3 Pt. II para. 22; 1984 Sch. 3 para. 25(2)(*c*).
26	1948 Sch. 3 Pt. II para. 23.
27 and 28	1948 Sch. 3 Pt. II paras. 24, 25; 1984 Sch. 3 para. 25(2)(*d*).
Sch. 8	
Pt. I.	
para. 1 to 3	1948 Sch. 4 Pt. I paras. 1, 2, 4.
4 to 6	1948 Sch. 4 Pt. I paras. 5 to 7; S.I. 1978/742 Sch. para. 1.
Pt. II.	
para. 7	1948 Sch. 4 Pt. II para. 8.
8	1948 Sch. 4 Pt. II para. 9; 1984 Sch. 3 para. 26.
9	1948 Sch. 4 Pt. II para. 10.
10	1948 Sch. 4 Pt. II para. 11; S.I. 1951/2168 art. 3(1); S.I. 1985/1947 art. 3(2).
11	1948 Sch. 4 Pt. II para. 12; S.I. 1978/742 Sch. para. 2; S.I. 1985/1947 art. 3(3).
Sch. 9	
Pt. I.	
para. 1(1)	1948 s. 36(1).
(2)	1948 s. 35(2).
(3)	1948 s. 36(1).
(4)	1948 s. 36(2).
(5)	1948 s. 43(3).
2(1)	1948 s. 37; 1984 Sch. 3 para. 10.
(2)	1948 s. 43(1).
3	1948 s. 38.
4(1)(2)	1948 s. 39(1).
(3)	1948 s. 39(2).

TABLE OF DERIVATIONS

5(1)	1948 s. 44.
(2)	1948 s. 45.
Pt. II	
paras. 1 to 15	1948 Sch. 2 Pt. I paras. 1, 2, 4 to 11, 13 to 17.
16	1948 Sch. 2 Pt. II.
Sch. 10	
paras. 1 to 5	1948 Sch. 5 paras. 1 to 5.
Sch. 11	
para. 1(1)	1948 Sch. 6 para. 1(1); 1984 s. 8(1)(2).
(2)	1984 s. 8(3)(4).
(3)	1948 Sch. 6 para. 1(1A); 1984 s. 8(2), Sch. 3 para. 28(2).
(4)	1948 Sch. 6 para. 1(2); 1984 s. 8(2).
(5)	1948 Sch. 6 para. 1(3); 1958 Sch. 1 Pt. I para. 20.
2	1948 Sch. 6 para. 2.
3	1948 Sch. 6 para. 2A; 1984 Sch. 3 para. 28(3).
4	1948 Sch. 6 para. 3; 1984 Sch. 3 para. 28(4).
5	1948 Sch. 6 para. 4.
6	1948 Sch. 6 para. 5; 1984 s. 8(2), Sch. 3 para. 28(5).
7	1948 Sch. 6 para. 6; 1984 Sch. 3 para. 28(6).
8	1948 Sch. 6 para. 7.
9	1948 Sch. 6 para. 8.
10	1948 Sch. 6 para. 9.
11(1)	1948 Sch. 6 para. 10(1)(2).
(2)(3)	1948 Sch. 6 para. 10(1).
(4)	1948 Sch. 6 para. 10(3).
12(1)(2)	1948 Sch. 6 para. 11(1).
(3)(4)	1948 Sch. 6 para. 11(2).
13	1948 Sch. 6 para. 12.
14(1)	1948 Sch. 6 para. 13; 1963 s. 20.
(2)	1948 Sch. 6 para. 13; 1984 s. 8(2).
15	1948 Sch. 6 para. 14.
16	1948 Sch. 6 para. 16.
17	1948 Sch. 6 para. 17.
18	1948 Sch. 6 para. 18.
19	1948 Sch. 6 para. 19.
20	1948 Sch. 6 para. 20.
21	1948 Sch. 6 para. 20A; 1984 Sch. 3 para. 28(7).
22	1948 Sch. 6 para. 20B; 1984 Sch. 3 para. 28(7).
23	1948 Sch. 6 para. 21.
24	1948 Sch. 6 para. 22; 1984 Sch. 3 para. 28(8).
25	1948 Sch. 6 para. 23.
26	1948 Sch. 6 para. 24; 1958 Sch. 1 Pt. I para. 21(1).
27(1)	1948 Sch. 6 para. 25(1).
(2)	1948 Sch. 6 para. 25(2); 1972 s. 15(1).
28(1) to (4)	1948 Sch. 6 para. 25A(1) to (4); 1984 Sch. 3 para. 28(9).
29	1948 Sch. 6 para. 26.
30	1958 Sch. I Pt. I para. 21(2).

TABLE OF DERIVATIONS

31	1948 Sch. 6 para. 29; 1984 s. 8(2), Sch. 3 para. 28(10).
32	1984 s. 8(5).
Sch. 12	
para. 1	1948 s. 2(1).
2	1948 s. 3(3).
3	1948 ss. 13(5)(*a*), 67(1)(*b*); 1984 Sch. 3 para. 16.
4	1977 s. 1(2)(*d*), (3), (3A), (4); Transport Act 1981 (c.56) s. 5; London Regional Transport Act 1984 (c. 32) Sch. 6 para. 13.
5	1948 s. 47(1)(*a*).
6	1948 s. 47(1)(*c*), (2); 1977 Sch. 1 para. 1.
7	S.I. 1951/2168 art. 4.
8	1948 ss. 56(4), 63(2), 64, 65(2); S.I. 1951/2168 art. 4.
9	Saving.
10	1948 s. 67(1)(2)(3).
Sch. 13	
para. 1 -	
2	1948 s. 96(2).
3-5 -	
6, 7	1984 Sch. 5 para. 5.
8 -	
9	1984 Sch. 5 para. 7.
10	1984 Sch. 5 para. 8.
11, 12 -	
13	1984 Sch. 5 para. 10.
14	Insolvency Act 1985 (c. 65) Sch. 9 para. 11.
15	1984 Sch. 5 para. 14.
16	1984 Sch. 5 para. 4(*d*).
Sch. 14	
para. 12	1948 Sch. 7 para. 2.
44	1968 s. 10(8).
53(4)	1968 s. 10(3)(8).
remainder -	
Sch. 15 -	

TABLE OF DESTINATIONS

This table was printed separately by HMSO.

TABLE OF DESTINATIONS

TABLE OF DESTINATIONS

A.176

HILL FARMING ACT 1946

1946	1986
s.9(2)(4)	s.68(3)(4)

THE AGRICULTURAL HOLDING ACT 1948

1948	1986	1948	1986	1948	1986
s.1(1)	s.1(1)	9(1)	ss.13(1), (2), (4), (8), 98	(2)	Sch. 9, Pt. I, para. 1(2)
(1A), (1B)	1(2), (3)	(2)	s.13(3)	36(1)	Sch. 9, Pt. I, para. 1(3), Sch. 9, Pt. I, para. 1(1)
(2)	1(4)	(4)	13(7)		
2	2	10(1)	ss.14(1), (2), 98		
2(1)	Sch. 12, para. 1	(2)(a)	s.14(3)	(2)	Sch. 9, Pt. I, para. 1(4)
3(1)	s.3(1), (4)	(b)	14(4), (5)		
(2)	3(2)	11(1)	ss.15(1), (4), (5)	37	Sch. 9, Pt. I, para. 2(1)
(3)	3(3), Sch. 12, para. 2	(2)	s.15(4), (5)	38	Sch. 9, Pt. I, para. 3
(4)	5(1)	(3)	15(6)		
3A(1)	4(1)	(4)(a), (b)	15(2)	39(1)	Sch. 9, Pt. 1, para. 4(1), (2)
(2), (3)	4(1), (2), (4)	(c)	82(1)		
(4)	4(3)	(5)	15(7)		
3B	5(2), (3)	12(1)	15(3)	(2)	Sch. 9, Pt. I, para. 4(3)
4(1)–(3)	21(1)–(3)	(2)	15(7)		
5(1)	ss.6(1), 98	13(1)	10(1), (2)	43(1)	Sch. 9, Pt. I, para. 2(2)
(2), (3)	s.6(2)	(2)–(4)	10(3)–(5)		
(4), (6)	6(5)	(4A)	10(1), (8)	(3)	Sch. 9, Pt. I, para. 1(5)
(5)	6(6)	(4B)	10(6)		
6(1)	ss.7(1), (3), 98	(5)(a)	10(7) Sch. 12, para. 3	44	Sch. 9, Pt. I, para. 5(1)
(2)	8(1), (2), (6), 98	(b)	10(2)	45	Sch. 9, Pt. I, para. 5(2)
(3)	s.8(3)	14(1)	20(1)–(3)		
(4)	94(1), (2)	(2)	20(4)	46(1)	ss.64(1), (3), 65(1), (3)
7(1)	9(1), (2)	(3)	20(5)		
(2)	9(3)	15	24	(2)	s.64(2)
(3)	ss.6(3), 8(4)	16(1)	22(1)	47(1)	ss.64(1), 65(1)
(4)	s.9(4)	(2)	22(2)	(a)	Sch. 12, para. 5
(5)	ss.6(4), 8(5)	(3)	22(3)		
8(1), (2)	s.12(1), (2)	17	23	(b)	s.65(2)
(3), (4)	Sch. 2, para. 1(1)–(3)	18	16	s.47(1)(c), (2)	Sch. 12, para. 6
		19(1)	18(2)–(5)	48	s.66(1)
(5)	Sch. 2, para. 1(3)	(2), (3)	18(2)–(4)	49(1)	67(1), (2)
(6)	Sch. 2, para. 2(1)	(4)	18(5)	(2)	67(2)
		20(1)	18(1)	50(1)–(4)	67(3)–(6)
(7)	Sch. 2, para. 3	(2)	18(5)	(3)	ss.67(7), 94(1), (2)
(8)	Sch. 2, para. 4(1)	s.21(1), (2)	19(1)		
(9)	Sch. 2, para. 5(1)	(3)	19(2)	51(1)	s.66(2)
		(4)	19(3)	(2)	66(4)
(10)	Sch. 2, para. 5(2)	22	17	(3)	66(3)
		34(1)	ss.60(1), (2), 61(1), (6)	52	68(1)
(11)	Sch. 2, para. 6			53	66(5)
s.8(12)	Sch. 2, para. 4(2)	(2)	s.60(5)	54	69(1)
		(a), (d)	60(3)	55(1), (2)	69(2), (3)
(13)	s.12(3)	(b), (c)	60(6)	56(1)	70(1)–(3)
8A(1)	98	(2A)	63(1)	(2), (3)	70(4), (5)
(2)	12(4)	(3)	63(2)	(4)	Sch. 12, para. 8
(3)–(5)	Sch. 2, para. 2(2)–(4)	(4)	63(3), (4)		
		(5)	60(7)	57(1)	s.71(1)
		35(1)	64(4)	(2)	71(2)
				(3)	71(3), (4)

1235

TABLE OF DESTINATIONS

THE AGRICULTURAL HOLDING ACT 1948—cont.

1948	1986	1948	1986	1948	1986
(4)	71(5)	94(1)	ss.1(5), 94(1), (2), 96(1)	9	Sch. 8, Pt. II, para. 8
58	72	(3), (4)	s.96(4), (5)	Sch. 4, Pt. II	
59	73	(5)	94(6)	para. 10	Sch. 8, Pt. II para. 9
60(1)	74(1), (2)	96(2)	Sch. 13, para. 1	11	Sch. 8, Pt. II, para. 10
(2)	74(3)	101	97	12	Sch. 8, Pt. II, para. 11
(3)	74(4)	Sch. 1,			
61	75	paras. 1–5	Sch. 1, paras. 1–5	Sch. 5,	
63(1)	76(1), (2)	8	Sch. 1, paras. 6 and 7	paras. 1–5	Sch. 10 paras. 1–5
(2)	76(3), Sch. 12 para. 8			Sch. 6,	
64	77, Sch. 12, para. 8	9	Sch. 1, para. 8	para. 1(1)	Sch. 11, para. 1(1)
65(1)	78(1), (2)	10	Sch. 1, para. 9	(1A)	Sch. 11, para. 1(3)
(2)	78(3), Sch. 12, para. 8	Sch. 2, Pt. I, paras. 1, 2, 4–11, 13–17	Sch. 9, Pt. I, paras. 1–15	(2)	Sch. 11, para. 1(4)
67(1)	79, Sch. 12, para. 10	Pt. II	Sch. 9, Pt. II, para. 16	(3)	Sch. 11, para. 1(5)
(b)	Sch. 12, para. 3	Sch. 3, Pt. I		2	Sch. 11, para.2
(2)	Sch. 12, para. 10	para. 1	Sch. 7, Pt. I, para. 1	2A	Sch. 11, para.3
(3)	s.79, Sch. 12, para. 10	2	Sch. 7, Pt. I, para. 2	3	Sch. 11, para.4
(4)	79			4	Sch. 11, para.5
68(1)	80(1), (2)	3–7	Sch. 7, Pt. I, paras. 3–7	5	Sch. 11, para.6
(2)	80(3), (4)			6	Sch. 11, para.7
(3)	80(5)	7A	Sch. 7, Pt. I, para. 8	7	Sch. 11, para.8
(4)	80(6), (7)			8	Sch. 11, para.9
(5)	80(8)	Pt. II,		9	Sch. 11, para. 10
(6)	ss.80(9), 96(2)	para. 8	Sch. 7, Pt. II, para. 9	10(1)	Sch. 11, para. 11(2), (3)
69	s.81				
70(1), (2)	83(1)–(3)	paras. 8A	Sch. 7, Pt. II, para. 11	(1),	
(3)	83(4)			(2)	Sch. 11, para. 11(1)
(4)	83(5)	9–12	Sch. 7, Pt. II, paras. 12–15	(3)	Sch. 11, para. 11(4)
(5)	83(6)				
71	85(1)				
72	85(2)	13	Sch. 7, Pt. II, paras. 16	11(1)	Sch. 11, para. 12(1), (2)
73	85(3)				
77(1)	84(1)	14–21	Sch. 7, Pt. II, paras. 17–24	(2)	Sch. 11 para. 12(3), (4)
(2)–(4),(6)	84(2)–(5)				
(5)	94(1), (2)	22	Sch. 7, Pt. II, para. 25		
78	91			12	Sch. 11, para. 13
(1)	94(1), (2)	23	Sch. 7, Pt. II, para. 26		
79	92			13	Sch. 11, para. 14(1), (2)
80	88	24, 25	Sch. 7, Pt. II, paras. 27, 28		
81(1)	89(1)				
(2)	89(2)	Sch. 4, Pt. I, paras. 1, 2		14	Sch. 11, para. 15
s.82(1), (2)	86(1)–(3)				
83	87	4	Sch. 8, Pt. I, para. 1–3	16	Sch. 11, para. 16
86	90				
87	95	5–7	Sch. 8, Pt. I, paras. 4–6	17	Sch. 11, para. 17
89	86(4)				
92(1)	93(1)	Pt. II		18	Sch. 11, para. 18
(2), (3)	93(2), (3)	para. 8	Sch. 8, Pt. II, para. 7	19	Sch. 11, para. 19
(4)	93(4)				
(5)	93(5)				
(2)	96(3)				

TABLE OF DESTINATIONS

The Agricultural Holding Act 1948—cont.

1948	1986	1948	1986	1948	1986
20	Sch. 11, para. 20	24	Sch. 11, para. 26	28(7)	Sch. 11, para. 21
20A	Sch. 11, para. 21	25(1)	Sch. 11, para. 27(1)	Sch. 6, para. 29	Sch. 11, para. 31
20B	Sch. 11, para. 22	(2)	Sch. 11, para. 27(2)	Sch. 7, para. 2	Sch. 14, para. 12
21	Sch. 11, para. 23	Sch. 6 para. 25A		4	s. 68(3), (4)
22	Sch. 11, para. 24	(1)–(4)	Sch. 11, para. 28(1)–(4)		
Sch. 6, para. 23	Sch. 11, para. 25	26	Sch. 11, para. 29		

The Agriculture (Miscellaneous Provisions) Act 1949

1949	1986
s.10(1)	s.82(1)
(2)	(2), (3)

Arbitration Act 1950

1950	1986
s.44(3)	s.84(1)

Crown Estate Act 1956

1956	1986
Crown Estate Act 1956	s.95

The Agriculture Act 1958

1958	1986	1958	1986	1958	1986
s.4(1)	s.11(1), (2)	Sch. 1, Pt. I		Sch. 1, Pt. I	
(2)–(4)	11(3)–(7)	para. 6	s.14(1)–(5)	para. 20	Sch. 11, para.1(5)
(5)	13(2)–(6)	7	15(4), (5)	21(1)	Sch. 11, para. 26
(6)	68(2)	14	62(3)–(6)	(2)	Sch. 11, para. 30
(7)	ss.11(8), 13(5), (6)	15	ss.67(7), 94(1), (2)		
(8)	s.96(3)	16	s.76(1)		
9(1)	96(1)	17	80(1), (2), (6)		
59	73				

Crown Estate Act 1961

1961	1986
Crown Estate Act 1961	s.95

The Agriculture (Miscellaneous Provisions) Act 1963

1963	1986
s.20	Sch. 11, para. 14(1)

Universities and College Estates Act 1964

1964	1986
Sch. 3, Pt. I	s.89(2)

TABLE OF DESTINATIONS

THE AGRICULTURE (MISCELLANEOUS PROVISIONS) ACT 1968

1968	1986	1968	1986	1968	1986
s.9(1)	ss.60(1), (2), (7), 61(1), 63(1), (3), 74(1), (2)	s.10(4)	s.78(1), (2)	s.15(2)	ss.62(1), (2), 74(2)
(1A)	s.74(3)	(5)	ss.63(2), 75, 83(1)–(3), 85(1)–(3), 86(1)–(4), 87, 88, 93(1), (4), 95, 96(6), 97	(4)	63(2), 75, 83(1)–(3), 85(1)–(3), 86(1)–(4), 87, 88, 93(1), (4), 95, 96(6), 97
(2)	ss.60(4), 74(1), (2)	(8)	s.61(3), (4), Sch. 14, paras. 44(4), 53(4), 61(6)	(5)	s.62(3)
10(1)(b), (c)	s.61(3), (4)			17(1)	96(1)
(1)(d), (e)	61(2)			(2)	74(4)
(2)	61(3)–(5)				
(3)	Sch. 14, para. 53(4)				

THE AGRICULTURE ACT 1970

1970	1986
Sch. 4	s.82(1)

COURTS ACT 1971

1971	1986
Sch. 9, Pt. I	s.19(2)

THE AGRICULTURE (MISCELLANEOUS PROVISIONS) ACT 1972

1972	1986
s.15(1)	Sch. 11, para. 27(2)
(2)	s.7(2)

THE AGRICULTURE (MISCELLANEOUS PROVISIONS) ACT 1976

1976	1986	1976	1986	1976	1986
s.17	Sch. 1 para. 9	(6B)	Sch. 6, Pt. I para. 5(4)	(3)	47(2)
18(1)	ss.35(1), (2), 36(1)		(5)	(4)	47(3)
(2)	1(4), 35(2), 36(3), (4), 39(1), 41, 96(1)	s.18(7)	s.96(1)	(5)–(7)	45(5)–(8)
		(8)	95	(8)	ss.45(5)–(8), 94(1), (2)
		19	43	(9)	s.46(3)
(3)	Sch. 6, Pt. I, para. 2	20(1)	ss.36(1), 39(1)	s.24(1)	s.48(1)
(3A)	Sch. 6, Pt. I, para. 3	(2)	s.39(2)	(2)	48(2)
(3B)	s.94(1), (2) Sch. 6, Pt. I, para. 4	(3)	39(3)	(3)	48(3), (4)
		(4)	39(4)	(4)	48(11)
		(5)	39(5)	(a)	48(5)
		(6)	39(6)	(b)	48(6)
		(7)–(9)	39(7)–(9)	(c)	48(7)
		(9A)	39(10)	(5)	48(8)
(4)(a)	38(1)	(10)–(14)	40(1)–(5)	(6)	48(9)
(b)	38(2)	(15)	42	(7)	48(10)
(c)	38(3)	21	41	(8)	48(12)
(d)	36(2)	22(1)	44(1)	(9)	84(1)
(e)	37(1), (9)	(2)	44(2)	Sch. 3A,	
(f)	38(4)	(3)	44(3)	para. 1	Sch. 6, Pt.I para. 1
(g)	38(5)	(4)	44(4)		
(5)	37(2), (3), (9)	(5)	44(5)	2	Sch. 6, Pt. I, para. 6
		(6)	44(6)		
(5A)	37(4), (5)	(7)	44(7)	3	Sch. 6, Pt. I, para. 8(1)
(6)	Sch. 6, Pt. I para. 5(1), (2)	23(1)	45(1)	4(1)–	
		(1)	47(1)		
		(1A)	45(2)–(4)	(3)	Sch. 6, Pt. 1, para. 7
(6A)	Sch. 6, Pt. I, para. 5(3)	(2)	46(1)		
		(2A)	46(2)		

TABLE OF DESTINATIONS

THE AGRICULTURE (MISCELLANEOUS PROVISIONS) ACT 1976—cont.

1976	1986	1976	1986	1976	1986
5	Sch. 6, Pt. 1, para. 9	Case I	Sch. 3, Pt. I, Case A, Pt. II, para. 1	(1A)	33(2)
6	Sch. 6, Pt. 1, para. 10			(2)	33(2), (3)
7	Sch. 6, Pt. 1, para. 5(2)	s.2(3A)	Sch. 3, Pt. II, para. 8	11(1), (2)	Sch. 5, para. 2
s.1(1)	s.25(1)	(4)	Sch. 3, Pt. II, para. 9(1)	(3), (4)	Sch. 5, para. 3
(2)	25(2)			(5)	Sch. 5, para. 4
(2)(d), (3), (3A), (4)	Sch. 12, para. 4	(4A)	Sch. 3, Pt. II, para. 9(2)	(6)	Sch. 5, para. 5
		(4B)	Sch. 3, Pt. II, para. 10(1), 11(2)	(7), (8)	Sch. 5, para. 6
(5)–(7)	s.25(3)–(5)	(5)	Sch. 3, Pt. II, para. 11(1)	(9)	s.94(1), (2)
2(1)	26(1)	(6)	Sch. 3, Pt. II, para. 10(2)	(10)	Sch. 5, para. 1
(2)	26(2)	3	s.27(1)–(5)	12(1)	ss.26(2), 96(1)
(3) Case B	Sch. 3, Pt. I, Case B	4(1)	28(1)	(1A)	s.96(2)
Case C	Sch. 3, Pt. I, Case C	(2)	28(2)–(4)	(2)(a)	ss.93(1), (5), 95, 96(1), (3)
Case D	Sch. 3, Pt. I, Case D Pt. II, para. 10(1)	(3)	28(2), (4)	Sch. 1,	
		(4)	28(5)	para.1–6	Sch. 12, para. 6
Case E	Sch. 3, Pt. I, Case E	(5)	28(6)	(3)(a)	s.60(1), (2)
		5(1)	Sch. 4	(3)(b)	61(1)
Case F	Sch. 3, Pt. I, Case F	(2)	s.94(1), (2)	(3)(c)	63(3)
		6(1)	27(6)	(5)	74(1)
Case G	Sch. 3, Pt. I, Case G, Pt. II, para. 12	(2)	27(8)	5	61(2)–(5)
		(3)	27(7)	7(2)(b)	38(1)
		(4)	27(9)	(c)	38(2)
Case H	s.96 Sch. 3, Pt. I, Case H	8(1)	31(1)	(d)	38(3)
		(2)	31(2)	(3)	43
		9	32	(4)	44(2)
		s.10(1)	s.33(1)	(5)	46(1)
				Sch. 1A paras. 1–6	Sch. 3, Pt. II, paras. 2–7

INTERPRETATION ACT 1978

1978	1986
s.25(2)	s.93(4)
78(3)	94(4)

TRANSPORT ACT 1981

1981	1986
s.5	Sch. 12, para. 4

LONDON REGIONAL TRANSPORT ACT 1984

1984	1986
Sch. 6, para. 13	Sch. 12, para. 4

THE AGRICULTURAL HOLDINGS ACT 1984

1984	1986	1984	1986	1984	1986
s.1	ss.12(1)–(4), 98, Sch. 2, paras. 1(1)–(3), 2(1)–(4), 3, 4(1), (2), 5(1), (2), 6	2(1), (2)	34(1), 35(1)		Sch. 6, Pt. I, paras. 3, 4
		(3)	s.34(2)	s.3(4)	Sch. 6, Pt. 1, para. 5(1)–(5)
		3(1)	45(2)–(4)		
		(2)(b)	36(4)		
		(3)	94(1), (2),	5	s.25(3)–(5)

TABLE OF DESTINATIONS

THE AGRICULTURAL HOLDINGS ACT 1984—*cont.*

1984	1986	1984	1986	1984	1986
6(3)	Sch. 3, Pt. I, Case C	(2) ...	42	10(1)	
(4), (8)	Sch. 3, Pt. II, para. 10(1)	6	44(6), (7)	(a)	34(1)
		7(3) ...	48(2)	(1)(b),	
(5)(a)	Sch. 3, Pt. I, Case G	8	Sch. 6, Pt. I, paras. 1(4), 5(2), 6, 8(2), 9, 10	(2) ...	37(6)
				Sch. 3,	
				para. 1(2) ...	1(1)
(b)	Sch. 3, Pt. II, para. 12	Sch. 2		(3) ...	1(2), (3)
		para. 1(1)	...ss.49(1), (2), 50(1)	2(1)(a)	3(1)
(6)	Sch. 3, Pt. I, Case A, Pt. II, paras. 2–7			(b)	5(1)
		(1)(a)	s.34(1)	(2)	...ss.4(1)–(4), 5(2), (3)
		(2)	...ss.1(4), 49(1)–(3), 50(2)(3), 53(2), 54(3), 96(1)	3(2) ...	s.6(1)
(7)	Sch. 3, Pt. I, para. 8			(3) ...	6(5), (6)
				para. 4	...ss.6(4), 8(5)
(8)	Sch. 3, Pt. II, paras. 9(2), 11(2)			5(2)(b)	s.13(2)
		(3)	...Sch. 6, Pt. I, para. 2 Pt. II	(c)	13(4)
				(3) ...	13(3)
(9)	s.43			6(2) ...	10(1)
7	28(5)	(4)	...Sch. 6, Pt. I, paras. 1(4), 3, 4, 5(1), 6, 9, 10, Pt. II	(3) ...	10(1), (6), (8)
8(1)	22(2), Sch. 11, para. 1(1)			7(2) ...	20(1)–(3)
				(3) ...	20(5)
(2)	ss.12(3), 22(2), Sch. 11, paras. 1(1), (3), (4), 6, 14(2), 31	(5)	...Sch. 6, Pt. I, para. 5(2)–(5), Pt. II	8(a) ...	22(1)
				(b) ...	22(2)
		(6)	...Sch. 6, Pt. II	9(2) ...	63(1)
		(7)	... s.93(1), (5)	(3)(a),	
		2(1)		(b) ...	63(3)
		(a)–(c)		(c) ...	63(4)
(3)	Sch.11, para. 1(2)	(f), (g)	51(1)	10	Sch. 9, Pt. I, para. 2(1)
		(d) ...	51(2)		
(4)	ss.94(1)–(3), 96(1), Sch. 11, para. 1(2)	(e),(3)	51(3)	11	66(5)
		(2) ...	49(3)	12	70(2), (3)
		(4) ...	51(1)	13(a) ..	71(2)
		(5) ...	51(4)	(b) ..	71(5)
(5)	s.22(5), Sch. 11, para. 32	(6) ...	51(5), (6)	14(a) ..	74(1)
		3(1),		(b) ..	74(3), (4)
9(2)	96(1), (3)	(2) ...	52(1), (2)	15	75
(3)	95	(3) ...	52(3), (4)	16	79, Sch. 12, para. 3
11(2)	Sch. 3, Pt. I, Case A	(4) ...	52(5)	17 (a) .	80(3), (4)
		4	54(1), (2)	(b)	..ss.80(9), 96(2)
Sch. 1,		5(1)	...ss.50(1), 53(1)	18(a) ..	93(4)
para. 1	ss.1(4), 35(2)	(2)–		(b) ..	83(5)
(a) ...	96(1)	(10) ..	s.53(3)–(11)	19(2) ..	84(1)
2(2) ...	38(1)	6(1)	...ss.55(1), 56(1)	(3)	..ss.84(2)–(5), 94(1), (2)
(3) ...	38(3)	(2)	...s.55(2)–(4)		
(5) ...	27(1), (9)	(3) ...	56(2)	21	s.93(1)
(6) ...	38(4)	(4)–		23 ..	96(1)
(7) ...	37(2)–(5), (9)	(7) ...	55(5)–(8)	25(1)	
		(6) ...	94(1), (2)	(b)	......Sch. 7, Pt. 1, para. 8
3	Sch. 6, Pt. I, para. 1	7(1)	...ss.46(1), 56(3), (4)		
(2) ...	s.43			(2)(b)	.Sch. 7, Pt. II, para. 16
(3)(a)	39(5), (6)	(2) ...	46(2), 56(3), (4)		
(b)	39(10)			(c)	..Sch. 7, Pt. II, para. 25
(4)(a)	44(2), (4)	(3) ...	s.84(1)		
(b)	44(5)	8	57	(d)	.Sch. 7, Pt. II, paras. 27, 28
(5) ...	46(3)	9	58, Sch. 6, Pt. I, para. 5(2)		
(6) ...	48(2)			26	Sch. 8, Pt. II, para. 8
4	39(2)				
5(1) ...	35(1)				

1240

TABLE OF DESTINATIONS

THE AGRICULTURAL HOLDINGS ACT 1984—*cont.*

1984	1986	1984	1986	1984	1986
27(*b*)	.. s.79	(1D)	......Sch. 11, para. 31	43	.....Sch. 3, Pt. II, para. 2–7
28(2)	.. Sch. 11, para. 1(3)	30	..... s.11(2)	Sch. 5,	
(3)	..Sch. 11, para. 3	31	..... 74(3)	para. 2(2)(*a*)	s.37(6), (7)
(4)	..Sch. 11, para. 4	32(1)		(*b*)	37(8)
		(*a*) ..	61(3), (4)	4(*d*)	...Sch. 13, para. 16
(5)	..Sch. 11, para. 6	(*b*) ..	61(2)		
		33	74(4)	5	.......Sch. 13, paras. 3–5
(6)	..Sch. 11, para. 7	34	38(2)		
		35	48(9)	7	.......Sch. 13, para. 9
		36	25(2)		
(7)	..Sch. 11, para. 22	37	.....Sch. 3, Pt. I, Case F	8	.......Sch. 12, para. 10
(8)	..Sch. 11, para. 24	38	.....Sch. 4	10	.....Sch. 13, para. 13
		39	s.31(2)		
(9)	..Sch. 11, para. 28(1)–(4)	40(*a*) ..	33(1)	14	.....Sch. 13, para. 15
		(*b*) ..	33(2)		
		(*c*) ..	33(2), (3)		
		41	.....Sch. 5, para. 3		
		42(*b*) ..	s.96(2)		

INSOLVENCY ACT 1985

1985	1986
Sch .8, paras. 9 and 30	s.96(2)
Sch. 9, para 11	Sch. 13, para 14

HOUSING ACT 1985

1985	1986
s.231(1)	ss.13(2)–(4), 68, 91, Sch. 7, Pt II, para 9

HOUSING (CONSEQUENTIAL PROVISIONS) ACT 1985

1985	1986
Sch.2, para. 34	Sch. 3, Pt. II, paras. 2–7

Destinations for Statutory Instruments

THE AGRICULTURAL HOLDINGS ACT (VARIATION OF FOURTH SCHEDULE) ORDER 1951

1951	1986
S.I. 1951 No. 2168,	
art. 3(1)	Sch. 8, Pt.II, para. 10
art. 4	Sch. 12, paras. 7, 8

THE TRANSFER OF FUNCTIONS (MINISTRY OF FOOD) ORDER 1955

1955	1986
S.I. 1955 No. 554,	
art.3	s.82(2), (3)

TABLE OF DESTINATIONS

THE TRANSFER OF FUNCTIONS (WALES) (NO. 1) ORDER 1978

1978	1986
S.I. 1978 No. 272	
art. 2(1), Sch. 1 …….	s.82(2), (3)

THE AGRICULTURAL HOLDINGS ACT 1948 (AMENDMENT) REGULATIONS 1978

1978	1986
S.I. 1978 No. 447,	
reg. 2(2) ……………	ss.76(1)

THE AGRICULTURAL HOLDINGS ACT 1948 (VARIATIONS OF FOURTH SCHEDULE) ORDER 1978

S.I. 1978 No. 742 Sch.
para. 1 ……………… Sch. 8.Pt I.
para. 4–6
    2 ……………… Sch. 8. Pt II,
                              para. 11

THE AGRICULTURAL HOLDINGS ACT 1948 (VARIATION OF FOURTH SCHEDULE) ORDER 1985

1985	1986
S.I. 1985 No. 1947 art.	
3(2) …………………	Sch. 8, Pt. II,
	para. 10
(3) …………………	Sch.8, Pt II,
	para. 11

REPORT OF THE LAW COMMISSION ON THIS ACT (CMND. 9665) RECOMMENDATIONS

R.1	…………	s.2
R.2	…………	68(3), (4)
R.3	…………	85(1), (3)
R.4	…………	88
R.5	…………	93(1), (5)

INDEX

Agent,
  service of notices, 588–589
Agreement,
  farm business tenancy, relating to, content of, 24–25
Agricultural holdings,
  Act of 1986,
    application exclusive of other codes, 151
    arbitration under. *See* arbitration, *below*
    definitions. *See* Words and phrases
    forms. *See full list of forms in* Part V
    general background, 9–10
    introduction to, 149–150
    status relating to consolidation, 150–151
    tenancy beginning on or after September 1, 1995,
      agreed succession by written agreement, 14
      agreed succession tenancies, 13–14
      Agricultural Land Tribunal succession direction, obtained by virtue of, 13
      Evesham custom, 14–15
      exclusions, 12–13
      parties agree 1986 Act shall apply, 13
      surrender and regrant in favour of tenant already protected, 15–16
    text, Part II
  agricultural land, meaning, 156–158
  Agricultural Land Tribunal. See Agricultural Land Tribunal
  agricultural use, abandonment of, 154–155
  arbitration,
    application of Schedule 11, 528
    appointment of arbitrator,
      agreement between parties, by, 529–530
      general, 529
      new appointment, 532
      President of RICS, by, 530–532
      revocation of, 532–533
    award,
      consent award, 555
      contents of, 555–556
      enforcement of, 559–560
      finality of, 558–559
      form of, 554–555
      interest on, 558
      interim, 554

Agricultural holdings—*cont.*
  arbitration—*cont.*
    award—*cont.*
      reasons, 556–558
      stamping of, 559
      time for making, 554
    communication with parties, 536
    compulsory, 524–525
    correct approach of arbitrator, 539–540
    costs,
      additional costs of apportionment, 573
      arbitrator has no jurisdiction, 573
      award set aside, 572
      date for payment, 573
      generally, 570–572
      special case, 572
    Council on Tribunals, supervision by, 570
    ex parte proceedings, 538–539
    fixing hearing, 537–538
    hearing, 552–554
    holding, arbitrator's inspection of, 550–551
    judicial control of reference,
      appeals, 561
      county court proceedings, 562
      direction to state case, 561
      drafting special case, 562
      error of law on face of award, 567–569
      judicial review, 569
      misconduct, 563–566
      mistakes of fact or law, no remedy for, 569
      nature of statement of case to court, 560
      remission of award for reconsideration, 567
      setting aside award, 563–566
    jurisdiction of arbitrator, challenge to, 536–537
    legal assistance by arbitrator, 551–552
    Lord Chancellor, formal powers of, 527–528
    nature of, 525–526
    procedure at hearing,
      arbitrator bound by own procedural directions, 549
      conduct of arbitration, 549–550
      construction agreed by parties, 548–549
      evidence, 542–543, 545–548

1243

Agricultural holdings—*cont.*
  arbitration—*cont.*
    procedure at hearing—*cont.*
      general points, 540–542
      parties to arbitration, 543
      valuer-advocate, 544–545
      witnesses at arbitration, 543–544
    remuneration of arbitrator, 533–534
    scope of, 524
    simultaneous, 526–527
    statement of case, 534–536
  building may be, 154
  change in use during tenancy,
    160–161
  compensation,
    custom, under, 360
    customary,
      abolition of, 410
      limitations on abolition of, 410–412
      no uniformity pre-1948, 410
      rules relating to, 412–413
    dilapidations and general deterioration, for,
      arbitration, 400
      assignment of reversion, effect of, 404
      claim for general deterioration, 405–406
      common law proceedings, 401–402
      construction of repairing obligations, 402
      contractual claim,
        common law action for damages, relating to, 398–399
        conditions of, 399
      damages,
        common law action for, 398–399 401–402
        limit to amount of, 403–404
        milk quota, loss of, 407
      election, 400
      forfeiture, action for, 401–402
      generally, 396
      good husbandry, meaning of rules of, 398
      high-tech farming methods, impact of, 404
      litigation designations, 407
      matters specified, 401
      measure of compensation, 402–403
      milk quota, loss of, 407
      model clauses, relevance of, 402
      opencast coal, 406
      preliminary notice, requirement of, 406
      record of holding, 407
      severance of reversion, claims of, 404–405
      standard of repair, 402
      statutes, application of, 406
      statutory claim, 397–398
      successive tenancies, 407
      time of making claim, 400
      written contract of tenancy, 399–400

Agricultural holdings—*cont.*
  compensation—*cont.*
    disturbance, for,
      additional compensation,
        exclusion of, 364–366
        meaning, 370
      availability of,
        additional compensation, and, 371
        counternotice of tenant, 362
        notice to quit entirety, 360–361
        tenant's death, termination by, 361–362
      basic compensation,
        actual loss of tenant, amount of, 367
        amount of tenant's actual loss, meaning, 368
        meaning, 367
        notice of claim, requirements relating to, 369
        one year's rent, amount equal to, 367
        right to, 366
        valuation, opportunity of making, 369–370
      circumstances where not available, 363–364
      claim,
        dealing with, 374–375
        how to make, 373–374
        notice of intention to claim, 374
        when to make, 373–374
      early resumption clause, extra compensation for operation of, 371
      exclusion, 364
      full compensation, tenant wishing to quit with, 375
      how to make claim, 373–374
      landlord's notice to quit part,
        followed by tenant quitting part only, 362–363
        tenant's counternotice to quit entirety, followed by, 362
      loss or expense, commentary on, 368–369
      notice of intention to claim, 374
      overview, 360
      reduced compensation, 372
      relevant previous notice, meaning, 373
      right to basic compensation, 366
      sub-letting, special provisions relating to, 371–372
      when to make claim, 373–374
    forms. *See full list of forms in* Part V
    game damage, for, 231–234
    general introduction, 353–354
    high farming claim,
      allowances and exclusions, 395–396
      conditions of claim, 395
      continuous adoption of special system of farming, 394–395
      difficulties in way of, 396
      measure of compensation, 395

INDEX

Agricultural holdings—*cont.*
compensation—*cont.*
improvements, for,
additional compensation, 390–391
assembling scheme of works, 386–387
classification of improvements, 386
consents,
not required, 389
requirements relating to, 387–388
distinction between old and new improvements, 376
generally, 375–376
hill farming, 394
improvement, meaning, 385
limitations on, 391–392
measure of compensation, 389–390
notices required, 387–388
old,
changes of tenancy during one occupation, 379
consents, 378–379
list of, 380
measure of compensation, 377–378
new improvements distinguished from, 376
right to compensation, 377
rules governing, 377
subrogation of incoming tenant to rights of outgoer, 379–380
planning permission, 387
relevant improvements, meaning, 380
restrictions on, 394
short term improvements, 389–390
sub-tenancies and work subject to direction, 393–394
subrogation of incoming tenant to rights of outgoer, 392–393
substituted compensation, 390–391
successive tenancies during one occupation, 392
works, 389
mandatory nature of, 354–356
mortgagee, tenancy not binding on, 360
non-statutory, unenforceable without agreement in writing, 356–357
part of holding, termination of tenancy of, 357–358
permanent pasture, relating to, 224
permitted exclusion of, 356
rent, set off against, 229
restrictions on, 359
reversionary estate in holding is severed, 358–359
settlement of claim on termination of tenancy,
agreement, period allowed for settlement by, 418–419
arbitration,
prescribed form of award, 420
scope of, 413–415
authority relating to claim, 416
enforcement of claim, 415–416

Agricultural holdings—*cont.*
compensation—*cont.*
settlement of claim on termination of tenancy—*cont.*
mandatory nature of s. 83 of the 1986 Act, 418
method of settlement, 413
notice of intention to claim, 416–418
occupation of part after termination, 419
writing down schemes, 419–420
tenant-right,
election on matters of,
pre-March 1, 1948 occupiers, 383
variations related to tenant's dates of occupation, 382–383
general entitlement, 382
generally, 375–376, 381–382
hill sheep, acclimatisation, hefting or settlement of, 383–384
measure of compensation, 389–390
sod fertility, 385
construction of repairing obligations, 209
contract for agricultural tenancy, meaning, 159–160
contract of tenancy, meaning, 156
contracting out of regulations,
arbitration, control by resort to, 208
award under s 8, 209
Crown land, 590
custom,
compensation under, 360
customary compensation,
abolition of, 410
limitations on abolition of, 410–412
no uniformity pre-1948, 410
rules relating to, 412–413
customary term days, 413
general rules relating to, 408
not relating to compensation, 408–410
recognition of, 407–408
scope for, 360
death, succession on. *See* Succession
dilapidations,
compensation for. *See* compensation, *above*
landlord's remedies for, 211–212
disposal of produce and cropping,
exclusions, 225
farming stock, 228
manure, position relating to, 226
mineral workings, 228
object of s. 15, 224–225
protection of holding, 226–227
remedies of landlord, 227
removal of other material, 226
sale of other material, 226
smallholdings, 227–228
dispute resolution,
Agricultural Land Tribunal. *See* Agricultural Land Tribunal
arbitration under Agricultural Holdings Act 1986. *See* arbitration, *above*

1245

INDEX

Agricultural holdings—*cont.*
  dispute resolution,—*cont.*
    generally, 510–511
  distress,
    compensation set off against rent, 229
    contracting out, 231
    generally, 228
    rent due more than year previously, 228–229
    settlement of disputes, 230–231
    third party, restrictions on distraining property of, 229–230
  disturbance, compensation for. See compensation, *above*
  emblements, extension of tenancies in lieu of claims to, 234–235
  entry, landlord's power of, 237–238
  exclusions,
    assured tenancies, 153
    leasehold reform, 152
    protected tenancies, 152–153
    relevant licences/tenancies, 152
    repairing obligations, 153
    secure tenancies, 153
  fixed equipment,
    condition of incorporation, 197–198
    contract of tenancy, 198–199
    contracting out, 222
    default by tenant, 202–203
    disputes under regulations, 207–208
    generally, 196–197
    insurance, 197
    landlord to carry out work on,
      conditions of successful application, 218–219
      excluded direction, 219
      extension of time, power to grant, 220
      generally, 217
      nature of direction, 220
      procedure, 217–218
      remedies of tenant, 220
    landlord's rights and liabilities, 199–201
    limited owners, 222
    maintenance, 197
    model clauses, incorporation of, 197
    money based on estimates, landlord's ability to demand, 202
    obsolete, 206
    redundancy of, disputes as to, 205–206
    regulations, 198–199
    repair,
      generally, 197
      meaning, 204–205
    replacement,
      landlord's failure to execute, 204
      meaning, 204–205
    service of counter-notices, time of essence for, 206
    subsidence relieving obligation to execute work, 207
    tenant's rights and liabilities, 201–202
    transitional arrangements, 209

Agricultural holdings—*cont.*
  fixed equipment—*cont.*
    underground water pipe, failure to execute repairs to, 203–204
  fixtures and buildings, tenant's right to remove,
    conditions for exercise of right, 215
    contracting out, 216
    custom, 216
    exceptions,
    general rule, 213–214
    generally, 213
    incoming tenant, position of, 216
    market garden tenants, 217
    non-compliance, effect of, 215–216
    opencast coal operations, 217
    property in fixture or building, 215–216
    record of, 217
  forms. See full list of forms in Part V
  game, damage by,
    arbitration, 234
    compensation, 231–234
  good estate management, 221–222, A.3
  good husbandry responsibilities, 221–222, A.3
  high farming claim. See compensation, *above*
  improvements, compensation for. See compensation, *above*
  intermediate tenant, direction to, 221
  Landlord and Tenant Act 1954, Part II, 151–152
  landlord's remedies for breach, restriction of, 238
  leasehold reform, 152
  life of tenancy, provisions arising in, 191–192
  limited owners. See Limited owners
  list of statutory definitions, 162–168
  market gardens. See Market gardens
  meaning, 155–156
  miscellaneous provisions, 575
  notice to quit,
    Agricultural Land Tribunal,
      consent to notice to quit, 295–296
      counter-notice, tenant's right to serve, 293–294
      grounds for consent, 295–296
      landlord's application to, 294–295
      reference to, 292
    agricultural unit, amalgamation or reshaping of, 344
    allotments, 299
    arbitration,
      extension of time under notice to remedy, 347–349
      machinery, scope of, 344–345
      postponement of notice after termination of, 347
      service of counter-notice, 346
      suspension of notice to quit during proceedings, 347

INDEX

Agricultural holdings—*cont.*
miscellaneous provisions—*cont.*
 arbitration—*cont.*
  time limit for appointment of
   arbitrator, 345–346
  when applicable, 345
 bad husbandry, 313–314
 Case A: smallholdings, 308–309
 Case B: non-agricultural use, 301, 309–313
 Case C: certificate of bad husbandry, 313–314
 Case D: non-payment of rent and remediable breach, 314–316
 Case E: non-remediable breach, 335–339
 Case F: insolvency, 339–340
 Case G: death of tenant, 340–344
 Case H: amalgamation or reshaping of agricultural unit, 344
 consent of Tribunal,
  conditions on, 303–304
  grounds for, 295–296
  not required, 305
 construction of, 289–292
 de minimis rule, use of, 292
 death of tenant,
  disturbance compensation, 344
  executors, notice from, 342
  generally, 340
  historical background, 340–341
  joint tenancies, 343
  modern position, 341–342
  response to notice to quit, 343
  serving notice to quit, 342–343
  succession, 343
 defective notice, effect of, 305
 drafting,
  clarity, requirement of, 288–289
  generally, 286–287
  use of general rubric, 287
 entry on parts at different dates, 278
 fair and reasonable landlord, 301–302
 forms. *See full list of forms in* Part V
 good husbandry, 296
 greater hardship, 299–301
 insolvency, 339–340
 invalidated by subsequent contract of sale, abolition of rule, 349
 jointly held estates, 285
 jurisdiction of courts,
  common law invalidity, 305–306
  fraud, 306–307
 landscaping,
  grazing, 312
  trees, 312
 less than twelve months,
  bad husbandry certificate, 277
  date of expiry, 278
  extended time, tenant's failure to do work within, 278
  historic agreement, 277
  insolvency of tenant, 275

Agricultural holdings—*cont.*
miscellaneous provisions—*cont.*
 less than twelve months—*cont.*
  Law of Property Act 1925 s. 149(6), 276–277
  length of notice, 278
  non-agricultural use, 275–276
  notice from tenant to sub-tenant, 276
  public purposes, 277
  statutory rent review, after, 277
 minimum twelve months, 273–275
 non-agricultural use, 301, 309–313
 non-payment of rent, 314–316
 non-remediable breach,
  assignor's dilemma, 338–339
  generally, 335–339
  material prejudice, meaning, 337–338
  meaning, 336–337
 other matters, 349
 part of agricultural holding,
  contractual clause, 281
  generally, 279
  notice to quit entirety, treated as, 283–284
  objects, 280
  purpose, 280
  reduction of rent, 284
  severance of reversion, 281–283
 postponement by Tribunal, 518
 procedural tables, 269–270, Part VI
 protection from eviction, 285
 remediable breach, 314–316
 second notice to quit, effect of, 278–279
 smallholdings, 298–299, 308–309
 sound management, 297–298
 sub-tenancy, 495–497
 waiver of defect in, 272–273
old tenancy, 161
opencast coal operations, 152
permanent pasture, variation of terms as to,
 compensation, 224
 generally, 222–223
 nature of award, 223–224
 procedure, 223
protected tenancies, 152–153
records,
 costs, 236
 disputes, 236
 effect of, 236–237
 entry on holding, 236
 form of, 237
 function of, 236–237
 generally, 236
 machinery for making, 236
 record-maker not an arbitrator, 237
recovery and charging of sums due,
 charges on holding,
  general provisions relating to, 578–579
  landlord's charge for repayment, 577
  obtaining charge on holding, 577
  tenant's charges, 575–576

1247

Agricultural holdings—*cont.*
recovery and charging of sums due—*cont.*
county court, 575
enforcement, 576
relevant licences/tenancies, 152
remedies,
dilapidations, for, 211–212
specific performance, orders for, 212–213
waste, tort of, 211
rent,
compensation set off against, 229
notice to pay,
availability of set-off, 320–321
compliance by tenant, 319–320
consequent notice to quit, 320
construction of, 316–317
procedure, 321
sufficient notice, requirements of, 318
review. *See* rent review, *below*
right to increase, 220–221
rent review,
acceptance of rent pending arbitration, 266
adjustment of boundaries, 262–263
agreement between landlord and tenant, 267
all relevant factors, meaning, 248
arbitrator,
appointment of, 241
deemed time of appointment, 243
expertise used in determining rent, 263–264
invalid appointment,
costs, 243
generally, 243
jurisdiction of, 265
replacement of, 243
boundaries, adjustment of, 262–263
capital outlay of landlord, tenant's agreement to pay interest on, 267–268
change of landlord, 266
comparable lettings,
determining rents for, 251
marriage value disregarded in relation to, 254
premiums disregarded in relation to, 257
scarcity disregarded in relation to, 251–252
current level of rents for comparable lettings, 250–251
dilapidation by tenant, 259
fixed equipment disregarded, 257–258
frequency of applications,
general rules, 260–261
matters not affecting, 261–262
generally, 239–240
high farming, 258
improvements,
grant aided element disregarded, 258

Agricultural holdings—*cont.*
rent review—*cont.*
improvements—*cont.*
landlord's right to increase rent for, 266–267
jurisdiction of arbitrator, 265
landlord,
agreement between tenant and, 267
capital outlay, tenant's agreement to pay interest on, 267–268
change of, 266
improvements, right to increase rent for, 266–267
promise not to increase rent, 265
marriage value,
comparable lettings, disregarded in relation to, 254
subject holding, relating to, 254–255
matters to be disregarded,
comparable lettings, determining rents for, 251
generally, 251
milk quotas, disregard of certain rent increases due to, 259–260
new tenancy, rent awards not normally creating, 264
open market, omission of reference to, 245–248
opencast coal,
Act of 1958, 265
activities, 268
productive capacity, meaning, 248–249
prudent, meaning, 244–245
quotas, treatment of, 260
rates, no provision relating to, 260
reduction of increases for contributions, 267
related earning capacity, meaning, 248–249
rent properly payable,
analysis, 244
meaning, 243–244
scarcity,
comparable lettings, disregarded in relation to, 251–252
subject holding, whether disregarded in relation to, 252–254
valuation in conditions where there is none, 256–257
value, techniques in ascertaining, 252
severed part of reversion, contract with persons entitled to, 262
specific factors enumerated, 248
tenant's improvements,
disregarded, 257–258
high farming as, 258
tenant,
dilapidation by, 259
own occupation of holding disregarded, 259
time limits,
arbitrator to determine rent, 242

INDEX

Agricultural holdings—*cont.*
rent review—*cont.*
time limits—*cont.*
condition of effectiveness, 241–242
date of demand for arbitration, 241
date of reference, 241, 242
demand for arbitration, 241–242
generally, 241
invalid appointment, 243
replacement of arbitrator, 243
valuation date, 241
variation of terms, 262–263
willing, meaning, 244–245
repairing obligations,
construction of, 209–210
enforcement of covenants, 210
exclusions, 153
specific performance, order for, 212–213
retirement, succession on. See Succession
secure tenancies, 153
security of tenure,
agreement made before March 1, 1948,
exclusion from s. 2 of the 1986 Act, 180
jurisdiction of court and arbitrator, 181–182
problems in construing agreement, 180–181
transactions not caught, 182–183
contemplation, meaning, 176–177
contracting out,
construing Minister's approval, 188
failure to satisfy conditions, effect of, 189
generally, 187
historic policy, 189
procedural requirements, 187
writing, requirement of, 188–189
conversion of licences, 171–173
exclusion of, 307
exemption from conversion,
agreement made before March 1, 1948, 180
grantor with interest less than tenancy from year to year, 179
grazing agreement, 175–176
prior approval by Minister, 175
general object of s. 2, 170
Gladstone v. Bower agreement, 183–184
grazing, use of land for, 178
grazing agreement,
exemption from conversion, 175–176
following tenancy from year to year, 179
mandatory nature of conversion, 183
mechanisms for, 169–170
mowing, use of land for, 178
nature of, 169–170
necessary modifications under s. 2, meaning, 173–175
origins, 270
prior approval by Minister, 175
scheme of, 270–272

Agricultural holdings—*cont.*
security of tenure—*cont.*
scope of s. 2, 170–171
some specified period of year, meaning, 177
tenant's death before term date,
assignees, position of, 186
date of termination, 186
generally, 185–186
termination of tenancies for two years or more,
agreement made before January 1, 1921, 185
operation of s. 3, 184–185
restricted ability to contract out, 185
scope, 184
service of notices. See Service of notices
size of, 153–154
smallholdings. See Smallholdings
specific performance, order for, 212–213
*statutory control over interests granted.
See* security of tenure, *above*
statutory definitions, list of, 162–168
statutory instruments. See full list *in* Part III
statutory rent review. See rent review, *above*
sub-tenancy. See Sub-tenancy
sublet dwelling-houses, 210–211
succession on death or retirement. See
Succession
termination of, meaning, 161–162
termination of tenancy,
arbitration on notice to do work,
availability of, 327–328
generally, 327
options of tenant, 328
date of, on failure to do work, 330–331
forms. *See full list of forms in* Part V
mandatory nature of protection, 272
members of reserve and auxiliary forces, protection of,
concessions, 350–351
conditions, 350
generally, 350
notice to do work,
arbitration on,
availability of, 327–328
generally, 327
tenant's options on, 328
extension of time for doing work, 330
liability, distinction between questions as to, 328–329
non-compliance with,
general effect of notice, 332
procedure, 333
tribunal's consent, 333–334
recovery of cost of work, 331
special provisions regarding, 331–332
subsequent events making time unreasonable, 329–330

1249

INDEX

Agricultural holdings—*cont.*
termination of tenancy—*cont.*
notice to do work—*cont.*
undisputed work must be done without delay, 329
notice to pay rent,
availability of set-off, 320–321
compliance by tenant, 319–320
consequent notice to quit, 320
construction of, 316–317
procedure, 321
sufficient notice, requirements of, 318
notice to quit. *See* notice to quit, *above*
notice to remedy,
construction of, 316–317
generally, 323–327
other than notice to do work, 334–335
statutory forms and procedure, 321–323
postponement of, 304
security of tenure. *See* security of tenure, *above*
settlement of claim on,
agreement, period allowed for settlement by, 418–419
arbitration,
prescribed form of award, 420
scope of, 413–415
authority relating to claim, 416
enforcement of claim, 415–416
mandatory nature of s 83, 418
method of settlement, 413
notice of intention to claim, 416–418
occupation of part after termination, 419
writing down schemes, 419–420
tied holdings, exclusion of, 151
Tribunal. See Agricultural Land Tribunal
waste, tort of, 211
arbitrator, duty of, 195
assignment, 195, 196
dates on which rent payable, 194
drainage rates, 194
effect of award, 195–196
fire, destruction by, 194
matters within Schedule 1, 193
names of parties, 193
particulars of holding, 193
rates, 194
re-entry, power of, 195
reference to arbitration, 192–193
rent, 194
right to, 192
term, 194
Agricultural land,
meaning, 156–158
Tribunal. See Agricultural Land Tribunal
Agricultural Land Tribunal,
case stated procedure, 520–523
constitution, 511–512
costs, 523–524
details of, 513–515
how to find, 512–515

Agricultural Land Tribunal—*cont.*
judicial review, 519–520
market gardens,
Evesham custom, 504
special privileges relating to, 503–504
notice to quit, postponement of operation of, 518
procedure, 515–518
reasons for decisions, 519
retirement succession, 488–490
statutory instruments. See Part III
succession,
conduct of hearing, 464–466
direction, 13, 466–467, 469–471
landlord and applicant in agreement, 467
rejection of application, 485
retirement, 488–490
rules, 461–464
taxation of costs, 523–524
Agricultural Tenancies Act 1995,
exclusions,
Agricultural Holdings Act 1986, tenancies protected by, 12–13
tenancy beginning before September 1, 1995, 11–12
farm business tenancy. See Farm business tenancy
Landlord and Tenant Act 1954,
relationship with, 11
territorial extent of, 10–11
text, Part II
Agricultural use,
abandonment of, 154–155
Agriculture,
Act of 1947 (part), Part II
Act of 1986,
milk quotas and. *See* Milk quotas
text of part, Part II
agricultural, meaning, 20
Agriculture (Miscellaneous Provisions) Act 1954 (part), Part II
condition, farm business tenancy, 19–21
statutory instruments. See full list in Part III
Allotment,
farm business tenancy excluded from definition of, 25
Small Holdings and Allotments Act 1908, 25
Amount,
meaning, 43
Appeal,
arbitration, reference to, 561
Arbitration,
Act of 1996, Part VII
Agricultural Holdings Act 1986, under.
See Agricultural holdings
farm business tenancy, dispute resolution relating to. See Farm business tenancy
forms. See full list of forms in Part V
milk quotas, relating to, 608–611
notice to do work, on,
availability of, 327–328

INDEX

Arbitration—*cont.*
notice to do work, on—*cont.*
generally, 327
options of tenant, 328
procedural tables. See Part VI
statutory instruments. See Part III
Arbitrator,
Agricultural Holdings Act 1986, arbitration under. See Agricultural holdings
Council on Tribunals, supervision by, 570
farm business tenancy, rent review under,
appointment of arbitrator, 54–55
breach of covenant or default, disregard of, 64–65
occupation of tenant, disregard of, 63–64
tenant's improvement, having regard to, 61–63
See also Dispute resolution

Bad husbandry,
certificate, 277
notice to quit, 313–314
Boundaries,
adjustment of, 262–263
Break clause,
following rent review, 41–42
Buildings,
Agricultural Tenancies Act 1995, tenant's right to remove under,
buildings, meaning, 74–75
buildings acquired, 75
content of rights, 71–73
exclusions,
building already compensated for, 70–71
consent of landlord, 71
replacement of building belonging to landlord, 70
works done in pursuance of obligation, 69–70
exhaustive nature of s. 8, 68
forfeiture clauses, 76
general, 67–68
landlord's right to purchase items, prohibition of, 68–69
mandatory nature of s. 8, 68
manner of exercise of rights, 75–76
Business tenancy,
farm. See Farm business tenancy

Charges on holding,
enforcement, 576
general provisions relating to, 578–579
landlord,
charge for repayment, 577
power to obtain charge on holding, 577
tenant, of, 575–576
Coal. *See* Opencast coal
Commencement date,
farm business tenancy, of, 11

Common Agricultural Policy,
legal framework of, 595–599
milk quotas. See Milk quotas
Compensation,
agricultural holdings, relating to. See Agricultural holdings
Evesham custom, meaning, 14–15
farm business tenancy, relating to,
Evesham custom, 14–15
exclusion from rights, 25
improvements for business tenant, 25–27
supplementary provisions, 36
tenant, rights of, 27
termination of tenancy, on,
acclimatisation or hefting of sheep, 101
amount of compensation,
planning permission, for, 103
tenant's improvement, for, 104
arbitration,
appointment of arbitrator, 105–106
machinery of, 101
reference to, where no satisfactory consent from landlord, 98–99
task of arbitrator, 101–102
benefit, meaning, 104
conditions of eligibility for claim, 94
contractual compensation, availability of, 88–89
essential right to, 93–94
fixed equipment of tenant, status of, 92–93
forms. *See full list of forms in* Part V
generally, 85–86
hefting of sheep, 101
making claim, 105
mandatory nature of Part III, 86–87
non-routine improvements, 100
planning permission,
amount of compensation, 103
conditions relating to, 94–96
resumption of possession of part of holding, 106–107
reversion severed, termination of entire tenancy where, 107–108
routine improvements, effect of providing, 100–101
service of notice, 105
settling claim, 105
sheep, acclimatisation or hefting of, 101
sub-tenancies, 91–92
successive tenancies, 106
tenant's improvement,
amount of compensation for, 104
intangible advantages, 90–91
meaning, 89–91
not being planning permission, 96–98
physical improvement, 89–90
forms. See full list of forms in Part V
milk quotas, relating to, 630–644

1251

INDEX

Contract,
agricultural tenancy, for, meaning, 159–160
farm business tenancy, 35–36
tenancy, of, meaning, 156
Costs,
Agricultural Land Tribunal, 523–524
arbitration,
  additional costs of apportionment, 573
  arbitrator has no jurisdiction, 573
  award set aside, 572
  date for payment, 573
  generally, 570–572
  special case, 572
Council on Tribunals,
supervision of arbitrators by, 570
County court,
arbitration reference, judicial control of, 562
recovery by order of, 575
Covenants,
arbitrator's disregard of tenant's breach of, 64–65
farm business tenancy, relating to,
  assigning underletting etc., 29
  implied covenants, 31–33
  new tenancy, 29
  repairing covenants, forfeiture for breach of, 27
  usual covenants, 33–34
implied, farm business tenancy, 31–33
usual, farm business tenancy, 33–34
Crown land,
Agricultural Holdings Act 1986, within, 590
farm business tenancy, 30, 145
Custom,
compensation under, 360
customary compensation,
  abolition of, 410
  limitations on abolition of, 410–412
  no uniformity pre-1948, 410
  rules relating to, 412–413
customary term days, 413
general rules relating to, 408
not relating to compensation, 408–410
recognition of, 407–408
scope for, 360

Dairy Produce Quota Tribunal,
milk quota allocated by, 640
See also Milk quotas
Damages,
common law action for, 398–399, 401–402
limit to amount of, 403–404
milk quotas, loss of, 407
Death,
succession on. See Succession
Definitions. *See* Words and phrases
Deterioration,
compensation for. See Agricultural holdings

Dilapidations,
compensation for. See Agricultural holdings
remedies for, 211–212
rent review, 259
Dispute resolution,
Agricultural Holdings Act 1986, arbitration under. See Agricultural holdings
Agricultural Land Tribunal. See Agricultural Land Tribunal
farm business tenancy, relating to. See Farm business tenancy
generally, 510–511
Distress,
compensation set off against rent, 229
contracting out, 231
generally, 228
rent due more than year previously, 228–229
settlement of disputes, 230–231
third party, restrictions on distraining property of, 229–230
Disturbance,
compensation for. See Agricultural holdings
Diversification,
farm business tenancy, relating to, 22–23
meaning, 22–23
Duchy of Cornwall,
farm business tenancy, 30
Duchy of Lancaster,
farm business tenancy, 30

EEC Regulations. *See* Part IV
Electronic means,
service of notices by, 587–588
Emblements,
extension of tenancies in lieu of claims to, 234–235
Enforcement,
arbitration award, of, 559–560
farm business tenancy, enforceable contractual timetable for rent review under,
  generally, 48–49
  landlord, rent trigger notice only available to, 49–50
  rent trigger notice, 49–50
  time of essence, 49
recovery and charging of sums due, 576
repairing covenants, of, 210
Enfranchisement. *See* Leasehold enfranchisement
Entry,
landlord's power of, 237–238
parts, on, at different dates, 278
Error of law,
arbitration, reference to, 567–569
Estate management,
good, 221–222, A.2

INDEX

European Union (EU),
Common Agricultural Policy, legal framework of, 595–599
milk quotas. See Milk quotas
regulations. See Part IV
Treaty of Rome as amended by Treaty of Amsterdam, Part IV

Evesham custom,
market gardens, relating to. See Market gardens
meaning, 14–15

Evidence,
farm business tenancy, rent review under, 65–66

Farm business tenancy,
agreed succession tenancy,
  beginning on or after September 1, 1995, 13–14
  written agreement, 14
agreement, content of, 24–25
agricultural holding, assimilating position to that of, 27
Agricultural Holdings Act 1986,
  general background, 9–10
  tenancy beginning on or after September 1, 1995,
    agreed succession by written agreement, 14
    agreed succession tenancies, 13–14
    Agricultural Land Tribunal succession direction, obtained by virtue of, 13
    Evesham custom, 14–15
    exclusions, 12–13
    parties agree 1986 Act shall apply, 13
    surrender and regrant in favour of tenant already protected, 15–16
agricultural land, mortgage of, 141
Agricultural Tenancies Act 1995,
  exclusions,
    tenancies beginning on or after September 1, 1995 protected by Agricultural Holdings Act 1986, 12–13
    tenancy beginning before September 1, 1995: s 2(1)(a), 11–12
  relationship with Landlord and Tenant Act 1954, 11
  territorial extent of, 10–11
agriculture condition, 17, 19–21
allotments,
  compensation rights, exclusion of farm business tenant from, 25
  definition, exclusion of farm business tenancy from, 25
alternative dispute resolution, 139
arbitration. See dispute resolution, *below*
business conditions, 17, 18
business tenancy, relationship with, 28
capital money, power to apply and raise, 142

Farm business tenancy—*cont.*
commencement date, importance of, 11
compensation,
  Evesham custom, 14–15
  exclusion from rights, 25
  improvements for business tenant, 25–27
  supplementary provisions, 36
  tenant's right to, 27
  termination of tenancy, on,
    acclimatisation or hefting of sheep, 101
    amount of compensation,
      planning permission, for, 103
      tenant's improvement, for, 104
    arbitration,
      appointment of arbitrator, 105–106
      machinery of, 101
      reference to, where no satisfactory consent from landlord, 98–99
      task of arbitrator, 101–102
    benefit, meaning, 104
    conditions of eligibility for claim, 94
    contractual compensation, availability of, 88–89
    essential right to, 93–94
    fixed equipment of tenant, status of, 92–93
    generally, 85–86
    hefting of sheep, 101
    making claim, 105
    mandatory nature of Part III, 86–87
    non-routine improvements, 100
    planning permission,
      amount of compensation, 103
      conditions relating to, 94–96
    resumption of possession of part of holding, 106–107
    reversion severed, termination of entire tenancy where, 107–108
    routine improvements, effect of providing, 100–101
    service of notice, 105
    settling claim, 105
    sheep, acclimatisation or hefting of, 101
    sub-tenancies, 91–92
    successive tenancies, 106
    tenant's improvement,
      amount of compensation for, 104
      intangible advantages, 90–91
      meaning, 89–91
      not being planning permission, 96–98
      physical improvement, 89–90
consents, power of limited owners to give, 141–142
content of agreement, 24–25
contract, relative freedom of, 35–36
covenants,
  assigning underletting etc., 29
  implied, 31–33
  new tenancy, 29
  repairing, forfeiture for breach of, 27

1253

INDEX

Farm business tenancy—*cont.*
  covenants—*cont.*
    usual, 33–34
  Crown land, application to, 30, 145
  definitions in s 4(3), 17
  dispute resolution,
    additional award, 133
    agreement in writing, 126
    alternative, 139
    appeal on point of law, 134
    appointment of arbitrator, 126–127, 134–135
    arbitral institutions, immunity of, 124
    Arbitration Act 1996, 114
    arbitration agreement, meaning, 126
    assessors, appointment of, 130
    authority of arbitrator, revocation of, 127
    awards on different issues, 131
    chairman, 127
    challenging award, 124
    commencement of arbitral proceedings, 126
    compensation dispute, 119
    competence of tribunal, 128
    concurrent hearings, 129
    consolidation of proceedings, 129
    correction of award, 133
    costs of award, 133
    court powers, exercise of, 131
    court's power to remove arbitrator, 121
    date of award, 132
    death of arbitrator, effect of, 121, 128
    default of parties, 130–131
    default to appoint sole arbitrator, 127
    determination of preliminary point of law, 131
    domestic arbitration agreement, modification of Part I relating to, 118
    effect of award, 133
    enforcement of award, 123
    enforcement of peremptory orders of tribunal, 131
    expenses of arbitrator, 121 123
    experts, appointment of, 130
    extension of time for making award, 132
    failure of appointment procedure, 127
    fees, liability of parties for, 121
    filling of vacancy, 128
    form of award, 132
    frustration of appointment process, 137
    general arbitration, 119
    general powers exercisable by tribunal, 130
    generally, 109–110
    honest award, whether possible to upset, 137–138
    immunity of arbitrator, 121–122
    independent expert, by, 135–136
    interest, 132
    intervention of court, experts and, 138
    legal advisers, appointment of, 130
    legal or other representation, 130

Farm business tenancy—*cont.*
  dispute resolution—*cont.*
    Limitation Acts, application of, 121
    loss of right to object, 124
    non-payment, withholding award in case of, 123
    notification of award, 132
    Order 73, application under, 124
    parties, general duty of, 123
    payment of costs, effectiveness of agreement for, 123
    place where award treated as made, 132
    preliminary point of jurisdiction, determination of, 122
    procedural and evidential matters, 128–129
    procedure and powers under arbitration, 120
    production of expert determination, 136
    provisional awards, power to make, 130
    recoverable costs of arbitration, 133
    recoverable fees and expenses, 133
    remedies, 132
    rent review arbitration, 119
    requirement for writing, 119–120
    resignation of arbitrator, 127–128
    saving for rights of person taking no part, 124
    section 28,
      concurrent jurisdiction of court, 117–118
      generally, 110–111
    section 29,
      application of Arbitration Act to arbitration under, 115
      non-binding mediation not within, 114
      scope of, 112–114
      status of reference, 114
    section 30,
      scope and terms, 111–112
      status of arbitration, 112
    separability of arbitration agreement, 126
    service of documents, 134
    service of notices, 134
    settlement, 132
    solicitors' costs, charge to secure payment of, 124
    statutory arbitration,
      application of Arbitration Act, 115–116
      mandatory sections, 121–124
      modifications of Arbitration Act, 116–117
      non-mandatory sections, 125–134
    stay of legal proceedings, 121
    substance of dispute, rules applicable to, 131
    substantive jurisdiction of tribunal, objection to, 122
    summary of legislation, 119
    tailoring provision, 37
    time limits, 134
    Tribunal, general duty of, 122–123

INDEX

Farm business tenancy—*cont.*
dispute resolution—*cont.*
  umpire, 127
  witnesses, securing attendance of, 123
diversification, 22–23
Duchy of Cornwall, land within, 30
Duchy of Lancaster, land within, 30
enfranchisement, 28
estimation of best rent, 142
Evesham custom, 14–15
exclusions,
  protection of Rent Act, 28
  repairing obligations, 28
  tenancies beginning on or after
   September 1, 1995 protected by
   Agricultural Holdings Act 1986,
   12–13
  tenancy beginning before September 1,
   1995: s. 2(1)(a), 11–12
failure to serve notices, 23
*fixtures and buildings, tenant's right to
  remove,*
  buildings, meaning, 74–75
  content of rights, 71–73
  exclusions,
   consent of landlord, 71
   fixture or building already
    compensated for, 70–71
   replacement of fixture or building
    belonging to landlord, 70
   works done in pursuance of obligation,
    69–70
  exhaustive nature of s. 8, 68
  fixtures, meaning, 73
  fixtures or buildings acquired, meaning,
   75
  forfeiture clauses, 76
  general, 67–68
  landlord's right to purchase items,
   prohibition of, 68–69
  mandatory nature of s. 8, 68
  manner of exercise of rights, 75–76
floating charges over farming stock, 27
forms. See full list of forms in Part V
general background, 9–10
government department, land held by, 30
implied covenants, 31–33
land used in breach of terms of, 19
Landlord and Tenant Act 1954,
  Agricultural Tenancies Act 1995,
   relationship with, 11
  amendments to, 28
length of term, 30–31
meaning, 17
milk quotas, 645–646
miscellaneous forms, 145–146
miscellaneous provisions, 141
no qualification as to size of, 11
notice conditions,
  failure to serve notice, 23
  requirements relating to, 21–22
Opencast Coal Act 1958, application of, 28
other statutes, 29–30

Farm business tenancy—*cont.*
rebuttable presumption as to use, 18–19
relative freedom of contract, 35–36
Rent Act 1977, application of, 28
rent review,
  amount, meaning, 43
  arbitrator,
   appointment of, 54–55
   breach of covenant or default,
    disregard of, 64–65
   occupation of tenant, disregard of,
    63–64
   tenant's improvement, having regard
    to, 61–63
  breach of covenant or default, arbitrator
   disregarding, 64–65
  break clause following, 41–42
  determination of initial rent, 47–48
  different rents for different parts of
   holding, 40–41
  enforceable contractual timetable for,
   generally, 48–49
   landlord, rent trigger notice only
    available to, 49–50
   rent trigger notice, 49–50
   time of essence, 49
  evidence relating to, 65–66
  exemption,
   amount, written agreement stipulating,
    43–44
   cumulative availability of exemptions,
    47
   formula, written agreement providing
    timetable and stipulating, 44–47
   no rent review, written agreement
    stipulating, 42
   timetable, written agreement
    providing,
    stipulating amount, 43–44
    stipulating formula, 44–47
  fine, taking capital sum by way of,
   40
  fixed equipment,
   meaning, 60
   tenant, of, 60
  formula, meaning, 43, 44–45
  general, 39–40
  implementing,
   arbitrator, appointment of, 54–55
   general, 53
   valid statutory review notice,
    requirements of, 53–54
  initial rent, determination of, 47–48
  notice to quit following, 41–42
  occupation of tenant, arbitrator having
   disregard of, 63–64
  open market valuation, 56–59
  percentage, meaning, 44
  premium, taking capital sum by way of,
   40
  purely contractual clause, scope for,
   51–52
  statutory review notice, 39

1255

Farm business tenancy—*cont.*
  rent review—*cont.*
    tenant,
      breach of covenant or default,
        arbitrator disregarding, 64–65
      fixed equipment of, 60
      improvements of,
        arbitrator having regard to, 61–63
        valuation difficulties, 63
    timetable,
      enforceable contractual,
        generally, 48–49
        landlord, rent trigger notice only available to, 49–50
        rent trigger notice, 49–50
        time of essence, 49
      written agreement providing, 44–47
    timing of, 39
    valuation,
      basis of, 55
      open market, 56–59
      tenant's improvements, 63
    written agreement,
      providing timetable and stipulating amount, 43–44
      stipulating for no rent review, 42
      stipulating formula, 44–47
      timetable, provision of, 44–47
  repairs,
    exclusion of obligations, 28
    forfeiture for breach of covenant, 27
  reserve and auxiliary forces, protection of, 27, A.12
  resolution of disputes. See dispute resolution, *above*
  secure tenancy, precluded from being, 28
  service of notices,
    dispute resolution, 134
    due service,
      agent or servant managing, holding or carrying on business there, 144–145
      body corporate, service on, 144
      change of landlord, 145
      contract, as authorised by, 143–144
      delivery to recipient, 143
      leaving document at recipient's proper address, 143
      generally, 142–143
  size of, 11
  Small Holdings and Allotments Act 1908, application of, 25
  succession tenancy. See Succession.
  surveyors, preparation of documents etc. by, 23–24 142
  tenancy, meaning, 17
  tenancy beginning on or after September 1, 1995,
    agreed succession by written agreement, 14
    agreed succession tenancies, 13–14
    Agricultural Land Tribunal succession direction, obtained by virtue of, 13

Farm business tenancy—*cont.*
  tenancy beginning on or after September 1—*cont.*
    Evesham custom, 14–15
    exclusions, 12–13
    parties agree 1986 Act shall apply, 13
    surrender and regrant in favour of tenant already protected, 15–16
  termination of,
    compensation on,
      acclimatisation or hefting of sheep, 101
      amount of compensation,
        planning permission, for, 103
        tenant's improvement, for, 104
      arbitration,
        appointment of arbitrator, 105–106
        machinery of, 101
        reference to, where no satisfactory consent from landlord, 98–99
        task of arbitrator, 101–102
      benefit, meaning, 104
      conditions of eligibility for claim, 94
      contractual compensation, availability of, 88–89
      essential right to, 93–94
      fixed equipment of tenant, status of, 92–93
      generally, 85–86
      hefting of sheep, 101
      making claim, 105
      mandatory nature of Part III, 86–87
      non-routine improvements, 100
      planning permission,
        amount of compensation, 103
        conditions relating to, 94–96
      resumption of possession of part of holding, 106–107
      reversion severed, termination of entire tenancy where, 107–108
      routine improvements, effect of providing, 100–101
      service of notice, 105
      settling claim, 105
      sheep, acclimatisation or hefting of, 101
      sub-tenancies, 91–92
      successive tenancies, 106
      tenant's improvement,
        amount of compensation for, 104
        intangible advantages, 90–91
        meaning, 89–91
        not being planning permission, 96–98
        physical improvement, 89–90
    notice, by,
      ascertainment of length of fixed term, 83
      break clause,
        fixed term agreement of two years or less, 79
        fixed terms of more than two years, 80–81

INDEX

Farm business tenancy—*cont.*
termination of—*cont.*
  notice, by—*cont.*
    break clause—*cont.*
      grounds on which exercised, 82
      periodic tenancies, 79
    disputes, 84
    exclusions,
      Law of Property Act 1925, terms within, 81–82
      tenant's counter-notice, 81 83
      fixed term farm business tenancy of two years or less, 78
    general, 77–78
    jointly held estates, 80, 82, 84
    jurisdiction of courts, 84
    monthly periodic tenancy, 78
    notice to quit,
      annual tenancies, 82
      valid, requirements of, 82–83
    protection from eviction, 83–84
    quarterly periodic tenancy, 78
    security of tenure, lack of, 83
    tenancy for more than two years,
      generally, 79
      jointly held estates, 80
      mandatory nature of s 5, 80
      who may give notice, 80
    weekly periodic tenancy, 78
    who may give notice, 80, 82, 84
  territorial extent of Agricultural Tenancies Act 1995, 10–11
  use, rebuttable presumption as to, 18–19
  usual covenants, 33–34
  valuers, preparation of documents etc. by, 23–24, 142
Fax,
  service of notices by, 587–588
Fine,
  farm business tenancy, rent review under, 40
Fixed equipment,
  Agricultural Holdings Act 1986, rights relating to. See Agricultural holdings
  rent review, 257–258
Fixtures,
  Agricultural Holdings Act 1986, rights relating to. See Agricultural holdings
  Agricultural Tenancies Act 1995, tenant's right to remove under,
    content of rights, 71–73
    exclusions,
      consent of landlord, 71
      fixture already compensated for, 70–71
      replacement of fixture belonging to landlord, 70
      works done in pursuance of obligation, 69–70
    exhaustive nature of s 8, 68
    fixtures, meaning, 73
    fixtures acquired, meaning, 75
    forfeiture clauses, 76
    general, 67–68

Fixtures—*cont.*
Agricultural Tenancies Act 1995, tenant's right to remove under,—*cont.*
    landlord's right to purchase items, prohibition of, 68–69
    mandatory nature of s 8, 68
    manner of exercise of rights, 75–76
  fixed equipment, meaning, 60
  rent review under Agricultural Tenancies Act 1995, 60
  statutory instruments. See Part III
Forfeiture,
  action for, 401–402
  buildings and fixtures, tenant's right to remove, 76
Forms. *See full list of forms in* Part V
Formula,
  meaning, 43, 44–45

Game damage,
  arbitration, 234
  compensation, 231–234
Gardens. *See* Market gardens
Good husbandry,
  meaning of rules of, 398
  notice to quit, 296
Government department,
  land held by, farm business tenancy, 30

Hearing,
  arbitration under Agricultural Holdings Act 1986. See Agricultural holdings
High Court,
  Agricultural Land Tribunal, control of, 519–520
High farming,
  compensation, claim for,
    allowances and exclusions, 395–396
    conditions of claim, 395
    continuous adoption of special system of farming, 394–395
    difficulties in way of, 396
    measure of compensation, 395
  rent review, 258
High-tech farming methods,
  impact of, 404
Hill farming,
  improvements, compensation for, 394
Holding,
  meaning, 53, 605

Improvements,
  compensation for,
    additional compensation, 390–391
    assembling scheme of works, 386–387
    classification of improvements, 386
    consents,
      not required, 389
      requirements relating to, 387–388
    distinction between old and new improvements, 376
    generally, 375–376
    hill farming, 394

1257

Improvements—*cont.*
  compensation for—*cont.*
    limitations on, 391–392
    measure of compensation, 389–390
    notices required, 387–388
    old improvements,
      changes of tenancy during one occupation, 379
      consents, 378–379
      list of, 380
      measure of compensation, 377–378
      new improvements distinguished from, 376
      right to compensation, 377
      rules governing, 377
      subrogation of incoming tenant to rights of outgoer, 379–380
    planning permission, 387
    relevant improvements, meaning, 380
    restrictions on, 394
    short term improvements, 389–390
    sub-tenancies and work subject to direction, 393–394
    subrogation of incoming tenant to rights of outgoer, 392–393
    substituted compensation, 390–391
    successive tenancies during one occupation, 392
    works, 389
  forms. See full list of forms in Part V
  meaning, 385
  relevant, meaning, 380
  rent review,
    grant aided element disregarded, 258
    landlord's right to increase rent, 266–267
  short term, 389–390

Insolvency,
  notice to quit, 339–340
  tenant, of, 275

Interest,
  arbitration award, on, 558

Judicial review,
  Agricultural Land Tribunal, decision of, 519–520
  arbitration, reference to, 569–570

Jurisdiction,
  arbitrator, of, challenge to, 536–537

Land,
  farm business tenancy, use in breach of terms of, 19
  transfer of milk quota without, 614–615

Landlord,
  Agricultural Holdings Act 1986, under. See Agricultural holdings
  fair and reasonable, 301–302
  farm business tenancy. See Farm business tenancy

Landlord and Tenant Act 1954,
  agricultural Tenancies Act 1995, relationship with, 11

Landscaping,
  grazing, 312
  trees, 312

Leasehold enfranchisement,
  farm business tenancy, 28

Limited owners,
  capital money,
    application of, 579–580
    compensation, not to be applied directly in, 580
    redemption of charges out of, 581–582
  consent, powers relating to, 579
  lease at best rent, 583
  tenant for life,
    direct expenditure by, 582–583
    may obtain charge, 581
    ultimate liability between remainderman and, 582
  Trusts of Land and Appointment of Trustees Act 1996, 579

Livestock,
  farm business tenancy, exemption relating to, 25

Lord Chancellor,
  arbitration, powers relating to, 527–528

Market gardens,
  Agricultural Land Tribunal, direction by, 503–504
  Evesham custom,
    agreement, compensation substituted by, 506
    conditions for compensation, 505
    custom, operation of, 505–506
    generally, 504
    measure of compensation, 506
  generally, 492
  meaning, 499–500
  special privileges relating to,
    fixtures, removal of, 500–501
    fruit trees and bushes, removal of, 501
    generally, 500
    improvements purchased by tenant, 501
    qualification, 502–504
    tenant's improvements, 500
  treatment of, 499

Milk quotas,
  Agriculture Act 1986, under,
    compensation to outgoing tenants, 630–644
    definitions, 626–627
    farm business tenancy, 645–646
    generally, 625–626
    rent arbitration, treatment of milk quota on, 628–630
    service of notices, 645
    severance of reversion, 645
    structure of statute, 626
    termination of tenancy of part of tenanted land, 645
  apportionment of quota, 611–613
  arbitration relating to, 608–611

Milk quotas—*cont.*
Common Agricultural Policy, legal framework of, 595–599
compensation of outgoing tenants, 630–644
Dairy Produce Quota Tribunal, allocated by, 640
damages for loss of, 407
disposal of quota on break up or sale of holding, 619–620
domestic level in UK, general implementation at, 601
domestic regulations, scheme of, 606–607
EEC Regulations, Part IV
economic purpose of, 594–595
generally, 593–594
holding, meaning, 605
land, transfers of quota without, 614–615
mortgages,
  created after March 1, 1948, but before September 1, 1995, 623
  created on or after September 1, 1995, 623–624
non-active quota holders, 603–604
partnership, and,
  cross-accounting,
    no tenancy, 622
    tenancy, where there is, 622
  equitable cross-accounting, 621
permanent transfers of,
  generally, 615–616
  market in, 616–617
procedural tables. See Part VI
producer, meaning, 602–603
protection clauses,
  absence of, 620–621
  efficacy, 618–619
  reservations on sale, 619
  types, 617–618
purchaser, meaning, 604–605
rent arbitration, treatment on, 628–630
rent increases, disregard of, 259–260
rent review, 260
roll over of compensation, 477
S.L.O.M. quota, 605–606
service of notices, 645
severance of reversion, 645
statutory instruments. See Part III
system at Community level, 599–601
temporary transfers of, 613–614
termination of tenancy of part of tenanted land, 645
transfers of,
  permanent, 615–617
  temporary, 613–614
  without land, 614–615
Misconduct,
arbitration, reference to, 563–566
Mortgage,
milk quotas and, 623–624

Northern Ireland,
Agricultural Tenancies Act 1995, territorial extent of, 10–11
Notice conditions,
farm business tenancy, 21–22
Notice to do work,
arbitration on,
  availability of, 327–328
  generally, 327
  tenant's options on, 328
extension of time for doing work, 330
liability, distinction between questions as to, 328–329
non-compliance with,
  general effect of notice, 332
  procedure, 333
  tribunal's consent, 333–334
recovery of cost of work, 331
special provisions regarding, 331–332
subsequent events making time unreasonable, 329–330
undisputed work must be done without delay, 329
Notice to pay rent. *See* rent
Notice to quit,
Agricultural Holdings Act 1986, under. See Agricultural holdings
farm business tenancy,
  following rent review under, 41–42
  termination of. *See* Farm business tenancy
forms. See full list of forms in Part V
procedural tables, 269–270, Part VI
Notice to remedy
construction of, 316–317
generally, 323–327
other than notice to do work, 334–335
statutory forms and procedure, 321–323

Open market,
farm business tenancy, rent review under, 56–59
meaning, 56, 245–248
rent review, 245–248
Opencast coal,
Act of 1958, 265
activities, 268
compensation relating to, 406
operations, 152
Owners,
limited. See Limited owners

Partnership,
milk quotas and. See Milk quotas
Pasture,
permanent, variation of terms as to,
  compensation, 224
  generally, 222–223
  nature of award, 223–224
  procedure, 223
Percentage,
meaning, 44
Planning permission,
improvements, compensation for, 387

INDEX

Post. *See* Service of notices
Premium,
  farm business tenancy, rent review under,
    40
Procedural tables. *See* Part VI
Producer,
  meaning, 602–603
Productive capacity,
  meaning, 248–249
Property,
  Law of Property Act 1925 (part), Part II
Protection clauses. *See* Milk quotas
Prudent,
  meaning, 244–245
Purchaser,
  meaning, 604

Records,
  costs, 236
  disputes, 236
  effect of, 236–237
  entry on holding, 236
  form of, 237
  function of, 236–237
  generally, 236
  machinery for making, 236
  record-maker not arbitrator, 237
Recovery,
  county court, order of, 575
Remedies,
  dilapidations, for, 211–212
  specific performance, orders for, 212–213
  waste, tort of, 211
Remuneration,
  arbitrator, of, 533–534
Rent,
  compensation set off against, 229
  notice to pay,
    availability of set-off, 320–321
    compliance by tenant, 319–320
    consequent notice to quit, 320
    construction of, 316–317
    procedure, 321
    sufficient notice, requirements of, 318
  review. See Rent review
  right to increase, 220–221
Rent review,
  Agricultural Holdings Act 1986, under.
    See Agricultural holdings
  farm business tenancy,
    amount, meaning, 43
    arbitrator,
      appointment of, 54–55
      breach of covenant or default,
        disregard of, 64–65
      occupation of tenant, disregard of,
        63–64
      tenant's improvement, having regard
        to, 61–63
    breach of covenant or default, arbitrator
      disregarding, 64–65
    break clause following, 41–42
    determination of initial rent, 47–48

Rent review—*cont.*
  farm business tenancy—*cont.*
    different rents for different parts of
      holding, 40–41
    enforceable contractual timetable for,
      generally, 48–49
      landlord, rent trigger notice only
        available to, 49–50
      rent trigger notice, 49–50
      time of essence, 49
    evidence relating to, 65–66
    exemption,
      amount, written agreement stipulating,
        43–44
      cumulative availability of exemptions,
        47
      formula, written agreement providing
        timetable and stipulating,
        44–47
      no rent review, written agreement
        stipulating, 42
      timetable, written agreement
        providing,
          stipulating amount, 43–44
          stipulating formula, 44–47
    fine, taking capital sum by way of, 40
    fixed equipment,
      meaning, 60
      tenant, of, 60
    formula, meaning, 43 44–45
    general, 39–40
    implementing,
      arbitrator, appointment of, 54–55
      general, 53
      valid statutory review notice,
        requirements of, 53–54
    initial rent, determination of, 47–48
    notice to quit following, 41–42
    occupation of tenant, arbitrator having
      disregard of, 63–64
    open market valuation, 56–59
    percentage, meaning, 44
    premium, taking capital sum by way of,
      40
    purely contractual clause, scope of,
      51–52
    statutory review notice, 39
    tenant,
      breach of covenant or default,
        arbitrator disregarding, 64–65
      fixed equipment of, 60
      improvements of,
        arbitrator having regard to, 61–63
        valuation difficulties, 63
    timetable,
      enforceable contractual,
        generally, 48–49
        landlord, rent trigger notice only
          available to, 49–50
        rent trigger notice, 49–50
        time of essence, 49
      written agreement providing, 44–47
    timing of, 39

1260

INDEX

Rent review—*cont.*
farm business tenancy—*cont.*
  valuation,
    basis of, 55
    open market, 56–59
    tenant's improvements, 63
  written agreement,
    providing timetable and stipulating amount, 43–44
    stipulating for no rent review, 42
    stipulating formula, 44–47
    timetable, provision of, 44–47
forms. See full list of forms in Part V
Repairs,
farm business tenancy,
  exclusion of obligations, 28
  forfeiture for breach of covenant, 27
fixed equipment, to, 197
meaning, 204–205
repairing obligations,
  construction of, 209–210
  enforcement of covenants, 210
  exclusions, 153
  specific performance, order for, 212–213
Reserve and auxiliary forces
protection of, 27, A.12
Resolution of disputes. *See* Dispute resolution
Retirement,
succession on. See Succession
Royal Institution of Chartered Surveyors,
appointment of arbitrator by President of, 530–532

Scotland,
Agricultural Tenancies Act 1995, territorial extent of, 10
Secure tenancy,
farm business tenancy precluded from being, 28
Security of tenure,
agreement made before March 1, 1948,
  exclusion from s. 2 of the 1986 Act, 180
  jurisdiction of court and arbitrator, 181–182
  problems in construing agreement, 180–181
  transactions not caught, 182–183
contemplation, meaning, 176–177
contracting out,
  construing Minister's approval, 188
  failure to satisfy conditions, effect of, 189
  generally, 187
  historic policy, 189
  procedural requirements, 187
  writing, requirement of, 188–189
  conversion of licences, 171–173
exclusion of, 307
exemption from conversion,
  agreement made before March 1, 1948, 180
  grantor with interest less than tenancy from year to year, 179

Security of tenure—*cont.*
exemption from conversion—*cont.*
  grazing agreement, 175–176
  prior approval by Minister, 175
general object of s. 2, 170
Gladstone v. Bower *agreement,* 183–184
grazing, use of land for, 178
grazing agreement,
  exemption from conversion, 175–176
  following tenancy from year to year, 179
mandatory nature of conversion, 183
mechanisms for, 169–170
mowing, use of land for, 178
nature of, 169–170
necessary modifications under s. 2, meaning, 173–175
origins, 270
prior approval by Minister, 175
scheme of, 270–272
scope of s. 2, 170–171
some specified period of year, meaning, 177
tenant's death before term date,
  assignees, position of, 186
  date of termination, 186
  generally, 185–186
termination of tenancies for two years or more,
  agreement made before January 1, 1921, 185
  operation of s. 3, 184–185
  restricted ability to contract out, 185
  scope, 184
Servant,
service of notices, 588–589
Service of notices,
due service,
  agent, on, 588–589
  change of landlord, 590
  delivery to recipient, 584
  electronic means, transmission by, 587–588
  fax, transmission by, 587–588
  ordinary post, use of, 586–587
  proper address of recipient, leaving document at, 585
  recorded delivery service, sending by, 585–586
  registered delivery service, sending by, 585–586
  servant, on, 588–589
farm business tenancy, relating to. see Farm business tenancy
generally, 583
milk quotas, relating to, 645
Severance,
apportionment of conditions on, A.2
Sheep,
acclimatisation or hefting of, 101
Size,
farm business tenancy, of, no qualification as to, 11

1261

INDEX

Smallholdings,
  Agricultural Holdings Act 1986, within, 506
  disposal of produce, 506–507
  freedom of cropping, 506–507
  generally, 492
  other matters, 507–508
  termination of schemes, 507
Specific performance,
  orders for, 212–213
Statutes. *See* Part II
Statutory control over interests granted. *See* Security of tenure
Statutory instruments. *See* Part III
Statutory rent review. *See* Rent review
Sub-tenancy,
  Agricultural Holdings Act 1986, protected by, 493
  collusive activity between head landlord and head tenant, 497–498
  compensation relating to, 91–92
  concurrent lease, 493–494
  forfeiture of head tenancy, 497
  generally, 492
  meaning, 492–493
  merger of head tenancy, 497
  notice to quit, position of sub-tenant and, 495–497
  section 25, 494–495
  section 26, 495
  security of tenure, avoidance of, 498
  sub-tenants, special provisions for, 494
  surrender of head tenancy, 497
Succession,
  agreed succession tenancy,
    beginning on or after September 1, 1995, 13–14
    written agreement, 14
  Agricultural Land Tribunal direction, 13
  death, on,
    Agricultural land Tribunal,
      conduct of hearing, 464–466
      direction to more than one applicant, 466–467
      effect of direction by, 469–471
      landlord and applicant in agreement, 467
      notice to quit, consent to operation of, 468–469
      succession rules, 461–464
    analysis of historical events, 477–478
    applicable tenancies, 423
    arbitration,
      award, 473–474
      demand for, 471–472
      rent, as to, 473
      scope of, 472
      terms of new tenancy, 471
      time-limit, 471–472
      variation in terms of tenancy, 472–473
    close relative of deceased tenant, 434
    contracting-in tenancies, 424–425
    direction,
      tenancies granted following, 424

Succession—*cont.*
  death, on—*cont.*
    direction—*cont.*
      tenancies obtained by virtue of, 424
    eligibility,
      close relative of deceased tenant, 434
      conditions for, 434
    exclusions,
      close relative, tenancy granted by landlord to, 427
      direction,
        tenancy granted by landlord following, 427
        tenancy obtained by virtue of, 426–427
      ex-servicemen settled in agriculture, 430
      fixed term tenancy, 426
      generally, 425
      Gladstone v. Bower tenancy, 426
      notice to quit, 429
      retirement at age 65 or over, 429
      smallholding, 429–430
      succession inter vivos by agreement, 427–428
      tenancy obtained by virtue of direction, 426–427
      tenant deriving title by operation of law, 425
      two previous successions having occurred, 426
    forms. *See full list of forms in* Part V
    general scheme of Part IV, 423
    grant to existing tenant, 425
    landlord's response,
      completion of form, 432–433
      form, 432
    livelihood condition,
      accommodation, benefit of, 444–445
      agricultural unit of which holding forms part, 438–440
      agricultural work, meaning, 437
      applicant demonstrating eligibility,
        discovery, 441–442
        livelihood, 441
      complex land holdings, effect on figures of, 444
      full time higher education, 441
      generally, 435
      livelihood, meaning, 436
      principal source of livelihood, 440
      relevant period, 436
      source of livelihood, 437, 442–444
      succession planning, principles for, 445–446
      wife, agricultural work by deceased counting as work by, 440
      work on holding, 437
    making application,
      amending forms, 433–434
      completion of form, 431–432
      filing forms, 433–434
      form, 430–431

1262

INDEX

Succession—*cont.*
  death, on—*cont.*
    making application—*cont.*
      serving forms, 433–434
      time limits, 430
      treated as eligible, 434
    milk quota compensation, roll over of, 477
    new tenancy, changeover and adjustment to, 474–476
    non-eligible family members, 435
    notice to quit,
      restriction on operation of, 467
      seeking consent to operation of, 468–469
    occupancy condition,
      application to be treated as eligible, availability, 455–456
        exercise of Tribunal's discretion, 456–457
        meaning, 455–456
      commercial unit of agricultural land, 446
      deemed occupation, 451, 454–455
      disapplication of disregard, 451
      disregarded occupation, 449–451
      generally, 446
      joint occupation,
        cases apparently not covered, 452–453
        cases covered, 451–452
      limitation to appropriate share, meaning, 453–454
      material dates for fulfilment of, 446
      mathematical test, 447
      ministerial statements as to net annual income,
        extent to which binding, 448
        making request, 447–448
        who may make request, 447
      objective element, 447
      occupation which counts for purposes of, 448–449
      subjective element, 446–447
    priority of applications, 459–461
    procedural tables. *See* Part VI
    succession tenancy, 476–477
    suitability,
      discovery, 458
      discussion, 458–459
      relevant matters, 457–458
    surrender and re-grant, 425
    tenancies granted on or after July 12, 1984, 423–424
  forms. *See full list of forms in* Part V
  planning,
    principles for, 445–446
    retirement succession, 487–488
  procedural tables, 422–423, Part VI
  retirement, on,
    Agricultural Land Tribunal, 488–490
    arbitration on terms of new tenancy, 485–486

Succession—*cont.*
  retirement, on—*cont.*
    availability of retirement where tenant is under 65 but infirm, 480–481
    direction based on greater hardship, refusal of, 484
    fate of application, 484–485
    forms. *See full list of forms in* Part V
    generally, 478
    miscellaneous, 488
    nominated successor, application by, 481–484
    notice to quit, inter-relationship of retirement notice and, 481
    procedure tables. *See* Part VI
    relevant time, meaning, 487
    retirement notice,
      death of tenant after giving, 486–487
      notice to quit, inter-relationship with, 481
    retirement scheme,
      conditions for operation of, 479
      exclusions from, 479–480
    succession planning, 487–488
    Tribunal direction, effect of, 487
  statutory instruments. *See* Part III
Surveyor,
  farm business tenancy, preparation of documents relating to, 23–24, 142

Table of derivations, A.175
Table of destinations, A.176
Tenancy,
  farm business. *See* Farm business tenancy
  forms. *See full list of forms in* Part V
  meaning, 17
  termination of. *See* Termination of tenancy
Tenant,
  fixed equipment of, 60
  fixtures and buildings, removal of,
    buildings, meaning, 74–75
    content of rights, 71–73
    exclusions,
      consent of landlord, 71
      fixture or building already compensated for, 70–71
      replacement of fixture or building belonging to landlord, 70
      works done in pursuance of obligation, 69–70
    exhaustive nature of s. 8, 68
    fixtures, meaning, 73
    fixtures or buildings acquired, meaning, 75
    forfeiture clauses, 76
    general, 67–68
    landlord's right to purchase items, prohibition of, 68–69
    mandatory nature of s. 8, 68
    manner of exercise of rights, 75–76
  rent review. *See* Rent review

INDEX

Termination of tenancy,
Agricultural Holdings Act 1986, under.
See Agricultural holdings
Agricultural Tenancies Act 1995, notice under,
ascertainment of length of fixed term, 83
break clause,
fixed term agreement of two years or less, 79
fixed terms of more than two years, 80–81
grounds on which exercised, 82
periodic tenancies, 79
disputes, 84
exclusions,
Law of Property Act 1925, terms within, 81–82
tenant's counter-notice, 81, 83
fixed term farm business tenancy of two years or less, 78
general, 77–78
jointly held estates, 80, 82, 84
jurisdiction of courts, 84
monthly periodic tenancy, 78
notice to quit,
annual tenancies, 82
valid, requirements of, 82–83
protection from eviction, 83–84
quarterly periodic tenancy, 78
security of tenure, lack of, 83
tenancy for more than two years,
generally, 79
jointly held estates, 80
mandatory nature of s. 5, 80
who may give notice, 80
weekly periodic tenancy, 78
who may give notice, 80, 82, 84
compensation,
acclimatisation or hefting of sheep, 101
amount of compensation,
planning permission, for, 103
tenant's improvement, for, 104
arbitration,
appointment of arbitrator, 105–106
machinery of, 101
reference to, where no satisfactory consent from landlord, 98–99
task of arbitrator, 101–102
benefit, meaning, 104
conditions of eligibility for claim, 94
contractual compensation, availability of, 88–89
essential right to, 93–94
fixed equipment of tenant, status of, 92–93
forms. *See full list of forms in* Part V
generally, 85–86
hefting of sheep, 101
making claim, 105
mandatory nature of Part III, 86–87
non-routine improvements, 100
planning permission,
amount of compensation, 103

Termination of tenancy—*cont.*
compensation—*cont.*
planning permission—*cont.*
conditions relating to, 94–96
resumption of possession of part of holding, 106–107
reversion severed, termination of entire tenancy where, 107–108
routine improvements, effect of providing, 100–101
service of notice, 105
settling claim, 105
sheep, acclimatisation or hefting of, 101
sub-tenancies, 91–92
successive tenancies, 106
tenant's improvement,
amount of compensation for, 104
intangible advantages, 90–91
meaning, 89–91
not being planning permission, 96–98
physical improvement, 89–90
forms. See full list of forms in Part V
Tied holdings,
exclusion of, 151
Tort,
waste, of, 211
Tribunal. *See* Agricultural Land Tribunal

Valuation,
farm business tenancy, rent review under,
basis of valuation, 55
open market, 56–59
tenant's improvements, 63
Valuer,
farm business tenancy, preparation of documents relating to, 23–24, 142

Waste,
tort of, 211
Words and phrases,
1951 Act, 168, A.9
accepted proportion, 163, A.9
additional compensation, 163, 370, A.9
aftercare condition, 163, A.9
agisted livestock, 163, A.9
agreed, 163, A.9
agreement, 163, A.9
agricultural, 20, 163, A.9
agricultural holding, 155, 163, A.9
agricultural land, 156–158, 163, A.9
agricultural unit, 163, A.2, A.9
agriculture, 163, A.9
all relevant factors, 248
amalgamation, 163
amount, 43
amount of tenant's actual loss, 163, 368, A.9
arable land, 163, A.9
basic compensation, 163, 367, A.9
benefit, 104
Board, 163, A.9
body corporate controlled by close relative, 163, A.9

1264

INDEX

Words and phrases—*cont.*
buildings, 74–75, 163, A.9
case, 163, A.9
close relative, 164, A.9
commercial unit of agricultural land, 164, A.9
connected person, 164, A.9
contemplation, 176–177
contract for agricultural tenancy, 159–160, 164, A.9
contract of tenancy, 156, 164, A.9
contracting-in tenancies, 424–425
county court, 164, A.9
current level of rents for comparable lettings, 250–251
date of any relevant notice, 164, A.9
date of death, 164, A.9
date of insolvency, 164, A.9
date of reference, 242
deceased, 164, A.9
district, 164, A.9
dwelling-house, 164, A.9
eligible person, 164, A.9
Evesham custom, 14–15, 164, A.9
excess qualifying leys, 164, A.9
excluded matters, 164, A.9
fair and reasonable landlord, 301–303
farm business tenancy, 17
farmed under competent management, 446–447
farming of land, 164, A.9
fixed equipment, 60, 164, A.9
fixtures, 73
fixtures or buildings acquired, 75
formula, 43, 44–45
high farming, 258
hill land, 165, A.9
hill sheep, 165, A.9
holding, 53, 164, 605, A.9
housing authority, 165, A.9
improvement, 385
insolvent, 165, A.9
intangible advantages, 90–91
landlord's improvements, 165, A.9
landlord, 165, A.9
leys, 165, A.9
livelihood, 436
livelihood condition, 165, A.9
livestock, 165, A.9
local government funds, 165, A.9
long term improvements, 165, A.9
market garden, 499–500
matters specified, 401
minister, 165, A.9
model clauses, 165, A.9
modifications, 165, A.9
necessary modifications, 173–175
new holding, 165, A.9
nominated successor, 165, A.9
notice to do work, 165, A.9
occupancy condition, 165, A.9
old improvements, 165, A.9
open market, 56, 245–248

Termination of tenancy—*cont.*
original holding, 165, A.9
original landlord, 166, A.9
pasture, 166, A.9
percentage, 44
period of residence protection, 166, A.9
person validly designated by deceased in his will, 166, A.9
physical improvement, 89–90
prescribed, 166, A.9
prescribed period, 166, A.9
President, 166, A.9
prisoner, 166, A.9
producer, 602–603
productive capacity, 166, 248–249, A.9
prudent, 244–245
purchaser, 604–605
qualifying leys, 166, A.9
question (a), 166, A.9
question (b), 166, A.9
reasonable cost of work, 166, A.9
related earning capacity, 166, 248–249, A.9
related improvement, 166, A.9
relevant compensation, 166, A.9
relevant improvements, 166, 380, A.9
relevant land, 166, A.9
relevant notice, 166, A.9
relevant period, 166, A.9
relevant previous notice, 167, 373, A.9
relevant service, 167, A.9
relevant time, 167, A.9
rent, 167, A.9
rent properly payable, 167, A.9
repair, 204–205
replacement, 204–205
restoration condition, 167, A.9
retirement date, 167, A.9
retirement notice, 167, A.9
retiring tenant, 167, A.9
roots, 167, A.9
rules of good estate management, 167, A.9
rules of good husbandry, 167, A.9
service man, 167, A.9
short period of training, 167, A.9
short term improvements, 167, A.9
some specified period of year, 177
sub-tenancy, 492–493
tenancy, 17, 167, A.9
tenant, 168, A.9
tenant right matters, 168
tenant's fixed equipment, 168, A.9
tenant's improvement, 89, 168, A.9
tenant's pasture, 168, A.9
term date, 168, A.9
termination, 161–162, 168, A.9
termination date, 168, A.9
tribunal, 168, A.9
use of land for agriculture, 168, A.9
willing, 244–245
year, 168, A.9

Written agreement,
Agricultural Holdings Act 1986, under.
See Agricultural holdings
farm business tenancy, rent review under,
providing timetable and stipulating amount, 43–44

Written agreement—*cont.*
farm business tenancy, rent review under—*cont.*
stipulating for no rent review, 42
stipulating formula, 44–47
timetable, provision of, 44–47